TO THE STUDENT: A Study Guide for this textbook is available
through your college bookstore under the title *Study Guide for
Cost Accounting: Concepts and Managerial Applications* by
Harold Bierman, Jr., Thomas R. Dyckman, and Ronald W. Hilton.
The Study Guide can help you with course material by acting as a
tutorial, review, and study aid. If the Study Guide is not in stock,
ask the bookstore manager to order a copy for you.

Cost
Accounting

Concepts and Managerial Applications

The KENT Series in Accounting

Cost Accounting

Concepts and Managerial Applications

Harold Bierman, Jr.
Nicholas H. Noyes Professor of Business Administration

Thomas R. Dyckman
Ann Whitney Olin Professor of Accounting

Ronald W. Hilton
Professor of Accounting

*All of the Johnson Graduate School of Management
Cornell University*

PWS-KENT Publishing Company
Boston

PWS-KENT
Publishing Company

20 Park Plaza
Boston, Massachusetts 02116

This book is dedicated to our families.

PWS-KENT Publishing Company is a division of Wadsworth, Inc.

Library of Congress Cataloging-in-Publication Data

Bierman, Harold.
    Cost accounting : concepts and managerial applications / Harold Bierman, Jr., Thomas R. Dyckman, Ronald W. Hilton.
        p.   cm.
    ISBN 0-534-92176-0
    1. Cost accounting.   2. Managerial accounting.   I. Dyckman, Thomas R.   II. Hilton, Ronald W.   III. Title.
    HF5686.C8B467   1990
    657'.42—dc20   89-16295
                                                                CIP

Printed in the United States of America.

  91 92 93 94 95 – 10 9 8 7 6 5 4 3

Sponsoring Editor: Rolf A. Janke
Production Editor: Susan M. C. Caffey
Manufacturing Coordinator: Marcia A. Locke
Assistant Editor: Deirdre A. Lynch
Interior Designer: Catherine L. Johnson
Cover Designer: Vanessa Piñeiro-Robbins
Interior Illustrator: Boston Graphics, Inc.
Compositor: Bi-Comp, Inc.
Text Printer/Binder: Arcata Graphics/Halliday
Cover Printer: New England Book Components, Inc.

Material from Uniform CPA Examination, Questions and Unofficial Answers, Copyright (1978, 1980, 1982, 1983, 1984) by the American Institute of Certified Public Accountants, Inc. is adapted with permission.

Materials from the Certificate in Management Accounting Examinations (Copyright 1977, 1978, 1979, 1980, 1981, 1982, 1983, 1984, 1985, 1986, 1987, 1988, 1989 by the National Association of Accountants) are adapted with permission.

About the Authors

Harold Bierman, Jr. is the Nicholas H. Noyes Professor of Business Administration at the Johnson Graduate School of Management, Cornell University. A graduate of the U.S. Naval Academy, Annapolis, he received his MBA and his Ph.D. from the University of Michigan.

A Cornell faculty member since 1956, Professor Bierman formerly taught at Louisiana State University, the University of Michigan, and the University of Chicago. He has also taught at INSEAD in Fountainebleau, France.

He is a recent recipient of the Dow Jones Award from the American Assembly of Collegiate Schools of Business for his outstanding contributions to collegiate business education. In 1985 he served as a financial consultant at Prudential Bache Securities in New York. His industrial experience includes consulting for Corning Glass Works, Eastman Kodak, Sun Oil Company, Exxon Oil Corporation, IBM, and Xerox Corporation. He has written numerous books, including *The Capital Budgeting Decision* (with Seymour Smidt), *Financial Accounting, Managerial Accounting, Quantitative Analysis for Business Decisions,* and more than a hundred journal articles.

Thomas R. Dyckman is the Ann Whitney Olin Professor of Accounting at the Johnson Graduate School of Management, Cornell University. Since 1984 he has served as the school's associate dean for academic affairs. Professor Dyckman received his B.A., M.B.A., and Ph.D. degrees from the University of Michigan.

On the Cornell faculty since 1963, Professor Dyckman has also taught at the University of California, Berkeley. His industrial experience includes work with IBM Corporation, GTE Service Corporation, Goodyear Tire & Rubber Company, and General Foods Corporation.

Professor Dyckman has been an active member of the American Accounting Association, serving both as president and director of research. In 1987 he received the Outstanding Educator Award from the American Accounting Association. He has served numerous times on the faculties of both the Doctoral Consortium and the New Faculty consortium sponsored by the American Accounting Association.

Thomas R. Dyckman is the author of over fifty journal articles on topics in accounting and quantitative methods. He has served on many editorial boards, including the *Journal of Accounting Research,* The *Accounting Review,* and the

Journal of Accounting and Economics. He is co-author of several books, including *Managerial Cost Accounting, Accounting for Long-Lived Assets, Management Decision Making under Uncertainty, Algebra and Calculus for Business, Efficient Capital Markets, Statistical Analysis for Business,* and *Intermediate Accounting: A Case Book*. His book *Efficient Capital Markets* won the Notable Contributions to the Accounting Literature Award presented by the American Institute of Certified Public Accountants.

Professor Dyckman is currently serving as a consultant to the Financial Accounting Standards Board.

Ronald W. Hilton is a professor of accounting at the Johnson Graduate School of Management, Cornell University. With bachelor's and master's degrees in accounting from The Pennsylvania State University, he received his Ph.D. from The Ohio State University.

A Cornell faculty member since 1977, Professor Hilton has also taught accounting at Ohio State and the University of Florida, where he held the position of Walter J. Matherly Professor of Accounting. Prior to pursuing his doctoral studies, Hilton worked for Peat, Marwick, Mitchell and Company and served as an officer in the United States Air Force.

Professor Hilton is a member of the National Association of Accountants and has been active in the American Accounting Association. He is currently associate editor of *The Accounting Review,* and was formerly a member of its editorial board. Hilton has served on the resident faculties of both the Doctoral Consortium and the New Faculty Consortium sponsored by the American Accounting Association.

With wide-ranging research interests, Hilton has published articles in many journals, including the *Journal of Accounting Research, The Accounting Review, Contemporary Accounting Research, Management Science, Decision Sciences,* the *Journal of Mathematical Psychology* and the *Journal of Economic Behavior and Organization*. He has also published a monograph in the AAA *Studies in Accounting Research* series and is a co-author of *Budgeting: Profit Planning and Control*.

Preface

Cost accounting systems provide vital information to accountants and other business managers in a wide variety of organizations. This book presents the major concepts of cost accounting and focuses on decision-making situations that require accounting data. Decision makers and others interested in the design of cost accounting systems will find this book useful in the analysis and application of cost accounting data.

Flexible Organization

This book is designed so that chapters can be assigned out of order if the instructor so desires. The material requires a working knowledge of financial accounting and can be used immediately after a first course in financial accounting or after an introductory managerial accounting course. We have included more chapters in the book than can be covered comfortably in a single semester or quarter. In fact, the first thirteen chapters can easily form the basis of a one-semester (or quarter) introductory course in cost accounting. The instructor can choose chapters that fit both the students' preparation and the objectives of the course.

If students already have taken a managerial accounting course, some chapters can be used to review that introductory material. There are sufficient advanced topics to fill a semester. If the book is used immediately after an introductory financial accounting course, the introductory cost accounting chapters can be used with selected advanced topics.

Pedagogical Features

The text has many features to make cost accounting interesting and accessible to a wide range of readers.

Real-World Illustrations

Experience has convinced us that student interest in cost accounting is increased considerably when they read real-world illustrations of concepts and techniques throughout the course. To stimulate interest we have included numerous illustrations of cost accounting issues from well-known companies and organizations. We obtained most of the information for these illustrations directly from the organizations; in other instances we obtained information from published case studies, used here with the permission of the publishers.

Financial statements that include cost accounting data are shown for Delta Air Lines, Inc., F. W. Woolworth Co., and The Maytag Company. Cost-volume-profit illustrations are provided for Delta Air Lines, Inc. and Dunkin' Donuts. Alternative product-costing systems are illustrated with information from The Walt Disney Company, McDonnell Douglas Corporation, and Hewlett-Packard Company. We have included a process-costing illustration from Hewlett-Packard Company and an illustration of cost variances from Chrysler Corporation. A master budget is constructed based on data obtained from The Firestone Tire & Rubber Company, and responsibility accounting is illustrated for the Marriott Corporation (Marriott Hotels). We illustrate the use of relevant costs in making decisions about athletic programs at Wright State University. Other major illustrations include cost allocation at Mayo Clinic, linear programming by Exxon Company, U.S.A., transfer pricing at Cornell University, learning curves by The Boeing Company, inventory control at Ford Motor Company, uncertainty in decision making at the Environmental Protection Agency, and productivity accounting at the New York City Sanitation Department.

In addition to major illustrations, we include dozens of excerpts and summaries from published business sources describing cost accounting issues in well-known companies and organizations. Short excerpts and summaries are included for 3M, Emerson Electric, Federal Express, General Motors, Michigan National Bank, American Express, Citibank, United Parcel Service, Harvard Medical Center, Hewlett-Packard, A&P, General Electric, J. C. Penney, ARCO, The Firestone Tire & Rubber Company, Lockheed, Florida Power and Light, Honeywell, Ingersoll Rand, Monsanto, United States government, Sony, Dow, B. F. Goodrich, City of Charlotte, North Carolina, and Chesebrough Ponds.*

The real-world examples are included in the book to illustrate the ideas developed and, we hope, enhance the reader's interest in cost accounting, rather than to teach relevant cost-accounting techniques. We believe that heightened interest results in a more effective learning process.

Balance Among Manufacturing, Service, and Nonprofit Illustrations

Coverage of cost accounting techniques is provided for manufacturing companies, service-industry firms, nonprofit organizations, and international firms. The partial list of real-world illustrations given above suggests the variety and scope of this balanced coverage.

* All company logos used within this text are registered trademarks.

Up-to-Date Coverage

We have taken great pains to keep our coverage up to date, and have included discussions of executive incentive programs, just-in-time (JIT) inventory systems, material requirements planning (MRP), flexible manufacturing, computer-integrated manufacturing (CIM), automation and robotics, emphasis on productivity and product quality, nonfinancial performance data, cost drivers and non–labor-based cost assignment, ethics, and computerized systems. We also note the criticisms levied against contemporary cost accounting systems by such scholars as Robert S. Kaplan and acknowledge the limitations of these systems where appropriate. In doing so, we endeavor to provide a balanced view of the issues involved.

Learning Objectives

Each chapter begins with a list of learning objectives to guide students in their study. Instructors may find it worth reviewing these objectives with students at the conclusion of each chapter.

Clarity, Exhibits, and Step-by-Step Instruction

Clarity of exposition has been a key objective in writing this text. In addition to precise definitions and explanations, we include many graphs, tables, flow charts, and step-by-step instructions to make the material more easily understood by the reader.

Review Problems and Key Terms

Most chapters contain a review problem followed by a solution, which can help readers determine how well they have mastered the material. A list of key terms is also given at the end of each chapter with references to the page where each term is defined. In addition, all of the book's key terms are listed and defined in the glossary at the end of the text.

Questions, Exercises, and Problems

The questions, exercises, and problems are an integral part of each chapter. In answering them, students will find it necessary to refer back to the text material. Indeed, problem solving is an essential step in understanding the main ideas in each chapter. A first reading will not give anyone a full command of the material. Problem solving followed by an additional reading of the chapter is strongly recommended.

Suggested Readings

In some respects, this volume is only an introduction to the topics covered. The reader who wishes to pursue more deeply an interest in any of the subject areas is encouraged to refer to the suggested readings provided at the end of each chapter.

Supplements

A full set of supplements is available to assist the instructor in designing and implementing a successful cost accounting course.

Instructor's Manual   The Instructor's Manual provides valuable suggestions for organizing and teaching a cost accounting course and using the text.

Solutions Manual   The Solutions Manual contains answers to all review questions, exercises, and problems. Also included are time estimates for solving the exercises and problems.

Study Guide   The Study Guide is designed to help students master the material presented in the text, and provide a means of testing this mastery through self-tests.

Test Bank   The Test Bank supplies an ample variety of testing materials to permit the preparation of several exams without repeating exam questions or problems. A computerized test bank is also available.

Cost Accounting Problems Using Lotus 1-2-3   The computer supplement contains approximately 30 problems, and helps students develop skill in using personal computers and electronic spreadsheets in performing cost accounting activities. Two levels of problems challenge students to build upon their knowledge of cost accounting by completing formatting and template problems.

Coverage of Product Costing

We have devoted two early chapters (Chapters 4 and 5) to basic product-costing systems and job-order costing. This in-depth coverage introduces students to the overall structure within which product-costing systems may be classified, including the basic differences among actual, normal, and standard costing; between job-order and process costing; and between variable and absorption costing. We have found that students benefit from having an overall framework to which they can relate various product-costing concepts as they are discussed in detail throughout subsequent chapters. The two chapters on job-order costing provide thorough coverage of these product-costing concepts.

Sequence of Topics

Recognizing that instructors often disagree on the optimal sequencing of topics in a cost accounting course, we have written the text in a modular and flexible style to facilitate a rearrangement of the topics to suit individual needs. Most chapters can easily be pulled out of their current sequence and assigned at other points in a course. The current chapter sequence makes sense to us, but we recognize that others may disagree. Several possibilities for topic rearrangement are listed below.

**Chapter 3
Cost-Volume-
Profit Analysis**

We have found that the placement of this topic differs widely across the cost accounting texts and course syllabi, and therefore, we wrote the chapter so that it can easily be moved to a point later in the course. One common placement for Cost-Volume-Profit (CVP) analysis is near the coverage of relevant costs. We cover relevant costs in Chapter 10, and our CVP chapter can easily be moved to that point in the sequence.

**Chapter 6
Process Costing**

We place process costing immediately after job-order costing in our sequence of topics because these are the two polar extremes of product-costing systems. Some instructors view process costing as an advanced or specialized topic and defer it to late in the course or even to a second-semester cost-accounting course. Chapter 6 can easily be extracted from the current sequence and delayed until any point in the course.

**Chapter 9
Variable and
Absorption
Costing**

Some instructors treat this issue as a special topic late in the course. To allow for this approach, Chapter 9 has been written so that it may be covered anytime after Chapters 7 and 8 (on standard costing systems) have been covered.

**Chapter 10
Budgeting and
Responsibility
Accounting**

We cover budgeting after the two chapters on standard costing systems (Chapters 7 and 8) in recognition of the dual role of standard costing systems: product costing *and* control. Chapters 4 through 6 are primarily product-costing chapters, and Chapters 9 and 10 are primarily planning and control chapters. Placing the two chapters on standard costing between the product costing and control modules enables us to emphasize the dual role of standard costing.

Because some instructors may prefer to cover budgeting and responsibility accounting prior to standard costing, Chapter 10 (Budgeting and Responsibility Accounting) is designed to be able to be covered prior to Chapters 7 and 8. When placed in this sequence, the discussion of budgets as control devices can be used to motivate the subsequent discussion of standard costing. Although the term *standard cost* is mentioned near the beginning of Chapter 10, there is no substantive use of standard costing concepts in Chapter 10. Moreover, standard costing systems are introduced briefly, early in Chapter 4, as one of several alternative product-costing systems.

**Chapter 16
Accounting for
Spoiled and
Defective Units**

We have placed this topic in the latter half of the text as a specialized topic. Some instructors prefer to discuss this topic along with process costing, however, and with this in mind, we wrote Chapter 16 so that it may be completed anytime after Chapter 6 (Process Costing).

**Chapter 14   Cost
Allocation and
Chapter 15
Joint Costs and
Joint Products**

We cover these topics in the latter part of our course, but some instructors prefer to include them with the product-costing chapters. We have therefore written Chapters 14 and 15 so that they may be covered anytime after Chapters 4 and 5 (Job-Order Costing).

**Chapter 26
Behavioral and
Economic
Implications of
Budgeting and
Responsibility
Accounting**

Budgeting and responsibility accounting is an important topic that requires two chapters to cover thoroughly. We introduce the basics of these topics in Chapter 10, where we demonstrate how to construct a master budget and discuss both performance reports and responsibility-accounting centers.

Budgeting and responsibility-accounting systems have important behavioral and economic implications. These topics are covered in Chapter 26, since most instructors treat these issues as an advanced or specialized topic, but it also can easily be used immediately after Chapter 10. In fact, that is how we use this material when we teach the course.

Chapter 27 Learning Curves and Cost Behavior

We cover this topic late in the text. For instructors who prefer to discuss learning effects along with cost estimation, Chapter 27 can be moved up and assigned immediately after Chapter 13 (Cost Estimation).

Behavioral and Economic Issues

Elementary economic theory, introductory statistical methods, and topics in organizational behavior are woven throughout the text, reflecting the interaction of cost-accounting systems with the economic and behavioral forces that shape an organization. Students need no prior background in these topics. Several decision-making topics that are especially relevant to practicing accountants and managers receive particularly detailed treatment. A report of the Committee on Education and Experience Requirements for Certified Public Accountants describes the cost-accounting requirement and states that "it is believed important that students know how cost accounting can contribute to decision making and planning. Typical problems might involve make-or-buy, product mix, capital budgeting, and inventory decisions. The methodologies might include present-value analysis, models, and incremental analysis." The report of the American Accounting Association's Committee to Compile a Revised Statement of Educational Policy reaches a similar conclusion: "Management has come to recognize that accountants are in a strategic position to make significant contributions in the area of resource planning."

Many of the topics in this book might be covered elsewhere in a business curriculum, but we also include topics for which no other functional area in business has an obvious first claim. We believe these topics are highly relevant for cost accountants and managers using cost-accounting information.

Acknowledgments

We owe debts to many individuals for the ideas contained in this volume, and occasionally their names appear in the footnotes. Foremost among our debts, however, is that owed to our colleagues at Cornell, who refined many of our ideas; our students, who challenged us; and our families.

We are indebted to people employed in the following organizations who generously provided information to be used in our real-world illustrations: Delta Air Lines, Inc., F. W. Woolworth Co., The Maytag Company, Dunkin' Donuts, The Walt Disney

Company, McDonnell Douglas Corporation, Hewlett-Packard Company, Chrysler Corporation, The Firestone Tire & Rubber Company, Marriott Corporation, Exxon Company, U.S.A., Mayo Clinic, Cornell University, The Boeing Company, and Ford Motor Company.

We acknowledge the National Association of Accountants for allowing us to use excerpts from *Management Accounting* and cases from their series, *Cases from Management Accounting Practice* from the NAA/AAA Management Accounting Symposium Series. We acknowledge the Institute of Certified Management Accountants of the National Association of Accountants for permission to use problems from Certified Management Accountant (CMA) examinations. We also acknowledge the American Institute of Certified Public Accountants for permission to use problems from the Uniform CPA Examinations, Questions and Unofficial Answers. Acknowledgment is also given to the President and Fellows of Harvard College, from whom we obtained permission to use several published Harvard Business School cases. We are indebted to Gerald Zimmerman and David Solomons for allowing us to use some of their materials in the text. We are grateful to the literary executor of the late Sir Ronald A. Fisher, F.R.S., to Dr. Frank Yates, F.R.S., and to the Longman Group, Ltd., London, for permission to reprint tables from their book *Statistical Tables for Biological Agricultural and Medical Research* (6th ed., 1974).

The following individuals reviewed various versions of the manuscript, and we owe them a debt of gratitude for their many helpful suggestions: Michael A. Crosby, *University of Toledo;* Fred A. Jacobs, *Georgia State University;* Robert E. Jensen, *Trinity University;* Douglas A. Johnson, *Arizona State University;* Yow-Min R. Lee, *California State University–Northridge;* Thomas W. Lin, *University of Southern California;* Robert E. Malcom, *Pennsylvania State University;* Garry Marchant, *University of Texas–Austin;* Joseph W. Milligan, *College of DuPage;* Richard J. Murdock, *The Ohio State University;* William Rotch, *University of Virginia;* Leopold Schachner, *City University of New York;* and Thomas Selling, *Dartmouth College.*

The following individuals at Cornell helped us with typing, proofreading, and problem-checking tasks: Barbara Guile, Kenneth Beck, David Steinman, Francis Rivkin, Joseph Fergus, Martha Turner, and Mark Shea.

We sincerely welcome any comments or suggestions from those who use this text.

Harold Bierman, Jr.
Thomas R. Dyckman
Ronald W. Hilton

Ithaca, New York

Brief Contents

Contents

10 Budgeting and Responsibility Accounting   334

16   *Accounting for Spoilage, Rework, and Scrap*   *570*

Cost Accounting and Control in Decentralized Organizations

Cost
Accounting

Concepts and Managerial Applications

PART ONE

Cost Accounting Fundamentals

1

The Role of Managerial Accounting

LEARNING OBJECTIVES

After studying this chapter, you should be able to:

1 Discuss the purposes of and differences among financial accounting, managerial accounting, and cost accounting.

2 Describe the users of financial accounting information and managerial accounting information.

3 Explain the role of managerial accountants in an organization.

4 List and describe four major objectives of cost accounting.

5 Describe six steps in a typical decision process.

6 Explain why managerial accountants should be familiar with economic theory and behavioral science.

7 Identify and describe several professional organizations and the certification process for managerial accountants.

The Impact of Managerial Accounting Excellence

The number of U.S. corporations with track records of perennial success and excellence has diminished in the last few years. The recent spate of "megabuck" mergers and acquisitions, decreasing productivity, economic downturns, and stiffer foreign competition have damaged companies' chances for sustained growth and profitability. A few exceptions, however, have survived these adversities and continue to achieve stellar performances. Minnesota Mining and Manufacturing Company (3M) is a prime example.

In the top 50 of the Fortune 500, 3M is an $8 billion giant which made *Fortune* magazine's list of America's most admired corporations — recently rising to No. 2, just behind IBM.

What is 3M's formula for success? Chronicled along with 61 other high achievers in the best-seller, *In Search of Excellence,* by Thomas J. Peters and Robert H. Waterman, Jr., then revisited in *A Passion for Excellence* by Peters and Nancy Austin, 3M is heralded as a model for product innovation. 3M also is a model for managerial accounting excellence.

Readers of the two books may have come away with a mental image of teams of 3M employees dashing through the hallways, spewing forth new product ideas to anyone who would listen, then plunging ahead with a frenzy of new product developments, all in a state of almost uncontrolled chaos. Highly charged creativity does abound in 3M, but an underlying thread of good financial planning and tight cost control also permeates the entire organization. It extends from top management down through the center of every operating unit and through every product and service created. It is a vital part of everyday decision making.

New products are the lifeblood of 3M, and the company carefully nurtures its product champions, taking every step possible to see that its entrepreneurs have the best conditions under which to create. At the same time, centralized legal, engineering, human resources, and finance departments keep the entrepreneurial spirits headed in the right direction.

Financial expertise, long recognized as one of 3M's greatest assets, is a major contributor to the corporation's success. 3M uses its financial control system to encourage rather than curtail innovation and creativity. Numbers are used to set goals and measure performance rather than to deny expenditures or punish for unmet expectations.

Management accountants — whether from the controller, treasurer, or internal auditing area — all serve as a check and balance for corporate activities. The accountants from the controller's area are closest to daily operations. "3M management wants a good, objective financial reading as to what's really going on. Therefore we have a controllers' group to serve in that capacity," Roger W.

Roberts, vice president and controller, explains. "That's one of our big functions — to provide an independent, objective viewpoint of the financial performance of 3M's various organizations.

"Yet we get intimately involved with day-to-day activities . . . with forecasting and planning activities of the business units. As an example, in new product development we try to lay out for the managers the cost implications of bringing on a new product and what it means in relation to their total business and whether or not they can still reach their financial targets. We work with them, developing the analysis to help them prioritize what products they want to go after. We also develop alternatives as far as facilities for the general manager. . . . Our controllers view their roles as not to always challenge management, but as being a cooperative effort to develop a better business."[1]

What is managerial accounting, and how can it contribute to the overall success of an organization? What is the role of cost accounting in helping managers achieve an organization's goals? These fundamental questions are answered in this textbook.

Financial versus Managerial Accounting

Accounting is the means used to communicate the nature and financial impact of an organization's economic activities. **Financial accounting** is typically described in terms of providing financial information for *external* reporting to shareholders, governmental units, and other outside parties. **Managerial accounting** is typically described in terms of providing financial information for *internal* reporting to managers for use in planning and controlling operations, in making decisions, and in formulating overall policies and long-range plans.

The distinction between financial and managerial accounting is often less clear than these definitions suggest. In part, managerial accounting procedures are designed to meet financial accounting objectives. Moreover, both financial and managerial accounting rely on the information provided by the cost accounting system.

Purposes of Financial, Managerial, and Cost Accounting Systems

Accounting systems are an organization's major means of accumulating financial information. Some type of accounting system can be found in virtually any organization, whether it is a corporate giant such as 3M, a governmental unit like the City of New York, or a private, nonprofit organization such as the Red Cross.

The data accumulated by an organization's accounting system is used for both external and internal purposes. As noted above, information used externally is generated by the organization's financial accounting system. The annual financial statements prepared by General Electric provide an example of the results of financial accounting. The users of financial accounting information include current and pro-

1. This description of managerial accounting at 3M is an excerpt from an article in *Management Accounting* published with permission from the National Association of Accountants. See K. Williams, "The Magic of Managerial Accounting Excellence," *Management Accounting* (February 1986): 20–27.

spective corporate stockholders, lenders, investment analysts, governmental agencies, unions, consumer groups, and virtually anyone with an interest in the financial position and results for an organization. If a company's stock is publicly traded, its financial statements must be prepared in conformity with both generally accepted accounting principles (GAAP) and certain Securities and Exchange (SEC) regulations.

EXHIBIT 1-1

Relationships Among Financial, Managerial, and Cost Accounting Systems

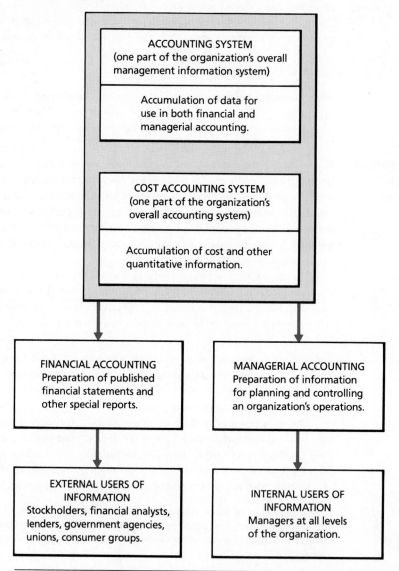

ACCOUNTING SYSTEM
(one part of the organization's overall management information system)

Accumulation of data for use in both financial and managerial accounting.

COST ACCOUNTING SYSTEM
(one part of the organization's overall accounting system)

Accumulation of cost and other quantitative information.

FINANCIAL ACCOUNTING
Preparation of published financial statements and other special reports.

MANAGERIAL ACCOUNTING
Preparation of information for planning and controlling an organization's operations.

EXTERNAL USERS OF INFORMATION
Stockholders, financial analysts, lenders, government agencies, unions, consumer groups.

INTERNAL USERS OF INFORMATION
Managers at all levels of the organization.

Information used internally is generated by an organization's managerial accounting system. Managers at all levels of an organization use managerial accounting information for a variety of purposes related to planning and controlling the organization's activities. Preparing the annual budget at General Motors, determining the cost of the Chicago to Los Angeles flight by United Airlines, and estimating net contributions by the United Way are all examples of managerial accounting.

Cost accounting is the part of an organization's accounting system that accumulates cost and other quantitative data for the purposes described above in both financial and managerial accounting. Thus, cost accounting is a set of procedures and tools that are used in gathering information for both financial and managerial accounting purposes. Exhibit 1-1 depicts the relationships among financial, managerial, and cost accounting systems.

This book focuses on the concepts and procedures of cost accounting and on the managerial accounting applications of cost accounting information. From time to time, the financial accounting implications and uses of cost accounting data are also discussed.

The Role of Cost Accounting

Cost accounting information is instrumental in helping an organization reach its goals and objectives by maintaining a record of relevant events. Events such as the purchase and use of material, labor, and capital resources are recorded by the cost accounting system. Maintaining such a record of events is an essential task because it facilitates several functions of the organization's managerial accounting system.

Emerson Electric Company

As an illustration, we focus on Emerson Electric Company, which manufactures a broad range of electrical products. Based in St. Louis, Emerson is cited as an outstanding United States company by Peters and Waterman.[2] Emerson's objectives and policies were defined by the firm's chairman and chief executive officer in a letter to shareholders accompanying the firm's annual report. Those objectives and policies are quoted below:

- *Above-average growth.* The Company's consistent management approach over the past twenty-five years has resulted in above-average growth. For each of the restated five-year periods the Company's five-year compound growth rates have substantially exceeded the average of all manufacturers for the same periods.... The average of the Emerson five-year growth rates ... is 16.3 percent for net earnings and 14.8 percent for sales. The same comparison of relative performance for the ten-year period 1972 to 1982 shows a compound growth rate for Emerson of 13.1 percent in sales versus

---

2. T. Peters and R. Waterman, Jr., *In Search of Excellence: Lessons From America's Best-Run Companies* (New York: Harper & Row, 1982).

a 9.8 percent sales growth for all manufacturers and 14.7 percent growth rate for Emerson in net earnings versus a 9.3 percent net earnings growth rate for all manufacturers.

- **Commitment to planning.** Planning the Company's businesses in detail allows Emerson to maximize its growth potential and implement budget contingency plans during economic downturns.

- **Diversification.** Operating in broadly diversified electrical-product markets around the world, Emerson has strategically positioned itself in faster growing market niches and contracyclical markets.

- **Product-market leadership.** Approximately 80 percent of the Company's sales come from products that are number one or number two in their market. The Company's strategy to accelerate the internal growth rate is based on strong market leadership, developing new products, responding to technological opportunities, and reposturing the core businesses into faster growing markets.

- **Strong financial position.** Emerson is one of a select few industrial companies rated AAA by all services. As a result, the Company is well positioned to fund future growth opportunities.

- **High levels of profitability.** Emerson's rate of return on total capital and equity continue at historically high levels, and the Company has targeted further improvements.

- **Low cost producer strategy.** The Company continues to increase its resource commitment to cost reduction and productivity-improvement programs as part of an overall program to ensure a competitive cost position in its major markets.

- **Flexible organization approach.** Stressing division autonomy, Emerson plans and controls profits at divisional levels, utilizing tight-loose controls to encourage entrepreneurial action on the part of division management.

- **A simple but effective management process.** The process involves setting tough targets, developing plans and programs to meet these targets, involving managers at all levels in implementation and follow-up, and compensating for results.

As noted previously, the record of relevant events maintained by the cost accounting system facilitates several functions of the company's managerial accounting system. Those functions can be represented by three critical questions often asked of a company's management team:

1. How well has the firm done in terms of its established goals, and how can it do better?

2. What problems does the firm have, and what additional information will help the firm understand and resolve those problems?

3. Of the solutions available, which will best serve the company's stated objectives and goals?

Take another look at Emerson's letter to its shareholders and notice that its focus correlates closely to these three critical questions. For example, Emerson focuses on growth rates, product-market leadership, financial position, and profitability. These objectives are all measures of performance and address the first question by asking, "How well are we doing and how can we do better?" Emerson targets two areas for improvement: level of profitability and competitive costing and productivity. We will show how cost accounting information can provide insights about how those objectives can be achieved by Emerson. Finally, Emerson identifies two solutions: a flexible organization approach and a targeted management process.

These questions and answers are not independent of one another. Improving on past performance, for example, often follows the recognition and resolution of several complex and technically challenging problems.

The Role of Managerial Accountants

Understanding the organizational structure of a large corporation helps clarify the role of cost accounting and of managerial accountants within an organization. At the very top of a corporation are the owners or shareholders. The shareholders exercise control by electing the board of directors, who in turn choose the executives responsible for administering the general policies established by the board of directors. The top-management structure of Emerson Electric Company is illustrated in Exhibit 1-2, which can be generalized to many other large corporations.

Liaison between the senior executives in the office of the chief executive officer and the operating executives is provided by the corporate staff. At Emerson sixteen executives are included as members of the corporate staff. One of these senior executives is the vice president of finance and comptroller. This individual, often called the **controller** in other companies, is the chief managerial accountant in the organization. This position on the corporate staff reflects the value of the accounting profession to the corporation.

The corporate staff includes several individuals who engage in managerial accounting activities. For Emerson these individuals include the vice president and comptroller, the senior vice president and treasurer, and three assistant treasurers. The **treasurer** of a company is usually responsible for the custody of funds and other assets, arranging financing, and managing investments and receivables.

Managerial accountants are also likely to work with operating executives. Most large corporations have complex organizational structures in which decentralized operating units, such as divisions and plants, are present. In such cases, a division controller provides information and advice to a division manager, and a plant controller provides information and advice to a plant manager.

Managerial accountants are in key positions in many organizations, and controllers, who are aware of what is happening in virtually every facet of the business, have risen to the top of their organizations. In recent years, former accountants have served as the top executives of General Electric, General Motors, Chrysler, Allied Chemical, Freuhauf, Singer, Pfizer, and Bethlehem Steel.[3]

3. For some management accounting success stories, see R. L. Shultis and K. Williams, *From Management Accountant to CEO: A Challenging, Rewarding Path to the Top* (New York: National Association of Accountants, 1984).

EXHIBIT 1-2

EXHIBIT 1-2

Top-Management Structure of Emerson Electric Company

Board of Directors

Five Inside Directors:

　　　Chairman and chief executive officer
　　　Vice chairman
　　　Vice chairman and chief financial officer
　　　President and chief operating officer
　　　Executive vice president and chief administrative officer

Executive Committee　　　　　　　　　　　　　　　**Finance Committee**

Office of the Chief Executive

Chairman and chief executive officer
Vice chairman
Vice chairman and chief financial officer
President and chief operating officer
Executive vice president and chief administrative officer
Senior vice president–corporation development

Corporate Staff

Executive vice president–corporate sales
Senior vice president and treasurer
Assistant treasurer
Assistant treasurer
Assistant treasurer
Senior vice president–international
Senior vice president–law
Group vice president–technology
Group vice president–corporate services
Vice president–corporate manufacturing
Vice president–manpower development
Vice president–financial services
Vice president–development
Vice president–industrial relations
Vice president of finance and comptroller[a]
Secretary and general counsel

Operating Executives

---

[a] Chief managerial accounting position.

Objectives of Cost Accounting

The information needs of managerial accountants suggest four major objectives of cost accounting activity:

1. Measuring income and financial position,

2. Assisting in cost control,

3. Motivating managers toward organizational goals,

4. Providing information for planning and decision making.

The relative importance of these objectives varies across organizations.

1. *Measuring income and financial position.* One objective of cost accounting is the measurement of a company's income and financial position. This requires the recording and allocation of many costs, including labor, materials, and overhead.

Emerson Electric's focus on growth rates, financial position, and profitability requires measures of income and financial position, which are necessarily inexact and subject to numerous assumptions. An important function of cost accounting known as **product costing** determines how the costs of such productive inputs as material, labor, and electricity should be associated with an organization's products or services.

2. *Assisting in cost control.* Emerson Electric's objective of being a low-cost producer implies the importance of controlling costs, and the control or reduction of costs requires a detailed cost accounting system. It is necessary to know when and in what department costs are incurred and the nature of those costs. Equally important, the actual amount of the costs needs to be compared with a predetermined estimate of what costs should have been. Unless all of this information is available, the cost accounting system cannot be effective in the control of costs.

Cost accounting information is collected in conjunction with a system of **responsibility accounting.** Under this system, a specific subunit of a company, such as a department, is assigned to a manager who is held accountable for its operations. To each of those defined subunits, costs and revenues (and sometimes assets and liabilities) are specifically traced. The designated manager of each subunit is held accountable only for the financial results that the manager controls or influences.

Cost control also holds individuals responsible for actual performance that differs from what was expected. A comparison of budgeted (or expected) costs with actual costs is illustrated in Exhibit 1-3 for the catering department of a restaurant. (Unfavorable differences are indicated by parentheses.) Such comparisons can be made for particular periods of time and over all management levels. Managers can then focus on items that are out of line with expectations.

Determining budgeted (or expected) costs for different levels of activity can be difficult. Just how these determinations are made, and how conclusions are drawn and reported in performance reports, are subjects that are frequently discussed in this text.

3. *Motivating managers toward organizational goals.* Cost accounting systems provide performance measures that influence actions, choices, and careers. Several

---

EXHIBIT 1-3

Budgeted and Actual Cost Comparison: Catering Department

Item	Expected Cost	Actual Cost	Difference
1	$ 300	$ 400	$(100)[a]
2	280	290	(10)
3	420	330	90
Totals	$1,000	$1,020	$(20)

[a] Parentheses denote unfavorable differences.

---

features of these accounting systems are reflected in Emerson Electric's description of "a simple but effective management process," which "involves setting tough targets, developing plans and programs to meet those targets, involving managers at all levels in implementation and follow-up, and compensating for results."

Large organizations like Emerson Electric tend to delegate decision-making authority to the managers of departments, divisions, groups, and subsidiary companies. Because managers have diverse goals that may differ from those of the organization, performance measurements and incentive systems are devised to encourage managers to act in the best interests of the organization or at least to discourage them from acting contrary to those interests. In designing such performance-evaluation systems, firms relate the goals of the organization to the managers within it so that managers have an appropriate set of instructions. Moreover, managers are encouraged to focus on these goals by measuring their performance and basing rewards on the measures obtained.

4. Providing data for planning and decision making. Achieving an organization's goals — such as Emerson Electric's objectives of growth, diversification, product-market leadership, strong financial position, profitability, and low-cost production — requires managers to plan ahead. Cost accounting provides information that assists managers in formulating plans and making decisions. The cost accountant must often choose the best way to provide the information needed by management. Such a choice requires a cost-benefit analysis, in which the additional cost of better information is weighed against the benefits associated with the likelihood of better decisions. The costs and benefits of cost accounting information, and the information choices that the cost accountant must make, are discussed throughout this text.[4]

---

4. For a discussion of the factors that affect the benefits obtained from better information, see R. W. Hilton, "The Determinants of Cost Information Value: An Illustrative Analysis," *Journal of Accounting Research* (Autumn 1979): 411–435 or R. W. Hilton, "The Determinants of Information Value: Synthesizing Some General Results," *Management Science* (January 1981): 57–64.

The Decision-Making Process

The process of making decisions generally involves the following six steps:

1. Clarify the problem.

2. Establish a criterion.

3. Identify alternatives.

4. Develop a decision model.

5. Collect data.

6. Make a choice.

These steps may influence one another, and the decision maker may cycle through them several times before completing the task of solving a problem.

1. Clarify the problem.   Problems seldom arrive on a manager's desk neatly defined with ready solutions. Yet time and effort must be applied to formulate the problem correctly before an effective plan can be devised for resolving the issue.

2. Establish a criterion.   To judge the relative merits of different courses of action, a measuring unit or criterion is needed. The most commonly used measure is dollars, although this measure may not be appropriate in all situations. Often the criterion is to choose the action that maximizes some measure of profit or minimizes some measure of cost. Various measures of profit and cost can be derived from the data recorded and maintained by cost accounting systems. Thus, cost accounting systems facilitate decision making in organizations by providing measures that can be used in judging alternative courses of action.

3. Identify alternatives.   Choices are limited by the alternatives that are considered. Generating alternatives is a creative process. However, sometimes alternatives and attributes of a decision must be ignored if a timely decision is to be made. Managers must abstract from a decision situation those factors that are most important to their circumstances. Abstraction is a necessary step in analyzing and solving any decision problem.

4. Develop a decision model.   In this step the critical factors or variables in the decision situation are identified. What are the alternatives, and what consequences or outcomes are likely to be associated with each alternative? What aspects or attributes of these consequences are meaningful, and what measures can be used to describe their importance and to facilitate comparisons and trade-offs?

After managers have selected the critical factors that comprise a decision situation, these factors are combined in a logical manner to form a model of the actual problem. A **decision model** is a simplified, mathematical representation of a decision situation. Ideally, it strips the situation of its bewildering complexity and duplicates the important characteristics of the situation with a few variables that are simply related. The simple model is best, provided it serves as a reasonably reliable abstraction of the situation.

In analyzing decisions, managers are encouraged to focus on the future costs or revenues (cash flows) that various actions are expected to produce. Providing the basis for obtaining this information is the most important justification for a detailed cost accounting system.

5. Collect data.   A decision maker typically needs to search out the data needed to reach a decision. The data may be available in the firm's records or from outside sources or may require generation. In obtaining the data, the manager should avoid biases and lack of precision and should seek data that are relevant to the current decision. Historical data may not be useful if economic or social conditions have changed.

6. Make a choice.   Once managers have identified the alternative outcomes of a decision, validated the logic of the decision model, and obtained the relevant data, then their solution to the problem should be effective. However, the conclusion derived from the decision model is subject to a degree of error because of the abstraction process: The manager must judge the point at which the error becomes so large that the conclusion must be modified before it can be adopted as a solution. Decision analysis is an aid to judgment; it is not a substitute for judgment. Moreover, effective decision making does not ensure effective implementation.

Examples of the decision process include capital budgeting, cost control, performance evaluation, product pricing, and setting inventory levels. Mathematical model building is a powerful technique that can be applied in these decision-making processes; it relates relevant variables and derives logical conclusions that would otherwise elude the decision maker.

Two cautions should be observed, however. First, the consequences of decisions are usually expressed in monetary terms that may not reflect the full effect of events. For example, suppose that one event, a loss of $1 million, will lead to a firm's certain bankruptcy but a loss of $500,000 will not lead to bankruptcy. Under these conditions, the first loss is more than twice as serious as the second because it would result in the termination of the enterprise.

Second, nonmonetary factors (such as growth, market size, and prestige), indirect contributions to society (such as the creation of jobs), or costs to society (such as pollution) usually cannot be easily expressed in monetary terms. Decision analysis can effectively measure quantifiable aspects of decision situations, but managers must use intuition to assess various qualitative variables. Managers must establish a balance between the quantitative and qualitative factors.

Adapting to Change

Cost accounting is an essential tool in the successful management of any organization, but cost accounting systems must be adapted continually as the business environment changes. Several recent changes that have significantly affected cost accounting practice are identified in the following sections, and the impact of these changes on various topics in cost accounting are discussed throughout this book.

Service versus Manufacturing Firms

Although manufacturing continues to be a major sector in the economy of the United States, the role of service industries is growing. Companies such as airlines, hotels, insurance companies, and banks produce services rather than inventoriable goods. Nevertheless, many of the cost accounting techniques that were originally developed by manufacturers have been successfully adapted to the service sector.

Computer-Integrated Manufacturing

As manufacturing processes become increasingly automated, robotic manufacturing equipment has taken over many functions previously done manually. In **computer-integrated manufacturing,** or **CIM,** a manufacturing facility is fully automated, and computers control the entire production process. CIM has important implications for the types of costs that a manufacturer incurs.

Just-in-Time Inventory Management

Most production processes require several stages, and materials must be available at each stage before that production step can begin. The recent trend in manufacturing has been to reduce the inventories of materials available at each production step in order to save costs associated with holding inventory: Materials are acquired just in time to be used in the production process. **Just-in-time,** or **JIT, inventory management** systems are becoming more common throughout the world.

Productivity and Product Quality

In order to compete internationally, many U.S. companies have needed to improve their productivity and product quality. As a result, cost accountants have become increasingly involved in measuring productivity and the costs of ensuring product quality.

Importance of Economic Theory and Behavioral Science

Virtually all decisions or analyses made by any organization — whether large or small, public or private, profit-seeking or not-for-profit, manufacturing, service or retail — require some recognition of economic principles. Because economic forces shape the analyses and decisions of managers, the cost accountant needs to understand not only cost accounting concepts and applications but also the economic principles that shape an organization's actions. Moreover, the cost accountant needs to understand how economic principles relate to cost accounting principles. Economic principles and analyses are woven throughout this textbook in discussions of cost accounting concepts and applications.

Behavioral relationships are as important as economic relationships in most organizations. Individual and group reactions to cost accounting information shape actions taken by the organization. How will a department head react to a budget?

What incentives will a division manager have when divisional performance is measured in a certain way? Will marketing personnel be motivated to set product prices too low if product costs are calculated in a particular manner? Will the demands placed on the computer department by operating personnel be too great if computer costs are apportioned among operating departments in a particular way?

These questions are as important to an effective cost accountant as are economic questions about demand and competition. Behavioral science and the implications of human motivation and limitations are essential ingredients of a well-designed cost accounting system, and this text frequently refers to the behavioral implications of cost-accounting information and analyses. On completing this text, you should understand not only how to produce cost accounting data but also how the people in an organization are likely to react to that data.

The next chapter introduces some basic features of cost accounting, including how costs are classified, the economic characteristics of costs, and how costs are used in decision making.

Summary

Cost accounting systems contribute to a successfully managed organization by maintaining a record of relevant events that can be used to measure income and financial position, by providing various performance measures that can be used to assess how well the organization has done in achieving its established goals and how it can do better, and by providing incentives so that managers are encouraged to strive toward these goals. Cost accounting systems also provide data that managers can use to control costs, to identify problems that should be examined, to assess alternative ways of solving problems, and to select and implement the best solutions.

Management accountants typically occupy staff positions in which they provide information and advice to senior executives and to operating managers. Management accountants play a major role in the targeting process, in cost control efforts, in performance evaluation, and in decision making.

To use data from cost accounting systems in analyzing and making decisions, management accountants must be familiar with the various decision models and techniques used by operating managers. In addition, management accountants must understand their organizations' technical operations. Furthermore, management accountants should be aware of the potential behavioral and motivational effects of their activities. They need to understand all areas of management to provide useful services to operating managers and assist the organization in attaining its goals and objectives.

Review Problem

COST ACCOUNTING OBJECTIVES

For each activity a through j, indicate which of the following four objectives of cost accounting activity is involved (some of the activities involve more than one objective of cost accounting):

Objectives:

1. Measuring income and financial position,

2. Assisting in cost control,

3. Motivating managers toward organizational goals,

4. Providing information for planning and decision making.

Activity:

a. Holding city government officials accountable for the public property entrusted to their management.

b. Preparing a report from the mayor to the city council regarding costs incurred in police and fire protection.

c. Determining the bonus to be paid to an airline executive. The bonus is based on reported profit.

d. Measuring the inventory values in a manufacturing firm.

e. Controlling the costs of aircraft fuel in an airline, food and beverage in a hotel, or asphalt used in repairing a city's streets.

f. Providing information about the costs of locating a new golf course and country club on each of three different sites.

g. Comparing the costs incurred by a car rental company with budgeted costs for the period.

h. Measuring the losses from shoplifting in a department store.

i. Providing information on the cost of several alternative methods of manufacturing furniture.

j. Preparing an income statement for a hotel, a department store chain, or a manufacturing firm.

Solution to Review Problem

a. 1, 3	d. 1	g. 2, 3	j. 1, 3
b. 1, 3	e. 2	h. 2	
c. 3	f. 4	i. 4	

Key Terms to Review

computer-integrated manufacturing (CIM), p. 15
controller (or comptroller), p. 9
cost accounting, p. 7
decision model, p. 13
financial accounting, p. 5

just-in-time (JIT) inventory management, p. 15
managerial accounting, p. 5
product costing, p. 11
responsibility accounting, p. 11
treasurer, p. 9

APPENDIX
Professional Organizations and Certification

Managerial accountants often belong to one or more professional organizations. These organizations help members keep informed about new developments in their field. Some of these organizations also provide certification programs that recognize educational achievement and professional competence in the field.

The National Association of Accountants (NAA) is the largest association of cost or managerial accountants in the United States. The NAA publishes the monthly journal *Management Accounting* and also publishes research studies on various managerial accounting issues. The NAA established the Institute of Certified Management Accountants, which administers a program that qualifies Certified Management Accountants (CMA). The qualifying examination for this certification process measures knowledge and competence in the field of managerial accounting, including economics and business finance, organization and behavior, public reporting, periodic reports for internal and external purposes, and decision analysis (such as modeling and information systems). Many problems adapted from CMA examinations are included in this text.[5]

The Financial Executives Institute (FEI) is an organization composed primarily of financial executives, such as controllers, treasurers, and financial vice presidents. The FEI publishes special studies on accounting and issues in financial reporting.

Similar organizations are found in other western industrial nations. In Canada the major professional organization is the Society of Management Accountants of Canada (La Société des Comptables en Management du Canada). In Great Britain the major organization is the Institute of Cost and Management Accountants. Organizations in Canada, Great Britain, and several other countries have long had professional certification programs. In Canada, for example, a management accountant can become a Registered Industrial Accountant (RIA) by completing certain educational requirements and passing an examination administered by the Society of Management Accountants.

Management accountants in the United States also may belong to several other professional organizations. A management accountant who is a Certified Public Accountant (CPA) may belong to the American Institute of Certified Public Accountants (AICPA), the major professional association of independent auditors in the United

---

5. For information about the CMA examination, write to the Institute of Certified Management Accountants, 10 Paragon Drive, P.O. Box 405, Montvale, N.J. 07645.

States. The AICPA publishes a monthly periodical called the *Journal of Accountancy,* establishes the rules about independence and professional standards of practice for independent auditors, and prepares and administers the CPA examination. Many problems adapted from CPA examinations are included in this text.[6]

Management accountants who are internal auditors may belong to the Institute of Internal Auditors (IIA), the professional organization of internal auditors. IIA publishes a journal entitled the *Internal Auditor* and research studies in internal auditing. The IIA also establishes criteria for and administers the Certificate in Internal Auditing (CIA) program. Federal, state, or local government management accountants may belong to the Association of Government Accountants, which publishes the *Government Accountant's Journal.*

Some management accountants belong to the American Accounting Association (AAA), an organization composed primarily of college professors and practicing accountants. The AAA publishes *The Accounting Review* as well as monographs on accounting issues. The Managerial Accounting Section of the AAA focuses on managerial accounting thought and practice.

Several professional organizations influence the establishment of accounting standards or principles. Financial accounting standards, commonly referred to as *generally accepted accounting principles* (GAAP), are currently established by the Financial Accounting Standards Board (FASB). The FASB is a private, seven-member, full-time board that operates in full view of the public through a due-process system that provides ample opportunity for interested parties to comment on pending pronouncements. The Securities and Exchange Commission (SEC) is an independent regulatory agency of the United States government. The SEC publishes *Financial Reporting Releases* (FRRs) and various regulations about filing financial statements. The SEC also makes decisions on cases that come before it. The Internal Revenue Service (IRS) derives its authority from the Internal Revenue Code, its amendments and legal interpretations. The FASB, SEC, and IRS have been instrumental in the development of financial accounting standards that often overlap with topics relevant to cost and managerial accounting. The Government Accounting Standards Board (GASB) was established in 1984 to examine governmental financial reporting, measurement focus and the basis of accounting, pension accounting, and financial reporting. Pronouncements of the GASB are also likely to overlap with topics in cost or managerial accounting.

From 1970 to 1980 the Cost Accounting Standards Board (CASB) influenced the development of cost accounting terminology and practice in the United States. The CASB was established as a federal agency by the United States Congress to promote uniformity and consistency in cost accounting practices for defense contracts. Although Congress dissolved the CASB in 1980, the cost accounting standards issued by the CASB remain in force.

---

6. For information about the CPA examination, write to the AICPA, 1211 Avenue of the Americas, New York, N.Y. 10036.

Suggested Readings

Anthony, R., and R. Herzlinger. *Management Control in Nonprofit Organizations.* Rev. ed. Homewood, Ill.: Irwin, 1980.

"The Controller: Inflation Gives Him More Clout with Management." *Business Week* (Aug. 15, 1977): 84.

Deakin, E., M. Maher, and J. Cappel. *Contemporary Literature in Cost Accounting.* Denton, Tex.: Institute of Petroleum Accounting, 1988.

Demski, J. *Information Analysis,* Reading, Mass.: Addison-Wesley, 1980.

Figler, H. R. "What Should the Management Accountant Know?" *Management Accounting* (June 1978): 27.

Geneen, H. S. "The Case for Managing by the Numbers." *Fortune* (October 1, 1984): 78–81.

Goldratt, E.M., and J. Cox. *The Goal: A Process of Ongoing Improvement.* Rev. ed. Croton-on-Hudson, N.Y.: North River Press, 1986.

Kiani, A. R. "Do Corporate Controllers Use Quantitative Tools Currently Taught in Managerial Accounting?" *Accounting Journal* (Winter 1977–78): 278.

Jacobs, S. L. "This Company Is Run Better Because It Nearly Went Under." *Wall Street Journal,* Sept. 30, 1985, p. 23.

Kirk, D. "The Impact of Managerial Accounting on GAAP." *Management Accounting* (July 1985): 26–59.

"The Money Chase." *Time* (May 4, 1981): 58–65.

Shultis, R. L., and K. Williams. *From Management Accountant to CEO: A Challenging, Rewarding Path to the Top.* New York: National Association of Accountants, 1984.

Thomas, W. E. *Readings in Cost Accounting, Budgeting and Control.* Cincinnati: South-western, 1983.

Williams, K. "Ed Hennessy Reshapes Allied." *Management Accounting.* (January 1985): 18–25.

Williams, K. "The Magic of Management Accounting Excellence." *Management Accounting* (February 1986): 20–27.

Review Questions

1-1 Define and distinguish among the following terms: *financial accounting, managerial accounting,* and *cost accounting.*

1-2 Accounting is one type of information system. Name several other systems supplying information to business managers.

1-3 The early role of accounting was described as a "judiciary" one in which accountants kept records to verify the honesty of those in control of valuable resources. How well does this role describe the present functioning of managerial accountants?

1-4 The president of Speedy Commuter Airlines has suggested to her controller that costs be classified and recorded according to whether or not they are relevant to decisions. What should be the controller's response?

1-5 List and discuss the four objectives of cost accounting activity.

1-6 How might an accountant determine the information needs of an operating department or manager? Do you see any problems in the methods you specified?

1-7 It is often stated that the responsibility of management is to maximize the wealth of owners of the firm. Discuss some general factors that make this a difficult responsibility to define and carry out.

1-8 Is managerial cost accounting in a better position to suggest alternative courses of action or to assist in the evaluation of alternatives already identified?

1-9 Planning and performance evaluation are important functions in managing a firm. With respect to these activities, why might the study of human behavior be useful to an accountant?

1-10 Does the form of the organization determine the appropriate accounting information system, or does the information system determine the best organizational form?

1-11 Is an elaborately detailed cost accounting system a necessary part of the financial reporting function? Should the cost accounting system be integrated into the management planning and control function? Explain your answer.

1-12 Firms are beginning to use more complex approaches to problem solving, including, for example, operations research techniques. How does this affect the function of the management accountant?

1-13 In a not-for-profit organization where the goal is, by definition, not profit maximization, what role does the cost accountant play?

1-14 Jones has a bias for action; she fires and then takes aim. Smith always makes a very careful study of the facts before taking action. Under what conditions would Jones be a better manager than Smith?

1-15 Emerson Electric Company sets "tough targets." Using an analogy for the game of golf, what would be a tough target?

1-16 List and briefly discuss the six steps in the decision-making process.

1-17 Discuss the importance of quantitative analysis and qualitative factors in making a decision.

1-18 Define the following terms as they relate to the field of cost accounting: *CMA, NAA,* and *CASB.* (See the appendix.)

Exercises

1-19 **Credit Manager's Decision** A credit manager of the Chase Manhattan Bank has to decide whether to offer credit to a small manufacturer. There is a significant risk that the firm will fail, but it is more likely that the loan will be repaid and return a profit for the bank. Discuss the considerations that might affect the credit manager's decision.

1-20 Factors Relevant to a Decision   The manager of the grinding department of a manufacturing plant has recommended acquiring a new machine that is fully automatic and is fed information from a central computer station. The computer is currently being used for a variety of purposes in the company. The analysis used to justify the acquisition compared the direct economic savings (essentially savings in labor) with the cost of the equipment. Assume the basic investment analysis was done in a reasonable manner. What other factors might be considered in making this decision?

1-21 Relevance of Historical Information   Accounting reports indicate what has happened in the past; what we want is information relating to the future. The past is gone and not relevant to the present. Discuss this statement.

1-22 Responsibility of Plant Manager   A plant manager oversees a factory that produces covers for convertible automobiles. In recent years the profits of the plant have been decreasing. To what extent should the plant manager be held responsible for the profit decrease?

1-23 Accounting-System Design   Managerial accounting is an information processing operation whose ultimate objective is to assist internal decision making. List the decisions that must be made by the management accountant who designs such a system.

1-24 Low-Cost Producer   Timothy Williams, president of Erie Machine Tool Company, has just read a consulting report presenting the recommended strategy for his corporation. The prime recommendation is that the firm become the low-cost producer in the industry. How does a firm become the low-cost producer? What decisions must be made?

1-25 Productivity Through People   The statement that a business gains "productivity through people" is emotionally appealing. Give a good argument in favor of this position. Give a good argument for modifying the statement.

1-26 Planning versus Action   One of Emerson's main strengths is its planning process. Management spends a large amount of time preparing for the annual planning meeting. These plans are updated throughout the years as circumstances change. Is this planning process inconsistent with the bias for action?

1-27 Cost Accounting Information and a New-Product Decision   Bradley Ronaldson, president of the Quick Snacks Company, has read *In Search of Excellence* and is particularly impressed with the authors' advice to "Stick to your knitting." To him, this means that the product research department was wrong in suggesting that the company explore a new health food product line. The company's only products have been so-called junk food (potato chips, pretzels, cookies, and so forth), and it knows how to make a profit with this product line. Discuss the issues. How can managerial accounting information help managers make such a decision about new products?

1-28 Objectives of Cost Accounting   For each of the following activities, designate which of the four objectives of cost accounting is involved. In some cases, multiple objectives are involved.

   1. Measuring the cost of each compact disk stereo system produced during the year.

   2. Determining the amount of labor cost that will be saved if a new aircraft-refueling truck is purchased.

3. Comparing the actual and planned costs of servicing the checking accounts at a bank.

4. Measuring the cost of the inventory of skis on hand on December 31 at an outdoor sports store.

5. Devising a bonus system for the restaurant managers of a national pizza chain.

6. Determining the actual cost of conducting an audit by a large CPA firm.

Problems

1-29 Line versus Staff Relationships and the Controller The controller of the Krocks and Pots Company received the following letter and has asked you to draft a response.

Ms. Meg Johnstone, Controller
The Krocks and Pots Company
13 Morningside Avenue
Sashay, Ohio

Dear Ms. Johnstone:

I hesitate to write you even before your arrival, but a problem has come up in the controller's department about which you should be informed.

As you know we have just recently overhauled our entire organization and have brought in a number of new people. One of these new people is Ann Smith who has taken over our Putter, Pennsylvania, activities. Ann is a professional who is well suited to our decentralized operations.

About the same time we hired Ann, Fred Ritter, one of our staff members, took over our new performance-analysis staff. This staff operates out of the controller's office.

It is Fred Ritter's responsibility to prepare reports showing budgeted performance, actual performance, and explanations for any differences for both divisions. Fred has staff members who work with each division. These staff members have consulted and are acquainted with each division's line and staff executive personnel.

Until yesterday we thought all was going well. Yesterday afternoon, however, Ann Smith stormed into my office quite unhappy about the whole setup.

I can't recall her exact words, but the gist of her comments indicated that she feels Fred's staff is usurping her responsibilities. She feels that they snoop around asking too many questions and generally waste her staff's time. Ann feels that it is her job to analyze and explain her division's performance.

From your experience, can you think of any reason for Ann's position, and what would you suggest we do, if anything, about her complaint?

Sincerely,

I. M. Thebos
Manager

REQUIRED:

Prepare a memorandum for Johnstone to send to Thebos.

1-30 Role of the Divisional Controller The Arjohn Corporation is a multidivisional firm. Each division has a manager who is responsible for division operations. The controller for each division is assigned to the division by the corporate controller's office. The division controller manages the division's accounting system and provides analysis of financial information for the division management. The division manager evaluates the performance of the division controller and makes recommendations for salary increases and promotions. However, the final responsibility for promotion evaluation and salary increases rests with the corporate controller.

Each division of Arjohn is responsible for product design, sales, pricing, operating costs and expenses, and profits. However, corporate management exercises tight control over the financial operations of the divisions. For example, all capital expenditures above a very modest amount must be approved by corporate management. The method of financial reporting from the division to corporate headquarters provides further evidence of the degree of financial control. The division manager and the division controller submit to corporate headquarters separate and independent commentary of the financial results of the division. The corporate management states that the division controller is there to provide an independent view of the division's operations and not as a spy.

REQUIRED:

a. Discuss the concept of line, staff, and functional reporting using the facts presented in the question as examples of each.

b. Arjohn Corporation's dual reporting systems for divisions may create problems for the division controller.

  1. Identify and discuss the factors that make the division controller's role difficult in this type of situation.

  2. Discuss the effect of the dual reporting relationship on the motivation of the division controller. (*CMA adapted*)

1-31 Financial Objectives, Operating Strategy, and Cost Accounting Quaker Oats Company is a worldwide marketer of consumer products and services, whose principal businesses (grocery products and toys) account for over 90 percent of its sales. In the geographic markets in which it competes, Quaker is a major producer of cereals, mixes, syrup, corn products, edible oils, and pet foods. Through its Fisher-Price Division, Quaker is also one of the world's leading toy makers. Other businesses include specialty chemicals, specialty retailing and mail order marketing companies, and electronic games. The company has plant facilities in many states in the United States, as well as Western Europe, Canada, Latin America, Australia, and Taiwan.

The operations review discussion in an annual report of Quaker Oats included the following list of financial objectives and operating strategies:

FINANCIAL OBJECTIVES	*OPERATING STRATEGIES*
1. Achieve "real" earnings growth (after inflation, as measured by the GNP deflator) averaging 5 percent per year over time.	1. Be a leading supplier of strong consumer brands of goods and services.
2. Improve return on equity over time to 19 to 20 percent.	2. Continue to support growth in Quaker's largest and most profitable businesses—worldwide grocery products and worldwide toys.

3. Increase Quaker's dividend (our shareholders' current return) at a rate which is at least consistent with the growth in earnings and recognizes the impact of inflation.

4. Maintain a strong financial position as represented by Quaker's current strong bond and commercial paper ratings.

3. Improve profitability of low-return businesses.

4. Establish a new line of business beyond grocery and toys, participating in markets benefitting from favorable demographic and life-style trends, which could amount to approximately 20 percent of Quaker's portfolio by the end of the decade.

In addition to a review of this year's results for each of our businesses, this year's operations review section focuses on the opportunities to achieve real growth. The charts attempt to demonstrate the dynamics favoring real earnings growth in our major lines of business in support of our first financial objective.

REQUIRED:

How can cost accounting help Quaker Oats accomplish its financial objectives and operating strategies?

1-32 Quality Control; Ethical Behavior   FulRange Inc. produces complex printed circuits for stereo amplifiers. The circuits are sold primarily to major component manufacturers, and any production overruns are sold to small manufacturers at a substantial discount. The small manufacturer market segment appears very profitable because the basic operating budget assigns all fixed expenses to production for the major manufacturers, the only predictable market.

A common product defect that occurs in production is a "drift" that is caused by failure to maintain precise heat levels during the production process. Rejects from the 100 percent testing program can be reworked to acceptable levels if the defect is drift. However, in a recent analysis of customer complaints, Scott Richardson, the cost accountant, and the quality control engineer have ascertained that normal rework does not bring the circuits up to standard. Sampling shows that about one-half of the reworked circuits will fail after extended, high-volume amplifier operation. The incidence of failure in the reworked circuits is projected to be about 10 percent over one to five years' operation.

Unfortunately, there is no way to determine which reworked circuits will fail because testing does not detect this problem. The rework process could be changed to correct the problem, but the cost-benefit analysis for the suggested change in the rework process indicates that it is not feasible. FulRange's marketing analyst has indicated that if the problem is not corrected it will significantly affect the company's reputation and customer satisfaction. Consequently, the board of directors would interpret this problem as having serious negative implications on the company's profitability.

Richardson has included the circuit failure and rework problem in his report that has been prepared for the upcoming quarterly meeting of the board of directors. Due to the potential adverse economic impact, Richardson has followed a long-standing practice of highlighting this information.

After reviewing the reports to be presented, the plant manager and his staff are upset and indicate to the controller that he should control his people better. "We can't upset the board with this kind of material. Tell Richardson to tone that down. Maybe we can get it by this meeting and have some time to work on it. People that buy those cheap systems and play them that loud shouldn't expect them to last forever."

The controller calls Richardson into his office and says, "Scott, you'll have to bury this one. The probable failure of reworks can be referred to briefly in the oral presentation, but it should not be mentioned or highlighted in the advance material mailed to the board."

Richardson feels strongly that the board will be misinformed on a potentially serious loss of income if he follows the controller's orders. Richardson discusses the problem with the quality control engineer, who simply remarks, "That's your problem, Scott."

REQUIRED:

a. Discuss the ethical considerations that Scott Richardson should recognize in deciding how to proceed in this matter.

b. Explain what ethical responsibilities should be accepted in this situation by the

1. Controller

2. Quality control engineer

3. Plant manager and his staff

c. What should Scott Richardson do in this situation? Explain your answer. (*CMA adapted*)

1-33 Ethical Code for Managerial Accountants Kristin Leigh, corporate controller for Wuster Company, is concerned because her company has no code of professional ethics for the management accountants. Based on her reading, she believes that a code of professional ethics should be established for the management accountants at Wuster Company. The steps she intends to follow in developing such a code are as follows:

- Review the role of the managerial accounting function within the company.

- Determine the objectives of such a code and what it would accomplish.

- Establish general ethical standards classified according to the nature of the obligations of managerial accounting.

- Review specific situations in order to develop guidelines that would enable management accountants to interpret and apply ethical standards.

REQUIRED:

a. Formulate a statement of objectives for a code of professional ethics, including an identification of expected company benefits from such a code, which Kristin Leigh would be likely to present in order to justify establishing such a code for Wuster Company's management accountants.

b. Three activities are considered a normal part of managerial accounting responsibility:

- Preparation of quarterly financial statements for distribution to external parties (such as stockholders and lending institutions).

- Approval for payment of corporate employees' expense reimbursements.

- Accumulation and reporting of cost data for a nonrecurring decision such as a special order of raw materials.

For each of the three activities presented above,

    1. Describe a specific ethical situation that might arise in relation to the activity.

    2. Identify and prepare a specific provision that would appear in a code of professional ethics for management accountants. (*CMA adapted*)

2

Basic Cost Terms and Concepts

After studying this chapter, you should be able to:

1 Name and define several different kinds of costs.

2 Describe how various definitions and classifications of costs are used for different purposes.

3 Explain how product costs and period costs are treated in manufacturing, retail, and service companies.

4 Define the concept of a relevant cost and be able to determine which costs are relevant to a particular decision.

*M*anagers in organizations seek answers to many questions. Which products should be manufactured and sold? What services should be provided? How many units of each product should be produced and marketed? What prices should be set? Should the organization manufacture a component or acquire it from an outside supplier? How can costs be controlled? Should the organization provide a particular service or hire an outside contractor? Would it be wise to obtain new, improved equipment? Should the manufacturing process be changed? Should the marketing approach for the product or service be changed? All these questions require reasonable measures of cost to be answered correctly. This chapter defines several types and classifications of costs that are used throughout the book. These cost terms constitute a large part of the language of cost accounting.

Different Costs for Different Purposes

Managers use different cost classifications for different purposes, and data recorded and classified to achieve one objective may not be appropriate for other objectives. For example, data accumulated to measure income and financial position may not be useful in cost control, motivating managers toward organizational goals, or providing data for decision making. Understanding how costs are classified for specific purposes makes it easier to reclassify them for other purposes.

Cost Classifications

Management accountants classify costs in many different ways. Some important classifications are listed in Exhibit 2-1, and each is defined, discussed, and illustrated in the following sections.

Management accountants do not use every one of the above classifications each time cost accumulation is necessary. In fact, it would not be desirable to do so. Management accounting systems are both flexible and a ready source of cost data. However, analysis and rearrangement of the data using these classifications generally are necessary for specific decisions. In some cases, cost data that might be useful for decision purposes are not currently gathered and processed by the organization's management-accounting system. When this is true, a study of the costs and benefits of obtaining and processing the desired cost data should be undertaken. An implication of this recommendation is that the costs and benefits of data currently gathered and processed by the management-accounting system also should be reviewed periodi-

---

EXHIBIT 2-1
Cost Classifications

Cost Classification	Basis for Classification
Fixed cost, variable cost	Cost behavior (relationship between total cost and activity)
Direct cost, indirect cost	Traceability
Controllable cost, uncontrollable cost	Whether or not the specified subunit can control or significantly influence the cost
Manufacturing costs, marketing costs, administrative costs, merchandise costs, costs of producing a service	Functional characteristics of the costs
Direct material, direct labor, manufacturing overhead	Types of manufacturing costs
Product costs, period costs	Timing of recognition
Opportunity cost, sunk cost, incremental cost, marginal cost	Economic characteristics of costs
Average cost	
Relevant costs	Decision for which the costs will be used

---

cally. Such a review may reveal that some of the information currently being produced is not needed by management. Eliminating such data can reduce the costs of information production. Moreover, additional savings may result because managers do not have to spend their time reviewing and analyzing unnecessary information. The following example from the Dow Chemical Company illustrates this scenario.

Costs and Benefits of Information at the Dow Chemical Company

The controller for the Dow Chemical Company had the feeling that the company was producing more internal accounting information than managers could use. The company was currently producing a complete set of financial statements on a monthly basis for managers at all levels in the company. By the eighth working day following the close of business of the previous month, the controller's office had prepared financial statements combining the latest results from the company's more than 200 foreign and domestic subsidiaries. "Great pride was taken in being able to compress and integrate the accounting closing cycle to the point that management could feel the pulse of current operations."

Following his instincts, the controller conducted an extensive review of how the monthly information was being used and by whom. The controller knew that with each increase in the speed of generating monthly accounting reports, "more time was being devoted to analysis of the data; but he questioned whether too much analysis was taking place. Were better decisions being made as a result of the faster information flow? Was the flow of information the most efficient?" Should less frequent internal accounting reports be considered? If so, what about quarterly, rather than monthly reports?

This review revealed that a great deal of unnecessary reports were being generated and, as a result, much valuable management time was being lost on reading and responding to the reports. (Some people have called this phenomenon *paralysis by analysis*.) It became apparent that the company's management could perform its function just as effectively with quarterly reporting. The reporting cycle was changed, and considerable savings were achieved in information production and managerial analysis. The company recently reviewed its decision to change to less frequent reporting, and the decision was reaffirmed by top management.[1]

Cost Behavior: The Relationship Between Cost and Activity

It is often useful to classify costs according to how they vary in relation to changes in activity levels. *Activity* refers to the number of units of the organization's product or service that are produced. The terms *fixed* and *variable* are generally used to describe how a cost reacts to changes in activity. A **fixed cost** does not change in total when the volume of activity changes. The graph of a fixed cost is shown in Exhibit 2-2 (Panel *a*). A **variable cost,** on the other hand, does change proportionately with changes in activity. Thus, total variable cost increases as activity increases. A variable cost is graphed in Exhibit 2-2 (Panel *b*). A **semivariable cost** has both a fixed and a variable component. This cost behavior pattern is graphed in Exhibit 2-2 (Panel *c*). A **step-fixed cost** is constant in total over a given range of activity, but the total cost increases with any further increase in activity. Thereafter, the cost remains constant in total over a different range of activity. A step-fixed cost is graphed in Exhibit 2-2 (Panel *d*). In specifying cost behavior, the managerial accountant often limits the description to a specific range of activity. This is called the **relevant range.**

A fixed cost that may be eliminated under some circumstances is termed an *avoidable fixed cost.* For example, if an organization ceases to exist or its activities are scaled down, fixed costs associated with some staff functions may be avoidable.

Sometimes the terms *avoidable* and *unavoidable* are used in place of the words *variable* and *fixed,* respectively, but these terms are better used to describe costs associated with particular decisions. For example, the salary of an additional supervisor may be avoidable if the supervisor has not yet been hired. Once the supervisor is hired, however, the supervisor's salary is fixed regardless of the level of activity (assuming that the supervisor is paid even if there is a decrease in activity). Faced with a decrease in activity, the firm has the option of not replacing the next supervisor that leaves the organization. The term *variable cost* should not be used interchangeably with *avoidable cost* because a fixed cost also may be avoidable over some time period. An avoidable fixed cost is graphed in Exhibit 2-3.

1. Dennis Dankoski, "Dow Opts for Less — and Gains," *Management Accounting* (June 1986): 56, 57.

EXHIBIT 2-2

Cost Behavior

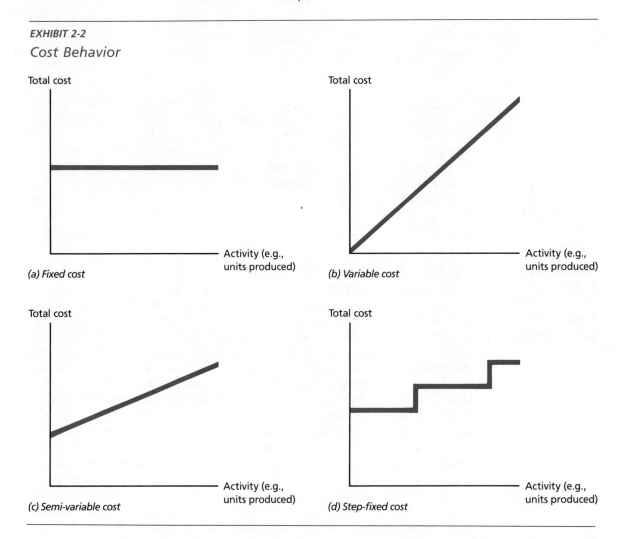

(a) Fixed cost

(b) Variable cost

(c) Semi-variable cost

(d) Step-fixed cost

Examples of each type of cost behavior defined above are given in Exhibit 2-4. Assign each cost item in Exhibit 2-4 to the associated graph displayed in Exhibit 2-2.

Organizations frequently find it useful to compute costs on a unit basis rather than in total. Unit costs are often used in pricing and other decisions. Exhibit 2-5 shows the cost per unit for a fixed cost and for a variable cost. Panel *a* of Exhibit 2-5 displays the amount of fixed cost incurred per unit of production, as production volume increases. Thus, as more and more units are produced, the constant fixed cost (shown in Panel *a* of Exhibit 2-2) is divided by a larger and larger denominator. This yields a fixed cost per unit that decreases as production volume increases.

The unit cost curve for a fixed cost requires careful interpretation because total cost does not change with respect to the number of units produced. If a cost is fixed,

EXHIBIT 2-3

Avoidable Fixed Cost

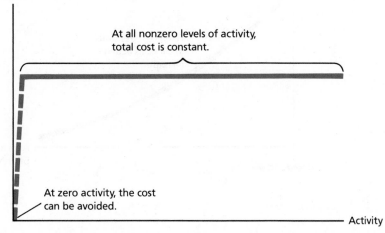

Cost

At all nonzero levels of activity, total cost is constant.

At zero activity, the cost can be avoided.

Activity

EXHIBIT 2-4

Examples of Cost Behavior

Cost Item	Activity Measure	Type of Cost Behavior
Salary of the administrative staff of a Sears store	Merchandise sold	Fixed
Cost of sheet metal used in manufacturing automobiles at a Chrysler Motors Corporation plant	Automobiles produced	Variable
Cost of telephone service at Mayo Clinic in Rochester, Minnesota	Telephone calls made	Semi-variable (fixed monthly service charge plus costs incurred per call)
Total cost of compensating dining room personnel in the restaurant at a Holiday Inn	Food and beverages sold	Step-fixed (Personnel are paid fixed salaries; number of personnel on duty depends on anticipated range of activity.)

SEARS

Chrysler

mayo

Holiday Inn

EXHIBIT 2-5

Fixed and Variable Cost per Unit

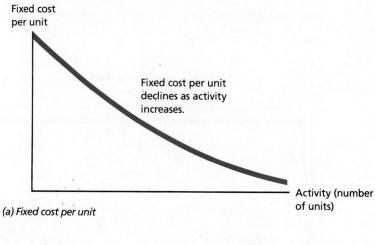

(a) Fixed cost per unit

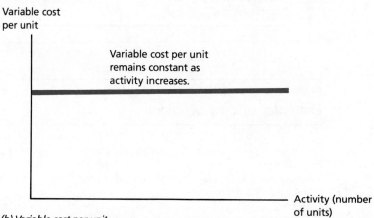

(b) Variable cost per unit

	Total cost	Cost per unit
Variable cost	Increases with an increase in activity	Constant
Fixed cost	Constant	Decreases with an increase in activity

(c) Comparison of fixed and variable costs

the cost of one more unit is zero. The graph of total fixed cost in Exhibit 2-2 (Panel *a*) suggests this conclusion.

In contrast, for a variable cost, the cost per unit is equal to the cost of one more unit. This is because the cost per unit is a constant, as shown in Exhibit 2-5 (Panel *b*). The graph in Exhibit 2-2 (Panel *b*) also indicates this result because the slope is constant.

The appropriate graph of a cost depends on whether the information desired by the manager relates to unit costs or total costs. The wrong graph can confuse rather than clarify the behavior of costs.

Responsibility and Traceability

In attempting to control costs, managers want to know who incurs costs and where they are incurred. Hence costs are classified by units of activity or responsibility, which provides the basis for cost control. **Responsibility accounting** is the process of identifying organizational units of activity or responsibility (such as strategic business units, departments, segments, or divisions), tracing costs (and sometimes revenues) to these units, and assigning responsibility for decisions and outcomes. For example, the costs incurred in a department store are traced to individual departments, such as Sporting Goods and Housewares.

In addition to tracing costs to the organization's departments for the purpose of responsibility accounting, managerial accountants also trace costs to specific units of product or service. Such tracing of costs is called *product costing*. A **cost objective** is the entity (either a department or a unit of product or service) to which costs are assigned. The relationship between these cost objectives is depicted in Exhibit 2-6.

A cost that can be traced to a specific cost objective is called a **direct cost,** with respect to that cost objective. A cost that cannot be traced to a particular cost objective is called an **indirect cost,** with respect to that cost objective. For example,

EXHIBIT 2-6
Tracing Objectives

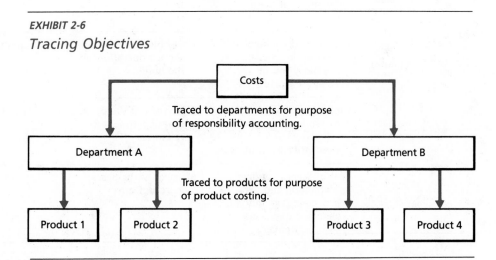

the cost of the materials in the car and the wages of those who assemble it are direct costs of manufacturing. Alternatively, the president's salary and the rental expense on the plant cannot be traced to a specific car or production lot and are considered indirect.

In addition to tracing a cost to one or more cost objectives, management accountants classify costs by the degree to which they can be influenced by specific managers. **Controllable costs** are those that result directly from decisions that particular managers make or influence. The costs of raw materials, labor, and variable manufacturing costs are often considered controllable by the managers of production departments.

The idea that managers should be held accountable only for those costs they can control is appealing. Individuals typically do not believe they should be held responsible for something they cannot control. In large organizations, however, few costs are entirely controlled by any one manager. The costs resulting from many decisions are affected by several different departments and by several managers.

Exhibit 2-7 provides examples of direct, indirect, controllable, and uncontrollable costs.

EXHIBIT 2-7

Responsibility for and Traceability of Costs

	Cost Item	Cost Objective or Subunit Manager	Type of Cost
DELTA	Cost of the pilot's salary on Delta Air Lines' Atlanta to St. Louis route	Cost objective: route from Atlanta to St. Louis	Direct cost
Holiday Inn	Cost of landscaping and grounds maintenance at a Holiday Inn in Orlando, Florida	Cost objective: the food service operations in the hotel	Indirect cost
HEWLETT PACKARD	Cost of raw material used to produce hand-held calculators at a Hewlett-Packard plant	Supervisor of the production department for calculators	Controllable cost
SEARS	Cost of Sears's national accounting and data processing operation allocated to a Sears store in Denver	Manager of the Sears store in Denver	Uncontrollable cost

Functional Characteristics of Costs

Functional cost classification refers to the functional area of the organization in which the costs are incurred. Several broad functional categories are used in most organizations:

   1. Administrative cost.   Cost of running the organization. Includes such costs as top management salaries, accounting, data processing, personnel, and employee training.

   2. Marketing (or selling) cost.   Cost of marketing the organization's product or service. Includes such costs as salaries and commissions of sales personnel, depreciation on company-owned cars used by sales personnel, advertising and promotion of the organization's product or service.

   3. Merchandise cost.   Cost of acquiring merchandise for resale in a merchandising firm (both retailers and wholesalers). Includes the purchase cost of the merchandise plus transportation and handling costs.

   4. Manufacturing cost.   Cost of manufacturing a product for resale. Manufacturing costs are considered in detail in the next section.

   5. Cost of service production.   Cost of producing a service such as air transportation, equipment rental, insurance, hotel accommodations, or food and beverage service.

Manufacturing Firms   Manufacturing firms generally classify production costs into three categories:

   1. Direct material.   Raw material that is physically incorporated into the manufactured product. The steel used in a General Motors car, the wiring in an RCA television, and the fabric in an Arrow shirt are examples of direct materials.

   2. Direct labor.   The cost of personnel (including wages, salaries, bonuses, and fringe benefits) who work directly on the manufactured product. Examples include wages of workers who assemble Zenith stereos, of U.S. Steel workers who operate the blast furnaces, and of personnel who assemble Toyota automobiles.

   3. Overhead (or burden).   All other costs of manufacturing. Includes three elements:

   a. *Indirect material.*   The cost of materials of two types: (1) materials that are consumed in production but are not physically incorporated in the product (such as the cost of lathe blades in a Pennsylvania House furniture plant); (2) the cost of minor materials, even if they are physically incorporated in the product (such as glue, some paints and laquers, small amounts of wire).

   b. *Indirect labor.*   The cost of compensating employees who are necessary for production, but do not work directly on the product. For example, the wages of security personnel at a Dow Chemical plant and the wages of custodial personnel at a Standard Oil Company refinery are indirect labor costs.

c. *Other manufacturing costs.*   All other manufacturing costs, including depreciation of plant and manufacturing equipment, utilities such as natural gas and electricity, property taxes, and insurance on plant and equipment. Also includes service department costs, such as costs incurred in the maintenance department or the engineering department.

Manufacturing costs also include *prime cost,* such as direct material and direct labor, and *conversion cost,* which is direct labor plus overhead.

Service Industry Firms   The three production cost categories used in manufacturing firms are less widely used in service industry firms, but the same classifications can be applied. In a hotel business, for example, the salaries of employees who have direct contact with hotel guests can be classified as direct-labor costs. Examples include the front desk personnel and table service employees in the hotel's restaurant. The labor costs of employees such as custodians, cooks, and landscape personnel are classified as indirect-labor costs. Direct materials in a hotel business include food and beverages consumed and hotel stationery used by guests. Materials such as soap used to wash dishes in the kitchen are indirect materials. Hotel overhead costs include energy costs and the costs of maintaining the hotel's elevator, air-conditioning system, and swimming pool. Thus, the various cost categories described above can be useful in classifying costs in nonmanufacturing organizations also.

Computer-Integrated Manufacturing: Changing Cost Structure

The introduction of computer-integrated manufacturing (CIM) systems has important implications for the cost structure of a manufacturing firm. The *cost structure* refers to the relative proportions of different types of costs incurred by the firm. Thus, a manufacturer using a CIM system still incurs direct material, direct labor, and manufacturing overhead costs, but the relative proportions of these costs are different from those in other firms. A highly automated factory has a much lower proportion of direct labor costs relative to other manufacturing costs. Moreover, the labor costs that are incurred are associated with different kinds of employees. For example, a CIM system requires highly skilled computer programmers, computer systems experts, and computer maintenance technicians, rather than drill-press operators and manual laborers. Manufacturing overhead costs typically are much higher when a CIM system is used. Depreciation and maintenance of sophisticated industrial robots and the computers that control them are examples of the overhead costs associated with CIM.

Product Costs, Period Costs, and Expenses

The terms *product cost* and *period cost* describe the point in time when costs incurred to acquire assets or services are recognized as expenses. A **product cost** is a cost that is identified with goods manufactured or purchased for resale. Product costs are used to value the inventory of manufactured products until they are sold, at which time the cost of the units sold is recognized as an expense called *cost of goods sold.*[2] Product costs are also called *inventoriable costs* because these costs are held in

---

2. Expenses are subtracted from revenue to determine the income of a firm.

inventory until the inventory is sold. For example, the labor cost of a production employee at Chrysler Corporation is assigned to the products on which the employee works. These costs remain attached to those products until they are sold. Product costing is discussed in detail in Chapters 4, 5, and 6.

An **expense** is the cost of an asset that has been used up or sold for the purpose of generating revenue; the asset and hence its cost are no longer associated with the organization. When revenue is recognized at the time of sale, the cost of acquiring the goods (which previously have been considered an asset or part of inventory) becomes an expense.[3]

All costs that are not product costs are *period costs*. A **period cost** is identified with a period of time rather than with units of production. Period costs are recognized as expenses during the period of time to which they have been assigned. Some period costs, such as salaries of sales personnel, are assigned to the period during which the costs are actually incurred. Other costs, such as the cost of automobiles assigned to sales and administrative personnel, are incurred at the time the assets are acquired but are then allocated as period costs across several time periods through depreciation expense.

The distinction between product costs and period costs is emphasized in Exhibit 2-8, which displays recent income statements for three companies. These companies are from three very different industries. The Maytag Company is a *manufacturer* of household appliances. F. W. Woolworth Co. is a large *retail* firm with merchandising operations throughout the nation. Delta Air Lines, Inc. represents the *service* industry with flight operations throughout the United States and Europe. Let's examine these three income statements carefully and compare them.

In all three statements, selling, administrative, and general costs are period costs. These costs are assigned to periods of time and expensed during those periods. In the Maytag Company, the costs of manufactured products are stored in inventory as product costs until those products are sold. These product costs then are expensed as "cost of products sold," another term for cost of goods sold.

Product costs in F. W. Woolworth Co. consist of the cost of acquiring merchandise inventory for resale. F. W. Woolworth is a merchandising firm and does not engage in production. The product costs of acquiring merchandise are stored in inventory until the merchandise is sold. Then the costs are expensed as *cost of sales*, another term for cost of goods sold.

Delta Air Lines, Inc. has no inventoried product costs. This firm does engage in productive activity, but the service it produces, air transportation service, is consumed as soon as it is produced. Hence, there are no product costs to inventory. In service-industry firms such as Delta Air Lines, Holiday Inns, Burger King, and Hertz, the costs of producing the firm's service are usually called *operating expenses*. Operating expenses are period costs; they are expensed during the periods to which they are assigned.

---

3. The accounting profession does not universally recognize the distinction between *cost* and *expense* in its terminology. *Cost of goods sold* is used to describe an expense rather than the more exact *expense of goods sold* or *cost of goods sold expense*.

EXHIBIT 2-8

Product Costs and Period Costs in a Manufacturing Company

THE MAYTAG COMPANY

MAYTAG®

The Maytag Company
Statement of Consolidated Income
for a Recent Year

Product Costs and Period Costs
in a Manufacturing Firm

Net sales	$642,560,925
Interest	7,759,202
Miscellaneous	1,459,232
Total revenue and other income	651,779,359
Cost of products sold	421,516,206
Selling, administrative, and general expenses	109,477,912
Interest expense	4,144,684
Total expenses	535,138,802
Income before taxed on income	116,640,557
Federal and state taxes on income	53,500,000
Net income	$ 63,140,557

Product costs

Period costs

Products are manufactured

Product costs are incurred and attached to manufactured products (i.e., inventoried). These costs are carried in work-in-process and finished goods inventories.

Some of the products manufactured in both previous years and the current year are sold in the current year

Product costs attached to manufactured products in both previous years and the current year become an expense of the current year. The expense is called *cost of products sold.*

Previous years

Current year

Period costs assigned to previous years were expensed in previous years.

Period costs assigned to the current year are expensed in the current year.

(continued)

F. W. WOOLWORTH CO.

F. W. Woolworth Co.
Consolidated Statement of Income
for a Recent Year

Revenues:		
Sales, including sales from leased departments	$5,737,000,000	
Other income	26,000,000	
Total sales revenue and other income		5,763,000,000
Costs and expenses:		
Cost of sales	3,853,000,000	
Selling, general, and administrative expenses	1,472,000,000	
Depreciation and amortization	105,000,000	
Interest expense	82,000,000	
		5,512,000,000
Income from continuing operations before income taxes		251,000,000
Income taxes		110,000,000
Net income from continuing operations		141,000,000

Product costs

Period costs

Product Costs and Period Costs in a Retail Firm

Merchandise inventory is purchased.

⇨ Some of the merchandise purchased in both previous years and the current year is sold in the current year

The purchase price plus transportation and handling costs are product costs of the merchandise. These costs are carried as an asset in merchandise inventory.

Product costs attached to merchandise inventory in both previous years and the current year become an expense of the current year. The expense is called *cost of sales*.

Previous years

Current year

Period costs assigned to previous years were expensed in previous years.

Period costs assigned to the current year are expensed in the current year.

(*continued*)

EXHIBIT 2-8 Continued

DELTA AIR LINES, INC.

Delta Air Lines, Inc.
Consolidated Statement of Income
for a Recent Year

Operating revenues:	
Passenger	$4,376,986,000
Cargo	235,199,000
Other, net	71,930,000
Total operating revenues	4,684,115,000
Operating expenses:	
Salaries and related costs	1,856,243,000
Aircraft fuel	892,182,000
Aircraft maintenance materials and repairs	66,022,000
Aircraft rentals	57,090,000
Other rentals	92,839,000
Landing fees	60,908,000
Passenger service	170,163,000
Passenger commissions	350,690,000
Other cash costs	422,840,000
Depreciation and amortization	349,128,000
Total operating expenses	4,318,105,000
Operating income	366,010,000
Other income (expense):	
Interest expense	(84,081,000)
Less interest capitalized	22,028,000
	(62,053,000)
Gain on disposition of flight equipment	94,343,000
Miscellaneous income, net	6,863,000
	39,153,000
Income before income taxes	405,163,000
Income taxes (provided) credited	(186,624,000)
Amortization of investment tax credit	40,914,000
Net income	$ 259,453,000

Period Costs in a
Service Industry Firm

There are no product costs. The company produces a service, air transportation, which is consumed at the time of production.

Previous years ——————— Current year

Period costs assigned to previous years were expensed in previous years.

Period costs assigned to the current year are expensed in the current year.

Schedule of Cost of Goods Manufactured and Sold   Manufacturing firms generally prepare a *schedule of cost of goods manufactured and sold* for the use of management. This schedule is an internal report and generally is not made available to the public. It shows the cost of materials, labor, and overhead incurred during the current year. An example of such a schedule is shown in Exhibit 2-9.

To determine the cost of materials used, the year's beginning balance in materials inventory is added to material purchases for the year, and then the year's ending inventory is subtracted. This yields the cost of materials used during the year.

To the cost of materials used are added the costs of direct labor and manufacturing overhead for the year. The result is the total manufacturing cost incurred for the year.

To determine the cost of products finished during the year, the accountant adds the cost of beginning work-in-process inventory to total manufacturing costs incurred, and then subtracts the cost of ending work-in-process inventory. The result is the cost of goods finished during the year, called *cost of goods manufactured.*

EXHIBIT 2-9

Schedule of Cost of Goods Manufactured and Sold

THE MAYTAG COMPANY
Schedule of Cost of Goods Manufactured and Sold for a Recent Year[a]

Materials and supplies:	
Inventory, January 1	$ 13,146,870
Plus: purchases	xx
Cost of materials and supplies available	xx
Less: inventory, December 31	13,279,764
Cost of materials and supplies used	xx
Direct labor	xx
Manufacturing overhead	xx
Total manufacturing costs incurred	xx
Plus: work-in-process inventory, January 1	32,161,543
Total manufacturing costs to account for	xx
Less: work-in-process inventory, December 31	34,407,438
Cost of goods manufactured	xx
Plus: finished-goods inventory, January 1	30,339,584
Cost of goods available for sale	xx
Less: finished-goods inventory, December 31	29,996,513
Cost of products sold	$421,516,206

[a] This partially completed Schedule of Cost of Goods Manufactured and Sold shows the general format that would be used for such a schedule by a manufacturing firm. The numbers included were taken from the company's annual report. The missing numbers are not available to the public.

To calculate the cost of goods sold, the accountant adds the cost of beginning finished-goods inventory to the cost of goods manufactured and then subtracts the cost of ending finished-goods inventory. The result is cost of goods sold, which is then included on the income statement as an expense. The Maytag Company calls this expense *cost of products sold*.

Exhibit 2-8 focuses on the income statement, but the balance sheets of manufacturers and retailers are also affected by product costs. The Maytag Company and F. W. Woolworth Co. included the following inventory values under current assets on their balance sheets for a recent year. These inventory values are the product costs that have been assigned to the inventories.

THE MAYTAG COMPANY
Inventories from the Current Asset Section of the
Balance Sheet for a Recent Year

Materials and supplies inventory	$13,279,764
Work-in-process inventory	34,407,438
Finished appliances inventory	29,996,513

F. W. WOOLWORTH CO.
Inventory from the Current Asset Section of the
Balance Sheet for a Recent Year

Merchandise inventory	$1,108,000,000

Economic Characteristics of Costs

Management accountants classify costs in many ways. Ideally they like to record costs as relevant or irrelevant to specific decisions. Because this classification depends on the particular decision being made, however, guidance is needed in classifying costs as relevant or irrelevant. The concepts of opportunity cost, sunk cost, and incremental cost provide this guidance.

Opportunity Cost   An **opportunity cost** is the cost of one course of action in terms of the opportunities that are precluded by taking that course of action. This concept is central to the analysis of accounting data and to business decision making. If an asset can be used to perform only one function and cannot be sold or used in other ways, the opportunity cost of that asset is zero. For example, the opportunity cost of using the underground gas line of a gas company in the city of Chicago is zero if the pipe is going to carry either natural gas or nothing. With no alternative opportunity, the use of the pipe has a zero opportunity cost.

A machine used to make ice cream has an opportunity cost if the machine can be sold or if it also can be used to make yogurt. Assume that one period's production of yogurt can be sold for $100,000 and that the costs of yogurt that vary directly with production are $80,000. The period's opportunity cost of not producing yogurt is $20,000 ($100,000 − $80,000). Assuming that producing yogurt is the next best alternative use of the machine, the $20,000 net proceeds that are foregone by producing ice cream instead of yogurt is the opportunity cost of producing ice cream.

Suppose a company can use its manufacturing capacity either to produce a special order for 100,000 units or to rent its capacity to another company for $150,000. The use of the capacity to produce the special order has an opportunity cost of $150,000.

The opportunity-cost concept is extremely useful when deciding on the best use of productive facilities. Yet management accountants generally do not record opportunity costs because these costs generally depend on the alternative uses of the resources or facilities at the time of a particular decision. Because these alternative uses are known fully only at the time a decision is made, it is impossible to record them in advance.

From an economic viewpoint, opportunity costs should be treated as equivalent to out-of-pocket costs. *Out-of-pocket* or *outlay costs* are costs that require the payment of money (or other assets) as a result of their incurrence. Studies by behavioral scientists and economists suggest that individuals tend to pay more attention to outlay costs than to opportunity costs.

Sunk Cost   The term **sunk cost** is frequently used to refer to a cost incurred in the past, such as the acquisition cost of a machine. This acquisition cost, once incurred, is not relevant for subsequent decisions about whether to use or sell the machine because it cannot be altered by any future decision. Suppose a retail clothes store, Midtown Wardrobe Center, purchased 100 pairs of bellbottom pants for $20 per pair (total cost of $2,000). Ten pairs of pants were sold at $35 per pair, and suddenly bellbottoms went out of style. When the owner exclaimed, "How am I going to get my money back for these blasted pants?," a salesperson suggested charging only $15 per pair for the pants. The owner screamed, "What? And lose $5 per pair? Never!" The owner will lose money on his initial investment if they are sold for $15 per pair. However, the initial cost of the pants is a sunk cost; it is not relevant for decisions about how much should be charged for the pants now. What is relevant in this situation is that only a few individuals (who aren't concerned with looking fashionable) will buy the bellbottoms now and only if they can be purchased at a reduced price. The owner should heed the salesperson's advice or risk having 90 pairs of obsolete pants in stock forever. Except for the fashion knowledge gained, the owner should not consider the initial purchase when pricing the pants.

In spite of these economic considerations, there are several situations in which managers may be motivated to justify past losses or costs. Under responsibility accounting systems, managers are held responsible for actual outcomes. The prospects of negative consequences from previous actions may lead managers to try to justify those decisions, especially if there is a perceived need to demonstrate competence to themselves or others.

Incremental Cost   The **incremental cost** of an action is the additional cost that is incurred when the action is taken, assuming that all other activities of the organization remain the same. For example, the additional cost incurred by Hertz when one more car rental facility is opened in Boston, assuming that all other activities of the firm remain the same, is the incremental cost of the new rental facility. Consider the additional cost incurred by General Motors when it accepts a special order to sell five hundred vehicles to the U.S. government. This cost is the incremental cost of the special order, assuming that General Motors' other activities are unaffected.

Incremental cost differs from **marginal cost,** which is the cost of producing one more unit during a specified time period. Suppose, for example, that IBM produced one hundred computers of a particular type during a one-month period. The cost of manufacturing one additional computer during that period is the marginal cost.

The term *differential cost* sometimes is used to refer to the difference in the cost between two alternatives. If the cost of action A is $150 and the cost of action B is $400, the differential cost is $250 ($400 − $150).

Relevant Costs

Accountants specify the correct cost in any particular business situation by saying that the *relevant* cost is required. Unfortunately, different costs are relevant for different purposes.

To illustrate costs relevant for specific decisions, consider the situation faced by Tompco Products, Inc., which has recently received an order for an industrial chemical it does not normally produce. Tompco has sufficient capacity to fill this one-time order, and its managers wish to accept the special order if the order's cost is less than the price the firm has been offered. To assist them in making this decision, they have asked the controller to estimate the order's relevant cost with regard to each of the following items:

1. ***The order requires 10,000 pounds of TSX.***   Tompco recently ceased production of its only product requiring TSX but still has some on hand. The best offer for its remaining supply of 15,000 pounds is $30,000. Inventory records reflect an average acquisition cost of $4.00 per pound. The purchasing department manager estimates that 10,000 pounds of TSX can be purchased on the open market for $4.80 per pound.

What economic sacrifice will Tompco incur if it uses 10,000 pounds of TSX for the special order? Is the relevant cost $2.00 per pound, $3.00 per pound, $4.00 per pound, $4.80 per pound, or some other amount? What assumptions underlie the choice of a relevant cost for TSX?

The market price of $4.80 per pound is relevant if Tompco intends to replace the 10,000 pounds to be used in this order, but the facts indicate that TSX is no longer needed and the material used will not be replaced. As a result, the replacement cost of $4.80 per pound is not relevant to this situation.

The inventory cost of $4.00 per pound reflects past acquisition costs that will not change because of a decision about the special order. This inventory cost is a sunk cost but will be charged to cost of goods sold for financial statement purposes if the order is accepted.[4]

The "best offer" of $2.00 per pound ($30,000/15,000 pounds) reflects the opportunity cost of foregoing the option of selling the TSX. The opportunity cost is the relevant cost in measuring Tompco's economic sacrifice resulting from the use of TSX to produce the special order, assuming the other 5,000 pounds not needed in the order can be sold. If Tompco can sell the remaining 5,000 pounds at $2.00 per pound, the total relevant cost of the TSX used for the special order is $20,000 (10,000 pounds × $2.00). If Tompco cannot sell the remaining 5,000 pounds (because its only buyer wants either 15,000 pounds or none), the total relevant cost of the TSX is $30,000, since that is the total revenue foregone by completing the special order.

Relevant cost of
TSX
{
$2.00 × 10,000 pounds — $20,000, if the remaining 5,000 pounds can be sold

Entire bid price for 15,000 pounds of TSX — $30,000, if the remaining 5,000 pounds cannot be sold
}

2. **The special order requires 20,000 gallons of TA-1000, which is used regularly by Tompco.** Currently, 50,000 gallons are in stock. The average inventory cost is $2.50 per gallon. The purchasing manager estimates that if the special order is accepted, the company will be forced to place its next regular order for 100,000 gallons of TA-1000 one month earlier than expected. (Smaller orders are not feasible.) Seasonal patterns in the price of TA-1000 are expected to result in a minimum price of $2.20 per gallon at the regular order point. An earlier order will result in a price of $2.40 per gallon. Future orders can be placed on the previous schedule. Storage and carrying costs of inventory are expected to be $0.04 per month on each dollar of inventory, and order costs (preparation, receiving, and inspection) are expected to amount to $5,000 per order.

What economic sacrifice will Tompco incur if it uses 20,000 gallons of TA-1000 for this special order? The facts suggest that TA-1000 has to be replaced if it is used for this order. Therefore, the relevant cost is the incremental cost of the additional

---

4. The difference between the inventory cost of $4.00 per pound and the best offer of $2.00 per pound ($30,000/15,000 pounds) is a loss that has already been incurred and not a cost of this special order.

20,000 gallons. The average inventory cost of $2.50 per gallon will be charged to cost of goods sold if the order is accepted. Tompco will have to incur a cost of $2.40 per gallon, instead of $2.20 per gallon, and will have to hold the extra gallons for an additional month if the order is accepted. The replacement cost is relevant in this case. The relevant cost of TA-1000 is as follows:

Cost of TA-1000 used:	
$2.40 × 20,000 gallons	$48,000
Additional cost of extra gallons ordered:	
($2.40 − $2.20) × 80,000 gallons	16,000
Cost of carrying extra gallons:	
$0.04 × $2.40 × 80,000 gallons	7,680
Incremental cost of TA-1000	$71,680

The order cost is not an incremental cost because no additional orders will be processed.[5] Instead, the next regular order will be processed a month earlier.[6]

The decision faced by Tompco Products illustrates how situation-specific the relevant cost of a productive input can be. The relevant cost of TSX is an opportunity cost; this cost is measured by the amount that Tompco would forego if the order is accepted. The relevant cost of TA-1000 is an incremental cost; this cost is the amount by which total cost would increase if the order is accepted.

Summary

Not all cost classifications are relevant for every decision. The concept of a relevant cost is an important reminder that costs are measured depending on how those costs will be used.

Accountants classify costs in several ways. Classifications based on cost behavior include fixed, variable, semivariable, and step-fixed costs. Costs that are traceable to a particular cost objective are called direct costs. Costs that are not traceable to a cost objective are indirect costs. Controllable and uncontrollable costs are classifications used to indicate the extent to which a manager is able to influence costs. Accountants also classify costs according to their functional characteristics. Common classifications include administrative, marketing, merchandise, manufacturing and service production costs. Manufacturing costs are classified further into direct material, direct labor, and overhead. Product costs are stored in inventory until the related goods are sold, whereas period costs are assigned to a time period and expensed immediately. Economic characteristics of costs also provide an important basis for classification. Accountants help managers make decisions by identifying opportunity costs, sunk costs, and incremental costs.

5. However, any cost of incurring the regular order cost one month earlier than normal should be included as an incremental cost of this order. One such cost is the lost interest on $5,000 for one month. At a 10 percent interest rate, this amounts to about $42, a minor factor.

6. In this case, if it is possible to buy 20,000 gallons on the market it would be best to do so, since 20,000 (2.40) + 5,000 = 53,000, which is less than $71,680.

The cost classifications discussed in this chapter do not imply that business decisions can be made using only management accounting data. Information from management accounting systems can help managers make decisions but does not replace judgment. Managers often must look beyond the accounting information and analysis to choose the best course of action.

For many purposes it is useful to assign costs to the products and services that an organization produces. Product and service costing is the subject of Chapters 4, 5, and 6.

Key Terms to Review

controllable cost, p. 36	period cost, p. 39
cost objective, p. 35	product cost, p. 38
direct cost, p. 35	relevant range, p. 31
expense, p. 39	responsibility accounting, p. 35
fixed cost, p. 31	semivariable cost, p. 31
incremental cost, p. 45	step-fixed cost, p. 31
indirect cost, p. 35	sunk cost, p. 45
marginal cost, p. 46	variable cost, p. 31
opportunity cost, p. 44	

Review Problem

Listed below are various costs incurred by Niagra Tire Company. For each cost, indicate which of the following terms best describes that cost. More than one cost term may apply to the same cost item.

Cost Terms

a. Product cost
b. Period cost
c. Variable cost
d. Fixed cost
e. Semivariable cost
f. Step-fixed cost
g. Direct material
h. Direct labor
i. Manufacturing overhead
j. Opportunity cost
k. Sunk cost

Cost Items

1. Depreciation on the cars used by sales personnel

2. Rubber used in the tires

3. Wages of factory employees

4. Cost of purchasing new robotic production equipment two years ago

5. Cost of telephone service in the company president's office, which includes a flat monthly fee plus a charge for each phone call.

6. Cost of supervisory personnel (one production supervisor for each eight-hour shift)

7. Cost of renting space in a nearby warehouse (incurred when part of the factory building was taken over by the sales department)

Solution to Review Problem

1. b   5. b, e

2. a, g   6. a, f

3. a, h   7. j*

4. k

Suggested Readings

Black, H. A., and J. D. Edwards, eds. *The Managerial and Cost Accountant's Handbook.* Homewood, Ill.: Dow-Jones-Irwin, 1979.

Colvin, G. "Federal Express Dives into Air Mail." *Fortune* (June 15, 1981): 106–108.

Govindarajan, V., and R. N. Anthony. "How Firms Use Cost Data in Price Decisions." *Management Accounting* (July 1983): 30–36.

Hartman, B. P. "The Management Accountant's Role in Deleting a Product Line." *Management Accounting* (August 1983): 63–66.

Kaplan, R. and A. Atkinson. *Advanced Management Accounting,* 2d ed. Englewood Cliffs, N.J.: Prentice-Hall, 1989.

Magee, R. P. *Advanced Managerial Accounting.* New York: Harper & Row, 1986.

Sias, R. "Pricing Bank Services." *Management Accounting* (July 1985): 48–49.

Review Questions

2-1 Is the cost of a commuter airline pilot's salary a direct or indirect cost of the airline's operations in Atlanta? Why?

2-2 Are the following costs incurred in a pizza business variable, fixed, semivariable, or step-fixed?

a. Cost of pepperoni

b. Monthly cost of renting a vacant lot for overflow parking across the street

c. Labor cost of personnel to serve tables

d. Cost of telephone service

---

* The warehouse rental cost is the opportunity cost associated with using the factory space for the sales department instead of storage.

2-3 Discuss some basic differences among manufacturing, merchandising, and service companies.

2-4 Would the cost terms and concepts defined in this chapter be applicable in not-for-profit organizations such as the American Red Cross or New York City? Why?

2-5 Explain why the fixed cost per unit graphed in Exhibit 2-5 declines as volume increases. Give an example.

2-6 Why is cost of goods sold called an expense on the income statement of a television manufacturer?

2-7 List some costs that might be part of the incremental cost incurred when a bank adds automatic-teller services.

2-8 Give examples of variable overhead costs and fixed overhead costs.

2-9 List and give examples of types of manufacturing costs in a tennis racket factory.

2-10 Define the terms *prime cost* and *conversion cost.*

2-11 The new president of an insurance company remarked to the controller, "From now on, I want your department to collect only relevant costs. Forget about the others." Comment on this remark.

2-12 Assume a situation where you can hire workers when you need them but you cannot fire them when they are not needed, except at a very large cost. How would this information affect decision making?

2-13 It is difficult for a firm to classify its costs separately as fixed or variable, but it can be done. As an illustration, divide the costs of owning and operating an automobile into fixed and variable classifications.

2-14 Consider education as a product. What are the direct and the indirect costs to a university of educating a student?

2-15 The concept of opportunity cost is important to decision making. Discuss the following:

  a. Deciding how space in a department store is to be used.

  b. Deciding how much salary to offer a college graduate being considered for employment.

  c. The importance of the reserve clause to professional baseball (a ballplayer plays only for the team he has signed with or he does not play).

  d. The decision of a student to obtain a college degree.

2-16 The president of the Aeros Company in an effort to find out why profits were down, closely inspected the variable costs incurred and compared the actual costs incurred with the costs that should have been incurred at the actual level of operations. He ignored the fixed-cost classification because fixed costs are "fixed." Discuss.

Exercises

2-17 Opportunity Costs of Ordering Inventory   The demand for a product can be 1 or 2 units. If one unit is ordered and the demand is one unit, the profit will be 10. If two units are ordered, and demand is two units, profit will be 20. If one too many or one too few units are ordered, the profit will be 5.

REQUIRED:

a. Assuming that one unit is ordered, what is the opportunity cost if demand is two units?

b. If two units are ordered and demand is two units, what is the opportunity cost?

c. What additional information would be useful in making this ordering decision?

2-18 Sunk Costs   The New York Oil Company has just bought 1 million barrels of oil. The vice president of production argues that the cost of the oil is a sunk cost and thus not relevant to any decision the company faces. The president of the firm realizes that the cost of his pipelines is a sunk cost but finds it difficult to consider his inventory to be sunk.

REQUIRED:

As an outside consultant, write a memorandum to the president expressing an opinion about this issue.

2-19 Finding Missing Amounts   Fill in the missing amounts in the following list of figures from a manufacturing company's records.

	Case I	Case II
Direct-material inventory, December 31, 19X3	$ 2,100	$ a
Direct-material inventory, January 1, 19X3	3,000	4,200
Direct-material purchases during 19X3	a	20,000
Cost of direct materials used during 19X3	42,900	22,800
Direct labor incurred during 19X3	21,700	70,000
Indirect labor incurred during 19X3	11,200	b
Indirect materials used during 19X3	2,100	9,000
Other manufacturing overhead incurred during 19X3	b	7,100
Total manufacturing costs incurred during 19X3	80,100	119,100
Work-in-process inventory, January 1, 19X3	2,900	11,400
Work-in-process inventory, December 3, 19X3	c	11,700
Cost of goods manufactured	69,000	c
Finished-goods inventory, January 1, 19X3	21,000	12,000
Finished-goods inventory, December 31, 19X3	11,500	8,500
Cost of goods available for sale	d	130,800
Cost of goods sold	78,500	d

2-20 Relevant Costs for Different Decisions   The salary of the president of a firm is usually considered a fixed cost. Is it a relevant cost when pricing the product for sale to the government? Is it a relevant cost in a decision to sell the company? Explain.

2-21 Controllable and Noncontrollable Costs Within an Organization Certain costs are controllable and others are uncontrollable. This is a meaningless statement unless we define the segment of the organization that is being discussed. Explain.

2-22 Salaries as Fixed Costs The Miner Company is considering eliminating an outlying plant. The elimination would result in increased efficiency because of savings in transportation of material and parts. The present plant, which is 40 miles from the main plant, would be replaced by a plant adjacent to the main plant. In preparing an analysis of the pros and cons of the elimination, a consultant suggests that a portion of the salaries of the executives of the plant and headquarters should be considered — that is, the portion reflecting the amount of time spent traveling during company hours between the plants. Another consultant responds, "The salaries should not be considered because they are a fixed cost. The executives would be paid the same amount whether they traveled or not; thus the cost is not relevant."

REQUIRED:

    a. Should the time the executive spent traveling be considered in making the decision whether or not to replace the present plant?

    b. What other information would you want if you were going to make the decision?

2-23 Question on Disposal of Assets The Miller Company is considering the sale of the physical assets of a subsidiary company. The president of the Miller Company has requested an analysis of the costs of the subsidiary and has been given a breakdown of costs (assuming normal operations) into fixed and variable classifications.

REQUIRED:

    a. Name some fixed costs that would be avoidable if the subsidiary were sold.

    b. Name some fixed costs that would be avoidable if the subsidiary were retained but not operated.

    c. Name some costs that would continue even if the subsidiary were not operated (assuming that it were not sold).

2-24 Opportunity Costs A star professional football player has asked you for advice. His club has offered him a contract paying $500,000 for a season. He wants to know whether he should sign. His club has a viable backup player. What do you advise him?

2-25 Pricing Policy Decisions A professor charges $1,500 per day for consulting. If she charged $200 per day, she would obtain many more days of consulting and thereby substantially increase her total take-home pay (while still performing her teaching responsibilities). Why may her current pricing policy be reasonable?

2-26 Opportunity Costs of School A student graduating from engineering college is thinking of entering a graduate school of business. She has been offered a job as an engineer at a salary of $24,000 per year. If she returns to school, tuition will be $8,000 per year (it is a two-year program) and living costs $6,000 per year. To live in a comparable style will cost $15,000 if she takes the job. What is the cost of continuing her education? Ignore income taxes.

2-27 Costs of Inventory   The following statement was taken from a managerial report.

> During the year a Merchandise Control Section was established whose function has been to hold a tight rein on inventory position and to plan for the maximum turnover of merchandise. The success of this function has been apparent in the approximately four-time turnover of inventories during the year. In addition, short-term seasonal borrowings have been held to a minimum, since funds were not unnecessarily tied up in inventory.

REQUIRED:

Comment on the statement.

2-28 Questions on Fixed and Variable Costs   Comment on the following:

a. Despite the fact that direct labor is commonly thought of as a variable cost and depreciation is commonly thought of as a fixed cost, circumstances may call for a completely opposite treatment in budgeting. Can you give an example of such a situation?

b. Why do many companies refrain from reporting fixed costs in performance reports?

c. Graph the behavior of the following costs versus volume per period:

(1) Total depreciation computed on a sum-of-the-years digits method.

(2) Variable cost per unit of output.

(3) Total power cost where a minimum amount is supplied at a specified total charge. Additional usage is at a constant rate per kilowatt hour, until a given number of kilowatt hours is used, after which the hourly rate is cut in half.

d. Is the pricing policy of c(3) desirable?

Problems

2-29 Interpretation of Accounting Reports   Refer to Exhibit 2-8, and answer the following questions.

REQUIRED:

a. Identify the major differences between the income statements for The Maytag Company and Delta Air Lines, Inc.

b. Identify the major differences between the income statements for The Maytag Company and F. W. Woolworth Co.

c. How was cost-accounting data used to prepare all three income statements?

d. On the income statement for The Maytag Company, where are the wages of a factory worker represented? the cost of sheet metal used in washing machines? the salaries of the sales personnel?

e. On the Delta Air Lines, Inc. income statement, where are the salaries of the pilots represented? the costs of the replacement parts used in aircraft maintenance?

2-30 **Using Cost Data in an Acquisition Decision**   The Morusty Manufacturing Company is considering expanding by acquiring a plant currently being operated by the Talmadge Company. The Talmadge Company has submitted the following list of costs for a normal level of operations:

Direct labor	$100,000
Direct material	200,000
Indirect manufacturing costs, fixed	
Plant and equipment depreciation	150,000
Salaries of personnel (includes allocation	
of central office salaries, $100,000)	200,000
Indirect manufacturing costs, variable	40,000
	$690,000

The plant is designed to produce only widgets. Widgets sell for a price of $1 per unit, and because the widget industry is very competitive, a price change is unlikely. At a normal level of operations, the plant produces 500,000 widgets.

The Talmadge Company has operated the plant efficiently, and it is unlikely that the Morusty Company can introduce additional efficiencies. Selling costs are nominal. The Morusty Company would not have to add to its central office staff.

REQUIRED:

a. In computing the maximum price that the Morusty Company should offer for the plant, what income figure should be used? (Assume normal sales.)

b. If the Talmadge Company cannot sell the plant, should it be closed? Explain.

2-31 **Costs and Volume of Sales**   The president of a company described his situation as follows: "My problem is having too low a volume of sales. I have fixed costs of $100,000 and variable costs of $1 per unit of product. With my present volume of 10,000 units, the average cost of product is $11 per unit. If I could sell 100,000 units, the average cost would be $2 per unit. My selling price is $11 per unit."

REQUIRED:

a. Compute the income presently being earned by the firm.

b. Assume that the firm could increase its volume to 200,000 units by decreasing its price to $1.80 per unit. Would this price reduction be desirable, assuming that the present plant capacity is adequate?

c. The generalization is often made that "With high fixed costs, increase production and sales." Discuss the validity of this statement.

2-32 **Schedule of Cost of Goods Manufactured and Sold**   Using the following data for Gator Company, construct a schedule of cost of goods manufactured and sold.

Direct-materials inventory, December 31, 19X5	$10,000
Direct-materials inventory, January 1, 19X5	1,300
Direct-material purchases during 19X5	20,000
Direct labor incurred during 19X5	11,000
Indirect labor incurred during 19X5	1,700
Indirect materials used during 19X5	2,900
Other manufacturing overhead during 19X5	3,200
Work-in-process inventory, December 31, 19X5	700
Work-in-process inventory, January 1, 19X5	2,200
Finished-goods inventory, December 31, 19X5	1,400
Finished-goods inventory, January 1, 19X5	600

2-33 Using Relevant Costs in Formulating Bids   The Marshall Company is about to bid on a government contract for 10,000 units. The president of the firm desires to know the minimum bid that the company can make in order for the firm to be no worse off than if the firm did not get the order. Assume that the firm has adequate capacity to produce the product for the government without adding to plant. The analyst presented the president with the following report:

	Per Unit	Total
Direct-material costs	$ 1.30	$ 13,000
Direct-labor costs	4.60	46,000
Overtime incurred because of contract	0.10	1,000
Overhead		
Variable overhead	1.00	10,000
Fixed overhead	2.00	20,000
Special equipment (to be purchased)	4.00	40,000
Allocation of selling and administrative expenses		
(fixed costs)	3.00	30,000
Safety factor (100% of the overhead rate)	3.00	30,000
Minimum price	$19.00	$190,000

REQUIRED:

Prepare a supplemental report for the president.

2-34 Costs and Make-or-Buy Decisions   The Make-or-Buy Company uses machine tools that it manufactures. The company currently has excess capacity, and the tools are being manufactured in a part of the plant that would otherwise lie idle.

A salesman has been attempting to sell machine tools to the Make-or-Buy Company and has prepared the following analysis in cooperation with company personnel:

	Cost of Manufacturing the Next Year's Supply of Tools	Cost of Buying the Next Year's Supply of Tools
Cost of purchasing tools		$210,000
Cost of parts and material	$100,000	
Labor (especially hired for this type of work)	40,000	
Labor (distribution of labor costs of regular hourly workers based on hours of actual labor)	30,000	
Labor (allocation of labor costs of salaried employees)	20,000	
Variable overhead	10,000	
Fixed overhead (includes $20,000 of depreciation of equipment especially purchased for this purpose in the past)	40,000	
	$240,000	$210,000

The purchased machine tools will have no operating advantage over the tools made by the plant itself.

REQUIRED:

Prepare an analysis showing whether the Make-or-Buy Company should purchase or make its machine tools to fill its needs.

2-35 **Interpretation of Accounting Reports**   Refer to Exhibit 2-9 to answer the following questions.

   a. What types of costs are included in "manufacturing overhead" on the Schedule of Cost of Goods Manufactured and Sold for The Maytag Company? Give some examples.

   b. Suppose the company's production volume had been 5 percent higher. Would total direct-labor costs have been greater or about the same? Would the total cost of depreciation of the company's production equipment have been greater or about the same? Explain your answer.

   c. Again suppose that production volume had been 5 percent higher. Would the direct-labor cost per unit have been greater or about the same? Would depreciation cost per unit have been greater or about the same? Explain your answer.

   d. Is it likely that all of the costs included in the amount "cost of products sold" were actually incurred during the year for which the statement was prepared? Explain your answer.

2-36 **Costs and Pricing**   The Spring Manufacturing Company is considering accepting a special order for 50,000 cushions that it received from a large chain of department stores. The order specified a price of $30 per unit. This compared unfavorably to the company's regular price of $33 per unit. The accounting department prepared the following analysis to show that there would be cost saving resulting from the additional sales:

	Cost per Unit without the Additional Sales (100,000 units)	Cost per Unit with the Additional Sales (150,000 units)
Variable costs	$20	$20
Fixed costs	9	6
	$29	$26

No additional fixed costs would be incurred because the company had excess capacity. Since the average cost per unit will be reduced from $29 to $26, the president of the firm believes he would be justified in reducing the price by $3 to sell to the department store chain.

REQUIRED:

Should the order for the 50,000 units at a price of $30 be accepted? Explain. Ignore any legal considerations.

3

Cost-Volume-Profit Analysis

LEARNING OBJECTIVES

After studying this chapter, you should be able to:

1 Explain the fundamentals of conventional break-even analysis.

2 Discuss price and output decisions and their relationship to cost-volume-profit analysis.

3 Conduct break-even analysis with multiple products.

4 Describe the Robinson-Patman Act and its impact on cost-price relationships.

5 Explain the relationship between the accountant's and the economist's approaches to cost-volume-profit analysis.

*T*he preceding chapter discussed different types of costs and the behavior of costs as output changes. These cost concepts are used in this chapter to analyze changes in profit as the volume of output changes. The product-pricing decision is also discussed in this chapter, since the way in which prices are set affects sales volume and profit. Moreover, the cost concepts developed in Chapter 2, and applied in this chapter, are also important in the price-setting process.

Decisions involving price, volume, and cost can be classified as those decisions made after the long-lived assets necessary for production have been acquired and those made in connection with the acquisition of plant and equipment. Consider-ations relevant for one may not be relevant for the other, and applying the same procedures in both situations can lead to incorrect decisions. This chapter discusses cost-volume-profit relationships, pricing, and output decisions when the capital assets are already owned. Such decisions are often referred to as short-run decisions. The problems of decision making when the capital assets have not yet been acquired are capital-budgeting decisions. These decisions are examined in Chapters 19 and 20.

Break-Even Analysis

Pricing and output decisions are made jointly. One common approach to pricing and output decisions is break-even analysis. By examining the changes in revenues and costs across various output levels and estimated prices, management can determine the level of output sales needed to recover its costs for any given price. The analysis is illustrated in Exhibit 3-1 for the case of a single product.

In Exhibit 3-1, fixed costs are assumed to be constant over the relevant output range. The analysis also assumes that the total-cost line can be approximated by a straight line.[1] The curves in Exhibit 3-1 give values for zero activity even though the nature of the relationships is suspect in this region. The total-cost line is of limited use over regions of activity not previously experienced. Very low activity levels provide examples of such a region.

The **break-even point,** Q_b in Exhibit 3-1, is located where the total-cost curve intersects the total revenue curve, or, equivalently, where total revenue equals total cost.

The use of straight lines in the graph presumes that output and sales can be increased without changing price over the range graphed and that the firm operates at the same efficiency at all levels. Thus, to increase profit it is necessary merely to increase the number of units sold. If the assumptions that the quantity sold can be

---

1. The total-cost relationship may be established using the regression techniques discussed in Chapter 13.

EXHIBIT 3-1 ·

Break-even Graph

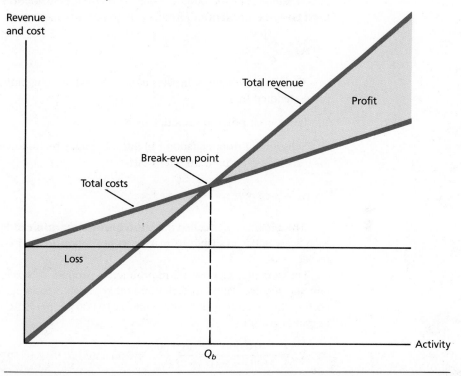

increased with the price remaining unchanged and that efficiency will remain constant no longer hold, the graphs of total revenue and total costs are no longer straight lines. This situation is discussed in the appendix.

Finding the Break-Even Point

The following discussion can be related to Exhibit 3-1. To break even, sales revenue must be sufficient to cover all related variable and fixed costs. Sometimes the fixed costs include an assigned profit as well, but a profit figure is not included in this analysis. The break-even output is given by

Sales revenues = Variable costs + Fixed costs

or, alternatively,

$$\text{Price} \times \left(\begin{array}{c}\text{Break-even}\\ \text{output}\end{array}\right) = \left(\begin{array}{c}\text{Unit variable}\\ \text{cost}\end{array}\right) \times \left(\begin{array}{c}\text{Break-even}\\ \text{output}\end{array}\right) + \left(\begin{array}{c}\text{Fixed}\\ \text{cost}\end{array}\right)$$

Solving for the break-even output yields:

$$\text{Break-even output} = \frac{\text{Fixed cost}}{\text{Price} - \text{Unit variable cost}} = \frac{\text{Fixed cost}}{\text{Unit contribution margin}}$$

The price less the unit variable cost is known as the **contribution margin per unit.** Each unit sold contributes this amount to cover fixed cost and profit. Letting X_b denote the break-even output, c denote the unit contribution margin, and F denote fixed cost, the break-even formula can be rewritten as

$$X_b = \frac{F}{c} \tag{1}$$

The break-even point in sales dollars, S_b, is found by multiplying X_b by the sales price, denoted by p:

Break-even point in sales dollars $= S_b = pX_b$ (2)

Substituting from equation (1) into (2) yields the following equivalent formula for the break-even point in sales dollars:

$$S_b = pX_b = p\frac{F}{c} = \frac{F}{c/p}$$

The amount c/p is called the **contribution margin ratio.** It is the percentage of each sales dollar available to make a contribution toward covering fixed cost and profit.

For example, suppose a firm produces a product or service that sells for $100 a unit and requires labor, material, and other variable costs per unit of $60. The fixed costs of the required facilities amount to $10,000 per period. One period's break-even output is given by

$$X_b = \frac{\$10,000}{\$100 - \$60} = \frac{\$10,000}{\$40} = 250 \text{ units}$$

$$S_b = \frac{\$10,000}{\dfrac{\$40}{\$100}} = \frac{\$10,000}{.4} = \$25,000$$

and $c/p = .4$.

Break-even quantities are calculated for a particular time period. The relevance of those calculations relies on several assumptions, some of which have been discussed earlier. Nevertheless, it is worth repeating the assumptions noted earlier and augmenting the list.

Assumptions Underlying Break-Even Analysis   The assumptions previously noted include the following:

1. All related costs have been identified accurately, quantified, and reasonably dichotomized between fixed and variable.

2. Unit variable cost is constant across volume changes and total variable costs are a function only of the volume of activity.

3. Selling prices remain constant across the levels of output considered in the analysis.

4. Efficiency and productivity remain unchanged.

Additional assumptions follow:

5. If more than one product is considered in a single analysis, the sales mix remains the same. (The *sales mix* is the relative proportion of sales of each product.)

6. Inventory levels are constant.

7. Accounting procedures for measuring results are not altered.

8. Fixed costs will generally be constant in total (decreasing per unit) over the relevant production range.

These assumptions require the cost and revenue functions to be linear, which may be an adequate assumption over a limited relevant range of output. If the analysis extends beyond this range, or if any other assumptions are substantively violated, the analysis must be adjusted to reflect the altered conditions. Conventional break-even analysis also assumes certainty about all of the parameters in the analysis. Break-even analysis under uncertainty is covered in Chapter 21.

Sales Required to Earn a Given Profit

The analysis above can be extended to determine the number of units required to earn a given before-tax profit level. To do so, the desired before-tax profit level, denoted π, is added to fixed cost in the break-even formula. Let X_π denote the number of units of sales required to earn a profit of π, and let S_π denote the sales dollars required to earn a profit of π.

$$X_\pi = \frac{F + \pi}{c} \tag{3}$$

$$S_\pi = \frac{F + \pi}{\dfrac{c}{p}} \tag{4}$$

Using the numerical example in the previous section and a desired profit level of $5,000, the following calculations can be made:

Price $(p) = \$100$

Unit variable cost $= \$60$

Unit contribution margin $(c) = \$40$

Fixed cost $(F) = \$10,000$ per period

Desired before-tax profit $(\pi) = \$5,000$

$$X_\pi = \frac{\$10,000 + \$5,000}{\$40} = 375 \text{ units}$$

$$S_\pi = \frac{\$10,000 + \$5,000}{\dfrac{\$40}{\$100}} = \$37,500$$

Income Taxes   Cost-volume-profit analysis can also be used to determine the sales (in units or dollars) required to earn a given after-tax level of profit. Let t denote the income tax rate, Y denote the desired after-tax profit level, and π denote before tax profit. The following relationship exists between Y and π:

After-tax profit $= Y = (1 - t)\pi$

Equivalently,

$$\pi = \frac{Y}{(1 - t)} \tag{5}$$

Let X_Y denote the number of sales units required to earn an after-tax profit of Y, and let S_Y denote the dollars of sales required to earn Y after taxes. Then, substituting from formula (5) into (3) and (4), respectively:

$$X_Y = \frac{F + \dfrac{Y}{(1 - t)}}{c}$$

$$S_Y = \frac{F + \dfrac{Y}{(1 - t)}}{\dfrac{c}{p}}$$

Referring again to the numerical example used above, if the tax rate is 40 percent and the firm desires an after-tax profit of $3,000, then

$$X_Y = \frac{\$10,000 + \dfrac{\$3,000}{(1 - .4)}}{\$100 - \$60} = \frac{\$15,000}{\$40} = 375 \text{ units}$$

$$S_Y = \frac{\$10,000 + \dfrac{\$3,000}{(1 - .4)}}{\dfrac{\$100 - \$60}{\$100}} = \frac{\$15,000}{.4} = \$37,500$$

The results for X_Y and S_Y are unchanged because a $5,000 before-tax profit is equivalent to an after-tax profit of 3,000 with a tax rate of 40 percent.

To verify the result:

Sales (500 units)	$37,500
Variable cost	22,500
Aggregate contribution margin	$15,000
Fixed cost	10,000
Before-tax profit	$ 5,000
Income tax (40%)	2,000
After-tax profit	$ 3,000

Break-Even Analysis and Cost Control

Break-even charts are used extensively in reviewing and analyzing past results because they show at a glance when favorable or unfavorable variances exist. One popular type of break-even chart used for this kind of analysis is shown in Exhibit 3-2. This presentation — a **profit-volume (PV) chart** — plots the difference between revenue and budgeted costs for different levels of sales. The actual profit for the period (a month here) is marked on the graph. The location of the actual profit in relation to the budgeted profit determines whether the budgeted profit for the actual level of activity has been attained. In Exhibit 3-2 the profit for January is more than budgeted, and the profit for February is less. One explanation for this discrepancy is that costs may not have been reduced rapidly enough in the face of a sales decline. The expected variability around the line is useful in evaluating the significance of the observed deviations.

An alternative presentation (see Exhibit 3-3) shows only the budgeted costs for the different levels of sales and the actual costs for the different time periods. This type of graph is useful for a manager who has responsibility for costs but not revenues.

In addition to showing the budgeted and actual total costs, charts should show breakdowns for the totals by types of cost, by departments, and by product lines. Charts may be prepared for any of these breakdowns so that the budgeted and actual results may be compared for any level of operations. For many costs, measures of nonsales activity are the most appropriate explanatory variables. Several variables may be employed, using the regression techniques described in Chapter 13, to construct graphs that illustrate the net effect of each independent variable. Direct-labor costs then can be plotted against the number of units of product actually produced or machine hours used and the wage costs of accounts payable clerks plotted against invoices processed or hours worked. One or more appropriate measures of activity should be determined for each cost classification. Examining these charts can direct efforts toward areas where possible savings can be achieved.

EXHIBIT 3-2

PV Chart

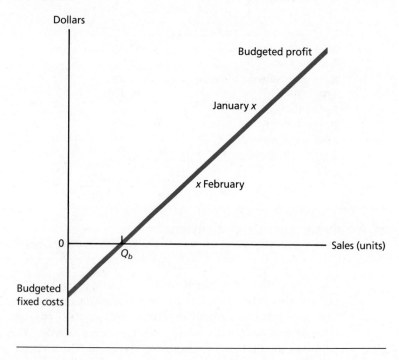

EXHIBIT 3-3

Budgeted and Actual Costs

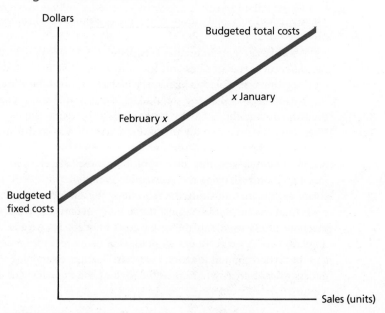

Illustrations of Break-Even Analysis

This section presents several illustrations of break-even analysis as it has been adapted to the needs of different industries. They are included not to teach the basics of break-even analysis but rather to provide a sense of how break-even analysis is applied by actual companies.

Delta Air Lines

Delta Air Lines computes a break-even load factor for each flight. The break-even load factor is the percentage of available passenger seats that need to be occupied on a flight in order for that flight to break even. The following explanation of Delta's procedures was supplied by the director of accounting at Delta Air Lines.

Available Seat Miles (ASMs)   An *ASM* is defined as the seating capacity of an aircraft multiplied by the great-circle mileage between airports. For example, a B-767 (204 seats) flight between Orlando and San Francisco via Dallas/Ft. Worth generates $499,392 = 204 \times (983 + 1465)$ ASMs, given great-circle distances of 983 miles between Orlando and Dallas/Ft. Worth and 1,465 miles from Dallas/Ft. Worth to San Francisco.

Revenue Passenger Miles (RPMs)   *RPMs* are defined as the number of passengers multiplied by the mileage flown. If, in the example above, 190 passengers were on the Orlando–Dallas/Ft. Worth segment and 130 passengers traveled from Dallas/Ft. Worth to San Francisco, the total RPMs for the flight would have been $377,220 = 190(983) + 130(1465)$.

Passenger Load Factor   The passenger load factor is given by RPMs divided by ASMs, which is simply a seat occupancy rate weighted by distance. In this example, the passenger load factor for the flight was $.7554 = \dfrac{377,220}{499,392}$, with individual segment load factors of 93.14 and 63.73 percent.

Passenger Mile Yield   Passenger mile yield is the average fare received per mile, computed by dividing passenger revenue by revenue passenger miles.

Break-Even Load Factor   The break-even load factor is the passenger load factor at which operating revenues will equal operating expenses. There are variations of the break-even calculation throughout the industry, but for public reporting on a system basis, Delta uses a fairly simple approach. The RPMs required to break-even are computed by dividing passenger expenses (total operating expenses less nonpassenger expenses) by the passenger mile yield. This figure is then divided by actual available seat miles to give a break-even load factor.

In a recent annual report, Delta Air Lines reported its average, systemwide passenger load factor as 56.28 percent and its average, systemwide break-even load factor as 51.57 percent.

Dunkin' Donuts

DUNKIN' DONUTS®
It's worth the trip.

This section includes edited excerpts from the training manual used by Dunkin' Donuts to familiarize its new franchise owners with financial control procedures. The excerpt illustrates how the firm relates its break-even analysis to its budgeting process. The numbers in the excerpt are illustrative for training purposes only. They are not the actual numbers for a Dunkin' Donuts shop. An illustrative budget from the training manual is displayed in Exhibit 3-4.

Illustrative Break-Even Calculation   The break-even point is the amount of sales that permits the shop to meet all of its obligations and show no profit or loss. The standard formula for computing the break-even point is:

$$\text{Break-even point (sales dollars)} = \cfrac{\text{Fixed costs}}{100\% - \begin{bmatrix} \text{Variable} \\ \text{cost as a} \\ \text{percentage} \\ \text{of sales} \end{bmatrix}}$$

This formula is not easily adapted to the donut business because some items are neither clearly fixed nor clearly variable. The following steps may be followed:

1. Refer to the budget.

2. Total the fixed expenses, as follows:

Operating expenses	$ 90,030
Payroll[a]	81,500
Principal payments[b]	15,000
Total	$186,530

[a] Payroll is considered a fixed expense because it is related to a given sales volume based on the break-even point.

[b] Principal payments must be made from profit after taxes. We have assumed a tax rate of 20 percent in this illustration. Consequently, the franchise owner must have total before-tax income of $15,000 [$12,000 ÷ (1 − .20)] to make principal payments of $12,000 after taxes.

3. Variable expenses (as a percentage of sales):

Food	26.5%
Supplies	3.3
Premiums	.8
Advertising	4.0
Service fee	4.9
Total	39.5%

EXHIBIT 3-4

Illustrative Budget from Dunkin' Donuts Training Manual

Percentage	Annual Budget	Item	August	Corrected August
100.0%	$343,200	Sales	$25,030	$25,030
		Cost of sales:		
26.5		Food		
23.7		Payroll		
3.3		Supplies		
.8		Premiums		
4.0		Advertising		
4.9		Service fee		
63.2	217,080	Total cost of sales	15,820	15,820
	126,120	Gross profit	$ 9,210	$ 9,210
		Less operating expenses:		
	670	Bakery		
	340	Cash short		
	3,990	Cleaning		
	8,630	Depreciation/amortization		
	240	Employment expense		
	1,940	Insurance, casualty		
	3,510	Insurance, Worker's Compensation		
	3,290	Interest paid		
	770	Laundry and uniforms		
	500	Licenses and permits		
	600	Travel		
	1,500	Legal and professional		
	580	General expense		
	700	Office expense		
	18,900	Rent		
	12,500	Rental override		
	4,140	Repairs and maintenance		
	160	Equipment rental		
	650	Serving expense		
	50	Sales expense		
	8,150	Taxes, payroll		
	3,400	Taxes, real estate		
	530	Taxes, other		
	800	Telephone		
		Utilities		
	8,650	Electric		
	4,400	Gas		
	440	Water		
26.2%	$ 90,030	Total operating expenses	$ 6,560[a]	$ 6,930[b]
	36,090	Net operating profit	2,650	2,280
	1,400	Other income	120	120
	$ 37,490	Net profit before taxes	$ 2,770	$ 2,400
	(7,500)	Provision for taxes	(580)	(580)
	$ 29,990	Net profit after taxes	$ 2,190	$ 1,820
	8,630	Add back depreciation	660	660
	$ 38,620	Gross cash flow from operations	$ 2,850	$ 2,480
	(12,000)	Principal and other payments	(1,000)	(1,000)
	$ 26,620	Net cash flow from operations	$ 1,850	$ 1,480

[a] Operating expenses at 26.2 percent of sales.
[b] Operating expenses as budgeted in cash flow budget (27.7 percent of sales).

4. Break-even calculation:

$$\text{Break-even sales} = \frac{\$186,530}{100\% - 39.5\%} = \frac{\$186,530}{1.00 - .395} = \$308,310$$

Multiproduct Break-Even Analysis

Break-even analysis is most easily used when efficiency is constant, the price is set, and only one product is being sold. The problem of efficiency and price changes were discussed. The problem of product mix is more complex: The total output may vary, and the amount of each product sold may change from period to period. If the different products have different contribution margins, the profit per dollar of sales will differ for each product, and the break-even point for the firm becomes a function of the sales mix.

One possibility is to draw break-even charts by product line. The costs that can be identified directly with the product line are plotted to obtain a break-even point for direct costs (direct in terms of the product line). The costs that are allocated to the product as the result of indirect-cost allocations are plotted on top of the direct costs. This approach gives a second break-even point.

An alternative approach that can be used is to assume a standard sales mix. This approach is appropriate if one multiproduct break-even chart is desired. The analysis then proceeds in the conventional way except that the sales price, unit variable cost, and unit contribution margin used in the analysis are weighted averages based on the standard sales mix.

To illustrate, assume that the Montrose Corporation produces three products, denoted by *A, B,* and *C.* A firm's **sales mix** is the relative proportion of sales of each of its products. The standard sales mix for Montrose's products is 50 percent for *A,* 30 percent for *B,* and 20 percent for *C.* Price and cost data for the products, along with fixed costs, are given in Exhibit 3-5:

EXHIBIT 3-5

Three-Product Break-Even Analysis

Product	Standard Proportion of Total Sales	Sales Price	Variable Cost	Unit Contribution Margin
A	50%	$10.00	$6.00	$4.00
B	30%	8.00	4.00	4.00
C	20%	5.00	3.00	2.00
Weighted average		$ 8.40	$4.80	$3.60
Fixed cost		$72,000		

The weighted average contribution margin is determined by multiplying each product's unit contribution margin by its standard sales proportion. The break-even point in units is found using this equation:

$$X_b = \frac{\$72{,}000}{\$3.60} = 20{,}000 \text{ units}$$

The 20,000 unit break-even point represents aggregate sales across all three product lines. Assuming that the standard mix holds true, the break-even point implies that the firm must sell 10,000 units of *A*, 6,000 units of *B*, and 4,000 units of *C*.

Changes in the Cost Structure

The break-even sales volume is determined in part by the level of fixed costs. Many possibilities for measuring these costs exist, including historical cost allocations, adjusted historical costs, current costs, and replacement costs. The choice may be viewed as an approximation of the opportunity costs of using the fixed factors of production. In the conventional analysis, historical costs are used.

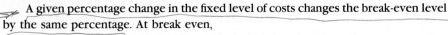

A given percentage change in the fixed level of costs changes the break-even level by the same percentage. At break even,

$$cX_b = F$$

where *c* denotes the unit contribution margin (assumed to remain constant), X_b denotes the break-even sales level, and *F* denotes the fixed cost. A change of *y* percent in fixed cost yields a new fixed-cost level of $(1 + y)F$. This requires that cX_b be increased to $(1 + y)cX_b$, so that

$$(1 + y)cX_b = (1 + y)(F)$$

or

$$c[(1 + y)X_b] = (1 + y)(F)$$

This means, considering the term in brackets, that the break-even point also increases by *y* percent, given that *c* remains constant.

Computer-Integrated Manufacturing (CIM)

A high-technology manufacturing system significantly affects a firm's cost structure. Typically a CIM system results in substantially higher fixed costs and somewhat lower variable costs. Fixed manufacturing overhead costs, such as depreciation and maintenance on robotic equipment, usually are much higher. Labor costs are lower in total, and a larger portion of labor is associated with highly skilled employees, such as computer programmers and systems analysts.

The effect of these changes on the firm's break-even point depends on the specific numbers involved. Suppose, for example, that a manufacturer of electronic equipment installs a CIM system. Scenario I below shows the firm's cost structure before automation. Scenarios II and III are two alternative cost structures after automation. Both scenarios II and III entail higher fixed costs and lower variable costs than scenario I.

	I	II	III
Sales price per unit	$ 600	$ 600	$ 600
Variable cost per unit	400	100	350
Fixed cost	1,000,000	2,000,000	1,500,000
Break-even point	5,000	4,000	6,000

The break-even point declined when the firm's cost structure changed from scenario I to II. However, the break-even point increased when the change was from scenario I to III. Thus, when both fixed and variable costs change, due for example to the installation of CIM, the break-even point can move either up or down.

Profit-Value Ratio as a Decision Aid

Assume that a company wants to decide which product is worthy of additional sales effort and productive capacity. Some firms use the ratio of the contribution margin to sales (the excess of revenues over variable costs, divided by sales) to make this decision. This ratio is called by various names, but the exact title is unimportant; PV ratio (PV standing for "profit-value") is used here.

The PV ratio fails as a reliable guide for the decisions being considered for two reasons. First, it relies on the excess of revenue over variable cost for the present manufacturing process. The manufacturing process being considered for the additional productive capacity may use a different technology and may have a different PV ratio. The PV ratio fails to consider the capital outlays required by the additional productive capacity and the additional fixed costs that are added (for example, the additional accountants, quality-control personnel, and supervisors required for the operation whose salaries may become fixed costs). Second, the PV ratio fails to consider competition, the market, and hence the number of units that are sold or that can be sold.

Inspection of the PV ratios of products can suggest profitable product lines that might be emphasized and unprofitable lines that should be reevaluated and possibly eliminated from the company's offerings. But until the analysis is broadened to take into consideration other factors including all incremental costs, avoidable costs and revenue changes, as well as their likelihoods, a decision cannot be made regarding whether or not to expand or contract a product line.

The PV ratio is a questionable device for decision making, but it does indicate the relative profitability of the different profit lines, if all other things are equal. For example, an automobile manufacturer may make ten models of a low-priced car. Should a particular model be pushed by sales because of the high PV ratio? If the fixed costs connected with producing additional cars are truly fixed, the model with the highest PV ratio may be the most desirable one to sell, other things being equal. But the conclusion may not be correct, for the PV ratio generally uses average revenues and average-variable costs. The decision of whether to push one model should be made using a marginal analysis. Even PV ratios defined in terms of marginal profits per marginal dollar of costs should not be used in decisions that are not marginal in nature (such as one involving plant expansion). The PV ratio, as generally computed, is useful for forming impressions but not for making decisions.

Price-Volume Relationships

The effect of pricing on sales volume is an important element of cost-volume-profit analysis. Consider the Scott Company, which manufactures garden equipment. The firm's management is considering the marketing strategy for its top-of-the-line lawn mowers. Scott Company owns a new plant, which is fully equipped with the latest-model machinery. Among other issues management must decide is the price it should charge and the output level at which it should produce. These decisions will affect Scott's costs and profits. Profit is the ultimate result of the price charged, the costs incurred, and the production level undertaken.

The company decides on a price and an output and attempts to produce the goods efficiently. It does not decide on a profit. If the planning process is effective and is efficiently carried out, a profit may result. But management does not select a profit level. In this situation management cannot say that it needs a profit of 20 percent on an investment of $1 million and therefore must have a dollar profit of $200,000. Profit is a result of planning and the execution of the adopted plan, but it is a consequence of other decisions and not the result of a profit decision.

Often the profits that are implied under a given plan are not considered satisfactory by management. In such cases management searches for a better plan. If it is feasible, management alters the factors it inputs to the process in the hope of producing an acceptable result. But if the "best" plan has already been chosen, unsatisfactory profits may be unavoidable.

The Scott Company can budget costs for various levels of output, attempt to control these costs, improve efficiency, and use inventories to stabilize production. However, one basic element of the cost structure is determined by the characteristics of the machinery and plant purchased: overtime. Whether overtime is necessary is a decision to be made in each period, but to some extent the decision is made when the plant is built. If demand for the product is high, it may be necessary to incur overtime. But the decision that determined the size of the plant and in turn resulted in the need for overtime, was made previously when the plant was acquired.

Other decisions by management also influence costs. For example, a company policy that stresses quality or service, as is true at McDonald's, IBM, and Frito-Lay, has implications for costs as well as for revenues. Among these decisions is the choice of a price. The pricing decision is a crucial decision made by management and often is misunderstood. Two commonly used pricing methods are the cost-plus and return-on-investment methods, which are discussed in the following section. Both methods have limitations.

Cost-Plus and Return-on-Investment Pricing

Under **cost-plus pricing** and **return-on-investment pricing,** the cost of the product is computed and a "required" or "fair" profit is added to obtain the price. If a government cost-plus contract is in hand, this may be a justifiable procedure, but in a competitive situation (as in bidding for a government contract) cost-plus pricing can lead to undesirable results.[2] One difficulty is computing the average unit cost, since this computation requires deciding on the level of activity that should be used to apply fixed costs to product. A second problem in determining unit price is deciding what constitutes a "reasonable" profit.

To illustrate the problem of determining average unit cost, assume that the Scott Company can produce 10,000 lawn mowers per month when operating at capacity. The monthly fixed costs are $200,000, and the variable costs are $30 per lawn mower. What is the cost of one lawn mower? One reasonable answer is $50 (the variable costs of $30 plus average per-unit fixed costs of $20). The application of $20 of fixed costs is based on production capacity. But suppose that the company expects to produce and sell only 5,000 lawn mowers during the month. Are the unit costs to be used for pricing now $70 (the variable costs of $30 plus fixed costs per unit of $40)? Carrying this issue to one extreme, if only one unit is to be produced, the total cost per unit is $200,030. At the other extreme, the cost of one unit is $30 if the fixed costs are not considered to be part of the unit cost.

With a cost-plus pricing system, a reasonable profit is added to the unit cost. The profit added can be based on costs per unit or on the investment that is used. A company can attempt to recover all costs and to earn as much profit as possible in a competitive environment. But this desire does not necessarily mean that all costs will be recovered or that the company will earn a profit. The first step in determining a price is to set a price that leads to the desired profit at the planned level of sales. The second step is to adjust the price for the realities of competition.

Fixed-Cost Calculation   One method of handling the costing problem is to base the application of fixed costs on normal-activity-level costs without regard to the expected or actual level of operations. This method of applying fixed costs is called *absorption costing* and is discussed in detail in Chapters 4 and 5. When fixed costs are handled in this manner, the pricing method is called **normal pricing.** This procedure is more effective than adjusting the cost per unit upward or downward as output decreases or

---

2. For some results in this area, see S. Colantoni, R. Manes, and A. Whinston, "Programming, Profit Rates and Pricing Decisions," *Accounting Review* (July 1969): 567–581.

increases. In fact, average unit cost based on normal activity can be used to set a standard price that must be obtained to maintain the productive facilities and earn the required return on the capital employed. Nevertheless, using a standard price is not likely to be desirable. In some situations, the firm may be able to charge more than the standard price. This can occur, for example, when the firm is introducing a new product that has little if any competition. In other situations, it may be desirable or even necessary to set a price less than the standard price because of the level of competition. In fact, complementary products are often priced below variable cost in order to increase sales of a related product. Camera film is an example of a complementary product priced low to make camera sales more attractive. Another example is the low pricing of razor blades by a company that also manufactures razors.

Another method for treating fixed costs under cost-plus pricing is to ignore fixed costs altogether and base prices entirely on variable costs. This method is sometimes referred to as **direct pricing.**

The pricing decision is complex, and the information required for a complete analysis is costly to obtain. Therefore, managers often resort to simplified pricing approaches such as cost-plus pricing. Prices set in this manner are based on information from the cost-accounting system. From an overall cost-benefit perspective, such simplified approaches to the pricing problem, using less costly information, may be best. A profit-maximizing price may not result, but the costs of information and decision analysis are saved, thereby resulting in higher returns to the firm. A recent survey of the *Fortune* 1,000 companies revealed that normal pricing (cost-plus pricing with fixed costs included in the unit cost) is the prevailing pricing approach in practice.[3]

The use of cost-plus pricing based on costs that include fixed costs is often mentioned in articles about well-known companies.

Pricing the Overnight Letter at Federal Express	When Federal Express entered the market for overnight letters, the firm was already well established as an express package carrier. Federal Express was the first private firm to compete with the U.S. Postal Service for air mail letter business. The founder and chairman of Federal Express stated that the company's new express mail service would have the potential to destroy the firm's competitors. The reason? Federal Express already was incurring very low unit costs for its express package service and was able to set an extremely low, cost-based price for the new overnight letter service. The chairman of Federal Express stated that no other company would be able to make the overnight letter profitable, because no other firm had the low unit costs of Federal Express.[4]

3. V. Govindarajan and R. Anthony, "How Firms Use Cost Data in Price Decisions," *Management Accounting* (July 1983): 30–36.

4. "Federal Express Dives into Air Mail," *Fortune* (June 15, 1981): 106–108.

Normal Pricing at General Motors

The pricing policy of General Motors was stated as early as 1927 by Albert Bradley (who later became chairman of the board for the firm) in a NACA Bulletin. Many people believe the company's pricing policy is essentially the same today. Bradley described General Motors' pricing policy as pricing to achieve a target average rate of return on investment over a long period of time. To determine the cost basis for this pricing policy, the firm established a normal average rate of capacity utilization. This rate of operation was used to apply fixed cost to product for the purpose of determining the product cost.[5]

Sebrite Corporation

Normal pricing in the financial services industry Sebrite Corporation, a national insurance and financial services company, measures its output in ATMs (average transactions per sales person per month). The company determines the cost of an ATM at differing levels of ATM output. These normal costs, based on different levels of ATM output, are then used to determine the company's origination fee (price) for certain types of financial services at different output levels. If Sebrite expects a given number of ATMs for the planning period in question, the firm adjusts its origination fees to enable Sebrite to earn a certain target profit on each transaction.[6]

Michigan National Bank

The role of the cost accounting function in setting prices for banking services at Michigan National Bank was described in a recent article written by a company executive as an "essential catalyst to a successful pricing framework."[7]

Pricing Under the Robinson-Patman Act

 The **Robinson-Patman amendment** to the *Clayton Act* is concerned with unlawful price discrimination. Price discrimination is considered unlawful where the effect "may be to substantially lessen competition or tend to create a monopoly in any line

5. NACA Bulletin, 1927. See also "Flexible Pricing," *Business Week* (December 12, 1977): 78.

6. This illustration is an excerpt from R. Possett, "Measuring Productive Costs in the Service Sector," *Management Accounting* (October 1980): 16–24.

7. This illustration is an excerpt from R. Sias, "Pricing Bank Services," *Management Accounting* (July 1985): 48–59.

of commerce." The law is administered by the Federal Trade Commission and is specifically designed to prevent *predatory pricing*, wherein prices are temporarily cut to limit supply in order to raise prices later.[8]

The amended act makes it easier to establish a violation and more difficult to achieve a defense than was the case under the Clayton Act. For a firm to be subject to the Act, several conditions must be satisfied. The price must

- Occur in interstate commerce,

- Be related to "commodities of like grade and quality,"

- Have the requisite effect on competition,

- Be other than price changes occurring because of market conditions such as seasonal clearances,

- Not be justified as a means of meeting an equally low price of a competitor,

- Not be justified by cost differences of equal or greater magnitude.[9]

Defenses by firms faced with lawsuits under the Robinson-Patman Act have attempted to show that one or more of these conditions are not satisfied. In general, this has been very difficult to do. The concept of interstate commerce has been expanded until this section of the law offers little if any defense. Goods can be considered of like grade and quality even though they are not identical. Once price differences have been established, the presumption of at least a potentially undesirable effect on competition is nearly automatic, and it has been extremely difficult to rebut this charge by the defense of meeting an equally low competitor's price.[10]

Complaints involving distress merchandise have been rare, and this sort of activity is unlikely to bring action by the Commission. Nevertheless, it is desirable not to come under the investigatory scrutiny of the Commission. Contrary to normal legal proceedings, a defendant under the Robinson-Patman Act is presumed guilty unless a successful defense can be established. Furthermore, if the firm is unable to establish a successful defense, it may be subject to triple damages.

The most successful defense against a complaint brought by the Federal Trade Commission under the Robinson-Patman Act has been by cost justification of the price differences. Even in this area success is an elusive goal. Although about 50 percent of the cost defenses made in public proceedings have been at least partially successful, relatively few cases have reached the stage of public proceedings.[11] Most

---

8. For a more complete description of the Robinson-Patman Act, see H. E. Taggart, "Cost Justification: Rules of the Game," *Journal of Accountancy* (December 1958): 52–60; and H. E. Taggart, *Cost Justification* (Michigan Business Studies, vol. 14, no. 3) (Ann Arbor: University of Michigan, 1959; and supplements 1 and 2, 1964 and 1967). See also the ABA Antitrust Section, Antitrust Law Developments (2nd ed., 1984) and the Legal Developments sections of the *Journal of Marketing* for recent case law.

9. Taggart, "Cost Justification," 548.

10. The meeting-of-competition defense has been used successfully by very few firms in public proceedings. One successful defense took seventeen years.

11. Taggart, "Cost Justification," 544–545.

complaints have been settled by informal hearings before the Commission's staff. The number of successful cost defenses in informal hearings, however, is not known because the results of such hearings are not available to the public.

Use of the cost defense has been limited by the time-consuming nature of the work involved, the expense of making cost-justification studies, and perhaps most important by the difficulty anticipated in convincing the Commission's accountants that adequate cost justification exists. Nevertheless, cost calculations have been accepted in both formal and informal proceedings — evidence that this defense is not completely illusionary.

In 1984 variable cost information was used to successfully defend selective price cuts in the case of *Adjustor's Replace-a-Car Inc. v. Agency Rent-a-Car.* The court held that Agency did not engage in price discrimination because its prices always exceeded its average variable cost. This conclusion was not affected by the plaintiff's claim that Agency reported a net loss from operations after overhead allocation. Nonetheless, cost defenses are suspect, and the support provided by some cases should be treated with caution since the specific defense particulars are not part of the law.

An analysis of the cases that have been open to the public suggests several basic principles that can help firms avoid or successfully answer complaints by the Federal Trade Commission. Any cost-justification defense must convince the Commission's accountants, and one important means of accomplishing this objective is to provide evidence that a firm has considered price differentials in light of the related costs prior to offering the prices to customers. Cost analyses prepared in advance and, perhaps, if possible, after consultation with the Commission, can provide evidence of this good faith. Because the effect of the Commission's actions can be severe, the best management talent available should be put on the job. This is not a place for the second team.

Several additional points can also be gleaned from the public cases:[12]

- Time is the only satisfactory means of allocating labor services.

- Sales dollars cannot be used to allocate overhead.

- Differential costing is not acceptable.

- Cost methods and classifications already in use by a firm need not be accepted by the Commission.

- Management cost estimates are not acceptable.

- Sampling methods may be used, but samples must be demonstrably representative (small samples are suspect).

Example   Ten thousand units of a product are being produced and sold at a price of $10. The product costs $5 per unit (variable costs are $3, and fixed costs are $2 per unit and $20,000 in total). An order for 10,000 more units can be obtained if units are

12. A good source is Taggart, "Cost Justification," particularly chaps. 20 and 21.

sold at a price of $8 each. Should the order be taken, from the point of view of economic considerations (assuming that the order will not reduce present sales)? Because the price per unit of $8 exceeds the variable cost per unit, the additional business is desirable from an economic point of view.

Should the order be taken from the point of view of legality under the Robinson-Patman Act? Can the $2 difference in price be explained by a "saving" of $2 in fixed costs? The answer is no. The defense would be rejected. If the company wants to accept the business, it will have to change its basic price to all customers to $8 per unit or change the price for the order to $10 per unit or find another defense. One possible defense would be to show that the fixed cost of $20,000 should reasonably be allocated to the other sales. For example, assume that the $20,000 is related to packaging equipment that will not be used with the new order because shipment will be in bulk. In this case a price difference might be justified by real cost savings.

Summary

Break-even analysis can be useful, during pricing decisions and can be broadened from its conventional use to take a variety of factors into account. In this way, the analysis can be used to answer "what if" questions such as "What if unit price were decreased by 10 percent?" Changes in one variable may affect other variables. Changes in price may lead in turn to changes in the amount demanded and thereby change the amount of fixed overhead applied to product. Methods are suggested in later chapters for dealing with uncertainty about demand and other factors. Nevertheless, any analysis of prices, costs, and volume makes important assumptions, and these assumptions should be kept in mind if the limitations in the results are to be appreciated.

The output and pricing decision may be made to maximize profits, but a firm does not know if it is going to make a profit. It may very well at best minimize a loss. Whether a profit is made requires a comparison of actual costs and revenues. But a pricing and output decision analyses should still be made to improve the firm's future position, whether a profit is earned or a loss reduced in any given period.

Key Terms to Review

break-even point, p. 60
contribution margin per unit, p. 62
contribution-margin ratio, p. 62
cost-plus pricing, p. 74
direct pricing, p. 75

normal pricing, p. 74
profit-volume chart, p. 65
return-on-investment pricing, p. 74
Robinson-Patman amendment, p. 76
sales mix, p. 70

Review Problem

COST-VOLUME-PROFIT ANALYSIS

The following data pertains to the single product of the Dexter Electronics Company:

Fixed costs	$500,000
Sales price per unit	50
Variable cost per unit	40

REQUIRED:

a. Calculate the unit contribution margin.

b. Compute the firm's break-even point in (1) units and (2) sales dollars.

c. Prepare a break-even graph and label the axes, all lines, and the break-even point.

d. What is the break-even point if fixed costs rise by 10 percent?

e. Suppose the company's income tax rate is 40 percent. How many units must the firm sell to achieve an after-tax profit of $24,000? (Assume the total fixed cost is $500,000.)

Solution to Review Problem

a. $$\text{Unit contribution margin} = \text{Sales price per unit} - \text{Unit variable cost}$$
$$= \$50 - \$40 = \$10$$

b. Break-even point:

(1) In units:

$$\text{Break-even point} = \frac{\text{Fixed cost}}{\text{Unit contribution margin}}$$

$$= \frac{\$500,000}{\$10} = 50,000 \text{ units}$$

(2) In sales dollars:

$$\text{Break-even sales dollars} = \text{Break-even units} \times \text{Sales price}$$

$$= 50,000 \times \$50 = \$2,500,000$$

c. Revenue and cost

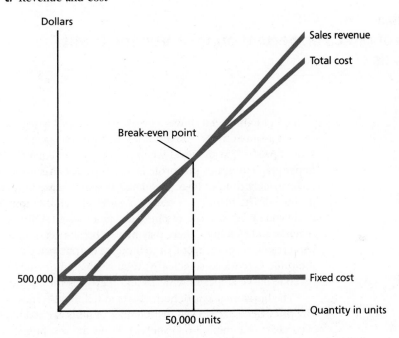

d. If fixed costs increase by 10 percent, the break-even point rises by 10 percent, from 50,000 units to 55,000 units.

Proof: New break-even point $= \dfrac{\$550,000}{\$10} = 55,000$ units

e. X_Y denotes the sales in units required to earn an after-tax profit of Y; F denotes fixed cost; t denotes the tax rate; and c denotes the unit contribution margin.

$$X_Y = \frac{F + \dfrac{Y}{1-t}}{c} = \frac{\$500,000 + \dfrac{\$24,000}{1-.4}}{\$10} = \frac{\$500,000 + \$40,000}{\$10}$$

$$= 54,000 \text{ units}$$

APPENDIX
An Economic Perspective on Cost-Volume-Profit Analysis

Panel A of Exhibit 3-6 shows a break-even analysis when the revenue and cost curves are not assumed to be straight lines. Exhibit 3-6 is useful in explaining why the firm should produce at the level where marginal cost equals marginal revenue, since the upper graph indicates that profit is maximized at an output of Q_m. (The marginal cost, at a particular output level, is defined as the increase in total cost if one more unit is produced. The marginal revenue, at a given level of output, is defined as the increase in revenue from the sale of one more unit.) Panel A also shows that, with nonlinear revenue and cost lines, there may be two break-even points, X_1 and X_2. This phenomenon results from the fact that to increase output, price must be reduced. However, if the price is reduced sufficiently, total revenue ultimately decreases. Thus, the total-revenue curve slopes downward and recrosses the total-cost curve.

The horizontal axis of both charts in Exhibit 3-6 shows the number of units sold. The price necessary to sell that number of units is obtained from Panel B. The break-even chart of Exhibit 3-6 (Panel A) shows the revenue, cost, and profit for different levels of unit sales and different prices (though for only one level of sales at each price).

Panel B of Exhibit 3-6 graphs the marginal cost, marginal revenue, and average revenue curves. The two graphs are related in the following ways. The output where marginal cost equals marginal revenue, Q_m, is the output where the difference between the total-revenue and total-cost curves is greatest. (Profit is maximized and the slope of the total-cost curve equals the slope of the total-revenue curve.) The price, P, at which profit is greatest on the break-even chart in Panel A is the price determined by the intersection of the vertical line through the point where marginal cost equals marginal revenue (point B) and the average-revenue curve. The point where total revenue reaches a maximum, point A, is where the marginal revenue is equal to zero. The marginal-cost curve attains a minimum at the point where the total-cost curve changes from concave downward to concave upward (point C). Finally, the two break-even points, Q_{b1} and Q_{b2} (neither of which appears in Panel B), bracket the optimal level of activity, Q_m.

The presentation of a break-even chart with changing prices is not meant to suggest that the conventional break-even chart with its assumption of constant prices is not useful. In many cases it is the more useful presentation. However, if the need is for a chart showing the results of different possible price-quantity relations, a figure similar to Exhibit 3-6 should be used.

A common managerial practice is to draw a break-even chart assuming the present price will continue, and to show that a decrease in price requires greater sales in order to break even. There is no question that the lower the price, the higher the

EXHIBIT 3-6

Break-even Chart (Panel A) and Output-Price Chart (Panel B)
When Revenue and Cost Curves Are Nonlinear

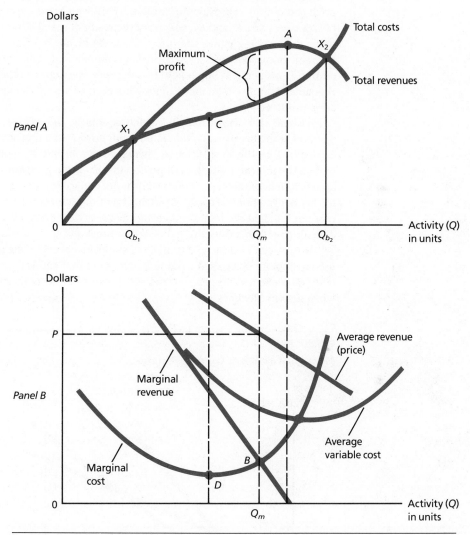

break-even point in terms of units sold and total revenues, assuming no gains in efficiency. The lowest conceivable break-even point is the sale of one unit with a price equal to the sum of the variable cost of one unit and the total fixed cost. Thus, only one unit would have to be sold to break even. But could that unit be sold? Probably not.

Exhibit 3-6 shows that the optimal price and output are determined by reference to the marginal-cost, marginal-revenue, and average-revenue curves. The effect on the break-even point is not considered in determining the optimum price, nor should it be. The conventional break-even analysis is inadequate for determining the optimal price and output. For example, Exhibit 3-7 shows a break-even chart with two possible revenue lines, R_1 and R_2, which are the result of two different prices, P_1 and P_2. All other things being equal, the price that leads to the revenue line R_1 appears more desirable because it gives a lower break-even point and higher profits at every point of output. However, it is impossible to determine the better of the two prices until the probable revenues to be earned following each of the two suggested pricing policies are considered.

Assume that with price P_1, which results in the revenue curve R_1, the firm operates at the break-even point B, but with price P_2 the firm sells an amount equal to capacity, Q. In this case, price P_2, which results in line R_2, is more desirable, even though the indicated break-even point with that price is higher. The fact that a larger dollar amount of sales (or of units sold) is needed to break even does not indicate that the break-even point is harder to attain. Again, a price equal to the sum of the variable cost per unit and the total fixed cost gives the lowest break-even point, but it may be difficult to sell that one unit necessary to break even.

Break-even analysis is essentially a static analysis. The diagram cannot easily be used to explore changes in circumstances over time. This is the result of the irreversibility of efficiency changes and the sticky nature of costs that tend not to decrease when activity declines.

EXHIBIT 3-7

Comparing Two Selling Prices

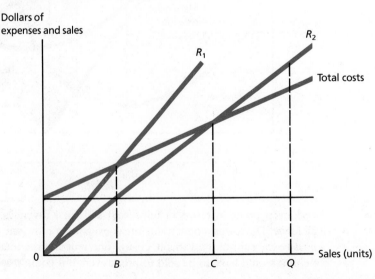

**Cost and
Benefit of
Information
and Decision
Analysis**

Although the logic of marginal analysis is correct, it is not commonly used in practice because the required information is often costly to obtain. The average-revenue, the marginal-revenue, and the marginal-cost curves are seldom known. If these curves are not known, then the solution to the problem of output and price cannot be solved precisely. For example, it might be argued that if prices were reduced, competitors would also reduce prices and output would not be increased. When plotting a firm's average-revenue curve, the actions of competitors should be taken into consideration.

The informational and analytical requirements of a complete marginal analysis make it a costly procedure to employ. The analytical demands are costly in terms of managerial time and effort, and the data needed for the analysis require a sophisticated and costly information system. The marginal-cost curve is neither readily available nor can it be established easily from the accounting records. This is not merely an oversight on the part of the management accountant. The informed management accountant appreciates the importance of marginal costs but also recognizes the expense and feasibility of accumulating this information. It is very difficult to measure the change in cost caused by adding or dropping a single unit of production. Instead,

EXHIBIT 3-8

Information and Decision Analysis

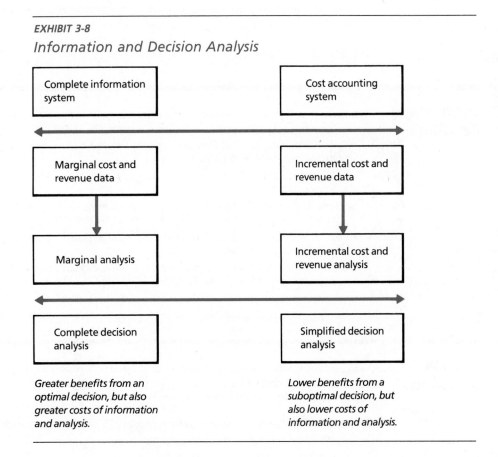

the management accountant compromises and substitutes a technique that uses incremental costs.

The economic approach is concerned with the increase in revenues and expenses arising from the additional production and sale of one unit. The management-accounting approach concerns itself with the increase in revenues and expenses arising from the additional sale of a block or group of units. This approach is known as *incremental-cost* analysis. For instance, what is the effect of a sale of 1,000 units at a price of $5 a unit? To answer this question, the total cost without the sale is compared to the total cost if the sale is made. The difference is the incremental cost of making the sale. If the revenue of $5,000 is greater than the incremental cost, the sale will increase total profit.

Although the incremental cost and revenue approach may not yield the optimal decision in terms of a profit-maximizing price, it may be best in a broader sense. When the cost of a somewhat inferior pricing decision, resulting from using the accountants' approximate methods, is weighed against the cost of the informational and analytical requirements of a marginal analysis, it is quite possible that the simplified approach is the most effective when both costs and benefits are considered. The cost/benefit trade-offs associated with information and decision analysis are summarized in Exhibit 3-8.

Suggested Readings

Areeda, P., and D. Turner. "Predatory Pricing and Related Practices under Section 2 of the Sherman Act." *Harvard Law Review* (Volume 88, 1975). 697–733.

Hilton, R. "Determinants of Cost Information Value: An Illustrative Analysis." *Journal of Accounting Research* (Autumn 1979).

Ijiri, Y., and H. Itami. "Cost-Volume Relationship and Demand Information." *Accounting Review* (October 1973): 724–737.

Jaedicke, R. K., and A. Robichek. "Cost-Volume-Profit Analysis Under Conditions of Uncertainty." *Accounting Review* (October 1964): 917–926.

Kaplan, R. and A. Atkinson. *Advanced Management Accounting*, 2nd ed. Englewood Cliffs, N.J.: Prentice-Hall, 1989.

Shih, W. "A General Decision Model for Cost-Volume Profit Analysis Under Uncertainty." *Accounting Review* (October 1979): 687–706.

Review Questions

3-1 In a situation where a corporation desires a 20 percent return on the plant assets it owns, would it be correct to start the budgeting process by computing the necessary profit and then conceiving decisions that will lead to the desired profit?

3-2 Assume that the cost-accounting system produces a cost per unit of $50. What questions may be raised relative to this cost measure?

3-3 In establishing an optimal price, should the firm take into consideration fixed costs of production?

3-4 The conventional break-even analysis shows total cost and total revenues as straight lines. What are the assumptions and limitations of using straight lines in this type of analysis?

3-5 Explain how the following curves are interrelated:

a. Total revenue and marginal revenue.

b. Total cost and marginal cost.

3-6 Discuss the following statement: "If you lower your price, the break-even point will increase."

3-7 Assuming that a firm is currently pricing its product optimally, should it change its price if it is able to shift its average variable-cost curve downward? Assume that the average-revenue curve slopes downward.

3-8 "Costs are simply a function of output. They increase when output increases and decrease when output decreases." Comment.

Exercises

3-9 **Sales-Mix Decisions** An automobile executive wants to expand the sales of the firm's deluxe model because its ratio of gross margin to sales is higher than that of any other model. This expansion would require additional plant facilities. Discuss.

3-10 **Target Profit Level; Taxes** The Brywood Corporation sells a single product. Fixed costs are $240,000, the unit variable cost is $1.75, the unit sales price is $3.55, and the tax rate is 40 percent.

REQUIRED:

Compute the number of units of sales required to earn after-tax profit of $72,000.

3-11 **Mean Sales and Expected Profit** The Brickbat Corporation is about to market a new whiffle bat that has fixed costs of $100,000 and variable costs of $3 per unit at a level of production of 100,000 units. (There are changes in efficiency for different levels of sales.) The company is considering selling the bats at a price of $4 per unit. The probabilities of different sales levels, as estimated by the sales manager, and the profit for the different levels of sales are as follows:

Sales	Probability of Sales	Profit Given Sales
$ 50,000	0.10	$(25,000)
100,000	0.50	0
150,000	0.30	40,000
200,000	0.10	75,000

REQUIRED:

a. Compute the mean sales. (The mean is a weighted average, with each sales level weighted by its probability.)

b. Compute the expected profit (weighting each profit level by the likelihood it will occur and adding the products).

3-12 **Effects of Pricing on Revenue**   The demand for a product is said to have an elasticity greater than 1 if a decrease in the sales price of the product will result in an increase in total revenues. The economist hired by the Roger Corporation has come up with the following schedule, which shows that the elasticity of the product being sold by the Roger Corporation is greater than 1 (the demand is relatively elastic). The capacity of the plant is 150,000 units per year.

	Present Policy	If Price Is Reduced 10%	If Price Is Reduced 20%
Price per unit	$ 1.00	$ .90	$ .80
Unit sales (per year)	100,000	120,000	150,000
Fixed manufacturing costs (per year)	15,000	15,000	15,000
Variable manufacturing costs	.50 (per unit)		

REQUIRED:

a. Compute the total revenues following the three alternatives.

b. What are the break-even points?

c. What price should the firm charge?

3-13 **Pricing Decisions**   A corporation has fixed costs of $250,000 and variable costs of $2 per unit. The company is attempting to choose the best of three possible prices. The prices and estimated sales are as follows:

Price	$ 2.50	$ 3.00	$ 3.50
Estimated sales (units)	500,000	280,000	200,000

REQUIRED:

Based on expected profit, what price should be charged? Compute the break-even points for the three prices.

3-14 **Effect of Production on Sales Prices**   An automobile company in England slows its production of automobiles and shifts to a four-day work week. The company is considering increasing its export of cars. It states that a good export position requires a strong home market because large production reduces unit costs. If the sales in the home market slow down, unit costs rise, putting pressure on export sales prices.

REQUIRED:

Comment on the company's point of view.

3-15 Explaining Increases in Break-Even Volume The American Dynamics Company experienced an increase in its break-even volume as sales expanded sharply over the period 19x2–19x5. The expansion in sales occurred despite the fact that prices were increased enough to cover the direct increases in unit variable cost resulting from increases in direct material prices, wage rates, and related items. Can you suggest a reason for this occurrence?

3-16 Interpreting Profit-Volume Graphs A profit-volume or P/V graph is sometimes used in place of or along with the break-even chart. An example of such a graph is given here:

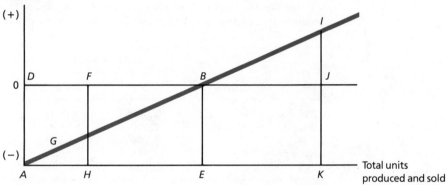

REQUIRED:

a. What does *JK* represent?

b. What is represented by the point *E?*

c. What is represented by *IJ?* (Be precise.)

d. What is represented by *GH?*

e. What does *IK ÷ AK* represent?

f. What does *IJ ÷ DJ* represent?

g. If variable cost per unit decreases (other factors constant), what would happen to the ratio *IJ/DJ?* Why?

h. If fixed costs were to increase but sales prices were also increased to the extent necessary to retain the prior breakeven, what would be the effect on profits at a level of output (sales) *K* and how would this appear on the graph?

i. Order the following in terms of their absolute effect on the slope of the line *AI*. (Give a 1 to the greatest change and a 3 to the smallest change.)

(1) Variable cost per unit declines 10 percent.

(2) Selling price per unit declines 10 percent.

(3) Fixed costs decline 10 percent.

j. What, in your opinion, is the most significant limitation to traditional break-even analysis and why do you think so?

Problems

3-17 **CVP Analysis; Explaining Fluctuations in Income**   The Brake-Even Company manufactures two general types of brakes — automobile and truck. The management of the Brake-Even Company is concerned because fluctuations in income have been experienced in the past few years. Some members of management have also suggested that one of the product lines should be dropped.

The company has made an analysis of its sales and income by product line (each of the products is organized as a department for manufacturing and sales purposes).

		Sales of Brakes		Income Before Taxes	
Year	Quarter	Auto	Trucks	Auto	Trucks
19x4	1	$2,000ᵃ	$ 500	$ 200	$(450)
	2	2,400	600	440	(440)
	3	3,200	1,200	920	(380)
	4	1,500	2,000	(100)	(300)
19x5	1	2,100	1,500	260	(350)

ᵃ All dollar figures in thousands.

An analysis of the expenses associated with the sales of the product disclosed the following information:

	Auto Dept.	Truck Dept.
Variable costs per dollar of sales, 19x4		
Material	$ .10	$ .25
Direct labor	.21	.50
Variable overhead	.05	.10
Variable selling expenses	.04	.05
	$ .40	$ .90
Fixed costs for 19x4		
Directly associated with the department:		
Avoidable (foremen's salaries, etc.)	$1,600,000	$ 80,000
Unavoidable (depreciation of special equipment, etc.)	400,000	320,000
Allocated from other departments (including administrative costs)	2,000,000	1,600,000
	$4,000,000	$2,000,000

The unavoidable costs cannot be avoided by sale of the equipment because the removal costs would approximately equal the sales price. General overhead would not be reduced by elimination of any one of the product lines.

For internal reporting purposes, the company charges all fixed costs to the period in which they are incurred, and only variable costs are considered a cost of product.

REQUIRED:

a. Prepare an analysis explaining the fluctuations in income.

b. Make recommendations as to the desirability of continuing the sale and production of any of the products.

c. Prepare a break-even chart for the auto department. Explain the difficulties connected with preparing one break-even chart for the company as a whole.

d. Assume that during the first quarter of 19x5 the auto brakes were sold at a price of $20 per unit. If the price were dropped to $15 per unit, 200,000 would be sold (according to the company's economist). Is the reduction in price desirable? Assume that the variable costs are $8 per unit.

3-18 CVP Analysis; Special-Order Decision   The New York Company manufactures folding chairs for sale to clubs, commercial establishments, and individual consumers. At this level, the company produces 60,000 chairs, which it sells at an average price per chair of $8.40. Total costs at the 40 percent level are made up of $216,000 for fixed items and $360,000 for variable items. Variable costs are known to change exactly in proportion to output.

REQUIRED:

a. If the average selling price remains the same as it has been in the past, at what level of activity will the company break even?

b. What would the company's profit be if it could operate (and sell) at capacity?

c. Assume that the company computes the fixed cost per unit using their capacity level of operations. What is the average total cost per unit?

d. Assume that a new customer offers the New York Company $6.80 per unit for its product. Provided that there are no effects on sales to old customers (and no legal complications), should the New York Company accept an order for 40,000 chairs? Briefly justify your answers.

3-19 Robinson-Patman Act   The Winter Company is considering offering one of its customers a quantity discount, but the president of the firm is concerned about the possibility of the government bringing action under the Robinson-Patman Act. The usual method of shipment for the Winter Company is to pack its product individually in boxes and ship by truck. If a customer would be willing to buy in larger quantities (such as 1,000 units), larger containers could be used. In fact, it would be possible to ship the product loose in a railroad freight car. The estimated packing saving would be $0.20 per unit.

REQUIRED:

Would the cost savings described be acceptable grounds for having price differentials for customers who ordered in 1,000-unit lots?

3-20 Justifying Price Differentials   The Fall River Paper Company sells to two different customers. One customer is charged a price of $2 per unit and the other customer is charged
a price of $3 per unit. In defense of its pricing policy, the following schedule was prepared
by the company:

	Unit Revenue and Cost Schedules for Selling to:			
	Company A		Company B	
Net margin[a]	$1.00	100%	$2.00	100%
Distribution costs (allocations based on net margin)	.60	60	1.20	60
Net income	$ .40	40%	$ .80	40%

[a] Net margin is after deducting the cost of product sold, $1.

Because the profit per dollar of net margin was the same for sales to both companies,
the Fall River Paper Company argued that it was reasonable to charge Company *A* a price
of $1 and Company *B* a price of $2.

REQUIRED:

Comment on whether the price differentials are justified. What additional information
would you want before advising Fall River's management?

3-21 Charges of Illegal Price Discrimination   "Because the cost defense against a charge of illegal
price discrimination provided by Section 2(a) of the Clayton Act as amended by the
Robinson-Patman Act has proved largely illusory in practice, the prudent company is
advised to charge the same price on commodities of similar grade and quality." Do you
agree with this statement? Why or why not?

3-22 Cost-Volume-Profit   Siberian Ski Company recently expanded its manufacturing capacity
that will allow it to produce up to 15,000 pairs of cross-country skis of the mountaineering
model or the touring model. The sales department assures management that it can sell
between 9,000 and 13,000 of either product this year. Because the models are similar,
Siberian Ski will produce only one of the two models.

The following information was compiled by the accounting department:

	Model	
	Mountaineering	Touring
Selling price per unit	$88.00	$80.00
Variable costs per unit	$52.80	$52.80

Fixed costs will total $369,600 if the mountaineering model is produced but will be only $316,800 if the touring model is produced. Siberian Ski Company is subject to a 40 percent income tax rate.

REQUIRED:

a. Calculate the contribution margin rate on the touring model.

b. If Siberian Ski Company desires an after-tax net income of $24,000, how many pairs of touring model skis will the company have to sell?

c. Compute the total sales revenue at which Siberian Ski Company would make the same profit or loss regardless of the ski model it decided to produce.

d. How much would the variable cost per unit of the touring model have to change before it had the same break-even point in units as the mountaineering model?

e. If the variable cost per unit of touring skis decreases by 10 percent and the total fixed cost of touring skis increases by 10 percent, compute the new break-even point. (*CMA adapted*)

3-23 Break-Even Point; Multiple Products The J. J. Finley Company produces three lines of suntan lotion:

	Product Line	Sales Ratio
A	Sun block (provides maximum protection)	40%
B	Sun screen (provides moderate protection)	30
C	Sun tan (provides minimal protection)	30

J. J. Finley's fixed costs amount to $279,000. The prices and unit variable costs of the three products are as follows:

	Price	Unit Variable Cost
A	$6.20	$4.20
B	$5.30	$3.80
C	$4.80	$3.80

REQUIRED:

Compute the company's break-even point in units. How many units of sales of each product would be predicted at the break-even point?

3-24 Break-Even; Changes in Variable Costs   Maxwell Company manufactures and sells a single product. Price and cost data regarding Maxwell's product and operations are as follows:

Selling price per unit	$ 25.00
Variable costs per unit	
Raw materials	$ 11.00
Direct labor	5.00
Manufacturing overhead	2.50
Selling expenses	1.30
Total variable costs per unit	$ 19.80
Annual fixed costs	
Manufacturing overhead	$ 192,000
Selling and administrative	276,000
Total fixed costs	$ 468,000
Forecasted annual sales volume (120,000 units)	$3,000,000
Income tax rate	40%

REQUIRED:

a. Compute Maxwell's break-even point in units.

b. How many units would Maxwell Company have to sell in order to earn $156,000 after taxes?

c. Maxwell Company estimates that its direct-labor costs will increase 8 percent next year. How many units will Maxwell have to sell next year to reach break even?

d. If Maxwell Company's direct-labor costs increase 8 percent, what selling price per unit of product must it charge to maintain the same contribution margin ratio? (*CMA adapted*)

3-25 Understanding CVP Graph; Multiple Choice   The SAB Company uses a profit-volume graph similar to the one shown on the following page to represent the CVP relationships of its operations. The vertical (y-axis) is the profit in dollars and the horizontal (x-axis) is the volume in units. The diagonal line is the contribution margin line.

REQUIRED:

Complete statements a through e by selecting the correct response.

a. Point *A* on the profit-volume graph represents

(*1*) the point where fixed costs equal sales.

(*2*) the point where fixed costs equal variable costs.

(*3*) a volume level of zero units.

(*4*) the point where total costs equals total sales.

(*5*) the point where the rate of contribution margin increases.

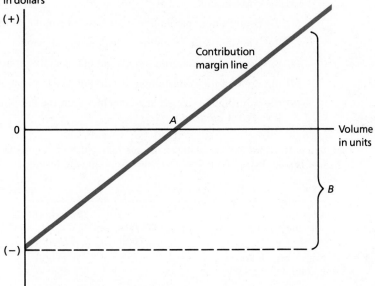

Profit in dollars

b. The vertical distance from the dotted line to the contribution margin line denoted as *B* on the profit-volume graph represents

(1) the total contribution margin.

(2) the contribution margin per unit.

(3) the contribution margin rate.

(4) total sales.

(5) the sum of the variable and fixed costs.

c. If SAB Company's fixed costs increase,

(1) the contribution margin line shifts upward parallel to the present line.

(2) the contribution margin line shifts downward parallel to the present line.

(3) the slope of the contribution margin line is more pronounced (steeper).

(4) the slope of the contribution margin line is less pronounced (flatter).

(5) the contribution margin line coincides with the present contribution margin line.

d. If SAB Company's variable costs per unit increase but its unit selling price stays constant,

(1) the contribution margin line shifts upward parallel to the present line.

(2) the contribution margin line shifts downward parallel to the present line.

(3) the slope of the contribution margin line is more pronounced (steeper).

(4) the slope of the contribution margin line is less pronounced (flatter).

(5) the slope of the contribution margin line changes but how it will change is not determinable.

e. If SAB Company increases its unit selling price to offset exactly the increase in the variable cost per unit,

   (1) the contribution margin line shifts upward parallel to the present line.

   (2) the contribution margin line shifts downward parallel to the present line.

   (3) the slope of the contribution margin line is more pronounced (steeper).

   (4) the slope of the contribution margin line is less pronounced (flatter).

   (5) the contribution margin line coincides with the present contribution margin line. (*CMA adapted*)

3-26 Straightforward CVP Calculations; Income Taxes   Laraby Company produces a single product. It sold 25,000 units last year with the following results:

Sales		$625,000
Variable costs	$375,000	
Fixed costs	150,000	525,000
Net income before taxes		$100,000
Income taxes (45%)		45,000
Net income		$ 55,000

To improve its product, Laraby is considering replacing a component part in its product that has a cost of $2.50 with a new and better part costing $4.50 per unit in the coming year. A new machine also would be needed to increase plant capacity. The machine costs $18,000 and has a useful life of six years and no salvage value. The company uses straight-line depreciation on all plant assets.

REQUIRED:

a. What was Laraby Company's break-even point in number of units last year?

b. How many units of product would Laraby Company have to sell in the last year to earn $77,000 in net income after taxes?

c. If Laraby Company holds the sales price constant and makes the suggested changes, how many units of product must be sold in the coming year to break even?

d. If Laraby Company holds the sales price constant and makes the suggested changes, how many units of product does the company have to sell to match last year's net income after taxes?

e. If Laraby Company wishes to maintain the same contribution margin ratio, what selling price per unit of product must it charge next year to cover the increased material costs? (*CMA adapted*)

3-27 Retail; CVP Analysis with Changes in Costs   DisKing Company is a retailer for video disks. Its projected after-tax net income for the current year is $120,000 based on a sales volume of 200,000 video disks. DisKing has been selling the disks at $16 each. The variable costs consist of the $10 unit purchase price of the disks and a handling cost of $2 per disk. DisKing's annual fixed costs are $600,000, and DisKing is subject to a 40 percent income tax rate. Management expects that in the coming year the unit purchase price of the video disks will increase 30 percent.

REQUIRED:

   a. Compute DisKing Company's break-even point for the current year in number of video disks.

   b. An increase of 10 percent in projected unit sales volume for the current year results in an increased after-tax income for the current year of what amount?

   c. Compute the volume of sales in dollars that DisKing Company must achieve in the coming year to maintain the same after-tax net income as projected for the current year, if unit selling price remains at $16.

   d. In order to cover a 30 percent increase in the disk's purchase price for the coming year and still maintain the current contribution margin ratio, DisKing Company must establish a selling price per disk for the coming year of what amount? (*CMA adapted*)

3-28 CVP; Determine Price   The Bodine Company produces a single product, which currently sells for $5.00. Fixed costs are expected to amount to $60,000 for the year, and all variable manufacturing and administrative costs are expected to be incurred at a rate of $3.00 per unit. Bodine has two sales employees who are paid strictly on a commission basis. Their commission is 10 percent of the sales dollars they generate.

REQUIRED:

   a. If Bodine alters its current plans by spending an additional amount of $5,000 on advertising and increases the selling price to $6.00 per unit, compute the before-tax profit on 60,000 units.

   b. The Sorde Company has just approached Bodine to make a special one-time purchase of 10,000 units. These units would not be sold by the sales force, and therefore no commission would have to be paid. Compute the price Bodine would have to charge per unit on this special order to earn additional profit of $20,000 before taxes. (*CMA adapted*)

3-29 Agribusiness; CVP with Changing Costs and Prices   The statement of income for Central Florida Groves, Inc. is presented below. It represents the operating results for the year just ended. The company had sales of 1,800 tons of orange juice during the current year. The production capacity of the company's facilities is 3,000 tons of product.

CENTRAL FLORIDA GROVES, INC.
Statement of Income
for the Year Ended December 31, 19x0

Sales	$900,000
Variable costs	
Manufacturing	$315,000
Selling costs	180,000
Total variable costs	$495,000
Contribution margin	$405,000
Fixed costs	
Manufacturing	$ 90,000
Selling	112,500
Administration	45,000
Total fixed costs	$247,500
Net income before income taxes	$157,500
Income taxes (40%)	63,000
Net income after income taxes	$ 94,500

REQUIRED:

Answer each of the following questions independently.

a. Compute the break-even volume in tons of product for 19x0.

b. If the sales volume is estimated to be 2,100 tons in the next year, and if the prices and costs stay at the same levels and amounts next year, compute the after-tax net income that the company can expect for 19x1.

c. Central Florida Groves has a potential foreign customer that has offered to buy 1,500 tons at $450 per ton. Assume that all of the company's costs would be at the same levels and rates as in 19x0. What net income after taxes would the firm make if it took this order and rejected some business from regular customers so as not to exceed capacity?

d. Central Florida Groves's management plans to market its product in a new territory. It estimates that an advertising and promotion program costing $61,500 annually will need to be undertaken for the next two or three years. In addition, a $25 per ton sales commission over and above the current commission to the sales force in the new territory will be required. How many tons have to be sold in the new territory to maintain the company's current after-tax income of $94,500?

e. The firm is considering replacing a highly labor-intensive process with an automatic machine, which would result in an increase of $58,500 annually in fixed manufacturing costs. The variable manufacturing costs would decrease $25 per ton. Calculate the new break-even volume in tons.

f. Ignore the facts presented in requirement **e** and now assume that the company estimates that the per-ton selling price will decline 10 percent next year, variable costs will increase $40 per ton, and the fixed costs will not change. What sales volume in dollars will be required to earn an after-tax net income of $94,500 next year? (*CMA adapted*)

3-30 Break-Even Calculation; Return on Assets, Income Taxes Madden Company has projected its income before taxes for next year as shown below. Madden is subject to a 40 percent income tax rate.

Sales (160,000 units)		$8,000,000
Cost of sales		
Variable costs	$2,000,000	
Fixed costs	3,000,000	
Total costs		5,000,000
Income before taxes		$3,000,000

REQUIRED:

a. Compute Madden's break-even point in units sold for the next year.

b. If Madden wants $4,500,000 of income before taxes, compute the required sales in dollars.

c. Madden's net assets are $36,000,000. Compute the dollar sales that must be achieved for Madden to earn a 10 percent after-tax return on assets. (*CMA adapted*)

3-31 CVP; Income Taxes; Determine Selling Price Pawnee Company operated at normal capacity during the current year, producing 50,000 units of its single product. Sales totaled 40,000 units at an average price of $20 per unit. Variable manufacturing costs were $8 per unit, and variable marketing costs were $4 per unit sold. Fixed costs were incurred uniformly throughout the year and amounted to $188,000 for manufacturing and $64,000 for marketing. There was no year-end work-in-process inventory.

REQUIRED:

a. Compute Pawnee's break-even point in sales dollars for the current year.

b. If Pawnee is subject to an income tax rate of 30 percent, compute the number of units required to be sold in the current year to earn an after-tax net income of $126,000.

c. Pawnee's variable manufacturing costs are expected to increase 10 percent in the coming year. Compute Pawnee's break-even point in sales dollars for the coming year.

d. If Pawnee's variable manufacturing costs increase 10 percent, calculate the selling price that would yield Pawnee the same contribution margin rate in the coming year. (*CMA adapted*)

3-32 Break-Even; Taxes; Changes in Fixed Costs   Budget data for the Bidwell Company are as follows:

Sales (100,000 units)			$1,000,000
Costs	*Fixed*	*Variable*	
Raw material	$ –0–	$300,000	
Direct labor	–0–	200,000	
Factory costs	100,000	150,000	
Selling and administrative costs	110,000	50,000	
Total costs	$210,000	$700,000	910,000
Budgeted operating income			$ 90,000

REQUIRED:

a. Based on the above data, compute the break-even sales in units.

b. If Bidwell Company is subject to an income tax rate of 40 percent, compute the number of units Bidwell needs to sell to earn an after-tax profit of $90,000.

c. If fixed costs increased $31,500 with no other cost or revenue factors changing, calculate the break-even sales in units. (*CMA adapted*)

3-33 CVP Considerations in Decision Making; Retail   Condensed monthly operating income data for Cosmo, Inc. for November 19x4 is presented below. Additional information regarding Cosmo's operations follows the statement.

	Total	Mall Store	Town Store
Sales	$200,000	$80,000	$120,000
Less variable costs	116,000	32,000	84,000
Contribution margin	$ 84,000	$48,000	$ 36,000
Less direct fixed expenses	60,000	20,000	40,000
Store segment margin	$ 24,000	$28,000	$ (4,000)
Less common fixed expenses	10,000	4,000	6,000
Operating income	$ 14,000	$24,000	$(10,000)

(1) One-fourth of each store's direct fixed expenses would continue through December 31, 19x5, if either store were closed.

(2) Cosmo allocates common fixed expenses to each store on the basis of sales dollars.

(3) Management estimates that closing the Town Store would result in a 10 percent decrease in Mall Store sales, while closing the Mall Store would not affect Town Store sales.

(4) The operating results for November 19x4 are representative of all months.

REQUIRED:

a. A decision by Cosmo, Inc. to close the Town Store would result in a monthly increase (decrease) in Cosmo's operating income during 19x5 of what amount?

b. Cosmo is considering a promotional campaign at the Town Store that would not affect the Mall Store. Increasing annual promotional expenses at the Town Store by $60,000 in order to increase Town Store sales by 10 percent would result in a monthly increase (decrease) in Cosmo's operating income during 19x5 of what amount?

c. One-half of Town Store's dollar sales are from items sold at variable cost to attract customers to the store. Cosmo is considering the deletion of these items, a move that would reduce the Town store's direct fixed expenses by 15 percent and result in the loss of 20 percent of the remaining Town Store's sales volume. This change would not affect the Mall Store. A decision by Cosmo to eliminate the items sold at cost would result in a monthly increase (decrease) in Cosmo's operating income during 19x5 of what amount? (*CMA adapted*)

3-34 CVP Relationships in Equation Form   Able Company has one department that produces three replacement parts for the company. However, only one part can be produced in any month because of the adjustments that must be made to the equipment. The department can produce up to 15,000 units of any one of the three parts in each month. The company expresses the monthly after-tax CVP relationships for each part using an equation method. The format of the equations and the equation for each replacement part are given below:

Equation Format

$$(ATR) \times [(SP - VC) \times U - FC]$$

ATR = after-tax rate

SP = selling price

VC = variable cost

U = units

FC = fixed costs

Part	Part Equations
AL45	$.6[(\$4.00 - \$1.25)U - \$33,400]$
BT62	$.6[(\$4.05 - \$2.55)U - \$15,000]$
GM17	$.6[(\$4.10 - \$2.00)U - \$22,365]$

REQUIRED:

a. Compute the contribution margin per unit for Part BT62.

b. Compute the break-even volume in units for Part GM17.

c. If Able Company produces and sells 13,000 units of Part AL45, compute the amount of Able's after-tax net income attributable to this product.

d. Calculate the number of units of Part BT62 required to be produced and sold to contribute $4,140 to Able's net income after tax.

e. Calculate the production and unit sales volume level at which Able Company will profit equally from Parts BT62 and GM17. (*CMA adapted*)

3-35 **Break-Even; Alternative Production Methods; Computer-Integrated Manufacturing** Candice Company has decided to introduce a new product. The new product can be manufactured by either its new computer-integrated manufacturing (CIM) system or a labor-intensive method. The manufacturing method will not affect the quality of the product. The estimated manufacturing costs by the two methods are as follows:

	CIM System		Labor Intensive Method	
Raw materials		$5.00		$5.60
Direct labor	.5DLH[a] @ $12	6.00	.8DLH @ $9	7.20
Variable overhead	.5DLH @ $6	3.00	.8DLH @ $6	4.80
Directly traceable incremental fixed manufacturing costs		$2,440,000		$1,320,000

[a] DLH denotes *direct labor hours*.

Candice's market research department has recommended an introductory unit sales price of $30. The incremental selling expenses are estimated to be $500,000 annually plus $2 for each unit sold regardless of the manufacturing method.

REQUIRED:

a. Calculate the estimated break-even point in annual unit sales of the new product if Candice Company uses the

　(1) CIM system.

　(2) labor-intensive manufacturing method.

b. Determine the annual unit sales volume at which Candice Company profits equally from the two manufacturing methods. (*CMA adapted*)

3-36 Hospital; Break-Even; Capacity Decision   Melford Hospital operates a general hospital but rents space and beds to separately owned entities rendering specialized services such as pediatrics and psychiatric. Melford charges each separate entity for common services such as patients' meals and laundry and for administrative services such as billings and collections. Space and bed rentals are fixed charges for the year, based on bed capacity rented to each entity.

Melford charged the following costs to pediatrics for the fiscal year ended June 30, 19x2.

	Patient Days (Variable)	Bed Capacity (Fixed)
Dietary	$ 600,000	—
Janitorial	—	$ 70,000
Laundry	300,000	—
Laboratory	450,000	—
Pharmacy	350,000	—
Repairs and maintenance	—	30,000
General and administrative	—	1,300,000
Rent	—	1,500,000
Billings and collections	300,000	—
Totals	$2,000,000	$2,900,000

During the year ended June 30, 19x2, pediatrics charged each patient an average of $300 per day, had a capacity of 60 beds, and had revenue of $6,000,000 for 365 days. In addition, pediatrics directly employed the following personnel:

	Annual Salaries
Supervising nurses	$25,000
Nurses	20,000
Aides	9,000

Melford has the following minimum departmental personnel requirements based on total annual patient days:

Annual Patient Days	Aides	Nurses	Supervising Nurses
Up to 21,900	20	10	4
21,901 to 26,000	26	13	4
26,001 to 29,200	30	15	4

These staffing levels represent full-time equivalents. Pediatrics always employs only the minimum number of required full-time equivalent personnel. Salaries of supervising nurses, nurses, and aides are therefore fixed within ranges of annual patient days.

Pediatrics operated at 100 percent capacity on ninety days during the year ended June 30, 19x2. It is estimated that during these ninety days the demand exceeded twenty patients more than capacity. Melford has an additional twenty beds available for rent for the year ending June 30, 19x3. Such additional rental would increase pediatrics' fixed charges based on bed capacity.

REQUIRED:

a. Calculate the minimum number of patient days required for pediatrics to break even for the year ending June 30, 19x3, if the additional twenty beds are not rented. Patient demand is unknown, but assume that revenue per patient day, cost per patient day, cost per bed, and salary rates remain the same as for the year ended June 30, 19x2.

b. Assume that patient demand, revenue per patient day, cost per patient day, cost per bed, and salary rates for the year ending June 30, 19x3, remain the same as for the year ended June 30, 19x2. Prepare a schedule of increase in revenue and increase in costs for the year ending June 30, 19x3, in order to determine the net increase or decrease in earnings from the additional twenty beds if pediatrics rents this extra capacity from Melford. (*CPA adapted*)

Product and Service Costing

4

Product-Costing Systems and Job-Order Costing

LEARNING OBJECTIVES

After studying this chapter, you should be able to:

1 Diagram the flow of costs through the accounts in a product-costing system.

2 Describe the various approaches to product and service costing.

3 Accumulate, classify, and assign costs to products in a job-order costing system.

4 Explain the three main steps in accounting for overhead.

Overview of Product-Costing Systems

Product costing is the process of accumulating and classifying costs and then assigning those costs to products. For external reporting purposes, a firm must develop product costs to value inventory and determine income. Inventory is an asset that is valued at its cost under Generally Accepted Accounting Principles. When the inventory is subsequently sold, its cost becomes an expense called *cost of goods sold*.

Product costs are also used in various managerial decisions. In product-mix decisions, pricing decisions, inventory-control procedures, make or buy decisions, bidding, and a host of other decisions, managers use product-cost data in one way or another.

There is an ever-growing need for product-cost information in various relationships between firms and outside organizations. Regulated firms, such as electrical utility companies, need information about the cost of providing their services to justify customer rate increases to regulatory boards. Manufacturing firms use product-cost information to determine the contract price in cost-plus production contracts. Hospitals are reimbursed by insurance companies, such as Blue Cross/Blue Shield, or by the government, under the Medicare program, on the basis of the estimated cost of the health care services provided.

Product Costing in Manufacturing Firms

As a result of the many uses of product-cost and service-cost information, organizations have developed elaborate procedures for accumulating and assigning production costs. In manufacturing firms, product-costing systems use several manufacturing accounts. Throughout the manufacturing process, production costs are added to a *work-in-process inventory* account. This increases the cost-based value of the asset represented by the partially completed production. When products are completed, their cost is transferred from the work-in-process inventory account to the *finished-goods inventory* account by crediting work-in-process inventory and debiting finished goods inventory. When finished products are sold, their cost is transferred to the expense account called *cost of goods sold* by crediting finished goods inventory and debiting cost of goods sold. The cost-of-goods-sold account is subsequently closed into the *income summary* account at the end of the accounting period. This flow of costs through the manufacturing accounts is summarized in Exhibit 4-1.

Product Costing and Service Costing in Nonmanufacturing Firms

The previous description of cost flows relates to a manufacturing operation. These same cost flows are also generally applicable to nonmanufacturing firms that engage in production of a good that is inventoriable. Examples of such production operations are the harvesting of grapes and subsequent production of wine by Ernest and Julio Gallo and the lumber harvesting and finishing operations of Weyerhauser.

Service-industry firms employ different procedures because they generally have no work-in-process or finished-goods inventory. The services of firms such as Pizza Hut (restaurant food service), Avis (car rental), Ramada Inn (lodging), Aetna (insur-

EXHIBIT 4-1

Cost Flows in a Manufacturing Firm

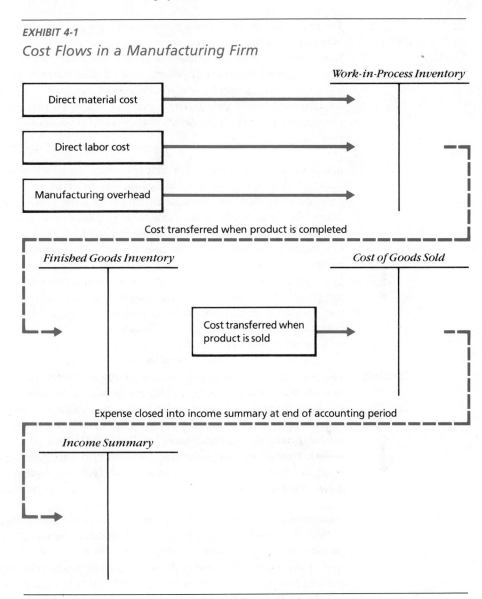

ance), Amtrak (transportation), American Express (financial services), Sloan Kettering Memorial Institute (health care), and Chase Manhattan Bank (banking services) are consumed as they are produced. In such organizations, determining the costs of providing services is also vital to effective management. Many of the procedures of cost accumulation, classification, and assignment for manufacturing firms are applicable to service organizations as well.

Different Types of Product-Costing Systems

The choice of a product-costing system depends on many factors, including the type of industry, the needs of management, and the nature of the product or service. Three basic characteristics distinguish product-costing and service-costing systems: (1) whether actual or estimated costs are used, (2) the treatment of fixed-overhead costs, and (3) the procedures by which costs are accumulated. These three characteristics are discussed briefly below. The remainder of this chapter and the following four chapters are devoted to the details of the various product-costing and service-costing systems.

Actual or Estimated Costs   The first dimension on which product-costing and service-costing systems may be distinguished is the type of cost that is assigned to products or services. In an **actual costing** system the actual costs of direct material, direct labor, and overhead are assigned to products or services. This costing procedure can be used only after the production costs have been incurred and are known. In a **normal costing** system the actual costs of direct material and direct labor are assigned to products or services, but *estimated overhead* is assigned on the basis of a **predetermined overhead rate.** The details of this procedure are discussed later in this chapter. In a **standard costing** system the estimated (rather than actual) costs of direct material, direct labor, and overhead are assigned to products or services. These estimated costs are referred to as *standard costs.* The details of standard costing systems are discussed in Chapters 7 and 8.

The three types of costing systems described above are illustrated in Exhibit 4-2. The Walt Disney Company, located in Burbank, California, is a major producer of movies. Walt Disney uses an actual costing system for film production. McDonnell Douglas Corporation, headquartered in St. Louis, is a large aerospace and information-systems company. Among its products are the DC-10 and the F-15 aircraft. For its aircraft production contract work, McDonnell Douglas uses a normal job costing system. Hewlett-Packard Company, based in Palo Alto, California, produces a wide range of computing and other sophisticated electronic equipment. Hewlett-Packard uses a standard costing system for its personal computer production operation.

Treatment of Fixed Overhead   The manner in which fixed overhead is treated is the second dimension on which product-costing and service-costing systems are distinguished. In an **absorption costing** system, both variable and fixed overhead are treated as product costs, and both are assigned to products or services. In a **variable costing** system, only variable overhead is treated as a product cost. Fixed overhead is treated as a period cost under variable costing. Exhibit 4-3 summarizes the difference between absorption and variable costing. The implications and relative merits of absorption and variable costing are discussed in more detail in Chapter 9.

Cost Accumulation Procedures   The third dimension on which product-costing systems may be distinguished relates to the detailed accounting procedures used to accumulate costs and assign them to products. The two basic costing approaches are called **job-order costing** and **process costing.** Job-order costing is used by firms in which goods are produced in distinct batches. For example, printers, furniture manufacturers, custom machining firms, aircraft manufacturers, shipbuilders, and construction companies use job-order costing. Many service industry firms also use job-order costing procedures, although these firms have no work-in-process or finished goods inventories. In an architectural firm for example, costs are accumulated and assigned to projects in much the same way that they are accumulated for a batch of manufactured items in a job shop.

Process costing procedures are employed by firms producing large quantities of relatively homogeneous products. These firms tend to engage in either continuous or repetitive production operations. Examples of firms using process costing include

---

EXHIBIT 4-2

Actual, Normal, and Standard Costing Systems

ACTUAL COSTING
The Walt Disney Company

The Walt Disney Company. ©

	Productions in Process	Completed Productions	Amortization of the Cost of Productions[b]
Direct material: actual cost of material used in the production of a film	→		
Direct labor: actual cost of direct labor incurred during the production of a film	→	Transferred at actual cost →	Expense recognized at actual cost →
Overhead: allocation of actual overhead to a film	→		
Development cost: actual cost of developing the story and script[a]	→		

(continues)

EXHIBIT 4-2 Continued

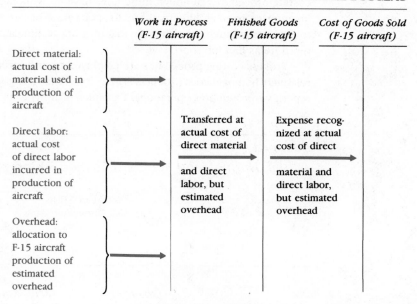

NORMAL COSTING
McDonnell Douglas Corporation

MCDONNELL DOUGLAS

	Work in Process (F-15 aircraft)	Finished Goods (F-15 aircraft)	Cost of Goods Sold (F-15 aircraft)

Direct material: actual cost of material used in production of aircraft

Direct labor: actual cost of direct labor incurred in production of aircraft

Overhead: allocation to F-15 aircraft production of estimated overhead

Transferred at actual cost of direct material and direct labor, but estimated overhead

Expense recognized at actual cost of direct material and direct labor, but estimated overhead

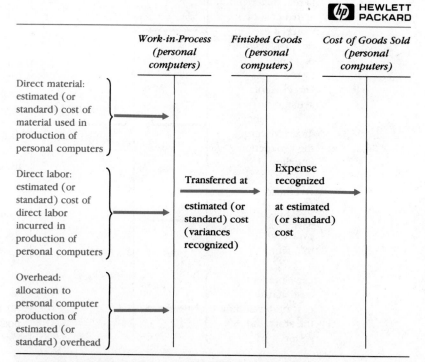

STANDARD COSTING
Hewlett-Packard Company

(hp) HEWLETT PACKARD

	Work-in-Process (personal computers)	Finished Goods (personal computers)	Cost of Goods Sold (personal computers)

Direct material: estimated (or standard) cost of material used in production of personal computers

Direct labor: estimated (or standard) cost of direct labor incurred in production of personal computers

Overhead: allocation to personal computer production of estimated (or standard) overhead

Transferred at estimated (or standard) cost (variances recognized)

Expense recognized at estimated (or standard) cost

[a] Development cost is largely unique to the film industry as a product cost.

[b] The cost of a completed production is recognized as an expense (amortized) over several time periods as the revenue from the film is recognized.

EXHIBIT 4-3

Absorption and Variable Costing

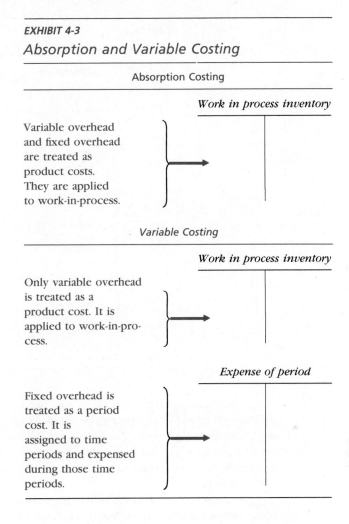

Absorption Costing

Work in process inventory

Variable overhead
and fixed overhead
are treated as
product costs.
They are applied
to work-in-process.

Variable Costing

Work in process inventory

Only variable overhead
is treated as a
product cost. It is
applied to work-in-pro-
cess.

Expense of period

Fixed overhead is
treated as a period
cost. It is
assigned to time
periods and expensed
during those time
periods.

chemical firms, paint manufacturers, food processing firms, oil companies, and some electronics firms.

Exhibit 4-4 reviews two basic characteristics on which product-costing or service-costing systems may be distinguished. As the exhibit suggests, there are six basic costing systems.

{actual, normal, standard}   {absorption, variable}

$$3 \qquad \times \qquad 2 \qquad = 6$$

Each of these costing systems may be employed with the procedures of either job-order costing or process costing. This yields twelve possible cost-approach combinations.

EXHIBIT 4-4

Combinations of Costing Approaches

	Absorption costing	Variable costing
Actual costing	Actual absorption costing	Actual variable costing
Normal costing	Normal absorption costing	Normal variable costing
Standard costing	Standard absorption costing	Standard variable costing

---

In practice, the same firm often uses two or more of these combinations for different plants and production processes. For example, Hewlett-Packard uses a standard, absorption, job-order costing system for its production of electronic instruments in its Loveland Instrument Division. However, the company uses a standard, absorption, process costing system for its production of printed circuit boards in its Boise Division.

Some companies use a **hybrid costing system** that does not perfectly match any of the twelve possible systems listed in Exhibit 4-4. A hybrid costing system combines certain features of a variety of costing approaches in order to tailor the system to the company's special needs. One such hybrid system, called **operation costing,** is covered in Chapter 6, along with process costing systems.

The remainder of this chapter and the next chapter are devoted to a detailed discussion of job-order cost accounting systems.

Job-Order Cost Accounting Systems

Job-order cost accounting systems accumulate costs by jobs or batches. Industries such as construction, furniture, machinery, and printing typically employ production processes that are not repetitive. Such production processes generally yield batches of products that are more or less distinctive. The details of job-order costing discussed below assume that either normal or actual costing is in use. Standard costing is discussed in Chapters 7 and 8.

The Job-Cost Sheet

In a manufacturing firm, each production job or batch is given a job number. Direct material, direct labor, or overhead costs that are incurred for a job are recorded in the work-in-process account in the general ledger and also in a *subsidiary ledger* that maintains the cost of each job. This subsidiary ledger typically takes the form of a document called a **job-cost sheet.** In the past, job-cost sheets were printed paper documents, but today many firms maintain their job-cost sheets as computer files. They can be viewed on a computer screen or printed out when paper copies are required. An example of a job-cost sheet is presented in Exhibit 4-5.

Accounting for Prime Costs

Each job is likely to require different kinds and amounts of direct materials, direct labor, and overhead. **Material requisition documents** are used to authorize the release of materials to production and trace their costs to the appropriate job-cost sheets. **Labor distribution documents,** or time cards, are used to charge jobs for direct labor. These *source documents* for material and labor may be printed paper forms or computer files. In highly automated factories, material requisitions may be made by entering a material request into a computer terminal on the shop floor, and the request is communicated by the computer system to the material stores department or warehouse. Similar procedures are used for direct labor by many firms. For many manufacturing operations at McDonnell Douglas, for example, factory workers enter the time that they start and stop working on each production job into a time clock that is connected to the company's computer. The computer then automatically records the time each worker spends on each job directly on the appropriate job-cost sheets, which are also maintained as computer files. Thus, computerization of source documents and job-cost sheets can minimize the flow of paper in the factory, reduce delays, and cut down on clerical errors. Exhibit 4-6 displays highly simplified examples of a material requisition form and a labor time card. A real labor time card and a real material requisition form used by McDonnell Douglas Corporation are reproduced in Exhibits 4-7 and 4-8.

Overhead Accounting: An Overview

All production costs other than direct material and direct labor are classified as overhead. Some typical overhead costs are listed below.

1. Depreciation of factory buildings and equipment,

2. Utilities and insurance,

3. Supplies, such as lubricants, cleaning supplies, small tools, and gloves,

4. Indirect labor, such as material handling, supervision, idle time, and overtime premiums (idle time is unproductive time, such as scheduled rest breaks and down-time due to power failures; an overtime premium is the *extra* compensation an employee receives while working overtime),

EXHIBIT 4-5

Job-Cost Sheet (Subsidiary Ledger Account)

Job number_____

Description_____

Date_____ Date to be completed_____

Specifications_____

Department_____

		Direct material		
Date	Requisition number	Quantity	Unit price	Cost

		Direct labor		
Date	Work record number	Hours	Rate	Cost

		Overhead application		
Date	Activity base	Quantity	Application rate	Cost applied

Cost summary	
Cost item	Amount
Total direct material Total direct labor Total overhead Total cost	

EXHIBIT 4-6

Simplified Material Requisition Form and Time Card

MATERIAL REQUISITION FORM

Department _____ Job number _____ Date _____

Item	Quantity	Unit cost	Amount

TIME CARD

Employee name _____

Employee number _____

Date	Time started	Time stopped	Job number	Uncharged (idle time)

5. Taxes, such as property taxes on manufacturing facilities and payroll taxes,

6. Service department costs, such as plant accounting, personnel, research and development, engineering, and equipment repair (service departments are departments in which no work is done directly on the product; they are, however, necessary in order for production to take place).

As with a product's prime costs, overhead costs must be applied to products. The three steps in this process, described below, are diagrammed in Exhibit 4-9.

1. **Cost distribution** (sometimes called cost allocation) involves the assignment of overhead costs to *department overhead centers.* For example, the total cost of electricity is distributed among all of the departments that use electricity.

2. **Service department cost allocation** involves identifying and allocating costs incurred by service departments back to the production departments that

EXHIBIT 4-7
Labor Time Card and Instructions Used by McDonnell Douglas Corporation

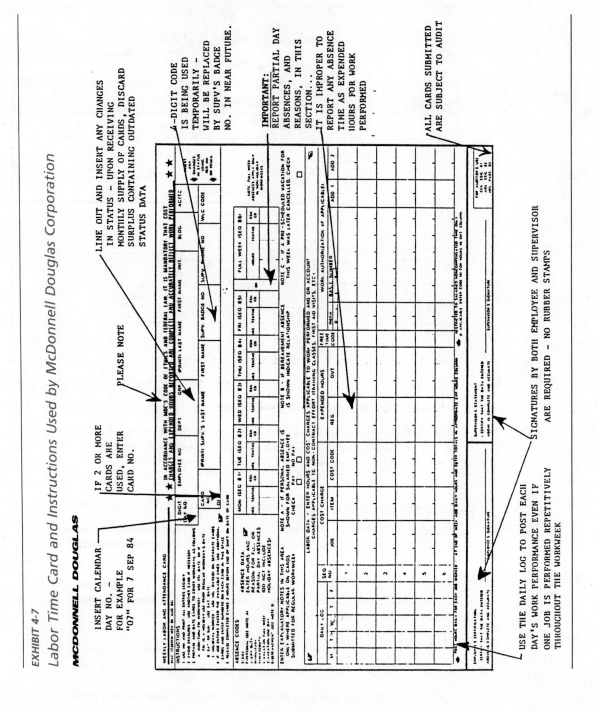

EXHIBIT 4-8

Material Requisition Form Used by McDonnell Douglas Corporation

MCDONNELL DOUGLAS

SERIAL NO.	REQUESTING		ASSEMBLY NO.	VALID DATE	DOCUMENT CONTROL NO.
	STOREROOM	DEPT. NO.			

010243

						MATERIAL CONTROL AUTHORITY

DELIVER TO		BLDG. NO.	POST NO.	REQUESTED BY	DATE PREPARED	

OWN	MATERIAL CODE	UNIT	QUANTITY REQ'D	QUANTITY DEL'VD	PART NUMBER AND MATERIAL TYPE	FACTORY ORDER NO.		
						JOB	ITEM	COST CODE

REMARKS

	DATA REFERENCE			
P.O. OR CROSS REF.				
ITEM			MNP	

SERIAL NO. **010243**

IF USED FOR PRODUCTION MATERIAL THIS MUST BE COUNTERSIGNED BY MATERIAL CONTROL

FILLED BY	MO	DAY	YR	MATERIAL REQUISITION	COPY	RECEIVED BY	MO	DAY	YR
				MCDONNELL DOUGLAS CORPORATION MAC 282 (REV 14 OCT 83)	1				

benefited from those services. After this step is completed, all manufacturing overhead costs have been assigned to the firm's production departments.

3. **Overhead application** (sometimes called *overhead absorption*) involves each production department in applying or assigning some portion of its total department overhead costs to its work-in-process inventory account.

The methods for allocating overhead costs from service departments to production departments and of applying overhead to production vary from company to company and even within different plants or facilities of the same company. This chapter describes several accounting procedures for recording and applying overhead to production. A detailed discussion of service department cost allocation is deferred until Chapter 14.

EXHIBIT 4-9

Overhead Distribution, Service Department Cost Allocation, and Overhead Application

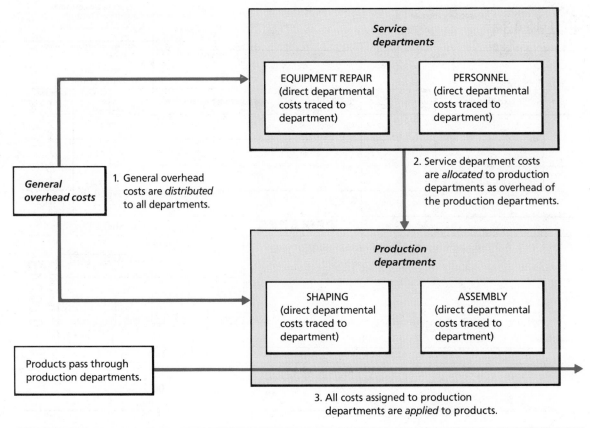

An Illustration of Job-Order Costing

This section illustrates basic job-order costing procedures for a hypothetical plastic fabrication firm called Great Lakes Fabricators, Inc. The firm uses normal costing, so actual direct material and direct labor and estimated overhead costs are applied to units of production. Great Lakes also uses absorption costing, so both fixed and variable overhead are treated as product costs and applied to production (a review of Exhibit 4-2 is recommended).

Each job produced by Great Lakes Fabricators requires different materials and is routed through departments differently. A separate work-in-process account is maintained for each department. For every cost recorded in a work-in-process account, an entry for the same amount is made on a job-cost sheet. Thus, the work-in-process accounts act as control accounts over the subsidiary record, the job-cost sheets. The

EXHIBIT 4-10

Great Lakes Fabricators: Sheet Plastic Department Transactions

Entry Number	Transaction	Source of Entry Data
1.	Material purchased	Invoice
2.	Material placed into production	Summary of material requisitions
3.	Direct labor cost incurred	Labor distribution sheet
4.	Actual overhead costs incurred	Various invoices, time cards, requisitions, etc.
5.	Overhead applied to production	The overhead rate per direct labor hour
6.	Job orders finished	Job-cost sheet

sum of the costs recorded on the individual job-cost sheets must equal the sum of the balances in the related work-in-process account.

Several transactions have occurred during one week in the Sheet Plastic Department of Great Lakes Fabricators. General journal entries for the transactions in Exhibit 4-10 are presented below. It is useful to trace each journal entry to the general ledger accounts shown in Exhibit 4-12.

All purchases of materials and supplies are charged to a material inventory account at their actual cost. Subsidiary records (inventory cards) are maintained for each item. The following journal entry (also shown in Exhibit 4-12) is made to record material purchases:

1.	Direct Material Inventory	20,000	
	Accounts Payable		20,000
	To record material purchases.		

Material requisitions are used as a basis for charging departments (and individual jobs) for the costs of direct materials. A summary of material requisitions is presented below:

SHEET PLASTIC DEPARTMENT
Summary of Material Requisitions

Date	Requisition No.	Job No.	Quantity	Cost	Type of Material
Jan. 21	26	556	600 lbs.	$ 6,000	Plastic powder
Jan. 21	27	557	400 lbs.	$ 4,000	Binding agent
				$10,000	

The following entry (also shown in Exhibit 4-12) is made to record the cost of materials requisitioned:

2. Work in Process — Sheet Plastic Department   10,000
        Direct Material Inventory   10,000
    To record materials issued.

Direct-labor distribution sheets are the basis for charging departments (and individual jobs) for the cost of direct labor. A direct-labor distribution summary is presented below. The wage rate is $10 per hour.

SHEET PLASTIC DEPARTMENT
Direct Labor Distribution Summary

Date	Job No.	Hours	Wages
Jan. 21	556	1,400	$14,000
Jan. 21	557	600	$ 6,000
			$20,000

The following entry (also shown in Exhibit 4-12) is made to record the cost of direct labor:

3. Work in Process — Sheet Plastic Department   20,000
        Salaries and Wages Payable   20,000
    To record payroll costs.

The actual overhead cost incurred was $17,000. This cost is debited to the Actual Overhead account, and the related credits are entered in the appropriate accounts.

4. Actual Overhead — Sheet Plastic Department   17,000
        Salaries and Wages Payable   4,000
        Factory Supplies Inventory   1,000
        Accumulated Depreciation — Equipment   2,000
        Accumulated Depreciation — Building   7,000
        Electric Utility Payable   3,000
    To record actual overhead costs.

Since Great Lakes Fabricators, Inc. uses a normal costing system, a *predetermined overhead rate* is used to apply overhead to work-in-process. The predetermined overhead rate per machine hour is the amount of overhead that is assigned to the firm's products for every machine hour incurred in the production process. Great Lakes' predetermined overhead rate is $8.00 per machine hour. The origin and nature of this overhead rate is discussed in greater detail in the next chapter.

EXHIBIT 4-11

Job-Cost Sheets for Great Lakes Fabricators, Inc.

JOB COST SHEET
Job No. 556

	Material			Labor			Overhead	
Date	Requisition No.	Quantity, lb.	Cost, $	Hours	Dollars	Machine Hours	Rate	Dollars
1/21	26	600	$6,000	1,400	$14,000	1,400	$8.00	$11,200

JOB COST SHEET
Job No. 557

	Material			Labor			Overhead	
Date	Requisition No.	Quantity, lb.	Cost, $	Hours	Dollars	Machine Hours	Rate	Dollars
1/21	27	400	$4,000	600	$6,000	600	$8.00	$4,800

Because the predetermined overhead rate is $8.00 per machine hour, the amount of overhead applied to each job depends on the number of machine hours used on that job. Computerized production records indicate that a total of 2,000 machine hours were actually used during the week. The following entry is made to apply overhead to the jobs in process. This entry is also shown in Exhibit 4-12.[1]

5.	Work in Process — Sheet Plastic Department	16,000	
	Applied Overhead — Sheet Plastic Department		16,000
	To record application of manufacturing overhead		
	(2,000 machine hours × $8.00 predetermined		
	overhead rate).		

As the individual jobs are completed, the job-cost sheets are totaled. The job-cost sheets for Jobs 556 and 557 are presented in Exhibit 4-11. There is a column on each job-cost sheet for overhead. If a job is completed during the accounting period, the

---

[1] The amount entered in the Actual Overhead account (entry number 4) and the amount entered in the Applied Overhead account (entry number 5) are not the same. The reconciliation of these accounts is discussed in the next chapter, which treats overhead accounting in detail.

EXHIBIT 4-12

Relationships Among Accounts in Job-Order Costing System

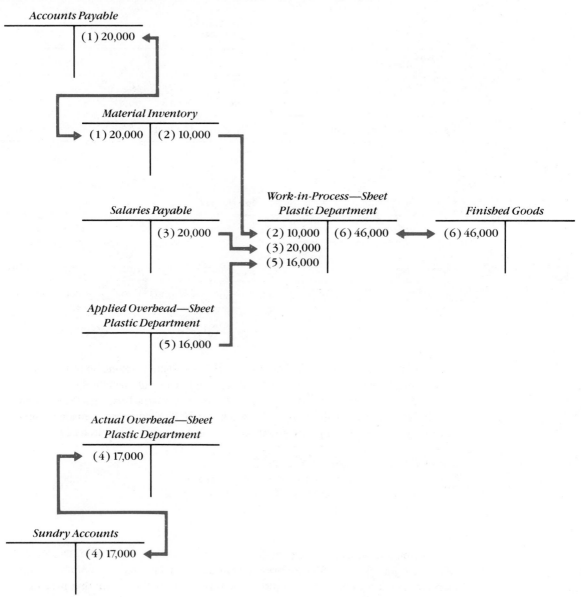

overhead can be computed once for the entire job, rather than on a daily basis as machine hours are used. If the period ends before a job is completed, the overhead is computed at that time based on the number of machine hours used to date on that job.

The total costs of $46,000 recorded on the job-cost sheets equal the total costs recorded in the work-in-process account.

Work in Process					
Material	$10,000				
Direct labor	20,000				
Overhead	16,000				
Balance	$46,000				

Job Cost Sheets Summary
(from Exhibit 4-9)

Job	*Material*	*Labor*	*Overhead*	*Total Costs*
556	$ 6,000	$14,000	$11,200	$31,200
557	4,000	6,000	4,800	14,800
Totals	$10,000	$20,000	$16,000	$46,000

When the jobs are completed, the job-cost sheets are removed from the work-in-process account files and included with the finished goods account file. The completed job-cost sheets serve as a subsidiary ledger for the finished goods account. The following entry (also shown in Exhibit 4-12) is then made to transfer the total cost of the jobs from work-in-process inventory to finished-goods inventory:

6.	Finished Goods	46,000	
	Work in Process — Sheet Plastic Department		46,000
	To record completion of jobs 556 and 557.		

A diagram of the relationships among the accounts is presented in Exhibit 4-12.

The $46,000 amount in the finished-goods account represents the costs assigned to the products manufactured. When these goods are sold, $46,000 will be transferred to the cost-of-goods-sold account. This completes the Great Lakes Fabricators example. In the next chapter, overhead accounting is discussed in greater detail.

Computer-Integrated Manufacturing

As production processes become more heavily automated, direct labor occupies a smaller role. In a computer-integrated manufacturing (CIM) environment, total direct-labor cost may be very small relative to overall production costs. In such a production setting, it may not be necessary (or even possible) to trace labor costs to specific production jobs. The kinds of labor costs that remain, such as the cost of computer programmers and operators, are properly associated with all production. Hence, they are included as part of manufacturing overhead.

Summary

Product costing is the process of accumulating and classifying costs and then assigning those costs to the products or services produced. Product and service costs are important for income determination, inventory valuation, and various managerial decisions.

Several types of product-costing systems are currently in use. Job-order and process-costing systems differ mainly in the procedures used to accumulate costs. Absorption and variable costing systems differ in their treatment of fixed overhead costs. Actual, normal, and standard costing systems differ in their use of actual or estimated costs.

Direct-material costs are accumulated on the basis of information from material requisition documents and are then recorded on job-cost sheets for the various production jobs. Direct-labor costs are accumulated using information from labor time records. These costs are also then recorded on job-cost sheets. Overhead costs are first distributed to departmental overhead centers. Then service-department costs are allocated to production departments. Finally, the overhead costs associated with the production departments are applied to the products or services produced in those departments.

Key Terms to Review

absorption costing, p. 110
actual costing, p. 110
cost distribution, p. 117
finished goods inventory, p. 108
hybrid costing system, p. 114
job-cost sheet, p. 115
job-order costing, p. 110–111
labor distribution document, p. 115
material requisition document, p. 115
normal costing, p. 110

operation costing, p. 114
overhead application, p. 119
predetermined overhead rate, p. 110
process costing, p. 110–111
product costing, p. 108
service department cost allocation, p. 117
standard costing, p. 110
variable costing, p. 110
work-in-process inventory, p. 108

Review Problem

JOB-ORDER COSTING

Prepare journal entries to record the following events, which relate to Ready Chef Kitchen Appliances, Inc. The company uses a normal costing system. Direct material and direct labor are added to Work-in-Process Inventory at their actual amounts. Manufacturing overhead is applied using a predetermined overhead rate, which is $4 per direct-labor hour. The following events occurred during September 19x8.

1. Purchased raw material for $20,000 on account.

2. Put $10,000 of direct material into production.

3. Used 300 direct-labor hours at $20 per hour.

4. Applied overhead using the predetermined overhead rate.

5. Received an invoice (bill) for rent on the factory building, $18,000.

6. Used 25 hours of indirect labor at $20 per hour.

7. Finished a production job with total accumulated costs of $18,000.

8. Sold goods with a product cost of $12,000 for $20,000 cash.

9. Paid sales commissions of $1,000.

Solution to Review Problem

The following journal entries are made to record the events listed above.

1.	Direct Material Inventory	20,000	
	Accounts Payable		20,000
2.	Work in Process	10,000	
	Direct Material Inventory		10,000
3.	Work in Process	6,000	
	Salaries and Wages Payable		6,000
4.	Work in Process	1,200	
	Applied Overhead		1,200

The amount of overhead applied to Work in Process, based on the usage of direct labor specified in event number 3, is computed below.

Direct labor hours used	300 hours
Predetermined overhead rate	× $4 per hour
Overhead applied	$1,200

5.	Actual Overhead	18,000	
	Rent Payable		18,000
6.	Actual Overhead	500	
	Salaries and Wages Payable		500
7.	Finished Goods	18,000	
	Work in Process		18,000
8.	Cost of Goods Sold	12,000	
	Finished Goods		12,000
	Cash	20,000	
	Sales Revenue		20,000
9.	Selling and Administrative Expense	1,000	
	Cash		1,000

Suggested Readings

Anthony R., and R. Herzlinger. *Management Control in Nonprofit Organizations.* Rev. ed. Homewood, Ill.: Irwin, 1980.

Capettini, R., and D. K. Clancy, ed. *Cost Accounting, Robotics, and the New Manufacturing Environment.* Sarasota, Fl.: American Accounting Association, 1987.

Carbone, F. J. "Automated Job Costing Helps Mulach Steel Stay Competitive." *Management Accounting* (June 1980): 29.

Goldratt, E. M., and J. Cox. *The Goal: A Process of Ongoing Improvement.* Rev. ed. Croton-on-Hudson, N.Y.: North River Press, 1986.

Imhoff, E. A. "Management Accounting Techniques: A Survey." *Management Accounting* (January 1980): 239.

Kaplan, R. "One Cost System Isn't Enough." *Harvard Business Review* (January–February 1988): 61–66.

Kaplan, R., and H. T. Johnson. *Relevance Lost.* Boston: Harvard Business School Press, 1987.

Lee, J. Y. *Managerial Accounting for the 1990's.* Artesia, Calif.: McKay Business Systems, 1987.

Noreen, E. "Commentary on H. T. Johnson and R. Kaplan's Relevance Lost." *Accounting Horizons* (December 1987): 110–116.

Possett, R. W. "Measuring Productive Costs in the Service Sector." *Management Accounting* (October 1980): 16–24.

Riley, K. "Productive Hours Analysis for a Small Shop." *Management Accounting* (January 1973): 7.

Worthy, F. S. "Accounting Bores You? Wake Up." *Fortune* (October 12, 1987): 43–53.

Review Questions

4-1 Distinguish among actual, normal, and standard costing.

4-2 Distinguish between absorption and variable costing.

4-3 What is a job-cost sheet?

4-4 Using T-accounts, diagram the flow of manufacturing costs in a job-order costing system.

4-5 Distinguish between direct and indirect labor.

4-6 Describe a material requisition form and discuss its purpose.

4-7 Describe a labor time card and discuss its purpose.

4-8 The City Steel Company sells five different product lines and regularly incurs the following costs:

Cost of sales	Selling
Purchasing	Credit and collection
Ordering processing	Bad debts

Material handling	General administrative
Delivery (including shipping)	Public relations
Storage	Auditing (fee to public
Advertising	accounting firms)

For product-costing purposes, discuss how each cost should be assigned to the five product lines. If a cost should not be assigned, indicate why.

4-9 The labor cost of material handlers is generally treated as indirect labor.

  a. How are such costs generally applied to product for costing purposes?

  b. Suggest an alternative solution and explain why one might be useful.

  c. What is the major reason such costs are treated as indirect labor?

Exercises

4-10 **Applying Overhead Using Direct-Labor Dollars**   The Absorption Corporation is in the process of changing its cost-accounting system. It has decided on the use of direct-labor dollars as the basis for applying overhead to work in process.

Budget Information for Coming Year

Budgeted Direct-Labor Dollars	Budgeted Fixed Overhead	Budgeted Variable Overhead
90,000	450,000	180,000

REQUIRED:

  a. Compute the overhead applied in January if $10,000 direct-labor dollars of cost were incurred. Fixed overhead actually incurred was $38,000, and variable overhead was $22,000.

  b. Explain the difficulties connected with determining the "actual" cost of a product.

  c. In this problem overhead is applied using direct-labor dollars. What other measures of activity could be used?

4-11 **Use of Costs in Oil Distribution**   The Ithaca Oil Company prepares income statements by product line and by customers for each product. It sells directly to gasoline stations, to wholesalers, and to jobbers. The following report was prepared for the sale of gasoline to gasoline stations.

ITHACA OIL COMPANY
Income Statement
for Month Ending March 31

Sales (400,000 gallons)		$200,000
Expenses:		
Cost of product sold[a]	$120,000	
Local delivery	8,000	
Storage and handling	2,000	
Selling costs	1,000	
Accounting and credit	800	
Administrative	1,200	
Advertising and sales promotion	4,000	
Headquarters	10,000	
Total expenses		147,000
Net income		$ 53,000

[a] Transfer price from the manufacturing division times 400,000 gallons.

REQUIRED:

a. For each expense discuss the nature of the assignment of the cost. Was it a direct cost or an allocation?

b. Assume that you are attempting to measure the performance of the manager in charge of sales of gasoline to gasoline stations. Would you use the figure of $53,000? Explain.

c. Assume that you are considering the construction of an additional gasoline station. What quantitative factors would you take into consideration?

d. Assume that the cost of product sold was $190,000 instead of $120,000. Should the sale of the product to gasoline stations be dropped? Assume that the present prices of the product sold and purchased are expected to continue in the foreseeable future.

4-12 **Cost-Allocation Concepts**   The following is taken from the *Progress Report to the Congress 1973* (Cost Accounting Standards Board):

Cost-Allocation Concepts

The Board's primary goal is increased uniformity and consistency in treatment of costs as they are related to negotiated defense contracts. Set forth herein are discussions of a number of important concepts which the Board will use in developing cost-accounting standards.

Cost accounting for negotiated government contracts has long been on the basis of full allocation of costs, including general and administrative expenses and all other indirect costs. The allocation of all period costs to the products and services of the period is not a common practice either for public reporting or for internal management purposes; yet this has long been the established cost principle for costing defense procurement. The Board will adhere to the concept to full costing wherever appropriate.

A cost objective is "a function, organizational subdivision, contract, or other work unit for which cost data are desired and for which provision is made to accumulate and measure the cost of processes, products, jobs, capitalized projects, etc." This definition has been promulgated by the Board.

Cost-accounting systems are developed to provide a means for assigning all costs to appropriate cost objectives. Under the full costing concept, all costs initially allocated to intermediate cost objectives are reallocated to final cost objectives. Costs which are identified for special treatment (unreasonable costs, or costs unallowable for other reasons) may be assigned to final cost objectives established for that purpose.

Even with the foregoing concept, there are occasional difficult questions as to whether specified units of an organization or its work should be allocated cost on a full costing basis. The Board will attempt to identify and dispose of such questions in individual cost-accounting standards.

REQUIRED:

Evaluate the cost-allocation concepts.

4-13 Effect of Overhead Rates on Formulating Bids A large dairy company relies heavily on competitive bidding for securing contracts for the production of private-label dairy products. Small errors in calculating costs can be disastrous because competition for contracts is keen.

Included in the calculation of its bid, the company uses an overhead application rate that last year was

$$\frac{\text{Overhead}}{\text{Direct labor cost}} = \frac{\$150,000}{\$75,000} = \$2.00$$

Of the $150,000 overhead, $50,000 is variable overhead. Since this application rate was developed, direct laborers earned a 5 percent increase in wages and related benefits. In submitting a recent bid, the plant manager failed to consider this wage increase. What effect will this have on his bid?

Problems   **4-14 Budgeted versus Actual Costs** The Hall Corporation has made an analysis of how the salaries of supervisors should react to changes in activity.

	Total Cost of Supervisors' Salaries
From plant shutdown to 20,000 direct-labor hours per month	$20,000 (monthly)
From 20,000 direct-labor hours to 22,000 direct-labor hours per month	$20,000 + ($2.50 per direct-labor hour in excess of 20,000)
From 22,000 direct-labor hours to 23,000 direct-labor hours per month	$25,000 (monthly rate)

A core of supervisors will be retained even if the plant is temporarily closed. If production requires more than 20,000 hours of direct-labor hours per week but less than 22,000, then these supervisors can handle the extra work by taking overtime. If the direct-labor hours increase above 22,000 hours, it is expected that a new supervisor will be hired.

The actual costs for the first quarter are as follows:

	Direct-Labor Hours per month	Total Cost of Supervisors' Salaries
January	20,400	$24,000
February	22,400	28,000
March	19,600	24,500

REQUIRED:

a. Plot the budgeted costs and the actual costs for the first quarter.

b. Comment on the level of supervisors' salaries for each of the first three months.

4-15 Controlling Indirect Labor Costs   A flexible budget is a budget that adjusts the indirect labor (and other variable-overhead costs) to the actual level of activity. This is necessary if variable indirect costs are to be effectively controlled. Usually, direct-labor hours, direct-labor dollars, machine hours, or some other one basis is used to adjust all indirect costs. In recent years the weakness of this procedure has been noted. Many indirect costs do not vary directly with direct-labor hours. In the long run, there may be a good correlation, but in the short run there may be leads and lags. For example, the receiving department may have to expand to receive raw material before the direct-labor force is expanded. The accounts receivable department may not have to expand, although the direct-labor force has been expanded.

To secure better control of indirect labor, attempts have been made in recent years to obtain types of work measurement more immediately related to the work than direct labor. For example, the accounts payable labor cost is related to the number of invoices processed.

REQUIRED:

Name several types of indirect labor and the measures of work that can help to control these indirect labor costs.

4-16 Expected Profit and Budgeted Profit   The Sell-More Company followed a strict budgeting procedure for advertising expenditures. The president of the firm received a forecast of sales from the sales vice president and a forecast of expenses from the controller. He computed the profit without deducting advertising expense and compared it to a budgeted profit (based on a reasonable return on investment). The difference between the two profits was then allocated to advertising (assuming that the expected profit was greater than the budgeted profit).

REQUIRED:

Comment on the policy described above.

4-17 Use of Direct and Indirect Costs The College Textbook Company was regularly faced with accept or reject decisions concerning the possible printing of books. To make this decision, it completed a projected income per copy of the book that assigned no general overhead and that excluded editorial work on the book. Included were the printing costs and advertising and distribution costs of a direct nature (the salaries of the sales force were excluded).

REQUIRED:

Comment on the policy described above.

4-18 Allocating Production Costs to Departments The Williams Manufacturing Company's production activities involve three producing departments and a factory office. All materials are added at the start of process 1. Processed material moves from process 1 through process 2, then through process 3, where the product is completed.

The following account balances reflect costs of the Williams Company for the month of January:

Materials used	$ 8,200
Direct labor	11,600
Indirect labor	1,700
Sales salaries	4,200
Taxes, properties	2,100
Depreciation of factory building	714
Depreciation of equipment	550
Advertising	1,455
Factory office labor	900

Direct-labor costs were as follows:

Process 1	$4,900
Process 2	2,700
Process 3	4,000

Indirect labor is primarily janitorial in nature, and distribution is made to the three producing departments and the factory office, giving double weight to the producing departments. Floor space is as follows:

Process 1	2,500 ft^2
Process 2	3,500
Process 3	2,000
Factory office	1,000

Property tax valuations are as follows:

Process 1	$13,000
Process 2	16,000
Process 3	10,000
Factory office	3,000

Depreciation is charged at a uniform rate on all equipment. The cost of equipment in each department is as follows:

Process 1	$ 7,500
Process 2	5,500
Process 3	13,000
Factory office	1,500

Because the factory office is maintained primarily for timekeeping and employee services, the cost of operating the office is distributed to the producing departments on the basis of the number of workers in each department. They are as follows:

Process 1	10 workers
Process 2	4
Process 3	6
Factory office	2

REQUIRED:

Prepare a schedule allocating production costs other than direct materials to the three producing departments. Set up overhead accounts for each of the four departments. Make entries to these accounts showing the results of the allocation.

4-19 **Ledger Entries in Job Cost Accounting** The Matson Manufacturing Co. specializes in producing machine tools according to specifications provided by its customers. It uses a job-order system of accounting.

REQUIRED:

Enter the following information directly into the manufacturing accounts. Make all necessary entries on the job-cost sheets.

   a. Materials inventory, October 1 $82,500

   b. Supplies inventory, October 1 $15,750

   c. Unfinished cost sheets, October 1, as follows:

Job No.	Materials	Direct Labor		Overhead (rate is $8.00/DLH)
1115	$ 6,625	400 hr	$4,000	$3,200
1118	4,050	250 hr	2,500	2,000
1120	3,825	300 hr	2,375	2,400
	$14,500		$8,875	$7,600

d. Materials used during October were as follows:

Requisition No.	Job No.	Cost
56	1118	$ 2,575
57	1120	3,325
58	1121	4,550
59	1124	3,600
		$14,050

e. The balance in the manufacturing overhead account on October 1 was $300 (Dr.).

f. Material purchases during October amounted to $19,450.

g. A summary of labor costs is as follows (ignore taxes):

Job No.	No. of Hours	Cost
1115	50	$ 475
1118	120	1,075
1120	85	800
1121	65	600
1124	30	325
Total direct labor	350	$3,275
Indirect labor	72	575
	422	$3,850

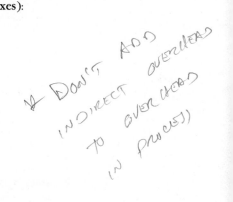

h. Supplies purchased during October were $2,200.

i. Supplies consumed during October were $2,725.

j. Miscellaneous other overhead charges for October were $525.

k. The overhead rate is the same as in previous periods ($8.00/DLH).

l. The following jobs were completed in October and delivered to the customers: Jobs 1115, 1118, and 1120.

m. The accounts in the factory ledger are

- Materials, Inventory

- Supplies, Inventory

- Overhead

- Material in Process

- Labor in Process

- Overhead in Process

- General Ledger

The form to use for the job-cost sheets is as follows:

JOB-COST SHEET
Job No. _____

Material		Direct Labor		Overhead	
Requisition No.	Cost	Hours	Cost	Rate	Cost

4-20 Determining Cost of Goods Manufactured   Hamilton Company uses job-order costing. Factory overhead is applied to production at a predetermined rate of 150 percent of direct-labor cost. Any over- or underapplied factory overhead is closed to the cost of goods sold account at the end of each month. Additional information is available as follows:

a. Job 101 was the only job in process at January 31, with accumulated costs as follows:

Direct materials	$4,000
Direct labor	2,000
Applied factory overhead	3,000
Total	$9,000

b. Jobs 102, 103, and 104 were started during February.

c. Direct materials requisitions for February totaled $26,000.

d. Direct-labor cost of $20,000 was incurred for February.

e. Actual factory overhead was $32,000 for February.

f. The only job still in process at February 28, was Job 104, with costs of $2,800 for direct materials and $1,800 for direct labor.

REQUIRED:

Determine the cost of goods manufactured during February. (Hint: In addition to the concepts covered in Chapter 4, you may wish to refer back to Chapter 2.) *(CPA adapted)*

4-21 Understanding Basic Product Cost Flows Selected data concerning the past fiscal year's operations of the Televans Manufacturing Company are presented below (in thousands).

	Inventories	
	Beginning	*Ending*
Raw materials	$75	$ 85
Work in process	80	30
Finished goods	90	110

Other data

Raw materials used	$326
Total manufacturing costs charged to production during the year (includes raw materials, direct labor, and factory overhead applied at a rate of 60% of direct-labor cost)	686
Cost of goods available for sale	826
Selling and general expenses	25

REQUIRED:

a. Compute the cost of raw materials purchased during the year.

b. Calculate the direct-labor cost charged to production during the year.

c. Compute the cost of goods manufactured during the year.

d. Determine the cost of goods sold during the year.

4-22 Job-Cost Sheet   Milligan Company incurred the following costs to produce Job Number N68, which consisted of 1,000 pillows.

Direct Material:

- 6/1/x0 requisition number 201, 400 yards of fabric at $.75 per yard

- 6/5/x0 requisition number 208, 500 cubic feet of stuffing at $.25 per cubic foot

Direct Labor:
- 6/15/x0 time card number 65, 500 hours at $12 per hour

Manufacturing Overhead:
- Applied on the basis of direct-labor hours at $2.00 per hour.

On June 30, 800 of the pillows were shipped to a local furniture store.

REQUIRED:

Prepare a job-cost sheet and record the information given above. (Use Exhibit 4-5 as a guide.)

4-23 Manufacturing Cost Flows; T-Accounts; Financial Statements   Caroline Company incurred the following costs during 19x8.

Direct material	$258,000
Direct labor	340,000
Manufacturing overhead	180,000

During 19x8, products costing $120,000 were finished, and products costing $132,000 were sold for $190,000. The beginning balances in the firm's inventory accounts are shown below.

Raw materials	$321,000
Work in process	18,000
Finished goods	40,000

REQUIRED:

The company uses actual costing.

a. Prepare T-accounts to show the flow of costs through the company's manufacturing accounts during 19x8.

b. Prepare a partial balance sheet and a partial income statement to reflect the information given above.

4-24 Concepts from Chapters 2 and 4; Schedule of Cost of Goods Manufactured   Matyo Company's cost of goods sold for the month ended March 31, 19x4, was $345,000. Ending work-in-process inventory was 90 percent of beginning work-in-process inventory. Factory overhead applied was 50 percent of direct-labor cost. Other information pertaining to Matyo Company's inventories and production for the month of March is as follows:

Beginning inventories, March 1	
Direct materials	$ 20,000
Work in process	40,000
Finished goods	102,000
Purchases of direct materials during March	110,000
Ending inventories, March 31	
Direct materials	26,000
Work in process	?
Finished goods	105,000

REQUIRED:

a. Prepare a schedule of cost of goods manufactured for the month of March.

b. Prepare a schedule to compute the prime cost incurred during March.

c. Prepare a schedule to compute the conversion cost charged to work in process during March. *(CPA adapted)*

4-25 Steps in Applying Overhead Costs; Hospital   Suppose you are the controller for a hospital. Think carefully about the three steps in overhead accounting depicted in Exhibit 4-9. Give examples of these steps in the hospital setting. The hospital's service departments do not directly treat patients. Its "production" departments do treat patients. Given an example of each in the hospital setting.

4-26 Journal Entries; Job-Order Costing   The following events relate to Myers Company, which uses a normal costing system. The predetermined overhead rate is $7 per direct-labor hour.

1. Purchased raw material for $60,000 on account.

2. Used $41,000 of direct material in production.

3. Used 200 direct-labor hours at $15 per hour.

4. Applied overhead using the predetermined overhead rate.

5. Recorded depreciation on factory equipment of $11,000.

6. Used indirect material costing $3,200.

7. Paid rent of $8,000 on the vehicles used by sales personnel.

8. Finished products costing $30,000.

9. Used 15 hours of indirect labor at $12 per hour.

REQUIRED:

a. Prepare journal entries to record the events listed above.

b. Why are production costs added to work-in-process inventory instead of being recorded as expenses?

4-27 Comprehensive Product-Costing Problem This problem is a continuation of the Great Lakes Fabricators illustration in the chapter. Review that illustration before proceeding. The following events occurred in the Sheet Plastic Department during one week in February.

1. Direct material purchased for $38,000 on account.

2. The following requisitions for material were received.

Date	Requisition No.	Job No.	Quantity	Cost	Type of Material
Feb. 1	28	559	800 lbs.	$ 8,000	Plastic powder
Feb. 1	29	560	500 lbs.	5,000	Binding agent
Total				$13,000	

3. Direct labor of $30,000 was incurred, but not yet paid, in the Sheet Plastic Department. Half of the direct-labor cost was incurred for each of the jobs, 559 and 560. The wage rate is $10 per hour.

4. Actual overhead cost was $19,500. This account was comprised of the following costs.

- Indirect labor, $4,100

- Indirect material, $1,200

- Depreciation — equipment, $2,000

- Depreciation — building, $7,000

- Utilities, $3,500

- Property taxes, $1,700

5. The predetermined overhead rate is $8.00 per machine hour. Computerized production records indicate that 3,000 machine hours were used in the Sheet Plastic Department during the week. Half of the machine hours were used on each of the jobs, 559 and 560.

REQUIRED:

a. Prepare journal entries to record the events listed in items (1) through (5) above.

b. Prepare job-cost sheets, similar to those in Exhibit 4-11, for jobs 559 and 560.

c. Products costing $38,000 were finished during the week. Prepare the required journal entry.

4-28 Ledger Entries in Job-Order Costing Refer to the preceding problem.

REQUIRED:

Post the journal entries made in that problem to the appropriate T-accounts. (Refer to Exhibit 4-12 for guidance.)

4-29 Job-Order Costing; Journal Entries   Watkins Electronics Corporation manufactures peripheral devices for computers. The firm uses a normal, job-order costing system, and manufacturing overhead is applied on the basis of direct-labor hours. Estimated manufacturing overhead for 19x6 is $300,000, and the expected level of direct-labor usage is 40,000 hours. The following events occurred during March of 19x6.

1. The firm purchased on account 3,000 square feet of plastic casing at $9 per square foot.

2. Twenty disk drive controls were requisitioned for production. Each control cost $35.

3. Five rolls of metallic tape were requisitioned for production. The tape cost $20 per roll. Tape is treated as an indirect material.

4. Depreciation on the plant building for March was $10,000.

5. A $600 utility bill was paid in cash.

6. Time cards showed the following usage of labor.

   ■ Job Number T21: 10 disk drives, 80 hours of direct labor

   ■ Job Number W42: 50 printers, 600 hours of direct labor

   The direct-labor personnel earn $18 per hour.

7. The March property tax bill for $1,100 was received but not yet paid in cash. The tax bill was related to the factory building.

8. The firm employs laborers who perform various tasks such as material handling and shop cleanup. Their wages for March amounted to $3,000.

9. Job Number T21, which was started in January, was finished in March. The total cost of the job was $24,000.

10. Six of the disk drives from Job Number T21 ~~were sold in~~ March for $3,000 each. *THAT COST $1k each.*

REQUIRED:

The company's predetermined overhead rate for 19x6 is $7.50 per direct-labor hour. Prepare journal entries to record the events described above.

4-30 Continuation of Preceding Problem   Show how your answer to the preceding problem would have been different if the company had used actual costing instead of normal costing.

5

Overhead Accounting Under Job-Order Costing

LEARNING OBJECTIVES

After studying this chapter, you should be able to:

1 Explain how cost distribution is used to assign overhead costs to departmental overhead centers.

2 Describe the process of allocating service-department costs to production departments.

3 Carry out the procedures of applying overhead to production.

4 Explain the treatment of underapplied or overapplied overhead.

5 Define several concepts of activity and use them to compute a predetermined overhead rate.

Overhead Accounting

*P*rime costs — direct material and direct labor — are accumulated in a job-order cost accounting system (as was discussed in Chapter 4). All production costs other than direct costs are classified as overhead costs and also must be applied to production. **Overhead** — a pool of indirect costs — is accounted for using three steps:

1. Cost distribution (or allocation): distributing overhead costs to department overhead (or burden) centers (including both service and production departments).

2. Service department cost allocation: allocating the costs of service departments to production departments.

3. Cost application: applying (or absorbing) overhead costs to production.

These steps, which were illustrated in Exhibit 4-9, are discussed in detail in this chapter.

Cost Distribution

Overhead costs are initially distributed (or allocated) to department overhead (or burden) centers. Each production or service department has at least one such overhead center. Although overhead cannot be traced directly to specific units of production, some overhead costs can be traced directly to departments. For example, indirect labor costs, such as a department supervisor's salary, often can be traced to a specific department but not to specific units of production.

Some overhead costs are not traceable to specific departments. For example, the cost of depreciation on the factory building is not traceable to any factory department. These overhead costs must be distributed (or allocated) to departments using some reasonable basis. There are no generally accepted rules for choosing the **allocation base.** Instead, the management accountant allocates overhead costs to the departments that are logically related to the incurrence of the overhead costs. Some common allocation bases for general overhead costs include the following:

Overhead Cost to Be Allocated	Allocation Base
Electricity cost	Rated amperage (or horsepower) of electrical equipment in departments
Heating cost	Cubic feet of space in departments
Water cost	Engineering study of water usage in departments
Depreciation on factory building	Square feet of space in departments

General Ledger Account for Actual Overhead   As overhead costs are distributed to departments, either by tracing or by allocating, they are recorded in the Departmental

Actual Overhead accounts maintained by each department. The Actual Overhead account accumulates all actual overhead costs in one account in order to more easily access this information. It would be inconvenient to have to look at the accounts for every overhead item or at all of the departmental overhead accounts in order to determine the total actual overhead costs. These departmental actual overhead accounts comprise the subsidiary ledger for the Actual Overhead Control account in the general ledger. All actual overhead costs are debited to this account as they are incurred.

Journal entry number (4) in the Great Lakes Fabricators example of the preceding chapter illustrates the overhead distribution procedure. This entry is repeated below:

Actual Overhead — Sheet Plastic Department	17,000	
Indirect Salaries Payable		4,000
Factory Supplies Inventory		1,000
Accumulated Depreciation — Equipment		2,000
Accumulated Depreciation — Building		7,000
Electric Utility Payable		3,000

To record actual overhead costs for indirect salaries, indirect materials, depreciation on plant and equipment, and electrical utility cost.

How were the credit amounts in this journal entry determined? Indirect salaries and factory supplies were traced directly to the Sheet Plastic Department using labor time cards and material requisitions as source documents. Depreciation on the Sheet Plastic Department equipment is likewise traceable directly to the department.

The other two overhead items in the journal entry are not traceable to departments; they were allocated. The total depreciation expense on the factory building for the week was $28,000. Because the Sheet Plastic Department occupies one-quarter of the building, 25 percent of the cost was allocated to that department. The total electric utility cost for the factory for the week being illustrated was $6,000. Because half of the total rated amperage for all of the firm's factory equipment relates to Sheet Plastic Department equipment, half of the total cost was allocated to that department.

Allocation of Service Department Costs

Distributing overhead costs to departments is the first step in accounting for overhead costs. The next step is to allocate service department costs to production departments. For example, assume that in the Western Furniture Company the overhead costs of maintaining and running a factory building are first accumulated in a service department called the Buildings and Grounds Department. For product costing purposes, these service department costs must be allocated to the various production departments. What would be a reasonable basis for allocating these costs? The floor space occupied by each production department is one likely choice.

Assume that the following actual overhead costs have been debited to the Buildings and Grounds Department Actual Overhead account:

Depreciation	$10,000
Repairs	150
Cleaning supplies	100
Labor	2,750
Total	$13,000

Each of the four production departments in the Western Furniture Company's plant occupies the floor space indicated in Exhibit 5-1, and the Buildings and Grounds Department cost is allocated as shown.

The journal entry to record the allocation of overhead is as follows:

Production Department 1: Actual Overhead	3,900	
Production Department 2: Actual Overhead	2,600	
Production Department 3: Actual Overhead	5,200	
Production Department 4: Actual Overhead	1,300	
Buildings and Grounds Department Actual Overhead		13,000

To allocate Buildings and Grounds Department cost to production departments.

The specific methods for allocating service-department costs are discussed in detail in Chapter 14.

EXHIBIT 5-1

Allocation of Buildings and Grounds Department Cost to Production Departments

Production Department	Floor Space		Building Costs	Allocation of Buildings and Grounds Department Cost
	Square Feet	Percentage		
1	3,000	30%	$13,000	$ 3,900
2	2,000	20	13,000	2,600
3	4,000	40	13,000	5,200
4	1,000	10	13,000	1,300
	10,000	100%		$13,000

Overhead Application (or Absorption)

The third step in overhead accounting is to apply overhead costs to work in process. Under the normal costing approach used in this chapter, this step is accomplished using a *predetermined overhead rate.* The general formula for calculating the predetermined overhead rate is shown below:

$$\text{Overhead rate} = \frac{\text{Budgeted overhead for a selected level of production activity}}{\text{Selected level of production activity}}$$

The numerator in this formula is budgeted overhead costs, not actual overhead costs. Because managers need timely product-cost information throughout the accounting period for such purposes as pricing, inventory valuation, and income measurement, overhead rates generally are computed before the actual costs of the period are known. The use of a predetermined overhead rate for overhead application makes the system a normal costing system (review Exhibit 4-2).

The denominator of the predetermined overhead rate, sometimes referred to as the **denominator activity,** is a measure of production activity. Common choices include the following:

- Direct labor dollars

- Direct labor hours

- Hours of machine operation

- Units of production

- Total time in the production process

- Dollars of material used

Machine hours and process time are rapidly increasing with the expansion of factory automation. The appropriateness of a measure depends on the situation. For example, machine hours is not a good measure of activity where machines play a small role in the manufacturing process. The same is true of direct labor where extensive automation is present. Units of production does not provide a sensible measure of activity for a multiproduct firm. Adding units of different products to get total units produced results in a meaningless number. In some cases, the information required to compute the best measure, such as direct labor hours, is not readily available. In this case, an alternative such as direct labor dollars is used instead.

Using the Predetermined Overhead Rate   To illustrate the use of the predetermined overhead rate, consider a manufacturing firm that budgets its total overhead cost at $500,000, for an anticipated level of 100,000 machine hours. The predetermined overhead rate for this firm is computed as follows:

$$\frac{\text{Budgeted overhead}}{\text{Budgeted level of activity}} = \frac{\$500,000}{100,000 \text{ machine hours}} = \$5 \text{ per machine hour}$$

The $5 rate then is used for applying overhead costs to the individual jobs processed. For example, assume that the job-cost sheet for Job Number 246 reflects direct material cost of $450, direct labor cost of $750, and 50 machine hours. The overhead costs applied to Job Number 246 is computed as follows:

50 machine hours × $5 per machine hour = $250 applied overhead

The total cost of Job Number 246 is

Direct material	$ 450	
Direct labor	750	
Overhead applied	250	(50 machine hours × $5)
Total job cost	$1,450	

The application of overhead to Job Number 246 is recorded in the Applied Overhead account as follows:

Work in process	250	
Applied overhead		250

The entry in the Applied Overhead account is posted to the general ledger as follows:

Applied Overhead
250

Some companies break the predetermined overhead rate into a fixed overhead rate and a variable overhead rate (see Appendix 5A). Overhead rates are also calculated on a departmental basis by some firms (see Appendix 5B).

Actual versus Applied Overhead

The **Actual Overhead** account in the general ledger is debited for actual overhead costs; the **Applied Overhead** account is credited for overhead applied to work in process.[1] At the end of an accounting period, the balances in these two accounts typically differ because the credits to the Applied Overhead account use a predetermined overhead rate based on budgeted, not actual, overhead and production activity. Actual overhead and production activity typically differ from the budgeted

---

1. In practice, two overhead accounts are generally used. However, it is not really necessary to have two different overhead accounts. One account called Overhead could be maintained in which actual overhead cost is debited and applied overhead cost is credited, as shown below.

Overhead

Actual Overhead} → Debit	Credit ← {Applied Overhead

amounts, and therefore applied and actual overhead usually will differ. The procedure used to reconcile these two accounts is explained in the next section.

Underapplied or Overapplied Overhead   The overhead cost recorded in an actual overhead account rarely equals the amount credited to an applied overhead account. For example, assume that a company has actually incurred $120,000 of overhead costs during the month of January and has applied $105,000 of this overhead to production using a predetermined rate. The $15,000 difference ($120,000 − $105,000) is referred to as underapplied (or underabsorbed) overhead. **Underapplied overhead** occurs when the balance in the applied overhead account is less than the balance in actual overhead account. **Overapplied overhead** occurs when the balance in the applied overhead account is greater than the balance in the actual overhead account.

The actual and applied overhead accounts are closed periodically into an account called Over- or Underapplied Overhead.

Referring to the example above, the following entry is made:

	Actual Overhead		Applied Overhead	
Overhead accounts before closing entry	120,000			105,000

Closing entry	Underapplied Overhead	15,000	
	Applied Overhead	105,000	
	Actual Overhead		120,000

	Actual Overhead		Applied Overhead		Underapplied Overhead
Overhead accounts after closing entry	120,000	120,000	105,000	105,000	15,000
	0			0	

This entry has isolated the discrepancy between actual and applied overhead in a special account. The appropriate disposition of a balance in Under- or Overapplied Overhead depends on whether this amount is considered to be a product cost (inventoriable cost) or a period cost (noninventoriable cost).

It can be argued that because the products produced during the period were costed by using an annual predetermined overhead rate instead of the period's actual overhead rate, the difference is a product cost. Thus, all products worked on during the period should be adjusted from normal costs to actual costs. Assume that all of the products worked on in January were finished and that a third of the products made during the period are still in finished goods inventory. The following journal entry assigns one-third of the $15,000 balance in Underapplied Overhead to the finished goods inventory and the other two-thirds to cost of goods sold:

Finished Goods Inventory	5,000	
Costs of Goods Sold	10,000	
Underapplied Overhead		15,000

To prorate underapplied overhead.

The proration of underapplied or overapplied overhead is more complicated if some of the products are still in process at the end of the period. Ideally, proration of underapplied or overapplied overhead is done in proportion to the overhead cost in work in process, finished goods, and cost of goods sold. Some companies prorate in proportion to total product costs, but this approach is sensible only if the proportions of direct materials, direct labor, and overhead costs are the same in work in process, finished goods, and cost of goods sold.

Most companies treat underapplied or overapplied overhead as a period cost by closing it directly into cost of goods sold at the end of the accounting period. Once again using the illustration given above, the following entry is made:

Cost of Goods Sold	15,000	
Underapplied Overhead		15,000

The treatment of the balance in underapplied or overapplied overhead depends on whether there is an error in the predetermined overhead rate. If so, the balance should be prorated to work in process, finished goods, and cost of goods sold. Alternatively, if this balance is the result of inefficiency or idle capacity, it should not be inventoried but written off as an expense of the period by closing it into cost of goods sold.[2]

Levels of Activity

Significant changes in the overhead rate can be caused by fluctuations in the anticipated level of activity used in the denominator of the predetermined overhead rate. To avoid the possibility that unit costs will be affected merely by short-run changes in the level of activity, the overhead rate often is based on an activity measure that reflects the production facility's capacity. If actual operations are then at less than this measure of capacity, the overhead will be underapplied. The underapplied overhead is then considered to be a cost of idle capacity.

Normal Activity Normal activity is the average expected activity over several time periods, often three to five years. The common use of normal activity as the

---

2. The regulations set forth by the Cost Accounting Standards Board during its existence require that underapplied or overapplied overhead be prorated by firms engaged in certain cost-plus contracts with the federal government.

denominator in the predetermined overhead rate gives rise to the term *normal costing,* which is the product-costing method emphasized in this chapter. Some management accountants believe that overhead should be applied entirely each period at the expected level of activity for that period. As a result, many different capacity measures are used in predetermined overhead rates in practice. Among the more common approaches are those listed below. There is no general agreement as to which of these bases is the best one to use.

- **Practical (or attainable) capacity:** the activity level at which long-run and short-run marginal costs are equal. If the firm wants to produce more than practical capacity, it should obtain more fixed factors of production.

- **Normal (or average) activity:** the level of output necessary to satisfy average consumer demand. Typically, this concept represents a long-run notion covering cyclical influences; it often represents an average over several years.

- **Expected activity:** the level of output anticipated for a particular period.

- **Actual activity:** the level of output experienced over the period in question. This approach can be used only in an actual costing system and not in a normal costing system.

- **Theoretical (or ideal) capacity:** the level of activity that can be obtained by operating at peak output (larger than practical capacity).

To illustrate the effects of the choice of different activity levels on overhead rates, consider the information given below for the month of April. Assume that overhead is applied using machine hours. Different overhead rates for each level of activity are computed by dividing the second column (b) by column (a).

	(a) Machine Hours at Given Activity Level	(b) Total Budgeted Overhead at Given Activity Level	(c) Overhead Rate
Practical capacity	100,000	$340,000	$3.40/machine hour
Normal (or average) activity	60,000	300,000	5.00/machine hour
Expected activity	50,000	290,000	5.80/machine hour
Actual activity	40,000	280,000	7.00/machine hour

The overhead applied to work in process in April, based on actual activity of 40,000 machine hours, is as follows:

- Using practical capacity $3.40 × 40,000 = $136,000

- Using normal (or average) activity   5.00 × 40,000 =   200,000

- ▪ Using expected activity　　　　　　　　5.80 × 40,000 =　232,000

- ▪ Using actual activity　　　　　　　　　7.00 × 40,000 =　280,000

The wide differences in overhead costs applied to work in process affect the income for the period and the valuation of inventories. This demonstrates the importance of the choice of activity level for the computation of the overhead rate. In practice, companies tend to compute predetermined overhead rates based on normal activity for one or more years. Using such overhead rates smooths out fluctuations in monthly activity. If normal activity changes from month to month, any overhead rate based on monthly activity will differ from month to month and the application of overhead costs also will differ from month to month.

Smoothing Fluctuations in Overhead Costs　　The use of annual overhead rates also smooths out fluctuations in budgeted overhead costs over time. Overhead rates based on monthly budgeted overhead costs can differ from month to month because some overhead costs are incurred in different amounts at different times during the year.

Comprehensive Review Problem: Job-Order Costing

Malott Company is a manufacturer of custom metal office furniture. The firm begins operations in January 19x1. Because Malott Company's product is produced in distinct batches, management decides to implement a job-order costing system. Management also decides to use normal costing with a predetermined overhead rate based on normal, annual machine hours. Finally, management decides to use absorption costing and apply both fixed and variable overhead to production.

The following events take place in 19x1. Exhibit 5-2 shows the ledger accounts. Each entry below can be traced to the ledger accounts in Exhibit 5-2.

1. Malott purchases 100,000 pounds of direct materials for $330,000.

Direct Material Inventory	330,000	
Accounts Payable		330,000

To record purchase of materials.

2. Requisitions for 90,000 pounds of direct materials costing $3.30 per pound are processed in 19x1.

Work in Process	297,000	
Direct Material Inventory		297,000

To record requisitions of materials.

EXHIBIT 5-2

Ledger Accounts for Malott Company Review Problem

	Materials Inventory					Accounts Payable					Other Credits	
(1)	330,000	(2)	297,000				(1)	330,000		(5)	483,000
										(8)	70,000

	Salaries Payable					Work in Process					Finished Goods		
		(3)	777,750	(2)	297,000	(6)	1,584,750	(6)	1,584,750	(7)	1,267,800
				(3)	777,750			(11)	5,400		
				(4)	510,000						

	Applied Overhead					Overapplied Overhead					Cost of Goods Sold		
(10)	510,000	(4)	510,000	(11)	27,000	(10)	27,000	(7)	1,267,800		
								(11)	21,600		
										(12)	1,246,200

	Actual Overhead					Accounts Receivable					Sales Revenue		
(5)	483,000	(10)	483,000	(9)	1,500,000			(12)	1,500,000	(9)	1,500,000

	Selling and Administrative Expenses							Income Summary		
(8)	70,000	(12)	70,000					(12)	183,800

3. 85,000 hours of direct labor are used at a cost of $777,750.

Work in Process	777,750	
Salaries and Wages Payable		777,750

To record direct labor cost.

4. The predetermined overhead rate is based on budgeted fixed overhead costs of $300,000 and budgeted variable overhead costs of $3.00 per machine hour. A level of 100,000 machine hours is chosen as an annual, normal activity level. These estimates result in total budgeted overhead of $600,000, and the following calculation establishes the predetermined overhead rate:

$$\frac{\text{Total budgeted overhead at 100,000 machine hours}}{\text{Annual normal activity of 100,000 machine hours}} = \frac{\$600,000}{100,000} = \$6.00 \text{ per machine hour}$$

Since 85,000 machine hours actually are used in 19x1, the following entry is made to apply overhead to work in process.

Work in Process	510,000	
Applied Overhead		510,000

To apply overhead to products (85,000 machine hours × $6.00 per hour).

5. Actual overhead incurred is $483,000 in 19x1.

Actual Overhead	483,000	
Accumulated Depreciation — Plant		220,000
Accumulated Depreciation — Equipment		60,000
Salaries and Wages Payable		35,000
Supplies Inventory		42,000
Utilities Payable		41,000
Property Taxes Payable		62,000
Insurance Payable		23,000

To record actual overhead.

6. Twelve production jobs of office furniture are completed in 19x1. There is no work-in-process inventory at the end of the year. All of the costs previously recorded in work-in-process inventory are now transferred to finished-goods inventory.

Finished Goods	1,584,750	
Work in Process		1,584,750

To record completed production ($297,000 + $777,750 + $510,000).

7. Furniture with a total cost of $1,267,800 is sold in 19x1.

Cost of Goods Sold	1,267,800	
Finished Goods		1,267,800

To record cost of products sold.

8. Selling and administrative expenses are $70,000 in 19x1.

Selling and Administrative Expenses	70,000	
Miscellaneous Credits (Wages Payable, Cash, etc.)		70,000

To record selling and administrative expenses.

9. Total sales revenue for 19x1 amount to $1,500,000. All sales are on account.

Accounts Receivable	1,500,000	
Sales Revenue		1,500,000

To record sales on account.

10. The actual and applied overhead accounts are closed.

Applied Overhead	510,000	
Actual Overhead		483,000
Overapplied Overhead		27,000

To close actual and applied overhead and isolate overapplied overhead.

11. Malott prorates overapplied overhead to work in process, finished goods, and cost of goods sold on the basis of the total manufacturing costs applied to production during the year that remain in those accounts at the end of the year.

Manufacturing costs applied in 19x1 that remain in work in process at year end	–0–	
Manufacturing costs applied in 19x1 that remain in finished goods at year end	$ 316,950	20% of total
Manufacturing costs applied in 19x1 in cost of goods sold at year end	1,267,800	80% of total
Total costs applied in 19x1	$1,584,750	100% of total

The required entry is shown below ($27,000 \times 20\% = \$5,400$; $27,000 \times 80\% = \$21,600$).

Overapplied Overhead	27,000	
Finished Goods		5,400
Cost of Goods Sold		21,600

To prorate overapplied overhead.

12. Revenue and expense accounts are closed into income summary.

Sales Revenue	1,500,000	
Cost of Goods Sold		1,246,200
Selling and Administrative Expenses		70,000
Income Summary		183,800

To close revenue and expense accounts.

The following income statement results from these entries:

MALOTT COMPANY
Income Statement
for the Year Ended December 31, 19x1

Sales revenue	$1,500,000
Less: cost of goods sold	1,246,200
Gross margin	$ 253,800
Less: selling and administrative expenses	70,000
Net income	$ 183,800

The Malott Company example uses a single actual overhead account and a single applied overhead account. Some companies use subsidiary ledger accounts to record overhead costs on a departmental basis. This procedure is discussed in Appendix 5C.

Cost Drivers and Overhead Cost Pools

The basic objective in accounting for overhead costs is to assign overhead costs to each product or service based on the extent to which that product or service causes overhead cost to be incurred. In many production processes that objective may not be achieved when overhead is assigned to products using a single predetermined overhead rate based on any single activity measure. The managerial accountant should ask, "What drives overhead costs?" A **cost driver** is an activity or procedure that causes costs to be incurred. Examples of overhead cost drivers are machine set-ups, material handling operations, or the number of steps in a manufacturing process. Examples of drivers in nonmanufacturing organizations include hospital beds occupied, the number of take-offs and landings for an airline, or the number of rooms occupied in a hotel.

The most accurate method for assigning overhead costs to products or services is to separate overhead costs into **overhead cost pools,** where each cost pool is associated with a different cost driver. Then a predetermined overhead rate is computed for each cost pool and each cost driver. Suppose, for example, that Midwest Metals Company has established the following overhead cost pools and cost drivers:

Overhead Cost Pool	Budgeted Overhead Cost	Cost Driver	Predicted Level for Cost Driver	Predetermined Overhead Rate
Machine set-ups	$200,000	Number of set-ups	100	$2,000 per set-up
Material handling	100,000	Weight of raw material	50,000 pounds	$2 per pound
Hazardous waste control	50,000	Weight of hazardous chemicals used	10,000 pounds	$5 per pound
Quality control	75,000	Number of inspections	1,000	$75 per inspection
Other overhead costs	$200,000	Machine hours	20,000	$10 per machine hour
Total	$625,000			

Job Number N17 consists of 1,000 specially coated chemical drums with the following requirements:

Machine set-ups	4 set-ups
Raw material required	10,000 pounds
Hazardous materials required	2,000 pounds
Inspections	10 inspections
Machine hours	500 machine hours

The overhead assigned to Job Number N17 is computed below.

Overhead Cost Pool	Predetermined Overhead Rate	Level of Cost Driver	Assigned Overhead Cost
Machine set-ups	$2,000 per set-up	4 set-ups	$ 8,000
Material handling	$2 per pound	10,000 pounds	20,000
Hazardous waste control	$5 per pound	2,000 pounds	10,000
Quality control	$75 per inspection	10 inspections	750
Other overhead costs	$10 per machine hour	500 machine hours	5,000
Total			$43,750

The total overhead cost assigned to Job Number N17 is $43,750, or $43.75 per drum. Compare this with the overhead cost that is assigned to the job if the firm uses a single predetermined overhead rate based on machine hours:

$$\frac{\text{Total budgeted overhead cost}}{\text{Total predicted machine hours}} = \frac{\$625,000}{20,000}$$

$$= \$31.25 \text{ per machine hours} = \text{predetermined overhead rate}$$

Under this approach, the total overhead cost assigned to Job Number N17 is $15,625 ($31.25 per machine hour × 500 machine hours). This is only $15.625 per drum, which is less than half the overhead cost per drum computed when multiple cost drivers are used.

What has happened here? The specially lined drums require a relatively large number of machine set-ups, a sizable amount of hazardous materials, and several inspections. Thus, they are relatively costly in terms of driving overhead costs. Use of a single predetermined overhead rate obscures that fact.

Misestimating the overhead cost per drum to the extent illustrated above can have serious adverse consequences for the firm. For example, it can lead to poor decisions about product prices, adding or dropping product lines, or making bids. The cost accountant needs to weigh carefully such considerations in designing a product-costing system. A costing system using multiple cost drivers is more costly to implement and use, but it may save millions through improved decisions.

Illustration of Multiple Overhead Cost Pools

Hewlett-Packard Company's Personal Office Computer Division uses two overhead application rates.[3] One rate is based on direct labor and assigns overhead costs associated with production. The second rate is based on material cost and assigns overhead

3. This description is based on J. Patell, "Cost Accounting, Process Control and Product Design: A Case Study of the Hewlett-Packard Personal Office Computer Division," *Accounting Review* (October, 1987): 808–837.

EXHIBIT 5-3

Multiple Overhead Cost Pools—Hewlett-Packard Company:
Personal Office Computer Division

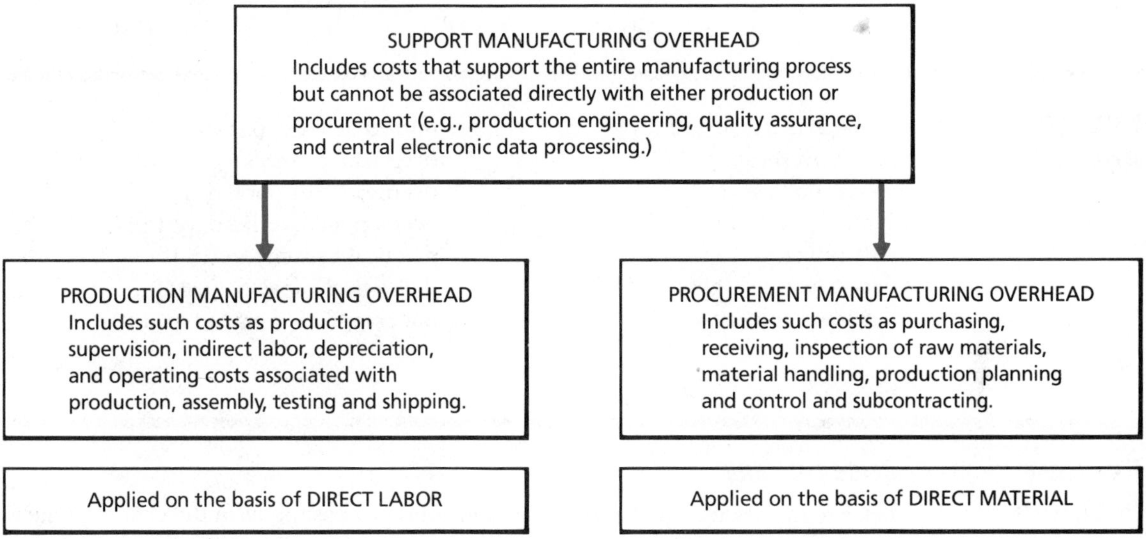

SUPPORT MANUFACTURING OVERHEAD
Includes costs that support the entire manufacturing process
but cannot be associated directly with either production or
procurement (e.g., production engineering, quality assurance,
and central electronic data processing.)

PRODUCTION MANUFACTURING OVERHEAD
Includes such costs as production
supervision, indirect labor, depreciation,
and operating costs associated with
production, assembly, testing and shipping.

Applied on the basis of DIRECT LABOR

PROCUREMENT MANUFACTURING OVERHEAD
Includes such costs as purchasing,
receiving, inspection of raw materials,
material handling, production planning
and control and subcontracting.

Applied on the basis of DIRECT MATERIAL

---

costs associated with procurement. Exhibit 5-3 illustrates these systems. Overhead costs are initially categorized into three cost pools or *buckets,* in the company's terminology. Then the overhead costs associated with overall manufacturing support functions are allocated between the production cost pool and the procurement cost pool. This allocation is based on the number of employees and the estimated percentage of time spent on these two types of activities.

Summary

Job-order cost accounting systems are common in manufacturing situations in which products differ substantially from item to item or batch to batch. These systems are used to accumulate costs for product costing purposes. Cost control under a job-order cost accounting system requires that costs be recorded twice, once by job and once by department or cost center.

Control of overhead is accomplished by recording overhead costs by cost centers or departments and by identifying costs in detail. The overhead cost of products, on the other hand, is determined by using overhead rates. These rates can be separated into their fixed and variable components so that costs can be computed for different purposes. Using departmental overhead rates results in more realistic unit-cost figures, since the cost of the product includes costs that are identified with the product either directly or indirectly, using appropriate allocation bases. Using multiple overhead cost pools and cost drivers, although more costly, provides the most accurate method of assigning overhead costs.

Key Terms to Review

actual activity, p. 150
actual overhead, p. 144
allocation base, p. 145
applied overhead, p. 147
cost driver, p. 155
denominator activity, p. 146
expected activity, p. 150

normal activity, p. 149
overhead, p. 145
overhead cost pool, p. 155
overapplied overhead, p. 148
practical capacity, p. 150
theoretical capacity, p. 150
underapplied overhead, p. 148.

Review Problem

COST DRIVERS

Refer to the discussion of cost drivers and overhead cost pools in the chapter. Calculate the unit cost of Midwest Metals Company's Job Number Z67, which consists of 100 coated plates used in producing batteries. Job Number Z67 has the following requirements:

Machine set-ups	2
Raw material required	800
Hazardous materials required	300
Inspections	3
Machine hours	50

Solution to Review Problem

Overhead Cost Pool	Predetermined Overhead Rate	Level of Cost Driver	Assigned Overhead Cost
Machine set-ups	$2,000 per set-up	2	$4,000
Material handling	$2 per pound	800	1,600
Hazardous waste control	$5 per pound	300	1,500
Quality control	$75 per inspection	3	225
Other overhead costs	$10 per machine hour	50	500
Total			$7,825

The unit cost for Job Number Z67 is $78.25 per plate ($7,825 ÷ 100).

APPENDIX 5A
Variable and Fixed Overhead Rates

In calculating predetermined overhead rates, management accountants sometimes classify overhead items into fixed and variable categories. Then two overhead rates are computed: a fixed overhead rate and a variable overhead rate. For example, assume that a manufacturing department budgets fixed overhead costs of $200,000 and variable overhead costs of $300,000 for a level of activity of 100,000 machine hours. The fixed, variable, and total predetermined overhead rates for this department are as follows:

$$\text{Fixed overhead rate} = \frac{\$200,000}{100,000} = \$2.00 \text{ per machine hour}$$

$$\text{Variable overhead rate} = \frac{\$300,000}{100,000} = \$3.00 \text{ per machine hour}$$

$$\text{Total overhead rate} = \frac{\$500,000}{100,000} = \$5.00 \text{ per machine hour}$$

If, instead of operating at 100,000 machine hours, the department expects to operate at 50,000 machine hours, the fixed, variable, and total overhead rates would be the following:

$$\text{Fixed overhead rate} = \frac{\$200,000}{50,000} = \$4.00 \text{ per machine hour}$$

$$\text{Variable overhead rate} = \frac{\$150,000}{50,000} = \$3.00 \text{ per machine hour}$$

$$\text{Total overhead rate} = \frac{\$350,000}{50,000} = \$7.00 \text{ per machine hour}$$

The variable overhead rate is unchanged, but the fixed overhead rate changed from $2.00 per machine hour to $4.00 per machine hour.[4] The choice of the budgeted activity level always affects the fixed overhead rate. By affecting this rate, the budgeted activity level affects the total overhead rate.

---

4. This example assumes that when activity changes, variable overhead changes proportionately. Although this may not be exactly true, when activity is cut in half, variable overhead declines substantially.

APPENDIX 5B

Departmental Overhead Rates

Different overhead rates may be appropriate for each production department, and several rates may be needed in the same department for different types of overhead. The potential importance of applying overhead to production using *departmental overhead rates* can be demonstrated by an example. Consider two production departments that have the following characteristics:

	Production Department 1	Production Department 2
Direct-labor hours (at normal activity)	10,000	10,000
Machinery and equipment depreciation	None	$50,000
Floor space	1,000 sq. ft.	29,000 sq. ft.
Power cost	$100 (lighting only)	$ 5,000

If only one overhead rate is used for the entire plant and both departments work at normal activity, the same amount of overhead will be applied to the products in both departments. Assume that the following costs are budgeted for the year and are the basis for one *plantwide overhead rate:*

Depreciation of machinery and equipment	$50,000
Building costs	30,000
Power costs	5,100
	$85,100

The plantwide overhead rate is $4.255 per machine hour ($85,100 divided by 20,000 hours). Assume that each unit of product produced in either Department 1 or Department 2 requires one hour of direct labor and $5.00 of costs other than overhead. Each unit of product, whether produced in Department 1 or in Department 2, is then assigned a cost of $9.255 ($5.00 of direct costs, $4.255 of overhead); at 10,000 machine hours, $42,550 of overhead costs are applied to production in each department. Department 2, however, should bear a larger share of the overhead costs than Department 1 because Department 2 uses more floor space, more equipment, and more power. If overhead is first allocated to departments and separate overhead rates are computed for the two departments, Department 2 has a higher overhead rate. The product produced in Department 2 then bears a larger (and more appropriate) overhead cost.

Departmental overhead rates are computed below. The cost of the product made in Department 1 is now $5.11 ($5.00 of direct cost plus $.11 of applied overhead). The cost of the product made in Department 2 is now $13.40 ($5.00 of direct cost plus $8.40 of applied overhead).

	Dept. 1	Dept. 2
Depreciation of machinery and equipment	$ 0	$50,000
Building costs (allocation based on floor space)	1,000	29,000
Power	100	5,000
Total	$1,100	$84,000
Overhead rates (based on 10,000 direct-labor hours in each department)	$ .11	$ 8.40

APPENDIX 5C
Subsidiary Ledger Accounts

An accounting system that uses a single actual overhead account to record overhead costs omits information. The natural classification of overhead costs has not been recorded. Thus, information about how much of the actual overhead cost is represented by such costs as supplies, depreciation, indirect labor, and electrical utility cost is not easily accessible. In addition, because the departments in which the overhead costs were incurred are not indicated, the department managers responsible for the costs are not identified.

The first omission can be addressed by initially recording the actual overhead costs incurred by their natural classification and then transferring the balances in these accounts to a single "actual overhead control" account. The second omission can be handled by assigning the overhead costs as they are incurred to departmental overhead accounts, so the managers responsible for each department can be held accountable for the costs incurred in their departments.

For example, assume that supplies costing $1,000 were used as follows:

Personnel Department	$200
Grinding Department	300
Polishing Department	500

The following entry is made in the general ledger:

Actual Overhead	1,000	
Factory Supplies Inventory		1,000

The debit for this transaction also is recorded in detail in the appropriate departmental subsidiary cost ledgers as indicated below:

Personnel Department Overhead Cost Ledger

Indirect Labor	Allocation from Service Depts.		Supplies Used		(Other Columns)	
			$200			

Grinding Department Overhead Cost Ledger

Indirect Labor		Allocation from Service Depts.		Supplies Used		(Other Columns)	
				$300			

Polishing Department Overhead Cost Ledger

Indirect Labor		Allocation from Service Depts.		Supplies Used		(Other Columns)	
				$500			

Overhead classifications are even more useful if they are broken down into finer divisions. Types of supplies can be identified as cleaning supplies, office supplies, first aid supplies, tools, and so on. The recording of such information used to be quite burdensome, but the use of computers has greatly facilitated the recording of detailed overhead information, both by natural classifications and by departments.

Suggested Readings

Capettini, R. and D. K. Clancy, ed. *Cost Accounting, Robotics, and the New Manufacturing Environment.* Sarasota, Fl.: American Accounting Association, 1987.

Chin, J., and Y. Lee. "A Survey of Current Practice in Overhead Accounting and Analysis." *Proceedings of the 1980 Western Regional Meeting,* edited by O. R. Wittington. San Diego State University, School of Accounting, 1980, p. 239.

Cooper, R. "You Need a New Cost System When. . . ." *Harvard Business Review* (January–February 1989):77–82.

Goldratt, E. M., and J. Cox. *The Goal: A Process of Ongoing Improvement.* Rev. ed. Croton-on-Hudson, N.Y.: North River Press, 1986.

Hunt, R., L. Garrett, and C. M. Merz. "Direct Labor Cost Not Always Relevant at H-P." *Management Accounting* (February 1985): 58–62.

Kaplan, R. "Measuring Manufacturing Performance: A New Challenge for Managerial Accounting Research." *Accounting Review* (October 1983): 686–705.

———. "One Cost System Isn't Enough." *Harvard Business Review* (January–February 1988): 61–66.

Kaplan, R., and H. T. Johnson. *Relevance Lost.* Boston: Harvard Business School Press, 1987.

Lammert, D., and D. Stratis. "Uniform Capitalization Rules Are Here to Stay." *Management Accounting* (December 1987): 31–33.

Lee, J. Y. *Managerial Accounting for the 1990's.* Artesia, Calif.: McKay Business Systems, 1987.

Noreen, E. "Commentary on H. T. Johnson and R. Kaplan's Relevance Lost." *Accounting Horizons* (December 1987): 110–116.

Patell, J. "Cost Accounting, Process Control and Product Design: A Case Study of the Hewlett-Packard Personal Office Computer Division." *Accounting Review* (October 1987): 808–837.

Schonberger, R. J. *Japanese Manufacturing Techniques.* New York: Macmillan, 1982.

Wise, R. L. "Cost Reporting for the Small and Medium Size Job Shop Operation." *Management Accounting* (February 1970): 20.

Worthy, F. S. "Accounting Bores You? Wake Up." *Fortune* (October 12, 1987): 43–53.

Review Questions

5-1 Define *cost distribution.*

5-2 Define *cost allocation.*

5-3 Define *cost application.*

5-4 How is a predetermined overhead rate computed, and what is it used for?

5-5 During a severe business recession throughout the manufacturing industry, a division manager for a large heavy-machinery company is confused and unhappy. He is distressed with the controller, whose cost department keeps providing him with cost data that is of little use. Production costs are high, but the manager has to quote low prices in order to get business.

   a. What activity base is probably being used for the application of overhead?

   b. How might overhead be applied in order to make the cost data more useful in making price quotations?

   c. Would the product costs furnished by the cost department be satisfactory for costing the annual inventory?

5-6 Respond to the following questions concerning the accounting treatment of overhead costs.

   a. "The practical problems of applying various elements of overhead to physical units are fraught with trouble spots. An understanding of the limitations of overhead application should accompany an understanding of the technique." What is the primary reason for these problems?

   b. "Overhead is applied to product because of the managerial need for a close approximation of costs of different products prior to the end of the fiscal period." Give two purposes why this need exists.

   c. "Accountants have chosen an averaging process for attaching overhead to product." What is this process, and in what way is it an averaging process?

> *d.* "The total forecasted overhead is related to some common denominator or base." Name three such bases, and give in one sentence the reason for the existence of more than one basis.
>
> *e.* "Overhead costs are also accumulated weekly or monthly on departmental cost sheets without regard to their application to specific jobs." What is the purpose of such cost accumulation, and what three additional steps or precautions are necessary to effect this purpose?

5-7 What factors should be considered in deciding on bases for allocating service department costs to producing departments?

5-8 If overtime is incurred in a job-cost shop, how should the overtime be charged to the jobs? Does it make any difference if the job worked on during the overtime period was accepted after the regular work hours of the shop had been scheduled?

5-9 Would you use a fixed basis (that is, determined at the beginning of the budget period) or a variable basis (that is, based on some measure of actual activity) to allocate the following corporate costs to divisions?

> *a.* Corporate controller's costs
>
> *b.* President's salary and staff costs
>
> *c.* Trucking costs (assuming the corporate office handles all divisional transportation)

5-10 If a company acquires excess capacity (say it builds a boiler twice as large as is currently needed), should the cost of that excess capacity be considered a cost of product during the early periods, when that part of the capacity is not being used?

5-11 A corporate controller was pleased that the overhead variances for the year were very small. He said, "This shows that we effectively predicted costs and activity in setting our overhead rates." Comment on this statement.

Exercises

5-12 The Universal Corporation uses a flexible budget procedure to control variable overhead costs. Each month the actual cost incurred is plotted, using direct labor hours as a measure of activity. At the end of the year, the points are plotted and a regression line is calculated. The equation of the line is determined in order to obtain the fixed and variable components of the cost. This equation is used as the basis for the flexible budget for the next year.

REQUIRED:

> *a.* Comment on the effectiveness of the procedure followed.
>
> *b.* How could the procedure be improved? Could the monthly plottings of cost be used for cost-control purposes? Explain.

5-13 **Allocating Cost Pools**   The following is taken from the Progress Report to the Congress 1973 (Cost Accounting Standards Board):

Hierarchy for Allocating Cost Pools

Costs not directly identified with final cost objectives should be grouped into logical and homogeneous expense pools and should be allocated in accordance with a hierarchy of preferable techniques. The costs of like functions have a direct and definitive relationship to the cost objectives for which the functions are performed, and the grouping of such costs in homogeneous pools for allocation to benefitting cost objectives results in better identification of cost with cost objectives.

The Board believes there is a hierarchy of preferable allocation techniques for distributing homogeneous pools of cost. The preferred representation of the relationship between the pooled cost and the benefitting cost objectives is a measure of the activity of the function represented by the pool of cost. Measures of the activities of such functions ordinarily can be expressed in such terms as labor hours, machine hours, or square footage. Accordingly, costs of these functions can be allocated by use of a rate, such as a rate per labor hour, rate per machine hour, or cost per square foot, unless such measures are unavailable or impractical to ascertain. In the latter cases, the basis for allocation can be a measurement of the output of the supporting function. Output is measured in terms of units of end product produced by the supporting functions, as for example, number of printed pages for a print shop, number of purchase orders processed by a purchasing department, number of hires by an employment office.

Where neither activity nor output of the supporting function can be measured practically, a surrogate for the beneficial or causal relationship should be selected. Surrogates used to represent the relationship are generally measures of the activity of the cost objectives receiving the service. Any surrogate used should be a reasonable measure of the services received and should vary in proportion to the services received.

Pooled costs which cannot readily be allocated on measures of specific beneficial or causal relationship generally represent the cost of overall management activities. These costs should be grouped in relation to the activities managed and the base selected to measure the allocation of these indirect costs to cost objectives should be a base representative of the entire activity being managed. For example, the total cost of plant activities managed might be a reasonable base for allocation of general plant indirect costs. The use of a portion of a total activity, such as direct labor costs or direct material costs only, as a substitute for a total activity base, is acceptable only if the base is a good representative of the total activity being managed.

REQUIRED:

Evaluate the suggested procedures.

5-14 Capacity Measurement   The following cost information applies to a product:

Units	Total Cost for a Week
100	$10,000
200	25,000
300	50,000

The fixed-cost component of cost is $5,000 per week, and this would not increase if additional units are produced. Additional equipment can be obtained. The unit cost (excluding fixed costs, which should be incurred in any event) would be $150 per unit for the additional units if the new equipment is obtained.

REQUIRED:

What is the practical capacity of the present long-lived assets?

5-15 **Under- (Over-) Applied Overhead** The Pokerface Playing Card Company uses an overhead rate of $3.00 per direct labor hour, based on expected variable overhead of $100,000 per year, and expected fixed overhead of $200,000 per year. Data for the year's operations are as follows:

	Direct Labor Hours Used	Overhead Costs Incurred[a]
First 6 months	60,000	$168,000
Last 6 months	36,000	136,000

[a] Fixed costs equaled budgeted fixed costs throughout the year, and were incurred uniformly over the year.

a. What is the under- (over-) applied overhead for each six-month period in total and broken down by fixed and variable components?

b. Give plausible reasons for the amounts or any subamounts of the figures determined in question a.

Problems

5-16 **Differences Between Companywide and Departmental Overhead Rates** Able Body Products, Ltd., produces two models of exercising machines. Each model begins processing in the Assembly Department and then is transferred to the Finishing Department where the final touches are added. Model 1 requires the assembly of several small components, but it requires little in the way of finishing. Thus each unit requires three hours of direct labor in the Assembly Department but only one hour in the Finishing Department. Model 2 requires little in the way of assembly, but the machine is given a high polish in the Finishing Department that requires about five hours of direct labor. Model 2 requires about two hours of direct labor in the Assembly Department.

For the year just ended, Able Body used a companywide overhead application rate based on direct labor hours for determining product costs. The company developed the rate from the following budget information:

	Budgeted Overhead	Normal Capacity[a]
Assembly Department	$ 50,000	10,000
Finishing Department	200,000	20,000

[a] Direct labor hours.

The budgeted level of activity was met exactly and the only ending inventories for the year were 100 units of Model 1 and 800 units of Model 2 in finishing goods.

REQUIRED:

a. Find the overhead application rate used by the company.

b. Find departmental overhead rates.

c. How would the company's net income change if it used departmental overhead application rates?

5-17 **Departmental Overhead Rates**   The Overhead Company has five departments, two of which are producing departments. Overhead costs are first identified with the department responsible for the costs, and then all costs are allocated to the two producing departments. Producing Department 1 has a normal capacity of 50,000 direct labor hours, and Producing Department 2 has a normal capacity of 100,000 direct labor hours. Factory office costs are all fixed costs and are budgeted at $110,500. Costs for the materials handling departments are all fixed and are budgeted at $75,000. Costs for the machinery repairs department are budgeted as follows:

Fixed costs	$14,000
Variable costs per hour	2.20

Producing Department 1 is scheduled for 1,200 hours of machinery repairs, and Producing Department 2 is scheduled for 3,000 hours. Budgeted overhead costs for the two producing departments are as follows:

	Variable[a] Costs	Fixed Costs
Producing Department 1	$.52	$125,000
Producing Department 2	.65	198,000

[a] Per direct labor hour.

Factory office costs are allocated on the basis of direct labor hours. Producing Department 1 is budgeted to requisition 5,000 units of material, and Producing Department 2 is budgeted to requisition 10,000 units of material.

REQUIRED:

Compute overhead application rates for each of the two producing departments.

5-18 **Diagram of Plant Capacity**   Using average total cost, average variable cost, marginal cost curves, and any other curves that you think useful, indicate on a diagram the practical capacity of a plant.

5-19 **Overhead: From Determination of Rate to Absorption by Product**   The Webster Corporation uses normal activity for determining overhead rates. Overhead is applied to product, using direct-labor hours.

Part I. Determining Overhead Rates

	Dept. 1 Normal Activity	Dept. 2 Normal Activity
Budgeted direct labor dollars	$200,000	$400,000
Budgeted direct labor hours	100,000	200,000
Budgeted fixed overhead	$ 50,000	$ 40,000
Budgeted variable overhead	$150,000	$180,000

REQUIRED:

a. Compute the fixed and variable overhead rates for the two departments.

b. Explain briefly how the amounts of fixed overhead were obtained for the two departments.

c. Explain how the above computations would be changed by the use of practical capacity instead of normal activity.

Part II. Recording Overhead in Burden Centers
During the month of January the following overhead costs were incurred.

	Building Dept.	Dept. 1	Dept. 2
Indirect labor (fixed)	$200	$ 4,000	$ 2,000
Indirect supplies (fixed)	100	1,000	1,200
Indirect labor (variable)		10,000	11,000
Indirect supplies (variable)		2,000	3,000

REQUIRED:

a. Record the given information in general ledger accounts.

b. Record the given information in departmental subsidiary ledgers.

c. If the direct labor hours actually worked during the month are 9,000 in Department 1 and 18,500 in Department 2, are the variable overhead costs under or over the budgeted amounts? Prepare a schedule.

Part III. Allocation of Overhead to Operating Departments

The Building Department costs are allocated to the two operating departments, based on the floor space used:

Department	Floor Space Used (ft²)
1	30,000
2	10,000

REQUIRED:

a. Record the allocation of the Building Department overhead to the two operating departments in the departmental subsidiary ledgers.

b. Would the allocation of Building Department costs be relevant for controlling the costs of the Building Department or the operating departments? Explain.

Part IV. Absorption of Overhead by Product

During the month of January there are 9,000 direct labor hours worked in Department 1 and 18,500 worked in Department 2.

REQUIRED:

a. Record the absorption of overhead by product in the general ledger.

b. What factors caused the amount of overhead absorbed by product to be different from the amount incurred?

c. What disposition do you suggest for the overhead variances?

5-20 Overhead Accounting   Baehr Company is a manufacturing company with a fiscal year that runs from July 1 to June 30. The company uses a job order accounting system for its production costs.

A predetermined overhead rate based on direct labor hours is used to apply overhead to individual jobs. A flexible budget of overhead costs was prepared for the 19x7 and 19x8 fiscal year as shown below:

Direct labor hours	100,000	120,000	140,000
Variable overhead costs	$325,000	$390,000	$455,000
Fixed overhead costs	216,000	216,000	216,000
Total overhead	$541,000	$606,000	$671,000

Although the annual ideal capacity is 150,000 direct labor hours, company officials have determined 120,000 direct labor hours as normal capacity for the year.

The information presented below is for November 19x7. Jobs 77-50 and 77-51 were completed during November.

Inventories November 1, 19x7

Raw materials and supplies	$ 10,500
Work in process (Job 77-50)	54,000
Finished goods	112,500

Purchases of raw materials and supplies

Raw materials	$135,000
Supplies	15,000

Materials and supplies requisitioned for production

Job 77-50	$45,000
Job 77-51	37,500
Job 77-52	25,500
Supplies	12,000
	$120,000

Factory direct labor hours

Job 77-50	3,500 DLH
Job 77-51	3,000 DLH
Job 77-52	2,000 DLH

Labor costs

Direct labor wages	$ 51,000
Indirect labor wages (4,000 hours)	15,000
Supervisory salaries	6,000

Building occupancy costs (heat, light, depreciation, etc.)

Factory facilities	$ 6,500
Sales offices	1,500
Administrative offices (occupied by company president and vice presidents of finance and sales)	1,000
	$ 9,000

Factory equipment costs

Power	$ 4,000
Repairs and maintenance	1,500
Depreciation	1,500
Other	1,000
	$ 8,000

REQUIRED:

a. Calculate the predetermined overhead rate to be used to apply overhead to individual jobs during the 19x7 and 19x8 fiscal year.

Note: Without prejudice to your answer to **a** assume the predetermined overhead rate is $4.50 per direct labor hour. Use this amount in answering **a** through **f.**

b. Compute the total cost of Job 77-50.

c. Calculate the factory overhead costs applied to Job 77-52 during November.

d. Determine the total amount of overhead applied to jobs during November.

e. Compute the actual factory overhead incurred during November 19x7.

f. At the end of the last fiscal year (June 30, 19x7), Baehr Company had the following account balances:

Over applied overhead	$ 1,000
Cost of goods sold	980,000
Work-in-process inventory	38,000
Finished-goods inventory	82,000

What is the most common treatment of the firm's overapplied overhead? (*CMA adapted*)

5-21 Departmental Overhead Rates in Production Costing   Fine Products, Inc. wants to develop departmental overhead rates for product costing. The company has prepared the following budgeted overhead for next year based on normal capacity:

Department	Budgeted Overhead
Buildings and Grounds	$ 50,000
Cafeteria	25,000
Personnel	10,000
Power	100,000
Material Stores	45,000
Producing: 1	50,000
Producing: 2	75,000
Total	$355,000

In order to determine departmental overhead application rates, service department overhead must be allocated to the two producing departments.

The following data are available for choosing allocation bases:

	Producing: 1	Producing: 2
Direct labor hours — Normal capacity	10,500	15,000
Number of employees	50	75
Square feet of space	25,000	10,000
Metered power — Last year	5,500	3,200
Number of material requisitions — Last year	500	250

REQUIRED:

    a. Allocate the service department budgeted costs to the producing departments.

    b. Compute departmental overhead allocation rates based on direct labor hours.

5-22 Job-Order Costing; Overhead Accounting   Targon, Inc. manufactures lawn equipment and uses a job-order system because the products are manufactured on a batch rather than a continuous basis. Targon employs a full-absorption accounting method for cost accumulation. The balances in selected general ledger accounts for the eleven-month period ended August 31, 19x2, are presented below:

Stores inventory	$ 32,000
Work-in-process inventory	1,200,000
Finished-goods inventory	2,785,000
Factory overhead control	2,260,000
Cost of goods sold	14,200,000

The work-in-process inventory consists of two jobs:

Job No.	Units	Items	Accumulated Cost
3005-5	50,000	Estate sprinklers	$ 700,000
3006-4	40,000	Economy sprinklers	500,000
			$1,200,000

The finished-goods inventory consists of five items:

Items	Quantity and Unit Cost	Accumulated Cost
Estate sprinklers	5,000 units @ $22 each	$ 110,000
Deluxe sprinklers	115,000 units @ $17 each	1,955,000
Brass nozzles	10,000 gross @ $14 per gross	140,000
Rainmaker nozzles	5,000 gross @ $16 per gross	80,000
Connectors	100,000 gross @ $ 5 per gross	500,000
		$2,785,000

    The factory cost budget prepared for the 19x1 and 19x2 fiscal year is presented below. The company applies factory overhead on the basis of direct labor hours.

The activities during the first eleven months of the year are quite close to the budget. A total of 367,000 direct labor hours have been worked through August 31, 19x2.

FACTORY COST ANNUAL BUDGET
for the Year Ending September 30, 19x2

Direct materials	$ 3,800,000
Purchased parts	6,000,000
Direct labor (400,000 hours)	4,000,000
Overhead	
Supplies	190,000
Indirect labor	700,000
Supervision	250,000
Depreciation	950,000
Utilities	200,000
Insurance	10,000
Property taxes	40,000
Miscellaneous	60,000
Total factory costs	$16,200,000

The September 19x2 transactions are summarized below.

1. All direct materials, purchased parts, and supplies are charged to stores inventory. The September purchases are as follows:

Materials	$410,000
Purchased parts	285,000
Supplies	13,000

2. The direct materials, purchased parts, and supplies are requisitioned from stores inventory as shown in the table below.

	Purchased Parts	Materials	Supplies	Total Requisitions
3005-5	$110,000	$100,000	$ —	$210,000
3006-4	—	6,000	—	6,000
4001-3 (30,000 gross rainmaker nozzles)	—	181,000	—	181,000
4002-1 (10,000 deluxe sprinklers)	—	92,000	—	92,000
4003-5 (50,000 ring sprinklers)	163,000	—	—	163,000
Supplies	—	—	20,000	20,000
	$273,000	$379,000	$20,000	$672,000

3. The payroll summary for September is as follows:

	Hours	Cost
3005-5	6,000	$ 62,000
3006-4	2,500	26,000
4001-3	18,000	182,000
4002-1	500	5,000
4003-5	5,000	52,000
Indirect	8,000	60,000
Supervision	—	24,000
Sales and administration	—	120,000
		$531,000

4. Other factory costs were incurred during September:

Depreciation	$62,500
Utilities	15,000
Insurance	1,000
Property taxes	3,500
Miscellaneous	5,000
	$87,000

5. Jobs completed during September and the actual output were as follows:

Job No.	Quantity	Items
3005-5	48,000 units	Estate sprinklers
3006-4	39,000 units	Economy sprinklers
4001-3	29,500 gross	Rainmaker nozzles
4003-5	49,000 units	Ring sprinklers

6. The following finished products were shipped to customers during September:

Items	Quantity
Estate sprinklers	16,000 units
Deluxe sprinklers	32,000 units
Economy sprinklers	20,000 units
Ring sprinklers	22,000 units
Brass nozzles	5,000 gross
Rainmaker nozzles	10,000 gross
Connectors	26,000 gross

REQUIRED:

a. (1) Calculate the over- or underapplied overhead for the year ended September 30, 19x2. Be sure to indicate whether the overhead is over- or underapplied.
(2) What is the appropriate accounting treatment for this overapplied or underapplied overhead balance? Explain your answer.

b. Calculate the dollar balance in the work-in-process inventory account as of September 30, 19x2.

c. Calculate the dollar balance in the finished goods inventory as of September 30, 19x2, for the estate sprinklers using a FIFO basis. (*CMA adapted*)

5-23 Cost Drivers   Refer to the discussion at the end of the chapter regarding the Midwest Metals Company. Job Number P78, consisting of 2,000 metal plates, has the following requirements:

Machine set-ups	1 set-up
Raw material required	2,000 pounds
Hazardous materials	None
Inspections	1 inspection
Machine hours	400 machine hours

REQUIRED:

a. Compute the overhead cost assigned to Job Number P78, in total and per unit, under each of these approaches:

(1) Using the multiple overhead cost pools and cost drivers described in the chapter.

(2) Using a single predetermined overhead rate based on machine hours.

b. Comment on the implications of the different answers obtained in a(1) and a(2) above.

5-24 Understanding Product-Costing Systems; Multiple Choice   Cincinnati Castings is a job-order shop that uses a normal absorption costing system to account for its production costs. The overhead costs are applied on a direct labor hour basis.
a. The firm's choice of a production volume as a denominator for calculating its factory overhead rate

(1) has no effect on the fixed factory overhead rate for applying costs to production.

(2) has an effect on the variable factory overhead rate for applying costs to production.

(3) has an effect on the fixed factory overhead rate but not on the variable factory overhead rate.

b. Which of the following costs does the company's system treat as variable when determining the inventory value of manufactured products?

(1) Only variable manufacturing costs

(2) Only variable manufacturing costs and variable selling costs

(3) Only variable manufacturing costs and semi-variable (mixed) manufacturing costs

(4) All manufacturing costs and no selling costs

(5) All manufacturing costs and variable selling costs

c. The amount of fixed factory overhead that the firm would apply to finished production would be

(1) the actual direct labor hours times the predetermined fixed overhead rate per direct labor hour.

(2) the actual units of output times the predetermined fixed overhead rate per unit of output.

(3) the actual fixed overhead cost per direct labor hour times the actual direct labor hours worked on finished production. (*CMA adapted*)

5-25 Predetermined Overhead Rate with Various Bases The following data pertains to Geller Company for 19x1.

Budgeted machine hours	10,000
Budgeted direct labor hours	20,000
Budgeted direct labor rate	$14
Budgeted manufacturing overhead	$364,000
Actual machine hours	11,000
Actual direct labor hours	18,000
Actual direct labor rate	$15
Actual manufacturing overhead	$320,000

REQUIRED:

a. Compute the firm's 19x1 predetermined overhead rate using each of the following common bases: (1) machine hours, (2) direct labor hours, and (3) direct labor dollars.

b. Calculate the overapplied or underapplied overhead for 19x1 using each of the bases listed above.

5-26 Actual versus Normal Costing Refer to the data for the preceding problem.

REQUIRED:

Prepare a journal entry to add to work-in-process inventory the total manufacturing overhead cost for 19x1, assuming:

a. The firm uses actual costing.

b. The firm uses normal costing, with a predetermined overhead rate based on machine hours.

5-27 Underapplied or Overapplied Overhead   Refer to the data given in Problem 4-20 of the preceding chapter.

Compute the overapplied or underapplied overhead to be closed into Cost of Goods Sold on February 28, 19x2. (*CPA adapted*)

5-28 Tastee-Treat Company prepares, packages, and distributes six frozen vegetables in two different size containers. The different vegetables and different sizes are prepared in large batches. The company employs an actual-cost, job-order costing system. Manufacturing overhead is assigned to batches by a predetermined rate on the basis of direct labor hours. The manufacturing overhead costs incurred by the company during two recent years (adjusted for changes using current prices and wage rates) are presented below:

	19x1	19x2
Direct labor hours worked	2,760,000	2,160,000
Manufacturing overhead costs incurred (adjusted for changes in current prices and wage rates)		
Indirect labor	$11,040,000	$ 8,640,000
Employee benefits	4,140,000	3,240,000
Supplies	2,760,000	2,160,000
Power	2,208,000	1,728,000
Heat and light	552,000	552,000
Supervision	2,865,000	2,625,000
Depreciation	7,930,000	7,930,000
Property taxes and insurance	3,005,000	3,005,000
Total overhead costs	$34,500,000	$29,880,000

REQUIRED:

a. Tastee-Treat Company expects to operate at a 2,300,000 direct labor hour level of activity in 19x3. Using the data from the two recent years, calculate the rate Tastee-Treat should employ to assign manufacturing overhead to its products. (Hint: Divide the difference between the 19x1 and 19x2 total cost amounts by the difference between the 19x1 and 19x2 direct labor hours.)

b. Explain how the company can use the information it developed for calculating the overhead rate for

(1) evaluation of product pricing decisions.

(2) cost control.

(3) development of budgets. (*CMA adapted*)

5-29 Plantwide versus Departmental Overhead Rates; Effect on Product Pricing Medical Testing Systems Corporation manufactures two types of medical testing equipment for hospitals. Cost estimates for the two products for the year 19x8 are shown below.

	Product I	Product II
Direct material	$ 400	$ 800
Direct labor (20 hours at $15 per hour)	300	300
Manufacturing overhead[a]	600	600
Total	$1,300	$1,700

[a] The predetermined overhead rate is $20 per direct labor hour.

Each product requires 30 hours of direct labor. Product *I* requires 10 hours in Department *A* and 20 hours in Department *B*. Product *II* requires 20 hours in Department *A* and 10 hours in Department *B*. The costs incurred in these two production departments are as follows:

	Department A	Department B
Variable cost	$16 per direct labor hour	$4 per direct labor hour
Fixed cost	$200,000	$200,000

The firm's management expects to operate at a level of 20,000 direct-labor hours in each production department during 19x8.

REQUIRED:

a. Show how Medical Testing Systems' predetermined overhead rate was determined.

b. If the firm prices each computer model at 10 percent over its cost, what is the price of each product?

c. Suppose the company were to use departmental predetermined overhead rates. Calculate the rate for each of the two production departments.

d. Compute the cost of each product using the departmental overhead rates calculated in requirement **c.**

e. Compute the price to be charged for each product, assuming the company continues to price each product at 10 percent above cost. Use the revised product costs calculated in requirement **d.**

f. Make a recommendation as to whether the firm should use a plantwide overhead rate or departmental rates. Consider the potential implications of the overhead rates on the firm's pricing policy. How might these considerations affect the firm's ability to compete?

5-30 **Overapplied or Underapplied Overhead** The following information was compiled for Morrison Industries for 19x6:

Budgeted direct labor cost: 85,000 hours at $16 per hour	
Actual direct labor cost: 80,000 hours at $17 per hour	
Budgeted manufacturing overhead: $969,000	
Actual manufacturing overhead:	
Depreciation	$140,000
Property taxes	22,000
Indirect labor	82,000
Supervisory salaries	300,000
Utilities	49,000
Insurance	130,000
Rental of space	200,000
Indirect material (see data below)	
Indirect material:	
Beginning inventory, December 31, 19x5	32,000
Purchases during 19x6	100,000
Ending inventory, December 31, 19x6	54,000

REQUIRED:

a. Compute the firm's predetermined overhead rate, which is based on direct labor hours.

b. Calculate the overapplied or underapplied overhead for 19x6.

c. Prepare journal entries to (1) close out the Actual and Applied Manufacturing Overhead accounts and (2) close the balance in overapplied or underapplied overhead into Cost of Goods Sold.

6

Process Costing

LEARNING OBJECTIVES

After studying this chapter, you should be able to:

1 Explain the concept of equivalent units.

2 Calculate equivalent units.

3 Accumulate, classify, and assign costs to products in a process-costing system.

4 Use the first-in, first-out (FIFO) and weighted-average methods of process costing.

*T*he job-order cost accounting system described in Chapters 4 and 5 illustrates how cost data are accumulated for service and production departments and ultimately applied to products for the purposes of product costing and cost control. Job-order cost accounting systems are used in situations where manufacturing operations are not repetitive and where each product or group of products receives varying amounts of direct materials, direct labor, and overhead. The basic document used by these systems is a job-cost sheet. These job-cost sheets are used to both accumulate and control costs.

The type of system described in this chapter is the process cost accounting system. Industries such as chemicals, petroleum, food processing (canneries and flour mills), glass, paints, rubber, steel, and textiles engage in production in which relatively homogeneous products are mass produced in continuous fashion. **Process costing** systems make no attempt to account for the costs of individual units or specific groups of units. Instead, all costs are accumulated by operations or processes, and these costs are subsequently allocated to products on a systematic basis. Because no attempt is made to distinguish among specific units of production, process-costing systems are generally less expensive to operate than job-order costing systems.

In a sequential production process, every major step or operation in the sequence has a work-in-process account in which costs are accumulated. For example, in flour production, grinding, milling, refining, and other production departments each have a work-in-process account. The flow of costs from one work-in-process account to the next is illustrated in Exhibit 6-1. The journal entries used to record the costs of direct material, direct labor, and overhead in each department's work-in-process account are the same under both job-order and process costing.

EXHIBIT 6-1

Transfer of Costs in a Process-Costing System

Work in Process: Milling		Work in Process: Refining	
Direct materials Direct labor Overhead	Transfer cost of partially completed product to next department	Costs transferred in from Milling Department	Transfer cost of completed product to finished-goods inventory

EXHIBIT 6-2

Job-Order versus Process Costing

JOB-ORDER COSTING: Accumulates costs by job

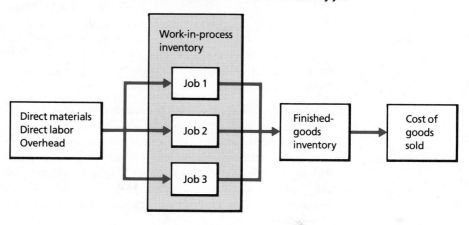

PROCESS COSTING: Accumulates costs by production department

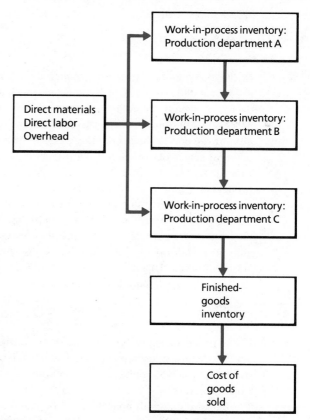

The basic formula for product costs in a process-costing system is as follows:

$$\frac{\text{Total costs incurred in production}}{\text{Total units produced}} = \text{Unit cost of product}$$

The basic difference between job-order and process costing lies in the fact that job-order costing focuses on jobs, which are specific batches of production, and process costing focuses on production departments or steps in the production process. Exhibit 6-2 summarizes this difference.

As in the case of job-order costing systems, a process-costing system may be used in conjunction with actual, normal, or standard costing. The distinction among these three costing approaches involves the type of costs for direct labor, direct material, and overhead that are entered into the work-in-process accounts associated with the various major production operations. (Exhibit 4-2 summarizes the distinctions among actual, normal, and standard costing.) In this chapter, the focus is on process costing in conjunction with normal and actual costing. Chapters 7 and 8 examine standard costing systems.

Equivalent Units: A Key Concept

In many production processes, materials, labor, and overhead are applied to the product at different rates. Material is often added at discrete points in time. Labor and overhead, which are called **conversion costs,** are often applied to a production process continuously, in a relatively uniform way, throughout the production process. At the end of the accounting period, the partially completed product may be at different stages of completion with respect to material and conversion. Exhibit 6-3 summarizes this situation. At the end of an accounting period, the partially completed products are only two-thirds complete with respect to the conversion activity (labor and overhead) that must be done before the units are finished.

Suppose there are 300 partially completed physical units in process at the end of the accounting period. The amount of conversion activity already applied to these units at the period's end is equivalent to the activity that is necessary to completely finish 200 units. This is determined as follows:

300 partially completed physical units

$$\times \frac{2}{3} \text{ complete with respect to conversion} = 200$$

In process costing, the term **equivalent units** is used to measure the production activity that has been accomplished on a batch of partially completed products. Thus, the 300 partially completed physical units represent 200 equivalent units of conversion activity.

Because materials are added at the beginning of the production process in this example, the 300 partially completed physical units are complete with respect to

EXHIBIT 6-3

Application of Materials and Conversion in a Production Process

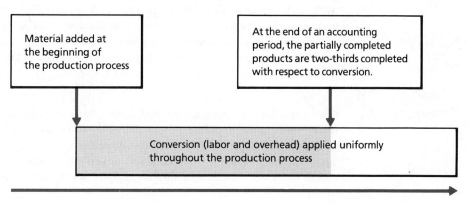

materials. Thus, these units represent 300 equivalent units of materials (300 physical units × 100% complete with respect to materials = 300 equivalent units).

In process-costing systems, product costs are assigned to equivalent units rather than to physical units.

An Illustration

The most effective way to describe process cost accounting systems is by using an extended example. This example describes and illustrates the steps required to account for both units of production and total costs.

The Wing Chemical Company manufactures a single industrial chemical that requires two processes: Process No. 1 and Process No. 2. Process No. 1 is a heating operation in which several dry chemicals are combined and melted. Process No. 2 is a blending operation in which the melted chemicals are mixed and then combined with a liquid chemical.

Direct materials are introduced at the beginning of Process No. 1. For each unit of Process No. 1 output, one unit of raw material is placed in process at the start of processing. As units in Process No. 1 are completed, they are immediately transferred to Process No. 2.

Direct materials are added at the end of Process No. 2. For each unit of Process No. 2 output, one unit of raw material is placed in process at the end of processing. As units of Process No. 2 are completed, they are immediately transferred to finished goods. When these units are sold, their costs are transferred to cost of goods sold. The work of converting materials into finished goods is assumed to occur uniformly throughout both processes. The production sequence employed by the Wing Chemical Company is depicted in Exhibit 6-4.

Two methods of process costing are in use — first-in, first-out (FIFO) and weighted average — and each method is explained in this illustration. Wing Chemical Company uses the FIFO process-costing method in Process No. 1 and the weighted-average process-costing method in Process No. 2.

The data presented in Exhibit 6-5 are for the month of December. The contents of this exhibit are explained as the illustration proceeds.

Process No. 1

The steps used to account for the costs incurred in each process are listed in Exhibit 6-6. These steps focus on an analysis of (1) units of production worked on in each process (steps 1 and 2), costs distributed to each process (step 3), and the unit and total costs of work completed and in process at month's end (steps 4 and 5). These steps are used to structure an analysis of the data in Exhibit 6-5 for Process No. 1.

Analysis of Units In and Units Out   Step 1 focuses on the physical flow of units of production. An analysis of Units In provides the total number of units to be accounted for; an analysis of Units Out provides an accounting for these units. Exhibit 6-7 analyzes the flow of units for Process No. 1.

Process No. 1 had 2,000 units in process at the beginning of the period and an additional 23,000 units were started during the period. The Total Units In represents

---

EXHIBIT 6-4

Sequential Production Processes in Wing Chemical Company

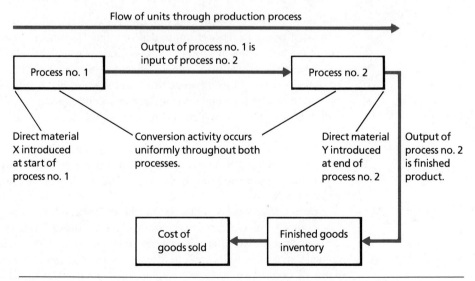

EXHIBIT 6-5

Data for Wing Chemical Company

	Process No. 1		Process No. 2		Finished Goods	
	Beg.	End	Beg.	End	Beg.	End
Units	2,000	3,000	2,000	4,000	7,000	6,000
Fraction completed	$\frac{1^a}{2}$	$\frac{1^a}{3}$	$\frac{1^a}{2}$	$\frac{3^a}{4}$		
New units started	23,000 units		11,000 units			
Units transferred out	22,000 units		9,000 units			
Beginning inventory costs:						
Materials	$ 3,000		-0-			
Conversion	$ 12,000		$ 25,000			
Transferred in			$ 63,000		$455,000	
Direct materials						
costs added	$ 69,000		$135,000			
Transferred from Process						
No. 1			327,000			
Conversion costs added:						
Direct labor	176,000		165,000			
Overhead	88,000[b]		110,000[c]			
Total costs	$348,000		$825,000			

[a] Fraction completed relative to conversion activity. This is the proportion for each process of the total conversion work to be done on the units that has been accomplished at the indicated date.

[b] The predetermined overhead rate in Process No. 1 is $.50 per direct labor dollar.

[c] The predetermined overhead rate in Process No. 2 is $10.00 per direct labor hour.

the total units that could have been completed during the period (2,000 + 23,000 = 25,000 units) and therefore the total number of units for which an accounting is required.

Process No. 1 had 3,000 units in process at the end of the period and 22,000 units were completed and transferred out (to Process No. 2) during the period. The Total Units Out represents an accounting of the total units that could have been completed

EXHIBIT 6-6

Steps in Accounting for Costs Incurred in a Process

Steps	Procedures
1.	Analysis of units in and units out
2.	Computation of equivalent units (the concept of equivalent units will be explained as the illustration proceeds)
3.	Analysis of costs in
4.	Computation of unit costs
5.	Analysis of costs out

EXHIBIT 6-7

Analysis of Units In and Units Out for Process No. 1

Units In:
Work in Process, Beginning	2,000
New Units Started	23,000
Total Units In	25,000

Units Out:
Transferred Out (to Process No. 2)	22,000
Work in Process, Ending	3,000
Total Units Out	25,000

---

during the period (3,000 + 22,000 = 25,000 units). The Total Units In should equal the Total Units Out. Stated another way, the units in the beginning inventory plus the units started should equal the units completed and transferred plus the units in the ending inventory.

Computation of Equivalent Units   The second step is the computation of equivalent units. An equivalent unit is a measure of inputs applied to the production process. For example, one equivalent unit of conversion is the amount of conversion work required to completely convert one physical unit from start to finish. The concept of an equivalent unit enables the management accountant to calculate the amount of inputs applied to batches of partially completed units. The accountant typically keeps track of equivalent units of input separately for material and conversion, because material and conversion inputs are generally applied to the production process at different rates. Material is typically added at discrete points in the process, whereas conversion activity generally occurs more evenly throughout a process.

Consider the beginning inventory in Process No. 1. This inventory consists of 2,000 physical units, but each one of them is only 50 percent complete with respect to conversion. Therefore, the 2,000 physical units represent only 1,000 equivalent units of conversion activity. This conclusion is the result of the following computation:

2,000 physical units × 50% complete = 1,000 equivalent units of conversion

How many equivalent units worth of material are represented in the beginning work-in-process inventory in Process No. 1? The answer is found by the following calculation:

2,000 physical units × 100% complete with = 2,000 equivalent units
                        respect to   of materials
                        materials

Because materials are entered at the beginning of Process No. 1, the 2,000 physical units represent 2,000 equivalent units of material input.

The procedure for the calculation of equivalent units depends on what inventory method or flow of costs is assumed. Process No. 1 uses the **first-in first-out (FIFO)** method. This method assumes that the beginning inventory is a separate batch that is distinct from the units that were started during the current period. In computing equivalent units, only equivalent units of work done during the current period are included. As a result, unit costs reflect work done during the current period only.

Consider the work done in Process No. 1 in December. Because direct materials are placed in process at the start of processing, all units processed in December include direct materials. However, the 2,000 physical units in the beginning inventory had direct materials added to them in the preceding period, and only the 23,000 new units started had direct materials added to them *this* period. Thus, 23,000 equivalent units of direct materials were applied in December.

The 22,000 units transferred out (to Process No. 2) include essentially two batches of units. One batch is the 2,000 units in beginning inventory that were begun prior to December but completed during December. The units in this batch were half complete in terms of direct labor and overhead (conversion) as of December 1. Thus, this batch received 1,000 equivalent units of conversion in December. The second batch is the 20,000 units that were both started and completed during December. This batch received all of its conversion work in December, resulting in 20,000 equivalent units of conversion during December. Finally, the 3,000 units in the ending work-in-process inventory were one-third complete with respect to conversion. These units received 1,000 equivalent units of conversion during December. The total equivalent units for conversion is therefore 22,000 units.

1,000	+	20,000	+	1,000	=	22,000
Equivalent units of conversion done in December on the beginning work-in-process inventory		Equivalent units of conversion done in December on the units that were both started and completed in December		Equivalent units of conversion done in December on the ending work-in-process inventory		Total equivalent units of conversion done during December

Two computations of equivalent units for Process No. 1 are presented in Exhibit 6-8. The 23,000 total equivalent units for direct materials includes only direct materials used in units started in December. The 22,000 units transferred out, less the 2,000 units in the beginning inventory, results in 20,000 units started and completed during December. These 20,000 units, plus the 3,000 units in the ending work-in-process inventory, equals the 23,000 equivalent units for direct materials.

Similarly, the 22,000 equivalent units of conversion includes only the conversion input applied in December. The 22,000 units transferred out received only 21,000 equivalent units of direct labor and overhead *during December*. This 21,000 equivalent units, plus the 1,000 equivalent of conversion done in December on the ending work in process, yields a total of 22,000 equivalent units for conversion.

EXHIBIT 6-8

Computation of Equivalent Units for Process No. 1 (FIFO Method)

		Materials	Conversion
(1) Analysis of Units In and Units Out			
Units In:			
Work in Process, Beginning	2,000 (1/2)	(2,000)	(1,000)
New Units Started	23,000		
Total Units In	25,000		
Units Out:			
Transferred Out	22,000	22,000	22,000
Work in Process, Ending	3,000 (1/3)	3,000	1,000
Total Units Out	25,000		
(2) Equivalent Units		23,000	22,000

There is an alternative method of calculation of equivalent units:

	Materials	Conversion
Equivalent Units Required to Finish Units in Beginning Inventory		
2,000(1/2)		1,000
Equivalent Units Required for Units Started and Finished		
20,000 units started and finished	20,000	20,000
Equivalent Units Required to Start Units in Ending Inventory		
3,000(1/3)	3,000	1,000
Equivalent Units	23,000	22,000

Analysis of Costs In   The direct materials and conversion costs charged to Process No. 1 are summarized in Exhibit 6-2. The beginning balance in the work-in-process account for Process No. 1 is $15,000 ($3,000 of materials costs and $12,000 of conversion costs). These costs were incurred during a prior period and assigned to the partially completed units as product costs. During December, direct materials costing $69,000 and direct labor of $176,000 were charged to the work-in-process account for Process No. 1. Because Wing Chemical uses normal costing, the overhead charged to the work-in-process account in Process No. 1 is as follows:

$$\$176,000 \times \$.50/\text{direct labor dollar} = \$88,000$$

Direct Labor Dollars × Predetermined Overhead Rate = Overhead Applied

Wing Chemical makes the following journal entries for December to account for production costs in Process No. 1:

Work in Process — Process No. 1	69,000	
Materials Inventory		69,000
To record materials requisitions.		
Work in Process — Process No. 1	176,000	
Salaries Payable		176,000
To record direct labor costs.		
Work in Process — Process No. 1	88,000	
Applied Overhead		88,000
To record overhead applied.		

An analysis of costs in for Process No. 1 is presented in Exhibit 6-9. The total costs in of $348,000 represent the total costs for which we need to account. The costs incurred in December of $333,000 ($69,000 + $176,000 + $88,000) do not include the costs attached to the beginning balance in work in process.

Computation of Unit Costs   The fourth step is the computation of unit costs for Process No. 1. This analysis is presented in Exhibit 6-10. The cost of direct materials of $69,000, divided by the 23,000 equivalent units for materials, results in a material

---

EXHIBIT 6-9

Analysis of Costs In for Process No. 1 (FIFO Method)

			Materials	Conversion
(1)	Analysis of Units In and Units Out			
	Units In:			
	Work in Process, Beginning	2,000 (1/2)	(2,000)	(1,000)
	New Units Started	23,000		
	Total Units In	25,000		
	Units Out:			
	Transferred Out	22,000	22,000	22,000
	Work in Process, Ending	3,000 (1/3)	3,000	1,000
	Total Units Out	25,000		
(2)	Equivalent Units		23,000	22,000
(3)	Analysis of Costs In:			
	Work in Process, Beginning	$ 15,000		
	Current Costs:			
	Material	69,000	$69,000	
	Conversion	264,000		$264,000
	Total Costs In	$348,000	$69,000	$264,000

EXHIBIT 6-10

Computation of Costs per Equivalent Unit for Process No. 1 (FIFO Method)

		Materials	Conversion
(1) Analysis of Units In and Units Out			
Units In:			
Work in Process, Beginning	2,000 (1/2)	(2,000)	(1,000)
New Units Started	23,000		
Total Units In	25,000		
Units Out:			
Transferred Out	22,000	22,000	22,000
Work in Process, Ending	3,000 (1/3)	3,000	1,000
Total Units Out	25,000		
(2) Equivalent Units		23,000	22,000
(3) Analysis of Costs In:			
Work in Process, Beginning	$ 15,000		
Current Costs:			
Material	69,000	$69,000	
Conversion	264,000		$264,000
Total Costs In	$348,000	$69,000	$264,000
(4) Computation of Unit Costs:		$ 3.00[a]	$ 12.00[b]
(a) Material $\dfrac{\$69,000}{23,000} = \$ 3.00$			
(b) Conversion $\dfrac{\$264,000}{22,000} = \$12.00$			
Total	$15.00		

cost per equivalent unit of $3.00. Similarly, the conversion costs of $264,000, divided by the 22,000 equivalent units for conversion, results in conversion cost per equivalent unit of $12.00. *In both calculations, the cost of the beginning inventory and the equivalent units of work done in the preceding period are excluded.* These costs and equivalent units are excluded because the beginning inventory is treated as a separate batch that is distinct from the goods started and completed during December.

Analysis of Costs Out   The final step is to allocate the total costs in to the units transferred out and the ending work-in-process inventory. An analysis of costs out for Process No. 1 is presented in Exhibit 6-11. Because the FIFO inventory method is used, the cost of the beginning work-in-process inventory is calculated separately. The cost of the 2,000 physical units of beginning work-in-process inventory incurred prior to December is $15,000. Additional conversion costs of $12,000 are incurred in December to complete these units. Thus, the costs to be transferred out for these 2,000 units are $27,000. The 20,000 units that are started and completed this period

EXHIBIT 6-11

Analysis of Costs for Process No. 1 (FIFO Method)

			Materials	Conversion
(1)	Analysis of Units In and Units Out			
	Units In:			
	Work in Process, Beginning	2,000 (1/2)	(2,000)	(1,000)
	New Units Started	23,000		
	Total Units In	25,000		
	Units Out:			
	Transferred Out	22,000	22,000	22,000
	Work in Process, Ending	3,000 (1/3)	3,000	1,000
	Total Units Out	25,000		
(2)	Equivalent Units		23,000	22,000
(3)	Analysis of Costs In:			
	Work in Process, Beginning	$ 15,000		
	Current Costs:			
	Material	69,000	$ 69,000	
	Conversion	264,000		$264,000
	Total Costs In	$348,000	$ 69,000	$264,000
(4)	Unit Costs		$ 3.00	$ 12.00
(5)	Analysis of Costs Out:			
	Work in Process, Beginning	$ 15,000		
	Conversion Costs (costs to complete) (1,000 × $12.00)	12,000	$ 27,000	
	Costs of Units Started and Completed (20,000 × $15.00)[a]		300,000	
	Total Cost of Goods Transferred Out (to Process No. 2)			$327,000
	Work in Process, Ending:			
	Material Cost (3,000 × $3.00)		$ 9,000	
	Conversion Cost (1,000 × $12.00)		12,000	
Total Cost of Work in Process, Ending				21,000
Total Costs Out				$348,000

[a] Total cost per equivalent unit = $3.00 + $12.00 = $15.00.

had a total cost of $300,000 (20,000 × $15.00). The total cost of units transferred out is therefore $327,000 ($27,000 + $300,000 = $327,000).

The 3,000 units in the ending work-in-process inventory include all of the materials applied in Process No. 1 but only one-third of the conversion costs for completed units. The total costs of the ending work-in-process inventory are $21,000, as indicated in Exhibit 6-11. The total costs out equal the total costs in.

Process No. 2   The five steps listed in Exhibit 6-6 provide a systematic approach for analyzing the data about units of product and costs for Process No. 1. The same overall approach can be used to analyze the data for Process No. 2. However, three features of Process No. 2 require some changes in the details of the analysis. The first of these features is the transfer of units of product from Process No. 1 into Process No. 2. The second feature is the introduction of direct materials at the end of processing in Process No. 2. The third feature is the use of the weighted-average process-costing method in Process No. 2.

Analysis of Units In and Units Out   Exhibit 6-12 analyzes the flow of units of Process No. 2. There were 2,000 physical units already in process at the beginning of December, and 11,000 units were transferred in from Process No. 1. However, two units of Process No. 1 output are placed in production at the start of Process No. 2 for each unit Process No. 2 started. That is, two units of product, as measured in Process No. 1, become one unit of product, as measured in Process No. 2.[1] This relationship is summarized in the following diagram.

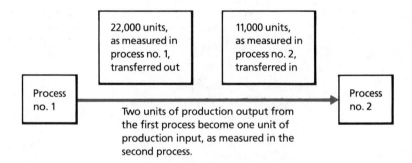

The 13,000 total physical units to be accounted for are reflected in the 9,000 units transferred out of Process No. 2 (to finished goods) and the 4,000 units in the ending work-in-process inventory. Review the accounting for physical units in Process No. 2 shown in Exhibit 6-12 (left numerical column).

Computation of Equivalent Units   The computation of equivalent units for Process No. 2 is also presented in Exhibit 6-12. Only units transferred out have the Process No. 2 materials applied to them because direct materials are introduced at the *end* of processing in Process No. 2. The equivalent units for transferred-in work, direct materials, and conversion reflect the equivalent units in the physical units transferred

---

[1] Such a change in units of measurement is common in sequential processing operations. The change may result from a difference in the natural unit of measure in the two processes. For example, Process No. 1 may be a "dry process," where units are naturally measured in kilograms. Process No. 2 may be a "wet process," where units are naturally measured in liters. In the example, two kilograms of Process No. 1 output are entered into Process No. 2 for every one liter of Process No. 2 production.

EXHIBIT 6-12

Analysis of Units In and Units Out and Computation of Equivalent Units in Process No. 2 (Weighted-Average Method)

	Transferred	Materials	Conversion
(1) Analysis of Units In and Units Out			
Units In:			
Work in Process, Beginning	2,000 (1/2)		
Units Transferred In	11,000		
Total Units In	13,000		
Units Out:			
Transferred Out	9,000	9,000	9,000 9,000
Work in Process, Ending	4,000 (3/4)	4,000	3,000
Total Units Out	13,000		
(2) Equivalent Units		13,000	9,000 12,000

out of Process No. 2 and the equivalent units in the Process No. 2 ending work-in-process inventory. Work done in the preceding period on the beginning work-in-process inventory is *not* treated separately. The weighted-average, process-costing method comingles the beginning work-in-process inventory and the units started and completed during December. As a result, the equivalent units include *both* the work completed *before* December as well as the work completed *during* December. The important difference between the **weighted-average** and FIFO methods is that the equivalent units calculated under the weighted-average method include all work done to date, and the equivalent units calculated under FIFO include work done in the current period only.

Notice that in Exhibit 6-12 there is an additional type of input. In Process No. 1, the only inputs were materials and conversion. In Process No. 2, the inputs are material, conversion, and "transferred." The "transferred" input represents the partially completed products that were transferred from Process No. 1 to Process No. 2. The transferred input is similar to a material input. The only difference between the transferred input and raw materials is that the transferred input has already been worked on by Wing Chemical Company. The cost of the transferred input is the cost that was assigned to it by the process-costing system for Process No. 1.

Analysis of Costs In The transferred-in, direct materials and conversion costs charged to Process No. 2 are summarized in Exhibit 6-13. Exhibit 6-5 shows that the beginning balance in the work-in-process account for Process No. 2 is $88,000 ($25,000 of conversion costs plus $63,000 of transferred-in costs). The $63,000 of transferred-costs were assigned to these units in Process No. 1 in a previous period. Thus, these Process No. 1 costs have been inventoried and transferred to Process No. 2 where additional costs will be assigned to them.

EXHIBIT 6-13

Analysis of Costs In and Computation of Costs per Equivalent Unit for Process No. 2 (Weighted-Average Method)

		Transferred	Materials	Conversion
(1) Analysis of Units In and Units Out				
Units In:				
Work in Process, Beginning	2,000 (1/2)			
Units Transferred In	11,000			
Total Units In	13,000			
Units Out:				
Transferred Out	9,000	9,000	9,000	9,000
Work in Process, Ending	4,000 (3/4)	4,000		3,000
Total Units Out	13,000			
(2) Equivalent Units		13,000	9,000	12,000
(3) Analysis of Costs In:				
Work in Process, Beginning	$ 88,000	$ 63,000		$ 25,000
Current period costs:				
Transferred In	327,000	327,000		
Materials	135,000		$135,000	
Conversion	275,000			275,000
Total Costs In	$825,000	$390,000	$135,000	$300,000
(4) Computation of Unit Costs:		$ 30.00[a]	$ 15.00[b]	$ 25.00[c]

$$^a \text{Transferred In } \frac{\$390,000}{13,000} = \$30.00$$

$$^b \text{Materials } \frac{\$135,000}{9,000} = \$15.00$$

$$^c \text{Conversion } \frac{\$300,000}{12,000} = \$25.00$$

Total $70.00

During December, transferred-in costs of $327,000 were transferred from Process No. 1 to Process No. 2. These costs were incurred in Process No. 1 in December. The costs were inventoried and passed on to Process No. 2 where additional product costs will be assigned to the units. The $327,000 of transferred-in costs was calculated in Exhibit 6-11.

Also during December, $135,000 of direct material costs and $165,000 of direct labor costs (for 11,000 direct labor hours) were incurred in Process No. 2. In Process No. 2, Wing Chemical Company uses normal costing with a predetermined overhead rate of $10 per direct labor hour. Thus, the overhead cost applied to production in Process No. 2 during December is calculated as follows:

$$11,000 \times \$10.00/\text{direct labor hour} \qquad = \$110,000$$

Direct Labor Hours $\times$ Predetermined Overhead Rate $=$ Overhead Applied

During December, the following journal entries are made to apply costs to work-in-process in Process No. 2:

Work in Process — Process No. 2	327,000	
Work in Process — Process No. 1		327,000
To record costs of units transferred.		
Work in Process — Process No. 2	135,000	
Materials Inventory		135,000
To record materials requisitions.		
Work in Process — Process No. 2	165,000	
Salaries Payable		165,000
To record direct labor costs.		
Work in Process — Process No. 2	110,000	
Applied Overhead		110,000
To record overhead applied.		

The transferred-in costs and conversion costs already assigned to the beginning work-in-process inventory are added to the transferred-in and conversion costs for December. The weighted-average method averages the costs of work done in the preceding period with the costs of the current period. Thus, both the computation of equivalent units and the analysis of costs comingle the beginning work-in-process inventory with the work of the current period.

Computation of Unit Costs   The computation of unit costs for Process No. 2 is also presented in Exhibit 6-13. The total cost of units transferred in, $390,000, divided by the equivalent units of transferred-in work, 13,000, results in a cost per equivalent unit of $30.00 for transferred-in costs. The cost of direct materials of $135,000 divided by the 9,000 equivalent units for materials result in a material cost per equivalent unit of $15.00. Conversion costs of $300,000 divided by the 12,000 equivalent units for conversion result in a conversion cost per equivalent unit of $25.00. The numerator for each of these calculations includes costs of both the preceding and current periods, and the denominator for each calculation includes equivalent units of work for both the preceding and current periods.

Analysis of Costs Out   The final step is to account for the total costs in by determining the cost of the goods transferred out to finished goods and the cost of the ending work-in-process inventory. An analysis of costs out for Process No. 2 is presented in Exhibit 6-14. The computations for Process No. 2 are much simpler than for Process No. 1 because all of the units transferred out are multiplied by a single average unit cost of $70.00.

EXHIBIT 6-14

Analysis of Costs for Process No. 2 (Weighted-Average Method)

		Transferred	Materials	Conversion
(1) Analysis of Units In and Units Out				
Units In:				
Work in Process, Beginning	2,000 (1/2)			
Units Transferred In	11,000			
Total Units In	13,000			
Units Out:				
Transferred Out	9,000	9,000	9,000	9,000
Work in Process, Ending	4,000 (3/4)	4,000		3,000
Total Units Out	13,000			
(2) Equivalent Units		13,000	9,000	12,000
(3) Analysis of Costs In:				
Work in Process, Beginning	$ 88,000	$ 63,000		$ 25,000
Current period costs:				
Transferred In	327,000	327,000		
Materials	135,000		$135,000	
Conversion	275,000			275,000
Total Costs In	$825,000	$390,000	$135,000	$300,000
(4) Unit Costs		$ 30.00	$ 15.00	$ 25.00
(5) Analysis of Costs Out:				
Cost of Units Transferred Out				
(9,000 × $70.00)[a]				$630,000
Work in Process, Ending:				
Transferred-in Costs				
(4,000 × $30.00)		$120,000		
Conversion Costs (3,000 ×				
$25.00)		75,000		
Total Cost of Work in Process, Ending				195,000
Total Costs Out				$825,000

[a] Total cost per equivalent unit = $30 + $15 + $25 = $70.

The following journal entry is made in December to record the transfer of units of finished product from Process No. 2 to finished goods inventory.

Finished-Goods Inventory	630,000	
Work-in-process — Process No. 2		630,000

To transfer cost of units completed in Process No. 2 to finished goods.

Relationships Among Ledger Accounts The extended example discussed in the previous section can now be used to provide an overview of the ledger relationships of a process-costing system. The data in Exhibits 6-5, 6-11, and 6-14 provide the basis for the following summary events or transactions that took place in December. Wing Chemical Company made the typical general journal entries for a process cost accounting system. Exhibit 6-15 shows the ledger account relationships. Each entry below can be traced to the accounts in Exhibit 6-15:

1. Process No. 1 requisitioned direct materials costing $69,000.

Work in Process — Process No. 1	69,000	
Materials Inventory		69,000
To record requisition of materials.		

2. Process No. 1 incurred direct labor costs of $176,000.

Work in Process — Process No. 1	176,000	
Salaries Payable		176,000
To record direct labor.		

3. Process No. 1 applied overhead costs of $88,000 to production.

Work in Process — Process No. 1	88,000	
Applied Overhead		88,000
To apply overhead to products.		

4. Units completed and transferred out of Process No. 1 were transferred to Process No. 2.

Work in Process — Process No. 2	327,000	
Work in Process — Process No. 1		327,000
To record transfer of units of product.		

5. Process No. 2 requisitioned direct materials costing $135,000.

Work in Process — Process No. 2	135,000	
Materials Inventory		135,000
To record requisition of materials.		

6. Process No. 2 incurred direct labor costs of $165,000.

Work in Process — Process No. 2	165,000	
Salaries Payable		165,000
To record direct labor cost.		

7. Process No. 2 applied overhead costs of $110,000 to production.

Work in Process — Process No. 2	110,000	
Applied Overhead		110,000

To record overhead applied to production.

8. Finished products costing $630,000 were transferred from Process No. 2 to finished-goods inventory.

Finished-Goods Inventory	630,000	
Work in Process — Process No. 2		630,000

To record transfer of units of finished product to Finished-Goods Inventory.

9. Finished goods costing $665,000 were sold.

Cost of Goods Sold	665,000	
Finished-Goods Inventory		665,000

To record cost of units sold.

Actual Costing in a Process Cost Accounting System

In the preceding example, Wing Chemical Company used a normal-costing approach for the application of product costs to work in process in both Process No. 1 and Process No. 2. It is also possible to use actual costing with a process cost accounting system. If Wing Chemical Company had used an actual costing system, then the process cost accounting procedures used in both Process No. 1 and Process No. 2 would remain exactly the same as in the example, except that applied overhead costs would be replaced with actual overhead costs in each process. Refer again to Exhibit 6-5, which summarizes the current-period costs in Process No. 1 of the Wing Chemical Company. In that exhibit, the current-period costs in Process No. 1 are as follows:

Materials	$ 69,000
Direct labor	176,000
Overhead	88,000

The overhead cost of $88,000 was determined by multiplying the Process No. 1 predetermined overhead rate ($.50 per direct labor dollar) by the Process No. 1 direct labor cost ($176,000 direct labor dollars). This calculation of applied overhead

EXHIBIT 6-15

Diagram of Ledger Relationships for Process Cost Accounting System

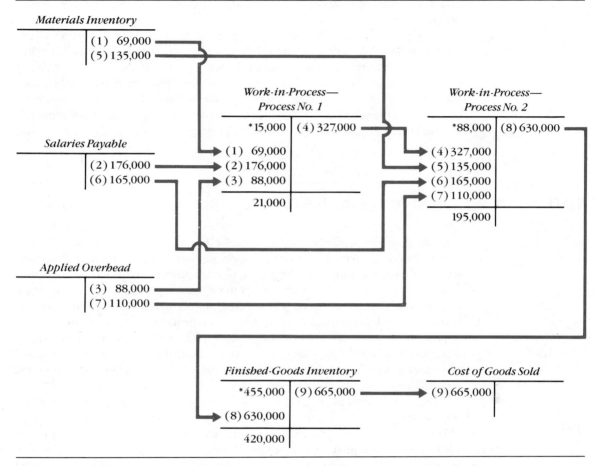

ª Beginning account balances.

reflects Wing's use of normal costing. If Wing were to use actual costing instead, the $88,000 of applied overhead costs would be replaced with actual overhead costs. Suppose the current-period actual overhead cost amounted to $92,300 in Process No. 1. Then the current-period costs in Exhibit 6-5 for Process No. 1 would be as follows:

Direct material	$ 69,000
Direct labor	176,000
Overhead	92,300

From that point onward, the process-costing calculations proceed in exactly the same manner as illustrated in Exhibits 6-6 through 6-11. Under actual costing, the current-period's conversion cost for Process No. 1 is $268,300 (direct labor of $176,000 plus actual overhead of $92,300) instead of the $264,000 of conversion costs under normal costing.

Process costing can also be used in conjunction with standard costing. (Refer again to Exhibit 4-2, which compares actual, normal, and standard costing.) The only difference in the way a process-costing system operates under actual, normal, or standard costing is in the way the current period's total costs are determined for each process. Under standard costing, the costs of direct material, direct labor, and overhead are determined as estimated amounts based on studies of what costs should be incurred in the production process. Standard costing is the topic of Chapters 7 and 8.

FIFO versus Weighted Average: A Graphical Approach

A graphical approach may be used to highlight the differences between the FIFO and weighted-average methods of process costing. Suppose that on February 1 a company has 1,000 physical units in its beginning work-in-process inventory. Each of these units is 40 percent complete with respect to conversion. During February the beginning work-in-process inventory is completed, and, in addition, 8,000 more physical units are started and finished. On February 28 there are 3,000 physical units in work-in-process, and each of these is 80 percent complete with respect to conversion. In Exhibit 6-16, groups of physical units are shown along the horizontal dimension, and the relevant percentage of completion with respect to conversion is shown on the vertical dimension.

Area I represents the equivalent units of conversion work done on the work-in-process inventory during the *prior* period (400 equivalent units = 40% × 1,000 physical units). Area II represents the equivalent units of conversion work done on the beginning work-in-process inventory during the *current* period [600 equivalent units = (1 − 40%) × 1,000 physical units]. Area III represents the equivalent units of conversion work done during the current period on the units started *and* completed during the current period (8,000 equivalent units = 100% × 8,000 physical units). Area IV represents the equivalent units of conversion work done during the *current* period on the ending work-in-process inventory (2,400 equivalent units = 80% × 3,000 physical units). Area V represents the equivalent units of conversion work to be done *next period* on the ending work-in-process inventory [600 equivalent units = (1 − 80%) × 3,000 physical units].

In computing the conversion cost per equivalent unit under FIFO, the conversion costs associated with the units in areas II, III, and IV is divided by the total number of equivalent units of conversion work represented by areas II, III, and IV. The costs and equivalent units in area I are *not* included in this calculation. They are kept separate.

To compute the conversion cost per equivalent unit under the weighted-average method, the conversion costs associated with areas I, II, III, and IV are divided by the

EXHIBIT 6-16

Difference Between FIFO and Weighted-Average Process-Costing Methods

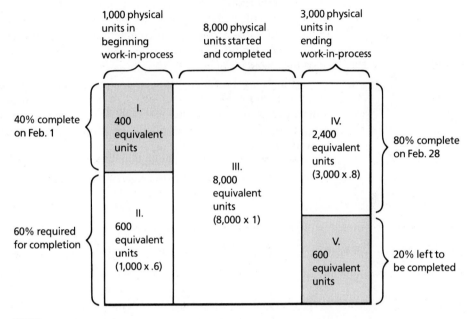

FIFO:

$$\frac{\text{Cost per equivalent}}{\text{unit for conversion}} = \frac{\text{Total conversion costs for work done in areas II, III, IV}}{\text{Total equivalent units of conversion work in areas II, III, IV}}$$

Weighted Average:

$$\frac{\text{Cost per equivalent}}{\text{unit for conversion}} = \frac{\text{Total conversion costs for work done in areas I, II, III, IV}}{\text{Total equivalent units of conversion work done in areas I, II, III, IV}}$$

total number of equivalent units of conversion work in areas I, II, III, and IV. Hence, the costs and equivalent units from the prior period (area I) and the current period (areas II, III, and IV) are comingled under the weighted-average method. This comingling gives rise to the name of the method, since the resulting conversion cost per equivalent unit is a weighted average of costs incurred during two periods of time.

The difference between the FIFO and weighted-average methods hinges on the treatment of the costs and equivalent units associated with area I in the graph. A similar graphical analysis could be done for materials.

Complications in Process Costing

Various complications may occur that are not reflected in this example. The extent of completion of the work-in-process inventory is given for each process in the example. Yet estimating this percentage of completion may be difficult in practice, especially where large quantities are in process, and production operations are not easily divided into standard operations or time periods.

Materials can be added at the start or end of processing, or they may be added when the product is partially completed. A portion of the production may be spoiled or defective, which complicates calculations, especially when the spoilage is in excess of the normal amount. The cost of normal spoilage is spread over the good units of product and inventoried, but abnormal spoilage cost is considered a loss of the period. The techniques for dealing with these complications are discussed in Chapter 16. They are logical extensions of the techniques described in this chapter.

Operation Costing

Many different types of production processes are used, and a product-costing system is often tailored to the specific characteristics of the process employed. The result is that some organizations use hybrid product-costing systems that have some characteristics of job-order costing and some characteristics of process costing. One popular hybrid is **operation costing.** This product-costing method is used in manufacturing processes where the conversion activities are very similar across all of the different types of products but the materials used in the various products differ significantly. An example is the manufacture of some types of clothing, where the labor and overhead inputs are similar across product lines but the material (such as denim, silk, or polyester) differs significantly. In an operation-costing system, conversion costs are accumulated by production department or process. A unit conversion cost is then computed and assigned to each unit of product passing through the department. Thus, conversion costs are handled in the same manner as under process costing.

Direct-material costs are treated differently under operation costing. Material costs are traced to specific jobs or batches of production, just as they are under job-order costing. Exhibit 6-17 summarizes the key features of operation costing.

Process Costing at Hewlett-Packard

As a final illustration of process costing, this section offers a description of the process-costing system used by Hewlett-Packard Company at its Boise Division. Also included are two of the reports prepared by the cost accounting department. This

EXHIBIT 6-17
Operation Costing

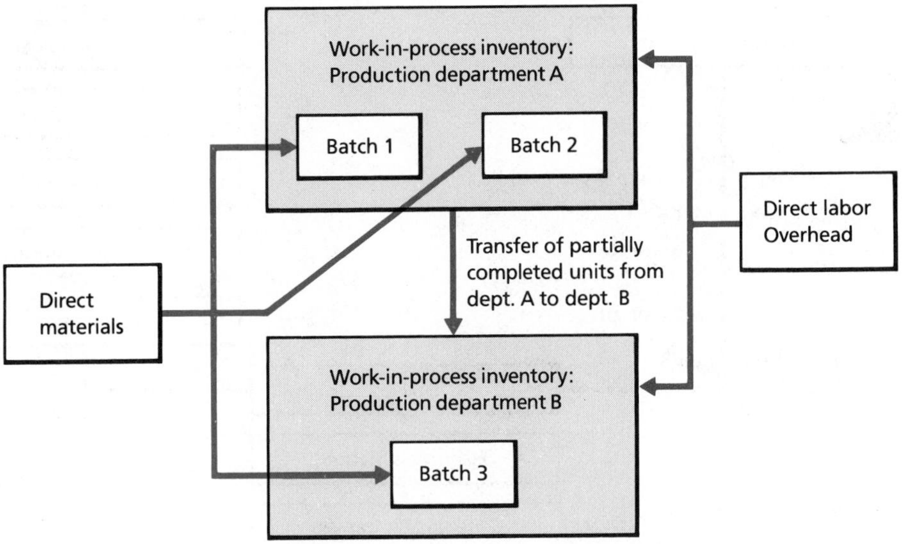

material is presented not for the purpose of learning the details of process costing but rather to help relate this chapter to real-world cost accounting practices.

Product

The product consists of raw printed circuit boards that are used to hold the electronic parts for many other HP products. Although each printed circuit board is different, each board moves through one of four major processes in a standard lot size. Each lot uses approximately the same number of labor and machine hours. Material cost is basically the same for each lot and each process. Each product varies in size.

Process

The four major processes consist of movement through some or all of the ten work centers in the manufacturing area. The ten work centers are grouped into four departments that are used to define levels of expense management. The four major processes are designated on the process diagram displayed in Exhibit 6-18.

Accounting System

Because the environment consists of several major processes, HP focuses on averaging labor and overhead costs among the products that move through each process. Material cost is traced directly to each product, however, leading to a combined process and job-order costing system. The key cost parameters in the processes are yield, material usage (how well each product fits on the standard panel within the standard lot), and utilization of fixed overhead (volume).

Direct labor is oriented toward monitoring the process rather than driving the product through the production process, and HP deemphasizes the traditional focus

EXHIBIT 6-18

Process Diagram for Production of Circuit Boards by Hewlett-Packard

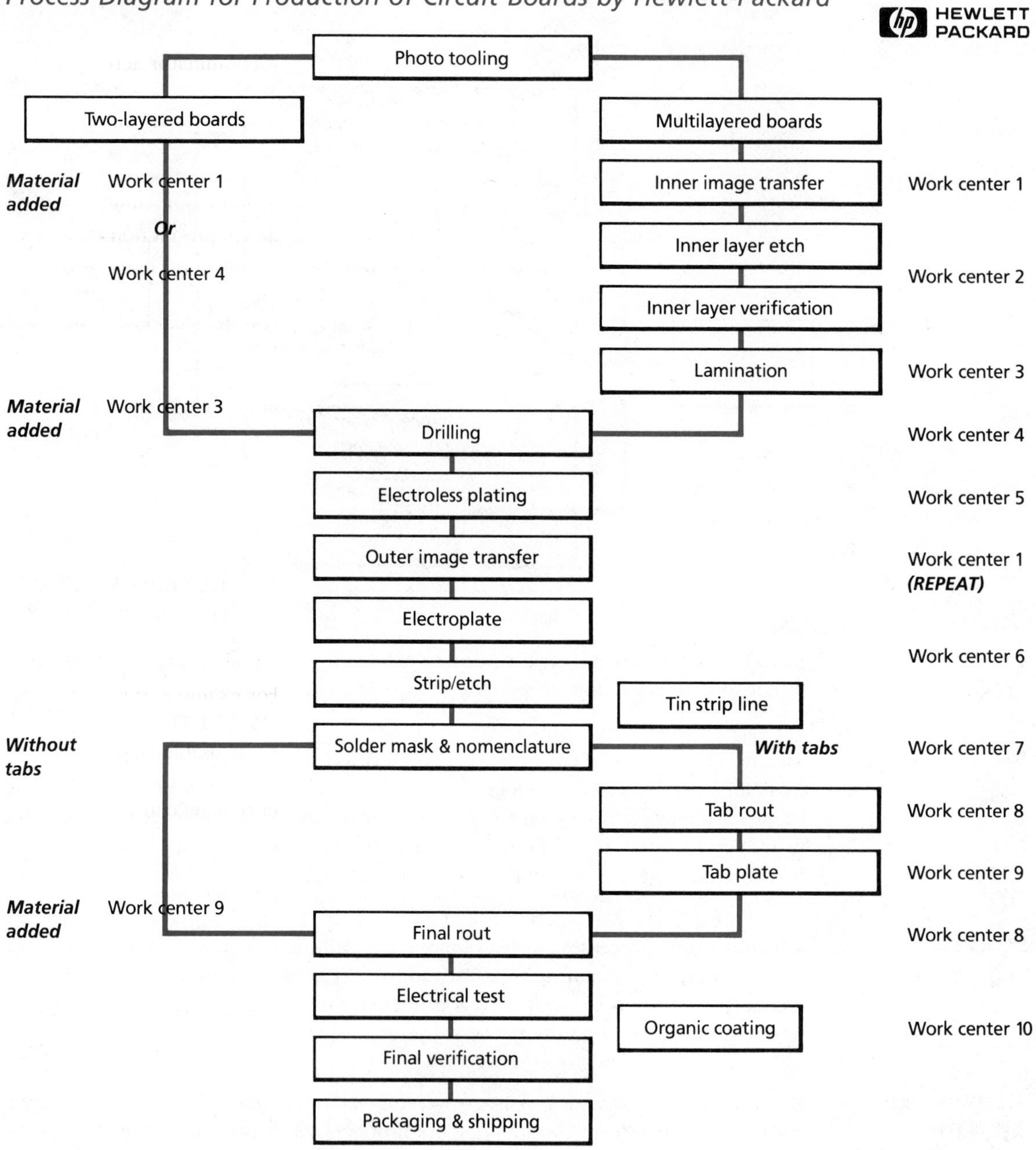

hp HEWLETT PACKARD

	Photo tooling	

Two-layered boards		Multilayered boards

Material added   Work center 1

| | Inner image transfer | Work center 1 |

Or

Work center 4

| | Inner layer etch | Work center 2 |

| | Inner layer verification | |

| | Lamination | Work center 3 |

Material added   Work center 3

Drilling	Work center 4

| Electroless plating | Work center 5 |

| Outer image transfer | Work center 1 **(REPEAT)** |

| Electroplate | |

| Strip/etch | Work center 6 |

| Tin strip line |

Without tabs | Solder mask & nomenclature | **With tabs**   Work center 7 |

| Tab rout | Work center 8 |

| Tab plate | Work center 9 |

Material added   Work center 9

| Final rout | Work center 8 |

| Electrical test | |

| Organic coating | Work center 10 |

| Final verification | |

| Packaging & shipping | |

BASIC PROCESSES
Process 1: Basic two-layer
Process 2: Basic multilayer
Process 3: Two-layer with gold tabs
Process 4: Multilayer with gold tabs

on labor utilization by including direct labor with indirect labor as part of overhead. HP uses volume-based process time as the method of applying overhead costs to production because labor is no longer a feasible base (denominator activity).

The cost accounting system focuses on the efficiency of the process at the work-center level through unit yields and actual volume. In addition, HP manages total costs and reduces product costs through better utilization of the standard processes.

Inventory levels are minimal due to the just-in-time method of manufacturing. Under this approach to manufacturing, inventories of materials and component parts are purchased in small amounts just before they are needed in production.[2] Inventory is costed on the basis of completed cost at each work center. A perpetual inventory record is kept by product number.

HP uses a standard-costing system in conjunction with process costing (review Exhibits 4-2 and 4-4). The description here focuses on the process-costing dimension only (standard costing is the subject of Chapters 7 and 8).

Exhibit 6-19 displays a *cost sheet* for the multilayer circuit board, and Exhibit 6-20 shows a *daily unit summary.* Referring to the top of the cost sheet, the heading "CUSTOMER DIVISION 48" means that the multilayer circuit board was produced for another HP division, the Disk Memory Division, also located in Boise. The information at the top of the cost report also indicates that the circuit boards to which the report refers are eight-layer boards requiring four lithographic imaging steps in their production. Moreover, the cost report refers to a production run in which 4,409 image square feet (ISF) of circuit board were produced, and there were sixty-four images per lot. Each circuit board required four images, so there were sixteen circuit boards per lot. The other information at the top of the report refers to specific characteristics of the circuit boards produced. For example, this production run did not require a solder mask or tabs. The heading "MATL UTIL %" refers to the percentage of the surface area of each circuit board that was usable after holes were cut in the board to mount various electronic components. For the circuit boards produced in this run, 58 percent of the image square feet remained at the end of the production process.

Moving to the middle part of the cost report, we see that eleven steps were required in the production of the circuit boards. Each step has a work center (WCNTR) code and a yield percentage (YIELD %). Thus, the operation in work center 4712000 yielded 99.7 percent usable material. The headings "MATL/LOT" and "MATL/BD" refer to the direct material cost per production lot and per circuit board, respectively. The heading "YLD ML/BD" refers to the portion of the material cost per board relating to the usable portion of the board. "PT/LOT" refers to process time per lot. For the operation designated as SEQ 010, for example, the process time per lot was 2.1 hours. The heading "MOH/BD" refers to the manufacturing overhead cost per circuit board. The heading "SEQ COST/BD" refers to the total cost of a particular

---

[2] Just-in-time inventory systems are discussed further in Chapter 18.

EXHIBIT 6-19

Cost Sheet for Multilayer Board Produced by Hewlett-Packard

```
PCF7001R - COSTING REPORT FOR     07940-80095
            CUSTOMER DIVISION     48                    LAYERS          3
                                                        IMAGES          4
                                                        ISF         .4409
                                                        IMAGES/LOT     64
                                                        1
```

SEQ	WCNTR	YIELD%	MATL/LOT	MATL/BD	*	YLD ML/BD	*	PT/LOT
010	4712000	99.7000	247.2832	3.8638	*	3.8393	*	2.1000
020	4714222	99.0000	.0000	.0000	*	.0000	*	2.0000
030	4718999	99.5000	113.6512	1.7758	*	1.7645	*	4.0000
040	4716666	99.5000	.0000	.0000	*	.0000	*	2.0000
050	4714333	99.8000	.0000	.0000	*	.0000	*	1.5000
060	4712000	99.0000	.0000	.0000	*	.0000	*	.4000
070	4714444	97.0000	.0000	.0000	*	.0000	*	2.2500
080	4712111	100.0000	.0000	.0000	*	.0000	*	.1000
090	4716777	99.5000	.0000	.0000	*	.0000	*	.6500
100	4716888	108.0000	.0000	.0000	*	.0000	*	4.7500
110	4717000	100.0000	.0000	.0000	*	.0000	*	.0000
TOTALS		100.6377	360.9344	5.6396	*	5.6038	*	19.7500

```
                    MATERIAL PERIOD EXPENSE      2.4250
                       TOTAL MATERIAL COST       8.0288
```

```
        DETAILED MATERIAL USED:
            SEQ   PART DESCRIPTION    QUANTITY   UNIT COST   EXTENSION
            010   PLSTC-MET CLD KT      .0158    247.6800     3.8638
            030   EPOXY BNDG SHTS       .0625     18.0000     1.1250
            030   COPPER FOIL KIT       .0156     41.7200      .8508

            1. Yielded Material Cost
            2. Yielded Overhead Cost (Labor Included)
            3. Yielded Cost for Each Process
               *Cumulative cost is calculated and saved in costing file
```

EXHIBIT 6-19 Continued

```
                                                            DATE

SUBPANEL      N    TABS            0
SOLDER MASK   0    SIDES W/ TABS   0
NOMENCLATURE  0    RECESSED TABS   0
MATL UTIL %  58
                                         2                3
   MOH/LOT     PT/BD     MOH/BD   *YD OH/BD *     **SEQ COST/BD**
 --------------------------------------------------------------------
   146.4750    .0328     2.2887   *  2.2742 *     **   6.1135 **
   139.5000    .0313     2.1797   *  2.1659 *     **   2.1659 **
   279.0000    .0625     4.3594   *  4.3318 *     **   6.0963 **
   139.5000    .0313     2.1797   *  2.1659 *     **   2.1659 **
   104.6250    .0234     1.6348   *  1.6244 *     **   1.6244 **
    27.9000    .0063      .4359   *   .4331 *     **    .4331 **
   156.9375    .0352     2.4521   *  2.4366 *     **   2.4366 **
     6.9750    .0016      .1090   *   .1083 *     **    .1083 **
    45.3375    .0102      .7084   *   .7039 *     **    .7039 **
   331.3125    .0742     5.1768   *  5.1440 *     **   5.1440 **
      .0000    .0000      .0000   *   .0000 *     **    .0000 **
 --------------------------------------------------------------------
  1377.5625    .3088    21.5245   * 21.3881 *     **  26.9919 **
 --------------------------------------------------------------------

         MOH PERIOD EXPENSE    .0000
         TOTAL MOH COST    21.3881
              TOTAL BOARD COST ***    29.4169
```

EXHIBIT 6-20

Daily Unit Summary at Boise Division of Hewlett-Packard

```
                              PC FABRICATION - SHOP SUMMARY
                                 WEDNESDAY - 860409
                              DAILY TOTALS
```

WORKCENTER	SCRAP LOTS	PLAN LOTS	GOOD LOTS	PROTO LOTS	WIP LOTS	IMAGE-SQ-FT IN	IMAGE-SQ-FT OUT	YIELD %
INNER IMAGE	0	50	54	1	12	2141	2141	100.00
INNER ETCH	0	50	56	1	8	2194	2177	99.22
LAMINATION	0	50	52	2	50	2242	2225	99.24
DRILL	0	72	73	1	56	2811	2802	99.67
ELECTROLESS	0	72	72	1	30	2744	2741	99.89
OUTER IMAGE	1	72	86	4	25	3194	3152	98.68
ELECTROPLATE	1	72	73	3	19	2620	2576	98.32
S.MASK/NOMENCL	0	72	73	8	55	2396	2378	99.24
ROUT	0	92	102	5	57	3477	3468	99.74
TAB PLATE	0	20	25	0	8	805	802	99.62
E.T.	0	72	93	5	19	3298	3094	93.81
Q.A.	0	72	102	4	13	3508	3344	95.32

			DAILY TOTALS			
	2 SIDED	MULTILAYER 4L	6L	8L	ML TOTAL	GRAND TOTAL
PRODUCTION:						
ISF-IN	1659	903	1132	283	2318	3977
ISF-OUT	1537	767	846	195	1808	3345
PLAN ISF	650	617	505	234	1356	2006
YIELD %	92.64	84.93	74.73	68.90	77.99	84.10
PLAN YIELD %	88.00	80.00	79.00	65.00	77.04	80.59
GOOD LOTS	40	26	28	8	62	102
PLAN LOTS	22	22	18	10	50	72
SCRAPPED LOTS	0	0	2	0	2	2
MATERIAL USAGE %	86.40	72.35	78.61	73.69	75.45	79.66
OUTPUT MIX %	45.94	22.92	25.29	5.82	54.05	
SHIPMENTS:						
ISF SHIPPED	1322	815	494	62	1371	2693
SHIP MIX %	49.09	30.26	18.34	2.30	50.90	
WIP LOTS:						
PRODUCTION	94	108	83	57	248	342
PROTO	4	1	5	0	6	10
TOTAL LOTS	98	109	88	57	254	352
PROTO LOTS:						
GOOD LOTS	3	0	1	0	1	4
SCRAPPED LOTS	0	0	0	0	0	0
YIELD % (IMAGES)	98.69	.00	75.00	.00	75.00	97.96

EXHIBIT 6-20 Continued

SCRAP LOTS	PLAN LOTS	GOOD LOTS	PROTO LOTS	IMAGE-SQ-FT IN	OUT	YIELD %
			MONTH TO DATE TOTALS			
0	363	373	12	13848	13848	100.00
0	354	375	12	13912	13850	99.55
0	361	373	12	13729	13583	98.93
0	556	538	18	19495	19461	99.82
0	538	523	20	18918	18912	99.96
1	531	523	21	18815	18634	99.03
3	540	514	20	18285	17975	98.30
1	538	515	20	17865	17705	99.10
0	671	632	23	21400	21314	99.59
1	167	141	3	4478	4431	98.95
1	523	478	22	16541	15527	93.86
3	527	462	22	15099	14232	94.25

2 SIDED	MULTILAYER 4L	6L	8L	ML TOTAL	GRAND TOTAL
		MONTH TO DATE TOTALS			
5416	4789	4712	2269	11770	17186
4886	4140	3743	1501	9384	14270
4520	4291	3507	1638	9436	13956
90.21	86.44	79.43	66.15	79.72	83.03
88.00	80.00	79.00	65.00	77.04	80.59
143	138	121	61	320	463
153	153	125	70	348	501
2	2	6	0	8	10
77.81	71.26	77.29	77.49	74.75	75.69
34.23	29.01	26.22	10.51	65.76	
4714	4879	4121	1571	10571	15285
30.84	31.92	26.96	10.27	69.15	
12	2	4	4	10	22
0	0	0	0	0	0
92.10	100.00	52.00	61.41	63.27	85.18

production step. Thus, the operation designated as SEQ 010 costs a total of $6.1135 per multilayer board.

Below the main part of the cost report is the heading "MATERIAL PERIOD EXPENSE," which refers to indirect material costs (per board) that are treated as period expenses rather than being inventoried. Adding the total "YLD ML/BD" of $5.6038 and the "MATERIAL PERIOD EXPENSE" of $2.4250 gives $8.0288 as the total material cost of a multilayer circuit board. Adding this to the total manufacturing overhead cost per board (denoted TOTAL MOH COST) of $21.3881 gives $29.4169 as the total cost of a multilayer circuit board. The other information on the cost report provides detail for some of the numbers given in the main part of the report.

Exhibit 6-20 is a production report for the PC Fabrication operation. In the upper left part of the report, the various work centers are listed. For each work center the number of scrapped production lots, planned lots, good lots, prototype lots, and in-process lots is shown. Prototype lots refer to products used in a Hewlett-Packard lab as part of the research and development process. The headings "IMAGE—SQ FT" ("IN" and "OUT") refers to the number of square feet of circuit board put into the production process and removed from the production process in each step. Finally, the "YIELD %" refers to the portion of the good production at each step that is usable at the completion of that step.

The summary information in the lower right corner of the report provides similar information for two-sided circuit boards and for the four-layer, six-layer, and eight-layer multilayer boards. In this part of the report "ISF" refers to image square feet of circuit board.

Summary

Like job-order costing, process costing is an averaging process. However, process costing, unlike job-order costing, uses broad averages and applies them to large quantities of identical units. Job-order costing methods concentrate on single jobs, where each job or batch is different in important ways from the others. In process costing, accumulated costs are divided by a production measure, and the resulting unit cost is used to transfer costs. In this chapter, five steps are used to analyze the units of product being worked on in each process, to analyze the costs charged to each process, and to calculate the unit and total costs of work completed and remaining in process. These steps were illustrated for both first-in, first-out (FIFO) and weighted-average process costing.

The process cost accounting illustration in this chapter used normal costing. Actual costing and standard costing may also be used in conjunction with process costing. Standard costing, as it may be applied to either job-order or process cost accounting, is discussed in Chapters 7 and 8.

Key Terms to Review	conversion costs, p. 184	operation costing, p. 204
	equivalent unit, p. 184	process costing, p. 182
	first-in, first-out (FIFO), p. 189	weighted-average, p. 195

Review Problem

PROCESS COSTING

To review the concepts in this chapter, solve the process-costing problem on your own, using the data in Exhibit 6-5. Concentrate first on Process No. 1, and do each of the five steps in solving the process-costing problem. Use the FIFO method. Then check your computations in Step 5, which is the Analysis of Costs, by comparing your answer with Exhibit 6-11.

After successfully completing the work for Process No. 1, do the same steps for Process No. 2. Use the weighted-average method. Check your answer to Step 5 by comparing it with Exhibit 6-14.

Suggested Readings

Dinius, S. H. "A Matrix Solution to Process Cost Problems." *Issues in Accounting Education* (Spring 1987): 44–56.

Franke, R. "Process Model for Costing." *Management Accounting* (January 1975): 45.

Horngren, C. T. "Process Costing in Perspective: Forget FIFO." *Accounting Review* (July 1967): 593.

Hunt, R., L. Garrett, and C. M. Merz. "Direct Labor Cost Not Always Relevant at H-P." *Management Accounting* (February 1985): 58–62.

Kaplan, R. S. "Measuring Manufacturing Performance: A New Challenge for Managerial Accounting Research." *Accounting Review* (October 1983): 686–705.

Partington, G. H. "Teaching Process Costing." *Issues in Accounting Education* (1984): 75–80.

Schonberger, R. J. *Japanese Manufacturing Techniques* (New York: Macmillan, 1982).

Stallman, J. C. "Framework for Evaluating Cost Control Procedures for a Process." *Accounting Review* (October 1972): 774.

Wilner, N. "A Simple Teaching Approach for Process Costing Using Logic and Pictures." *Issues in Accounting Education* (Fall 1987): 388–396.

Review Questions

6-1 What is meant by an *equivalent unit?* Give a numerical example.

6-2 "Standard costing would not be applicable if process costing is used." True or false? Explain briefly.

6-3 "Process costing is only appropriate for the production of chemicals or other 'continuous' production processes. Process costing could not be used in a discrete production process such as the manufacture of hand-held calculators." True or false? Explain.

6-4 "Transferred-in costs are costs incurred in a previous period of time." True or false? Explain.

6-5 Briefly explain the chief difference between FIFO and weighted-average process costing.

6-6 How could process-costing concepts be applied in a service firm, such as a bank?

Exercises

6-7 Weighted-Average Process Costing Information for the month of January concerning Department *A*, the first stage of Ogden Corporation's production cycle, is as follows:

	Materials	Conversion
Work in process, beginning	$ 8,000	$ 6,000
Current costs	40,000	32,000
Total costs	$ 48,000	$38,000
Equivalent units using weighted-average method	100,000	95,000
Average unit costs	$ .48	$ .40
Goods completed		90,000 units
Work in process, end		10,000 units

Materials are added at the beginning of the process. The ending work in process is 50 percent complete as to conversion costs.

REQUIRED:

How would the total costs accounted for be distributed, using the weighted-average method? (Select one.)

	Goods Completed	Work in Process, End
a.	$79,200	$6,800
b.	$79,200	$8,800
c.	$86,000	$0
d.	$88,000	$6,800 *(CPA adapted)*

6-8 Weighted-Average Process Costing   During April 19x3 Clayton Company's Department *B* equivalent unit product costs, computed under the weighted-average method, were as follows:

Materials	$1
Conversion	3
Transferred-in	5

Materials are introduced at the end of the process in Department *B*. There were 2,000 units (40 percent complete as to conversion costs) in work-in-process at April 30, 19x3.

REQUIRED:

The total costs assigned to the April 30, 19x3 work-in-process inventory should be (select one):

  a. $12,400

  b. $13,600

  c. $14,400

  d. $18,000 *(CPA adapted)*

6-9 Weighted-Average Process Costing   Empire Company adds materials at the beginning of the process in Department *M*. Conversion was 75 percent complete as to the 8,000 units in work in process on July 1 and 50 percent complete as to the 6,000 units in work in process at July 31. During July, 12,000 units were completed and transferred to the next department. An analysis of the costs relating to work in process on July 1 and to production activity for July is as follows:

	Costs	
	Materials	*Conversion*
Work in process, 7/1	$19,200	$ 7,200
Costs added in July	31,200	21,600

REQUIRED:

Using the weighted-average method, what was the total cost per equivalent unit for July? *(CPA adapted)*

6-10 Transferred-In Costs   Roy Company manufactures product *X* in a two-stage production cycle in Departments *A* and *B*. Materials are added at the beginning of the process in Department *B*. Roy uses the weighted-average method. Conversion for Department *B* was 50 percent complete as to the 6,000 units in the beginning work in process and 75 percent complete as to the 8,000 units in the ending work in process. During February, 12,000 units were completed and transferred out of Department *B*. An analysis of the costs relating to work in process (WIP) and a production analysis in Department *B* for February 19x0 follow:

	Costs		
	Trans-ferred In	Materials	Conversion
WIP, February 1:			
Costs attached	$12,000	$2,500	$1,000
February activity:			
Costs added	29,000	5,500	5,000

REQUIRED:

The total cost per equivalent unit transferred out for February 19x0 of product *X*, rounded to the nearest penny, was:

  a. $2.75

  b. $2.78

  c. $2.82

  d. $2.85 *(CPA adapted)*

6-11 FIFO Process Costing   Walden Company has a process-cost system using the FIFO cost flow method. All materials are introduced at the beginning of the process in Department One. The following information is available for the month of January:

	Units
Work in process, 1/1/x3 (40% complete as to conversion)	500
Started in January	2,000
Transferred to Department Two during January	2,100
Work in process, 1/31/x3 (25% complete as to conversion)	400

REQUIRED:

What are the equivalent units of production for the month of January 19x3? *(CPA adapted)*

6-12 Calculation of Units-In   Bronson Company had 6,000 units in work in process at January 1, which were 60 percent complete as to conversion. During January, 20,000 units were completed. At January 31, 8,000 units remained in work in process which were 40 percent complete as to conversion. Materials are added at the beginning of the process.

REQUIRED:

a. Using the weighted-average method, what were the equivalent units for January for conversion costs?

b. How many units were started during January? *(CPA adapted)*

6-13 FIFO and Weighted-Average Process Costing

a. Department *A* is the first stage of Mann Company's production cycle. The following information is available for conversion for the month of April:

	Units
Work in process, beginning (60% complete)	20,000
Started in April	340,000
Completed in April and transferred to Department *B*	320,000
Work in process, ending (40% complete)	40,000

Using the FIFO method, the equivalent units for the conversion-cost calculation are:

(1) 320,000

(2) 324,000

(3) 336,000

(4) 360,000

b. Barnett Company adds materials at the beginning of the process in Department *M*. Conversion was 75 percent complete as to the 8,000 units in work in process at May 1, and 50 percent complete as to the 6,000 units in work in process at May 31. During May, 12,000 units were completed and transferred to the next department. An analysis of the costs relating to work in process at May 1 and to production activity for May is as follows:

	Costs	
	Materials	Conversion
Work in process, 5/1	$ 9,600	$ 4,800
Costs added in May	15,600	14,400

Using the weighted-average method, the total cost per equivalent unit for May was:

(1) $2.47

(2) $2.50

(3) $2.68

(4) $3.16 *(CPA adapted)*

6-14 FIFO and Weighted-Average Process Costing   Richardson Company computed the flow of physical units completed for Department *M* for the month of March as follows:

Units completed:	
From work in process on March 1, 19x2	15,000
From March production	45,000
	60,000

Materials are added at the beginning of the process. The 12,000 units of work in process at March 31, 19x2, were 80 percent complete as to conversion. The work in process at March 1, 19x2, was 60 percent complete as to conversion.

REQUIRED:

Using the FIFO method, the equivalent units for March conversion costs were (select one):

a. 55,200

b. 57,000

c. 60,600

d. 63,600

6-15 Allocating Labor Costs

a. Compute the equivalent units of labor performed on the following products:

Product	Beginning Inventory in Process	Completed Production	Ending Inventory in Process
1	100 units (1/4 completed)	200	None
2	—	200	100 units (1/4 completed)
3	100 units (1/4 completed)	200	100 units (1/2 completed)
4	100 units (1/2 completed)	200	100 units (1/4 completed)

b. If the labor cost incurred in making product 2 during the period was $10,000, compute the amount of labor in the ending inventory of labor in process for product 2.

c. If the labor cost incurred during the period in manufacturing product 3 was $20,000, compute the amount of labor in the ending inventory of labor in process of product 3. The beginning inventory of labor in process was $2,600. Assume a FIFO flow of costs.

6-16 Process Costs   The Allison Manufacturing Company produces a single product. Raw material *A* is committed to the production process at the start of process 1. Operating data for the period just ended are as follows:

	Process 1		Process 2	
Beginning inventories	270 lb	$1,152	160 lb	$1,972
	(1/3 finished)		(1/2 finished)	
Raw material *A* used	650 lb	1,170		
Direct labor and overhead		5,616		
Ending inventories	200 lb		90 lb	3,774
	(3/4 finished)		(1/3 finished)	

The weight of the finished product is exactly equal to the weight of the material used.

REQUIRED:

a. How many pounds of product were transferred from process 1 to process 2 during the period? How many equivalent units of labor were performed in process 1? What is the cost per equivalent unit of labor and overhead in process 1 for the period?

b. Set up T-accounts for process 1, process 2, and finished goods, and enter therein the operating results for the period. Assume a FIFO flow.

c. What was the labor and overhead cost per pound of product (cost per equivalent unit) in process 2 for this period?

d. How do labor costs for the period just ended compare with those of the preceding period for process 1? Assume that material costs were the same in each period and that a constant overhead rate is used throughout the year.

6-17 Equivalent Units and Costs   The following information applies to the only product produced by the May Company:

Work in process, January 31 inventory — 900 units, 1/3 completed.	
Work in process, January 1 inventory — 800 units, 1/2 completed.	
Product finished during January — 1,000 units.	
Direct labor cost for January	$2,205
Material used during January	$3,850
Direct labor in process, January 1	$ 800
Material in process, January 1	$3,200
Overhead in process, January 1	$1,600

The material is introduced at the beginning of the production process. The labor is applied evenly throughout the production process. The overhead rate is $2 per direct labor dollar. The company treats labor and overhead as separate categories in the process-costing calculations instead of combining them in the single category "conversion costs."

REQUIRED:

a. Compute the equivalent units of labor performed during January.

b. Determine the number of units of product started during January.

c. Find the weighted-average cost of an equivalent unit of product started and produced during January. The following two parts assume a FIFO flow of costs:

d. Find the cost of goods finished during January.

e. The cost of the January 31 inventory is (supply dollar amount):
_____ direct labor in process, January 31
_____ material in process, January 31
_____ overhead in process, January 31

6-18 Process-Costing Procedures   Firehouse Company uses a LIFO method for inventory. The company does not use a finished-goods account but transfers the cost of product sold directly from work in process to the "Cost of Goods Sold" account.

The following information applies to the month of July:

- July 1 inventory of labor in process: 1,000 equivalent units with a cost of $2,000

- Production for July: 100 equivalent units

- Direct labor cost for the month: $300

- During the month, 900 units were shipped

The amount of labor cost to be transferred to cost of goods sold was computed as follows:

$$\text{Labor costing rate} = \frac{\text{Direct labor cost for July}}{\text{Equivalent units produced}} = \frac{\$300}{100} = \$3/\text{unit}$$

$$\text{Transfer to cost of goods sold} = \text{Units shipped} \times \text{labor costing rate}$$
$$= 900 \times \$3 = \$2,700$$

REQUIRED:

Comment on the procedure followed.

Problems

6-19 Deriving Costs from Limited Information   Fabian Manufacturing Company produces low-quality musical records under the brand name "Sough." Orders in units of 1,000 are accepted for specific quantities of a given record, which has been prerecorded, and are processed by order. The single process by which the records are made is a continuous one. Materials consist of blank, labeled records that are processed to match the master record and then automatically packaged in batches of 1,000. Records are kept of actual costs (no standard cost system is employed).

The accounting office is destroyed by an earthquake on April 1 and only certain facts are salvaged from the ruins (fortunately the "Artist" and the manufacturing plant were saved). The following facts are known for the first quarter of operations:

a. Wages paid in cash since Jan. 1 — $10,000 (Debit Accrued Wages Payable)
  Wages accrued payable Jan. 1 — $5,000
  Wages accrued payable April 1 — $15,000
  (Wages are for both direct labor (at $2.50 per hr) and indirect labor (at $1 per hr)

b. Total overhead for the period — $10,000
  Overhead applied ($2 per Direct Labor Hour) — $12,000

c.

Orders Worked On	Completion Jan. 1	Labor Completion April 1
#10 Screech Records (1000 rec.)	0	100%
#11 Stamp Studios (2000 rec.)	0	80%
#12 Farce Films (1000 rec.)	0	?

No other orders were in process Jan. 1 or in Finished Goods.

d. Materials Stores Card

Records				Bal. Jan. 1 39,000 (13,000 x $3.00)
Date	Ref.	Rec.	Issued	Balance
1/10	#10		2000 lbs. @ 3.00	11,000 @ 3.00
2/15	#11		4000 lbs. @	7,000
3/5	#12			

All materials enter at the beginning of the process for each order.

e. Finished-Goods Inventory April 1: Job #10 $15,000.

REQUIRED:

a. What was the total labor expense applicable to production for the quarter?

b. What was the total direct labor expense for the quarter?

c. How many indirect labor hours were used this quarter?

d. What is the best estimate for the dollar value of materials charged to work in process for the quarter?

e. From what accounting record would the $15,000 finished goods figure for Job #10 most likely be obtained?

f. Assume (see **e**) that this record was destroyed (but the $15,000 figure is known in total). Derive the $15,000 figure. (Hint: Use the overhead rate given above and try to determine the hours of direct labor spent on this job.)

g. What costs are relevant to the Stamp Studio Job? (Assume the information supplied by the answer to **f** is relevant here.)

h. Determine the labor percentage completion of the Farce Films Job.

6-20 Understanding How Procedures Affect Information   The plant manager of the Waterhouse Company is confused by accounting reports of income. According to the production reports, it appears recently that the more inefficient workers are, the higher the profit reported by the accounting department. He has called in an expert (you).

The Waterhouse Company manufactures dashboard assemblies for a large automobile producer. Beginning in July the company starts building up an inventory so that when the new model year starts in October, it can supply a steady stream of product without resorting to an excessive amount of overtime.

The company has adopted a process cost-accounting system, using actual costs. Because the stock is handled so that the oldest goods are shipped first, a FIFO assumption as to the flow of costs is followed. As is common with many manufacturers, the Waterhouse Company keeps all product in the work in process account until it is shipped and does not use a finished-goods account (work in process is credited and manufacturing cost of goods sold is debited when goods are shipped).

The following information is made available to you for the month of September (all the information refers to direct labor in process):

Beginning work in process inventory (Sept. 1):		$2,250
Units of goods completed	850	
Units of goods one-half completed	100	
Units shipped during the month	100	
Ending work in process inventory:		
Units of goods completed	975	
Units of goods one-half completed	50	
Direct labor costs for the month	$600	
Equivalent units of production during September	200	

The amount of direct labor cost transferred to cost of goods sold was computed by the following procedures:

Ending Inventory, equivalent units:		
Goods completed	975	
Goods in process (50 × 1/2)	25	
Total equivalent units in inventory	1,000	
Direct labor cost per unit produced during the period		
($600 ÷ 200)	$ 3.00	
Direct labor cost of ending inventory (assuming that the most		
recently produced goods are still in inventory) 1,000 × $3.00	$3,000	
Computation of transfer to cost of goods sold:		
Work in process, beginning of period		$2,520
Plus costs incurred		600
		$3,120
Less ending inventory		3,000
Amount to be transferred to cost of goods sold		$ 120

a. Why does the above procedure give misleading information?

b. If the direct labor costs for the month had been $800 (assuming the same production), what would have been the transfer to cost of goods sold?

c. Compute the transfer to cost of goods sold, following a reasonably correct FIFO procedure.

6-21 Equivalent-Unit Schedules The Felix Manufacturing Company uses a process-cost system to account for the costs of its only product, known as "Nino." Production begins in the fabrication department where units of raw material are molded into various connecting parts. After fabrication is complete, the units are transferred to the assembly department. There is no material added in the assembly department. After assembly is complete, the units are transferred to the packaging department where the units are packaged for shipment. At the completion of this process the units are complete, and they are transferred to the shipping department.

At year end, December 31, 19x7, the following inventory of "Ninos" is on hand:

- No unused raw material or packing material

- Fabrication department: 6,000 units, 25% complete as to raw material and 40% complete as to direct labor

- Assembly department: 10,000 units, 75% complete as to direct labor

- Packaging department: 3,000 units, 60% complete as to packing material and 75% complete as to direct labor

- Shipping department: 8,000 units

REQUIRED:

Prepare schedules showing the following at December 31:

a. The number of equivalent units of raw material in all inventories.

b. The number of equivalent units of fabrication department direct labor in all inventories.

c. The number of equivalent units of packaging department material and direct labor in the packaging department inventory. *(CPA adapted)*

6-22 Equivalent Units and Weighted-Average Costing The Alpha Company manufactures a single product and uses a weighted-average process-costing system. The product is composed of Material 1 and Material 2. Material 1 is added at the beginning of the process while Material 2 is added when the process is 50 percent complete. Conversion costs are applied uniformly throughout the production process. The data on the following page apply to the month of July.

	Units	Amounts
Beginning inventories (30% complete)[a]	100	
Material 1		$ 542
Material 2		327
Conversion costs		551
Material 1 used		2,542
Material 2 used		3,984
Direct labor		2,680
Variable overhead		1,623
Fixed overhead		5,907
Ending inventories (40% complete)[a]	150	
Started in July	500	
Completed in July	450	

[a] Refers to conversion.

REQUIRED:

a. Prepare a schedule computing the equivalent units of production in July for Material 1, Material 2, and conversion.

b. Calculate the cost per equivalent unit for each type of material and for conversion.

PART THREE

Standard Costing and Budgeting

7

Standard Costing: Direct Material and Direct Labor

LEARNING OBJECTIVES

After studying this chapter, you should be able to:

1 Explain how standard costs are set.

2 Calculate direct material and direct labor variances.

3 Interpret direct material and direct labor variances.

4 Explain how differences between standard and actual costs can be analyzed to determine their causes.

5 Calculate and interpret mix and yield variances for materials and labor.

6 Calculate and interpret sales mix and quantity variances.

*T*he job-order and process-costing systems described in Chapters 4, 5, and 6 are used to accumulate the costs of direct materials, direct labor, and overhead and to apply these costs to units of production. This chapter describes standard-cost accounting systems, which may be used in conjunction with either job-order or process-costing systems. A **standard-cost accounting system** uses predetermined costs instead of actual costs and highlights performance that deviates from predetermined levels. It allows managers to employ **management by exception,** an approach that investigates only the most significant deviations from predetermined levels of performance and helps managers allocate their energies to those areas that can benefit most from their attention.

Cost Control

A **control system** has three basic components: (1) a predetermined or *standard level of performance,* (2) a measurement of *actual performance,* and (3) a *comparison* of standard level of performance with actual performance. An automatic thermostat provides a good example of such a control system: The thermostat is set to a predetermined (or standard) temperature, it measures the actual temperature in the room, and someone compares the predetermined temperature with the actual temperature. The thermostat then goes one step further and employs a form of management by exception by turning on a heating source when the actual temperature falls below the predetermined temperature. A control system is illustrated in Exhibit 7-1.

A standard costing system may be used in much the same way as a thermostat for the control of costs. Under a standard costing system, predetermined or standard cost levels are established, the actual cost level is measured, and a comparison is made between actual and standard performance. The difference between standard cost and actual cost is called a **cost variance.** An unfavorable variance exists when actual cost exceeds standard cost; a favorable variance exists when actual cost is less than standard cost. Cost variances are identified according to their causes and are recorded in variance accounts. The three basic types of cost variances are direct material variances, direct labor variances, and overhead variances. This chapter discusses direct material and direct labor variances, and Chapter 8 analyzes overhead variances.

Direct materials have two types of variance accounts: price variances and quantity variances. Direct material may be purchased from several suppliers who have different prices, transportation charges, and discounts for quantity purchases, and the resulting cost is often different from the standard. A **price variance** occurs when the amount of material used is equal to the standard, but the amount paid is not. **Quantity variances** are caused by using more or less material than was budgeted.

EXHIBIT 7-1

Elements of a Control System

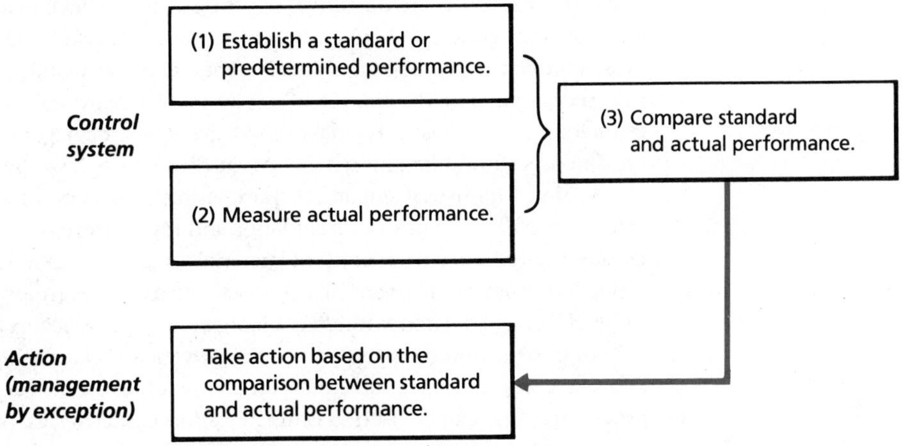

For direct labor, there are also two types of variance accounts: rate variances and efficiency variances. Workers with different pay grades are often able to perform the same function. When workers are employed whose rates do not reflect the mixture of pay rates provided for in the budget, a *labor rate variance* results. *Efficiency variances* are caused by using more or less labor hours than budgeted for a production task.

Under a standard-cost system, as with the actual or normal costing systems discussed in Chapters 4 and 5, the amounts in the work-in-process and finished-goods inventory account are used for determining inventory values. These values are needed in the determination of a company's financial position and its periodic profit. But these amounts, particularly on a unit basis, are also important for pricing, bidding, and other managerial decisions. Because such decisions often must be made before production is complete, predetermined or standard costs are necessary. For these reasons, standard costs commonly are reflected in a company's budgeting process.

Before discussing the details of cost variances, we will consider the process of setting standard costs.

Setting Standards

Standard costs are predetermined costs that should be attained or incurred. Setting standard costs requires an assessment of how a production task should be accomplished and how much the task should cost. Estimates of future costs can be derived by using a combination of historical analysis, expert advice, and managerial insight.

Perhaps the most common method of estimating future costs is to look at past costs. This process often reveals cyclical trends and is particularly useful for estimating direct costs. In fact, it is common for managers to rely excessively on an analysis of past costs. Past costs are objective, but they do not relieve managers from the need to forecast. Managers' insights into the raw materials market, the effect of economywide events on prices, the impact of local events on the availability of labor, the effect of a new technology, or the impact of a new intermediate goods supplier are critical in estimating future costs. To make good decisions, managers need to estimate what future costs should be and not just what these costs have been.

At times industrial engineers, purchasing managers, or market researchers can provide useful estimates of direct labor and raw materials costs. If indirect costs are closely related to either units of material or direct labor hours, they too can be estimated using the relevant direct costs. For example, fringe benefit costs are likely to be closely associated with direct labor hours. Historical relationships also may be helpful in determining whether a sufficiently close relationship exists between other indirect costs and units of either direct materials or direct labor. Some technical procedures that can be used to estimate or forecast costs are discussed in Chapter 13.

Setting standard costs also requires an assessment of how efficiently a production task should be accomplished. Should cost standards be very difficult to attain or relatively easy to attain? An entire range of possibilities reflects different expectations about performance. The problem of setting standards is analogous to the problem of setting par for a golfer.

A **theoretical standard** (or ideal standard) is analogous to shooting an eighteen-hole golf course in eighteen strokes. Although this feat is theoretically possible, it is extremely unlikely to occur. A theoretical standard can be attained only under the best of conditions. Setting standards that will not be attained is discouraging to workers and should be avoided.

A **practical standard** (or attainable standard) is analogous to completing an eighteen-hole golf course in par. Par is difficult to attain, but a very good golfer can attain it and sometimes do even better. A standard that is difficult but attainable is preferable to a theoretical standard that is almost impossible to attain.

A **normal standard** is analogous to setting a par consistent with the golfer's ability, often by means of a handicap. Par for a course may be seventy-two strokes, but a golfer who is just a duffer may have a par of ninety-eight strokes. *Par* is here used in the sense of a goal or standard of performance based on an individual's ability. The standard is an achievable value for the golfer's score.

It may be beneficial to use standards that take into consideration not only the present state of experience and skill of workers but also the variability in their performance across time. Ideally, the skill of workers should increase until the standard finally approaches a high level of performance (the seventy-two strokes for the golf course analogy). (The concept of a learning curve discussed in Chapter 15 is relevant here.)

Setting cost standards typically is the responsibility of operating managers who are directly involved in production activities. The relative tightness or looseness of the standards is determined in a process of bargaining and negotiation among the operating managers and others. Management accountants, industrial engineers, purchasing managers, and market researchers can provide information and advice to the managers who set cost standards, but the operating managers must accept and live with these standards.

The relative tightness or looseness of the standards that result from the bargaining and negotiation process affects the interpretation of any differences observed between actual and standard costs. A standard that is almost impossible to attain (a theoretical standard) will virtually always yield unfavorable variances. A difficult to attain, or practical, standard produces mostly unfavorable variances.

Use of Standards in the Service Industry

Standards exist in service industry firms as well as manufacturing firms. Banks, fast food chains, rental car companies, airlines, and insurance companies all use standards in their budgeting, cost control, and service costing activities. An article in *Business Week* described the development of standards by Ruth Finley, who at the time was a vice president of American Express, a large financial services company.

Standards at American Express

Business Week reported that Finley's approach to speeding up and improving service at American Express was similar to the approach used in industrial engineering studies of manufacturing operations. The firm's financial-service operations were broken up into their basic tasks. For each of these tasks, performance standards were set, and means were devised for achieving the standards. The approach was based on viewing the firm's end product (financial services) as though it were as tangible as a new car.[1]

Waffle House, Inc. has used standards for cost control and analysis in the restaurant industry. As part of this analysis an "efficiency report" was produced that monitored food and labor costs by comparing actual costs, at a given sales volume, with standard costs based on past experience.[2]

The use of standards by Dutch Pantry, Inc. was described in the following excerpt from *Management Accounting:*[3]

Dutch Pantry, Inc. operates 53 full service family restaurants in 12 eastern states. To assure consistent quality, many of the items served in the restaurants are prepared in a central commissary called the Kemberling Foods plant. The commissary also produces many items which are sold to hospitals and other institutions through the food service division of Dutch Pantry.

[1] "Boosting Productivity at American Express," *Business Week* (October 5, 1981).

[2] E. Sasser, "Waffle House, Inc. (J)" (a management case) (Boston: President and Fellows of Harvard College, 1972), p. 5.

[3] D. Boll, "How Dutch Pantry Accounts for Standard Costs," *Management Accounting* (December 1982), p. 32.

Because the commissary produces more than 150 different items, it requires a cost accounting system that allows the costs for the many products to flow through the various operations involved in product preparation. The Kemberling Foods plant uses a standard cost system based on the production of a batch of product.

Six Flags, Inc., which operates large theme parks in several states, also uses standards. A management case described the firm's financial control system, part of which was a "monthly financial packet" composed of nineteen different reports. These reports compared standard and actual expenses in each of the firm's five major cost categories: operations, maintenance, general services, marketing, and finance.[4]

[4] J. Reece, "Six Flags, Inc." (a management case) (Boston: President and Fellows of Harvard College, 1973), p. 5.

Cost Variances

In standard cost accounting systems, direct materials and direct labor are applied to production using standard costs. As production occurs, actual costs are accumulated and compared with standard costs to reveal variances. Management accountants analyze these variances, which is the first step toward identifying the factors that caused the differences between actual and standard costs. Identifying these factors can provide a basis for finding better ways to adhere to the standards or to alter the standards to reflect changed conditions since the standards were set.

Consider the following facts about direct materials and direct labor for Bradley Corporation for 19x1.

	Standard Allowances and Prices
Direct materials	1 pound per unit of product, at $3.00 per pound
Direct labor	1 hour per unit of product, at $9.00 per hour

Assume that the following data about actual costs incurred and actual quantities used are available for 19x1.

	Actual Results
Good units produced	80,000
Cost of direct material used	$297,000
Pounds of direct material used	90,000
Actual price per pound	$3.30
Direct labor cost incurred	$777,750
Direct labor hours used	85,000
Actual labor rate per hour	$9.15

These data about actual and standard costs can be summarized as follows:

	Total Actual Costs	Total Standard Costs	Variances
Direct material	$297,000	$240,000	$57,000 *U*
Direct labor	777,750	720,000	57,750 *U*
U denotes unfavorable.			

The variances for direct material and direct labor are unfavorable because the actual cost exceeds the standard cost. Why do the actual costs differ from the standard costs? How can these variances be analyzed?

Direct Material Variances

The *direct material variance* of $57,000 can be divided into the material price variance (the part caused by paying a price for materials different than standard) and the material quantity variance (the part that was caused by using more or less than the standard amount of material). The **material price variance** is the difference between the actual and standard prices per unit of material multiplied by the actual quantity of material used:

$$\text{Material price variance} = \text{Actual quantity used} \times (\text{Actual price} - \text{Standard price})$$
$$= Q_A(P_A - P_S)$$

The actual cost per pound is equal to the total actual cost incurred, divided by the actual quantity used ($297,000/90,000 = $3.30). The material price variance for the data presented above is calculated below.

$$\text{Material price variance} = Q_A(P_A - P_S) = 90,000(\$3.30 - \$3.00) = \$27,000 \ U$$

The **material quantity variance** is equal to the difference between the actual quantity used and the amount that should have been used (given actual output), valued at the standard price.

$$\text{Material quantity variance} = \text{Standard price} \times (\text{Actual quantity} - \text{Standard quantity})$$
$$= P_S(Q_A - Q_S)$$

The material quantity variance for the data presented above is

$$\text{Material quantity variance} = P_S(Q_A - Q_S) = \$3.00(90{,}000 - 80{,}000)$$
$$= \$30{,}000 \ U$$

The standard quantity (Q_S) of 80,000 pounds was obtained by multiplying the units produced by the standard allowance for materials as follows:

$$\text{Standard quantity} = 80{,}000 \text{ units} \times 1 \text{ pound} = 80{,}000 \text{ pounds}$$

The material price and material quantity variances are presented graphically in Exhibit 7-2. Both the actual prices and actual quantities exceed the standards. When this occurs, the additional cost due to the higher price paid for the extra quantity used is arbitrarily assigned to the material price variance, as shown in Exhibit 7-2.

An alternative approach is to use a three-way breakdown of the total direct material variance. This breakdown isolates the additional cost due to the higher price paid for the extra quantity used. The three-way breakdown of the total direct material variance is illustrated in Exhibit 7-3 and uses the following definitions:

Pure material price variance $= Q_S(P_A - P_S)$
Material quantity variance $= P_S(Q_A - Q_S)$
Joint price/quantity variance $= (P_A - P_S)(Q_A - Q_S)$

The three-way breakdown for the data presented above follows:

$$\text{Pure material price variance} = Q_S(P_A - P_S) = 80{,}000(\$3.30 - \$3.00)$$
$$= \$24{,}000 \ U$$

$$\text{Material quantity variance} = P_S(Q_A - Q_S) = \$3.00(90{,}000 - 80{,}000)$$
$$= \$30{,}000 \ U$$

$$\text{Joint price/quantity variance} = (P_A - P_S)(Q_A - Q_S)$$
$$= (\$3.30 - \$3.00)(90{,}000 - 80{,}000) = \$3{,}000 \ U$$

The three-way breakdown reveals that $3,000 of the $27,000 material price variance in the two-way variance breakdown occurs because of the higher price paid for the extra quantity used. This distinction may be important in assigning responsibility for this portion of the total variance.

Because the standard quantity of material used is equal to the units produced times the standard material allowed per unit of product, the importance of an accurate count of units produced cannot be overstated. Companies often have difficulty getting accurate production counts because of errors or intentional misstatements. Mechanical counts can serve as a check but also are subject to manipulation. Sometimes the best check on reported production is the inventory of finished goods. If

EXHIBIT 7-2

Material Price and Quantity Variances

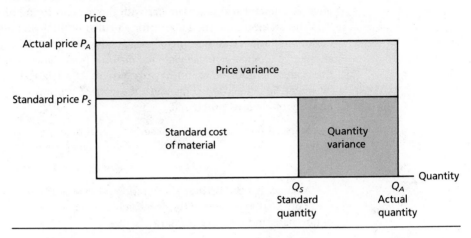

production reports are inflated, the ending inventory of finished goods discloses this fact.

Equally important to good production counts are reliable material usage standards. If these standards are not carefully set, they can lead to inaccurate financial statements that ultimately reduce the usefulness of the management accounting system as a management tool. One way to ensure that the standards are reasonable is for management accountants to learn about the firm's production operations. In an actual

EXHIBIT 7-3

Material Variances: Three-Way Breakdown

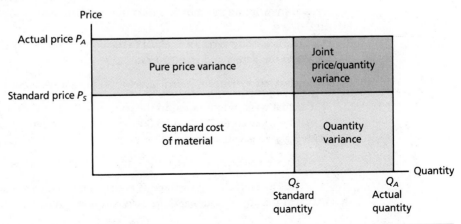

situation, the management accountant was using a material usage standard of five pounds per unit of product when the usage standard should have been 0.5 pounds. The error in placing the decimal point could have been caught sooner if the management accountant had been familiar with the manufacturing process.

The method described above for calculating the material price variance determines this variance at the time of usage and is based on the actual material used. An alternative method is to calculate the material price variance at the time of purchase. Under this method, the **material purchase price variance** is equal to the difference between the actual unit price and the standard unit price multiplied by the actual quantity of material purchased.

$$\text{Material purchase price variance} = \text{Actual quantity purchased}$$
$$\times (\text{Actual price} - \text{Standard price})$$
$$= Q_P(P_A - P_S)$$

Assume that the Bradley Corporation purchases 100,000 pounds of material and uses only 90,000 pounds. If the firm calculates the material price variance at the time of purchase, the result is as follows:

$$\text{Material purchase price variance} = Q_P(P_A - P_S)$$
$$= 100{,}000(\$3.30 - \$3.00)$$
$$= \$30{,}000 \ U$$

In many instances the material purchase price variance may be more useful than the price variance calculated at the time of usage, since the purchase price variance is determined at the time when the price differential occurs. The more timely variance that results may help management to react to the variance in an effective manner.

Direct Labor Variances

Direct labor variances are similar to the direct material variances discussed in the preceding section. The total direct labor variance is comprised of the variance caused by paying more or less than the standard rate of pay (*rate variance*) and the variance caused by working more or less than the standard number of hours (*efficiency variance*).

The labor rate variance is equal to the hours actually worked times the difference between the actual and standard rates:

$$\text{Labor rate variance} = \text{Actual hours} \times (\text{Actual rate} - \text{Standard rate}) = H_A(W_A - W_S)$$

The actual wage rate is equal to the total actual labor cost incurred, divided by the actual hours used ($\$777{,}750/85{,}000 = \$9.15$). The rate variance for the data presented above is calculated as follows:

$$\text{Labor rate variance} = H_A(W_A - W_S) = 85{,}000(\$9.15 - \$9.00) = \$12{,}750 \ U$$

The labor efficiency variance is equal to the standard rate times the difference between the actual hours and the standard hours allowed:

Labor efficiency variance = Standard rate × (Actual hours
− Standard hours allowed)

$$= W_S(H_A - H_S)$$

The efficiency variance for the Bradley Corporation is calculated as follows:

Labor-efficiency variance = $W_S(H_A - H_S)$ = $9.00(85,000 − 80,000) = \$45,000 \, U$

The labor rate variance is that portion of the labor variance caused by paying an amount per hour other than the standard rate. The efficiency variance discloses the extra cost incurred because of hours worked in excess of standard hours (or the savings because fewer than the standard number of hours were worked). If labor hours in excess of standard are worked, they are valued at the standard wage rate for purposes of computing the efficiency variance. The wage rate and efficiency variances are pictured graphically in Exhibit 7-4. It can again be argued that the upper right-hand area in Exhibit 7-4, which is caused by both the excess hours and excess rate, should be isolated as a third variance.

The total standard hours allowed is obtained by multiplying the units produced during the period by the work standard expressed in hours per unit. Before a product goes into production, engineers compute how many hours (or minutes) of labor are required to produce each end product and each component part. Assume the standard time required to produce a product is 10 minutes per unit. If 600 units of product are produced during the period, the standard amount of labor allowed is 6,000 minutes, or 100 hours.

EXHIBIT 7-4

Labor Rate and Efficiency Variances

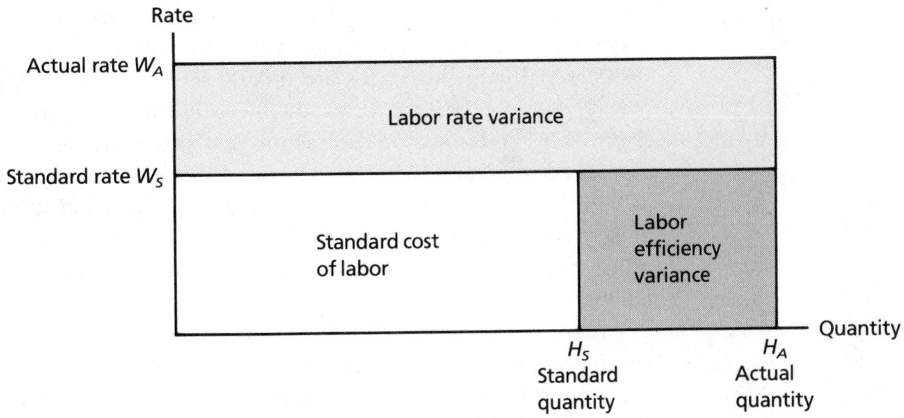

Interpretation of Material and Labor Variances

The variances described thus far for direct materials and direct labor are measured in dollar terms. Physical measures also can be used for the material quantity and labor efficiency variances. Because the standard labor rates and the standard material prices are reasonably easy to establish, the dollar measures of the material quantity and labor efficiency variances are likely to be useful.

The sign of a variance indicates whether the variance is favorable or unfavorable, although logic always yields the right interpretation. An arbitrary convention specifies a positive variance as unfavorable. It is generally (but often incorrectly) assumed that an unfavorable variance reflects inefficiency and a favorable variance indicates unusual efficiency. Yet both favorable and unfavorable variances may reflect conditions that have changed since the standards were established or, alternatively, the effects of random factors over which the manager has little or no control.

Frequently, even large cost variances are not controllable by the managers whose performances are being measured. Material price standards usually are based either on expected prices or on prices prevailing at the time the standards are set. Material price variances can be computed at the time materials are acquired or at the time the materials are placed into production. Purchasing managers are often held responsible for unfavorable material price variances, yet actual material prices can be affected by external factors that cannot be accurately predicted. Companies can try to obtain the lowest possible material prices by obtaining several quotations, buying in optimum lots, arranging for economical transportation, or taking advantage of cash and other discounts. Even when these actions are taken, however, material prices are frequently difficult to control. For example, import quotas may increase the cost of steel throughout the country after material price standards have been set, creating an unfavorable price variance for the users of steel; purchasing managers of companies using steel have no control over this event. In addition, rush orders or changes in production schedules can result in material price variances caused by using substitute materials or paying premiums for rush deliveries.

Material usage standards are usually set by industrial engineers or production managers on the basis of formal engineering studies, sample production runs under controlled conditions, or data about past use. Material quantity variances can be computed while production is in process, based on inspection reports or requisitions of additional materials, or after production is completed. Material usage often is closely controlled by operating managers. Many companies compare actual material usage with standards on a daily or weekly basis, and some companies make hourly comparisons.

Labor rates result from labor negotiations as well as the supply and demand for labor. Because labor rate standards are typically changed to reflect changes in actual wage rates, labor rate variances from contract alterations are often relatively small. However, the actual wage rates for individual workers may differ because of differences in seniority, experience, or skill levels. Using workers with wage rates that differ from the standard for a particular operation produces labor rate variances, and such variances are considered the responsibility of operating managers.

Labor efficiency standards are often set by industrial engineers or production managers on the basis of time and motion studies. Allowances are made for fatigue and rest periods, but efficiency standards are intended to provide incentives for efficient performance of individual operations. Both favorable and unfavorable labor efficiency variances may reflect either changes in operating methods or working conditions or factors unrelated to the efficiency of workers. For example, an unfavorable labor efficiency variance that reflects a statewide power failure reflects a situation that is not preventable by any cost center manager. Operating managers and management accountants should realize that reports of cost variances indicate where actual costs differ from standard costs and not that abnormal efficiencies or inefficiencies necessarily exist.

Sometimes interactions occur among the direct material and direct labor variances. If a company purchases low-quality materials but the material standards call for high-quality materials, unexpected shrinkage or spoilage may occur, thereby causing more downtime, which in turn has to be made up for with the use of highly skilled labor. In this situation, a favorable material price variance results in unfavorable material quantity, labor efficiency, and labor rate variances. If the unfavorable material quantity, labor efficiency, and labor rate variances exceed the favorable material price variance, the decision to purchase low-quality materials may be a poor one, even though the material price variance is favorable. Alternatively, if the favorable material price variance exceeds the unfavorable material quantity, labor efficiency, and labor rate variances, the decision may be a good one, even though several unfavorable variances resulted. Often managers can reduce the total cost of accomplishing a particular task by trading off favorable variances against unfavorable ones. Such interactions among variances makes the interpretation of individual variances both difficult and important.

Significance of Cost Variances

Managers cannot investigate every cost variance. They generally follow company-established criteria that determine whether a variance is sufficiently important to be investigated. In the absence of criteria, managers examine variances they believe their superiors consider important, often employing simple rules of thumb (such as the variance exceeds 10 percent of standard). The absolute size of a variance is one factor to be considered, and the size of the variance relative to the total cost incurred in that cost category is another. Other factors include the nature of the cost, how much control can be exercised over its incurrence, and the benefits to be obtained from managerial action. The specific criteria are best established by someone other than the managers responsible for the operations affected, preferably by someone with a knowledge of statistics because statistical techniques can help determine how unusual a variance is. The use of statistical techniques in variance analysis is discussed in Chapter 28.

The analysis of the variances illustrated in this chapter is only a first step. Once the variances are computed, the causes of the variances need to be investigated in detail. Variance analysis generates questions but does not provide answers; it is an example of the *attention directing* role of managerial accounting. Once variances have been investigated, corrective action may be undertaken but may take some time to be effective. Some variances may not be controllable.

Behavioral and Economic Effects of Variances

Variances are used for a variety of management purposes. In addition to being useful in diagnosing performance and clarifying the details behind the numbers that characterize a business, variances are used to evaluate the performance of both people and departments. Because variances are used in performance evaluation, they can have an important influence on managerial rewards such as promotions, salary raises, and additional responsibilities. At General Electric, for example, managers are evaluated in what is referred to as a "performance screen" on how well they achieve various financial and nonfinancial goals. This performance evaluation process provides one of many criteria by which managers are ranked for their annual salary reviews and the awarding of incentive compensation.[5] At Corning Glass Works, the performance of divisional managers is measured largely on the basis of the variance from the budgeted divisional operating profit. This performance measure figures prominently in Corning's executive compensation system. In calculating salary bonuses for managers not of officer rank, equal weight is given to the variance from budgeted operating profit and other individual performance factors.[6]

Using standards and variances for performance evaluation and for providing incentives can profoundly affect the behavior of people in an organization. We examine these effects from the perspective of behavioral science in Chapter 26.

Computer-Integrated Manufacturing: Real-Time Variance Data

A computer-integrated manufacturing (CIM) system can compile and transmit variance data to management on a real-time basis. It is a **real-time information system** and generates data instantaneously, as soon as the relevant events have occurred. In a computerized manufacturing environment, cost variances can be computed even as production takes place. A real-time information system also permits management to simulate the effects on costs of material, labor-scheduling, and engineering design changes. Before such changes are implemented, the computer can show implications of the changes in terms of predicted cost variances.

[5] P. Browne, "General Electric Company — Background Note on Management Systems: 1981" (a management case prepared under the direction of R. Vancil) (Boston: President and Fellows of Harvard College, 1981), p. 85.

[6] T. Clough, "Corning Glass Works — Tom MacAvoy" (a management case prepared under the supervision of R. Vancil and with the cooperation of T. MacAvoy, president of Corning Glass Works) (Boston: President and Fellows of Harvard College, 1978), p. 25.

Summary

A standard cost accounting system uses predetermined costs for budgeting and cost accumulation purposes. Standard costs can be determined by a combination of historical perspective, expert advice, and managerial insight. Standards that represent efficient but attainable performance levels are most useful. Final responsibility for setting standards rests with operating managers; management accountants advise operating managers how to control costs.

A standard costing system provides data about cost variances by comparing actual costs with standard costs. These variances can be used to control costs. Actual costs can differ from standard costs for many reasons, but variances for material and labor generally are classified as price or rate variances and quantity or efficiency variances. Material price and labor rate variances are caused by the payment of materials prices and labor wage rates that are higher or lower than the standard material prices and wage rates, respectively. Material quantity and labor efficiency variances are caused by using a different amount of material and direct labor hours than the standard amounts necessary to accomplish a task. Material quantity and labor efficiency variances are usually more subject to control by operating managers than are material price and labor rate variances.

Review Problem

DIRECT MATERIAL AND DIRECT LABOR VARIANCES

The following data pertains to Hang Ten Corporation, a manufacturer of surf boards, for the month of April.

	Standards
Direct material	20 pounds per unit, at $5.00 per pound
Direct labor	2 hours per unit at $15.00 per hour

	Actual Results
Good units produced	900
Cost of direct material used	$90,650
Quantity of direct material used	18,500
Actual direct material price	$4.90 per pound
Direct labor cost incurred	$27,200
Direct labor hours used	1,700
Actual direct labor rate	$16.00 per hour

REQUIRED:

Calculate the following variances for April. Indicate whether each variance is favorable or unfavorable.

a. Direct material variance

b. Material price variance

c. Material quantity variance

d. Direct labor variance

e. Labor rate variance

f. Labor efficiency

Solution to Review Problem

a. Direct material variance:

$$\text{Actual cost} - \text{Standard cost, given actual production} = \$90,650 - (900)(20)(\$5.00)$$
$$= \$90,650 - \$90,000$$
$$= \$650 \text{ Unfavorable}$$

b. Material price variance:

$$\text{Actual quantity} \times (\text{Actual price} - \text{Standard price}) = 18,500(\$4.90 - \$5.00)$$
$$= \$1,850 \text{ Favorable}$$

c. Material quantity variance:

$$\text{Standard price} \times (\text{Actual quantity} - \text{Standard quantity, given actual production}) = \$5.00(18,500 - 18,000)$$
$$= \$2,500 \text{ Unfavorable}$$

d. Direct labor variance:

$$\text{Actual cost} - \text{Standard cost, given actual production} = \$27,200 - (900)(2)(\$15)$$
$$= \$200 \text{ Unfavorable}$$

e. Labor rate variance:

$$\text{Actual hours} \times (\text{Actual rate} - \text{Standard rate}) = 1,700(\$16.00 - \$15.00)$$
$$= \$1,700 \text{ Unfavorable}$$

f. Labor efficiency variance:

$$\text{Standard rate} \times (\text{Actual hours} - \text{Standard hours, given actual production})$$
$$= (\$15.00)(1,700 - 1,800)$$
$$= \$1,500 \text{ Favorable}$$

Key Terms to Review

material purchase price variance, p. 236

normal standard, p. 230

practical standard, p. 230

price variance, p. 228

pure material price variance, p. 234

quantity variance, p. 228

real-time information system, p. 240

standard costs, p. 229

standard-cost-accounting system, p. 230

theoretical standard, p. 230

Suggested Readings

Barnes, J. "How to Tell If Standard Costs Are Really Standard." *Management Accounting* (June 1983): 50–54.

Boll, D. "How Dutch Pantry Accounts for Standard Costs." *Management Accounting* (December 1982): 32–35.

Demski, J. S., and S. Baiman. "Economically Optimal Performance Evaluation and Control Systems." *Journal of Accounting Research* (Supplement 1980): 184–220.

Hilton, R. "The Determinants of Cost Information Value: An Illustrative Analysis." *Journal of Accounting Research 17* (Autumn 1979): 411–35.

Itami, H. *Adaptive Behavior: Management Control and Information Analysis* (Sarasota, Fl.: American Accounting Association, 1977).

Lere, C. "Explaining Alternative Standard Cost Entries." *Journal of Accounting Education* (Fall 1985): 187–93.

Littrell, E. "The High-Tech Challenge to Management Accounting." *Management Accounting* (October 1984): 33–36.

Magee, R. *Advanced Managerial Accounting* (New York: Harper & Row, 1986).

Mister, W. G. "A Note on the Interpretation of Standard Cost Variances." *Journal of Accounting Education* (Fall 1983): 51–56.

National Association of Accountants. *Research Reports Nos. 11, 15, 17, 22,* and *28.*

Peles, T. "A Note on Yield Variance and Mix Variance." *Accounting Review* (April 1986): 325–29.

APPENDIX 7A
Mix and Yield Variances for Material and Labor

In some manufacturing situations, factors of production may be substituted for each other. Thus, in an emergency or during slack activity, a highly paid worker may be used in a task that ordinarily requires a worker of lower skill grade, or one grade of steel may be substituted for another grade. This type of event gives rise to mix and yield variances. A *mix variance* is caused when one factor of production is substituted for another factor of production. The variance caused by differences in wage rates (or prices) can be determined relatively easily, but the change in efficiency that results from the substitution is more difficult to establish because the necessary information to compute it is often not available. Thus, it is often difficult to measure the total effect of a shift in the mix of productive factors. A *yield variance* results when the total actual material or labor input differs from the total standard amount allowed.

This appendix illustrates the calculation of mix and yield variances in the context of direct material variances; similar calculations apply to the direct labor input. Midwest Metals, Inc. manufactures a range of metallic alloys for use in the aircraft industry. In the manufacture of one product, raw materials A, B, and C are used in the following standard amounts:

Material	Standard Input Proportion	Price per Pound
A	.2	1.00
B	.3	2.00
C	.5	6.00

When the manufacturing process is running normally, 100 pounds of material input results in only 95 pounds of good output. The other 5 percent of the material inputs evaporate during the production process. During June, the following actual results were observed:

	Input	
Material	Actual Input Quantity	Actual Price
A	190	$1.10
B	280	1.95
C	510	6.10
	Output	

855 pounds of good output were obtained.

First we calculate direct material price and efficiency variances. The procedure is identical to that illustrated earlier but now we sum across the three types of material.

DIRECT MATERIAL VARIANCES

$$\text{Price variance} = \Sigma \,(\text{Actual price} - \text{Standard price}) \times \text{Actual quantity inputs}$$
$$= (\$1.10 - \$1.00) \times 190 + (\$1.95 - \$2.00) \times 280 + (\$6.10 - \$6.00) \times 510$$
$$= \$56 \text{ Unfavorable}$$

$$\text{Quantity variance} = \Sigma \,(\text{Actual quantity} - \text{Standard quantity}) \times \text{Standard price inputs}$$
$$= (190 - 180^*) \times \$1.00 + (280 - 270^*) \times \$2.00 + (510 - 450^*) \times \$6.00$$
$$= \$390 \text{ Unfavorable}$$

* The standard quantities for the three materials were calculated as follows:

Good output $= .95 \times \text{Input} = 855$ pounds

This implies the following:

$$\text{Standard input} = \frac{\text{Good output}}{.95} = \frac{855}{.95} = 900 \text{ pounds}$$

Using the standard input proportions given above, we have

Material	Standard Input Proportion	Total Standard Input	Standard Input
A	.2	900	180
B	.3	900	270
C	.5	900	450

Mix and Yield Variances

The mix and yield variances result from breaking the quantity variance up into two components as follows:

Quantity variance
— Yield variance
— Mix variance

$$\text{Yield variance} = \left(\begin{array}{c}\text{Total actual} \\ \text{quantity}\end{array} - \begin{array}{c}\text{Total standard} \\ \text{quantity}\end{array}\right)\left(\begin{array}{c}\text{Weighted average} \\ \text{standard price}\end{array}\right)$$

$$\text{Mix variance} = \sum_{\text{inputs}} \left(\begin{array}{c}\text{Actual} \\ \text{quantity}\end{array} - \begin{array}{c}\text{Standard} \\ \text{quantity}\end{array}\right)\left(\begin{array}{c}\text{Standard} \\ \text{price}\end{array} - \begin{array}{c}\text{Weighted average} \\ \text{standard price}\end{array}\right)$$

These formulas include a term called the *weighted average standard price.* This is the average of the input prices weighted by the standard input proportions as follows:

Weighted average standard price

$$= \sum_{\text{inputs}} (\text{Input price}) \times (\text{Standard input proportion})$$

We can now compute the yield and mix variances for the Midwest Metals example. These calculations are shown below:

Weighted average standard price $= (\$1.00)(.2) + (\$2.00)(.3) + (\$6.00)(.5)$
$$= \$3.80$$

Yield variance $= (980 - 900)(\$3.80) = \$304$ Unfavorable

Mix variance $= (190 - 180)(\$1.00 - \$3.80)$
$$+ (280 - 270)(\$2.00 - \$3.80)$$
$$+ (510 - 450)(\$6.00 - \$3.80)$$
$$= \$86 \text{ Unfavorable}$$

The sum of the yield and mix variances is $390 ($304 + $86), which is equal to the quantity variance.

Interpretation

The yield variance is unfavorable because the *total* actual quantity of material used was greater than the *total* standard quantity allowed. This variance focuses on the total quantity effect, or the yield of the raw materials. In this variance, the input mix is held constant by multiplying by the weighted average standard price, which incorporates the standard input proportions.

The mix variance focuses on changes in the mix of inputs. To determine the overall sign of the variance, we examine each of its components. The first (material A) component $(190 - 180)(\$1.00 - 3.80)$ is favorable because when the input mix shifted, a greater amount than standard was used of a *relatively* inexpensive input. Material A is relatively inexpensive because its standard price is less than the weighted average standard price. The second (material B) component $(280 - 270)(\$2.00 - \$3.80)$ is favorable for the same reason. The third (material C) component $(510 - 450)(\$6.00 - \$3.80)$ is unfavorable because in this case more than the standard was used of a relatively expensive input. Because the unfavorable component is numerically larger than the sum of the two favorable components, the overall mix variance is unfavorable.

In summary, the mix and yield variances are components of a direct material quantity variance (or a direct labor efficiency variance) that are calculated when there are multiple inputs of these types. The yield variance focuses on the total quantity usage effect, while holding constant the input mix. The mix variance focuses on shifts in the input mix. These variances are designed to provide a more complete picture of the effects of changing the mix of factor inputs in a production process.

APPENDIX 7B
Mix and Quantity Variances for Analyzing Sales Performance

When a financial plan is prepared at the beginning of the planning period, management generally forecasts certain levels of sales for each of the company's products. Multiplying each product's planned sales level by its planned unit contribution margin (planned sales price minus standard variable cost) yields that product's planned aggregate contribution margin.

Later, when actual sales are known, management can determine what the aggregate contribution margin should be based on *actual,* rather than forecasted, sales. A variance may then be calculated between the aggregate contribution margin in the original plan (based on forecasted sales) and the aggregate contribution margin that should be attained given actual sales. Suppose that Midwest Metals sells three grades of sheet metal with the following forecasted and actual levels of sales:

	Forecast Sales	*Actual Sales*
Grade 1	1,000 units	1,200 units
Grade 2	2,000 units	1,900 units
Grade 3	5,000 units	4,800 units

The projected contribution margins for the three products are as follows:

Grade 1	$20/unit
Grade 2	$10/unit
Grade 3	$ 6/unit

The aggregate contribution margins for both forecasted and actual sales are as follows:

	Aggregate Contribution Margin Based on Forecasted Sales	*Aggregate Contribution Margin Based on Actual Sales*
Grade 1	1,000 × $20 = $20,000	1,200 × $20 = $24,000
Grade 2	2,000 × $10 = 20,000	1,900 × $10 = 19,000
Grade 3	5,000 × $ 6 = 30,000	4,800 × $ 6 = 28,800
Total	$70,000	$71,800

Variance = $1,800 Favorable

The $1,800 favorable variance calculated above is called a *sales-volume variance* and is caused by a differential between planned and actual sales volume.[7] The variance has nothing to do with sales prices or production costs because these are held constant in the standard contribution margin.

The sales volume variance may be decomposed into two parts. One part focuses on the change in the *total* sales quantity, and the other part focuses on the change in the sales mix. The formulas, given below, are analogous to those for the material mix and yield variances discussed in Appendix 7A:

$$
\text{Sales-volume variance}
\begin{cases}
\text{Sales-quantity variance} \\
\\
\text{Sales-mix variance}
\end{cases}
$$

$$\text{Sales-volume variance} = \sum_{\text{products}} \left(\begin{array}{l} \text{Forecasted} \\ \text{quantity} \end{array} - \begin{array}{l} \text{Actual} \\ \text{quantity} \end{array} \right) \left(\begin{array}{l} \text{Projected contribution} \\ \text{margin} \end{array} \right)$$

$$\text{Sales-quantity variance} = \left(\begin{array}{l} \text{Total} \\ \text{forecasted} \\ \text{quantity} \end{array} - \begin{array}{l} \text{Total} \\ \text{actual} \\ \text{quantity} \end{array} \right) \left(\begin{array}{l} \text{Weighted average} \\ \text{projected contribution} \\ \text{margin} \end{array} \right)$$

$$\text{Sales-mix variance} = \sum_{\text{products}} \left(\begin{array}{l} \text{Forecasted} \\ \text{quantity} \end{array} - \begin{array}{l} \text{Actual} \\ \text{quantity} \end{array} \right)$$

$$\left(\begin{array}{l} \text{Weighted average} \\ \text{projected contribution} \\ \text{margin} \end{array} - \begin{array}{l} \text{Projected contribution} \\ \text{margin} \end{array} \right)$$

The weighted average projected contribution margin, which holds the sales mix constant at its forecast level, is calculated as follows:

$$
\begin{array}{l} \text{Weighted average projected} \\ \text{contribution margin} \end{array} = \frac{\sum_{\text{products}} \left(\begin{array}{l} \text{Planned} \\ \text{quantity} \end{array} \right) \times \left(\begin{array}{l} \text{Projected contribution} \\ \text{margin} \end{array} \right)}{\sum_{\text{products}} \left(\begin{array}{l} \text{Planned} \\ \text{quantity} \end{array} \right)}
$$

For Midwest Metals, the weighted average projected contribution margin is calculated as follows:

$$
\begin{array}{l} \text{Weighted average projected} \\ \text{contribution margin} \end{array} = \frac{(1,000)(\$20) + (2,000)(\$10) + (5,000)(\$6)}{1,000 + 2,000 + 5,000}
$$

$$= \$8.75$$

We can now calculate the following variances for Midwest Metals:

$$
\begin{aligned}
\text{Sales-volume variance} = \ & (1,000 - 1,200) \times \$20 \\
& + (2,000 - 1,900) \times \$10 \\
& + (5,000 - 4,800) \times \$6 \\
= \ & \$1,800 \text{ Favorable}
\end{aligned}
$$

---

[7] Some authors refer to this variance as a *budget adjustment variance,* but this term is not used in practice.

$$\text{Sales-quantity variance} = (8,000 - 7,900) \times \$8.75 = \$875 \text{ Unfavorable}$$

$$\begin{aligned}
\text{Sales-mix variance} = \quad & (1,000 - 1,200) \times (\$8.75 - \$20) \\
+ \, & (2,000 - 1,900) \times (\$8.75 - \$10) \\
+ \, & (5,000 - 4,800) \times (\$8.75 - \$6) \\
= \, & \$2,675 \text{ Favorable}
\end{aligned}$$

Interpretation

The sales-volume variance is favorable because the aggregate contribution margin based on actual sales exceeds the aggregate contribution margin based on forecast sales. The volume variance is due to *both* quantity and mix changes in sales.

The sales quantity variance is unfavorable. Holding constant the sales mix at its forecast level, the quantity variance reflects the fact that the firm sold 100 fewer units *in total*.

The sales mix variance is favorable reflecting the fact that the change in the firm's sales mix had a favorable effect on aggregate contribution margin. To see why this occurred, let us examine each component in the sales-mix variance.

The component for product grade 1 is favorable because the firm sold more than the forecast amount of this relatively high contribution margin product. The product's individual unit contribution margin of $20 exceeds the weighted average projected contribution margin of $8.75. The component for product grade 2 is unfavorable because here the firm sold fewer units than were forecast of this relatively high contribution margin product. The component for product grade 3 is favorable because in this case the firm sold fewer units than were forecast of this relatively low contribution margin item. Because the sum of the two favorable components of the sales-mix variance exceeds the unfavorable component, the sales-mix variance is favorable.

Sales-quantity and sales-mix variances are used to analyze sales performance and are sometimes used in the evaluation of sales and marketing personnel.

Review Questions

7-1 List the three components of a control system and give a brief explanation.

7-2 What is meant by the total standard cost of material? How is it computed?

7-3 List three possible causes for an unfavorable labor efficiency variance.

7-4 How might an unfavorable material price variance and a favorable labor efficiency variance be related?

7-5 What is meant by a theoretical (or ideal) standard?

7-6 How can standard costs be used in the financial services industry?

7-7 The typical way to calculate a material price variance does not yield a pure price variance. Explain.

7-8 Should standard costs be used for planning purposes?

7-9 Should cost standards be easy or difficult to attain? Discuss.

7-10 "Standard direct labor hours allowed for work done are superior to actual direct labor hours as an activity measure." Comment.

Exercises   **7-11 Analysis of Cost Variances**   Prepare an analysis of labor rate and labor efficiency variances from the following information:

Process	Workers	Standard Hours	Standard Costs per Hour	Total
1	Jones	1	$12.00	$12.00
2	Smith	3	$16.00	48.00
				$60.00

During January, Jones worked 40 hours and Smith worked 180 hours. Jones earned $520 and Smith $3,060. Fifty units of product were produced. All of Smith's and Jones's time was assigned to this product. Smith filled in and worked on process 1 for 8 hours.

7-12 Computing Variances   The Bobb Company makes one product. The following data are accumulated for the month of July. Overhead is applied using standard direct labor hours.

	Standard	Actual	Budgeted
Hours of direct labor	95,000	90,000	100,000
Dollars of direct labor cost	$760,000	$740,000	$800,000
Pounds of material A used	76,000	75,000	80,000
Dollar amount of material A used	$228,000	$228,000	$240,000
Variable manufacturing overhead		$ 82,000	$100,000
Fixed manufacturing overhead		$ 47,500	$ 50,000
Units of production		38,000	40,000

REQUIRED:

Compute the material and labor variances.

7-13 Material and Labor Variances   The Stewart Aluminum Company manufactures aluminum cans for tennis balls. The following data is available for January.

	Direct Material	Direct Labor
Actual price	$8.00/pound	$15.00/hour
Standard price or rate	$7.50/pound	$14.00/hour
Standard quantity allowed	.10/pound	.25/hour
Actual quantity used	1,300 pounds	2,850 hours
Actual output	12,000 cans	12,000 cans

REQUIRED:

a. Compute the material price and quantity variances and the labor rate and efficiency variances.

b. Compute the joint price quantity variance and the pure price variance for material.

7-14 Labor and Material Variances   The Archer Company produces one product. For the month of September, the following information is accumulated:

	Actual Usage	Standard Hours and Tons	Actual Cost	Standard Cost per Unit
Direct labor	11,000 hrs	10,000 hrs	$225,000	$ 21.00/hr
Direct material	530 tons	540 tons	52,650	100.00/ton

	Budgeted Overhead for Year[a]	Actual Overhead for Month
Variable	$288,000	$20,900
Fixed	144,000	13,200

[a] Equal amount each month.

The overhead is budgeted for average (normal) activity of 144,000 hours of direct labor per year and 12,000 hours per month.

REQUIRED:

Compute the labor and material variances.

7-15 Favorable and Unfavorable Variances The Auburn Company manufactures one product, Bypo. The standards for one unit of Bypo are as follows:

10 lb. of material X at $1/lb	$10
3 hr. of direct labor at $9/hr	27
Overhead:	
Fixed: $2/DLH	6
Variable: $1/DLH	3
Total standard cost for one unit of Bypo	$46

Material X is added at the beginning of the manufacturing process. Overhead is budgeted on the basis of direct labor hours.

The inventory of work in process on February 1 consisted of 900 units of Bypo, $66\frac{2}{3}$ percent complete with regard to labor and overhead. A purchase of 92,000 pounds of material X was made during February at a cost of $1.05 per pound. During the month, 26,000 hours of direct labor were worked at an average wage of $9.30 per hour. February plant capacity was 30,000 direct labor hours. Actual fixed overhead costs amounted to $63,000 during February, and actual variable overhead costs amounted to $26,000 during the month.

During February, 8,900 units of Bypo were completed. The inventory of work in process as of February 28 consisted of 1,000 units of Bypo, 80 percent with regard to labor and overhead.

The entire 92,000 pounds of material purchased was used during February.

REQUIRED:

Compute labor and material variances for the month of February. Indicate whether the variances are unfavorable or favorable.

Problems

7-16 Developing Standards Associated Media Graphics (AMG) is a rapidly expanding company that mass reproduces instructional materials. Ralph Boston, owner and manager of AMG, has tried to provide a quality product at a fair price with delivery on the promised due date. Expanding sales have been attributed to this philosophy. Boston finds it increasingly difficult to supervise personally the operations of AMG and is beginning to institute an organizational structure that would facilitate management control.

Recently operating departments were renamed cost centers, with control over departmental operations transferred from Boston to each departmental manager. However, quality control still reports directly to Boston, as do the finance and accounting functions. A materials manager was hired to purchase all raw materials and to oversee the inventory handling (such as receiving and storage) and record keeping functions. The materials manager also is responsible for maintaining an adequate inventory based on planned production levels.

The loss of personal control over the operations of AMG led Boston to look for a method of efficiently evaluating performance. Dave Cress, a new cost accountant, proposed the use of a standard cost system. Variances for material, labor, and manufacturing overhead could then be calculated and reported directly to Boston.

REQUIRED:

a. Assume that Associated Media Graphics is going to implement a standard cost system and establish standards for materials and labor. Discuss how each of the following cost components should be incorporated into the cost system:

(1) The individuals who should be involved in setting the standards.

(2) The factors that should be considered in establishing the standards.

b. Describe the basis for assignment of responsibility under a standard cost system. *(CMA adapted)*

7-17 Computing Material Variances The following information applies to one day's production:

Units of good product started and finished	5,000
Standard material per unit	2 lbs
Actual material used	11,000 lbs
Standard price per pound of material	$2.25/lb
Actual price per pound of material	$2.35/lb

REQUIRED:

a. Compute the material quantity variance.

b. Compute the material price variance.

c. Compute the total variance from standard cost.

d. Part of the variance was caused by a higher price paid for units that should not have been used. Compute this amount. Compute a price and quantity variance to accompany it so that the total variance is equal to the answer for c. Explain the difference in results in relation to a and b and discuss the value, if any, of the refinement in calculation.

7-18 Explaining Material Variances

Memorandum

To: The Controller, Krocks and Potts Company
From: Thebos
Subject: Price Variance — Ball Clay, April

I note that the total material variance for the month of April amounted to $1,050 despite continuance of our normal production level of 36 units. Can you give me any explanation of why this occurred?

The data in the controller's records indicate

1. Equivalent units of work (material, Ball Clay) in mixing: April	36
2. Standard pounds of Ball Clay required per unit	875
3. Standard purchase price per April budget	$0.80/lb
4. Purchases of Ball Clay (30,000 lbs)	$23,100
5. Requisitions by Mixing Departments (@ average April price)	35,000 lbs
6. Inventories of Ball Clay at Average Prices	
April 1, 30,000 lbs	$21,900
May 1, 25,000 lbs	$18,750

The periodic inventory method is used to value raw materials and to cost out requisitions on a first-in, first-out (FIFO) basis.

REQUIRED:

As controller write a brief reply to the boss. In your response indicate (a) how the $1,050 figure was derived, (b) what — if any — modifications you would make to this figure, and (c) any reasons that might explain (regardless of your personal knowledge of their actual occurrence) the price variance.

7-19 Material Mix and Yield Variance   (see Appendix 7A) Energy Products Company produces a gasoline additive, Gas Gain. This product increases engine efficiency and improves gasoline mileage by creating a more complete burn in the combustion process.

Careful controls are required during the production process to ensure that the proper mix of input chemicals is achieved and that evaporation is controlled. If the controls are not effective, there can be loss of output and efficiency.

The standard cost of producing a 500-liter batch of Gas Gain is $135. The standard materials mix and related standard cost of each chemical used in a 500-liter batch are as follows:

Chemical	Standard Input Quantity in Liters	Standard Cost per Liter	Total Cost
Echol	200	$.200	$ 40.00
Protex	100	.425	42.50
Benz	250	.150	37.50
CT-40	50	.300	15.00
	600		$135.00

The quantities of chemicals purchased and used during the current production period are shown in the schedule below. A total of 140 batches of Gas Gain were manufactured during the current production period. Energy Products determines its cost and chemical usage variations at the end of each production period.

Chemical	Quantity Purchased	Total Purchase Price	Quantity Used
Echol	25,000 liters	$ 5,365	26,600 liters
Protex	13,000 liters	6,240	12,880 liters
Benz	40,000 liters	5,840	37,800 liters
CT-40	7,500 liters	2,220	7,140 liters
Total	85,500 liters	$19,665	84,420 liters

REQUIRED:

a. Calculate the purchase price variances by chemical for Energy Products Company.

b. Calculate the total material quantity variance related to Gas Gain for Energy Products Company and then analyze this total quantity variance into the following two components:

(1) Mix variance.

(2) Yield variance. *(CMA adapted)*

7-20 Material and Labor Variances H. T. Johnson and Sons, Inc. employs a standard cost system. Raw materials inventory is carried at standard cost. The company's standards for the prime costs of one unit of product are as follows:

	Standard Quantity	Standard Price	Standard Cost
Direct material	12 lbs	$ 2.00/lb	$24.00
Direct labor	.5 hr	$15.00/hr	7.50
			$31.50

During September, the company purchased 340,000 pounds of direct material at a total cost of $714,000. The total direct labor cost for September was $169,400. The company manufactured 20,000 units of product during September using 252,000 pounds of direct material and 11,000 direct labor hours.

REQUIRED:

Compute the following variances for September:

a. The direct material purchase price variance.

b. The direct material quantity variance.

c. The direct labor rate variance.

d. The direct labor efficiency variance.

7-21 Sales Mix and Quantity Variances (see Appendix 7B) The Mount Pleasant Sports Company produces balls for racquet ball, squash and hand ball. The forecast and actual sales for 19x3 are the following:

	Forecast Sales	Actual Sales
Racquet balls	5,000	4,000
Squash balls	10,000	11,000
Hand balls	10,000	12,000
Total	25,000	27,000

The projected contribution margins for the three products are as follows:

Racquet balls	$.20
Squash balls	$.10
Hand balls	$.15

REQUIRED:

Compute the following for 19x3:

a. The sales-volume variance.

b. The sales quantity variance.

c. The sales-mix variance.

7-22 Reporting Procedures to Control Indirect Labor Costs   The Small Automobile Company (sales, $1 billion per year) is very much concerned with the control of indirect labor. To help control this cost, the following report is prepared monthly:

Plant _____   **Department** _____   **Month** _____

Code Number	Account Title	Budgeted for Month	Actual Exp. for Month	Variance	Budgeted for Year	Actual Exp. for Year

This report is expensive to prepare ($400,000 per year) and has several weaknesses. The timing of the report is not good. It is distributed twenty working days after the end of the month. Some executives feel that by the time they receive the report, it is too late to take action.

Another difficulty has to do with sick leave and vacations. When a person on sick leave or vacation is replaced by a temporary worker, the wage cost of this extra worker appears as a variance because it has not been budgeted for the month. This annoys executives who have to explain why they had an unfavorable variance.

The company has a procedure that strictly ties the wage rates to the type of work being done. A higher grade of labor cannot be used for a job other than that approved without the personnel department's written permission. Changes in wage rates (increases in wages) are also strictly controlled, requiring the permission of the head of the department, the immediate supervisor, the personnel department, and the budget control officer.

Because wage rates are so tightly controlled, wage rate variances appear only because some authorized wage rate changes are not yet incorporated into the budget figure. The significant variances in labor expense are caused by an excessive number of hours worked in proportion to the amount of direct labor activity budgeted.

An analyst in the budget control group has recommended that the present report be replaced by a report that compares budgeted manpower with actual manpower (a head-count basis). Overtime would be controlled by a separate but accompanying report. These reports could be distributed on the second working day following the end of the month.

REQUIRED:

Assuming that you are controller of the Small Automobile Company, what action will you take?

7-23 **Analyzing Sales Performance Using Variances** (see Appendix 7B) Budgeted and actual income statements for Xerbert Company for 19x2 are shown below.

XERBERT COMPANY
Budgeted and Actual Income Statements
for the Year Ended December 31, 19x2
(000s omitted)

	Budget			Actual		
	Xenox	Xeon	Total	Xenox	Xeon	Total
Unit sales	150	100	250	130	130	260
Net dollar sales	$900	$1,000	$1,900	$780	$1,235	$2,015
Variable expenses	450	750	1,200	390	975	1,365
Contribution margin	$450	$ 250	$ 700	$390	$ 260	$ 650
Fixed expenses:						
Manufacturing			$ 200			$ 190
Marketing			153			140
Administration			95			90
Total fixed expenses			$ 448			$ 420
Income before taxes			$ 252			$ 230

REQUIRED:

a. Compute the percentage difference between actual and budgeted breakeven in units.

b. The 19x2 budgeted total volume of 250,000 units was based on Xerbert achieving a market share of 10 percent. Actual industry volume reached 2,580,000 units. Calculate the portion of Xerbert's increased volume due to improved market share.

c. Compute the variance of actual contribution margin from budgeted contribution margin attributable to sales price.

d. Compute the variance of actual contribution margin from budgeted contribution attributable to unit variable cost changes.

e. Xerbert Company considers Xenox and Xeon as substitutes for each other. Therefore, it separates the portion of the variance in contribution margin due to changes in volume into a mix variance and a quantity variance. These two variances are based on budgeted unit contribution margins.

(1) Compute the variance in contribution margin from budgeted contribution margin attributed to a change in mix.

(2) Compute the variance in contribution margin from budgeted contribution attributed to a change in quantity. *(CMA adapted)*

8

Flexible Budgeting and Standard Overhead Costs

LEARNING OBJECTIVES

After studying this chapter, you should be able to:

1 Explain the concept of a flexible budget for overhead.

2 Calculate variances for variable and fixed overhead.

3 Interpret overhead variances.

4 Explain how differences between standard (predetermined) and actual costs are accounted for at the end of an accounting period.

5 Use a standard costing system to accumulate, classify, and assign costs to products.

6 Explain how standard costs are used for both product costing and cost control purposes.

*T*his chapter turns from direct material and direct labor variances to overhead variances. Overhead variances for indirect costs are usually computed separately for variable overhead and fixed overhead. There are two variable overhead variances, the spending variance (or budget variance) and the efficiency variance. A **spending variance** occurs when the variable overhead incurred differs from the variable overhead budgeted for the actual level of operations. An **efficiency variance** occurs when the actual amount of the production activity measure on which overhead application is based differs from the standard amount of that activity.

There are also two fixed overhead variances: the budget variance, and the volume variance (or denominator variance). The **budget variance** is the difference between the budgeted fixed cost and the actual fixed overhead for the period. The **volume variance** is the difference between the fixed overhead applied to production and the budgeted fixed overhead.

Overhead Budgets

Standard costs are useful in controlling direct materials and direct labor costs; an overhead budget is useful in controlling indirect costs. In developing an overhead budget, managers estimate the overhead costs that should be incurred at different levels of production activity. Actual overhead costs are then compared to the estimated amount for that production level. This overhead budget is called a **flexible budget** because it is adjusted to the actual level of activity. Using a flexible budget avoids the problem of using a budget set for one level of production activity to evaluate the actual results for another level of production activity.

Flexible Budgets

A flexible overhead budget for the Bradley Corporation for 19x1 is presented in Exhibit 8-1. (The Bradley Corporation illustration is a continuation of the illustration used in Chapter 7.) This budget includes different dollar amounts for different amounts of direct labor hours. Other common measures of activity include machine hours, amount of materials used, and number of units produced. The activity measure used should be easily understood, readily available at a reasonable cost, and subject to adequate control.

Notice that there are really five overhead budgets in Exhibit 8-1, based on different levels of direct labor hours ranging from 80,000 hours to 100,000 hours.

Exhibit 8-1 includes both variable and fixed overhead items. The variable overhead items include indirect labor, lubricants and supplies, utilities, and other variable overhead items. The usage of these items is expected to vary in proportion to changes in direct labor hours. The fixed overhead items include supervision, depreciation, and

EXHIBIT 8-1

Flexible Overhead Budget

	Direct Labor Hours				
	80,000	85,000	90,000	95,000	100,000
Variable overhead:					
Indirect labor ($1.00/hr)	$ 80,000	$ 85,000	$ 90,000	$ 95,000	$100,000
Lubricants, supplies					
($.60/hr)	48,000	51,000	54,000	57,000	60,000
Utilities ($.40/hr)	32,000	34,000	36,000	38,000	40,000
Other variable					
overhead ($1.00/hr)	80,000	85,000	90,000	95,000	100,000
Total variable					
overhead ($3.00/hr)	$240,000	$255,000	$270,000	$285,000	$300,000
Fixed overhead:					
Supervision	$ 80,000	$ 80,000	$ 80,000	$ 80,000	$ 80,000
Depreciation	160,000	160,000	160,000	160,000	160,000
Other fixed	60,000	60,000	60,000	60,000	60,000
Total fixed	$300,000	$300,000	$300,000	$300,000	$300,000
Total overhead	$540,000	$555,000	$570,000	$585,000	$600,000
Variable overhead rate	$3.00	$3.00	$3.00	$3.00	$3.00
Fixed overhead rate	3.75	3.53	3.33	3.16	3.00
Total overhead rate	$6.75	$6.53	$6.33	$6.16	$6.00

other fixed overhead. These items are expected to remain constant over the different levels of direct labor hours for which the costs have been computed.

The data presented in Exhibit 8-1 are for activity levels ranging from 80,000 to 100,000 direct labor hours, but the formula underlying these data can be used for other activity levels as well. The flexible budget for other activity levels can be calculated by using the following relationship:

Flexible overhead budget = Fixed overhead + Variable overhead

= $300,000 + ($3.00 per hour)(Direct labor hours)

The general formula for the flexible budget is as follows:

$$Y = a + bX$$

where Y = total overhead cost, a = fixed overhead cost, b = unit variable overhead cost, and X = the activity level on which the overhead budget is based (such as direct labor hours).

The predetermined overhead rates for different levels of activity are also presented in Exhibit 8-1. The variable overhead rate remains constant at $3.00 per direct labor hour across the different levels of activity because variable overhead costs are assumed to vary in proportion to changes in activity levels. The variable overhead rate is computed by dividing the total variable overhead cost by the number of direct labor hours. The expected total variable overhead is $240,000 at 80,000 direct labor hours and $300,000 at 100,000 direct labor hours, reflecting the constant variable overhead rate of $3.00 per direct labor hour.

The fixed overhead rate changes for different levels of activity. The total fixed overhead cost does not change over the levels of activity presented in Exhibit 8-1. At each level of activity, the total fixed overhead cost is expected to be $300,000. However, the fixed overhead rate does change. The total fixed overhead rate is computed by dividing the total fixed overhead cost by the number of direct labor hours. The higher the level of activity, the lower the fixed overhead rate. The selection of the appropriate activity level, sometimes referred to as the denominator level, is important because it affects the fixed overhead rate. Selection of the appropriate level of activity (denominator level) for calculating fixed overhead rates requires judgment.

The flexible overhead budget presented in Exhibit 8-1 represents a simplification of reality. Not all overhead costs can be conveniently and easily categorized as variable or fixed. As was discussed in Chapter 2, some costs (semivariable costs and step-fixed costs) have both fixed and variable elements. Ideally, the fixed and variable elements should be separated and budgeted individually. Even fixed overhead items can change if activity changes are large enough.

Only a single measure of activity, direct labor hours, was used to estimate the overhead costs presented in Exhibit 8-1. Some overhead items may not be sufficiently predicted by one measure of activity. Several measures of activity (such as direct labor hours, machine hours, and amount of materials used) may have to be used to estimate overhead costs at different activity levels. Exhibit 8-1 assumes a linear (straight-line) relationship between variable overhead costs and direct labor hours. However, the relationships between some overhead costs and measures of activity may reflect other than linear behavior patterns. Finally, estimating overhead costs for different activity levels is limited to a range of activity that is relevant to the company's experience. Companies seldom operate at all possible levels of activity. Rather, their experience is limited to a range of activity levels, and it may be difficult to estimate overhead costs outside of this range. Cost estimation procedures are explored in depth in Chapter 13.

Variable Overhead Variances

Flexible overhead budgets provide the basis for calculating variable overhead variances. The two variable overhead variances — the spending variance and the efficiency variance — are analogous to the labor rate and labor efficiency variances discussed in Chapter 7. A spending variance results when the actual variable overhead cost for a certain level of production activity differs from the variable overhead specified by the flexible budget for that level of activity.

Variable overhead spending variance = Actual variable overhead
$$- \text{(Actual hours}$$
$$\times \text{Standard variable overhead rate)}$$
$$= H_A V_A - H_A V_S = H_A(V_A - V_S)$$

Assume that the actual variable overhead cost incurred by Bradley Corporation in 19x1 totaled $238,000, that 85,000 direct labor hours were actually incurred, and that the standard direct labor hours allowed for the output obtained totaled 80,000 hours. The actual variable overhead rate for the direct labor hours incurred is computed by dividing the actual variable overhead cost of $238,000 by the 85,000 actual direct labor hours. Thus we obtain $2.80 per direct labor hour. The variable overhead spending variance is computed as follows:

Variable overhead spending variance $= H_A(V_A - V_S)$
$$= 85,000(\$2.80 - \$3.00)$$
$$= \$17,000\ F$$

where H_A = actual hours, V_A = actual variable overhead rate, and V_S = standard variable overhead rate. The actual variable overhead cost is equal to $H_A \times V_A$.

An efficiency variance occurs because the actual hours worked differ from the standard hours:

Variable overhead efficiency variance = Standard variable overhead rate
$$\times \text{(Actual hours} - \text{Standard hours)}$$
$$= V_S(H_A - H_S)$$

The efficiency variance is computed as follows:

Variable overhead efficiency variance $= V_S(H_A - H_S)$
$$= \$3.00(85,000 - 80,000)$$
$$= \$15,000\ U$$

The actual and budgeted variable overhead costs for Bradley Corporation for 19x1 are compared in Exhibit 8-2. Column (1) shows the actual overhead cost incurred in 19x1. Column (2) shows the budgeted amount for the 85,000 direct labor hours actually incurred in 19x1. The difference between the total for column (1), the variable overhead incurred, and the total for column (2), the variable overhead budgeted for the actual level of direct labor hours incurred, was defined earlier as a spending variance. An item by item analysis reveals that the $17,000 favorable spending variance resulted because the reduced spending for indirect labor, lubricants and supplies, and other variable overhead more than offset the increased spending for utilities.

Columns (2) and (3) in Exhibit 8-2 compare the budgeted variable overhead cost at the actual and standard hours for the work completed. The difference between

EXHIBIT 8-2

Comparison of Actual and Budgeted Variable Overhead Costs

	(1) Actual	(2) Budgeted Variable Overhead at Actual Direct Labor Hours	(3) Budgeted Variable Overhead at Standard Direct Labor Hours Allowed
Direct labor hours	85,000	85,000	80,000
Variable overhead:			
Indirect labor	$ 80,000	$ 85,000	$ 80,000
Lubricants, supplies	44,000	51,000	48,000
Utilities	36,000	34,000	32,000
Other variable	78,000	85,000	80,000
Total variable	$238,000	$255,000	$240,000

$17,000 F	$15,000 U
Spending variance	Efficiency variance

$2,000 F
Total variable overhead variance

these budgeted amounts was defined earlier as an efficiency variance. The $2,000 favorable total variable overhead variance reflects the difference between the favorable spending variance of $17,000 (obtained because of reduced costs) and the unfavorable efficiency variance of $15,000 (obtained because 5,000 additional direct labor hours were needed to achieve the work completed).

If variable overhead costs were applied to production on the basis of the direct labor hours incurred, only the budget in column (2) would be used to evaluate the variable overhead cost incurred and only a spending variance would be identified. There would be no efficiency variance. The budget in column (3) is used if variable overhead costs are applied to production on the basis of standard hours. Column (3) focuses on the variable overhead costs that should have been incurred based on the direct labor hours that should have been used to achieve the work completed. The standard hours allowed are based on the output achieved, not the inputs consumed. The column (3) amount is the flexible budget.

A graphic approach also can be used to analyze variable overhead variances. This approach is especially useful for visualizing the relationships among the variances that have been discussed. The variable overhead variances are shown in Exhibit 8-3. Line OB is the variable overhead budgeted for the different levels of activity and also shows the amount of overhead applied to production for different standard hours of activity.

EXHIBIT 8-3

Variable Overhead Variances

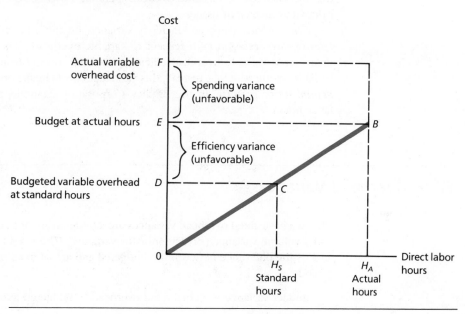

Thus, for any number of standard direct labor hours, the amount of variable overhead to be applied to production may be found by the intersection of *OB* and a vertical line (*H$_s$C*) extended up from the appropriate number of standard direct labor hours on the horizontal axis. The amount of overhead applied to production is *OD*. In the Bradley Corporation example, this is equal to 80,000 standard direct labor hours times the $3.00 variable overhead rate, or $240,000. For any number of actual direct labor hours, the variable overhead that should have been incurred (the budgeted amount) can be found by the intersection of *OB* and a vertical line (*H$_A$B*) extended up from the actual direct labor hours measured on the horizontal axis, *H$_A$*. The amount of budgeted variable overhead, given actual direct labor hours, is *OE*. For the example, this is $255,000. The difference *OE − OD* is the variable overhead efficiency variance of $15,000. It is unfavorable because the standard hours allowed, given actual output, are less than the actual hours worked. We have also incorporated the actual variable overhead cost in Exhibit 8-3 to illustrate the spending variance *FE*. It also is unfavorable in this case.

Of the two variances described above for variable overhead, the spending variance is the most useful for control purposes. An unfavorable spending variance means that more money was spent for variable overhead costs than was anticipated, after making an adjustment for the actual direct labor hours worked. The company may have paid higher prices for some variable overhead items than was anticipated, as, for example, when electric rates per kilowatt hour rise unexpectedly. Alternatively, the company may have used some variable overhead items inefficiently, relative to the variable overhead standards, as when electricity is wasted. Of course, it is possible that the unfavorable variable overhead spending variance resulted from both higher prices and inefficient usage.

The variable overhead efficiency variance, on the other hand, does not have a control interpretation with respect to variable overhead. It is *not* the case that an unfavorable variable overhead efficiency variance results from inefficient usage of variable overhead items. Instead, this variance reflects inefficiency in the usage of the *denominator activity*. In the Bradley Corporation example, this activity is direct labor hours.

Fixed Overhead Variances

The two basic fixed overhead variances are a budget variance (or spending variance) and a volume variance (or denominator variance). The fixed overhead budget variance is the difference between the budgeted and actual fixed overhead costs for the period:

Budget variance = Actual fixed overhead − Budgeted fixed overhead

The volume variance is the difference between the fixed overhead applied to production and the budgeted fixed overhead costs for the period:

Volume variance = Fixed overhead applied − Fixed overhead budgeted

= Fixed overhead rate × (Budgeted hours − Standard hours)

Assume that the fixed overhead costs incurred by Bradley Corporation in 19x1 totaled $245,000, that 85,000 direct labor hours were used, and that the standard direct labor hours that should have been used totaled 80,000 hours. Also assume that the budgeted fixed overhead costs were $300,000 and that the normal activity level (denominator level) was 100,000 direct labor hours. Therefore, the fixed overhead rate was $3.00 per direct labor hour ($300,000/100,000 hours). The fixed overhead budget variance for Bradley Corporation for 19x1 was

Budget variance = Actual fixed overhead − Budgeted fixed overhead

= $245,000 − $300,000

= $55,000 *F*

The volume variance for Bradley Corporation for 19x1 is

Volume variance = Fixed overhead rate × (Budgeted hours − Standard hours)

= $3.00 × (100,000 − 80,000)

= $60,000 *U*

The actual and budgeted fixed overhead costs for Bradley Corporation in 19x1 are compared in Exhibit 8-4. Column (1) shows the fixed overhead costs incurred for 19x1. Column (2) shows the budgeted fixed overhead costs for 19x1. These budgeted costs would be the same at activity levels of either 85,000 or 80,000 direct labor hours because the flexible budget for fixed overhead costs is constant across different levels of activity. The difference between the total for column (1) and the total for column (2) is the budget variance. The actual costs incurred for supervision, depreciation, and other fixed overhead are less than the budgeted amounts, resulting in a favorable budget variance of $55,000.

Column (3) in Exhibit 8-4 shows the amount of fixed overhead costs applied to production. The fixed overhead rate was $3.00 at an assumed denominator level of 100,000 direct labor hours. The standard hours allowed for the output achieved were 80,000 hours. As a result, $240,000 ($3.00 × 80,000 hours) of fixed overhead costs are applied to production. The volume variance, the difference between the total for column (2) and the total for column (3), arises whenever the standard hours allowed differ from the denominator level used for computing the fixed overhead rate. At 100,000 standard direct labor hours, all of the budgeted fixed overhead costs would have been applied to production: $3.00 × 100,000 hours = $300,000.

A graph that can be used to analyze fixed overhead variances is given in Exhibit 8-5. In this case, line *OB* has a more limited significance than line *OB* in Exhibit 8-3 for variable overhead costs. In Exhibit 8-5 line *OB* no longer represents the budgeted overhead costs for different levels because fixed overhead costs are constant over the

---

EXHIBIT 8-4

Comparison of Actual and Budgeted Fixed Overhead Costs

	(1) Actual	(2) Budget	(3) Applied
Direct labor hours	80,000	85,000	80,000
Fixed overhead:			
Supervision	$ 65,000	$ 80,000	$ 64,000
Depreciation	150,000	160,000	128,000
Other fixed	30,000	60,000	48,000
Total fixed	$245,000	$300,000	$240,000

| $55,000 F | $60,000 U |
| Budget variance | Volume variance |

| $5,000 U |
Total fixed overhead variance

EXHIBIT 8-5

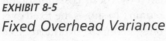

Fixed Overhead Variance

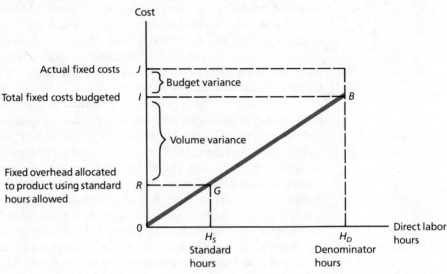

entire range of activity being considered. Instead, the line *OB* in Exhibit 8-5 represents the amount of fixed overhead costs *applied* to production at different levels of standard direct labor hours. Note that in Exhibit 8-5, the budget variance is unfavorable, rather than favorable as in the Bradley Corporation example.

Interpretation of Overhead Variances

The overhead variances for Bradley Corporation for 19x1 are summarized in Exhibit 8-6. The $3,000 unfavorable total overhead variance reflects the amount of overhead underapplied to production in 19x1. The reasons for this underapplication are reflected in the four overhead variances: variable overhead spending and efficiency variances, and fixed overhead budget and volume variances. These variances explain why the actual overhead costs incurred in 19x1 differ from those applied to production, but they differ in their significance for cost control.

In Exhibit 8-6 the variable overhead spending variance and the fixed overhead budget variance have been combined to form a single variance called a budget variance, which results in three overhead variances and sometimes is referred to as a **three-way analysis** of overhead variances. The budget and efficiency variances also

EXHIBIT 8-6

Summary Analysis of Overhead Variances

	Actual	Budget Actual Hours	Budget Standard Hours	Applied
Variable overhead	$238,000	$255,000	$240,000	$240,000
Fixed overhead	245,000	300,000	300,000	240,000
Total overhead	$483,000	$555,000	$540,000	$480,000

| $72,000 F | $15,000 U | $60,000 U |
| Budget variance | Efficiency variance | Volume variance |

| $3,000 U |

Total overhead variance
(Underapplied overhead)

may be combined, which results in only two overhead variances and is referred to as a **two-way analysis** of overhead variances.

The $72,000 favorable budget variance reflects a $17,000 favorable variance for variable overhead and a $55,000 favorable variance for fixed overhead. Budget variances are considered controllable by operating managers, at least to some extent. The budgeted amounts for the direct labor hours incurred reflect the use of a flexible budget to control overhead costs. However, budget variances can reflect conditions that have changed since the flexible budget was established or the effects of random factors over which operating managers have relatively little control.

The $15,000 unfavorable efficiency variance for variable overhead is also considered to be controllable by operating managers. This efficiency variance is tied to the labor efficiency variance because the measure of activity used for variable overhead is direct labor hours. Essentially, the unfavorable efficiency variance estimates the additional variable overhead that should be incurred because of the inefficiency of direct labor. There is no efficiency variance for fixed overhead because fixed overhead costs are not expected to be affected by changes in levels of activity within the relevant range of production activity.

The $60,000 unfavorable volume variance is not considered to be controllable by operating managers. This variance resulted because the company did not operate at the denominator level of activity. Because the denominator level often reflects a normal level of activity, questions can be raised about why the corporation failed to achieve this level. For whatever reasons, however, the primary mechanism for controlling fixed overhead costs is the fixed overhead budget variance. Applying fixed overhead costs to production facilitates product costing but not cost control.

Product Costing

Up to this point, the discussion of variances has focused on the use of standard costs for cost control. The calculation and interpretation of variances is critical in this activity. Now attention is turned to the use of standard costing systems for product costing. It may be helpful at this time to review the first section of Chapter 4, entitled Overview of Product Costing Systems. In a standard product-costing system, the standard costs of production are entered into work in process and flow through the manufacturing accounts to finished goods and ultimately to cost of goods sold. The Bradley Company illustration used throughout this and the preceding chapter is based on a job-order costing system. The use of standards under a process-costing system is illustrated in Appendix 8B.

Disposition of Cost Variances

The disposition of cost variances is relevant for product costing and financial statement preparation but not for cost control. It is essential to keep in mind the distinction between product costing and cost control. Cost variances may be disposed of by following either of two procedures. First, cost variances can be considered period costs (noninventoriable costs). These variances are treated as costs of inefficiency (or benefits of unusual efficiency) and not costs of product. Thus, they are charged against the revenues of the period. Alternatively, cost variances can be considered product costs (inventoriable costs). These variances are treated as a cost of production and are allocated to work in process, finished goods, and cost of goods sold.

Of more importance than the treatment of specific variances is an appreciation of what is affected by the choice of the procedure. Both the inventory valuation and the measurement of income are affected. The control of costs is not directly affected because the cost variances are analyzed in the same manner regardless of their ultimate disposition for financial statement purposes. Practical considerations, such as the costs of record keeping, may result in expensing all variances as period costs. Under this approach, all variances are simply closed into cost of goods sold.

The details of prorating cost variances to work-in-process inventory, finished-goods inventory, and cost of goods sold are covered in Appendix 8C.

Overview of Standard Costing Systems

The following example illustrates standard cost accounting systems. The data is consistent with that presented throughout Chapters 7 and 8 for Bradley Corporation for 19x1. Typical general journal entries for a standard cost accounting system are provided. It is assumed that direct materials, direct labor, and overhead are charged to work in process using standard costs. Exhibit 8-7 shows the relationships among the accounts. It is useful to trace each entry to the accounts in Exhibit 8-7. The Actual Overhead account is a control account for accumulating actual overhead costs.

1. The Bradley Corporation purchased 100,000 pounds of direct materials for $330,000. The company computes the material price variance at the time of usage, so the actual cost of the material is debited to material inventory.

EXHIBIT 8-7

Diagram of Ledger Relationships for Standard Cost Accounting System

Material Inventory

(1)	330,000	(2) 297,000
(B)	33,000	

Material Price Variance

(2) 27,000	(11) 27,000

Material Quantity Variance

(2) 30,000	(11) 30,000

Accrued Payroll

	(3) 777,750

Labor Rate Variance

(3) 12,750	(11) 12,750

Labor Efficiency Variance

(3) 45,000	(11) 45,000

Variable Overhead Efficiency Variance

(10) 15,000	(11) 15,000

Variable Overhead Spending Variance

(11) 17,000	(10) 17,000

Fixed Overhead Volume Variance

(10) 60,000	(11) 60,000

Fixed Overhead Budget Variance

(11) 55,000	(10) 55,000

Actual Overhead

(5) 483,000	(10) 483,000

Applied Overhead

(10) 480,000	(4) 480,000

Selling and Administrative Expenses

(8) 270,000	

Sales Revenues

	(9) 1,500,000

Work in Process

(2)	240,000	(6) 1,440,000
(3)	720,000	
(4)	480,000	

Finished Goods

(6)	1,440,000	(7) 1,080,000
(11)	29,437	
(B)	389,437	

Cost of Goods Sold

(7)	1,080,000
(11)	88,313
(B)	1,168,313

(B) denotes account balance.

Direct Material Inventory   330,000
   Accounts Payable   330,000

To record purchase of materials.

2. Requisitions for 90,000 pounds of direct material were processed in 19x1. The standard allowance for materials is one pound per unit of product; the standard cost is $3.00 per pound. Notice in the entry below that material is removed from the material inventory account at its *actual* price and amount, but it is charged to work in process at its *standard* price and amount.

Work in Process   240,000
Material Price Variance   27,000
Material Quantity Variance   30,000
   Direct Material Inventory   297,000

To record requisitions of materials.

3. 85,000 hours of direct labor were used at a cost of $777,750. The standard allowance for direct labor is one direct labor hour per unit of product; the standard rate is $9.00 per hour. Note that labor cost is entered into work in process at its *standard* rate and quantity.

Work in Process   720,000
Labor Rate Variance   12,750
Labor Efficiency Variance   45,000
   Salaries and Wages Payable   777,750

To record direct labor cost.

4. The predetermined overhead rate of $6.00 per direct labor hour was based on estimated fixed overhead costs of $300,000, estimated variable overhead costs of $3.00 per direct labor hour, and a denominator level of 100,000 budgeted direct labor hours for 19x1. Because there were 80,000 *standard allowed hours,* given actual output, the overhead entered into work in process is 80,000 hours times $6.00 per hour.

Work in Process   480,000
   Applied Overhead   480,000

To apply overhead to products.

5. Actual overhead incurred was $483,000 in 19x1, of which $245,000 was fixed overhead and $238,000 was variable overhead.

Actual Overhead   483,000
   Miscellaneous Credits   483,000

To record overhead incurred.

6. 80,000 units of finished product were produced in 19x1. There was no work in process inventory at December 31, 19x1. Note that finished goods is increased by the *standard* cost of the units finished.

Finished Goods	1,440,000	
Work in Process		1,440,000

To record completed production.

7. 60,000 units of product were sold in 19x1. The cost of goods sold reflects the *standard* cost of the units sold.

Cost of Goods Sold	1,080,000	
Finished Goods Inventory		1,080,000

To record cost of units sold.

8. Selling and administrative expenses were $270,000 in 19x1.

Selling and Administrative Expenses	270,000	
Miscellaneous Credits		270,000

To record selling and administrative expenses.

9. Total sales revenues for 19x1 amounted to $1,500,000. All sales were on account.

Accounts Receivable	1,500,000	
Sales Revenue		1,500,000

To record sales on account.

10. The Actual Overhead and Applied Overhead accounts are closed in order to isolate the overhead variances.

Applied Overhead	480,000	
Variable Overhead Efficiency Variance	15,000	
Fixed Overhead Volume Variance	60,000	
Variable Overhead Spending Variance		17,000
Fixed Overhead Budget Variance		55,000
Actual Overhead		483,000

To record overhead variances.

11. The company prorates all variances across the manufacturing accounts. In this case, the variances are only prorated to finished goods and cost of goods sold because there was no ending work-in-process inventory.[1] The total variance is $117,750 (unfavorable). The proration calculation follows.

[1] A more complicated illustration of variance proration is given in Appendix 8C.

	Standard Cost	Per- centage	Total Variances	Prorated Variances
Finished Goods	$ 360,000	.25	117,750	$ 29,437[a]
Cost of Goods Sold	1,080,000	.75	117,750	88,313[a]
Total	$1,440,000			$117,750

[a] Rounded to whole numbers.

The following journal entry is made to close all variance accounts and prorate the variances to finished goods and cost of goods sold.

Finished Goods	29,437	
Cost of Goods Sold	88,313	
Variable Overhead Spending Variance	17,000	
Fixed Overhead Budget Variance	55,000	
Variable Overhead Efficiency Variance		15,000
Fixed Overhead Volume Variance		60,000
Material Price Variance		27,000
Material Quantity Variance		30,000
Labor Rate Variance		12,750
Labor Efficiency Variance		45,000

To close and prorate variance accounts.

The following income statement would result from these entries:

BRADLEY CORPORATION
Income Statement
for the Year Ended December 31, 19x1

Sales revenue	$1,500,000
Less cost of goods sold	1,168,313
Gross margin	$ 331,687
Less selling and administrative expenses	270,000
Net income	$ 61,687

Advantages of Standard Costing

The standard costing system in Exhibit 8-7 accounts for standard costs. Standard costs are charged to work in process and then transferred to finished goods and ultimately to cost of goods sold. The use of standard costs provides three important advantages.

First, standard costs *provide a basis for management by exception.* Exceptions (variances) can be isolated and responsibility for these exceptions assigned. The materials price, materials quantity, labor rate, and labor efficiency variances are used to isolate exceptions to what was expected about direct costs in advance of production. Consideration of these exceptions can result in changes in how products are manufactured or priced.

Second, standard costs *provide a basis for better comparisons.* Companies that use actual costing systems often compare actual results for the current period with the actual results for previous periods. The current month's results may be compared with those for the same month a year ago or the year-to-date results may be compared with those for the previous year. Comparisons with previous periods are usually inappropriate and often misleading. Almost every period is unique and atypical for various reasons. However, these reasons are usually overlooked when interperiod comparisons are made. Companies that use standard costing systems compare the actual results with the standards set for the current period. How good or useful this comparison is depends on how good the standards are. The use of standard costs provides the basis for comparing actual results with those expected for the current period and thereby avoids the problem of interperiod comparisons.

Third, standard costs *provide the basis for isolating unanticipated costs at various points in the production process.* An actual costing system results in all direct material, direct labor, and overhead costs being charged to work in process, and these costs are then passed along to finished-goods inventory and cost of goods sold. Changes in material prices are passed on to work-in-process departmental accounts. Material quantity, labor rate, and labor efficiency fluctuations are passed along to finished-goods inventory and cost of goods sold. Passing along actual costs results in cost fluctuations all along the production process. A standard costing system isolates changes in material prices so that these changes are not passed on to work in process departmental accounts. Moreover, material quantity, labor rate, and labor efficiency fluctuations are isolated in work-in-process accounts. They are not passed along to finished-goods inventory and cost of goods sold.

Standard Costing and Variance Analysis at Chrysler Motors Corporation

The final illustration of standard costing and variance analysis included here is a description provided by Chrysler Motors Corporation of the variances calculated in one of its automobile plants.

Material Price Variance

Chrysler establishes a standard cost per unit for each of its assembly components. When parts are purchased, the price actually paid is compared to the standard cost and a material price variance is computed. For example:

Part No. 04221448 — Windshield Wiper Cover

Standard cost per unit	.63
Actual cost per unit	.675
Number of units purchased	576
Material price variance = 576(.675 − .63) = $25.92 Unfavorable	

Material Quantity Variance

Chrysler has material quantity variances arise principally on indirect materials such as paints. For most direct materials, such as car hoods, there is a one-to-one relationship between materials and finished product. Any excessive use of these materials is generally characterized as a scrap, spoilage, or an inventory adjustment. Nevertheless, the concept of a quantity variance results from a comparison of actual quantity used with standard quantity, priced at standard cost, which is the price at which material enters raw material inventory. The variance is based on a periodic count of inventories. For example:

Material — Primer Gray Paint

Standard quantity per unit	.5 gallon
Actual production	4,000 units
Actual quantity used	2,080 gallons
Standard price per gallon	$2.30
Material quantity variance = (2,080 − 2,000)$2.30 = $184 Unfavorable	

Labor Rate Variance

Chrysler sets standard labor rates for departments based on rates set by union contracts and department worker classifications. Variances can arise due to the signing of a new contract or by the use of "out-of-class" labor. The labor rate variance is computed by comparing the actual and standard rates, multiplied by the actual hours worked. For example:

Department AA

Actual hours worked in the department	4,000 hours
Actual labor cost	$92,000
Actual labor rate	$23 per hour
Standard labor rate	$20 per hour
Labor rate variance = 4,000($23 − $20) = $12,000 Unfavorable	

Labor Efficiency Variance

Chrysler sets work standards based on an evaluation of the direct labor required to produce each assembly. The labor efficiency variance is computed by comparing actual and standard labor hours, multiplied by the standard wage rate. For example:

Department AA

Actual hours worked in the department   4,000 hours
Standard hours   4,200 hours
Standard labor rate $20
Labor efficiency variance = (4,000 − 4,200)$20 = $4,000 Favorable

Standard Variable Overhead Rate

Variable overhead costs are budgeted at Chrysler based on a standard production volume. An overhead rate is computed by dividing the total of these budgeted variable costs by budgeted direct labor dollars.

Chrysler computes separate standards and variances for indirect labor and other major components of variable overhead. The company does not separate out spending and efficiency variances.

Standard Fixed Overhead Rate

Fixed overhead costs are budgeted at Chrysler based on a standard production volume. An overhead rate is computed by dividing the total of these budgeted fixed costs by budgeted direct labor dollars.

Fixed Overhead Budget Variance

The fixed overhead budget variance is computed by comparing actual and budgeted fixed overhead. For example:

Actual fixed overhead $82,000
Budgeted fixed overhead $90,000
Fixed overhead budget variance = $82,000 − $90,000 = $8,000 Favorable

Fixed Overhead Application Variance

The fixed overhead application variance is computed by comparing budgeted fixed overhead with applied fixed overhead. For example:

Budgeted fixed overhead $90,000
Direct labor dollars $92,000
Standard fixed overhead rate $1.00 per direct labor dollar
Fixed overhead application variance = $90,000 − ($92,000)($1.00)
                                     = $2,000 Favorable

This variance was referred to as a volume or denominator variance earlier in the chapter.

Summary

Flexible overhead budgets are used to control overhead costs and to develop predetermined overhead rates for product costing. Overhead variances are usually divided into variable and fixed overhead variances. The variable overhead spending variance indicates the difference between the actual variable overhead incurred and the variable overhead budgeted given the actual level of the denominator activity. The variable overhead efficiency variance indicates the amount of variable overhead that should be incurred because the actual level of denominator activity differed from the standard level of denominator activity for the actual production achieved. The fixed overhead variances include a budget variance, which indicates the difference between the actual fixed overhead and budgeted fixed overhead, and a volume variance, which reflects the difference between the standard level of denominator activity and the denominator level used in calculating the predetermined fixed overhead rate. The variable overhead spending variance and the fixed overhead budget variance are controllable by operating managers, at least to some extent, and are useful in controlling overhead costs. The volume variance is not controllable by operating managers and is not useful for controlling costs.

If cost standards are properly set, the identification of significant cost variances is an important first step in controlling costs. The selection of those variances to be investigated and the determination of the causes are essential subsequent steps. For financial accounting purposes, individual cost variances can be treated as product costs and prorated among various inventory accounts and cost of goods sold, or they may be treated as period costs and credited to cost of goods sold. How cost variances are treated will affect inventory valuation and income determination.

Key Terms to Review

budget variance, p. 260
efficiency variance, p. 260
flexible budget, p. 260

spending variance, p. 260
three-way analysis, p. 268

two-way analysis, p. 269
volume variance, p. 260.

Review Problem

OVERHEAD VARIANCES

The following flexible budget pertains to the Jacksonville Foundry for one month. The company applies overhead on the basis of direct labor hours.

Direct labor hours	10,000	15,000	20,000
Variable overhead ($8 per hour)	$ 80,000	$120,000	$160,000
Fixed overhead	150,000	150,000	150,000

The standard quantity of direct labor per unit of product is 2.5 hours per unit. The fixed overhead rate is $7.50 per hour, based on an assumed denominator activity level of 10,000 direct labor hours.

During May, 6,000 units of product were produced. The actual quantity of labor used was 16,000 hours. Actual overhead costs amounted to $271,200, of which $140,000 related to fixed costs.

REQUIRED:

Calculate the following variances by drawing diagrams similar to those in Exhibits 8-2 and 8-4.

a. Variable-overhead spending variance.

b. Variable-overhead efficiency variance.

c. Fixed-overhead budget variance.

d. Fixed-overhead volume variance.

Solution to Review Problem

	Actual	Budgeted Variable Overhead at Actual Direct Labor Hours	Budgeted Variable Overhead at Standard Direct Labor Hours Allowed
Direct labor hours	16,000	16,000	15,000
Variable overhead	$131,200	$128,000[a]	$120,000[b]

| $3,200 U | $8,000 U |
| Spending variance | Efficiency variance |

| $11,200 U |
| Total variable overhead variance |

[a] 16,000 hours × $8.00 per hour = $128,000
[b] 15,000 hours × $8.00 per hour = $120,000

	Actual	Budget	Applied
Direct labor hours	16,000	20,000	15,000
Fixed overhead	$140,000	$150,000	$112,500[a]

| $10,000 F | $37,500 U |
| Budget variance | Volume variance |

| $27,500 U[b] |
| Total fixed overhead variance |

[a] 15,000 hours × $7.50 per hour = $112,500
[b] ($10,000) favorable budget variance
   37,500 unfavorable volume variance
  $27,500 unfavorable total fixed overhead variance

Suggested Readings

Baiman, S. "Agency Research in Managerial Accounting: A Survey." *Journal of Accounting Literature 1* (1982): 154–210.

Horngren, C. T. "A Contribution Margin Approach to the Analysis of Capacity Utilization." *Accounting Review* (April 1967): 254–64.

Itami, H. *Adaptive Behavior: Management Control and Information Analysis.* Sarasota, Fl.: American Accounting Association, 1977.

Magee, R. *Advanced Managerial Accounting.* New York: Harper & Row, 1986.

National Association of Accountants. *Research Reports Nos. 11, 15, 17, 22, and 28.*

Pollard, W. B. "Teaching Standard Costs: A Look at Textbook Differences in Overhead Variance Analysis." *Journal of Accounting Education* (Spring 1986): 211–20.

Ronen, J. "Capacity and Operating Variances: An Ex Post Approach." *Journal of Accounting Research* (Autumn 1970): 232–52.

APPENDIX 8A
Other Fixed Overhead Variances

Two fixed overhead variances, a budget variance and a volume variance, were described in the chapter. Some companies break the volume variance into a *fixed overhead efficiency variance* and a *fixed overhead activity variance.* The fixed overhead efficiency variance is calculated by multiplying the fixed overhead rate times the difference between the actual input hours and the standard hours allowed given actual output:

$$\text{Fixed overhead efficiency variance} = \text{Fixed overhead rate} \times (\text{Actual hours} - \text{Standard hours allowed})$$

Some managers believe that the fixed overhead efficiency variance provides a measure of how effectively the actual activity was used. For example, an unfavorable fixed overhead efficiency variance may indicate poorly motivated or poorly skilled workers.

The activity variance is calculated by multiplying the fixed overhead rate times the difference between the budgeted and actual hours as follows:

$$\text{Activity variance} = \text{Fixed overhead rate} \times (\text{Budgeted hours} - \text{Actual hours})$$

The activity variance represents the failure of actual activity to correspond to the denominator level. An unfavorable variance may be due to insufficient sales or equipment breakdowns that prevented the company from achieving the denominator level. A graphical solution for these additional fixed overhead variances is shown in Exhibit 8-8.

For the Bradley Corporation example used in this chapter, the actual direct labor hours were 85,000, the standard direct labor hours were 80,000, and the fixed overhead rate was $3.00 per direct labor hour for a denominator level of 100,000 direct labor hours for 19x1. The fixed overhead efficiency variance for 19x1 is calculated as follows:

$$\text{Fixed overhead efficiency variance} = \$3.00(85,000 - 80,000) = \$15,000 \; U$$

The activity variance for 19x1 is computed below:

$$\text{Activity variance} = \$3.00(100,000 - 85,000) = \$45,000 \; U$$

The total of the unfavorable fixed overhead efficiency variance of $15,000 and the unfavorable activity variance of $45,000 is the unfavorable volume variance of $60,000 shown in Exhibit 8-4.

Exhibit 8-9 illustrates an additional breakdown of the activity variance for fixed overhead for the Bradley Corporation for 19x1. Assume that the denominator level

EXHIBIT 8-8

Other Fixed Overhead Variances

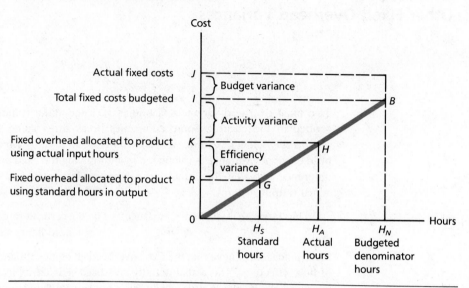

for Bradley Corporation for 19x1 was set at the practical capacity level, and assume that the normal level of activity was 90,000 direct labor hours.

The capacity variance is the difference between the practical capacity level and the normal level of activity (100,000 − 90,000 = 10,000 hours). Practical capacity is, however, difficult to define. Sometimes it is defined as the most efficient point of operation, or the point where average variable costs are at a minimum for a given set of fixed factors of production. However, many companies have relatively flat average variable cost and average total cost curves over a wide range of activity and thus can

EXHIBIT 8-9

Fixed-Overhead Variance Analysis

Standard hours allowed 80,000		Actual hours 85,000		Normal activity in hours 90,000		Practical capacity in hours 100,000
	Efficiency variance		Idle activity variance		Capacity variance	
			←——— Activity variance ———→			
	←——————————— Volume variance ———————————→					

produce past that point with little loss of efficiency. Practical capacity can also be defined as the minimum of the average total cost curve or the point at which the company would operate if there were no shortage of orders. The latter makes practical capacity equivalent to the point where marginal cost equals marginal revenue. A common practice is to base practical capacity on normal industry usage. Thus, if the industry works six days a week, twenty hours a day, this becomes practical capacity. Another industry may commonly work only eight hours a day, five days a week, and this becomes practical capacity. Practical capacity is defined here as the output at which long- and short-run costs are equal. If the company wants to produce more than the amount where this equality exists, it needs to obtain more fixed factors of production. When a company operates below practical capacity, as is often the case, the use of overhead rates based on practical capacity for product costing causes some of the budgeted fixed costs to be expensed.

Because a company can produce at its practical capacity level without expansion of facilities, the capacity variance is a measure of the slack in the system. Large and persistent variances here reflect on long-range planning decisions, the ability of the marketing activity to penetrate potential markets, or perhaps changes in economic conditions.

The normal level of activity to be encountered over a period of several years should be an important input to the design of a plant, and thus there should be a close relationship between normal activity and practical capacity. The relationship would probably be closer than that suggested by the figures for Bradley Corporation, although because of the nonsymmetric nature of cost behavior and opportunity losses, practical capacity would be planned to exceed normal demand for capacity. Wide differences between normal activity and practical capacity might reflect poor long-run activity forecasts in the past. If, on the other hand, use of an asset is expected to increase through time, the normal activity level in the early years could easily be less than the practical capacity.

The idle activity variance is the difference between the normal and actual levels of activity (90,000 − 85,000 = 5,000 hours). This variance represents the failure of actual activity to reach the normal level and could be due to poor scheduling or equipment breakdowns. It also may result from disruptions in marketing plans, inaccurate economic projections, or difficulties such as strikes.

The variances in Exhibit 8-9 are all expressed in physical units of output or input (actual or standard direct labor hours). These physical units can be converted to dollar measures by multiplying them by the fixed overhead rate of $3.00 for Bradley Corporation for 19x1. The resulting breakdown of the unfavorable volume variance of $60,000 would be as follows:

Efficiency variance	$15,000
Idle activity variance	15,000
Capacity variance	30,000
Volume variance	$60,000

These variances are not ideal measures. The real cost of idle activity (and perhaps inefficiency as well) is the contribution margin foregone because the facilities are not being used fully and effectively. The sum of these cost-based measures is at best an approximation of the opportunity cost of failing to make the most effective use of the fixed facilities.

APPENDIX 8B
Using Standard Costs with Process Costing

Our presentation of standard costing in Chapters 7 and 8 has been based on an illustration in which a job-order costing system was used. However, standard costing can also be used in conjunction with a process-costing system. Under standard costing, the costs of direct material, direct labor, and overhead entered into work-in-process inventory are all calculated at standard cost. Thus, the costs of material and conversion used in the process-costing calculations are standard costs.

The combined use of standard costing and process costing is illustrated using the data given in Exhibit 8-10. The Gator Company manufactures a single product using one department. The single direct material is introduced at the beginning of the production process. Each unit of product requires two pounds of direct material and three hours of direct labor.

EXHIBIT 8-10

Data for Process-Costing Illustration: Gator Company
STANDARDS

Direct material:	
Standard quantity allowed per product unit	2 pounds
Standard price per pound	× $1.00
Standard material cost per product unit	$2.00/unit
Conversion Costs	
Direct labor:	
Standard hours allowed per product unit	3 hours
Standard rate per hour	× $15.00
Standard labor cost per product unit	$45.00/unit
Overhead (applied on the basis of direct labor hours):	
Standard hours allowed per product unit	3 hours
Standard overhead rate per hour (half variable and half fixed)	× $6.00
Standard overhead cost per product unit	$18.00

Total standard conversion cost per product unit:

Direct labor	$45.00
Overhead	18.00
Total	$63.00

Total standard cost per product unit:

Direct material	$ 2.00
Conversion cost	63.00
Total	$65.00

Budgeted direct labor hours (denominator activity)	24,000 hours

(continued)

EXHIBIT 8-10   Continued

INVENTORIES

Work-in-process inventory, beginning, 5,000 units, each 20 percent complete
  with respect to conversion:

Standard material cost (5,000 × $2/unit)	$10,000
Standard conversion cost (5,000 × 20% × $63/unit)	63,000
Total standard cost of beginning work in process	$73,000
Units completed and transferred out during the period	8,000
Units started during the period	4,000

Work-in-process inventory, ending, 1,000 units, each 10 percent completed
  with respect to conversion.

The process-costing calculations under standard costing are much simpler than
they are under actual or normal costing. Under standard costing, there is no need to
calculate the cost per equivalent unit. The standard cost *is* the cost per equivalent
unit. This is true for both material and conversion costs. Under standard costing, no
distinction is made between the weighted-average and FIFO methods of process
costing. These two approaches to process costing are different methods of calculating
the cost per equivalent unit for material and conversion. But under standard costing,

---

EXHIBIT 8-11

Process Costing Calculations: Gator Company

	Total	Material	Conversion
Standard cost per equivalent unit		$2.00	$63.00
Equivalent units of activity during the current period[a]		4,000	7,100
Current cost (using standard costs of material and conversion)	$455,300	$ 8,000	$447,300
Cost of beginning work-in-process inventory	73,000	10,000	63,000
Total cost to be accounted for	$528,300		
Cost of units completed and transferred out (8,000 × $65.00)	$520,000		
Cost of ending work-in-process inventory:			
Material (1,000 × $2.00)	2,000		
Conversion (1,000 × 10% × $63.00)	6,300		
Total costs accounted for	$528,300		

[a] Calculation of equivalent units:

Completed and transferred out	8,000	8,000
Ending work-in-process inventory	1,000	100
Total	9,000	8,100
Beginning work-in-process inventory	5,000	1,000
Current-period equivalent units	4,000	7,100

these unit costs are already known. They are the standard costs. Hence there is no need to calculate unit costs using either weighted-average or FIFO.

The process-costing calculations for the Gator Company data are presented in Exhibit 8-11.

To complete the Gator Company illustration, suppose that the actual results for the period are those given in the upper portion of Exhibit 8-12. The variances for the period are calculated in the lower portion of the exhibit.

The total standard cost for the period was $455,300 (see current cost line in Exhibit 8-11). The total actual cost incurred was $480,400 (see Exhibit 8-12: $9,900 + $341,000 + $62,000 + $67,500). Thus, the total variance for the period is $25,100 U ($480,400 − $455,300). Adding up the eight variances in Exhibit 8-12 also yields a total variance of $25,100 U. This reconciles the actual costs and standards in the illustration.

EXHIBIT 8-12

Variance Analysis: Gator Company

ACTUAL RESULTS

Actual production:
  Direct material, 4,000 equivalent units
  Conversion, 7,100 equivalent units
Direct material:
  Actual quantity used, 9,000 pounds
  Actual price per pound, $1.10
  Actual cost, $9,900

Conversion Costs

Direct labor:
  Actual hours used, 22,000 hours
  Actual labor rate per hour, $15.50
  Actual cost, $341,000
Overhead:
  Actual variable overhead cost, $62,000
  Actual fixed overhead cost, $67,500

VARIANCES

Direct material:
  Standard allowed materials, 4,000 equivalent units × 2 lb/unit = 8,000 lb
  Quantity variance, (9,000 − 8,000) × $1.00 = $1,000 U
  Price variance, ($1.10 − $1.00) × 9,000 = $900 U
Direct labor:
  Standard allowed hours, 7,100 equivalent units × 3 hrs/unit = 21,300 hrs
  Efficiency variance, (22,000 − 21,300) × $15.00 = $10,500 U
  Rate variance, ($15.50 − 15.00) × 22,000 = $11,000 U
Variable overhead:
  Efficiency variance, (22,000 − 21,300) × $3.00 = $2,100 U
  Spending variance, $62,000 − (22,000 × $3.00) = $4,000 F
Fixed overhead:
  Budgeted fixed overhead, 24,000 hrs × $3.00/hr = $72,000
  Budget variances, $67,500 − $72,000 = $4,500 F
  Volume variance, (24,000 − 21,300)$3.00 = $8,100 U

APPENDIX 8C
Cost Variance Proration

This appendix provides a more comprehensive illustration of cost-variance proration. The data for the illustration is given in Exhibit 8-13.

Of the 10,000 pounds of materials purchased during the period, 3,000 pounds remained in material inventory at the end of the period. The standard allowed quantity of materials, given actual production activity is shown below.

Standard Allowed Quantity of Direct Materials	
In work in process	1,000
In finished goods	1,500
In cost of goods sold	2,500

EXHIBIT 8-13

Data for Variance Proration Illustration

Direct material:	
Purchases (debited to material inventory at standard price), 10,000 lbs @ $1.00/lb	$10,000
(1) Purchase-price variance, 10,000 lbs @ $.15	1,500 U
(2) Quantity variance, 2,000 lbs @ $1.00	2,000 U
Direct labor:	
Standard cost, 500 hrs @ $25.00/hr	12,500
(3) Rate variance, 600 hrs @ .50/hr	300 U
(4) Efficiency variance, 100 hrs @ $25.00/hr	2,500 U
Variable overhead (applied on the basis of direct labor hours):	
Standard cost, 500 hrs @ $10.00/hr	5,000
(5) Spending variance	600 F
(6) Efficiency variance, 100 hrs @ $10.00/hr	1,000 U
Fixed overhead (applied on the basis of direct labor hours):	
Budgeted cost, 700 hrs @ $20.00/hr	$14,000
(7) Budget variance	1,200 F
(8) Volume variance, 200 hrs @ $20.00/hr	4,000 U
Total of variances	9,500 U

EXHIBIT 8-14
Proration of Variances

Type of Variance	Total Variance	Direct Material Inventory	Direct Material Quantity Variance	Work-in-Process Inventory	Finished-Goods Inventory	Cost-of-Goods-Sold Expense
Proportion of quantity of materials purchased:		30%	20%	10%	15%	25%
(1) Direct material purchase price	$1,500 U	$450	$ 300	$ 150	$ 225	$ 375
(2) Direct material quantity (unadjusted)	2,000 U		2,000			
Direct material quantity (adjusted)			$2,300	460	690	1,150
Proportion of Standard Allowed Direct Labor Hours:				20%	30%	50%
(3) Direct labor rate	300 U			$ 60	$ 90	$ 150
(4) Direct labor efficiency	2,500 U			500	750	1,250
(5) Variable overhead spending	600 F			(120)	(180)	(300)
(6) Variable overhead efficiency	1,000 U			200	300	500
(7) Fixed overhead budget	1,200 F			(240)	(360)	(600)
(8) Fixed overhead volume	4,000 U			800	1,200	2,000
Total proration	$9,500 U	$450	—	$1,810	$2,715	$4,525

The remaining 2,000 pounds of the 10,000 pounds purchased was consumed by inefficiency and is reflected in the unfavorable material quantity variance. Hence, we can account for the 10,000 pounds of material purchased as follows:

Accounting for Material Purchased	
Still in material inventory	30%
In the quantity variance	20%
In work-in-process inventory	10%
In finished-goods inventory	15%
In cost of goods sold	25%
	100%

A similar analysis reveals that 20 percent of the standard allowed direct labor hours for the period were related to the units remaining in work-in-process inventory at the period's end; 30 percent of the standard allowed direct labor hours were related to finished-goods inventory; and 50 percent of the hours were related to cost of goods sold.

The proration of variances is illustrated in Exhibit 8-14. The eight variances are prorated to each manufacturing account in proportion to the standard amount of the period's inputs remaining in that account at the end of the period. For example, 30 percent of the 10,000 pounds of material purchased remained in the direct material inventory account. Hence, 30 percent of the unfavorable direct material purchase-price variance is prorated to the material inventory account. The balance in the account will be raised by $450 (30% × $1,500). Since the direct material quantity variance is calculated using the standard price, the quantity variance is adjusted to reflect the actual price of the materials before the quantity variance is prorated. Thus, the actual cost of inefficiently consuming 2,000 pounds of material is not $2,000 but rather $2,300 (2,000 pounds @ $1.15/pound). The adjusted quantity variance is then prorated to the accounts affected by efficiency — namely, the work-in-process, finished-goods, and cost-of-goods-sold accounts. The adjusted quantity variance is not prorated to the material inventory account because efficiency is a concept that applies only to the production process and not to materials sitting in a warehouse.

Review Questions

8-1 What is meant by a flexible overhead budget?

8-2 Give the "formula" for a flexible budget, and provide a brief explanation.

8-3 How should an unfavorable variable overhead spending variance be interpreted?

8-4 An unfavorable variable overhead efficiency variance means that the organization was inefficient in using variable overhead items such as electricity. True or false? Explain.

8-5 A favorable fixed-overhead volume variance does not really measure the benefit of having operated at greater than planned activity. True or false? Explain.

8-6 What could be misleading about the term *flexible overhead budget?*

8-7 Why is the total variance for a company disaggregated into variances for material, labor, and overhead and then further broken down into several component variances?

8-8 What is meant by *denominator volume?*

8-9 Describe how costs are entered into work-in-process inventory under standard costing.

8-10 Discuss some advantages and disadvantages of standard-cost systems.

Exercises

8-11 **Analysis of Cost Variances** Complete the list below:

No.	Item	Amount
1.	Variable overhead rate per standard hour	$.85
2.	Fixed overhead rate per standard hour	
3.	Total overhead rate per standard hour for product costing	
4.	Total overhead incurred	$11,425
5.	Total variable cost incurred at actual hours worked	
6.	Total fixed overhead incurred	
7.	Actual hours worked	7,000
8.	Standard hours of (or allowed for) work done	6,500
9.	Standard hours at normal capacity	
10.	Overhead applied to product using standard rates only	$10,400
11.	Budget variance fixed	$425 F
12.	Budgeted variable overhead for actual hours	
13.	Budgeted fixed overhead	
14.	Spending variance variable	$100 F

8-12 Refer to the data presented in Exercise 7-12. Compute (a) the variable overhead spending and efficiency variances and (b) the fixed overhead budget and volume variances.

8-13 **Computing Variances** The Thrower Company produces one product. For the month of March, the following information is accumulated:

	Actual Hours and Tons	Standard Hours and Tons	Actual Cost	Standard Cost per Unit
Direct labor	10,500 hr	10,000 hr	$215,000	$ 21.00/hr
Direct material	550 tons	540 tons	52,250	100.00/ton

	Budgeted Overhead for Year[a]	Actual Overhead for Month
Variable	$216,000	$15,200
Fixed	72,000	6,200

[a] Equal amount each month.

The overhead is budgeted for average (normal) activity of 144,000 standard direct labor hours per year (12,000 hours per month).

REQUIRED:

a. Compute the labor and material variances for March.

b. Compute the overhead variances for March.

8-14 Refer to the data presented in Exercise 7-14. Compute (a) the variable overhead spending and efficiency variances and (b) the fixed overhead budget and volume variances.

8-15 Refer to the data presented in Exercise 7-15. Compute (a) the variable overhead spending and efficiency variances and (b) the fixed overhead budget and volume variances.

8-16 Analysis of Variances   The I. C. Thelite Company has accumulated the following information in an effort to explain the differences between standard and actual cost for the month of March. Overhead is applied, using standard direct labor hours. All the actual costs given are for March. There is no beginning or ending balance in work in process.

PRODUCTION FOR MARCH

Product	Units Produced	Direct Labor Standards	Direct Labor Cost per Hour	Material Standards	Standard Material Cost per Ton
A	900,000	6.0 min/unit	$8.40	1.0 lb/unit	$1000.00
B	800,000	4.8 min/unit	$8.80	3.0 lb/unit	$2000.00

ACTUAL DIRECT LABOR AND MATERIAL

Product	Direct Labor Hours	Direct Labor Dollars	Material, tons	Material, $
A	80,000	$656,000	530	$ 545,000
B	70,000	$760,000	1,248	2,590,000

BUDGET INFORMATION

Product	Budgeted Fixed Cost, March	Budgeted Production, March	Budgeted Variable Overhead, March	Budgeted Direct Labor Hours, March
A	$ 600,000	1,000,000	$800,000	100,000
B	$1,360,000	850,000	$680,000	68,000

ADDITIONAL INFORMATION

Product	Actual Fixed Cost, March	Actual Variable Cost, March
A	$ 592,000	$840,000
B	$1,372,000	$672,000

REQUIRED:

Prepare an analysis of all variances.

8-17 **Cost of Units and Related Variances; Equivalent Units** (see Appendix 8B) The DeBrosse Company produces a single product and uses a standard cost system. Direct materials are added at the beginning of the production process; labor and overhead costs are applied uniformly throughout the manufacturing process. The following standards apply to the product:

	Standard Cost per Unit
Material	$2.66
Direct labor and burden	3.22
Total	$5.88

Production data for February are as follows:

	Units	Costs
Beginning inventory (50% complete)	100	
Materials		$ 266
Direct labor and overhead		161
Units completed	800	
Ending inventory (10% complete)	200	
Material costs incurred for February		2,316
Actual direct labor and overhead for February		2,752

REQUIRED:

a. Compute the standard cost of units completed and the standard cost of the ending work in process.

b. Compute the total material variance and the variance for conversion costs (labor and overhead) for February.

8-18 **Standard Costs and Monthly Capacity** Pashaw and Co. produces a single product in a single department under a standard cost system. Standard costs per finished unit include $48.00 for direct material and $27.00 for direct labor. Four units of direct material are required per finished unit. The standard direct labor rate is $9.00 per hour. Condensed monthly flexible budget data is provided on the following page.

	Operating Levels		
Direct labor standard hours per month	60,000	80,000	100,000
Supplies	$ 27,000	$ 36,000	$ 45,000
Indirect labor	99,000	132,000	165,000
Other variable overhead	18,000	24,000	30,000
	$144,000	$192,000	$240,000
Depreciation	$180,000	$180,000	$180,000
Supervision	150,000	150,000	150,000
Other fixed overhead	52,500	52,500	52,500
	$382,500	$382,500	$382,500

The company uses a combined overhead rate of $20.70 per finished unit for product costing. Data for the month of June follow:

- Units produced: 31,000.

- Units sold: 26,000.

- Inventory June 1 (at standard): 50,000 units (raw material).

- Direct material purchased: 100,000 units @ $12.60.

- Direct materials used: 126,000 units.

- Direct labor: 96,000 actual hours, $843,840.

- Total overhead incurred: $609,000.

REQUIRED:

a. Compute the cost of sales for June (at standard).

b. Compute normal monthly capacity in standard direct labor hours.

8-19 T Accounts and Ledger Entries   The Newcastle Corporation makes one model of a product. The following information is available for the month of April:

	Actual Costs Incurred	Work-in-Process Inventory, Beginning of Period at Standard Cost	Goods Finished During April at Standard Cost	Work-in-Process Inventory, End of Period at Standard Cost
Direct material (requisitioned)	$ 43,400	$12,000	$ 40,000	$13,000
Direct labor	84,300	20,000	80,000	20,400
Fixed overhead	21,000	5,000	20,000	5,100
Variable overhead	163,000	40,000	160,000	40,800

There was $7,500 of finished goods (500 units) in inventory at the beginning of the period. During the month of April, 20,000 units were completed and 19,000 units were shipped to customers.

The company uses separate work-in-process accounts for material, labor, variable overhead, and fixed overhead. Also, the company uses four variance accounts:

- Direct material variance

- Direct labor variance

- Fixed overhead variance

- Variable overhead variance

The overhead rates used are

Variable overhead = $2 × direct labor dollars

Fixed overhead = $.25 × direct labor dollars

REQUIRED:

Set up T accounts and prepare summary entries to record the information given.

8-20 **Standard Costs, Overhead Rates and Accounting for Work-in-Process Inventory** **Part I.** The Stan-low Corporation makes products *A* and *B*. The company uses two work-in-process accounts, one for product *A* and one for product *B*.

The following standard costs have been established and are used in the cost-accounting system:

	Product A	Product B
Material:		
Standard cost of wood	$.20	$ .30
Standard cost of paint	—	.02
Labor:		
Cutters (standard cost per unit)	.40	.60
Finishers (standard cost per unit)	.25	.30
Overhead rates:		
Variable (varnish, power, glue, etc.)	.25[a]	.50[a]
Fixed (supervisor, depreciation, etc.)	.75[a]	1.00[a]

[a] Per direct labor dollar. Cutters earn $10.00 per hour; finishers, $12.50 per hour.

REQUIRED:

a. Compute the standard cost per unit for each product.

b. If the total fixed costs budgeted for the year are $30,000, and if $7,500 of these costs are allocated or identified with product *A*, what amount of direct labor dollars was used in computing the fixed overhead rate? What is the fixed overhead rate if the level of activity used to compute the rate is 200,000 units of product *A*?

Part II. The following information relates to the month of May for product *B*:

Cost of wood used	$310
Cost of paint used	$21
Direct labor, cutters	$620
Direct labor, finishers	$290
Overhead incurred:	
Variable	$450
Fixed	$1,000
Units finished during May	950
Units in process May 31 (units assumed to be one-half completed, labor and paint; all completed, wood)	250
Units in process May 1 (units assumed to be one-half completed, labor and paint; all completed, wood)	150

The work in process at the beginning of May was valued at standard cost.

REQUIRED:

Set up a work-in-process account for product *B*. Record the beginning work in process, the costs incurred, the transfer to finished goods, and the closing of the variances to an account called Variances from Standard Costs. Overhead is to be applied to product using direct labor dollars.

8-21 Cost Variances ·Prepare as complete an analysis of cost variances as possible from the following information:

STANDARD COSTS PER UNIT

Direct labor (5 hr @ $4)	$20.00
Material (20 lb at @ $2)	40.00
Variable overhead ($1.50 × 5)	7.50
Fixed overhead ($3 × 5)	15.00
	$82.50

BUDGET INFORMATION FOR THE YEAR

Variable overhead	$150,000
Fixed overhead	300,000
Normal activity for year	100,000 direct labor hours
Practical activity for year	120,000 direct labor hours

The actual results of January's operations were as follows:

Variable overhead	$11,000
Fixed overhead	$26,000
Actual activity	8,000 direct labor hours
Actual production	1,450 units
Actual labor cost	$33,600
Actual material cost (30,000 pounds)	$66,000

8-22 Equivalent Units and Cost of Goods Under Standard Costing (see Appendix 8B) The Carter Corporation makes one product, widgets, and uses a standard cost system to record the costs of making that product. On December 1 manufacturing inventory accounts had balances as follows:

Finished goods	$30,000	1,000 units
Work in process, labor	8,000	500 units one-half completed with respect to conversion
Work in process, material	5,000	500 units completed as far as material is concerned
Work in process, overhead	1,000	overhead rate $2.00/DLH

The standard cost of a widget is:

Direct labor	$16
Direct material (20 lb of material)	10
Overhead:	
Fixed	3
Variable	1
	$30

The current work standard is two direct labor hours per unit of product. The fixed overhead rate is $1.50 per direct labor hour, and the variable overhead rate is $0.50 per direct labor hour.

The normal activity for a month is 200,000 direct labor hours, and the overhead rates are based on normal activity. The fixed manufacturing costs budgeted for a month are $300,000, and the variable manufacturing overhead costs are $100,000.

The following transactions took place during December:

Direct labor costs incurred (180,000 hr of work)	$1,520,000
Material requisitioned and used (1,800,000 lb)	1,150,000
Fixed overhead incurred	320,000
Variable overhead incurred	95,000
Selling expenses incurred	1,000,000
Administrative expenses incurred	800,000
Income taxes	100,000
Sales on account (95,000 widgets)	4,800,000

During the month of December, the plant completed 100,000 units of product. The work in process on December 31 consisted of 400 units, 50 percent completed with respect to labor and 100 percent completed with respect to material.

REQUIRED:

a. Prepare a schedule computing the equivalent units of production in December for materials and conversion.

b. Using standard costing, compute (1) the cost of goods completed and transferred to finished goods, and (2) the cost of the ending work-in-process inventory.

c. Compute (1) the direct-material quantity variance, (2) the direct labor rate variance, (3) the variable overhead efficiency variance, and (4) the fixed overhead budget variance.

8-23 **Comprehensive Standard Costing**   Cain Company has an automated production process, and machine hours are used to describe production activity. A full absorption costing system is employed by the company.

The annual profit plan for the coming fiscal year is finalized in April of each year. The profit plan for the fiscal year ending May 31, 19x2, called for 6,000 units to be produced requiring 30,000 machine hours. The full absorption costing rate for the 19x1 to 19x2 fiscal year was determined using 6,000 units of planned production.

Cain develops flexible budgets for different levels of activity for use in evaluating performance. A total of 6,200 units were actually produced during the 19x1 to 19x2 fiscal year, requiring 32,000 machine hours. The schedule presented below compares Cain Company's actual costs for the 19x1 to 19x2 fiscal year with the profit plan and the budgeted costs for two different activity levels.

CAIN COMPANY
Manufacturing Cost Report
for the Fiscal Year Ended May 31, 19x2
(in thousands of dollars)

| | Flexible Budgets for | | | |
Item	Profit Plan (6,000 units)	31,000 Machine Hours	32,000 Machine Hours	Actual Costs
Direct material:				
G27 aluminum	$ 252.0	$ 260.4	$ 268.8	$ 270.0
M14 steel alloy	78.0	80.6	83.2	83.0
Direct labor:				
Assembler	273.0	282.1	291.2	287.0
Grinder	234.0	241.8	249.6	250.0
Manufacturing overhead:				
Maintenance	24.0	24.8	25.6	25.0
Supplies	129.0	133.3	137.6	130.0
Supervision	80.0	82.0	84.0	81.0
Inspector	144.0	147.0	150.0	147.0
Insurance	50.0	50.0	50.0	50.0
Depreciation	200.0	200.0	200.0	200.0
Total cost	$1,464.0	$1,502.0	$1,540.0	$1,523.0

Use the above data in answering the following items (all answers have been rounded to the second decimal place when necessary):

REQUIRED:

a. Compute the budgeted number of machine hours needed to produce one unit of product.

b. Compute the actual cost of material used in one unit of product.

c. Calculate the cost of material that should be processed per machine hour.

d. What is the budgeted direct labor cost for each unit produced?

e. The company uses a three-way analysis of overhead variances. Compute the manufacturing overhead budget variance for 19x1.

f. Actual production was 6,200 units, although the original profit plan was to produce 6,000 units. What is the effect on the variable cost per unit of this change in volume?

g. Using the flexible budget formula, compute the total budgeted manufacturing cost (in thousands of dollars) for an output of 6,050 units. *(CMA adapted)*

8-24 Variance Proration   (see Appendix 8C) The following information is available for the Ellis Hollow Toy Company for the month of August.

Direct material:	
Purchases (debited to material inventory at standard price), 20,000 lbs @ $2.00/lb	$40,000
Purchase-price variance, 6,000 lbs @ $.25	1,500 *U*
Quantity variance, 1,000 lbs @ $2.00	2,000 *U*
Direct labor:	
Standard cost, 1,000 hrs @ $20.00/hr	20,000
Rate variance, 1,200 hrs @ $1.00/hr	1,200 *U*
Efficiency variance, 200 hrs @ $20.00/hr	4,000 *U*
Variable overhead (applied on the basis of direct labor hours):	
Standard cost, 1,000 hrs @ $5.00/hr	$5,000
Spending variance	1,400 *F*
Efficiency variance, 200 hrs @ $5.00/hr	1,000 *U*
Fixed overhead (applied on the basis of direct labor hours):	
Budgeted cost, 1,300 hrs @ $7.00/hr	9,100
Budget variance	1,900 *U*
Volume variance, 300 hrs @ $7.00/hr	2,100 *U*
Accounting for material purchased (as of August 31):	
Still in material inventory	40%
In the quantity variance	10%
In work-in-process inventory	25%
In finished-goods inventory	10%
In cost of goods sold	15%
Analysis of standard allowed direct labor hours (as of August 31):	
Related to work-in-process inventory	50%
Related to finished-goods inventory	20%
Related to cost of goods sold	30%

REQUIRED:

Prorate all eight variances to the appropriate accounts.

8-25 Missing Values Refer to the data presented in Problem 8-24. Supply the following missing values:

    a. Actual material price per pound.

    b. Actual material quantity used.

    c. Actual labor rate per hour.

    d. Actual labor hours used.

    e. Actual variable overhead cost.

    f. Actual fixed overhead cost.

    g. Underapplied overhead.

8-26 Alternative Computation of Fixed Overhead Variances (see Appendix 8A) Refer to the data presented in Exercise 7-12. Compute the fixed overhead efficiency, activity, and budget variances.

8-27 Alternative Computation of Fixed Overhead Variances (see Appendix 8A) Refer to the data presented in Exercise 7-14. Compute the fixed overhead efficiency, activity, and budget variances.

8-28 Alternative Computation of Fixed Overhead Variances (see Appendix 8A) Refer to the data presented in Exercise 7-15. Compute the fixed overhead efficiency, activity, and budget variances.

8-29 Planned Financial Statements and Variances (see Appendix 8A)* Each December the Kracked Bat Company prepares a financial plan for the coming year. The complete plan has the following components:

- Sales and selling expenses

- Production

- Material and labor

- Manufacturing overhead

- Cash

- Projected financial statements

    The Kracked Bat Company's only products are baseball bats. The bats are all produced at one plant. There are four sales offices. The company uses a last-in, first-out (LIFO) procedure for pricing inventory and cost of goods sold expense.

---

* This comprehensive problem also may be assigned with Chapter 10, to integrate the topics of standard costing, variance analysis, and budgeting. If assigned with Chapter 8, Part V (on cash budgeting) may be omitted.

Part I. Sales and Selling Expense

The sales and selling expense plans are prepared by the sales department with the assistance of the controller's office. The sales forecasts are based on reports from the salesmen and information from the company economist, whose task it is to incorporate into the forecast such things as changes in prices, population, age of the population, and income. The following projections were made for the year:

SALES PROJECTIONS FOR YEAR

Sales District	Number of Bats	Sales	Planned Selling Expense
New England	500,000	$15,000,000	$200,000
Middle West	300,000	9,000,000	180,000
South	150,000	4,500,000	100,000
South West	50,000	1,500,000	120,000
Total	1,000,000	$30,000,000	$600,000

REQUIRED:

What additional information should be contained in the completed sales and selling expense plan?

Part II. Production Plan

The production department receives from the sales department a breakdown of forecasted sales by months.

SALES PROJECTIONS FOR YEAR BY MONTHS
(number of bats)

January	200,000	July	Vacation
February	200,000	August	60,000
March	100,000	September	60,000
April	100,000	October	100,000
May	50,000	November	40,000
June	50,000	December	40,000

The company follows a policy of stabilizing employment throughout the year. If it did not follow this policy, it would probably lose its skilled workers to other plants in the area. Studies and experience indicate that the plant can produce 60,000 bats per month when it is operating without overtime and employing only the basic workforce. By working overtime and adding temporary workers, production can be upped to 120,000 bats per month. The entire plant and sales force is given a month's vacation in July. Normal activity for budget purposes is 100,000 bats per month.

There will be a January 1 beginning inventory of 180,000 bats. The company tries to keep a basic minimum inventory of 20,000 finished bats, and it builds up the inventory to 180,000 bats as of the beginning of each year. Where there is conflict between inventory control and employment policy, the stabilized employment policy has priority.

REQUIRED:

Plan the production (number of bats to be produced) in each month.

Part III. Projected Material and Labor

The material and labor standards for the type of bat being produced are as follows:

Wood (standard rough weight)	2 lbs
Standard cost per pound	$1.00
Standard cost of wood used in bat	$2.00
Direct labor:	
Cutters	0.25 hr at $10.00/hr = $ 2.50
Finishers	0.50 hr at $15.00/hr = 7.50
Standard direct labor cost per bat	= $10.00

REQUIRED:

Compute the total direct labor and material to be used during the year and for each of the first three months of the year.

Part IV. Projected Manufacturing Overhead

The manufacturing overhead costs are projected as follows:

FIXED OVERHEAD

Equipment depreciation	$ 240,000
Salaries of supervisors	1,800,000
Building rent	960,000
Manufacturing labor, indirect	360,000
Manufacturing supplies	240,000
	$3,600,000

VARIABLE OVERHEAD
(for normal activity of
1,200,000 bats per year)

Indirect labor	$ 960,000
Power	240,000
Indirect supplies	480,000
	$1,680,000

REQUIRED:

a. What additional information should be presented in the detailed plan?

b. Compute the fixed and variable overhead rates to be used. Overhead is to be applied using standard direct labor hours.

c. What is the standard overhead per unit of product?

Part V. Cash

The only sources of cash in the next period are sales and the collections of accounts receivable. Past experience indicates that the following schedule of collections holds true:

Collections in month of sale	20%
Collections in month following sale	70
Collections in second month following sale	9
Uncollectible accounts	1
	100%

The accounts receivable balance as of January 1 is expected to consist of the following items:

Source	Accounts Receivable	Expected Uncollectibles
December sales	$320,000	$ 4,000
November sales	30,000	3,000
October sales	10,000	10,000
September sales	5,000	5,000
	$365,000	$22,000

Payments of cash are expected to be equal to the sum of

- Selling expenses

- Cost of direct material used

- Direct labor cost incurred

- Out-of-pocket overhead costs

There is a cash balance of $1,000,000 on January 1.
No income tax payments are due in the coming year.

REQUIRED:

Prepare a cash budget for the year.

Part VI. Projected Income Statement

The January 1 balance sheet is expected to include the following items:

Assets		Equities	
Cash	$1,000,000	Accounts payable	$2,000,000
Accounts receivable	365,000	Capital stock	4,000,000
Allowance for uncollectibles	(22,000)	Retained earnings	1,543,000
Inventories	4,000,000		
Equipment	3,000,000		
Accumulated depreciation	(800,000)		
	$7,543,000		$7,543,000

REQUIRED:

Prepare a projected income statement for the year. Assume that the income tax rate is 50 percent and that the taxable income (if any) is the same as the income per books.

Part VII. Variances

Assume that certain price (wage) and usage (efficiency) variances can be forecasted. Which of the plans will be affected by these items? Explain briefly.

Part VIII. Actual Costs in January

The following events occurred during January:

Bats produced		125,000
Cutters worked 30,000 hrs and earned		$375,000
Finishers worked 62,000 hrs and earned		$1,250,000
Cost of wood used (260,000 lbs)		$280,000
Fixed overhead:		
Equipment depreciation	$ 20,000	
Salaries of supervisors	150,000	
Building rent	80,000	
Indirect labor	45,000	
Indirect supplies	25,000	
		$320,000
Variable overhead:		
Indirect labor	$90,000	
Power	20,000	
Indirect supplies	50,000	
		$160,000
Selling expense		$50,000

REQUIRED:

a. Compute the material price and quantity variances; labor efficiency and rate variances; variable overhead spending and efficiency variances; and fixed overhead variances.

b. Assuming that all the bats produced could be sold for $30 per bat, analyze the results of operations for January. What actions could be taken to improve the profit picture?

9

Variable and Absorption Costing

LEARNING OBJECTIVES

After studying this chapter, you should be able to:

1 Explain the difference between variable costing and absorption costing.

2 Prepare income statements under variable costing and absorption costing.

3 Reconcile reported income under variable costing and absorption costing.

4 Evaluate variable and absorption costing for product-costing and decision-making purposes.

*P*roduct costing is an important purpose of any cost accounting system. One important dimension of product-costing systems is the treatment of fixed manufacturing overhead. Under **variable costing** fixed manufacturing costs are treated as a period expense and are not inventoried as product costs. Variable costing is also called **direct costing.**

The alternative approach to product costing, with respect to the treatment of fixed manufacturing costs, is **absorption costing.** Under this product-costing approach, fixed manufacturing costs are inventoried as product costs, attached to units of product, and included in the cost of work in process, finished goods, and cost of goods sold. Absorption costing is also called **full costing.**

Only fixed manufacturing costs are handled differently under variable and absorption costing. Selling and administrative costs, both fixed and variable, are always treated as period costs. This is true under both variable costing and absorption costing.

The distinction between fixed and variable costs is useful for decision-making purposes. However, determining the nature of costs for purposes of decision making is not dependent on the method of accounting for fixed costs for financial reporting purposes. Under generally accepted procedures of financial accounting, absorption costing is used, under which the fixed manufacturing cost is absorbed as a product cost. As a result, the income reported for a period is affected not only by sales and efficiency but also by the amount of production and by the change in inventory. Thus the reported income of a period may be increased not only by additional sales or improved efficiency but also by producing more units and putting the excess units into inventory.[1]

Illustration of Variable and Absorption Costing

Assume that the Geneva Company sells 5,000 units at $8 each in both March and April. The production costs are identical for both months:

Fixed manufacturing costs	$90,000 per month
Variable manufacturing costs	$1 per unit

[1] A survey of *Fortune* 500 firms revealed that roughly 65 percent of the American companies that use standard costing also use absorption costing for internal reporting purposes. See J. Chiu and Y. Lee, "A Survey of Current Practice in Overhead Accounting and Analysis," Proceedings of the 1980 Western Regional Meeting of the American Accounting Association. All companies must use absorption costing for external reporting purposes.

Production for March is 10,000 units and for April 20,000 units. The normal production for both months is 15,000 units per month.

A variety of income statements can be prepared for the two months, depending on the treatment of fixed manufacturing costs. These statements are shown in Exhibits 9-1, 9-2, and 9-3.

Absorption Costing

Actual absorption costing and normal absorption costing yield the same reported income figures if the underapplied overhead is prorated to cost of goods sold and finished-goods inventory, and a LIFO (last-in, first-out) cost-flow assumption is used. Both procedures result in the reported income of the period being a function of the level of production as well as of sales. The results of these procedures are shown in Exhibit 9-1.

EXHIBIT 9-1

Geneva Company
Income Statements Using Actual Absorption Costing and Normal Absorption Costing

| | Actual Absorption Costing | | Normal Absorption Costing (overhead variance prorated) | |
	March	April	March	April
Sales	$40,000	$40,000	$40,000	$40,000
Less: Variable costs	5,000	5,000	5,000	5,000
Fixed costs	45,000[a]	22,500[b]	45,000[c]	22,500[d]
Total costs	$50,000	$27,500	$50,000	$27,500
Income (loss)	($10,000)	$12,500	($10,000)	$12,500

---

[a] The fixed cost per unit produced was $90,000/10,000, or $9 per unit. There were 5,000 units sold; thus the fixed costs charged to expense were $45,000. The remainder are inventoried.

[b] The fixed cost per unit produced was $90,000/20,000 or $4.50 per unit. There were 5,000 units sold. Thus, the fixed costs charged to expense were $22,500. This statement assumes a LIFO cost flow.

[c] On the basis of normal activity, the fixed cost per unit was $90,000/15,000, or $6 per unit. There were 10,000 units produced in March. Thus, the fixed cost applied to product was $60,000 and the underapplied fixed cost was $30,000. Half of the underapplied overhead, $15,000, is charged to inventory and half to expense because 5,000 units were sold and 5,000 units remain in finished-goods inventory. The total fixed cost charged to expense was the $15,000 of allocated, underapplied overhead and $30,000 of applied overhead (one half of the applied fixed costs of $60,000).

[d] During April production was 20,000 units. Thus, there was $120,000 (20,000 × $6) of fixed overhead applied to product. There was a favorable volume variance of $30,000 = $6(20,000 − 15,000). The fixed cost charged to expense was the number of units sold times the overhead rate of $6 (this assumes a LIFO flow of costs), minus one-quarter (5,000/20,000) of the $30,000 volume variance.

Frequently, volume variances are treated as expenses of the period in which they are incurred instead of being prorated to cost of goods sold and ending inventory. Typically, they are included with other expenses of the period and allowed to affect operating income. Alternatively, they can be subtracted from operating income so that operating income is not affected by the level of activity. The latter procedure is rarely observed in practice. The results are shown in Exhibit 9-2.

Variable Costing

Under variable costing, all fixed manufacturing costs are accounted for as expenses of the period in which they are incurred, and only variable manufacturing costs are considered to be inventoriable. Variable costing is illustrated in Exhibit 9-3.

Under variable costing, the reported incomes of the two periods are the same. This treatment is consistent with the fact that sales, unit variable cost, and total fixed cost are the same for the two periods. The only difference in the two periods is the level of production: The absorption costing method arrives at a reported income for one period and a loss for the other, but the variable costing procedure shows the same loss for both periods. The total reported loss is also larger than under either of the other methods because no fixed costs have been inventoried.

The primary advantage of variable costing is that reported income is not affected by changes in inventory and production levels. To increase reported income, either total sales must increase or some meaningful change must be achieved in the cost-revenue relationship. Fixed costs of production for the period are not inventoried, and the final reported income figure is not influenced by fluctuations in inventory

---

EXHIBIT 9-2

Geneva Company
Absorption-Costing Income Statements with Different Treatment of the Volume Variance

	Normal Absorption Costing (volume variance treated as a period expense)		Normal Absorption Costing (volume variance subtracted from the reported operating income)	
	March	April	March	April
Sales	$40,000	$40,000	$40,000	$40,000
Less: Cost of goods sold[a]	35,000	35,000	35,000	35,000
Volume variance	30,000	(30,000)		
Total	$65,000	$ 5,000		
Operating income (loss)	($25,000)	$35,000	$ 5,000	$ 5,000
Less: Volume variance			30,000	(30,000)
Income (loss)			($25,000)	$35,000

[a] The $35,000 is equal to $5,000 of variable overhead cost and $30,000 applied fixed overhead (5,000 units times the predetermined fixed overhead rate of $6 per unit).

EXHIBIT 9-3

Geneva Company
Variable Costing Income Statement

	Variable Costing	
	March	April
Sales	$40,000	$40,000
Less: Variable costs	5,000	5,000
Contribution margin	$35,000	$35,000
Less: Fixed costs	90,000	90,000
Income (loss)	($55,000)	($55,000)

levels. This result is desirable because an increase in inventory may reflect inefficiency if excess inventory gives rise to additional (and undesirable) handling, storage, and carrying costs. Moreover, increasing inventory levels may suggest the existence of marketing problems. Unfortunately, the inventory values obtained by omitting fixed costs may give little indication as to the inventory's real value, or even the inventory's cost, when these values exclude the opportunity costs of fixed factors of production.

A policy of including only variable costs as product costs biases the valuation of the inventory in the direction of being less than its market value measured in terms of net sales value, value in use, or replacement cost. This conclusion is based on the assumption that some fixed factors of production have opportunity costs because they are in limited supply and have alternative uses. The absorption of fixed costs in inventory values may be incorrect because such costs are based on historical costs, but the inclusion of fixed costs can be considered as an attempt to include an estimate of the opportunity costs of the factors of production that result in fixed costs. Such costs include depreciation on plant and equipment, property taxes, and so forth.

Another argument advanced in favor of inventorying fixed costs is the concept of matching expenses with the revenues that they are incurred to earn. If the fixed costs are valid costs of production, it is argued that they should not be considered an expense until the product is sold. The accounting treatment of the variable costs and fixed costs identified as product costs should be the same under this argument.

Evaluating Variable Costing for Internal Decision Making

Absorption costing is required for financial statements prepared under generally accepted accounting principles (GAAP). However, the decision concerning whether to use variable or absorption costing for internal financial reporting should be made on the basis of which approach is more useful for decision making. The costs of preparing the information are not likely to be significantly different under either the variable costing or absorption costing procedure.

Is variable costing useful for decision making? The question is better phrased in terms of what costs are appropriate for the decision at hand. Fixed costs may or may not be relevant in a particular decision situation. It is better to address the question directly in each decision than to assume that some method such as variable costing always provides the correct values.

If only variable manufacturing costs are inventoried, the unit value of the inventory is unaffected by fluctuating production levels. Under variable costing the inventory presented in the balance sheet includes only variable costs. In the absence of input price changes or changes in efficiency, the inventory reported in the balance sheet would reflect changes in the number of physical units on hand. This result may be preferred over fluctuations in the cost per unit caused by variations in the level of production when absorption costing is used. Such fluctuation occurs if the cost per unit is determined by dividing the actual costs by actual production or if the volume variance is prorated to both finished-goods inventory and cost of goods sold.

Reconciliation of Variable and Absorption Costing

The differences between variable and absorption costing are revealed by reconciling the income amounts reported under the two methods. Exhibit 9-4 highlights the differences between Aurora Company's income statements prepared under variable and absorption costing. The data used to develop Exhibit 9-4 are the following:

Sales	1,000 units
Sales price	$200
Standard variable manufacturing cost per unit	$50
Budgeted fixed overhead	$100,000
Budgeted production	10,000 units
Actual production	9,000 units
Variable selling and administrative expenses	$1,000
Fixed selling and administrative expenses	1,000

The chief differences in the income statements shown in Exhibit 9-4 appear in the following three places:

- *Cost of goods sold* contains a fixed-cost component on the absorption costing statement but not on the variable costing statement.

- *Manufacturing variances* include a volume variance on the absorption costing statement but not on the variable costing statement.

EXHIBIT 9-4

Aurora Company
Reconciliation of Absorption Costing and Variable Costing Income
Variable Costing Income Statement

Sales	$200,000
Variable cost of goods sold	50,000[a]
Variable selling and administrative expenses	1,000
Total variable expense	51,000
Contribution margin	149,000
Manufacturing variances:	
Material variance (unfavorable)	1,200
Labor variance (unfavorable)	1,500
Variable overhead spending variance (unfavorable)	1,000
Variable overhead efficiency variance (unfavorable)	2,000
Total variances	$5,700
Contribution margin (adjusted for variances)	$143,300
Period expenses:	
Fixed manufacturing overhead (budgeted)	100,000
Fixed overhead budget variance	2,300
Fixed selling and administrative expenses	1,000
Operating income	$40,000

Absorption Costing Income Statement

Sales	$200,000
Cost of goods sold	60,000[b]
Gross margin (at standard)	$140,000
Manufacturing variances:	
Material variance (unfavorable)	$1,200
Labor variance (unfavorable)	1,500
Fixed overhead budget variance (unfavorable)	2,300
Variable overhead spending variance (unfavorable)	1,000
Variable overhead efficiency variance (unfavorable)	2,000
Volume variance (unfavorable)	10,000
Total variances	$18,000
Gross margin (adjusted for variances)	$122,000
Selling and administrative expenses	2,000
Operating income	$120,000

[a] $50,000 = 1,000 \times \$50 =$ Sales in units $\times$ Variable manufacturing cost per unit

[b] $\$60,000 = 1,000 \times \left(\$50 + \dfrac{\$100,000}{10,000} \right) =$ Sales in units $\times$ (Variable cost per unit + Fixed cost per unit)

■ **Period expenses** include fixed manufacturing overhead on the variable costing statement but not on the absorption costing statement.

The income amounts reported on the two statements in Exhibit 9-4 can be reconciled as follows:

Income under absorption costing	$120,000
− Income under variable costing	40,000
Income difference	$80,000
Cost of goods sold under absorption costing	$60,000
− Cost of goods sold under variable costing	50,000
Subtotal	$10,000
+ Volume variance on absorption costing statement	10,000
Subtotal	$20,000
− Fixed overhead period expense on variable costing statement	100,000
Total: absorption costing income exceeds variable costing income	($80,000)

The predetermined fixed overhead rate is $10 per unit ($100,000 ÷ 10,000 units). Because production was only 9,000 units, there is an unfavorable volume variance of $10,000 or (10,000 units − 9,000 units) × $10 per unit. Moreover, production exceeded sales by 8,000 units. Under absorption costing, $80,000 of fixed overhead is inventoried as a product cost (8,000 unit inventory increase times $10 fixed overhead per unit), but under variable costing that $80,000 in fixed overhead cost is expensed as a period cost. Thus, there is an $80,000 difference in reported income under the two methods.

Shortcut Formula

Another way to reconcile reported income under variable and absorption costing is to use the following formula:

$$\begin{array}{ccc} \text{Difference between} & \text{Change} & \text{Fixed overhead} \\ \text{variable costing and} \quad = & \text{in} \quad \times & \text{rate per} \\ \text{absorption costing income} & \text{inventory} & \text{unit} \end{array}$$

$$\$80,000 = (8,000 \text{ units}) \times (\$10 \text{ per unit})$$

Aurora Company produced 9,000 units but sold only 1,000 units. Thus inventory increased during the period by 8,000 units. For each of these units that remained in inventory, Aurora Company inventoried $10 of fixed overhead costs under absorption costing. However, under variable costing all of the period's fixed overhead costs were expensed.

Contribution Format

Notice that the variable-costing income statement in Exhibit 9-4 uses a different format than the absorption costing statement. The absorption costing statement highlights the **gross margin,** which is defined as sales revenue less all manufacturing costs assigned to the units sold. The variable costing statement is prepared using the **contribution format.** This format highlights the **contribution margin,** which is defined as sales revenue less all variable expenses. Included in the variable expenses are the variable cost of goods sold (manufacturing costs) and the variable selling and administrative expenses.

Use of Actual Costing

The example in Exhibit 9-4 uses standard costing. A similar analysis is possible under actual costing. Appendix 9A provides formulas for reconciling income under variable and absorption costing if actual costing is used.

Variable Costing and Performance Evaluation

Firms commonly prepare financial reports for purposes of evaluating performance in divisions and departments, and often these reports use a variable costing approach to focus attention on the contribution of a subunit. Variable costing is most appropriate when a department's performance is measured by its profitability.

Not all departments of an organization should have a profit goal. Cost minimization, subject to an assigned output level in terms of quantity and quality, is more appropriate for some departments. For these departments, cost control is the primary long-run objective of internal reporting. Variable costs, however, may only approximate controllable costs. Differences occur between variable costs and controllable costs to the extent that expenditures that are fixed in relation to the level of activity are under the control of a department manager. Internal reports can create problems in performance evaluation and in motivation if the reports are prepared reflecting inappropriate goals, or if the reports include costs over which the manager is not able to exercise any control. Interdependencies among departments and fuzzy lines of responsibility for decisions and expenditure authorization add to the difficulties.

A common error made by managers is to assume that a method used to report on performance for external reporting purposes is equally relevant to internal performance measurement and cost-control needs. The two objectives should be addressed separately. There are advantages and disadvantages to both variable costing and absorption costing. A different inventory valuation procedure is suggested in Appendix 9B.

Summary

Variable and absorption costing are two approaches to product costing that differ in their treatment of fixed manufacturing costs. Under absorption costing, fixed manufacturing cost is inventoried as a product cost and is included in work in process, finished goods, and cost of goods sold. Under variable costing, fixed manufacturing cost is treated as a period expense. Absorption costing is required for external reporting under generally accepted accounting principles. However, variable costing is in many cases preferable for internal decision-making purposes. Under variable costing, changes in income from period to period reflect changes in sales or efficiency rather than changes in inventory levels.

Key Terms to Review

absorption costing, p. 306
contribution format, p. 313
contribution margin, p. 313
direct costing, p. 306

full costing, p. 306
gross margin, p. 312
variable costing, p. 306

Review Problem

VARIABLE AND ABSORPTION COSTING

Two alternative annual income statements are presented below for Grady Corporation. Prepare a reconciliation of these income amounts. The company uses a standard costing system. The denominator production volume is 18,000 units per year, but only 15,000 units were actually manufactured and 10,000 units were sold.

VARIABLE COSTING INCOME STATEMENT

Sales	$45,000
Variable cost of goods sold	(21,000)[a]
Variable selling and administration expenses	(1,500)
Contribution margin (at standard)	22,500
Manufacturing variances:	
Material variance (unfavorable)	(1,000)
Contribution margin (adjusted for variances)	21,500
Period expenses:	
Fixed manufacturing overhead	(9,000)
Fixed selling and administrative expenses	(2,000)
Operating income	$10,500

[a] $21,000 = 10,000 × $2.10 = Sales in units × Variable cost per unit

ABSORPTION COSTING INCOME STATEMENT

Sales	$45,000
Cost of goods sold	(26,000)[a]
Gross margin (at standard)	19,000
Manufacturing variances:	
Material variance (unfavorable)	(1,000)
Volume variance (unfavorable)	(1,500)
Total variances	(2,500)
Gross margin (adjusted for variances)	16,500
Selling and administrative expenses	(3,500)
Operating income	$13,000

$$^a \ \$26,000 = 10,000 \times \left(\$2.10 + \frac{\$9,000}{18,000}\right) = \text{Sales in units} \times \left(\begin{array}{c}\text{Variable} \\ \text{cost per} \\ \text{unit}\end{array} + \begin{array}{c}\text{Fixed} \\ \text{cost per} \\ \text{unit}\end{array}\right)$$

Solution to Review Problem

Income under absorption costing	$13,000
− Income under variable costing	10,500
Income difference	$ 2,500
Cost of goods sold under absorption costing	$26,000
− Cost of goods sold under variable costing	21,000
Subtotal	5,000
+ Volume variance on absorption costing statement	1,500
Subtotal	6,500
− Fixed overhead period expense on variable costing statement	9,000
Total: absorption costing income exceeds variable costing income	$ 2,500

Using the shortcut formula,

$$\frac{\text{Difference}}{\text{in income}} = \left(\begin{array}{c}\text{Inventory} \\ \text{change}\end{array}\right) \times \left(\begin{array}{c}\text{Fixed cost} \\ \text{per unit}\end{array}\right)$$

$$\$2,500 = (5,000 \text{ units}) \times (\$.50)$$

Suggested Readings

Ajinkya, B., R. Atiase, and L. S. Bamber. "Absorption versus Direct Costing: Income Reconciliation and Cost-Volume-Profit Analysis." *Issues in Accounting Education* (Fall 1986): 268–81.

Chen, J. T. "Full and Direct Costing in Profit Variance Analysis." *Issues in Accounting Education* (Fall 1986): 282–92.

Govindarajan, V., and R. Anthony. "How Firms Use Cost Data in Price Decisions." *Management Accounting* (July 1983): 30–36.

Hilton, R., R. Swieringa, and M. Turner. "Product Pricing, Accounting Costs, and Use of Product-Costing Systems." *Accounting Review* (April 1988): 195–218.

Horngren, C. T., and G. H. Sorter. "Direct Costing for External Reporting." *Accounting Review* (January 1961): 84–93.

Ijiri, Y., R. Jaedicke, and J. Livingstone. "The Effect of Inventory Costing Methods on Full and Direct Costing." *Journal of Accounting Research* (Spring 1965): 63–74.

Kaplan, R., and A. Atkinson. *Advanced Management Accounting,* 2d ed. Englewood Cliffs, N.J.: Prentice-Hall, 1989, chap. 8.

Lere, J. "Product Pricing Based on Accounting Costs." *Accounting Review* (April 1986): 318–24.

Turner, M., and R. Hilton. "Use of Accounting Product Costs in Making Production Decisions." *Journal of Accounting Research* (Autumn 1989).

APPENDIX 9A
Reconciling Variable and Absorption Costing Income — Actual Costing

---

EXHIBIT 9-5

*Absorption and Variable Costing:
Formulas for Reconciling Income*

Notation:*

A = income under absorption costing
V = income under variable costing
B = fixed cost inventoried in beginning inventory
F = fixed manufacturing cost of current period
O = opening inventory quantity
E = ending inventory quantity
Q = quantity produced in current period
S = quantity sold in current period
f = standard fixed cost per unit

Inventory Costing Method	Income Difference $A - V$
FIFO actual, $S > O$	$E\left(\dfrac{F}{Q} - \dfrac{B}{E}\right)$
FIFO actual, $S < O$	$S\left(\dfrac{F}{S} - \dfrac{B}{O}\right)$
LIFO actual, $S > Q$	$(E - O)\dfrac{B}{O}$
LIFO actual, $S < Q$	$(E - O)\left(\dfrac{F}{Q}\right)$
Standard costing,	$f(E - O)$

---

* The formulas in this appendix are explained in detail in
Y. Ijiri, R. Jaedicke, and J. Livingstone, "The Effect of Inventory Costing Methods on Full and Direct Costing," *Journal of Accounting Research* (Spring 1965): 63–74.

APPENDIX 9B
An Alternative Valuation Procedure

A paradoxical situation often exists where inventory values are best approximated by absorption costing while income is more appropriately measured using variable costing. This appendix suggests a means by which both objectives can be accomplished simultaneously. Income is measured by an accounting procedure that considers all fixed costs as expenses of the time period. Fluctuations in income caused by changes in production and inventory are thereby eliminated.

To avoid an understatement of inventory values relative to market values, the often undesirable by-product of a variable costing procedure, the inventory can be presented at full cost. The fixed overhead in the inventory of the present period is compared to the amount of fixed overhead in the inventory of the previous period, and the change is recorded in the retained earnings account. The change in fixed costs included in inventory at the end of the period appears in the reconciliation of retained earnings but does not affect the reported income of the period.

A reconciliation is needed, however, because both absorption and variable costing assume that income is being measured in terms of the difference between revenues and expenses of the period. If income is redefined in terms of the change in the stockholders' equity at the beginning and end of the accounting period, excluding new capital raised and capital distributions, the need for the special adjustment to retained earnings is eliminated. If production is treated as increasing the well-being of the stockholders, the increased well-being is then reflected in the income statement. However, as long as accountants consider that realization of income is accomplished only by a completed sale and historic cost is the basis of asset accounting, then the basic inconsistency between absorption and variable costing will continue to exist.

A possible objection to the suggested procedure is that it makes use of the retained earnings reconciliation to adjust the amount of fixed costs remaining in inventory and considers the fixed costs an asset after they have been expensed. Against this objection can be balanced an improved measure of income, compared with that of generally accepted accounting procedures, as well as an improved valuation of inventories. The following example shows how the suggested procedure works. The results are compared with those from conventional accounting and variable costing.

Dryden Company produces a single product. The budgeted and actual fixed manufacturing costs in each year are $10,000. The standard and actual variable manufacturing costs are $2 per unit. The company has a normal capacity of 10,000 units and uses normal capacity to apply fixed overhead to product. The fixed-overhead rate is $1 per unit. There is no work-in-process inventory. The company's January 1 balance sheet is shown in Exhibit 9-6.

EXHIBIT 9-6

Balance Sheet as of January 1

				Year 1
Finished goods	$ 0	Retained earnings		$20,000
Other assets	40,000	Capital stock		20,000
Total assets	$40,000	Total equities		$40,000

During year 1 the company finished 10,000 units of product and sold 4,000 units at a price of $3.10 per unit. During year 2 the company finished 2,000 units and sold 4,000 units, also at $3.10 per unit. Dryden Company's selling and administrative expenses in both year 1 and year 2 can be ignored in this example without affecting the point being made.

Under the suggested procedure, the reports in Exhibit 9-7 could be prepared.

EXHIBIT 9-7

Accounting Reports for Dryden Company

Income Statements

	Year 1		Year 2	
Sales revenues (4,000 × $3.10)		$12,400		$12,400
Manufacturing costs:				
Variable costs (4,000 × $2)	$ 8,000		$ 8,000	
Fixed costs	10,000	18,000	10,000	18,000
Operating loss		($ 5,600)		($ 5,600)

Balance Sheets

	Dec. 31 Year 1	Dec. 31 Year 2		Dec. 31 Year 1	Dec. 31 Year 2
Finished goods	$18,000	$12,000	Retained earnings	$20,400	$12,800
Other assets	22,400	20,800	Capital stock	20,000	20,000
Total assets	$40,400	$32,800	Total equities	$40,400	$32,800

Retained Earnings Reconciliation

	Dec. 31 Year 1	Dec. 31 Year 2
Retained earnings, January 1	$20,000	$20,400
Less: Operating loss for year	5,600	5,600
Subtotal	$14,400	$14,800
Plus: Adjustment for changes in amount of fixed costs in inventory	6,000	(2,000)
Retained earnings, December 31	$20,400	$12,800

The fixed costs are charged to expense in the period in which they are incurred. However, generally accepted accounting principles assign to the cost of manufactured goods a share of the fixed manufacturing costs incurred. This procedure adjusts the inventory and retained earnings for the amount of fixed costs considered to be associated with the goods in inventory (six-tenths of $10,000 in year 1 and four-tenths of $10,000 in year 2).

Because the second year begins with $6,000 of fixed costs in inventory and ends with $4,000 in inventory, a credit of $2,000 to the inventory account and a debit of $2,000 to the retained earnings account are required. The journal entries are as follows:

December 31, Year 1		
Finished goods	6,000	
Retained earnings		6,000
Adjustment for fixed cost in inventory.		
December 31, Year 2		
Retained earnings	2,000	
Finished goods		2,000
Adjustment for fixed cost in inventory.		

These entries adjust the amount of fixed costs included in inventory to be consistent with the number of units in inventory as of December 31. They do not affect the income of the present or future periods. The procedure accomplishes several goals. The inventory is stated at full historical cost, satisfying the concern with the omission of fixed costs from inventory values. Furthermore, the income amounts for the two periods are equal, as would be expected for two accounting periods where the revenues are equal, the total number of units sold are the same, and there are no changes in cost efficiency. Under the conventional variable costing procedure, the income statements would be exactly the same as above, but the inventories would include only the variable costs. The income statements under absorption costing are given in Exhibit 9-8. Generally accepted accounting procedures lead to the interest-

---

EXHIBIT 9-8

Income Statements Using Absorption Costing

	Year 1	Year 2
Revenues	$12,400	$12,400
Manufacturing costs:		
Standard cost of product	12,000	12,000
Activity variance (loss)	0	8,000
Total expenses	$12,000	$20,000
Net income (loss)	$ 400	($ 7,600)

ing, although misleading, conclusion that there is an income of $400 in year 1, and a loss of $7,600 in year 2, when the only difference between the two years is the level of production and the associated change in inventory.

Review Questions

9-1 Briefly explain the difference between variable costing and absorption costing.

9-2 Name the three places where differences will appear when reconciling income on variable costing and absorption costing statements.

9-3 Will inventory on a balance sheet be higher under variable costing or absorption costing?

9-4 During a period when inventory increases, will reported income be higher under variable costing or absorption costing?

9-5 Three terms (variable costing, direct costing, and marginal costing) are sometimes used for the accounting procedure that expenses all fixed costs and considers only variable costs to be inventoriable. Which name do you consider most appropriate and why?

9-6 What advantages for financial reporting of overhead does absorption costing using normal activity have over actual costs and actual activity?

9-7 When do normal activity and fixed overhead application result in a distortion of the measure of income? How can this distortion be corrected?

9-8 Is the use of variable costing reasonable from the point of view of financial accounting?

9-9 Should cost factors that are conventionally classified by the accountant as being fixed ever be considered a cost of product from an economic point of view? Explain.

9-10 Should revenues be recognized as the production takes place or when the product is sold? Should income be a function of the level of production rather than sales? Should the cost per unit for reporting inventory levels and determining income be a function of the level of production? Explain.

Exercises

9-11 Straightforward Variable- and Absorption-Costing Income Calculations Kallman-Dykes Corporation produces a single product. The selling price is $12.00 per unit, the unit variable cost is $9.00 per unit, total fixed cost is $180,000, and the denominator activity is 90,000 units. Production for the period was 93,000 units and 90,000 units were sold.

REQUIRED:

Calculate net income under variable and absorption costing. Any volume variance under absorption costing is closed directly into income for the period.

9-12 Straightforward Reconciliation of Variable Costing and Absorption Costing Income   Refer to the data in the preceding exercise.

REQUIRED:

Reconcile the income amounts reported under variable and absorption costing.

9-13 Interpreting Financial Statements   The Rao Company was organized on January 1, 19x2.

	Statement of Financial Position		
	Jan. 1, 19x2	*Jan. 1, 19x3*	*Jan. 1, 19x4*
Cash	$10,000	$ 6,000	$20,000
Inventories	0	15,000ᵃ	5,000ᵇ
	10,000	21,000	25,000
Capital stock	10,000	10,000	10,000
Retained earnings	0	11,000	15,000
	$10,000	$21,000	$25,000

ᵃ Includes $3,000 of fixed overhead.
ᵇ Includes $1,000 of fixed overhead.

REQUIRED:

a. What were the reported incomes for 19x2 and 19x3, assuming that no dividends were declared?

b. What would income have been if variable costing had been used in both years?

9-14 Understanding Published Financial Statements   The annual report of a corporation included the following note:

> Inventories are priced, for the most part, at the lower of cost or market of materials plus direct labor and other direct costs, including overhead; however, in continuation of practices adopted by certain companies merged into the Corporation in prior years, overhead has been omitted from a portion of the inventories. The omission of such overhead ($6,826,618 this year and $5,609,148 last year) resulted in a reduction in net income (after taxes of *approximately* $600,000) for this year.

REQUIRED:

Comment on the procedure followed. How was the net income after taxes of $600,000 probably computed? (The corporate tax rate was 48 percent.)

9-15 Preparing an Absorption-Costing Income Statement   The Ruck Company produces one product, which it sells for $5.00 per unit. The production costs are as follows:

Fixed cost per year	$200,000
Variable costs per unit	$1

Normal activity is 100,000 units per year. At the beginning of 19x4 the company has the following balance sheet:

Other assets	$45,000	Capital stock	$30,000
Finished goods[a]	30,000	Retained earnings	45,000
	$75,000		$75,000

[a] Represents 10,000 units ($10,000 of variable costs and $20,000 of fixed costs).

The information for the year 19x4 is as follows:

Sales (units)	Sales (dollars)	Production (units)
50,000	$250,000	140,000

The manufacturing costs were the same as specified above. The company uses a LIFO inventory procedure.

REQUIRED:

Prepare an income statement using absorption costing and normal activity as the basis of overhead application. Allocate variances to inventory and cost of goods sold.

9-16 Preparing a Variable-Costing Income Statement Refer to the data in the preceding exercise.

REQUIRED:

Prepare an income statement using variable costing.

9-17 Reported versus Budgeted Income Explain the difference between the reported income of $10,000 and the income of $22,000 budgeted for sales of 10,000 units (see the accompanying break-even chart).

THE GRIPPER COMPANY
Income Statement for Month Ending July 31, 19x4

Sales (10,000 units sold for $10 apiece)			$100,000
Expenses:			
Manufacturing cost of sales (see note 1)		$60,000	
Selling expenses:			
Variable	$10,000		
Fixed	15,000	25,000	
Administrative expenses		5,000	
			90,000
Income (before taxes)			$ 10,000

(continued)

Income Statement *Continued*

Note 1:
Standard cost:

Material	$ 8,000	
Labor	15,000	
Variable overhead	3,000	
Fixed overhead (based on a fixed-overhead rate of $2 per direct labor dollar)	30,000	
		$ 56,000
Material usage, price and labor efficiency, and wage-rate variances	$19,000	
Volume variance (favorable)	15,000	4,000
Total		$ 60,000

Note 2: The budgeted fixed costs for the month were:

Manufacturing overhead	$25,000
Selling	12,000
Administrative	5,000
Total	$42,000

Note 3: The budgeted variable selling expense is 10% of sales.

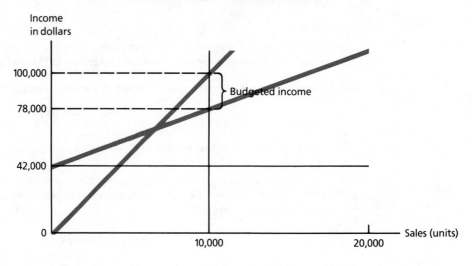

GRIPPER COMPANY BREAK-EVEN CHART

Problems

9-18 Preparing Financial Statements   The Bennett Company produces one product, which it sells for a price of $4.80 per unit. The production costs are as follows:

Fixed costs per year	$150,000
Variable cost per unit	$1

Normal activity is 100,000 units per year. At the beginning of 19x3 the company has the following balance sheet:

BALANCE SHEET JANUARY 1, 19x3

Other assets	$50,000	Capital stock	$30,000
Finished goods[a]	25,000	Retained earnings	45,000
	$75,000		$75,000

[a] Represents 10,000 units ($10,000 of variable costs and $15,000 of fixed costs).

The information for the years 19x3 through 19x5 is as follows:

Year	Sales (units)	Sales (S)	Production (units)
19x3	50,000	240,000	80,000
19x4	50,000	240,000	40,000
19x5	50,000	240,000	120,000

The manufacturing costs of each year were as indicated previously.

REQUIRED:

a. Prepare income statements for the three years, using normal activity as the basis of overhead absorption.

b. Prepare income statements for the three years, using variable costing as the basis of overhead accounting.

9-19 Refer to the data given in the preceding problem.

REQUIRED:

a. Prepare retained earnings reconciliations for the three years, assuming that inventory is presented on the balance sheets using normal activity as the basis of overhead absorption while variable costing is used for measuring the income of the period.

b. Prepare a balance sheet as of December 31, 19x5.

9-20 **Comparative Income Statements** The Capable Company includes its activity variance based on normal capacity in its cost of sales. The income statements for January and February were as follows:

Sales	January	February
Sales	$900,000	$900,000
Less: Manufacturing cost of sales	750,000	950,000
Manufacturing margin	$150,000	$(50,000)
Less: Selling and administrative expenses	25,000	25,000
Net income	$125,000	$(75,000)

During the month of January the company produced 500,000 units of product and sold 300,000. During the month of February the company produced and sold 300,000 units.

The variable costs of manufacturing are $1.50 per unit. There were no spending (expense) or efficiency variances during either of the two months. The fixed costs budgeted and incurred for each of the two months were $500,000. The normal capacity of the plant is 500,000 units (used for determining the fixed-overhead rate).

REQUIRED:

Present comparative income statements for the two months that could be more useful in appraising the results of operations during these months

a. Using variable costing,

b. Using absorption costing.

9-21 **Reconciling Income**   The can industry is an industry in which fluctuations in production and sales occur because of the seasonal nature of the products being canned. The United States Can Company has two plants, one in San Francisco and one in New York. The physical characteristics of the plants are similar, and the results of operations of the two plants are compared each month to judge the performance of the two managements. The March income statements for the two plants were as follows:

	San Francisco Plant	New York Plant
Sales	$1,000,000	$1,000,000
Less:		
Manufacturing cost of sales	$ 700,000	$ 800,000
Selling and administrative expenses	200,000	200,000
Total expenses	$ 900,000	$1,000,000
Net income	$ 100,000	0

Each plant sells their product for the same price. During the month of March, both plants sold and shipped 20,000,000 cans. The production for the month at the two plants was as follows:

	San Francisco Plant	New York Plant
Opening inventory (number of cans)	50,000	50,000
Production during month	30,000,000	20,000,000
	30,050,000	20,050,000
Cans shipped during month	20,000,000	20,000,000
Ending inventory	10,050,000	50,000

The San Francisco plant built up its inventory in March in anticipation of the canning season, which begins in April on the West Coast. The East Coast canning season begins in the middle of May.

The standard cost card for the type of can sold in March discloses the following information:

Standard Cost Card
(for both plants):
Can No. 4593

	Cost per 1,000 Cans
Direct material	$20
Direct labor	4
Overhead:	
Variable	1
Fixed	10
Total	$35

For both plants the manufacturing fixed costs budgeted for the month were $300,000. There were no spending (budget) or efficiency variances. All selling and administrative expenses were fixed.

REQUIRED:

Write a report relative to the operations of the two plants during the month of March. Explain the differences in income, and prepare a revised statement that helps managers appraise the results of the operations of the two plants.

9-22 Constructing Comparative Income Statements   For several months management has been puzzled by fluctuations in the income reported by its western division. The results for February, March, and April were as follows:

	February	March	April
Sales	$1,000,000	$1,000,000	$500,000
Less manufacturing cost of sales	$1,000,000	$ 800,000	$250,000
Selling and administrative expenses	200,000	200,000	200,000
Total expenses	$1,200,000	$1,000,000	$450,000
Net income (loss)	$ (200,000)	$ 0	$ 50,000

There has been no change in sales price during the three-month period. During the months of February and March the plant sold and shipped 20,000,000 units. In April it shipped half that total. The production for the three months was as follows:

	February	March	April
Opening inventory	20,050,000	50,000	50,000
Production during month	—	20,000,000	40,000,000
	20,050,000	20,050,000	40,050,000
Units shipped during month	20,000,000	20,000,000	10,000,000
Ending inventory	50,000	50,000	30,050,000

The standard cost card for the type of product sold discloses the following information:

	Cost per 1,000 Units
Direct material	$20
Direct labor	4
Overhead:	
Variable	1
Fixed	10
	$35

The fixed manufacturing costs budgeted for each of the months were $300,000. There were no spending (expense) or efficiency variances during the three months. All selling and administrative expenses were fixed.

REQUIRED:

Present comparative income statements for the three months that help managers appraise the results of operations for the three months.

9-23 **Preparing Income Statements**   The Gulf Box Company has decided to use a variable costing procedure for internal accounting reports. Following this procedure, all fixed costs are considered a cost of the period, and only variable costs are inventoried.

Manufacturing costs incurred:	
Variable manufacturing costs	$ 500,000
Fixed manufacturing costs	$ 250,000
Selling costs incurred:	
Variable selling costs	$ 50,000
Fixed selling costs	$ 80,000
Administrative costs incurred:	
Fixed administrative costs	$ 100,000
Number of boxes produced	25,000,000
Number of boxes sold	24,000,000
Revenues from sales	$1,000,000

REQUIRED:

a. Prepare two income statements, one following conventional overhead absorption accounting techniques and the other using variable costing. Assume that there was no beginning inventory of finished goods and that the fixed overhead application rate is $10 per 1,000 boxes. Except for fixed overhead, actual costs are used in determining the cost of product.

b. Prepare two additional income statements, one assuming that the fixed-overhead application rate is $5 per 1,000 boxes and that the company does not close out the activity variance monthly; the other assuming that the plant uses normal activity of 20,000,000 boxes as the basis for computing the fixed overhead rate, an application rate of $12.50 per 1,000 boxes, and the company does close the variance account monthly to cost of goods sold.

c. It is possible to use absorption costing and still retain the benefits of variable costing. Explain.

9-24 **Income Statements Using Different Overhead and Costing Systems**   The Bandura Company had sales of $200,000 in both May and June (this represents 50,000 units at $4 per unit). The production costs for each of the two months are as follows:

Fixed costs per month	$150,000
Variable costs per unit	$1

The production for May was 50,000 units and for June 150,000 units (the plant operated at capacity). The May 1 finished goods inventory is zero.

REQUIRED:

Prepare income statements for May and June based on

a. Actual costs and actual activity for the month.

b. Overhead absorption using normal activity of 100,000 units as the basis of overhead absorption.

c. Overhead absorption using practical capacity of 150,000 units as the basis of overhead absorption.

d. Variable costing.

9-25 **Direct versus Absorption Costing**   The vice president for sales of Huber Corporation has received the income statement for November 19x9. The statement has been prepared using variable costing and is reproduced below. The firm has just adopted a variable costing system for internal reporting purposes.

HUBER CORPORATION
Income Statement
for the Month of November 19x9
(000s omitted)

Sales		$2,400
Less: Variable standard cost of goods sold		1,200
Manufacturing margin		$1,200
Less: Fixed manufacturing costs at budget	$600	
Fixed manufacturing cost spending variance	0	600
Gross margin		$ 600
Less: Fixed selling and administrative costs		400
Net income before taxes		$ 200

The controller attached the following notes to the statements.

(1) The unit sales price for November averaged $24.

(2) The standard unit manufacturing costs for the month were

Variable cost	$12
Fixed cost	4
Total cost	$16

The unit rate for fixed manufacturing costs is a predetermined rate based on a normal monthly production of 150,000 units.

(3) Production for November was 45,000 units in excess of sales.

(4) The inventory at November 30 consisted of 80,000 units.

REQUIRED:

a. The vice president for sales is not comfortable with variable costing and wonders what the net income would have been with an absorption costing basis.

    (1) Present the November income statement on an absorption costing basis.

    (2) Reconcile and explain the difference between the variable-costing and the absorption-costing net income figures.

b. Explain the features associated with variable-costing income measurement that should be attractive to the vice president for sales. (*CMA adapted*)

9-26 Variable-Costing Income Statement BBG Corporation is a manufacturer of a synthetic element. Gary Voss, president of the company, has been eager to get the operating results for the just completed fiscal year. He was surprised when the income statement revealed that income before taxes has dropped to $885,000 from $900,000 even though sales volume had increased 100,000 kg. This drop in net income had occurred even though Voss had implemented the following changes during the past twelve months to improve the profitability of the company:

- In response to a 10 percent increase in production costs, the sales price of the company's product was increased by twelve percent. This action took place on December 1, 19x1.

- The managements of the selling and administrative departments were given strict instructions to spend no more in fiscal 19x2 than in fiscal 19x1.

BBG's Accounting Department prepared and distributed to top management the following comparative income statements. The accounting staff also prepared related financial information to assist management in evaluating the company's performance. BBG uses absorption costing and the FIFO inventory method for finished goods.

BBG CORPORATION
Statements of Operating Income
for the Years Ended November 30, 19x1 and 19x2
(000s omitted)

	19x1	19x2
Sales revenue	$9,000	$11,200
Cost of goods sold	$7,200	$ 8,320
Manufacturing volume variance	(600)	495
Adjusted cost of goods sold	$6,600	$ 8,815
Gross margin	$2,400	$ 2,385
Selling and administrative expenses	1,500	1,500
Income before taxes	$ 900	$ 885

BBG CORPORATION
Selected Operating and Financial Data
for 19x1 and 19x2

	19x1	19x2
Sales price	$ 10/kg	$11.20/kg
Material cost	$1.50/kg	$ 1.65/kg
Direct labor cost	$2.50/kg	$ 2.75/kg
Variable overhead cost	$1.00/kg	$ 1.10/kg
Fixed overhead cost	$3.00/kg	$ 3.30/kg
Total fixed overhead costs	$3,000,000	$3,300,000
Selling and administrative (all fixed)	$1,500,000	$1,500,000
Sales volume	900,000 kg	1,000,000 kg
Beginning inventory	300,000 kg	600,000 kg

REQUIRED:

a. Explain to Gary Voss why BBG Corporation's net income decreased in the current fiscal year despite the sales price and sales volume increases.

b. A member of BBG's Accounting Department has suggested that the company adopt variable costing for internal reporting purposes. Do You agree?

(1) Prepare an operating income statement through income before taxes for the year ended November 30, 19x2, for BBG Corporation using the variable costing method.

(2) Present a numerical reconciliation of the difference in income before taxes using the absorption costing method as currently employed by BBG and the variable costing method as proposed.

c. Identify and discuss the advantages and disadvantages of using the variable costing method for internal reporting purposes. (*CMA adapted*)

9-27 Variable and Absorption Costing; CVP Analysis   Pralina Products Company is a regional firm that markets three major product lines — cereals, breakfast bars, and dog food. The income statement for 19x8 is shown below; the statement was prepared by product line using absorption (full) costing. Explanatory data follow the income statement.

PRALINA PRODUCTS COMPANY
Income Statement for 19x8
(in thousands)

	Cereals	Breakfast Bars	Dog Food	Total
Sales in pounds	2,000	500	500	3,000
Revenue from sales	$1,000	$400	$200	$1,600
Cost of sales:				
Raw materials	$ 330	$160	$100	$ 590
Direct labor	90	40	20	150
Factory overhead	108	48	24	180
Total cost of sales	$ 528	$248	$144	$ 920
Gross margin	$ 472	$152	$ 56	$ 680
Operating expenses:				
Selling expenses:				
Advertising	$ 50	$ 30	$ 20	$ 100
Commissions	50	40	20	110
Salaries and related benefits	30	20	10	60
Total selling expenses	$ 130	$ 90	$ 50	$ 270
General and administration expenses:				
Licenses	$ 50	$ 20	$ 15	$ 85
Salaries and related benefits	60	25	15	100
Total general and administrative expenses	$ 110	$ 45	$ 30	$ 185
Total operating expenses	$ 240	$135	$ 80	$ 455
Operating income before taxes	$ 232	$ 17	$(24)	$ 225

1. Cost of sales.   The company's inventories of raw materials and finished products do not vary significantly from year to year. The inventories at year end were essentially identical to those on January 1. Factory overhead was applied to products at

120 percent of direct labor dollars. The factory overhead costs for the year were as follows:

Variable indirect labor and supplies	$ 15,000
Variable employee benefits on factory labor	30,000
Supervisory salaries and related benefits	35,000
Plant occupancy costs	100,000
Total	$180,000

There was no overapplied or underapplied overhead at the end of the year.

2. *Advertising.* The company has been unable to determine any direct causal relationship between the level of sales volume and the level of advertising expenditures. However, because management believes advertising is necessary, an annual advertising program is implemented for each product line. Each product line is advertised independently of the others.

3. *Commissions.* Sales commissions are paid to the sales force at the rates of 5 percent on the cereals and 10 percent on the breakfast bars and dog food.

4. *Licenses.* Various licenses are required for each product line and are renewed annually.

5. *Salaries and related benefits.* Sales and general and administrative personnel devote time and effort to all product lines. Their salaries and wages are allocated on the basis of management's estimates of time spent on each product line.

REQUIRED:

a. The controller of Pralina Products Company has recommended that the company do a cost-volume-profit analysis of its operations. As a first step the controller has requested that you prepare a revised income statement for Pralina Products Company that employs a product contribution margin format, which will be useful in CVP analysis. The statement should show the profit contribution for each product line and the net income before taxes for the company as a whole.

b. How would significant increases in inventories affect net income before taxes determined in problem a? Explain your answer.

c. The controller of Pralina Products Company is going to prepare a report to present to the other members of top management explaining CVP analysis. Identify and explain the following points, which the controller should include in the report:

(1) The advantages that CVP analysis can provide to a company.

(2) The difficulties Pralina Products Company could experience in the calculations involved in CVP analysis.

(3) The dangers that Pralina Products Company should be aware of in using the information derived from the CVP analysis. (*CMA adapted*)

10

Budgeting and Responsibility Accounting

LEARNING OBJECTIVES

After studying this chapter, you should be able to:

1 List and explain the major purposes of budgets.

2 Describe some different types of budgets.

3 Prepare a master budget.

4 Explain the purpose of a responsibility accounting system.

5 Define and give examples of *cost centers, revenue centers, profit centers,* and *investment centers.*

6 Explain how performance is measured in cost, revenue, profit, and investment centers.

Budgeting

A **budget** is an important management tool that is a quantitative statement of a plan of action for some specified period of time. It is used to plan for the organization's future activities and also to control current operations.

Many of the topics covered in previous chapters are closely related to the topic of budgeting. For example, the cost classifications discussed in Chapter 2 are often used to classify costs in a budget. Classifications such as variable and fixed costs or controllable and uncontrollable costs provide important distinctions in the planning process. Cost-volume-profit analysis, discussed in Chapter 3, is also related to budgeting; changes in activity on cost, revenue, and profit affect the development of a financial plan. Similarly, the product-costing systems discussed in Chapters 4, 5, and 6 provide data used in budgeting for an organization's production activities. Finally, the standard costs discussed in Chapters 7 and 8 are really budgets for the production of one unit of product or service. Standard costs are the building blocks for the budgeting process in companies that use standard costing systems. Moreover, just as standard costing systems provide a means of controlling operations, budgets also serve as a control device. Managers compare actual levels of cost, revenue, or goal achievement with budgeted levels to evaluate and diagnose performance.

Types of Budgets

Most large companies use several types of budgets and develop budgets for different time periods, purposes, and parts of the organization. The budget that ties all of these budgets together into a unified plan for the organization is called a **master budget.** An **operating budget** specifies the organization's plan for carrying out operating activities such as production and sales. A **financial budget,** which specifies the organization's plans for financing its activities, shows how financial resources will be generated and how they will be used. **Pro forma financial statements** are budgets that show how the organization's financial reports will appear if the organization carries out its planned activities. A **cash budget** shows planned sources and uses of cash. A **capital budget** quantifies the organization's plans for acquisition and disposal of capital assets (such as buildings and equipment).

Budgets may be developed for short periods of time, such as a week, month, or year. Alternatively, budgets may cover a longer period, such as five years. Most organizations have both *short-range budgets* and *long-range budgets.* Many organizations use a **revolving budget** (also called a *rolling* or *continuous budget*) — a new budget periodically developed for some specified period of time. For example, a business may develop an operating budget for the next year every three months. Under this budgeting system, the organization is continually in the process of developing its budget. As events unfold, plans are updated to reflect new information.

Budget Administration

A **budget director** or *budget officer* generally determines and directs the procedures by which the organization's budget is constructed and implemented. A **budget committee,** composed of senior line or staff executives, is often appointed to act in an advisory role in the budgetary process. Many organizations have a **budget manual** that details the procedures by which the budget is constructed. The authority to approve an organization's budget is generally reserved to the board of directors or some similar body governing the organization's overall activities.

Purposes of Budgeting

Force Planning   Budgets force managers to plan ahead for the activities of the organization. The budgeting process compels managers at every level in the organization, from chairman of the board to a departmental supervisor, to plan.

Facilitate Communication and Coordination   The budgeting process requires that managers of different departments or divisions communicate about the plans they have made. In a manufacturing firm, for example, production cannot be planned until the sales manager has communicated the sales plan to the production manager. Similarly, the purchasing manager cannot plan raw material acquisition until the production manager has communicated the production plan to the purchasing department. The budgeting process forces the managers of the various parts of the organization to communicate with one another and coordinate their plans for action.

Allocate Resources   Most organizations face shortages of labor, equipment, materials, capital investment funds, computer time, and so forth. The budget provides management with a means to allocate such scarce resources.

Provide Control   Budgets are important control tools; they are the benchmark against which actual performance is compared. When needed, *flexible budgets* are employed to adjust budgeted cost levels to reflect actual activity. A unit standard cost is a *unitized budget* — the budget for one unit of production. Multiplying the unit standard by actual production provides the flexible budget cost, which is the standard cost against which actual cost is compared. Then variance analysis is employed, as described in Chapters 7 and 8, to determine how and why actual performance differed from the budget. Thus, the budget is a tool used in analyzing, diagnosing, and controlling performance.

Evaluate Performance and Provide Incentives   Related to the control purpose of budgets is evaluation of performance. Because a manager's performance is evaluated, at least in part, on the basis of performance relative to a budget, incentives are created for managers to meet the standards established by the budget. This chapter concentrates on the procedures of budgeting, while Chapter 26 discusses the behavioral implications of budgets.

Master Budget

To illustrate the steps involved in preparing a master budget, we use data supplied by The Firestone Tire & Rubber Company. Firestone is a well-known manufacturer of high-quality tires and related products. The example is a highly simplified illustration of the steps in the budgeting process used by Firestone. The numbers used in the example are for illustrative purposes; they were supplied by the company, but some numbers have been altered to protect confidential information.

Exhibit 10-1 depicts the six basic steps used to prepare the master budget at Firestone. The budgeting process begins with a sales budget or forecast for each product (1). Based on the sales forecast, together with an ending inventory budget, a production budget is developed stating the number of units of each product to be produced (2). In addition, a selling and administrative expense budget is developed (3). On the basis of the production budget, it is possible to prepare budgets for the acquisition of direct material (4a and 4b) and direct labor (4c) and for factory

---

EXHIBIT 10-1

Preparing the Master Budget: A Simplified Illustration

Firestone

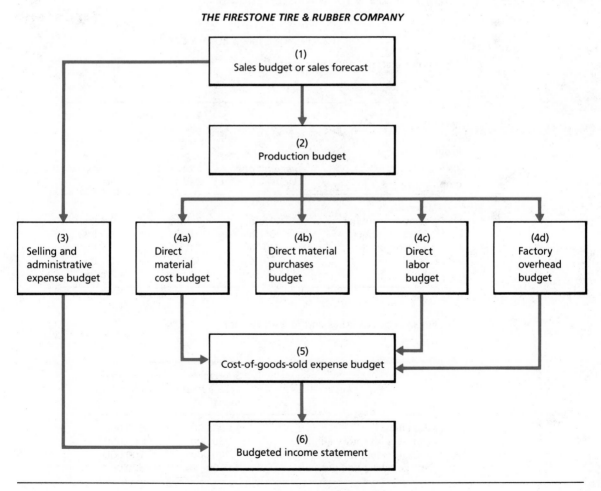

THE FIRESTONE TIRE & RUBBER COMPANY

overhead costs (4d). Using these budgets, the cost-of-goods-sold budget (5) and budgeted income statement (6) are prepared.

Forecast Sales   Notice that the budgeting process begins with a sales forecast. Although this is a critical step in the budgeting process, it is very difficult to do. In forecasting sales, companies try to take the following factors into account: past sales, sales trends, general economic conditions, political and legal considerations, planned advertising and product promotion, and the expected actions of the firm's competitors. Many companies have a high-level staff that is devoted exclusively to forecasting.

Illustration   Now let's see how these individual budgets are prepared, using the data in Exhibit 10-2.

EXHIBIT 10-2
Illustrative Data for a Master Budget

Firestone

THE FIRESTONE TIRE & RUBBER COMPANY

1. Direct material and labor costs

		Standard Usage per Tire	
	Standard Cost per Unit of Input	Supreme® Steel Belted Radial	Deluxe Champion® Bias
Materials:			
Synthetic rubber	$ .55/lb	7.0 lbs	9.0 lbs
Natural rubber	.65/lb	6.0 lbs	3.0 lbs
Carbon black	.20/lb	7.0 lbs	7.5 lbs
Steel	2.50/lb	3.0 lbs	1.0 lbs
Labor	15.00/hr	11 mins	7 mins

2. Finished goods: sales and inventory data

	Supreme® Steel Belted Radial	Deluxe Champion® Bias
Sales (units)	3,000,000	500,000
Beginning inventory (units)	750,000	85,000
Desired ending inventory (units)	700,000	100,000
Average sales price per unit	$48.00	$29.00

EXHIBIT 10-2 Continued

3. Direct materials inventory data

	Synthetic Rubber	Natural Rubber	Carbon Black	Steel
Beginning inventory (pounds)	2,000,000	5,000,000	3,000,000	1,000,000
Desired ending inventory (pounds)	2,500,000	4,000,000	3,000,000	1,000,000

4. Factory overhead (applied to product on the basis of direct labor hours)

Indirect labor	$20,000,000
Supplies	2,500,000
Group employee benefits	7,500,000
Utilities	5,000,000
Maintenance	14,000,000
Taxes and insurance	4,000,000
Depreciation	15,000,000
Other	2,000,000
Total	$70,000,000

5. Selling and administrative expenses

Administrative expense	$ 3,000,000
Selling expense	5,250,000
Advertising expense	2,250,000
District office expense	1,125,000
Retail operating expense	375,000
Total	$12,000,000

6. Corporate tax rate: 50 percent

The first step in preparing the master budget is the sales budget or forecast. A sales budget can be prepared as follows:

Schedule 1
Sales Budget

	Units	Price	Sales Dollars
Supreme® Steel Belted Radial	3,000,000[a]	$48.00[a]	$144,000,000
Deluxe Champion® Bias	500,000[a]	$29.00[a]	14,500,000
Total			$158,500,000

[a] From Exhibit 10-2, Finished goods: sales and inventory data.

The sales forecast coupled with the inventory data is then used to develop the production budget. The following equation is used to determine the required production quantity:

$$\begin{bmatrix} \text{Required} \\ \text{production} \end{bmatrix} = \begin{bmatrix} \text{Budgeted} \\ \text{sales} \end{bmatrix} + \begin{bmatrix} \text{Desired ending} \\ \text{inventory} \end{bmatrix} - \begin{bmatrix} \text{Beginning} \\ \text{inventory} \end{bmatrix}$$

The production budget follows:

Schedule 2
Production Budget

	Supreme® Steel Belted Radial	Deluxe Champion® Bias
Budgeted sales (units)	3,000,000	500,000
Add: Desired ending inventory (units)	700,000	100,000
Finished goods needed (units)	3,700,000	600,000
Less: Beginning inventory (units)	750,000	85,000
Required production (units)	2,950,000	515,000

The production budget is then used to budget raw material and labor.

Schedule 3
Raw Material Cost Budget

	Materials for Production				
	Supreme® Steel Belted Radial (2,950,000 units)[a]	*Deluxe Champion® Bias (515,000 units)[a]*	*Total Usage*	*Price per Pound*	*Raw Material Cost*
Synthetic rubber Supreme (7 lb)[b] Deluxe Champion (9 lb)[b]	20,650,000[c]	4,635,000[c]	25,285,000	$ .55	$13,906,750
Natural rubber Supreme (6 lb)[b] Deluxe Champion (3 lb)[b]	17,700,000[c]	1,545,000[c]	19,245,000	$ .65	12,509,250
Carbon black Supreme (7 lb)[b] Deluxe Champion (7.5 lb)[b]	20,650,000[c]	3,862,500[c]	24,512,500	$ .20	4,902,500
Steel Supreme (3 lb)[b] Deluxe Champion (1 lb)[b]	8,850,00[c]	515,000[c]	9,365,000	$2.50	23,412,500
Total			—		$54,731,000

[a] Is determined in the Production Budget, Schedule 2.

[b] From Exhibit 10-2, Direct Material and Labor Costs, Standard Usage per Tire.

[c] Standard usage per tire multiplied by required production in units.

The amount of each raw material to be purchased is computed using the following equation:

$$\begin{bmatrix} \text{Required} \\ \text{purchase} \end{bmatrix} = \begin{bmatrix} \text{Amount needed} \\ \text{for production} \end{bmatrix} + \begin{bmatrix} \text{Desired ending} \\ \text{inventory} \end{bmatrix} - \begin{bmatrix} \text{Beginning} \\ \text{inventory} \end{bmatrix}$$

Schedule 4
Raw Material Purchases Budget

	Synthetic Rubber	Natural Rubber	Carbon Black	Steel
Budgeted for production (lbs)	25,285,000[a]	19,245,000[a]	24,512,500[a]	9,365,000[a]
Desired ending inventory (lbs)	2,500,000[b]	4,000,000[b]	3,000,000[b]	1,000,000[b]
Materials needed (lbs)	27,785,000	23,245,000	27,512,500	10,365,000
Less: Beginning inventory (lbs)	2,000,000[b]	5,000,000[b]	3,000,000[b]	1,000,000[b]
Required purchases (lbs)	25,785,000	18,245,000	24,512,500	9,365,000
Price per pound	× $.55[c]	× $.65[c]	× $.20[c]	× $2.50[c]
Dollar purchases	$14,181,750	$11,859,250	$ 4,902,500	$23,412,500

[a] From Schedule 3, Raw material cost budget (column b).
[b] From Exhibit 10-2, Direct materials inventory.
[c] From Exhibit 10-2, Direct material and labor costs.

The production budget is also used as the basis for the direct labor budget.

Schedule 5
Direct Labor Budget

	Units Produced	Direct Labor Hours per Unit	Hours Required	Direct Labor Cost (Q $15.00/hr)
Supreme® Steel Belted Radial	2,950,000[a]	11/60[b]	540,830[c]	$8,112,450
Deluxe Champion® Bias	515,000[a]	7/60[b]	60,080[c]	901,200
Total			600,910	$9,013,650

[a] From Schedule 2.
[b] From Exhibit 10-2, Direct material and labor costs.
[c] These figures were rounded.

The factory overhead budget is given below:

Schedule 6
Factory Overhead Budget

Indirect labor	$20,000,000
Supplies	2,500,000
Group employee benefits	7,500,000
Utilities	5,000,000
Maintenance	14,000,000
Taxes and insurance	4,000,000
Depreciation	15,000,000
Other	2,000,000
Total	$70,000,000

The predetermined overhead rate (rounded) is

$$\frac{\text{Total budgeted overhead}}{\text{Total budgeted direct labor hours}} = \frac{\$70,000,000}{600,910} = \$116.50 \text{ per hour}$$

The unit cost data for direct materials, direct labor, and overhead is summarized below.

Schedule 7
Unit Cost Summary

	Supreme® Steel Belted Radial			*Deluxe Champion® Bias*		
	Quantity[a]	*Price[a]*	*Unit Cost*	*Quantity[a]*	*Price[a]*	*Unit Cost*
Direct material:						
Synthetic rubber	7	$ .55	$ 3.85	9	$ .55	$ 4.95
Natural rubber	6	.65	3.90	3	.65	1.95
Carbon black	7	.20	1.40	7.5	.20	1.50
Steel	3	2.50	7.50	1	2.50	2.50
Total materials			16.65			10.90
Direct labor	11/60	15.00	2.75	7/60	15.00	1.75
Factory overhead	11/60	116.50[b]	21.36	7/60	116.50[b]	13.59
Total unit cost			$40.76			$26.24

[a] From Exhibit 10-2, Direct material and labor costs.
[b] From Schedule 6, Predetermined overhead rate.

Cost of goods sold can now be calculated as follows:

Schedule 8
Cost-of-Goods-Sold Expense Budget

	Sales (units)	Unit Cost	Cost of Goods Sold
Supreme® Steel Belted Radial	3,000,000[a]	$40.76[b]	$122,280,000
Deluxe Champion® Bias	500,000[a]	$26.24[b]	13,120,000
Total			$135,400,000

[a] From Schedule 1, Sales budget.
[b] From Schedule 7, Unit cost summary.

The selling and administrative expense budget is prepared as follows:

Schedule 9
Selling and Administrative Expense Budget[a]

Administrative expense	$ 3,000,000
Selling expense	5,250,000
Advertising expense	2,250,000
District office expense	1,125,000
Retail operating expense	375,000
Total	$12,000,000

[a] From Exhibit 10-2, Anticipated selling and administrative expenses.

Finally, the budgeted (or pro forma) income statement can be prepared, using information from Schedules 1, 8, and 9.

Schedule 10
Budgeted Income Statement

Sales (Schedule 1)	$158,500,000
Less: Cost of goods sold (Schedule 8)	135,400,000
Gross margin	$ 23,100,000
Less: Selling and administrative expenses (Schedule 9)	12,000,000
Income before taxes	$ 11,100,000
Less: Income tax expense (50%)	5,550,000
Net income	$ 5,550,000

This illustration of the budgeting process has focused on the master budget for operations. Appendix 10A concentrates on cash budgeting.

Widespread Use and Diversity of Budgeting Procedures

Almost all organizations — manufacturing firms, retailers, service industry firms, educational institutions, health care facilities, and governmental units — use budgets. Even many small businesses benefit from implementing some type of budgeting process. Because the organizations in which budgets are used are diverse, the budgeting procedures found in practice tend to vary widely across organizations. Several current issues related to budgeting processes are described below in the context of real-world organizations.

Budgeting Using Representative Products   Many companies produce thousands of products and find it impractical to develop detailed budget data for each product. As a result, many large companies classify products into a small number of categories and then develop detailed production budgets for a representative product in each category.

The following excerpt from *Management Accounting* indicates how Chesebrough-Ponds, Inc. budgets the cost of sales for its hundreds of products by using a representative sample of products. The excerpt also describes the use of a rolling budget. Each quarter (three months) a new annual budget is developed, and the quarter just completed is dropped from the budget.

Chesebrough-Ponds

We began automation of our established cost of sales projection system within the Health and Beauty Products division of Chesebrough-Ponds, Inc. This system projects an expected product cost for future accounting periods. Several key products are used to represent the division's most cost-impactive items. These products are broken down to their most detailed elements (material packaging parts, raw ingredients for formulas, direct labor and overhead) and each element projected outward for four quarters of the upcoming operating year.

Our system does not employ sophisticated techniques beyond what is required to choose a representative sample of products. Each selected product acts as the model for its respective product line and the quarter by quarter changes in total cost are used for all products within the line. The steps involved in the overall process are:

(1) The annual sales forecast is evaluated on a product line basis to highlight where the major activity will take place in the upcoming year.

(2) Sample products are selected for detailed cost projection. The resulting increases or decreases in these samples are applied to their respective product lines.

(3) An evaluation is made of the results to ensure that the proper attention is given to all product lines.

The projection system does not end once it has delivered cost data for the sample. A monitoring exercise is carried out for the entire operating year. At the end of each quarter the actual performance of the sample is measured against its original projection. Any large deviations can be investigated for the effect they may have on the parent product line. Also at this time, new projections are made. The system projects on a rolling four quarter basis while the prior quarter is dropped and a future quarter is picked up.[1]

---

[1] D. Worrell, "Cost of Sales: A Budgeting Priority," *Management Accounting* (August 1983): 67.

Long-Range and Short-Range Budgeting   Many organizations develop budgets covering different time periods as a routine part of the planning process. Short-range budgets are highly detailed and are designed to guide day-to-day operations. Long-range budgets contain less detail and are more strategic in nature. The following excerpt from *Management Accounting* describes the use of such budgets at UNYSIS (formerly Burroughs Corporation).

UNYSIS

We developed a manufacturing plant forecast to give our managers a comprehensive but consolidated view of future plant operations. . . . The long-range forecast, the annual plan, and the quarterly and monthly outlook forecasts are prepared at various times of the year for management's review. Each plan has its own purpose and objective. The purpose of the long-range forecast is to evaluate and determine what the future financial needs will be for an individual product or an entire program for the next three to five years. Based on information from product management, the forecast projects a product's anticipated financial performance and the impact it will have on existing corporate resources. . . .

The annual forecast plan covers a two-year period and focuses on reviewing dynamic operational issues and marketing forecasts of current and soon-to-be-released products.[2]

Management by Objectives   Often used in conjunction with a budgeting process in a service or not-for-profit organization is the concept of **management by objectives (MBO).** Under this approach, the organization's mission or primary goal is broken down into specific objectives. Budgets are then developed to meet each of these objectives. The following excerpt from *Management Accounting* describes the use of MBO in budgeting for the transportation-services department of the city of Charlotte, North Carolina.

City of Charlotte, North Carolina

Services provided are broken down into six areas: (1) community development, (2) environmental health and protection, (3) protection of persons and property, (4) transportation, (5) leisure-time opportunities, and (6) policy formulation and administration. Within each of these areas specific work objectives are determined, specific program changes are recommended to meet changing cir-

---

[2] D. Janusky, "Plant Forecasting at Burroughs," *Management Accounting* (March 1985): 59, 60.

cumstances, resources are determined in terms of dollars and manpower, and recommendations are determined for city council action.

Illustration The transportation service area will be reviewed to illustrate how the individual service areas are presented in the budget. Each of the major service areas is handled in a similar manner.

The transportation budget starts with the overall objectives of the transportation service area and a recommendation of resources needed to meet the transportation objectives. The recommended resources are presented in terms of dollars and employment positions in a two-year comparison. The overall objectives are stated in general terms. For instance, the overall objectives of the transportation program are stated as follows:

> Plan and provide for the safe, convenient, economical and expeditious movement of people and goods, as desired and needed by residents and businesses in the Charlotte area. Furnish this capability through projects in new construction, capital improvement and maintenance which will facilitate a variety of transportation modes including automobiles, trucks, buses, airplanes and bicycles, and their associated traffic controls and facilities. Provide updated studies of feasible options for meeting immediate, short-term, and long-range transportation needs to guide the community and elected officials in making decisions that promote a highly usable, coordinated, effective, economical, and safe transportation network of facilities and services. Incorporate measures that demonstrate sensitivity and concern for potential impact on the environment and adjacent neighborhoods in all transportation undertakings.

The transportation budget is broken down into several areas such as airport, automotive services, traffic control, transportation planning and traffic engineering. Each of the areas such as traffic engineering is detailed in terms of general objectives, target clients, achievement and performance objectives, objective linkages, resources to meet the objectives, and recommended city council action.[3]

Zero-Base Budgeting The concept of **zero-base budgeting (ZBB)** has been applied in a variety of organizations, including Texas Instruments, Southern California Edison, and the State of Georgia. Under this budgeting approach, the initial budget for every activity in the organization is set at zero. Then funds are budgeted for the activity at whatever level its further existence can be justified. The concept of ZBB and its use in a suburban Rochester public school district is summarized in the following excerpt from *Management Accounting.*

[3] C. H. Gibson, "Budgeting by Objectives: Charlotte's Experience," *Management Accounting* (January 1978): 39, 40.

Zero-Base Budgeting in a Public School District

Zero-base budgeting is not a magic formula, but an attitude, woven into a structured analytical process. As most administrators know, the usual approach to budgeting is to begin with the present level of operation and spending and then carefully justify the new programs or additional expenditures desired for next year. In zero-base budgeting there are no "givens." It starts with the basic premise that the budget for next year is zero — and that every expenditure, old and new, must be justified on the basis of its cost and benefit. . . . Virtually everything you do resolves to a selection among alternatives. In zero-base budgeting, the process of alternatives is more rigidly defined. Having measured the effect of eliminating a function, you next must define what would happen if the function were reduced to a lower level of service. What would be saved? What would be the consequence of providing less or delayed service?[4]

Responsibility Accounting

Many organizations are divided into smaller subunits, such as divisions, business units, segments, or departments. Each subunit has a manager in charge of that subunit's activities. If the managers of an organization's subunits have the authority to make substantive decisions concerning their subunits, the organization is said to be *decentralized.* There are several benefits of decentralization. Some of the most important ones are listed below:

- Managers of subunits are better informed than top management about the subunits' activities and can make better decisions to optimize the subunits' activities.

- Subunit managers can react more quickly than top management as events unfold to adapt their subunits' activities to changing conditions.

- Decentralized decision making provides training for subunit managers who may one day become part of top management.

- Most organizations' activities are too complex for top management to make all of the detailed decisions affecting subunit operations.

- Relying on subunit managers to make some operational decisions frees top management for strategic planning.

[4] A. F. Brueningsen, "SCAT — A Process of Alternatives," *Management Accounting* (November 1976): 56.

The major disadvantage of decentralization is that a subunit manager who chooses an optimal action for that subunit may be unaware of the effects on that action on other subunits. Thus, the optimal action for a subunit may not be beneficial for the organization as a whole.

Most organizations are to some degree decentralized. A **responsibility accounting system** accumulates information about the activities of each organizational subunit for planning, control, evaluation of performance, and provision of incentives to managers. A responsibility accounting system should be designed to measure the performance of each subunit manager in a way that provides incentives for the manager to make decisions that are in the best interest of the overall organization. When the goals of the manager and the entire organization mesh in this fashion, **goal congruence** exists.

Cost, Profit, Revenue, and Investment Centers

A responsibility accounting system designates each subunit in the organization as a cost center, profit center, revenue center, or investment center. A **cost center** incurs costs but does not generate revenue. The cost center manager is held responsible only for costs. Examples of cost centers would include a particular production department at a General Motors plant and the security department at a Citibank facility. A **profit center** incurs costs and generates revenue. The profit center manager is held responsible for revenue minus cost (profit). Examples of profit centers include the jewelry department at a Sears department store and a particular restaurant owned and operated by McDonald's Corporation. A **revenue center** is an organizational subunit for which the manager is held responsible only for revenue. The most common examples are given by the geographical sales territories of manufacturing and wholesaling firms. An **investment center** incurs costs, generates revenue, and is assigned assets. The manager of the investment center, rather than being held accountable for profit alone, is held responsible for the relationship of the center's profit to the capital resources invested in the subunit. Investment center performance measurement is covered in Chapters 22 and 23.

Managers in profit centers and investment centers are evaluated differently, but in practice people often use the term *profit center* to refer to both true profit centers and investment centers. Thus, it is important to clarify how performance is being evaluated when the term *profit center* is used.

The use of profit centers by Corning Glass is described in the following excerpt from *Management Accounting*.

Corning Glass Works

Since Corning Glass Works is basically a manufacturing operation, our major budget control effort is centered on manufacturing operations where we use a full standard cost and flexible budget system. . . . Corning's management control system decentralizes profit responsibility to the plant and division level. Each plant, division, and subsidiary is accountable for the sales it produces and the costs it controls or influences. The consolidation of operating results at the end of each accounting period involves 50 manufacturing plants, 12 operating divisions, 10 staff divisions, and 18 subsidiary companies.[5]

Illustration of Responsibility Accounting

An illustration of a responsibility accounting system is provided by the Marriott Corporation, which is engaged in the hospitality services industry throughout the world. Exhibit 10-3 shows a highly simplified organization chart for the firm.

Concentrate on the shaded boxes in the organization chart of Exhibit 10-3. Starting at the lowest level, the kitchen is a cost center. Its manager, the executive chef, is held responsible for food and food preparation costs in addition to the quality of the meals provided. The Food and Beverage Department is a profit center, and its director is held responsible for the cost of providing food and beverage service as well as the revenue generated from food and beverage sales. The general manager of the Marriott Hotel in Boston is held responsible for the profit earned by that entire Marriott facility. The hotel is a profit center.

Each of the other shaded boxes in the organization chart of Exhibit 10-3 is an investment center. The northeastern regional vice president (Marriott Hotels and Resorts), the area executive vice president, the president (Hotel Division), and the president and chief executive officer (Marriott Corporation) manage organizational units in which performance is measured by relating the profit generated by the subunit to the assets employed in the subunit. These managers have the authority to make substantive economic decisions regarding capital expenditures for their subunits.

Subunits versus Subunit Managers

In any responsibility accounting system a distinction is made between organizational subunits and the managers of those subunits. Managers should be evaluated in terms of all of the financial results that they control or substantially influence. In many cases, costs and revenues can be traced to a particular subunit but are not subject to any control or influence by that subunit's manager, and therefore should be excluded from the manager's evaluation. In contrast, when evaluating the economic performance of the subunit itself, all costs and revenues that are traceable to that subunit should be included in the evaluation. By maintaining the distinction between subunit's and their managers, top management can determine when a subunit's economic viability should be questioned, apart from the issue of how effective the manager of the subunit has been. In many instances, the most able managers in an organization are given the task of managing the weakest subunits. Such a manager should not be penalized for the weak performance of a subunit that is beyond the manager's control.

[5] J. C. Kostolansky, "Budget Control at Corning Glass Works," *Management Accounting* (November 1977): 21.

EXHIBIT 10-3

Partial Organization Chart for the Marriott Corporation

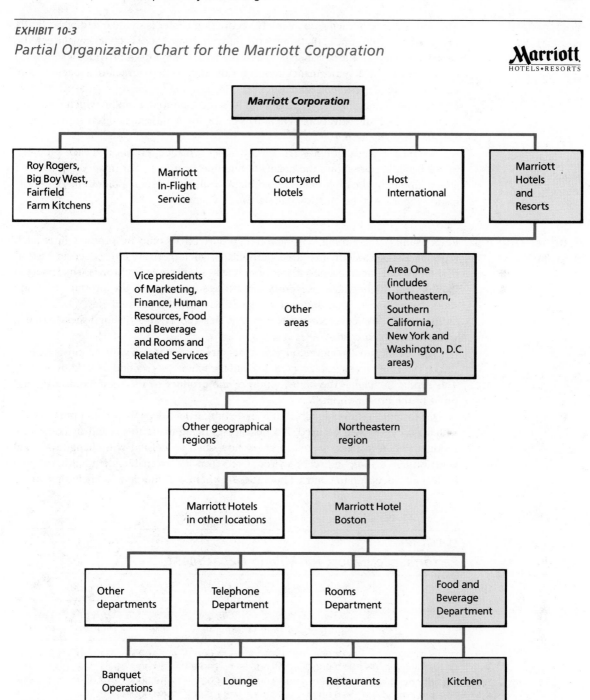

Performance Reporting

The performance of each responsibility accounting center is summarized periodically in a **performance report** that shows the budgeted amount of each financial item, the actual amount, and the variance between the two. Exhibit 10-4 provides a simplified example of a typical performance report for the milling department of a machine tool company. The department is a cost center. Management receives many such performance reports and employs management by exception to determine which variances require further investigation. (See Chapter 28 for a thorough discussion of cost-variance investigation.)

A typical organization has a hierarchy of performance reports, and each subunit's performance report shows the details of one line item in a performance report for a larger subunit in the organization. Exhibit 10-5 illustrates such a hierarchy of performance reports for the Quality Manufacturing Company.

Product-Line Reports

Responsibility accounting systems often report on income by product line. Such reports must be carefully prepared, particularly when there are indirect costs. Instead of showing one income amount, it is desirable to show several subtotals. The report in Exhibit 10-6 highlights those costs directly associated with the product line and subordinates those costs indirectly associated with the product line. (Direct and indirect costs are covered in Chapter 2.) This report also distinguishes between variable and fixed costs.

Instead of initially subtracting the costs directly identified with the product line, the variable costs can be subtracted first and the fixed costs second, as in Exhibit 10-7. This report highlights the contribution of the product to the total fixed costs and profit of the organization.

Choosing a report (Exhibit 10-6 or Exhibit 10-7) depends on the purpose for which the report will be used. If a decision is being made to expand or contract a product line, a manager wants to know how such a decision will change the total contribution. If some indirect or direct fixed costs are avoidable, then neither report is ideal for a decision to contract operations. Other considerations — including future

---

EXHIBIT 10-4

Performance Report for Milling Department

	Flexible Budget		Actual		Variance	
	Current Month	Year to Date	Current Month	Year to Date	Current Month	Year to Date
Direct labor	$13,000	$ 65,000	$14,000	$ 73,000	$ 1,000	$ 8,000
Direct material	7,000	39,000	6,000	40,000	(1,000)	1,000
Variable overhead	26,000	130,000	24,000	132,000	(2,000)	2,000
Fixed overhead	10,000	50,000	11,500	50,000	1,500	0
Total	$56,000	$284,000	$55,500	$295,000	$ (500)	$11,000

EXHIBIT 10-5

Hierarchy of Performance Reports

	Flexible Budget		Actual		Variance	
	Current Month	Year to Date	Current Month	Year to Date	Current Month	Year to Date
Sales department	$ 51,000	$245,000	$ 50,000	$ 250,000	$(1,000)	$ 5,000
Production department	131,000	650,000	131,500	665,000	500	15,000
Engineering department	21,000	100,000	23,000	100,000	2,000	0
Total	$203,000	$995,000	$204,500	$1,015,000	$ 1,500	$20,000
Production Department						
Cutting department	$ 12,000	$ 61,000	$ 13,000	$ 68,000	$ 1,000	$ 7,000
Milling department	56,000	284,000	55,500	295,000	(500)	11,000
Grinding department	42,000	200,000	41,000	195,000	(1,000)	(5,000)
Assembly department	21,000	105,000	22,000	107,000	1,000	2,000
Total	$131,000	$650,000	$131,500	$ 665,000	$ 500	$15,000
Milling Department						
Direct labor	$ 13,000	$ 65,000	$14,000	$ 73,000	$ 1,000	$ 8,000
Direct material	7,000	39,000	6,000	40,000	(1,000)	1,000
Variable overhead	26,000	130,000	24,000	132,000	(2,000)	2,000
Fixed overhead	10,000	50,000	11,500	50,000	1,500	0
	$ 56,000	$284,000	$ 55,500	$ 295,000	$ (500)	$11,000

EXHIBIT 10-6

Income Statement for Product A

Sales	$5,000
Less: Direct variable costs (materials, etc.)	2,000
	$3,000
Direct fixed costs (managers' salaries, etc.)	800
Excess of revenues over direct costs	$2,200
Less: Indirect variable costs (repairs, etc.)	1,000
	$1,200
Indirect fixed costs (rent, etc.)	400
Net income for product A	$ 800

EXHIBIT 10-7

Income Statement for Product A

Sales		$5,000
Less: Direct variable costs	$2,000	
Indirect variable costs	1,000	3,000
Excess of sales over variable costs (the contribution)		$2,000
Less: Direct fixed costs	$ 800	
Indirect fixed costs	400	1,200
Net income for product *A*		$ 800

---

market expectations, complementarity with other product lines, other opportunities, and the time value of money — also are relevant to a given decision situation.

Cost Reduction   The pressures of inflation and international competition have led many businesses and other organizations to cut costs while maintaining the high levels of service or product quality. Such cost reduction programs can be facilitated by a responsibility accounting system that identifies those in a position to control or significantly influence costs. The following excerpt from *Management Accounting* reports on the benefits of using budgeting and responsibility accounting at JKL, Inc., a New York-based advertising agency.

JKL, Inc., an Advertising Agency

Since devising the budgeting system, JKL has become aware of which specific accounts are unprofitable and the reasons why. Since the budgeting and control system has been instituted, the agency has resigned several unprofitable accounts that otherwise would have gone unnoticed. Account managers and supervisors now feel responsible for the profitability of their accounts and carefully monitor actual hours used to make sure that they are being managed and run as efficiently as possible. For example, an account manager noticed a large amount of supervisory creative time was being spent on her account and decided to investigate further. It turned out that the supervisors were doing the actual creative work (rather than the creative department). She pointed this out to her superiors and a junior creative team was appointed to her account, saving a great deal of money.[6]

---

[6] W. B. Mills, "Drawing Up a Budgeting System for an Ad Agency," *Management Accounting* (December 1983): 59.

Nonfinancial Information

Many organizations use a responsibility accounting system to collect important nonfinancial information that supplements the financial information available to top management. For example, airlines collect information on the percentage of available seats occupied; restaurants collect information on the number of patrons eating breakfast, lunch, and dinner; and manufacturing firms collect information on factors such as units of energy consumption and percentage of defective units produced. Such nonfinancial information helps management understand what is happening at all levels of an organization.

Summary

Budgeting is an important tool that is used in virtually all organizations. Types of budgets are distinguished by the time period covered, the organizational subunit for which the budget is prepared, and the purpose for the budget. Budgets typically are administered by a senior executive called the budget director with the advice of a budget committee. Approval of the budget is generally reserved to the board of directors.

Budgets can help management force planning, facilitate communication and coordination, allocate resources, control organizational subunits, and evaluate performance. A master budget is an overall budget covering an organization's operational activities from sales forecasting to pro forma financial statements.

A responsibility accounting system reports on the operating results of an organizational subunit. Cost center managers are held responsible for costs; revenue center managers for revenue; and profit center managers for both costs and revenue. Managers of investment centers are evaluated based on the relationship between the investment center's profit and the capital invested in it. A responsibility accounting systems must distinguish between the performance of subunits and the performance of subunit managers. A manager's performance can be good even when the subunit is a poor economic investment. Conversely, a subunit with high economic potential may be managed by a poorly performing manager. Many organizations use their responsibility accounting systems to collect important nonfinancial information to assist management in understanding and diagnosing organizational performance.

Review Problem

BUDGETING

Review the budgeting illustration in this chapter. Try to reconstruct each budget schedule by using only the information in Exhibit 10-2.

Key Terms to Review

budget, p. 335
budget committee, p. 335
budget director, p. 335
budget manual, p. 336
capital budget, p. 335
cash budget, p. 335
cost center, p. 349
financial budget, p. 335
goal congruence, p. 349
investment center, p. 349

management by objectives (MBO), p. 346
master budget, p. 335
operating budget, p. 335
performance report, p. 352
profit center, p. 349
pro forma financial statements, p. 335
responsibility accounting system, p. 349
revenue center, p. 349
revolving budget, p. 335
zero-base budgeting (ZBB), p. 347.

Suggested Readings

Baber, B. "Budget-Based Compensation and Discretionary Spending." *Accounting Review* (January 1985): 1–9.

Blanchard, G., C. Chow, and E. Noreen. "Information Asymmetry, Incentive Schemes, and Information Biasing: The Case of Hospital Budgeting Under Rate Regulation." *Accounting Review* (January 1986): 1–15.

Brownell, P. "Role of Accounting Data in Performance Evaluation, Budgetary Participation, and Organizational Effectiveness." *Journal of Accounting Research* (Spring 1982): 12–27.

Gershefski, G. W. "Building a Corporate Financial Model." *Harvard Business Review* (July–August 1969): 61–72.

Gilchrist, M., D. D. Pattison, and R. J. Kudla. "Controlling Indirect Costs with Headcount Forecast Algorithms." *Management Accounting* (August 1985): 46–51.

Janusky, D. R. "Plant Forecasting at Burroughs." *Management Accounting* (March 1985): 59–62.

Kenis, I. "Effects of Budgetary Goal Characteristics on Managerial Attitudes and Performance." *Accounting Review* (October 1979): 707–21.

Merchant, K. "The Design of the Corporate Budgeting System: Influences on Managerial Behavior and Performance." *Accounting Review* (October 1981): 813–29.

Mickle, C. E., J. D. Reed, and D. L. Butler. "Analyzing the Profitability of Branch Banks." *Management Accounting* (December 1985): 61–65.

Miller, E. L. *Responsibility Accounting and Performance Evaluation.* New York: Van Nostrand Reinhold, 1982.

"TRW Leads a Revolution in Managing Technology." *Business Week* (November 15, 1982): 124–28.

Tucker, F. G., and S. M. Zivion. "A Xerox Cost Center Imitates a Profit Center." *Harvard Business Review* (May-June 1985): 1610–74.

Weberman, B. "Smart Answers to Dumb Questions." *Forbes* (May 19, 1986): 110–13.

Welsch, G., R. Hilton, and P. Gordon. *Budgeting: Profit Planning and Control,* 5th ed. Englewood Cliffs, N.J.: Prentice-Hall, 1988.

" 'What If' Help for Management." *Business Week* (January 21, 1980): 73–74.

Wheelwright, S. C., and S. Makridakis. *Forecasting Methods for Management,* 3d ed. New York: Wiley-Interscience, 1980.

APPENDIX
Cash Budgeting

Cash budgeting is a critical aspect of any organization's financial planning process. It helps businesses and other organizations ensure that sufficient cash is available to pay bills. Moreover, the careful planning of cash receipts and disbursements avoids cash balances that are larger than necessary and allows excess cash to be reinvested in operations or other assets.

Illustration of Cash Budgeting

As an illustration of cash budgeting, consider the following information relating to the Seneca County Hospital.[7] A wide range of health services is provided to the community by the Seneca County Hospital, a nonprofit facility. The hospital's board of directors has authorized the following capital expenditures:

Interaortic balloon pump	$1,100,000
CT scanner	700,000
X-ray equipment	600,000
Laboratory equipment	1,400,000
	$3,800,000

The expenditures are planned for October 1, 19x4, and the board wishes to know the amount of borrowing, if any, necessary on that date. The hospital controller has gathered the following information to be used in preparing an analysis of future cash flows:

Billings Billings made in the month of service, for the first six months of 19x4 are listed below.

Month	Actual Billings
January	$4,400,000
February	4,400,000
March	4,500,000
April	4,500,000
May	5,000,000
June	5,000,000

[7] The illustration of cash budgeting on which this appendix is based is adapted from a CMA examination problem, adapted with permission.

Ninety percent of the hospital's billings are made to third parties such as Blue Cross, federal or state governments, and private insurance companies. The remaining 10 percent of the billings are made directly to patients. Historical patterns of billing collections are presented below:

	Third Party Billings	Direct Patient Billings
Month of service	20%	10%
Month following service	50	40
Second month following service	20	40
Uncollectible	10	10

Estimated billings for the last six months of 19x4 are listed below. The same billing and collection patterns that have been experienced during the first six months of 19x4 are expected to continue during the last six months of the year.

Month	Estimated Billings
July	$4,500,000
August	5,000,000
September	5,500,000
October	5,700,000
November	5,800,000
December	5,500,000

Purchases   The purchases that have been made during the past three months and the planned purchases for the last six months of 19x4 are presented in the following schedule.

Month	Amount
April	$1,100,000 (actual)
May	1,200,000 (actual)
June	1,200,000 (actual)
July	1,250,000 (planned)
August	1,500,000 (planned)
September	1,850,000 (planned)
October	1,950,000 (planned)
November	2,250,000 (planned)
December	1,750,000 (planned)

All purchases are made on account, and accounts payable are remitted in the month following the purchase.

Expenses

1. Salaries for each month during the remainder of 19x4 are expected to be $1,500,000 per month plus 20 percent of that month's billings. Salaries are paid in the month of service.

2. The hospital's monthly depreciation charges are $125,000.

3. The hospital incurs interest expense of $150,000 per month and makes interest payments of $450,000 on the last day of each calendar quarter.

Endowment Income   Endowment fund income is expected to continue to total $175,000 per month.

Other

1. The hospital has a cash balance of $300,000 on July 1, 19x4, and has a policy of maintaining a minimum end-of-month cash balance of 10 percent of the current month's purchases.

2. The hospital employs a calendar year reporting period.

Using the information presented above, the hospital controller is able to prepare for the third quarter of 19x4 (1) a schedule of budgeted cash receipts and (2) a schedule of budgeted cash disbursements. These schedules are displayed in Exhibits 10-8 and 10-9.

Explanation of Cash Receipts Budget

The cash receipts budget displayed in Exhibit 10-8 lists the actual or estimated billings for each month. The billings are then multiplied by 90 percent to determine the amount billed to third parties. This amount is in turn multiplied by the percentage of those expected to be collected during that month. For example, total billings during May were $5,000,000. Because 90 percent of these billings were to third parties, the amount billed to third parties in May was $4,500,000 ($5,000,000 × 90%). For third-party billings, 20 percent of the billings are collected in the second month following service. Therefore, $900,000 ($4,500,000 × 20%) of the May billings to third parties will be collected during July. Thus, $900,000 is shown in the upper right corner of Exhibit 10-8 as the amount collected during July from May billings to third parties.

Similar calculations are made each month for direct patient billings.

Explanation of Cash Disbursements Budget

Budgeted cash disbursements are shown in Exhibit 10-9. The variable salary cost for each month is budgeted at 20 percent of the month's estimated billings. Thus, July's billings are projected at $4,500,000 and the variable salary cost is budgeted at $900,000 ($4,500,000 × 20%). Each month's cash disbursements for purchases are

EXHIBIT 10-8

Schedule of Budgeted Cash Receipts

SENECA COUNTY HOSPITAL
Schedule of Budgeted Cash Receipts for the Quarter Ending September 30, 19x4
(000s omitted)

Billings				Receipts		
	Actual or Estimated	Percentages				
Month	Amount	Classification	Timing	July	August	September
May	$5,000	Third party	20%	$ 900		
May	5,000	Direct patient	40	200		
June	5,000	Third party	50	2,250		
June	5,000	Direct patient	40	200		
June	5,000	Third party	20		$ 900	
June	5,000	Direct patient	40		200	
July	4,500	Third party	20	810		
July	4,500	Direct patient	10	45		
July	4,500	Third party	50		2,025	
July	4,500	Direct patient	40		180	
July	4,500	Third party	20			$ 810
July	4,500	Direct patient	40			180
August	5,000	Third party	20		900	
August	5,000	Direct patient	10		50	
August	5,000	Third party	50			2,250
August	5,000	Direct patient	40			200
September	5,500	Third party	20			990
September	5,500	Direct patient	10			55
Total receipts from billings				$4,405	$4,255	$4,485
Endowment fund income				175	175	175
Total cash receipts				$4,580	$4,430	$4,660

equal to the prior month's purchases. Hence, July's cash disbursement for purchases is equal to June's purchases of $1,200,000.

Use of the Cash Budget for Planning

The cash budget is useful to management for a variety of planning and decision-making purposes. For example, the controller can use the cash budget to prepare the analysis displayed in Exhibit 10-10. The analysis shows the amount of borrowing that will be necessary in order for the board of directors to meet its objective of purchasing equipment in October.

EXHIBIT 10-9

Schedule of Budgeted Cash Disbursements

SENECA COUNTY HOSPITAL
Schedule of Budgeted Cash Disbursements
for the Quarter Ending September 30, 19x4
(000s omitted)

	Disbursements		
	July	*August*	*September*
Salaries:			
Variable salaries			
$4,500 × 20%	$ 900		
$5,000 × 20%		$1,000	
$5,500 × 20%			$1,100
Total variable	$ 900	$1,000	$1,100
Fixed salaries	1,500	1,500	1,500
Total salaries	$2,400	$2,500	$2,600
Purchases of previous month	1,200	1,250	1,500
Interest			450
Total cash disbursements	$3,600	$3,750	$4,550

EXHIBIT 10-10

Analysis of Borrowing Required for Planned Capital Expenditures

Cash balance — July 1, 19x4		$ 300[a]
Cash receipts in third quarter:		
July	$4,580	
August	4,430	
September	4,660	13,670
Total cash available		$13,970
Cash disbursements in third quarter:		
July	$3,600	
August	3,750	
September	4,550	11,900
Projected cash balance — September 30, 19x4		$ 2,070
Minimum end-of-month cash balance required ($1,850 × 10%)		185
Cash available to acquire capital items		$ 1,885
Capital expenditures planned for October 1, 19x4		(3,800)
Amount of borrowing necessary on October 1, 19x4		$(1,915)

[a] 000s omitted.

Review Questions

10-1 List and briefly describe three types of budgets.

10-2 List and briefly explain the purposes of budgets.

10-3 Define the terms *cost center, revenue center, profit center,* and *investment center.*

10-4 Give examples of cost, revenue, profit, and investment centers.

10-5 Why is it important to distinguish between subunits and subunit managers in responsibility acounting?

10-6 Give a brief explanation of management by objectives (MBO).

10-7 Briefly describe the concept of zero-base budgeting.

10-8 Give some examples of nonfinancial information that might be collected by the responsibility accounting system at a bank.

10-9 What is meant by a rolling budget?

10-10 What is the role of an organization's budget director?

Exercises

10-11 Budgeting Material Purchases for an Airline   Tri-State Commuter Airlines provides commuter service to Maryland, Delaware, and Virginia. The company expects its aircraft to fly 950,000 air miles during the second quarter of 19x1 (April, May, and June). The inventory of aircraft fuel on April 1 is 12,000 gallons, and the airline's management wishes to have 8,000 gallons on hand on June 30. An average of .1 gallons is required per air mile flown. How many gallons of fuel must be purchased during the quarter?

10-12 Budgeting Production in a Restaurant   The Crescent Beach Pizzeria prepares pizza crusts each morning to cover anticipated sales for the day. Crusts left over at the end of the day are frozen for use the next day. On Tuesday morning, the restaurant has twenty-one frozen pizza crusts that were made on Monday. Management desires to end the day with ten crusts. Anticipated sales for Tuesday are 127 pizzas. How many crusts should be prepared on Tuesday?

10-13 Budgeting Production in a Manufacturing Plant   The Flagler Athletic Company manufactures wooden tennis rackets. The sales budget for the first seven months of 19x7 is given below:

	Sales Forecast
January	2,000
February	3,000
March	4,000
April	5,000
May	5,000
June	8,000
July	4,000

The company's management desires to have 10 percent of the following month's sales on hand at the end of each month. The inventory on December 31, 19x6, is 200 rackets. Prepare a production budget for each month from January through June.

10-14 Purchases Budget for a Manufacturer   Refer to the data for the preceding exercise. Racket production requires the following primary materials:

Material	Requirement for One Racket	Inventory on December 31, 19x6
Wood	2 pounds	1,000 pounds
String	10 feet	6,600 feet

Material equal to 20% of the next month's requirement is to be on hand at the end of each month. Prepare a purchases budget for each material for the first *three* months of 19x7.

10-15 Budgeting for Personnel in a Bank   The management of the Alachua County Trust Company expects the bank to process 124,800 transactions during the first quarter of 19x4. The average amount of clerical time required per transaction is ten minutes. If each clerical employee works a forty-hour week, how many clerical personnel will the bank need during this period? (Assume that there are thirteen weeks in the quarter.)

10-16 Production Budget   Betz Company's sales budget shows the following projections for the year ending December 31, 19x3:

Quarter	Units
First	60,000
Second	80,000
Third	45,000
Fourth	55,000
Total	240,000

Inventory at December 31, 19x2, was budgeted at 18,000 units. The quantity of finished-goods inventory at the end of each quarter is to equal 30 percent of the next quarter's budgeted sales in units. How much should the production budget show for units to be produced during the first quarter? (*CPA adapted*)

10-17 Responsibility Accounting Centers   A segment of an organization is referred to as a profit center if it has (choose one):

   a. Authority to make decisions affecting the major determinants of profit including the power to choose its markets and sources of supply.

   b. Authority to make decisions affecting the major determinants of profit including the power to choose its market and sources of supply and significant control over the amount of invested capital.

    c. Authority to make decisions over the most significant costs of operations including the power to choose the sources of supply.

    d. Authority to provide specialized support to other units within the organization.

    e. Responsibility for combining the raw materials, direct labor, and other factors of production into a final output. (*CMA adapted*)

10-18 Responsibility Accounting Centers   A segment of an organization is referred to as an investment center if it has (choose one):

    a. Authority to make decisions affecting the major determinants of profit including the power to choose its markets and sources of supply.

    b. Authority to make decisions affecting the major determinants of profit including the power to choose its market and sources of supply and significant control over the amount of invested capital.

    c. Authority to make decisions over the most significant costs of operations including the power to choose the sources of supply.

    d. Authority to provide specialized support to other units within the organization.

    e. Responsibility for developing markets for and selling the output of the organization. (*CMA adapted*)

10-19 Responsibility Accounting Centers   A segment of an organization is referred to as a cost center if it has (choose one):

    a. Responsibility for developing markets for and selling of the output of the organization.

    b. Authority to make decisions affecting the major determinants of profit including the power to choose its markets and sources of supply.

    c. Authority to make decisions over the most significant costs of operations including the power to choose the sources of supply.

    d. Authority to provide specialized support to other units within the organization.

    e. Responsibility for combining the raw materials, direct labor, and other factors of production into a final output. (*CMA adapted*)

10-20 Types of Budgets   A rolling budget (choose one):

    a. Drops the current month or quarter and adds a future month or a future quarter as the current month or quarter is completed.

    b. Presents a statement of expectations for a period of time but does not present a firm commitment.

    c. Presents the plan for only one level of activity and does not adjust to changes in the level of activity.

    d. Presents the plan for a range of activity so that the plan can be adjusted for changes in activity levels. (*CMA adapted·*)

10-21 Types of Budgets A flexible budget (choose one):

a. Classifies the budget requests by activity and estimates the benefits arising from each activity.

b. Presents a statement of expectations for a period of time but does not present a firm commitment.

c. Presents the plan for only one level of activity and does not adjust to changes in the level of activity.

d. Presents the plan for a range of activity so that the plan can be adjusted for changes in activity levels. (*CMA adapted*)

10-22 Budgeting Merchandise Purchases by a Retailer The Russon Corporation is a retailer whose sales are all made on credit. Sales are billed twice monthly, on the tenth of the month for the last half of the prior month's sales and on the twentieth of the month for the first half of the current month's sales. The terms of all sales are 2/10, net 30. Based on past experience, the collection experience of accounts receivable is as follows:

Within the discount period	80%
On the 30th day	18%
Uncollectible	2%

The sales value of shipments for May 19x0 and the forecasts for the next four months are:

May (actual)	$500,000
June	600,000
July	700,000
August	700,000
September	400,000

Russon's average markup on its products is 20 percent of the sales price.

Russon purchases merchandise for resale to meet the current month's sales demand and to maintain a desired monthly ending inventory of 25 percent of the next month's sales. All purchases are on credit with terms of net 30. Russon pays for one-half of a month's purchases in the month of purchase and the other half in the month following the purchase.

All sales and purchases occur uniformly throughout the month.

REQUIRED:

a. How much merchandise should Russon plan to purchase during June 19x0?

b. What amount should Russon budget in August 19x0 for the payment of merchandise? (*CMA adapted*)

10-23 Budgeting Cash Collections and Inventories; Retailer   Refer to the data given in the preceding exercise.

REQUIRED:

   a. How much cash can Russon Corporation plan to collect from accounts receivable collections during July 19x0?

   b. How much cash can Russon plan to collect in September from sales made in August 19x0?

   c. What will be the budgeted dollar value of Russon's inventory on August 31, 19x0? (*CMA adapted*)

10-24 Segment Performance Measurement; Financial Services Firm   John Arnston recently has been appointed chief operating officer of Parton Co. Arnston has a background in banking and most recently managed the consumer financial services segment of the company. The business segments of Parton range across banking, insurance, and security brokerage.

In a recent conversation with the company's chief financial officer, Arnston suggested that segment managers be evaluated on the basis of the segment data appearing in Parton's annual financial report. This report presents revenues, earnings, identifiable assets, and depreciation for each segment for a five-year period. He raised this issue because he thought that evaluating segment managers by using the same type of information often used to evaluate the company's top management would be appropriate.

Parton's chief financial officer has expressed his reservations to Arnston about using segment information from the annual financial report for this purpose. He has suggested that Arnston consider other ways to evaluate segment management performance.

REQUIRED:

   a. Identify the characteristics of segment information in the annual financial report that would lead Parton's chief financial officer to have reservations about its use for the evaluation of segment management performance.

   b. Is it in the best interests of the company to evaluate segment managers on the basis of segment information in the annual financial report? Explain your answer.

   c. Identify and explain the financial information you would recommend Arnston obtain when evaluating segment management performance. (*CMA adapted*)

Problems

10-25 Production and Labor Budgets   Roletter Company makes and sells frames for pictures of weddings, graduations, christenings, and other special events. Controller Bob Anderson is responsible for preparing Roletter's master budget and has accumulated the following information for 19x5:

	19x5				
	January	February	March	April	May
Estimated unit sales	10,000	12,000	8,000	9,000	9,000
Sales price per unit	$50.00	$47.50	$47.50	$47.50	$47.50
Direct labor hours per unit	2.0	2.0	1.5	1.5	1.5
Wage per direct labor hour	$ 8.00	$ 8.00	$ 8.00	$ 9.00	$ 9.00

Labor related costs include pension contributions of $.25 per hour, workers' compensation insurance of $.10 per hour, employee medical insurance of $.40 per hour, and social security taxes. Assume that as of January 1, 19x5, the base figure for computing social security taxes is $37,800 and that the rates are 7 percent for employers and 6.7 percent for employees. The cost of employee benefits paid by Roletter on its employees is treated as a direct labor cost.

Roletter has a labor contract that calls for a wage increase to $9.00 per hour on April 1, 19x5. New labor-saving machinery has been installed and will be fully operational by March 1, 19x5.

Roletter expects to have 16,000 frames on hand at December 31, 19x4, and has a policy of carrying an end-of-month inventory of 100 percent of the following month's sales plus 50 percent of the second following month's sales.

REQUIRED:

a. Prepare a production budget and a direct labor budget for Roletter Company by month and for the first quarter of 19x5. Both budgets may be combined in one schedule. The direct labor budget should include direct labor hours and show the detail for each direct labor cost category.

b. For each item used in Roletter's production budget and its direct labor budget, identify the other component(s) of the master budget that would also use these data. (*CMA adapted*)

10-26 Preparing the Master Budget   The Scarborough Corporation manufactures and sells two products, Thingone and Thingtwo. In July 19x7 Scarborough's budget department gathered the following data in order to project sales and budget requirements for 19x8.

19x8 Projected Sales

Product	Units	Price
Thingone	60,000	$ 70
Thingtwo	40,000	$100

19x8 Inventories (in units)

Product	Expected January 1, 19x8	Desired December 31, 19x8
Thingone	20,000	25,000
Thingtwo	8,000	9,000

In order to produce one unit of Thingone and one unit of Thingtwo, the following raw materials are used:

		Amount Used per Unit	
Raw Material	Unit	Thingone	Thingtwo
A	lbs	4	5
B	lbs	2	3
C	each		1

Projected data for 19x8 with respect to raw materials is as follows:

Raw Material	Anticipated Purchase Price	Expected Inventories January 1, 19x8	Desired Inventories December 31,19x8
A	$8	32,000 lbs	36,000 lbs
B	$5	29,000 lbs	32,000 lbs
C	$3	6,000 each	7,000 each

Projected direct labor requirements and rates for 19x8 are as follows:

Product	Hours per Unit	Rate per Hour
Thingone	2	$3
Thingtwo	3	$4

Overhead is applied as the rate of $2 per direct labor hour.

REQUIRED:

Based on the above projections and budget requirements for 19x8 for Thingone and Thingtwo, prepare the following budgets for 19x8:

a. Sales budget (in dollars).

b. Production budget (in units).

c. Raw-materials purchase budget (in quantities).

d. Raw-materials purchase budget (in dollars).

e. Direct labor budget (in dollars).

f. Budgeted finished-goods inventory at December 31, 19x8 (in dollars). (*CPA adapted*)

10-27 Budgeting and Performance Evaluation; Selling-Expense Budget Wielson Company employs flexible budgeting techniques to evaluate the performance of several of its activities. The selling-expense flexible budgets for three representative monthly activity levels are shown below:

REPRESENTATIVE MONTHLY FLEXIBLE BUDGETS FOR SELLING EXPENSES

Activity measures:			
Unit sales volume	400,000	425,000	450,000
Dollar sales volume	$10,000,000	$10,625,000	$11,250,000
Number of orders	4,000	4,250	4,500
Number of salespersons	75	75	75
Monthly expenses:			
Advertising and promotion	$ 1,200,000	$ 1,200,000	$ 1,200,000
Administrative salaries	57,000	57,000	57,000
Sales salaries	75,000	75,000	75,000
Sales commissions	200,000	212,500	225,000
Salesperson travel	170,000	175,000	180,000
Sales office expense	490,000	498,750	507,500
Shipping expense	675,000	712,500	750,000
Total selling expenses	$ 2,867,000	$ 2,930,750	$ 2,994,500

The following assumptions were used to develop the selling-expense flexible budgets.

■ The average size of Wielson's salesforce during the year was planned to be seventy-five people.

■ Sales personnel are paid a monthly salary plus commission on gross dollar sales.

■ The travel costs are best characterized as a step variable cost. The fixed portion is related to the number of sales personnel, while the variable portion tends to fluctuate with gross dollar sales.

■ Sales office expense is a mixed cost with the variable portion related to the number of orders processed.

■ Shipping expense is a mixed cost with the variable portion related to the number of units sold.

A salesforce of 80 people generated a total of 4,300 orders resulting in a sales volume of 420,000 units during November. The gross dollar sales amounted to $10.9 million. The selling expenses incurred in November were as follows:

Advertising and promotion	$1,350,000
Administrative salaries	57,000
Sales salaries	80,000
Sales commissions	218,000
Travel by sales personnel	185,000
Sales office expense	497,200
Shipping expense	730,000
Total	$3,117,200

REQUIRED:

  a. Explain why flexible budgeting is a useful management tool.

  b. Explain why the selling-expense flexible budgets presented above are not appropriate for evaluating Wielson Company's November selling expenses, and indicate how the flexible budget would have to be revised.

  c. Prepare a selling expense report for November that the company's management can use to evaluate its control over selling expenses. The report should have a line for each selling-expense item showing the appropriate budgeted amount, the actual selling expense, and the monthly dollar variation. (*CMA adapted*)

10-28 Income Statements for Segments   Caprice Company manufactures and sells two products—a small portable office file cabinet that it has made for over fifteen years and a home/travel file introduced in 19x1. The files are made in Caprice's only manufacturing plant. Budgeted variable production costs per unit of product are as follows.

	Office File	Home/Travel File
Sheet metal	$ 3.50	—
Plastic	—	$3.75
Direct labor (@ $8 per DLH)	4.00	2.00
Variable manufacturing overhead (@ $9 per DLH)	4.50	2.25
	$12.00	$8.00

Variable manufacturing overhead costs vary with direct labor hours. The annual fixed manufacturing overhead costs are budgeted at $120,000. A total of 50 percent of these costs are directly traceable to the Office File Department and 22 percent of the costs are traceable to the Home/Travel File Department. The remaining 28 percent of the costs are not traceable to either department.

Caprice employs two full-time salespersons — Pam Price and Robert Flint. Each salesperson receives an annual salary of $14,000 plus a sales commission of 10 percent of his or her total gross sales. Travel and entertainment expense is budgeted at $22,000 annually for each salesperson. Price is expected to sell 60 percent of the budgeted unit sales for each file, and Flint the remaining 40 percent. Caprice's remaining selling and administrative expenses include fixed administrative costs of $80,000 that cannot be traced to either file plus the following traceable selling expenses.

	Office File	Home/Travel File
Packaging expenses per unit	$ 2.00	$ 1.50
Promotion	$30,000	$40,000

Data regarding Caprice's budgeted and actual sales for the fiscal year ended May 31, 19x4, are presented below. There were no changes in the beginning and ending balances of either finished-goods or work-in-process inventories.

	Office File	Home/Travel File
Budgeted sales volume in units	15,000	15,000
Budgeted and actual unit sales price	$29.50	$19.50
Actual unit sales:		
Pam Price	10,000	9,500
Robert Flint	5,000	10,500
Total units	15,000	20,000

Data regarding Caprice's operating expenses for the year ended May 31, 19x4, follow:

1. There were no increases or decreases in raw-materials inventory for either sheet metal or plastic, and there were no usage variances. However, sheet metal prices were 6 percent above budget and plastic prices were 4 percent below budget.

2. The actual direct labor hours worked and costs incurred were as follows:

	Hours	Amount
Office file	7,500	$ 57,000
Home/Travel file	6,000	45,600
Total	13,500	$102,600

3. Fixed manufacturing overhead costs attributable to the office file department were $8,000 above the budget. All other fixed manufacturing overhead costs were incurred at the same amounts as budgeted, and all variable manufacturing overhead costs were incurred at the budgeted hourly rates.

4. All selling and administrative expenses were incurred at budgeted rates or amounts except the following items.

Nontraceable administrative expenses		$ 34,000
Promotion:		
Office files	$32,000	
Home/Travel files	58,000	90,000
Travel and entertainment:		
Pam Price	$24,000	
Robert Flint	28,000	52,000
Total		$176,000

REQUIRED:

a. Prepare a segmented income statement of Caprice Company's actual operations for the fiscal year ended May 31, 19x4. The report should be prepared in a contribution-margin format by product and should reflect total income (loss) for the company before income taxes.

b. Identify and discuss any additional analyses that could be made of the data presented that would be of value to Caprice Company. (*CMA adapted*)

10-29 Performance Report   Refer to the information about Caprice Company given in the preceding problem.

REQUIRED:

Prepare a performance report for the year ended May 31, 19x4, that would be useful in evaluating the performance of Robert Flint. (*CMA adapted*)

10-30 Production, Labor, Materials, and Overhead Budgets   The Wyoming Division of Reid Corporation produces an intricate component part used in Reid's major product line. The division manager has been concerned recently by a lack of coordination between purchasing and production personnel and believes that a monthly budgeting system would be better than the present system.

Wyoming's division manager has decided to develop budget information for the third quarter of the current year as a trial before the budget system is implemented for an entire fiscal year. In response to the division manager's request for data that can be used to develop budget information, the division controller accumulates the following data.

Sales   Sales through June 30, 19x7, the first six months of the current year, are 24,000 units. Actual sales in units for May and June and estimated unit sales for the next four months are detailed as follows:

May (actual)	4,000
June (actual)	4,000
July (estimated)	5,000
August (estimated)	6,000
September (estimated)	7,000
October (estimated)	7,000

Wyoming Division expects to sell 60,000 units during the year ending December 31, 19x7.

Direct Material   Data regarding the materials used in the component are shown in the schedule below. The desired monthly ending inventory for all direct materials is to have sufficient materials on hand to produce the next month's estimated sales.

Direct Material	Units of Direct Materials per Finished Component	Cost per Unit	Inventory Level 6/30/x7
#101	6	$2.40	35,000 units
#211	4	3.60	30,000 units
#242	2	1.20	14,000 units

Direct Labor   Each component must pass through three different processes to be completed. Data regarding the direct labor is presented below:

Process	Direct Labor Hours per Finished Component	Cost per Direct Labor Hour
Forming	.80	$8.00
Assembly	2.00	5.50
Finishing	.25	6.00

Factory Overhead   The division produced 27,000 components during this six-month period through June 30, 19x7. The actual variable overhead costs incurred during this six-month period are shown below. The division controller believes the variable overhead costs will be incurred at the same rate during the last six months of 19x7.

Supplies	$ 59,400
Electricity	27,000
Indirect labor	54,000
Other	8,100
Total variable overhead	$148,500

The fixed overhead costs incurred during the first six months of 19x7 amounted to $93,500. Fixed overhead costs are budgeted for the full year as follows:

Supervision	$ 60,000
Taxes	7,200
Depreciation	86,400
Other	32,400
Total fixed overhead	$186,000

Finished-Goods Inventory The desired monthly ending inventory in units of completed components is 80 percent of the next month's estimated sales. There are 5,000 finished units in the inventory on June 30, 19x7.

REQUIRED:

a. Prepare a production budget in units for the Wyoming Division for the third quarter ending September 30, 19x7.

b. Without prejudice to your answer in requirement a, assume that Wyoming Division plans to produce 18,000 units during the third quarter ending September 30, 19x7, and 60,000 units for the year ending December 31, 19x7.

   (1) Prepare a direct materials purchased budget in units and dollars for the third quarter ending September 30, 19x7.

   (2) Prepare a direct labor budget in hours and dollars for the third quarter ending September 30, 19x7.

   (3) Prepare a factory overhead budget for the six-month period ending December 31, 19x7.

c. Assume Wyoming Division actually produced 38,000 components during the six-month period of July 1 through December 31, 19x7, and incurred variable overhead of $203,300 and fixed overhead of $95,000. Evaluate Wyoming Division's performance for the last six months of 19x7 with respect to its control of factory overhead costs. Show and explain briefly any supporting calculations used in your evaluation. (*CMA adapted*)

10-31 Budgeted Income Statement Rein Company, a compressor manufacturer, is developing a budgeted income statement for the calendar year 19x2. The president is generally satisfied with the projected net income for 19x1 of $700,000 resulting in an earnings per share figure of $2.80. However, next year he would like earnings per share to increase to at least $3.

Rein Company employs a standard absorption cost system. Inflation necessitates an annual revision in the standards as evidenced by an increase in production costs expected in 19x2. The total standard manufacturing cost for 19x1 is $72 per unit produced.

Rein expects to sell 100,000 compressors at $110 each in the current year (19x1). Forecasts from the sales department are favorable, and Rein Company is projecting an annual increase of 10 percent in unit sales in 19x2 and 19x3. This increase in sales will occur even though a $15 increase in unit selling price will be implemented in 19x2. The selling-price increase was essential to compensate for the increased production costs and operating expenses. However, management is concerned that any additional sales-price increase would curtail the desired growth in volume.

Standard production costs are developed for the two primary metals used in the compressor (brass and a steel alloy), the direct labor and manufacturing overhead. The following schedule represents the 19x2 standard quantities and rates for material and labor to produce one compressor:

Brass	4 pounds @ $5.35/lb	$21.40
Steel alloy	5 pounds @ $3.16/lb	15.80
Direct labor	4 hours @ $7.00/hr	28.00
Total prime costs		$65.20

The material content of the compressor has been reduced slightly, hopefully without a decrease in the quality of the finished product. Improved labor productivity and some increase in automation have resulted in a decrease in labor hours per unit from 4.4 to 4.0. However, the significant increases in material prices and hourly labor rates more than offset any savings from reduced input quantities.

The manufacturing overhead cost-per-unit schedule has yet to be completed. Preliminary data are as follows:

	Activity Level (units)		
Overhead items	100,000	110,000	120,000
Supplies	$ 475,000	$ 522,500	$ 570,000
Indirect labor	530,000	583,000	636,000
Utilities	170,000	187,000	204,000
Maintenance	363,000	377,500	392,000
Taxes and insurance	87,000	87,000	87,000
Depreciation	421,000	421,000	421,000
Total overhead	$2,046,000	$2,178,000	$2,310,000

The standard overhead rate is based on direct labor hours and is developed by using the total overhead costs from the above schedule for the activity level closest to planned production. In developing the standards for the manufacturing costs, the following two assumptions were made:

- The cost of brass is currently selling at $5.65/pound. However, this price is historically high, and the purchasing manager expects the price to drop to the predetermined standard early in 19x2.

- Several new employees will be hired for the production line in 19x2. The employees will be generally unskilled. If basic training programs are not effective and improved labor productivity is not experienced, then the production time per unit of product will increase by fifteen minutes over the 19x2 standards.

Rein employs a LIFO inventory system for its finished goods. Rein's inventory policy for finished goods is to have 15 percent of the expected annual unit sales for the coming year in finished-goods inventory at the end of the prior year. The finished-goods inventory at December 31, 19x1, is expected to consist of 16,500 units at a total carrying cost of $1,006,500.

Operating expenses are classified as selling, which are variable, and administrative, which are all fixed. The budgeted selling expenses are expected to average 12 percent of sales revenue in 19x2, which is consistent with the performance in 19x1. The administrative expenses in 19x2 are expected to be 20 percent higher than the predicted 19x1 amount of $907,850.

Management accepts the cost standards developed by the production and accounting departments. However, they are concerned about the possible effect on net income if the price of brass does not decrease, or the labor efficiency does not improve as expected. Therefore, management wants the budgeted income statement to be prepared using the standards as developed but assuming the worst possible situation for 19x2. Each resulting manufacturing variance should be separately identified and added to or subtracted from budgeted cost of goods sold at standard. Rein is subject to a 45 percent income tax rate.

REQUIRED:

Prepare the budgeted income statement for 19x2 for Rein Company as specified by management. Round all calculations to the nearest dollar. *(CMA adapted)*

10-32 Budgeting Travel Cost; Research and Development Lymar Products is a divisionalized corporation in the agribusiness industry with its corporate headquarters in Philadelphia. The R&D Division is located in central Illinois and is responsible for all of the corporation's seed, fertilizer, and insecticide research and development. The research and development is conducted primarily for the benefit of Lymar's other operating divisions. The R&D Division conducts contract research for outside firms when such research does not interfere with the division's regular work or does not represent work that directly competes with Lymar's interests.

Lymar's annual budget preparation begins approximately five months before the beginning of the fiscal year. Each division manager is responsible for developing the budget for his or her division within the guidelines provided by corporate headquarters. Once the annual budget procedure is completed and the budget is accepted and approved, the division managers have complete authority to operate within the limits prescribed by the budget.

The budget procedures apply to the R&D Division. However, because this division does work for other Lymar divisions and for the corporate office, careful coordination between the R&D Division and the other units is needed to construct a budget for the R&D Division. Further, the costs associated with the contract research require special consideration by Lymar's management. In the past, good cooperation has resulted in sound budget preparation.

R&D's management always has presented well-documented budgets for both the internal and contract research. Budget revisions are the result of review, discussion, and agreement between R&D's management and corporate management.

Staff travel is a major item included in R&D's budget. Some twenty-five to thirty-five trips are made annually to corporate headquarters for meetings by R&D's employees. In addition, the division's technical staff makes trips related to their research projects and are expected to attend professional meetings and seminars. These trips always have been detailed in a supporting schedule presented with the annual budget.

Lymar's performance for the current year is considered reasonable in light of current and expected future poor economic conditions, but corporate management has become extremely cost conscious in order to maintain corporate performance at the best possible level. Divisions have been directed to cut down on any unnecessary spending. A specific new directive has been issued stating that any travel in excess of $500 must now be approved in advance by corporate headquarters. In addition, once a division's total dollar amount budgeted for travel has been spent, no budget overruns will be allowed. This directive is effective immediately, and corporate management has indicated that it will continue to be in effect for at least the next two years.

The R&D Division manager is concerned because this directive appears to represent a change in budget policy. Travel was thought already approved because it was included in the annual budget but now must be reapproved before each trip. In addition, some scheduled trips previously approved may have to be cancelled because travel funds are likely to run out before the end of the year. R&D staff members already have had to make five special trips to corporate headquarters that were not included in the current year's budget.

The new directive probably will increase costs. The approval process may delay the purchase of airline tickets, reducing the opportunity to obtain the lowest fares. Further, the R&D Division will have a major increase in paperwork because virtually every trip exceeds the $500 limit.

REQUIRED:

    a. The directive requiring "the reapproval of all travel in excess of $500" could have far-reaching effects for Lymar Products.

        (1) Explain how this directive could affect the entire budget process, especially the validity of the annual budget.

        (2) Explain what effect this directive is likely to have on the care with which divisions prepare their annual travel budgets in the future.

    b. Explain what effect the directive on "reapproval of travel costs" is likely to have on the morale and motivation of the division manager and research staff of the R&D Division. *(CMA adapted)*

10-33 Overview of Responsibility Accounting   Kelly Petroleum Company has a large oil and natural gas project in Oklahoma. The project has been organized into two production centers (Petroleum Production and Natural Gas Production) and one service center (Maintenance).

Maintenance Center Activities and Scheduling   Don Pepper, Maintenance Center manager, has organized his maintenance workers into work crews that serve the two production centers. The maintenance crews perform preventive maintenance and repair equipment both in the field and in the central maintenance shop.

Pepper is responsible for scheduling all maintenance work in the field and at the central shop. Preventive maintenance is performed according to a set schedule established by Pepper and approved by the production center managers. Breakdowns are given immediate priority in scheduling so that downtime is minimized. Thus, preventive maintenance occasionally must be postponed, but every attempt is made to reschedule it within three weeks.

Preventive maintenance work is the responsibility of Pepper. However, if a significant problem is discovered during preventive maintenance, the appropriate production-center supervisor authorizes and supervises the repair after checking with Pepper.

When a breakdown in the field occurs, the production centers contact Pepper to initiate the repairs. The repair work is supervised by the production center supervisor. Machinery and equipment sometimes need to be replaced while the original equipment is repaired in the central shop. This procedure is followed only when the time to make the repair in the field would result in an extended interruption of operations. Replacement of equipment is recommended by the maintenance crew supervisor and approved by a production center supervisor.

Routine preventive maintenance and breakdowns of automotive and mobile equipment used in the field are completed in the central shop. All repair and maintenance activities taking place in the central shop are under the direction of Pepper.

Maintenance Center Accounting Activities   Pepper has records identifying the work crews assigned to each job in the field, the number of hours spent on the job, and parts and supplies used on the job. In addition, records for the central shop (jobs, labor hours, parts, and supplies) have been maintained. However, this detailed maintenance information is not incorporated into Kelly's accounting system.

Pepper develops the annual budget for the Maintenance Center by planning the preventive maintenance that will be needed during the year, estimating the number and seriousness of breakdowns, and estimating the shop activities. He then bases the labor, part, and supply costs on his plans and estimates and develops the budget amounts by line item. Because the timing of the breakdowns is impossible to plan, Pepper divides the annual budget by 12 to derive the monthly budget.

All costs incurred by the work crews in the field and in the central shop are accumulated monthly and then allocated to the two production cost centers based on the field hours worked in each production center. This method of cost allocation has been used on Pepper's recommendation because he believes that it is easy to implement and understand. Furthermore, he believes that a better allocation system is impossible to incorporate into the monthly report due to the wide range of salaries paid to maintenance workers and the fast turnover of materials and parts.

The November cost report for the Maintenance Center (provided by the Accounting Department) is shown just above the requirements for this problem.

Production Center Manager's Concerns   Both production center managers have been upset with the method of cost allocation. Furthermore, they believe the report is virtually useless as a cost-control device. Actual costs always seem to deviate from the monthly budget, and the proportion charged to each production center varies significantly from month to month. Maintenance costs have increased substantially since 19x0, and the production managers believe that they have no way to judge whether such an increase is reasonable.

The two production managers, Pepper, and representatives of corporate accounting have met to discuss these concerns. They conclude that a responsibility accounting system can be developed to replace the current system. In their opinion, a responsibility accounting system would alleviate the production managers' concerns and accurately reflect the activity of the Maintenance Center.

OKLAHOMA PROJECT
Maintenance Center Cost Report
for the Month of November 19x2
(in thousands of dollars)

	Budget	Actual	Petroleum Production	Natural Gas Production
Shop hours	2,000	1,800	—	—
Field hours	8,000	10,000	6,000	4,000
Labor — electrical	$ 25.0	$ 24.0	$ 14.4	$ 9.6
Labor — mechanical	30.0	35.0	21.0	14.0
Labor — instrumentation	18.0	22.5	13.5	9.0
Labor — automotive	3.5	2.8	1.7	1.1
Labor — heavy equipment	9.6	12.3	7.4	4.9
Labor — equipment operation	28.8	35.4	21.2	14.2
Labor — general	15.4	15.9	9.6	6.3
Parts	60.0	86.2	51.7	34.5
Supplies	15.3	12.2	7.3	4.9
Lubricants and fuels	3.4	3.0	1.8	1.2
Tools	2.5	3.2	1.9	1.3
Accounting and data processing	1.5	1.5	.9	.6
Total	$213.0	$254.0	$152.4	$101.6

REQUIRED:

a. Explain the purposes of a responsibility accounting system, and discuss how such a system could resolve the concerns of the production center managers of Kelly Petroleum Company.

b. Describe a report format for the Maintenance Center that is based on an effective responsibility accounting system, and explain which, if any, of the Maintenance Center's costs should be charged to the two production centers. (*CMA adapted*)

10-34 **Pro forma Income Statement**   George Paige, chief executive officer of Valan Glass Co., has been reviewing the forecasted results for 19x3. The 19x3 forecast combines the actual results for the first ten months of the current year with management's expectations for the last two months of the year. Although there has been growth and improvement in 19x3, the financial results are less than had been planned for the year. The schedule below compares a summary of the forecasted data with the actual results of the prior two years.

	19x1 Actual	19x2 Actual	19x3 Forecast
Net sales (in millions)	$182.9	$182.6	$202.5
Net income (in millions)	$ 8.6	$ 8.4	$ 9.0
Earnings per share (5 million shares)	$ 1.72	$ 1.68	$ 1.80
Total liabilities (in millions)	$ 46.5	$ 40.8	$ 50.0
Total stockholders' equity (in millions)	$ 99.8	$105.7	$112.0
Total assets (in millions)	$146.3	$146.5	$162.0
Return on average equity	8.2%	8.2%	8.3%

Paige called a meeting of some of his staff to discuss the current financial situation and plan a strategy for 19x4 based on the 19x3 forecasted financial results. The following conversation took place at the meeting:

Paige: "I'm not pleased with the progress we made this year. I believe that our earnings per share and return on equity are too low. I'm afraid that the price of our stock has remained low because we haven't been able to raise them. Therefore, I'd like to see the following results in 19x4:

- Increase real sales volume by 10 percent.

- Increase earnings per share by 15 percent.

- Increase the return on average equity to at least 8.5 percent.

- Continue to pay out 30 percent of our net income as cash dividends.

- Maintain assets at a level consistent with the historical turnover ratio of about 1.25 times.

At the same time, I would like the following to occur:

- Generate at least $20 million of net cash flows from operations after payment of cash dividends.

- Total liabilities should not exceed 35 percent of total assets.

What do you think of these ideas?"

Mike Ford (budget manager): "George, what about cost increases? Have you considered their impact? The production people have indicated to me that their variable manufacturing costs are expected to increase 8 percent in each of the next two years. Furthermore, the fixed manufacturing cost, exclusive of the noncash expenditures, are expected to increase 10 percent in each of the next two years."

Scott Dean (vice president for sales): "Our promotional campaign and related expenses are expected to increase 10 percent next year. This campaign was designed to achieve the 10 percent increase in our unit sales volume that you requested. However, if we try to pass any more than 75 percent of those variable manufacturing cost increases on to our customers, our growth will be affected and we won't make the 10 percent real growth."

Paige: "OK, any other comments? I guess we need some figures to look at to see if my ideas are possible. Mike, prepare a pro forma income statement for 19x4 and calculate the related performance measures using my guidelines. Be sure to incorporate the cost increases. Let's assume we can pass on three-fourths — that is, 6 percent of the 8 percent — of the increase in variable manufacturing costs. We'll have to hope that the increased volume will offset the increased fixed costs. Incidentally, Mike, general administration expenses exclusive of depreciation and amortization are also going to increase 10 percent. Let's get this group together after Mike gets the numbers cranked out."

The 19x3 forecasted income statement that George Paige has been reviewing is reproduced below.

VALAN GLASS CO.
Forecasted Income Statement
for the Year Ended December 31, 19x3
(in millions of dollars)

	Amount	Percent
Net sales	$202.50	100.0
Costs and expenses:		
Variable manufacturing	$125.00	61.7
Fixed manufacturing	25.00[a]	12.4
Sales commissions	4.05[b]	2.0
Sales promotion and administration	18.45	9.1
General administration	15.00[a]	7.4
Total costs and expenses	$187.50	92.6
Income before taxes	$ 15.00	7.4
Income taxes (40%)	6.00	3.0
Net income	$ 9.00	4.4

[a] The fixed manufacturing and general administration expenses include depreciation and amortization of $10 million and $5 million respectively.

[b] Sales commissions are paid on net sales dollars.

REQUIRED:

Using the guidelines outlined by George Paige, develop a budgeted income statement for 19x4. *(CMA adapted)*

10-35 Interpretation of Master Budget; Budgeted Balance Sheet Einhard Enterprises has a comprehensive budgeting program. Pro forma statements of earnings and financial position are prepared as the final step in the budget program. Einhard's projected financial position as of June 30, 19x2, is presented below. Various 19x2 and 19x3 master budget schedules based on the plans for the fiscal year ending June 30, 19x3, are also provided.

All sales are made on account. Raw material, direct labor, factory overhead, and selling and administrative expenses are credited to vouchers payable. The federal income tax rate is 40 percent and the expense is charged to income taxes payable.

EINHARD ENTERPRISES
Pro forma Statement of Financial Position
as of June 30, 19x2
(000s omitted)
Assets

Cash	$ 800
Accounts receivable	750
Direct material inventory	506
Finished goods inventory	648
Total current assets	$ 2,704
Land	$ 1,500
Property, plant, and equipment	11,400
Less accumulated depreciation	(2,250)
Total long-term assets	$10,650
Total assets	$13,354

Liabilities and Equity

Vouchers payable	$ 1,230
Income taxes payable	135
Notes payable (due 12/30/-2)	1,000
Total liabilities	$ 2,365
Common stock	$10,200
Retained earnings	789
Total equity	$10,989
Total liabilities and equity	$13,354

Sales Schedule in Units and Dollars

Unit Sales	Selling Price per Unit	Total Sales Revenue
2,100,000	$16	$33,600,000

Production Schedule in Units and Dollars

Production in Units	Cost per Unit	Total Manufacturing Cost
2,110,000	$12.00	$25,320,000

Raw Material Purchases Schedule in Units and Dollars

Purchases in Pounds	Cost per Pound	Total Purchase Cost
4,320,000	$2.75	$11,880,000

Two pounds of raw material are needed to make one unit of finished product.

Direct Labor Schedule in Units and Dollars

Production in Units	Direct Labor Cost per Hour	Total Direct Labor Cost
2,110,000	$8	$8,440,000

Each unit requires one-half hour of direct labor time.

Manufacturing Overhead Schedule in Dollars (expected activity level — 1,055,000 direct labor hours)

Variable expenses	$2,954,000[a]
Depreciation	600,000
Other fixed expenses	1,721,000[a]
Total manufacturing overhead	$5,275,000

* All require cash expenditures. The manufacturing overhead rate is $5.00 per direct labor hour ($5,275,000 ÷ 1,055,000).

Selling and Administrative Expense Schedule in Dollars

Selling expenses	$2,525,000
Administrative expenses	2,615,000
Total	$5,140,000

All selling and administrative expenses require the expenditure of cash.

Beginning Inventory Schedule in Units and Dollars

	Quantity	Cost per Unit	Total Cost
Direct material	184,000 pounds	$ 2.75 per lb.	$506,000
Finished goods	54,000 units	$12.00 per unit	$648,000

Cash Receipts and Disbursements Schedule
(000s omitted)

Cash balance 7/1/-2 (estimated)	$ 800	
Cash receipts:		
Collection of accounts receivable	33,450	
Total cash available		$34,250
Cash disbursements:		
Payment of vouchers payable:		
Direct material	$11,900	
Direct labor	8,400	
Manufacturing overhead	4,650	
Selling and administrative expenses	5,200	
Total vouchers payable	$30,150	
Income taxes	1,100	
Purchase of equipment	400	
Cash dividends	820	
Total cash disbursements		$32,470
Excess cash		$ 1,780
Financing:		
Repayment of note payable 12/30/-2	$ 1,000	
Interest expense	50	
Total financing cost		$ 1,050
Projected cash balance 6/30/-3		$ 730

REQUIRED:

Construct a Budgeted Statement of Financial Position for Einhard Enterprises as of June 30, 19x3. *(CMA adapted)*

10-36 Budgeted Contribution; Alternative Production Plans   Poe Corp. has manufacturing plants in Boston and Chicago. Both plants produce the same product, Xoff, which sells for $20 per unit. Budgeted revenues and costs for the year ending December 31, 19x5 are as follows:

	(000s omitted)		
	Total	*Boston*	*Chicago*
Sales	$6,200	$2,200	$4,000
Variable factory costs:			
Direct material	1,550	550	1,000
Direct labor	1,660	660	1,000
Factory overhead	1,140	440	700
Fixed factory overhead costs	1,600	700	900
Fixed regional promotional costs	200	100	100
Allocated home office costs	310	110	200
Total costs	6,460	2,560	3,900
Operating income (loss)	$(260)	$(360)	$ 100

Home office costs are fixed and are allocated to manufacturing plants on the basis of relative sales levels. Fixed regional promotional costs are discretionary advertising costs needed to obtain budgeted sales levels. Because of the budgeted operating loss, Poe is considering the possibility of ceasing operations at its Boston plant. If Poe ceases operations at its Boston plant, proceeds from the sale of plant assets would exceed their book value and exactly cover all termination costs; fixed factory overhead costs of $50,000 would not be eliminated. Poe is considering the following plan: Expand Boston's operations from the budgeted 110,000 units of Xoff to a budgeted 170,000 units. It is believed that this can be accomplished by increasing Boston's fixed regional promotional expenditures by $120,000.

REQUIRED:

a. Without considering the effects of implementing the new plan, compute the number of units of Xoff required by the Boston plant to cover its fixed factory overhead costs and fixed regional promotional costs.

b. Prepare a schedule by plant, and in total, computing Poe's budgeted contribution margin and operating income resulting from the implementation of the new plan. *(CPA adapted)*

10-37 Cash Budgeting; Nonprofit Fitness Club (see Appendix) The Triple-F Health Club (Family, Fitness, and Fun) is a nonprofit family-oriented health club. The club's board of directors is developing plans to acquire more equipment and expand the club facilities. The board plans to purchase about $25,000 of new equipment each year and wants to begin a fund to purchase the adjoining property in four or five years. The adjoining property has a market value of about $300,000.

The club manager, Jane Crowe, is concerned that the board has unrealistic goals in light of its recent financial performance. She has sought the help of a club member with an accounting background to assist her in preparing a report to the board supporting her concerns. The club member reviewed the club's records, including the cash basis income statements presented below. The review and discussions with Jane Crowe disclosed the additional information that follows the statement.

TRIPLE-F HEALTH CLUB
Statement of Income (Cash Basis)
for Years Ended October 31
(000s omitted)

	19x7	19x6
Cash revenues:		
Annual membership fees	$355.0	$300.0
Lesson and class fees	234.0	180.0
Miscellaneous	2.0	1.5
Total cash received	$591.0	$481.5
Cash expenses:		
Manager's salary and benefits	$ 36.0	$ 36.0
Regular employee's wages and benefits	190.0	190.0
Lesson and class employee wages and benefits	195.0	150.0
Towels and supplies	16.0	15.5
Utilities (heat and light)	22.0	15.0
Mortgage interest	35.1	37.8
Miscellaneous	2.0	1.5
Total cash expenses	$496.1	$445.8
Cash income	$ 94.9	$ 35.7

Additional Information

1. Other financial information as of October 31, 19x7:

- Cash in checking account, $7,000.

- Petty cash, $300.

- Outstanding mortgage balance, $360,000.

- Accounts payable arising from invoices for supplies and utilities that are unpaid as of October 31, 19x7, $2,500.

2. No unpaid bills existed on October 31, 19x6.

3. The club purchased $25,000 worth of exercise equipment during the current fiscal year. Cash of $10,000 was paid on delivery, and the balance was due on October 1 but has not been paid as of October 31, 19x7.

4. The club began operations in rental quarters. In October of 19x3 it purchased its current property (land and building) for $600,000, paying $120,000 down and agreeing to pay $30,000 plus 9 percent interest annually on November 1 until the balance was paid off.

5. Membership rose 3 percent during 19x7. This is approximately the same annual rate the club has experienced since it opened.

6. Membership fees were increased by 15 percent in 19x7. The board has tentative plans to increase the fees by 10 percent in 19x8.

7. Lesson and class fees have not been increased for three years. The board policy is to encourage classes and lessons by keeping the fees low. The members have taken advantage of this policy, and the number of classes and lessons have grown significantly each year. The club expects the percentage growth experienced in 19x7 to be repeated in 19x8.

8. Miscellaneous revenues are expected to grow at the same percentage as experienced in 19x7.

9. Operating expenses are expected to increase. Hourly wage rates and the manager's salary will need to be increased 15 percent because no increases were granted in 19x7. Towels and supplies, utilities, and miscellaneous expenses are expected to increase 25 percent.

REQUIRED:

a. Construct a cash budget for 19x8 for the Triple-F Health Club.

b. Identify any operating problem(s) that this budget discloses for the Triple-F Health Club. Explain your answer.

c. Is Jane Crowe's concern that the board's goals are unrealistic justified? Explain your answer. *(CMA adapted)*

10-38 Quarterly Cash Budget; Sports Club (see Appendix) Prime Time Court Club (PTCC) has been in business for five years. The club has experienced cash-flow problems each year, especially in the summer when court use is low and new membership sales are insignificant. Temporary loans have been obtained from the local bank to cover the summer shortages. Additional permanent capital also has been invested by the owners.

The owners and the bank have decided some action needs to be taken at this time to improve PTCC's net cash-flow position. They want to review a quarterly cash budget based on a revised fee structure that hopefully will increase club revenues. The purpose of the cash budget is to better anticipate both the timing and amounts of the probable cash flow of the club and to determine whether the club can survive.

John Harper, club manager, recommends that the membership dues be increased and that the hourly court-time fees be replaced with a monthly charge for unlimited court use. He believes that this plan will increase membership and reduce the cash-flow and timing problems. The proposed fee schedule, which is consistent with rates at other clubs, is presented on the following page. In his opinion, the proportions of the different membership categories should not change, but the total number of members will increase by 10 percent. Court use also will increase an estimated 20 percent as a result of this new program. The pattern of use throughout the year is not expected to change.

The present fee structure, the distribution among membership categories, and the projected 19x3 operating data (including membership status, court usage, and estimated operating costs) are presented below. The projected operating data presented in the table were based on the present fee structure before Harper's proposed fee schedule was recommended.

Proposed Fee Schedule

Membership Category	Annual Membership Fees	Monthly Court Charges
Individual	$ 75	$10
Youth	45	8
Family	150	18

Present Fee Structure

Annual Membership Dues	
Individual	$ 45
Youth	30
Family	100

Court Time Fees	
Prime	$10 per hour
Regular	6 per hour

Membership Distribution

Individual	50%
Youth	20
Family	30
	100%

Projected Operating Data

Quarter	Membership Renewal or New Memberships	Court Time in Hours		Costs	
		Prime	Regular	Fixed Costs[a]	Variable Costs
1	600	5,500	6,000	$ 56,500	$ 57,500
2	200	2,000	4,000	56,500	30,000
3	200	1,000	2,000	56,500	15,000
4	600	5,500	6,000	56,500	57,500
	1,600			$226,000	$160,000

[a] Includes a quarterly depreciation charge of $12,500.

REQUIRED:

a. Construct a quarterly cash budget for one year for PTCC assuming the new fee structure is adopted and John Harper's estimates of increases in membership and court use occur. Assume the transition from the old to the new fee structure is immediate and complete when preparing the budget.

   b. Will John Harper's proposal solve the summer cash-shortfall problem? Explain your answer.

   c. Will John Harper's proposal support a conclusion that the club can become profitable and survive in the long run? Explain your answer. *(CMA adapted)*

10-39 Problem 8-29 may also be assigned with this chapter. The problem integrates the topics of budgeting and standard costing.

Identifying and Estimating Relevant Costs for Decisions

11

Decision Making: Analysis of Differential Costs and Benefits

LEARNING OBJECTIVES

After studying this chapter, you should be able to:

1 Evaluate decision alternatives by focusing on differential costs.

2 Calculate the contribution margin per unit of scarce resource to make certain kinds of decisions.

3 Use sensitivity analysis and calculate the cost of prediction errors.

4 Understand the role costs play in the decision process.

5 Select relevant costs for various decisions.

Decision Making

Cost accounting systems provide information to managers who make decisions. Several chapters in this book have concentrated on the accumulation of cost information; this chapter's focus is on how that information is used in the decision-making process. The process is applied to several specific decision problems to illustrate the general principles involved. Some managers are able to make good decisions without the aid of books or courses of study. Yet even capable managers can improve their ability to make decisions and their general understanding of the decision process by learning new techniques designed for specific situations. Using systematized approaches to decision making avoids ad hoc methods that often neglect relevant considerations and increases the likelihood of better decisions.

Decisions imply multiple alternative outcomes are possible. In nearly all decisions, uncertainty (about sales, costs, collections, product quality, and so forth) is present. Finding ways to incorporate uncertainty into the decision process increases understanding of the problem and the probability that better decisions will be made. Moreover, it is useful to have an approach for valuing information that may be obtained to reduce such uncertainty. This chapter discusses the impact of uncertainty, but a discussion of the more complex aspects of this topic is delayed until Chapter 21.

Unique versus Repetitive Decisions

Decisions may be classified in many ways. One classification is based on the frequency of decisions: unique versus repetitive decisions (with or without random intervals between decisions).

All decisions are unique in the sense that sequential circumstances are never exactly the same. Yet similarities among decisions (successive-day production runs, for example) occur, and it is reasonable to treat them as repetitive. Both unique and repetitive decisions are important. Even a one-time decision may have consequences that make it worthwhile to spend considerable time and effort in making the decision.

Many decisions are repetitive in nature, and a store of information from the past may be available for the next occasion. Complex decisions become routine through familiarity. A New Yorker of average intelligence can choose the correct subway; a visitor of superior intelligence may head in the wrong direction. Determining the value of a proposed investment is a complex task for a new employee. After several such computations, the same employee may complain of the routine work load.

A decision that becomes repetitive can draw on information accumulated for similar decisions in the past and use that information in the current situation. In other words, it is helpful when the decision becomes routine. However, not all repetitive decisions are routine. Repetitive decisions may be classified by whether the decisions are unique in some manner. For example, a manager establishing a decision rule for ordering a specific inventory item is faced with a type of repetitive decision. Yet different inventory items require special considerations. Even in the case of the same item, the manager must be alert to changes in production, delivery, and other factors that affect the appropriateness of the previous best decision. Some inventory items, for example, involve quantity discounts, and others entail variable lead times. Consider personnel decisions: hiring of individuals for managerial jobs and promoting individuals are both examples of repetitive decisions where each decision is different. Thus, different decision approaches may be required.

Importance of Decision Outcomes

Decisions also may be classified by the importance of the outcomes. If the future existence of the firm depends on the outcome of a decision, this decision should receive a different degree of consideration than relatively less important decisions. Fortunately for a manager's peace of mind, most decisions are not crucial; that is, no matter how the decision turns out, the organization and the decision maker will survive. Continued poor decisions, however, ultimately spell failure for both.

The more important a decision is, assuming time permits, the more likely it is that the decision maker will seek additional information. Often, additional information can improve the decision process as well as the decision itself. Placing the decision in perspective is extremely important when deciding whether additional information should be obtained. Several considerations are important: How much information should be obtained? What is its value, and is the additional information worth its cost? Can it be obtained in sufficient time? Is the information relevant, or have conditions changed sufficiently to render the information useless? It is of no value to reach a decision based on irrelevant data or to reach a decision based on relevant data but too late to be implemented.

Decisions Under Certainty

Many decisions are formulated as if there is no uncertainty. This simplifies the analysis and may result in a perspective close enough to the actual situation that little is lost by the assumption of certainty. If the cost of making a component for a product is $100 per unit and the cost of buying the component is $90, it appears that the firm should buy rather than make. However, is it certain that the actual cost will be $100? Is there a possibility that the cost will be reduced as more experience is gained? Is the cost accurately measured? Generally, certainty is assumed in this type of decision.

It has been suggested that a manager's time should be devoted to decisions of substantive impact and that the degree of uncertainty involved can influence the managerial effort expended. Attention must be focused on identifying the problem, assuring the relevance of the data, and resolving the action choice in time to be effective. In addition, what is important to one individual may not be critical to a superior, unless the organization's and the manager's goals are compatible (see Chapter 26 for an extended discussion of this issue). Moreover, additional analysis may allow the manager to cope more effectively with the inherent uncertainty, but it will not remove the uncertainty.

Differential Cost Analysis

Certain standard approaches are often used in making decisions under the assumption of certainty. One of these approaches is **differential cost analysis**—the process of selecting the least-cost alternative and ignoring costs that are the same across alternatives. Suppose there are two alternative methods of producing a product: method A and method B. The costs of producing the required quantity of the product under each alternative method are given in Exhibit 11-1.

Using a complete analysis, the decision maker sums the production costs under each method and chooses the one with the lowest total cost. Under the differential-cost approach, the decision maker calculates the cost differences under the two methods. The decision is based on those costs that differ among alternatives, and all costs that are the same under both alternatives are ignored. The differential-cost approach is illustrated in Exhibit 11-2, where all the costs are incremental.

Under the differential-cost approach in this case, the decision maker focuses on only the difference in the costs of direct labor, direct material, and electricity while ignoring indirect labor and other costs that are not influenced by the alternatives adopted. The differential cost of $(50) favors method B. Differential-cost analysis can be useful in situations where the decision maker has a large number of cost items to be considered and can substantially reduce the number examined by ignoring costs that are not expected to differ between alternatives.

One additional benefit of this method is that it permits a value to be attached to nonquantified factors that differ between the alternatives. For example, suppose method A offers safety factors not available with B but that are hard to assign a dollar value. If this is the only such difference, the manager can now decide whether the safety advantage to method A exceeds the $50 cost advantage currently attributable to method B.

Contribution Margin per Unit of Scarce Resource

Another standard approach to some kinds of decisions under certainty is to base the decision on the contribution per unit of scarce resource (or constraining factor). Suppose a firm is trying to decide whether to produce and sell product X or product Y. The price, variable costs, and required machine time for the two products are given in Exhibit 11-3.

EXHIBIT 11-1

Production Costs for Two Production Methods

	Method A	Method B
Direct labor	$1,000	$1,200
Direct material	2,100	1,800
Electricity	200	250
Indirect labor	400	400
Other costs	750	750
Total cost	$4,450	$4,400

EXHIBIT 11-2

Differential Costs of Two Production Methods

	Method A	Method B	Differential Costs
Direct labor	$1,000	$1,200	$200
Direct material	2,100	1,800	(300)
Electricity	200	250	50
Indirect labor	400	400	0
Other costs	750	750	0
Total cost	$4,450	$4,400	$(50)

The **unit contribution margin** of a product is the excess of the product's sales price over its unit variable cost. It is the amount contributed by one unit of sales of the product to covering fixed cost and making a profit. In this example, product X has a higher unit contribution margin than product Y. If the factors of production used to produce X and Y are in unlimited supply, both products should be produced because both earn a positive contribution. However, suppose that machine time is constrained and is, therefore, a scarce resource. With a single constrained resource, the relevant measure of profitability is the contribution margin per unit of the scarce resource, and not the contribution margin per unit of product. Suppose that only 100 machine hours are available for the production of either X or Y. If all 100 machine hours are used for the production of X, 500 units can be produced (100 hours ÷ .2 hours per unit), and the aggregate contribution margin will be 500 × $4.00 or $2,000. If all 100 hours are used to produce product Y, 1,000 units can be produced (100 hours ÷ .1 hours per unit), and the aggregate contribution margin will be 1,000 × $3.00 or

EXHIBIT 11-3

Contribution Margins and Production Times for Two Products

	Product X	Product Y
Sales price	$10.00	$8.00
Direct material	$ 1.00	$2.00
Direct labor	3.00	1.50
Variable overhead	2.00	1.50
Total variable cost per unit	$ 6.00	$5.00
Contribution margin per unit	$ 4.00	$3.00
Machine time required	.2 hours	.1 hour

$3,000. Hence, it is better to use the constrained resource of machine time to produce product Y than to produce product X given demand is sufficient. A more direct way to reach the same conclusion is to compare the contribution margin per unit of scarce resource for products X and Y as shown in Exhibit 11-4.

Because product Y contributes more to fixed cost and profit per machine hour than product X, it is better to produce Y than X. This is true in spite of the fact that product X has a higher contribution margin per unit. But the analysis does not stop here. The data also suggest that management consider expanding machine capacity.

Sensitivity Analysis

Managers often make calculations assuming certainty even when they know that uncertainty exists about one or more aspects (such as data items) in the problem. In such cases, managers can perform a **sensitivity analysis** to determine how sensitive the calculation is to errors in predicting one or more input values. Consider the production-decision example given in Exhibit 11-3. As Exhibit 11-4 shows, the best decision is to manufacture product Y. But suppose there is uncertainty about the direct material cost of product Y. Previously, the decision maker was willing to establish the unit cost as though the product Y material cost is known precisely and use the single-valued estimate of $2.00 per unit in the decision analysis.

The issue addressed in sensitivity analysis is "How sensitive is the decision to manufacture product Y to errors in predicting the product Y material cost?" Stated in terms of break-even analysis, the question becomes "What range of values for the product Y material cost indicates that it is preferable to manufacture product Y instead of product X?" The range of values for the product Y material cost are those for which the contribution margin per machine hour for product Y exceeds that for product X.

Because the contribution per machine hour for product Y already exceeds that for X (when the Y material cost is estimated at $2.00 per unit), any decrease in the Y material cost will increase its contribution margin. Hence, a decrease in the Y material cost will not alter the optimal decision to manufacture product Y.

If the product Y material cost increases to $3.00, the unit contribution margin of product Y declines to $2.00, and the contribution margin per machine hour for product Y drops to $20.00, the same as that for product X. Hence, any value for the product Y material cost in the range $0 to $3.00 (and assuming no change in other

---

EXHIBIT 11-4

Contribution per Machine Hour for Two Products

	Product X	Product Y
Unit contribution margin	$ 4.00	$ 3.00
Machine hours per unit	.2	.1
Contribution margin per machine hour	$20.00[a]	$30.00[b]

[a] $4.00/.2 = $20.00.
[b] $3.00/.1 = $30.00

factors, such as quality) results in the same optimal decision — namely, to manufacture product Y. If the Y material cost exceeds $3.00, it is better to manufacture X.

The decision to manufacture product X or Y is insensitive to the accuracy with which the product Y material cost is predicted. Any decrease or an increase of up to 50 percent in the cost, relative to the estimate of $2.00, does not result in a changed optimal decision. Such information can be useful to the cost accountant when deciding which parameters are most important to be predicted accurately.

Cost of a Prediction Error

One type of sensitivity analysis involves the calculation of the **cost of a prediction error.** A prediction error occurs when the value chosen for a particular variable, such as material cost, turns out to be in error. Using the production-decision example in Exhibits 11-3 and 11-4 again, suppose the cost accountant has predicted a value of $2.00 for the product Y direct material cost. The optimal decision is to manufacture product Y, and the predicted total contribution margin is 1,000 × $3.00 or $3,000. Suppose this material cost prediction proves wrong, and the product Y material cost is actually $3.50. What is the cost of this prediction error? What did it cost the firm to act on a $2.00 prediction, when $3.50 is the actual material cost?

If the production manager had known that $3.50 would be the actual product Y material cost, the manager would have calculated a unit contribution margin of $1.50 for product Y instead of $3.00 (see Exhibit 11-3). The contribution margin per unit of scarce resource for product Y would then have been $15.00 ($1.50 per unit ÷ .1 machine hours per unit). This is less than the $20.00 contribution margin per unit of scarce resource for product X, so the optimal decision would have been to produce 500 units of X and earn a total contribution margin of 500 × $4.00 or $2,000.

Given that the manager based the decision on a prediction of $2.00 for the product Y material cost, and the manager produced 1,000 units of Y, and then the actual cost turned out to be $3.50, the actual total contribution margin achieved will be 1,000 × $1.50 or $1,500. Hence, the cost of this prediction error is $2,000 − $1,500 or $500. The calculation is summarized in Exhibit 11-5.

EXHIBIT 11-5

Cost of a Prediction Error

	Value of Product Y Material Cost	Optimal Action (Based on Given Value of Product Y Material Cost)	Contribution Margin (Given Optimal Action and $3.50 Actual Product Y Material Cost)
(a)	$3.50	Product 500 units of X	$2,000 (500 × $4.00)
(b)	$3.50	Product 1,000 units of Y	$1,500 (1,000 × $1.50)
(c)	Cost of prediction error:	Difference between contribution margins in rows (a) and (b):	
		$2,000 − $1,500 = $500	

The calculation of the cost of the prediction error assumes that the cost of material to manufacture product X remains unchanged. However, this may not be true. And even if it is true, the changes observed may not have been reasonably expected: A good decision can still be followed by an undesirable outcome, something that senior managers must realize when evaluating the decisions of subordinates.

Appropriate or Relevant Costs

To be relevant in a given decision context, a cost must have two characteristics. A **relevant cost** must lead to a future cash flow, and the cash flow must differ across available alternatives. Under this definition, an **opportunity cost** is a relevant cost of an alternative action not explicitly considered in the analysis. For example, suppose a manager desires to know the relevant cost of an electrician's time in performing a particular task. If the electrician could perform another activity instead of the task under consideration, the analysis could either

1. Measure the relevant cost of the electrician as the foregone contribution from the alternative task; or

2. Simply use the electrician's wage as an estimate of the electrician's value in performing the alternative task.

The term *relevant costs* generally is used because some costs are not considered in analysis. Costs of past decisions, for example, are generally of no relevance to current decisions. The first exception to this rule relates to taxes. Prior costs can and do influence current and future tax consequences, and hence the real economic flows, of current decisions. A decision should not be made without a consideration of the tax implications.

Past costs also may constrain a firm's actions through legal constraints or the perceptions of those on whom the firm relies. For example, current costs may restrict available pricing alternatives under the Robinson-Patman Act (see Chapter 3). Also, a firm's reported profits, which are based in part on past costs, may constrain the firm's ability to borrow. Large profits caused by inflation-driven prices, matched with low historical costs, can invite government scrutiny and action, as was the case in the late 1970s when the government levied an excess-profits tax on major oil companies.

For a final example, consider the impact of past costs on a decision maker's performance evaluation, which is closely tied to the bottom line. Suppose the purchase of a new machine is being considered. Last year a machine was purchased for $1,000,000 to do the same task. It has been depreciated very little for book purposes but does not do a satisfactory job. The old machine could be traded in toward a new machine for $600,000. The manager will be quick to point out that this trade will cause a loss of about $400,000 to be included in the manager's performance report. If the old machine is kept, the manager can prevent this loss from appearing in the performance report. If forced to show the loss, the manager may elect not to obtain the new machine. Thus, performance evaluation based on past costs can affect a manager's decision in an undesirable manner. The logic that a historical cost is not relevant for decision making is basically valid. The person who buys a new car for $10,000 in the morning and immediately drives it into a tree should probably not reject an offer of $4,000 for the wreck simply because the car cost $10,000 in the morning.

It is equally dangerous to assume that full cost is always the appropriate term or figure to use in a decision context. Full cost or full product cost includes the variable costs to produce a product as well as a share of the organization's fixed costs. For example, suppose a local electrical contracting firm has for some time costed its electrical service calls at their full cost while pricing its services competitively. A consultant is hired to explore the option of eliminating services that show a loss. The analysis shows that eliminating these service calls actually would decrease company profit rather than increase it because only some of the costs allocated to the service calls would be saved by eliminating the calls. For example, the general overhead costs of the firm's office, which have been allocated to service calls, would continue. The consultant's recommendation is to evaluate services on the basis of their contribution to overhead and profit. Those that make a positive contribution should be continued.

The inappropriateness of using full-cost data does not mean that fixed costs are always irrelevant. If a decision will alter fixed costs, then the change in total fixed cost is an incremental cost associated with the decision and should be considered. Thus, continuing the prior example, if eliminating service calls allows the firm to get by with one less secretary, or if adding service calls results in increased expenditures for data processing, these incremental costs should be included in the analysis of the proposed change.

Finding the Relevant Costs for Various Decisions

Any decision problem involving cost data requires careful analysis to establish costs that are relevant and costs that should be excluded from the analysis. This section provides several examples that reinforce the topics discussed in this chapter.

The Special Order

Suppose the Nash Company currently has excess capacity and is considering the acceptance of a one-time order for its product. Management wishes to know the cost of filling the order. If the price offered for the special order exceeds its cost, the order should be accepted. Otherwise, it should be rejected. Assume for simplicity that there are no taxes.

First, it is critical to establish what management means by *cost*. Several alternative interpretations are possible. They include the following:

1. The accounting cost based on the historical accounting records,

2. The cost figure on which a price choice would be made (such as in a cost-plus pricing contract), or

3. The cost that actually will be incurred to fill the order.

These concepts are not the same, as the example illustrates. The discussion here is concerned with the third interpretation of cost given above — that is, the actual cost to be incurred in filling the order.

One element required for the special order, creolite, is highly perishable. The firm has 1,000 gallons on hand, of which 800 will be required for the special order. The current supply was purchased at $10 a gallon and is inventoried on the firm's books at $10,000. The current market price for creolite is $10.50 and this price is expected to hold for a while. The firm uses creolite in its current operations. What is the cost of creolite in the special order?

The answer to this question is, as is often true, "It depends." In this case, it depends on the assumption made (or facts determined) about the potential uses of the 1,000 gallons of creolite currently in inventory. If the current stock will be used in the ordinary course of business, the value that must be sacrificed if the order is accepted is $8,400 (the $10.50 current market price times the 800 gallons needed to fill the order). The creolite must be replaced for the company's other operations if the special order is accepted.

On the other hand, if the creolite's perishability will cause it to become valueless before it can be used, it costs nothing to use it in the special order. The cost is zero. Management may wish to talk to the purchasing manager or production manager to see why the extra material is on hand, but this does not alter the relevant cost; it is still zero. The **book value** of the creolite, defined as the historical cost value at which the material is inventoried ($8,000 = $10 × 800), is not relevant to the decision.[1]

Sale of Inventory

Consider again the special order discussed above. Suppose a second material, culman, is also required. This material no longer is used by the firm, but a stock of 1,000 pounds remains from prior orders. The material is currently on the books at its historical cost of $20 a pound, a total of $20,000. Nine hundred pounds of culman

---

1. If we had assumed instead that Nash Company must pay income taxes, then the relevant cost of the creolite is reduced. The company will include the book value of the creolite as a production cost included in cost of goods sold, an expense. Thus, income will be reduced by the book value of the creolite, in this case $8,000 (800 × $10 per gallon). Assuming a tax rate of 40 percent, this will save the company $3,200 ($8,000 × 40%) in taxes. Therefore, the net relevant cost of the creolite would be calculated as follows:

Replacement cost	$8,400
Less: tax savings	3,200
Net relevant cost	$5,200

The tax effects of decisions are covered more extensively in Chapters 19 and 20.

would be required by the special order. Currently, management has an offer from another corporation to purchase the entire inventory of culman for $12 a pound. The current market price of culman is $15 a pound, and the purchasing manager indicates that the company could buy the required 900 pounds at that price. What is the cost of the culman?

Again, as you might expect, there is more than one answer to this question. In the current context, cost means value sacrificed to fill the order. The opportunity to sell the culman provides the alternative that establishes the value at $12 per pound, and hence the cost, to be assigned to the required material. Because 1,000 pounds of the material is on hand but only 900 pounds are needed, the ability of the firm to buy it outside is not relevant. The book value is a historical (sunk) cost and also is not relevant.

If the outside buyer's $12 offer price is valid, the relevant cost of the culman required for the order is $10,800 ($12 × 900). If all the 1,000 pounds could be sold for $12 per pound but the additional 100 pounds not needed for the special order cannot be sold and must be dumped at no cost, the relevant cost of the required culman is $12,000 ($12 × 1,000). In this case, the sale of all 1,000 pounds is foregone even though only a portion of it is needed for the special order.

Make or Buy

To decide whether to make a component part or purchase the part outside, management first compares the total differential costs. For example, suppose the Boheed Airframe Corporation is considering whether to manufacture or purchase the landing gear assembly needed in a modified version of one of its current aircraft. The modified aircraft will be used on natural-surface airfields.

The initial cost for 100 assemblies is estimated as follows:

	Total Cost	Unit Cost
Direct labor	$ 500,000	$ 5,000
Direct material	250,000	2,500
Variable overhead	250,000	2,500
Fixed overhead	300,000	3,000
	$1,300,000	$13,000

The Beck Manufacturing Company has offered to supply the landing gear assemblies for $12,000 each or a total of $1,200,000 for 100 assemblies. Because this price is below Boheed's costs, purchase might appear to be the best option. However, it is necessary first to consider whether the Boheed facilities will be idle if the landing gear is not made internally.

If the facilities are already available at Boheed and will be idle if Beck manufactures the landing gear assemblies, then Boheed must examine its allocated fixed and variable overhead to see what portion, if any, can be avoided if it decides to buy outside. Suppose a quarter of the fixed overhead items are unavoidable costs related to property taxes, insurance, central staff salaries, and depreciation. Then one-fourth of $300,000, or $75,000, should be removed from the cost allocations. This amount will not be influenced by the decision. Likewise, suppose one-fifth of the variable overhead is related to supervisory labor, maintenance, and related items, which will be incurred regardless of the current decision. Then one-fifth of $250,000 or $50,000 also should be removed from the cost allocations.

Now the cost of making the 100 landing gear assemblies is reduced from $1,300,000 to $1,175,000 ($1,300,000 − $75,000 − $50,000). It is less expensive to make the landing gear than to buy it.

This example emphasizes that differential-cost analysis should focus on costs that a particular decision can avoid. These costs are relevant. It also points out that the right question needs to be asked. The proper question is not whether to make or buy but rather how to best use available production facilities. (If the facilities do not already exist, the question is how to best obtain the landing gear assembly.) Boheed's managers should explore whether, if the assemblies are purchased, the idle production facilities should be used to produce some other item. Indeed, the same issue exists whether the facilities are currently idle or not. However, if the facilities are not expected to be idle, other factors, such as lost contribution from current operations or incremental costs from shifting current activities, must be considered. Boheed's management has several alternatives to analyze, including the following:

1. Make,

2. Buy and leave current facilities idle,

3. Buy and use current facilities for another purpose.

A third lesson to be learned from this example is to be wary of unit-cost figures. They may include costs that are irrelevant. Moreover, the application of fixed over-head costs depends on the assumed volume of activity; computations should be made using total costs, which can be unitized later if necessary.

Finally, the Boheed analysis has dealt only with quantitative factors, but decisions seldom rest on such an analysis alone. For Boheed the monetary difference is small enough that the most important elements in the final decision may be qualitative factors such as

1. Control over supply,

2. Quality,

3. Expected future activity levels,

4. Morale,

5. Flexibility in purchasing the assembly in the future.

Book Values and Decisions

The Nash example, discussed earlier in this chapter, illustrated the irrelevance of historical book values in decision making. This irrelevance is true for the book values of inventories, equipment, goodwill, and other assets. This concept is worth review and enforcement. To do so, consider several factors that relate to the decision to replace a machine:

1. The historical book value determined by deducting book depreciation (usually determined using the straight-line method) from the asset's original cost,

2. The book loss or gain on the disposal or replacement,

3. The disposal market value of the old machine,

4. The market value (not necessarily the list price) of the new machine as measured by the value sacrificed to obtain it. The market value is the actual cash needed to acquire the new machine.

Items 1 and 2 are not relevant to the replacement (or to a disposal) decision. They cannot be changed by a current action. The original investment is a sunk cost, and the current loss or gain on disposal exists whether the decision to get rid of the equipment is made or not. Whether the loss has been formally recognized in the financial books is not relevant. The old equipment will be written off under either alternative (either as a write-off at disposal or through depreciation). The question is one of timing, and because this is a bookkeeping entry only, no cash flows are involved. Therefore, it does not matter for decision analysis when this is done; there is no differential cost.

Items 3 and 4 are relevant. They entail cash outlays and the sacrifice of resources that could be used for other purposes. The amounts affect the costs under the two alternatives available: replace or do not replace the machine.

Two caveats to the above discussion are required. The first deals with taxes. The disposal of an asset can affect the timing of the tax deductions available from depreciation and on any recognized gain or loss. Assets are often depreciated differently (more quickly) for tax purposes, and hence the relevant numbers are not necessarily those based on the company's financial books. The decision to replace a machine is really a capital-budgeting decision, which is the subject of Chapters 19 and 20, The timing of tax flows and the tax effects of investment decisions are covered more extensively in those chapters.

Second, management performance reports reflect any loss (or gain) from disposal in the period. Because the loss (or gain) can influence managers' compensation and promotion prospects, managers consider the impact of major decisions on their own well being.

Analysis of Relevant Costs and Benefits in a University

Identification of the costs and revenues relevant to decisions is also important in not-for-profit institutions. The following case illustrates an analysis of the relevant financial benefits of athletic programs at Wright State University.[2]

2. Copyright © 1983 by the President and Fellows of Harvard College. The case was prepared by Robert N. Anthony as the basis for class discussion rather than to illustrate either effective or ineffective handling of an administrative situation. Reprinted by permission of the Harvard Business School.

Relevant Costs and Benefits of University Athletic Programs

Wright State University

Wright State University is a state-supported institution of 12,000 students located in Dayton, Ohio. The data in this case are derived from a study of the sports of baseball, soccer, softball, men's and women's swimming, men's tennis, volleyball and wrestling. These sports are used because they are considered non-revenue generating sports, they receive limited scholarship aid, and they have been eliminated at several other institutions.

Dr. Michael J. Cusack, Director of Athletics at Wright State University, described a way of evaluating certain athletics programs in a paper presented at a conference on college sports sponsored by Skidmore College. This paper is summarized below. Dr. Cusack's men's basketball team has won the national championship in Division II of the National Collegiate Athletic Association. He stated that his method of analysis would be useful as Wright State debated whether or not to move to NCAA's Division I.[3]

The current state of the economy is causing most institutions to scrutinize their budgets very closely. The demographics for the remainder of the decade and into the next are very disturbing. They are especially disturbing, however, within education. As federal aid reductions are coupled with a diminishing student pool, budgetary cuts in the form of retrenchment and program elimination will become more and more likely at various institutions.

In many colleges and universities, cost-effective programs could be the difference between the existence and extinction of the institution. In situations where programs and expenditures are examined and cuts are indicated, the first place that often comes to mind is the athletic program. Cuts made within the athletic program are often made in the form of elimination of one or more sports. The activities eliminated typically fall in the category of "non-revenue" or so-called minor sports. The people making the decisions point to the savings generated by the elimination of the operating budget and the scholarship allotment for those sports. They will often combine these budgetary savings with the position that the programs serve a limited number of students and generate little or no fan support or public interest.

If the examination of athletic programs is limited to that level, it might be a logical conclusion to eliminate particular programs. It should be noted, however, that there are several factors worthy of consideration before such a conclusion is drawn. Among these factors are a determination as to whether the non-revenue sports are, in fact, generating no revenue. In addition, consideration should be given to the benefits

3. Dr. Cusack used as an illustration both Wright State University and Mercyhurst College (where Dr. Cusack was formerly athletic director), but in the interest of brevity only the data for Wright State University are presented here.

the Athletic Department provides to the Admissions Office through the recruiting efforts of the athletic staff. Furthermore, the retention rates of student athletes should be examined to determine the difference between their retention rates and those of students who do not participate in intercollegiate athletics. Finally, the publicity value of each program should be computed and considered in determining its financial impact on the institution.

Revenue Generation Intercollegiate athletic programs conducted on a partial or non-scholarship basis will provide revenue to the institution through the amount paid by each student-athlete above the athletic or other institutional aid provided. This amount will vary according to the cost of attendance, the amount of athletic and other institutional aid provided, and the amount of federal and state aid received by the student-athletes.

With the help of the Financial Aid Office, the maximum amount of aid to which each student is entitled can be determined. Coaches should be instructed that every student-athlete recruited must complete the financial aid forms before they will receive any institutional aid. Regardless of the amount of athletically-related aid a coach anticipates providing an individual, the completion of the appropriate forms should be required. Every dollar received from outside sources is that much more available to the institution.

We found that the tuition generated in the sports under discussion totalled an amount substantially greater than the costs involved in conducting the programs. In baseball, for example, the average revenue received per student-athlete was $1,415. There were 37 athletes, so the total revenue generated was $52,355. The total budget for baseball was $40,020, so the net revenue generated was $12,335. The results of similar calculations for the other sports are shown in the first column of Exhibit 11-6.

EXHIBIT 11-6

Wright State University
Total Revenue Generated by Non-Revenue Sports

Sport	Revenue Generated	Retention Benefits	Publicity Value	Total Financial Benefits
Baseball	+ $12,335	$ 775	$ 6,685	+ $19,795
Soccer	+ 6,607	− 100	4,315	+ 10,822
Softball	+ 23,105	+ 300	585	+ 23,990
Swimming (Men)	− 7,488	− 200	454	− 7,234
Swimming (Women)	− 21,684	+ 150	370	− 21,164
Tennis	+ 11,815	+ 100	370	+ 12,285
Volleyball	− 16,526	+ 175	745	− 15,606
Wrestling	+ 1,500	+ 300	396	+ 2,196
Total	$ 9,664	$1,500	$13,920	$25,084

Admissions Benefits   Coaches are, by virtue of their recruiting efforts, an arm of the admissions office. The recruitment of student-athletes, who will be a positive factor on the campus, is as essential to their programs as it is for the admissions department. Furthermore, the contacts usually enjoyed by coaches and the specificity of their needs provides them with an excellent position to generate students for an institution.

In some cases it is possible to determine the unit cost incurred by the Admissions Office in the recruitment of students. When this is possible, the actual savings generated by the coaches, who recruit student-athletes and add to the institutional population without the Admissions Office's involvement, can be computed.

Due to the nature of the student body and the various populations the Admissions Office works with, the development of a recruiting figure was not possible at Wright State University. At Mercyhurst College we found that the average cost of recruiting a student by the admissions office was $500. During a recent academic year, we found that ten student-athletes were recruited by the athletic staff in the non-revenue sports. At $500 per student, this would represent a savings to the institution of $5,000.

Retention Benefits   It is generally accepted that students who are involved in an activity at an institution are more likely to remain at that institution. Furthermore, admissions offices are constantly attempting to find a match between what their institution has to offer, and the needs and interests of the prospective students.

An athletic program provides the opportunity for students to become involved in an activity, and the recruitment efforts of the coaching staff are predicated upon matching the needs of the athletic program with the abilities of the prospective student-athletes. It would seem, therefore, that members of the athletic teams are more likely to remain at the institution than the non-athletic students. If there are, in fact, a greater proportion of student-athletes remaining at the institution than other students, then the athletic program is generating revenue to the institution. The retention rate at Wright State University in a recent year was 65% for the whole freshman class; for the student-athlete population it was 75%.

An indication of the financial benefit generated by these retention rates can be determined by multiplying the cost of attendance for the fall term by the number of student-athletes who would have left the university if their rates were at the same level as the general student population. The cost of enrollment for the fall term of a recent year was $500, the average cost of tuition and fees. The number of student-athletes who would have left the university in order to reach the level of the general student population was 3. The financial impact of the higher retention rate for student-athletes was, therefore, $1,500.

Publicity Value   The sports pages of every newspaper in the country provide college results in almost every sport each day. Institutions have long pointed to the publicity value of an athletic program, and they have generally pointed to the high-visibility sports as an example. All sports, however, generate some publicity for which an institution would otherwise have to pay. By simply measuring the amount of space generated in the sports pages for each activity, and multiplying the figure by the cost of advertising space, the value of each sport can be computed. For example, baseball generated 538 inches of space during the year, with a value of $6,685. It should be noted that no attempt was made to evaluate the space generated in the student-athletes' home newspapers, releases generated by other institutions, or any other form of media.

Formula for Calculating the Financial Impact of "Non-Revenue" Sports Utilizing the figures generated in each of the sports categories discussed, it is possible to objectively assess the financial impact of "non-revenue" sports. The formula that can be used to compute the collective impact of the program, or of each individual sport, is as follows:

$$\text{Tuition Generation} + \text{Admissions Savings} + \text{Retention Benefits} + \text{Publicity Value}$$

The benefits that Wright State derived from non-revenue sports during a recent academic year totalled $25,084, not counting the value of admission savings. (The benefits for Mercyhurst College, calculated in the same manner, were $85,714 for tuition revenue generated, $5,000 for admissions savings, $13,200 for retention benefits, and $1,742 for publicity value, for a total of $105,656.)

Reduced Use of Retention and Counseling Services Counseling services typically attempt to help students connect with some part of the institution, with the expectation that this will help students attain a more positive feeling about their roles at the institution. Student-athletes already have a connection with the institution through their teams. They also have a relationship with a coach that often transcends the field of competition. Often this relationship approaches that of a parent or counselor.

We have found that student-athletes use counseling and retention services significantly less than the general student population. We feel that this reduced usage is due to the relationship within the teams and with the coaches. We have not attempted to quantify this effect, but the reduced usage of the services frees the counselors to spend more time with other students.

Unit-of-Delivery Cost It is essential that an institution provide activities for their students throughout the school year. The student-services area of an institution is budgeted to provide entertainment and activities that will help enhance the quality of life of the student body. Most of those activities require a financial outlay by the institution. Dances, concerts, lectures and the like cost Student Services something to stage, and the activities are cost efficient in terms of the number of students who attend them. The unit of delivery cost can be determined by dividing the cost of an activity by the number of students who attend that activity. For example, a dance that costs $500 to run and is attended by 500 students would have a unit-of-delivery cost of $1.

Athletic events are generally paid for through the athletic budget, and they typically are free to the students. There would, therefore, be no unit-of-delivery cost to the Student Services budget, or any other budget of the institution, with the exception of the athletic department. Since we have already shown that the programs examined more than offset the budgets provided, there would also be no unit-of-delivery cost in this area. While the actual financial value of sports programs (in unit-of-delivery costs) is not easily computed, the value to the Admissions Office (in recruiting) and to the institution's student body (in entertainment and spirit) is substantial.

In examining an individual activity or an entire program, the number of students attending those events and the cost to the institution of staging them should be considered. It is generally accepted that events usually cost the institution something to stage, and that those costs are worth incurring if they improve the atmosphere on the campus. If, however, those activities are costless to the institution, and are in fact proving to be financially rewarding, then those programs would appear to be valuable assets to the institution.

Beyond justifying a program's existence, the use of the formula presented above, and an examination of the categories discussed, has several potential values to an institution. The formula could serve to identify areas within a program that are in need of improvement or which show particular strength. Coaches could be given a report showing how they have performed in each area, and where they might consider working toward improvement. The formula could serve as a major component of a planning process. Activities could be evaluated on their revenue-generating potential, admissions benefits and the other areas discussed above. The results of these studies could be used in making decisions such as initiating new programs or eliminating or curtailing existing programs.

An analysis of full-scholarship programs could also be conducted using the formula to determine the actual cost of those programs. Traditionally, full-scholarship programs have been justified by their revenue production through gate receipts and media contracts. It might turn out that scholarship programs that do not generate this type of revenue actually do offset much of their cost in other areas.

Finally, the approach and formula outlined above could serve as the basis for studying other areas within an institution. As financial accountability becomes more necessary, all programs will come under close scrutiny. Every program has variables that are important to their existence, and many of these variables could be quantified. This would establish the total value of the programs to the institution. Conversely, where programs show weakness in various areas, administrators would have a basis for determining means of improving them or deciding to eliminate them.

Summary

This chapter has examined costs from a decision-making perspective by focusing on those costs that differ among the available alternatives. Total costs are preferable to unit costs in a differential-cost analysis; the unit-cost figures can be obtained later if needed. Sensitivity analysis can be used to incorporate uncertainty into decision

...ts of prediction errors can be estimated, but it is important to ...d decisions can be followed by bad outcomes.

...to be cautious in assuming that variable costs are always avoidable ...e not. The best answer as to what costs are relevant often is "it ...cision and the circumstances. A careful analysis is often required ...costs are relevant in a particular situation.

...levant costs in the analysis is, however, only the first step. Many ...ors such as product quality, business strategy, and security of ...determine the best course of action. Nevertheless, the quantita-...s some factors from speculation and provides a benchmark that ...luating the significance of the qualitative items.

...nt is understanding the firm's decision process. Who are the ...at data do they require, how should it be presented, and what ...e made for follow-up and feedback? A critical element here is ...ppreciating the relevance of the data to managers' performance

...decisions, including special orders, sale of inventory and the ...n have been examined in some detail. These decision analyses ...the application of differential costing and the determination of ...nt under different circumstances.

...intenance Organization is considering disposing of its main-...nd renting the required capacity outside. The following data ...on are available. This decision is evaluated yearly.

	$100,000
	60,000
...ue	20,000
...ue	30,000
...ting costs (est.)	4,000
...l costs (est.)	15,000
...e year	25,000

...items are relevant in evaluating the decision? Are there other ...ns?

...omic viewpoint, the original cost (a) and current book value (b) are not ...e values are often called sunk costs. The tax depreciable base (c) will be ...r time, but if the asset is sold, this tax base will influence cash flows immediately. The timing difference is relevant because a tax saving today is worth more than one obtained later. The decline in disposal value $(d - c)$ is a relevant cost of keeping the machine one more year. The increased operating cost $(f - e)$ is also a relevant cost. If the manager making the decision is evaluated on a bottom-line profit-type figure, the manager might behave as if the loss due to writing off the book value (b) is relevant to the decision.

Other relevant considerations for which dollar magnitudes are difficult to establish include the availability of capacity on a timely basis from the outside contractor, the difficulties of reestablishing a computer system if outside prices increase substantially, morale problems if current employees are affected, and the technological system that can best serve the changing needs of the organization.

Key Terms to Review

book value, p. 402
cost of a prediction error, p. 399
differential cost analysis, p. 396
opportunity cost, p. 400

relevant cost, p. 400
sensitivity analysis, p. 398
unit contribution margin, p. 397

Suggested Readings

Goetz, J. "The Pricing Decision: A Service Industry Experience." *Journal of Small Business Management* (April 1985): 61–67.

Hartman, B. "The Management Accountant's Role in Deleting a Product Line." *Management Accounting* (August 1983): 63–66.

Kaplan, R. S. "Application of Quantitative Models in Managerial Accounting: A State of the Art Survey." In *Management Accounting — State of the Art,* Beyer Lecture Series. Madison: University of Wisconsin, 1977; reprinted in *Accounting Journal* (Winter 1977–78): 218–42.

———, *Advanced Managerial Accounting.* Englewood Cliffs, N.J.: Prentice-Hall, 1982, chap. 3.

Lund, D., K. Monroe, and P. Choudhury. "Pricing Policies and Strategies: An Annotated Bibliography." Chicago: American Marketing Association, 1982.

Magee, R. *Advanced Managerial Accounting.* New York: Harper & Row, 1986.

Review Questions

11-1 Describe several ways into which decisions can be classified. What important distinctions exist between these categories — that is, why is the classification useful?

11-2 Name the method that was discussed in the chapter that allows the decision maker to incorporate uncertainty into the analysis and discuss the major assumption of the approach.

11-3 Can a cost that will not change across alternatives be omitted from the decision analysis? Why or why not?

11-4 In a decision situation why might a given fixed-cost item be relevant but perhaps at a different level than that charged to a product or service line? Give an example.

11-5 The unit contribution margin of service 1 exceeds that of service 2. If only one of the two can be done, it should be service 1. Do you agree? Explain.

11-6 Should a junior analyst be concerned with how the manager's performance is evaluated when presenting decision alternatives? Explain.

11-7 In selecting among alternatives, how can a numerical value be placed on qualitative factors?

11-8 Is an opportunity cost a relevant cost? Explain.

11-9 If a firm considers contracting out a task it can currently do in house, on what basis should the best alternative be determined (that is; lowest cost, highest revenue or some other criterion)?

Exercises

11-10 **Prediction Errors**   In the example of products X and Y (see Exhibit 11-5 and surrounding text), what are the costs of the following prediction errors? Do each part separately.

 a. The cost of product X's material should be $.50 not $1.00.

 b. The direct labor of product X is $2 (rather than $3) and for product Y the $1.50 estimate is only 75 percent of what it should be.

 c. It takes twelve minutes to make a unit of Y rather than six minutes.

11-11 **Disposal Value, Book Value, and the Loss on Disposal**   David James is CEO of a local printing company. The firm is considering replacing a special-purpose printer with a new and more efficient machine whose useful life is forecast to be seven years. It will cost $13,200 but will result in cash operating expenses of $45,000 per year versus $48,386 for the current machine.

  The old machine's cost was $27,000 four years ago and has a current book value of $15,000 based on straight-line depreciation and no estimated salvage value. The best alternative use of the old machine is to sell it for scrap for $4,600. Management currently estimates salvage values at

Old machine in 7 more years	$ 400
New machine in 7 years	$1,300

Linda Danile, the firm's controller, favors retention of the old machine based on the following analysis:

Investment cost	$13,200
Loss on old printer	15,000
Total cost	$28,200
Savings $3,386 × 7	23,702
Loss on replacement	$ 4,498

Evaluate the current option ignoring tax effects and the time value of money.

11-12 Estimating Benefits of Alternative Decisions   Stewart Industries has been producing two bearings, components B12 and B18, for use in production. Data regarding these two components are presented in the columns labeled B12 and B18.

	B12	B18
Machine hours required per unit	2.5	3.0
Standard cost per unit:		
Direct material	$ 2.25	$ 3.75
Direct labor	4.00	4.50
Manufacturing overhead:		
Variable[a]	2.00	2.25
Fixed[b]	3.75	4.50
	$12.00	$15.00

[a] Variable manufacturing overhead is applied on the basis of direct labor hours. All variable overhead is incremental to production.
[b] Fixed manufacturing overhead is applied on the basis of machine hours.

Stewart's annual requirement for these components is 8,000 units of B12 and 11,000 units of B18. These requirements cannot be altered. Recently, Stewart's management decided to devote additional machine time to other product lines resulting in only 41,000 machine hours per year that can be dedicated to the production of the bearings. An outside company has offered to sell Stewart the annual supply of the bearings at prices of $11.25 for B12 and $13.50 for B18. Stewart wants to schedule the otherwise idle 41,000 machine hours to produce bearings so that the company can minimize its costs (maximize its net benefits).

The net benefit (loss) per machine hour that would result if Stewart Industries accepts the supplier's offer of $13.50 per unit for component B18 is (choose one):

a. $.50.

b. $(1.00).

c. $1.50.

d. $(1.75).

e. some amount other than those given above. (*CMA adapted*)

11-13 Selecting among Purchase Options (continuation of Exercise 11-12). Stewart Industries will maximize its net benefits by (choose one):

a. purchasing 4,800 units of B12 and manufacturing the remaining bearings.

b. purchasing 8,000 units of B12 and manufacturing 11,000 units of B18.

c. purchasing 11,000 units of B18 and manufacturing 8,000 units of B12.

d. purchasing 4,000 units of B18 and manufacturing the remaining bearings.

e. purchasing and manufacturing some amounts other than those given above. (*CMA adapted*)

11-14 Selecting the Optimal Price (continuation of Exercise 11-13). Without affecting your answers to Exercises 11-13 and 11-14, assume that Stewart Industries' idle capacity of 41,000 machine hours has a traceable avoidable annual fixed cost of $44,000 that will continue if the capacity is not used to produce product B18. The maximum price Stewart Industries would be willing to pay a supplier for component B18 is (choose one):

a. $10.50.

b. $14.00.

c. $14.50.

d. $18.00.

e. some amount other than those given above. (*CMA adapted*)

11-15 Dropping a Product RBW Corporation is considering dropping one product that requires special equipment. Unit data regarding the product are as follows:

Selling price		$14.00
Costs:		
Raw materials	$2.40	
Direct labor	3.60	
Manufacturing overhead:		
Variable	2.75	
Fixed	2.25	
Depreciation — special equipment	.50	11.50
Net amount		$ 2.50

Fixed and variable manufacturing overhead are applied on the basis of direct labor hours. The unit charge for special equipment depreciation cost ($.50 per unit) is determined by dividing the annual depreciation charge on the equipment ($20,000) by the normal annual volume for the product.

If production of this product is discontinued, the special equipment can be sold for $15,000. If production continues, the equipment will be useless for further production at the end of one year and would have no salvage value. The equipment had an original cost of $100,000 four years ago and will be fully depreciated at the end of one more year. The fixed overhead manufacturing costs ($2.25 per unit) represents the capacity costs of the plant and will continue to be incurred whether or not production ceases.

RBW Corporation is subject to a 40 percent income tax rate. Depreciation expense is the same for book and tax purposes.

a. The sum of the raw material, direct labor, and variable overhead costs ($8.75) are the total variable costs of the product. These costs can also be characterized in this situation as (choose one):

   (1) prime costs.

   (2) allocated costs.

   (3) avoidable costs.

   (4) opportunity costs.

   (5) sunk costs.

b. The fixed manufacturing overhead costs in this situation are referred to as (choose one):

   (1) joint costs.

   (2) opportunity costs.

   (3) incremental costs.

   (4) avoidable costs.

   (5) allocated costs.

c. The original cost of the equipment ($100,000) in this situation is referred to as (choose one):

   (1) a sunk cost.

   (2) an opportunity cost.

   (3) a fixed cost.

   (4) an incremental cost.

   (5) an avoidable cost.

d. The sales price of the equipment that will not be realized if RBW continues production is referred to as (choose one):

   (1) a sunk cost.

   (2) an opportunity cost.

   (3) a fixed cost.

   (4) an incremental cost.

   (5) an avoidable cost.

e. If RBW Corporation discontinues production of the product and sells the special equipment, it will no longer have the advantage of an annual tax saving from the depreciation of (choose one):

(1) $6,000.

(2) $20,000.

(3) $8,000.

(4) $12,000.

(5) some amount other than those given above.

f. If RBW Corporation discontinues the product and sells the special equipment, the cash flow (considering tax savings) from the sale of the equipment will be (choose one):

(1) $15,000.

(2) $17,000.

(3) $13,000.

(4) $9,000.

(5) some amount other than those given above. (*CMA adapted*)

11-16 Excess Capacity   Atway Company has met all production requirements for the current month and has an opportunity to produce additional units of product with its excess capacity. Unit selling prices and unit costs for three models of one of its product lines are as follows:

	Plain Model	Regular Model	Super Model
Selling price	$60	$65	$80
Direct material	18	20	19
Direct labor	10	15	20
Variable overhead	8	12	16
Fixed overhead	16	5	15

Variable overhead is applied on the basis of direct labor dollars and is incremental to production, while fixed overhead is applied on the basis of machine hours. There is sufficient demand for the additional production of any model of the product line to be sold at the given prices.

a. If Atway Company has excess machine capacity and can add more labor as needed (that is, neither machine capacity nor labor is a constraint), the excess production capacity should be devoted to producing (choose one):

(1) the plain model.

(2) the regular model.

(3) the super model.

(4) an equal number of regular and super models.

(5) an equal number of plain and regular models.

b. If Atway has excess machine capacity but a limited amount of labor time available, the excess production capacity should be devoted to producing (choose one):

(1) the plain model.

(2) the regular model.

(3) the super model.

(4) an equal number of regular and super models.

(5) an equal number of each model. (*CMA adapted*)

Problems   **11-17** **Selecting Among Several Alternatives**   Auer Company received an order for a piece of special machinery from Jay Company. Just as Auer Company completed the machine, Jay Company declared bankruptcy, defaulted on the order, and forfeited the 10 percent deposit paid on the selling price of $72,500.

Auer's manufacturing manager identified the costs already incurred in the production of the special machinery for Jay as follows:

Direct materials used		$16,600
Direct labor incurred		21,400
Overhead applied:		
Manufacturing:		
Variable	$10,700	
Fixed	5,350	16,050
Fixed selling and administrative		5,405
Total cost		$59,455

Another company, Kaytell Corp., would be interested in buying the special machinery if it is reworked to Kaytell's specifications. Auer offered to sell the reworked special machinery to Kaytell as a special order for a net price of $68,400. Kaytell has agreed to pay the net price when it takes delivery in two months. The additional identifiable costs to rework the machinery to the specifications of Kaytell are as follows:

Direct materials	$ 6,200
Direct labor	4,200
	$10,400

A second alternative available to Auer is to convert the special machinery to the standard model. The standard model lists for $62,500. The additional identifiable costs to convert the special machinery to the standard model are

Direct materials	$2,850
Direct labor	3,300
	$6,150

A third alternative for the Auer Company is to sell, as a special order, the machine as is, without modification, for a net price of $52,000. However, the potential buyer of the unmodified machine does not want it for sixty days. The buyer offers a $7,000 down payment with final payment on delivery.

The following additional information is available regarding Auer's operations:

1. Sales commission rate on sales of standard models is 2 percent while the sales commission rate on special orders is 3 percent. All sales commissions are calculated on net sales price (that is, list price less cash discount, if any).

2. Normal credit terms for sales of standard models are 2/10, n/30 (2/10 means a discount of 2 percent is given if payment is made within 10 days; n/30 means full amount is due within 30 days).

3. Customers take the discounts except in rare instances. Credit terms for special orders are negotiated with the customer.

4. The application rates for manufacturing overhead and the fixed selling and administrative costs are as follows:

Manufacturing:	
Variable	50% of direct labor cost
Fixed	25% of direct labor cost
Selling and administrative:	
Fixed	10% of the total of direct material, direct labor, and manufacturing-overhead costs

5. Normal time required for rework is one month. A surcharge of 5 percent of the sales price is placed on all customer requests for minor modifications of standard models. Auer normally sells a sufficient number of standard models for the company to operate at a volume in excess of the break-even point. Auer does not consider the time value of money in analyses of special orders and projects whenever the time period is less than one year because the effect is not significant.

REQUIRED:

a. Determine the dollar contribution that each of the three alternatives will add to the Auer Company's before-tax profits.

b. If Kaytell makes Auer a counteroffer, what is the lowest price Auer should accept for the reworked machinery from Kaytell? Explain your answer.

c. Discuss the influence that fixed factory overhead costs should have on the sales prices quoted by Auer Company for special orders when (1) a firm is operating at or below the breakeven point and (2) a firm's special orders constitute efficient utilization of unused capacity above the breakeven volume. (*CMA adapted*)

11-18 Making a Bid   Jenco, Inc. manufactures a combination fertilizer/weedkiller under the name Fertikil. This is the only product Jenco produces at the present time. Fertikil is sold nationwide through normal marketing channels to retail nurseries and garden stores.

Taylor Nursery plans to sell a similar fertilizer/weedkiller compound through its regional nursery chain under its own private label. Taylor has asked Jenco to submit a bid for a 25,000-pound order of the private brand compound. Although the chemical composition of the Taylor compound differs from Fertikil, the manufacturing processes for the two are similar.

The Taylor compound would be produced in 1,000 pound lots. Each lot requires sixty direct labor hours and the following chemicals:

Chemicals	Quantity in Pounds
CW-3	400
JX-6	300
MZ-8	200
BE-7	100

The first three chemicals (CW-3, JX-6, MZ-8) are all used in the production of Fertikil. The chemical BE-7 was used in a compound that Jenco has discontinued; it has not been sold or discarded because it does not deteriorate and Jenco has adequate storage facilities. Jenco could sell BE-7 at the prevailing market price less $.10 per pound selling/handling expenses.

Jenco also has on hand a chemical called CN-5, which was manufactured for use in another product that is no longer produced. CN-5, which cannot be used in Fertikil, can be substituted for CW-3 on a one-for-one basis without affecting the quality of the Taylor compound. The quantity of CN-5 in inventory has a salvage value of $500.

Inventory and cost data for the chemicals that can be used to produce the Taylor compound are as shown below:

Raw Material	Pounds in Inventory	Actual Price per Pound When Purchased	Current Market Price per Pound
CW-3	22,000	$ .80	$ .90
JX-6	5,000	$ .55	$ .60
MZ-8	8,000	$1.40	$1.60
BE-7	4,000	$ .60	$ .65
CN-5	5,500	$ .75	(salvage)

The current direct labor rate is $7.00 per hour. The manufacturing overhead rate is established at the beginning of the year and is applied consistently throughout the year using direct labor hours (DLH) as the base. The predetermined overhead rate for the current year, based on a two-shift capacity of 400,000 total DLH with no overtime, is as follows:

Variable manufacturing overhead	$2.25 per DLH
Fixed manufacturing overhead	3.75 per DLH
Combined rate	$6.00 per DLH

Jenco's production manager reports that the present equipment and facilities are adequate to manufacture the Taylor compound. However, Jenco is within 800 hours of its two-shift capacity this month before it must schedule overtime. If necessary, the Taylor compound can be produced on regular time by shifting a portion of Fertikil production to overtime. Jenco's rate for overtime hours is one-and-one-half the regular pay rate or $10.50 per hour. There is no allowance for any overtime premium in the manufacturing overhead rate. The variable overhead is all incremental to production.

Jenco's standard markup policy for new products is 25 percent of full manufacturing cost.

REQUIRED:

a. Assume that Jenco Inc. has decided to submit a bid for a 25,000 pound order of Taylor's new compound. The order must be delivered by the end of the current month. Taylor has indicated that this is a one-time order that will not be repeated. Calculate the lowest price Jenco can bid for the order and not reduce its net income.

b. Next, assume that Taylor Nursery plans to place regular orders for 25,000 pound lots of the new compound during the coming year. Jenco expects the demand for Fertikil to remain strong again in the coming year. Therefore, the recurring orders from Taylor will put Jenco over its two-shift capacity. However, production can be scheduled so that 60 percent of each Taylor order can be completed during regular hours or Fertikil production can be shifted temporarily to overtime so that the Taylor orders can be produced on regular time. Jenco's production manager has estimated that the prices of all chemicals will stabilize at the current market rates for the coming year and that all other manufacturing costs are expected to be maintained at the same rates or amounts.

Calculate the price Jenco, Inc. should quote Taylor Nursery for each 25,000-pound lot of the new compound assuming that there will be recurring orders during the coming year. (*CMA adapted*)

11-19 Make or Buy Gian Auto Corporation manufactures automobiles, vans, and trucks. Among the various Gian Auto plants around the United States is the Denver Cover Plant. Coverings made primarily of vinyl and upholstery fabric are sewn at the Denver Cover Plant and are used to cover interior seating and other surfaces of Gian Auto products.

Ted Vosilo is the plant manager for Denver Cover. The Denver Cover Plant was the first Gian Auto plant in the region. As other area plants were opened, Vosilo, in recognition of his management ability, was given responsibility for managing them. Vosilo functions as a regional manager, although the budget for him and his staff is charged to the Denver Cover Plant.

Vosilo has just received a report indicating that Gian Auto could purchase the entire annual output of Denver Cover from outside suppliers for $30 million. Vosilo was astonished at the low outside price because the budget for Denver Cover's operating costs for the coming year was set at $52 million. Vosilo believes that Gian Auto will have to close down operations at Denver Cover in order to realize the $22 million in annual cost savings.

The budget for Denver Cover's operating costs for the coming year is presented below. Additional facts regarding the plant's operations are as follows:

1. Due to Denver Cover's commitment to use high-quality fabrics in all its products, the purchasing department was instructed to place blanket purchase orders with major suppliers to ensure the receipt of sufficient materials for the coming year. If these orders are canceled as a consequence of the plant closing, termination charges will amount to 15 percent of the cost of direct materials.

2. Approximately 700 plant employees will lose their jobs if the plant is closed. This includes all the direct laborers and supervisors as well as the plumbers, electricians, and other skilled workers classified as indirect plant workers. Some will be able to find new jobs, while many others will have difficulty doing so. All employees will have difficulty matching Denver Cover's base pay of $9.40 per hour, which is the highest in the area. A clause in Denver Cover's contract with the union may help some employees; the company must provide employment assistance to its former employees for twelve months after a plant closing. The estimated cost to administer this service is $1 million for the year.

3. Some employees probably will elect early retirement if the plant closes because Gian Auto has an excellent pension plan. In fact, $3 million of the 19x6 pension expense will continue whether Denver Cover is open or not.

4. Vosilo and his staff will not be affected by the closing of Denver Cover; they still will be responsible for administering three other area plants.

5. Denver Cover considers equipment depreciation to be a variable cost and uses the units-of-production method to depreciate its equipment; Denver Cover is the only Gian Auto plant to use this depreciation method. However, Denver Cover uses the customary straight-line method to depreciate its building.

DENVER COVER PLANT
Budget for Operating Costs
for the Year Ended December 31, 19x6
(000s omitted)

Materials		$12,000
Labor:		
Direct	$13,000	
Supervision	3,000	
Indirect plant	4,000	20,000
Overhead:		
Depreciation — equipment	$ 5,000	
Depreciation — building	3,000	
Pension expense	4,000	
Plant manager and staff	2,000	
Corporate allocation	6,000	20,000
Total budgeted costs		$52,000

REQUIRED:

a. Without regard to costs, identify the advantages to Gian Auto Corporation of continuing to obtain covers from its own Denver Cover Plant.

b. Gian Auto Corporation plans to prepare a numerical analysis that will be used in deciding whether to close the Denver Cover Plant. Identify

(1) The recurring annual budgeted costs that can be avoided by closing the plant,

(2) The recurring annual budgeted costs that are not relevant to the decision, and explain why they are not relevant,

(3) Any nonrecurring costs that arise due to the closing of the plant, and explain how they affect the decision,

(4) Any revenues or costs not specifically mentioned in the text that Gian Auto should consider before making a decision. (*CMA adapted*)

11-20 Production Decisions   Calen Co. manufactures and sells three products. The three products are manufactured in a factory consisting of four departments. Both labor and machine time are applied to the products as they pass through each applicable department. The nature of the machine processing and labor skills required in each department is such that neither machines nor labor can be switched from one department to another.

Calen's management is attempting to plan its production schedule for the next several months. The planning is complicated by the fact that there are labor shortages in the community and some machines will be down several months for repairs.

The following information regarding available machine and labor time by department and the machine hours and direct labor hours required per unit of product has been accumulated to aid in the decision. These data should be valid for at least the next six months.

	Department			
Monthly Capacity Availability	*1*	*2*	*3*	*4*
Normal machine capacity in machine hours	3,500	3,500	3,000	3,500
Capacity of machine being repaired in machine hours	(500)	(400)	(300)	(200)
Available machine capacity in machine hours	3,000	3,100	2,700	3,300
Labor capacity in direct labor hours	4,000	4,500	3,500	3,000
Available labor in direct labor hours	3,700	4,500	2,750	2,600

Labor and Machine Specifications per Unit of Product		Department			
Product	*Labor and Machine Time*	*1*	*2*	*3*	*4*
401	Direct labor hours	2	3	3	1
	Machine hours	1	1	2	2
403	Direct labor hours	1	2	—	2
	Machine hours	1	1	—	2
405	Direct labor hours	2	2	2	1
	Machine hours	2	2	1	1

The sales department believes that the monthly demand for the next six months will be as follows:

Product	*Monthly Sales Volume in Units*
401	500
403	400
405	1,000

Inventory levels are at satisfactory levels and need not be increased or decreased during the next six months. The unit price and cost data that will be valid for the next six months are presented on the following page.

	Product		
	401	*403*	*405*
Unit costs:			
Direct material	$ 7	$ 13	$ 17
Direct labor			
Department 1	12	6	12
Department 2	21	14	14
Department 3	24	—	16
Department 4	9	18	9
Variable overhead	27	20	25
Fixed overhead	15	10	32
Variable selling	3	2	4
Unit selling price	$196	$123	$167

REQUIRED:

a. Calculate the monthly requirement for machine hours and direct labor hours for the production of products 401, 403, and 405 to determine whether the monthly sales demand for the three products can be met by the factory.

b. What monthly production schedule should Calen Co. select in order to maximize its dollar profits? Explain how you selected this production schedule, and present a schedule of the contribution to profit that would be generated by your production schedule.

c. Identify the alternatives Calen Co. might consider so it can supply its customers with all the product they demand. (*CMA adapted*)

11-21 Cost Analysis and Qualitative Considerations VAR Association is a professional educational organization with affiliates located throughout the United States. The organization publishes a monthly magazine, offers continuing education courses, and conducts research that is published in report or monograph form. All of these operations are provided out of VAR's office in Los Angeles.

VAR has over 250 research reports and monographs in print. These are available to members and the general public at selling prices ranging from $2.50 to $35.00 each. Approximately twelve to twenty titles are released during each fiscal year. The printing of all publications takes place in the Los Angeles metropolitan area.

The association processes an average of 1,500 orders a month. The processing and filling of orders has become an increasingly burdensome task for the association staff. The association's publication director has suggested that VAR contract with an outside service to handle the inventorying, order processing, shipping, and billing for publication orders.

VAR has contacted ProEd Book Service to determine the kind of service it offers and the cost. ProEd is located in Cincinnati and inventories and distributes books and monographs for several other professional organizations. ProEd is willing to inventory VAR's complete stock of research publications and process, ship, and bill all direct mail orders. ProEd would charge VAR an inventory storage fee, processing and record-keeping fees at the rate of $10.00 per hour, and the cost of mailing supplies and shipping charges.

VAR's publication director asked a member of the association's staff to prepare an analysis to determine the feasibility of using ProEd Book Service. The preliminary cost analysis and narrative report follow.

MONTHLY COST SAVINGS ANALYSIS
ProEd Book Service

Rental savings:		
1. Outside warehouse (4,000 square feet @ $8.40 per square foot ÷ 12)	$2,800	
2. Basement storeroom (900 square feet @ $12.00 per square foot ÷ 12)	900	
3. Stockroom (100 square feet @ $21.00 per square foot ÷ 12)	175	$3,875
Labor savings:		
4. Order clerk (150 @ $8.50 per hour)	$1,275	
5. Shipping clerk (150 hours @ $7.00 per hour)	1,050	
6. Storeroom clerk (60 hours @ $7.50 per hour)	450	
7. Stockroom clerk		
a. Inventory function (16 hours @ $8.50 per hour)	136	
b. Replenishing stock room (30 hours @ $8.50 per hour)	255	
8. Mailroom supervisor (50 hours @ $10.00 per hour)	500	3,666
Total savings		$7,541
Costs:		
9. ProEd storage fees (4,000 square feet @ $4.20 per square foot ÷ 12)	$1,400	
10. Process/recordkeeping fees (456 hours @ $10.00 per hour)	4,560	
11. Additional supplies (1,500 orders @ [$.50 − .40])	150	6,110
Net monthly savings		$1,431

Rental Savings   If the services of ProEd Book Service are used, the outside warehouse would no longer be required. Space in the basement storeroom and the upstairs stockroom now used for research publications would be used to provide additional space for storage of affiliate supplies and educational materials. Currently, these items are stored in space too crowded for easy access. The quantities of affiliate and educational supplies would not be increased, but the accessibility to materials would be improved. The cost used in the analysis is based on the current rental charge for the space.

Labor Savings   The services of an order clerk and a shipping clerk would not be needed if ProEd's services are employed. The activities of the other three positions identified in the analysis cannot be combined. The stockroom clerk would still be required to take inventory of all materials and replenish stock when needed. A portion of the released time of the mailroom supervisor would be devoted to shipping new titles to ProEd. The remaining released time of these individuals would allow them to do their other regularly assigned duties on a more timely basis. The labor analysis is based on the hourly wage plus employee benefits of each individual and a normal work month of 150 hours.

Storage Costs   ProEd has indicated that the VAR inventory can be stored in 4,000 square feet in its warehouse. The annual charge for this space is $4.20 per square foot.

Processing and Recordkeeping Costs   Order processing and recordkeeping would be charged at the actual hours required. ProEd has not provided an estimate of the time required for these activities. Therefore, the labor hours saved by the VAR staff were used in the analysis.

Supply Costs   VAR uses three different shipping packages depending on the size of the order, such as envelope (cost of $.10 each), corrugated mailing pouch (cost of $.30 each), or cardboard carton (cost of $.75 each). An average cost of $.40 per order was used in the analysis. The carton ProEd uses costs $.50 each.

Other Information   Shipping costs to customers were not included in the analysis. These should be reduced because ProEd is more centrally located.

The start-up cost related to the movement of the present inventory to ProEd's warehouse in Cincinnati would consist of costs related to loading, shipping and unloading. Total cost should not exceed $3,500.

Conclusions   Considering all costs, VAR should save over $17,000 exclusive of start-up costs, during the course of a year by using ProEd. Due to ProEd's central location, shipping costs should be less. Thus, these cost savings along with the freeing of storage space and personnel time for other purposes are excellent reasons for using the services of ProEd Book Service.

REQUIRED:

Review the cost analysis and narrative report regarding the use of ProEd Book Service by VAR Association.

a. For each of the eleven items identified in the cost analysis, discuss whether the item and amount is appropriate or inappropriate for the analysis.

b. Identify and explain cost items, if any, that were omitted but should have been incorporated into the cost analysis and narrative report.

c. Identify and explain additional qualitative items, if any, that VAR Association should consider in its analysis. (*CMA adapted*)

11-22 **Machine Installation Decision**   William Company owns and operates a nationwide chain of movie theaters. The 500 properties in the William chain vary from low-volume, small-town, single-screen theaters to high-volume, big-city, multiscreen theaters.

The management is considering installing machines that make popcorn on the premises. These machines allow theaters to sell popcorn that is freshly popped daily rather than the prepopped corn that they currently purchase in large bags. This proposed feature will be properly advertised and is intended to increase patronage at the company's theaters.

The machines can be purchased in several different sizes. The annual rental costs and the operating costs vary with the size of the machines. The machine capacities and costs are shown on the following page.

	Popper Model		
	Economy	*Regular*	*Super*
Annual capacity	50,000 boxes	120,000 boxes	300,000 boxes
Costs:			
Annual machine rental	$8,000	$11,000	$20,000
Popcorn cost per box	.13	.13	.13
Other costs per box	.22	.14	.05
Cost of each box	.08	.08	.08

REQUIRED:

a. Calculate the volume level in boxes at which the Economy Popper and Regular Popper would earn the same profit (loss).

b. The management can estimate the number of boxes to be sold at each of its theaters. Present a decision rule that will enable William's management to select the most profitable machine without having to make a separate cost calculation for each theater.

c. Could the management use the average number of boxes sold per seat for the entire chain and the capacity of each theater to develop this decision rule? Explain your answer. (*CMA adapted*)

11-23 Direct-Mail Advertising Decision   Everhope Company has acquired a large tract of land bordering the ocean and has subdivided it into lots. Three types of lots are designed to sell at three different prices as shown below:

Lot Type	Selling Price
Oceanfront	$50,000
Oceanview	30,000
Ocean access	15,000

Due to the relatively complex sewage requirements for oceanfront lots, the variable costs for developing this type of property total approximately $12,000 each. Oceanview lots are the least costly to develop, with variable costs amounting to $6,000 each. Ocean-access lots require more road construction costs than the others, bringing the total variable development cost for this type of lot to $8,000.

Everhope sells lots for a 10 percent down payment and then conveys the buyer's promissory note for the balance, with recourse, to a financial institution in exchange for the remaining 90 percent of the cash. If the buyer defaults, Everhope must pay the 90 percent back to the financial institution, but Everhope keeps the 10 percent down payment and takes the lot back into its inventory.

The variable costs do not have to be incurred again to resell a defaulted lot. However, a buyer who defaults typically does some alterations that require restoration. In addition, legal costs are involved in a repossession. The average amounts of both these costs are shown on the following page.

Default Cost	Amount
Restoration	40% of selling price
Legal costs	$2,000 per repossession

Everhope uses several methods for attracting potential customers. They have gained sufficient experience to permit estimation of the cost and default risk associated with each method of attracting customers.

Method of Attracting Customers	Annual Cost	Probability of Default
Direct mail	$20,000	.30
National magazine ads	50,000	.10
National newspaper ads	30,000	.10
Agents[a]	—	.10
Local promotion	10,000	.05

[a] Sales made through agents require payment of a 6 percent commission at the time of the sale. This commission is not recovered in the event of a default.

Everhope is also in a position to estimate the number of each type of lot which would be sold to customers attracted by each method during the next year. These estimates are shown below.

Method of Attracting Customers	Number of Lots Sold			
	Oceanfront	Oceanview	Ocean Access	Total
Direct mail	0	10	40	50
National magazine ads	5	20	20	45
National newspaper ads	5	10	20	35
Agents	5	10	20	35
Local promotion	5	10	5	20
Total	20	60	105	185

Even though the present supply of lots will carry the firm far into the future, the president is reluctant to use direct mail because of the high probability of default and the low average value of a sale to one of these customers.

REQUIRED:

a. Based on the information presented and ignoring interest and the time value of money, perform an analysis to determine the before tax profit or loss to Everhope Company of selling lots by direct mail.

b. If Everhope Company could legally limit direct-mail customers to purchasing only ocean-access lots, would this be a desirable action for the company to take? Support your answer with an appropriate analysis.

c. Everhope Company has used its experience to estimate the cost and default risk associated with the various methods of attracting customers.

(1) Discuss the problems Everhope could encounter by basing its estimates entirely on past experience.

(2) Identify information that Everhope could obtain from external sources that would be of value in making estimates of costs and default risk. (*CMA adapted*)

11-24 Pricing to Maximize Contribution   Systems Planners Institute (SPI) is a professional educational association for systems analysts and programmers. The organization has approximately 50,000 members.

SPI holds an annual convention each October and planning for the 19x6 convention is progressing smoothly. The convention budget for such items as promotional brochures, fees and expenses for twenty speakers, equipment rental for presentations, the travel and expenses of twenty-five staff people, consultant fees, volunteer expenses, and so forth is $330,000. This amount does not include any of the hotel charges for meeting rooms, luncheons banquets, or receptions.

SPI has always priced each function at the convention separately — that is, members select and pay for only those functions they wished to attend. Members receive a ticket for each registered function, and the ticket is surrendered at the function. If members attend the convention, they pay a registration fee that also gives them the right to attend the annual reception and annual meeting at no additional charge.

The Annual Convention Committee, consisting of volunteer members of SPI, has recommended that SPI consider setting a single flat fee for the entire convention. The official convention name badge would be issued only to convention attendees, and a registered member would be entitled to attend all functions at the convention if the member displayed the badge.

The table below lists the convention functions, the percentage of people expected to attend each function, the price SPI would charge for each function if it priced each function separately, and the hotel charges for food service and meeting halls and rooms. The percentage of persons that can be expected to attend each function is based on past experience and is expected to hold regardless of the pricing scheme used.

Function	Percentage of Attendees who will Participate	Price of Function	Hotel Charge
Registration fee	100%	$ 50	None
Wednesday:			
Reception	100	Free	$25/attendee
Thursday:			
Annual meeting	100	Free	$2,000 for meeting hall
Keynote luncheon	90	$ 40	$25/attendee
Six concurrent sessions[a]	70	60	$200/room or $1,200 in total
Friday:			
Plenary session	70	50	$2,000 for meeting hall
Six workshops[a]	50	100	$200/room or $1,200 in total
Banquet	90	50	$30/attendee

[a] Attendee selects one session for the fee.

The hotel's package of services to SPI and the convention attendees are as follows:

1. Three free rooms are provided for convention headquarters and storage.

2. A 20 percent discount is granted off posted room rates for all convention attendees who stay in the hotel during the three-day convention. Attendees are to make room reservations directly with the hotel, and all hotel room charges are the responsibility of the attendees. The types of rooms, posted rate, and the proportion of each type of room taken by attendees are as follows:

Type	Posted Rate/Night	Proportion Renting This Type
Single	$100	10%
Studio	105	10
Double	125	75
Suite	200	5

3. SPI is given credit for one free double room for three days for every fifty convention registrants who stay at the convention hotel. The credit will be applied to the room charges of staff and speakers. No fractional credit is awarded.

4. Meeting rooms and halls are free if food is served at the function.

5. Meeting rooms and halls for professional sessions are free if 1,000 members are registered at the hotel.

6. Meal costs given in the table include all taxes and gratuities.

7. The hotel receives all revenue from cash bar sales at the reception, and before the luncheon and banquet. The hotel estimates that the average consumption at each

of these functions will be one cocktail per attendee at a contribution of $1.50 per cocktail.

If SPI continues to price each convention function separately, the prices given in the prior table will apply. Expected attendance under this type of pricing scheme would be 2,000, as shown below.

Number of Attendees		Probability		Expected Value
1,650	×	.2	=	330
1,900	×	.3	=	570
2,150	×	.4	=	860
2,400	×	.1	=	240
				2,000

The Annual Convention Committee has estimated the convention attendance for three different single flat fee structures as follows.

Proposed Single Flat Fee	Estimated Number of Attendees
$325	1,600
300	1,750
275	1,900

SPI estimates that 60 percent of the persons who attend the convention will stay in the convention hotel. Furthermore, convention attendees will not share hotel rooms — that is, each attendee will need a room. The average stay at the hotel will be three nights.

REQUIRED:

SPI wants to maximize its contribution from its annual convention. Recommend whether SPI should price each function at the convention separately or charge one of the three single flat fees for the convention. Support your recommendation with an appropriate analysis. (*CMA adapted*)

11-25   Hartwell Jewelers was established in 19x2 when Keith Richmond purchased two small jewelry stores that were going out of business. Three additional stores have since been added to the chain. Richmond built Hartwell's reputation by offering fair prices for quality engagement and wedding rings, and these items currently comprise 60 percent of Hartwell's sales.

In 19y0, eight years later, Hartwell began offering discounts on wedding rings to purchasers of engagement rings in order to stimulate follow-up business. A couple that purchases one wedding ring within one year of the purchase of the engagement ring receives a 20 percent discount. For the purchase of two wedding rings, the couple receives a 30 percent discount. The discount program has been successful, and Hartwell's sales have increased steadily.

In order to offer the discounts and maintain Hartwell's profit margin, Richmond must plan the purchase of engagement and wedding rings carefully. To take advantage of wholesale discounts, Richmond purchases, each January and July, all the engagement and wedding rings that Hartwell expects to sell in the coming six months. Richmond has decided to develop a model based on Hartwell's past sales experience to enable him to more accurately forecast the sales of engagement and wedding rings. He has gathered the following information from his analysis of historical data.

1. Of the couples who purchase silver engagement rings at Hartwell, 35 percent return to purchase a single wedding ring, while 45 percent return for a pair of wedding rings.

2. Purchasers of gold engagement rings return to buy a single wedding ring 45 percent of the time and buy a pair of wedding rings 50 percent of the time.

3. The average period between the sale of engagement rings and the follow-up sale of wedding rings is six months.

4. Customers do not switch to a different type of ring once they have purchased an engagement ring — that is, a customer who purchases a gold engagement ring will only purchase gold wedding rings, if any, and not silver wedding rings.

5. The demand for gold or silver rings is affected by the market price of gold at the time of the initial purchase of a ring. If the market price of gold rises above a certain level, customers are more likely to buy silver rings rather than gold rings. If the market price of gold drops below a certain level, gold rings become more popular than silver rings.

6. Additional wedding ring sales are derived from customers who did not purchase engagement rings at Hartwell. These sales equal 80 percent of the number of wedding rings sold by Hartwell as follow-up business in both the silver and gold categories.

7. Total unit sales of engagement rings (gold and silver combined) have increased at a 5 percent growth rate for each six-month period since the discount plan was adopted.

Richmond's model is a function of engagement ring sales during each prior six-month period before he buys rings in January and July. Richmond has been able to quantify the impact of the market price of gold as an adjustment factor and incorporate this adjustment factor into the model. Richmond's model and the adjustment factors for the market price of gold are presented below:

$$W_s = 1.25 \sum_{n=-1}^{-6} S_n + .8\left[\left(1.25 \sum_{n=-1}^{-6} S_n\right) + X\right]$$

$$W_g = 1.45 \sum_{n=-1}^{-6} G_n + .8\left[\left(1.45 \sum_{n=-1}^{-6} G_n\right) + Y\right]$$

$$E_s = 1.05\left[\left(\sum_{n=-7}^{-12} S_n\right) + X\right]$$

$$E_g = 1.05\left[\left(\sum_{n=-7}^{-12} G_n\right) + Y\right]$$

where

W_s = sales forecast for silver wedding rings for the next six months,

E_s = sales forecast for silver engagement rings for the next six months,

S_n = actual monthly sales for silver engagement rings,

X = adjustment factor that quantifies the impact of the market price of gold on the demand for silver rings,

W_g = sales forecast for gold wedding rings for the next six months,

E_g = sales forecast for gold engagement rings for the next six months,

G_n = actual monthly sales for gold engagement rings,

Y = adjustment factor that quantifies the impact of the market price of gold on the demand for gold rings.

Adjustment Factors for the Market Price of Gold

Market Price of Gold per Ounce	X	Y
$305 and below	−880	+1,240
$305.01–315.00	−480	+750
$315.01–325.00	−0−	−0−
$325.01–335.00	+600	−500
Above $335.00	+1,100	−1,800

Hartwell's actual sales of engagement and wedding rings for the past twelve months are presented below. The average price of gold for the first six months of 19x6 was $340.00 per ounce. Richmond estimates that the average price of gold will drop to $333.00 per ounce during the last six months of 19x6.

	Engagement Rings		Wedding Rings	
	Silver	Gold	Silver	Gold
July 19x5	400	350	820	790
August	450	400	900	900
September	350	350	700	810
October	350	350	590	750
November	300	350	620	·770
December	450	500	880	1,120
January 19x6	350	400	730	880
February	300	400	600	850
March	300	350	650	840
April	400	400	840	750
May	400	450	790	1,010
June	450	600	920	1,350

REQUIRED:

a. Keith Richmond plans to use his new model to estimate the number of rings Hartwell Jewelers should purchase in July 19x6 for resale during the last six months of 19x6. Using the model, calculate the estimated purchases that would be made in July 19x6 of

(1) Silver wedding rings.

(2) Gold engagement rings.

b. A colleague of Keith Richmond's has suggested that the gold price adjustment factor is too dependent on a single price prediction and should consider sensitivity analyses. For example, the model could consider predictions based on pessimistic, most likely, and optimistic predictions. Would this change improve the accuracy of Richmond's model?

c. Describe how Keith Richmond could test the accuracy of his new model. (*CMA adapted*)

12

Analysis and Control of Nonmanufacturing Costs

After studying this chapter, you should be able to:

1 Describe cost analyses in service-type firms and understand the similarities to those of manufacturing companies.

2 Incorporate distribution costs into decision situations and explain how these costs are controlled.

3 Understand how administrative costs are controlled.

4 Understand the similarities and differences between research and development costs as well as distribution and administrative costs.

5 Cost jobs in a nonmanufacturing environment.

6 Describe work measurement as a means for controlling nonmanufacturing costs.

*T*raditionally, cost accountants have been primarily concerned with manufacturing costs. Because of the increased level of service activities in the economy and the relative importance of these costs as a percentage of total costs, however, more attention has been directed to nonmanufacturing costs. This chapter examines several types of nonmanufacturing costs and standard setting for nonmanufacturing activities.

The techniques used for decision making and control of manufacturing costs are, in large part, also relevant to nonmanufacturing costs. Thus, the notions of cost-variance analysis (Chapters 7 and 8), cost-volume-profit analysis (Chapter 3), and budgeting (Chapter 10) are all appropriate, in varying degrees, to the analysis of nonmanufacturing costs. However, the benefits from incurring nonmanufacturing costs are often more difficult than manufacturing costs to measure.

Service Organizations and Departments

Some organizations are entirely of a service nature; service is their final product. Examples include utilities, education, insurance and financial services, transportation, recreation, lodging, spectator sports, legal services, consulting, communications, personal services, and health-care organizations. Service departments also are found in manufacturing firms; they supply service to other parts of the organization but not directly to ultimate consumers. Examples include power, maintenance, repair, engineering, cafeteria, administration, and building and grounds.

In analyzing service organization costs it is first necessary to distinguish the services offered. Seldom does a service organization offer only a single service. Whether these services are provided in a market context or offered by not-for-profit organizations, it is important to know their cost. Pricing, cost control, and performance evaluation are all fundamentally tied to cost measures.

The methods discussed in earlier chapters are equally relevant to the costing problems of service organizations. Standard costs of such operations can be estimated and combined to obtain costs for various activities. In banking, for example, a number of tasks, such as opening an account and posting entries, can be studied and costed. These tasks can then be combined when determining the cost of servicing a checking or commercial account. Types of customers or activities can be evaluated for profitability, and departments can be monitored over time to ensure that their costs remain in control.

In order to cost the output of service organizations it may be necessary, as with manufacturing organizations, to allocate common costs. For this reason meaningful relationships need to be found between the various activities performed by the organization and the requirements of the final service to be provided. Establishing cause-and-effect relationships is desirable where they exist. The bases traditionally used to establish such relationships include physical identification, service supplied, capacity provided, actual benefits received, ability to recover costs, and fairness or equity. Sometimes combinations of these bases are appropriate. Each type of relationship for a consulting firm is listed below:

Physical identification	cost of traveling to the client
Service supplied	billing time of the consultant
Capacity provided	computer costs allocation based on usage by a particular project
Actual benefits received	recovery on a lawsuit on which the consulting firm acted as an advisor
Ability to recover costs	contractual specifications of cost recovery based on client cash flows or return on assets
Fairness or equity	allocation of office space overhead costs across clients

Physical identification is preferable where a direct relationship between the final product and the input activities exists. This is common in the manufacture of physical goods, where direct materials can be physically traced to the product. It is not nearly as relevant for service operations; however, it can be used to allocate the use of physical items to final service operations. This would be true, for example, of blood transfusions and intravenous feedings in a hospital.

Service supplied is an appropriate basis for cost allocation for such activities as repair, engineering, and power. Charges can be made at standard rates based on efficiency considerations for such service. Typically this charge can be made when the service is requested. However, the fixed costs of establishing and maintaining these indirect service activities must be allocated as well. Separate cost-allocation rates are appropriate for these fixed costs based on the needs of the operating departments that justified incurring the fixed costs.

A key point in the discussion of cost allocation is that different allocation rates are often appropriate for the fixed and variable components of indirect service department costs. A second key point is that the cost-allocation process need not allocate all costs either from a costing or from a control point of view. Inefficiencies should be detected where they occur if control is to be maintained. This can occur only if the costs caused by the inefficiency remain in the offending department.

For planning and for control, flexible budgets based on realistic activity measures (that is, those measuring cost incurrence) should be used. Standard unit prices and rates (not actual costs) are required. Fixed-cost and variable-cost components are best handled separately. Finally, the costs allocated to one activity should not be influenced by those allocated to some other activity.

Sales revenue is often a convenient basis used to allocate service costs. The method is often applied to property taxes, building depreciation, and related items. Although cause and benefit are hard to establish for these items, long-run operations require these expenditures, and accounting requires that the costs be allocated. The result is that such costs are often allocated on the basis of the revenue-producing ability of each operating unit or product. The implication is that the costs incurred have contributed to the value to the final product in proportion to the product's sales value, but this is often not the case. The sales-revenue method is, in many respects, a default solution that is opted for when other more convincing criteria are lacking.

The ability to recover costs and the fairness criteria are other arbitrary bases in use that leave a thoughtful manager uneasy about the usefulness of the final cost allocations. These methods should be avoided except perhaps for costing in cost-plus contracts, where prior agreement is obtained on how the cost allocations are to be made.

Where substantive damage will not be done — that is, in the case of relatively small cost allocations — similar costs may be grouped and allocated using a single method.

Service organizations need to establish a basic charge unit. Consulting organizations typically use time with different hourly rates for different service types. Hospitals must determine the cost of several types of service, including room, laboratory, and surgical. Airlines base their rates on miles traveled and type of flight as well as special services provided.

Distribution Cost Analysis and Control

The distribution function generally begins before the manufacture of the product or delivery of the service and continues after the cash is collected. Under this broad time horizon, distribution costs include the following:

1. The costs (including advertising costs) of promoting customer goodwill and obtaining sales of products or services,

2. The costs of handling and storing the completed product and of shipping it to the customer and the costs of delivering the service,

3. The costs of recording and collecting the amounts owed to the company by its customers,

4. The costs of handling the returns and servicing guarantees (a more generous guarantee being a way to enhance the marketability of the product or service).

The purpose of the distribution function is to increase the long-run contribution of the firm's primary activities to fixed costs and profits. (Short-run goals may include market penetration and establishing markets for new products; performance evaluation should note these short-run goals when they are operative and considered consistent with long-run profit maximization.) The analysis of distribution costs should, then, be directed toward decisions that can be made to improve the overall contribution. This implies that such costs should be broken down by product or service line, customer type, sales personnel, geographical location, or in other ways to identify their contribution to ongoing activities. The classification in Exhibit 12-1 suggests four distinct possibilities.

EXHIBIT 12-1

Possible Breakdowns of Distribution Costs

Sales Outlets (customer type)	Methods of Selling
Wholesalers	Mail order
Retailers	Company sales personnel, outside
Discount houses	Company sales personnel, inside
Chain stores	Manufacturers' agents

Product Line	Geographical Location
Line I	Cities over 1,000,000
Product *A*	Cities over 100,000
Product *B*	Cities over 10,000
Product *C*	Cities under 10,000
Line II	or
Product *D*	Sales districts, counties, states,
Product *E*	countries

The discussion in Chapter 11 concerning the relevance of historic cost data is relevant to nonmanufacturing costs as well. Historical cost figures should be carefully analyzed before they are used in any decision context. First, the data may reflect arbitrary cost allocations and costs that would not be altered by the decision being contemplated (the contraction or expansion of some activity, for example). Distribution costs are usually common to several functions, and allocation therefore must often be made on a relatively arbitrary basis. In decision making and control, it is important to recognize the common nature of these costs and the effect of this commonality on decisions. Second, future costs are relevant, and historical data provide reliable indications of the future only when conditions remain essentially unaltered. In determining future costs, the use of statistical techniques (such as regression analysis) and experimentation (such as controlling the variation of marketing effort across products or consumer types) and decision-making techniques can be particularly helpful.

Decision Making and Distribution Costs

Many decisions in the distribution area are made intuitively, and it is unlikely that distribution cost analysis will completely eliminate the need to make decisions in this manner. For example, it will probably never be possible for the accounting department, using historical costs, to tell the marketing staff that they are spending too much or too little on advertising or to establish beyond a doubt that an alternative amount is optimal. But the accounting department can tell top management that the revenue of a product or service is not recovering the manufacturing and distribution costs, including advertising, directly associated with it. This may lead indirectly to a decision to alter advertising expenditures or drop the product or service.

In the type of cost analysis being considered, it is useful to think of three layers of costs:

1. **Direct costs** are costs that can be directly identified with the service or product, division, geographical unit, and so on. For example, people providing the service such as a clerk are considered direct costs.

2. **Allocated costs with traceable benefits** are costs that cannot be directly identified but have a close correlation with the activity of a unit. For example, costs of writing bills usually are affected by the number of lines on an invoice.

3. **Allocated costs with indirect benefits** are costs that cannot be identified directly with the activity and have little correlation with changes in the level of the activity. For example, the benefits derived from the sales manager's salary may not be closely identified with any one service or product line and must be arbitrarily allocated across several service or product lines.

These three classifications also take on different meanings according to whether they are used to analyze distribution costs or manufacturing costs. In manufacturing cost analysis, interest centers on how costs react to changes in manufacturing activity. With distribution costs, interest centers on how costs react to changes in sales or a given type of promotional effort. In addition to the above three classifications, it often is useful to know whether a cost is fixed or variable. A variable distribution cost, for example, is a sales commission; a fixed distribution cost is the salary of the sales manager. The problem is complicated, however, by costs that may be fixed in one sense but not in another. Thus, advertising cost may be fixed by a managerial decision, but in order to increase sales it may be necessary to increase the amount spent on advertising. (Advertising is often treated as a residual factor in budgeting; this treatment implicitly assumes that advertising is a function of sales and does not acknowledge the effect of advertising on sales.) Alternatively, an increase in sales may result from lowering the sales price with no change in advertising. Thus, advertising may be considered fixed when the firm is considering a change in sales price, or the firm may vary both advertising and sales price at once. A cost such as advertising is sometimes called a **discretionary fixed cost.** A discretionary fixed cost can be avoided at the decision maker's election. The amount of advertising may be initially budgeted as a function of an activity such as sales. Once set, however, the amount does not necessarily vary with changes in sales. Many costs whose level is established by a specific decision do not vary with activity. The president's salary is an example.

The decisions made with the help of distribution-cost analysis are varied. Some important ones follow:

- Setting prices of the product or service,

- Expanding, contracting, or abandoning product or service lines or sales effort,

- Expanding, contracting, or abandoning specific customer outlets or geographical locations,

- Establishing warehouses and supply points,

- Determining the relative merits of different sales efforts (including performance of sales personnel),

- Selecting media,

- Altering bill collection and warrantee servicing policies.

The above decisions require that cost and revenue information be classified in several ways. For example, where possible, each cost must be identified as to a service or product line and geographical location. Also of interest is the relation of the cost to any particular type of sales outlet, its functional classification (such as delivery, warehousing, billing, collecting, and sales), and its natural classification (such as labor, supplies, and utilities).

Costs that cannot be directly identified with product or service lines, geographical locations, and so on, present a problem. Should they be allocated? All costs may be allocated, but for decision making the manager should carefully distinguish among the direct costs, the allocated costs with traceable benefits, and the allocated costs that have no close relation with the unit to which the cost is being allocated.

For example, assume a situation where White's Tree and Landscaping Service offers two different types of service. Management is reviewing the profitability of the tree cutting and removal service. The income statement for the most recent period is given in Exhibit 12-2. Assume that all of the fixed costs are unavoidable and would be incurred even if the service were abandoned and that the $2,500 of allocated costs includes $1,000 of costs that are variable and closely related to the tree-cutting activity. (These include hauling expense, which is allocated by weight, bulk, and mean distance of travel.)

What action, if any, should management take? When the income statement is rearranged, management finds that the tree cutting service is contributing $2,500 to the recovery of common and fixed costs and should not be abandoned. This is shown in Exhibit 12-3. Allocated costs in the amount of $1,000 are considered relevant to

---

EXHIBIT 12-2

Tree Service Income Statement (for year ending December 31)

Sales	$30,000	
Personnel costs of activity (includes fixed costs of $3,000)	25,000	
Gross margin		$5,000
Distribution costs directly identified with delivering of the service (includes fixed costs of $2,000)	$ 6,500	
Allocated costs	2,500	9,000
Net loss		($4,000)

EXHIBIT 12-3

Revised Tree Service Income Statement

Sales		$30,000
Variable costs:		
Personnel	$22,000	
Distribution ($1,000 + $4,500)	5,500	27,500
Contribution to recovery of fixed costs		$ 2,500
Fixed costs:		
Personnel	$ 3,000	
Distribution	3,500	6,500
Net loss		($ 4,000)

this decision. The income statement in Exhibit 12-3 is often called a **contribution income statement;** it provides a measure of the income foregone if the activity had not been conducted.

The fact that the service is recovering more than its avoidable (here variable) costs does not mean that no action is required. A company may recover variable costs every day right up until it files for bankruptcy. The analysis does indicate that, assuming the fixed costs are unavoidable, the company is better off with the tree cutting business than it would be without it. It is possible that more or less marketing effort is required or that the price should be changed or some other activity should be considered. The income statement presented shows that management should not be complacent; it does not indicate the nature or the direction of managerial action.

In recommending a decision not to drop the service, neither the unavoidable fixed costs nor the allocated costs not closely related to the product were included. If some fixed costs can be avoided by dropping the service, these costs become relevant to a decision to abandon.

If the problem is changed so that there is an option to dispose of the tree cutting portion of the business, then most of the fixed costs can be avoided. The price that can be obtained for the business becomes a type of opportunity cost, a cost to be recovered if the business is retained. This problem can be solved by capital-budgeting methods (Chapter 19) that compare the present value of the cash flows resulting from retaining the business to the present value of the cash flows that would result from the disposing of the business. (Again, alternative uses of the firm's resources should be considered.)

Recently operations research models have been introduced in distribution decisions. Consider advertising costs. This is one of several decision areas in the distribution area for which formal mathematical models have been used. Mathematical programming and decision-theory models have been applied to the media-selection and message-effectiveness problems. The models typically attempt to minimize advertising cost subject to a limitation (constraint) on the minimum benefit provided. Although substantial portions of the cost, such as the cost per unit of an advertising medium, are externally set, there is a tendency to ignore the associated internal cost.

The cost of advertising should include the cost of supportive activities (accounting being an example) even if they can be allocated to the advertising function only on relatively arbitrary bases, if these costs are altered by the decision of how much to invest in advertising. The allocation also should include the fixed cost of providing service where such costs may be considered as opportunity-cost approximations for using the committed resources.

Formal mathematical models also have been used to make distribution decisions, such as the location of warehouses and the establishment of supply centers. Costs play a central role in all of these decisions, and the managerial accountant should understand these models and the cost-information requirements they entail.

Management faces a variety of decisions, and these decisions often require different types of cost information. Not all costs are relevant for all decisions. Costs worth paying special attention to are costs that are fixed but avoidable and costs that are common to many products. The inclusion or exclusion of these costs depends on the exact nature of the decisions. Neither the inclusion nor exclusion of fixed or common costs should be automatic.

Distribution Cost Control

Control of distribution costs is especially difficult because unlike many manufacturing operations distribution provides no easily measurable and assignable output. Standards of performance are difficult to set but can be effective enough to assist in controlling distribution costs.

For purposes of cost control, it is useful to separate distribution costs into those involved with obtaining sales and those involved with filling orders. The techniques of control are somewhat different.

Control of Order-Filling Costs   Order-filling costs include the costs of order processing, storage, packing, delivery, billing, credit, and collection. Where a task is repetitive and uniform in nature and the benefits are easily measured, the setting of standards for performance is relatively well defined. Thus, the billing department may be judged on how much it costs to turn out invoices, with due consideration for the characteristics of the invoices and changes therein. The shipping and receiving departments may be judged on the number of items handled and the weight of the items or by delays that it causes in production or breakage. The credit and collection departments may be effectively controlled in a manner similar to that used in the control of manufacturing costs.

Consider, for example, the situation in a billing department. Suppose that a firm employs twenty individuals in the billing department. Each can handle (the standard at normal activity levels) 500 billings per week. The twenty employees are all paid $200 per week. Suppose that in a given week, 9,700 billings are made. If the twenty employees worked at the standard rate, the expectation is that 10,000 billings would have been made. What is the explanation of the variance of 300 billings?

An analysis similar to that in Chapter 8 is relevant. First it is necessary to know how the standard was determined because this affects the interpretation of the variance. Suppose that the standard of 10,000 billings was established on the basis of normal activity. Under these conditions, the actual sales level may explain some of the variance. For example, there may have been only 9,700 billings requiring processing, the employees may have been inefficient in performing their jobs (assuming that more than 9,700 billings required processing), or the bills may have been more complex than the average bills. The activity variance in this case is 10,000 − 9,700, or 300 billings. Analyzing these factors can assist in week-to-week activity evaluation leading to better performance.

The approach, or attitude, taken by management toward cost control can influence cost-reduction programs. Cost savings are not likely to be achieved in areas where management considers costs to be uncontrollable. Suppose that in the above example only 9,700 billings actually required processing. Even when activity and expectations match, there still may be valuable information available for cost control. Because the workforce could process 10,000 billings, there is presently overcapacity in the billing task — at least for the week in question. But this may represent only a necessary safety factor to handle variable activity levels. It would be useful to know the standard activity level and the activity's variability.

The cost of the difference between the normal capacity (10,000 billings) and the actual output level (in this case, 9,700 billings) is $120:

$$\frac{\$200}{500}(10,000 - 9,700) = \$120$$

Alternatively, the average unit cost of billing (assuming that capacity is used as the basis of the calculation) is $.40 ($4,000/10,000). Because 300 billings less than 10,000 were processed, the cost of the idle capacity is $0.40 × 300, or $120. This amount might represent the investment required to maintain the stable workforce necessary to meet fluctuating activity levels, or it might indicate an opportunity for cost reduction.

Management must decide the employee level for each task and whether to meet peak activity levels by hiring part-time employees, by overtime, by delays, or by shifting employees from other tasks. Each reasonable alternative should be examined in terms of its cost, considering a full cycle of activity and the frequency associated with the various activity levels. If this has not been done previously, large cost variances suggest that currently it may be profitable to consider the alternatives.

The process of controlling the incremental cost of billings involves the concept of work measurement, which is discussed later in this chapter. In distribution-cost control, measurement difficulties may center about the diversity of tasks performed by individuals in a group or, instead, on the difficulty of isolating an output measure (such as the number of billings). Sometimes the nature of the output is difficult to measure. For example, how should the output of the market research staff be measured for cost-control purposes, and how can the output of the legal or of the economic-analysis staff be computed?

Control of Order-Getting Costs Controlling the costs of selling is complicated by variables beyond the control of the sales department — including general business conditions, the actions of competitors, the design of the product, the price of the product, and the changing habits of consumers. In the control of selling costs, even more than with most other areas, quantitative measures should be tempered by qualitative judgments as to whether the sales department or a particular salesperson is doing a good job. Furthermore, the measurement and control of these costs becomes more complex as advertising becomes more general, selling more personal, products more interrelated, and economic conditions quickly change. Hence, for example, control of institutional advertising cost is not facilitated by allocating it to specific products even though measuring the profitability of product lines requires an allocation.

Companies frequently use measures such as selling cost per order, selling cost per call, or calls per day as control devices. Comparing sales personnel where the geographical and economic characteristics of the sales areas differ considerably can be misleading, but used with discretion these measures can help managers form impressions of a salesperson's effectiveness. An analysis of trends may also prove useful.

Control of order-getting costs is more effective in the cost-planning stage than in the implementation stage. Still, ex post analysis is important as a step in improving resource allocation. Analysis can highlight those areas (such as product or service line, selling method, advertising medium) where the contribution is large, either on a unit basis or in total, and thereby identify possibilities that may deserve greater (or less) effort on the part of the firm. A comparison of actual costs to the figures used in decision making can help determine the limitations of the decision model or provide cost information for future decisions.

Distribution Costs and Financial Reporting

Most distribution costs are considered to be expenses of the time period in which the costs are incurred, and little attempt is made to assign these costs to the periods that benefit from their incurrence. Thus, advertising costs generally are considered an expense in the period in which the advertising medium displays a message rather than a cost to be allocated over the periods that benefit from the advertising. In like manner, selling costs connected with obtaining unfilled orders are only infrequently carried over to the periods in which the orders are filled. These are considered to be conservative accounting procedures. In part, the accounting treatment reflects the impact of taxes; because such expenses are deductible for tax purposes, they are usually treated as tax expenses in the earliest period permitted by law. For simplicity and consistency, this treatment is then typically used in the firm's financial records regardless of its effect on the data supplied to decision makers.

Administrative Costs

A distinction between administrative and distribution costs is somewhat artificial, at least from an analysis and control point of view. All of what has been said concerning distribution costs is relevant to administrative costs. Those distinctions that can be drawn are essentially ones of degree and not of substance.

Administrative costs are basically fixed in the short run. They are sometimes called **programmed costs** or discretionary fixed costs. In this sense, they are similar to promotional expenditures. Few of these costs exhibit any variability with short-run changes in the physical activity of the firm.

As was true in the case of distribution decisions, formal models also have been applied in recent years to several problems in the administrative area. These include problems of the optimal-size workforce and the related problems of absenteeism, pay incentive plans, vacations, and so on. These decisions usually are based on cost considerations because the contribution of these activities to profit is extremely difficult to establish. The decisions, when formalized, are often based on minimizing the expected cost to perform some given level of service. An analogous case is found in pollution-control equipment investments. Management seeks the minimum cost method of meeting governmental standards.

Often an analysis of cost behavior informs management of improvements in costs that can be obtained by the introduction of corrective action; that is, management needs a cost-benefit analysis. For example, knowing the relationship between the absentee rate and total-period costs and estimating the effect of various strategies (such as a bonus for a good employment record) on the absentee rate can facilitate the choice among several strategies to lower absenteeism.

The accountant is in a position to analyze cost behavior, predict the effect of strategic variables on costs, and thereby assist in the initiation and implementation of administrative cost-reduction programs. Control is usually achieved through budgets based on the type and amount of service anticipated for the period in question. Some tasks, including clerical activities, lend themselves to the use of standards based on some measure of task activity. Where this is the case, the control methods found in the production area can be applied. Generally, however, administrative services are rendered indirectly to many different departments, and it is practically impossible to establish input-output relationships that permit overall evaluations.

The tendency of new administrative services, regardless of their actual value, to become permanent once initiated argues strongly for a full analysis of suggested new activities. Stringent criteria should be applied to the benefits alleged to be associated with new administrative services before they are adopted, even though objective measures of the benefits may not always be available. Moreover, the value and cost of present administrative services should be reviewed periodically; it should not be assumed that all present services should be continued.

Research and Development Costs

Much of what has been said about distribution and administration costs is relevant to the research and development area. Nevertheless, additional factors call for some discussion.

The difficulty of measuring the results or output of an activity is perhaps most pronounced in this area. An indication of the success of research and development activities usually can be obtained only over an extended period of time. In addition, benchmarks against which to measure the effectiveness of research and development activities are not easily established. Conditions may change appreciably over time, and disentangling a research department's contribution from that of sales, production, and so on makes it difficult to use historical data in research analysis. Information concerning similar activities in other firms is neither easily obtained nor adjustable to permit comparisons.

Budgets are used as a control mechanism for research and development costs, but the approach suffers from several shortcomings common to other activities as well. First, a strong incentive to stay within budgeted levels is usually built into the control system. Such budgets restrict management's opportunity to take advantage of unexpected opportunities that develop. Second, department managers are periodically moved to other positions. They may be motivated more by the easily seen short-run budget controls than by the long-run research contribution to the firm, which is more difficult to evaluate. Finally, research and development budgets, like many promotional expenditures, indirectly affect the level of sales and thereby cash flows. Thus, they interact with the very factors that often determine the budgeted level for research; this interrelationship, although indirect, is nevertheless important.

Research and development expenditures (like promotion expenditures) should not usually be treated as residual budget allocations made after investment, production, and similar outlays have been determined. Indeed, in many industries, the single most important activity affecting the future prosperity of the firm is the success of its research and development activities.

Given the importance of research and development and the unreasonableness of short-run evaluations, management should foster a climate where research has an optimal chance of success. Accomplishing this objective requires balancing the unusual character of the creative individual, the frustration of delays resulting from inadequate facilities or lack of adequate research assistants, the importance of minimizing paperwork and reports, and the tendency for many creative individuals to be unconcerned with time and cost considerations.

A useful approach to control and analysis is to organize a research department by projects with each project under the supervision of a department member. The supervisor then takes responsibility for administration and personnel evaluation. Cost control is achieved through the comparison of periodic reports listing percentage completion and expenditures of time and resources, as well as estimates of time and resources needed to finish the project. Typically, it will be necessary to divide projects into well-defined tasks in order to maximize the effectiveness of this control procedure. Even the mere fact that control is considered important can often encourage real savings in both costs and time.

Job Costing in Nonmanufacturing Firms

Many of the product-costing concepts discussed in earlier chapters are also applicable in nonmanufacturing firms. However, the terminology used in these costing systems is often different from that used in manufacturing settings. Rather than jobs, health care institutions may assign costs to "cases," architectural firms to "contracts," advertising firms to "clients," public accounting and consulting firms to "engagements," and engineering firms to "projects." Although the terms differ, the need to assign costs to the firm's output is nearly universal. Another significant difference in costing procedures is that service firms do not inventory their output and direct materials are generally a rather small component of total cost. Labor is usually a significant cost component in such firms, and all other costs generally are classified as overhead.

Contract Costing

As an illustration of costing procedures in nonmanufacturing firms, consider the information given below for Upstate Architectural Services, Inc.

	Budgeted overhead for 19x1:
Indirect labor (custodial, security, secretarial)	$ 76,000
Travel	15,000
Entertainment	3,000
Postage	2,500
Supplies	9,000
Photocopying	1,500
Computer time-sharing	11,000
Equipment rental	10,500
Utilities	14,500
Building depreciation	25,000
Total	$168,000
Budgeted direct professional labor	$ 84,000

Budgeted overhead rate:

$$\frac{\text{Budgeted overhead}}{\text{Budgeted direct labor}} = \frac{\$168,000}{\$84,000} = 200\%$$

An overhead rate of 200 percent of direct labor costs will be used to load overhead onto each architectural contract on which the firm works. Suppose the firm performs a contract involving part of the design of a library building, and the professional labor cost associated with the contract is $9,000. Then the contract cost is calculated as follows:

Contract J101: Partial design of library

Direct professional labor	$ 9,000
Overhead (200% × $9,000)	18,000
Total contract cost	$27,000

In some cases a contract may involve specific costs that are not generally included in overhead and do not fall in the category of direct labor. Such costs are then added to the contract cost. For example, suppose that Upstate Architectural Services,

Inc. hires an engineering consulting firm as a subcontractor to assist in the completion of the library contract. Now the contract cost is determined as follows:

Contract J101: Partial design of library

Direct professional labor	$ 9,000
Overhead (200% × $9,000)	18,000
Subtotal: in-house work	$27,000
Subcontracted engineering consulting	3,000
Total contract cost	$30,000

Refinements of the costing system described above are also possible. It could be, for example, that Upstate has two grades of professional architectural personnel: senior architects and architectural associates. Each of these types of professional personnel may require different levels of support services, and hence the firm might wish to have two different overhead rates. The rate for senior architects' time may be 250 percent of direct labor cost, while the rate for architectural associates' time may be 160 percent of direct labor cost. Then each contract's cost is the sum of the labor costs in the two professional categories plus the overhead costs "loaded" onto each type of professional labor.

Contract Pricing

The way in which contracts or engagements are priced varies across organizations, but a common method is to establish a markup rate on the basis of budgeted revenue and budgeted direct labor cost. Referring again to our example of the architectural firm, suppose that the revenue budgeted for the year is $378,000. The markup rate for contract pricing is established as follows:

$$\frac{\text{Budgeted revenue}}{\text{Budgeted direct professional labor}} = \frac{\$378,000}{\$84,000} = 450\%$$

Using this approach the contract price for the library-design work would be determined as follows:

Direct professional labor	$ 9,000
Markup rate	× 450%
Contract price	$40,500

The profit on the contract is:

Contract price	$40,500
Contract cost	30,000
Profit on contract	$10,500

The subcontracted engineering is included in the cost, resulting in a net profit of $10,500.

Often firms are in competition with other firms to provide their services. Therefore, pricing policies have to reflect not only costs but also the market for the firms' services. For example, Upstate might use the $40,500 price calculated on the previous page as an initial negotiating position. To better its competition, however, Upstate may be willing to settle for less, or, alternatively, might add the $3,000 of engineering consulting costs and charge a price of at least $43,500.

Work Measurement

Work measurement is the systematic analysis of nonmanufacturing tasks to determine the resources (people, time, computer access) necessary to perform a task. It has become increasingly important in a variety of industries for improving efficiency of administrative, service, clerical, and other tasks. Some examples of work measurement applications are listed below:

Activity	Work Measure
Material procurement	Number of orders placed or number of vendor bids obtained
Billing	Invoices or invoice lines
Ledger postings	Number of amounts posted
Proofreading	Lines read
Customer relations	Customer complaints or comments handled

Several prominent service firms have adopted work measurement techniques with favorable results in productivity. Some examples are detailed below.

American Express Company

Business Week reported that American Express Company has launched a productivity-improvement program for the firm's customer service operations. The program was similar to a traditional industrial engineering analysis. Customer service tasks, such as replacing a lost American Express card, were broken up into the steps required to perform the activity. Then standards were set for the amount of time required to complete each step, and measures were constructed for evaluating how well the standards were met. According to an American

Express executive, as reported by the *Business Week* article, the program has increased both customer satisfaction and the bottom line.[1]

Citibank

An article in the *Wall Street Journal* described Citibank's efforts to increase efficiency through work measurement methods. The bank's Operating Group performs the routine tasks of banking, such as preparing customers' bank statements, sending checks to other banks, and debiting or crediting depositors' accounts. In a year, over $2 trillion in transactions are processed.

Every task has a performance standard, and employees know exactly what is expected of them. Performance is measured as frequently as daily or hourly in some cases. A deviation of as little as 2 percent from forecasted performance is considered significant. According to the *Wall Street Journal* article, employees have their own terminology for describing their performance. An employee "blips" when a goal is not met; a "save" is made when an employee cuts a cost. An employee "wins," "passes," or "fails" according to whether a standard is beaten, met, or not met, respectively. According to Citibank executives, the program has cut costs and improved customer service.[2]

United Parcel Service

The *Wall Street Journal* reported that at United Parcel Service, over 1,000 industrial engineers use engineering time studies to set performance standards for a variety of UPS tasks. For example, UPS drivers are expected to walk to a customer's door at the pace of three feet per second and knock rather than lose valuable seconds looking for a doorbell button. According to the *Wall Street Journal* article, a UPS executive stated that the standards are used to give accountability rather than as "hammers." The executive went on to say that the company's "ability to manage labor and hold it accountable" is the key to its success.[3]

1. "Boosting Productivity at American Express," *Business Week* (October 5, 1981): 66–68.

2. "Moving Money: In the Back Office of a Bank, 'Blipping Is Not Appreciated,'" *Wall Street Journal,* June 6, 1975.

3. "Up to Speed: United Parcel Service Gets Deliveries Done by Driving Its Workers," *Wall Street Journal,* April 22, 1986: 1, 23.

Concepts of work measurement are also being applied in the health care industry to develop standard-cost levels for certain types of patient diagnoses. Under one approach, the production measure used for a health care facility is the number of patients treated in each of 383 diagnosis related groups or DRGs. Each DRG is a classification of patient diagnoses in which patients are expected to require similar services and therefore incur similar costs. By developing a cost structure for each DRG, the health care facility's management team can improve budgeting and cost analysis.[4]

Another approach to controlling health care costs focuses on greater individualization of the costs incurred by the patients using a health care facility, as illustrated in the following example.

Massachusetts Eye and Ear Infirmary (a Harvard Medical Center Hospital)	The *Harvard Business Review* reported that the Massachusetts Eye and Ear Infirmary instituted a cost accounting system that traces the use of health care labor and other resources directly to each patient's true requirements. The traditional approach to charging for the use of an operating room is to refer to a list of charges based on various surgical procedures. At the Massachusetts Eye and Ear Infirmary, a patient's charges for the use of an operating room are based on the length of time a patient is in the operating room, thereby tying the charges to a precise measure of the patient's use of the facility's resources. The hospital also measured the average amount of clinical care received by patients in each diagnosis classification on each day of their hospital stay. The result was a declining curve of "clinical care units" per day as a hospital stay lengthened. For example, a cataract patient with a one-day hospital stay is charged with thirty-nine care units, but a cataract patient with a two-day hospitalization is billed for fifty-three care units. Thus, during the second day of hospitalization the patient receives, and is charged for, less intensive care.[5]

Summary

Cost analyses of nonmanufacturing operations apply costs to the specific services performed and not to products manufactured. Service firms use little or no direct materials and do not inventory their service product, but job-costing procedures are basically the same in both service and manufacturing organizations.

The significant cost components in such firms are labor and overhead. In some cases, costs are involved that are not usually included in overhead and do not fall in

4. J. Thompson, R. Averill, and R. Fetter, "Planning, Budgeting, and Controlling — One Look at the Future: Case-Mix Cost Accounting," *Health Services Research* (Summer 1979): 111–25.

5. C. Wood, "Relate Hospital Charges to Use of Services," *Harvard Business Review* (March-April, 1982): 123–30.

the direct labor category. These costs can be applied on a rate basis — such as 160 percent of direct labor and in some cases 100 percent of direct costs.

Work measurement techniques are used to determine the resources necessary to perform a task. Examples include people, time, and computer access. Several prominent service firms like American Express, Citibank, and United Parcel Service have successfully adopted work measurement techniques with favorable results in productivity.

The accountant should be alert both to the relationship of nonmanufacturing costs to activity and other variables and to alternatives for cost reduction. Further, the accountant should be familiar with the cost requirements of formal models that have been used in decision making involving nonmanufacturing activities, especially difficulties associated with measuring the relevant costs required by those models.

In some cases, cost control may be achieved by the same methods that are used in the area of production costs. Generally, however, output measures and standards are not easily established in nonmanufacturing sectors, where control tends to be exercised more through comparing budgeted and actual costs. The elements of these indirect-control systems should be designed so that they motivate employees toward achieving the goals of the organization.

Review Problem

EVALUATING DISTRIBUTION EFFORT

Suppose two door-to-door salespeople are equally capable and hardworking. Which of the following variables might inappropriately affect a comparative performance evaluation?

1. Household income levels in their territories,

2. Traffic congestion,

3. Product quality,

4. Personality differences of the salespersons,

5. Advertising campaigns,

6. Number of buying units,

7. Length of time the areas have been represented by each salesperson,

8. Allocated costs with traceable benefits.

Solution to Review Problem

Item 3 should be the same in either area and hence have no effect. Traffic, item 2, could be different and limit calls, and differential advertising, item 5, of a local nature also could cause differences not attributable to the salesperson. Indeed, even general advertising can have an effect, particularly if it is on television; the income levels of the areas could be different, and one area could have a smaller portion of residents that own televisions, or a relation could exist between income level and what is watched. Item 6 combines with item 1 to establish potential sales volume. Item 7 may help or hurt the current sales effort, inappropriately affecting comparisons. Trends and percentage changes could be used to mitigate the effect. Item 4 would likely affect comparisons, but it would be considered appropriate that personality differences be reflected in results. Item 8 also can produce differences, but if they represent judicious use of the firm's resources by the salesperson, they would be properly included in the comparison because increased sales could result.

Key Terms to Review

allocated costs with indirect benefits, p. 441

allocated costs with traceable benefits, p. 441

contribution income statement, p. 443

direct costs, p. 441

discretionary fixed costs, p. 441

programmed costs, p. 446

work measurement, p. 451

Suggested Readings

Anthony, R., and R. Herzlinger. *Management Control in Nonprofit Organizations,* rev. ed. Homewood, Ill.: Irwin, 1980.

"Boosting Productivity at American Express." *Business Week* (October 5, 1981): 66–68.

Charles, A., W. W. Cooper, J. K. DeVoe, D. B. Learner, and W. Reinecke. "A Goal Programming Model for Media Planning." *Management Science* (April 1968): 423–30.

Jones, R. L., and H. J. Trentin. "Budgeting General and Administrative Expenses: A Planning and Control System." *Management Bulletin 74.* New York: American Management Association, 1966.

Kaplan, R. S. and A. Atkinson. *Advanced Managerial Accounting,* 2d ed. Englewood Cliffs, N.J.: Prentice-Hall, 1989.

King, W. R. "Performance Evaluation in Marketing Systems." *Management Science* (July 1964): 659–66.

Rayburn, L. G. "Marketing Costs — Accountants to the Rescue." *Management Accounting* (January 1981): 32–41.

Sloan, S. "How Milliken Measures Training Program Effectiveness." *Management Accounting* (July 1981): 37–41.

"Up to Speed: United Parcel Service Gets Deliveries Done by Driving Its Workers." *Wall Street Journal* (April 22, 1986): 1.

Wood, C. "Relate Hospital Charges to Use of Services." *Harvard Business Review* (March-April 1982): 123–30.

Review Questions

12-1 It has been said that the primary function of the accountant relative to distribution costs is to record the costs so that the information is available for analysis. Comment.

12-2 Why is distribution-cost analysis more difficult than manufacturing-cost analysis?

12-3 Is it possible for fixed-distribution costs to be avoidable?

12-4 How would you allocate billing department costs to different product lines?

12-5 How would you allocate shipping department costs to different product lines?

12-6 Are advertising expenditures properly considered expenses in the period in which the advertising is distributed?

12-7 Would it ever be reasonable to consider costs associated with selling to be an asset at the end of a period rather than an expense?

12-8 As a business manager, would you want an income statement for a product line that included allocations of joint distribution and manufacturing costs not controllable by the manager in charge of the product line?

12-9 How should service department costs be treated from a cost-control and decision-making viewpoint?

12-10 Consider education as a product. What are the direct costs to a university of facilitating the education of a student?

Exercises

12-11 Evaluating Decisions about Group versus Individual Support Staff   Stenographic pools often handle all dictation and typing required by executives because money can be saved by cutting down on the total number of typists and/or stenographers required by a department or company. A pool eliminates private secretaries, however, and executives generally dislike pools in part for convenience reasons and in part because private secretaries are considered status symbols. How would you analyze the problem of whether or not to have a stenographic pool? Assume that the pool does not presently exist. How would you estimate the costs and savings? What other factors should be considered?

12-12 Allocation of National Advertising Costs   The Elson Company is considering a suggestion to allocate national magazine advertising costs to sales territories on the basis of magazine circulation weighted by an index of relative buying potential in each territory. Is this a good method for

   a. Deciding whether to discontinue an unprofitable territory?

   b. Measuring the performance of a district sales manager?

   c. Controlling advertising costs?

12-13 Estimating Service and Operating Costs   A firm is considering the purchase of a special type of duplicating machine. Two costs that must be estimated are service and operating costs (other than material used in duplication). Service is supplied at a fixed monthly fee. Operating costs are controllable by the firm. How would you estimate the total of these costs?

12-14 Selecting Strategies to Increase Sales   The Automated Tank Company reports the following results for operations in the past two years:

	19x0	19x1
Sales revenues	$3,000,000	$3,300,000
Cost of sales	1,500,000	2,250,000
Gross margins	$1,500,000	$1,050,000
Operating expenses	900,000	300,000
Net profit	$ 600,000	$ 750,000

During 19x1, $675,000 of depreciation expense on manufacturing equipment was transferred from operating expense to cost of sales because management felt that the decrease in the value of manufacturing equipment should be considered a cost of the manufactured product. There has been no essential change in either the manner in which operations are conducted or in prices for the above two years.

The company is considering two alternatives:

1. Pursuing an intensive sales campaign expected to increase sales by $750,000. This effort requires nine additional salespeople at a salary of $12,000 each.

2. Opening a new branch expected to increase sales by $675,000. The operating costs for the new branch include rent, $4,500; office employees, $30,000; branch manager (who is presently employed at the home office and whose present duties would be allocated to other present employees), $25,000; and other expenses, $10,000. All figures are yearly.

Which alternative do you favor and why? Assume that the figures are accurate as given.

Problems

12-15 Research Cost Performance   The Argo Company has an extensive and well-organized research program. Each project is broken down into its phases with the completion times and the cost of each phase estimated. The project descriptions and related estimates are the basis for developing the annual research department budget.

The schedule on the following page presents the costs for the approved research activities for a recent year. The actual costs incurred by projects or overhead category are compared to the approved activity and the variances noted on this same schedule.

The director of research prepared a narrative statement of research performance for the year to accompany the schedule. The director's statement follows the schedule.

ARGO COMPANY
Comparison of Actual with Budgeted Research Costs
(000 omitted)

	Approved Activity for the year	Actual Costs for the year	(Over) Under Budget
Projects in progress:			
74-1	$ 23.2	$ 46.8	$(23.6)
75-3	464.0[a]	514.8	(50.8)
New projects:			
78-1	348.0	351.0	(3.0)
78-2	232.0	257.4	(25.4)
78-3	92.8	—	92.8
Total research costs	$1,160.0	$1,170.0	$(10.0)
General research overhead costs (allocated to projects in proportion to their direct costs)			
Administration	$ 50.0	$ 52.0	$ (2.0)
Laboratory facilities	110.0	118.0	(8.0)
Total	$ 160.0	$ (170.0)	$10.0)
Allocated to projects	(160.0)	(170.0)	(10.0)
Balance	$ 0	$ 0	$ 0
Total research costs	$1,160.0	$1,170.0	$(10.0)

[a] Phases 3 and 4 only.

The year has been most successful. The two projects, 74-1 and 78-1 scheduled for completion in 19x8 were finished. Project 78-2 is progressing satisfactorily and should be completed in 19x9 as scheduled. The fourth phase of Project 75-3, with estimated direct research costs of $100,000 and the first phase of Project 78-3, both included in the approved activity for the year, could not be started because the principal researcher left our employment. They were resubmitted for approval in next year's activity plan.

Director of Research

REQUIRED:

a. From the information given, prepare an alternative schedule that provides the management of Argo Company with better information than the existing schedule by which to judge the research cost performance for the given year.

b. On the basis of the data in the problem, identify and explain an important weakness in Argo Company's system of controlling research costs. (*CMA adapted*)

12-16 Maintenance Cost Control   The Stevenson Works is a medium-sized manufacturing plant in a capital-intensive industry. Because the corporation's profitability is very low at the moment, it has limited investment funds and restricted hiring, which have strained the plant's repair and maintenance program. The result has been a reduction in work efficiency and cost-control effectiveness in the repair and maintenance area.

The assistant controller proposes the installation of a maintenance work order system to overcome these problems. This system would require a work order to be prepared for each repair request and for each regular maintenance activity. The maintenance superintendent would record the estimated time to complete a job and send one copy of the work order to the department in which the work was to be done. The work order would also serve as a cost sheet for a job. The actual cost of the parts and supplies used on the job as well as the actual labor costs incurred in completing the job would be recorded directly on the work order. A copy of the completed work order with the actual costs would be the basis of the charge to the department in which the repair or maintenance activity occurred.

The maintenance superintendent opposes the program on the grounds that that added paperwork will be costly and nonproductive. The superintendent states that the departmental clerk who now schedules repair and maintenance activities is doing a good job without all the extra forms the new system would require. The real problem, in the superintendent's opinion, is that the department is understaffed.

REQUIRED:

a. Discuss how such a maintenance work order system would aid in cost control.

b. Explain how a maintenance work order system might assist the maintenance superintendent in gaining authorization to hire more mechanics. *(CMA adapted)*

12-17 **Incentives for Sales Personnel** Betterbuilt Corporation manufactures a full line of windows and doors, including casement windows, bow windows, and patio doors. The bow windows and patio doors have a significantly higher profit margin per unit than casement windows, as shown in the schedule below.

	Unit Price and Cost Data		
	Casement Windows	*Bow Windows*	*Patio Doors*
Sales price	$130	$250	$260
Manufacturing costs:			
Direct material	$ 25	$ 40	$ 50
Direct labor	20	35	30
Variable overhead[a]	16	28	24
Fixed overhead[b]	24	42	36
Total manufacturing costs	$ 85	$145	$140
Gross margin	$ 45	$105	$120

[a] Variable manufacturing overhead is applied at the rate of 80 percent of direct labor cost.

[b] Fixed manufacturing overhead is applied at the rate of 120 percent of direct labor cost.

The company sells almost entirely to general contractors of residential housing. Most of these contractors complete and sell fifteen to fifty houses per year. Each contractor builds tract houses that are similar, with some variations in exteriors and rooflines.

When contractors contact Betterbuilt, they are likely to seek bids for all the windows in the houses they plan to build in the next year. At this point, the Betterbuilt salespeople have an opportunity to influence the window configuration of these houses by suggesting patio doors or bow windows as variations for one or more casement windows for each of the several exteriors and rooflines built by the contractor.

The bow windows and patio doors are approximately twice as wide as the casement windows. A bow window or a patio door usually is substituted for two casement windows. Casement windows are usually ordered in pairs and placed side-by-side in those houses that could be modified to accept bow windows and patio doors.

Joseph Hite, president of Betterbuilt Corporation, is perplexed with the company's profit performance. In a conversation with his sales manager he declared, "Our total dollars sales volume is growing but our net income has not increased as it should. Our unit sales of casement windows have increased proportionately more than the sale of bow windows or patio doors. Why aren't our salespeople pushing our more profitable products?" The sales manager responded with a sense of frustration, "I don't know what else can be done. The salespeople have been told which type of windows we want sold due to the greater profit margin. Furthermore, they have the best compensation plan in the industry, with $500 monthly drawn against their commissions of 10 percent on sales dollars."

REQUIRED:

   a. Identify the need(s) of the salespeople that would seem to be met by Betterbuilt's current compensation program.

   b. Explain why Betterbuilt's present compensation program for its salespeople does not support the president's objectives to sell the more profitable units.

   c. Identify and explain alternative compensation program(s) that may be more appropriate for motivating Betterbuilt Corporation's salespeople to sell the more profitable units. *(CMA adapted)*

12-18 **Behavioral Implications of Sales Compensation Plans**   Pre-Fab Corporation, a relatively large company in the manufactured housing industry, is known for its aggressive sales promotion campaigns. Pre-Fab's innovative advertising and sales strategies have resulted in generally satisfactory performance in the last few years.

One of Pre-Fab's objectives is to increase sales revenue by at least 10 percent annually. This objective has been attained. Return on investment is considered good and had increased annually until last year, when net income decreased for the first time in nine years. The latest economic recession could be the cause of the change, but other factors such as sales growth discount this reason.

A significant portion of Pre-Fab's administration expenses are fixed, but the majority of the manufacturing expenses are variable in nature. The increases in selling prices have been consistent with the 12 percent increase in manufacturing expenses. Pre-Fab has consistently been able to maintain a companywide manufacturing contribution margin of approximately 40 percent. However, the manufacturing contribution margin on individual product lines varies from 25 to 55 percent.

Sales commission expenses increased 30 percent over the past year. The prefabricated housing industry has always been sales oriented, and Pre-Fab's management has believed in generously rewarding the efforts of its sales personnel. The salesforce compensation plan consists of three segments:

   1. A guaranteed annual salary, which is increased annually at about a 6 percent rate. The salary is below the industry average.

2. A sales commission of 9 percent of total sales dollars. This is higher than the industry average.

3. A year-end bonus of 5 percent of total sales dollars to each salesperson when the salesperson's total sales dollars exceed the prior year by at least 12 percent.

The current compensation plan has resulted in an average annual income of $42,500 per sales employee compared with an industry annual average of $30,000. However, the compensation plan has been effective in generating increased sales. Further, the sales department employees are satisfied with the plan. Management, however, is concerned about the financial implications of the current plan. They believe the plan has caused higher selling expenses and a lower net income relative to the sales revenue increase.

At the last staff meeting the controller suggested that the sales compensation plan be modified so that sales employees could earn an annual average income of $37,500. The controller believed that such a plan still would be attractive to its sales personnel and, at the same time, allow the company to earn a more satisfactory profit.

The vice president for sales strongly objected to altering the current compensation plan because employee morale and incentive would drop significantly if there were any change. Nevertheless, most of the staff believed that the area of sales compensation merited a review. The president stated that all phases of a company operation can benefit from a periodic review, no matter how successful they have been in the past.

Several compensation plans known to be used by other companies in the manufactured housing industry include

- Straight commission as a percentage of sales,

- Straight salary,

- Salary plus compensation based on sales to new customers,

- Salary plus compensation based on contribution margin,

- Salary plus compensation based on sales unit volume.

REQUIRED:

a. Discuss the advantages and disadvantages of Pre-Fab Corporation's current sales compensation plan with respect to

(1) The financial aspects of the company.

(2) The behavioral aspects of the sales personnel.

b. For each of the alternative compensation plans known to be used by other companies in the manufactured housing industry, discuss whether the plan would be an improvement over the current plan in terms of

(1) The financial performance of the company and

(2) The behavioral implications for the sales personnel. *(CMA adapted)*

13

Cost Estimation

LEARNING OBJECTIVES

After studying this chapter, you should be able to:

1 Explain the limitations of the account-classification method of cost estimation.

2 Use the high-low method of cost estimation and describe its limitations.

3 Perform and interpret simple regression analyses as they are applied to cost estimation.

4 Describe some methods for determining the reliability of a regression analysis.

5 Understand some problems associated with statistical cost estimation.

An important element in controlling costs is determining how costs change or "behave" in relation to other measurable factors. Virtually all managerial decisions are affected in some way by predictions of cost behavior. For example, preparation of a valid operating budget for the city of Chicago, pricing decisions by American Airlines, the development of standard costs by General Motors, performance reporting in the Department of Defense, and the evaluation of cost variances by General Electric all require reliable cost estimates.

In many organizations, cost estimates are frequently obtained through what might be called off-the-cuff or rule-of-thumb methods. These methods sometimes use average historical data with adjustments for the plans of the organization and relevant economic or technological trends. New developments in mathematical, engineering, and management methods have led to the development of several improved techniques for analyzing cost behavior. An important technique used to estimate direct materials, labor, and machine time is based on industrial engineering methods. For example, time-and-motion studies analyze the underlying physical variables influencing costs. Once the relation between time and cost is known, the final results can be converted into cost estimates. Thus, if it is found that a particular task requires two hours of a skilled worker's time and the worker is paid $15 per hour, the cost estimate for this imput is 2 × $15 or $30.

For a number of reasons, it is usually more difficult to estimate the costs of service, supervision, and the other indirect costs of operation. First, these cost factors may be common to several products or departments. In addition, there may be slack in one or more of the factors of production, allowing an increase in output without an increase in the factor's cost. (Alternatively, a small increase in output may result in a large increase in cost.) Further, because of indirect relationships with the activity levels of other departments, it may not be feasible to use the same engineering methods for estimating costs that are usually employed on direct or easily traceable costs.

In addition to engineering approaches, accountants also attempt to understand cost behavior by analyzing historical and standard-cost data. The technique, called the **account classification method,** concentrates on the distinction between fixed and variable costs. Although this approach represents an improvement over ad hoc approaches, it makes several assumptions that can substantially reduce its value. First, account classification assumes that only one factor influences cost. Typically, this factor is related to the level of activity, such as units produced. Second, the technique assumes a linear relationship between output and cost over a reasonable range of output levels. Third, although cost predictions can be obtained, the accuracy of these predictions is not known. Fourth, the approach tends to ignore indirect costs that are influenced by the activity. Fifth, account classification relies on the initial classification of costs as either fixed or variable. Finally, even if the analysis is carried out for several periods, it is not clear whether the mean, the median, or some other measure of average cost over these periods is the best measure for the manager to use.

Consider the application of the account classification technique to operating a delivery vehicle. One reasonable choice for the variable related to activity is miles driven. Costs such as insurance and perhaps depreciation are considered fixed. The manager then attempts to estimate variable costs such as gasoline, oil, repairs, and others as so many dollars per mile. The estimated cost for a period or a project is established by multiplying the variable costs per mile by the level of activity expected and then adding the fixed costs to this amount.

High-Low Method

An alternative method of estimating the costs of an activity is the **high-low method**. Under this procedure, illustrated in Exhibit 13-1, two points are estimated. One of these represents the highest activity level (in, say, units of service) anticipated. Cost is then estimated or measured at this activity level because activity is believed to be the cause of cost, not vice versa. Alternatively, this cost could be measured at some activity level — say, 20 percent — above the normal activity level or at a "representative high" activity point to avoid extreme cases. The second cost estimate is made at a symmetrically located activity level equally far below the normal operating level. These two points are connected with a straight line. The straight line is then used to estimate costs for any activity level. The procedure is illustrated by the solid line in Exhibit 13-1 connecting point *B* to point *C*. The method is quickly and easily applied,

EXHIBIT 13-1

High-Low Method of Cost Estimation

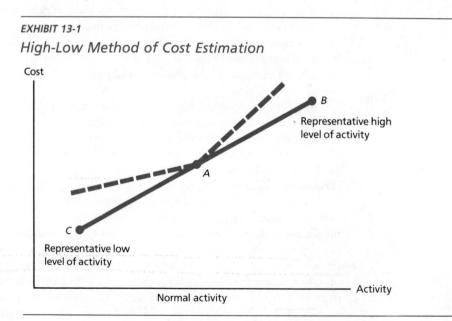

and it can provide inexpensive and useful approximations in cases where costs are closely related to the variability of a single activity measure.

If, however, costs exhibit sharper increases and smaller decreases as activity departs from the normal level at which the process is designed to operate, the broken line in Exhibit 13-1 yields a better estimate in the most likely region of operation, assuming that point A represents the present cost level at the normal activity level. It is typical for costs to behave in this asymmetrical pattern. Costs tend to be "sticky" when activity declines (costs tend not to decrease) but increase more rapidly than the high-low method suggests when activity increases. The result is the V-shaped relationship depicted by the broken line in Exhibit 13-1. The procedure gives poor estimates when several variables affect the cost being estimated. Further, the analysis uses a limited set of the available data; in the most extreme case, only two data points are used even when the organization has data on cost at other output levels.

An example is useful at this point. Suppose that the normal level of activity expected in a department over a specified time period is 10,000 units of product. Some other measure of activity could be used, such as labor or machine hours, but units will do nicely for this example. The department foreman, working with the cost accountant, estimates costs for the department based on both past experience and knowledge of future trends at 20 percent above and below the 10,000 unit figure to be:

Cost Factor	Activity Level (Units)	
	8,000	12,000
Fixed	$57,000	$ 57,000
Variable	90,000	150,000

Based on this information the linear cost function can be estimated in the form:

$$\text{Total cost} = \text{Fixed cost} + \left(\frac{\text{Variable cost}}{\text{per unit}}\right)\left(\frac{\text{Activity}}{\text{level}}\right)$$

or, in this case,

$$\text{T.C.} = \$57,000 + \left(\frac{150,000 - 90,000}{12,000 - 8,000}\right)(\text{units})$$

giving

$$\text{T.C.} = \$57,000 + \$15U.$$

The total cost for any activity level in the range 8,000 to 12,000 units is estimated using this relation. For example, at 9,000 units, the total cost would be estimated to be

$$\$57,000 + \$15(9,000) = \$192,000$$

Three aspects of this situation are noteworthy:

1. For the reasons discussed in this section and illustrated in Exhibit 13-1, the estimate for 9,000 units is likely to be in error.

2. The analysis could be more detailed by estimating the components of the fixed and variable costs separately using the different factors that drive each cost.

3. The relation should be examined for accuracy for

   a. Levels of activity beyond the range (8,000 − 12,000) over which the relation is estimated.

   b. Changes in technology or future methods of operation.

Regression Analysis: A Mathematical Approach

Regression analysis is a mathematical approach for estimating costs that overcomes the limitations inherent in the approaches discussed previously. Regression analysis measures the extent to which a dependent variable changes in relation to changes in one or more independent variables. Our high-low example has two variables — activity level and cost. Activity level is the **independent variable,** and cost is the **dependent variable.** Examining how these two variables reacted with each other in the past reveals that a higher level of activity brings a higher level of cost. Similarly, as activity level decreases, cost decreases. Thus, the level of cost is dependent on the level of activity.

A **simple regression analysis** uses past data to estimate the relationship between a single independent variable and the dependent variable. Such an analysis can accomplish two things:

1. Predict the value of the dependent variable, given the value of the independent variable. If the level of the independent variable (say, activity) is known, a prediction or estimate of the dependent variable (say, cost) can be made, based on the analysis of how changes in activity levels affected cost in the past.

2. Estimate the effect on the dependent variable of changes to the independent variable. Cost can be considered on a "what if" basis by making assumptions of various changes in the activity level.

Let's see how this last point works. Suppose we wish to predict total overhead cost based on the level of direct labor cost. The mathematical expression for this

EXHIBIT 13-2

Total Overhead Cost and Direct Labor Cost

Month	Y Total Overhead Cost	X Direct Labor Cost
1	$30,010	$20,050
2	$31,000	$21,000
3	30,500	20,800
4	29,300	19,700
5	27,050	17,000
6	30,200	20,300
7	33,100	22,100
8	37,100	24,100
9	29,000	19,900
10	29,900	20,100
11	27,800	17,100
12	30,400	20,300

linear relationship between a dependent and independent variable is the **regression equation.** For our example[1],

$$Y = b_0 + b_1 X \qquad (1)$$

where

Y = the dependent variable, total overhead cost in dollars,

X = the independent variable, direct labor cost in dollars,

b_0 = the intercept or the portion of total overhead cost that does *not* vary with respect to direct labor costs, as long as the firm operates within the range covered by the data,

b_1 = the regression coefficient or the rate at which overhead cost varies with direct labor cost within the relevant range — that is, the variable overhead rate.

An analysis of the last twelve months shows the information presented in Exhibit 13-2.

Exhibit 13-3 shows a **scatter plot** (a graph of the points) of the data tabulated in Exhibit 13-2. Exhibit 13-3 gives a visual perception of the relationship between these two variables.

In Exhibit 13-3 there appears to be a linear relationship between these two variables — that is, as the direct labor cost increases, so does the total overhead cost. Based on this history, the intercept (b_0) and the regression coefficient (b_1) can be

---

1. Equation (1) is often written with the addition of another term, U, as $Y = b_0 + b_1 X + U$. The last term is called the *error* (or *disturbance*) *term* and reflects the fact that all the historical data will not lie exactly on one straight line.

EXHIBIT 13-3

Scatter Plot of the Data in Exhibit 13-2

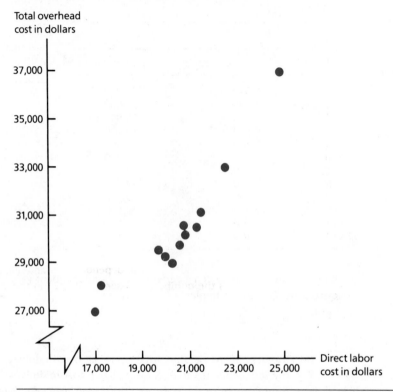

estimated. The value of b_1 is the dollar amount that overhead cost increased histori-cally when direct labor cost increased by one dollar. Hence, b_1 is an estimate of the variable overhead rate based on direct labor cost.

For the data in Exhibit 13-2, the least-squares estimates for b_0 and b_1 are 1445.600 and 1.435, respectively. The estimated regression equation is

$$\text{Total overhead cost} = 1445.600 + 1.435 \, (\text{direct labor cost}) \qquad (2)$$

The equation allows us to predict the average level of total overhead cost for any value of direct labor cost. For example, if $20,000 of direct labor cost is expected and the manager believes the historical relation given by equation (2) still holds, then total overhead cost is estimated to be $1,445.6 + 1.435(20,000) or $30,146.[2]

---

2. Confidence limits can be placed around cost prediction using the following relationship:

   Prediction $\pm \, tS_e$

where   *(footnote continues on page 469)*

The range of the independent variable within which the data used to run the regression was collected is called the **relevant range.** The estimate of the intercept term in the regression — 1445.600, in this case — may be interpreted as that portion of total overhead cost that does not vary with respect to direct labor cost, as long as the firm operates within the range covered by the data. (The assumption is made here that the data span the range of activity expected by management, the relevant range.) It is important to note, however, that the intercept may not be a good estimate of the fixed overhead cost in the example because it is estimated at levels of activity outside the range of the data set for the firm. There are no values of zero for direct labor cost in Exhibit 13-2.

The **regression coefficient** of direct labor cost, a positive 1.435 in this case, gives the rate at which overhead cost varies with direct labor cost within the relevant range. In other words, if direct labor cost rises $1.00, overhead costs increase by $1.44. Still another way to state the relation is that the variable overhead rate, based on direct labor cost is $1.435.

Many computer programs are available for solving regression problems, and many hand-held calculators also can perform simple regression analyses. The values of b_0 and b_1 in equation (1) can be computed by hand using the following formulas, where X stands for the values of the independent variable (direct labor cost in the example), Y stands for the values of the dependent variable (fixed overhead cost in the example), and n is the number of observations (12 in the example):

$$b_0 = \frac{(\Sigma Y)(\Sigma X) - (\Sigma X)(\Sigma XY)}{n(\Sigma X^2) - (\Sigma X)^2} \tag{3}$$

$$b_1 = \frac{n(\Sigma XY) - (\Sigma X)(\Sigma Y)}{n(\Sigma X^2) - (\Sigma X)^2} \tag{4}$$

The easiest approach to obtaining a line of relationship is to draw the line by using a straight edge. You may wish to try this on Exhibit 13-3. Because different analysts would draw slightly different lines, there is an advantage to using the mathematical technique that yields a unique line for any given set of data. The method of least-squares linear regression accomplishes this objective.

As the name suggests, a linear line is fitted to the data that reduces the sum of the squared vertical distances from the data points to the line to a minimum. The distance minimized for a single point is illustrated in Exhibit 13-4.

Computer regression programs provide an additional number that is useful in determining how well the equation accounts for changes in the dependent variable. This value is called the **coefficient of correlation** and is denoted by the letter R. We can interpret the number better after multiplying it by itself, $R \times R = R^2$. In squared form the number is called the **coefficient of determination.** The coefficient of

---

S_e = the standard deviation of the data points around the regression line (called the *standard error of estimate*) available from the computer output, and

t = the value of the t distribution for the desired confidence level (for example, $t = 4.64$ for a 99 percent confidence level, from Table F).

EXHIBIT 13-4

Illustration of Distance Minimized in Squared Form: Idealized

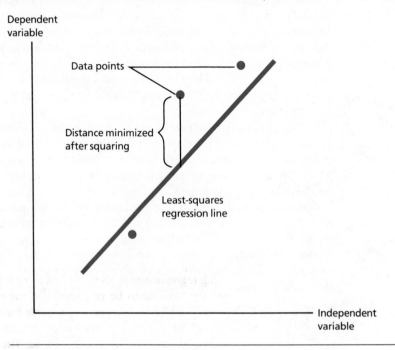

determination is the proportion of the variability in the dependent variable explained by the independent variable. Thus if $R = 0.9$ in our overhead example, we can say that about 81 percent ($0.9 \times 0.9 = 0.81$) of the variability in total overhead is accounted for by direct labor cost. This is a high percentage and leads us to conclude that direct labor cost should help predict total overhead quite accurately in the future as long as major changes do not occur in the cost relationship.

The value of the coefficient of determination varies between one and zero. A value of one occurs when all the data points fall exactly on the line, a rare situation. A value of zero results when there is no relationship between the two variables, also a rare situation. In this case the regression line will be horizontal, suggesting that changing the dependent variable has no effect on the dependent variable.

Multiple Regression Analysis

Although simple regression analysis can provide considerable insight into the relationship between two variables, the restriction to only one independent variable limits its usefulness. In **multiple regression analysis**, several independent variables are used as predictors of the dependent variable. The dependent variable in the analysis is generally the cost of the activity being analyzed. Occasionally, a physical measure such as units of material or labor hours may be used if the costs are a known function of the physical measure. The independent variables may include variables such as output, batch size, number of employees, number of products, and weather. An example of multiple regression is contained in Appendix 13B to this chapter.

Data Collection Issues

Computers can do the necessary computations, but selecting the appropriate variables and collecting the relevant data requires managerial judgment. The managerial accountant can help select appropriate data, understand limitations of data, and judge whether the linear regression equation captures the relationship. Therefore, the managerial accountant should understand the nature of regression analysis and not merely be familiar with its mechanics.

Nature of Regression Analysis

An early step in applying regression analysis to cost estimation is to think through the relationships between the variable to be predicted and the potential independent variable(s). We assume only a single independent variable for the rest of this discussion. Typically, the dependent variable is related to the independent variable through some unit of association, such as output, input, or time. The concept of a unit of association is important because the validity of the regression equation and the predicted costs are affected by the relevance and limitations that relate to the particular unit of association employed. In the example given in Exhibit 13-2, total overhead cost and direct labor cost are related by time in months.

Unit of Association

Regression analysis may be adapted to either **time-series** or **cross-sectional data.** Useful time-series data can be obtained only from a single, stable process observed over time. Cross-sectional data are obtained from several homogeneous processes during a single time period. Because it is unusual for a firm to have a large enough number of homogeneous processes to provide sufficient cost data for cross-sectional analyses, time-series data are usually more appropriate. The example given in Exhibit 13-2 involves time-series data.

In time-series analysis, the unit of association that connects the values of the dependent and independent variables is the time period. The time period is a convenient, but not necessarily ideal, unit of association. Suppose the objective is to predict direct labor cost using direct labor hours. If, as may often be the case, decisions concerning the independent variable (direct labor hours) and its impact on the dependent variable (direct labor cost) are time determined, then time would seem to be acceptable as the unit of association. However, the unit of association may, in fact, be output. In this case, labor cost and labor hours are related because of output decisions, and using time as the unit of association could produce misleading results.

Yet even using output may not give precise results. For example, the output of the period may be 100 units, and the labor cost incurred during the period may be $500. But labor costs also may be related to these same units incurred in other time periods. Relating the labor costs with output on the basis of a common time period under these conditions would not provide a meaningful predictive relationship.

Because accounting records are kept on a time-period basis, time often is used as the unit of association regardless of underlying causal relationships. The manager's knowledge about the process under investigation is indispensable to obtaining meaningful mathematical results. Only when the manager and the mathematician work jointly and understand each other's relative contributions are useful results likely.

Because time is typically the unit of association, attention should be given to influences that occur in various time periods. Perhaps the most common potentially cost-influencing factor associated with different calendar periods is the weather. This factor can be considered by using a different equation for each season considered. Accomplishing this task may mean looking outside the firm's information system for relevant data, and this should be encouraged. Other examples of time-dependent variables include seasonal factors, such as holiday season influences on production activity and overhaul activity, which may be high in periods of otherwise slack activity.

Length of the Time Period

The time period used to obtain measures of the dependent and independent variables must be long enough to permit bookkeeping procedures to record accurately the associated costs, labor hours, and other factors in the same time period used to measure the variable to be predicted. Leads and lags in recording can be particularly troublesome. If a cost relevant to one period's activity (a bonus, for example) is recorded in a later period, or if a cost relevant to several periods' activity is expensed in a single period (advertising is often treated this way), the resultant statistical relationships may be quite misleading.

The time period must be short enough, however, to avoid activity variations within the time period that tend to average out the very cost behavior that is of interest. For example, when predicting direct labor costs, differences may exist by days. If daily needs are to be forecast, daily relationships may be necessary, and cost records also must be adjusted to a daily format. The analysis of cost behavior should be one factor considered in the design of record-keeping procedures. Data lifted directly from cost records as normally maintained may yield misleading results.

Historical Data

The incorporation of, say, monthly or daily data over several years will add greatly to the data base and the reliance that can be placed in the regression equation. However, the managerial accountant should be careful to ensure that no substantive changes have occurred in the operations, prices, or productive apparatus underlying the data that would invalidate the relevance of the data to future predictions.

One example of a changing factor causing complications is inflation. Changes in the rate of inflation can obscure physical relationships. Increasing prices will offset increased productivity. Physical versus dollar measures can avoid confounding these two effects. A price-level deflator could be used to deflate the nominal dollar values.

Managers usually wish to predict or estimate costs for specific values of the independent variable. They prefer to construct the predictive relationship on the basis of these specific values. Usually, however, it is not feasible to assign values to the independent variable and then observe the resultant cost. More often, the available historical data must be used. Moreover, managers may not wish to discard past data merely because the data do not represent either the exact combinations of values for the two related variables that are expected to prevail in the future or the values that would be selected to be observed if conditions permitted. Relevant data are usually too scarce to discard. Yet this does not mean that all historical data will be used. Unusual circumstances surrounding past data may lead to rejection. For example, data from a period in which output was restricted due to a supplier strike should be omitted.

Problems in Applying Regression Analyses

Several problems arise in applying regression analysis. Again, the following discussion assumes a single independent variable.

Determining the Relevant Variable

Determining the relevant independent variable to be used in the analysis is not an easy task. Selection of an inappropriate independent variable can cause systematical over- or underpredictions from period to period. A useful variable may be overlooked because of a lack of recorded data or an inadequate understanding of the problem. It is imperative that managers consult with those involved in the operating process before attempting to establish the relevant variables. An example of a variable that is often omitted from consideration in regression studies is the external effect of an activity. Thus, adequate maintenance or an overhaul in one cost center may reduce the repair costs incurred in a second cost center. This occurs because better-quality products produced by the first cost center cause less wear and tear on the equipment in the second cost center. The best approach is to begin by carefully considering all variables thought to be relevant and for which good data can be obtained.

The appropriate independent variable depends on the activities of a cost center and may differ widely among cost centers. It is, therefore, important to associate each cost properly with the relevant cost center. Failure to do so may not affect plantwide relationships but can lead to poor decisions in the cost centers involved. Determining the appropriate variables is a job for the manager, in consultation with the statistician.

Care also must be taken to ensure that basic changes in the environment, such as substantial increase in the skills and abilities of the labor force or changes in technology, either did not occur over the period studied or are considered in some way in the analysis. One approach is to use a different equation for each period.

Specifying the Form of the Relationship

Cost relationships are not usually smooth, linear equations. Relationships are continuously undergoing change. Relationships also may change over time as a result of changes in economic conditions, technology, or learning. These factors need to be considered in any attempt to forecast cost behavior.

Under these conditions, what is known about the underlying technological or economic basis of the relationship is critical. The manager, not the accountant or mathematician, provides this information, with expert assistance. Typically, the simplest relationship consistent with the observed cost-behavior pattern is selected. The manager should examine the results produced by the mathematics to see if the relationship makes sense. Is the sign of coefficient on the independent variable, b_0 in equation (1), logical? Is its magnitude plausible? Do the data satisfy the linearity assumption? In the final analysis, it is not whether the relationship selected perfectly represents the actual situation, but whether it yields useful results.

Problems in Using Regression Cost Studies

The early stages of cost-behavior studies are often characterized by a search for relationships using both what is presumed to be known about the situation and by working with the available historical data. Variables are plotted against one another, and possible forms for meaningful relationships are examined. From this work, a belief emerges concerning the relevant independent variable and the functional form of the relationship. Such beliefs should be confirmed using new data. However, new data are generally not available. One way to circumvent this problem is to develop the beliefs from a randomly selected subset of the available historical data. The beliefs could be substantiated using the remaining data. Once the final relationship is established, all the relevant data should be used to estimate the coefficient b_1 of the independent variable. Anticipated changes in the environment must be considered in light of their impact on the relevant data to be used to estimate the final relationship.

The slope coefficient, which measures the marginal impact on average cost for a unit change in the independent variable, is useful only for recurring decisions in which the future can be assumed to be like the past (unless a means for incorporating additional information is appended). Furthermore, for predictive purposes an independent variable is useful only if it can be measured more easily than the dependent variable it supposedly is predicting.

The functional relationship should be used for prediction with caution. Two types of predictions are important: those that extrapolate the relationship and those that interpolate from the relationship. Generally, predictions based on extrapolating the relationship outside the range of data points studied can be made only when we can reasonably assume the functional form of the relationship holds beyond the historical range. One problem is that the range of data is difficult to determine because it involves the values of two variables simultaneously. In the example in Exhibit 13-2, for example, direct labor costs less than $20,000 are not observed jointly with overhead costs above $31,000. Each of these activity levels has been experienced individually, but they have not been experienced concurrently.

The problem of extrapolation extends immediately to the constant term. Unless the relationship holds, the constant term should not be viewed as a measure of the overhead cost at a zero activity level.

Interpolation, which is more common, may also be questionable in certain circumstances. The jointly observed values of the variables may result in interpolation or extrapolation, and the interpolation may or may not be valid. For example, if a product is typically made in batches of, say, 1,000 and if the predictive equation is derived thereon, it may not lead to useful predictions involving odd-lot batches that require special handling or other processing costs.

Care should be taken in extrapolation and interpolation using such relationships. In general, if it can be assumed that the relationships hold not only for the data points used to derive them but also for the new ones being examined, then predictions can be made. Predictions can be made if the assumptions underlying the methodology and discussed in this chapter are met. Nevertheless, sometimes predictions are required when the manager is not certain of the validity of the assumptions. In such cases, it is often necessary to forge ahead, while keeping in mind the tenuous nature of any predictions considered necessary.[3]

Computerized Cost-Estimation Systems

Many firms have developed sophisticated computer software that enables them to forecast the cost of a production job quickly and accurately. Such programs often use the techniques discussed in this chapter and appendices in conjunction with computerized cost data from past operations. The importance of timely and accurate cost predictions in preparing bids is described in the following excerpt from an article in *Management Accounting*.[4]

Cost Estimation in the Structural Steel Industry

Mulach Steel Corporation supplies structural and miscellaneous steel to general contractors in the tri-state area encompassing Western Pennsylvania, West Virginia, and Eastern Ohio. We are one of the major suppliers in the Pittsburgh area. . . .

In our industry, bidding is everything. The more darts you throw, the better are your chances of hitting the bull's-eye. We receive 15 to 20 requests for bids each week, which keeps our people on the phone to suppliers,

3. The meaningful data that regression analysis can yield, coupled with the existence of ready-made computer programs to handle the typically computerized input data quickly and relatively cheaply, provide strong arguments for its use. Nevertheless, regression analysis is not commonly used in cost-behavior studies. In part, this is due to the general distrust of statistical methods that are widely misunderstood and often misused.

4. F. Carbone, "Automated Job Costing Helps Mulach Steel Stay Competitive," *Management Accounting* (June 1980): 29–31.

subcontractors, and customers eight hours per day. Beyond a sheer volume effort, successful estimating and subsequent bidding require speed, accuracy, and consistency. . . .

Automation of our estimating affords two primary advantages over manual processing—time savings and accuracy. Bidding is always conducted against a tight deadline. We can receive a call on Thursday asking for a quote by Monday. If we miss the deadline, we are out of the running. Clearly, the speed of the computer—in cutting estimating time in half—gives us a competitive edge. . . . bidding is now more a science than a guess. We have checked our estimating program against completed jobs where we actually know the tonnage requirements. On a 2,000- to 3,000-ton job, the system is only a mere 50 pounds off!

Contractors requesting bids submit rough design drawings to us. Our estimators then process these, steel beam by steel beam. But it is not a mere counting process. A contractor cannot simply bolt pieces together like a giant erector set. Each piece must be milled and cut to the specified dimensions, holes drilled in the proper places for fastening, and any required plates must be bent to the proper angle and welded in a two-step process.

Our estimator crosses each piece off the drawing as he punches it into the computer, adding proper specifications, and using familiar steel industry nomenclature. Our estimating program automatically extends the weights and prints out how much steel we need to buy, how much labor will be required, and how much any special materials will cost. This provides the potential customer with the bottom line that he needs.

Summary

Regression analysis provides a powerful technique for estimating and predicting costs. Multiple regression, covered in Appendix 13B, is even more powerful although more difficult to use. If the assumptions are valid, predictions can be made of future cost levels. Moreover, the sensitivity of the predictions to errors in estimation can be investigated.

The technique is subject to several limitations resulting from errors in the data and the techniques presently used by accountants to record cost information. The effects of these limitations on the estimating equation and the cost predictions should be borne in mind, both in designing and in using cost-information systems. The more important cost predictions are, the more attention should be given to the length of the time period used to record costs, the establishment of cost centers, and the assignment of costs to time periods and cost centers.

The methods described are only as effective as the knowledge of the problem by those using the model and the quality of the data. For this reason, the manager and the statistician work with the accountant to avoid applying highly sophisticated techniques to relatively naive data.

Key Terms to Review

account classification method, p. 463
coefficient of correlation, p. 469
coefficient of determination, p. 469
cross-sectional data, p. 471
dependent variable, p. 466
high-low method, p. 464
independent variable, p. 466
multiple regression analysis, p. 470

regression analysis, p. 466
regression coefficient, p. 469
regression equation, p. 466
relevant range, p. 469
scatter plot, p. 467
simple regression analysis, p. 466
time-series data, p. 471

Review Problem

ESTIMATING COSTS

A regression analysis relating the cost of a service department to the number of set-ups is given by

$$Y = 16 + 200X \ (R = 0.5)$$
Y = monthly service cost in thousands of dollars
X = number of set-ups

a. Predict the monthly service cost if the department performs 100 set-ups in the month.

b. Should the manager have any misgivings about using this equation to predict costs?

Solution to Review Problem

a. Predicted monthly service costs are $Y = 16,000 + 200(100) = \$36,000$.

b. First, the coefficient of determination $.5 \times .5 = .25$ indicates that only one-quarter of the variability in cost is explained by the number of set-ups. Apparently, other factors affect cost and one of them might be a better predictor of cost. Second, if, for example, the maximum number of set-ups experienced in the past never reached 75, the manager may not be sure the given relation holds.

APPENDIX 13A
Exponential Smoothing

An alternate simple technique for forecasting costs (or other variables) is called *exponential smoothing*. In this approach the forecast is based on just two values: (1) the most recent value observed and (2) the (exponentially smoothed) weighted average calculated in the prior period. The formula for the new weighted average is

$$A_i = \alpha X_i + (1 - \alpha)A_{i-1} \tag{5}$$

where[5]

X_i = most recent observation,
A_i = (exponentially smoothed) weighted average in period i,
$0 \le \alpha \le 1$ is the smoothing constant.

The result of the technique is to give older observations less and less importance in determining the new average. The importance of the most recent observation to past observations in the average is determined by the value of the smoothing constant, α. The smaller this value is, the less weight the most recent observation carries in the determination of the new average.

Assume, for example, a set of cost values from the past of 100, 110, 125, 125, and 125, and a smoothing constant of 0.5. The data are given in Exhibit 13-5:

EXHIBIT 13-5

Cost Values

Period	X	A_{i-1}	A_i
1	100	—	100
2	110	100	105
3	125	105	115
4	125	115	120
5	125	120	122.5

---

5. Previous values of X are all included in the A_{i-1} term. Substitution will show that in period i, the $i - r$ value of $X(X_{i-r})$ is multiplied by the factor $\alpha(1 - \alpha)^r$ where r is the measure of the time before i:

$$A_i = \alpha X_i + \alpha(1 - \alpha)X_{i-1} + \alpha(1 - \alpha)^2 X_{i-2} + \ldots$$

As actual cost levels increase, so does the revised average, but it continually lags behind. The larger α, 0.5 here, the faster the series catches up, but the more sensitive it is to recent changes in the cost being estimated.

In most demand-prediction models, where exponential smoothing has received its major applications, α has been set below 0.1. In cost estimation this may or may not be appropriate. Equation (5) can be used with historical data to estimate α.

If there are no trend or seasonal factors to be considered, then the estimate for the next (or any future) period is given by A_i, as determined from equation (5). But the method is also powerful enough to allow for adjustments when a trend is present, or when a seasonal pattern is present, or both.

When a trend is present in the data, the result obtained using equation (5) will lag too far behind. An exponentially smoothed estimate of the trend is needed as a prediction base because an exponentially smoothed estimate is appropriate to apply to exponentially smoothed data. Such an estimate, call it b_i, is provided by

$$b_i = \alpha(A_i - A_{i-1}) + (1 - \alpha)b_{i-1} \tag{6}$$

Using b_i from equation (6), and some mathematics not reproduced here, the forecast for the next period is given by

$$A_i + \frac{1 - \alpha}{\alpha}b_i + b_i \tag{7}$$

Or for any period s time periods ahead, the forecast is

$$A_{i+s} = A_i + \frac{1 - \alpha}{\alpha}b_i + sb_i \tag{8}$$

Exponential smoothing is a relatively easy technique to use and is much less costly than regression analysis. However, it makes no attempt to discover the underlying causal relationships involved. Further, it is not possible to separate out the individual effects of the variables that underlie cost behavior. The method is most valuable in problems where quick and relatively cheap predictions are adequate.

The following excerpt from an article in *Management Accounting*[6] describes the use of exponential smoothing by Hewlett-Packard Company in forecasting the demand for replacement parts.

Exponential Smoothing at Hewlett-Packard	It is difficult to analyze the demand function for replacement parts in relation to the product life (most HP products are produced for at least three to five years, after which HP continues its parts support policy for an additional five to seven years). In addition, the Corporate Parts Center (CPC) currently stocks almost 65,000 different replacement parts, so 65,000 forecasts are needed.

6. R. Stanton, and E. Drury, "Forecasting at Hewlett-Packard: Finding a Better Way," *Management Accounting* (June 1981): 45–49.

To forecast parts demand, CPC uses an exponential smoothing model. On the last workday of each month, the Center runs an order point program. The first section of this program computes the new forecast demand and a current mean absolute deviation (MAD). The forecast demand (F_t) is calculated by multiplying the previous month's demand (D_t) by one minus an alpha factor, then adding that product to the product obtained by multiplying the current month's demand (D_t) by the alpha factor:

$$F_t = \alpha(D_t) + (1 - \alpha)D_{t-1}$$

The alpha factor is set at 0.3, as the formula is similar to a five-month moving average. The mean absolute deviation is calculated in a similar fashion, with $\alpha = 0.3$:

$$MAD_t = \alpha(F_t - D_t) + (1 - \alpha)MAD_{t-1}$$

Once these figures have been computed, the program uses them to operate the order point system, which calculates new order points, safety stock, and order quantities. The program also generates a variety of summary statistics, including the current distribution of parts according to value class, the total monthly sales volume, the new inventory levels, and the anticipated work loads for the schedulers (the employees who actually order the parts).

APPENDIX 13B
Multiple Regression Analysis

This appendix presents an example of multiple regression analysis involving several independent variables. The assumptions required by the procedure, beyond those in the case of linear regression analysis involving a single independent variable, are covered in any standard statistics text.

An Example

As an example, suppose that the tasks performed in a service center consist of the overhaul of several common business machines such as typewriters and desk calculators.[7] Suppose, further, the direct labor cost of operating this department is considered by management to be a linear function of the time spent overhauling the various types of equipment serviced during a given time period. Finally, assume the overhaul time differs depending on the type of machine involved In this example, labor hours rather than labor cost is the dependent variable. The independent variables are the number of machines of each type worked on in a week. Once a relationship has been established between the total hours worked and the hours required on each type of machine, total direct labor cost may be estimated by multiplying each term by the associated labor rate.

Suppose the overhaul operation is characterized by a linear relationship of the following form:

$$Y_i = b_0 + b_1 X_{1i} + b_2 X_{2i} + b_3 X_{3i} + U_i \tag{9}$$

where

Y_i = total direct labor hours in period i,
b_0 = constant of regression,
b_1 = estimated overhaul time for a typewriter,
X_{1i} = number of typewriters overhauled in period i,
b_2 = estimated overhaul time for a desk calculator,
X_{2i} = number of desk calculators overhauled in period i,
b_3 = estimated overhaul time for a photocopier,
X_{3i} = number of photocopiers overhauled in period i,
U_i = error (or disturbance) term (incorporates the net effect of other factors in period i).

7. Based on an example found in P. R. McClenon, "Cost Finding Through Multiple Correlation Analysis, *Accounting Review* (July 1963): 540–47.

The weekly overhaul data in Exhibit 13-6 are drawn at random from the prior two years.[8]

EXHIBIT 13-6

Hours Worked by Week and Machine

Week	X_1 Typewriters Serviced	X_2 Calculators Serviced	X_3 Photocopiers Serviced	Y Total Hours
1	5	8	7	64
2	7	6	9	64
3	9	5	5	53
4	9	4	7	54
5	8	3	8	51
6	9	3	10	57
7	9	2	10	53
8	9	1	10	49
	65	32	66	445

Other conditions that might contribute to differences in the total hours required, such as technical abilities and labor intensiveness, are assumed to be constant. Whether in fact the assumption is valid requires careful consideration by management if the ensuing analysis is to be valid.

The estimated regression based on these data is

$$Y = 8.000 + 1.456X_1 + 4.016X_2 + 2.047X_3 \qquad (10)$$

The equation indicates that it takes 1.456 or about one and one-half hours, on the average, to overhaul a typewriter. This time differs substantially from that required for overhauling a calculator (about four hours). Estimates of future costs should reflect the difference in repair activity to be undertaken by the service center. Care should also be taken to recognize the uncertainty in the estimates resulting from errors such as faulty measurement of the dependent variable, the hours, and the limited data used to estimate the equation.

Assuming that one wage rate applies to all employees, the direct labor cost could be predicted by multiplying the estimated hours by the rate. If other variable costs in the department bear a constant relationship to the wage rate, total-variable cost can be approximated using an estimate of total hours obtained from the equation. How-

---

8. Only eight observations are used to simplify the mathematics. In general, much more data would be used. Random selection may help reduce serial correlation, discussed later in the chapter, because the level of activity in a week is likely to be related to that in the previous and the following weeks. *Serial correlation* refers to the fact that data observations at different points in time of the same series may be related to each other and hence not independent as strictly required by the statistical technique.

ever, if wage rates differ and an average rate is not relevant, the direct labor cost cannot be determined using equation (10). A new analysis that uses cost as the dependent variable may be required. Alternatively, a separate equation can be used for each type of labor. Furthermore, if other activities are performed in the service center (repairs) and the labor involved differs from that required by the overhaul activity, the relations may not be accurate if the mix of activities changes (or is expected to change) over time.

In the machine overhaul example, a week is the unit of association. This implicitly assumes that all costs associated with accomplishing repairs are incurred in the same time period as that leading to the need for the repairs. Alternatively, if the overhaul decision is related to previous machine usage or expected activity levels (and hence the need for repairs in the overhaul period), additional relationships can be developed that permit the values of the independent variables to be estimated with greater accuracy.

Multiple regression analysis attempts to determine the constants, the b_j's also called *parameter estimates,* involved in a functional relationship between a dependent variable and several independent variables. In general terms, such a relation can be written

$$Y = f(X_1, X_2, X_3, \ldots, X_j, \ldots, X_k) \tag{11}$$
$$= b_0 + b_1 X_1 + b_2 X_2 + \ldots + b_j X_j, \ldots + b_k X_k + U$$

Equation (11) is of this general form. The dependent variable, which often is cost, is written as a function of k factors, called *independent variables.* Rather than cost, the function could specify a relationship between output and several independent variables such as hours worked or machines used. The relationship formalized by equation (11) is called the regression equation. Determination of the regression coefficients, the b_j's, is the first task of the analysis. Once the variables are chosen and data sources determined, sample observations are collected. Each sample includes a value for each of the independent variables and the dependent variable related by the unit of association. For the machine overhaul example, the unit of association is the week, and each week provides one sample set of observations on each variable. The mathematical procedure by which the estimates of the b_j's are determined is the method of least-squares. A summary of the approach is contained in any statistics text. The resulting regression equation can then be used to predict the value of the dependent variable, cost, for a given set of values of the independent variables.

The data used to estimate the regression equation can also be used to estimate the reliability of the predictions. For this purpose, two additional measures are required. These two measures are estimates of the *standard error of the predicted individual value of Y* commonly called the *standard error of estimate* and written S_e; and the *standard error of the average value Y,* written $S_{\bar{Y}}$.

The assumption made in developing both measures is that the variability of the points around the regression line does not change as the independent variables change. Thus, overhead costs must be no more (or less) variable for the case of a high direct labor cost than for a low direct labor cost. Statisticians say the variance of the conditional distribution of the dependent variable is the same for any value of the independent variable. This condition is also called *homoscedasticity.*

The value of S_e measures the variability of the possible individual weekly overhead cost levels for a given direct labor cost value in the example.[9] The value $S_{\bar{Y}}$ measures the variability in an average week having the given direct labor cost. The value of $S_{\bar{Y}}$ is less than S_e. The relationship is equivalent to that of the standard deviation of the sample mean to the standard deviation of the individual values. The choice between S_e and $S_{\bar{Y}}$ depends on whether the desired prediction is for the average (or expected) cost in a week with direct labor cost (use $S_{\bar{Y}}$) or whether the prediction is for a specific week's cost (use S_e). The larger these values, the less reliable the predictions.

Two other measures obtained from the data are also useful. They are the standard errors of the regression coefficients, written S_j, and the estimated multiple correlation coefficient, written R. These measures are provided in the printouts from multiple regression computer programs. The standard error of a regression coefficient, S_j, is the standard deviation of that coefficient. It is a measure of the sampling error in the coefficient. A large value indicates less confidence in the value of that specific regression coefficient and hence of its influence on the dependent variable. The estimated multiple correlation coefficient, R, is a measure of how well the regression line fits the data. The square of the correlation coefficient, denoted R^2, is called the *multiple coefficient of determination.* The multiple coefficient of correlation is a measure of the percentage of the variation of the dependent variable about its mean that is explained by the variation of the independent variables about their means. A large value of R^2 suggests a successful analysis can occur even if there is no readily available logical explanation or when the analysis is faulty. In such a case, attempts to predict or even speculate on the nature of the underlying relationship should proceed only with the utmost caution. The cost accountant and the manager must use their knowledge of the actual situation to develop meaningful relations through the choice of variables, the choice of the unit of association and the time period used in the analysis. They should be able to explain the logical nature and economic interpretation of the regression equation to management.

Rewriting equation (11), the more complete form of the mathematical expression for the example discussed earlier, including the symbols for the computer output, gives

$$Y = 8.000 + 1.456X_1 + 4.016X_2 + 2.047X_3 \qquad (R) \qquad\qquad (12)$$
$$\qquad\quad (S_1) \qquad\quad (S_2) \qquad\quad (S_3) \qquad\quad (S_e)$$

The S_j's are the standard errors of the three regression coefficients, R is the multiple correlation coefficient, and S_e is the standard error of estimate.

To use the regression equation to predict values of the dependent variable requires only that

---

9. The statement assumes equal variability about the regression relation everywhere. When this is not the case, a usually modest correction is required; it is discussed in many statistics texts.

1. A linear relationship is a reasonable approximation over the relevant prediction range,

2. The assumed relationship makes sense, and

3. The statistical analysis has been conducted without error.

To use a regression equation to predict value of a dependent variable and make probabilistic and interpretive statements concerning the error associated with any prediction or test the regression coefficient depends on the validity of several additional assumptions. In their strongest form, these assumptions include the following:

1. The distribution of the disturbance term, U in equation (11), is normal with an expected value of zero.

2. The dependent variable has constant variance regardless of the values of the independent variables.

3. The disturbance terms (U's) are not correlated.

4. The variation in the dependent variable results only from the variation in the disturbance term. (The independent variables are measured without error and hence only the dependent variable is a random variable.)

5. The number of sample observations exceeds the number of parameters, the b_j's, to be estimated. (The excess should be large.)

6. The independent variables are not correlated with each other (called *multicollinearity*). Required for tests on regression coefficients.

When the independent variables and the dependent variable are the result of observation, rather than predetermined, they are *random variables*. Then the assumptions of the analysis apply to the joint probability distribution of the dependent and independent variables, rather than to just the conditional distribution of the independent variables. Fortunately, the same computations can be made whether the independent variables are considered to be random variables or not. Furthermore (subject to certain limitations described later), predictions of the relevant cost levels can be made using the estimated relationship. When all variables are random variables, the correlation coefficient can be interpreted either as a measure of the strength of association or, in squared form, as the proportion of variation in the dependent variable explained by the independent variables used in the analysis. When the dependent variable is random, only the latter interpretation applies. In the machine-overhaul example, values of the independent variables were not preselected. Thus, all variables were random variables.

If the second, third, and fifth assumptions hold, confidence intervals can be placed around the predicted value of the dependent variable. The prediction can be constructed as the average value of Y for the given X values or as a predicted individual value of Y. The confidence interval depends on which interpretation is relevant, and it is larger for individual estimates than for averages. The confidence interval given here applies to an individual value. Calculation of a confidence interval requires the value of the standard error of estimate. For example, if the standard error of estimate (S_e) were 2.112, the manager could be 99 percent confident (implying 4.64 t units for $n - k - 1$ or 4 degrees of freedom) that in week 9 (in which six typewriters, four calculators, and nine photocopiers were overhauled) the total number of hours (Y) would satisfy the following relationship:[10]

$$43.223 - tS_e \leq Y \leq 43.223 + tS_e$$
$$43.223 - 4.64(2.112) \leq Y \leq 43.223 + 4.64(2.112)$$

Or equivalently,

$$33.423 \leq Y \leq 53.023$$

Here n is the number of data points, and k is the number of independent variables in the regression. (A table of values for the t distribution is included in Table F at the end of the book.) The value 43.223 is obtained first by solving equation (10) for $X_1 = 6$, $X_2 = 4$, and $X_3 = 9$. Then the intervals are obtained by adding and subtracting 4.56 t units. The value 4.56 is taken from a table of the t distribution. If, instead, the manager wishes a confidence interval for an average week with the given X values; that is, for the average value of Y, denoted $\bar{Y}$, the only change is to replace $S_e = 2.112$ with $S_{\bar{Y}} S_e/\sqrt{n} - 1 = 2.112/\sqrt{8} - 1$ where n is the number of data points.

A confidence interval also may be constructed for each regression coefficient using its standard error. If the confidence level is set at 99 percent, a confidence interval for b_j is given by $b_j \pm 4.64 S_j$, where S_j is the standard error of coefficient b_j, and 4.64 is the t-value for a 99 percent confidence level with $n - k - 1$ (which is 4 in the example) degrees of freedom.

The manager can also test the null hypothesis that each coefficient, b_j, equals zero. (This tests the claim that a change in the specific independent variable has no effect on the dependent variable.) Computer print-outs for regression programs usually display the t-statistic (or t-value) for each regression coefficient. The t-statistic for regression coefficient b_j is defined as b_j/S_j. If b_j equals zero, then b_j/S_j has a t distribution with $(n - k - 1)$ degrees of freedom. Using a two-sided alternative test-hypothesis (i.e., $b_j \neq 0$) and a significance level of 99 percent, reject the null hypothesis that b_j is equal to zero if the t-value for b_j is greater than 4.64 or less than -4.64 (for $n - k - 1$ or 4 degrees of freedom). Rejection of the null hypothesis leads us to accept that a change in X_j does change Y.

The correlation coefficient indicates the closeness of the relationship. Suppose its value is 0.9 in the machine-repair example. The best way to interpret this value is to consider it in squared form — that is, .81. The *coefficient of determination,* as it is then called, indicates the percentage of the variability in total hours explained by the three independent variables used in the analysis. For the present case 81 percent of

---

10. Due to the small sample size and the fact that the underlying variability is unknown and, hence, must be estimated from the sample data, the t distribution is used in place of the normal. In fact, the value of 2.112 for S_e used in this example is smaller than the proper value. With a reasonably large sample (and for predictions near the center of the data), the downward bias is of little practical consequence.

the variation in total hours is explained by the repair activity on the three types of machines.

Discussion in the chapter pointed out several limitations with simple regression analysis using a single variable. Multiple regression allows the investigator to expand the explanatory set of variables but introduces additional problems, including, for example, the problems created when the explanatory variables are correlated.

A relatively new technique developed by Charnes and Rhodes in 1978, called *data envelope analysis,* can be used to solve questions related to the measurement of efficiency in the use of resources while avoiding some of the difficulties associated with regression analysis.[11] The technique is a linear programming approach to an ex post evaluation of the relative efficiency across decision-making units. The result of the process is an efficiency rating, based on actual inputs and outputs, for each decision unit that also identifies the sources and levels of inefficiency that a regression analysis would ignore. Further, it suggests the amount of input changes or output enhancements required to achieve parity among the decision-making units. Linear programming is discussed in Chapter 17.

Suggested Readings

Benston, G. J. "Multiple Regression Analysis of Cost Behavior." *Accounting Review* (October 1966): 657–72.

Borden, J. "An Assessment of the Impact of Diagnosis-Related Group (DRG)-Based Reimbursement on the Technical Efficiency of New Jersey Hospitals Using Data Envelopment Analysis." *Journal of Accounting and Public Policy* (Summer 1988): 77–96.

Carbone, F. J. "Automated Job Costing Helps Mulach Steel Stay Competitive." *Management Accounting* (June 1980): 29–31.

Charnes, A., and E. Rhodes. "Measuring the Efficiency of Decision Making Units." *European Journal of Operations Research* (November 1978): 429–44.

Dean, J. *Statistical Cost Estimation.* Bloomington: Indiana University Press, 1976.

Durbin, J., and G. Watson. "Testing for Serial Correlation in Least Squares Regression," pts. I and II. *Biometrica* (December 1950): 409–28; (June 1951): 159–78.

Geurts, M., and T. Buchman, "Accounting for 'Shocks' in Forecasts," *Management Accounting* (April 1981): 21–26.

Jensen, R. "Multiple Regression Models for Cost Control — Assumptions and Limitations." *Accounting Review* (April 1967): 265–72.

Johnston, J. *Econometric Methods,* 3d ed. New York: McGraw-Hill, 1984.

Kaplan, R. and A. Atkinson. *Advanced Managerial Accounting,* 2d ed. Englewood Cliffs, N.J.: Prentice-Hall, 1989, chap. 3.

Lovell, M. "Data Mining." *Review of Economics and Statistics* (February 1983): 1–12.

Magee, R. *Advanced Managerial Accounting.* New York: Harper & Row, 1986.

McClenon, P. "Cost Finding Through Multiple Correlation Analysis." *Accounting Review* (July 1963): 540–47.

11. A. Charnes, and E. Rhodes, "Measuring the Efficiency of Decision Making Units," *European Journal of Operations Research* (November 1, 1978): 429–44.

Stanton, R., and E. Drury. "Forecasting at Hewlett-Packard: Finding a Better Way." *Management Accounting* (June 1981): 45–49.

Troxel, R. B. "Variable Budgets Through Correlation Analysis — A Simple Approach." *National Association of Accountant's Bulletin* (February 1965): 48–55.

Review Questions

13-1 For what purpose might an organization want to know how costs react to changes in the level of activity?

13-2 Suppose the high-low method of cost estimation is applied by using actual daily data over a year. Total cost is related to the volume of activity. What problems, if any, might result? Can you offer an alternative approach to avoid the problems suggested but still using the high-low method?

13-3 A method regularly used to establish the fixed and variable fractions of a cost is the high-low method. The approach relies on the two extreme outputs to reflect the change in cost resulting from a change in activity. What limitations are present in this method?

13-4 Suppose that the true unit of association between cost and labor input measured by direct labor hours is the output level decision. Why might a misleading relationship result if time were used as the unit of association?

13-5 Cost and related data that might be used in a regression analysis are available for given-length time periods. Usually, these time periods are established for purposes other than cost analysis (tax purposes, for example). What problems can be encountered because of the failure to consider the analysis function in the design of the firm's information system?

13-6 Two independent variables are being considered for use in a regression analysis. Only one will be used. The ranges of observations on each are as follows:

$$X_1: \quad 15–83 \qquad X_2: \quad 25–52$$

a. Assuming that each independent variable would have the same regression coefficient, which one is most important if the objective is to predict changes in the dependent activity variable? Why?

b. Suppose variable X_1 is selected. Would it be appropriate to use the regression equation to predict the activity level of the dependent variable for a value of X_1 of 90?

c. What reasons could be offered for selecting the variable you did not pick in **a**?

13-7 Would a linear relationship between the volume of activity and the total monthly cost of an input subject to quantity discounts be linear? Explain.

13-8 Suppose a cost, Y, and an activity measure, X, are negatively related — that is, when X increases, Y decreases. When one variable increases, the other declines. This is not just a chance situation. Answer the following with *true* or *false* or *uncertain*, and provide an example or reason for each:

a. Changes in activity cause changes in the cost Y.

b. If X causes changes in Y, then increases in X cause decreases in Y.

13-9 What does the least-squares criterion implicitly assume about the importance of the prediction error to the manager?

13-10 "If historically relevant and valid data on a variable are available for predicting a required cost, a regression equation will be useful." Evaluate this statement.

13-11 Costs that do not behave in a linear manner should not be treated as though they were linear. Comment.

13-12 (See Appendix 13B.) Suppose that a regression analysis in a service department uses two independent variables — namely, direct labor hours and dollar value of materials. What effects on the estimates of future cost levels (the dependent variable) might be expected?

Exercises

13-13 Interpreting Graphs   The accompanying graphs illustrate three different cost-volume relationships. Assume that the diagonal lines represent the least-squares regression line determined mathematically from the underlying data in each case. Note that the data range from activity levels of about 2,000 to 6,000 units.

a. Using the top graph, what might the manager estimate fixed costs to be? Would you be satisfied with his estimate? Why?

b. In which of the three cases does a change in activity have the greatest impact on cost?

c. In which case does the relationship permit the smallest error in prediction? What does this suggest about the value of the analysis?

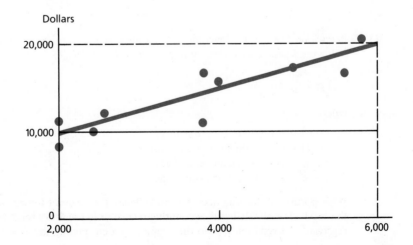

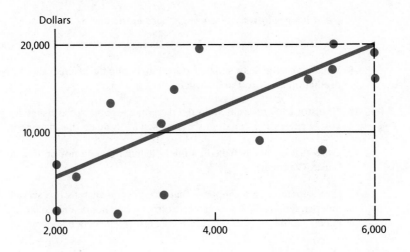

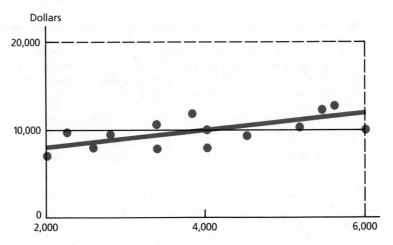

13-14 Regression Analysis and Inventories   Assume that an inventory-control model leads to the following formula for the economic order quantity (*EOQ*):

$$EOQ = \sqrt{\frac{2DP}{S}}$$

where

EOQ = economic order quantity,
D = annual quantity used in units,
P = cost of placing an order,
S = annual cost of storing one unit.

What portion of the data necessary to estimate the relevant future values needed to use this model is available in the accounting record or in the firm's records in general? How is regression analysis relevant to the problem of determining the EOQ?

13-15 Interpreting Cost Analyses   In a given cost analysis, data were gathered for each bimonthly period over the last four years. Plotting all the data available suggested a relationship between the activity and total employment that gave a very close estimate of total activity. On the basis of this preliminary investigation, the organization hypothesized that cost was a function of the total employment level and used that data for the previous four years to test the hypothesis. What conclusion concerning the hypothesis do you suppose they reached? What comments can you make concerning their methodology?

Problems **13-16 Significance of the Relationship and Independence**   Suppose a linear relation between cost and an activity measure shows no relationship — that is, the slope of the line is essentially zero. Can you be confident the two variables are not related? Ignore additional variables in your answer. Support your answer with an example.

13-17 Explaining Results   Control procedures in many organizations require written explanations when actual results are worse than projections. These explanations usually require indications of corrective action to be taken as well as an explanation of present discrepancies. What effects do such procedures have on obtaining accurate cost forecasts? What can be done, if anything?

13-18 Regression and Overhead Estimation   Turfland Corporation provides commercial landscaping services. Linda Dake, the firm's owner, wants to develop standard cost estimates that she can use to prepare bids on jobs. After analyzing her costs, Dake has developed the following preliminary cost standards for each 1,000 square feet of landscaping.

Direct material	$400
Direct labor (5 DLH @ $10/DLH)	50
Overhead (5 DLH @ $18/DLH)	90
Total cost per 1,000 square feet	$540

Dake is certain about the estimates for direct materials and direct labor, but she is not comfortable with the overhead estimate. The estimate for overhead is based on the overhead costs that were incurred during the past twelve months as presented in the schedule below. The estimate of $18 per direct labor hour (DLH) was determined by dividing the total overhead costs for the twelve-month period ($648,000) by the total direct labor hours (36,000).

	Total Overhead	Regular Direct Labor Hours	Overtime Direct Labor Hours	Total Direct Labor Hours
January	$ 47,000	2,380	20	2,400
February	48,000	2,210	40	2,250
March	56,000	2,590	210	2,800
April	54,000	2,560	240	2,800
May	57,000	3,030	470	3,500
June	65,000	3,240	760	4,000
July	64,000	3,380	620	4,000
August	56,000	3,050	350	3,400
September	54,000	2,910	190	3,100
October	53,000	2,760	40	2,800
November	47,000	2,770	30	2,800
December	47,000	2,120	30	2,150
Total	$648,000	33,000	3,000	36,000

Dake believes that the overhead is affected by the total monthly direct labor hours. The overtime premium, 50 percent of the direct labor rate, is not included in the total overhead. Instead, the overtime is regarded as a special item associated with each project and considered a rate variance. Dake decided to perform a least-squares regression of overhead (OH) on total direct labor hours ($TDLH$). The following regression results and statistics were obtained:

$$OH = 26,200 + 9.25\ TDLH$$

$$R = 0.92718$$

$$S_e = 2,434$$

REQUIRED:

a. The overhead rate developed from the least-squares regression is different from Linda Dake's preliminary estimate of $18 per direct labor hour. Explain the difference in the two overhead rates.

b. Using the overhead formula that was derived from the least-squares regression, determine a standard-cost estimate for each 1,000 square feet of landscaping on

1. A variable cost basis.

2. An absorption cost basis.

c. Linda Dake has been asked to submit a bid on a landscaping project consisting of 50,000 square feet. Dake estimates that 40 percent of the direct labor hours required for the project will be on overtime. Calculate the minimum bid that Dake should submit on this project if she uses the overhead formula that was derived from the least-squares regression.

d. Should Turfland Corporation rely on the overhead formula derived from the least-squares regression as the basis for the overhead component of its cost standard? Explain your answer. (*CMA adapted*)

13-19 Exponential Smoothing (see Appendix 13A) When using exponential smoothing, if the last observation is $1,250 and the smoothed average up to this point is $1,000, what is the prediction for the next period's cost level using a smoothing coefficient, α, of 0.2?

13-20 Selecting Variables (see Appendix 13B) Consider the cost of some activity. Suppose two independent variables are used, one in each of two simple single-variable regression equations, to explain the cost variability. If the trend of points for the first independent variable is "closer on the average" to the regression line than for the second, would you use the first regression relation line and reject the second?

13-21 Methods for Meaningful Cost Analysis In the machine-overhaul example discussed in the appendix to this chapter, suppose that during a week in July of a given past year one-half of the calculators were replaced by a new and more complex type of machine. What should be done at the time of installation and now to ensure a more meaningful cost analysis? Do any special factors need consideration?

13-22 Interpreting Regression Equations (see Appendix 13B) If the regression equation for two independent variables and one dependent has the form

$$C = 20 + 4X_1 + 2X_2$$

where

C = weekly cost for the activity,
X_1 = direct labor hours/week,
X_2 = number of orders processed/week,
S_e = 5 (standard error of estimate),
S_c = 6 (standard deviation of weekly costs).

REQUIRED:

a. Explain the exact meaning of the numbers 20 and 4.

b. Explain the exact meaning of the value for S_e and S_c.

c. Assuming normality, estimate the probability that the weekly cost of the activity will lie between 46 and 50 if $X_1 = 4$ and $X_2 = 5$.

d. Assuming normality, estimate the probability that the weekly cost will lie between 40 and 50 if $X_1 = 4$ and $X_2 = 5$.

e. Under what conditions would you be willing to use these estimates?

13-23 Selecting Regression Models The time spent adjusting and the set-up cost required on a piece of machinery depends on the experience and training of the machine operator. For this reason a ten-week training program has been set up. After ten weeks there will be a class of machinists in each week of the program. The manager of the department wishes to estimate the set-up time (and cost) based on the number of weeks of training. Two machinists are selected at random from each of the ten classes, and the set-up time on a typical job is measured. The results are shown in the table:

Weeks of Training W	1/W X	Set-up Times (minutes)[a]	
		Machinist 1 T	Machinist 2 T
1	1.00	9.5	10.2
2	0.50	9.0	6.4
3	0.33	5.5	7.1
4	0.25	5.8	6.8
5	0.20	6.6	5.3
6	0.17	5.5	7.3
7	0.14	5.2	5.4
8	0.12	4.9	7.6
9	0.11	5.9	4.2
10	0.10	4.5	6.3

[a] A different pair of machinists is observed for each week.

REQUIRED:

a. The manager cannot decide whether model A or model B is more appropriate.

Model A: $T = b_0 + b_1 W + U_A$

Model B: $T = b_0 + b_1 X + U_B$

The manager is willing to assume that U_A or U_B is normally distributed with zero mean and constant variance. Using scatter diagrams (T versus W and T versus X) and whatever else you think is reasonable, choose between the models.

b. Suppose that the manager selects model B. Obtain estimates of b_0, b_1. Use the following data and solve equations (3) and (4).

$$\Sigma X = 5.84 \qquad \Sigma T = 129 \qquad \Sigma X^2 = 3.0928$$
$$\Sigma TX = 44.439 \qquad \Sigma T^2 = 882.34$$
$$\Sigma T = nb_0 + b_1 \Sigma X \text{ and } \Sigma TX = b_0 \Sigma X + b_1 \Sigma X^2$$

c. Suppose that the statistician asserts that model B is more reasonable than A because A implies that a machinist with no experience (or training) can set up the equipment in a finite expected time while a machinist with a great deal of experience will be able to set up the equipment in a negative expected time. Model B, on the other hand, implies that a machinist with no experience cannot set up the equipment and that the machinist with a great deal of experience needs a finite time of at least b_0.

(1) Do you agree? Why or why not?

(2) If you agree, would you be willing to use model B to estimate set-up time for a machinist with fifteen weeks of training?

(3) If you disagree, would you be willing to use model A for this estimate?

d. Suppose that the study was made by observing the same two machinists in each of the ten weeks. What problems are created? Do any problems result if two different machinists for each week are used at a point in time when the program is ten weeks old?

    e. A machinist with five weeks of training set up the equipment in 3.8 minutes. Using the results of the study and the fact that S_e, based on the data given, can be computed to be .9587, answer the following:

        (1) Was the machinist unusual? Why or why not?

        (2) If so, what might explain this result?

    f. What verbal interpretation can be given the correlation coefficient in this problem?

13-24 Continuation of Problem 13-23 Using the High-Low Method   Use the high-low method to estimate model *B* for machinist one in Problem 13-23. Do you see any major differences in the resulting equations compared to the results in 13-23?

13-25 Continuation of Exercise 13-13   In which case is cost most closely related to changes in output? Defend your choice.

13-26 Using Multiple Linear Regression   (see Appendix 13B) A local firm is engaged in the process of applying a rust preventive coating to the underside of automobiles. It has data by months for five years on the amount of direct material and labor hours used as well as on the number of customers serviced and total costs.

    A multiple linear regression equation is fitted to this data and yields

$$T = 10 + 2M + 3L + C: \quad S_e = 4$$

where

       T = total monthly cost in thousands,
      M = direct material costs in hundreds,
      L = labor cost in hours,
      C = customers serviced in hundreds.

    A sentence or two at most is required.

REQUIRED:

    a. Interpret the figure 10 in the equation in terms of what cost concept it represents. Is it a meaningful figure by itself? Why or why not?

    b. Give the cost interpretation of the figure 3 in the equation. Why should one be careful of accepting this interpretation here?

    c. Should the company expand the equation to consider a seasonal effect if one exists, say, between summer or winter? Explain.

    d. Would it be reasonable to use this equation to predict costs if the process remains stable? Explain.

Cost Allocation

14

Cost Allocation

*H*ow should an airline allocate the costs of its aircraft repair facilities to the various routes flown by its aircraft? How should a hospital allocate the costs of its patient-reservation service among its departments? How should a manufacturer allocate the costs of its security department among its production departments? Indeed, should any of these allocations be made at all? And if the allocations should be done, for what purpose?

These difficult questions illustrate how pervasive the issue of cost allocation is and how subjective it can be. This chapter discusses the concept of allocation in general and examines the techniques of service-department cost allocation. Chapter 15 addresses the problem of allocating joint costs.

Cost Allocation: Definition and Purposes

Cost allocation is the systematic assignment of a cost or group of costs to products, services, or time periods. The recipient of the cost assignment is called the **cost objective.** The cost assigned is sometimes referred to as a **cost pool.** Exhibit 14-1 depicts the relationship among cost pools, cost objectives, and cost allocation.

For example, the cost pool for fixed-asset depreciation is the asset's depreciable cost (its acquisition cost minus its estimated salvage value), and the cost objectives are the time periods to which the depreciable cost is assigned. The cost assignment method might be to assign equal cost to each period — the straight-line cost allocation method. In overhead accounting, the cost pool consists of overhead costs (indirect material, indirect labor, utility costs, property taxes, and so forth), and the cost objectives are the manufactured products or services produced. The cost assignment method might be to use a constant cost per unit of direct labor time used to make the product.

EXHIBIT 14-1

Cost Allocation Relationship

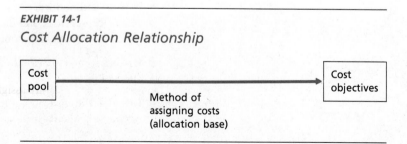

EXHIBIT 14-2

Multistage Allocation

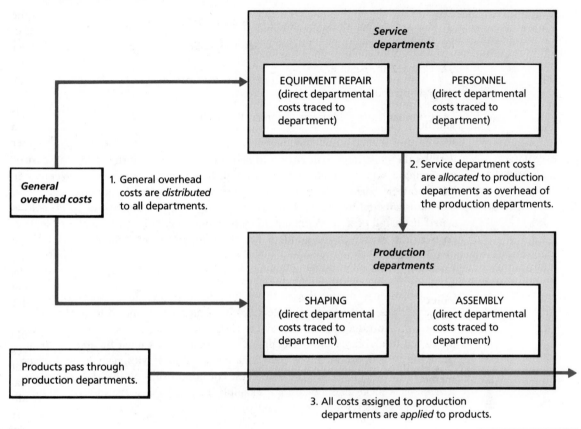

Sometimes the allocation of a cost pool to the cost objectives takes place in several stages. In overhead accounting, for example, overhead costs may first be assigned to service departments and producing departments. In this stage, the cost pool is overhead cost and the cost objectives are departments. In the second stage, the service department costs are assigned to producing departments; there is a cost pool for each service department, and the cost objectives are the producing departments. In the third stage, the producing department costs are assigned to the products or services produced; there is a cost pool for each producing department, and the manufactured products or services produced are the cost objectives. Exhibit 14-2 depicts such a multistage allocation process.

Purposes of Cost Allocation

Costs are allocated for a number of reasons, including

1. Inventory valuation and income determination,

2. Cost reimbursement,

3. Pricing and bidding, and

4. Communicating the costs of internally produced services.

Inventory Valuation and Income Determination

Perhaps the most important reason to allocate costs is to determine the full cost of producing a service or manufactured good. In a manufacturing firm, inventory is valued on the balance sheet at its full production cost. On the income statement, income is affected by the value of cost of goods sold, and the cost of goods sold is stated at the full cost of producing the goods sold. Thus, allocation of all production costs to the manufactured goods is necessary for inventory valuation and income determination.

Cost Reimbursement

Cost allocation is also necessary to justify reimbursement in a variety of settings. Public utilities, such as gas and electric companies, are required to justify rate increases with production cost analyses. Health care institutions must justify their prices for insurance reimbursement. Defense contractors must be able to demonstrate the costs of producing defense equipment. Public service agencies and governmental units often must justify tax increases or bond issues on the basis of the costs they incur. A local school board, for example, may use a cost analysis to gain public support for an increase in school taxes.

Pricing and Bidding

Cost allocation is needed in order to determine the full cost of providing products and services. These costs are often used as the basis for pricing and bidding decisions. Economic theory suggests that prices are optimally set by equating marginal revenue and marginal cost. However, such an approach to pricing is costly because marginal-revenue and marginal-cost information is very difficult to obtain. Due to the cost of such information, firms often rely instead on pricing and bidding policies based on production cost plus some markup for profit.

Communicating the Costs of Internally Produced Services

Costs are also allocated as a means of communicating to the users of internally produced services that such services are costly. For example, the manager of a specific production line will have no control over the cost of the organization's accounting or legal staff. Yet it may prove useful to allocate these costs to individual managers to ensure they are aware of overhead costs that must be covered through sales if the organization is to prosper over time.[1]

Proxies for Externalities

Another possible reason for cost allocation is that allocated costs can serve as proxies or surrogates for various difficult-to-observe opportunity costs resulting from decentralization.[2]

> Consider the following simplified example. The firm leases from the telephone company a WATS (Wide Area Telephone Service) line for $3,800 per month, expecting to use the line 100 hours per month. This service allows the firm unlimited toll-free long distance calls within the United States. Although each individual long distance call is not billed by the phone company, only one call at a time can be placed. The $3,800 is a "fixed" cost; the "variable" cost of a call is zero. Should the firm allocate this $3,800 internally among the users?
>
> One argument goes that the cost should not be allocated, for any charge will discourage use and since the marginal cost is zero, the value of the resource is not being maximized. However, the "correct" marginal cost (i.e., the opportunity cost) of using the resource is not zero. It equals the cost imposed by forcing others who want to use the WATS line to either wait or place a regular toll call. Hence, the correct price to charge is the cost which the user imposes on others by tying up the scarce resource. But this cost varies between zero (if no one is delayed) to, at most, the cost of a regular toll call if a user cannot use the WATS line. This cost changes from instant to instant throughout the day. To measure it exactly is not easy,[3] requiring either a real-time information system or a sophisticated statistical analysis of hourly arrival rates, distribution of calls, etc. Both of these solutions are costly. An alternative to either charging a zero price or charging a price based on an elaborate (costly) system is to charge $38 per hour (i.e., a constant price based on the full allocated cost of the $3,800 divided by the expected utilization of 100 hours). A side benefit of such a full-cost allocation is that information is generated regarding the value of the service. If more than $3,800 in overhead is absorbed, the purchase of an additional WATS line should be investigated. If less than $3,800 is absorbed, then discontinuance of the service might be warranted.

The example illustrates the existence of opportunity costs that are hard to observe and to quantify. Cost allocations can be used to proxy for these opportunity costs. Further, these cost allocations can provide a means of pricing the resource to improve its use by the firm.

1. Zimmerman argues that cost allocation may be used to "tax" the consumers of internally produced services and thereby reduce consumption of these services. The argument relies on viewing managers as agents of the stockholders concerned with both their monetary rewards and the consumption of nonmonetary services (such as staff support or computer time). J. Zimmerman, "The Costs and Benefits of Cost Allocations," *Accounting Review* (July 1979): 504–21.

2. The example is taken from J. Zimmerman, "The Costs and Benefits of Cost Allocations," *Accounting Review* (July 1979): 504–21.

3. See R. J. Dolan, "Incentive Mechanisms for Priority Queuing Problems," unpublished manuscript, University of Chicago, 1977.

Widespread Use of Allocations

Whatever the reasons for cost allocations, their use is pervasive in almost all organizations. Such allocations are often justified and useful; in other cases they can be very misleading. Several illustrations of cost allocation issues follow.

Cost Allocation and Store Closing at A&P

An article in *Fortune* magazine reported that, due to a cost-allocation system that failed to reflect true costs, A&P executives could not determine whether some stores were profitable or not. Transportation costs, for example, were allocated equally to the stores in each marketing area without regard to each store's distance from the central warehouse. Such problems made it very difficult for the company's strategists to make rational decisions about store closings when the grocery chain experienced a decline in profits.[4]

Allocation of Corporate Interest Expense at General Electric

An article in *Forbes* reported that many companies prorate corporate interest expenses among their divisions, leading to intercorporate hostility. General Electric has recently changed its practices in this area. For nearly twenty years the company had allocated interest expenses to divisions based on changes in their overall asset position. Recently, GE began making a distinction between short-term and long-term investments. Divisions that use capital for new equipment and facilities are not charged as heavily for interest costs as those that use capital primarily for inventory. The new system, according to a GE consultant, provides an incentive to division managers to update old, inefficient plant and equipment, and to simultaneously reduce inventories. According to the GE consultant, the firm now gets better overall results.[5]

4. *Fortune* (November 6, 1978).
5. R. Morais, "None for Me, Thanks," *Forbes* (October 22, 1984): 134.

Allocation of Corporate Personnel, Legal, and Auditing Costs at J. C. Penney Co.

A *Business Week* article reported that J. C. Penney Co. recently adopted an allocation plan in which corporate costs for internally produced personnel, legal, and auditing services are allocated to J. C. Penney's subsidiaries on the basis of the actual time spent providing such services to the subsidiaries. The subsidiaries had previously been charged for these services on the basis of the revenues the subsidiaries generated. The subsidiaries had argued that they should be charged less for these services because they had their own departments for legal and personnel services. The new allocation system resulted in lower charges to the subsidiaries than they had previously been charged, but higher charges than they had argued for. The new plan was easily implemented.[6]

The following excerpt from an article in *Management Accounting* describes the cost allocation practices used by ARCO Oil and Gas Company, a division of Atlantic Richfield Company, at its oil operation in Prudhoe Bay, Alaska.

Cost Allocation by ARCO at Prudhoe Bay

Control of costs implies the ability to influence or change cost. Motivation to control costs falls off sharply as the ability to influence costs diminishes. If noncontrollable costs are reported under a given supervisor, he should be fully aware that he is not "responsible" for them.

At Prudhoe Bay, separation of controllable and noncontrollable costs became defined by the system of cost assignment peculiar to the operation. All costs are either charged directly to an end cost center or collected at an intermediate facility and allocated on an equitable basis. Maintenance personnel can charge time and materials directly where applied when identifiable. If not directly identifiable with a cost center, the costs are charged to the maintenance employee's shop cost center. These accumulated charges then are allocated based on direct labor hours incurred in the prior month. For purposes of the responsibility accounting system, we at AOGC determined that costs could be controlled only by a supervisor at the point of original charge. Costs that are further allocated were not considered controllable.[7]

6. "Teamwork Pays Off at Penney's," *Business Week* (April 12, 1982).

7. M. E. Scott, "ARCO Establishes Responsibility Accounting at Prudhoe Bay," *Management Accounting* (March 1980): 15.

Allocation of Service Department Costs

Service departments such as the power department, maintenance and repair, heat, and the cafeteria are necessary to production but not involved directly in the making of a product. To obtain the full cost of items produced, the costs of service departments must be allocated to the production departments as a first step in assigning these costs to units of production.

Three basic methods may be used to allocate service department costs:

1. Direct method,

2. Step-down method,

3. Reciprocal-services method.

In the direct allocation method, service department costs are allocated directly to producing departments. The fact that one service department renders service to another is ignored. This method is the most commonly employed approach. The step-down allocation method, widely used by hospitals, recognizes the service given by one service department to another service department. The step-down method can become quite involved where reciprocal services are involved. **Reciprocal services** occur when two or more service departments serve each other. The order in which the service department costs should be allocated must be established. The most common solution is to allocate first the costs of that service department that serves the greatest number of other service departments. An alternative (which could also be used in cases where no choice is indicated by the first solution) is to select first that service department with the largest total value to be allocated. Another method is to select for initial allocation the department that gives the greatest percentage of its service to other service departments versus production departments.

For example, let's assume that the ABC Company has five departments: three service departments and two producing departments. ABC Company allocates the costs of its service departments directly to its producing departments, ignoring the fact that one service department may use the services of another.

Here's a breakdown of the costs and usage of the three service departments of ABC Company:

EXHIBIT 14-3

ABC Company

Service Departments

| Department | Total $ Incurred | Service Use Measured by | Total Units Used | Usage by Department | | | | |
				A	B	S.D.I	S.D.II	S.D.III
Power (S.D.I)	$ 800	Kilowatt hours	1,000	600	200	0	100	100
Maintenance (S.D.II)	600	Labor hours	120	30	30	20	0	40
Building and grounds (S.D.III)	900	Square footage	100	75	25	0	0	0
	$2,300		1,220	705	255	20	100	140

As Exhibit 14-3 shows, of the total possible units of activity that were produced by the service departments (1,220), only 960 units were used by producing departments A and B (705 + 255). What happened to the other 260 units (1,220 − 960)? They were used up among the three service departments. But if the direct allocation method is used, the activity among the service departments is ignored. The total cost of the service department is allocated to the producing departments based on the ratio of their usage alone.

Direct Method

We want to allocate the total $2,300 of cost of the three service departments to the two producing departments. The first step is to determine the ratio of consumption for each producing department. The ratios for the direct method are determined as follows for operating department A:

Power (S.D.I)	$600 \div (600 + 200) = 6/8$	
Maintenance (S.D.II)	$30 \div (30 + 30)$	$= 3/6$
Building and grounds (S.D.III)	$75 \div (75 + 25)$	$= 3/4$

EXHIBIT 14-4

Direct Allocation Method

Service Departments	Total	Producing Departments			
		A		**B**	
		Ratio	Amount	Ratio	Amount
I	$ 800	6/8	$ 600	2/8	$ 200
II	600	3/6	300	3/6	300
III	900	3/4	675	1/4	225
Direct costs	2,200		1,000		1,200
Total costs	$4,500		$2,575		$1,925

Step-Down Method

The step-down allocation method, which recognizes the service given by one department to another, is illustrated in Exhibit 14-5. The cost of power (S.D.I) is allocated first because it has more cost to be allocated than maintenance (S.D.II). The allocation ratios for power (S.D.I) are

Power to Maintenance	$100/1,000 = 1/10$
Power to Building and grounds	$100/1,000 = 1/10$
Power to A	$600/1,000 = 6/10$
Power to B	$200/1,000 = 2/10$

The maintenance cost is allocated second. The total cost to be allocated is $680, which includes the $600 allocated from service department I (see Exhibit 14-5). The allocation ratios are calculated as follows:

Maintenance to Building and grounds $40/100 = 4/10$

Maintenance to A $30/100 = 3/10$

Maintenance to B $30/100 = 3/10$

No building and grounds costs are allocated to the power or maintenance, since building and grounds does not serve any other service departments. The ratios for building and grounds are given below:

Building and grounds to A 75/100

Building and grounds to B 25/100

No building and grounds costs are allocated to power or maintenance, since building and grounds does not serve any other service departments. The ratios for building and grounds are given below:

Reciprocal-Services Method

When two or more service departments serve each other, a more accurate allocation method is the reciprocal-services allocation method. In this method, each service department is allocated some of the cost of any other department from which it receives service. To simplify the calculations, this method is illustrated for only two service departments in the example to follow.

Assume that the building department cost should be allocated as follows (percentages are based on the use of floor space):

- 20 percent to repair department

- 70 percent to producing department 1

- 10 percent to producing department 2

EXHIBIT 14-5

Step-Down Allocation Method

	Service Department				Producing Department				
	Maintenance		Building and Grounds		A		B		
Service Department	Ratio	Amount	Ratio	Amount	Ratio	Amount	Ratio	Amount	Total
Power	1/10	$ 80	1/10	$ 80	6/10	$ 480	2/10	$ 160	$ 800
Maintenance[a]			4/10	272	3/10	204	3/10	204	680
Building and grounds[b]					3/4	939	1/4	313	1,252
Traceable costs		600		900		1,000		1,200	
Total		$680		$1,252		$2,623		$1,877	

[a] $600 + $80 is allocated.

[b] $900 + $80 + $272 is allocated.

The repair department should be allocated as follows (percentages are based on this period's repairs):

- 80 percent to building department

- 20 percent to producing department 1

The traceable costs incurred in the building department were $5,960. The traceable costs incurred in the repair department were $2,000. Thus, the total costs to be allocated are $7,960 ($5,960 + $2,000). Computation of the total costs of the building and repair departments, and the allocation of these costs to the two operating departments, is shown below.

B = total building costs (costs incurred directly in the building department plus the allocation from the repair shop)

R = total repair costs (costs incurred directly in repair shop plus the allocation from the building department)

Then, the following equations specify the cost and service relationships among the departments.

$$B = 5,960 + 0.8R$$
$$R = 2,000 + 0.2B$$

The next step is to solve for B and R.

$$
\begin{aligned}
B &= 5,960 + 0.8R \\
  &= 5,960 + 0.8(2,000 + 0.2B) \\
  &= 5,960 + 1,600 + 0.16B \\
0.84B &= 7,560 \\
B &= \$9,000 \text{ (``total'' building department cost)} \\
R &= 2,000 + 0.2B \\
  &= 2,000 + (0.2 \times 9,000) \\
  &= \$3,800 \text{ (``total'' repair department cost)}
\end{aligned}
$$

Finally, the "total" costs of the building and repair departments are each allocated to the remaining three departments. The results are shown in Exhibit 14-6.

The total of the building department cost ($9,000) and the repair department cost ($3,800) is greater than the total cost incurred in the two departments ($7,960). This occurs because of the reallocation of building cost to the repair department and then repair cost back to the building department, and so on. The total overhead allocated to the operating departments is $7,960, which is equal to the costs incurred in the two service departments ($5,960 plus $2,000).

The journal entries to record the allocation of the service department costs are shown on the following page.

Overhead — repair department	1,800	
Overhead — producing department 1	6,300	
Overhead — producing department 2	900	
Overhead — building		9,000
Overhead — building	3,040	
Overhead — producing department 1	760	
Overhead — repair department		3,800

Dual Allocation

A refinement of the three allocation procedures discussed above is to treat variable and fixed costs separately. This "dual" allocation approach can be used in combination with the direct, step-down, or reciprocal-services methods of service department cost allocation. The rationale behind dual allocation is that the proportions of a service department's output used by various other departments in the short run may be quite different from the proportions used by those departments in the long run. Because the scope and size of service facilities are often designed to satisfy the long-run needs of the using departments, there is some merit to using the long-run usage proportions to allocate service department costs that are incurred because of the size and scope of the service facility. Short-run usage proportions are used to allocate the costs incurred in the service department due to current usage. Most of the costs due to the scale and size of the service facility are fixed costs, whereas variable costs are generally incurred as a result of short-run usage. Thus, under dual allocation fixed costs are allocated using long-run usage proportions, and variable costs are allocated using short-run usage proportions.

We illustrate the dual allocation approach in combination with the direct allocation method. The data for the illustration are given in Exhibit 14-7.

EXHIBIT 14-6

Reciprocal-Services Allocation Method

	Service Department		Producing Department	
	Building Department	Repair Department	Department I	Department II
Traceable costs before allocation	$5,960	$2,000		
Building department	(9,000)	1,800 (20%)	$6,300 (70%)	$900 (10%)
Repair department	3,040 (80%)	(3,800)	760 (20%)	
	$ 0	$ 0	$7,060	$900

Total costs
allocated   = $7,960

EXHIBIT 14-7
Data for Dual Allocation Illustration

| | Users of Service | | | |
| | Service Departments | | Producing Departments | |
Providers of Service	I	II	A	B
Service department I:				
Proportion of output consumed in the current period	—	.25	.15	.60
Proportion of output consumed in the long run	—	.20	.30	.50
Service department II:				
Proportion of output consumed in the current period	.10	—	.80	.10
Proportion of output consumed in the long run	.50	—	.40	.10
Variable cost	$ 4,000	$ 9,000		
Fixed cost	20,000	32,000		
Total cost	$24,000	$41,000		

The results of applying dual allocation in combination with the direct method are shown in Exhibit 14-8. Because the direct method is being used, no service department costs are allocated to either service department. The service department costs are allocated to the producing departments in proportion to the producing departments' service-usage proportions. Variable costs are allocated using short-run proportions, and fixed costs are allocated using long-run proportions.

EXHIBIT 14-8
Dual Allocation in Combination with the Direct Allocation Method

| Service Departments | Variable Cost Allocation | | | | Fixed Cost Allocation | | | | Total Costs |
| | A | | B | | A | | B | | |
	Ratio	Amount	Ratio	Amount	Ratio	Amount	Ratio	Amount	
I	15/75	$ 800	60/75	$3,200	30/80	$ 7,500	50/80	$12,500	$24,000
II	80/90	8,000	10/90	1,000	40/50	25,600	10/50	6,400	41,000
Total service department cost allocated									$65,000

The dual allocation approach may be used in combination with the step-down and reciprocal-services allocation method also. The techniques are applied exactly as illustrated earlier, but variable costs are allocated using short-run usage proportions and fixed costs are allocated using long-run usage proportions.

The dual allocation approach can provide a better picture of the full cost of operating each producing department because service department costs are allocated on the basis of why those costs are being incurred. Since dual allocation provides a clearer picture of the cost of operating producing departments, it also yields more accurate product costs.

Dual allocation provides an incentive for producing department managers to understate their departments' long-run service needs in order to ensure a lower proportion is used in allocating fixed service department costs to their departments. If these understatements are significant, they can lead to faulty decisions about the optimal size and scale of service facilities. For example, an organization may acquire too small a computer if the using department managers have understated their long-run service needs. The possibility of this dysfunctional result can be minimized by instituting a cost penalty to a using department for short-run consumption of service-department output that is above the using department's stated long-run needs. This approach, however, may discourage a using department manager from consuming the optimal amount of service in the short run in those instances when short-run needs are greater than long-run average needs. For example, a manager may decide not to use the computing department's services, when it would actually be in the best interests of the organization for those services to be used.

Probably the only way to avoid dysfunctional behavioral consequences from service department cost allocation is to be sure that departmental managers are evaluated on costs that do not include such allocations. Thus, cost allocation would be used for product-costing purposes but not for control and incentive purposes.

Service-Department Cost Allocation at Mayo Clinic

On the following page is an illustration of service-department cost allocation provided by Mayo Clinic. Mayo Clinic is a world-renowned health care facility operated by the Mayo Foundation and located in Rochester, Minnesota. Mayo Clinic allocates the costs of its administrative and support services (referred to as overhead) using the step-down method of cost allocation. The sequence begins with the cost center that renders service to the greatest number of cost centers. The telephone cost center is allocated first, then accounting, then library, and finally clinical support services. Clinical support services performs numerous patient care functions ranging from scheduling patient appointments to billing and collections. Mayo Clinic employs two bases for allocating its overhead: full time equivalents (FTEs) and dollars of patient care revenue (bookings). An example of how the step-down method works is shown in Exhibit 14-9.

EXHIBIT 14-9

Example of Step-Down Cost Allocation at Mayo Clinic

mayo

	Telephone	Accounting	Library	Clinical Support Services	Patient Care Department		Total
					Surgery	Lab	
Number of FTEs	40	30	30	100	500	200	900
Patient care revenue	—	—	—	—	$30,000	$16,000	$46,000
Costs before allocation of overhead	$500	$400	$700	$1,200	$24,000	$13,000	$39,800
Allocations:							
Telephone	($500)	$ 17	$ 17	$ 58	$ 293	$ 115	—
Basis: FTEs							
Numerator of allocation ratio		30	30	100	500	200	
Denominator of allocation ratio		860	860	860	860	860	
Accounting		($417)	$ 15	$ 50	$ 252	$ 100	—
Basis: FTEs							
Numerator of allocation ratio			30	100	500	200	
Denominator of allocation ratio			830	830	830	830	
Library			($732)	$ 92	$ 457	$ 183	—
Basis: FTEs							
Numerator of allocation ratio				100	500	200	
Denominator of allocation ratio				800	800	800	
Clinical support services				($1,400)	$ 913	$ 487	—
Basis: Bookings							
Numerator of allocation ratio					$30,000	$16,000	
Denominator of allocation ratio					$46,000	$46,000	
Total department costs including overhead	—	—	—	—	$25,915	$13,885	$39,800

Summary

Cost allocation pervades almost all organizations. Allocation is used to determine full product costs for pricing bidding, cost reimbursement, inventory valuation, and determination of cost of goods sold. Allocations also can communicate to users the costs of internally produced services and can act as proxies for difficult-to-estimate opportunity costs. Common methods of service department cost allocation include the direct, step-down, and reciprocal services methods. The dual approach to cost allocation may be used in combination with any of these methods. There can be important behavioral implications of cost allocations, and these must be taken into account in designing a cost accounting system. In most cases, allocations should be removed from cost data before the data is used for economic decision making.

Key Terms to Review

cost allocation, p. 500   cost pool, p. 500
cost objective, p. 500   reciprocal services, p. 506

Review Problem

COST ALLOCATION

Consider the following service department situation and establish the cost allocation based on the step-down approach.

Department Providing Service	Measure of Service	Department Cost ($000 omitted)	Service Used by Department[a]					
			S.D.I	S.D.II	S.D.III	PI	PII	Total
S.D.I	Labor dollars	100	—	20	40	70	70	200
S.D.II	Labor hours	200	40	—	120	120	120	400
S.D.III	Units serviced	400	160	240	—	200	200	800

[a] P stands for production department.

Solution to Review Problem

S.D.III is selected first because it has the largest cost to distribute. Then S.D.II is allocated second.

S.D.III to S.D.I $(160/800)\$400 = \$\ 80$

S.D.III to S.D.II $(240/800)\$400 = \$120$

S.D.III to PI $(200/800)\$400 = \$100$

S.D.III to PII $(200/800)\$400 = \$100$

There is now $200 + $120 of costs in S.D.II to allocate.

S.D.II to SI $(40/280)(\$200 + \$120) = \$\ 45.71$

S.D.II to PI $(120/280)(\$200 + \$120) = \$137.14$

S.D.II to PII $(120/280)(\$200 + \$120) = \$137.14$

There is now $100 + $80 + $45.71 of costs in S.D.I to allocate.

S.D.I to PI $(70/140)(\$100 + \$80 + \$45.71) = \$112.85$

S.D.I to PII $(70/140)(\$100 + \$80 + \$45.71) = \$112.85$

This yields the total costs to each of the two producing departments of

$100 + 137.14 + 112.85 = \$350$

Because each service department provides the same ratio of service to each of the production departments (50–50 here), the solution can be obtained by adding the total cost of the three service departments to be allocated and multiplying by the ratio:

Cost allocated to PI   ($100 + $200 + $400)1/2 = $350

Cost allocated to PII   ($100 + $200 + $400)1/2 = $350

The reciprocal service ratios between service departments will not matter. The reciprocal allocation method yields the same result. This case is, however, a very special one.

APPENDIX
Cost Accounting Standards Board

The Cost Accounting Standards Board (CASB) was chartered by the United States Congress in 1970 as a federal agency. The CASB was created in response to large cost overruns by defense contractors and spent ten years establishing cost accounting standards that must be used by defense contractors to determine contract costs for contracts priced on a cost-reimbursement or cost-plus basis. The CASB developed costing standards for a wide range of issues including the allocation of administrative costs, research and development costs, and pension costs. The charter of the CASB was not renewed by Congress in 1980 because its work was largely completed. However, the CASB regulations remain in effect and have the force of federal law. Opinions by cost accounting experts in government and industry on the success of the CASB vary.

Cost Accounting Standards Board	A *Business Week* article reported that many people, including Senator William Proxmire (Democrat-Wisconsin) lamented the termination of the CASB since it was unclear who would then enforce the agency's standards. Others, however, scoffed at claims that the CASB saved the government money on defense contracts. Some people claimed that the CASB disrupted the procurement process and actually cost the taxpayers money due to the expenses of ensuring compliance with the regulations.[8]

Nineteen of the cost accounting standards issued by the CASB during its ten-year life are still in effect. They are listed in Exhibit 14-10.

The Federal Acquisition Regulation, effective since 1984, governs the cost accounting procedures that must be followed by contractors selling to the federal government. The cost accounting standards issued by the CASB provide the detail for these accounting practices. The production costs referred to in cost-reimbursement or cost-plus contracts, which govern many major federal purchases, must be calculated in accordance with these standards. In a cost-reimbursement or cost-plus contract, the contractor is allowed to recover the actual costs incurred in completing the contract.

8. "Can a Dead Watchdog Growl" *Business Week* (March 2, 1981).

EXHIBIT 14-10

Cost Accounting Standards Issued by CASB

CAS	401	Consistency in Estimating, Accumulating and Reporting Costs
CAS	402	Consistency in Allocating Costs Incurred for the Same Purpose
CAS	403	Allocation of Home Office Expenses to Segments
CAS	404	Capitalization of Tangible Assets
CAS	405	Accounting for Unallowable Costs
CAS	406	Cost Accounting Period
CAS	407	Use of Standard Cost for Direct Material and Direct Labor
CAS	408	Accounting for Costs of Compensated Personal Absence
CAS	409	Depreciation of Tangible Capital Assets
CAS	410	Allocation of Business Unit General and Administrative Expense to Final Cost Objectives
CAS	411	Accounting for Acquisition Costs of Material
CAS	412	Composition and Measurement of Pension Costs
CAS	413	Adjustment and Allocation of Pension Cost
CAS	414	Cost of Money as an Element of the Cost of Facilities Capital
CAS	415	Accounting for the Cost of Deferred Compensation
CAS	416	Accounting for Insurance Costs
CAS	417	Cost of Money as an Element of the Cost of Capital Assets under Construction
CAS	418	Allocation of Direct and Indirect Costs
CAS	420	Accounting for Independent Research and Development Costs and Bid and Proposal Costs

---

Procedures for allocating costs are specified in several of the CASB's cost accounting standards. For example, CAS 418 covers the allocation of direct and indirect costs, CAS 410 specifies allocation procedures for general and administrative expenses, and CAS 403 covers the allocation of home office expenses. In these standards, the CASB specified the allowable allocation bases for various types of expenses. For example, CAS 403 suggests that personnel administration costs be allocated to segments of the company on the basis of the number of personnel employed in those segments.

Suggested Readings

Atkinson, A. *Intrafirm Cost and Revenue Allocations: Theory and Practice.* Society of Management Accountants of Canada and Canadian Academic Accounting Association Research Monograph, 1987.

Baiman, S., and J. Noel. "Noncontrollable Costs and Responsibility Accounting." *Journal of Accounting Research* (Autumn 1985): 486–501.

Clark, J. M. *Studies in the Economics of Overhead Costs.* Chicago: University of Chicago Press, 1923.

Demski, J. "Cost Allocation Games." In S. Moriarity, ed., *Joint Cost Allocations.* Norman: University of Oklahoma, 1981.

Demski, J., and G. Feltham. *Cost Determination: A Conceptual Approach.* Iowa City, Iowa: Iowa State Press, 1976.

Dopuch, N. "Some Perspectives on Cost Allocations." In *Joint Cost Allocations.* Norman: University of Oklahoma, 1981.

Finkler, S. "The Future of Product Costing and Cost Allocation." *Hospital Cost Accounting Advisor* (June 1985).

Fremgen, J., and S. Liao. *The Allocation of Corporate Indirect Costs.* New York: National Association of Accountants, 1981.

Hamlen, S. S., and W. A. Hamlen. "The Concept of Fairness in the Choice of Joint Cost Allocation." In S. Moriarity, ed., *Joint Cost Allocations.* Norman: University of Oklahoma, 1981.

Haskins, T., and D. Crum. "Cost Allocations: A Classroom Role Play in Managerial Behavior and Accounting Choices." *Issues in Accounting Education* (1985): 109–30.

Jensen, M. C., and W. H. Meckling, "Theory of the Firm: Managerial Behavior, Agency Costs and Ownership Structure." *Journal of Financial Economics* (October 1976): 305–60.

Kaplan, R. "Application of Quantitative Models in Managerial Accounting: A State-of-the-Art Survey." In *Management Accounting — State of the Art.* University of Wisconsin Press (January 25, 1977): 30–71.

Kaplan, R., and U. P. Welam. "Overhead Allocation with Imperfect Markets and Non-Linear Technology." *Accounting Review* (July 1974): 477–84.

Moriarity, S. "Some Rationales for Cost Allocations." In S. Moriarity, ed., *Joint Cost Allocations.* Norman: University of Oklahoma, 1981.

Thomas, A. "The Allocation Problem in Financial Accounting Theory." Sarasota, Fla.: American Accounting Association, 1969.

———. "The Allocation Problem: Part II." Sarasota, Fla.: American Accounting Association, 1974.

———. *A Behavioral Analysis of Joint-Cost Allocation and Transfer Pricing.* Stipes, 1980.

Young, H. P., ed. *Cost Allocation: Methods, Principles, Applications.* Elsevier Science Publishers B.V. (North Holland), 1985.

Zimmerman, J. "The Costs and Benefits of Cost Allocations." *Accounting Review* (July 1979): 504–21.

Review Questions

14-1 Define the term *cost allocation.*

14-2 Define the terms *cost pool* and *cost objective.* Give an example of each.

14-3 What are some purposes of allocation?

14-4 Give an example of allocation in financial accounting.

14-5 What is meant by *reciprocal services?*

14-6 What is the purpose of dual allocation?

14-7 Describe a potential behavioral problem resulting from dual allocation.

14-8 What is an allocation base?

14-9 A single basis for allocation of one service department's costs is not theoretically justifiable. Do you agree? If not, why not? If so, then why is a single basis the most common method for allocation of such costs?

14-10 Briefly explain the intended purpose of the CASB.

Exercises

14-11 Reciprocal-Services Allocation Method The Tompkins Corporation has two operating departments and two service departments. The building department is allocated as follows:

- 10 percent to utility department
- 45 percent to operating department 1
- 45 percent to operating department 2

The utility department should be allocated as follows:

- 50 percent to building department
- 40 percent to operating department 1
- 10 percent to operating department 2

The costs incurred in the building department were $90,000; in the utility department, $10,000.

REQUIRED:

a. Compute the allocation of the service departments and prepare journal entries to accomplish the allocation to the operating departments. Use the reciprocal-services allocation method.

b. Discuss the usefulness of the allocation from the point of view of controlling costs and determining unit costs of product.

14-12 Direct Method of Allocation Hartwell Company charges its service department overhead costs directly to producing departments without allocation to the other service department. Information for the month of January is shown below.

	Service Departments	
	Maintenance	*Utilities*
Overhead costs incurred	$18,700	$9,000
Service provided to:		
Maintenance department	—	10%
Utilities department	20%	—
Producing department *A*	40%	30%
Producing department *B*	40%	60%
Total	100%	100%

What amount of utilities department costs should be charged to producing department B for January? (*CPA adapted*)

14-13 Direct Method of Allocation   Given the service relationships in the following table, allocate costs to the producing departments using the direct method of allocation.

From:	To: Producing Department A	Producing Department B	Service Department 1	Service Department 2	Service Department 3
Operating department A	100%	—	—	—	—
Operating department B	—	100%	—	—	—
Service department 1	30%	30%	—	10%	30%
Service department 2	20%	40%	20%	—	20%
Service department 3	50%	20%	20%	10%	—
Total period costs	$40,000	$35,000	$10,000	$4,500	$9,500

14-14 Step-Down Allocation Method   Refer to the data given for Exercise 14-13. Use the step-down method to allocate the service-department costs. Allocate the service-department costs in the order of the department that yields the greatest percentage of its service to the producing departments.

14-15 Step-Down Allocation Method   Refer to the data given for Exercise 14-13. Use the step-down method to allocate the service-department costs. Allocate the service-department costs in the order of the department with the greatest cost to be allocated.

14-16 Step-Down Allocation Method   Refer to the data given for Exercise 14-13. Use the step-down method to allocate the service-department costs. Allocate the service-department costs in the order of the service department with the least cost to be allocated.

14-17 Step-Down Allocation Method   Refer to the data given for Exercise 14-13.

  a. Allocate the service department costs in order of which service department has the greatest absolute difference between what is owed to it by other service departments less what it owes other service departments.

  b. Repeat **a** using the inverse order to allocate the costs of service departments.

14-18 Evaluation of Allocation Methods   Which service-department cost allocation method do you believe to be the best? Why?

14-19 Direct Allocation Method   The Palmer Company has two service departments and two production departments. The costs and usage of services in these departments follows.

| | Using Department | | | |
| | Service Departments | | Production Departments | |
Supplying Department	S1	S2	P1	P2
S1	—	50%	20%	30%
S2	40%	—	20%	40%
Traceable costs	$10,000	$20,000	$40,000	$60,000

REQUIRED:

Allocate the service-department costs to the producing departments using the direct method.

14-20 Step-Down Allocation Method Refer to the data given for Exercise 14-19. Allocate the service-department costs using the step-down allocation method. Allocate the costs of service department S1 first.

14-21 Reciprocal Services Allocation Method Refer to the data given for Exercise 14-19. Allocate the service-department costs using the reciprocal-services allocation method.

14-22 Direct Allocation and Dual Allocation Methods Refer to the data given for Exercise 14-19. The usage percentages provided there relate to the short-run usage of service-department output. The long-run rates of usage are expected to be as follows:

| | Using Department | | | |
| | Service Departments | | Production Departments | |
Supplying Department	S1	S2	P1	P2
S1	—	50%	10%	40%
S2	50%	—	25%	25%

Half of the traceable costs indicated in Exercise 14-19 for each department are variable costs, and half are fixed costs.

REQUIRED:

Allocate the service-department costs using the direct method combined with the dual method.

14-23 Step-Down Allocation and Dual Allocation Methods Refer to the data given for Exercise 14-19. The usage percentages provided there relate to the short-run usage of service-department output. The long-run rates of usage are expected to be as follows:

	Using Department			
	Service Departments		Production Departments	
Supplying Department	S1	S2	P1	P2
S1	—	50%	10%	40%
S2	50%	—	25%	25%

Half of the traceable costs indicated in Exercise 14-19 for each department are variable costs, and half are fixed costs.

REQUIRED:

Allocate the service-department costs using the step-down method (S1 first) combined with the dual method.

Problems

14-24 Step-Down Cost Allocation The Havid Crimson Corporation mass produces certain standardized-quality products that are consumed by large businesses. Each of its two main products is produced in a separate department. Product Embiary is manufactured in the Beeskule Department, which employs sixty laborers, and product Jaydee is manufactured in the Ellskule Department, which employs sixty-five laborers.

A recent financial squeeze has caused management to desire to know the "full cost" of its products. This information will then be used in an attempt to justify proposed higher prices. Therefore, they want to have the costs of their service departments allocated to the operating departments.

The manager of building and grounds reported that in the last period 25,000 workhours were spent taking care of the Beeskule Department and 20,000 workhours were used by the Ellskule. The employee cafeteria requires 5,000 workhours for maintenance. The total actual expenses of building and grounds was $150,000 during that period and this division employed twenty-five people.

It was reported by the utilities manager that his division, which employed ten, had total expenses of $120,000 during that period. It was further reported that building and grounds had consumed 30,000 kilowatt hours of power; the cafeteria had used 10,000 kilowatt hours; the Beeskule used 40,000 kilowatt hours; and the Ellskule used 40,000 kilowatt hours.

The manager of the cafeteria reported that his total expenses for this period were $80,000.

REQUIRED:

Given that the manufacturing expenses for the Beeskule and the Ellskule were $230,000 and $310,000, respectively, compute the total costs allocating those of the service departments in the step-down method. Allocate first by number of departments serviced and second using department cost.

14-25 Allocation Procedures   Columbia Company is a regional office-supply chain with twenty-six independent stores. Each store has been responsible for its own credit and collections. The assistant manager in each store is assigned the responsibility for credit activities including the collection of delinquent accounts because the stores do not need a full-time employee assigned to credit activities. The company has experienced a sharp rise in uncollectibles the last two years. Corporate management has decided to establish a collections department in the home office to be responsible for the collection function companywide. The home office of Columbia Company will hire the necessary full-time personnel. The size of this department will be based on the historical credit activity of all of the stores.

The new centralized collections department was discussed at a recent management meeting. A method to assign the costs of the new department to the stores has been difficult because this type of home office service is somewhat unique. Alternative methods are being reviewed by top management.

The controller favored using a predetermined or standard rate for charging the costs to the stores. The predetermined rate would be based on budgeted costs. The vice president of sales had a strong preference for an actual-cost charging system.

In addition, the basis for the collection charges to the stores was also discussed. The controller identified the following four measures of services (allocation bases) that could be used:

1. Total dollar sales,

2. Average number of past-due accounts,

3. Number of uncollectible accounts written off,

4. One twenty-sixth of the cost to each of the stores.

The executive vice-president stated that he would like the accounting department to prepare a detailed analysis of the two charging methods and the four service measures (allocation bases).

REQUIRED:

a. Evaluate the two methods identified (predetermined (standard) rate versus actual cost) that could be used to charge the individual stores the costs of Columbia Company's new collections department in terms of

(1) Practicality of application and ease of use, and

(2) Cost control.

Also indicate whether a centralized or decentralized type of organization structure would be more conducive for each charging method.

b. For each of the four measures of services (allocation bases) identified by the Controller of Columbia Company,

(1) Discuss whether the service measure (allocation base) is appropriate to use in this situation, and

(2) Identify the behavioral problems, if any, that could arise as a consequence of adopting the service measure (allocation base). (*CMA adapted*)

14-26 Overhead Allocation Herbert Manufacturing Co. is a manufacturer of custom-designed restaurant and kitchen furniture. Herbert Manufacturing uses a job-order cost accounting system. Actual overhead costs incurred during the month are applied to the products on the basis of actual direct labor hours required to produce the products. The overhead consists primarily of supervision, employee benefits, maintenance costs, property taxes, and depreciation.

Herbert Manufacturing recently won a contract to manufacture the furniture for a new fast-food chain, which is expanding rapidly in the area. In general, this furniture is durable but of a lower quality than Herbert Manufacturing normally manufactures. To produce this new line, Herbert Manufacturing must purchase more molded plastic parts for the furniture than for its current line. Through innovative industrial engineering, an efficient manufacturing process for this new furniture has been developed that requires only a minimum capital investment. Management is very optimistic about the profit improvement the new product line will bring.

At the end of October, the start-up month for the new line, the controller has prepared a separate income statement for the new product line. On a consolidated basis the gross profit percentage was normal; however, the profitability for the new line was less than expected.

At the end of November the results were somewhat improved. Consolidated profits were good, but the reported profitability for the new product line was less than expected. John Herbert, president of the corporation, is concerned that knowledgeable stockholders will criticize his decision to add this lower-quality product line at a time when profitability appeared to be increasing with their standard product line.

The results as published for the first nine months, for October, and for November follow.

HERBERT MANUFACTURING COMPANY
(000s omitted)

	Fast Food Furniture	Custom Furniture	Consolidated
Nine months, year-to-date, 19x8:			
Gross sales	—	$8,100	$8,100
Direct material	—	$2,025	$2,025
Direct labor:			
Forming	—	758	758
Finishing	—	1,314	1,314
Assembly	—	558	558
Overhead	—	1,779	1,779
Cost of sales	—	$6,434	$6,434
Gross profit	—	$1,666	$1,666
Gross profit percentage	—	20.6%	20.6%
October 19x8:			
Gross sales	$400	$ 900	$1,300
Direct material	$200	$ 225	$ 425
Direct labor:			
Forming	17	82	99
Finishing	40	142	182
Assembly	33	60	93
Overhead	60	180	240
Cost of sales	$350	$ 689	$1,039
Gross profit	$ 50	$ 211	$ 261
Gross profit percentage	12.5%	23.4%	20.1%
November 19x8:			
Gross sales	$800	$ 800	$1,600
Direct material	$400	$ 200	$ 600
Direct labor:			
Forming	31	72	103
Finishing	70	125	195
Assembly	58	53	111
Overhead	98	147	245
Cost of sales	$657	$ 597	$1,254
Gross profit	$143	$ 203	$ 346
Gross profit percentage	17.9%	25.4%	21.6%

Ms. Jameson, cost accounting manager, has stated that the overhead allocation based only on direct labor hours is no longer appropriate. On the basis of a recently completed study of the overhead accounts, Ms. Jameson feels that only the supervision and employee benefits should be allocated on the basis of direct labor hours and the balance of the overhead should be allocated on a machine-hour basis. In her judgment the increase in the profitability of the custom-design furniture is due to a misallocation of overhead in the present system.

The actual direct labor hours and machine hours for the past two months are shown below.

	Fast Food Furniture	Custom Furniture
Machine hours:		
October		
Forming	660	10,700
Finishing	660	7,780
Assembly	—	—
	1,320	18,480
November:		
Forming	1,280	9,640
Finishing	1,280	7,400
Assembly	—	—
	2,560	17,040
Direct labor hours:		
October:		
Forming	1,900	9,300
Finishing	3,350	12,000
Assembly	4,750	8,700
	10,000	30,000
November:		
Forming	3,400	8,250
Finishing	5,800	10,400
Assembly	8,300	7,600
	17,500	26,250

The actual overhead costs for the past two months were

	October	November
Supervision	$ 13,000	$ 13,000
Employee benefits	95,000	109,500
Maintenance	50,000	48,000
Depreciation	42,000	42,000
Property taxes	8,000	8,000
All other	32,000	24,500
Total	$240,000	$245,000

REQUIRED:

a. Based on Ms. Jameson's recommendation, allocate the overhead for October and November using direct labor hours as the allocation base for supervision and employee benefits. Use machine hours as the base for the remaining overhead costs.

b. Support or criticize Ms. Jameson's conclusion that the increase in custom-design profitability is due to a misallocation of overhead. Use the data developed in requirement **a** to support your analysis.

c. Ms. Jameson has also recommended that consideration be given to using predetermined overhead absorption rates calculated on an annual basis rather than allocating actual costs over actual volume each month. She stated that this is particularly applicable now that the company has two distinct product lines. Discuss the advantages of predetermined overhead rates. (*CMA adapted*)

14-27 **Allocation of Data Processing Costs**   The Independent Underwriters Insurance Co. (IUI) established a Systems Department two years ago to implement and operate its own data processing systems. IUI believed that its own system would be more cost effective than the service bureau it had been using.

IUI's three other departments — Claims, Records, and Finance — have different requirements with respect to hardware and other capacity-related resources and operating resources. The system was designed to accommodate these differing needs. In addition, the system was designed to meet IUI's long-term capacity needs. The excess capacity designed into the system would be sold to outside users until needed by IUI. The estimated resource requirements used to design and implement the system are shown in the following schedule.

	Hardware and Other Capacity-Related Resources	Operating Resources
Records	30%	60%
Claims	50	20
Finance	15	15
Expansion (outside use)	5	5
Total	100%	100%

IUI currently sells the equivalent of its expansion capacity to a few outside clients.

At the time the system became operational, management decided to redistribute total expenses of the Systems Department to the user departments based on actual computer time used. The actual costs for the first quarter of the current fiscal year were distributed to the user departments as follows:

Department	Percentage Utilization	Amount
Records	60%	$330,000
Claims	20	110,000
Finance	15	82,500
Outside	5	27,500
Total	100%	$550,000

The three user departments have complained about the cost distribution method since the Systems Department was established. The Records Department's monthly costs have been as much as three times the costs experienced with the service bureau. The Finance Department is concerned about the costs distributed to the outsider-user category because these allocated costs form the basis for the fees billed to the outside clients.

James Dale, IUI's controller, decided to review the distribution method by which the Systems Department's costs have been allocated for the past two years. The additional information he gathered for his review is reported in Exhibits 14-11, 14-12, and 14-13.

Dale has concluded that the method of cost distribution should be changed to reflect more directly the actual benefits received by the departments. He believes that the hardware and capacity-related costs should be allocated to the user departments in proportion to the planned, long-term needs. Any difference between actual and budgeted hardware costs would not be allocated to the departments but remain with the Systems Department.

The remaining costs for software development and operations would be charged to the user departments based on actual hours used. A predetermined hourly rate based on the annual budget data would be used. The hourly rates that would be used for the current fiscal year are shown below.

Function	Hourly Rate
Software development	$ 30
Operations:	
Computer related	$200
Input/output related	$ 10

Dale plans to use first-quarter activity and cost data to illustrate his recommendations. The recommendations will be presented to the Systems Department and the user departments for their comments and reactions. He then expects to present his recommendations to management for approval.

REQUIRED:

a. Calculate the amount of data processing costs that would be included in the Claims Department's first-quarter budget according to the method James Dale has recommended.

b. Prepare a schedule to show how the actual first-quarter costs of the Systems Department would be charged to the users if James Dale's recommended method was adopted.

EXHIBIT 14-11

Systems Department Costs and Activity Levels

| | Annual Budget | | First Quarter | | | |
| | | | Budget | | Actual | |
	Hours	Dollars	Hours	Dollars	Hours	Dollars
Hardware and other capacity-related costs	—	$ 600,000	—	$150,000	—	$155,000
Software development	18,750	562,500	4,725	141,750	4,250	130,000
Operations:						
Computer related	3,750	750,000	945	189,000	920	187,000
Input/output related	30,000	300,000	7,560	75,600	7,900	78,000
		$2,212,500		$556,350		$550,000

EXHIBIT 14-12

Historical Utilization by Users

| | Hardware and Other Capacity Needs | Software Development | | Operations | | | |
| | | | | Computer | | Input/Output | |
		Range	Average	Range	Average	Range	Average
Records	30%	0–30%	12%	55–65%	60%	10–30%	20%
Claims	50	15–60	35	10–25	20	60–80	70
Finance	15	25–75	45	10–25	15	3–10	6
Outside	5	0–25	8	3–8	5	3–10	4
	100%		100%		100%		100%

EXHIBIT 14-13

Utilization of Systems Department's Services in Hours, First Quarter

| | Software Development | Operations | |
		Computer Related	Input/ Output
Records	425	552	1,580
Claims	1,700	184	5,530
Finance	1,700	138	395
Outside	425	46	395
Total	4,250	920	7,900

c. Explain whether James Dale's recommended system for charging costs to the user departments will

(1) Improve cost control in the Systems Department,

(2) Improve planning and cost control in the user departments,

(3) Be a more equitable basis for charging costs to user departments. (*CMA adapted*)

14-28 **Plantwide versus Departmental Overhead Rates** MumsDay Corporation manufactures a complete line of fiberglass attaché cases and suitcases. MumsDay has three manufacturing departments — Molding, Component, and Assembly — and two service departments — Power and Maintenance.

The sides of the cases are manufactured in the Molding Department. The frames, hinges, locks, and so forth are manufactured in the Component Department. The cases are completed in the Assembly Department. Varying amounts of materials, time, and effort are required for each of the various cases. The Power Department and Maintenance Department provide services to the three manufacturing departments.

MumsDay has always used a plantwide overhead rate. Direct labor hours are used to assign the overhead to its product. The predetermined rate is calculated by dividing the company's total estimated overhead by the total estimated direct labor hours to be worked in the three manufacturing departments.

Whit Portlock, manager of cost accounting, has recommended that MumsDay use departmental overhead rates. The planned operating costs and expected levels of activity for the coming year have been developed by Portlock and are presented by department in the following schedules.

	Manufacturing Departments (000s omitted)		
	Molding	Component	Assembly
Departmental activity measures:			
Direct labor hours	500	2,000	1,500
Machine hours	875	125	–0–
Departmental costs:			
Raw materials	$12,400	$30,000	$ 1,250
Direct labor	3,500	20,000	12,000
Variable overhead	3,500	10,000	16,500
Fixed overhead	17,500	6,200	6,100
Total departmental costs	$36,900	$66,200	$35,850
Use of service departments:			
Maintenance:			
Estimated usage in labor hours for coming year	90	25	10
Power (in kilowatt hours):			
Estimated usage for coming year	360	320	120
Maximum allotted capacity	500	350	150

	Service Departments	
	Power	*Maintenance*
Departmental activity measures:		
Maximum capacity	1,000 KWH	Adjustable
Estimated usage in coming year	800 KWH	125 hours
Departmental costs:		
Materials and supplies	$ 5,000	$1,500
Variable labor	1,400	2,250
Fixed overhead	12,000	250
Total service department costs	$18,400	$4,000

REQUIRED:

a. Calculate the plantwide overhead rate for MumsDay Corporation for the coming year using the same method as used in the past.

b. Whit Portlock has been asked to develop departmental overhead rates for comparison with the plantwide rate. The following steps are to be followed in developing the departmental rates.

(1) The Maintenance Department costs should be allocated to the three manufacturing departments using the direct method.

(2) The Power Department costs should be allocated to the three manufacturing departments using the dual method — that is, the fixed costs allocated according to long-term capacity and the variable costs according to planned usage.

(3) Calculate departmental overhead rates for the three manufacturing departments using a machine-hour base for the Molding Department and a direct-labor-hour base for the Component and Assembly Departments.

c. Should MumsDay Corporation use a plantwide rate or departmental rates to assign overhead to its products? Explain your answer. (*CMA adapted*)

14-29 Allocation of Costs to Promotion Department   The Promotion Department of the Doxolby Co. is responsible for the design and development of all promotional materials for the corporation. This includes all promotional campaigns and related literature, pamphlets, and brochures. Top management is reviewing the effectiveness of the Promotion Department to determine if the department's activities could be managed better and more economically by an outside promotion agency. As a part of this review, top management has asked for a summary of the Promotion Department's costs for the most recent year. The following cost summary was supplied.

PROMOTION DEPARTMENT
Costs for the year ended November 30, 19x8

Direct department costs	$257,500
Charges from other departments	44,700
Allocated share of general administrative overhead	22,250
Total costs	$324,450

The direct department costs consist of those costs that can be traced directly to the activities of the Promotion Department (such as staff and clerical salaries, including related employee benefits and supplies). The charges from other departments represent the costs of services provided by other departments of Doxolby at the request of the Promotion Department. The company has developed a charging system for such interdepartmental uses of services. For instance, the "in-house" Printing Department charges the Promotion Department for the promotional literature printed. All such services provided to the Promotion Department by other departments of Doxolby are included in the "Charges from Other Departments." General administrative overhead is comprised of such costs as top management salaries and benefits, depreciation, heat, insurance, and property taxes. These costs are allocated to all departments in proportion to the number of employees in each department.

REQUIRED:

Discuss the usefulness of the cost figures as presented for the Promotion Department of Doxolby Co. as the basis for a comparison with a bid from an outside agency to provide the same type of activities as Doxolby's own promotion department. (*CMA adapted*)

15

Joint Costs and Joint Products

LEARNING OBJECTIVES

After you have studied this chapter, you should be able to:

1 Explain the distinction between joint and indirect costs.

2 Describe joint products and by-products.

3 Allocate joint costs using a physical-measure, net-realizable-value, or gross-sales-value method.

4 Value by-product inventories.

5 Make better decisions in situations involving joint production processes and joint products.

6 Examine the optimal price and production decisions for joint-product production processes.

*T*his chapter discusses many of the problems that arise from joint processes. A **joint process** is one that results in two or more outputs or products. The production of gasoline, for example, leads to several additional products, including oil and chemicals. The provision of airline service typically includes both passenger and freight activities.

Joint processes lead to two similar but basically different types of costs: joint costs and indirect costs. **Joint costs** relate to situations in which the factors of production, by their basic nature, result in two or more products. These products are the result of the method of production or the nature of the raw material rather than a decision by management to produce both products. Gasoline production is an example. **Indirect costs** result from an explicit management decision to produce multiple products using the same factors of production. Airline service provides an example. This chapter examines the problem of allocating joint costs to the various products generated in a joint process.

Examples of Joint and Indirect Costs

An example of a joint cost is the cost of a barrel of crude oil purchased by a refining company. Several products, including gasoline, fuel, oil, tar, and chemicals, result from processing a barrel of crude oil. These products all have a common cost, the cost of the oil, so the cost of the oil is joint to these products. Another example of a joint cost is the cost of cocoa beans used in the production of chocolate by companies such as Nestlé Corporation. Processing cocoa beans results in two products: cocoa powder and cocoa butter. Frequently, in joint-cost situations, it would be uneconomical to produce a single product. Joint costs can be found in chemicals, tobacco, soap making, meat packing, grain milling, and food processing and result when the appearance of one product is accompanied by one or more additional (or joint) products in either constant or variable proportions.

Joint products are generally visually identifiable, separate products that emerge in reasonably predictable portions from a joint production process. But this is not always the case. In the semiconductor industry, memory chips of differing quality or grade may be considered joint products from the same chip production process. The relative proportion of high-grade and low-grade chips is neither determinable nor predictable with any certainty by management, and the different classes of joint products are not readily identifiable. The following excerpt from a *Management Accounting* article describes this joint process.

Joint Products in the Semiconductor Industry

The application of joint product costing techniques in the extractive, agricultural, and chemical industries is well established. In these situations, the joint products are clearly distinguishable from one another in terms of their physical appearance at the split-off point. However, there also are cases where jointness exists among products in terms of other, less obvious, attributes. Typically, in these situations, the products have not been viewed as joint for costing purposes. In the semiconductor industry, the production of memory chips of differential quality represents such a case.

The production of memory chips may be viewed as a joint processing situation because the output consists of different quality chips from a common production run. The manufacturing operation is composed of three phases: fabrication, assembly, and a "stress test." The first and second steps are mandatory. The third is optional and necessary to produce memory with a longer life expectancy. Of the three cases, only fabrication represents a joint production process; assembly and stress testing are separable steps.

The input to the fabrication phase is raw silicon wafers which are first photolithographed and then baked at high temperatures. Each wafer will yield multiple chips of identical design. Upon completion of the fabrication process, the finished wafer is tested to identify usable and unusable chips. The test also classifies usable chips according to density (the number of good memory bits) and speed (the time required to access those bits).

The input to the assembly process is usable chips which are encapsulated in ceramic and wired for use on a memory board. The encapsulation process varies according to the number of chips which constitute a finished module. Modules of a given density may be composed of one all-good chip or multiple partially-good chips. The finished modules are subjected to a nondestructive functional test to identify defective output.

If an extended life expectancy is not required, the good modules are not processed any further. A small sample of the good modules is subjected to the destructive reliability test before the finished product is considered salable. This destructive reliability test is a traditional quality control step designed to establish the "time-to-failure" distribution of the output. The profile of this distribution will depend, in part, upon whether the modules were subjected to the optional stress test.

If a longer life expectancy is desired, the modules are stressed before being tested for reliability. This optional step exposes the modules to extreme conditions and those that survive are labeled extended-life modules. The proportion of the modules selected to undergo the stress test is under management control and can be varied with market conditions.[1]

---

1. W. Cats-Baril, J. Gatti, and D. J. Grinnell, "Joint Product Costing in the Semiconductor Industry," *Management Accounting* (February 1986): 28–35.

Indirect costs result from the production of more than one product when management decides to use the factors of production to produce several products. Any indirect cost factor can be directed to the production of a single product instead of several products. For railroads the cost of the rails is an indirect cost of both freight and passenger travel.

Another example of indirect costs occurs when a plant produces beer and soda cans. Some of the same equipment is used to produce both products, yet both products need not be produced. Other examples include the machinery used in processing timber (the cost of the logs, on the other hand, is a joint cost), and telephone switching equipment used to carry different types of phone calls. Perhaps the most common illustration, however, is the overhead cost of an organization (depreciation, insurance, and so on) required for general operations.

Two types of costs (joint and indirect), then, cannot be directly identified with the end products or services when two or more types of products or services are being produced. In fact, the term **common costs** is sometimes used to describe both of these types of costs.

Products resulting from joint-cost processes are called joint products if they are approximately of equal importance to the firm. Joint products of relatively small importance to the firm are called **by-products.** The distinction is typically based on relative total sales value. A product may have a high unit value but still be considered a by-product if the total revenue generated is small in comparison with other related products or services.

An example of a by-product is the scrap metal resulting from the production of an airplane. This scrap has considerable value in absolute amount, but compared to the value of the primary product, airplanes, it is of small value. The scrap results from the airplane production process and hence satisfies the definition of a by-product. If the value of the end product were nearly equivalent to the value of the scrap produced, the scrap metal would be considered a joint product by accountants, although common usage might still refer to it as a by-product.

In practice, the distinction between a joint product and a by-product is primarily a result of accounting convention and of minimal use to management in decision situations. Furthermore, the distinction could be eliminated by considering all products to be joint products. There need be no loss in reporting accuracy. In fact, it could be argued that reporting would be improved.

Joint Costs and Inventory Valuation

Joint costs cannot be split up and traced to the products and services to which they attach, except arbitrarily. There is no single right way to split the cost of a barrel of crude oil among the products made from it. The total cost of a barrel is known, but the costs of the several products processed from it cannot be known with certainty. The same is true of indirect costs.

Accountants allocate joint costs to attach costs to the products and services produced. In regulated industries, prices (the rates charged) usually depend on these cost allocations.[2] Moreover, government contracts typically require that specific cost-allocation procedures be followed. Accounting for the determination of income taxes also necessitates cost allocation. Accountants use the same procedures to determine both income and, simultaneously, inventory values for the financial statements of the organization. Even recognizing the arbitrariness of the cost-assignment task, the accountant must still determine inventory values. The income figures not only are required for external reporting but often are used to evaluate performance and determine production levels. This creates problems, as is shown later.

Joint costs must be allocated so that the costs of different products can be assigned for income determination, for contract bidding, for cost-based pricing decisions, for utility rate-regulation requests, and for figuring taxes. A number of methods can be used to allocate joint costs. One must be selected. Let's consider the alternatives. They are based on physical units and profitability.

Joint costs are frequently allocated using physical measures, such as the number of units produced, or their relative weights. For example, it is fairly common in the petroleum industry to use BTU's (British thermal units) to allocate joint costs to the various joint products. A limitation of the physical-measure allocation method is that the contribution established for each product is influenced by the physical characteristic of the product used to allocate the joint cost rather than by the product's economic characteristics. For this reason, alternative methods based on profitability are favored by most organizations. Two allocation methods are common: the net-realizable-value method and the gross-sales-revenue method. The following example illustrates both of these methods as well as the procedure using physical-unit measures.

Example of Joint-Cost Allocation Methods

Suppose a raw material costs $200 per unit, and three joint products are made from each unit. The basic characteristics of the three products are given in Exhibit 15-1.

Allocation Based on Physical Measures   The pounds of product given in Exhibit 15-1 can be used to allocate the joint costs of $200. Using the proportion of the raw material, the allocation in Exhibit 15-2 would result. Product *A* receives $140 (70 percent of the $200 common costs) despite the fact that its net sales value is only $100. This procedure seems strange to many managers because the allocations are made on a basis completely unrelated to the value of the product. Managers generally favor allocation methods using relative sales values. Such methods ensure that all end products show some profit under normal market conditions.

2. Regulated industries can present particularly complex situations. For example in the energy area, crude oil and natural gas result from the same joint process but only natural gas is regulated in the United States. See J. Crespi and J. Harris, "Joint Cost Allocation Under the Natural Gas Act: An Historical Review," *Journal of the Extractive Industries* (Summer 1983): 133–42, for a case study of allocating joint costs in this area.

EXHIBIT 15-1

Product Characteristics: Three-Product Example

Product	Pounds of Raw Material Required	Product Sales Revenue	Percentage of Total Sales Revenue	Cost to Finish and Sell[a]	Net Realizable Value Col. 3– Col. 5[b]	Percentage of Total Net Realizable Value
A	35	$130	26.5%	$30	$100	25%
B	10	210	43.0%	50	160	40%
C	5	150	30.5%	10	140	35%
	50	$490	100 %	$90	$400	100%

[a] Cost other than that of the raw material identified with the product.
[b] Selling price less costs to finish and sell.

Allocation Based on Net Realizable Value   The most common profitability-based method used to allocate joint costs is **net realizable value.** The net realizable value per unit is the selling price less the costs of completion and sale, after the split-off point. The **split-off point,** in turn, is that point where the joint products can be separately identified, and where the decision to sell or process any one of them further can be made independently of the other products.

The net realizable value for each product is shown in Exhibit 15-1. Exhibit 15-3 shows the cost allocations resulting from the use of net realizable value.

Using the net realizable value to allocate the $200 of joint costs, product A would be charged with 25 percent (or $50) of the joint costs, product B with 40 percent (or $80), and product C with 35 percent (or $70).

Now let's look at the income statements if the units are sold for the expected prices. Assuming net realizable value is used to allocate the $200 of costs, the results are shown in Exhibit 15-4.

EXHIBIT 15-2

Use of Physical Measure (Pounds) to Allocate Joint Costs

Products	Pounds	Percentage of Total	Total Joint Cost	Allocated Cost
A	35	70%	$200	$140
B	10	20%	200	40
C	5	10%	200	20
				$200

EXHIBIT 15-3

Use of Net Realizable Value to Allocate Joint Costs

Product	Net Realizable Value	Percentage of Total	Total Joint Cost of Raw Material	Allocated Joint Cost
A	$100	25%	$200	$ 50
B	160	40%	200	80
C	140	35%	200	70
	$400	100%		$200

In this example finishing costs are not a constant proportion of sales values. (They are: Product A, $30 \div 130 = 23\%$; Product B, $50 \div 210 = 24\%$; and Product C, $10 \div 150 = 7\%$.) The result is that the percentage of gross profit to sales, given at the bottom of Exhibit 15-4, differs among the three products.

Now assume a new set of finishing costs that are proportional to sales values. This results in the product income statements shown in Exhibit 15-5.

The ratio of gross profits to sales is now the same for all three products. The gross profit percentages will be different only where there are direct material or finishing costs that can be directly identified with the end product, and where these costs are not in proportion to the net realizable value of the product. The arbitrariness of the joint-cost allocations warns against placing excessive faith in product-line profit figures. Furthermore, this net-realizable-value method becomes quite cumbersome

EXHIBIT 15-4

Product Income Statements: Net-Realizable-Value Method (Direct Material and Finishing Costs Not in Proportion to Sales Value)

	Product A	Product B	Product C
Sales value per unit[a]	$130	$210	$150
Finishing costs[b]	$ 30	$ 50	$ 10
Joint cost of raw material	50	80	70
Total cost	$ 80	$130	$ 80
Gross profit	$ 50	$ 80	$ 70
Gross profit as percentage of sales	38.5%	38.1%	46.7%

[a] From Exhibit 15-1.

[b] From Exhibit 15-3.

EXHIBIT 15-5

Product Income Statements: Net-Realizable-Value Method (Direct Material and Finishing Costs in Proportion to Sales Value)

	Product A	Product B	Product C
Sales value[a]	$130	$210	$150
Raw material and finishing costs	$ 65	$105	$ 75
Gross profit	$ 65	$105	$ 75
Gross profit as percentage of sales	50%	50%	50%

[a] From Exhibit 15-1.

EXHIBIT 15-6

Use of Gross Sales to Allocate Costs

Product	Sales Revenue[a]	Percent of Total[a]	Total Joint Cost	Allocated Cost
A	$130	26.5%	$200	$ 53
B	210	43.0%	200	86
C	150	30.5%	200	61
	$490	100.0		$200

[a] From Exhibit 15-1.

when multiple split-off points are involved or when products, once split, merge at a later point in the production process perhaps only to be split again.[3]

Allocation Based on Gross Sales Values   If gross sales and the information presented in Exhibit 15-1 are used, the related statements in Exhibits 15-6 and 15-7 result. There is an increase in the apparent contribution per unit of product C due to the impact of the allocation method on the distribution of the joint cost across products.

---

3. Indeed in one study of joint-cost allocation in the oil industry in England, most firms considered the process too complex "to establish any meaningful cost apportionment between products." K. Slater and C. Wooton, *A Study of Joint and By-Product Costing in the U.K.* (London: Institute of Cost and Managerial Accountants, 1984): 101.

EXHIBIT 15-7

Product Income Statements: Gross-Sales-Revenue Method

	Product A	Product B	Product C
Sales[a]	$130	$210	$150
Finishing costs[a]	$ 30	$ 50	$ 10
Cost of raw materials (joint cost allocation)[b]	53	86	61
Total cost	$ 83	$136	$ 71
Gross profit	$ 47	$ 74	$ 79
Gross profit as percentage of sales	36.2%	35.2%	52.7%

[a] From Exhibit 15-1.

[b] Column 4 of Exhibit 15-1 is used to allocate the $200 joint cost.

When the gross-sales-value method is used, the income statements in Exhibit 15-7 result. The contribution per unit of product C is the largest of the three products.

Comparison of Allocation Methods

Each joint-cost allocation method makes implicit assumptions about the importance of finishing costs in generating a contribution to fixed costs and profit. The gross-sales-revenue method assumes that all costs are equally effective in generating a contribution to fixed costs and profit. The net-realizable-value method, on the other hand, assumes that the finishing costs generate revenue sufficient only to cover the finishing costs. Finishing costs are implicitly assumed to contribute nothing toward fixed cost and profit. Neither assumption is likely to be in accord with the facts. Using the physical measure (number of pounds), product A receives 70 percent of the $200 of joint cost (or $140), despite the fact that its net realizable value is only $100. In summary, managers have favored the net-realizable-value method because it is based on the economic characteristics of the joint products.

Recognizing the arbitrary nature of all procedures in allocating joint costs, some companies elect to carry their joint-product inventories at net realizable value, calculated at the split-off point. Although this approach avoids the allocation problem, it too presents difficulties. Using net realizable values causes inventories to be overstated and for profit to be recognized prior to sale. Costs are attached to inventories rather than included in the cost-of-goods-sold figure. As inventories increase, so do reported profits. Accountants generally disapprove of any procedure that recognizes profit resulting from production and inventory increases rather than sales. The net-realizable-value procedure produces less of this type of distortion when margins are low, disappearing entirely when margins are zero. Perhaps this explains its popularity in the meat packing, canning, and mining industries.

By-products

By-products are those products with relatively minor total sales value. Products classified as by-products can change over time. Kerosene, once a by-product, is now a joint product. Glycerin, a by-product of soap manufacturing, became a joint product during wartime. Furthermore, by-products may be altered over time to other, more profitable uses. For example, furniture companies that once experienced a waste of up to 50 percent of the wood used, now process that waste into cultured board and incorporate it into their product as drawer bottoms, dresser backs, and similar items.

An accepted procedure with by-product costs is to deduct their net-realizable value, at the time the by-product is produced, from the cost of the main or joint products. The by-products are then inventoried at their net-realizable value and, if prices are as anticipated, by-product sales show no profit. This procedure may recognize profit before sale, but the amount is typically minor for a true by-product.

An alternative and somewhat simpler procedure, although less often used, is to deduct the net-realizable value from the main product's inventory value when the by-product is sold rather than when it is produced. In this situation, the inventory of the by-product is recorded at a zero value. The value of the by-product inventory is typically not well matched to the production and sale of the main products using this approach. If inventory turnover is high or the level of productive activity is uniform, little distortion results.

Assume that in addition to products A, B, and C in the previous example, there is another product, Z, that is relatively small in total sales value. For example, Z could be perhaps scrap metal that is accumulated and sold to scrap dealers. Assume that 50 pounds of Z is generated from each unit of raw material, that Z sells for $.40 per pound, and that it costs $.10 per pound to dispose of the scrap.

Each unit of raw material results in $(50)($.40)$, or $20, worth of Z. However, preparing Z costs $.10 per pound, or $5. The net value of the scrap is $20 less $5, or $15. Using the method that deducts the net realizable value from the main products at the time of production, the by-product would be inventoried at $15, and the main product cost would be reduced by $15. Under the alternate procedure, no inventory adjustment would be made until the by-product is sold. Any sale of the by-product would result in a credit, in the amount of the sale, to the inventory of the main products.

If the dollar value of the by-product becomes significant in size, then the procedure described above will distort the relative performance of the by-product compared to the main products, since the approach tends to show no profit for the by-product when it is sold. To avoid this result product Z could be treated as a joint product.

An alternative and common practice is to assign no material cost to by-products. If the amounts are small, this procedure can be excused because the difference is not material. Finally, it should be emphasized that these costing procedures typically do not provide the kinds of costs needed for decision making. The distinction between by-products and main products is arbitrary, and it would be logical to eliminate the by-product classification altogether. The advantage of by-product accounting is that it is somewhat less complex than accounting for joint products.

Joint Costs and Decision Making

Given the arbitrary nature of all cost allocations, they should not be used for decisions on pricing, further processing, accepting special orders, or emphasizing product lines. Instead, marginal or incremental analysis should be used. One exception is the case of decisions made in a regulated environment. Regulations often indicate precisely how a contracting firm must allocate its joint costs for pricing purposes. Whenever the allocation procedure is fixed, it constitutes a constraint to the decision problem faced by management.

Suppose that a firm makes two products (*A* and *B*) from a raw material that costs $2 per pound and weighs 10 pounds. The 10 pounds of raw material yield one unit of *A* at 4 pounds and one unit of *B* at 6 pounds. The direct finishing costs are $1.25 per pound of *A* and $.50 per pound of *B*. Indirect finishing (joint processing) costs that apply to both *A* and *B* amount to $.70 per pound of the raw material. These facts are summarized in Exhibit 15-8. Management wishes to determine how much of each product to produce.

Both the direct and indirect finishing costs indicated above are of an incremental nature. (Any fixed costs have been omitted because they do not affect the production decision to be made.) Neither the cost of *A* nor *B* can be determined with certainty because they have common costs of $20 for material and $7 for indirect processing costs. However, the cost of making both *A* and *B* can be determined. It costs a total of $35 to manufacture 4 pounds of *A* and 6 pounds of *B*, as shown below:

Raw material	$20
Joint processing costs	7
Direct cost of A ($1.25)(4)	5
Direct cost of B ($.50)(6)	3
	$35

EXHIBIT 15-8

Summary Statistics: Products A and B

Item	Product A	Product B
Weight of product resulting from 10 lbs of raw material (cost $20.00)	4 lbs	6 lbs
Direct finishing costs	$1.25/lb	$.50/lb
Indirect finishing costs $7	(applies jointly to *A* and *B*)	

Also, if the company made just *A* and did not finish *B*, the cost would be $32 (made up of $20 plus $7 plus $5). If the company made just *B* and did not finish *A*, the cost would be $30 (made up of $20 plus $7 plus $3).

From the above information, several initial conclusions can be drawn that do not depend on an allocation of joint costs and that are theoretically sound:

1. If the revenue from the sale of *A* plus *B* is in excess of $35, the firm should produce at least one of the products. It does not follow that if the revenue is less than $35, it should not produce.

2. If the revenue from the sale of *A* is greater than $32, the firm should produce *A*. It should not finish *B* unless the revenue arising from the sale of *B* is in excess of $3, the direct cost of finishing *B*.

3. If the revenue from the sale of *B* is greater than $30, the firm should produce *B*. It should not finish *A* unless the revenue arising from the sale of *A* is in excess of $5, the cost required to finish *A*.

4. If the revenue from the sale of one unit (4 lbs) of *A* and one unit (6 lbs) of *B* is less than $30 for each product and, in total, less than $35, the firm should not produce either *A* or *B*.

Although products *A* and *B* are made from a common raw material and are joint products, the manufacturer may choose not to produce one or the other or both. Thus, a chemical company may find that it is commercially sound to produce one joint product but that the demand for another of the joint products has decreased, with a resulting decrease in price, so that its production is no longer economically sound. This discussion is expanded in Appendix 15.A.

Illustration of Joint-Cost Allocation

An illustration of joint-cost allocation is provided by the following discussion of the Memory Manufacturing Company. The case describes an actual situation in a real company, but the firm's name has been changed to protect its confidentiality.[4] The term **separable cost** used in the illustration refers to those costs that are not joint costs and that can be identified directly with the final product such as the cost of the materials used to package the separate products.

---

4. This case was prepared by the company described for the National Association of Accountants and the Management Accounting section of the American Accounting Association. It originally appeared in *Cases from Management Accounting Practice,* vol. 2, S. Moriarity, ed. (Montvale, N.J.: National Association of Accountants, 1986). It is adapted and reproduced here with permission.

Allocation of Joint Costs in Computer-Chip Production

Memory Manufacturing Company produces and markets many different kinds of memory modules for the computer industry for high-, medium-, and low-priced end products. The manufacturing processes for high-technology products have advanced tremendously over the past several years. Memory chips, the major component of memory modules, result from a single process. Although identical in composition, the chips are separated after production into good or usable chips and bad or unusable chips. The good or usable chips are further divided, through testing, into various grades according to their density and speed.

Because the different grades are produced simultaneously, only the total cost of the process, and not that of the individual chips, is known. The cost incurred for any specific chip cannot be separately traced.

The "average cost technique" (good chips divided by the total cost of the process), used for the much simpler chips produced by earlier processes, no longer provides a satisfactory cost allocation if consideration is given to the density, speed, reliability, and the relative market value of the individual chips. Of the two grades of chips mentioned in this case, "standard" chips are worth far less in the market than "deluxe" chips. These differences in value, however, are masked in the chip manufacturing process.

The Manufacturing Process

Memory modules are the output from two basic manufacturing processes: chip fabrication and module assembly/testing. A raw silicon wafer is the input in the chip fabrication process. Each wafer yields multiple chips of identical design.

After as many as 200 different manufacturing operations during chip fabrication, the finished chips are ready for testing. The finished chips are first tested to distinguish between the good/usable chips and the bad/unusable ones. Subsequently, good chips are classified according to their density (the number of good memory bits on each chip) and their speed (the time required to access the good bits). The chip testing process can determine density and speed only. Reliability is determined when testing the completed module assembly. The cost of the chips amounts to approximately 80 percent of the cost of the completed module.

Good chips of various densities and speeds are the input to the module assembly process. The chips are then processed through a series of separable manufacturing operations (cost can be identified at each module assembly operation and for each part number).

The output of the module assembly process, as determined by the final module test, consists of memory modules of different quality along a number of different dimensions. The dimensions include number of chips per module, chip density, chip speed, and reliability. A simplified flow of the manufacturing processes for chip fabrication and module assembly/testing is shown in Exhibit 15-9.

EXHIBIT 15-9

The Module Manufacturing Process

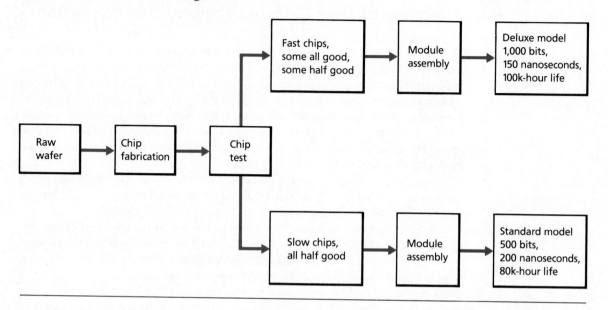

EXHIBIT 15-10

Product and Cost Data for a Batch of Modules

Production Data

	Production Quantity
Modules:	
Deluxe	500
Standard	500
Chips:	
Fast all good (1,000 bits)	200
Fast half good (500 bits)	600
Slow half good (500 bits)	500

	Production Cost
Modules:	
Deluxe assembly cost	$ 2,000
Standard assembly cost	$ 1,000
Chips:	
Total fabrication cost	$20,000
Market value:	
Deluxe module	$45.00
Standard module	$20.00

EXHIBIT 15-11

Description of Memory Modules

Memory Products	Density (Bits)	Speed (Nano Seconds)	Reliability of Module (Power on Hours)
Deluxe module	1 all good 1,000 bits or 2 half good 500 bits	Fast 150 nanosec	Long life 100K hrs
Standard module	1 half good 500 bits	Slow 200 nanosec	Short life 80K hrs
Deluxe module	Contains 1,000 bits (1 all good or 2 half good chips), with 150 nanosecond speed, and is rated for 100K power on hrs		
Standard module	Contains 500 bits (1 half good chip), with 200 nanosecond speed, and is rated for 80K power on hrs		

For the purposes of this illustration, only two memory modules, which command different prices in the marketplace, are considered. The two memory modules are referred to as *standard* and *deluxe*. Production quantity and cost data are shown in Exhibit 15-10. Exhibit 15-11 describes the product characteristics.

There are three possible allocation methods to consider: (1) treating one of the products as a by-product, (2) using a physical measure for the allocation basis, and (3) using a market-value measure as the allocation basis.

The use of a by-product costing approach seems inappropriate in this case. Both of the products are in high demand and eventually generate significant revenues. There are several easily measured physical attributes that could be used, such as the number of chips, the number of good bits per chip, speed, and reliability. However, in each case, the physical measure relates to only one aspect of the chip that contributes to its value. The value of a chip as determined by the marketplace is a function of each of the physical measures.

In this case a market exists for each of the joint products. This allows the firm to easily cost the modules in proportion to their value as dictated by the marketplace. Further, by doing so, the firm obtains a cost figure for each product that approximates the opportunity cost for using the products internally versus selling them externally. Thus a relative market value allocation appears to be a reasonable choice for the firm.

Using the data supplied in Exhibit 15-10, the market-value approach would yield the following allocation of the total fabrication cost:

Module	Selling Price	Proportion	Allocation	Separable Cost	Total Cost	Cost per Unit
Deluxe	$22,500	22.5/32.5	$13,846	$2,000	$15,846	$31.69
Standard	10,000	10/32.5	6,154	1,000	7,154	14.31
Total	$32,500		$20,000			

The above allocation is based on market values. The net realizable value would yield the following allocation:

Module	Selling Price	Separable Cost	Realizable Value	Proportion	Allocation
Deluxe	$22,500	$2,000	$20,500	20.5/29.5	$13,898
Standard	10,000	1,000	9,000	9/29.5	6,102
Total			$29,500		$20,000

This would yield the following unit costs:

Module	Allocated Cost	Separable Cost	Total Cost	Unit Cost
Deluxe	$13,898	$2,000	$15,898	$31.79
Standard	6,102	1,000	7,102	14.20

Because the resulting unit costs are so similar, the extra effort required to use the net-realizable-value method probably cannot be justified.

The firm recognized that using a simple average cost per chip (all chips valued at the same unit cost) for these high-technology products, did not provide a satisfactory cost allocation. Therefore, they commissioned a study to focus on the total manufacturing process and to review applicable costing methodologies that could be utilized in costing memory products. The recommendation of the study was to use market value to allocate joint costs. Management reviewed the recommendation and after determining that there was no major impact on their current control and measurement systems, decided that the market-value method satisfied their requirements. Market values have been established based on competitive products where such products exist. Where there are no comparable products in the market, an estimated price has been established, based on a price of a substitute product with appropriate adjustments for quality, density, speed, and reliability.

Summary

Common costs arise when the factors of production lead to two or more products. Although it is not possible to determine a precise cost for each product, it is possible to make economically sound pricing and production decisions. Accountants can assist in this process if they understand the nature of joint costs. Accountants must also establish inventory values for the firm's financial statements. Three widely used methods of cost allocation for inventory valuation are

1. Physical measures (such as weight),

2. Sales value,

3. Net realizable value.

The difficulty with physical measures is that value and weight may not be closely related. Sales value is not reliable because it fails to consider any processing (finishing) costs. Net realizable value is the most reasonable of the three methods. Its main fault is that the results reflect an average calculation that implicitly assumes all units can be sold at a well-defined price.

A theoretical method of valuing the inventory of joint products uses the marginal revenue of the joint products to allocate costs is covered in the appendix. It does not make unrealistic implicit assumptions concerning the revenue-generating ability of specific costs that are made by the gross-sales-value and net-realizable-value methods. This appendix also examines a means of making pricing and output decisions in the case of joint products when competitive conditions are such that prices must be lowered to increase sales.

Key Terms to Review

by-products, p. 536
common costs, p. 536
indirect costs, p. 534
joint costs, p. 534
joint process, p. 534

joint products, p. 534
net realizable value, p. 538
separable cost, p. 544
split-off point, p. 538

Review Problem

ALLOCATING JOINT COSTS

The Cayuga Salt Company processes raw salt into several finished products. The company allocates the cost of the salt it buys to three products — chlorine, table salt, and a by-product. The by-product and table salt are further refined after the split-off point, at which time the three products described above are separated from the raw salt. Cayuga allocates joint cost using net realizable values. In August Cayuga bought and processed 30,000 tons for $67 a ton.

Production for August resulted in the following:

	Processed Tons	Price per Ton[a]
Table salt	10,000	$100
Chlorine	15,000	80
By-product	5,000	—

[a] Sale value per ton at the split-off point except for the by-product, which must be further processed at a cost of $10 per ton before it can be sold for $30 per ton.

a. Determine the cost allocation for August using net realizable values for all three items.

b. Is Cayuga currently making a contribution toward covering its fixed costs?

c. Suppose the price of the by-product declines. How far can it decline before the by-product should not be finished?

Solution to Review Problem

a.

	Sales Price	Net Finishing Costs	Net Realizable Value	Percentage	Allocated Cost (000)[a]
Table salt	$100	—	$100	43.48	$ 873,948
Chlorine	80	—	80	52.17	1,048,617
By-product	30	10	20	4.35	87,435
Total				100%	$2,010,000

[a] (30 × $67) times the percentage in the previous column. The figures are in thousands of dollars.

b. Total costs in thousands are

Raw material: joint 30 × $67 =	$2,010
By-product: processing 5 × $10 =	50
Total	$2,060

Total revenues are:		
Table salt	10 × $100 =	$1,000
Chlorine	15 × $80 =	1,200
By-product	5 × $30 =	150
Total		$2,350

Revenues exceed costs. Therefore a contribution is being made to fixed costs. This is the case even though two of the products sell for less per ton than the cost of the raw material.

c. If the sales value of the by-product drops below its finishing costs of $10, it should not be finished.

APPENDIX
Determining the Price of Joint Products[5]

It is frequently assumed that the pricing policy for joint products requires an arbitrary cost allocation. This is not true. It is possible to establish a theoretically sound framework for determining price and production decisions for joint products. The price determines the cost allocation; the cost allocation does not determine the price. Because price is usually established by competitive market conditions and not by a firm's cost structure, this is important.

The example discussed in the chapter, dealing with products A and B produced in fixed proportions, may be used. The analysis included in the chapter holds under conditions of perfect competition. However, when the competitive situation requires that prices must be reduced to increase sales (the demand curve is no longer horizontal), the analysis becomes more complex. This is the topic of this appendix.

The Problem   Assume that the two products have independent demand curves (average-revenue or price curves) (see Exhibit 15-12). The demands for the two products may be independent or mutually dependent. For simplicity, however, it is assumed here that the prices and total sales, at different prices of the two products, are independent of each other. The only additional assumption made in this appendix is that each demand curve slopes downward to the right. The number of units sold increases as the price is decreased.

From the numerical example, each unit of A weighs 4 pounds and each unit of B weighs 6 pounds. Let Q and P denote quantity and price, respectively. The demand equations represented in Exhibit 15-12 for products A and B are

$$Q_A = 100 - 2P_A \tag{1}$$

$$Q_B = 20 - .5P_B \tag{2}$$

Solving equations (1) and (2) for P_A and P_B yields

$$P_A = 50 - .5Q_A \tag{3}$$

$$P_B = 40 - 2Q_B \tag{4}$$

Using equations (3) and (4), the total-revenue equations, R_A and R_B, are obtained by multiplying price by quantity:

$$R_A = P_A Q = 50Q_A - .5Q_A^2 \tag{5}$$

$$R_B = P_B Q_B = 40Q_B - 2Q_B^2 \tag{6}$$

5. This appendix uses differential calculus.

EXHIBIT 15-12

Demand Curves for Two Joint Products

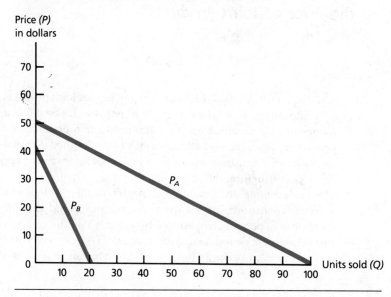

Because optimal solutions are found by equating marginal revenue with marginal cost, the next step is to obtain the marginal-revenue expressions (MR_A and MR_B) for each product. This is done by differentiating equations (5) and (6) with respect to Q_A and Q_B, as shown below:

$$MR_A = \frac{dR_A}{dQ_A} = 50 - Q_A \tag{7}$$

$$MR_B = \frac{dR_B}{dQ_B} = 40 - 4Q_B \tag{8}$$

Equating marginal revenue and marginal cost is not so easily accomplished, however, because the joint material and processing costs cannot be allocated to the products. Yet these costs increase with output.

An Initial but Not Necessarily Optimal Solution

Instead of separate demand curves for the two products, consider the 10 pounds of raw material as making one unit of a new joint product defined as one unit (4 pounds) of A and one unit (6 pounds) of B. Denote this joint product by AB. Average-revenue and marginal-revenue curves for this new product can then be obtained. The average-revenue curve for one unit of AB consists of the revenue from selling one unit of AB (4 pounds of A and 6 pounds of B). Thus, 20 pounds of raw material yield 2 units of AB with a price of $50 - .5(2) + 40 - 2(2) = 85$. This is the sum of equations (3) and (4). Adding equations (3) and (4):

$$P_{AB} = 90 - 2.5Q_{AB} \tag{9}$$

Total revenue is given by

$$Q_{AB}(P_{AB}) = 90Q_{AB} - 2.5Q_{AB}^2 \tag{10}$$

and differentiating (10) with respect to Q_{AB} yields the marginal revenue curve (11):

$$MR_{AB} = 90 - 5Q_{AB} \tag{11}$$

Both equations (9) and (11) are graphed in Exhibit 15-13.

The only cost curve shown in Exhibit 15-13 is the marginal-cost curve for the production of both A and B. The curve is assumed to be a horizontal line. Hence, it also serves as an average variable-cost curve. Exhibit 15-13 suggests that the optimal solution to the problem of setting the output level is Q_{AB} equal to eleven units, where the units are expressed in terms of 4 pounds of A and 6 pounds of B. At this output, marginal revenue equals marginal cost. The prices charged result in average revenue of R. However, R is not the price, since Q_{AB} units are not sold. Rather, units of products A and B are sold. To find the prices at which the units are sold, it is necessary to return to Exhibit 15-12 and find the prices for A and B that clear the market at the

EXHIBIT 15-13

Marginal Analysis for Two Joint Products

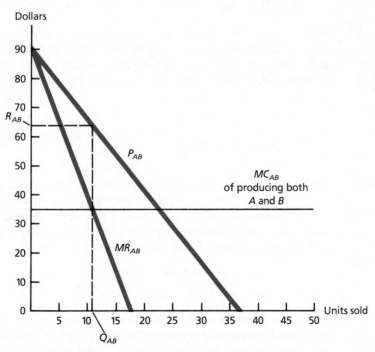

level of eleven units that will be produced. The price of A times the number of units of A, plus the price of B times the number of units of B, is equal to R times Q_{AB} (the number of units of AB) from Exhibit 15-13.

The same solution can also be obtained using equations (7) and (8). Again, consider a single unit of A (4 pounds of A) and a single unit of B (6 pounds of B) to be the result of processing one unit of raw material (10 pounds). Then the revenue of the joint product AB is:

$$R_{AB} = R_A + R_B = 50Q_A - .5Q_A^2 + 40Q_B - 2Q_B^2 \tag{12}$$

Because one unit of AB yields one unit (4 pounds) of A and one unit (6 pounds) of B, the following equation holds:

$$Q_{AB} = Q_A = Q_B \tag{13}$$

Therefore, the total-revenue equation for the product AB is given by

$$R_{AB} = 50Q_{AB} - .5Q_{AB}^2 + 40Q_{AB} - 2Q_{AB}^2 = 90Q_{AB} - 2.5Q_{AB}^2 \tag{14}$$

Taking the derivative, marginal revenue is obtained:

$$MR_{AB} = 90 - 5Q_{AB} \tag{15}$$

This is also the sum of equations (7) and (8).

Equating the marginal revenue to the marginal cost of completing both products yields

$$90 - 5Q_{AB} = 35 \tag{16}$$

Both the joint costs and the direct costs of finishing are incorporated in the \$35 marginal cost figure of equation (16). Solving equation (16) yields 11 for Q_{AB}. In other words, the initial solution (omitting finishing costs) is to produce eleven units of both A and B. The prices to be charged are obtained from equations (3) and (4), using $Q_A = Q_B = 11$. The prices are

$$P_A = 50 - .5Q_A = \$44.50 \tag{17}$$

$$P_B = 40 - 2Q_B = \$18.00 \tag{18}$$

Checking for an Optimal Solution

Although marginal revenue equals marginal cost for the production level and prices determined above, this is not necessarily the optimal solution. Because the direct costs of finishing are not common to both products, to have an optimal solution, the marginal revenue for each product separately must at least equal its marginal finishing cost. The marginal revenues for products A and B are given by equations (7) and (8):

$$MR_A = 50 - Q_A = 50 - 11 = \$39 \tag{19}$$

$$MR_B = 40 - 4Q_B = 40 - 44 = -\$4 \tag{20}$$

The marginal revenue of B is less than its finishing cost of \$3. In fact, here it is negative. If the marginal revenue of each product had equaled or exceeded its marginal finishing cost, the solution given by solving equation (16) would have been optimal. However, this is not the case here.

Equating the marginal revenue of product B to its $3 finishing cost yields:

$$40 - 4Q_B = 3 \tag{21}$$

Solving for Q_B indicates that only 9.25 units of B should be finished. The rest should be sold for whatever can be obtained for them (possibly as scrap) at the split-off point.[6] The 9.25 finished units of B should be priced, using equation (4), at

$$P_B = 40 - 2Q_B = 40 - 2\left(9\frac{1}{4}\right) = \$21.50 \tag{22}$$

Equating the marginal revenue of B with its marginal finishing cost means that the costs of the joint raw material and processing costs of the last unit must be recovered by product A. Therefore, the marginal cost of producing a unit of A is \$32 (\$20 + \$7 + \$5). Equating marginal revenue and marginal cost for product A yields

$$MR_A = MC_A \text{ or } 50 - Q_A = 32 \text{ and } Q_A = 18 \tag{23}$$

The optimal quantity of product A is 18 units. Using equation (3), it should be priced at \$41 per unit ($50 - .5Q_A$).

To summarize, for this example, the optimal solution is to produce and sell 18 units of product A and price it at \$41 per unit (or \$41/4 = \$10.25 per lb). The production of A will yield 18 units of product B, of which 9.25 units should be finished and sold for \$21.50 per unit (or \$21.50/6 = \$3.58 per lb). The remaining 8.75 units of B should be disposed of at the split-off point without finishing them.

Summary of Steps for Pricing Joint Products

The steps necessary to solve this joint price-output problem for any number of products follow:

1. Derive the total-revenue and marginal-revenue functions for each product.

2. Add the marginal-revenue functions to obtain a single joint marginal-revenue function that assumes equivalent units of all products will be sold. (Four pounds of A and 6 pounds of B are made equivalent units in the example.)

3. Set the joint marginal-revenue function equal to the joint marginal-cost function (where the joint marginal-cost function is obtained in the same way as the joint marginal-revenue function) and solve for the quantity of the joint product.

4. Determine the marginal revenue for each separate product using the equations determined in step (1) and the quantity determined in step (3).

5a. If the marginal revenue for all separate products is equal to or greater than the direct finishing costs, the solution obtained in step (3) is optimal.

---

6. It is interesting to note that in this case the same product may have the attributes of both a by-product and a joint product. However, if B can be sold at a profit at split-off, this would reduce the number of units finished. For example, if the incremental profit from the sale of 1 unit of B at split-off is \$5, only 8 units of B would be finished ($40 - 4Q_B = 3 + 5$ and $Q_B = 8$). The return to finishing B must more than cover the opportunity cost available were B to be sold at split-off.

5b. If the marginal revenue less finishing costs for a product is negative, equate the marginal-revenue function for that product to its finishing costs to determine the optimal output. Steps (1) through (5a) must be repeated for all products with nonnegative marginal revenues.

The analysis given here includes the case where the production involves by-products because the same dependencies in output and profit exist.

A manager may object to a pretense of accuracy in the solution offered because the information necessary for this solution is seldom known in practice. In particular, the methodology described is appropriate only when demand is the sole limiting factor.[7] The objection has merit, but the importance of the presentation is not in terms of its being applied exactly as illustrated but rather in terms of a method of reasoning. This reasoning shows that the allocation of joint costs is not essential when making output and pricing decisions for joint products.

Allocating Joint Costs Based on Decision Values

An alternative method of allocating common costs is suggested by the use of such costs in a decision-making context. The marginal revenues of the individual products can be used to obtain the inventory values. Suppose, consistent with Exhibit 15-13 (but not the earlier numerical example), that the marginal revenues of two products C and D are equal to or exceed their finishing costs.

Exhibit 15-14 shows the marginal-revenue curves of products C and D as well as the combined marginal-revenue curves. The marginal-cost curve includes finishing costs. The total marginal cost of the two products at the point of optimal output is equal to $35. It is reasonable to divide the marginal cost into two parts based on the marginal revenue of each product. At the optimal level of output, the marginal revenue of product D in this example is $15, and the marginal revenue of C is $20. The marginal revenue and the marginal cost of the joint product is $35. Dividing the $35 of cost between products C and D results in $20 being allocated to C and $15 to D. This procedure is somewhat different from earlier methods of allocation, which based the allocation on the price (average revenue) less any finishing costs. The two procedures would be equivalent if the average-revenue curve were horizontal because the average-revenue and marginal-revenue curves would then coincide.

If a firm has one unit of C and one unit of D in inventory at the end of a period, and if these units would otherwise be produced next period, then the value of these units is the cost that can be saved (less holding costs) from not making these units in the next period. The value of these units is the marginal cost of the units to be produced in the next period. Marginal revenue will be equated to marginal cost, so the marginal-revenue figures can be used to split the marginal costs among the joint products.

---

7. Nonlinear programming techniques could be applied to this type of problem when additional constraints are incorporated. These extensions are not explored here.

EXHIBIT 15-14

Determining Marginal Revenue of Products C and D

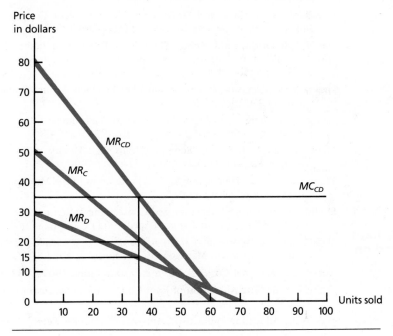

If the productive facilities are not available in the next period, or if the demand will expand so that without the existing inventory of finished products the total demand would not be met, then the value of the units in inventory would depend on the revenue they could earn and not on their cost of replacement. (The actual cost is sunk and is not relevant to the decision to sell.)

Two final points should be made:

1. Suppose that the raw material has been purchased and all of product E has been sold while some product F is still on hand (E and F are joint products). If the firm could not economically store any more F nor sell F, then the cost of product E is the entire cost of the raw material. The cost (and value) of product F's raw material is zero.

2. If the firm has purchased a small amount of raw material, it is reasonable to split the cost of the raw material between the joint products using the expected marginal revenues of the products. These costs would be relevant for decision making (although the price would be set by reference to the average-revenue curves), since they give a reasonable estimate of both the cost and value of the last units made.

Suggested Readings

Baumol, W. J., et al. "The Role of Cost in the Minimum Pricing of Railroad Services." *Journal of Business* (October 1962): 1–10.

Cats-Baril, W., J. Gatti, and D. Grinnell. "Joint Product Costing in the Semiconductor Industry." *Management Accounting* (February 1986): 28–35.

Hardy, J., B. Orton, and L. Pope. "The Sales to Production Ratio: A New Approach to Joint Cost Allocation." *Journal of Accountancy* (October 1981): 105–10 (replies appear in the September 1982 issue of the same journal).

Hatley, R. V. "Decision Making When Joint Products Are Involved." *Accounting Review* (October 1971): 746–55.

Jensen, D. L. "The Role of Cost in Pricing Joint Products: A Case of Production in Fixed Proportions." *Accounting Review* (July 1974): 465–76.

Manes, R., and V. L. Smith. "Economic Joint Cost Theory and Accounting Practice." *Accounting Review* (January 1965): 31–35.

Pfouts, R. W. "The Theory of Cost and Production in the Multi-product Firm." *Econometrica* (October 1961): 650–58.

Shubik, M. "Incentives, Decentralized Control, the Assignment of Joint Costs, and Internal Pricing." *Management Science* (April 1962): 325–43.

Slater, K., and C. Wootton. *A Study of Joint and By-Product Costing in the U.K.* London: Institute of Cost and Management Accountants, 1984.

Turvey, R. "Marginal Cost." *Economic Journal* (June 1969): 282–99.

Walters, A. A. "The Allocation of Joint Costs." *American Economic Review* (June 1960): 419–32.

Weil, R. L. "Allocating Joint Costs." *American Economic Review* (December 1968): 1342–45.

Review Questions

15-1   It is sometimes said that joint-cost allocations are worthless because they cannot be used for decision making. Comment.

15-2   The costs of operating and maintaining a building are common costs with several products resulting. Do you think that it is useful to allocate building-department costs to operating departments and to product lines?

15-3   Distinguish joint costs and indirect costs.

15-4   Distinguish between joint products and by-products from an accounting point of view.

15-5   Assuming the presence of joint costs, what types of decisions may be made using cost-revenue information?

15-6   A firm makes two products that are normally of equal value. Because of a temporary overabundance of one product, it is sold for scrap, resulting in a zero profit per unit. How should the cost of the raw material be allocated during that period of overabundance?

15-7   Is it reasonable for the accountant to allocate joint costs to different products despite the acknowledged impossibility of proving that the allocation is *the* correct allocation?

Exercises   **15-8 Allocating Costs to Joint Products Using Net Sales Values** The Fidler Company has an accounting problem resulting from the production of joint products. How much of the raw material and other joint costs of $3,000 should be assigned to each of the joint products A, B, and C?

Joint Products	Pounds[a]	Sales Value (price × units)	Direct Finishing Costs
A	150	2,000	400
B	50	3,000	900
C	200	4,000	1,700

[a] Product resulting from one unit of raw material and joint cost of $3,000.

REQUIRED:

Compute a reasonable allocation of the $3,000 to the three joint products, using the net sales values.

15-9 Allocating Costs to Joint Products and By-products Referring to Exercise 15-8, assume that a by-product has a value of $100 (per $3,000 of joint costs) and processing costs of $20. Compute the allocation of the $3,000 to the joint products and to the by-product.

15-10 Production and Sales Decisions Referring to Exercise 15-8, assume that the market prices of the factors of production remain unchanged but that the sales prices of the joint products A, B, and C change to $2,500, $2,000, and $1,000 for A, B, and C, respectively. What would be your decision relative to producing and selling each type of product?

15-11 Influence of Manufacturing Procedures on Costs The Capital Corporation stamps a component part, called X. From a roll of steel 100 feet long it is expected that 50 units of X will be obtained. The cost of 100 feet of the steel is $25, and the standard material cost of a unit of X has been set at $.50. X uses approximately 90 percent of the total metal.

In April 1986 an engineer found that by cutting the metal scraps from the production line of X into easily handled shapes, a product Y could be made. For the remainder of 1986, Ys were made from this scrap. It is estimated that one unit of Y could be obtained per foot of steel. Y used approximately one-tenth of the total metal; the cost per unit was established at $.025. To record the manufacture of 1 million units of Y from 1,000,000 feet of steel, the following journal entry was made for the material component of Y (a standard cost system was in use for material):

Inventory — Y	$ 25,000	
Material		$ 25,000

To record the manufacture of 500,000 units of X, the following entry was made:

Inventory — X	$250,000	
Material		$250,000

REQUIRED:

Comment on the procedure followed.

15-12 Allocating Expenses of Scrap Operation   The Skyle Company has an extensive scrap operation, and the pieces of metal resulting from stamping operations have a high value on the
scrap market. Total scrap sales amount to approximately $4 million per year. The total
sales of the corporation are approximately $1 billion per year. The expenses of operating
the scrap-processing center (where the scrap is sorted and baled) are approximately
$300,000 of direct costs.

The controller has argued that the scrap operation should be charged with part of the
cost of raw material; the production manager, who is in overall charge of the scrap
operation, argues that it should not be charged because there is no reasonable method of
assigning material costs to the operation.

REQUIRED:

Comment on the positions of the controller and the production manager. What, if any, are
the accounting problems?

15-13 Role of Cost in the Minimum Pricing of Railroad Services   The following summary is from
W. J. Baumol, et al., "The Role of Cost in the Minimum Pricing of Railroad Services,"
Journal of Business (Vol. 35, No. 4).

1. In the determination of cost floors as a guide to the pricing of particular railroad
services, or the services of any other transport mode, incremental costs of each
particular service are the only relevant costs.

2. Rates for particular railroad services should be set at amounts (subject to the
regulation maximum rates and to legal rules against unjust discrimination) that
will make the greatest total contribution to net income. Clearly, such maximizing rates would never fall below incremental costs.

3. Pricing which is not restricted by any minimum other than incremental cost
can foster more efficient use of railroad resources and capacity and can therefore encourage lower costs and rates. This same principle applies to other
modes of transportation.

4. The presence of large amounts of fixed costs and unused capacity in railroad
facilities makes it especially important that railroad rates encourage a large
volume of traffic.

5. Reduced rates which more than cover incremental costs and are designed by
management to maximize contribution to net income do not constitute proof
of predatory competition.

6. "Fully distributed" costs derived by apportioning unallocable costs have no
significance in determining rate floors for particular railroad services. The application of such a criterion would arbitrarily force the railroads to maintain rates
above the level which would yield maximum contribution to net income and
would deprive them of much traffic for which they can compete economically.
For similar reasons, restriction of railroad minimum rates according to the "full
cost of the low-cost carrier" is economically unsound.

REQUIRED:

Comment on the conclusions.

15-14 Applying Conclusions for Services to Manufacturing The following argument can be found in an article by W. J. Baumol, et al, in the *Journal of Business* (Vol. 35, No. 4).

"Fully Distributed" Cost—
An Invalid Basis for Minimum Pricing

The relevant incremental costs constitute all the cost information pertinent to the determination of floors in the pricing of particular railroad services. "Fully distributed" cost, measured by some kind of arbitrary statistical apportionment of the unallocable costs among the various units or classes of traffic, is an economically invalid criterion for setting minimum rates, from both a managerial and a regulatory standpoint. No particular category of traffic can be held economically responsible for any given share of the unallocable costs. Whether any particular rate is above or below some fully distributed cost is without real economic significance for minimum pricing.

Stated differently, the appropriate aim of the railroads is to determine that margin above incremental costs, traffic volume considered, at which a rate produces the maximum total contribution toward fixed costs and net income. Fully distributed costs cannot serve this vital economic purpose. They present an entirely false picture of traffic profitability. Their use would drive away great quantities of profitable, volume-moving traffic now handled at rates below fully distributed costs.

REQUIRED:

Is the statement valid for a manufacturing firm?

Problems   **15-15 Joint Product Decisions** Lorimar Paint Company buys a by-product from Gulf Oil Corporation for $17 a barrel. Lorimar then converts each barrel through various chemical processes into two gallons of paint thinner and two gallons of paint remover. The chemical process results in separation of the products at the end of the process and costs $8 to run. Each product requires separate finishing costs before it can be sold. These costs are $4 per gallon for the paint thinner and $6 per gallon for the paint remover.

REQUIRED:

a. Assume the following market prices:

Paint thinner	$20 per gallon
Paint remover	$25 per gallon

What allocation of the *joint* cost would be made *per gallon* based on the ultimate sales prices?

b. What allocation of the joint cost would be made per gallon using a method that is based on the estimated product values at split-off?

c. What allocation of the *joint* cost would be made per gallon if inventories are to reflect revenue generation ability when all costs (whether joint or not and regardless of which product they relate to) are equally productive?

d. Answer the following questions based on units of *one* gallon (ignore the prices in part 1 above):

(1) If the price of one gallon of paint thinner plus the price of one gallon of paint remover exceeds _____, production of at least one product will be profitable.

(2) If the price of one gallon of paint thinner plus the price of one gallon of paint remover is less than _____, neither product should be produced.

(3) If the price of one gallon of paint remover is at least _____, then it will be profitable to produce it and it will be profitable to finish and market a gallon of paint thinner if the price of paint thinner exceeds _____.

(4) If the price of paint thinner is $6 per gallon and the price of paint remover is $7 per gallon, what product(s) should be produced (both, thinner, remover, neither)?

15-16 Joint Product Decisions　The Krayler Manufacturing Company purchases material for $50 per unit. This material is converted into two separate products, X and Y. Joint processing costs are $30. After separation of the products, it costs $14 to finish one unit of X and $6 to finish one unit of Y. Each unit of raw material yields one unit of X and one unit of Y. The marketing research group estimates monthly demand for the two products in units as follows:

$$X \quad \text{Quantity demanded} = 400 - 2 \text{ (price of } X)$$

$$Y \quad \text{Quantity demanded} = 75 - .5 \text{ (price of } Y)$$

REQUIRED:

Complete the following:

a. If the price of X plus the price of Y exceeds _____, the firm should produce.

b. If the price of X plus the price of Y is less than _____, in total, the firm should do nothing.

c. If the price of X exceeds _____, the firm should finish X and it should also finish Y if its price exceeds _____.

d. If the price of Y exceeds _____, the firm should finish Y and it should finish X if its price exceeds _____.

15-17 Assigning Joint Costs and Decisions

a. Johnson Computer Systems Company manufactures computer chips. The chips are produced in batches, and when they are completed, several of their parameters are tested. On the basis of these tests, some chips are scrapped, and the rest are classified according to particular combinations of their parameters (the production process cannot be controlled to the extent that the parameters of all the chips are the same). In a recent batch of 1,000, production costs of $4,000 were incurred. Eight hundred of the chips were estimated to have a net realizable value of $5 a piece (on the basis of their parameters) and the remaining 200, $10 a piece. These estimates were based on competitors' prices for chips with roughly similar parameters. How would you assign production costs to the chips? What are the limitations of your method?

b. The $10 chips meet all the electrical specifications of the $5 chips. Assume that all the $5 chips have been sold, but that 100 of the $10 chips remain in inventory. Should the $10 chips be sold at a net realizable value of $5 to meet additional demand for the cheaper chips, given the production cost assigned to them? Explain, indicating any assumptions required.

15-18 Main Products and By-products   Doe Corporation grows, processes, cans, and sells three main pineapple products—sliced pineapple, crushed pineapple, and pineapple juice. The outside skin is cut off in the Cutting Department and processed as animal feed. The skin is treated as a by-product. Doe's production process is as follows:

1. Pineapples first are processed in the Cutting Department. The pineapples are washed and the outside skin is cut away. Then the pineapples are cored and trimmed for slicing. The three main products (sliced, crushed, juice) and the by-product (animal feed) are recognizable after processing in the Cutting Department. Each product is then transferred to a separate department for final processing.

2. The trimmed pineapples are forwarded to the Slicing Department, where the pineapples are sliced and canned. Any juice generated during the slicing operation is packed in the cans with the slices.

3. The pieces of pineapple trimmed from the fruit are diced and canned in the Crushing Department. Again, the juice generated during this operation is packed in the can with the crushed pineapple.

4. The core and surplus pineapple generated from the Cutting Department are pulverized into a liquid in the Juicing Department. There is an evaporation loss equal to 8 percent of the weight of the good output produced in this department, which occurs as the juices are heated.

5. The outside skin is chopped into animal feed in the Feed Department.

The Doe Corporation uses the net-realizable-value method (relative-sales-value method) to assign costs of the joint process to its main products. The by-product is inventoried at its market value.

A total of 270,000 pounds were entered into the Cutting Department during May. The schedule presented below shows the costs incurred in each department, the proportion by weight transferred to the four final processing departments, and the selling price of each end product.

PROCESSING DATA AND COSTS
May

Department	Costs Incurred	Proportion of Product by Weight Transferred to Departments	Selling Price per Pound of Final Product
Cutting	$60,000	none	none
Slicing	4,700	35%	$.60
Crushing	10,580	28	.55
Juicing	3,250	27	.30
Animal feed	700	10	.10
Total	$79,230	100%	

REQUIRED:

a. The Doe Corporation uses the net-realizable-value method to determine inventory values for its main products and by-products. Calculate:

(1) The pounds of pineapple that result as output for pineapple slices, crushed pineapple, pineapple juice, and animal feed,

(2) The net realizable value at the split-off point of the three main products,

(3) The amount of the cost of the Cutting Department assigned to each of the three main products and to the by-product in accordance with corporate policy,

(4) The gross margins for each of the three main products.

b. Comment on the significance to management of the gross margin information by main product.

c. In the production of joint products either a by-product or scrap could be generated.

(1) Distinguish between a by-product and scrap.

(2) Would the proper accounting treatment for scrap differ from that for by-products? Explain your answer. (*CMA adapted*)

15-19 Joint Cost Allocation and Decision Making   Talor Chemical Company is a highly diversified chemical processing company. The company manufactures swimming pool chemicals, chemicals for metal processing companies, specialized chemical compounds for other companies, and a full line of pesticides and insecticides.

Currently, the Noorwood plant is producing two derivatives, RNA-1 and RNA-2, from the chemical compound VDB developed by Talor's research labs. Each week 1,200,000 pounds of VDB is processed at a cost of $246,000 into 800,000 pounds of RNA-1 and 400,000 pounds of RNA-2. The proportion of these two outputs is fixed and cannot be altered because this is a joint process. RNA-1 has no market value until it is converted into a product with the trade name Fastkil. The cost to process RNA-1 into Fastkil is $240,000. Fastkil wholesales at $50 per 100 pounds.

RNA-2 is sold as is for $80 per hundred pounds. However, Talor has discovered that RNA-2 can be converted into two new products through further processing. The further processing would require the addition of 400,000 pounds of compound LST to the 400,000 pounds of RNA-2. The joint process would yield 400,000 pounds each of DMZ-3 and Pestrol—the two new products. The additional raw material and related processing costs of this joint process would be $120,000. DMZ-3 and Pestrol would each be sold for $57.50 per 100 pounds. Talor management has decided not to process RNA-2 further based on the analysis presented in the schedule below. Talor uses the physical method to allocate the common costs arising from joint processing.

		Process Further		
	RNA-2	DMZ-3	Pestrol	Total
Production in pounds	400,000	400,000	400,000	
Revenue	$320,000	$230,000	$230,000	$460,000
Costs:				
VDB costs	$ 82,000	$ 61,500	$ 61,500	$123,000
Additional raw materials (LST) and processing of RNA-2	—	60,000	60,000	120,000
Total costs	$ 82,000	$121,500	$121,500	$243,000
Weekly gross profit	$238,000	$108,500	$108,500	$217,000

A new staff accountant who was to review the analysis above commented that it should be revised and stated, "Product costing of product such as these should be done on a net relative sales value basis not a physical volume basis."

REQUIRED:

a. Discuss whether the use of the net relative sales value method would provide data more relevant for the decision to market DMZ-3 and Pestrol.

b. Critique the Talor Company's analysis and make any revisions that are necessary. Your critique and analysis should indicate

(1) Whether Talor Chemical Company made the correct decision,

(2) The gross savings (loss) per week of Talor's decision not to process RNA-2 further, if different from the company's prepared analysis. (*CMA adapted*)

15-20 Allocation Based on Relative Sales Value Warfield Corporation manufactures products *C*, *D*, and *E* from a joint process. Joint costs are allocated on the basis of relative-sales-value at split-off. Additional information is as follows:

	Product			
	C	D	E	Total
Units produced	6,000	4,000	2,000	12,000
Joint costs	$ 72,000	?	?	$120,000
Sales value at split-off	?	?	$30,000	$200,000
Additional costs if processed further	$ 14,000	$10,000	$ 6,000	$ 30,000
Sales value if processed further	$140,000	$60,000	$40,000	$240,000

a. How much of the joint costs should Warfield allocate to product *D* (choose one)?

(1) $24,000

(2) $28,800

(3) $30,000

(4) $32,000

b. Assuming that the 2,000 units of product *E* were processed further and sold for $40,000, what was Warfield's gross profit on the sale (choose one)?

(1) $4,000

(2) $14,000

(3) $16,000

(4) $22,000 (*CPA adapted*)

15-21 Joint Cost Allocation　Grafton Company produces joint products *A* and *B* in Department 1 from a process that also yields by-product *W*. Product *A* and by-product *W* are sold after separation, but product *B* must be further processed in Department 2 before it can be sold. The cost assigned to the by-product is its market value less $0.40 per pound for delivery expense (net-realizable-value method). Information relating to a batch produced in July is as follows:

Product	Production (in pounds)	Sales Price per Pound
A	2,000 lbs	$4.50
B	4,000	9.00
W	500	1.50
Joint cost in Department 1		$18,000
Product B additional process cost in Department 2		$10,000

a. For joint cost allocation purposes, what is the net realizable value at the split-off point of product *B* (choose one)?

(1) $46,000

(2) $45,000

(3) $36,000

(4) $26,000

b. How much of the joint cost incurred in Department 1 should be allocated to the joint products (choose one)?

(1) $17,250

(2) $17,450

(3) $17,800

(4) $18,550 (*CPA adapted*)

15-22 **By-product; Process Costing** The Adept Company is a manufacturer of two products known as Prep and Pride. Incidental to the production of these two products, it produces a by-product known as Wilton. The manufacturing process covers two departments, Grading and Saturating.

The manufacturing process begins in the Grading Department when raw materials are started in process. On completion of processing in the Grading Department the by-product Wilton is produced, which accounts for 20 percent of the material output. This by-product needs no further processing and is transferred to finished goods.

The net realizable value of the by-product Wilton is accounted for as a reduction of the cost of materials in the Grading Department. The current selling price of Wilton is $1 per pound and the estimated selling and delivery costs total ten cents per pound.

The remaining output is transferred to the Saturating Department for the final phase of production. In the Saturating Department, water is added at the beginning of the production process, which results in a 50 percent gain in weight of the materials in production.

The following information is available for the month of November:

	November 1		November 30
Inventories	Quantity (pounds)	Amount	Quantity (pounds)
Work in process:			
Grading Department	None	—	None
Saturating Department	1,600	$17,600	2,000
Finished goods:			
Prep	600	14,520	1,600
Pride	2,400	37,110	800
Wilton	None	—	None

The work-in-process inventory (labor and overhead) in the Saturating Department is estimated to be 50 percent complete both at the beginning and end of November.

Costs of production for November are as follows:

Costs of Production	Materials Used	Labor and Overhead
Grading Department	$265,680	$86,400
Saturating Department	—	86,000

The material used in the Grading Department weighed 36,000 pounds. Adept uses the first-in, first-out method of process costing.

REQUIRED:

Prepare a cost of production report for both the Grading and Saturating Departments for the month of November. Show supporting computations in good form.

The answer should include

a. Equivalent units of production (in pounds),

b. Total manufacturing costs,

c. Cost per equivalent unit (pounds),

d. Dollar amount of ending work in process,

e. Dollar amount of inventory cost transferred out. (*CPA adapted*)

15-23 Production Decisions and Inventory Values **(see Appendix 15A)**   A raw material is used to produce two products. One unit of raw material costing $8.50 is turned into 1 unit of *A* and 1 unit of *B*. Additional information is as follows:

Joint cost of processing raw material $ 4
Direct cost of finishing product *A*   8
Direct cost of finishing product *B*   12

The price-quantity relationships of the two products are:

$$Q_A = 40 - \tfrac{1}{2}P_A \qquad Q_B = 80 - 4P_B$$

where *Q* is the number of units demanded in one day with price *P*.

REQUIRED:

a. How many units of raw material, product *A*, and product *B* should be processed daily?

b. If there were one unit each of *A* and *B* remaining in the finished-goods inventory, what would be the inventory value of those units?

c. Suppose that $P_A = 16$, $P_B = 18$ regardless of the firm's output, and either product can be sold for $7 at the split-off point. What should the firm do?

15-24 Pricing and Production Decisions **(see Appendix 15A)**   The Auston Company purchases a raw material for $50 per unit that is turned into two products, *A* and *B*. The joint costs of processing are $30. After the two products are separated, it costs $14 to finish *A* and $6 to finish *B*. One unit of *A* and one unit of *B* are obtained from each unit of raw material.

The following quantity-price relationships are expected to continue into the future (they relate the units of demand for a month):

$$P_A = 200 - \tfrac{1}{2}Q_A \qquad P_b = 150 - 2Q_B$$

REQUIRED:

a. What price and what output for each of the two end products would maximize profits?

b. Assuming that one unit of unfinished *A* and 20 units of unfinished *B* are on hand at the end of a month, how should these be valued?

15-25 Continuation of Problem 15-15 **(see Appendix 15A)**   Given the following demand equations (ignore the prices but not the costs given earlier), establish the optimal level of production (figures relate to gallons). You need not round your numbers.

Paint thinner: $D = 40 - .5P$

Paint remover: $D = 80 - 4P$

Also compute the profit for your solution.

15-26 Continuation of Problem 15-16 (see Appendix)

   a. What price and what output for each of the two products would maximize contribution on a monthly basis?

   b. Assume one unit of X at the split-off point and one unit of Y at the split-off point (i.e., they are not finished) are on hand at the end of a given month. How should they be valued for internal decision making? (Ignore production level questions relating to the next month.)

   c. In part 1, what assumption made in the problem statement would be most difficult to establish in fact?

15-27 Production and Pricing Decisions (see Appendix)   The Microtheory Company uses a joint process for the production of three goods: A, B, and C. For each unit of raw material, one unit of each of the three end products is obtained. The total joint costs of both purchasing the raw material and processing it into the intermediate stages of the three goods is $20. The additional costs of finishing the products are: A, $10; B, $20; C, $20. The company has done a study of price-quantity relationships for the three goods, and it is believed that over the relevant range of output (50,000 to 100,000 units of each product) the following demand functions will apply for the next period:

$$P_A = 200 - Q_A$$
$$P_B = 400 - 2Q_B$$
$$P_C = 260 - 2Q_C$$

In each case, the Qs represent thousands of units.

REQUIRED

What quantity of each product should be produced for the next period, and what should the prices be? (The intermediate products have no scrap value.)

16

Accounting for Spoilage, Rework, and Scrap

LEARNING OBJECTIVES

After studying this chapter, you should be able to:

1 Define *normal* and *abnormal spoilage, reworked units,* and *scrap*.

2 Account for normal and abnormal spoilage under process costing.

3 Account for normal and abnormal spoilage under job-order costing.

4 Account for normal and abnormal spoilage under standard costing.

5 Determine the amount of normal spoilage.

6 Account for the costs of reworked units.

7 Account for the costs of scrap materials.

*C*ontrolling the costs of spoilage, reworked units of product, and scrap is important in any manufacturing process. In order to make a reasonable profit, manufacturers must do everything possible to keep these costs in check. Moreover, recent years have seen increased concern on the part of manufacturers regarding the quality of the products they sell. Controlling product quality is closely related to the problem of controlling the costs of spoilage, reworked units, and scrap.

Properly controlling the costs of spoiled or reworked units and scrap requires a system for measuring these costs. Moreover, most production processes normally include some amount of spoiled and reworked units and scrap. Because these costs are a normal consequence of the production process, the costs should be inventoried and considered part of the cost of good units produced. This chapter discusses the cost accounting systems used (1) to measure the costs of spoiled and reworked units and scrap and (2) to allocate properly these costs to the good units produced.[1]

Terminology

Scrap results when the raw material being processed is not of the exact length, width, or thickness required for the product being made and some part of the raw material is not usable in making the product. To some extent, scrap may be reduced and controlled, but there is likely to be "skeletons" created in a process where pieces are punched from a metal strip or bar ends when metal bar stock is being cut into pieces. Scrap generally has relatively minor economic value and may either be sold or reused in some way in the production process. The term **waste** is often used to refer to the portion of material inputs that either disappears in the production process or has no economic value. Examples include evaporated liquids, sawdust, metal shavings, and shrinkage.

Spoilage results when either the material being processed or the finished product is discovered to be unusable because of defects in workmanship or material. Like scrap, the spoilage occurs after the raw material has entered the production process, but spoilage is not inherent in the design of the product or in the characteristics of the raw material. With sufficient care, spoilage can be avoided entirely or at least reduced to very small amounts. However, achieving this reduction in spoilage is costly, and the benefit of reducing the spoilage rate may not be worth the cost.

The amount of spoiled product may be normal or abnormal. **Normal spoilage** is the amount expected, given the production technology. The technology embodies such factors as the production machinery, grade of material and labor, and sequence of operations. **Abnormal spoilage** is spoilage above that considered normal for the

1. This chapter may be studied after Chapter 6 or after Chapter 8.

production technology. Defining normal spoilage is a management responsibility. This determination should be reviewed periodically because new techniques, better inputs, or improved controls may lead to a reduction in the normal level of spoilage. The determination of normal and abnormal spoilage is dependent on the production technology that has been chosen by management. A better, and usually more costly, production process may result in lower expected levels of normal spoilage, whereas greater normal spoilage may result from a less costly or less sophisticated production process.

Reworked units are those that do not initially meet product-quality specifications but have subsequently been reworked so that they may be sold as good units.

Spoilage

This section presents the methods of accounting for normal and abnormal spoilage under process costing, job-order costing, and standard costing.

Treatment of Spoilage Under Process Costing[2]

When a process-costing system is used in conjunction with either actual or normal costing, the costs of normal and abnormal spoilage are identified and accounted for in the process-costing calculations. The cost of abnormal spoilage is treated as a period cost and is charged against the income of the period.

The cost of normal spoilage is treated as a product cost. This approach reflects the fact that normal spoilage is part of the normal cost of producing good units of product. If the ending work-in-process inventory is at a stage of completion prior to the point where product units are inspected, the normal spoilage cost is allocated entirely to the cost of good units completed and transferred out. If the ending work-in-process inventory is at a stage of completion after the point where product units are inspected, the cost of normal spoilage is allocated between the good units completed and the ending work-in-process inventory. These two situations are depicted in Exhibit 16-1.

Examples are the best way to illustrate the process-costing calculations for both of the situations depicted in Exhibit 16-1.

Situation I: Ending Work-in-Process Not Yet Inspected   The data for the example is given in Exhibit 16-2. The material is introduced at the beginning of the process. The normal spoilage is 8 percent of the good units completed and transferred out. Thus, normal spoilage is 1,600 units (20,000 good units $\times$ 8 percent), and abnormal spoilage is 400 units.

Suppose that inspection occurs when the units are one-half converted. Because the units in ending work in process are only one-third converted, they have not yet

---

2. This section assumes that Chapter 6 on process-costing has been completed.

EXHIBIT 16-1

Treatment of Normal Spoilage Costs Under Process Costing

Situation I

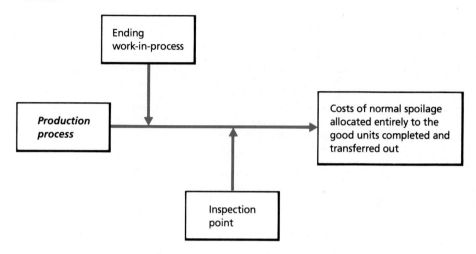

Situation II

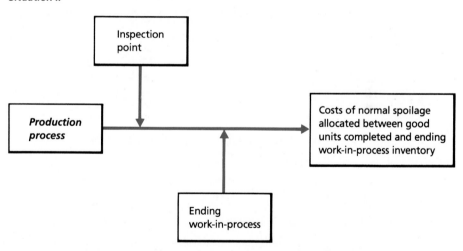

^aIn both situation I and situation II, the cost of abnormal spoilage is treated as a period cost.

---

passed the inspection point. Hence, no spoilage costs will be allocated to the ending work-in-process inventory.

The calculations for FIFO process costing are shown in Exhibit 16-3. The calculations are similar to those done when no spoilage had occurred (covered in Chapter 6).

EXHIBIT 16-2

Data for Illustration of Situation I: Ending Work-in-Process Inventory Not Yet Inspected

	Beginning	Ending
Units	2,000	3,000
Fraction completed	$1/2^a$	$1/3^a$
New units started	23,000 units	
Good units transferred out	20,000 units	
Normal spoilage	1,600 units	
Abnormal spoilage	400 units	
Beginning inventory costs:		
Materials	$ 3,000	
Conversion	$ 12,000	
Direct material costs added	$ 69,000^b	
Conversion costs added:		
Direct labor	$170,000^b	
Overhead	92,500^b	
Total costs	$346,500	

[a] Fraction completed with respect to conversion activity. This is the proportion of the total conversion work to be done on the units that has been accomplished at the indicated date. (Refer back to Chapter 6 for a discussion of equivalent units.)

[b] Actual costs incurred during the month.

EXHIBIT 16-3

FIFO Process-Costing Calculations for Situation I

		Materials	Conversion
1. Analysis of units in and units out			
Units in:			
Work in process, beginning	2,000 (1/2)	(2,000)	(1,000)
New units started	23,000		
Total units in	25,000		
Units out:			
Good units transferred out	20,000	20,000	20,000
Normal spoilage	1,600	1,600	800
Abnormal spoilage	400	400	200
Work in process, ending	3,000 (1/3)	3,000	1,000
Total units out	25,000		
2. Equivalent units		23,000	21,000

EXHIBIT 16-3   *Continued*

	Materials	Conversion
3. Analysis of costs in		
Work in process, beginning	$ 15,000	
Current costs:		
Material	69,000	$ 69,000
Conversion	262,500		$262,500
Total costs in	$346,500	$ 69,000	$262,500
4. Unit costs		$ 69,000	$262,500
		23,000	21,000
		equals	equals
		$3.00	$12.50
5. Analysis of costs out		
Work in process, beginning	$ 15,000	
Conversion costs		
(costs to complete)		
(1,000 × $12.50)	12,500	$ 27,500
Cost of units started		
and completed		
(28,000 × $15.50[a])		279,000
Total cost of good units		
transferred out before allocation		
of normal spoilage		$306,500
Normal spoilage:		
Material cost (1,600 × $3.00)		4,800
Conversion cost (800 × $12.50)		10,000
Total cost of normal spoilage		14,800
Abnormal spoilage:		
Material cost (400 × $3.00)		1,200
Conversion cost (200 × $12.50)		2,500
Total cost of abnormal spoilage		3,700
Work in process, ending:		
Material cost (3,000 × $3.00)		9,000
Conversion cost (1,000 × $12.50)		12,500
Total cost of work in process, ending		21,500
Total costs out		$346,500
6. Allocation of normal spoilage cost		
Total cost of good units transferred out		
before allocation of normal spoilage		$306,500
Cost of normal spoilage		14,800
Total cost of units transferred out in-		
cluding allocation of normal spoilage		$321,300

[a] Total cost per equivalent unit = $3.00 + $12.50 = $15.00

The differences in the calculations in Exhibit 16-3 relate to the units that were spoiled. In step 1, analysis of units in and units out, two more categories of units have been added to fully explain what happened to all of the units in process. These categories are normal spoilage and abnormal spoilage. Because materials are added at the beginning of the process, the 1,600 physical units of normal spoilage represent 1,600 equivalent units of material input, and the 400 physical units of abnormal spoilage represent 400 equivalent units of material input. Inspection occurs when units are one-half converted, however, so the conversion activity on a unit stops when it is discovered to be spoiled. Hence, the 1,600 physical units of normal spoilage only received 800 (1,600 × 50 percent) equivalent units of conversion activity, and the 400 physical units of abnormal spoilage received only 200 (400 × 50 percent) equivalent units of conversion activity.

The purpose of step 2 in Exhibit 16-3 is to determine the total equivalent units of materials and conversion accomplished during the current period. Steps 3 and 4 determine the costs per equivalent unit of materials and conversion. All of these steps are identical to those performed with no spoilage involved.

Step 5 is to compute the cost of each of the categories of physical units. This is done by multiplying the number of equivalent units of conversion by the unit conversion cost, multiplying the number of equivalent units of materials by the unit material cost, and then adding the two. Costs are computed for normal and abnormal spoilage as well as for the good units completed and transferred out and ending work-in-process inventory. Because FIFO is in use, the costs associated with the beginning work-in-process inventory are kept separate and associated as a lump sum with the units completed and transferred out.

The final step in Exhibit 16-3 is to allocate the costs of normal spoilage. None of the units in the ending work-in-process inventory has yet been inspected, so all of the normal spoilage costs are added to the cost of the good units completed and transferred out.

The journal entries used to record the flow of costs during the month are:

Work-in-Process Inventory	331,500	
Materials Inventory		69,000
Salaries Payable		170,000
Actual Overhead		92,500
To put costs of direct material, direct labor, and overhead into work in process.		
Normal Spoilage	14,800	
Work-in-Process Inventory		14,800
To remove the cost of normal spoilage from work in process.		
Loss from Abnormal Spoilage	3,700	
Work-in-Process Inventory		3,700
To remove the cost of abnormal spoilage from work in process and designate it as a loss of the period.		

Finished-Goods Inventory	306,500	
Work-in-Process Inventory		306,500

To remove the costs of good units completed
and transferred from work-in-process inventory
and add these costs to finished-goods inventory.

Finished-Goods Inventory	14,800	
Normal Spoilage		14,800

To add the costs of normal spoilage to finished-
goods inventory.

Income Summary	3,700	
Loss from Abnormal Spoilage		3,700

To close the loss from abnormal spoilage into
income for the period, thereby reducing
income.

The process-costing calculations using the weighted-average method are displayed in Exhibit 16-4. The same differences occur between FIFO and weighted-average process costing regardless of whether any spoilage is involved. Under the weighted-average method, the costs associated with the beginning work-in-process inventory are added to the current-period costs. The cost per equivalent unit is then computed by dividing that total cost figure by the total equivalent units of input, which includes both the input activity of the current period as well as the equivalent units of input associated with the beginning work in process. Once the cost per equivalent unit has been calculated, for both materials and conversion, the treatment of spoilage is the same under both FIFO and weighted-average process costing.

Situation II: Ending Work-in-Process Has Been Inspected When the ending work-in-process inventory has already passed the inspection point, the cost of normal spoilage is allocated between the ending work-in-process inventory and the good units completed and transferred out. The data for our example of this situation are given in Exhibit 16-5.

Because materials are added to the process at the beginning, each spoiled unit represents one whole equivalent unit of material input. However, conversion activity stops when a spoiled unit is discovered at the half-way point in the production process. Hence, each spoiled unit represents only .5 equivalent unit of conversion activity. The costs of normal and abnormal spoilage are calculated below:

Normal spoilage:	
Material cost $(100 \times \$3.00)$	$300
Conversion cost $(100 \times .5 \times \$8.00)$	400
Total cost of normal spoilage	$700
Abnormal spoilage:	
Material cost $(60 \times \$3.00)$	$180
Conversion cost $(60 \times .5 \times \$8.00)$	240
Total cost of abnormal spoilage	$420

EXHIBIT 16-4

Weighted-Average Process-Costing Calculations for Situation I

		Materials	Conversion
1. Analysis of units in and units out			
Units in:			
Work in process, beginning	2,000 (1/2)		
New units started	23,000		
Total units in	25,000		
Units out:			
Good units transferred out	20,000	20,000	20,000
Normal spoilage	1,600	1,600	800
Abnormal spoilage	400	400	200
Work in process, ending	3,000 (1/3)	3,000	1,000
Total units out	25,000		
2. Equivalent units		25,000	22,000
3. Analysis of costs in:			
Work in process, beginning	$ 15,000	$ 3,000	$ 12,000
Current costs:			
Material	69,000	69,000	
Conversion	262,500		262,500
Total costs in	$346,500	$72,000	$274,500
4. Unit costs		$72,000	$274,500
		25,000	22,000
		equals	equals
		$2.88	$12.4773[a]
5. Analysis of costs out:			
Cost of good units transferred out before allocation of normal spoilage (20,000 × $15.3573[b])			$307,146[a]
Normal spoilage:			
Material cost (1,600 × $2.88)		$ 4,608	
Conversion cost (800 × $12.4773)		9,982[a]	
Total cost of normal spoilage			14,590
Abnormal spoilage:			
Material cost (400 × $2.88)		1,152	
Conversion cost (200 × $12.4773)		2,495[a]	
Total cost of abnormal spoilage			3,647
Work in process, ending			
Material cost (3,000 × $2.88)		$ 8,640	
Conversion cost (1,000 × $12.4773)		12,477[a]	
Total cost of work in process, ending			21,117
Total costs out			$346,500
6. Allocation of normal spoilage cost:			
Total cost of good units transferred out before allocation of normal spoilage			$307,146
Cost of normal spoilage			14,590
Total cost of units transferred out including allocation of normal spoilage			$321,736

[a] Rounded.

[b] Total cost per equivalent unit = $2.88 + $12.4773 = $15.3573.

EXHIBIT 16-5

Data for Illustration of Situation II: Ending Work-in-Process Inventory Has Been Inspected

---

Good units completed and transferred out	6,000 units
Ending work-in-process inventory (75% complete with respect to conversion)	2,000 units
Normal spoilage	100 units
Abnormal spoilage	60 units

Inspection point is when units are 50 percent converted.
Materials are added at the beginning of the process.
Cost per equivalent unit (assumes weighted-average process costing):

Material	$ 3.00
Conversion	8.00
Total unit cost	$11.00

The abnormal spoilage cost is treated as a period cost. The normal spoilage cost is allocated as shown in Exhibit 16-6.

The cost of normal spoilage is allocated between ending work-in-process inventory and good units completed and transferred out in proportion to the number of units in those two categories that have passed the inspection point.

EXHIBIT 16-6

Allocation of Normal Spoilage Costs: Situation II

	Material	Conversion
Good units completed and transferred	6,000	6,000
Ending work-in-process inventory:		
Material (2,000 × 100%)	2,000	
Conversion (2,000 × 75%)		1,500
Total equivalent units	8,000	7,500

Normal spoilage cost:
Allocated to good units completed and transferred out:

Material (6,000/8,000) × $300	= $225
Conversion (6,000/8,000) × $400	= 300
Total	$525

Allocated to ending work-in-process inventory:

Material (2,000/8,000) × $300	= $ 75
Conversion (2,000/8,000) × $400	= 100
Total	$175

Treatment of Spoilage Under Job-Order Costing

Under job-order costing, the costs of abnormal spoilage are considered a period cost, just as they are under process costing. There are two methods used to account for the costs of normal spoilage under job-order costing. In method I the cost of the normal spoilage associated with a particular job is considered a product cost of that job. Under method II the cost of normal spoilage for all jobs is added to actual overhead, and then this normal spoilage cost is spread over all jobs through the application of overhead.

Suppose that the normal spoilage in the production of a type of circuit board (Job Number A27) is 5 percent of good output. When 1,050 boards were manufactured, 60 of them were spoiled, so that normal spoilage was 50 units and abnormal spoilage was 10 units. Assume that the cost incurred in producing each spoiled circuit board is $4 and that $1 worth of usable material can be salvaged from a spoiled board. The two methods of accounting for the spoilage costs are shown below.

- *Method I:*   Normal spoilage considered a cost of the particular job in which it occurs.

Material Inventory (60 boards × $1.00)	60	
Loss Due to Abnormal Spoilage (10 boards × $3.00)	30	
Work-in-Process Inventory (Job #A27)		90

This journal entry reduces the job cost in work-in-process inventory by the salvage value of the usable material in the spoiled boards plus the net cost of the abnormally spoiled units (10 boards at $3 per board, where $3 = $4 production cost incurred − $1 salvage value). The effect is to leave the net cost of the normally spoiled units in work in process where it is associated with Job A27. The net cost of the normal spoilage is $150 (50 boards at $3 per board).

- *Method II:*   Normal spoilage added to overhead cost to be spread among all production jobs.

Material Inventory (60 boards × $1.00)	60	
Loss Due to Abnormal Spoilage (10 boards × $3.00)	30	
Actual Overhead (50 boards × $3.00)	150	
Work-in-Process Inventory (Job #A27)		240

This journal entry differs from the previous one in that an additional $150, the net cost of normal spoilage, is removed from work in process and is no longer associated specifically with Job A27. This $150 is added to actual overhead. Under this approach, normal spoilage costs are estimated and included in budgeted overhead. Then the costs of normal spoilage are spread across all jobs through the application of overhead.

The choice between method I and method II depends on the nature of the normal spoilage. If it is specific to a particular job, in the sense that it is due to the characteristics of that job, then method I is most sensible. If, on the other hand, normal spoilage is common to all jobs, then the inclusion of such costs in overhead is a reasonable procedure.

Treatment of Spoilage Under Standard Costing

Under standard costing, the cost of normal spoilage is incorporated into the standards. Following this procedure, the cost of normal spoilage is not reported separately. The unit standard cost of the product includes the cost of normal spoilage and is not affected by the actual amount of spoilage. Assume, for example, that normal spoilage in a manufacturing process is 25 percent of the good product. Thus, with the production of 80 units of good product, 20 units of spoiled product are expected. By adding 25 percent to the standard cost of each unit, a new standard can be obtained that incorporates the cost of normal spoilage. (This illustration assumes that spoilage occurs at the end of the production process after all costs have been incurred.)

	Standard Cost per Unit (without spoilage)	Standard Cost per Unit (with spoilage)
Direct material	$1.00	$1.25
Direct labor	0.60	0.75
Overhead (rate is $.50 per direct labor dollar)	0.30	0.375
Unit standard cost	$1.90	$2.375

The total standard cost for 80 units of good product is $2.375 per unit times 80 units, or $190. The $190 figure is also equal to 100 units times $1.90 (the standard cost, not considering normal spoilage, times the total units, including the normal spoilage). The $2.375 standard cost is applied to only good product, while the $1.90 standard cost is applied to both good product and normal spoilage.

At the end of each period the normal spoilage (25 percent of the good product) is computed to determine whether the actual spoilage is higher or lower than normal. If the actual spoilage is different from the normal spoilage, the difference might be helpful in the analysis of labor efficiency. For example, a decline in spoilage to less than the normal amount may result from workers slowing down and being especially careful, which in turn may result in an unfavorable labor efficiency variance. The decrease in spoilage may or may not be desirable, depending on the additional cost resulting from the unfavorable efficiency variance. Thus, the breakdown of spoilage into normal and abnormal spoilage should be an integral part of cost-variance analysis. Although the analysis and control of spoilage can be carried out using just physical-unit measures, it is useful to have dollar measures to evaluate the importance of spoilage and its effect on profit.

Example Suppose that normal spoilage is 25 percent of good product. Standard direct labor cost is $.75 per unit. The standard cost includes normal spoilage cost of $.15 per unit. In July 1,100 units were produced, of which 800 were good units and 300 were spoiled. The direct labor cost was $700. In August 950 units were produced, of which 800 were good and 150 were spoiled. The direct labor cost was $900. The analysis of this situation follows on the next page.

Analysis of July Performance

Actual spoilage	300 units
Normal spoilage (25% × 800)	200
Abnormal spoilage: unfavorable	100
Standard direct labor (800 × $.75)	$600
Actual direct labor	700
Unfavorable labor variance	$100

In July there is both an unfavorable labor variance and 100 units of abnormal spoilage:

Analysis of August Performance

Actual spoilage	150 units
Normal spoilage (25% × 800)	200
Abnormal spoilage: favorable	(50)
Standard direct labor (800 × $.75)	$600
Actual direct labor	900
Unfavorable labor variance	$300

In August there is an unfavorable labor variance. At the same time, spoilage is below expectations.

Isolating Spoilage   Rather than conceding that there has to be normal spoilage, we can determine the standard cost assuming zero spoilage and treat all spoilage as an unfavorable variance. Using the same information for July as was given above, the standard direct labor cost per unit (without spoilage) is now $.60 ($600/1,000 units). Thus, the following analysis is appropriate:

Actual direct labor		$700
Standard direct labor:		
Good product	800 × $.60 = $480	
Spoilage	300 × $.60 = 180	660
Unfavorable labor variance		$ 40

The unfavorable labor variance is now $40, the labor spoilage cost is $180, and the labor cost assigned to good product is $480. If we subtract the $480 from $700, we obtain $220 that is to be allocated between the cost of good product, cost of spoilage, and the unfavorable labor variance. The exact allocation will depend on the assumptions made. This example assumes that all spoilage is controllable and only $480 of labor costs is assigned to good product. Consistent with the above calculations, $480 is charged to work in process, $180 to spoilage loss, and $40 to an unfavorable labor variance. The spoilage loss is considered a period cost, and the labor variance is either closed to cost of goods sold or prorated.

Some firms charge only direct costs to spoilage and do not absorb any overhead in this charge; others charge only the variable cost. The latter procedure is based on a desire to isolate the incremental cost associated with spoilage. Where there is a shortage of productive facilities, it is reasonable to include the opportunity cost of the fixed facilities in the spoilage cost if the cost data are to be used for decision purposes regarding the control of spoilage.

Responsibility for Spoilage　If the abnormal spoilage in July was caused by noncontrollable external factors, then for control purposes the standard cost of the good product for July could be defined to be $660 ($480 + $180), and only the $40 of unfavorable labor variance would be considered to be the fault of the cost center's management. Rather than redefine the standard cost, the inventoriable cost could be kept at $480, and all of the standard cost of spoilage ($180) plus the unfavorable labor variance ($40) could be expensed. The cost center would not be held accountable for the cost of the spoilage.

In order to have effective control over a production process, the amount of spoilage should be analyzed. Was it normal and within the allowed level of spoilage for the operation? Was it caused by the workers in the cost center, or were the spoiled units caused by the purchased material? Should the spoilage have been avoided?

In order to reduce spoilage in the future, it must be classified by its causes and by the department or operation responsible. If the material vendor was responsible, the spoilage should be reported to the accounts-payable section and, in particular, to the purchasing department. Steps may then be initiated to recover damages from the supplier and to examine alternative sources of future supply.

Determining Normal Spoilage

The determination of normal spoilage is necessary if normal spoilage is considered a cost of product, and its cost is inventoriable (while abnormal spoilage is expensed as a period cost). From the point of view of control, the determination of normal spoilage is needed if the amount of abnormal spoilage is to be known.

Normal spoilage should be determined by applying a percentage representing the normal spoilage per good unit to the number of good units produced. Assume that normal spoilage is 25 percent of good units produced, and 100 units of raw material are placed into production. If the output is 80 good units and 20 units are spoiled, the normal spoilage is determined by multiplying the 80 units of good product by the normal spoilage percentage of 25 percent to obtain 20 units. There is no abnormal spoilage in this situation.

It would be incorrect to argue that 20 percent multiplied by the input of 100 units gives a normal spoilage of 20 units. The weakness of this position is illustrated by assuming that 200 units of raw material were required to produce 80 good units, where the normal spoilage is 25 percent of the good units. The normal spoilage for 80 units of good product does not change: it is still 20 units (not 20 percent times 200). If the 25 percent figure is applied to the good product of 80 units, the normal spoilage remains at 20 units, and the abnormal spoilage increases by 100. This is consistent with the fact that an extra 100 units of raw material were required to produce 80 units of good product.

The correct procedure for computing normal spoilage is to apply the percentage of normal spoilage to the good product completed during the period. The abnormal spoilage is computed by subtracting the normal spoilage from total spoilage. Using units of input as the base for the computation of normal spoilage can give an incorrect measure of normal spoilage.

Interpretation of Normal Spoilage

For the computations made in this chapter, normal spoilage is defined in terms of one number, a percentage of good product. Normal spoilage may be thought as the mean (or expected) amount of spoilage. Assuming that the number of spoiled units may be approximated by a normal probability distribution, spoilage is expected to exceed this value 50 percent of the time.[3] The next step would be to obtain an idea of spoilage variability by estimating the standard deviation of this distribution. This may be accomplished using past data, perhaps adjusted for management's subjective judgments. Having determined the standard deviation, the probability of any amount of spoilage occurring can be computed.

Example   Assume, based on past data, that the mean or expected amount of normal spoilage per 100 units is 18 units, and the standard deviation is 6 units. The actual spoilage is 30 units.

The actual spoilage is two standard deviations above the mean $[(30 - 18)/6 = 2]$. With a normal probability distribution, the probability of a deviation of this size or larger (above or below the mean) is .0456 (see Table E), and the probability of this level of spoilage or a larger level is .0228 (one-half of .0456).[4] Thus, the spoilage of this period was an unlikely event, and it should probably be investigated, subject to a comparison of the costs of investigation with the potential savings.

---

3. Spoilage is, in fact, a discrete variable, but continuous approximations are often quite adequate in estimating discrete probabilities. The statement also holds for any symmetrical distribution. (In such distributions the mean and the median are identical, and it is the median that divides the distribution into two equal portions.)

4. Because the normal curve represents a continuous probability distribution, but measurement here is discrete (number of defective units), spoilage might be calculated as $(29.5 - 18)/6 = 1.83$ standard deviation units. Normally this correction for continuity can be ignored.

Accounting for Reworked Units

Reworked units are units that were originally identified as spoiled or defective but that have subsequently been reworked to make them acceptable as good output. As in the case of accounting for normal spoilage under job-order costing, there are two methods of accounting for reworked units. In method I, the costs of rework are added to the cost of the particular job from which the reworked units came. Under method II, the costs of rework are added to actual overhead. Rework costs are estimated each period and included in budgeted overhead. The result is that rework costs are spread across all production through the overhead rate.

Suppose, for example, that the costs of reworking some units in Job Number 2526 are as follows:

Direct material	$100
Direct labor	70
Applied overhead (200% × direct labor dollars)	140
Total	$310

■ *Method I:* Costs of rework added to cost of a particular job.

Work-in-Process Inventory	310	
Material Inventory		100
Salaries Payable		70
Applied Overhead		140

■ *Method II:* Costs of rework added to overhead costs to be spread across all production.

Actual Overhead	310	
Material Inventory		100
Salaries Payable		70
Applied Overhead		140

The choice between method I and method II depends on whether the reasons for the rework were (1) specific to the particular job in which the rework was done or (2) a reflection of characteristics common to all production. In the former case, method I is more appropriate. In the latter case, method II is best.

Accounting for Scrap

Scrap is material that emerges from the production process but has little economic value. As in the cases of normal spoilage (under job-order costing) and reworked units, there are two methods of accounting for scrap. In both cases, when scrap is collected, it is returned to the warehouse and inventoried at a zero value.

Under method I the sales proceeds of the scrap are deducted from the cost of the job that yielded the scrap. Under method II the sales proceeds of the scrap are deducted from actual overhead. Under this approach the value of scrap is estimated at the beginning of the period and deducted from budgeted overhead. The result is that the benefits from selling scrap are spread across all production through a lower overhead rate.

Suppose, for example, that $100 worth of scrap material is sold.

- *Method I:* Proceeds from the scale of scrap deducted from the cost of the job.

Cash (from sale of scrap)	100	
Work-in-Process Inventory (reduction in the cost on a specific job-cost sheet)		100

- *Method II:* Proceeds from the sale of scrap deducted from actual overhead.

Cash (from sale of scrap)	100	
Actual Overhead		100

As in the cases of normal spoilage and rework, the choice of method I or method II depends on whether (1) the scrap resulted from characteristics specific to a particular job (method I) or (2) the scrap resulted from general characteristics of the firm's production process common to all production jobs (method II).

Summary

Control procedures that make use of efficiency variances and the cost per unit are incomplete unless control is also exercised over the amount of spoiled product. Spoilage should be rigorously controlled, and the control should be coordinated with the control of labor costs. Otherwise labor efficiency may be increased at the expense of an increase in spoilage.

The computation of product costs is complicated by the fact that the cost of product should include the normal spoilage costs but not the abnormal spoilage costs. The abnormal spoilage should be considered a cost of the period. A further complication occurs because the determination of normal spoilage should be based on the good output rather than on the input. Although a rough control of spoilage may be implemented by a report of the number of units spoiled, a more refined report would include the cost of the spoiled units and the cost of abnormal spoilage. Above all, the control of spoilage is a matter of balancing the cost of spoilage with the cost arising from more careful production procedures. A procedure that results in little or no spoilage may be just as bad as a procedure that results in too much spoilage. Some spoilage is usually acceptable to obtain optimal production levels.

To control labor, it is necessary to control both labor-efficiency variances (or actual cost for equivalent units of labor) and spoilage. If only one or the other is controlled, it is possible that undesirable incentives will arise from the control procedure. For example, the cost per unit of labor may be decreased by an increase in work tempo, and this in turn may result in a greater loss through increased spoilage. Thus, the behavioral implications of the spoilage-control procedure should be considered when the procedure is designed.

Key Terms to Review

abnormal spoilage, p. 571
normal spoilage, p. 571
reworked units, p. 572

scrap, p. 571
spoilage, p. 571
waste, p. 571

Review Problem

SPOILAGE COSTS UNDER PROCESS COSTING

To review the concepts in this chapter, solve the process costing problem on your own. First, concentrate on situation I, using the data in Exhibit 16-2. Check your answer by comparing it to the analysis of costs in Exhibit 16-3 (FIFO) and Exhibit 16-4 (weighted average).

After successfully completing the work for situation I, solve the same problem for situation II, using the data in Exhibit 16-5. Use weighted-average process costing. Check your answer by comparing it with Exhibit 16-6.

Suggested Readings

Fertakis, J. P. "Responsibility Accounting for By-Products and Industrial Wastes." *Journal of Accountancy* (May 1986): 138–47.

Hayes, R. "Why Japanese Factories Work." *Harvard Business Review* (July–August 1981): 57–66.

Kaplan, R. "Measuring Manufacturing Performance: A New Challenge for Managerial Accounting Research." *Accounting Review* (October 1983): 686–705.

Reich, R. "The Next American Frontier." *Atlantic Monthly* (March 1983): 43–58 and (April 1983): 97–108.

Rogoff, D. L. "Scrap into Profits: How to Fully Exploit Scrap as a Revenue Source." *Journal of Accountancy* (February 1987): 106–13.

Roth, H. P., and W. J. Morse. "Let's Help Measure and Report Quality Costs." *Management Accounting* (August 1983): 50–53.

Review Questions

16-1 Distinguish between scrap and spoilage.

16-2 Distinguish between normal and abnormal spoilage.

16-3 Define the term *reworked units.*

16-4 Should spoilage be considered (1) a cost of product and thus inventoriable or (2) a cost of inefficiency and thus an expense of the period?

16-5 With an actual cost system, if normal spoilage is considered a cost of product, how might the cost per good unit be affected by changes in product quality control?

16-6 How is normal spoilage computed assuming that the units of input and output are given?

16-7 What costs are relevant in computing the real costs of spoilage?

16-8 What alternatives are available to account for the costs of rework? When would each alternative be appropriate?

16-9 Under what circumstances is the cost of normal spoilage allocated between ending work-in-process inventory and good units completed and transferred out?

16-10 What is the justification for including the cost of normal spoilage in standard costs?

Exercises

16-11 Spoiled Units and Weighted-Average Process Costing The Simmons Company uses weighted-average process costing. Inspection takes place when units are 75 percent complete, and materials are added at the beginning of the process. The following data are available:

Beginning work-in-process inventory (50% converted)	10,000 units
Good units completed and transferred	30,000 units
Ending work-in-process inventory (70% converted)	4,000 units
Normal spoilage	2,000 units
Abnormal spoilage	400 units

REQUIRED:

Prepare a schedule of equivalent units.

16-12 Spoiled Units and FIFO Process Costing Refer to the data in Exercise 16-11. Assuming that FIFO process costing is used, prepare a schedule of equivalent units.

16-13 Cost per Equivalent Unit; Weighted-Average Process Costing Refer to the data in Exercise 16-11. Assume the following additional information.

Beginning work-in-process inventory:	
Materials	$ 57,280
Conversion	$ 35,580
Current period costs:	
Materials	$132,000
Conversion	$251,600

Compute the cost per equivalent unit for materials and conversion.

16-14 Cost per Equivalent Unit; FIFO Process Costing Refer to the data in Exercises 16-11 and 16-13. Compute the cost per equivalent unit for materials and conversion.

16-15 Computing the Cost of One Spoiled Unit Refer to the data given in Exercises 16-11 and 16-13. What is the cost associated with one spoiled unit of production? Use the weighted-average method of process costing.

16-16 Allocation of Normal Spoilage Costs to Ending Work in Process The Raintree Corporation manufactures 3.5-inch computer disks. The company inspects units when they are 80 percent complete with respect to conversion. Materials are added at the beginning of the process, and the company uses weighted-average process costing. The following information relates to production in November:

Good units completed and transferred out	20,000 units
Ending work-in-process inventory (90% complete with respect to conversion)	6,000 units
Abnormal spoilage	400 units
Normal spoilage	800 units
Weighted-average cost per equivalent unit:	
Material	$ .50
Conversion	.90
Total unit cost	$1.40

a. Calculate the costs of normal and abnormal spoilage.

b. Calculate the cost of ending work-in-process inventory and good units completed and transferred, including an allocation of normal spoilage costs. In allocating the normal spoilage cost, carry out the answer to two decimal places (that is, dollars and cents).

16-17 Journal Entries for Spoilage Costs Refer to the data given in the preceding exercise. Prepare journal entries to (1) isolate normal and abnormal spoilage costs and (2) allocate normal spoilage costs.

16-18 **Normal and Abnormal Spoilage; Job-Order Costing**   The Sante Fe Company produces a variety of balls for various sports. In Job 11B, which consisted of 1,200 footballs, 40 balls were spoiled. Normal spoilage is 2.5 percent of good output. The cost of each spoiled football was $6.00, of which $2.00 worth of material is salvageable. Prepare journal entries to record the spoilage, assuming

     a. Normal spoilage cost is associated with a particular job.

     b. Normal spoilage cost is added to overhead.

16-19 **Cost of Reworked Units**   The Yonatus Corporation manufactures billiard tables. In Job Number 18W, seven tables required rework consisting of the following costs:

Direct labor	$ 750
Direct material	470
Applied overhead (300% × direct labor dollars)	2,250
Total	$3,470

Prepare journal entries to record the costs of rework, assuming

     a. Costs of rework are added to the cost of a particular job.

     b. Costs of rework are added to overhead.

16-20 **Accounting for Scrap**   Suwanee Steel Fabricators produces automobile parts. During October $8,000 worth of scrap metal was sold. Prepare journal entries to record the sale of scrap metal, assuming

     a. Proceeds from scrap metal sales are deducted from the cost of a particular job.

     b. Proceeds from scrap metal sales are deducted from actual overhead.

16-21 **Standard Costs Including Spoilage**   The normal spoilage in a manufacturing process is 10 percent of the good product. The standard cost per unit, without a spoilage allowance, is as follows:

	Standard Cost per Unit (without spoilage)
Direct material	$ 6.00
Direct labor (1 hour)	9.00
Overhead (the rate is $12.60/DLH)	12.60
	$27.60

In July 1,000 units were produced, of which 900 were good units. The actual direct labor costs were $9,900. There was no labor rate variance. Compute the standard cost per unit, including normal spoilage in the cost.

16-22 **Analysis of Spoilage and Direct Labor Costs**   Refer to the data given in Exercise 16-21. Analyze the spoilage and direct labor cost for the month.

16-23 **Analysis of Spoilage and Direct Labor Costs**   Assume the same basic situation as in Exercises 16-21 and 16-22. In August 1,000 units were produced, of which 800 were good units. The actual direct labor costs were $7,200. There was no labor rate variance.

    a. Analyze the spoilage and direct labor costs for the month.

    b. Compare the operations of July and August (Exercise 16-21 gives the data for July).

Problems

16-24 **Costs per Unit and Abnormal Spoilage**   The normal spoilage of a manufacturing process is 10 percent of the good product. Inspection takes place at the end of the production process. The data for three months were as follows:

	Total Equivalent Units of Labor	Good Units	Spoiled Units	Total Labor Costs
March	99	90	9	$79.20
April	99	99	0	79.20
May	99	80	19	79.20

REQUIRED:

    a. For each of the three months compute the labor cost per equivalent unit of product and the cost per good unit.

    b. Compute the units of abnormal spoilage for each of the three months.

16-25 **Computing Costs and Abnormal Spoilage**   The normal spoilage of a manufacturing process is 25 percent of the good product. The inspection for spoilage takes place when 60 percent of the conversion has been performed. In September 115 units were processed, of which 80 complete units were good. The direct labor cost for the month was $3,535.

REQUIRED:

    a. Compute the labor cost per equivalent unit of product and the labor cost per good unit of output.

    b. Compute the units of abnormal spoilage and the direct labor cost included in the abnormal spoilage cost.

16-26 **Normal and Abnormal Spoilage**   The normal spoilage is 10 percent of the good product or 9.09 percent of the input (assuming that the spoilage is normal). Units of input and good product are shown on the following page for March through June.

	Input	Good Product
March	88	80
April	100	80
May	500	80
June	500	100

REQUIRED:

Compute the normal and abnormal spoilage for each of the months shown.

16-27 **Probability of Abnormal Spoilage**   The normal spoilage is estimated to be 10 percent of good product; this is the mean or expected value of the spoilage. The standard deviation of the spoilage is 2 percent of good product. Assume the percentage of spoiled units is normally distributed. During the first three months of the year, the actual spoilage was as follows:

	Good Product	Actual Spoilage
January	1,000	120
February	1,500	195
March	2,000	160

REQUIRED:

a. For each month compute the probability of the spoilage being as large or larger than the spoilage incurred.

b. For January and February compute the probability of *unfavorable* spoilage that is as large or larger than the amounts actually incurred.

16-28 **The Influence of Labor on Spoilage Rates**   The Grinding Department of Spoilow Company has experienced a spoilage rate in the past months on a particular product that has averaged 20 percent of the good units. The supervisor of the department notes that this spoilage rate is the highest for any department in the company. She believes that she can reduce this normal spoilage rate to 10 percent by adding seven more workers to her department.

REQUIRED:

Assuming that you are the plant manager, what would you tell the supervisor?

16-29 **Cost of Good Product and Abnormal Spoilage**   Westwood Manufacturing Company produces a single product which begins processing in Department 1 and completes production in Department 2. In January, Department 1 began work on 1,000 units and transferred 1,000 partially completed units to Department 2. The total Department 1 production cost associated with the 1,000 units was $5,000, and Department 2 costs incurred were as follows:

Direct materials	$2,000
Direct labor	500
Overhead	1,000

REQUIRED:

Assuming that inspection occurs at the end of Department 2 processing and that normal spoilage is 25 percent of the good units, compute the cost per unit of good product and the total cost of abnormal spoilage for January in each of the following situations (there was no beginning or ending inventory for January):

  a. The number of good units completed was 1,000.

  b. The number of good units completed was 800.

  c. The number of good units completed was 500.

16-30 Computing Standard Costs The standard costs per thousand units of a product manufactured by the Aurora Company (without normal spoilage) are as follows:

Direct materials	20 lbs @ $0.20	= $ 4.00
Direct labor	10 hours @ $10.00 =	100.00
Overhead	10 hours @ $1.10 =	11.00
Total		$115.00

In the production process, the materials are added at the beginning, and all other costs are assumed to be incurred evenly throughout the process. Inspection occurs when the production process is 70 percent complete, and normal spoilage is 25 percent of the good units produced.

The following data apply to the December production process:

Beginning work in process	0 units
Completed and transferred	1,000,000 units
Spoilage	400,000 units
Ending work in process — 50% complete	600,000 units

Aurora Company uses weighted-average process costing in conjunction with a standard cost system.

REQUIRED:

  a. Compute the standard cost of the abnormal spoilage.

  b. Compute the standard cost of the units completed and transferred.

16-31 Spaghetti Sauce Costs and Spoilage; Probabilities Sauce Italiano Company makes a popular brand of spaghetti sauce, which is sold in supermarkets in eight-ounce cans. In making one batch of sauce, 100 pounds of ingredients are mixed together, and the mixture is cooked for several hours. During the cooking, the mixture loses 20 percent of its initial weight. If the mixture is not carefully watched during cooking and canning, spoilage may occur that would be detected after all the sauce is canned. Past experience suggests that the number of eight-ounce cans spoiled through improper processing is normally distributed with a mean of 5 percent of the good cans and a standard deviation of 1 percent of the good cans. In March, 500 batches of sauce were begun and 72,500 good cans of sauce were produced.

REQUIRED:

Assuming that there was no beginning or ending work in process for March, determine

a. The cost per good can of sauce if the total cost associated with cooking and canning the 500 batches was $50,000,

b. The probability that spoilage this great could occur if the spoilage process was distributed according to the normal distribution given above.

16-32 Computing Unit and Abnormal Spoilage Costs   Rockaway Corporation manufactures a product that is inspected when the production process is 60 percent complete. At inspection, all defective units are destroyed. Normal spoilage is 10 percent of the units that pass inspection. Direct materials are added at the beginning of the manufacturing process, whereas labor and overhead are applied at a constant rate throughout the process. There was no beginning inventory for July, and the ending inventory was 50 percent completed. The company uses weighted-average process costing. Production and cost information for July is as follows:

Costs incurred in July:	
Direct materials used	$ 5,200
Direct labor	21,315
Overhead	9,555
July production information:	
Units started	8,000
Units passing inspection	6,500
Units in ending inventory	500

REQUIRED:

a. Compute the cost of the units that were completed.

b. Compute the cost of the units in the ending work-in-process inventory.

c. Compute the cost of the abnormal spoilage.

16-33 Computing Costs from Work-in-Process Information   A manufacturing company produces a single product and uses weighted-average process costing for product costing. Materials for the product are added at the beginning of the process while labor and overhead costs are assumed to be added evenly throughout the production. The beginning inventory for May was one-half complete with respect to labor and overhead, and the ending inventory was one-fourth complete. Inspection occurs when units are 75 percent complete, and normal spoilage is 10 percent of the good product. The following information applies to the May work in process:

Beginning inventory:	
Materials	$ 948
Labor	1,544
Overhead	690
Costs incurred in May:	
Materials	$11,400
Labor	36,225
Overhead	7,007
Inventory and production information:	
Units in beginning inventory	1,000
Units completed	8,000
Units in ending work-in-process inventory	800
Spoilage	1,000

REQUIRED:

a. Compute the cost of the goods completed.

b. Compute the cost of the ending inventory.

c. Compute the cost of the abnormal spoilage.

16-34 Spoilage Losses; Job-Order Costing Harper Company's Job 501 for the manufacture of 2,200 coats was completed during August at the following unit costs:

Direct materials	$20
Direct labor	18
Factory overhead (includes an allowance of $1 for spoiled work)	18
Total	$56

Final inspection of Job 501 disclosed 200 spoiled coats, which were subsequently sold to a jobber for $6,000.

REQUIRED:

a. Assume that spoilage loss is charged to all production during August. What would be the unit cost of the good coats produced on Job 501?

b. Assume instead that the spoilage loss is attributable to the exacting specifications of Job 501 and is charged to this specific job. What would be the unit cost of the good coats produced on Job 501? (*CPA adapted*)

Using Cost Information in Making Decisions

17

Linear Programming and Cost Accounting

LEARNING OBJECTIVES

After studying this chapter, you should be able to:

1 Explain how linear programming is used to solve management problems.

2 Describe how the opportunity cost concept arises in the context of a linear program.

3 Explain how cost information is used in linear programming formulations.

*T*he book has stressed the importance of monitoring opportunity costs. Linear programming (LP) addresses a particular set of problems in a way that quantifies opportunity costs and, as such, provides a powerful decision aid for situations where it satisfies the constraints of the problem. LP is appropriate to use when allocating a set of scarce resources to reach a specified objective such as minimizing costs.

This chapter describes the use of linear programming techniques to solve selected managerial problems. It derives a linear programming solution that can measure the cost of fixed factors of production. The chapter also conveys the importance of cost information in many linear programming formulations that may arise in the organization.

Costs that are not avoidable are not relevant to a decision. These costs are incurred regardless of managerial actions with respect to the decision being considered. Even while the managerial economist stresses that such costs as building depreciation are not decision relevant, however, the accountant is simultaneously allocating depreciation costs to different processes and products. The development of linear programming has generated a technique for quantifying the opportunity costs associated with the use of fixed factors of production. This technique gives rise to measures that originally were called *accounting prices* but now are more commonly known as *shadow prices*. These prices are by-products of the solution to an alternate way of formulating the basic linear programming decision problem.

This chapter discusses the formulation of linear programming problems and illustrates the graphical solution process. The complexity of more realistic problems requires a more complex solution method (called the simplex method of solution).[1] Linear programming problems are well suited to being solved on computers, and linear programming software is widely available.

Linear Programming

Linear programming is a technique designed to accomplish the best (optimal) allocation of scarce resources. Product choices are usually thought of as short-run decisions because in the short run capacity is fixed but in the long run capacity can be changed. As such, a small CPA firm may have to choose between performing work for client *A* or for client *B* in the short run. In the long run, however, the small CPA firm may be able to serve both *A* and *B* by hiring more professional staff or by enlarging its facility.

---

1. For more complete explanations of the material in this chapter including the simplex approach, see H. Bierman, Jr., C. P. Bonini, and W. H. Hausman, *Quantitative Analysis for Business Decisions,* 7th ed. (Homewood, Ill.: Irwin, 1986): 286–361.

EXHIBIT 17-1

Woodmode-Boise

Revenues and Variable Costs

	Oak Cabinets	Pine Cabinets
Sales per unit	$50.00	$40.00
Less: variable costs per unit		
Materials	25.00	20.00
Labor	15.00	12.00
Variable overhead	6.00	6.00
Contribution margin per unit	$ 4.00	$ 2.00

In the short run, then, capacity limitations require that choices be made. Let's work with an example involving only one constraining factor — machine hours.

Woodmode Manufacturing is a multidivision company that makes several types of kitchen cabinets. For now, assume that one division of Woodmode manufactures oak and pine cabinets and that this division, Woodmode-Boise (located in Boise, Idaho), can sell all the cabinets it can currently produce. Woodmode's variable cost and revenue information is presented in Exhibit 17-1.

Woodmode can sell all of the cabinets it produces, but should it produce oak cabinets, pine cabinets, or some combination of the two? The answer depends on the capacity constraint. Suppose, for example, that Woodmode's capacity is limited to eight machine hours per day on each of several identical machines. Suppose, further, that one oak cabinet requires six hours of machine time and one pine cabinet requires only two hours of machine time.

In this case, the important measure of profitability is not the contribution margin per unit of product given in Exhibit 17-1 but the contribution margin per unit of scarce resource used. There is a single constrained resource — machine hours. Pine cabinets are more profitable than oak cabinets.

Perhaps the most interesting feature of the solution is that the product with the greater contribution margin, oak cabinets, should not be produced. This result occurs because the objective is to maximize the total contribution, and the contribution the firm can make is constrained by the hours of machine time available. The firm wants to maximize the contribution that can be made by the scarce resource. Oak cabinets contribute $4 per unit but require six hours per unit to produce. Thus, oak cabinets contribute $.67 per machine hour. Pine cabinets contribute $2 per unit but require only two hours to produce. So pine cabinets contribute $1 per hour. Hence, the firm can do better by concentrating on pine cabinets. Pine cabinets make better use of the scarce resource — machine hours. For each machine, the firm makes the following contribution to fixed costs and profit per eight-hour period:

Type of Cabinet	Number of Cabinets per Eight Hours	Profit per Eight Hours
Oak cabinets	(8 hours ÷ 6 hours per cabinet) × $4	= $5.33
Pine cabinets	(8 hours ÷ 2 hours per cabinet) × $2	= $8.00

The technique used here did not consider fixed costs. This approach is appropriate if the level of fixed costs is unaffected by the solution. A cost that does not change regardless of the alternative selected can be ignored in making the decision. In some cases, however, a sufficient alteration in activity can lead to changes in the level of fixed costs. If, for example, production is terminated, certain fixed costs may be avoided. A plant or a machine may be sold.

The opportunity cost notion can also be illustrated by the Woodmode Company example. If the firm had one more hour of machine time available per eight-hour day, it could produce one additional pine cabinet, the better choice, every two days. This would yield a net contribution of $2 or one extra dollar per day. This is the opportunity value of one more hour of machine time or the opportunity cost from losing one hour of machine time.

Objective Function

Woodmode wishes to maximize the contribution of its operations to covering fixed costs and profits. In the short run fixed overhead will not change and is not relevant to the current decision. What we have done so far is to pick the production level per machine of oak and pine cabinets to maximize total contribution. Mathematically the objective has been to make the following function as large as possible:

Maximize contribution =

Maximize output times contribution per unit =

Maximize: $f = 4X_1 + 2X_2$

where

X_1 = number of oak cabinets made in 8 hours

X_2 = number of pine cabinets made in 8 hours

The function, f, to be maximized (or in other problems sometimes minimized) is called the **objective function**. The function represents the total contribution where A_i is the net contribution of product i, and X_i is the number of units of product i.

More generally we can write:

$$f = A_1X_1 + A_2X_2 = \sum_{i=1}^{2} A_iX_i$$

or for N outputs:

$$f = \sum_{i=1}^{N} A_iX_i$$

where in the Woodmode example,

f = total contribution

A_1 = contribution per oak cabinet

A_2 = contribution per pine cabinet

X_1 = number of oak cabinets produced in 8 hours

X_2 = number of pine cabinets produced in 8 hours

Constraints

With a single constraint on machine hours from one type of machine, Woodmode maximized the contribution to fixed costs and profits by producing only pine cabinets. Because it could produce four per machine in an eight-hour day, the solution yields (4 units) × ($2 per unit) or $8 per machine.

The single constraint faced by Woodmode up to this point is that the number of oak and pine cabinets made cannot require more than eight hours. Mathematically,

$$6X_1 + 2X_2 \leq 8$$

Also, negative quantities of cabinets cannot be produced, so two additional constraints are:

$$X_1 \geq 0 \text{ and } X_2 \geq 0$$

Graphical Solution

Exhibit 17-2 shows several possible production alternatives and the resulting contribution of each to profit.[2] The greatest contribution for the product combinations shown in the table results when four units of product 2, pine cabinets, and zero units of product 1, oak cabinets, are produced. This gives a total profit of $8. It turns out that this is also the maximum possible (feasible) contribution under the constraints of the problem. No other feasible solution produces an equal or greater contribution.

Exhibit 17-3 graphs the possible production levels. All possible production possibilities (solutions to the problem) lie in the hatched (feasible) region. This hatched region is called a **convex polygon**. The feasible solutions always lie within a convex polygon. (A convex polygon is a set of points such that the straight-line segment connecting any two points in the set of points is entirely contained in the polygon.) It turns out (and has been proven mathematically) that the best (optimal) solution is always at one of the corners of this polygon.[3]

While the origin ($X_1 = 0, X_2 = 0$) is a corner point and is therefore a feasible solution, this point yields no contribution. The solution $X_1 = X_2 = 0$ is dominated by the point $X_1 = 1.33, X_2 = 0$, and also by the point $X_1 = 0, X_2 = 4$. Exhibit 17-2 gives the contribution at these two corner points as well as at the point $X_1 = 1, X_2 = 1$. The point $X_1 = 0, X_2 = 4$, has the largest contribution. The point $X_1 = 0, X_2 = 4$, is the

---

2. Alternatives 3 and 4 involve partial units. The logic here is that producing one unit of product A, in two days can be thought of as producing one-half the unit each day.

3. If another optimal solution exists, it occurs at an adjacent corner point and all of the points on the line connecting these adjacent corner points will also be optimal solutions.

EXHIBIT 17-2

Production Alternatives and Contribution

Alternative	X_1	X_2	Total Hours	$f = 4X_1 + 2X_2 = $ Contribution
1	0	4	8	$f = 2(4) = 8$
2	1	1	8	$f = 4(1) + 2(1) = 6$
3	1.33	0	8	$f = 4(1.33) = 5.32$
4	0.5	0.5	4	$f = 4(.05) + 2(.5) = 3$

---

optimum solution as we have previously shown. Interior points ($X_1 = .5, X_2 = .5$, is an example) are never optimal.

Assume now that the firm also is faced by a constraint on the available time for a second machine — machine 2. Two hours of time are available per eight-hour day on each machine of type 2. Oak cabinets require one hour per unit and pine cabinets require two hours per unit. The new constraint can be written as

$$1X_1 + 2X_2 \leq 2$$

EXHIBIT 17-3

Woodmode (with one constraint)

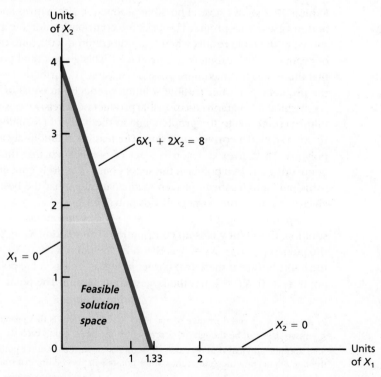

This constraint further restricts the feasible region since machine 2 has only two hours of available time. Now no more than one pine cabinet can be made per day rather than the four units that could be made with only the single constraint due to machine 1. The new situation is graphed in Exhibit 17-4. The feasible set of solutions is much smaller with two constraints than it was with one constraint. For example, solution alternative 1 ($X_1 = 0, X_2 = 4$) is no longer possible.

The two constraints intersect at the point $X_1 = 1.2, X_2 = .4$. This point is found by setting the two equations equal to each other, and solving. The value of f at that point is:

$$f = 4X_1 + 2X_2$$
$$= 4(1.2) + 2(.4)$$
$$= 4.8 + 0.8 = \$5.60$$

The other three corner points result in contributions of:

$$f = 4(1.33) = 5.32 \qquad X_1 = 1.33 \text{ and } X_2 = 0$$
$$f = 2(1.0) = 2 \qquad X_1 = 0 \text{ and } X_2 = 1$$
$$f = 0 \qquad X_1 = 0 \text{ and } X_2 = 0$$

EXHIBIT 17-4

Woodmode (with two constraints)

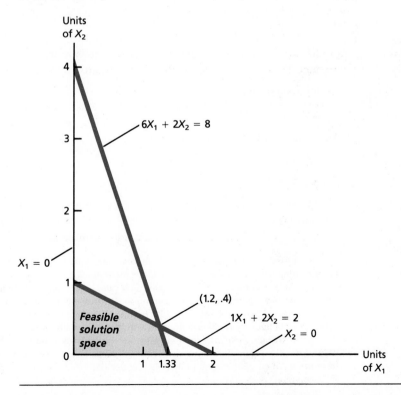

The point $X_1 = 0, X_2 = 0$ again yields zero profits. Thus, the optimum solution is now to produce 1.2 oak cabinets and .4 pine cabinets per day and earn a profit contribution of $5.60. The new constraint has altered the optimal solution.[4]

Dual Linear Programming Problem

The type of problem solved in the previous section is called the primary or **primal problem**. Every linear programming problem that is described as primal has a dual. If the primal problem is a maximization problem, the **dual problem** is the opposite, a minimization problem, and vice versa. For the example graphed in Exhibit 17-4, the dual is a problem in minimizing cost.

Continuing the above example, define:

U_1 = cost per hour of using machine 1

U_2 = cost per hour of using machine 2

C = total cost per hour of using the machines

Machine 1 has eight hours and machine 2 has two hours of available time; thus, the total cost of using the machines can be expressed in equation form as follows:

$$C = 8U_1 + 2U_2$$

Each unit of product should be produced up to the point where the total cost of production is at least equal to the net profit contribution ($4 for product 1 and $2 for product 2). Hence, the following two constraints can be written:

$$6U_1 + 1U_2 \geq 4$$
$$2U_1 + 2U_2 \geq 2$$

The costs U_1 and U_2 are also nonnegative:

$$U_1 \geq 0$$
$$U_2 \geq 0$$

There are routine methods for transforming primal problems into duals, but for our purposes it is more important to understand the economic interpretation of the dual rather than simply have a method for obtaining it.

---

4. When a fixed cost can be avoided (or, alternatively, must be added) at specific levels of activity, discontinuities are introduced to the linear-programming problem. In this case, only integer-valued variables can be used. Special algorithms (called mix-integer programming) are required to solve this problem. Furthermore, the solution to the problem is typically quite different from the solution obtained by rounding off the related linear-programming solution. To shift from the assumptions of linearity requires a nonlinear programming solution technique.

See H. Wagner, *Principles of Operations Research* (Englewood Cliffs, N.J.: Prentice-Hall, 1975), for a discussion of these extensions and R. Kaplan and A. Atkinson, *Advanced Management Accounting,* 2d ed. (Englewood Cliffs, N.J.: Prentice-Hall, 1989), for some applications to managerial accounting issues.

The inequality $6U_1 + 1U_2 \geq 4$ reflects the fact that oak cabinets take six hours of time on machine 1 and one hour of time on machine 2. Thus, the cost $(6U_1 + 1U_2)$ is either going to be equal to $4 (in which case the product should be produced) or greater than $4 (in which case the product should not be produced). The same type of analysis applies to the inequality for pine cabinets (which require two hours of time on each machine). The objective is to minimize the total cost subject to the imposed constraints. This is in contrast to the primal, which is a profit maximization problem.

This linear programming problem can be written:

In Primal Form	In Dual Form
Maximize: $f = 4x_1 + 2x_2$	Minimize: $C = 8U_1 + 2U_2$
Subject to: $6x_1 + 2x_2 \leq 8$	Subject to: $6U_1 + 1U_2 \geq 4$
$1x_1 + 2x_2 \leq 2$	$2U_1 + 2U_2 \geq 2$
$X_1 \geq 0$	$U_1 \geq 0$
$X_2 \geq 0$	$U_2 \geq 0$

EXHIBIT 17-5

The Dual to the Profit Maximization Problem Graphed in Exhibit 17-3

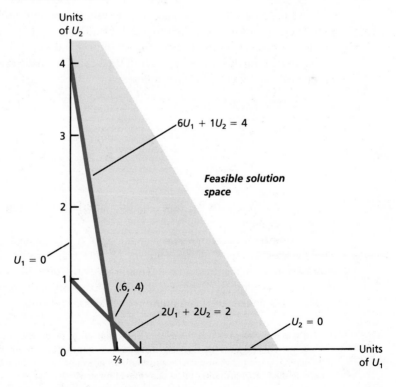

EXHIBIT 17-6

Machine Use Costs and Total Cost

U_1	U_2	$C = 8U_1 + 2U_2$
1	0	$8
0.6	0.4	$5.60
0	4	$8

Exhibit 17-5 graphs the dual (minimization) problem. The feasible solutions are to the right and above the constraints. Again, only the corner points need to be examined.

Exhibit 17-6 gives the costs associated with the three corner points. The exhibit shows that values of $U_1 = .6$, $U_2 = .4$, minimize the total cost at a value of $5.60. Referring back to the solution of the primal, the primal solution resulted in a contribution of $5.60. The objective function of the primal and the objective function for the dual are equal at their respective optimal solutions. This is always the case.

The solution to the dual in line 2 of Exhibit 17-6 indicates that the value of an hour of time on machine 1 is $.60, and the value of an hour of time on machine 2 is $.40. These results from the dual are called **shadow** (or accounting) **prices**. They are the economic costs of using these factors of production.

Suppose now that one more hour of time could be made available on machine 1. The primal can be formulated as follows:

Maximize $f = 4X_1 + 2X_2$

Subject to $6X_1 + 2X_2 \leq 9$

$\qquad\qquad 1X_1 + 2X_2 \leq 2$

$\qquad\qquad X_1 \geq 0$

$\qquad\qquad X_2 \geq 0$

Exhibit 17-7 graphs the new situation, and Exhibit 17-8 gives the profits at the three corner points.

Previously the maximum profit was $5.60. It is now $6.20, an increase of $.60. This increase is equal to the value of U_1 that was computed as the value of an additional hour of machine 1 time. That is, using the dual, the value of one more unit of time on machine 1 is determined to be worth $.60, and when one unit of time on machine 1 is added, the maximum profit increases by $.60.[5]

---

5. This statement assumes that the second constraint is not binding. If the second constraint were binding, it would prevent the increase in production. For this reason, the value only applies to a finite number of units because eventually another constraint will become binding. The range for which the dual variables hold can be determined by sensitivity analysis.

EXHIBIT 17-7

The Primal: Adding One Unit of Machine Time on Machine 1

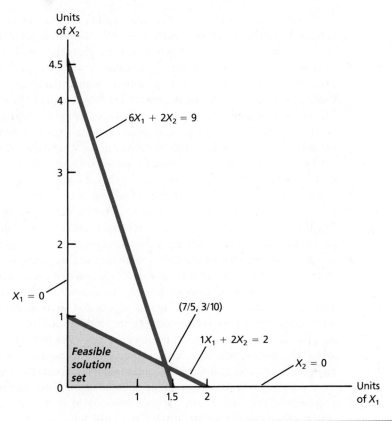

EXHIBIT 17-8

Primal with Two Constraints: Extra Unit of Machine Time

X_1	X_2	$f = 4X_1 + 2X_2$
1.5	0	$6
7/5	3/10	6.2
0	1	2

Implications for Managerial Accounting

Consider the above primal problem where $4 represents the contribution of one oak cabinet. In like manner the $2 in the objective function represents the contribution of one pine cabinet. This agrees with the basic marginal analysis presented earlier in Chapters 3 and 11. The constraint equations incorporate the fixed factors of production. Prior to the use of linear programming, managerial accountants used the opportunity cost concept to define the cost of the fixed factors of production for decisions. The linear programming technique introduces a new method of quantifying the opportunity cost. The linear programming approach ignores historical fixed costs. It considers only the amount of the resources available and the incremental benefits that can be gained from them. The primal is solved without reference to the historical cost of the machines (or of other fixed factors) being used. Nowhere in the formulation of the primal is there reference to the actual cost of the machines used. But the important cost, the opportunity cost, of these factors is very much present in the analysis. The linear programming solution automatically includes the opportunity cost of fixed factors of production in arriving at the solution.

If it is desired to place a dollar value on the cost of using fixed factors, the dual can do so. The dual gives the shadow prices for each of the constraints included in the analysis. These shadow prices represent the amount the firm could afford to pay to increase the amount of the factors of production so as to expand production. The analysis focuses on the constraining factor in the problem.

The accountant's intuition through the years has been good. When some maintained that fixed-cost factors have zero cost, the accountant resisted. There is usually an opportunity cost that must be considered. Fixed costs are allocated to production on the theory that it is not correct to say that only the variable costs are costs of production. The use of only variable costs could lead to excessive expansion and lower selling prices than are justified when the full costs are allocated to production. In the past the accountant had no way to estimate the opportunity costs of the many factors of production that are fixed in quantity and that service many different products. Now a better understanding exists of the relevant costs of the fixed factors (that is, of machine hours). The dual to the linear programming problem enables managers to calculate the shadow prices. Most important, the linear programming solution considers the opportunity cost of the factors of production.

Estimation of Variables

As with most techniques, a major limitation in using linear programming is building a model that is sufficiently rich to capture the essence of the problem. Moreover, it is also important to consider the effects of implementing the solution. Linear programming solutions rely on estimates of contribution margins and of the technological coefficients (such as the number of hours required to produce cabinets on each machine). These estimates are subject both to errors in estimation and to change. It is desirable to determine how the solution is affected by the use of different values. If the solution is not affected by large changes in these values, it is not necessary to spend large sums refining the estimates.

Finally, it may be possible to introduce a new method of production. This would require a new linear programming formulation to solve the new problem. The solution using the new data measures indicates the improvements in the objective function. Against this improvement the manager has to weigh the costs of changing the method of production.

Role of Cost Accounting Information

Linear programming and other optimization techniques are widely used to solve a variety of business problems ranging from the optimal assignment of vehicles among transportation routes to the blending of nutrients in the production of animal feed.[6] Much of the data directed into these decision models come from cost accounting systems. In the examples used throughout this chapter, the objective function of the primal problem is the maximization of aggregate contribution margin. The objective function is expressed as

$$f = A_1X_1 + A_2X_2 + \cdots + A_NX_N$$

The A_i values in this expression are unit product contribution margins. A unit contribution margin is equal to price minus variable cost, and the variable cost measurement typically comes from a managerial cost accounting system.

The constraints in the linear program illustrated in this chapter also include data that typically are produced by a managerial accounting system. The amounts of labor, machine time, and materials required by the firm's products, which are formalized in the constraints of a linear program, are often the quantities of these inputs based on a standard cost accounting system.

Other linear programming applications involve cost minimization in the primal problem, rather than profit maximization. Once again cost measurements are essential ingredients in the optimization procedure.

Illustration of Linear Programming at Exxon

As an illustration of the use of cost information in linear programming, consider the following example provided by Exxon Company, U.S.A. Exxon operates five refineries in the United States. Using a variety of processes, these refineries produce a wide range of petroleum products including motor gasoline, home heating oil, diesel fuel, jet fuel, kerosene, asphalt, and fuel oil. Each refinery's product mix changes

---

6. See also J. Moore and A. Reichert, "An Analysis of the Financial Management Techniques Currently Employed by Large U.S. Corporations," *Journal of Business Finance and Accounting* (Winter 1983): 623–45.

continuously according to individual product demands, such as a higher demand for home heating oil in the winter and for gasoline in the summer.

Motor gasoline normally constitutes the largest-volume product produced by the refineries, and significant optimization efforts are made to minimize its cost of production. The three major grades of gasoline (regular unleaded, premium unleaded, and regular leaded) are produced by combining some seven or more gasoline blending components. These components normally come from refinery production, but they also can be purchased on the open market or be delivered from production at one of Exxon's other refineries.

The components are blended in such a way as to meet numerous product specifications for each of the three grades. The two most important specifications are octane rating and volatility. *Octane rating* refers to the tendency, under certain conditions, for an engine using a particular gasoline to experience premature firing in the cylinder (commonly called *knocking*). *Gasoline volatility* refers to how rapidly the gasoline tends to vaporize and affects the ease with which an engine may be started. Volatility requirements for each grade of gasoline are changed throughout the year to satisfy the needs of the motoring public; for example, engines are more difficult to start in the winter than in the summer.

Exxon refineries use regularly updated linear programs to determine the optimal combination of blending components for each of the three grades of gasoline. The decision variables in the linear program are the amounts of each blending component to be used in producing each grade of gasoline. The objective function to be minimized is the total cost of the blending components and additives used. Some of these blending components, such as toluene, are quite costly because they have an alternative sales disposition as a high-value specialty chemical. Others, like straight-run naphthas, are relatively inexpensive.

The constraints in the linear program specify the relationships between the various blending components and the properties (such as octane and volatility) needed to produce gasolines that meet all product specifications. For example, an octane constraint row for each grade records the octane contribution from each component and requires that the optimal blend recipe meet or exceed the minimum octane specification. The linear programs are updated regularly to account for technical issues such as activity of the catalyst in refinery process units, relative demand for nongasoline products such as home heating oil, current inventory levels of the various blending components, and anticipated future gasoline blending requirements. A typical linear program used for this purpose may include up to 100 decision variables and 50 or more constraints.

Exhibit 17-9 summarizes Exxon's use of linear programming for its gasoline blending operations.

EXHIBIT 17-9

Use of Linear Programming for Gasoline Blending at Exxon

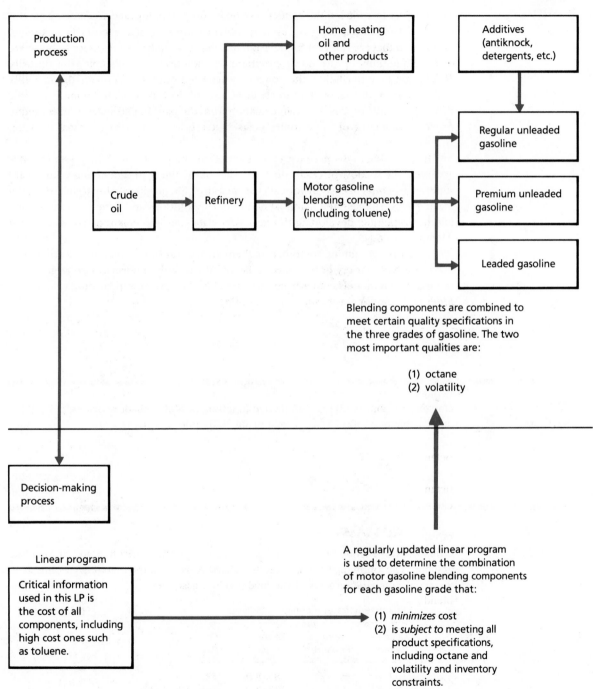

Blending components are combined to meet certain quality specifications in the three grades of gasoline. The two most important qualities are:

(1) octane
(2) volatility

Linear program

Critical information used in this LP is the cost of all components, including high cost ones such as toluene.

A regularly updated linear program is used to determine the combination of motor gasoline blending components for each gasoline grade that:

(1) *minimizes* cost
(2) is *subject to* meeting all product specifications, including octane and volatility and inventory constraints.

Summary

This chapter introduced the elements of linear programming, and discussed how the solutions to the dual may be used to obtain estimates of the costs of factors of production that are relevant for decision making. Although it is necessary to be aware of the limitations of any linear programming solution (for example, the linearity assumption may not hold), the concepts suggested open the door for the manager with help from the accountant to arrive at a set of decision-oriented numbers rather than relying only on cost-based information from the past. In particular, the technique provides estimates of opportunity costs that are key inputs to marginal decision analysis.

It is possible to disagree with the assumption of linearity, but if this assumption is accepted, the shadow prices or dual variables of the linear programming solution are superior to conventional historical-cost measures for purposes of marginal decision making. Nevertheless, the marginal nature of the solutions and difficulties in explaining the technique, developing the necessary data, and implementing solutions must be kept in mind.

Linear programming and other mathematical optimization techniques are widely used to solve a variety of business decisions. Much of the information that goes into these decision models comes from managerial costing systems, providing yet another important role for this branch of accounting.

Key Terms to Review

convex polygon, p. 603
dual problem, p. 606

objective function, p. 602
primal problem, p. 606

shadow prices, p. 608

Review Problem

LINEAR PROGRAMMING

Columbia Gas blends two types of gasolines into aviation gasoline and automobile gasoline. The following facts apply to the characteristics of the blending gasolines and the required characteristics of the final-product gasolines:

Characteristics of Blending Gasolines

Type	Octane Rating	Vapor Pressure	Barrels Available	Cost per Barrel
1	102	6	87,000	$37
2	96	9	113,000	28

Characteristics of Final-Product Gasolines

Final Product	Minimum Octane Rating	Maximum Vapor Pressure	Maximum Sales (barrels)	Price per Barrel
Aviation	100	7	45,000	$62.17
Automobile	98	8	Unlimited	41.29

Set up, but do not solve, the linear programming problem if Columbia wishes to maximize the contribution to fixed costs and profits. Use the following symbol definitions:

X_1 = Barrels of blending gasoline of type 1 used in aviation gasoline

X_2 = Barrels of blending gasoline of type 1 used in automobile gasoline

X_3 = Barrels of blending gasoline of type 2 used in aviation gasoline

X_4 = Barrels of blending gasoline of type 2 used in automobile gasoline

Solution to Review Problem

Maximize:

$$f = 62.17(X_1 + X_3) + 41.29(X_2 + X_4) - 37(X_1 + X_2) - 28(X_3 + X_4)$$

or

$$f = 25.17X_1 + 14.29X_2 + 34.17X_3 + 13.29X_4$$

subject to

$X_1 + X_3 \le 45{,}000$	Constraint on demand
$X_1 + X_2 \le 87{,}000$	Blending gasoline availabilities
$X_3 + X_4 \le 113{,}000$	
$2X_1 - 4X_3 \ge 0$	Octane rating constraints[a]
$4X_2 - 2X_4 \ge 0$	
$-X_1 + 2X_3 \le 0$	Vapor pressure constraints[b]
$-2X_2 + X_4 \le 0$	
$X_1, X_2, X_3, X_4 \ge 0$	Nonnegativity constraints

[a] The octane (and vapor pressure) constraints are satisfied by the weighted average of the input blended gasolines. For aviation gasoline,

$$\frac{102X_1 + 96X_3}{X_1 + X_3} \ge 100$$

Solving gives

$$2X_1 - 4X_3 \ge 0$$

For automobile gasoline,

$$\frac{102X_2 + 96X_4}{X_2 + X_4} \ge 98$$

or

$$4X_2 - 2X_4 \geq 0$$

b $$\frac{6X_1 + 9X_3}{X_1 + X_3} \leq 7 \qquad \text{for aviation gasoline}$$

$$\frac{6X_2 + 9X_4}{X_2 + X_4} \leq 8 \qquad \text{for automobile gasoline}$$

Blending gasolines was an early example of linear programming. Similar applications include paint mixtures, feed products for animals, and personal diets. This review problem involves four unknowns (X_1, X_2, X_3, and X_4) and hence cannot be solved using a two-dimension graphical approach. It can be solved easily by a computer.

APPENDIX
The Simplex Method

To this point the solution has been obtained by graphing the constraints and evaluating the various corner points to find the optimal mix of products. When the number of products increases beyond two, this graphical process becomes cumbersome and ultimately impractical. Fortunately, mathematicians have found a technical procedure for solving such problems called the *simplex method*.

The example discussed above can be used to illustrate the concept behind the linear programming solution. The objective function and constraints are as follows:

Maximize $\quad f = 4X_1 + 2X_2$

Subject to $\quad 6X_1 + 2X_2 \le 8$

$\qquad\qquad 1X_1 + 2X_2 \le 2$

$\qquad\qquad X_1 \ge 0$

$\qquad\qquad X_2 \ge 0$

Noninteger solutions are allowed because for this example it is assumed fractions of a product may be produced per day. Exhibit 17-10 is identical to Exhibit 17-4 except that a series of (dashed) constant-contribution lines have been drawn. The X_1 and X_2 axes measure units of contribution as well as units of products. These contribution lines are parallel. The contribution is the same for any point on one of the dashed lines. For example, using the dashed contribution line graphed furthest to the right, the contribution for $(X_1 = 2, X_2 = 0)$ is the same as for $(X_1 = 0, X_2 = 4)$, namely, $8.

These parallel contribution lines help to show why only corner points yield solutions of interest. Management desires the highest (largest) contribution that is feasible. The general form for the contribution line is obtained by solving the objective function for X_2 and inserting specific values for f:

$$X_2 = \frac{1}{2}f - 2X_1$$

The contribution line $f = \$5.60$ goes through the corner point $X_1 = 1.2, X_2 = .4$. Although $f = \$8$ is a more desirable contribution level, it does not touch any feasible-solution points. No level of production can be obtained that results in a contribution of $8. To reach that level, one of the constraints, $6X_1 + 2X_2 \le 8$ or $X_1 + 2X_2 \le 2$, would need to be relaxed.

The contribution may be increased by beginning with a line that goes through a feasible solution and moving the line upward, parallel, and to the right while always

EXHIBIT 17-10

The Primal with Contribution Functions (Contribution increases as dotted line shifts to right)

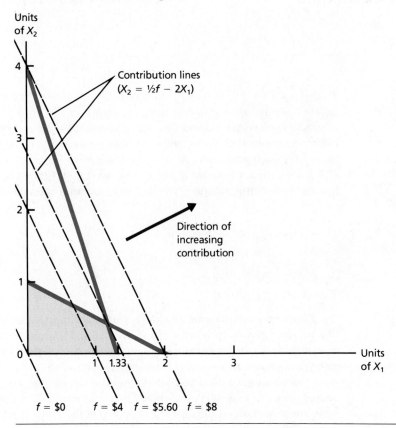

touching at least one point in the feasible-solution area. (Move from $f = \$0$ to $f = \$4$, for example.) This process always leads to a feasible solution represented by a corner point (or perhaps by the line segment connecting two adjacent corner points). That is why the corner points of the feasible-solution area are the points of interest.

The simplex method of solution is a method of systematically moving from one corner-point solution to an adjacent one and testing to determine whether a better solution has been found. When no better solution can be obtained by moving to an adjacent corner point, the method terminates. The optimal solution has been obtained.

If a third product (say, X_3) is added, it is more difficult to graph the solution process. To graph three products requires three-dimensional space. Conceptually, however, the same method of solution would be used.

More constraints can easily be incorporated in two dimensions. For example, if it is necessary that at least one unit of product 2 must be produced, the only feasible solution is to produce one unit of product 2 and zero units of product 1 ($X_1 = 0, X_2 = 1$, with a contribution of $2). This constraint is added to Exhibit 17-4 by drawing a horizontal line at $X_2 = 1$. All feasible solutions must be on or above this line. The addition of a constraint can only have the effect of either leaving the solution unaffected or reducing the attainable contribution. Adding a constraint, then, usually has a cost. This cost is the reduction in the attainable contribution due to the added constraint.

Suggested Readings

Baker, K., and R. Taylor. "A Linear Programming Framework for Cost Allocation and External Acquisition When Reciprocal Services Exist." *Accounting Review* (October 1979): 784–90.

Callahan, J. "An Introduction to Financial Planning Through Goal Programming." *Cost and Management* (January-February 1973): 7–12.

Charnes, A., W. W. Cooper, and Y. Ijiri. "Breakeven Budgeting and Programming to Goals." *Journal of Accounting Research* (Spring 1963): 16–41.

Demski, J. *Information Analysis,* 2d ed. Reading, Mass.: Addison-Wesley, 1980.

Dopuch, N., J. Birnberg, and J. Demski. *Cost Accounting.* New York: Harcourt Brace Jovanovich, 1974.

Feltham, G. *Information Evaluation.* Sarasota, Fla.: American Accounting Association, 1972.

Ijiri, Y., F. Levy, and R. Lyon. "A Linear Programming Model for Budgeting and Financial Planning." *Journal of Accounting Research* (Autumn 1963): 198–212.

Jaedicke, R. "Improving Break-even Analysis by Linear Programming Techniques." *NAA Bulletin* (March 1961): 5–12.

Jensen, R. "Optimal Allocation of Joint (Common Costs): A Parametric Programming Approach." *Decision Sciences* (July 1978): 436–51.

Kaplan, R. and A. Atkinson *Advanced Management Accounting,* 2d ed. Englewood Cliffs, N.J.: Prentice-Hall, 1989.

Kaplan, R., and G. Thompson. "Overhead Allocation via Mathematical Programming Models." *Accounting Review* (April 1971): 352–64.

Manes, R., S. Park, and R. Jensen. "Relevant Costs of Intermediate Goods and Services." *Accounting Review* (July 1982): 594–606.

Moore, J., and A. Reichert. "An Analysis of the Financial Management Techniques Currently Employed by Large U.S. Corporations." *Journal of Business Finance and Accounting* (Winter 1983): 623–45.

Wagner, H. *Principles of Operations Research.* Englewood Cliffs, N.J.: Prentice-Hall, 1975.

Review Questions

17-1 What is the objective of linear programming?

17-2 What important costs does linear programming reduce?

17-3 Comment on the following statements:

    a. "In a linear programming problem, fixed costs can be ignored."

    b. "When a linear programming formulation is appropriate to select output levels, the objective function results in selecting those products which make the largest contribution margin per unit."

17-4 What is a shadow price?

17-5 Is linearity a restrictive assumption?

17-6 Which of the following are true?

    a. $3 \leq 4$

    b. $3X \geq 12$ for $X \geq 4$

    c. If $3X \geq 12$, then $3(-X) \leq -12$

    d. If $2X_1 + X_2 \leq 10$, then if $X_1 \geq 0$; X_2 is ≤ 10

17-7 If the dual is a minimization problem, what type of problem is the primal?

Exercises

17-8 Finding Solutions Graphically Graph the following problems and find the optimum solution:

$$\text{Maximize} \quad f = 2X_1 + 4X_2$$
$$\text{Subject to} \quad X_1 + 3X_2 \leq 16$$
$$4X_1 + 2X_2 \leq 20$$
$$X_1 \leq 4$$
$$X_1 \geq 0$$
$$X_2 \geq 0$$

17-9 Allocating Free Machine Time Two products, cogs and wheels, have the following machine time and profit:

Product	Hours of Machine Time per Unit	Incremental Profit per Unit
Cogs	4	$2
Wheels	2	$4

The machine has four hours of free time.

    a. Formulate the primal and dual linear programming equations.

b. Graph the primal and the dual. What is the optimum mix?

c. Interpret the primal and the dual solution.

17-10 Continuation of Exercise 17-9   Repeat Exercise 17-9, parts **a** and **b**, assuming that the machine has five hours of free time.

17-11 Product Mix   Assume that two products are manufactured on two machines. Product one requires four hours on machine 1 and two hours on machine 2. Product two requires two hours on machine 1 and eight hours on machine 2. There are ten hours of excess capacity on machine 1 and eight hours on machine 2. Each unit of product one produces a net increase in profit of $4 and each unit of product two an incremental profit of $3.

a. Formulate the linear programming problem. Determine the maximum profit and the product mix which results in that profit.

b. Determine the value of each hour of machine time by solving the dual.

17-12 Continuation of Exercise 17-11   Repeat Exercise 17-11, part **a**, assuming that machine 1 has two more hours of machine time.

Problems

17-13 Allocation Machine Time   The Rosen Company has the option of producing two products during periods of slack activity. For the next period, production has been scheduled so that the milling machine is free ten hours and skilled labor will have eight hours of time available:

Product	Machine Time per Unit	Skilled Labor per Unit	Profit Contribution per Unit
A	4	2	$5
B	2	2	$3

REQUIRED:

a. Solve the primal problem (the number of units of *A* and *B* that should be produced).

b. Solve the dual problem (the cost of an hour of machine time and an hour of skilled labor).

17-14 Product-Mix Decisions   The Singh Company can produce two products on two machines. One product, whammos, sells for $4 and has variable costs of $3 per unit. A second product, blammos, sells for $4.60 and has variable costs of $4.10 per unit. Both products are made on a drill press (whammos require three hours and blammos require two hours of time per unit). Whammos also require five hours of time on a grinding machine. There are twelve hours on the drill press and ten hours available on the grinding machine.

REQUIRED:

a. Graph the problem. Solve the primal and the dual. What is the profit for the optimum production mix?

b. Assume that one hour of additional drill time can be obtained for no charge. What is the new production mix? The new profit?

c. Assume that one hour of additional grinding time can be obtained for no charge. What is the new production mix? The new profit?

d. Compare your answers to parts **b** and **c** with the dual variables obtained in part **a**. How much would you pay for an additional hour of time on each machine?

17-15 Product-Mix Decisions   The Alfa Company manufactures betas and gammas. Each beta sells for $15 and has a variable cost of $10. Gammas sell for $10 with a variable cost of $4. The traceable fixed costs for beta are $20,000 and for gamma they are $12,000.

REQUIRED:

a. Determine the break-even possibilities for the firm.

b. Suppose production of betas and gammas both require the use of machine delta. Each beta requires 6 hours and each gamma requires 7.5 hours. The available machine time is 30,000 hours. No other restraints on production and sale exist. What is the optimal output of betas and gammas?

c. Formulate as a linear programming problem.

17-16 Continuation of Problem 17-15   In Problem 17-15, suppose the estimate of variable costs for one beta is in error. Assume the correct value is $11 rather than $10.

REQUIRED:

a. Has the optimal solution changed? If so, what is it now?

b. What is the cost of the estimation error?

c. Do you see other similar errors that might be made? If so, indicate them.

d. Describe graphically how this change altered the solution.

17-17 Decisions Based on Capacity   Thomas & Company leased a production facility for $120,000 per year that provides 100,000 units of capacity. The lease costs (which are fixed) are allocated to products on the basis of the units of capacity required to make one unit of product.

Current production and sales information is presented below:

Products	Shirts	Pants	Shorts
Selling price	$11.00	$8.00	$6.00
Less:			
Variable costs	(5.00)	(5.00)	(5.00)
Allocated costs	(4.80)	(1.20)	(.60)
Contribution	$ 1.20	$1.80	$ .40
Demand limited to	20,000	80,000	20,000

REQUIRED:

a. How many shirts, pants, and shorts should Thomas produce?

Product	Quantity
Shirts	
Pants	
Shorts	

b. Set this problem up as a linear programming problem. Is it easy to tell whether the solution obtained in part **a** is reasonable? Are graphical methods helpful?

17-18 **Finding Solutions Graphically** A manufacturing firm produces two products, each of which must pass through two departments. Department 1 can process a maximum of fifteen units of product 1 per day and a maximum of twenty units of product 2 per day. Department 2 can process a maximum of twenty-five units of product 1 per day and a maximum of ten units of product 2 per day. Product 1 sells for $100 and has variable costs of $65 per unit, and product 2 sells for $110 and has variable costs of $70 per unit. The sales department of the firm notified the production foreman that no more than ten units of product 1 can be sold per day regardless of how many are produced.

REQUIRED:

Graph the problem. Find the optimal solution to this problem.

17-19 **Graphical Solutions** Delta Manufacturing Company manufactures two products. The firm has enough excess capacity to produce at most 500 units in any combination.

The manufacturing process is such that the number of units of product 2 produced must be no more than twice as great as the number of product 1 produced. No more than 400 units of product 1 can be sold.

REQUIRED:

Graph the feasible region implied by the problem and find the solutions that exist at each corner of the convex polygon.

17-20 **Which Cereal to Produce** Raisin bran and corn flakes are produced on two machines. One box of raisin bran requires five hours on machine 1 and seven hours on machine 2. One box of corn flakes requires six hours on machine 1 and three hours on machine 2. Machine 1 has thirty hours of excess capacity available while machine 2 has twenty-one. Raisin bran yields $7 of incremental profit per unit, and corn flakes yields $5 of incremental profit per unit.

REQUIRED:

a. Formulate the linear programming problem.

b. Graph and solve the problem.

c. Assuming that integer solutions are required, round the solution down to the nearest whole unit for each product. (Why do we round down instead of up?) Is this the optimal integer solution? If not, find a better integer solution.

17-21 Production-Mix Decisions A manufacturing company produces two products — double-sided tape and transparent tape — on two machines. The following facts apply to the two products.

	Double-Sided Tape	Transparent Tape
Per unit selling price	$10	$7.50
Per unit variable costs	6	2.50
Hours of machine 1 required per unit	5	2
Hours of machine 2 required per unit	5	8

Machine 1 has thirty hours of excess capacity available while machine 2 has forty hours.

REQUIRED:

a. Formulate the linear programming problem.

b. Graph and solve the problem.

17-22 Determining Optimal Production Schedule A manufacturing firm produces two grades of a product by blending different amounts of two ingredients. Grade *A* must be composed of at least 60 percent ingredient 1, while grade *B* must be composed of not more than 70 percent of ingredient 2. Grade *A* sells for $20 per gallon, while grade *B* sells for $10 per gallon. Ingredient 1 can be purchased for $10 per gallon but no more than 1,000 gallons per day are available. Ingredient 2 can be purchased for $3 per gallon but no more than 2,000 gallons can be purchased each day. Other variable costs associated with the production total $2 for each grade. The firm can sell as much as it can produce.

REQUIRED:

Formulate the problem of determining the optimal production schedule. Do not solve.

17-23 Solving LPs Two products — staples and paper clips — are manufactured on three machines. Product 1 requires four hours on machine 1, two hours on machine 2, and five hours on machine 3 for each unit produced. Product 2 requires one hour on machine 1, four hours on machine 2, and 2.5 hours on machine 3 for each unit produced. Machine 1 has twenty hours of excess capacity available per day, while machines 2 and 3 have ten hours and fifteen hours, respectively.

Each unit of product 1 produces a net increase in profits of $8, and each unit of product 2 produces an incremental profit of $5.

REQUIRED:

a. Formulate the linear programming problem.

b. Graph and solve the problem.

17-24 Determining Foregone Profit A manufacturing firm uses two machines for making two products, pins and nails. Each machine has twenty-four hours of excess capacity available each day. The production foreman scheduled pins and nails such that only four units of each are produced per day. The following facts apply to pins and nails:

	Pins	Nails
Per unit selling price	$30	$42
Per unit variable costs	22	28
Hours of machine 1 required per unit	2	2
Hours of machine 2 required per unit	1	3

REQUIRED:

Determine how much additional profit was foregone by the foreman's decision.

17-25 Production-Mix for Excess Capacity   Two products are produced on two machines. The following information applies to each unit of the products:

	X_1	X_2
Selling price	$30	$25
Materials	8	12
Direct labor	10	5
Variable overhead	2	1
Fixed overhead (applied on the basis of machine 1 hours at $0.50 per hour)	1.50	0.75

Machine 1 has twenty-one hours of excess capacity available per day and machine 2 has fifteen hours available. Product 1 requires three hours on machine 1 and product 2 requires 1.5 hours on machine 1. Product 1 requires one hour on machine 2 while product 2 requires three hours on machine 2.

REQUIRED:

Formulate the linear programming problem, and determine the optimal production mix for the excess capacity.

17-26 Considering Storage Necessities   A manufacturing firm has excess capacity that it is considering using to make two products, flim and flam. The selling price for flim is $25, and it requires $15 in variable costs for each unit produced. The selling price for flam is $22, and it requires $16 in variable costs for each unit produced. Storage space at the plant totals 10,000 cubic feet. Each unit of flim requires ten cubic feet for storage, and each unit of flam requires five cubic feet for storage. The firm has 4,500 hours of excess capacity available on its machines. Flim requires three hours for each unit and flam requires 4.5 hours for each unit. The sales department estimates that a maximum of 500 units of flim and 1,000 units of flam can be sold.

REQUIRED:

a. Formulate the linear programming problem to maximize the increase in profits.

b. Graph and solve the problem.

17-27 Malott Company   The Malott Company produces two main products, lounges and chairs. The following budget has been prepared for the next operating period:

	Lounges	Chairs
Sales in units	50,000	40,000
Price per unit	$ 10.00	$ 7.50
Revenue	$500,000	$300,000
Costs:		
Direct materials	$ 50,000	$ 40,000
Direct labor	100,000	50,000
Variable factory overhead	95,000	55,000
Fixed factory overhead allocated to products	38,000	25,000
Variable selling and administrative costs	50,000	30,000
Fixed selling and administrative costs allocated to products	73,000	54,000
	$406,000	$254,000
Profit by products	$ 94,000	$ 46,000

REQUIRED:

a. The president of Malott Company wants to know how many lounges and chairs must be sold to break even. The Controller responds that such a calculation would be meaningless for a multiproduct firm. Calculate the expected break-even point, and indicate your reasons for agreeing or disagreeing with the controller.

b. The sales manager believes that 60,000 units of each product can be sold under present market conditions and suggests that additional ways should be sought to increase the sales of lounges because they are more profitable than chairs. The production manager observes that the present operating budget (50,000 lounges and 40,000 chairs) is based on 100 percent use of the company's machine hour capacity and suggests that because each chair requires one hour of machine time and each lounge requires one-third more machine time than chairs, it is not clear which product is more profitable. Do you agree with the sales manager? Why or why not? Support your answer with the appropriate calculations.

c. The sales manager points out that the company has binding contractual agreements with several customers that require the company to produce at least 40,000 chairs during the next operating period. Given these agreements, the sales manager concludes that the projected sales mix is the best possible. Do you agree with the sales manager? Why or why not? Support your answer with a linear programming solution.

18

Inventory Valuation and Control

After studying this chapter, you should be able to:

1 Explain how inventory decisions help achieve profitability objectives.

2 Discuss the role played by cost accounting in supplying data for inventory control systems.

3 Summarize the traditional economic-order-quantity (EOQ) approach to inventory control and explain how the accountant uses costs to solve formal inventory models.

4 Explain how controlling inventories affects performance measurement.

5 List the fundamentals of material requirements planning (MRP) and just-in-time (JIT) manufacturing and inventory control systems.

*M*anagement desires to hold neither too much nor too little inventory. If acquisition of material, production, and delivery of finished goods took place instantaneously, there would be no reason to hold inventories, other than for price speculation. Japanese manufacturers have dramatically reduced the need for holding inventories through a policy of obtaining required items "just in time." **Just-in-time** (JIT) inventory policies that enforce minimal levels of inventories are now being implemented in the United States and other industrialized nations.[1] Nevertheless, most manufacturers still find it useful to hold some raw material, work-in-process, and finished goods inventories.

Determining and maintaining the optimal level of inventory involves balancing the acquisition cost against the carrying costs of inventory, as well as balancing the cost of having too much inventory against the cost of a shortage. Inadequate inventory levels can lead to disruptions in production or lost sales opportunities, while excessive inventories tie up cash that can be used to increase returns. Excess inventories can also become obsolete and lose value, as well as cause inefficient operations.

The importance of controlling inventory is reflected in the following three illustrations from the business press.

Firestone Tire & Rubber Co.	The *Wall Street Journal* reported on the inventory-cutting program at Firestone Tire & Rubber Co. Periods of high inflation or interest rates make it very expensive to keep inventory on hand, but cutting inventory levels is not easy or painless. Firestone Tire & Rubber Co. overhauled its entire inventory-control system in implementing a radical inventory-cutting program. To accomplish the task, Firestone hired A. T. Kearney, Inc., a Chicago management consulting firm. According to a Kearney executive, two very firm policies were in place at Firestone: (1) produce tires at as low a cost as feasible, and (2) never lose a sale. Both are sound policies, but together they tend to drive up inventories. Striving toward low unit costs suggests large production runs, but avoidance of lost sales means keeping every size and type of tire in inventory. As a result, Firestone has begun to change these policies.[2]

1. One production supervisor's comment illustrates the common misconception surrounding inventories in the United States. Faced with inventories of raw materials and finished items stacked to the ceiling in every square inch of free space and told that he had an inventory problem, he said, "I sure do. I've just got to find some more space."
2. *Wall Street Journal* (August 15, 1980): 15.

Business Week reported on inventory-ordering problems for Lockheed's L-1011 Tri Star airliner. Lockheed experienced a sudden surge in orders for the Tri Star airplane, resulting in drastically increased production costs.

Lockheed Corporation	According to an article in *Business Week,* higher-than-expected production costs for the Tri Star resulted largely from shortages and late deliveries of components for the rapidly expanding production of the aircraft. The increase in production of the Tri Star came after Boeing had already contracted for materials and subcontractors for its 757 and 767 aircraft. Lockheed had to purchase titanium, for example, at a premium from sources as far away as China. In retrospect, Lockheed's management felt that it should have ordered parts for the Tri Star much earlier.[3]

As a final illustration, consider the following examples from a report by *Business Week* on the cost savings from implementation of computerized inventory-control systems at Florida Power & Light Co., Shaklee Corporation, and National Airlines, Inc.

Florida Power & Light Co., Shaklee Corporation, National Airlines, Inc.	*Business Week* reported that clear efficiencies resulted from centralizing the inventory-distribution system at Florida Power & Light Company. As a result the Miami-based utility saved $13,500,000 in inventory-carrying costs in a single year. Managers at Shaklee Corporation anticipated one-year savings of $850,000 in operating costs due to a new computer system that allowed the firm to cut delivery time to customers by a third. A new computerized inventory system allowed National Airlines, Inc., to save fuel costs of $500,000 each month.[4]

Reasons for Holding Inventories

Companies hold inventories for three reasons: (1) transactional, (2) precautionary, and (3) speculative.

In a perfect world, a company would know exactly what demand for its products was going to be. In addition, the company would know exactly how many units of its

3. *Business Week* (July 28, 1980): 88.
4. *Business Week* (January 21, 1980): 73.

product could be produced, the exact availability of the materials, labor, and other resources needed, whether the prices of those resources were going to change and by how much, and whether the sale prices of its products were going to change and by how much. If all these factors were known, then the company would need to maintain only a **transactional level of inventory**—that is, only the exact amount of inventory to satisfy the demand for its products.

Unfortunately, perfect knowledge does not exist for any company. Uncertainty is a way of life for all businesses, and as a result, companies frequently maintain a **precautionary level of inventory** to avoid the costs associated with having too little inventory on hand. This precautionary level of stock is sometimes referred to as **safety stock.**

When input or output prices are expected to change, a **speculative level of inventory** may be maintained. For example, if prices of certain raw materials used in the production process are expected to fall, a firm should consider allowing its inventory to decline in the expectation of replacing it later at a lower price. The firm would, however, be limited in its actions by inventory needs for both transactional and precautionary purposes.

Establishing the optimal inventory level is one of the critical ongoing operating decisions facing firms today. The past two decades have seen the development of several formulas or models for determining optimal inventory levels and controls. Implementing these models requires a good deal of data that the accountant is equipped to provide.

Many inventory policies and models are used in manufacturing firms. These models range from the traditional *economic-order-quantity* (EOQ) model to the more contemporary just-in-time (JIT) approach to inventory management. Many firms use the EOQ model, and some of its extensions, in conjunction with JIT or other inventory-reducing policies.[5]

The Economic-Order-Quantity (EOQ) Model

The objective of the EOQ model is to determine the optimal quantity of inventory to order and the best time to place the order. In effect, the EOQ is balancing two inventory management costs: carrying costs and ordering costs. **Carrying costs** include out-of-pocket costs such as storage, insurance, security, taxes, and obsolescence as well as opportunity costs that relate to the cost of investing capital in inventory rather than in other income-producing assets. **Ordering costs** include out-of-pocket expenditures incurred every time an order is placed, such as handling, shipping, inspection, and so on.

Carrying costs and ordering costs demonstrate different cost behaviors relative to the level of inventory maintained. Carrying costs increase with the quantity of

5. A. Adkins, "EOQ in the Real World," *Production and Inventory Management* (Fourth Quarter, 1984): 50–54.

inventory maintained; ordering costs decrease with the quantity of inventory maintained. If we think about this difference, it makes sense. The more inventory kept on hand, the more storage, handling, security, and other such carrying costs are incurred. The larger the amount of inventory, the fewer number of orders needed to replenish the inventory and the smaller the amount of ordering costs.

Exhibit 18-1 illustrates this relationship. Line *OA* represents the carrying costs of inventory. We see that as the number of inventory units maintained increases, the amount of the carrying costs increases. Line *BC* represents the ordering costs of inventory. As the number of units per order increases, the amount of ordering costs decreases because fewer orders are required in any time period. Line *DE* represents the sum of lines *OA* and *BC*. Total cost first declines and then rises. The objective of the EOQ model is to identify that point at which line *DE* is the lowest. That point is called the **economic order quantity, *EOQ*.**

The following example illustrates the economic-order-quantity model.

EXHIBIT 18–1

Graphic Illustration of the Economic Order Quantity

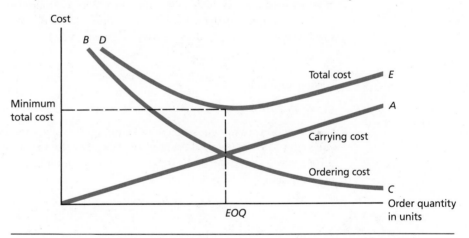

PYC Corporation produces a facial cleanser that it sells for $5 per bottle. The cleanser is packaged in six-ounce bottles purchased from the King Bottling Company. PYC expects to sell 5,000 bottles per month. Future inventory carrying costs should average $10 per month for every 100 bottles according to standards set by production and finance. According to the accounting department, the company incurred order costs of $80 based on ten orders but expects a 25 percent increase in future ordering costs. We need to establish the company's EOQ based on this information. The example is used first, however, to develop the EOQ formula.

Symbols for several costs essential to the model's structure are needed. Except for the ordering cost, these costs are a function of the time period (week, month, or year) under consideration. The monthly values of each variable for the example are given after the colon.

K = Cost per order: 1.25 [$80 ÷ 10] = $10
C = Carrying cost per unit of inventory per time period t: $10 ÷ 100 = $.10
D = Total demand expected during time period t: 5,000 units

The figures used are those expected to hold in the future.

If the optimal order size or EOQ is denoted by the letter E, then the average inventory on hand is $E/2$. Total period carrying costs for the period t can then be established as $C(E/2)$. This is $.10 times the average inventory level in the example. The number of orders required is D/E, which is 5,000/E here, and purchase order costs are $K(D/E)$, $250 (5,000/E). Total cost (TC) for period t, considering holding and ordering costs but ignoring stock-out or shortage costs, is given by

$$TC = C(E/2) + K(D/E) \qquad (1)$$

or

$$TC = \$.10\,(E/2) + \$10(5000/E) \text{ in the example}$$

Hence if E were to be 100, TC would be $.10 (100/2) + $10(5000/100) or $505 per month. We could keep trying values of E until the value is found that made monthly total cost as small as possible. But there is a better way.

The economic order quantity is the value of E that makes the total cost, TC, as small as possible.[6] This value is given by equation (2):

$$E = EOQ = \sqrt{2KD/C} \qquad (2)$$

For our example

$$E = \sqrt{2(10)(5000) \div .10} = 1,000 \text{ units}$$

Shortage costs are not considered. Substituting the value of E from equation (2) into equation (1) gives the total cost for this EOQ. For the PYC Corporation, total cost is $.10(1,000/2) + $10(5,000/1,000) or $100 per month. Alternatively, using equations (1) and (2),

$$TC = \frac{CE}{2} + \frac{KD}{E} = \frac{CE^2 + 2KD}{2E} = \frac{2KD + 2KD}{2E} = \frac{2KD}{E} = \frac{CE^2}{E} = CE \qquad (3)$$

which for our example gives $.10 (1,000) or $100 as before.

We must remember that certain assumptions are incorporated into the EOQ model. The important assumptions are:

1. A known, constant demand over the period,

2. No change in holding costs per unit,

---

6. This is accomplished using calculus. To minimize total cost, the derivative of TC with respect to E is taken, set equal to zero, and solved for E.

$$\frac{dTC}{dE} = \frac{C}{2} - \frac{KD}{E^2} = 0 \text{ and hence } E^2 = 2KD/C.$$

3. A constant order cost incurred with each order placed,

4. No change in the acquisition price per unit,

5. Immediate delivery or known delivery times.

These assumptions may not be precisely true for any given situation. As long as they are close enough, the EOQ model will provide a useful result. Familiarity with the operations of the firm is critical to deciding whether the model is "close enough."

As was discussed earlier, implementing inventory control models such as the EOQ model requires a good deal of data that the accountant is equipped to provide. Let's take a closer look at what information is needed and how the accountant goes about gathering it.

Inventory Costs

The costs associated with inventory arise from the processes of acquiring and carrying inventory, from being out of stock, and from having leftover inventory. The cost of acquiring inventory includes the incremental cost of placing and receiving orders, if the units are purchased. It includes the incremental cost of setting up production, if the units are made. In addition, the costs of inspection, shipping, handling, returning inferior goods, set-up, and paying bills must be added. Carrying costs are composed of storage cost, insurance, cost of spoilage and obsolescence, taxes, and the opportunity cost of the funds tied up in the inventory. Stock-out costs include the cost of lost customer goodwill during the stock-out, possibly resulting in the loss of both current and future sales.

It is the managerial accountant's task to supply the necessary cost data. To do so, the accountant must be aware of what data are needed and also of the likely measurement errors associated with the data.

Data relevant to stock-out costs are difficult to obtain with accuracy. Future lost sales caused by stock-outs are hard to estimate, and hence the figures used are not precise. If it is possible to fill a specific demand by incurring the cost of a special order, then the cost of the special order could be used as an estimate of the stock-out cost. Although somewhat easier to obtain than a direct estimate of the stock-out cost, special order costs also present problems because they often are influenced by the time and current conditions when the order is made, including activity levels, the availability of inventory, and order size.

It is also difficult to determine the costs of acquiring additional inventory, in part because these costs are common to other activities as well as acquisition of inventory. For example, inspectors may examine current production as well as incoming deliveries of raw materials. This makes it difficult to establish separately the time spent on and, hence, cost of each activity. Because several variables usually influence the incremental level of acquisition costs, some technique that can isolate the effect of each variable is required to obtain adequate estimates of these costs. (Regression analysis, covered in Chapter 13, is one possibility.)

Inventory carrying costs are perhaps the easiest cost to estimate, although even here the opportunity-cost measure of carrying inventory is subject to a wide range of error. Typically, carrying costs are estimated as a percentage rate per dollar of average inventory investment for a specified time period, based on the actual, estimated, or expected amounts for the component costs. For the PYC example, the carrying cost was estimated to be $.10 per unit per month. One of the most important carrying cost components is the capital cost. A common approach is to use the firm's after-tax borrowing rate or an average cost of capital. Some managers want this rate also to reflect the risk of similar investment opportunities. When required, this rate must be estimated by the appropriate financial manager based on current market borrowing rates for the period.

There would be no inventory carrying cost if no time elapsed between acquisition and use. Some manufacturers, particularly in Japan, have moved toward this position by scheduling deliveries just in time to be used in production. Yet even here a balancing of costs is required because costs are incurred when monitoring is increased in a system that strives to receive inventory items just in time. For inventory held, the carrying-cost rate should apply only to costs that vary with the number of units purchased and to costs that are incurred at the time the order is received. This implies that the accountant should include the direct costs of purchase or manufacture, freight costs, and inspection costs in the average inventory investment. The carrying-cost rate selected is then multiplied by the average inventory investment.

Assume the product inventoried is manufactured by the firm. It is reasonable to use historical book-cost figures in cases where a LIFO inventory cost-flow system is used or where a FIFO inventory system is used and turnover is reasonably quick. In this case, inventory values reflect recent production costs. An alternative measure of inventory value is its current replacement cost. Raw materials and finished goods often have reasonably active markets from which replacement costs can be estimated. For partially finished items, which typically constitute the largest segment of inventories for most manufacturing-oriented firms, an analogous measure would be the most recent costs of the resources committed to the goods in process. A question then arises concerning the inclusion of fixed costs in these inventory values.

Fixed Costs and Inventory Decisions

The adherents of including only variable costs in inventory believe that fixed costs would be incurred even without production and thus are period costs and not inventoriable. This position has merit but falls short of proving the case for using only variable costs. In some cases, a fixed cost may not be as inevitable or as irrelevant as the argument above suggests.

Consider the salary of a plant manager and the depreciation of the plant. These are fixed costs, but it is possible that if there were no intention of producing a product, the plant could be sold or diverted to producing another product. The plant manager could be moved to another job. The fixed costs of plant and equipment, and other factors of production may provide useful estimates of the opportunity costs associated with the factors of production and hence be relevant costs of the product. Thus, the value of the plant manager's services, if the manager could be performing other tasks, represents the opportunity cost of the manager's time used working on the present product. Similarly, the funds that would result from the sale of a plant or the net revenue that would result from other uses of the plant are the opportunity costs of using the plant to make the present product. The salary of the plant manager and the plant depreciation charge may or may not be reasonable estimates of the actual opportunity costs of these factors of production. Judgment is required as to whether a more accurate determination of these values is needed than conventional accounting measures can provide. The exclusion of all fixed costs from inventory, with no alternative estimate of opportunity cost, usually yields an understatement of inventory cost. This is the case unless the current opportunity cost is zero, as would be true of a machine with no alternative use and a zero net salvage value.

Sensitivity Analysis

The EOQ formula and the associated total cost equation provide the manager with the means of evaluating the sensitivity of total cost to changes in the inventory decision or data inputs. For example, if a different order level is proposed or the borrowing rate changes, the new total cost can be computed. This allows the manager to quantify the impact of a change in inventory policy and the value of attaining more accurate estimates for the input variables in the model.

Consider the types of errors that can occur in estimating the values used in the EOQ formula. The cost values are not easily established using the underlying accounting records. Some of the needed data inputs are not part of the accountant's responsibility. For example, the appropriate interest rate for measuring the carrying cost should be obtained from financial managers. The accountant is also not in a good position to estimate the cost of shortages. Marketing managers may be able to provide a useful estimate. It is fortunate that rather large estimation errors in demand or in the cost of placing an order lead to relatively small percentage changes in the EOQ. The EOQ model is relatively insensitive to these types of estimation errors. This result is due to the square-root relationship between the cost factors and the optimal order quantity.

For example, using equation (2), a 50 percent increase in the cost of placing an order, K, or in periodic demand, D, leads to a 22 percent change in the EOQ. A 50 percent increase in C, however, produces only an 18 percent decrease in the EOQ. Similar magnitudes of sensitivity exist for decreases in these estimates.

One other cost that should be estimated in some situations is the cost of using the wrong decision model. For example, if equation (2) is used when demand is uncertain and the cost of shortages is substantive, poor decisions are reached. The firm is using the wrong model. Uncertainty and shortages are not incorporated in the standard EOQ model given in equation (2). Particularly complex situations require more comprehensive models than are discussed in this chapter. Such models can incorporate the effects of factors such as uncertain production lead times, overtime premiums, emergency expediting, uncertain demand, and the cost of shortages among others. The cost of using the wrong (simpler) model is the cost saving that could have been attained using the correct model less the expense of implementing the more complex model.

Internal Control and Performance Measurement: Implications of Inventory Decisions

Accounting for inventories presents opportunities for fraud. For internal control purposes, the responsibilities for ordering, receiving, inspecting, vouchering, and paying should be assigned to different individuals. In addition, taking physical inventory should be assigned to yet another independent group to ensure that objective and independent measures are obtained. If a firm is to operate effectively, records need to be kept for prices, discounts, delays, quality, and responses to special requests. These activities require a formal record-keeping system. The accounting department should design the system and play the primary role in its implementation.

The performance measurement system in most firms relies heavily on measures of income and investment. Cost measures obtained from the accounting system are an integral part of the system. Formal accounting systems, however, often ignore some of the costs involved in inventory decisions. Not only may this create some difficulties in determining the optimal inventory policy, but in addition, these omissions can influence managers' behavior. This influence results from both the omission of certain costs and from the incentives of the production and marketing personnel.

Consider, for example, stock-out costs versus carrying costs. Stock-out costs are not explicitly included in the accounting system at the time they occur, whereas many of the carrying costs are reported and allocated to units of product. This procedure tends to cause the manager interested in improving short-run performance measures of profit to decrease inventory levels and, thereby, carrying costs, while allowing stock-out costs to increase. Such behavior is not likely to be in the best interest of the organization. Contrarily, production managers prefer large production runs in order to reduce set-up costs, and such large runs lead to high periodic inventory levels of the most recently produced item. The marketing department prefers large inventories of all products to avoid disappointed customers. Performance evaluation measures must take managerial incentives into account, in order to motivate managers toward behavior more in line with the best interests of the organization.

Inventory Control in Multistage Production Systems

In modern manufacturing facilities, production processes are highly coordinated through several production stages. Several approaches are currently in use to deal with such complex coordination problems. In this section, two of these approaches are briefly reviewed: the material requirements planning (MRP) system and the just-in-time (JIT) inventory system.

Material Requirements Planning (MRP)

A **material requirements planning or MRP system** is a method for coordinating detailed production plans in multistage production systems that involve many products, subassemblies, components, and materials. The idea behind an MRP system is to begin with a master schedule that details the production sequence for each end product and then work backwards to ascertain how much of each component part will be required and when the parts will be needed. Because the demand for subassemblies, components, and raw materials depends on the demand for the final product, they are said to exhibit **dependent demand.** This means that the production requirements in early production stages depend on planned production in the final stage of manufacture.[7] While this description implies that MRP considers only material needs, this is not the case. In their complete form, MRP systems also involve labor scheduling and capacity planning.

The simple EOQ model described in the preceding section does not take into account the dependent nature of inventory parts demands at each manufacturing stage. Nevertheless, the types of inventory costs that can occur in an MRP environment are the same as those described in the preceding section. Such costs as carrying costs, costs of down time, order costs, and stock-out costs are still the relevant parameters in an MRP system. The difference is that now the stock-out cost associated with a particular part may be due to the implications of a stock-out at a dependent manufacturing stage rather than on unsatisfied customer demand. In any case, the managerial accountant should be instrumental in supplying cost data necessary for the MRP system to be implemented. One fundamental cause of the failure of many MRP systems has been in the developing and updating of inventory reports.

Most MRP systems are complex enough that they require computerization using highly sophisticated software designed to control the flow of materials and parts through the complex multistage manufacturing operation. Managerial accountants can be integrally involved in the development of MRP software for two reasons. First, the accountant is most familiar with the firm's cost structure. Cost break-downs into material, labor, and overhead can be readily supplied. Second, the cost data files in the MRP system should reflect both financial and managerial accounting considerations, generally including the necessary cost information for both variable and absorption costing. (Variable costing and absorption costing are discussed in Chapter 4.)

There are two principal data files in an MRP system: an inventory master file and a product structure file. The **inventory master file** is a computerized listing of all items in inventory, both raw materials and component parts. The file typically contains information about each inventory item including both technological data (manufacturing or ordering lead times, economic order quantities, and quantity on hand) as well as cost accounting data such as the standard cost elements of each produced part.

The product structure file is a computer file that details the listing of materials and parts for every manufactured item, whether it is a subassembly or final assembled product. The use of the inventory master file and product structure file in the MRP

---

7. J. McClain, and L. J. Thomas, *Operations Management*, 2d ed. (Englewood Cliffs, N.J.: 1985): 360.

system is described in the following excerpt from an article in *Management Accounting:*[8]

> The product structure is a file which provides the part numbers of the component parts of each manufactured item. The relationships of all parts to each other is organized into a tier of inventory items in a hierarchy rising from simple raw materials to manufactured component parts, then to subassemblies and complex final assemblies. The system is integrated by software called a "Bill of Materials" processor. The product structure allows one to call out or retrieve a bill of material for any item.
>
> If the cost elements are provided, a detailed, costed bill of material can be generated. . . . By updating costs of the basic component parts, such as raw materials and purchased and manufactured parts, costs of all of the more complex upper-level assemblies can then be updated through a process called a cost explosion defined as level-by-level cost retrievals of all bills of material.
>
> With such sophisticated systems available, the revision of product costs is a relatively simple step-by-step process, usually performed annually. Now new costs of purchased raw materials and component parts can be developed. Labor and overhead rates also can be updated for manufactured parts and assembled components; these rates are calculated through the use of operations routings, which define each step in the manufacture or assembly of a part or finished product. When these basic costs are developed and the cost files are updated, the cost explosion process is used for updating the costs of the entire inventory item master.

Exhibit 18-2 displays an actual cost explosion sheet, of the type just described, from the Loveland Instrument Division of Hewlett-Packard.

The cost accounting data described above is an integral part of an MRP system. Such data is essential to conducting the day-to-day operational decisions involving production lot size, production scheduling, and product mix. In addition, the MRP data files become the basis for an ongoing review of the firm's cost structure for purposes of cost control, product costing, budgeting, and the revision of standard costs.

More recently MRP systems are evolving to provide a linkup between manufacturing and the financial systems of an organization. These new computerized data systems are called **material requirements planning II (MRPII).** To do so requires that the system include both marketing and financial activities. When this integration is successful MRPII can be used to establish inventory requirements and order material needs in addition to simply scheduling production. The system requires careful and thorough planning, but once computerized, the entire organization can operate from a single set of financial controls, thereby allowing management to simultaneously plan and monitor its resources.

8. B. Bowers, "Product Costing in the MRP Environment," *Management Accounting* (December 1982): 24–25.

EXHIBIT 18-2

Cost Explosion from Hewlett-Packard

HEWLETT PACKARD

PART NUMBER INSTRUMENT A	DESCRIPTION SYSTEM DMM	OPT	ITEM TYPE 0	SOURCE OF STD $	ACCT 1342	HOME DEPT 4220	KDX/CTLR 230	DATE EFFECTIVE 85/10/17 VS	COST TYPE ACT

LEVEL	PART NUMBER	OPT	DESC	HOME DEPT	SRC STD	STD QTY PER	ACT QTY PER	LABOR STD	LABOR ACT	MATERIAL/UNIT TIME STD	MATERIAL/UNIT TIME ACT	PRODUCTION COST STD	PRODUCTION COST ACT
0	INSTRUMENT A		SYSTEM DMM	4220	S	1.0000	1.0000	40.53	40.61	689.74	702.83	1158.71	1148.17
	0020 09-4221-220		A&W					11.12	11.36	1.2792	1.2792	1091.48	1096.53
	0050 09-4225-250		TEST					6.80	8.11	0.5290	0.6200	67.22	48.33
	0005 09-4292-002		PACKAGING,DEL.TO					.**	0.00	.****	0.0000	.**	3.31
1	0340-0122		BUSHING-NY	4270	S	4.0000	4.0000	0.00	0.00	0.06	0.06	0.06	0.08
1	PART A		NATL REF A	4240	S	1.0000	1.0000	0.80	0.81	9.65	10.53	18.81	19.58
	0005 09-4261-440		MATERIAL STAGING					0.00	0.00	0.0030	0.0030	10.94	14.78
	0010 09-4261-410		MATERIAL CHECKIN					0.00	0.00	0.0100	0.0100	0.00	0.00
	0025 09-4280-463		A,M					0.00	0.00	0.0000	0.0000	0.00	0.00
	0030 09-4261-470		STAGING/PERFORM					0.00	0.00	0.0000	0.0000	0.00	0.00
	0035 09-4243-420		LOADING					0.30	0.29	0.0350	0.0350	2.94	1.74
	0045 09-4243-430		ADDING					0.23	0.25	0.0300	0.0300	2.26	1.49
	0055 09-4246-450		REFERENCE TEST					0.27	0.26	0.0250	0.0250	2.67	1.56
2	PART B		PC BD-BLK(	2611	S	1.0000	1.0000	0.17	0.17	0.19	0.20	1.45	1.58
	0005 09-2610-100		KARDEX					0.00	0.00	0.0000	0.0000	0.23	0.24
	0010 09-2600-101		TOOLING VERIFICATION					0.00	0.00	0.0000	0.0000	0.02	0.02
	0015 09-2600-111		MATL ISSUE 22272					0.01	0.01	0.0006	0.0003	0.02	0.02
	0020 09-2600-122		D/S DRILL					0.01	0.01	0.0006	0.0006	0.04	0.04
	0025 09-2600-132		ELECTROLESS CU PLATE					0.02	0.02	0.0005	0.0005	0.03	0.03
	0030 09-2600-144		1.5 MIL DRY FILM PLAT RES					0.01	0.02	0.0020	0.0020	0.13	0.14
	0035 09-2600-136		ELECTRO PLATING					0.01	0.01	0.0004	0.0009	0.06	0.06
	0040 09-2600-151		STRIP & FINAL ETCH 1/2 OZ CU					0.01	0.01	0.0004	0.0004	0.03	0.03
	0050 09-2600-171		IN PROCESS INSPECTION					0.05	0.05	0.0051	0.0051	0.32	0.36
	0055 09-2600-167		AQUEOUS DRY FLM SLDR MSK					0.02	0.02	0.0020	0.0020	0.13	0.14
	0060 09-2600-113		FINAL FABRICATION					0.02	0.02	0.0027	0.0027	0.17	0.19
	0065 09-2600-173		FINAL INSPECTION & WRAP					0.03	0.03	0.0030	0.0030	0.19	0.21
	0070 09-2600-199		STOCK					0.01	0.01	0.0016	0.0016	0.10	0.11
3	TWO-LAYER-09		BD IMAGE	2660	E	0.0171	0.0171	0.00	0.00	0.0000	0.0000	0.00	0.00
	0005 09-2600-103		INPUT IMAGE SQUARE FEET										
4	TWO-LAYER		TWO LAYER	2660	E	1.0000	1.0000	0.00	0.00	0.0000	0.0000	0.00	0.00
	0005 09-2600-103		INPUT IMAGE SQUARE FEET										
3	4174-0463		PLSTC SHT-	2660	S	0.0260	0.0260	0.00	0.00	0.07	0.07	0.07	0.07
3	8500-0108		GOLD-SOFT	2660	S	0.1950	0.1950	0.00	0.00	0.07	0.07	0.07	0.07
3	8500-4227		SOLDER RES	2660	S	0.0606	0.0606	0.00	0.00	0.05	0.05	0.05	0.05
2	PART C		SEQ PARTS-	4280	S	1.0000	1.0000	0.00	0.00	0.24	0.23	0.27	0.33
	0010 09-4280-520		SEQ RUN										
3	0160-4808		C-F 39PF 1	4270	S	1.0000	1.0000	0.00	0.00	0.05	0.04	0.05	0.05

Just-in-Time Production System

The just-in-time (JIT) production system, made famous by Toyota,[9] has been hailed by many as the best way to manage manufacturing and inventories. The U.S. approach has been called the JIC system for just-in-case. A JIT system is based on the notion that inventory is a bad thing. Ideally, items would be received or produced just as they are required for the final product or service. Need for the item creates the production or order in sufficient time to ensure it is present when required. In this sense, the system has been described as a demand-pull system.

In a JIT system, failure to have the necessary item on hand interrupts the production process. When something is amiss, it then is readily apparent. This result has required management to involve their employees more directly in the production and control process. Quality control becomes a function of a continuous flow in the manufacturing operation. Workers are responsible for their activity. Vendors ensure the quality and reliability of their individual inputs.

Effective use of JIT systems can reduce the inventory investment and hence the costs of carrying inventories. The associated risk of obsolescence is smaller. Improved vendor quality is often required, resulting in lower labor costs, less rework and scrap, lower administrative costs, and fewer returns by customers. Commonly in such systems the substantial reduction in the number of suppliers (Xerox reduced its suppliers from 5,000 to 300) coupled with longer contracts has reduced costs while concurrently increasing quality.

The following illustrations from a recent article in *Production Engineering* report on the cost savings from JIT programs at Honeywell, Ingersoll-Rand, and A.P. Parts.[10]

JIT Savings at Honeywell, Ingersoll-Rand, and A.P. Parts

Chrysler, Ford, General Motors, Hewlett-Packard, Motorola, Westinghouse, and General Electric are among the large companies using JIT with considerable cost savings. At Honeywell's Process Control Division, a JIT program was installed in one of ten production lines resulting in a savings of $26,000. Large JIT projects at Ingersoll-Rand and A.P. Parts resulted in cost savings of $3.5 million and $10 million, respectively. The program at A.P. Parts even eliminated the need for a 460,000 square-foot warehouse.

The changes in inventory policy are relevant to the EOQ model discussed earlier in this chapter. If the cost of an order (K in the model) can be reduced substantially through smaller and more frequent orders and if the past cost of carrying inventories

9. Y. Monden, "What Makes the Toyota Production System Really Tick?," *Industrial Engineering* (January 1981): 36–46.
10. J. Swartley-Loush, "Just-in-Time: Is It Right for You?," *Production Engineering* (June 1985): 61–64.

(*C* in the model) has been substantially underestimated, as claimed by JIT advocates, the impact on the EOQ level is substantial. For example, cutting the order cost in half and doubling the carrying cost cause the EOQ to decline to half its prior level. However, the EOQ model continues to assume a constant order size, even at the reduced level. Using a JIT system, different order sizes can be adopted when needed. The approach is not tied to the EOQ.

The main features of JIT are that (1) it requires minimal set-up time, (2) it eliminates inefficient inventory safety stocks, which cost money and often hide inefficient production methods, and (3) it recognizes the inseparability of product quality and productivity. JIT is not possible if poor-quality parts are manufactured; if part quality is a problem, the firm needs to stock excess parts to be certain of having usable parts on hand when needed.

JIT is as much a philosophy of manufacturing as a set of techniques. The relationship between JIT and managerial accounting comes in the need for accurate data about production efficiency and product quality. Many firms that have implemented JIT have simultaneously implemented a system of almost continuously revised production efficiency and cost standards in order to facilitate movement toward greater and greater levels of product quality and production efficiency.[11]

A JIT system also has implications for accounting record keeping. The system is quite similar to that of process costing, but it is simpler. Under JIT costing, sometimes called *backflush costing*, entries for all production costs are made directly to an asset account called Inventory: Raw and In Process (denoted *RIP*), rather than to a Raw Materials or an Inventory Stores account. The second and final entry transfers the cost from RIP to Finished Goods Inventory. This entry is made when the activity is completed. The JIT system avoids those entries that issue materials from stores to operating departments and transfer work in process from one operation to another. Under JIT cost accounting there is no need for either work orders or the detailed tracking of the materials, labor, and variable overhead across operations. All manufacturing overhead, which now includes direct labor, is entered directly into finished goods.

An example will clarify the accounting entries made under JIT cost accounting. Schuyler Fabrics, Inc. produces synthetic fabric. The production process is highly automated and JIT purchasing and production systems are used. The following events and accounting entries relate to the month of March.

1. Raw materials are purchased on account for $125,000.

Inventory: Raw and In Process	125,000	
Accounts Payable		125,000

To record the purchase of raw material under
a just-in-time system.

11. R. Seglund, and S. Ibarreche, "Just-in-Time: The Accounting Implications," *Management Accounting* (August 1984): 43–45.

2. Finished goods with material costs of $120,000 are finished during March.

Finished-Goods Inventory	120,000	
Inventory: Raw and In Process		120,000

To transfer raw-material costs from RIP to finished goods.

3. Monthly labor costs amount to $20,000 and the overhead rate is $2.00 per direct labor dollar.

Finished Goods Inventory	60,000	
Salaries Payable		20,000
Applied Overhead		40,000

To add conversion costs to finished-goods inventory

The important point of this example is that under JIT costing, material costs are added directly to the RIP account when purchased rather than being inventoried first in Raw-Material Inventory.[12]

JIT costing leads to a simplification of the accounting system. The result is reduced involvement of the accountants in day-to-day plant operations, reduced administrative costs and a greater reliance on nonfinancial performance measures of a time, productivity, or quality nature (such as the ratio of the number of defective units produced to total production).

Flexible Manufacturing Systems

Still another new development that can reduce inventory requirements is the **flexible manufacturing system (FMS).** An FMS system is a computerized plant network based on a substantial investment in equipment and its operation. The key objective of such systems is to improve the firm's ability to process many variations of a single item easily and to foster expansion of existing product lines. For example, different automobile models—say, four-door and two-door versions — can be mixed as desired in production. It's not necessary to produce only four-door models in one run.

FMS systems should be designed to link engineering and manufacturing with materials requirements planning. When the FMS system is functioning properly, set-up times are reduced, lower inventory levels are possible, and reductions appear in labor costs, scrap, rework, and need for space.

Cost data plays an important role in establishing an FMS. Decisions must be made as to what products to produce and the division between internal system development or the use of external vendors to provide the system. Technical expertise, availability, and support concerns will modify any cost projections. Once the system

---

12. See G. Foster and C. Horngren, "Cost Accounting and Cost Management Issues," *Management Accounting* (June 1987): 19–25. Some companies using backflush costing systems treat conversion costs as period costs by charging them directly to cost of goods sold instead of first adding these costs to finished-goods inventory.

is operating, cost considerations may influence scheduling and cost calculations, including cost variances, can be used in evaluation and control. Moreover, when a new system is introduced, cost procedures such as the methods used to allocate indirect costs should be reevaluated.

Summary

MRP and JIT systems are developments of inventory decision models and suggest new reasons for cost accumulation and analysis. The accountant should strive to understand these new developments and to provide the necessary cost data. Not all of the parameters of the EOQ model are available from the accounting records. The inventory carrying-cost rate and estimates of demand are examples. Further, the accountants' data are subject to estimation errors. Fortunately, even proportionally large errors in cost estimates have relatively small effects on either the EOQ or total costs.

Material requirements planning should cause more attention to be directed to the dependent nature of the production process. The advent of new software packages in this area places additional demands on accountants, who should be involved in their selection and implementation. The concurrent development of JIT systems has placed increased emphasis on the costs of carrying inventory and producing goods of inferior quality. These costs must be monitored by accountants. These procedures have reduced operating and administrative costs while reducing the involvement of accountants in day-to-day operations.

The accounting system and internal control procedures play a substantive role in cost control. Furthermore, the fact that periodic accounting income measures are used in performance evaluation can influence managers' inventory decisions so that larger profits are reported.

Inventory values are also necessary inputs for external reporting. They affect asset values and income. The subject of financial reporting for external uses is separate from the internal decisions involving inventory control, but it involves many of the same elements. Inventory valuation for financial reporting deals with the dual problem of establishing inventory and income figures.

Key Terms to Review

carrying costs, p. 630
dependent demand, p. 637
economic-order-quantity (EOQ), p. 631
flexible manufacturing systems (FMS), p. 642
inventory master file, p. 637
just-in-time, p. 628
material requirements planning (MRP), p. 637

material requirements planning II (MRP II), p. 638
ordering costs, p. 630
precautionary level of inventory, p. 630
product structure file, p. 637
safety stock, p. 630
speculative level of inventory, p. 630
transactional level of inventory, p. 630

Review Problem

INVENTORY CONTROL

Cherry Computer Casings builds the box that houses a personal computer. Each box contains a screen on the front, which costs $30. Last year the company made fifty screen orders for a total cost of $5,000. Cherry Company expects labor costs to rise due to union activity and order costs to increase by 28 percent. Demand is forecasted at 10,000 units per month next year, and carrying costs are estimated at $.12 per dollar of yearly inventory. Establish Cherry Company's EOQ for screens and total cost on a monthly basis.

Solution to Review Problem

$$K = (\$5,000 \div 50)\ 1.28 = \$128$$

$$C = (\$.12 \div 12)(36) = \$.36$$

$$D = 10,000$$

$$EOQ = \sqrt{2(128)(10,000)/.36} = \$2,667$$

$$TC = .36(EOQ) = .36(\$2,667) = \$960 \text{ per month.}$$

APPENDIX
Inventory Policy at Ford Motor Company

Excerpts from a Ford Motor Company Supply Manual Procedure on inventory management illustrate modern manufacturing and inventory control systems.[13] This document describes in detail the inventory control procedures used by Ford. Some technical and procedural detail has been eliminated, and italicized type is used in some places to emphasize the role of costs in the overall inventory management program.

Supply Manual Procedure: Establishing and Maintaining Production Parts Floats*

I. Introduction and Summary

The Company's Manufacturing and Supply Directive entitled Inventory Management emphasizes the importance of managing inventory size and investment to support Company profitability objectives. The Directive identifies what the Company expects of its management personnel with regard to the development of an inventory plan and strategy that minimizes inventory investment.

Float is an integral part of inventory management and is the technique used to control the flow of material through the various stages of manufacture to the ultimate delivery of the product. This control is accomplished by advancing the forecasted requirements for each component of each plant's product to establish the time at which each scheduled process within the plant should take place and each supplier shipment should be made.

Float has four basic components (*shipping bank*, *system*, *operational reserve*, and *transit allowance*) and is most often expressed in whole or fractional days. When volume fluctuation does not affect quantity, as in the case of a constant quantity system, or when facilities limit storage, float may be expressed in pieces rather than days. Such instances are known as *fixed float.*

Shipping bank is usually composed of two elements. The first element is *safety stock*, which is the planned minimum number of days' requirement of a shipping item scheduled to be available for immediate shipment at any time. This availability protects the customer and the supplier against moderate but abrupt schedule changes,

13. This extended description is somewhat more detailed than prior examples from practice and introduces terminology specific to Ford.

* Copyright Ford Motor Company. Reprinted with permission.

stock losses, transit delays, and other associated problems. The second float element of the shipping bank is *manufacturing frequency allowance*, which provides stock for shipment when parts are not planned to be produced on days that parallel or precede scheduled shipment. This allowance is added to the safety stock. Shipping bank should not fall below the safety stock level during normal production periods.

System is normally expressed in days' or fractional days' requirements. System is the material needed between planned schedule points in manufacturing operations.

Operational reserve usually includes two elements. The first element is *safety stock*, which is the planned minimum number of day's requirement of a part to be available ahead of scheduled manufacturing operations at any time. Safety stocks protect against interruptions in the flow of parts and materials in the manufacturing process. The second element is *manufacturing frequency allowance*. The allowance is to provide material for use on the schedule production date when the material to be used is not planned to be produced or received on dates which parallel or precede scheduled usage. The allowance is added to the safety stock. The operational reserve is not to be depleted below the safety stock level during normal operations.

Transit allowance is usually composed of two elements. The first element is *workday transit* and represents the number of work days an incoming item is in transit from its source of supply. The second element is *shipping frequency allowance*, which must be calculated to provide stock for use on scheduled production dates when the parts to be used are not planned to be shipped on dates that parallel or precede scheduled use. This allowance is added to workday transit.

The scheduled quantity of each part to be on hand at any time is the result of the application of its float to forecast requirements. Therefore, *high value parts* are ideally scheduled with a *low float.* This results in frequent fabrication or shipment from suppliers. *Low value parts* should usually be scheduled with a *higher float* and less frequent fabrication or shipment. The float determined by this general rule may be adjusted when specific storage, facility utilization, procurement risk, or other problems require special consideration. The float decision for each production part should be the result of an evaluation between its required inventory investment and the benefits from holding inventory.

II. Organizational Components Affected

Central staffs: Purchasing and supply staff; production planning and control office.

Operations: All affected operations.

III. Responsibilities

A. General

1. Parts should be categorized into *float classes* according to their *value* as shown in Exhibit 18-3. Separate cost classes should be developed for shop-made parts and for purchased items.

2. Established floats should be reviewed during each model year. A schedule which provides for the review of 15 percent of established floats per month

---

EXHIBIT 18-3

How to Establish Float Class Codes and Assign Safety Stock Levels

---

Ford Motor Company

Float Class Codes

1. For each part, multiply the planning volume for one day times the *unit cost.*

2. Make separate lists for shop-made parts and for purchased parts.

3. List the parts according to the *cost* of one day's supply (highest to lowest).

4. Float classes generally incorporate *parts cost* as follows:

Float Class	Cost of One Day's Planning Volume
A	80%
B	10
C	8
D	2
	100%

5. Each plant should determine its own weighting and its own pattern of distribution that will permit optimum management of *inventory cost* combined with *total cost.*

Safety Stock Levels

1. Assign safety stock levels to provide highest protection to highest risk parts.

2. Assign a degree of risk to each part depending on its problem experience and on its importance to continued operation of the production line.

3. Each plant manager has the right and obligation to manage his plant's safety stocks in a way that will maximize the cost-benefit relationship to the Company.

---

for ten months is recommended. This should assure frequent review of large investment items. Exhibit 18-4 provides a recommended format to monitor review progress.

3. Operational staffs are to issue implementing instructions for the development and review of parts floats consistent with this procedure.

4. Operational staffs will ascertain that parts floats developed by the plants comply with their instructions.

EXHIBIT 18-4

Production Parts Float Review

Ford Motor Company

PRODUCTION PARTS FLOAT REVIEW
Model Year _____
(IN THOUSANDS $)

PLANT _____

COST CLASSIFICATION

	A	B	C	D	TOTAL
NUMBER OF PARTS BY CLASS					
EXTENDED VALUE – AT CALCULATING FLOAT DAYS, TIMES DAILY PLANNING VOLUME, TIMES STANDARD COST					
FLOAT CLASS DOLLARS ($) AS A PERCENT OF TOTAL					
NUMBER OF TIMES PARTS ARE TO BE REVIEWED DURING MODEL YEAR					

MONTH ENDING _____

NUMBER OF REVIEWS SCHEDULED					
NUMBER OF REVIEWS COMPLETED					
AHEAD (BEHIND) SCHEDULE					
NET FLOAT DOLLARS REDUCED/ (ADDED) THIS MONTH *					

PROGRAM YEAR TO DATE

NUMBER OF REVIEWS SCHEDULED					
NUMBER OF REVIEWS COMPLETED					
AHEAD (BEHIND) SCHEDULE					
EXTENDED VALUE – AT CALCULATING FLOAT DAYS (AFTER ADJUSTMENTS + OR – FOR REVIEWS), TIMES DAILY PLANNING VOLUME, TIMES STANDARD COST					
NET FLOAT DOLLARS REDUCED/ (ADDED) MODEL YEAR TO DATE					

*THE ATTACHMENT DETAILS FIVE PARTS WITH THE HIGHEST FLOAT CHANGE (IN $) FOR THE REPORTING MONTH.

PREPARED BY _____

DATE _____

July 23, 1980

B. Vehicle Assembly Operations

1. Determine system float needed between the point of installation and vehicle completion. Use fractional days where appropriate, rather than rounding to whole days.

2. Determine Operational Reserve as follows:

Determine safety stock days and inventory class code using the guidelines contained in Exhibit 18-3. When necessary due to specific storage, facility utilization, or procurement risk problems, or to provide for fluctuations in demand for optional customer selections, adjust and reclassify to applicable inventory class code.

3. Determine Transit Allowance as follows:

a. Obtain transit time from established Traffic sources. When transit time is greater than five days or travel time occurs over a weekend, delete non-working travel time.

b. Determine a shipping frequency by supplier, which will optimize costs of receiving, transportation, scheduling, and inventory. The shipping frequency allowance added to workday transit equals the number of days scheduled use prior to the day the part is scheduled to be received. Establish fixed leave days for supplier shipments to minimize potential excess inventories.

C. Manufacturing Operations Other Than Vehicle Assembly — Production Control

1. Determining Shipping Bank

a. *Safety Stock*: Determine safety stock days required to optimize shipping schedule protection. Consideration should be given to required inventory investment and planned operational reserves at customer locations. Formal identification and provision for bottleneck operations may allow reduced safety stocks.

b. *Manufacturing Frequency Allowance*: The manufacturing frequency allowance to be added to safety stock is equal to the number of days scheduled to be shipped prior to the day the part is planned to be produced. Allowances should be developed from a manufacturing plan. Averages should not be used. Fixed leave day agreements require that manufacturing frequency allowances be carefully considered to avoid disruption in planned transportation and manufacturing cycles.

2. Determining System

a. System float is material that moves between scheduled operations. Examples are material on conveyors, ahead of and in heat treat furnaces, or in wash cycles.

    b. Knowledge of applicable manufacturing processes is required to accomplish system floating. Production, Industrial Engineering, and Manufacturing Engineering requirements should be considered in developing system floats.

    c. For complex manufacturing systems, a process flow chart is an invaluable aid and should be used.

    d. Tenths of day's requirements should be used in establishing system floats rather than rounding to whole days.

    e. System floats require frequent review for potential improvement, particularly with newly installed manufacturing processes.

    f. Parts that require outside processing at a point in their manufacturing cycle are properly included in system float if the material moves to and from the processing service on a daily basis. If there is an accumulation of parts to permit economic processing or reduced freight cost, a manufacturing frequency allowance should be calculated and included in operational reserve.

3. Determining Operational Reserve

    a. Safety Stock: Determine safety stock days to be available ahead of scheduled operations at any time. Exhibit 18-3 provides guidelines in setting safety stock levels.

    b. Manufacturing Frequency Allowance: The manufacturing frequency allowance is additive to safety stock. It is equal to the number of scheduled production days preceding the day the part is planned to be produced or received. Operational reserve may apply to either purchased items or to shop-made parts, and may be utilized before or after the first operation.

4. Review manufacturing cycles with production supervision to confirm compatibility with float and inventory objectives.

5. Determining Transit Allowance

    a. Establish transit time for each incoming item from information provided by Traffic. When transit time is greater than five days or travel time occurs over a weekend, delete nonworking travel time.

    b. Shipping frequency allowances provide material to manufacturing operations when suppliers do not ship daily, and is equal to the number of days scheduled to be used in production prior to the day the part is scheduled to be shipped. Shipping frequency allowances permit spreading the Receiving Activity's workload more evenly, and can generate freight cost savings by permitting consolidation of shipments.

Suggested Readings

Chalos, P. "High-Tech Production: The Impact on Cost Reporting Systems." *Journal of Accountancy* (March 1986): 106–12.

Deis, P. "Using an MRP System for Financial Decision Support." *Journal of Accounting and EDP* (Winter 1986): 38–48.

Foster, G., and C. Horngren. "Cost Accounting and Cost Management Issues." *Management Accounting* (June 1987): 19–25.

———. "Cost Accounting and Cost Management in a JIT Environment." *Journal of Cost Management* (Winter 1988): 4–14.

Green, A. *Flexible Manufacturing Systems.* New York: American Management Association, 1986.

Hahn, C., P. Pinto, and D. Bragg. "Just in Time Production and Purchasing." *Journal of Purchasing and Materials Management* (Fall 1983): 2–10.

Kaplan, R., and A. Atkinson, *Advanced Management Accounting,* 2nd ed. Englewood Cliffs, N.J.: Prentice-Hall, 1989, chap. 8.

Morse, W., and J. Scheiner. "Cost Minimization, Return on Investment, Residual Income: Alternative Criteria for Inventory Control." *Accounting and Business Research* (Autumn 1979): 320–24.

Newmann, B., and P. Jaoven. "Kanban, Zips and Cost Accounting: A Case Study." *Journal of Accountancy* (August 1986): 132–41.

Patell, J. "Adapting a Cost Accounting System to Just-in-Time Manufacturing: The Hewlett-Packard Personal Office Computer Division." *The Accounting Review* (October 1987): 808–40.

Schonberger, R. *World Class Manufacturing.* New York: Free Press, 1986.

Vollum, R. "Cost of Accounting: The Key to Capturing Cost Information on the Factory Floor." *Journal of Accounting and EDP* (Summer 1985): 44–51.

Review Questions

18-1 The chapter refers to optimal inventory levels and not to maximizing turnover. Why?

18-2 Answer the following questions concerning inventory information.

    a. What fundamental data need exist for determining inventory valuation? What data are necessary for financial reporting but not needed for inventory-level decisions?

    b. Why are there differences between inventory-cost data for (1) inventory-level decisions, (2) financial reporting to outsiders, and (3) internal performance measurement?

18-3 Suppose that cash and cashlike assets (short-term securities, for example) are considered as an inventory. Using the EOQ equation (2), what would the symbols mean?

18-4 In decisions involving the level of cash and cashlike assets to hold, what related decisions involving cash must be considered?

18-5 The costs of an inventory policy, K and C (ordering costs and storage costs, respectively), are usually treated as linear functions of the inventory quantity (that is, K and C are constant per unit per time period over a rather wide range). Describe several components of these costs and how they vary with inventory quantity. Suggest methods of estimating each component.

18-6 Why do firms hold inventories?

18-7 Some accountants state that fixed costs should not be considered a cost of product (and hence should not be inventoried). Because these costs will be incurred regardless of production or sale, should they be treated as period expenses or as product costs?

18-8 Are managers likely to be more concerned about having too much inventory or having too little? Why?

18-9 What limitation to the basic EOQ model is highlighted by an MRP system?

18-10 Which of the phrases below are appropriate to a JIT system?

   a. The system is a cost-push versus a demand-pull system.

   b. Inventory is a good thing.

   c. When items are not on hand, production is likely to be interrupted, pointing often to the cause.

   d. Accountants are more involved in day-to-day production operations.

   e. Accounting systems are simplified.

18-11 If the JIT advocates are correct, the costs of carrying inventory have been underestimated. Do you agree?

18-12 The number of inventory items held by some companies often runs in excess of 50,000 types. Some companies follow a system of classifying these items into one of three categories for control purposes. What basis would you expect them to use and why?

Exercises

18-13 **Opportunity Loss**   Using the EOQ equation (2), it can be shown that the opportunity loss as a percentage of the minimal achievable total cost is given by

$$(E - E^*)^2 \div 2EE^*$$

where E^* is the optimal order quantity based on the correct values and E is the order quantity computed and (potentially) implemented based on incorrect values. Suppose order costs are underestimated by a factor of four. What is the percentage loss in total cost from using the incorrect value? What is the percentage opportunity loss if holding costs are underestimated by a factor of four?

18-14 **Determining Order Size and Total Cost** Ruck Company produces a product that it sells for $5 per unit. Production costs for this item are

Fixed costs per year $10,000

Variable costs per unit $1

Normal activity is $5,000 units per year. The following additional facts are known for this product:

1. The company inventories this item at full cost using normal activity to absorb fixed costs. A FIFO cost-flow system is used.

2. Inventory values during the year increased from $600 to $690.

3. The year's production was $4,650 valued in sales dollars.

4. Inventory holding costs should average $10 per unit according to standards set by production and finance.

5. All raw materials are purchased simultaneously from a single supplier.

This year Ruck Company incurred order costs of $2,000 based on ten orders but expects a 25 percent increase in future ordering costs. Other costs are not expected to change.

   a. Determine the optimal order quantity

   b. Compute the total yearly cost at the optimal order quantity.

18-15 **Using EOQ Logic without the Equation** Suppose you knew the ordering cost was $100 per order, the holding cost per unit was fifty cents per year, and the total units required (D = demand) during the year was 1,000 units. You never have heard of the EOQ formula. How could you proceed to find the best order quantity? (The EOQ is 632 units.)

18-16 **Order Times** Suppose the items of inventory in Exercise 18-15 are used uniformly across time and that it takes exactly a month (four weeks) to receive a shipment once ordered. How many items should be on hand at the time an order is placed? How long would there be between orders?

Problems 18-17 **JIT Accounting Entries** An electronics firm with a normal process costing system engages in the following activities for July 19x9:

   a. Materials purchased $500

   b. Materials issued   400

   c. Applied overhead   200

   d. Direct labor   300

   e. Costs transferred to finished goods   700

   f. Cost of goods sold   650

Assuming no inventories July 1, 19x9, make the appropriate journal entries. Now assume this firm adopts a JIT costing system. Give the entries for the following facts:

a. Materials purchased	$500
b. Materials to finished goods based on com- pleted product	260
c. Materials to cost of goods sold	230
d. Applied overhead (including direct labor)	500
e. Overhead in ending inventories:	
(1) Finished goods	20
(2) Work in process (RIP)	60

Show, using T-accounts, how the two sets of entries lead to the same work-in-process, finished-goods, and cost-of-goods-sold accounts.

18-18 Solving for an EOQ and Total Cost   Suppose that monthly demand is 3,000 units, the cost of carrying a unit for one month is estimated at $3, and ordering costs are $5.

REQUIRED:

a. Determine the optimal order quantity.

b. What happens to the optimal order quantity if the estimated demand in part **a** is understated by 50 percent?

18-19 Moving Toward a JIT Approach   (Continuation of Problem 18-18) Suppose the firm in Problem 18-18, part **a**, can lower its ordering cost to $1.25 by joining a buying group with an annual membership cost of $1,000. Should the firm join? If so, what is the optimal order quantity?

18-20 Inventory Costs and JIT Systems   Right-Help Drugs operates a number of discount drug stores. Among other items, it carries Classic Cola. At its Richmond store its monthly (four-week) demand has averaged 1,500 six-packs. Orders were placed when needed given a week's required lead time. The cost of an order was estimated at this time to be $50, and the carrying cost per six-pack per month was estimated to be $.50.

Two months later the carrying cost was reestimated to be $2.

During the following month Right-Help reduced the number of suppliers it used, provided those remaining with long-run contracts and required prompt delivery of exactly the amount ordered. Right-Help estimated these new contracts to cut ordering cost by 50 percent.

REQUIRED:

a. Calculate the EOQs for each situation.

b. Do the results support the drug store's move toward a JIT system?

c. Would you expect the EOQ to be the same across months? Explain.

19

Introduction to Capital Budgeting

After studying this chapter, you should be able to:

1 Explain and evaluate the four basic methods used in practice for investment decision making — payback, return on investment, net present value, and internal rate of return.

2 List the limitations of each of the four basic methods.

3 Describe the conditions under which the net-present-value and internal-rate-of-return methods provide correct guidance to the investment decision problem.

*B*usiness organizations are continually faced with the problem of deciding whether the commitment of resources involving time and money is worthwhile in terms of the expected benefits. A decision that involves outlays and benefits stretched out through time is called a **capital budgeting decision**. Capital budgeting includes searching for new and more profitable investment proposals, investigating engineering, marketing, and strategic considerations to predict the consequences of accepting a given investment, and performing economic analyses to determine the profit potential of each investment proposal. This chapter discusses four of the many ways companies evaluate capital budget decisions. Before we look at those methods, however, we first review the time value of money concept. In this chapter, we evaluate the underlying economic desirability of an investment; we do not discuss the method by which an investment is financed. Initially a zero tax rate and certainty are assumed so that the analysis can concentrate on the more fundamental capital budgeting issues.[1]

Time-Value Calculations: Present Value and Future Value

Money has value. A dollar in hand is worth more than a dollar to be received one year from today. This concept is called the **time value of money.** For example, if money can be borrowed or lent at an interest rate of 10 percent per year, then $100 held today (time 0) and invested to earn 10 percent will be worth $110 one year from today (time 1).

If the $110 is again invested at time 1 at 10 percent, then at the end of year 2 the firm will have $121. The $100 grows to $121 in 2 years. The general expression for any time period, n, is

$$F = P(1 + r)^n \tag{1}$$

where

r = the interest rate
n = the number of time periods
F = the future sum to be received after n periods
P = the present value or present equivalent of F

---

1. Any investment analysis should be performed using the after-tax cash flows of each period as the inputs in the calculations. Initially tax considerations are omitted but are considered in detail in the next chapter.

If r, n, and F are properly specified, then one is indifferent between F dollars at time n and P dollars now. Thus, when $r = 0.10$, $n = 1$, and the investor starts at time 0 with $100, at time 1:

$$F = \$100(1.10)^1 = \$110$$

For two time periods,

$$F = \$100(1.10)^2 = \$121$$

Future value factors are given in Table B at the end of the book.

Instead of computing the future value, managers frequently want to compute the present value of a future sum. Assuming a manager can lend and borrow at an interest rate of r, equation (2), obtained from equation (1) by multiplying both sides by $(1 + r)^{-n}$, enables present values to be obtained:

$$P = (1 + r)^{-n} F \tag{2}$$

For $F = \$121$, $r = 0.10$, and $n = 2$:

$$P = (1.10)^{-2}(\$121) = (1.21)^{-1}(\$121) = \$100$$

Using equation (2), the $121 to be received at time 2 at 10 percent interest has a present value at time 0 of $100.

The present value, P, is called a **discounted cash flow (DCF).** When a future cash flow is multiplied by $(1 + r)^{-n}$ we obtain its present value or discounted cash flow, and any calculation process using this transformation is called a **discounted cash flow method.** The present value factors $(1 + r)^{-n}$ are given in Table A at the end of the book for a wide range of values. For example, for $n = 2$ and $r = 0.10$, $(1.10)^{-2}$ is equal to 0.8264. Hence, if a firm anticipates a cash flow of $1,000,000 two years from now and if 0.10 is the appropriate interest rate, the present value of the cash flow is $826,400.

$$P = (1.10)^{-2}(\$1,000,000) = 0.8264(\$1,000,000) = \$826,400$$

The firm is indifferent between an investment offering $826,400 now or $1,000,000 in two years. The following calculations demonstrate why:

Initial sum at time 0	$826,400
Year 1 interest	+ 82,640
Sum at time 1	909,040
Year 2 interest	+ 90,904
Sum at time 2	$1,000,000 (rounded)

Rather than use Table A to find the present equivalent of a future value, calculators can be readily used to determine the values. Some calculators have the present value factors built into them. If not, a calculator that has the function y^x can be used to compute a future value by setting y equal to $(1 + r)$ and x equal to n. Then

$$y^x = (1 + r)^n$$

EXHIBIT 19-1

Present Value and Future Value at an Interest Rate of 10 Percent

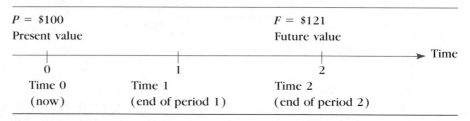

$P = \$100$
Present value

$F = \$121$
Future value

Time 0 (now)   Time 1 (end of period 1)   Time 2 (end of period 2)

By taking the reciprocal of y^x (that is, $\frac{1}{y^x}$), the present value factor can also be obtained.

Annuity Calculations

If identical payments are equally spaced, the series is called an **annuity.** The symbol $A(n, r)$ is used here to represent the present value of $1 per period for n periods discounted at an interest rate of r. The formula for calculating the present value of $1 per period for n periods, where the first payment is one period away, is

$$A(n, r) = \frac{1 - (1 + r)^{-n}}{r} \tag{3}$$

Table C at the end of the book gives the values of $A(n, r)$ for different values of r and n. The symbol $A(n, r)$ represents a single number and is not a multiplication of A times n and r. The fact that the n and r are separated by a comma indicates a functional relationship rather than a multiplication.

If $n = 3$ and $r = .10$, the value of $A(n, r)$ from Table C is 2.4869. Alternatively, Table A can be used to obtain the result that $(1 + r)^{-n} = 0.7513$. Then using equation (3),

$$A(3, .10) = \frac{1 - .7513}{.10} = 2.487$$

The future value of an n-year annuity is the amount that a level stream of cash flows will grow to over a period of n years. Table D provides the factors for the future value of a stream of $1 cash flows for n years at an interest rate of r.

To summarize, Table A gives the present value of $1 received at time n. Table B gives the future value of $1 at the end of n periods. Table C gives the present value of a series of n dollars when $1 is received at the end of each of n time periods. Table D gives the future value of a stream of $1 cash flows each received at the end of the period for n time periods.

Use of Cash Flows

Procedures using discounted cash flow (DCF) for investment decisions use the cash flows of the investments but exclude cash flows from financing. These methods of evaluating investments have now gained acceptability and are commonly found in all sizes of firms.

All firms face capital budgeting decisions where the timing of the cash flows and the uncertainty of the cash flows of an investment are important factors. For many years, managers either did not consider time value or did so incorrectly. Today two methods are widely used and they are both DCF methods.

One method, called the **net-present-value method,** applies a present value factor $(1 + r)^{-n}$ to each future cash flow (excluding financing cash flow) to bring it back to the present. The method computes the present value equivalent of each cash flow. The present values are then summed to obtain the net present value (NPV) of the project. The second method, called the **internal-rate-of-return method,** finds the rate of interest that causes the sum of the present values of the cash flows, including the investment but excluding financing cash flows, to be equal to zero. This rate of interest, called the *internal rate of return (IRR),* is also the average return on investment earned through the investment's life, although this average is of a very special type.

Assume an investment of $1,000 will pay $121 at time 1 and $1,121 at time 2. The NPV using .10 as a discount rate is

Time	Cash Flows	Present Value Factors	Present Values
0	$-1,000$	1.10^{-0}	$-1,000.00$
1	121	1.10^{-1}	110.00
2	1,121	1.10^{-2}	926.45
		NPV $	36.45

The IRR is .121 (found by trial and error).

Time	Cash Flows	Present Value Factors	Present Values
0	$-1,000$	1.121^{-0}	$-1,000.00$
1	121	1.121^{-1}	107.94
2	1,121	1.121^{-2}	892.06
		NPV $	0

Both of these methods will be discussed in greater detail later in this chapter.

Excluding Financing Cash Flows

It is instructive to see why it is appropriate to exclude the financing cash flows from the investment decision. Consider a simple one-time investment involving net cash flows of $10,000 during each of the next two years. The investment costs $17,355 now and has no residual value in two years. Assume the appropriate cost of money is 10 percent. Using a DCF approach, the present value of the future positive cash flows is

$$(\$10,000)0.9091 + (\$10,000)0.8264 = \$17,355$$

Because the present value of the positive cash flows equals the investment cost, this is a break-even investment.

To demonstrate that the investment breaks even, assume that the money to finance the investment is borrowed at 10 percent. At the end of the first year, interest of $1,736 or 0.10 ($17,355) is owed and paid. This leaves $10,000 − $1,736 or $8,264 for principal repayment. Using $8,264 to repay part of the initial loan leaves $17,355 − $8,264 or $9,091 outstanding on the loan at the end of the first year. Now at the end of the second year, interest of $909 or 0.10($9,091) is owed and paid. This leaves $10,000 − $909 or $9,091 for debt repayment. This is exactly enough to repay the amount left outstanding on the loan. Again this is a break-even situation. The cash proceeds just cover the borrowing. Had the interest payments (and/or the principal repayments) been deducted from the cash flows before discounting, the project would incorrectly have a negative net present value.

Investment Criteria versus Periodic Performance Measures

Why are cash flows rather than accounting profits used for the capital budgeting decision? The objective is to evaluate the investment over its entire life, and it is not necessary to determine the year-by-year profitability, as an accounting approach would do, in order to decide whether or not the investment is acceptable. Cash flow analysis is more simple and is likely to be more accurate.

Objectives of the Firm

When managers make capital budgeting decisions, their primary goal should be to maximize the present value of the stockholders' position. Because the investment decisions are made from the point of view of the stockholders, their interests are best served by a procedure that systematically assigns a cost to the capital that reflects the risks of the project being considered.

An investment evaluation process must incorporate (or adjust for) the risk of the projects being considered. The firm's investors have to be compensated both for the time value of money and for risk. In order to be acceptable, a project entailing more risk must offer the prospect of a higher return. Because capital budgeting decisions involve immediate outlays and uncertain benefits that are spread out through time, the primary decision problem facing management is to incorporate time value and risk considerations in such a manner that the well-being of the stockholders is maximized. Taking the time value of money into consideration is the easier problem. Much less is known about how to deal with the risk created by the uncertainty of the cash flows. Initially, certainty is assumed here for purposes of discussion.

Four Methods of Capital Budgeting

There are many methods of capital budgeting used by business firms, but most of them are based on one of the following four methods:

- Payback,
- Return on investment,
- Net present value,
- Internal rate of return.

It is common for firms to require that a variety of methods be used to evaluate each project proposed.

Payback

The most widely used method of making investment decisions is the payback method. It is still used by two-thirds of the *Fortune* 500 firms and by an even larger percentage of smaller firms. The **payback period** is the length of time required for an investment project's net cash inflows to recover the initial investment. In other words, the payback period is the time required for the total cash inflows to equal the cash outflows. For example, an investment costing $1,000,000 and yielding net cash inflows of $250,000 per year would have a payback period of four years.

The conventional payback approach without time discounting has two major drawbacks that are illustrated by the example above. First, a dollar of cash inflow today is given no more value than a dollar of cash inflow to be received in the future, in spite of the firm's ability to invest current dollars at a positive return. Second, the payback method ignores cash flows after the investment is recovered. Hence, two investments costing $1,000,000 and yielding net cash inflows of $250,000 per year, the first for five years and the second for ten years, are considered identically attractive because the payback periods are identical.

Some managers acknowledge these limitations but use the payback measure as an indication of the amount of an investment's risk. A payback of one year tends to indicate less risk than a payback of twenty years.

Managers like the payback approach for several reasons. First, it is simple to understand and explain. Second, early paybacks provide managers with flexibility to reinvest funds and do indicate less risk. Third, a manager who expects to be transferred in the near future and wants to see results while still managing the activity would prefer a short payback. Finally, managers are not comfortable attempting to predict the future very many periods forward. Payback appeals to them as a way around these difficulties. However, since payback considers neither the time value of money nor the economic contribution of an asset after its payback period, the method should be avoided as a primary investment evaluation tool.

The payback period calculation may highlight one type of game playing in the preparation of capital budgets. A payback calculation on an investment will expose any attempt to inflate the cash flows of the investment's later years, making the investment appear more desirable than it actually is, while not jeopardizing favorable performance measures in the project's early years (projecting low cash flows in the early years).

To adjust for the fact that the payback method does not consider the time value of money, a discounted variation of payback can be used. In this case the *discounted payback period* is the time required for the discounted cash flows to equal the investment. Assume an investment costs $379,000 and returns a $100,000 net cash inflow per year. Assume further that the appropriate cost of money is 10 percent. The undiscounted payback period is 3.79 years. The discounted payback period is five years because the present value of an annuity of $100,000 a year for five years is equal to the initial outlay of $379,000. If the forecasted cash flows occur over five years, the investment just breaks even economically. Investors would receive back their capital and the required return, 10 percent, on that capital. Discounted payback does not correct the omission of the cash flows after the payback period.

Return on Investment

The **return on investment (ROI)** of a project is the project's forecasted average income divided by its average required investment (the method is also called the *accounting or book rate of return method*). The computation is based on accounting values rather than cash flows, and it covers the entire life of the investment. Rather than the average investment (that is, a figure based on the depreciated or book value of the relevant plant assets), some companies use the initial investment (undepreciated plant assets). This alternate procedure adds a second flaw to an already flawed method. For an investment of finite life, the amount invested does not stay constant. Because the income and investment measures used are conventional accounting measures, the ROI measure also fails to take the time value of money into consideration. A dollar of benefits added in period 10 will affect the ROI calculation as much as a dollar of benefits added in period one. Thus, the conventional ROI measure is not an acceptable way of evaluating investments. Nevertheless it is in common use.

Assume an investment with the following cash flows:

Time Period		
0	1	2
−20,000	+11,000	+18,000

Using straight-line depreciation ($10,000), the income for year 1 is $1,000 and the ROI is $\frac{1,000}{20,000} = .05$. The income of year 2 is $8,000 and the ROI is $\frac{8,000}{10,000} = .80$.

Discounted cash flow (DCF) approaches avoid the problem of failing to consider the timing of the cash flows. These approaches yield more reliable measures of value than either the payback or the ROI measures described above.

Net Present Value

Use of the net-present-value (NPV) method of evaluating investments has been increasing for the past forty years. It is hard to find an industrial firm that does not employ the net-present-value method, generally in conjunction with other measures, somewhere in its organization.

The net present value of an investment is the amount the firm could afford to pay in excess of the cost of the investment and still break even on the investment. It is net of the present value of all future cash flows associated with the investment. If the net present value is positive, the investment is acceptable. However, strategic consider-ations and competitors' actions offer examples of factors not captured by the net-present-value calculation which may have a significant bearing on a capital budgeting decision.

The first step in the computation of the net present value of an investment is to choose an appropriate rate of discount. This may be a required return or *hurdle rate*, a minimum acceptable rate of return set by management. The second step is to compute the present value equivalents of all cash flows associated with the invest-ment, excluding the financing cash flows. These present-value equivalents are then summed to obtain the net present value of the investment.

Suppose the firm has an investment opportunity requiring a current cash outlay of $864,000 that promises net cash inflows of $1,000,000 one period from now and $100,000 two periods from now. Suppose the required return or hurdle rate is 10 percent. Using the present value factors for $r = 0.10$ yields:

EXHIBIT 19-2

NPV Example

Time Period	Cash Inflows (Outflows)	Present Value Factor (0.10)	Present Value Equivalents
0	$-864,000	1.00000	$-864,000
1	1,000,000	0.90909	909,090
2	100,000	0.82645	82,645
		Net present value	$ 127,735

The firm could pay $127,735 more than the $864,000 initial outlay and still break even; that is, it would just earn the 0.10 capital cost. Thus, the $127,735 is in a sense the "excess" incentive to invest, and it is a measure of the safety margin that exists for this two-year project.

Assume an investment which promises to earn proceeds of $20,000 at the end of period 1 and costs $10,000. The present value of the proceeds at 10 percent is $18,182 and the outlay is $10,000. The net present value of the investment using 10 percent is $8,182. The net present value of the investment can be plotted over a wide range of discount rates. The resulting graph is called a **present-value profile.** This example is shown in Exhibit 19-3.

The intersection of the graph with the x-axis determines the rate that equates the net cash flows to zero. This rate is called the internal rate of return of the investment. In this example, the internal rate of return is 100 percent.

EXHIBIT 19-3

Present Value Profile for a $10,000 Investment

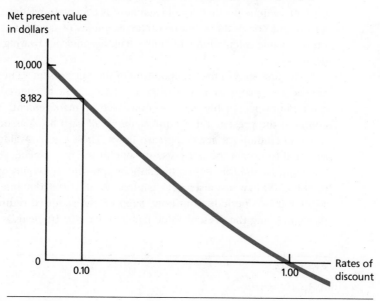

Internal Rate of Return

The net-present-value method provides a dollar measure of value. Some managers prefer a percentage measure. One such measure in frequent use is the investment's internal rate of return. Other terms applied to the same measure are the *yield, IRR* or *IROR* and *time-adjusted rate of return*. The internal rate of return is that rate of discount (interest) that equates the present value of the net cash flows, including the initial outlay, to zero. This rate can be found by trial and error using different rates of interest or by using a suitable hand calculator or a computer programmed to do the task.

What are the implications of the internal rate of return of an investment? If an investment requires an outlay of $173.55 and yields a single net cash flow of $210 at the end of two years, the rate of interest that equates the present value of $210 and an immediate outlay of $173.55 is the internal rate of return. The following equation can be solved for r since only two cash flows are involved:

$$210(1 + r)^{-2} - 173.55 = 0$$
$$(1 + r)^{-2} = 0.8264$$

Using Table A at the back of the book, or a calculator, r is found to be .10. The internal rate of return is .10 because using this rate the algebraic sum of the present value of the cash outlay and the present value of the cash proceeds is equal to zero.

Another interpretation of the internal rate of return is that it is the rate of growth of the investment. Thus, the investment of $173.55 may be thought of as growing in the following manner:

Original investment (time 0)	$173.55
0.10 return on $173.55	17.36
Investment plus interest (time 1)	$190.91
0.10 return on $190.91	19.09
Final value of investment (time 2)	$210.00

A third interpretation of the internal rate of return is that it is the highest rate of interest an investor could pay for borrowed funds to finance the investment being considered and be no worse off than if the investments were not undertaken. This interpretation assumes a conventional investment, which is an immediate outlay followed by a series of positive cash flows. The funds generated by the investment are used to repay the debt and interest on the debt.

If the investment results in several unequal cash inflows, the analysis is the same, although the computations become more complex. Assume, for example, that an investment requires an immediate outlay of $3,000 and has a life of two years. The forecasted net cash savings or proceeds are $1,100 for the first year and $2,420 for the second year as shown in Exhibit 19-4. Consider the implications of the internal rate of return illustrated in Exhibit 19-4.

At a discount rate of 10 percent, the present value of the cash proceeds is equated to the cost of the asset, $3,000. Thus, the internal rate of return is 10 percent. But what does this mean? The asset that cost $3,000 earns 10 percent the first year, and then $1,100 is withdrawn. The remaining investment of $2,200 again earns 10 percent and then $2,420 is withdrawn. At this time there will be no investment left. The asset earned a 10 percent return during its life. The calculations in Exhibit 19-5 show that the investment generates sufficient cash flows to pay for the funds invested, if those funds cost 10 percent.

The internal rate of return of an investment is frequently used to determine the desirability of an investment. All conventional independent investments with a return greater than some hurdle rate are considered to have passed this initial requirement. The internal rate of return can be used to make good accept or reject decisions involving independent investments. However, it is less reliable as a device for ranking investments, or for choosing the best of a set of mutually exclusive investments.

EXHIBIT 19-4

Internal Rate of Return Calculations: Investment with Net Cash Savings Evaluated at 10 Percent

Year	Cash Inflows (Outflows)	Present Value of a Dollar Discounted at 10%	Present Value of Cash Flows
0	− $3,000	$1.0000	− $3,000
1	1,100	.9091	1,000
2	2,420	.8264	2,000
		Sum of present values	−0−

EXHIBIT 19-5

Illustration of IRR

Original investment funds required (loan)	$3,000
Interest rate	× .10
Interest first year	300
Original debt	+3,000
Debt owed at time 1	3,300
Cash proceeds withdrawn to pay debt	−1,100
Debt beginning of second year	2,200
Interest rate	× .10
Interest second year	220
Debt beginning of second year	+2,200
Debt owed at time 2	2,420
Cash proceeds withdrawn to pay debt	−2,420
Debt remaining	$ −0−

Ranking of Investments: Capital Rationing

Management often wants to rank independent investments. The ranking of independent investments implies that a form of capital rationing is taking place. **Capital rationing** means that more dollars are needed for desirable investments than funds are available. For one reason or another, the firm chooses not to go to the capital market to raise new capital. The raising of capital would be the logical move, given that the firm has more good investment opportunities than it can finance. Despite this apparent inconsistency, managers do act as though capital rationing situations exist and rank investments to deal with such situations. Management, in rationing investments, acts as though the cost of raising new capital is prohibitively high. Often what is being rationed is not capital but some other scarce firm resource such as engineering or managerial talent.

Another reason for rationing capital is that top management does not accept the information regarding the expected profitability of the proposed investments. Frequently, the submissions are excessively optimistic.

Using any general method of ranking independent investments for purposes of capital rationing, a counterexample can be prepared that will indicate that the method is subject to failure. Fortunately, there are reasonable methods for making accept or reject decisions.

Evaluating the Methods of Investment Decision Making

Exhibit 19-6 illustrates three investment proposals, and the related cash inflows and outflows.

EXHIBIT 19-6

Investments A, B, and C

Investment Proposal	Initial Outlay (time 0)	Cash Flows (period 1)	Cash Flows (period 2)	Payback	ROI	IRR
A	− $10,000	$10,000	0	1 year	0%	0%
B	− 10,000	1,000	$11,000	1.82 years	20%	10%
C	− 10,000	5,762	5,762	1.74 years	15.2%	10%

The payback method would identify investment *A* as being the most desirable because it has a payback time of one period. The weakness of this position is indicated by the fact that investment *A* returns its original investment, but that is all. The payback method fails as an all-purpose device for making investment decisions because, among other factors, it does not take into consideration the life of the investment after the payback period. Another weakness, not illustrated by the above example, is that the payback method fails to take into consideration the timing of proceeds during the payback period.

The return on investment for project *A* is zero. Thus, *A* is eliminated from consideration if the return-on-investment method is used. The return-on-investment computations for the other two investments are given in Exhibit 19-6.

The return-on-investment computations shown in Exhibit 19-7 indicate that investment *B* is more desirable than investment *C*. However, the return-on-investment procedure fails to take into consideration the timing of the cash flows. This is one reason that the return-on-investment approach should not be used as a general method for making investment decisions.

When the internal rates of return of the two investments *B* and *C* are computed, both are found to be 10 percent. The internal rate of return of investment *A* is zero. Before deciding that investments *B* and *C* are equally desirable, the present value of the two investments should be considered, using several interest rates (different assumed costs of money). At a 10 percent rate of interest, the net present values of

EXHIBIT 19-7

Return-on-Investment Calculations for Investments B and C

Investment Proposal	Outlays	Total Cash Flows	Net Income for Two Years	Average Income	Average Investment	ROI (%)
B	− $10,000	$12,000	$2,000	$1,000	$5,000	20.0%
C	− 10,000	11,524	1,524	762	5,000	15.2

investments B and C are zero. Thus, if 10 percent is the hurdle rate for both projects, the investments are equally desirable.

With a discount rate of less than 10 percent, investment B has a higher net present value, although both investments have positive net present values. At a discount rate greater than 10 percent, investment C has a higher net present value than B, although both investments have negative net present values. Although the internal-rate-of-return and the net-present-value methods may give different rankings of investments, they lead to the same accept or reject decisions.

Are the rankings obtained using the net-present-value or the internal-rate-of-return methods the "correct" rankings? Unfortunately, the ranking is only a function of the method used and the assumptions made. Fortunately, for many investment decisions a firm does not have to rank investments, but only has to choose those investments that have an internal rate of return greater than the firm's cost of money.

If the investments are mutually exclusive, it is necessary to choose the investment that is the best of a group. This can be done because the failure to undertake a mutually exclusive investment does not invalidate the choice of the discount rate. If an independent investment with an internal rate of return greater than the required return is rejected because of capital rationing, the use of that required return to compute the net present value is invalid.

Economic Evaluation of Investment Projects

Independent and Dependent Projects

The classification of an investment is based on the way the benefits from the investment are affected by other possible investments. A given investment proposal may be either economically independent of or dependent on another investment proposal. The first investment proposal is **economically independent** of the second if the cash flows (or, more specifically, the costs and benefits) expected from the first investment are the same regardless of whether the second investment is accepted or rejected. With independent investments, the firm makes **accept or reject decisions** (accepts the investment or rejects it). If the cash flows associated with the first investment are affected by the decision to accept or reject the second investment, the first investment is **economically dependent** on the second. When one investment is dependent on another, decisions involving the first investment cannot be made separately from decisions about the second.

If one investment is to be economically independent of another investment, two conditions must be satisfied. First, it must be technically possible to undertake the first investment regardless of whether the other investment is accepted or not. For example, because it is not possible to build a school and a shopping center on the same site, the proposal to build one is not independent of a proposal to build the other. Second, the net benefits to be expected from the first investment must not be affected by the acceptance or rejection of the second. If the estimates of the cash outlays and the cash inflows for the first investment are not the same when the second is either accepted or rejected, the two investments are dependent. Thus, it is technically possible to build a toll bridge and operate a ferry across adjacent points on a river, but the two investments are not independent because the proceeds from one will be affected by the existence of the other.

Sometimes two investments cannot both be accepted because the firm does not have enough cash to finance both. In such a situation the acceptance of one investment may cause the rejection of the other, but the two investments are not referred to as economically dependent. To do so would cause all investments for such a firm to be dependent, and this does not yield a useful definition.

Two investments may be *economically independent*, but their sets of cash flows may not be *statistically independent*. If knowing something about the actual level of cash flow of one investment helps in predicting the cash flow of the second investment, there is statistical dependency. Investments in a Burger King franchise and an automobile dealership can be highly correlated (the price of gasoline affects both), but they are economically independent. The levels of both economic dependency and statistical dependency will affect a firm's willingness to undertake an investment.

Mutually Exclusive Investments

When the potential benefits to be derived from the first investment completely disappear if the second investment is accepted, or when it would be technically impossible to undertake the first if the second were accepted, the two investments are said to be **mutually exclusive investments**. Because the investments are mutually exclusive, only one can be accepted. We want to choose the **best of the set** of mutually exclusive investments. For example, assume that management is trying to decide where to build a new plant. It may be that either of two locations would be profitable, but because only one new plant is needed, management must decide which location is likely to be the more profitable. An oil company may need additional transport facilities for its products. Should it build a pipeline or acquire additional tankers and ship by water? Either of these alternatives may result in a net profit to the firm, but management will choose the one that is more profitable. In these situations, the choice is between mutually exclusive investments.

Mutually exclusive investment alternatives are common. For example, the situation often occurs in connection with the engineering design of a new installation. In the process of designing such an installation, the engineers are typically faced with alternatives that are mutually exclusive. Thus, any measure of investment worth that does not lead to correct choices among mutually exclusive alternatives is seriously deficient.

Timing Problem Assume that investments D and E in Exhibit 19-8 are mutually exclusive investments with 15 percent internal rates of return. Also assume that they are otherwise equally desirable projects. Management will select D or E. Assume a cost of money of 12 percent. The present values of the cash flows of the two investments are given in Exhibit 19-8, which illustrates the importance of the timing of the cash flows. The present value of the cash flows for investment D is greater than the present value of the cash flows for investment E.

EXHIBIT 19-8

Comparison of Investments D and E at 12 Percent: The Timing Problem Illustrated

Investment D

Period	Cash Inflows (Outflows)	Present-Value Factor (.12)	Present Value (0.12)
0	− $10,000	$1.0000	− $10,000
1	1,500	0.8929	1,339
2	11,500	0.7972	9,168
		Net present value	$ 507

Investment E

Period	Cash Inflows (Outflows)	Present-Value Factor (.12)	Present Value (0.12)
0	− $10,000	$1.0000	− $10,000
1	6,151	0.8929	5,492
2	6,151	0.7972	4,904
		Net present value	$ 396

The choice can also be made by evaluating the incremental cash flows, since the two alternatives have identical lives. Considering only the incremental cash flows yields the benefit to the firm from selecting one investment over another (see Exhibit 19-9).

EXHIBIT 19-9

Incremental Cash Flows and Their Present Values: Investments D and E

Period	Cash Flows Project D	Project E	[Project − Project] D E	Present-Value Factor	Difference in Present Values (D − E)
0	− $10,000	− $10,000	$ 0	1.0000	$ 0
1	1,500	6,151	−4,651	0.8929	−4,153
2	11,500	6,151	5,349	0.7972	4,264
			Net present value difference		$ 111

Exhibit 19-10, which gives the net-present-value profiles of investments D and E, shows that if the appropriate discount rate is 12 percent, then investment alternative D is preferred to E. If the lives of the investments compared using net present value or internal rate of return differ, each method makes an implicit assumption about the return available to the shorter-lived assets. The net-present-value approach compares the two projects assuming the shorter-lived project can be reinvested at the cost of money. The internal-rate-of-return approach assumes the funds from the shorter-lived investment can be invested at the same internal rate of return. Thus, the internal-rate-of-return method may not give correct rankings of mutually exclusive investments because the method fails to consider properly the reinvestment of the cash flows. It implicitly assumes that funds can be reinvested to earn the internal rate of return. If the rate at which funds generated by the investments are reinvested differs from the internal rates of return of the two investments, as will typically be the case, the internal rate of return of the investments cannot be used to evaluate mutually exclusive investments.

Scale Problem   Exhibit 19-11 illustrates a second problem involving mutually exclusive investments, the scale problem. The internal-rate-of-return criterion indicates that investment X is superior to investment Y. However, imagine that the differences between the cash flows of investments X and Y are the cash flows of another investment designated Z. Thus, investment Z would require an outlay of \$20,000 in period 0 and generate proceeds of \$23,000 in period 1, thereby yielding an internal rate of return of 15 percent. Assuming a cost of money of 12 percent, investment Z is desirable. The fact that the cash flows of investment Z are actually the differences

---

EXHIBIT 19-10

Present-Value Profile: Investments D and E

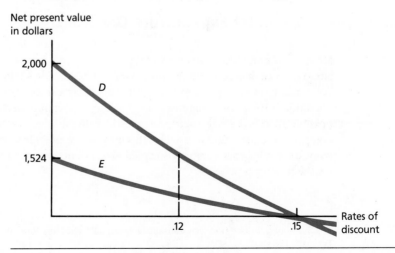

EXHIBIT 19-11

*Internal Rate of Return for Investments X and Y:
The Scale Problem*

Investment	Initial Investment: Time 0	Cash Proceeds: Period 1	Internal Rate of Return
X	− $10,000	$12,000	.200
Y	− 30,000	35,000	.167

Investment	Time 0	Period 1	Internal Rate of Return
X	− $10,000	12,000	.200
Y	− 30,000	35,000	.167
Z = Y − X	− 20,000	23,000	.150

---

between the cash flows of investments X and Y would indicate that investment Y is more desirable than X because by investing in Y an amount $20,000 greater than the investment required by X, a return of 15 percent may be earned. The internal-rate-of-return method may be used here to evaluate the incremental benefits, but it is awkward to employ if there are many investment possibilities. An elimination tournament is required. Thus, again the net-present-value method is preferred over the internal-rate-of-return method.

Approval Process for Capital-Expenditure Decisions

Most organizations have an elaborate approval process for evaluating and deciding on alternative capital-expenditure programs. Such processes can take months and involve many managers and much effort. This delay can be troublesome if economic conditions change or competitors exploit the opportunity in the meantime. It is not possible to characterize such processes in general because they vary greatly from company to company. An article written by a vice president at American Can Company, describing that company's capital investment approval process, is summarized on the following page.[2]

---

2. R. Marshuetz, "How American Can Allocates Capital," *Harvard Business Review* (January–February 1985): 82–91.

Capital Budgeting at American Can Company	The ideas for capital-investment projects are generated by business-unit managers. As part of the annual planning cycle, operating managers summarize their recommended investments by incorporating the projected cash flows from the investments in the financial projections for their business units. The corporate planning department then combines these financial projections. At the same time, the business-investment staff consolidates and ranks the major investment decisions from the perspective of the entire company. After reviewing the information from the business-unit managers, the business-investment staff recommends which projects to speed up, stretch out, or drop.

The continuous, ongoing nature of the evaluation and reevaluation decisions relating to capital projects is reflected in the following illustration from a *Wall Street Journal* article about capital budgeting in the Monsanto Company.[3]

Evaluating Capital Expenditures at Monsanto	A major capital-investment project, such as a new plant, is not completed until several years after it is approved. As a Monsanto executive explained, the company is betting its money on a market that could disappear by the time the new plant comes on line. As a result Monsanto emphasizes forecasts of the long-term potential of a product line before authorizing major capital expenditures. Decisions are made without placing too much emphasis on present economic conditions, according to the firm's director of corporate planning. In addition, project approval is done with greater care than in the past. Each of the company's forty-seven planning units prepare detailed "business direction papers" that outline the cash flows associated with proposed capital programs. Top management then culls through the proposals and assigns priorities to them. A three-year list of potential projects is always maintained.

Finally, a *Business Week* article explained what can happen to a firms' capital expenditure programs when high inflation and interest rates occur. The following illustration relates to Amfac, Inc., a Honolulu-based company engaged in mushroom, shrimp, and sugar cane production, and other food-related operations.[4]

3. D. Garino, "Firms Like Monsanto Give Capital Projects Tough Second Looks," *Wall Street Journal* (December 30, 1976): 1,7.

4. "High Rates Hit Amfac's Planning," *Business Week*, February 23, 1981, p. 120.

> *Higher Hurdle Rates at Amfac*   Amfac's controller wrote the company's operating managers to inform them that the firm would have to boost its "hurdle rate," the required rate of return that all new projects must meet in order to be funded. Every new project, whether repairing a truck or producing a new product, must show a projected rate of return at least two percentage points higher than was previously demanded.

Capital Budgeting in Nonprofit Organizations

The techniques of capital budgeting are also applicable to nonprofit organizations. Charitable organizations, such as the United Way and the American Red Cross, and governmental organizations at federal, state, and local levels are among the many nonprofit organizations that can benefit from capital budgeting analyses.

At the federal level, the use of capital-budgeting methods has been inconsistent among the various agencies of the government. The General Accounting Office recently conducted a study that ranked the United States Postal Service as the most effective federal user of capital-budgeting techniques. However, the lack of a capital-budgeting perspective (a long-run focus) in the overall federal budgeting process may be criticized, given the importance of the annual budget.

An illustration of capital budgeting in a nonprofit institution was provided by Cornell University.

Cornell University Dining Services

Cornell Dining Services conducted an analysis to determine the financial impact of implementing a comprehensive management information system. The proposed system was thoroughly analyzed to ascertain its impact on Cornell Dining at both the departmental and unit levels. This study involved research into the system's literature, analysis of Dining's historical records, and in-depth interviews with management and staff. The analysis identified immediate benefits to be realized from implementation of a customized system.

The system design encompasses computerized time and attendance, upgraded automation, and the installation and customization of a sophisticated accounting system. Time and attendance will provide electronic time recording, staff scheduling, and automated payroll processing. The upgrading of automation will include automated student billing and receivables, on-line menu planning, and computer-assisted buying and receiving. The accounting package will integrate these functions with budgeting, sales processing, accounts receivable, accounts payable, and general ledger functions.

The hardware configuration proposed to achieve these tasks include eight electronic time recording devices, fifteen magnetic stripe reading terminals, eight microprocessor communications devices, and one minicomputer with the necessary CRTs (terminals) and printers. The majority of peripheral components will be distributed to the operating units and networked to the mini-computer in the central office.

Dining personnel need access to the information and controls provided by the proposed system, as well as relief from the burdens of present manual operating systems. The management information system will

1. Improve on the quality and accessibility of information,

2. Reduce labor hours,

3. Eliminate expenditures for University support services,

4. Improve controls,

5. Provide management with better tools to significantly reduce labor, food, and other variable costs.

These benefits will be realized at a small incremental annual cost to operations beyond the initial development and implementation expenditures. Each module of the system enhances current operating methods by applying state-of-the-art technology. Estimates of quantifiable benefits predict a $183,400 annual savings from a $272,000 expenditure for development, hardware, software, and implementation. (See the following cost and benefit analysis for details.)

The value of the proposed management information system is dramatic when consideration is given to the alternatives. Rejection of this system would necessitate the purchase of either an upgraded version of the present system or the new Dining Services, Inc. package. These two alternatives offer the only available software and hardware systems in the industry that can compare with the proposed system.

All three alternatives offer significant differences in functions and hardware configurations. The proposed package, however, is superior because it provides more data-processing functions, a more integrated hardware and software design, and a substantially greater net present value. A summary of the financial analysis and general features of each package is provided on the following page.

The information that follows quantifies the cash flows of each alternative. The proposed alternative is presented in more detail than the other two alternatives to avoid redundancy. The analysis is inflation adjusted. A 10 percent discount rate is used for the analysis. This represents the estimated return on invested university funds, as obtained from the University Investment Office. A seven-year expected life has been used in this analysis.

Financial Analysis Summary

Year	PV Factor	Net Cash Flow: Proposed System	Net Cash Flow: Upgrade of Present System	Dining Services, Inc. System
0	1.000	(262,000)	(93,925)	(190,000)
1	.909	97,700	30,900	77,900
2	.826	135,400		
3	.751	171,400		
4	.683			
5	.621			
6	.564			
7	.513	171,400	30,900	77,900
Net present value		475,473	56,465	189,139

Proposed system: cost summary

1. **Hardware purchases**   Data-processing equipment purchases should include one minicomputer, disk drives, and tape drive, $80,000; 8 microprocessor communications devices, $25,000; printers, $10,000; 8 time-recording devices, $16,000; and 15 magnetic-stripe reading terminals, $21,000.

Total cost	$152,000

2. **Application software**   The costs of proposed software modules are summarized below:

Food management module	$30,000
Time and attendance module	25,000
Access control module	30,000
Accounting module	0
Total cost	$85,000

3. **Site preparation**   Installation of a sophisticated data-processing network requires a wiring network to provide power and to link peripheral devices and CRTs. Costs are summarized below:

Wiring and power	$25,000

4. **Hardware and software maintenance** Total cost to maintain all computer software and hardware will be $12,000.

Total annual maintenance cost	$12,000

5. **Miscellaneous** Initial consulting on special projects, miscellaneous travel expenses, and telephone data-communications charges should total approximately $10,000.

Total cost	$10,000

6. **Total costs:**

Total system investment cost	$272,000
Total annual recurring cost	12,000

Proposed system: benefit summary

1. **Menu management and planning:**

   a. **Reduced cost of goods sold** The new information system will offer expanded capabilities for improving recipe accuracy, enhancing forecasting precision, and monitoring and updating food prices. These changes will provide greater controls for meeting the food-cost budget, reducing waste, and improving purchasing decisions. In the context of these factors, it is estimated that food costs will be reduced by .006.

Present annual food cost	$5,900,000
Projected percentage reduction	× .006
Total annual benefit	$ 36,000 (rounded)

   b. **Improved inventory position** Improved inventory control and ordering procedures will increase inventory turnover and reduce inventory on hand. A one-half turn improvement per month will reduce average monthly inventory and improve university cash flow by $16,000.

Reduced inventory	$16,000
Number of months	× 12
Interest rate	× .10
Total annual benefit	$19,000 (rounded)

c. *Eliminate computing-service charges* The new system will eliminate annual computing charges for IBM 370 processing and keypunch for the current system.

Total annual benefit	$21,000

2. *Accounting*

a. *Reduced labor expense* Dining deals with many vendors and processes thousands of purchase orders, invoices, and credit memos annually. The new accounts-payable function will accommodate these activities by providing powerful tools to expedite purchase-order entry and vendor-statement reconciliation. These benefits will accrue to both Dining and the University Accounting Office. Labor savings of .2 percent of net sales are common. A reduction of .002 of total annual food purchases is incorporated in the following:

Total annual cost	$5,900,000
Percent labor reduction	$\times$ .002
Total annual benefit	$ 12,000 (rounded)

Flexibility to either manually or automatically enter billed charges, linkages to accounting and the bursar, and powerful reconciliation tools will dramatically reduce staff time on the receivables and cash-sales processing function. These savings will accrue to both Dining and the University Accounting Office. Reductions of .005 of total receivable sales are expected.

Annual receivable sales	$2,000,000
Labor reduction rate	$\times$ .005
Total annual benefit	$ 10,000

b. *Reduced bad-debt write-off* Monitoring hundreds of accounts and collecting outstanding bills pose an administrative hardship. The inevitable result is that follow-up activities are less than vigorous, and write-offs become unnecessarily large. The new system will provide a series of reports that greatly facilitate the follow-up effort, thereby reducing bad-debt expense. Savings of .005 of annual receivables are assumed.

Annual receivable sales	$2,000,000
Projected savings rate	$\times$ .005
Total annual benefit	$ 10,000

c. Payroll The new system will offer payroll processing which will monitor employee hours and time cards and perform payroll calculations. With 1,200 hourly employees, the annual savings to Dining and the University Payroll Office will be significant. It is estimated that .002 of the total payroll base would be saved in clerical time.

Total annual hourly payroll	$3,300,000
Projected savings rate	× .002
Total annual benefit	$ 6,600

d. Report generation Dining consumes hundreds of valuable labor hours each year in preparing financial and other analytical reports (sales reports, inventory reports, income statements, budgets, and so forth). Even then, these reports are often untimely and inaccurate. Flexible report writers, automated budgeting, and the use of the specialized language of the new system will save major blocks of time. Projected savings of .0006 of total labor expense are expected.

Total annual hourly labor expense	$3,300,000
Projected savings rate	× .0006
Total annual savings	$ 2,000 (rounded)

e. Time and attendance Some employees punch in early and punch out late, which presents serious time-theft problems. With the current mechanical time clocks, the cost of rounding errors are substantial. The new system will control employee clocking time and round with greater precision in time recording. Savings of .005 of total hourly labor expense are assumed.

Annual hourly labor expense	$3,300,000
Projected savings rate	× .005
Total annual savings	$ 16,500

f. Scheduling Each year thousands of labor hours in student and professional time are spent on employee scheduling. The scheduling function of 1,200 employees in 12 units is not a trivial task. The new system will provide an automated scheduling aid. Projected savings of .003 of total hourly labor expense is expected in reduced staff time.

Annual hourly labor expense	$3,300,000
Projected savings rate	× .003
Total annual benefit	$ 9,900

g. *Reduced labor costs*   Management of payroll processing and total labor hours for a department the size of Dining is a difficult undertaking. Calculation errors and untimely information inhibits management's ability to control costs. The new system will provide automated calculation, daily labor reports, and improved monitoring of productivity. Reduced labor costs arising from error prevention, increased scheduling efficiency, and improved overtime control are expected to be .005 of total annual labor expense.

Total annual labor expense	$3,300,000
Projected savings rate	$\times$ .005
Total annual benefit	$ 16,500

h. *Reducing billing errors*   Approximately 10,000 of an estimated 40,000 annual student billing transactions are processed manually. Most of these are processing of special adjustments and other account reconciliations. This magnitude of manual processing is conducive to significant errors, which cost Dining, since customers usually contest overbillings but not underbillings. The new system will reduce the number of manual transactions and provide improved tools for reconciling customer accounts. The estimated annual savings is $5,000 in reduced underbilling errors.

Total annual benefit	$5,000

i. *Reduced collection expenses*   Automation of student billing and receivables will significantly reduce the number of transactions on student accounts and provide an automated interface with the Bursar. The new system will reduce multiple transaction charges, eliminate keypunch and reduce the overall Bursar billing rate. Projected savings are .20 of annual collection expenses.

Total annual collection expense	$65,000
Projected savings rate	$\times$ .20
Total annual benefit	$13,000

j. *Reduced cost of goods sold*   The current system suffers from frequent down time with the result being weakened access control. During these periods, many ineligible customers gain access and are served. The new system will dramatically reduce down time by providing microprocessors and back-up at the unit level. The estimated annual saving in food costs are .001 of total cost of goods sold.

Total annual food costs	$5,900,000
Projected savings rate	× .001
Total savings	$ 5,900

k. Current system salvage value The salvage value of the current system is estimated from current market rates.

| Total one-time benefit | $10,000 |

l. Total benefits

| Total annual system benefits | $183,400 |
| Total one-time benefit | $ 10,000 |

Proposed system: summary of cash flows

This system will come on-line as developed over a two-year period. Consequently, full benefits will not begin to accrue until the beginning of the third year. The following cash flows reflect this implementation and development schedule.

Cash Flow

Year	Cost	Benefit	Net
0	(272,000)	10,000	(262,000)
1	(12,000)	109,700	97,700
2		147,400	135,400
3		183,400	171,400
4			
5			
6			
7	(12,000)	183,400	171,400
Net present value		$475,473	

Georgia-Pacific

Georgia-Pacific Corporation uses "rate of return." This is an internal rate of return calculation. The firm does not indicate how it evaluates mutually exclusive situations, but there is a large likelihood that it uses solutions similar to those illustrated in this book.

Georgia-Pacific Corporation's investment strategy, as stated in a recent annual report, is typical of the strategy of many corporations.

Capital Investment Strategy

Our ability to increase the value of our shareholders' investment in Georgia-Pacific depends to a large extent on the returns we earn on the capital investments we make. We have recently made substantial investments in our core forest products business to improve productivity, reduce costs and upgrade our product mix. We have also made several strategic acquisitions.

From 1984 through 1988, Georgia-Pacific spent $4.2 billion on capital assets, including almost $3.5 billion for property, plant and equipment and $760 million for timber and timberlands. These expenditures include approximately $1.5 billion for acquisitions. Approximately two-thirds of our investment in property, plant and equipment have been to expand our pulp and paper segment.

We categorize capital projects as defensive (those Georgia-Pacific must make to maintain our operations and stay in business) and as high-return (those that are justified on the basis of their discounted cash flow rate of return). Although some defensive expenditures for environmental, safety and other similar purposes have positive returns, they are undertaken primarily to maintain our operations. Our plants and mills are, for the most part, in superior condition but require defensive spending of approximately $200 to $250 million per year.

All proposed capital projects, both internal projects and acquisitions, are evaluated on the rate of return of free cash flow generated over the life of the investment. We define free cash flow as operating profits after taxes paid, plus noncash charges such as depreciation, minus any new investment in fixed assets or working capital. Our required return takes into account our cost of capital, the relative risk of the project and other variables which can affect the returns generated by a project. Post-completion audits are performed on all major high-return projects to measure achieved returns against targeted returns.

Capital expenditures of approximately $630 million are projected for 1989, excluding any major acquisitions. Consistent with the pattern of recent years, the majority of that amount is expected to be invested in the pulp and paper segment. We expect operating cash flow to be more than sufficient to finance these expenditures.

Summary

Investment expenditures need to be controlled and evaluated. The most widely used methods — payback and return on investment — are found to be inferior to the discounted cash-flow procedures — internal rate of return and net present value. For mutually exclusive investments, the net-present-value method is more easily applied and avoids problems of the internal-rate-of-return method. As long as it is assumed that the cash flows are known or estimated with little error, the net-present-value method deals effectively with the choice of acceptable independent investments and the selection of the best of a collection of mutually exclusive investments.

In the past forty years, there has been increasingly wide acceptance of the discounted cash-flow measures, internal rate of return, and net present value. One has to be careful because the internal-rate-of-return measure may yield faulty results in situations involving mutually exclusive investments. The net-present-value procedure is easier to apply and gives a more reliable indicator of value. Net present value is extensively used today, generally in conjunction with other methods.

Review Problem

CAPITAL BUDGETING

The following information applies to two mutually exclusive investments *A* and *B*.

	Net Present Value (.10)	*Internal Rate of Return*
A	$1,000	.21
B	1,818	.15

a. Draw the approximate present value profiles for the two investments.

b. Which is to be preferred if the discount rate is .10?

c. Although the cash flows for the two investments are not known, prepare one set of "correct" cash flows for each investment.

Solution to Review Problem

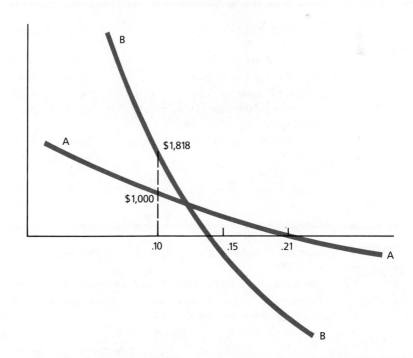

b. At .10, B is better.

c. For A,

$$-C_0 + C_1(1.21)^{-1} = 0$$

$$\underline{-C_0 + C_1(1.10)^{-1} = 1,000}$$

$$C_1[1.1^{-1} - 1.21^{-1}] = 1,000$$

$$C_1(1.10 - 1) = 1,210$$

$$C_1 = 12,100$$

$$C_0 = 10,000$$

For B,

$$-C_0 + C_1(1.15)^{-1} = 0$$

$$\underline{-C_0 + C_1(1.10)^{-1} = 1,818}$$

$$C_1[1.10^{-1} - 1.15^{-1}] = 1,818$$

$$(.90909 - .86957)C_1 = 1,818$$

$$C_1 = \$46,000$$

$$C_0 = 46,000(1.15)^{-1} = \$40,000$$

Key Terms to Review

accept or reject decisions, p. 668
annuity, p. 658
best of the set, p. 669
capital budgeting decision, p. 656
capital rationing, p. 669
discounted cash flow (DCF), p. 657
discounted cash flow method, p. 657
economically dependent projects,
    p. 668

economically independent projects,
    p. 668
internal-rate-of-return method, p. 659
mutually exclusive investments, p. 669
net-present-value method, p. 659
payback period, p. 661
present-value profile, p. 663
return on investment (ROI), p. 662
time value of money, p. 656

Suggested Readings

Bierman, H., and S. Smidt. *The Capital Budgeting Decision*, 7th ed. New York: Macmillan, 1988.

Brealey, R., and S. Myers. *Principles of Corporate Finance.* New York: McGraw-Hill, 1984.

Copeland, T., and J. Weston. *Financial Theory and Corporate Policy*, 2d ed. Reading, Mass.: Addison-Wesley, 1983.

Demski, J. *Information Analysis.* Reading, Mass.: Addison-Wesley, 1980.

Howell, R. A., and S. R. Soucy. "Capital Investment Analysis in the New Manufacturing Environment." *Management Accounting* (November 1987): 26–32.

Kaplan, R. and A. Atkinson *Advanced Managerial Accounting,* 2d. ed. Englewood Cliffs, N.J.: Prentice-Hall, 1989.

————, "Must CIM Be Justified by Faith Alone?" *Harvard Business Review* (March-April 1986): 87–93.

Klammer, T., and M. Walker. "The Continuing Increase in the Use of Sophisticated Capital Budgeting Techniques." *California Management Review* (Fall 1984): 137–48.

Magee, R. *Advanced Managerial Accounting.* New York: Harper & Row, 1986.

Rappaport, Alfred. *Creating Shareholder Value.* New York: Free Press, 1986.

Scott, D., and J. Petty. "Capital Budgeting Practices in Large American Firms: A Representative Analysis and Synthesis." *Financial Review* (March 1984): 111–23.

Van Horne, J. *Financial Management and Policy,* 7th ed. Englewood Cliffs, N.J.: Prentice-Hall, 1986.

Review Questions

19-1 Assume a .05 per year time value of money.

REQUIRED:

Compute the value of $100 received

a. One year from now,

b. Immediately,

c. At the *end* of five years,

d. At the *beginning* of the sixth year,

e. At the end of fifty years,

f. At the end of fifty years with an interest rate of .10.

19-2 Assume a .05 time value of money.

REQUIRED:

Compute the value of a *series* of equal payments of $100 a year received for

a. Five years, the first payment received one year from now;

b. Four years, the first of *five* payments received immediately;

c. Ten years, the first payment received one year from now;

d. Nine years, the first of *ten* payments received immediately.

19-3 Assume a .05 time value of money. The sum of $100 received immediately is equivalent to what amount received in ten equal annual payments, the first payment to be received one year from now? What would be the annual amount if the first of ten payments were received immediately?

19-4 Assume a .15 time value of money. We have a debt to pay and are given a choice of paying $1,000 now or some amount X five years from now. What is the maximum amount that X can be for us to be indifferent to defer payment for five years?

19-5 We can make an immediate payment now of $10,000 or pay equal amounts of R for the next ten years (first payment due one year from now). With a time value of money of .15, what is the maximum value of R that we would be willing to accept?

19-6 Assume a bank charges .01 interest per month. You borrow $50,000 to be paid by equal payments over a thirty-five-month period, first payment one month from now. How much will you have to pay each month?

19-7 Show that $F = P(1 + r)^n$.

19-8 An investment costs $1,000 and promises to return $1,210 two periods from now.

    a. Determine the internal rate of return of the investment.

    b. Explain in three different ways what is meant by the term internal rate of return. Use this example as the basis of your explanation.

19-9 Compute the net present value of an investment that costs $800 and promises to return $1,000 three periods from now. Assume that the time value of money is 0.05 per year. Explain what is meant by the term net present value of an investment.

19-10 Compute the net present value of an investment that costs $800 and promises to return $1,000 three periods from now. Assume that the time value of money is 0.10 per year.

19-11 Given the limitations of payback, why do you think it is so widely used in practice?

Exercises **19-12 Internal Rates of Return** Compute the internal rates of return of the following two investments:

    a. 0 − 9,089
        1 + 1,000
        2 +10,000
        3 + 1,000

    b. 0 − 7,118
        3 +10,000

19-13 Present Values Compute the present values of the investment of Exercise 19-12 if the appropriate rate of discount is .10.

19-14 Internal Rates of Return Compute the internal rates of return of the following three investments:

	0	1	2
A	−10,000	11,500	
B	−10,000	6,151	6,151
C	−10,000		13,226

19-15 Accumulating Funds for Exercise 19-14 Compute the amount the investor will have at time 2 if the funds earned at time 1 can earn .15.

19-16 Graphing Present-Value Profiles For each of the three investments of Exercise 19-14 graph the present-value profile.

19-17 Continuation of Exercise 19-14 Which investment is to be preferred in Exercise 19-14 if the rate of discount used by the firm is .10?

Problems   **19-18 Annuity Formula** Derive the relationship

$$A(n,r) = \frac{1 - (1+r)^{-n}}{r}$$

Hints:

1. Write $A(n, r)$ equal to the present value of a series of $1 cash flows. That is $A(n, r) = (1+r)^{-1} + (1+r)^{-2} + $ etc.

2. Multiply the equation you obtained in hint 1 by $(1+r)$ and subtract the basic equation from this result.

3. Solve for $A(n, r)$.

19-19 Present Values An investment has the following cash flows:

0	−11,712
1	10,000
2	5,000
3	1,000

Compute the net present value using 10 percent and the internal rate of return. Should the investment be undertaken?

19-20 Internal Rate of Return Compute the internal rate of return of the following investment:

0	$−3,477
1	1,000
2	1,000
10	10,000

19-21 Internal Rate of Return   Compute the internal rate of return of the following investment:

0	$-2,621
1	1,000
2	1,000
10	10,000

19-22 Choosing an Investment   There are two mutually exclusive investments:

	Cash Flows			Internal Rate of Return
Project	Period 0	Period 1	Period 2	
A	$-10,000	—	$11,664	0.08
B	-10,000	$5,608	5,608	0.08

You are to advise a client. What information do you need to choose between the two investments? Should the client be indifferent?

19-23 Investment Choices   The cost of money of the Blair Company is .10. The following mutually exclusive investments are available (ignore taxes):

	Cash Flows			Internal Rate of Return
Project	Period 0	Period 1	Period 2	
W	$-10,000	$ 6,545	$ 6,545	0.20
X	-10,000	—	14,400	0.20
Y	-10,000	12,000	—	0.20
Z	-30,000	19,400	19,400	0.19

For each of the following pairs of mutually exclusive investments, pick the better of the two.

a. W and X

b. W and Y

c. Y and X

d. W and Z

e. Z and Y

19-24 Using Payback   Given a twenty-year project with a payback period of 5.1 years, determine the project's internal rate of return assuming that the cash inflows are uniform over the project's life and the total investment is made immediately.

19-25 Investment Decisions Consider the following two mutually exclusive investments:

Investment	Cost	Cash Flows Year 1	Year 2	Internal Rate of Return
A	− $10,000	$5,608	$5,608	0.08
B	− $10,000	2,000	$9,504	0.08

What decision should the firm make?

19-26 The Milford Plant Warren Haford faced a major decision. The Milford plant was losing $1 million of cash per year and the operating income was negative to the extent of $1.8 million. The cash loss was expected to continue into the future unless change was implemented (assume it is a perpetuity).

One alternative was to close down the plant. The firm had an agreement with the union that would result in a one-time cash outlay of $10 million. There would be a $25,000,000 accounting loss.

A second alternative would be to invest $12 million to modernize the plant. This plan would convert the negative cash flow of $1 million to a positive cash flow of $600,000 per year (a perpetuity). Haford's assistant has computed the internal rate of return of this investment to be .05:

$$\frac{600,000}{12,000,000} = .05$$

The firm has a weighted average cost of capital of .15 and a borrowing cost of .12 (it has debt outstanding). The firm's tax rate is zero.

What should Mr. Haford do?

19-27 How does the answer to Problem 19-26 change if the cost of an immediate shut-down is only $4,000,000?

20

Additional Topics in Capital Budgeting

After studying this chapter, you should be able to:

1 Incorporate taxes properly in an investment analysis.

2 Establish the cash flows to be used in a capital-budgeting analysis.

3 Describe the determination of the discount rate and the difficulties in identifying the appropriate rate.

4 Evaluate nonconstant, perpetual cash-flow streams.

5 Define *annual equivalent costs* and use them in break-even analysis, in make-or-buy decisions, and to evaluate projects with unequal lives.

6 Discuss the postaudit and control process for an investment.

7 Describe the investment techniques of nonprofit organizations.

*T*his chapter continues the discussion of Chapter 19 by considering a number of special topics related to the analysis of capital-budgeting decisions. These topics are as follows:

- Effect of taxes,

- Estimating cash flows,

- Cost of money,

- Nonconstant cash flows,

- Annual equivalent cost,

- Unequal investment lives,

- Breakeven analysis considering the time value of money,

- Review process for capital-budgeting decisions,

- Capital budgeting in nonprofit organizations,

- Tracking projects.

Cash Flow and Taxes

Taxes are a key factor to be considered in any business decision. In capital-budgeting decisions, cash flows should be computed on an after-tax basis. (The term **cash flows** is used in this book to describe the change in cash during a period of time.) This requires that the taxable income be determined for each period of the investment. The amount of income tax arising because of the capital investment is then computed for each period and included as a decrease to the cash flows for that period. Only then should the resulting net cash inflows be discounted and compared to the required investment outlay.

An important complication in computing income taxes arises from the opportunity under the Internal Revenue Code to use accelerated depreciation to compute taxable income. The best depreciation method for a firm to use is determined by computing the present value of the tax deductions that result from following the different allowed procedures. The procedure resulting in the highest net present value is the best method.

The amount of depreciation allowable for tax purposes affects the cash flows. The amount of depreciation to be taken for book purposes does not affect cash flows. Hence depreciation taken for book purposes should not affect the investment decision. After-tax cash flows are needed for an investment analysis. Because income tax affects the cash flows, and is in turn affected by the amount of depreciation allowable for tax purposes, depreciation allowed for taxes is relevant for investment decisions.

Taxes: An Easy Solution

First, consider a systematic short-cut solution.

1. Compute the value of the after-tax cash flows without regard to depreciation expense.

2. Determine the present value of the best pattern of depreciation deductions and multiply by the tax rate to determine the depreciation tax savings.

3. Add the values in steps 1 and 2, and subtract the cost of the investment to compute the net present value of the investment.

Suppose, for example, that the acquisition of equipment costs $1,000,000. The investment is expected to earn net cash flows, after cash expenses but before taxes, of $500,000 per year. These cash flows are expected to continue for five years. Assume the corporate tax rate is 0.34 and that the firm has a .20 cost of money.

Applying the easy solution yields the following:

1. The after-tax net cash flow (before considering depreciation) is ($500,000)(1 − .34), or $330,000. The present value factor for the annuity is 2.9906, and the present value of the benefits is approximately $986,900.

EXHIBIT 20-1

Asset Classifications

(All lives refer to the midpoints of the class-life asset depreciation range, **CLADR**, a system defined by the IRS.)[a]

Class	Type of Property
Double declining balance method with switch to straight-line:	
3-year class	Tangible property with a life of four years or less excluding automobiles and light trucks.
5-year class	Tangible property with a life of at least four and less than ten years such as certain tools, research and development equipment, light duty trucks and autos.
7-year class	Machinery and equipment with a life of ten years or more but less than sixteen years.
10-year class	Machinery and equipment with a life of sixteen years or more but less than twenty years.
Declining balance at 150% method with switch to straight-line:	
15-year class	Tangible property with a life of twenty years or more and less than twenty-five years.
20-year class	Tangible property with a life of twenty-five years and more.
Straight-line:	
27.5-year class	Residential rental property
31.5-year class	Nonresidential real property with lives of 27.5 years or more.

[a] This is consistent with the 1986 and 1987 acts and is likely to change through time.

2. Assume the present value of the depreciation deductions is $621,100. The present value of the tax savings is ($621,100)(.34), or approximately $211,200. The calculation of the $621,100 will be illustrated in the next section.

3. The net present value of the investment is computed as follows:

$$NPV = \$986,900 + \$211,200 + (-\$1,000,000)$$

$$= \$198,100$$

The net present value is positive, and the investment passes this test. Whether it will be accepted or not depends on whether there are other factors not yet considered in the mathematical analysis.

The 1981, 1982, 1984, and 1986 tax acts changed the rules concerning depreciation expense. The 1986 act still allows an accelerated cost recovery system, but the tax allowances are not as generous as they were before the passage of the act. The 1986 act eliminated the previously allowed investment tax credit.

Exhibit 20-1 provides some of the key classifications under the 1986 law, and Exhibit 20-2 illustrates depreciation schedules for tangible property.

EXHIBIT 20-2

Depreciation Schedules: Tangible Property (consistent with 1986 tax reform act)

| Ownership Year | Class of Investment | | | | | |
	3-Year	5-Year	7-Year	10-Year	15-Year	20-Year
	%	%	%	%	%	%
1	33	20.0	14.3	10	05.0	03.8
2	45	32.0	24.5	18	09.5	07.2
3	15	19.2	17.5	14.4	08.6	06.7
4	07	11.5	12.5	11.5	07.7	06.2
5		11.5	08.9	09.2	06.9	05.7
6		05.8	08.9	07.4	06.2	05.3
7			08.9	06.6	05.9	04.9
8			04.5	06.6	05.9	04.5
9				06.5	05.9	04.5
10				06.5	05.9	04.5
11				03.3	05.9	04.5
12					05.9	04.5
13					05.9	04.5
14					05.9	04.5
15					05.9	04.5
16					03.0	04.5
17						04.5
18						04.5
19						04.5
20						04.5
21						01.7
	100	100	100	100	100	100

EXHIBIT 20-3

Present Values of $1 of Depreciation Tax Savings: Five-Year Asset

i	Depre-ciation	Present Value Factor $(1.2)^{-i}$	Present Value of Deduction	Tax Saving $(.34)$	Present Value of Tax Saving
1	$.200	.8333	$.1667	.0680	$.0567
2	.320	.6944	.2222	.1088	.0756
3	.192	.5787	.1111	.0653	.0378
4	.115	.4823	.0555	.0391	.0189
5	.115	.4019	.0462	.0391	.0157
6	.058	.3349	.0194	.0197	.0066
			$.6211		$.2113

Consider an asset costing $1,000,000 in the five-year class. The present value of the depreciation deductions for each $1 of asset using a .20 discount rate is given in Exhibit 20-3.

The $1,000,000 of depreciable asset base yields $621,100 of present value deductions. Given a .34 tax rate, each dollar of deductions is worth .34. The present value of the tax savings is ($621,100)(.34), or $211,300. The alternative calculation is ($1,000,000)(.2113) or $211,300.

Taxes: An Expanded Solution

Instead of the short-cut solution illustrated above, a longer solution may be used. This approach involves computing the net after-tax cash flows of each year. This approach is illustrated in Exhibits 20-4 and 20-5 with the same example solved in the previous section.

EXHIBIT 20-4

Calculation of After-Tax Cash Flows

	Year 1	Year 2	Year 3	Year 4	Year 5	Year 6
Net cash flow	$330,000	$330,000	$330,000	$330,000	$330,000	
Depreciation tax saving	68,000[a]	108,800[a]	65,300[a]	39,100[a]	39,100[a]	19,700[a]
After-tax cash flow	$398,000	$438,800	$395,300	$369,100	$369,100	$19,700

[a] Year 1: (.34)(.20) ($1,000,000); Year 2: (.34)(.32) ($1,000,000);
 Year 3: (.34)(.192)($1,000,000); Year 4: (.34)(.115)($1,000,000);
 Year 5: (.34)(.115)($1,000,000); Year 6: (.34)(.058)($1,000,000).

The net present value of the investment is calculated in Exhibit 20-5.

EXHIBIT 20-5
Calculation of the Net Present Value

Time	Cash Flow	Present Value Factor	Present Value[a]
0	$-1,000,000$	$1.20^{-0} = 1.0$	$-\$1,000,000$
1	$+\ 398,000$	$1.20^{-1} = 0.8333$	$331,700$
2	$+\ 438,800$	$1.20^{-2} = 0.6944$	$304,700$
3	$+\ 395,300$	$1.20^{-3} = 0.5787$	$228,800$
4	$+\ 369,100$	$1.20^{-4} = 0.4823$	$178,000$
5	$+\ 369,100$	$1.20^{-5} = 0.4019$	$148,300$
6	$+\ \ 19,700$	$1.20^{-6} = 0.3349$	$6,600$
Net present value			$\$\ \ 198,100$

[a] Rounded.

This is the same net present value that was obtained in the previous section.

Estimating the Cash Flows for Investment Decisions

A critical task in capital budgeting is the estimation of the cash flows used in the analysis. Estimating the cash flows that will occur in the future requires forecasting. Forecasting is a difficult business because it depends on a knowledge of markets, world trends, financial structures, and the strategic plans of the company as well as its competitors. Usually a team of several knowledgeable individuals is required to accomplish this task. Assumptions are inevitably required. Testing the impact of different assumptions with sensitivity analyses is a common part of the procedure for evaluating capital investment projects. The quality of the analysis and of any resulting decision is dependent on high-quality input data.

Cash flows provide the basis for capital-budgeting computations. The cash-flow procedure assumes that the moment of a cash disbursement or cash receipt is the moment at which the change in financial position associated with an investment should be measured. Only when the cash is disbursed has the firm experienced a decline in resources, since only then are real resources, which could be engaged in other earning activities, restricted to a particular investment project. For example, until sales result in cash, which the firm can put to other uses, there is assumed to be no benefit from the sales transaction. Thus, the legal sale and the creation of an account receivable are not important for purposes of analyzing the investment decision. The receipt or disbursement of cash is important.

For each period in the life of an investment, the analyst must compute the change in cash resulting from the investment under consideration. Exhibit 20-6 indicates how this might be accomplished for one period of time.

An additional computation would be necessary to compute the income taxes of the period associated with this investment. There may be differences between the cash-flow computations and the computations for tax purposes. The individuals making investment decisions should be familiar with the tax code or have access to expert tax advice.

EXHIBIT 20-6

Computation of Forecasted Cash Flow

Sales (as recorded by accountant)[a]		$100,000	
Less: Cost of goods sold[b]	$40,000		
Expenses of selling and administration[c]	20,000	60,000	
Net revenue after expenses			$40,000
Less: Investment outlays[d]	—		
Decrease in revenue from other products[d]	—		
Opportunity costs of factors of production[d]	$ 5,000		
Income tax caused by investment	10,000	$ 15,000	
Less: Change in working capital and noncash expenses[e]			
Decrease in current liabilities (change the sign for an increase)	$ 4,000		
Increase in current assets (including noncash expenses)	8,000	12,000	
Miscellaneous uses of cash			27,000
After-tax cash flow			$13,000

Explanations:

[a] Sales on the accrual basis are $100,000.

[b] This is the expense taken from the income statement. Usually it is not equal to the out-of-pocket cost of production because of changes in the level of inventories and the inclusion of costs not using cash. These items are picked up as adjustments.

[c] Selling and administrative expenses for which a current liability is incurred (or cash disbursed) and that result from the investment.

[d] Investment-type outlays, decrease in revenue from other products, and opportunity costs (including the use of executive time) associated with this venture are deducted as cash outlays, even though there may not be a cash disbursement, since they represent cash inflows lost elsewhere. The increase in income taxes associated with the investment is calculated after the deduction for any depreciation related to the investment under consideration.

[e] The adjustment for the change in working capital is necessary in order to determine the amount of cash needed to finance the investment. The $4,000 is the result of a decrease in current liabilities, thereby using cash. The $8,000 is an increase in current assets. The $12,000 represents the amount of new capital needs for the $12,000 increase in working capital.

Determining the Cost of Money

All capital has a cost. Whether cash is obtained via a gift, by retention of earnings, or by a tax break, does not alter the fact that funds have a cost. This **cost of money** is based on the ever-present opportunity to invest the funds and earn a return or, alternatively, to retire any outstanding debt. Determining the cost of money for a given project is difficult. This section provides no more than a brief introduction to the problem. The discounting carries with it an implicit assumption that funds may be borrowed or lent at one rate. One approach to selecting the proper rate is to separate the choice of a discount rate from the adjustment for the risk associated with the cash flows. Alternatively, the firm must find a means of establishing a discount rate that reflects the riskiness of the project.[1]

The cost of debt capital and of preferred stock are more easily measured than the cost of common stock. One solution is to use the cost of debt capital to discount for time and then apply a risk adjustment to the net present value before making a final decision. This adjustment reflects both the fact that equity capital is more expensive than debt and the riskiness of the project. Again the amount of this adjustment is not easily determined.

In practice there is a great deal of variation in the determination of the appropriate rate to be used in discounting future cash flows. Exhibit 20-7 shows the wide range of responses received by two researchers (Gitman and Forrester) who attempted to find out what discount rate firms used.[2]

EXHIBIT 20-7

Cost of Capital Used in Capital Investment Decisions

	Responses	
Rate	*Number*	*Percent*
Less than 5%	0	0.0
5 to 10%	9	9.5
10 to 15%	57	60.0
15 to 20%	22	23.1
More than 20%	7	7.4
Total Responses	95	100.0

1. A more complete prescription is beyond the scope of this book. For two alternative views, see R. A. Brealey and S. C. Myers, *Principles of Corporate Finance* (New York: McGraw-Hill, 1984), particularly chaps. 7–9; and H. Bierman, Jr. and S. Smidt, *The Capital Budgeting Decision,* 7th ed. (New York: Macmillan, 1988).

2. L. Gitman and J. Forrester, "A Survey of Capital Budgeting Techniques Used by Major U.S. Firms," *Financial Management* (Fall 1977): 66–71.

Nonconstant Cash Flows

The net present value of an investment requires estimating the cash flows of each period. Alternatively, it may be reasonable to assume the cash flows of the initial period change regularly over time. If so, different assumed rates of growth or decay applied to the projection of the initial period's cash flows can be used to approximate the net present value. Equation(1)gives the present value of positive cash flows, assuming a continuous rate of growth, g.[3]

To find the net present value of the investment, the initial outlay must be subtracted. All of the following formulas assume that the cash flows are on an after-tax basis. The assumptions are:

1. Constant rate of growth through time.

2. Cash flows in perpetuity (the cash flow growth continues forever).

3. The rate of discount exceeds the rate of growth. Otherwise the present value would be infinitely large.

These assumptions yield

$$\text{Present value} = \frac{A}{r - g} \tag{1}$$

A is the cash flow of the first period, g the rate of growth (if flows are declining, the rate of growth is negative), and r the rate of discount.

For an example involving increasing cash flows, assume that A equals $100, g equals .06, and r equals .10.

$$\text{Present value} = \frac{\$100}{.10 - .06} = \frac{100}{.04} = \$2,500$$

For an example involving decreasing cash flows, assume that A equals $100, g equals $-.15$, and r equals .10.

$$\text{Present value} = \frac{\$100}{.10 - (-.15)} = \frac{100}{.25} = \$400$$

---

3. Assuming r exceeds g, derivation of the formula for growing or decaying cash flows is found using calculus.

$$\text{Present value} = \int_0^\infty Ae^{gt}e^{-rt}dt$$

$$= A \int_0^\infty e^{(g-r)t}dt$$

$$= \frac{Ae^{(g-r)t}}{g - r}\Big|_0^\infty = 0 - \frac{A}{g - r} = \frac{A}{r - g}$$

If g equals zero (that is, constant cash flows), equation (1) becomes the present value of a perpetuity (constant cash flows):

$$\text{Present value} = \frac{\$100}{.10} = \$1,000$$

A table of values per dollar of initial cash flow can be developed. First, equation (1) is revised to obtain equation (2).

$$\text{Present value} = \frac{A}{i} \tag{2}$$

where $i = r - g$

A table of values of $1 divided by i, for different values of i, is given in Exhibit 20-8.

EXHIBIT 20-8

Table of Present Values

Values of i	Values of $\$1/i$
1.00	1.00
0.50	2.00
0.25	4.00
0.20	5.00
0.10	10.00
0.05	20.00
0.04	25.00
0.03	33.33
0.02	50.00
0.01	100.00

Annual Equivalent Cost

Investment outlays for assets are lumpy in that they normally occur at the front end of the project over a one- or two-year period, but the manager may desire to know the annual cost of using an asset. One solution is to compute an **annual equivalent cost,** wherein each year has the same cost and the present value of the annual costs is equal to the investment cost.

Assume an investment costs $10,000. This is the lumpy cost to be replaced with a series of equal annual costs, R, whose present value is also equal to $10,000. If the life of the investment is three years, and the cost of money is .10, then

$$A(3,0.10)R = \$10,000$$
$$2.487R = \$10,000$$
$$R = \$4,021$$

The result is graphed in Exhibit 20-9.

EXHIBIT 20-9

Time Diagram of End-of-Year Equivalent Annual Costs

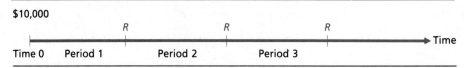

Exhibit 20-9 shows that the costs are assumed to be incurred at the end of each of the three years of life. If the costs are assumed to be incurred at the beginning of each of the three years, the alternative time diagram shown in Exhibit 20-10 is relevant.

EXHIBIT 20-10

Time Diagram of Beginning-of-Year Equivalent Annual Costs

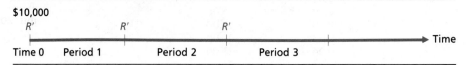

The value of R' is given by solving the following equation:

$$R' + R'A(2,0.10) = \$10,000$$
$$(1 + 1.7355)R' = \$10,000$$
$$R' = \$3,656$$

The annual equivalent cost under this approach is $3,656 per year.

In the next section, the annual equivalent cost concept is used to solve for the best of a mutually exclusive set of investments where the potential projects have unequal lives.

Comparing Projects with Unequal Lives

The net-present-value method gives the correct decision in judging mutually exclusive investments with unequal lives, but it may be necessary to consider what happens when the asset with the shorter life is retired. Assume there are just two mutually exclusive investments, C and D, with the characteristics given in Exhibit 20-11.

EXHIBIT 20-11

Cash Flows for Investments C and D

Investment	Initial Investment Period 0	Cash Proceeds		
		Period 1	Period 2	Period 3
C	− $10,000	$12,000		
D	− 10,000	5,000	$5,000	$5,000

Investments C and D may, for example, be different types of equipment, with investment C having a life of one year and investment D a life of three years. C can be a hand-held version of the equipment with the $10,000 cost representing 100 units of equipment. D can be an automatic more long-lived price of equipment, subject to breakdowns.

With a cost of money of 10 percent, the net present values of the cash flows of investments C and D are given in Exhibit 20-12. Investment D would seem to be the more desirable investment. However, this analysis is incomplete because it fails to take into consideration what will be done at the end of the first year if investment C were selected. The net-present-value method assumes reinvestment at 10 percent. But suppose that after one year, equipment of type C (or similar equipment) will again be available and could be purchased. When investment C can be repeated at the beginning of periods 2 and 3, the cash flows in Exhibit 20-13 would occur for investment C. The present value of the cash flows as now presented is $2,488 for investment C. Thus, C is more desirable than D.

The Reinvestment Assumption

Where the mutually exclusive investments have unequal lives, the reinvestment, possibly in similar equipment, must be taken into consideration.

EXHIBIT 20-12

Net Present Value of Cash Flows for Investments C and D at 10 Percent

Investment	Net Present Value of Cash Flows
C	$ 909
D	2,434

EXHIBIT 20-13

Cash Flows for Investment C Modified

| | Initial Investment | Cash Flows | | |
| | | Period 1 | Period 2 | Period 3 |
Investment	Period 0			
C	− $10,000	− $10,000	− $10,000	
		12,000	12,000	$12,000

Sometimes it may be difficult to find a common comparison time for two or more mutually exclusive investments. In some situations, the lowest common multiple of the lives of the investments results in a length of time longer than the life of the longest lived of the alternatives. For example, consider the relative merits of two types of equipment, one of which has a life of three years and the other eight years. In a situation of this nature, the equivalent return per year, the returns for **perpetuity** (a series of years that are infinite in number), or the net present value of the investment for twenty-four years (the lowest common multiple of years) could be computed. These three methods of computation all lead to the same decision. Alternatively, an attempt to forecast specific investment alternatives may be both feasible and appropriate.

For an example, assume that two pieces of equipment have the characteristics given in Exhibit 20-14 and that reinvestment in similar equipment may be assumed. An interest rate of 10 percent is used and the alternatives are mutually exclusive.

Exhibit 20-15 shows the net-present-value calculations for these two investments. The net-present-value results cannot be used directly to compare the two investments because their lives are not identical. This problem can be solved by taking the lowest common multiple of eight years and three years, twenty-four years, and computing the net present value assuming reinvestment. An alternative is to compute the net present value of each alternative and then find an equivalent yearly annuity.

Suppose a manager desires the annual equivalent costs of E and F. The first step is to find the level annuity, R, which when discounted at 10 percent equals $10,000 in

EXHIBIT 20-14

Cash Flows for Investments E and F

Investment	Expected Life (years)	Initial Cost	Net Cash Flows per Year
E	3	$10,000	$5,000
F	8	30,000	6,500

EXHIBIT 20-15

Present Value of Cash Flows for Investments E and F

Investment	Expected Life (years)	Initial Cost	Net Cash Proceeds per Year	Present Value Factor	Present Value of Proceeds	Net Present Value
E	3	− $10,000	$5,000	2.4869	$12,435	$2,435
F	8	− 30,000	6,500	5.3349	34,677	4,677

present value for investment E. Since $A(n, r)$ is the appropriate discount factor for a level annuity of n years at an interest rate of .10:

$A(n, r)R = \$10,000$

From Table B, $A(3, .10) = 2.4869$. Hence:

$2.4869R = \$10,000$, and

$R = \$4,021$

This is the three-year annual equivalent of $10,000 at 10 percent. It is the equivalent yearly payment an investor would be willing to substitute for an immediate outlay of $10,000. For investment F, the comparable figure is $5,623.

$A(8,0.10)R = 5.3349R = \$30,000$, and

$R = \$5,623$

The two investments can now be compared. See Exhibit 20-16. Investment E is preferred to investment F.

This example assumes that continued reinvestment in the selected alternative would ensue. Alternatively, these two investments can be compared assuming cash flows in perpetuity. To find the value in perpetuity, multiply the equivalent value per year by the present value of a perpetuity. The general formula for the present value of a perpetuity of $1 a period is the following:

$$\text{Present value of a perpetuity} = \frac{1}{r}$$

where r is the appropriate rate of interest.

EXHIBIT 20-16

Comparison of Investments E and F

Investment	Annual Benefits	Annual Equivalent Costs	Annual Net Benefits
E	$5,000	$4,021	$979
F	6,500	5,623	877

Since r is equal to .10 here, the factor in this example is 10. The present value of using E forever is 10(979), or $9,790. The present value of using F is 10(877), or $8,770. Since the equivalent yearly annuity of both alternatives is being multiplied by a constant factor of 10, the relative merits of the alternatives are not changed. Indeed the multiplication adds nothing new needed to make a choice between the two investments.

Investment E remains more desirable than investment F. Many factors have been omitted from this analysis, however, such as reinvestment flexibility and the likelihood of receiving the future returns. More important, the analysis also assumes that the equipment will be replaced in kind at the same cost. If other assumptions are more reasonable, their impact should be taken into account before a decision is reached.

Break-Even Analysis with Time Value

Firms commonly use break-even techniques when considering new investments. The notion of time value can be incorporated into these techniques. Assume some piece of equipment costs $1,000,000 with a life of twenty years. The cost of money is .10. The present value of an annuity of $1 for twenty years is 8.5136. Fixed operating costs are $25,000 per year. The price of the product to be produced with the equipment is $4.50 per unit, and the variable cost per unit is $3.50. Hence the unit contribution margin is $1.

The conventional break-even point would be based on annual fixed costs of $75,000 (depreciation of $50,000 that is equal to $1,000,000 ÷ 20 plus $25,000 of fixed operating costs).

The conventional break-even point, BE, is

$$BE = \frac{\text{Total fixed costs}}{\text{Price per unit} - \text{Variable cost per unit}}$$

$$BE = \frac{\$75,000}{\$4.50 - \$3.50} = 75,000 \text{ units}$$

The annual equivalent cost of using the equipment is

$$\frac{\$1,000,000}{8.5136} = \$117,459$$

The total fixed cost per year is $142,459 = ($117,459 + $25,000).

The **economic break-even point,** denoted EBE, is the break-even point obtained using the annual equivalent cost

$$EBE = \frac{\$142,459}{\$4.50 - \$3.50} = 142,459 \text{ units}$$

The difference in the two break-even points is even more dramatic if .20 is used as the discount rate (the present value of an annuity of $1 for twenty periods is now 4.8696). The annual equivalent cost is

$$\frac{\$1,000,000}{4.8696} = 205,356$$

The total fixed costs are

$$\$205,356 + \$25,000 = \$230,356$$

The economic breakeven point is now

$$EBE = \frac{\$230,356}{\$4.50 - \$3.50} = 230,356 \text{ units}$$

Unit Costs and the Make-or-Buy Decision

The ideas developed above are applicable to a wide class of decisions. One of these is the choice between making and buying. Consider the following three situations.

In situation 1 a firm is considering building a plant to make a product that can be bought for $2 per unit. The facts given in Exhibit 20-17 apply:

EXHIBIT 20-17

Investment Facts: Situation 1

	Cost	Life	Straight-Line Depreciation Cost	Annual Equivalent Cost Depreciation (Using .10)
Plant	$2,000,000	20 years	$100,000	$235,000
Equipment	4,000,000	10 years	400,000	651,000
Total			$500,000	$886,000

The other fixed costs are $114,000 per year, and the variable cost is $1.20 per unit. Should the product be made or bought for $2 per unit?

Assume 1,000,000 units can be sold each year. The annual cost per unit, using the straight-line method of depreciation to establish the depreciation cost, is computed in Exhibit 20-18:

The firm should buy rather than make, since $2 is less than $2.20. The same conclusion would result from the use of a straightforward present-value analysis. The calculations include the recovery of the initial investment over the twenty-year commitment, assuming the equipment is replaced for $4,000,000 after ten years.

EXHIBIT 20-18

Annual Cost per Unit: Situation 1

	Cost	Annual Equivalent Cost (.10)
Plant and equipment depreciation	$ .500	$ .886
Other fixed costs	.114	.114
Variable costs	1.200	1.200
Total	$1.814	$2.200

Including Working Capital

In situation 2 assume the product could only be bought for $3 per unit, but $2,000,000 of working capital is also required if the product is made.

The $2,000,000 of working capital adds $200,000 = (.10 × $2,000,000) of annual cost, or $.20 per unit. The total cost of making is now $2.40 = ($2.20 + $200,000/1,000,000), which is less than the $3 per unit cost of buying. Therefore, it is preferable to make rather than buy.

Sunk Costs

Now, in situation 3 assume that the project is undertaken and the actual costs turn out to be $2.40 as predicted in situation 2. Now the cost of buying changes to $2. Should the firm continue to make?

Assume the plant and equipment have no alternative use and no salvage value. The working capital is, however, salvageable. In this case, the plant and equipment costs are not relevant. The costs have already been incurred, thus are "sunk" and are not relevant. The relevant costs per unit are calculated in Exhibit 20-19:

EXHIBIT 20-19

Annual Cost per Unit: Situation 3

Variable costs	$1.200
Fixed operating costs	.114
Working capital	.200
Total	$1.514

The firm should continue to produce because the incremental costs are $1.514 per unit if the product is made, and $2 per unit if the product is bought. The sunk-cost nature of the plant and equipment are responsible for this new lower cost.

Review Process for Capital-Budgeting Decisions

After the capital-budgeting decision has been made, two control problems remain:

1. *Controlling* the amount of funds spent purchasing or constructing the investment,

2. *Reappraising* the investment decision once the investment starts operating.

Controlling Investment Expenditures

Capital expenditures are difficult to control because usually each investment project is unique, and neither standards nor past experience can be used in establishing the probable rate of expenditure. When actual costs vary from the costs originally estimated, the question arises as to whether the difference was caused by a bad original estimate, by changes in the prices of labor and material, or by inefficiency. The action taken by top management to prevent recurrence of the variance depends on the cause of the variance. Random uncontrollable events can also cause a difference from the estimate, further complicating the analysis. The reason that the actual expenditures exceed the budgeted expenditures are related to all the above items, and it is frequently impossible to isolate the causes with complete accuracy.

During installation or construction of an asset, reports of the percentage of completion, the estimated cost to complete, the time taken relative to the time budgeted for the stage of completion, and the estimated time to complete can enable management to take cost-saving actions. (For example, management could change the construction schedule.) Any such report should include the probable completion date. A delay in completion of an investment may be costly because interest payments have to be made even if operations have not yet begun. Thus, there are strong incentives to meet the planned date of completion. Any expected delay in completion should be explained, and differences between actual and budgeted costs should be investigated, whether they are favorable or unfavorable. Early completion of an investment may also be costly, and explanations are again in order.

If the actual costs are exceeding the budgeted costs significantly (say, by 20 percent), it may be necessary for the person in charge of the project to require additional funds. The decision to invest additional funds in the project is again a capital-budgeting decision, and the request should be treated like any other request. The funds already expended are sunk costs, and thus are not relevant to the decision concerning whether or not to invest additional funds in the project.

Control of capital expenditures is an inexact procedure because it is often difficult to establish benchmarks of performance. However, an estimate of cost is made and defended by the sponsor and the director of a project. This estimate is, at least in part, the basis of the decision to invest. It should be made with care and only after detailed investigation. It is reasonable to use this cost as the benchmark in the evaluation process. Large variances should be explained, not shrugged off by saying, "The estimate must have been off." The reason the estimate was off should be reviewed.

Furthermore, comparisons of actual and budgeted costs are useful in signaling the necessity for management action.

At a minimum, a review of purchase or construction costs gives an incentive for project sponsors to make careful estimates and for those in charge of construction to control costs and completion times. The choice of who should be responsible for the review is also important. Too often the entire review is left with the project initiator. Project reviews should be done by an independent group.

Cost Performance Reporting

One technique used extensively by the Department of Defense is a **cost-performance-reporting (CPR) system** that collects data on actual costs incurred, budgeted costs (adjusted to reflect unforeseen changes, say in prices), and the time activities are completed. This information assists in determining the overexpenditure and time-late-to-date, thereby providing an estimate of the overexpenditure and anticipated time late on the total project. Dividing a project into parts according to both the component activities and the responsible divisions of the firm permits the project manager to pinpoint trouble areas early and perhaps initiate corrective or ameliorating action. It also permits an evaluation of the statement so often made that: "Yes, I'm over the budget, but the work is substantially ahead of schedule." Exhibits 20-20, 20-21, and 20-22 suggest the essentials of this approach.

Exhibit 20-20 gives the overall picture of the project to date. The actual cost (the top curve) has been plotted up to the present time (b) and projected to the expected

---

EXHIBIT 20-20

Operating Schedule of Performance

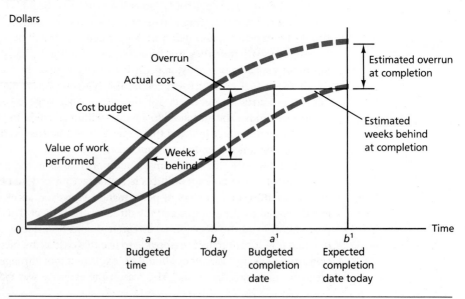

EXHIBIT 20-21

Expected Overrun Percentage

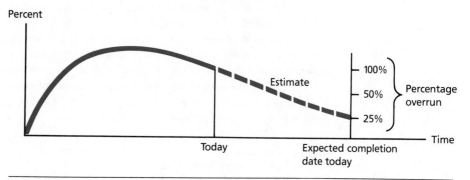

completion date (b'). The latter date is found by projecting the value-of-the-work-performed line (the bottom curve) until its height reaches the height of the cost-budget line (the middle curve) at the original budgeted completion date. This occurs at time b'. The value of the work performed is the budgeted value of those activities actually completed.

When actual costs exceed the value of the work performed, the difference is an overrun. The overrun in the present example (Exhibit 20-21) is quite large today but is expected to decrease by the time the project is completed. Actual cost less the value of the work performed as a ratio to the value of work performed gives the percentage overrun. This percentage is plotted and extrapolated to the expected completion data in Exhibit 20-21.

EXHIBIT 20-22

Expected Time Late

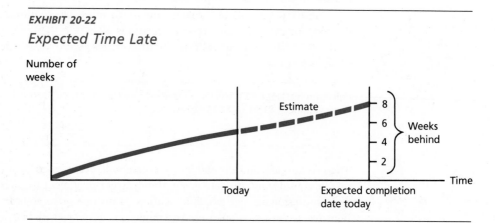

The cost-budget plot of Exhibit 20-20 indicates just when work should be done as well as its cost. In this case it has taken $b - a$ weeks longer to complete the work done to date than was budgeted. The amount, $b - a$, then, indicates the current time late. Exhibit 20-20 suggests that the project will be even further behind time when it is finished $b' - a'$. The weeks-late figure may also be considered important enough to diagram separately (Exhibit 20-22). The fact that the weeks-late figure is predicted to become worse may have some relation to the expected decline in cost overrun percentage. It would perhaps be surprising for the weeks-late figure to decline concurrently with a decline in the absolute value of the cost overrun.

The data on the entire project is perhaps most useful when broken down by tasks, departments, or both. Suppose, for example, that the following facts are available on a given activity as of the twenty-second week:

Actual cost at week 22	$4,400
Budgeted cost of work performed	$1,800
Budget time for value of work performed	11 weeks
Cost budget at week 22	$3,800
Estimated actual cost at completion	$5,400
Estimated time of completion (total)	36 weeks
Total budgeted cost at completion	$4,000
Budgeted completion time	23 weeks

The current overrun is $4,400 - $1,800 = $2,600. The above schedule of costs indicates that $2,200 of budgeted cost, $4,000 - $1,800, remains to be completed. However, the report simultaneously predicts that the manager can accomplish the production task for $1,000, $5,400 - $4,400. This optimistic forecast of doing $2,200 of budgeted activity and incur $1,000 (less than half) in actual expenditures should be questioned. Furthermore, this activity is currently eleven weeks beyond schedule, $22 - 11$, while estimating thirteen weeks behind at completion, $36 - 23$. This implies a much different level of performance than in the past. While feasible, this forecast, too, appears questionable in light of an estimate of less costs than budgeted for the remaining work to be completed.

The data can also be broken down into more conventional cost variances, if desired. For example, the present overrun is $2,600. If the budgeted cost per week were $150 while the actual cost (both averages) were $193, the following breakdown is possible.

Efficiency variance (11 weeks − 22 weeks) $150	=	$1,650U	
Price variance ($150 − $193) 22 weeks	=	950U	
		$2,600U	

These values are more useful and accurate when computed on a task level.

In considering the data given, the manager may elect to offer a revised budget and time estimate. For example, if there is no reason to assume performance will improve, a revised completion date might reflect the fact that it took 22 weeks to do

11 weeks of work. The new estimate for the total time would then be the total budgeted time of 23 weeks times two, 2(23) or 46 weeks, leaving 46 − 22 or 24 more weeks to go versus the 36 − 22 or 14 as shown in the above table. The alternative is to commit more resources to the project.

Further, the total cost could be reestimated based on the current result that it took $4,400 to do $1,800 work. At this rate, it would take ($4,400 ÷ $1,800) × $4,000 or about $9,800 to do the entire job versus the $5,400 initially budgeted. This would require additional expenditures after week 22 of $9,800 − $4,400 or $5,400 instead of the $5,400 − $4,400 or $1,000 currently projected. If management wishes to reduce the completion time, additional expenditures would be required.

If a new budget is established, performance should be compared to both the new and old budgets. There may not be a lot that can be done in the current case, but the lessons learned using the original budget will be useful for planning future projects while continued operational control is achieved using the new budget.

Evaluation of Computer-Integrated Manufacturing (CIM) Systems

The major thrust of change in manufacturing is towards the use of CIM. Can discounted cash flow methods of evaluation be used to evaluate state of the art manufacturing techniques? Are there errors to be avoided?

One major error is to use excessively high hurdle (discount) rates. One of the *Fortune* 500 manufacturing firms used .20 as a hurdle rate when debt cost .08 before tax and .04 after tax. It consistently rejected efficiency (CIM) type of investments while its competitors accepted the same opportunities. For example, consider a CIM project that would cost $10,000,000 and would earn after-tax cash flows of $1,000,000 of savings per year (in less labor, less spoilage, less inventory, less down time of product line charges, more output per unit time, and better quality) on an annual output of 500,000 units. The savings are $2.00 per unit. Assume the product sells for $10 per unit with incremental costs of $6 to produce. The competitor after investment has incremental costs of $4 per unit. When the price dropped to $6 per unit the *Fortune* 500 firm dropped the product (a price of $4 and incremental costs of $6 was not profitable). The competitor had a price of $6 and incremental costs of $4 and could show a profit. In fact, taking over the incremental sales of 500,000 units the competitor makes an incremental profit of 500,000 ($2) = $1,000,000, which can be added to its cost savings. In fact, with the elimination of a competitive producer, we can expect the price to increase further, adding to the value of the new equipment.

A second error is to specify incorrectly the cash flows of the status quo alternative. Any adverse effects from not having modern equipment should be included (such as lost sales from inferior quality or delayed delivery).

CIM tends to reduce the amount of inventory that must be held (flexibility in manufacturing reduces the need to stockpile work in process and finished goods). What is a $10,000,000 reduction in inventory worth in terms of present value? The reduction is worth $10,000,000 today. If sales are increasing, it is possible that there will be additional inventory savings in the future.

The final error considered here is the tendency to ignore the future generations of investments that will not be feasible unless the firm stays in the game today. There is a learning that takes place and is enhanced by making the efficiency (CIM) investment today. In the finance literature this type of consideration is called an *option*. The option to consider to invest in the future has value today and should be taken into consideration in valuing an investment in equipment today. Considering the future is a correct approach. But one must be careful because an excessively optimistic view of the value of the option to continue the process can be used to justify bad investments.

Thus, we conclude that net present value can and should be used to evaluate CIM alternatives. There are benefits that are difficult to measure that must be included, but this is true with most investments. DCF properly used (a reasonable discount rate) adjusts for the time value of money. But no DCF calculation is any better than the cash-flow inputs. The cash flows that are used must reflect all material costs and benefits over a valid time horizon. With CIM alternatives the relevant time horizon may be long and may include chains of alternatives and decisions.

Reappraisal or Postaudit of Operating Results

The sponsor of a capital-budgeting request makes estimates of future revenues and expenses in order to justify the proposed expenditure. If either the internal-rate-of-return method or the net-present-value method is used to evaluate the request, a key item needed is a forecast of net cash proceeds. After the investment has been placed in operation, a **postaudit** or reappraisal should compare the actual results to the estimated results, which formed the basis for the capital-budgeting decision, and any variances should be explained. Similarly, the director of the construction or installation of a project should be held accountable for the construction cost and time budget.

Reappraisal of capital-budgeting decisions results in three benefits:

1. The presentation of better information on capital-budgeting requests.

2. An incentive for operating departments to meet the income, cash-flow, and strategic goals implicit in a capital request.

3. An incentive for those charged with the installation or construction of a project to meet cost and time budgets.

Whether these benefits will occur depends on the care with which the reappraisal procedure is implemented.

The comparison of actual and predicted cash proceeds is a useful method of reappraising capital-budgeting decisions, but it cannot be used in all circumstances. Where the projected cash flow is an incremental value (as when equipment is being replaced), it may not be possible to determine the actual incremental cash flow after replacement, if the cash flows associated with the required investment cannot be separated from those of the firm's other activities.

Income is probably the most widely used measure of performance, and the return on investment (income divided by investment) is second. But unless they are carefully calculated, both measures are inferior to the use of actual cash flows as a means of reappraising capital-budgeting decisions.

By using cash flows the problem of allocating the cost of an investment to specific periods of use (depreciation expense) is avoided. If income is being used to measure performance, the depreciation cost of the investment must be computed and deducted from revenue because the cost of using the investment must be taken into consideration. However, the analysis of the decision to invest is clouded by the difficult issue of disengaging the effect of the depreciation method from the effect of the capital-budgeting process and the efficiency or inefficiency of operations.

Finally, capital-budgeting decisions are made under uncertainty. A good decision may turn out to be unsuccessful and still have been the correct decision given the information available. For example, most investors would pay $1 for an investment that had a .9 probability of an immediate return of $1,000 and a .1 probability of $0. However, if the event with a .1 probability occurred, the investment appraisal would cause the investment to appear to have been undesirable. This fact is often overlooked in a postaudit. Managers are aware of this down-side risk, and this causes them to be cautious, perhaps more cautious than stockholders desire. After all, rejected projects are not evaluated. If top management wants its lower-level managers to take risks, it must evaluate them with the understanding that an investment that appears to be good can turn out badly.

Summary

Time value must be considered whenever costs and benefits occur over several time periods. The cost of any product or service must reflect not only the wear and tear of the long-lived assets used but also the capital cost (interest) associated with these assets.

All economic evaluation must be made on an after-tax basis. The method of expensing long-lived assets may change, but economic evaluation always requires that the present value of the tax savings arising from expensing the asset through time be included in the cash flows.

Review Problem

AFTER-TAX COST OF AN ASSET

a. Assume an investment costs $100,000 and is to be depreciated as a three-year class asset using the following allowable accelerated depreciation:

Year	Depreciation (%)
1	33.33
2	44.44
3	14.82
4	7.41

What is the net cost of the asset (net of depreciation tax savings) if the tax rate is 34 percent? The firm uses a 10 percent discount rate.

b. If the above investment is a piece of equipment that produces a widget that sells for $10 per unit and has incremental expenses of $8 per unit, how many units have to be made and sold each year if the cost of money is 10 percent and the life of the equipment is five years?

Solution to Review Problem

a. The present value of the depreciation deductions is

$$33,330 \times 1.10^{-1} = 30,300$$
$$44,440 \times 1.10^{-2} = 36,727$$
$$14,820 \times 1.10^{-3} = 11,134$$
$$7,410 \times 1.10^{-4} = \underline{5,061}$$
$$83,322$$

The present value of the tax savings is

$$\$83,322 \times .34 = \$28,295$$

The net cost of the investment is

$$100,000 - 28,295 = \$71,705$$

b. The present value of an annuity with $r = .10$, $n = 5$ is 3.79079.

$$\frac{71,705}{3.79079} = \$18,916 \text{ after-tax income needed each year}$$

$$\frac{18,916}{1 - .34} = \$28,660 \text{ before-tax income needed each year}$$

Each unit contributes $2 per unit:

$$\frac{28,660}{2} = 14,330 \text{ units must be made and sold each year}$$

If 14,330 units are sold, the net (before tax) is $28,660. The after-tax amount is

$$\$28,660(1 - .34) = \$18,916.$$

The present value of $18,916 for five years is

$$PV = 18,916(3.79079) = \$71,705.$$

The $71,705 is the net cost of the investment.

Key Terms to Review

annual equivalent cost, p. 699
cash flows, p. 691
CLADR, p. 692
cost of money, p. 697
cost-performance-reporting (CPR)
    system, p. 708

economic break-even point,
    p. 704
perpetuity, p. 702
postaudit, p. 712

Suggested Readings

Anthony, R., and D. Young. *Management Control in Nonprofit Organizations,* 3d ed. Homewood, Ill.: Irwin, 1984.

Bierman, H., and S. Smidt. *The Capital Budgeting Decision,* 7th ed. New York: Macmillan, 1988.

Brealey, R., and S. Myers. *Principles of Corporate Finance.* New York: McGraw-Hill, 1988.

Comptroller General. *Federal Capital Budgeting: A Collection of Haphazard Practices.* Washington, D.C.: General Accounting Office, 1981.

Gitman, L., and J. Forrester. "A Survey of Capital Budgeting Techniques Used by Major U.S. Firms." *Financial Management* (Fall 1977): 66–71.

Kaplan, R. and A. Atkinson. *Advanced Managerial Accounting,* 2d ed. Englewood Cliffs, N.J.: Prentice-Hall, 1989.

Magee, R. *Advanced Managerial Accounting.* New York: Harper & Row, 1986.

McCarthy, C., D. Crambley, and P. Davis. *The Federal Income Tax: Its Sources and Applications.* Englewood Cliffs, N.J.: Prentice-Hall, current year's edition.

National Association of Accountants. *Practice and Techniques: Cost of Capital.* Montvale, N.J.: NAA, 1984.

VanHorne, J. *Financial Management and Policy,* 7th ed. Englewood Cliffs, N.J.: Prentice-Hall, 1986.

Review Questions

20-1 Explain how the cash flow of a typical period should be computed. Should interest payments be deducted? Do all the deductions require an explicit cash outlay?

20-2 How would a cash-flow computation differ from a fund-flow computation?

20-3 If the present value of the absolute cash flows of an investment is negative, is it possible for the present value of the relative cash flows of the investment to be positive (that is, the cash flows resulting from this investment being compared to an alternative)?

20-4 What are some difficulties involved in reviewing capital-budgeting decisions?

20-5 In making investment decisions, what factors other than those discussed in this chapter must be taken into consideration?

20-6 Some persons prefer to compute the present value of the cash flows of an investment, while others prefer to compute the terminal value. Will the choice of the method affect the acceptability of an investment?

Exercises

20-7 Equipment Purchase Assume that two pieces of equipment have the following characteristics:

Equipment	Expected Life	Initial Cost	Operating Cost per Year
X	5	$43,295	$4,500
Y	8	60,000	4,000

Assuming a cost of money of 0.05, which piece of equipment is the more desirable if both can do the same job equally well? Ignore taxes and uncertainty.

20-8 Investment Value The Auction Company uses a discount rate of .20. The following information applies to a projected investment (ignore taxes):

Time 0
Initial outlay of $1,000,000

Time 1	
Net revenue from sales (all cash sales)	$1,280,000
Interest paid	200,000
Net change in bank balance	$1,080,000

Should the investment be accepted?

20-9 Machine Replacement A product is currently being manufactured on a machine that results in incremental costs of $7.50 per unit. The rate of production expected in the future is 10,000 units per year, and the sales price per unit is $8.50. It is expected that the old machine can be used without repair for the next ten years.

An equipment manufacturer has agreed to accept the old equipment as a trade-in for a new version. The new machine would cost $200,000 plus the trade-in and would result in incremental costs of $5.50 per unit. It has an expected life of ten years, and an expected salvage of $10,000 at that time. The old equipment could be sold on the open market now for $55,000. Ten years from now it has an expected salvage of $1,000. Ignore income taxes. The appropriate time-discount rate for this company is .05. What do you recommend the company do?

20-10 Continuation of Exercise 20-9 Assume the same situation as in Exercise 20-9 except that the resale price of the old equipment is now $100,000. What do you recommend?

20-11 Equipment Purchase Decisions The Electrolite Company has a cost of money of .10. The following two mutually exclusive investments are available (two machines that do the same task). The task will be continued in the foreseeable future.

	X	Y
Initial cost	$10,000	$20,000
Other costs per year	2,000	1,000
Estimated life years	15	20

Which machine should be purchased? Ignore taxes.

20-12 Unit Costs The following facts apply to an investment the Dropdot Company is considering:

- Plant cost: $10,000,000 with a life of fifty years.

- Equipment cost: $2,000,000 with a life of twenty years.

- Annual fixed costs are $180,000 of which $100,000 are incremental with the decision (but excluding depreciation) and $80,000 are allocations from other departments and projects.

- The net revenue contribution per unit sold is $2 (this is after deducting variable manufacturing costs of $.20 per unit).

It is expected that 1,000,000 units of product will be used per year. Assume a zero tax rate and a time value of money of 10 percent.

a. How many units have to be produced and sold per year to break even?

b. If 1,000,000 units are produced, what will be the per unit cost?

20-13 Continuation of Exercise 20-12 Assume the plant and equipment described in Exercise 20-12 is purchased. One million units of the product are needed in the coming years. These units can be purchased at a cost of $.40 per unit from a reliable supplier. The variable-manufacturing costs per unit are $.20. If the units are purchased, the plant and equipment will be shut down (this can be done with little additional cost) and will be disposed of with zero salvage value. The book value of the plant and equipment is $12,000,000 less $2,000,000 accumulated depreciation.

Assume the probability of the product being supplied on time and the quality of the product are the same with either make or buy. There are no taxes. The $100,000 of fixed costs described above can be avoided if the product is purchased. Should the units be made or bought?

20-14 Continuation of Exercise 20-13 If the plant requires working capital of $1,500,000 (liquidation value), should the units be made or purchased?

20-15 Continuation of Exercise 20-13 Assume the plant and equipment have been purchased. There is a marginal tax rate of .4 and an after-tax time value factor of .06. Should the units be made or bought? Assume there are no other uses for the plant or equipment and their book value for taxes is $12,000,000. The annual out-of-pocket costs of making the product are $300,000. The annual costs of buying are $400,000. If retained, the plant and equipment will be depreciated over twenty years using the straight-line method of depreciation. Should the product be made or bought? The firm is highly profitable.

20-16 Write-Off Rates   Assume an investment costs $1,000,000 and is to be depreciated as a three-year class asset using the following allowable accelerated depreciation:

Year	Depreciation (%)
1	33.33
2	44.44
3	14.82
4	7.41

What is the net cost of the net-of-depreciation tax savings if the tax rate is 34 percent? The firm uses a 12 percent discount rate.

20-17 Equipment Evaluation   Which of the following three pieces of equipment is the most desirable? Assume that the investments are mutually exclusive.

Type of Equipment	Outlay	Life	Labor Savings per Year	Yield
A	$ 5,000	1	$ 6,000	.20
B	16,761	5	5,000	.15
C	42,883	7	10,000	.14

The cost of money of the firm is 10 percent. Assume a tax rate of zero.

20-18 Equipment Desirability   Assume that two pieces of equipment have the following characteristics:

Equipment	Expected Life	Initial Cost	Operating Cost per Year
X	5	$43,295	$4,500
Y	8	60,000	4,000

Assuming a cost of money of .08, which equipment is the more desirable? What assumption are you making? Ignore taxes.

20-19 Equipment Desirability   Assume that two pieces of equipment have the following characteristics:

Equipment	Expected Life	Initial Cost	Operating Cost per Year
X	3	$10,000	$4,500
Y	4	12,000	4,000

Assuming a cost of money of .05, which equipment is the more desirable? Ignore taxes.

20-20 Present Value of Cash Flows Assume the cash flow of the first year is $1,000,000 and that the rate of discount is .08. Compute the present value of the cash flows assuming that the

a. Cash flow decreases by .02 per year.

b. Cash flow is constant and continues forever.

c. Cash flow increases by .03 per year forever.

d. Cash flow increases by .09 per year forever.

20-21 Present Value of Cash Flows Assume that the cost of money is .10 and the first period's cash flow is $10,000. Compute the present value of cash flows assuming that

a. The $10,000 continues for perpetuity.

b. The $10,000 decays at the rate of .15 per year.

c. The $10,000 grows at the rate of .08 per year.

20-22 Equipment Replacement Procedures The controller of the Waditap Company has asked a member of his staff to prepare a report on the company's equipment-replacement procedure. One statement made by the staff member reads as follows: "Present procedure overestimates the profitability of replacement proposals because the investment in inventory, receivables, and working-cash balances is ignored. Two dollars are invested in these assets for every dollar invested in equipment, and, therefore, the average annual investment as computed (with the previously suggested changes) should be tripled in calculating the rate of return on investment." Evaluate this statement.

Problems

20-23 Equipment Purchase Decisions The Old Company is currently producing a product that sells for $7 per unit and the variable costs of manufacturing are $6 per unit. The company produces and sells 1,000,000 units per year and expects this level of production and sales in the future. The total market is 2,000,000 units. The fixed costs (including overhead) allocated to the product are $1,200,000 per year. The company has an opportunity to purchase new equipment costing $9,000,000 and having an expected life of twenty years. The IRS will accept the twenty-year life for taxes.

The equipment will reduce variable costs to $4.50 per unit. Because of the method of cost allocation, the fixed costs allocated (including the equipment depreciation) will increase to $1,600,000 per year.

The tax rate is .48. The appropriate rate of interest to be used in this type of investment decision has been determined by the company to be 6 percent. Maintenance expense will be constant throughout the equipment's life. The present value of the tax depreciation expense is .676799 per dollar of investment.

The board of directors of the company is very much concerned with an investment's payback, ROI, and its effect on earnings per share. However, it believes that all decisions should be made in the best interests of the firm's common stockholders.

REQUIRED:

Should the equipment be purchased? Explain.

20-24 Evaluation of Investment   The Farming Fan Company has an investment that costs $6,000 and has a life of three years. The tax rate is .48.

The asset will earn $10,000 the first year, $9,000 the second, and $7,000 the third. There are $5,500 of out-of-pocket expenses per year.

Working capital will be $1,000, then $1,600, then zero.

The time discount rate is 10 percent.

Assume the present value of the tax depreciation per dollar of asset is 0.855427 and, with a depreciable cost of $6,000, the present value of depreciation is $5,133.

	Period 1	Period 2	Period 3
Revenues or savings (cash and receivables)			
Out-of-pocket expenses	$	$	$
Income before taxes			
Taxes (0.48)			
Income after taxes	$	$	$
Plus: Net working capital decrease			
Less: Net working capital increase			
Cash flow	$	$	$
Present value factors			
Present values			

Total present value of savings $_____

Cost of investment $_____

Less:
  PV of depreciation times
    Tax rate   _____

    Net cost $_____

Net present value $_____

20-25 Retain versus Sell Decisions   The Happy Valley Hotel chain plans to close down one of its hotels. The hotel building was purchased sixty years ago for $500,000 and has been depreciated on a no-salvage, straight-line basis to a present book value of $200,000. The best offer for the hotel building at this time is an offer of $288,000. If the hotel is continued in operation for five more years, the after-tax accounting income will be $63,000 per year. At the end of five years, the hotel would be sold for $100,000. If the hotel were sold today, it would be possible to reduce certain expenditures, such as general administration, by $20,000 per year for the five years. Under all alternatives the furnishings would be retained standby use. The cost of moving the furnishings if sold now or later is $16,000. Assuming a 50 percent tax rate on all types of income, and considering the after-tax time value of money to be 16 percent, what decision should be made? Assume depreciation for tax purposes is the same as for book purposes.

20-26 Computer Purchase Decision   The Torng Advertising Agency is considering purchase of a small computer in order to reduce the costs of its manual operations. At the present time, the manual system in use involves the following direct cash expenses per month:

Salaries	$7,500
Payroll taxes and fringes	1,700
Supplies	600
	$9,800

Existing related furniture and equipment are fully depreciated in the accounts and for income taxes. The cost of the new computer, including alterations, installations, and accessory equipment, is $100,000. The entire amount can be depreciated for income-tax purposes on a double-declining-balance basis at the rate of .20 per year. The computer is expected to be obsolete in three years, at which time it is expected to have a salvage value of $20,000. (This is treated as a cash inflow at the end of year 3.) The current equipment has zero salvage value.

Year	Tax Basis	Tax Depreciation
1	100,000	20,000
2	80,000	16,000
3	64,000	12,800

Estimated annual costs of the new systems are

Salaries (supervisor)	$15,000
Salaries (other)	24,000
Payroll taxes and fringes	7,400
Supplies	7,200
	$53,600

REQUIRED:

a. Compute the cash savings using a 40 percent tax rate.

b. Should the computer be purchased assuming a 20 percent cost of debt before taxes?

20-27 Product Decisions   The Lytol Company prepares income statements by product line. It has one product (a cleaning liquid) that has the following income statement for the most recent year:

Revenues	$100,000,000
Less:	
Cash expenses, other	60,000,000
Advertising	45,000,000
Research	5,000,000
Loss	10,000,000

The firm has a .20 time value factor.

It is not expected that the economic situation for the product will turn around because competition is severe. With zero advertising cash flows, it would decrease by 30 percent per year.

The company has been offered $28,000,000 for the product. Lytol buys the product and markets it but does not make it. It does hold patents.

Note: The present value of a decaying cash flow stream is $P = \dfrac{D}{k - g}$ where k is the discount rate and g is the growth rate (decay would be negative).

REQUIRED:

Should Lytol sell the product? Explain your answer.

20-28 **Acquiring New Equipment**   Wyle Co. is considering a proposal to acquire new manufacturing equipment. The new equipment has the same capacity as the current equipment but will provide operating efficiencies in direct and indirect labor, direct material usage, indirect supplies, and power. The savings in operating costs are estimated at $150,000 annually.

The new equipment will cost $300,000 and will be purchased at the beginning of the year when the project is started. The equipment dealer is certain that the equipment will be operational during the second quarter of the year it is installed. Therefore, 60 percent of the estimated annual savings can be obtained in the first year. Wyle will incur a one-time expense of $30,000 to transfer the production activities from the old equipment to the new equipment. No loss of sales will occur, however, because the plant is large enough to install the new equipment without interfering with the operations of the current equipment. The equipment dealer states that most companies use a five-year life when depreciating this equipment.

The current equipment has been fully depreciated and is carried in the accounts at zero book value. Management has reviewed the condition of the current equipment and has concluded that it can be used an additional five years. Wyle Co. would receive $5,000 net of removal costs if it elected to buy the new equipment and dispose of its current equipment at this time.

Wyle currently leases its manufacturing plant. The annual lease payments are $60,000. The lease, which will have four years remaining when the equipment installation would begin, is not renewable. Wyle Co. would be required to remove any equipment in the plant at the end of the lease. The cost of equipment removal is expected to equal the salvage value of either the old or new equipment at the time of removal.

The company uses the sum-of-the-years-digits depreciation method for tax purposes. A full-year's depreciation is taken in the first year the asset is put into use. The present equipment is fully depreciated for tax purposes.

The company is subject to a 40 percent income tax rate and requires an after-tax return of at least 12 percent on any investment.

REQUIRED:

a. Calculate the annual incremental after-tax cash flows for Wyle Co.'s proposal to acquire the new manufacturing equipment.

b. Calculate the net present value of Wyle Co.'s proposal to acquire the new manufacturing equipment using the cash flows calculated in requirement a and indicate what action Wyle Co.'s management should take. For ease in calculation, assume all recurring cash flows take place at the end of the year. (*CMA adapted*)

20-29 **Machine Replacement** The WRL Company makes cookies for its chain of snack food stores. On January 2, 19x1, WRL Company purchased a special cookie cutting machine; this machine has been used for three years. WRL Company is considering the purchase of a newer, more efficient machine with a life of four years. If purchased, the new machine would be acquired on January 2, 19x4. WRL Company expects to sell 300,000 dozen cookies in each of the next four years. The selling price of the cookies is expected to average $.50 per dozen.

WRL Company has two options: (1) continue to operate the old machine or (2) sell the old machine and purchase the new machine. No trade-in was offered by the seller of the new machine. The following information has been assembled to help decide which option is more desirable.

	Old Machine	New Machine
Original cost of machine at acquisition	$80,000	$120,000
Salvage value at the end of the useful life for depreciation purposes	$10,000	$ 20,000
Useful life from date of acquisition	7 years	4 years
Expected annual cash operating expenses:		
Variable cost per dozen	$ .20	$ .14
Total fixed costs	$15,000	$ 14,000
Depreciation method used for tax purposes:	Straight-line	Sum-of-years'-digits
Estimated cash value of machines:		
January 2, 19x4	$40,000	$120,000
December 31, 19x7	$ 7,000	$ 20,000
Tax basis as of January 2, 19x4	$50,000[a]	$120,000

[a] Computed using a seven-year life and an estimated salvage value of $10,000.

WRL Company is subject to an overall income tax rate of 40 percent. Assume that all operating revenues and expenses occur at the end of the year. Assume that any gain or loss on the sale of machinery is treated as an ordinary tax item and will affect the taxes paid by WRL Company at the end of the year in which it occurred.

REQUIRED:

a. Use the net-present-value method to determine whether WRL Company should retain the old machine or acquire the new machine. WRL requires an after-tax return of 16 percent.

b. Without prejudice to your answer to requirement a, assume that the quantitative differences are so slight between the two alternatives that WRL Company is indifferent to the two proposals. Identify and discuss the nonquantitative factors that are important to this decision that WRL Company should consider.

c. Identify and discuss the advantages and disadvantages of using discounted cash flow techniques (such as the net-present-value method) for capital investment decisions. (*CMA adapted*)

20-30 Submitting a Bid   Wardl Industries is a manufacturer of standard and custom-designed bottling equipment. Early in December 19x3 Lyan Company asked Wardl to quote a price for a custom-designed bottling machine to be delivered on April 1, 19x4. Lyan intends to make a decision on the purchase of such a machine by January 1 so Wardl would have the entire first quarter of 19x4 to build the equipment.

Wardl's standard pricing policy for custom-designed equipment is to require a 50 percent markup on full cost. Lyan's specifications for the equipment have been reviewed by Wardl's Engineering and Cost Accounting Departments, and they made the following estimates for the raw materials and direct labor required to build the equipment.

Raw materials	$256,000
Direct labor 11,000 DLH @ $15	165,000

Manufacturing overhead is applied on the basis of direct labor hours. Wardl normally plans to run its plant 15,000 direct labor hours per month and assigns overhead on the basis of 180,000 direct labor hours per year. The overhead application rate for 19x4 of $9.00/DLH is based on the following budgeted manufacturing overhead costs for 19x4.

Variable manufacturing overhead	$ 972,000
Fixed manufacturing overhead	648,000
Total manufacturing overhead	$1,620,000

The Wardl production schedule (without the Lyan equipment) requires 12,000 direct labor hours per month during the first quarter. If Wardl is awarded the contract for the Lyan equipment, production of one of its standard products would have to be reduced. This is necessary because production levels can be increased only to 15,000 direct labor hours each month on short notice. Furthermore, Wardl's employees are unwilling to work overtime.

Sales of the standard product equal to the reduced production would be lost, but there would be no permanent loss of future sales or customers. The standard product whose production schedule would be reduced has a unit sales price of $12,000 and the following unit cost structure at 12,000 units.

Raw materials		$2,500
Direct labor	250 DLH @ $15	3,750
Overhead	250 DLH @ $ 9	2,250
Total cost		$8,500

Lyan needs the custom-designed equipment to increase its bottle-making capacity so that it will not have to buy bottles from an outside supplier. Lyan Company requires 5,000,000 bottles annually. Its present equipment has a maximum capacity of 4,500,000 bottles with a directly traceable cash outlay cost of $.15 per bottle. The new equipment has a cash outlay of $.14 per bottle. Lyan has had to purchase 500,000 from a supplier at $.40 each. The new equipment would allow Lyan to manufacture its entire annual demand for bottles and experience a raw material cost savings of $.01 for each bottle manufactured.

Wardl estimates that Lyan's annual bottle demand will continue to be 5,000,000 bottles over the next five years, the estimated economic life of the special-purpose equipment. Wardl further estimates that Lyan has an after-tax cost of capital of 15 percent and is subject to a 40 percent marginal income tax rate, the same rates as Wardl.

REQUIRED:

a. Wardl Industries plans to submit a bid to Lyan Company for the manufacture of the special-purpose bottling equipment.

(1) Calculate the bid Wardl would submit if it follows its standard pricing policy for special-purpose equipment.

(2) Calculate the minimum bid Wardl would be willing to submit on the Lyan equipment that would result in the same profits as planned for the first quarter of 19x4.

b. Wardl Industries wants to estimate the maximum price Lyan Company would be willing to pay for the special-purpose bottling equipment.

(1) Calculate the present value of the after-tax savings in directly traceable cash outlays that Lyan could expect to realize from the new special-purpose bottling equipment.

(2) Identify the other factors Wardl would have to incorporate in its estimate of the maximum price Lyan would be willing to pay for the equipment.

(3) Describe how the cost savings (requirement **b.1**) and the other factors (requirement **b.2**) would be combined to calculate the estimate of the maximum price Lyan would be willing to pay for the equipment. (*CMA adapted*)

20-31 Net-Present-Value Analysis   Hammond Industries is a toy manufacturer that will have excess capacity at its single plant after 1986. Hammond's management is currently studying two alternative proposals that would utilize this excess capacity.

Proposal 1:   Hammond has been approached by GloriToys, one of its competitors, to manufacture a partially completed doll. GloriToys, owner of the distribution rights for the doll, would finish the dolls in its plant and then market the dolls. The GloriToy doll would not compete directly with any of Hammond's products.

GloriToys would contract to purchase 5,000 unfinished dolls each month at a price of $7.50 each for the period of 1987 through 1990. Hammond's estimated incremental cash outlays to manufacture the doll would be $250,000 per year during the four-year contract period. In addition, this alternative would require a $400,000 investment in manufacturing equipment. The equipment would have no salvage value at the end of its useful life.

Proposal 2:   Hammond is considering the production of a new stuffed toy to be added to its own product line. The new stuffed toy would be sold at $15 per unit and the expected annual sales over the estimated six-year product life (19x1−19x6) for the toy is as follows.

Year	Annual Unit Sales
19x1	65,000
19x2	90,000
19x3	90,000
19x4	65,000
19x5	50,000
19x6	50,000

The variable unit manufacturing and selling costs are estimated to be $6 and $1, respectively, over this six-year period. The estimated annual incremental cash outlay for fixed costs would be $300,000. The manufacture and sale of the new stuffed toy would require a $700,000 investment in new manufacturing equipment; this equipment would have a salvage value of $50,000 at the end of the six-year period.

Additional information relative to a decision between the two proposals follows.

1. Manufacturing equipment for either proposal would be placed in service during December 19x0. Depreciation on the equipment would be recognized starting in 19x1. Straight-line depreciation over the life of each proposal would be used for book purposes and ACRS for three-year property would be employed for tax purposes. The ACRS personal property rates are presented below.

ACRS Tables for Three-Year Property

Year 1	25%
Year 2	38%
Year 3	37%

2. Hammond Industries is subject to a 30 percent income tax rate on all income.

3. Hammond's management assumes that annual cash flows occur at the end of the year for evaluating capital investment proposals. Hammond uses a 15 percent after-tax discount rate. Present value tables for 15 percent are presented below.

Year	Present Value of $1.00 Received at the End of the Period	Present Value of an Annuity of $1.00 Received at the End of Each Period
1	.87	.87
2	.76	1.63
3	.66	2.28
4	.57	2.85
5	.50	3.35
6	.43	3.78
7	.38	4.16

REQUIRED:

a. Calculate the net present value at December 31, 19x0, of the estimated after-tax cash flows of Hammond Industries' proposal of:

(1) Manufacturing unfinished dolls for GloriToys,

(2) Manufacturing and selling a new stuffed toy to be added to its own product line.

b. Without prejudice to the net-present-value calculations in requirement a and only considering the environment for Hammond Industries as described, identify other factors that increase the attractiveness of:

(1) Manufacturing the unfinished dolls for GloriToys,

(2) Manufacturing and selling a new stuffed toy. (*CMA adapted*)

20-32 **Cost Performance Reporting** Suppose that in a given network system the engineering subsystem has the following reported facts for a job that is done uniformly over time in terms of cost incurrence as well as actual activity: cost incurred to date, $6.6 million; cost of work completed (budget), $3.7 million; original budget for engineering, $6.0 million. The engineering department now estimates that it will cost a total (including past costs) of $8.1 million to complete its subsystem. The project was expected to take twenty-four weeks. It is now the twenty-second week. Engineering now predicts completion in ten more weeks.

REQUIRED:

a. What is the overrun percentage?

b. What is the value of the work left to be done in terms of the original cost budget?

c. How much more does the engineering department propose to spend to complete the task?

d. What is the predicted final overrun?

e. How far behind in weeks is the process now?

f. If engineering continued at its same rate, how many more weeks would you estimate until completion?

g. Comment on how realistic the engineering department's new predictions are?

20-33 **Cost Performance Reporting** What conclusions do you reach given the following project data?

Actual costs incurred to date	$80 thousand
Value of work performed	$60 thousand
Original budget time for work performed	12 weeks
Original cost budget today (week 10)	$50 thousand
Present estimated total costs at completion	$120 thousand
Present estimated total duration of project	16 weeks
Original estimated total budget at completion	$100 thousand
Original budget completion time	20 weeks

If they continued to work as they have to date, when would they finish and what would be the weeks-ahead figure?

20-34 **Cost Performance Reporting** The Jones Hangar Construction Company is building a new hangar for the Ithaca International Airport. The project's budget calls for a completion time of one year from its start on September 23, 19x6, and a cost of $9 million. (The budget is based on the assumption of a uniform expenditure and completion of work over the year.) As of May 23, 19x7, the company's industrial engineers estimate the budgeted value of the work completed to be $8 million although actual expenditures to date have reached $10 million.

Hap Hazard, the construction foreman, estimates he will be finished by July 23 and he estimates expenditures will run $2 million between now and then.

REQUIRED:

a. What is the overrun percentage 5/12/x7? What is the value of the work remaining to be done 5/23/x7?

b. How far behind schedule is the project now?

c. How much longer would you estimate the firm will take to complete the hangar if they continue to work as they have?

d. How much will they spend if they continue to work with the same efficiency as in the past?

e. What questions would you have for Mr. Hazard at this time, if any, concerning his estimates?

21

Using Cost Information in Making Decisions Under Uncertainty

LEARNING OBJECTIVES

After studying this chapter, you should be able to:

1 Describe how to include uncertainty in making decisions.

2 Understand why managers may make different decisions based on the same set of data.

3 Determine the expected value of perfect information.

4 Discuss the implications of utility analysis and risk aversion in making decisions.

5 Incorporate uncertainty into break-even analysis.

*B*ecause a primary role of the managerial accountant is to provide information to help managers make decisions, managerial accountants need to understand how decisions are made. The text has examined several types of decisions from the perspective of the accountant's role in providing information — primarily under the assumption of certainty. The consequences of alternative managerial actions were assumed to be known.

Yet real-world decisions are seldom made under certainty, and managers almost never can predict perfectly the outcomes of their decisions. This chapter examines the role of uncertainty in decision making. How can managers incorporate uncertainty into their decision analyses? How can managerial accountants provide information to help managers make their decisions?

Decisions Under Uncertainty

Despite the complexity of decision making under conditions of uncertainty, all decisions can be treated as having the following five common elements:

1. The possible *actions*. For example, in the context of an inventory-ordering problem, the possible actions would be the different possible order sizes.

2. The possible *states of nature* that may occur. For example, continuing the inventory example, the possible states of nature are that product demand will be $0, 1, 2, \ldots, n$.

3. The *probability of the states*. Each state is assigned a probability reflecting the likelihood of its occurrence.

4. The consequence or *outcome* for each action and state of nature. For example, if zero units are ordered, zero profits result for all possible demand levels, since there are no units to sell. If one unit is ordered and the amount demanded is one unit, profit equals the sale price minus the unit cost. If demand exceeds one, but only one unit is ordered, there will be less profit than could be attained with a different ordering policy.

5. The *payoff* for each consequence or outcome. The use of monetary measures may not be a sufficiently accurate reflection of the consequence of an action and a state of nature. The monetary outcome may need to be converted to a *preference* measure that reflects the *risk preferences* of the decision maker. Some decisions may not even involve monetary measures.

Example

The following example involving an inventory decision illustrates a general procedure for approaching a decision. The outcomes are indicated in the outcome table shown in Exhibit 21-1. In this case, the outcomes are profit levels, and the payoffs are the same as the outcomes. The outcome entries are conditional because they depend on the action that is taken and the state of nature that occurs. The accountant can play an important role in helping specify these outcomes. Initially, the consequences are assumed to be adequately reflected by units of money. Later this assumption will be relaxed. The state probabilities are indicated next to the states (the levels of demand). These probabilities must sum to 1; otherwise, some outcome has been incorrectly omitted or the probabilities have been incorrectly specified. A complete description of the reasonable actions that may be chosen by the decision maker is given across the top of the table (order is 0, 1, or 2 units). Down the side of the table are listed the possible states of nature that may occur (demand is 0, 1, or 2 units). In the body of the table are the outcomes (profits or costs or other values) for each action and state of nature. For example, if two units are ordered and one unit is demanded, the profit is $2.

Past experience and future expectations indicate that the demand for the product has the following probability distribution:

Demand	Probability of Demand
0	.50
1	.40
2	.10
Total	1.00

Any integer amount in the set [0, 1, 2] can be ordered, but no reorders may be placed in time to fill the demand. The purchase cost of a unit is $4, and the selling price is $10. If a unit is not sold during the period, it must be scrapped at a net value of zero. For each unit sold, there is profit of $10 − $4, or $6. For each unit purchased but unsold, there is a loss of $4. The outcome table of profit levels, conditional on action-state pairs, is given in Exhibit 21-1. The entries in the table are **conditional profit** or conditional costs since they depend on the decision and the state of nature.

EXHIBIT 21-1

Outcome Table

		Actions (Order Amounts)		
States of Nature (Demand Levels)	Probability	0	1	2
0	0.5	$0	− $4 - 2	− $8
1	0.4	0	6 2.40	2
2	0.1	0	6 .60	12
	Expected profit	$0	$1.00 1.14	− $2.00

EXHIBIT 21-2

Expected Value Calculation for Action: Order One Unit

State	(a) Probability		(b) Profit Resulting from Action "Order 1 Unit"		Column (a) × Column (b)
0	.50	×	− $4.00	=	− $2.00
1	.40	×	6.00	=	2.40
2	.10	×	6.00	=	.60
	1.00			Expected profit	$1.00

The bottom line of the outcome table is the **expected profit** (here the expected monetary value) of each action. The expected monetary value for each action is computed by multiplying the probability of each state by the outcome for the state, and then summing across states. For example, the expected monetary value for the action "order one unit" is calculated in Exhibit 21-2.

Comparison of the expected profits of each action suggests that the decision maker should order one unit because that action has the highest expected profit. Two units should not be ordered because the expected profit of that action is less than either ordering no units or ordering one unit. However, even if one unit is ordered (the optimal action), this can still result in a bad outcome if zero units are demanded (a .5 probability) or two units are demanded (a .10 probability). It is possible to have a good decision-making process, arrive at an optimal decision, and then after the actual outcome is determined, wish a different decision had been made. Good decisions ex ante can be followed by bad outcomes ex post.

The approach adopted here assumes it is reasonable to make a decision based on expected (average) profit. If the monetary amounts adequately reflect the consequences to the decision maker, this assumption has merit.

In most situations (which involve many states and action possibilities) the above approach to solving inventory problems would result in a great deal of arithmetic. Fortunately, there are more efficient techniques that can be used that bypass the need for payoff tables but that still yield optimal decisions.

The specialized technique that works in the current situation requires that:

1. The losses from misestimating the state be linear (that is, if the true state is demand equals 2, the loss of believing the state is demand equals 0 — $12 here — is twice the loss of believing the state is demand equals 1 — $6 here —), and

2. There is a unique best action choice for each state that has a positive probability.

The technique has three steps:

1. Compute the ratio of the cost of overestimating the state by one unit to the sum of this cost and the cost of underestimating the state by one unit;

2. Cumulate the state probabilities and find the largest state for which the cumulative probability exceeds the ratio calculated in step 2; and

3. The optimum choice is order an amount equal to this state.

For the current example, the procedure is illustrated below:

- C_u is the cost of underestimating the actual demand state by one unit,

- C_O is the cost of overestimating the actual demand state by one unit

Solution

1. C_u = $6 and increases linearly across states
C_O = $4 and increases linearly across states
Therefore $C_O/(C_O + C_u)$ = $4/($4 + $6) = .4

2.

State of Nature (Demand = d)	Cumulative Probability (Probability of Demand $\geq$ d)
0	1.0
1	.5
2	.1

A demand of 2 is the largest demand for which the cumulative probability exceeds the critical ratio of .4.

3. The best action choice is to order two units.

To better understand why $\dfrac{C_O}{C_O + C_u}$ defines the critical probability, let p be the critical probability that sales will be at least d. Then pC_u is the expected *profit* of the marginal unit ordered, and $(1 - p)C_O$ is the expected *cost* on average from ordering the marginal unit. We want pC_u to be equal to or larger than $(1 - p)C_O$ or

$$p \geq \frac{C_O}{C_O + C_u}$$

Thus the relationship $\dfrac{C_O}{C_O + C_u}$ is merely a shorthand method of equating the expected profits and expected costs.

A unit should be ordered as long as the probability of its sale is at least $\dfrac{C_O}{C_u + C_O}$. For the present example, C_U is the lost profit of $6, and C_O is the cost of a unit not sold or $4. The ratio is $4/($4 + $6) = .4. The probability of demand being one or more is .5 and two or more is only .1. Hence one unit should be ordered.

When there is time to do so, decision makers may elect to obtain additional information before selecting an action for important decisions. An upper limit on the value of such information is given by the value of perfect information, a quality of knowledge seldom attainable for actual problems, discussed later in this chapter.

Decision Trees

The previous section of this chapter used the decision criterion of expected monetary value and analyzed a decision using an outcome table and mathematical formulas. This section describes a general approach that is useful both for illustrating visually the decision problem and for finding a solution. The approach utilizes a decision tree.

To illustrate the basic ideas of the decision tree we will use the problem of the last section. Recall that the decision involves how many units to order. The decision point is represented by a square box or *decision node* in Exhibit 21-3. The alternatives are represented as *branches* emanating from the decision node.

Suppose the decision maker were to order two units. There are several possible events that can happen, each event representing a number of units that customers might demand. These are shown in Exhibit 21-4 as branches flowing from a round node. We are using the convention of a square box for a decision node and a circle for an event node. These branches represent uncertain events. However, probabilities are assigned to each event and are entered under each branch in parentheses. Because demand of three units has zero probability that branch can be eliminated.

At the end of each branch is the profit associated with the selected action and given event. The conditional profit thus represents the profit associated with the decisions and events along a specific path. For example, the $2 in Exhibit 21-4 is the profit associated with ordering two units and then experiencing a demand of one unit.

The **expected monetary value (EMV)** is calculated for each event node; that is, probabilities are multiplied by conditional profits and summed. The EMV is placed in the event node. Exhibit 21-5 shows the complete decision tree.

In Exhibit 21-5, the expected monetary values are shown in the event nodes. The decision maker must then choose which action to take, and this choice is to select the one with the highest EMV — namely, order one unit with EMV = $1. This is indicated in the tree by putting $1 in the decision node (square box) at the beginning of the tree. In addition, the mark ‖ is drawn across the nonoptimal decision branches, indicating that they are not to be followed.

EXHIBIT 21-3

Alternatives: A Decision Tree

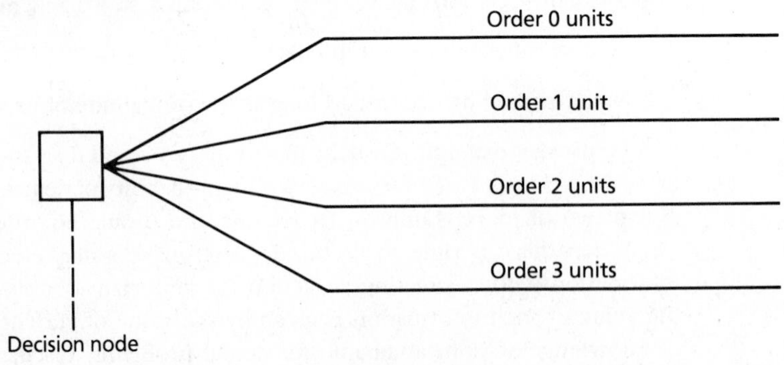

Order 0 units

Order 1 unit

Order 2 units

Order 3 units

Decision node

EXHIBIT 21-4

Events for Alternative "Order Two Units": A Decision Tree

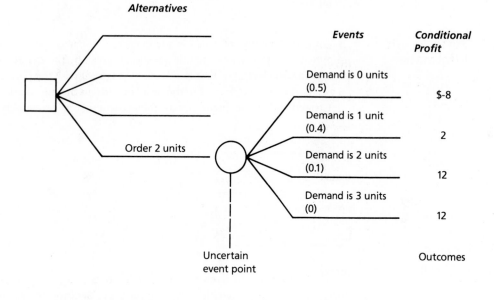

EXHIBIT 21-5

Complete Decision Tree

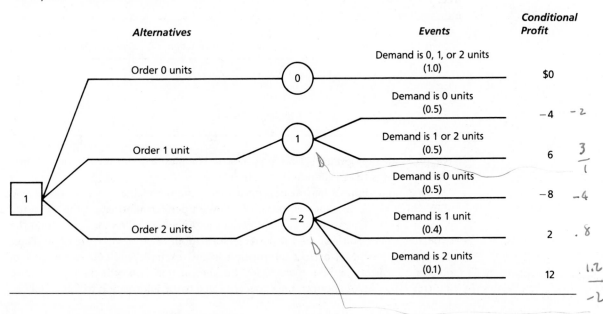

As the decision problem becomes more complex, the decision tree becomes more valuable in organizing the information needed to make the decision. This is especially true if the manager must make a sequence of decisions, rather than a single decision.

Perfect Information

Accountants supply information for decisions. What is the value of the information supplied? A partial answer to this question is given by the **expected value of perfect information (EVPI)** — that is, the expected profit with the perfect information compared to the expected profit of the best act without the information. This value can be illustrated using the inventory problem, where the probability distribution is as follows:

State (Demand)	Probability
0	.50
1	.40
2	.10

With **perfect information** we will find out what the outcome will be before we have to make the order decision. Suppose the decision maker knew the actual demand would be zero. The decision maker would order zero and make a profit of $0. If demand were known to be one, the decision maker would order one unit and make a profit of $6. For known demand of two, the decision maker would order two and make a profit of $12. The expected profit with perfect information would be:

State (Demand)	Probability	Profit with Optimal Action	Expected Profit
0	0.5	$ 0.00	$ 0
1	0.4	6.00	2.40
2	0.1	12.00	1.20
		Expected profit	$3.60

The profit for the optimal action in each state is multiplied by the state probability, which indicates the likelihood that state will occur.

Without additional information on demand, the optimal action is to order one unit, which yields an expected profit of $1. With perfect information the expected profit is $3.60. The expected value of perfect information is then the increase in the expected profit resulting from the perfect information: $3.60 − $1.00, or $2.60. Thus, the expected value of perfect information in this example is $2.60. If the cost of perfect information is less than $2.60, the information is worth buying. Because information is seldom perfect, the expected value of the information will generally be less than $2.60. Techniques exist for determining the expected value of imperfect information, but we do not explore them here. The expected value of perfect information provides an upper limit to the amount a manager would pay for imperfect information. Normally information is imperfect, and we have to make the decision without knowing which outcome will occur.

Imperfect Information

The expected value of perfect information sets an upper limit on the value of additional information in a decision situation. Most information is imperfect; it cannot help us predict with certainty which event will occur. Even so, imperfect information still has value if it improves the expected profit.

Taking a sample represents one method of obtaining information. This information is likely to be imperfect because the sample is not likely to represent exactly the population from which it is taken. There are ways of determining the reliability of samples and how sampling can add value by supplying imperfect information.

Unfortunately, the computation of the value of imperfect information requires insights beyond the appropriate scope of this book. A relevant reference is Bierman, Bonini, and Hausman (1986).

Utility Theory and Goal Congruence

The resolution of the inventory decision problem assumed that the proper decision could be made by selecting the action with the largest expected monetary value. However, suppose the payoffs for each outcome were a million times as large. Would the best decision still be to order one unit? Would the decision maker be willing to accept a .5 probability of a loss of $4 million? The decision rule used up to this point was to compute the expected monetary value of each action and choose the action with the largest expected monetary value. However, a decision maker may not wish to use the expected monetary value rule for all decisions. The monetary values in the outcome table may not adequately reflect the consequences of various action-state pairs. The consequences may be so large (positive or negative) that it is not sufficient to just take a weighted average of the possible dollar outcomes to reach a decision. An example would be an action and state combination leading to bankruptcy. In such cases, managers may find it useful to use utility theory. Utility theory transforms monetary outcomes to utility measures that reflect the decision makers' risk attitudes. If the utility of each possible outcome is multiplied by the probability of the outcome and added, we obtain the **expected utility.**

Managers have goals for their own careers and goals for the future of the segments of the firm they manage. A top manager has goals for the firm. If goals of the middle managers are consistent with the goals of the firm, the goals of the manager and of the firm are said to be *congruent.* Utility theory can help explain inconsistencies between the goals of top executives and lower-level managers. Second, utility theory provides an explanation of why some alternatives are attractive and other alternatives are not attractive to the same manager even though the latter alternatives appear to be attractive using monetary outcome measures.

The basic problem is that expected monetary values are not always reliable measures of the impact of the state-action outcomes when there is uncertainty. With certainty, $1,000,000 is to be preferred to $500,000. If uncertainty is added, the decision maker may *not* prefer an expected value of $1,000,000 to an expected value of $500,000. Consider a choice between the following two gambles:

Gamble A

Probability	Outcome	Expected Value
0.01	$100,000,000	$1,000,000
0.99	0	

Gamble B

Probability	Outcome	Expected Value
1	$500,000	$500,000

Would a manager choose gamble A with .99 probability of zero and .01 probability of $100,000,000, or gamble B with a certain outcome of $500,000? Most managers would choose B despite the fact that the expected monetary value of A is twice as large as that of B. However, the preference depends on the situation and perhaps the manager's wealth or budget. The easiest way of explaining the choice of B over A is to say the manager is risk averse and that the expected utility of B exceeds the expected utility of A. **Risk aversion** means the decision maker does not like risk. A risk averse person will pay less than a gamble's expected monetary value for the gamble.

A **utility function** takes money (or some other measure) and translates it into a new measure that reflects the value of the monetary outcomes to the manager. The use of utility functions enable managers to incorporate their risk attitudes into a decision analysis. Although the use of expected monetary value indicates a choice of gamble A, utility analysis offers an explanation of why gamble B may be chosen over gamble A.

Utility theory also helps explain why an intelligent, honest, and well-intentioned manager may act in a manner that is not considered to be consistent with the stated goals of the corporation. Thus, a manager of a division may select an investment project like gamble B over gamble A due to risk averseness, while a company president, with many divisions selecting similar projects, might prefer that all managers choose gamble A. The president may accept a gamble with low probability of a good outcome. A lower-level manager will generally prefer not to play than to accept an investment with .01 probability of success. Thus, it may not be reasonable to expect managers to use monetary expectations as the basis for decision making.

By investigating an individual's reactions to various decisions involving risk, a relationship can be obtained that enables utility numbers to be assigned to outcomes. Then the decision procedure uses the utilities and the probabilities of the different outcomes to compute the expected utility of each action. The action with the greatest expected utility is the optimal action. Almost all decisions are made under uncertainty, and many decisions involve large dollar amounts. Thus, there are many applications of utility analysis. The following decisions, which typically involve accountants, can make use of the concepts discussed in this section:

- Inventory control decisions,
- Cost-volume-profit decisions (including break-even analysis),
- Insurance decisions,
- Capital-investment decisions,
- Credit decisions,
- Marketable-security decisions,
- Use of alternative accounting procedures (such as LIFO versus FIFO).

The prime importance of the utility technique is not in its formal application in the above problems. Rather, its primary benefits may be as a general method for approaching a decision and as a means of explaining the reasons why a particular decision is reached. Two reasonable individuals may arrive at different decisions if they have different probability distributions associated with the possible states of nature. Alternatively, they may have different estimates of the losses associated with the events or different attitudes toward risk.

Because undesirable outcomes may follow correct decisions, it is important to judge the quality of the inputs into the decision-making process and the decision-making process itself rather than merely look at the resulting outcomes. It is also important to look at the results, but performance appraisal should reflect the uncertainties in risky decisions. If it is desirable that managers accept risk, then it is necessary for the evaluation of their performance to recognize the possibility that bad outcomes can follow good decisions. In the inventory problem described earlier, the decision maker who orders one unit, and has a loss of $4 when no units are demanded, made a better decision than a manager who would have ordered no units in the same situation. A result of this approach to performance evaluation is that it reduces top management's ability to reach definite conclusions relative to the performance of their subordinates. Performance evaluation is an extremely difficult process in a world of uncertainty.

Utility and Risk Attitudes

Assume that a manager is offered the choice between the following two alternatives (or gambles). Call them *A* and *B*.

Alternative A	Alternative B
.5 probability of $1,000 .5 probability of $0	1.0 probability of $X

For the manager to be indifferent between alternatives *A* and *B*, what value of *X* should be inserted in the description of alternative *B*? The expected monetary value of the gamble is .5($1,000) + .5($0), or $500. If the value of *X* is less than $500, the manager is averse to gambling, or risk averse, in this situation. Most managers are risk averse if the amounts are sufficiently large. A manager averse to gambling will be indifferent between a gamble and a certain value that is less than the gamble's monetary expectation. If the value of *X* is more than $500, the manager requires something in return for foresaking the opportunity of winning $1,000, and the manager is considered to be risk seeking. If the manager is indifferent between alternative *A* and $500 certain, the manager's *utility function is linear* in this range of values. Then the manager is said to be risk neutral. In this case, the expected monetary value may be used as the utility.

A utility function displaying risk aversion is shown in Exhibit 21-6. The horizontal axis in Exhibit 21-6 measures the monetary value, and the vertical axis measures the utility of the monetary value. The utility function shows the utility of different possible monetary values.

Consider again alternative *A*, which has a .5 probability of $0 and a .5 probability of $1,000. Assume that the utility of these uncertain payoffs can be read from the utility function in Exhibit 21-6 and the utility of $0 is 0 and the utility of $1,000 is 1.00. The expected utility is .5, .5(0) + .5(1.0), in this case. The next step is to determine the certainty equivalent of the gamble. A **certainty equivalent** is the sum of money that an investor will accept and be indifferent to participating in the gamble. The certainty equivalent is $300 because the utility of $300 is .5. The certainty equivalent can be obtained from the graph by finding the monetary value on the

EXHIBIT 21-6

Utility Function

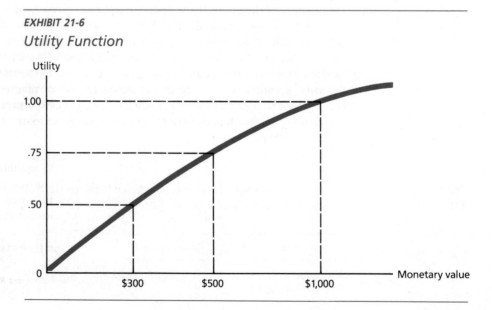

horizontal axis that has a utility of .5. The expected monetary value of alternative *A* is $500, .5($1,000) + .5($0). The gamble's certainty equivalent is $200 less than its expected monetary value. Thus, the manager attaches a $200 discount for risk to alternative *A*.

The discount for risk arises because the monetary values of $1,000 and $0 do not adequately represent the impact of these values on the manager. If they did, there would be no risk discount, and the utility function would be a straight line. Thus, if the utility function were linear, the expected monetary value of alternative *A* would have a certainty equivalent of $500 with a utility of 75. Uncertainty alone, then, is not sufficient to produce a discount for risk. There must also be an aversion to risk. The information could be presented as follows:

Expected monetary value of alternative	$500
Certainty equivalent	300
Discount for risk	$200

Appraisal of Utility Theory

The utility-theory approach described in this chapter has several weaknesses. First, it assumes that the same utility function is relevant for a series of decisions. This weakness can be corrected conceptually by changing the utility function as decisions are made. However, carrying this out operationally in a meaningful manner is likely to be quite difficult. Second, a corporation includes many individuals; the utility theory applies to an individual.

Making decisions on the basis of monetary expectations is reasonable if the dollar amounts involved are small. The underlying assumption is that the utility function is linear with respect to money when the dollar amounts are small. However, if the amounts are large in relation to the magnitude of operations of the entity making the decision, then considering factors (such as utility) beyond the expected profit is more appropriate for making decisions than only using expected monetary value. This can also be true if other factors surrounding an investment are important and not measurable in terms of marginal adjustments in the cash flows. No organization has a linear utility function over all possible outcomes. Thus, the theories presented in this chapter have relevance for all organizations. A decision analysis is incomplete unless it incorporates the impact of the outcomes on the firm.

An individual's aversion to risk seems to be related to amounts that are large in comparison to the size of expenditure that can be authorized rather than to the financial position of the firm.[1] This can induce conservative behavior that the firm would like to prevent. Perhaps one reason for this behavior lies in corporate control procedures that tend to be unduly hard on failures. The accountant should be aware of the behavioral effects of cost control techniques on the type of decisions made by

1. R. O. Swalm, "Utility Theory-Insights into Risk Taking," *Harvard Business Review* (November–December 1966): 123–35.

managers. Control techniques should be designed to motivate the behavioral pattern desired by the organization.

Decision Making Under Uncertainty: An Illustration

An illustration of a decision under uncertainty is provided by the following description of a decision faced by the Environmental Protection Agency.[2]

Environmental Protection Agency: Emergency Pesticide Exemptions

The Environmental Protection Agency (EPA) was set up with the goal of preventing significant deterioration of the environment, particularly with reference to man's industrial interference with it. Great attention had been directed by the agency toward pesticides, especially DDT, and the potential harm, often subtle, that they caused to flora and fauna. Not only may the indiscriminate use of pesticides affect the natural environment, but dairy cattle, human drinking water, and food are occasionally affected. The EPA is responsible for registering pesticides and only registered pesticides may be used. In some cases a pesticide may be registered for some types of applications but not for others. The EPA may also deregister previously registered pesticides.

Section 18 of the Federal Insecticide, Fungicide and Rodenticide Act, as amended by the Federal Pesticide Control Act had given the EPA the authority to permit Federal and State Agencies to use unregistered pesticides in emergency situations subject to case-by-case approval.

Exemptions can only be granted if the following three criteria are all met:

1. A pest outbreak has or is about to occur and no pesticide registered for the particular use, or alternative control method, is available to eradicate or control the pest.

2. Significant economic or health problems will occur without the use of the pesticide.

3. The time available from discovery or prediction of the pest outbreak is insufficient for a pesticide to be registered for the particular use.

2. Copyright © 1979 by the President and Fellows of Harvard College. This case was prepared by David E. Bell as the basis for classroom discussion rather than to illustrate either effective or ineffective handling of an administrative situation. Reprinted by permission of the Harvard Business School.

There are three categories of exemption requests. *Specific* exemption requests are those involving pests endemic to the United States. *Quarantine* exemption requests are those for pests foreign to the United States; a decision on these requests could take anywhere from a week to three months. A *crisis* exemption request involves a pest outbreak that was unpredictable and an immediate health or economic hazard, so that there is no time for filing for one of the other two exemptions. A crisis request is usually filed *after* application of the pesticide.

Graham Beilby[3] was in charge of all emergency exemption requests. The EPA rules and regulations largely dictated many mechanical aspects of handling requests. The requestor was required to submit a large amount of data supporting the claim as well as describing the expected detrimental effects of using the requested pesticide. While the EPA did not normally have enough time to collect its own data on a given situation, it was usually evident whether the claims of the requestor were basically true. Inflated claims were sufficient grounds for dismissal of the request. In any case, requestors would not wish to damage their credibility with the EPA for possible future requests.

Requests for crisis exemptions were often discussed on the telephone by Beilby and the head of the requesting agency involved before the official application was filed and before the pesticide was applied. This was because the requestor faced stiff legal penalties if a crisis exemption was not ultimately approved. Therefore, the discussion revolved around reaching an understanding as to what would or would not likely receive approval.

Beilby was concerned that this informal case-by-case evaluation was inadequate in the face of a growing volume of emergency exemption requests. Seven requests had been received in the first two years after the Pesticide Control Act, but thirty-six had been received by three years later, and even more seemed likely the following year. (Of these thirty-six requests, twelve were granted, fourteen were denied, two were crisis requests, seven were later withdrawn, and one was still pending.)

Three years after passage of the Pesticide Control Act, Graham Beilby received an application for a specific exemption request from the U.S. Forest Service to permit the use of DDT on its forests in the Pacific Northwest. The Tussock Moth, endemic to the region, was responsible for periodically defoliating Douglas fir trees. Until 1968 the U.S. Forest Service had used DDT to control the moth but then voluntarily discontinued its use. When they again wished to use DDT, by then deregistered, their request was denied by the EPA. This request, which projected losses of $13 million, was denied based on the belief that the nuclear polyhedrosis virus would cause a natural collapse of the moth. The moth, which did not collapse, instead became blamed for $77 million in losses.

Beilby was well aware of the difference between a bad decision and a bad outcome, but this event could not have helped EPA's credibility, which was already suffering from the outcome of an earlier exemption decision. In that case, a state had

3. This name and some dates have been altered by the author of the Harvard Business School case. The subjective opinions and probabilities expressed in this case are for illustration only. They do not necessarily reflect the opinion of any EPA staff member.

requested an exemption to use DDT, the EPA had granted the request, but the pest had disappeared naturally before doing any serious damage. Fortunately the pesticide had not been applied, but Beilby felt that this incident had undermined not only his own credibility but the image of the EPA in general. Both the U.S. Congress and the general public kept a watchful eye on EPA decisions. Certain exemption requests were politically explosive.

With this background in mind, Beilby looked over the current request. The Forest Service wished to use 490,000 pounds of DDT on 650,000 acres, which included parts of Washington, Oregon, and Idaho. Two-thirds of the land was federally owned, one-sixth was state land, and one-sixth was the Colville Indian Reservation. Forestry on the Indian land accounted for 40 to 50 percent of employment and 95 percent of the total income to the tribe. Their forests had been particularly hard hit by recent defoliation. Repeated defoliation leads to tree death, which is not only an economic loss but also substantially increases the chance of forest fires. This would be a severe hazard to the Colville Reservation.

The request was made conditional upon tests of egg mass samples to be taken after the next egg hatch. The tests would show whether the larval population was being controlled naturally by the nuclear polyhedrosis virus. If this natural control was not occurring and if the request for DDT was denied, the Forest Service projected economic losses of $67 million.

Even though the projected losses were high, Beilby was not comfortable with the thought of approving the request. But if he chose to deny the request, he would have to have his reasoning pretty explicit and defendable. It occurred to him that a study completed recently for the EPA by a well-known Cambridge consulting firm should be useful for his current decision. After rereading their report he drew the diagram shown in Exhibit 21-7. Because the request would be withdrawn by the Forest

---

EXHIBIT 21-7

Actions, Outcomes, and Probabilities

Actions		Outcomes and Probabilities
	.50	Outbreak collapses.
Deny	.40	Outbreak continues as predicted.
	.10	Outbreak is much worse than predicted (explodes).
	.75	Outbreak collapses.
Grant	.20	Outbreak continues as predicted.
	.05	Outbreak is much worse than predicted (explodes).

Service if the egg test proved favorable, the probabilities he estimated presupposed that the egg tests were unfavorable.

Beilby estimated economic losses in the best case (Outbreak collapses) at $3 million and in the worst case (Outbreak explodes) at $90 million. With these figures and the subjective probabilities that he had assessed he calculated expected losses of approximately $20.15 million for "grant" versus $37.3 million for "deny."

Break-Even Analysis Under Uncertainty

Techniques exist for incorporating uncertainty about the future level of product demand directly into break-even analysis. Assume two different break-even charts as shown in Exhibit 21-8. The slope of the line gives the contribution margin per unit. Situation *b* may be interpreted to be the same as situation *a* except that the profit line results from a higher price (or alternatively a lower variable cost). Assume *b* results from a higher price. Is the higher price in situation *b* more desirable than the price in situation *a*? The break-even point is lower, but this is the inevitable result of a higher contribution margin that accompanies a higher price. However, the graphs tell us nothing about the likelihood of occurrence of the different possible profit levels following either pricing policy. The change in the break-even point cannot be used as the criterion in making the pricing decision.

A more reasonable decision-making process first estimates the demand probability distribution for each pricing policy. This probability distribution gives the likeli-

EXHIBIT 21-8

Break-Even Charts at Two Different Prices for the Same Product

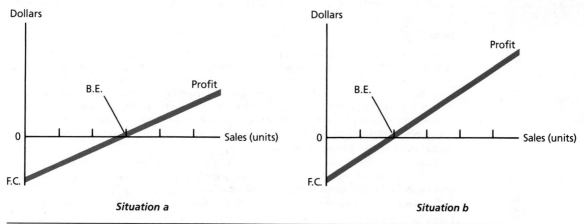

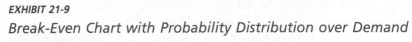

EXHIBIT 21-9

Break-Even Chart with Probability Distribution over Demand

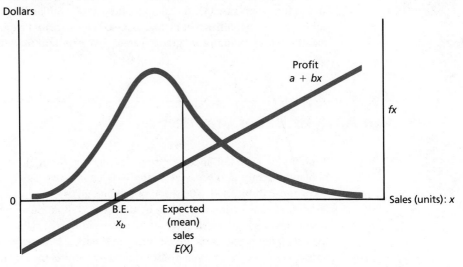

hood of selling different amounts of product as estimated by the firm.[4] See Exhibit 21-9, where such a function is superimposed on a break-even chart. The left vertical axis still records dollars while the right-hand vertical axis gives the probability of sales at that point.[5] The probability distribution is assumed for now to be continuous and unimodal (has one peak), but it is not assumed to be normal or even symmetrical.[6]

The continuous probability (density) function for demand (and thus, in this example, sales) shows the relative likelihood of each level of sales. The total area under the curve is equal to 1, and the area under the curve over any sales interval is equal to the probability that sales will be in that interval. Such a curve could be

---

4. In this section the probability distribution of the number of units sold is assumed to be the same as the number of units demanded. The possibility of the firm's being unable to fill an order because demand is in excess of the number of units on hand, with the result that the customer buys elsewhere, could be allowed, but the solution to this problem then becomes more complex because it combines pricing, production, and inventory decisions. The separation of pricing, production, and inventory decisions is unrealistic, but it is helpful in understanding one segment of the decision. Although optimizing part of the firm's problem is not the ideal solution, it is frequently an important feasible solution.

5. When the probability distribution is continuous, as it is here, the vertical axis gives the probability density. The text statement holds only for a probability mass function, which gives the probability for discrete values of the variable on the horizontal axis.

6. *Normality* refers to a particular probability density function. It will be explained more completely in a later chapter.

developed from historical data, although it might be substantially modified for circumstances management believes now exist, which are not adequately reflected by the historical data.

If the choice is made to produce, the profit (Y), for a given price policy, is $Y = a + bX$. Here a is the negative of the total fixed cost, b is the contribution margin, and X is the number of units sold. The expected profit is given by:[7]

$$E(Y) = a + bE(X)$$

The term a is equal to or less than zero and, where negative, measures the fixed cost. If management chooses not to produce, the return is a loss of a. Management computes the expected profit associated with the decision "produce." Management takes this action if the expected profit, $E(Y)$, is positive and sufficiently large to justify the associated risk.[8] The analysis presumes that the fixed cost represents opportunity costs that will be incurred even if the production facility is not used. Facilities that have zero opportunity costs have zero fixed costs, and their costs should be excluded in these computations.

The above analysis can be avoided and a decision made on the basis of the expected state value (such as expected demand) whenever the outcome functions for the actions are linear functions. For example, suppose that the payoffs for two different production alternatives involving linear payoffs, where X stands for sales, are given. Suppose further that the variable costs (b_1) of process I are larger, and the fixed costs (a_1) are smaller, than their process II counterparts. This assures that the two profit lines cross if plotted on one graph. (In this example, the outcome function for action 1 crosses that for action 2 from below, as X increases.)

Action	Outcome Function	
Produce using process I	$a_1 + b_1X$	$a_1 < a_2 \leq 0$
Produce using process II	$a_2 + b_2X$	$b_1 > b_2 \geq 0$

Assume, further, that the actual value of sales, X, is independent of the production process. The sales level where the payoffs are equal, X_b, is found by setting the two

---

7. Equivalently, the expected profit is equal to the product of the income at each level of sales and the probability density of that level of sales, integrated over all sales levels. That is, expected profit is given by

$$E(Y) = \int_0^\infty (a + bX)f(X)dX$$

where $f(X)$ is the probability density function of demand. Sometimes the evaluation of the integral given by this expression becomes rather complex, and it is therefore useful to know that the decision can be made on the basis of the expected level of sales when the payoff (profit) function is linear.

8. The assumption is implicitly made that the monetary values represent relevant measures of the impact of the outcomes on the manager. The decision maker's utility for money is linear.

equations equal to each other and solving for X_b. This yields

$$X_b = \frac{a_2 - a_1}{b_1 - b_2}$$

Process I is more desirable than process II if $E(X)$ is larger than X_b. Thus process I is more desirable if

$$E(X) > \frac{a_2 - a_1}{b_1 - b_2} = X_b$$

This equation indicates that if expected sales are greater than the break-even level, X_b, the expected payoff from process I exceeds that from process II. Process II is more desirable if the expected value of X is below X_b. This result is independent of the shape of the probability distribution of sales. It depends only on the value of expected sales, $E(X)$.

The expected level (mean) of future sales may not always be easy for management to estimate. The modal value of sales is the most likely level, and the median value is that level of sales for which the probabilities are equal that it will or will not be exceeded. These two values are perhaps relatively easy to visualize and discuss with the manager. Mean sales has no such simple interpretation or visualization. Furthermore, for skewed distributions such as the one in Exhibit 21-9, the mean tends to be slightly larger than the median. If median sales exceed the break-even level in this case, a preference for process I is still appropriate because the mean exceeds the median. But if median sales are less than but close to the indifference level, the better decision may not be clear. With moderately skewed distributions, as a general rule of thumb, the median falls about two-thirds of the distance from the mode toward the mean. Using this general relationship, the mean can be estimated for moderately skewed distributions by the following formula:

$$E(X) = \text{Mode} + \frac{3}{2}(\text{Median} - \text{Mode})$$

The manager first estimates the mode and median. If the probability distribution is assumed to be symmetrical, the mean, median, and mode are identical, and the decision process is again simplified.

Turning now to the choice between the two prices whose profit functions are graphed in Exhibit 21-10, preference is established by examining the expected profits because both payoff functions are linear. However, a different probability function applies to each price decision because price influences the amount sold. The distributions for the example are illustrated in Exhibit 21-10 and assume that a lower price (situation a) increases the likelihood of larger sales levels. In this situation, both distributions are assumed to have different means and variances. A preference results by selecting the price that yields the larger expected profit:

$$E(Y) = a + bE(X)$$

EXHIBIT 21-10

Break-Even Charts for Two Different Prices for the Same Product and Different Demand Distributions

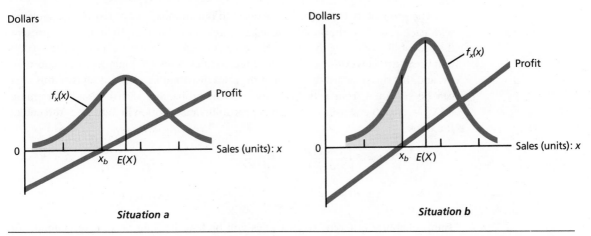

Situation a   Situation b

Equivalently, the expression for the expected profit given by the following equation can be used.[9]

$$\text{Expected profit} = E(Y) = b[E(X) - X_b]$$

Here b is the slope of the profit function (the contribution margin per unit), $E(X)$ is expected sales, and X_b is the break-even sales volume in units. The expected profit associated with any price is given by the product of the contribution margin with the amount by which expected sales exceed the break-even sales volume. Consider an example.

Assume that the contribution margin per unit is $2 with a price of $10 and $2.50 with a price of $10.50, fixed costs are $100,000, and expected sales are 60,000 units in case a and 46,000 units in case b. Then the break-even sales level (X_b) is 50,000 with a price of $10.00 and 40,000 with a price of $10.50. The expected profit is: $E(Y) = 2(60,000 - 50,000) = \$20,000$ in case a and $E(Y) = 2.50(46,000 - 40,000) = \$15,000$ with a price of $10.50. The lower price and contribution margin appears to be preferred. However, if the variance of sales with the $10 price is larger, this implies there may be more risk associated with this choice. If $E(X) < X_b$, the value of the expected profit would be negative. That is, an expected loss would be indicated.

In most practical problems, there are other uncertainties in addition to the level of sales. There will be uncertainty concerning the various costs to be experienced

9. If $Y = a + bX$, then $E(Y) = a + bE(X)$. At the break-even point, $Y = 0$, $a = -bX_b$. Therefore, $E(Y) = -bX_b + bE(X) = b[E(X) - X_b]$.

(even when suitable cost measures can be established), the performance of the employees, and the lives of the equipment. The levels of fixed costs and variable costs are also uncertain. Introduction of these complexities is beyond the scope of this text.[10]

The probability functions can be used to obtain measures of riskiness associated with each price distribution.[11] The shaded areas in Exhibit 21-10, *a* and *b*, represent the probability of failing to achieve the break-even level of sales. Consider the 50,000 unit break-even level for case *a* with expected sales of 60,000 units. Assuming normality, and that the standard deviation of the sales distribution, $\sigma(X)$, is known, this area can be obtained from a table of the normal probability distribution.[12] Assuming $\sigma(X) = 10,000$ and using the normal probability distribution in Table *E* at the end of the book:

$$P(X < X_b) = P\left(\frac{X - E(X)}{\sigma(X)} < \frac{X_b - E(X)}{\sigma(X)}\right)$$

$$= P\left(z < \frac{50,000 - 60,000}{10,000}\right) = P(z < -1) = 0.1587$$

The probability is about .16 that sales will be less than the break-even amount for situation *a*.

The choice between alternatives might be based on the size of these probabilities where expectations were considered inadequate. It is not clear, however, just how much of a difference in these probabilities is needed to compensate for a larger expectation. It is a matter of judgment, and most managers experience some difficulty in making a decision using this information.

Summary

The use of expected monetary values with no other factors considered is not likely to be appropriate except for alternatives involving relatively small resource commitments. One solution is to evaluate alternatives using utility analysis. Even when all of the results occur in a single time period, the application of utility analysis is difficult because of the need to derive the required utility function. The analysis becomes more complex when the consequences are spread through time and risk is not uniformly resolved over time, or where more than one person is involved. Nevertheless, utility analysis offers insights into the making of decisions under uncertainty

10. The interested reader is referred to R. Jaedicke and A. Robichek, "Cost-Volume-Profit Analysis Under Conditions of Uncertainty," *Accounting Review* (October 1964): 917–26. Also see R. Kaplan, *Advanced Management Accounting* (New York: Prentice-Hall, 1982, esp. 192–95.

11. The analysis assumes that the utility function is linear in money and that decisions can therefore be made using expected monetary values.

12. If $E(X)$ and $\sigma(X)$ are known or can be estimated and are finite, this probability can be estimated using Tchebychev's inequality for cases where the probability density function is not normal.

when the monetary values do not adequately capture the consequences of the outcomes to the decision maker.

These concepts appear useful in making rational decisions but are not widely used in practice. One explanation for this is that a substantial amount of information can be obtained from the simpler computations. However, the need for incorporating risk considerations into the analysis for major choices still exists. It is necessary to know how the firm will fare under a wide range of circumstances and, if an investment is undertaken, how the investment's performance is tied to the performance of other firm investments, both already undertaken and currently being considered.

Accountants supply information for decisions and for measuring performance. It is important that accountants realize that decision makers want more information than simply the most likely outcome. The conditional profit levels under different decisions and different states of nature are also required for good decision making. Although the expected monetary value is an appropriate point of departure for decisions, the manager might not be willing to base the decision only on that information.

Review Problem

UTILITY THEORY AND DECISION MAKING

Mr. Jones has the following utility function for money:

Change in Net-Asset Position

Dollars	Utility Measures
$-3,000	-3,000
-1,000	-1,150
-600	-500
-500	-350
0	0
100	100
500	150
1,000	200
2,000	350
4,000	500
9,000	680
10,000	700

Assume there is an investment that has a .5 probability of gaining $10,000 and .5 probability of losing $3,000. The expected monetary value is

Outcome	Probability	Expected Value
$10,000	.5	$5,000
-3,000	.5	-1,500
	EMV =	$3,500

Mr. Jones can either accept or pay an amount to avoid the investment.

a. What is the expected utility measure of the investment?

b. What is the amount Mr. Jones would be willing to accept for certain (or to pay out) to cause him to be indifferent to the two choices?

c. What is the certainty equivalent of the investment?

d. What is the expected monetary value of the gamble?

e. What is the discount for risk?

f. Would you describe Mr. Jones as being financially conservative?

g. Would you accept the investment with .5 probability of losing $3,000?

Solution to Review Problem

a.

Probability	Outcome	Utility	E(Utility)
.5	$10,000	700	350
.5	−3,000	−3,000	−1,500
		E(U) =	−1,150

b. Mr. Jones would be willing to pay $1,000 to avoid this investment.

c. A negative $1,000 since $−1,000 equates to a utility of −1,150.

d. EMV = .5($10,000) + .5($−3,000) $3,500.

e. The risk discount is $4,500.

f. He is risk averse.

g. Most of us would say no to the investment because of the large probability of a large loss. Some would say yes because it is a fair gamble (a positive EMV).

Key Terms to Review

Suggested Readings

Bierman, H., and S. Smidt. *The Capital Budgeting Decision.* New York: Macmillan, 1988.

Bierman, H., C. P. Bonini, and W. H. Hausman. *Quantitative Analysis for Business Decisions.* Homewood, Ill.: Irwin, 1986.

Brealey, R., and S. Myers. *Principles of Corporate Finance.* New York: McGraw-Hill, 1984.

Demski, J. *Information Analysis.* Reading, Mass.: Addison-Wesley, 1980.

Dyckman, T. R., and L. J. Thomas. *Fundamental Statistics for Business and Economics.* Englewood Cliffs, N.J.: Prentice-Hall, 1977.

Hartman, B. "The Management Accountant's Role in Deleting a Product Line." *Management Accounting* (August 1983): 63–66.

Hertz, D. "Investment Policies That Pay Off." *Harvard Business Review* (January–February 1968): 96–108.

Hilton, R. "The Determinants of Cost Information Value: An Illustrative Analysis." *Journal of Accounting Research* (Autumn 1979).

Hilton, R. "The Determinants of Information Value." *Management Science,* 1981.

Kaplan, Robert S. *Advanced Managerial Accounting.* Englewood Cliffs, N.J.: Prentice-Hall, 1982, chap. 3.

———. "Application of Quantitative Models in Managerial Accounting: A State of the Art Survey." In Management Accounting — State of the Art, Beyer Lecture Series. Madison: University of Wisconsin, 1977; reprinted in *Accounting Journal* (Winter 1977–78): 218–42.

Magee, R. *Advanced Managerial Accounting.* New York: Harper & Row, 1986.

Raiffa, H. *Introductory Lectures on Choices Under Uncertainty.* Reading, Mass.: Addison-Wesley, 1968.

von Neumann, J., and O. Morgenstern. *Theory of Games and Economic Behavior,* 1947.

APPENDIX
Economic Incentives and Managerial Accounting

This appendix considers the problem of providing the proper incentives to an economic agent to whom some decision-making authority has been delegated.[13] In its simplest form, the problem can be formulated in terms of two parties: a principal and an agent. The principal delegates some decision-making authority to the agent. The principal's problem is to design an incentive system such that when the agent makes a decision that the agent considers to be in his own best interest, the decision will be made by the agent in such a way as to optimize from the perspective of the principal. The agent's decision is made under uncertainty.

There are many interpretations that can be applied to the parties designated as principal and agent. They may be viewed, respectively, as a firm's ownership and management, a top-level manager and a divisional manager, a firm and an auditor, an insurer and an insured, and so forth. As with any economic analysis, the principal-agent problem is only a highly simplified model of reality. Many issues that are important determinants of managerial behavior and the construction of incentives are necessarily left out of the model. The complexity of these issues is too great to handle in any tractable way given the current state of our knowledge and available mathematical tools. Consequently, the conclusions of these analyses must be taken as tentative. Yet the issues addressed are so important that it is worthwhile to consider them even in their simplistic form. At the very least, an examination of the models should lead one to think carefully about the issues that are being addressed and their importance for managerial accounting. Moreover, in thinking about these issues, we should bear in mind two objectives of the inquiry. The first is to prescribe certain features of incentive systems. The second is to understand why we observe the incentive structures we do.

Review of Terms

Before proceeding further, it will be useful to review some terms.

Risk Aversion   A person is *risk averse* if the person's certainty equivalent for a gamble is less than the gamble's expected monetary value. The utility function (for money) given by $u(x) = x^{1/2}$ exhibits risk aversion. Suppose the person with this

---

13. This appendix draws heavily on the following sources: S. Ross, "The Economic Theory of Agency: The Principal's Problem," *American Economic Review* (May 1973): 134–39; J. Demski, "Uncertainty and Evaluation Based on Controllable Performance," *Journal of Accounting Research* (Autumn 1976): 230–45; B. Holmstrom, "Moral Hazard and Observability," *Bell Journal of Economics* (Spring 1979): 74–91; S. Baiman and J. Demski, "Economically Optimal Performance Evaluation and Control Systems," *Journal of Accounting Research* (Supplement 1980): 184–220.

utility function faces a 50-50 gamble of receiving either $49 or $100. The expected utility of the gamble is $(.5)(49)^{1/2} + (.5)(100)^{1/2}$, or 8.5. The *certainty equivalent* for the gamble is the certain payment for which the person would be indifferent between receiving the certain amount and facing the gamble. The certainty equivalent is $72.25, since $(72.25)^{1/2} = 8.5$. This is less than the *expected monetary value* of the gamble, $(.5)($49) + (.5)($100)$, or $74.50. Utility functions exhibiting risk aversion are concave as shown in Exhibit 21-11.

Risk Sharing *Risk sharing* implies that two or more parties share in the risky outcome from a gamble. Insurance is a common example of risk sharing in which the insured parties pool their risk of accidents, illness, fire, or death through premium payments and the settlement of claims.

Risk averse parties can always be made better off by sharing the risks they face. Consider the utility function in Exhibit 21-11. Suppose person A and person B each face the gamble of a 50-50 chance of receiving $49 or $100, and each has the utility function $u(x) = x^{1/2}$. Without risk sharing, each person has an expected utility of 8.5. Now suppose A and B pool their risk by agreeing to split equally the combined outcome of their gambles. There are three possible outcomes for the *combined gamble* faced by the two individuals.

Outcomes for A x(A)	Outcomes for B x(B)	Joint Outcomes x(A) + x(B)	Probability
49	49	98	.25
49	100	149 ⎫	
100	49	149 ⎬	.50
100	100	200	.25

Each individual now faces the following gamble:

Outcome	Probability
98/2 = 49	.25
149/2 = 74.50	.50
200/2 = 100	.25

The expected utility of each person is now $(.25)(49)^{1/2} + (.5)(74.50)^{1/2} + (.25)(100)^{1/2}$, or 8.56. This exceeds the expected utility of each person with no risk sharing, namely 8.50.

Pareto Optimality A *Pareto optimal solution* to a problem that affects several individuals is one where any *deviation* from the solution that makes one person

EXHIBIT 21-11

Utility Function Exhibiting Risk Aversion

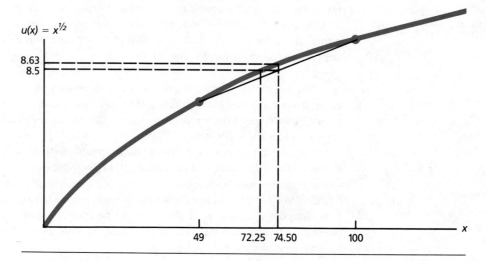

better off, would necessarily make at least one other person worse off. In discussing the optimality of incentive contracts, which by definition affect more than one person, Pareto optimality seems to be a reasonable requirement to impose on any solution. Any non-Pareto optimal contract could be improved on in a way that would make both parties better off.

First-Best and Second-Best Problems   Consider the following optimization problem:

Optimize: Objective function by choosing certain decision variables
Subject to: Constraints on decision variables

The optimized value of the objective function can never be improved by adding additional constraints, holding everything else constant. Let the following problem be called the *first-best problem:*

(I)   Optimize: Objective function
       Subject to: Constraint *A*

Then the following is a *second-best problem:*

(II) Optimize: Objective function
     Subject to: Constraint A and constraint B

Because the optimized value of the objective function in problem II can never be preferred to that in problem I, the second problem is second-best relative to problem I.

The Principal's Problem

Now we are ready to state the principal's problem. Both the principal and the agent are assumed here to be risk averse. The agent chooses some action. There is uncertainty in the agent's decision problem, and this is represented by an uncertain state of nature. The payoff to the firm — when the agent selects a particular action and a particular random state occurs — is a function of both the action and the state. The principal's problem is to select a contract that specifies the amount to be paid to the agent. The contract must be based on variables that are observable to both parties. The payoff is always observable to both parties. If the agent's action and the state of nature are observable, then the contract could be based on the outcome, the action, and the state. Given this contract, the agent could maximize his expected utility.

The agent presumably has other opportunities and can calculate his expected utility in the next best opportunity in the managerial labor market. Then the principal must choose a contract such that the agent has an expected utility of at least that level. Thus, the principal faces the following constraint in selecting the contract:

Agent's expected utility $\geq$ Expected utility available in next best employment opportunity

The principal will now want to maximize his own expected utility subject to the constraint given above.

The principal chooses a contract to maximize his expected utility. The problem specified here is not particularly interesting, however, because of the assumption that the agent's action is observable to the principal. In this case, the principal can also maximize his expected utility with respect to the agent's action and use a *forcing contract* to force the agent to take the desired action. Thus, the principal would specify a contract in which the agent receives nothing unless he chooses the action desired by the principal. The agent has no choice but to optimize by choosing the action desired by the principal. The only remaining problem for the principal is to choose a contract so as to optimally share the risk associated with the uncertain outcome. This is known as the first-best or *pure risk-sharing problem*. It is a pure risk-sharing problem because there is no difficulty in providing the proper incentives to the agent. It is easy to do so through the forcing contract.[14]

---

14. Actually, when both the action and state are jointly observable, the optimal contract will not be based on the action. We can ignore this technical point at this juncture.

The critical feature here is that the agent's action is observable by the principal. A more realistic scenario, descriptive of reality in decentralized organizations, is that the principal cannot observe the agent's action or the state of nature. The payoff is the only jointly observable variable; consequently the contract must be based on the payoff. Now the principal, in choosing the best contract, must take into account the fact that, given the contract, the agent will choose the action that maximizes the agent's expected utility.

As a result, the principal must solve what is known as the second-best problem. The objective function in the principal's problem is to maximize the principal's expected utility. The first constraint states that the agent's expected utility must be at least equal to that in the agent's next best opportunity. That is, the principal must "meet the market." The second constraint states that the principal must take account of the fact that the agent will maximize the agent's own self-interest given a particular contract. It is the "second-best problem" relative to the case where the principal can observe the agent's action, in that this second constraint has been added.

In this problem, the principal no longer faces a problem in pure risk sharing. The contract must now serve two purposes: (1) risk sharing and (2) provision of incentives to the agent to act in the principal's best interest. Thus, there is a trade-off in finding the best contract.

Two points may be made about this model. First, one of the main attributes of the formulation is the notion that there is a benefit to the principal and agent from sharing the risk associated with the outcome. This risk, of course, is the result of the uncertainty in the model. By sharing this risk, the manager is being evaluated (compensated) partially on the basis of factors beyond his control. This is contrary to one of the fundamental tenets of managerial accounting — that managers should be evaluated on the basis of controllable performance.

Second, there is a special case where the incentive problem mentioned above disappears, even when the agent's action is unobservable. This situation occurs when the agent's and principal's utility functions satisfy a condition known as *similarity*.[15] When this condition is satisfied, and the optimal incentive contract is selected by the principal, the agent and principal will agree on the optimal choice of an action. Once the principal and agent agree, there is no longer any incentive difficulty, and the problem reduces to one of pure risk sharing.

Disutility for Effort

A slightly different formulation of the principal-agent relationship assumes that the agent's action is some variable for which the agent has disutility, quite apart from the effect of the action on the payoff. One simple interpretation is that the action is effort expended by the agent. In this model, the agent's utility declines, other things being equal, with increases in effort. Moreover, the model assumes that the payoff to the firm is increasing in effort. Because the principal has no direct disutility for the agent's effort, and because the principal wants the payoff to be as large as possible, the principal prefers that the agent choose as large a value for effort as possible.

15. See S. Ross, "The Economic Theory of Agency: The Principal's Problem," *American Economic Review* (May 1973): 134–39.

The problem is very similar to the one in the previous section except that now the agent has disutility for effort. It is a "second-best" problem, in that the contract must serve a dual role: (1) risk sharing and (2) provision of incentives. This problem is characterized by a condition known as *moral hazard*. This term comes from the insurance literature and means that the agent has an incentive to shirk, contrary to the principal's wishes. (The agent acts differently because the principal is affected and not the agent.) However, such shirking is unobservable. After the agent has acted and the random state has occurred, the agent could claim that an unfavorable payoff was caused by a "bad state" rather than by the agent's shirking. A favorable payoff could be claimed by the agent to have resulted from high effort, rather than a "good state." Because the principal cannot observe either the action or the state, it is impossible for the principal to sort out the effects of these two factors on the payoff.

One special case is worth mentioning. If the agent is risk neutral, the solution is easy. Here the agent bears all of the risk. The principal pays the agent the outcome, less a fixed fee. Moreover, the principal does not care about the agent's effort level because the principal's payment is a fixed fee regardless of the payoff to the firm.

A Few Tentative Implications

Many variations of the models described above have been studied. Each was developed to address a slightly different issue. The main features of the models are largely the same, however. Rather than describing these models in detail, we summarize some of the more interesting results and speculate on the reasons they occur. The results discussed below are neither exhaustive nor presented rigorously.

Risk Sharing and Controllability As mentioned above, a basic precept of responsibility accounting is that managers should be evaluated on the basis of controllable performance. Yet in the context of the models described above, restriction of the contract to controllable events would preclude risk-sharing opportunities for the principal and agent. Because both parties can be made better off with such risk sharing, it would be a Pareto-inferior solution to preclude such a possibility. Demski examines this issue in some detail and gives two examples of contracts that admit risk-sharing possibilities and can make all parties better off while seemingly violating traditional managerial accounting "wisdom."[16]

The first example is essentially the one discussed earlier. The traditional wisdom of managerial accounting asserts that factors beyond a manager's control should be excluded from the manager's evaluation and reward structure. This implies that the random state should not affect the manager's share of the payoff. As was shown in the context of the model, to exclude such a risk-sharing possibility is suboptimal for both the principal and the agent.

The second example concerns intermanager effects. Managerial accounting tenets and casual intuition suggest that manager *A*'s reward structure should not be affected by manager *B*'s performance. Yet to the extent that both *A*'s and *B*'s performance can be affected by random states beyond their control, there can be risk-

16. Demski, J., "Uncertainty and Evaluation Based on Controllable Performance," *Journal of Accounting Research* (Autumn 1976): 230–45.

sharing benefits from compensating both on the basis of some pooled performance measure. Profit-sharing arrangements observed in business reflect this consideration.

Monitoring Information   In agency models, incentive difficulties arise because the principal is unable to observe the agent's action or the state. One would guess, then, that there would be a benefit to the principal from gathering some additional information about either the agent's action or the state or both. Such information could be viewed as a form of performance monitoring, a common occurrence in organizations. Suppose the principal can produce a performance report that can be jointly observed by the principal and the agent. The contract can now depend on both the payoff and the performance report. Suppose the report provides only imperfect information about the agent's action or the state — that is, the report is (imperfectly) correlated with the action or state. Will there always be value in producing the report? The answer is that there is always a benefit in producing the performance report as long as it is *informative*.[17] In casual terms, *informative* means that the report adds some information about the action or state *in addition to* that provided by the jointly observed payoff.

This may seem a very plausible and intuitive result, but the reasoning behind it is not trivial. If the performance report is produced and is only imperfectly correlated with the action or state, there are two opposite effects on the welfare of the parties involved. First, because the agent is risk averse, the introduction of another source of uncertainty (the report) results in a *decline* in the agent's expected utility. Because the principal must select a contract that provides the agent an expected utility sufficient to meet the market wage, the principal must counteract this decline in the agent's expected utility with a somewhat higher payment *across all uncertain states.* This, of course, is bad for the principal.

The second effect from producing the performance report is that it provides an additional incentive for the agent to select a high effort level and also affords an additional risk-sharing opportunity for the principal and agent. Thus, the first effect is a cost, and the second effect is a benefit. Fortunately, the benefit always exceeds the cost. Therefore, there always is a net benefit from the production of the monitoring report if it is informative. Because much of the data produced by cost-accounting systems can be viewed as monitoring information of one sort or another, this seems to be a rather important economic result for managerial accounting.

Costly Monitoring   Suppose it is costly to produce monitoring information. After all, cost accounting systems are not free goods. Baiman and Demski addressed the question of under what conditions the monitoring report should be produced.[18] One of their conclusions is that it is beneficial for the principal to wait and observe the payoff before producing the additional report, if it is costly to do so. For some values of the

17. See B. Holmstrom, "Moral Hazard and Observability," *Bell Journal of Economics* (Spring 1979): 74–91.

18. S. Baiman and J. Demski, "Economically Optimal Performance Evaluation and Control Systems," *Journal of Accounting Research* (Supplement 1980): 184–220.

payoff, the imperfect report will be produced; for other values of the payoff, it will not be. The intuition is that the payoff already provides the principal with some (albeit imperfect) information about the agent's action and the state variable. The performance report should be produced only if the *additional* information it provides over and above that implicit in the payoff has a benefit that exceeds the cost of producing it. Because this benefit can vary across levels of the payoff, the report will not always be produced. This is an important result for cost accounting because many types of cost-accounting data are typically produced only under certain circumstances, depending on some initial performance indicator such as profit.

Another result derived by Baiman and Demski is that if the agent's and principal's utility functions are of a certain special type, and if the payoff function and probability distribution satisfy certain properties, the values of the payoff for which the additional information will be produced fall only "in the tails." For some agent utility functions, monitoring information is produced only if the payoff is below a certain critical cut-off value. For other agent utility functions, the monitoring information will be produced only if the payoff is above a certain critical cut-off value. Moreover, it turns out that the more risk-averse agents are monitored only when the payoff is in the lower tail, and the less risk-averse agents are monitored only when the payoff is in the upper tail. These results are interesting from a cost accounting perspective because the conditional cost-variance investigation policies observed in practice often conform to the monitoring policy described above — that is, investigative cost variances only when they exceed certain prespecified cut-off levels. In this interpretation, the act of cost-variance investigation is viewed as the production of the additional performance report. (See Chapter 28 for a thorough discussion of cost-variance investigation.)

One final result of the Baiman-Demski analysis is that it always is optimal for the principal to "precommit" to a conditional investigation policy and this policy is nonrandom. That is, for every payoff the principal produces the monitoring information, with probability either zero or one. It is not optimal for the principal to investigate cost variances of a given magnitude randomly. To do so introduces additional risk into the agent's compensation function. This risk would have to be counteracted by higher payments, on average, and this would be bad from the principal's perspective. Once again, the theoretical result conforms with much of common cost accounting practice. Moreover, it affords us some modest insight into why such practices are observed.

Budgeting Demski and Feltham used an agency formulation to demonstrate that in some settings it is economically optimal to employ a *budget-based contract*.[19] A budget-based contract is one in which the agent is compensated based on the difference between the monetary outcome and a budgeted monetary outcome, rather than on the basis of the monetary outcome alone. This is an interesting result because budget-based contracts are widely observed in practice. We observe that organiza-

19. J. Demski and G. Feltham, "Economic Incentives in Budgetary Control Systems," *Accounting Review* (April 1978): 336–59.

tions often reward people (through pay raises, promotions, or other means of recognition) for their performance relative to a budget.

Magee used an agency model to address the economic characteristics of budget participation.[20] Behavioral approaches to this issue have generally found a benefit to participatory budgeting, and this benefit has been attributed to the motivational implications of participation. Workers internalize the goals of the organization when their input is sought in forming those goals. Magee's agency analysis showed that there is another potential benefit of budgetary participation. This benefit can be obtained when there is *information asymmetry* (unequal amounts of information) between the principal and the agent. Information asymmetry often occurs in organizations because the agent (subunit manager) is closer to, and better informed about, the subunit's technology and environment. When such information asymmetry is present, participatory budgeting can act to transfer information from the agent to the principal (top management). The principal can use this information to advantage in designing a contract to motivate the agent.

---

20. R. Magee, "Equilibria in Budget Participation," *Journal of Accounting Research* (Autumn 1980): 551–73.

APPENDIX SUMMARY

This appendix samples the issues in the economic theory of principal-agent relationships. Additional results are available in the literature, but the literature barely scratches the surface of the issues that need to be addressed. The models are simplistic, and the results are tentative. However, as theory in this area emerges, it will significantly change the way people think about performance evaluation and rewards. Its ultimate implications for managerial accounting are important.

Appendix Suggested Readings

Antle, R., and J. Demski. "The Controllability Principle in Responsibility Accounting." *Accounting Review* (October 1988): 700–18.

Baiman, S. "Agency Research in Managerial Accounting: A Survey." *Journal of Accounting Literature* (Spring 1982): 154–210.

Baiman, S., and J. Demski. "Economically Optimal Performance Evaluation and Control Systems." *Journal of Accounting Research* (Supplement 1980): 184–220.

Baiman, S., and H. Evans. "Predecision Information and Participative Management Control Systems." *Journal of Accounting Research* (Autumn 1983).

Baiman, S., and J. Noel. "Noncontrollable Costs and Responsibility Accounting." *Journal of Accounting Research* (Autumn 1985).

Blanchard, G. A., C. W. Chow, and E. Noreen. "Information Asymmetry, Incentive Schemes, and Information Biasing: The Case of Hospital Budgeting under Rate Regulation." *Accounting Review* (January 1986).

Demski, J., and G. Feltham. "Economic Incentives in Budgetary Control Systems." *Accounting Review* (April 1978): 336–59.

Holmstrom, B. "Moral Hazard and Observability." *Bell Journal of Economics* (Spring 1979): 74–91.

Lambert, R. "Variance Investigation in Agency Settings." *Journal of Accounting Research* (Autumn 1985).

Magee, R. "Equilibria in Budget Participation." *Journal of Accounting Research* (Autumn 1980): 551–73.

Waller, W., and C. Chow. "The Self-Selection and Effort Effects of Standard-Based Employment Contracts: A Framework and Some Empirical Evidence." *Accounting Review* (July 1985).

Young, M. "Participative Budgeting: The Effects of Risk Aversion and Asymmetric Information on Budgetary Slack." *Journal of Accounting Research* (Autumn 1985).

Review Questions

21-1   List the five common elements of a decision problem under uncertainty.

21-2   What is meant by perfect information? Imperfect information?

21-3   What is the expected value of perfect information?

21-4   What is a utility function?

21-5   Define *risk aversion*.

21-6   Define *certainty equivalent*.

21-7   What is a principal-agent relationship?

21-8   What is risk sharing?

21-9   A company estimates the expected cash flow of year 5 to be $10,000. If this figure is used in the investment analysis, what assumption is being made?

21-10   Why does the utility function for earnings (or for money) have an upper bound? Why does it have a lower bound?

21-11   Does the utility function of a firm change after making an investment? Why?

21-12   When is it reasonable for a firm to base decisions on the expected monetary values and to ignore utility considerations?

21-13   If an analysis did not try to incorporate utility considerations into its investment analysis, would the investment decisions of the firm still be affected by the utility functions of the individual corporate executives? Assume some degree of decentralization.

21-14   If a firm is small enough for the president (and owner) to make all decisions, is it necessary to make a formal analysis using utility functions? Explain.

Exercises

21-15   Evaluating a Gamble   What is the maximum amount you would pay for a gamble that involved the following two alternatives?

Alternative 1:   .5 probability of $1,000
Alternative 2:   .5 probability of $0

What does this imply about your utility function?

21-16   Calculation of Certainty Equivalent   For you to be indifferent between the following two gambles, what value of X must be inserted?

Gamble A	Gamble B
50% probability of $1,000	100% probability of $X
50% probability of $0	$500

What does this imply about your utility function? Compare your answer to the answer you gave to Exercise 21-15.

21-17 Assessing a Gamble Based on a Utility Function   The following utility function of Mr. Jay will be used for Exercises 21-17 and 21-18.

Change in Net-Asset Position

Dollars	Utility Measures
$-3,000	-3,000
-1,000	-1,000
- 600	- 500
- 500	- 350
0	0
100	100
500	150
1,000	200
2,000	350
4,000	500
9,000	680
10,000	700

Assume there is a gamble that has a .5 probability of $10,000 and .5 probability of $0.

REQUIRED:

a. What is the utility measure of the gamble?

b. What is the amount Mr. Jay would be willing to accept for certain to cause him to be indifferent to the two choices?

c. Would Mr. Jay be willing to pay $1,000 for this gamble?

d. What is the expected monetary value of the gamble?

e. What is the risk discount?

f. Would you describe Mr. Jay as financially conservative?

21-18 Continuation of Exercise 21-17   Assume that a gamble has a .5 probability of $4,000 and .5 probability of $1,000.

REQUIRED:

a. What is the utility measure of the gamble?

b. What is the amount Mr. Jay would be willing to accept for certain to cause him to be indifferent to the two choices?

    c. Would Mr. Jay be willing to pay $1,000 for this gamble?

    d. What is the expected monetary value of the gamble?

    e. What is the discount for risk?

21-19 **Investment Value Given Various Probabilities of Success**   Assume that the following utility function applies to the Arnot Corporation.

Change in Net-Asset Position

Dollars: Present Value	Utility Measures
$-20,000	-400
-10,000	-100
0	0
7,200	80
8,600	90
10,000	100
18,600	140
20,000	150
30,000	190
35,800	200
40,000	220
60,000	240

    a. Would the corporation accept an investment that requires an outlay of $10,000 and will either be a complete failure or generate cash flows of $30,000 within a week if each possibility has a .5 probability?

    b. What would you recommend if the probabilities were 0.65 of failure and .35 of success?

21-20 **Continuation of Exercise 21-19**   Assume the same utility function as in Exercise 21-19.

    a. Should the Arnot Corporation undertake the following investment? Assume that a .05 discount rate is appropriate.

Period	Cash Flow
0	$-10,000
1	$0 with .5 probability $30,000 with .5 probability

    b. What would be your recommendation if the probabilities were .6 of failure and .4 of success?

21-21 **Continuation of Exercise 21-19**   Assume the same utility function as in Exercise 21-19. The Arnot Corporation has been offered an investment in Exercise 21-19. The Arnot Corporation has been offered an investment that costs $20,000. The investment has .5 probability of not generating any cash the first day and .5 probability of generating $30,000. It can also generate $0 or $30,000 with the same probabilities the second day (the outcomes are independent of the day). Should the firm accept the investment?

21-22 **Continuation of Exercise 21-21** Assume the same investment as in Exercise 21-21, except the cash flows of the second day will be the same as the first day (the outcomes are dependent). Should the firm accept the investment?

21-23 **Mean, Variance, and Standard Deviation of Net-Present-Value Distribution** Assume that the expected cash flows of an investment are as follows:

Period	Mean Value	Variance
0	− $ 8,000	$ 250,000
1	$10,000	1,000,000
2	$10,000	4,000,000

Compute the mean and variance of the net-present-value distribution assuming that the cash flows of each period are independent. Use a .05 rate of discount. (Hint: The variance of the sum of two independent random variables is equal to the sum of their individual variances. The variance of a constant times a random variable is the constant squared times the variance of the random variable. Also, the mean of a sum of random variables is equal to the sum of the means of the random variables.)

Problems 21-24 **Determining the Expected Utility of an Investment** Determine the expected utility of the following investment:

Period	Cash Flows
0	− $1,000
1	0.5 probability of $2,100 cash flow
	0.3 probability of $1,050
	0.2 probability of $0

The firm has a cost of money of .05. The utility function of the corporation has the values shown on the following page (interpolate if you need other values).

Dollars: Present Value	Utility Measures
$-1,000	-300
0	0
500	50
1,000	70
1,050	75
1,300	85
1,500	90
2,000	100
2,100	101
3,000	125

(Hint: Calculate the present value of each cash flow, and then determine its utility value.)

21-25 Preparation of Payoff Table Jackston, Inc. manufactures and distributes a line of Christmas toys. The company has neglected to keep its dollhouse line current, so sales have decreased to approximately 10,000 units per year from a previous high of 50,000 units. The dollhouse has been redesigned recently and is considered by company officials to be comparable to its competitors' models. The company plans to redesign the dollhouse each year in order to compete effectively. Joan Blocke, the sales manager, is not sure how many units can be sold next year, but she is willing to place probabilities on her estimates. Blocke's estimates of the number of units that can be sold during the next year and the related probabilities are as follows:

Estimated Sales in Units	Probability
20,000	.10
30,000	.40
40,000	.30
50,000	.20

The units would be sold for $20 each.

The inability to estimate the sales more precisely is a problem for Jackston. The number of units of this product is small enough to schedule the entire year's sales in one production run. If the demand is greater than the number of units manufactured, then sales will be lost. If demand is below supply, the extra units cannot be carried over to the next season and would be given away to various charitable organizations. The production and distribution cost estimates are listed below.

	Units Manufactured			
	20,000	30,000	40,000	50,000
Variable costs	$180,000	$270,000	$360,000	$450,000
Fixed costs	140,000	140,000	160,000	160,000
Total costs	$320,000	$410,000	$520,000	$610,000

The company intends to analyze the data to facilitate making a decision as to the proper size of the production run.

REQUIRED:

a. Prepare a payoff table for the different sizes of production runs required to meet the four sales estimates prepared by Joan Blocke for Jackston, Inc. If Jackston, Inc. relies solely on the expected-monetary-value approach to make decisions, what size of production run will it select?

b. Identify the basic steps that are taken in any decision process. Explain each step by reference to the situation presented in the problem and your answer for requirement **a.** (*CMA adapted*)

21-26 **Probability of Operating at Less Than Break-Even Volume** A corporation has fixed costs of $250,000 and variable costs of $2 per unit. The company is attempting to choose the best of three possible prices. The prices, mean sales, and the standard deviations of sales are as follows:

Prices	$2.50	$3.00	$3.50
Mean sales (units)	600,000	280,000	100,000
Standard deviations	40,000	30,000	20,000

REQUIRED:

For each possible price, what is the probability of operating at less than break-even volume?

21-27 **Diagramatic Representation of Break-Even Analysis and Demand Functions** The following diagram combines a traditional break-even analysis with a probability density function for demand.

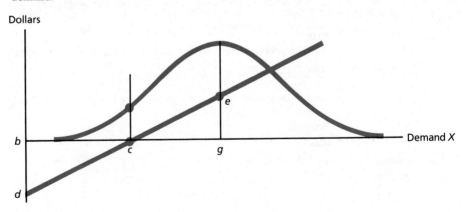

REQUIRED:

a. Give an expression using the letters in the graph for the unit contribution margin.

b. Give the break-even output.

c. Should this firm produce? Why or why not?

21-28 Use of Regression to Estimate Fixed-Cost Levels   One way to estimate fixed-cost levels is to fit a regression equation to the cost data and use the intercept term (the constant in the equation) as a measure of fixed costs. Is this a good procedure?

21-29 Combining Break-Even Analysis with Uncertain Demand   The following diagram combines a traditional break-even analysis with uncertainty concerning demand. The probability distribution of sales is skewed to the right. The letter *e* represents median sales (a value as likely to be exceeded as not reached), and *f* is expected sales.

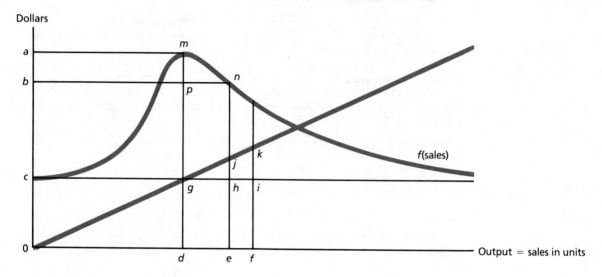

REQUIRED:

Using the letters to represent points on the graph,

a. Give an expression for the unit price.

b. Give an expression for the unit contribution margin used to construct this graph.

c. Indicate the break-even output level.

d. Indicate, in some way, the probability that the firm will fail to make a profit (define any new symbols used).

e. Give the line segment that best approximates the expected (profit, loss).

21-30 Interpreting Break-Even Chart   Consider the following break-even chart where cost is given on the left ordinate and the probability (density) function of sales on the right.

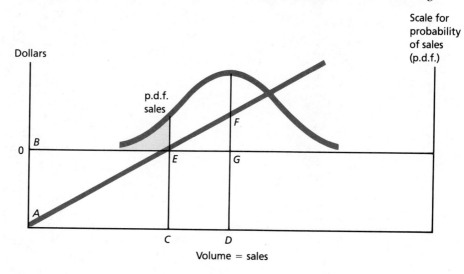

REQUIRED:

a. What does the slope of the line *AE* represent?

b. What is the output volume (also assumed sales) at the break-even point?

c. What does the darkened area represent?

d. Using the letters in the figure, which of the answers below gives expected profit if the probability function is symmetrical around the line *HFGD?*

   (1) *FG*

   (2) *FD*

   (3) *HG* ÷ *EG*

   (4) *EC*

   (5) *HG*

   (6) (*AD*)(*FG* ÷ *EG*)

21-31 Expected Utility   (see Appendix)   Assuming the utility function $u(x) = x^{1/2}$, which is graphed in Exhibit 21-11, what is the expected utility of a gamble involving a fifty-fifty chance of receiving $36 or $81?

21-32 Risk Sharing   (see Appendix)   Refer to Problem 21-31. Suppose *A* and *B* both have the utility function $u(x) = x^{1/2}$, and each individual faces the gamble given in Problem 21-31. What is the expected utility of each person if they share their risks equally? Compare this expected utility with that calculated in Problem 21-31, where there was no risk sharing.

21-33 Value of Perfect Information   Problem 28-26 on the value of perfect information in a cost-variance-investigation setting may be assigned with Chapter 21.

Cost Accounting and Control in Decentralized Organizations

22

Decentralization and Performance Measurement

LEARNING OBJECTIVES

After studying this chapter, you should be able to:

1 Describe the general problem of performance measurement in a decentralized organization.

2 Explain how managers set objectives for decentralized units.

3 Compute the investment turnover, operating rate, return on investment, and residual income of a decentralized organizational unit.

4 Identify the problems that arise in measuring the income and investment-base figures used in various performance measures.

5 Explain how performance measurement is conducted on different levels of an organizational structure.

*M*anagement's ability to react to change is determined by the timing and nature of the available information, the continuous nature of change, its limited familiarity with the operations of other units, and the difficulty of predicting the ripple effects of decisions and actions. As a partial solution, many firms resort to some degree of decision decentralization. This chapter examines the contribution of cost accounting to performance evaluation and control in decentralized organizations. It first describes the limitations of several widely used measures (including return on investment) and then introduces the very useful residual income measure.

Delegation of Decision Making

It is inefficient to attempt total decision control from the top level of a large firm. Decision making is delegated from top management to lower-level personnel to take advantage of their familiarity with operations and ability to respond quickly to local changes. This delegation may include the authority to make nearly all operating decisions or, alternatively, may limit the authority to a small range of decisions.

Still another reason division and plant-level managers are given decision responsibility is to encourage them to expend more effort and to feel committed to their portion of the business. Managers who feel they have the authority to run their business segment are likely to perform with more enthusiasm and to be willing to accept responsibility for the results achieved. It is good training for future top executives.

An article in *Business Week,* citing a study by McKinsey & Company that described the management practices of several of the world's most successful businesses, designated "autonomy to encourage entrepreneurship" as one of the key determinants of business success.

Decentralization to Encourage Entrepreneurship

As reported in *Business Week,* small top-management groups are common in some of the most successful companies. This is true, for example, of Digital Equipment Corporation and Emerson Electric Company. Dana Corporation, which is a $3 billion company, has fewer than 100 top-management personnel.

Successful companies do not force decisions for their operating managers. Companies such as 3M Company, Texas Instruments, IBM, and Johnson and Johnson tend to place more emphasis on the drive of their individual managers to make new programs and products successful than on detailed quantitative analyses of the market.[1]

1. "Putting Excellence into Management," *Business Week* (July 21, 1980): 196–205.

One danger of decentralization of control and decision making is that these decision-making subunits may take actions that are not consistent with the goals of the total entity. Decentralized management, if left on its own, may fail to consider economies external to its own local environment. Hence, a balance between control and decentralization is required.

Control may be achieved through goal setting and performance evaluation. The type of goals set and the manner in which performance is evaluated should depend on the degree of decision-making delegation. As decentralization increases, the measures used to evaluate performance should become more general.

The evaluation and control mechanism is influenced by the organizational structure of the firm. The firm's organizational structure and its accounting system must both be considered when designing an evaluation system. The accounting system should provide performance measures that reflect the consequences of decision making for the activity, and thereby allow top management to evaluate these decisions in light of the firm's goals. Incentives for managers should improve their performance and help them make decisions that increase the value of the firm. Unfortunately, it is not easy to decide how much control to exercise. Some organizations tightly control their subunits; others let the managers in the field run their own show, implying a belief by top management that the benefits of entrepreneurship outweigh those achieved by strict centralized control.

Setting Objectives

Managerial performance can be measured — by establishing the objectives of the activity over which the manager has decision-making authority and then determining how well these objectives are met. A primary objective of management should be to make the stockholders' value as large as possible. An alternative, but consistent, objective can be stated as maximization of profits subject to constraints (for example, continuity of existence).

The extent of success in attaining objectives may be assessed quantitatively or qualitatively. The qualitative criteria include relations with superiors and subordinates, training of subordinates, developing new products and new methods of production, professional attainments, civic activities, and a general ability to get things done. The qualitative factors are relevant in judging performance but traditionally are more the province of the industrial psychologist or the general manager than of the accountant. It should be recalled, however, that evaluating an individual affects motivation and the attainment of corporate objectives. Thus, it is important for the accountant to understand and work with the behavioral scientist in designing control reports and performance-measuring techniques. This chapter focuses on quantitative measures of performance. Qualitative factors are discussed in Chapter 26. Quantitative factors that can provide useful information include

- Return on equity (ROE)

- Investment turnover

- Income per dollar of sales (operating rate)

- Return on investment (ROI)

- Return on assets (ROA)

- Sales

- Income and cash flow

- Residual income (income after capital costs)

- Share of market

- Rate of growth

- Costs and cost variances

- Retention rate of employees

- Physical production (quantity and quality)

- Changes from period to period in any of the above measures

Objectives for any of these measures can be set, or standards may be established using the unit's past performance or objective measures of possible future performance (for example, engineering studies). An alternative procedure is to compare the performance of one unit of the firm with other similar units of the same or different firms. In practice, combinations of all of these methods are used.

Performance Evaluation and Managerial Incentives

Performance measures in decentralized firms are widely used as an important basis of managerial incentive compensation. An article in the *Wall Street Journal* described trends in the incentive plans of some well-known firms.

Managerial Incentive Plans at Honeywell and Champion International

As reported in the *Wall Street Journal*, executive compensation plans that tie executives' compensation to their performance in meeting corporate growth targets are used in a large number of the 100 largest U.S. companies. Such compensation plans are often referred to as "performance shares" or "performance units." For example, Champion International Corporation routinely compares the company's performance on growth in earnings per share with that of fifteen of its competitors. Honeywell also uses earnings per share as the basis for its growth performance determination.[2]

One of the earliest major incentive compensation plans was instituted by Alfred P. Sloan at General Motors Corporation. The plan was a classic managerial innovation.

---

2. "More Executive Bonus Plans Tied to Company Earnings, Sales Goals," *Wall Street Journal*, November 20, 1980, p. 1.

Incentive Compensation at General Motors	Incentive compensation at General Motors is designed to increase goal congruence of the firm's management and its shareholders.[3] "The most effective results and the maximum progress and stability of the business are achieved by placing its executives in the same relative position, so far as possible, that they would occupy if they were conducting a business on their own account. This provides opportunity for accomplishment through the exercise of individual initiative, and opportunity for economic progress commensurate with performance.

"Although the General Motors Bonus Plan was first adopted on August 27, 1918, its fundamental principles have never changed — that the interests of the corporation and its stockholders are best served by making key employees partners in the corporation's prosperity, and that each individual should be rewarded in proportion to his contribution to the profit of his own division and of the corporation as a whole."

Performance Measures

Seeking out the one best measure of performance and using it to the exclusion of all other measures can be dangerous. Frequently a single measure cannot do the job satisfactorily because a measure that is useful for one purpose may not be useful for another. The fact that a golf drive traveled 250 yards is useful in judging the force with which the ball was hit, but knowledge of the total distance covered is not sufficient to conclude whether the drive was good or bad. Information relating to the starting point and the location and distance of the hole is needed before this type of evaluation can be made. Knowledge of wind and course conditions also may be useful in comparisons with other drives.

Most of the quantitative measures listed in the previous section are not immune to distortion, manipulation, or misinterpretation. The manipulations may be a product of figure juggling or managerial actions designed to obtain the result sought by superiors. To the extent possible, measures of performance should be consistent with actions that improve performance and with the basic objectives of the firm. To obtain a valid measure of performance, several measures usually are needed, and the importance of each measure must be weighed. If this is not done, the resulting measure may not reflect performance, but rather the ability of a clever manager to obtain a favorable performance report through manipulation rather than performance.

Performance measures should reflect the nature of the responsibilities of the manager (or organization) whose performance is being measured. Where possible,

3. A. P. Sloan, Jr., *My Years with General Motors* (New York: Doubleday, 1964): 407.

items that are not controlled by the manager should be excluded from the measure. Further, actual results as well as methods used by a manager in decision making and control should be evaluated. The results are often a product, in part, of factors over which the manager has no control or influence. Uncertainty can cause excellent decision making to yield unsatisfactory results and vice versa.

The performance measure should indicate how well the manager is meeting predetermined objectives. More than one measure of performance is usually required, and different measures are typically needed for different situations, firms, and organization levels.

Investment Turnover

Investment turnover is defined as the sales of a period divided by the average investment:

$$\text{Investment turnover} = \frac{\text{Sales}}{\text{Average investment}}$$

The investment turnover gives an indication of how intensively an investment is being used. As sales increase, the turnover increases. Taken by itself, the investment turnover is not a reliable measure of a manager's performance. Total sales and turnover can be increased by increasing selling effort, lowering selling price, or a random change in general economic conditions. An increase in turnover may reflect not more efficient use of resources but instead factors that are not controllable. However, when used with other measures, investment turnover can be helpful in pointing out possible reasons for decreased or increased profits.

Operating Rate

The **operating rate** is the operating profit per dollar of sales:

$$\text{Operating rate} = \frac{\text{Operating profit}}{\text{Sales}}$$

The operating rate gives an indication of the production efficiency of operations. In addition to efficiency, the profit per dollar of sales is affected by

- Changes in the level of sales,
- Changes in the product mix sold,
- Changes in the prices of the products sold,
- Changes in the cost of materials and services used to produce the products sold,
- Changes in the level of production,
- The accounting methods used to determine operating profits.

If each of the above influences is isolated and the effect computed, then the operating rate is useful. If attention is focused on the operating rate, without proper analysis, incorrect conclusions may be drawn as to the causes of the changes in the rate. For example, assume the situation illustrated in Exhibit 22-1.

EXHIBIT 22-1

A Change in Operating Rates: Case 1

	Period 1	Period 2
Sales	$1,000,000	$1,500,000
Income	50,000	300,000
Operating rate	5%	20%

Here the operating rate increased from 5 to 20 percent. But this does not necessarily reflect increased production efficiency. (The term *production efficiency* is used here to describe a situation where the assets of the firm are being employed in such a manner to increase the income above the budgeted income for a given level of output, without adversely affecting future incomes.)

To know whether efficiency has been increased, it is first necessary to know what income should be for sales of $1,500,000. It may be that income should be $400,000 for sales of that level and that the operating rate of 20 percent for sales of $1,500,000 reflects inefficiencies. The increase in the operating rate may have occurred merely because of the increase in sales, for which the sales manager should receive primary credit. Moreover, assuming increased (even maximum) efficiency at this output, the increase in income could still have been attained at the expense of future periods. In other words, a good case can be made for the argument that to maximize profitability (a long-run notion), the firm should not merely maximize accounting income in any single period but should consider the effect on future incomes. For example, expensing research and development costs tends to reduce short-run profit measures, yet R&D is critical to most firms' future profitability. The effects of the factors responsible for the change in the operating rate also should be examined for their long-run effects. Taking advantage of short-run income-producing opportunities can sometimes have adverse long-run consequences.

Consider another situation. Sales have remained constant, but the opening rate has changed because a different product mix was sold. Assume this produced the changes indicated in Exhibit 22-2.

EXHIBIT 22-2

A Change in Operating Rates: Case 2

	Period 1	Period 2
Sales	$1,000,000	$1,000,000
Income	100,000	250,000
Operating rate	10%	25%

This situation also may not reflect increased production efficiency but may indicate merely a change in the composition of sales from low-margin items to high-margin items. This may or may not be due to managerial efficiency in production. It may instead indicate increased efficiency on the part of a manager responsible for sales-promotion decisions (a change in sales mix). Or it may merely reflect a fortuitous market phenomenon (a switch in consumer tastes) over which management had no control or influence. The surge in 1988 of oat bran sales is an illustration of this situation.

The operating rate is sometimes used to determine whether a profit is "fair." This practice has been common in defense contracts.

Consider the data in Exhibit 22-3:

EXHIBIT 22-3

Operating Rates of Two Firms

	Firm A	Firm B
Sales	$1,000,000	$15,000,000
Income	100,000	2,000,000
Operating rate	10%	13.33%

Firm *B*'s operating rate is larger than that of firm *A.* If *A*'s profits are "fair," then it would appear that *B*'s profits are excessive. However, suppose that *A* uses a much smaller amount of assets than does *B*. It is possible that *A*'s profits, given the amount of investment, are high and *B*'s profits are low.

Return on Investment

Return on investment (ROI) is calculated by dividing operating profit by average or beginning investment. Suppose *A* and *B* made the same product. Assume *A* produced 1,000,000 units at a cost of $1 per unit, and *B* produced 30,000,000 units at a cost of $.50 per unit. The operating-rate comparison would be a poor indicator of performance if the firms have unequal investments.

The return-on-investment (ROI) method of measuring performance is said to have several desirable features. First, it provides a single, comprehensive figure that incorporates the effect of a large number of events on the division or other activity unit and seems to be easy to understand. Furthermore, because it measures how effectively a division's assets are used to generate profits, ROI moves managers to make decisions involving those assets that improve the expected return. To attain these advantages without incurring disadvantages, ROI must be used carefully.

Return on investment can be computed by dividing income by investment or by multiplying the *investment turnover* (sales divided by investment) by the *operating rate* (income divided by sales):

$$\text{ROI} = \frac{\text{Sales}}{\text{Investment}} \times \frac{\text{Income}}{\text{Sales}} = \frac{\text{Income}}{\text{Investment}}$$

These three ratios (investment turnover, operating rate, and return on investment) are important efficiency measures of resource utilization. According to various surveys of actual practice, nearly all major companies use ROI to some extent in divisional performance measurement.

Return on investment, as a measure of performance, is only as good as the numbers used to compute it. It should not come as a surprise to anyone familiar with accounting that the problems of measuring sales, operating profit, and investment are numerous.

Measuring Sales   The measurement of sales is often identified with the problem of revenue recognition. Should revenue be recognized when the order is received, the product made, the product shipped, or the cash received? Because most companies are on the accrual basis of recognizing revenue, revenue is recognized when the goods are shipped or the services are performed. In some cases this method of accounting causes difficulties in computing the investment turnover. For example, consider ship construction. Shipbuilding firms that use the accrual method and recognize revenue only on a completed sale might have a low investment turnover in a period of great activity when no ships are completed and delivered. This particular difficulty might be readily solved by shifting to a production basis (percentage of completion basis) of revenue recognition, but the general problem of revenue recognition still exists.

Measuring Income   The problems of measuring the income of a corporate entity are many, and they increase when attention is focused on the component parts of an organization. The main problems are the pricing of transfers and the assignment of common costs to an organization's operating units. These problems become important when the segments of the company are compared to one another. Accounting procedures, which generally are accepted from a financial point of view, may result in a report of income that is worth little from the point of view of comparing different operating units. The report of income can be qualified by footnotes, but these qualifications tend to be lost when attention is focused on return on investment.

Several problems of income measurement are particularly relevant for the purpose of measuring return on investment:

- Revenue recognition and the matching of expenses with revenues,

- Treatment of repairs and maintenance costs,

- Accounting for inventory (during periods of fluctuating prices, income will be affected by the choice of the inventory-valuation basis, FIFO, LIFO, average cost, and so on, as well as by changing inventory levels),

- Treatment of nonproductive supplies (whether they should be expensed when purchased or inventoried),

- Choice of depreciation procedure (subunits would need to use depreciation procedures that permit meaningful comparisons of their calculated return on investment),

- Adjustments for changes in the price level,

- Allocation of common costs, especially central office expenses,

- The effects of changes in the level of production on income (these changes are caused by absorption costing combined with changes in production).

Techniques have been developed to handle all of these problems, but these techniques frequently are not applied uniformly to all plants and divisions of a company. One plant may use LIFO and another FIFO. One plant may use straight-line depreciation, while another uses some method of accelerated depreciation. For any of the items listed above, examples can be presented showing two plants or divisions (assumed to have the same physical characteristics) that will report a different return-on-investment figure, the difference being caused entirely by the accounting methods and not by variations in efficiency.

Two additional complexities involve financing and tax issues. If the objective of the ROI measure is to evaluate operating performance, then the effect on income caused by the method of financing should be eliminated (or at least analyzed). Interest payments and the tax effects of any interest expense should not affect the income measure if ROI is to remain unaffected by the method of financing. The performance measure should be consistent with the decision-making technique.

Taxes present a more difficult problem. All decisions should be made on an after-tax basis, thus the measure of performance also should be made on an after-tax basis. Otherwise the decision criterion and performance measure will be inconsistent, which is likely to lead to suboptimal decisions. This approach implies that when the tax law changes, the effects of the change should be analyzed to reflect the results of operations with and without the change in the tax law. For example, if the corporate income tax rate declines, an analysis of any increase in profit would identify the amount of the increase resulting from the tax-rate decrease.

Measuring Investment   Many of the problems of measuring investment are directly related to the problems of income measurement. The list is shortened here to focus attention on the three most important problems:

- Valuing long-lived assets,

- Valuing inventories,

- Allocation of assets administered directly from the central office.

Long-Lived Assets   There are three problems associated with the valuation of long-lived assets. The first is determining what items should be capitalized and what items charged to expense. This is particularly troublesome with repairs, overhauls, and any large expenditures for developing new procedures or products. For example, in the oil industry, the costs of drilling a dry well may be treated as an expense by some firms and as an asset by other firms. The case for treating the costs of drilling dry holes as assets rests on the argument that a certain number of dry holes usually must be drilled for every producing well. The costs of these dry holes are necessary to obtain the producing well and are therefore assets.

The second problem is to decide what to do about depreciation. Accumulated depreciation may be subtracted in computing the period's investment, or the initial investment may be used. This troublesome issue has no one best solution. However, several observations may be made. With constant revenue and maintenance charges, assets have an increasing return on investment through the periods of use if either straight-line depreciation or any one of the decreasing-charge methods of computing depreciation is used (and the accumulated depreciation is subtracted from the asset). With the above assumptions, the depreciable asset has an equal return on investment through the periods of use only if a present-value method (a depreciation method which is based on present values) of computing depreciation is used. (This depreciation method is discussed in Chapter 23.) The method is not used in practice, however.

When the straight-line (or one of the decreasing-charge) methods of depreciation is used, the investment shows a low initial return and an increasing return over time as the investment base declines. This phenomenon tends to discourage new investments that might decrease the return on investment simply because they are new. It also distorts comparisons across divisions when assets are obtained at different times or when price levels were substantially different.

Return on investment, as conventionally computed, does not provide a reliable check on investment performance. Discounted cash-flow techniques and portfolio considerations are involved in selecting investments. The accounting measures of profit (even ignoring tax problems) are not generally designed to be consistent with investment decision methods. As a result, the calculated return on investment differs from the projected rate of return, even when the actual cash flows are precisely as estimated.

Nearly all firms use some measure of book value for the fixed assets included in the investment base. Market values, although theoretically more correct, seem to present too many implementation problems for practical use. Some firms use gross book values rather than the net figures recommended here. When gross book values are used, the return on investment is likely to be less than the investment's internal rate of return (IRR).

Inflation is the third problem related to valuing long-lived assets for purposes of determining the investment. This is possibly the most important issue of the three, particularly in periods of rapid inflation. The purchasing power of the dollar changes significantly over time. It can be argued that the return-on-investment measure is not reliable if there are unexpected changes in the price level.

Valuing Inventories   The problem of measuring the value of inventories is related to the fact that LIFO is acceptable for accounting purposes. Under LIFO, the oldest goods purchased are the last goods to be charged as an expense, and the inventory value often represents goods dating back to the moment LIFO was adopted. The inventory resulting from the use of LIFO rarely gives an indication of the actual cost of the inventory, nor does it give an indication of its present value. In an inflationary period large inventories costed at LIFO can materially reduce the investment base compared to the value that would result from the use of FIFO.

Other problems of measuring inventory include writing down obsolete or spoiled items, taking a meaningful physical inventory, and, in the case of a manufacturing firm, deciding what costs are inventoried rather than expensed.

Allocation of Assets   Assets administered directly from the central office may or may not be allocated for purposes of computing the return on investment of a division or plant. If there are reasonable grounds for allocating the asset, it should be allocated. For example, if the payroll is paid out of a centrally administered payroll fund, the cash held in this fund should be considered an asset assignable to the individual plants. In this example the take-home pay of the workers of each plant would seem to be a reasonable basis for allocation.

Some companies do not allocate cash administered by the central office. This is not harmful if all of the operating units being compared have like characteristics, but if they are unlike (one plant having a large amount of long-lived assets, another a larger number of workers), the failure to allocate cash may give misleading results when operating units are compared.

Other Measures of Assets   In measuring ROI, the beginning investment is frequently used, but the average investment is also a useful measure. Many other possibilities are commonly used in practice and should be considered. These measures include the following:

- Gross investment (no deduction for accumulated depreciation),

- Beginning-of-period investment,

- End-of-period investment,

- Average investment,

- Replacement cost,

- Market value,

- Price-level adjusted cost,

- Liquidation value,

- Present value.

The use of gross investment tends to lead to ROI that is less than the internal rate of return earned by the investment. This downward bias in ROI is not welcomed by managers whose performance is being measured, nor should it be. The beginning-of-period investment is consistent with the internal-rate-of-return calculation, and its use is reasonable. The use of the end-of-period investment will overstate the ROI if no new assets are added. However, if new assets are added during the period, the use of the end-of-period investment tends to understate the ROI compared to the internal-rate-of-return approach.

Replacement cost is hard to measure and use effectively. It is rare that any asset in use for any period of time would be replaced exactly in kind. The advocacy of replacement cost has tended to decrease in recent years because of the difficulty of measuring the replacement cost of an asset that would be replaced by a different asset. The same practical difficulty works against using market value for tangible assets.

The use of price-level adjusted cost is discussed in Chapter 23. Although a set of assumptions can be defined that would cause price-level adjustments to be useful, it is just as likely that they will distort the evaluation of a manager's performance. Such measures are not currently in common use.

Liquidation (or resale) value is useful if the measure is available because it establishes an opportunity cost for the use of the asset. The opportunity cost of an asset is a useful measure since it should approximate the present value of the cash flows of the asset in its best alternative use. In practice, the liquidation-value measure is highly subjective and often not obtainable.

There is some confusion in practice about the inclusion or exclusion of working capital. Conceptually, all assets (including working capital) should be included in the asset base in computing ROI. If an ROI of 20 percent is required, and if $10,000,000 of working capital is used, then an income of $2,000,000 per year is necessary to justify the investment in working capital. When the residual income approach (discussed later in this chapter) is used, working capital can be treated separately from other long-lived assets, if it is desired to distinguish short-run and long-run capital costs.

If assets are leased, then the present value of the lease payments should be computed to obtain an equivalent asset value. The present value of the contractual lease payments, using the before-tax borrowing rate, gives an asset value approximating the value of a purchased asset. With a short-term lease this calculation does not capture the full value of the asset being used. It does, however, include the full value of the contractual obligations, which are a type of liability that matches the present value of the asset.

Return on Investment and Its Usefulness

The usefulness of return on investment for decision making or performance evaluation is very limited. Using ROI as the basis for rewarding management is difficult and unreliable because it can lead to managerial decisions that are not consistent with corporate goals. For example, if the manager of a division with the largest ROI earns the largest personal income, other divisions will aim at maximizing their ROIs rather than maximizing the firm's value.

Measuring Divisional Performance

A very important problem is caused by the use of return on investment to measure divisional performance. Assume that a high return on investment is considered desirable, and that division *A* has a return on investment of 35 percent and division *B* has a return on investment of 20 percent. Division *B* actually may be the better-managed division. If division *A* is rejecting all investment proposals of less than 35 percent when risk-justified investments returning, say, 30 percent are available, this leads to a higher return on investment but a less-than-optimal amount invested in the division from the point of view of the firm as a whole, assuming that the appropriate cost of money for the contemplated investment in division A is less than 35 percent. It is not desirable for a division to employ a high cutoff rate for investments when the rate is not justified by the investment's risk. This can occur if a firm (or even a division) uses one discount rate across all projects.

Managers know how they will be evaluated. If ROI is a key measure, they will focus their attention on it and possibly not take the best action from the organization's point of view. For example, investment A may promise a higher present value than equally costly alternate investment B. Yet if investment B produces a higher ROI, particularly in the early years when the manager is likely to still be in the same position, it may be preferred by the manager whose performance is measured on ROI.

The conflict of interests created by the use of a single measure of performance is not unique to return on investment. For example, one grocery chain employs profit per dollar of sales as a measure of their store managers' efficiency. Because certain items in the store have profit margins below the "standard required" margin, some store managers stock a smaller amount of these items and allow them to run out on busy days so that the profit-per-dollar-of-sales figure is not decreased. Although this decreases the profit of the store, the manager does it because the major emphasis is on the objective of earning the required profit per dollar of sales. The significant ratio for decision making here should be the total contribution per unit of the operation's scarce resource (probably floor or shelf space).

One method of counteracting the distortions just described is to include the rate of growth among the measures of performance. Since growth for growth's sake is not desirable, growth in income (or, perhaps, cash) rather than in sales should be the objective. If income is growing at the same time that return on investment is maintained at the desired level (or even increased), then, at least according to the quantitative measures, the manager is doing a reasonable job. Including the rate of growth in the performance measures puts the spotlight on the manager who is willing to be satisfied with the status quo. Balancing growth against return on investment ensures that the manager will not be obsessed with growth in sales at the expense of profit or return on investment at the expense of growth. Yet finding the correct mixture of ROI and growth is a difficult task.

Assume that the income, investments, growth rates, and ROIs of a firm in successive years are given in Exhibit 22-4.

EXHIBIT 22-4

ROI and Income Growth: An Example

Year	Operating Profit	Investment	Growth Rate	ROI
19x5	$10,000	$100,000	—	10.0%
19x6	11,000	110,000	10%	10.0%
19x7	14,300	125,000	30%	11.4%

Growth rates in operating profits:

$$19x5-19x6 \frac{1,000}{10,000} = 10\%$$

$$19x6-19x7 \frac{3,300}{11,000} = 30\%$$

$$19x5-19x7 \quad 14,300(1 + r)^{-2} = 10,000$$

$$(1 + r)^{-2} = \frac{10,000}{14,300} = 0.6993$$

$$r = 19.6\%$$

Return on investment:

$$19x5 \frac{10,000}{100,000} = 10\%$$

$$19x6 \frac{11,000}{110,000} = 10\%$$

$$19x7 \frac{14,300}{125,000} = 11.4\%$$

The manager is producing a profit growth and an increase in the return on investment simultaneously. It is still possible, however, that investment decisions may not be taking full advantage of the individual opportunities available or not be making adequate allowance for the interrelationships among the existing and proposed investments or that there may even be better investments. Investment policies, which are based on "portfolio" considerations, need to be examined in light of the return and risk goals of the firm as a whole, remembering the constraints within which both the firm and the division must operate.

All assets should not be expected to earn the same return because the required profitability may well differ across assets even in a single division if the risk associated with those returns differs. For the same reason, the returns appropriate to different divisions need not be identical, nor need they be identical to the average rate earned across the entire company. Some divisions are in more risky ventures than others. If performance is measured using a single rate, decisions that are inconsistent with the overall goals of the firm are likely.

Residual Income

Residual income is subject to substantially fewer problems. **Residual income** is income before capital costs, minus an implicit interest cost on all capital being employed. Residual income provides an alternative performance measure to ROI. Instead of measuring the percentage return achieved, it deducts an interest cost assumed to be required on the firm's capital and computes the income left over after the capital cost of the assets has been deducted.

Because common stock does not have an explicit cost, the accountant normally omits the cost of the stock of equity capital in computing accounting income. Residual income measures return after allowing for a return on equity as well as debt.

For example, suppose that a division has invested capital of $1,000,000, an implicit interest rate of 10 percent, and income before capital costs of $115,000. The residual income is calculated as follows:

Income before capital costs	$115,000
Invested capital × interest rate	100,000
Residual income	$ 15,000

Residual income has the desirable characteristic of having an expected positive present value for the incomes of an investment over its life (with an internal rate of return greater than its capital cost, if the cost of capital is used to compute the interest cost). The use of residual income to measure performance tends to give management an incentive to accept investments that have positive net present values. Residual income, as a performance measure, is discussed more extensively in the next chapter.

Measuring Performance on Different Levels of an Organization

The proper measures of performance are related to the degree of decentralization present and are a function of the level of organization under consideration. Several organizational levels are considered in this subsection. They include

- Department or cost center,
- Plant or operating unit,
- Division,
- Company.

Department or Cost Center

The term *department* is used here interchangeably with *cost center* or *burden center.* Assume that the performance of a manager, such as a foreman or department head, is to be measured. A manager's task is to accomplish a set objective with a minimum of cost. Recognizing that the task can be accomplished more expeditiously by incurring additional costs, a compromise between cost and time is required. Thus, a controller might be able to prepare the accounting reports two days sooner by hiring ten more accountants or by using a more powerful computer but still may not do so because the cost would be greater than the value of the expected benefits. To say that costs are too high must mean either that there is inefficiency and a waste of resources or that the benefits to be obtained are less than their cost, even if the operation is administered effectively.

In a research-and-development department, for example, the quantitative measurement of costs is reasonably accurate while the measurement of the benefits is not. Hence, it is very difficult to control or measure the performance of this type of department with purely quantitative measures. Contrarily, the direct costs and the benefits of a production department may be determined with relative accuracy, while the indirect costs are measured with less accuracy. The benefits in this case are the units produced. Generally, the costs are measured in terms of the labor, material, and overhead that are incurred by a department. The physical product may be converted into the amount of labor, material, and indirect costs that should have been used (the standard cost of the product), and the cost-control techniques suggested in Chapters 7 and 8 then can be used.

It is also necessary to control the scrap or spoilage that results from the manufacturing process. A high production level with low costs per unit may be desirable, but not if it results in large amounts of rework or unusable product. This undesirable outcome may be prevented by excluding bad units in computing the production of the period (if the bad production was caused within the department) and by controlling the amount of spoilage.

The main pitfall in measuring the performance of a department supervisor is one that applies to all levels of management — namely, the inclusion of items not controllable by the person whose performance is being measured. The supervisor should be held accountable for costs that can be directly identified with the department and over which control can be exerted. The measure of performance, for example, for the supervisor of an operating department should not include any departure from budgeted cost for the insurance on the machinery used in the department. Although this cost may be directly identified with the department, the variance is not a cost item controllable by the supervisor.

Plant or Operating Unit

This discussion assumes that the plant manager has no direct control over the sale of the product but is concerned with all phases of its production. Nevertheless, even though the production manager does not control sales, the manager can indirectly influence the level of sales. Availability of a product of good quality leads to satisfied customers, which in turn will influence the demand schedule. The same is true of service. When attempts are made to compute a profit and a return on investment for the plant under these conditions, this computation is likely to be dysfunctional and even misleading. The profit of the plant is a function of the level of sales, the sales price, and the cost of the product. If the plant manager has control over the last item only, performance should be measured only by the cost of product or, perhaps even better, by the costs incurred in relation to the level of production. Additional measures can and should be developed for the quality of the product, for service, and for product availability.

Computing a profit for a plant is generally thought to supply both a measure of performance and an incentive for improved performance. It may approximately accomplish this goal during prosperous periods, but in periods of slack activity the plant manager can blame a poor showing on low unit sales or a low sales price. These two items are probably the most dramatic of the causes of low profits, but there also may be inefficiencies that should be corrected.

A suitable measure of the performance of the plant manager is similar to the measure of performance of the department supervisor whose task is to complete a good product on time and at as low a cost as possible. Thus, the same measures used at the department level are also appropriate at the plant level. A desirable, but difficult to attain, situation is one in which the costs of production of one plant may be compared to the costs of similar plants.

In addition to the quantitative measures centering around the costs of production, the overall evaluation of performance should include the quality of the work performed and the timeliness of production — that is, ability to meet production schedules. Quality and service are particularly important in the service sector. For example, hotels and motels closely monitor physical appearance, cleanliness, lighting, and similar items. Although sometimes difficult to quantify, these factors can be extremely important in directly affecting the firm's profits. Evaluation should also consider any geographic and time differences involved in profit comparisons. Multiple performance measures are common, many of which are nonfinancial.

Because the authority of the plant manager is broader than that of the department head, more costs incurred in the plant are controllable by the manager. In fact, any out-of-pocket expenditures originating in the plant are usually subject to control and thus should be used in measuring performance. Whether expenses such as depreciation of plant and equipment should be included in the computation of the cost of product is a more difficult issue. Even a plant manager who did not have a voice in the original purchase of these assets does control their use, and the opportunity costs of these assets may well be included, perhaps as a separable item. The ideal measure of the opportunity cost would be the incremental revenues that would have resulted from the best alternative use of the assets. Depreciation may represent a reasonable surrogate for the opportunity cost.

Division

The measurement of the performance of the division manager who does not control sales is exactly analogous to that of the plant manager. The use of costs of production is a better measure of performance than a profit figure affected by items not controllable by the manager. When the division manager has control of the selling effort but not the level of plant investment, a different measure of performance is required — for example, the difference between revenues and costs controllable at the divisional level.

Where the division manager also controls the level of investment, the measurement of performance is further broadened. The division then becomes an entity very similar to a small corporation, and many of the measures of performance relevant for corporate organizations can be used. These may include total sales, profits, residual income, return on investment, investment turnover, operating profit per dollar of sales, share of market, and changes in any of the above items.

Two problems that are encountered with a division (and with plants and cost centers) but not with a separate corporation are the problem of common costs (or cost allocations) and the problem of pricing transfers to and from other divisions. The allocation of common costs has been discussed. Transfer pricing is the topic of Chapter 24.

In measuring the performance of a division, the allocations of central office costs should in general be excluded. The division manager has no control over these costs, and while the division may benefit from the incurrence of the expenses, more harm than good may be accomplished by including these costs in divisional income statements and in computations of return on investment. Yet it may be desirable to inform the division that a standard amount is billed for central office services and that for the corporation to be profitable these costs must be recovered. This can be done by calculating and displaying a second performance figure that incorporates these items. If services such as engineering or consulting are requested by a division from the central office, a charge based on a standard (or market) fee would be appropriate to reflect the use of scarce corporate resources. When more than one performance figure is used, management must be careful to make clear how each is to be used in the evaluation process.

Company

The measures of performance used in the case of a division that controls its sales and investment decisions can be used for the company. Several problems are eliminated, such as transfer pricing and the allocation of overhead costs, but many problems related to financial accounting still remain, including the question of what items to capitalize, the depreciation and inventory methods to use, and the treatment of leases. There are no shortages of accounting problems.

Other problems exist as well. If, for example, decreased sales are a result of general business conditions, does this absolve the company president (or division manager) from the blame of having a bad year? The president is responsible for how well the company does but cannot control the business cycle, yet over time, a good manager is expected to operate effectively through the ups and downs of the business cycle.

Perhaps the most common performance measures at the overall corporate level are those that reflect profitability. Paramount among these measures is the return-on-investment measure.[4] This measure has already been given substantial attention, and a number of its problems have been discussed.

Residual income is a theoretically correct measure of profitability. Determining residual income, however, necessitates a selection of the appropriate interest rate to use in charging implicit interest. The choice of a rate tends to be based in practice on some concept of the average required return, or cost of capital. Not only is this a difficult value to determine, but it may not be appropriate to use this rate to estimate the capital cost on incremental investments with risk characteristics quite different from those implicit to the existing asset mix. It may be necessary instead to use several different rates to reflect the different investment risks.

4. See R. Scapend, J. Sale, and P. Tikkas, *Financial Control of Divisional Capital Investment* (London: Institute of Cost and Management Accountants, 1982): 128.

Measures for Improving Performance

Good performance measures provide managers with figures that they can use to control operations. However, performance measures often represent the combined results of many subsidiary variables. Where possible, it is helpful to provide managers with indicators of the economic value of scarce resources to subactivities — that is, the opportunity costs of the scarce resources. These measures of opportunity cost provide the means by which managers can make better decisions concerning the activities on which to focus and which resources are in short supply. In some cases, the opportunity cost of resources can be obtained by noting the increase in contribution that can be achieved by switching one unit of a scarce resource to its best alternative use. The opportunity cost of other factors can be estimated by determining the contribution obtainable if another unit of the resource were available. Shadow prices resulting from the solution of mathematical programming formulations are measures of opportunity cost and may facilitate resource-allocation decisions when the assumptions of the mathematical technique are reasonable.[5] This evaluation is best made by the manager with help of an operations research expert.

Results of mathematical programming formulations are also relevant to controlling operations. If decisions are made using a linear programming model, the original solution adopted before the operating plan is implemented may be compared with a revised solution based on changes occurring in the data input to the model during the operating period. The value of the objective function using the now nonoptimal activity level with the new data can be determined and compared with the value of the objective function under the new optimal solution. The difference represents the gain from altering the program. If this difference exceeds the change-over cost, consideration should be given to altering the activity levels.

If it is too late to make the adjustments, the revised solution compared to the initial solution provides a rough measure of the forecasting error and hence the amount that might be expended on improving the forecasting activity. The difference between the actual results and the revised or ex post solution is an estimate of the opportunity cost associated with the actions taken. The differences or variances can be examined using the methods described in Chapters 7 and 8.

A distinction should be made between the performance of managers and the performance of the investment in an organizational subunit such as a plant or division. Managers should be evaluated on the basis of those costs, programs, and decisions under their control. A division may prove unsuccessful regardless of the efforts of its management.

---

5. Using the dual of the profit-maximization form of the problem, the optimal value of each ordinary or structural variable represents the increase in contribution if the associated activity is increased by one unit. The optimal value of each slack variable shows the decline in contribution if that activity is expanded by one unit. See Chapter 17 for a discussion of linear programming in cost analysis.

Exceptional managers are often shifted to the department or plant where troubles are plentiful. They may not be able to improve the performance to levels acceptable for that division. And even if they did improve performance, they might never achieve the return experienced by a segment of the organization facing better economic conditions. If top management relied solely on profit-performance comparisons to judge management, skillful managers would be reluctant to accept such trouble-plagued assignments. The current contribution to profit compared to past levels is one useful measure of the manager's performance (coupled with effects on morale, training, and so on). A measure of investment return would also be relevant to evaluating the unit's investment performance.

Cost Allocations

Assume each of five operating divisions of a firm shows positive income that add up to $15,000,000. However, the costs of the firm not associated directly with any operating unit are $18,000,000. The firm's president is not willing to indicate that all the operating units are profitable when the corporate entity as a whole is losing $3,000,000. The solution generally used is to allocate the $18,000,000 to the operating units on as reasonable bases as are feasible. But no matter what reasonable bases are chosen, the allocations can still be objected to on both theoretical and practical grounds.

Decisions being made can probably be made more correctly without the cost allocations where there is not a direct linkage between the cost incurrence and benefits received by the operating units. Decision models normally omit cost allocations based on accounting conventions and attempt to include the opportunity cost of using scarce resources using alternative analytical techniques (such as linear programming). At a minimum the decision maker should consider the decision with and without including the allocated costs.

Although the theoretical solution for decisions is relatively clear (the omission of cost allocations not based on a direct benefit relationship), the president's problem still remains. There is a strong temptation to allocate the costs but label the expense line item as being noncontrollable by the operating unit's management. This alerts division managers that they have to recover more than their own expenses if the firm is to survive. The head office expenses also have to be recovered. Top management can focus on both the contribution of each division to recovery of head office expenses as well as the net arising after the deduction of the noncontrollable (by the operating unit) expenses.

Nonfinancial Performance Measures

Many companies also make extensive use of nonfinancial measures in evaluating the performance of divisions or departments. Such information helps top management to understand the reasons behind changes in financial performance measures such as ROI or residual income. An illustration is given by the following information provided by General Electric Company.

General Electric Company	Measurement	Criteria
	Market Position	Market Share.
	Product Leadership	Comparison of design, features, quality, and cost with competing products.
	Productivity	The change from period to period in the relationship between output of goods and services and the resources consumed in their production. Output is measured by net sales billed. Input is measured by total cost of operations. Both output and input are adjusted to a constant-dollar basis by use of price and inflation indices, respectively.
	Employee Attitudes	Comparison of annual salaried-employee surveys with results from prior periods. Emphasis placed upon effectiveness of communications, fairness of management actions, working environment, and compensation.
	Number of Employees	Management, salaried, and hourly classifications of employees.
	Customer Service	The company is currently defining variables associated with customer service so that this area may be monitored in a quantitative manner.

Executive Compensation Plans

Executive compensation plans come in a variety of forms. Normally, the compensation is linked to both the profitability of the firm and the profitability of the manager's operating unit. This approach attempts to assure loyalty to the firm and increase firm profitability. This is the basic objective since one way to achieve the firm's profitability is to increase the profitability of the operating unit in which one works.

The measures on which the compensation is based are heavily weighted by the performance during the most recent time periods, but the past history of the firm is also frequently included (an effort to consider the long term rather than only the short term).

Although the accounting operating results are an important input, the compensation package frequently is affected by the performance of the firm's stock price. The entire calculation should not be dependent on market fluctuations, but ignoring market value (the maximization of shareholder value) is an error. Management should be rewarded for increasing shareholder value.

Too frequently the managerial compensation is determined by return on equity (ROE) or ROI calculations. As one of several inputs, the use of ROE or ROI may be useful (as long as the importance of ROE or ROI is not large compared to other measures). One way to neutralize negative aspects of return on investment is to include growth as one of the important facts. The limitations of ROI are discussed in detail in the next chapter, which also discusses an alternative basis of rewarding management.

As advanced manufacturing techniques (CIM) involving massive amounts of capital are used, it becomes extremely important that performance measures and managerial compensation plans be correctly structured so that the appropriate costs of using the capital are included in the calculations. The use of residual income offers a solution to this problem.

Summary

Quantitative measures of performance may assist in measuring performance, but they are not the complete answer. If enough measures are used, always in reference to trends and changes and with such factors as general business conditions considered, a reasonable indication of the performance of the management team can be obtained. For example, the use of market share can be a measure of performance when business conditions change, but this has to be supported by an analysis of changes in prices and selling expenditures to ensure the market share gain did not result in decreased profits. In addition to the record of performance, an analysis of the decision-making techniques used by the manager is extremely useful in evaluating managerial performance.

Key Terms to Review

investment turnover, p. 780
operating rate, p. 780

residual income, p. 789
return on investment (ROI), p. 782

Review Problem

USE OF ROI

The Southern Electric Company has been making electric motors for fifty years. Ten years ago it started a finance company to finance its receivables. The financial subsidiary has grown rapidly, and today the financing of receivables is an extremely small part of its activities.

The Motor Division is currently earning a 12 percent return on investment. The financial subsidiary is earning a 24.3 percent return on the Southern Company's investment.

The parent has a $700,000,000 investment in the financial subsidiary, as follows:

DOLLARS IN MILLIONS			
Assets	$5,000	Earnings before interest	$600
Liabilities	4,300	Interest	430
Stock equity	700	Income	$170

Based on the $700,000,000 investment of Southern Electric Company the ROI is:

$$\text{ROI} = \frac{170}{700} = .243$$

Based on the return-on-investment information above, top management has decided to shift capital resources from the Motor Division to the Financial Subsidiary. Evaluate the decision making.

Solution to Review Problem

a. The chapters on capital budgeting do not recommend using ROI or return on equity (ROE) to allocate capital.

b. Assume the Motor Division has the following balance sheet and income statement:

Assets	$5,000	Earnings before interest	$600
Liabilities	2,000	Interest	200
Stock equity	3,000	Income	$400

$$\text{ROI} = \frac{600}{5,000} = .12$$

$$\text{ROE} = \frac{400}{3,000} = .133$$

If the Motor Division had the same amount of .10 debt as the Financial Subsidiary, we would have

$$\text{ROI} = \frac{600}{5,000} = .12$$

which is identically the same as the financial subsidiary. Beware of ROI. Its use has pitfalls.

Suggested Readings

Abdallah, W., and D. Keller. "Measuring the Multinationals' Performance." *Management Accounting* (October 1985): 26–30.

Assessing Foreign Subsidiary Performance. New York: Business International Corporation, 1982.

Howell, R. A., and S. R. Soucy. "Operating Controls in the New Manufacturing Environment." *Management Accounting* (October 1987): 25–31.

Kaplan, R. "Accounting Lag: The Obsolescence of Cost Accounting Systems." *California Management Review* (Winter 1986): 174–99.

Kaplan, R., and A. Atkinson. *Advanced Managerial Accounting,* 2nd ed. Englewood Cliffs, N.J.: Prentice-Hall, 1989.

Scapend, R., J. Sale, and P. Tikkas. *Financial Control of Divisional Capital Investment.* London: Institute of Cost and Management Accountants, 1982, p. 128.

Simon, H. A., H. Guetzkow, G. Kozmetsky, and G. Tyndall. *Centralization vs. Decentralization in Organizing the Controller's Department.* New York: Controllership Foundation, 1954.

Sloan, A. P., Jr., edited by J. McDonald and C. Stevens. *My Years with General Motors.* New York: Doubleday, 1964.

Solomons, D. *Division Performance: Measurement and Control.* New York: New York Financial Executive Research Foundation, 1965.

Thompson, P., and G. Dalton. "Performance Appraisal: Management Beware." *Harvard Business Review* (January-February 1970): 149–57.

Review Questions

22-1 From the annual reports of three companies in the same industry, compute the

   a. Operating rates,

   b. Investment turnover,

   c. Return on investment.

   Describe the difficulties of using the computations. Would the same difficulties persist if you had access to the corporate records?

22-2 What additional information is required for evaluating performance in a profit center that is not required in a cost center?

22-3 To what extent can quantitative measures reflect the performance of a manager? Would it be reasonable to rely exclusively on quantitative measures?

22-4 Define the term *return on investment.*

22-5 Should accumulated depreciation be deducted in computing the investment for purposes of computing return on investment?

22-6 What are the difficulties of measuring the performance of a research and development department?

22-7 What two ratios may be multiplied together to compute the return on investment?

22-8 Managers are usually evaluated on their actual performance. What alternatives are there, and what is your evaluation of them?

22-9 Explain how the use of ROI as the sole measure of performance for divisions within a company can produce results different from those desired.

22-10 Compare and contrast ROI and residual income as performance evaluators. List some advantages and disadvantages associated with each measure.

Exercises

22-11 Return on Investment Charts as Control Devices   The Deep Well Machine Company has twenty divisions and is highly decentralized. Each division makes its own decisions as to price, output, and investments.

One of the primary means of measuring performance used by the company is the return-on-investment chart. Using a series of these charts, the performance of each division through time is noted as well as the comparison of each division with each other division.

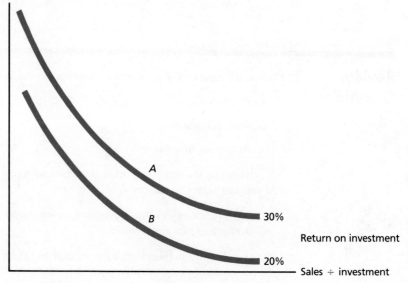

Top management is very enthusiastic about the charts because they show the relationship of profit to sales (operating profit per dollar of sales), sales to investment (the investment turnover), and the return on investment (profit divided by average investment).

The charts are relatively easy to construct because each return-on-investment curve is a smooth curve. Thus only three or four points have to be plotted for each return-on-investment value and a curve drawn to connect the points.

Comment on the effectiveness of these charts as control devices. Is division *A* more efficient than division *B* if the cost of money to the firm is 0.15? Explain.

22-12 Determining Growth Rates The Thistle Company has a policy of accepting only investments that have internal rates of return equal to or in excess of 0.10. It also pays out as dividends 60 percent of its earnings. Assuming that investments are financed entirely with funds generated from operations, at what minimum average rate would you expect the earnings of this firm to grow? Assume further that there are many investments available that return 10 percent.

22-13 Relationship Between Profit Margin and Return on Investment How is it possible for some companies to have very low profit margins and high returns on investment while other companies have very high profit margins and low returns on investment? Explain this phenomenon in terms of the formula for ROI.

22-14 Evaluating Performance The executives of a large company are attempting to construct measures to evaluate the performance of machining department foremen. One problem facing the executives is deciding which variables to include in the measures. They feel that no variable should be used in performance evaluation unless the variables can be affected by actions on the part of the foremen. The following list includes many of the variables that the executives have considered. State whether each variable is controllable or not controllable by the foremen.

a. Rework expenses

b. Lubricant expenses

c. Building rent

d. Supplies expenses

e. Repairs and maintenance expenses

f. Freight-in costs for materials

g. Direct-labor payment rates

h. Overtime expenses

i. Payroll taxes

j. Taxes on building and equipment

k. Insurance on building and equipment

l. Depreciation on equipment

m. Idle time

n. Clean-up labor

o. Heat in building

22-15 Fill in the Blanks   The following financial information applies to three companies in the same industry. Fill in the blanks.

	Company A	Company B	Company C
Sales	$1,000,000	$1,500,000	$———— (e)
Income	———— (a)	125,000	400,000
Average investment	———— (b)	1,000,000	———— (f)
Investment turnover	2	———— (c)	1.5
Return on investment	5%	———— (d)	10%

22-16 Return on Investment and Average Investment   A small firm has an operating rate of .06 and an investment turnover of 3.

REQUIRED

a. Compute the return on investment.

b. If sales are $100,000, what is the average investment?

c. If the president of the firm wishes to increase the return on investment without increasing the average investment, what major approaches are there?

22-17 Comparing Divisional Growth Rates and Return on Investment   The following data applies to two divisions in the same company:

	Division A		Division B	
	Operating Profit	Average Investment	Operating Profit	Average Investment
Year 1	$50,000	$500,000	$15,000	$ 90,000
Year 2	60,000	550,000	10,000	100,000
Year 3	65,000	600,000	20,000	150,000
Year 4	70,000	700,000	14,000	140,000

REQUIRED:

a. Compute growth rates in operating profits for each division for each year.

b. Compute the return on investment for each division for each year.

c. Based on **a** and **b**, which division has performed better? Do you need to qualify your answer? Why or why not?

22-18 Changing Prices to Achieve Return on Investment   In order to achieve a return on investment of 15 percent next year, a divisional manager of a large, diversified company is considering a price increase from $4 to $5 on each unit of the single product manufactured by his division. The applicable financial information projected for next year is as follows:

Average investment	$400,000
Variable cost per unit	3
Fixed expenses	100,000
Tax rate	40%

REQUIRED:

a. How many units must the division sell in order to achieve a 15 percent ROI for next year?

b. Compute the investment turnover and the operating rate associated with the 15 percent ROI.

22-19 **Comparing Divisional Return on Investment and Residual Income**   The following information concerns two divisions within a large manufacturing firm:

	Division A	Division B
Operating income	$ 500,000	$ 2,500,000
Operating assets	2,500,000	25,000,000

REQUIRED:

a. Compute the return on investment for each division.

b. Compute residual income using

(1)   5%

(2) 10%

(3) 15%

(4) 20%

c. Based on a and b, which division has the better performance?

22-20 **Evaluating Product Profit Using Return on Sales**   The Large Department Store uses return on sales to determine whether or not products are dropped from its product line. Two products are currently being evaluated.

	Product A	Product B
Sales	$200,000	$400,000
Merchandise cost	120,000	270,000
Gross margin	80,000	130,000

The inclusion of indirect costs results in the following statements:

	Product A		Product B	
Sales	$200,000		$400,000	
Merchandise cost	120,000		270,000	
Indirect costs	60,000		120,000	
Net income	$ 20,000	.10	$ 10,000	.025

It was decided that product B was inferior to A and should be dropped because its return per dollar of sales was only .025. Assume the investment for both products is $800,000. Is it possible that B is better than A? Explain.

Problems

22-21 How Evaluation Criteria Affect Investment Decisions   Brightbulb Manufacturing Company, a subsidiary of Acme Lighting, has prepared a schedule of investments that are proposed for the coming year. The following data apply to the investments:

Project	Required Investment	Projected First-Year Incremental Operating Income
A	$1,000,000	$ 10,000
B	1,000,000	40,000
C	1,000,000	150,000
D	2,000,000	200,000
E	2,000,000	200,000
F	2,000,000	250,000
G	2,000,000	300,000

The firm presently employs assets totaling $30,000,000, and with no additional investments the firm would expect operating income for the next year to total $5,000,000.

Assume that each project is independent of all others — that is, the fact that one project will be adopted and will not affect the projected incremental operating income for other projects considered here or presently in use.

REQUIRED:

a. Assuming that the president of Brightbulb knows the evaluation will be based on the maximum ROI delivered for the year, and ROI is to be maximized, what project or projects will be selected (use $30,000,000 plus the project investments as the base for computing ROI)?

b. Assuming that the president will be evaluated on the basis of next year's residual income using a 10 percent imputed interest charge, what project or projects will be selected?

c. How might the use of a one-year evaluation period affect the long-run performance of the firm?

22-22 Investment Evaluation Jim Smith is a young division manager (age thirty-four) employed by the Ace Corporation who hopes to become president of the firm before he is forty years old. Currently he is considering a major investment for his division. The following summary information has been prepared for him:

- Expected NPV (using .15) = − $10,000,000

- Expected IRR = .12

- The firm has a .15 required return.

Ordinarily, Jim would reject the investment using the conventional criteria of requiring a positive net present value or an IRR greater than the required return.

Jim knows the negative $10,000,000 of NPV is an expectation and the more detailed analysis indicates the following:

Event	Probability	NPV
Very good business condition	.3	$ 30,000,000
Good business condition	.5	2,000,000
Bad business condition	.2	− 100,000,000
	$E(NPV)$ =	− $10,000,000

With .8 probability of success and .3 probability of great success, Jim is inclined to accept the investment.

Last year in a good business condition year Ace Corporation earned $50,000,000, but a series of the kind of losses that occur with bad business conditions would jeopardize its existence.

REQUIRED:

a. Is the investment desirable?

b. What does this situation imply about the investment evaluation procedures?

22-23 Continuation of Problem 22-22 Jim Smith, recently fired by the Ace Corporation, has been hired by the Buzzell Corporation as a division manager. The Buzzell Corporation is a relatively conservative firm that likes to have a safety margin in its investments.

Jim's division has the chance to invest $10,000,000 in new equipment with known technology to produce a product with a steady demand and steady price.

The expected IRR is .14 and the net present value using .15 as a discount rate is a negative $1,000,000. The firm uses a weighted average cost of capital .15 as a discount rate.

Although most of the firm's investments have modest risk, this investment is relatively safe. Unless there is a major technological breakthrough the product will continue to sell, and it is not expected that the method of production will change drastically in the foreseeable future.

Because of his recent unhappy experience associated with promoting an unsuccessful project with the Ace Corporation, Jim is reluctant to advocate this project with an expected return of .14.

A study of the possible outcomes indicates the following:

Event	Probability	IRR Outcome
Very good business conditions	.3	.180
Good business conditions	.5	.150
Poor business conditions	.2	.055
	Expected IRR =	.14

Debt costs .12 and the after-tax cost of debt is .12(1 − .46) = .0648.

REQUIRED:

Should Jim advocate the project? What should the top managers of the firm want Jim to do?

22-24 Evaluating Compensation Plans   The Owens-Corning Fiberglas Corporation's Notice of Annual Meeting of Stockholders and Proxy Statement of April 16, 1981, included the following statement:

> The principal executive officers of the Company participate in the Company's stockholder-approved Additional Compensation Plan which provides for payment of additional compensation to participants based upon income before taxes of the Company in excess of $12\frac{1}{2}\%$ of capital invested. Some officers participate in part in this Plan and in part in other incentive compensation plans, or solely in those incentive compensation plans that are based upon achievement of performance goals set each year. All numbers in this column include payments under these plans for 1980.

REQUIRED:

Evaluate the plan. Assume a long-term debt cost of .16 in 1980.

22-25 Continuation of Problem 22-24   The Owens-Corning Fiberglas Corporation's Notice of Annual Meeting of Stockholders to be held on April 15, 1982, included the following statement:

> The Board of Directors terminated the Additional Compensation Plan effective for 1982. The Board concluded that this annual incentive compensation plan, first adopted in 1946, no longer served the best interest of the Company. All officers participate in one or more other incentive compensation plans, which are based generally upon achievement of performance goals set each year. All numbers in this column include payments under these plans for 1981.
>
> This column includes amounts expensed for financial reporting purposes for 1981 for contributions, payments, or accruals for the account of each named officer and all officers as a group for the stockholder-approved Savings and Stock Investment Plan.

In 1980 the stockholders of the Company adopted the Owens-Corning Fiberglas Corporation Long-Term Incentive Plan. The Compensation Committee of the board of directors selected participants in the plan for the 1980–83 and 1982–85 performance periods and granted each participant a target award for each period based on the participant's level of responsibility and the impact of his job on the company's success. The Committee also established target levels of company performance at which the target awards, and lesser or greater amounts, could be earned. The performance criteria for the 1980–83 performance period are based on both compounded growth in the company's annual earnings per share, compared with the average earnings per share for the years 1978 and 1979, and average annual return on the company's gross assets over the four-year period. The performance criteria for the 1982–85 performance period are based on both total net income and average annual return on the company's gross assets over the four-year period. Target awards are payable from 50 percent to 150 percent if compounded annual earnings per share or total net income and average annual return on gross assets reach specified levels for each performance period. Target awards payable may be adjusted up or down by 20 percent to reflect individual performance. In addition, any awards paid will be increased or decreased by one-half of the percentage change in the fair market value of common stock from the beginning to the end of the applicable performance period. Each officer is a participant in the plan for the 1980–83 and 1982–85 performance periods. No amounts were accrued under the plan in 1981.

REQUIRED:

Evaluate the new plan.

22-26 Evaluating Compensation Plans   The Boise Cascade Corporation's notice of its April 21, 1981, annual meeting included the following plan:

Performance Share Plan. The Company has a Performance Share Plan under which the board of directors grants performance shares (each performance share being equal to one share of the Company's common stock) to officers of the Company. The shares are credited to an account maintained for each officer over a five-year award period. Each performance share will have a value equal to the fair market value of one share of the Company's common stock. At distribution, however, no performance share may have a fair market value greater than three times the fair market value of a share of the Company's common stock on January 1 of the calendar year in which an award is granted.

There will be no payment under the Plan for an award period unless, for the five-year period, the Company achieves a return on equity of 10% or more and the Company's return on equity is at least 80% of the average of the returns on equity achieved by a key competitor group defined in the Plan.

If the Company meets the minimum return on equity and relative return on equity standards, payments to the executive officers for performance shares will be made in accordance with a schedule set forth in the Plan. Payments will normally be made one-half in cash and one-half in the Company's common stock. The following table illustrates the percent of performance shares to be paid to participants at certain levels of relative return on equity:

Relative Return on Equity	Percentage of Performance Shares to Be Paid to Participants
If the Relative Return on Equity is 80%	25
If the Relative Return on Equity is 90%	41
If the Relative Return on Equity is 100%	75
If the Relative Return on Equity is 117%	100

REQUIRED:

Evaluate the plan.

23

Return on Investment and Residual Income: Decision Effects and the Impact of Inflation

LEARNING OBJECTIVES

After studying this chapter, you should be able to:

1 Explain why performance evaluation measures and decision criteria must be consistent.

2 Describe the deficiencies of the return-on-investment measure.

3 Compute and evaluate the return-on-investment calculation.

4 Use the present-value depreciation method.

5 Explain the relative merits of return on investment and residual income as performance measures.

6 Describe the effects of inflation on performance measures and decision-making criteria.

7 Understand the implications of price-level–adjusted performance measures.

M ost people like to know how well they are doing, and managers are no exception. Furthermore, top managers like to know how those working below them are performing. This chapter is about performance measurement in situations where the manager controls the decisions to obtain, use, and dispose of the assets. The discussion explores issues related to the use of return on investment and residual income for segment performance measurement.

After an investment decision has been made and the asset has been acquired, it is sensible to evaluate management's performance in the utilization of the asset. To reduce potential misunderstandings, the term *asset* is used here in place of *investment*, since this evaluative process applies to all assets and not just those currently being acquired. Sometimes it is impossible to evaluate the performance of isolated assets. Because assets are used jointly, it is necessary to evaluate the use of groups of assets. Thus, the recommendations made in this chapter cannot always be applied precisely to single assets. One necessary condition for the application of the proposed methods is that the costs and benefits of the investment be measurable in dollars. The discussion applies equally to the operations of a firm, division, or other subunit that meets the definition of an investment center. An investment center both earns income (as does a profit center) and uses readily identified assets whose values can be measured.

Previous chapters have recommended the use of discounted-cash-flow evaluation procedures in making investment decisions. However, after an asset has been acquired, performance evaluation is likely to be based on return on investment (ROI). One measure that affects both the income and investment measures is depreciation. An objective of this chapter is to present a method involving depreciation, income, and investment to be used in performance evaluation that is consistent with the discounted-cash-flow procedure used in the investment decision-making process. Evaluations are more useful if they reflect the decision process that led to the investment initially.

Tools for Measuring Performance

Using ROI

If a firm earns $1,000,000 on an asset base of $1,000,000, it is earning an exceptional return on investment of 100 percent. If the same income is earned using $100,000,000 of assets, the return earned is only 1 percent, and this is not a good return. Both the dollar amount of assets used, as well as the income earned, must be known before anything can be concluded about management's performance. Return on investment is the most widely used method of evaluating the performance of an investment center, not only because it measures income relative to investment but also because the necessary inputs to the calculation are readily available in the financial records.

The ROI of a period is given by

$$ROI = \frac{Income}{Investment}$$

Suppose the firm is using a beginning-of-period definition of investment where accumulated depreciation is deducted and depreciation expense is computed using the straight-line method. The firm requires a 20 percent return on its investments, and an investment costing $21,065 is made with a life of three years. Management expects the investment to produce $10,000 of cash flows per year. If expectations are realized, this investment yields a 20 percent internal rate of return (IRR). Yet the yearly return-on-investment figures neither equal 20 percent (in any year) nor average 20 percent. Taxes are ignored here without any effect on the ideas presented in order to make the exposition easier.

Using straight-line depreciation, the income statements and the ROIs for each year, if expectations are realized, are given in Exhibit 23-1:

EXHIBIT 23-1

Investment ROIs

	Year 1	Year 2	Year 3
Cash flows	$10,000	$10,000	$10,000
Depreciation expense[a]	7,022	7,022	7,022
Income	$ 2,978	$ 2,978	$ 2,978
Beginning investment[b]	$21,065	$14,044	$ 7,022
ROI	$\dfrac{\$\,2,978}{\$21,065} = .14$	$\dfrac{\$\,2,978}{\$14,044} = .21$	$\dfrac{\$\,2,978}{\$\,7,022} = .42$

[a] Straight line: $21,065 ÷ 3.
[b] Initial cost less accumulated depreciation.

In year 1 the return on investment is .14. This is below the desired return of 0.20 even though expectations are precisely realized. Therefore, the manager's performance could easily be judged unsatisfactory. In year 2 the return is near the predicted level, but in year 3 the manager shows a ROI of .42, and hence performance may be considered exceptional. These results take place despite the fact that in all three years the forecasted income and the actual income are identical. The range of outcomes makes the use of ROI as a performance measure less than ideal. Further, if ROI is computed using accounting-based revenues and expenses as calculated in more realistic situations, additional discrepancies may be introduced.

The conventional ROI calculation is deficient in several respects, and thus it cannot be relied on always to give a useful measure of performance. To highlight its limitations, an example is used in which the conventional accounting does produce a ROI equal to the investment's internal rate of return.

Assume a firm is considering an investment with the cash flows given in Exhibit 23-2:

EXHIBIT 23-2

Investment Cash Flows

Time	Cash Flows
0	$-30,000 (investment)
1	16,000
2	14,000
3	12,000

This investment also has an internal rate of return (IRR) of .20. Using straight-line depreciation, the computation of the ROIs (assuming no other differences exist between accounting income and cash flows, except depreciation) also yields 20 percent, as is shown in Exhibit 23-3:

EXHIBIT 23-3

Return-on-Investment Calculations for the Investment in Exhibit 23-2

	Year 1	Year 2	Year 3
Cash flows	$16,000	$14,000	$12,000
Depreciation expense	10,000	10,000	10,000
Income	$ 6,000	$ 4,000	$ 2,000
Beginning investment	$30,000	$20,000	$10,000
ROI	$\dfrac{\$ 6,000}{\$30,000} = .20$	$\dfrac{\$ 4,000}{\$20,000} = .20$	$\dfrac{\$ 2,000}{\$10,000} = .20$

In this case the ROIs are equal for each year and are also identical to the investment's IRR. However, the sequence of cash flows is somewhat unusual. They decrease through time by an equal amount each year, and the amount of the decrease is equal to the depreciation expense multiplied by the IRR. This is the only set of cash-flow (accounting-income) numbers that will yield the 20 percent return implicit to the investment for each year of the asset's life.

A unique set of unusual cash flows is required to obtain the result. For any given set of cash flows, there is only one depreciation schedule that yields the return implicit to the asset (.20 here) when it is purchased. Further, the depreciation schedule may be quite unusual and is tied to the values of the asset through time. With increasing cash flows, the distortions introduced by conventional accounting are severe. For example, assume the cash flows in Exhibit 23-4:

EXHIBIT 23-4

Cash Flows

Time	Cash Flows
0	$-30,000 (investment)
1	12,000
2	14,400
3	17,280

The internal rate of return is again .20. The accounting incomes (assumed equal to cash flows reduced by depreciation) and ROIs of the three years are shown in Exhibit 23-5:

EXHIBIT 23-5

Return on Investment for an Asset with the Cash Flows in Exhibit 23-4

	Year 1	Year 2	Year 3
Cash flows	$12,000	$14,400	$17,280
Depreciation expense	10,000	10,000	10,000
Income	$ 2,000	$ 4,400	$ 7,280
Beginning investment	$30,000	$20,000	$10,000
ROI	$\frac{\$2,000}{\$30,000} = 0.067$	$\frac{\$4,400}{\$20,000} = 0.220$	$\frac{\$7,280}{\$10,000} = 0.728$

These ROI measures of performance are misleading. It is not useful to have an ROI of .067 in year 1 and .728 in year 3 when the actual results are exactly as forecasted, and the investment yields the .20 internal rate of return established at the time the investment was made.

Present-Value (or Economic) Depreciation

The economic depreciation expense for an asset is defined as the change in the value of the asset, where value is computed using the asset's cash flows. This is **present-value** or **economic depreciation.** The ROI continues to be calculated as income divided by beginning investment, but income is now computed using present-value depreciation. To avoid complications, the following example assumes that the actual decrease in value for each period is the same as the expected decrease. The tax rate is zero for this example.

Assume that an asset costs $17,355 and has expected net cash flows of $10,000 per year for two years. The cash is received at the end of each period and the time value of money is 10 percent. The IRR of this investment is 10 percent. (The present value of $10,000 for two years at 10 percent is $17,355.) Assume the actual cash flows also turn out to be $10,000 as expected.

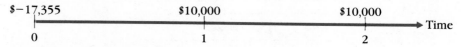

The value at time 0 is

$$\frac{\$10,000}{(1.10)^1} + \frac{\$10,000}{(1.10)^2} = \$17,355$$

The value of the asset at time 1 is

$$\frac{\$10,000}{1.10} = \$9,091$$

The value at time 2 is zero.

The present-value (or economic) depreciation expense measures are:

Period 1 depreciation = value time 0 − value time 1 = $17,355 − $9,091
$$= \$8,264$$

Period 2 depreciation = value time 1 − value time 2 = $ 9,091 − $0
$$= \$9,091$$

The incomes are:

Income for period 1 = $10,000 − $8,264 = $1,736

Income for period 2 = $10,000 − $9,091 = $909

The investment has the values, decreases in values, and performance measurements given in Exhibit 23-6 for the two years of its existence.

Using this depreciation procedure, the returns on investment of each period (cash flow less depreciation divided by net investment) are the same, and they equal the internal rate of return of the investment as anticipated upon purchase.

If the straight-line method of depreciation were used instead, as is common in accounting, the results in Exhibit 23-7 are obtained. The return on investment increases from an unsatisfactory (in that it is less than the cost of money) 7.6 percent to a satisfactory 15.2 percent for a situation in which the cash proceeds that were used to predict the expected IRR of 10 percent actually occur.

EXHIBIT 23-6

ROI Using Present-Value Depreciation

Period t	Investment, End of Period	Cash Flow	Present-Value Depreciation	Income: $10,000– Depreciation	Return on Investment
0	$17,355	—	—	—	—
1	9,091	$10,000	$8,264	$1,736	10%
2	0	$10,000	9,091	909	10%

There is a deficiency in a system that forecasts one thing and, when the forecasted event actually occurs, reports something different. The present investment promises a 10 percent return and constant proceeds, but only if the reporting method suggested in this subsection is used will the reported return be consistent with the interest rate used in the decision model. Hence, in a situation where the benefits are constant, the depreciation used in evaluating the investment should not be straight-line depreciation if return on investment is to be used in performance evaluation. Furthermore, accelerated depreciation would further distort the measurement problem. In fact, only a very special depreciation schedule is consistent with a given investment. Moreover, this schedule may not be related to any of the depreciation schemes commonly used by accountants. The objective is to develop a schedule of depreciation that is internally consistent with the investment decision, and at the same time that gives reasonable measures of income and return on investment for each year.

Other Difficulties with ROI

ROI can lead to bad decisions at the time an investment is being considered. Assume that a firm with a cost of money of .10 has a policy that rewards managers with higher ROIs. The manager of a division that earns an ROI of .30 is paid more than the manager of a division that earns .20. Both divisions have the same risk. Suppose the manager of a division had two assets, one earning .40 and the second earning .15, while on average the division is earning .20. If the asset earning .15 is sold, the

EXHIBIT 23-7

ROI Using Straight-line Depreciation

Period t	Investment, End of Period	Straight-line Depreciation	Income: $10,000– Depreciation	Return on Investment
0	$17,355.00	—	—	—
1	8,677.50	$8,677.50	$1,322.50	7.6%
2	0	8,677.50	1,322.50	15.2%

division then earns .40 on the remaining asset. The manager will then report a better record than the division manager earning .30.

Assume that the same manager now earning .40 can invest in new equipment of the same risk that is expected to earn an internal rate of return of .25. This investment is likely to be rejected by the manager since accepting it reduces the division's ROI from .40 to an average of .40 and the new investment's ROI of .25.

Thus, not only is there the depreciation problem described previously, but also the problem that using ROI encourages bad decisions (rejecting good investments and divesting of good investments). While the performance measure can be improved by taking the growth of assets into consideration as well as the level of the ROI, the problem in achieving this improvement is that it is very hard to administer. A firm can find its managers adding bad investments to achieve growth even though there is some erosion in ROI.

Although the use of ROI is attractive since the measure takes into consideration the value of the assets, its use tends to create incentives for managers to distort the decisions that are made. The interests of managers and owners are not likely to be congruent. This is true of top-level and lower-level managers as well.

Fortunately, there is an easily applied and theoretically correct solution available. While not used widely, it has been used by a few firms (the most famous being General Electric). The residual income technique, (introduced in Chapter 22), eliminates the difficulties of ROI, whenever it is used in combination with present-value depreciation.

Residual Income

Instead of using the return-on-investment calculation, the effect of asset utilization can be incorporated into the measurement of performance by deducting implicit interest figures on all capital from the operating income of the period. Thus, if $40,000,000 of capital is utilized during a period, and if the implicit interest cost is .20, an interest deduction of $8,000,000 is made from operating income. If the operating income is $9,000,000, the residual income would be $1,000,000 after the deduction of the implicit interest on the capital utilized.

Thus the accountant might report that:

1. The return on investment was $9,000,000/$40,000,000 = .225.

2. The amount of $1,000,000 was earned over and above the implicit interest cost charged on the assets utilized.

Assume the assets described in Exhibit 23-8 relate to a firm with a cost of money of .20. The firm has purchased an asset for $20,000. The depreciation and operating incomes of the two time periods are computed in Exhibit 23-9 in accordance with the present-value (economic) depreciation method developed earlier in this chapter. The returns on investment are .20 for both years (see Exhibit 23-9). If the firm computes the implicit interest cost for the two years, its residual income is zero in both years (see Exhibit 23-10).

Now assume that the firm's cost of money is .10. Exhibit 23-11 shows that the new residual incomes are positive. A positive residual income means that the firm

EXHIBIT 23-8
Revenues and Expenses by Periods

	Period 1	Period 2
Revenues	$29,000	$27,000
Less: Out-of-pocket expenses	15,000	15,000
Revenues less out-of-pocket expenses	$14,000	$12,000

EXHIBIT 23-9
Present-Value Depreciation and Operating Income

Time	Value (using .20)	Revenues Less Out-of-Pocket Expenses	Depreciation	Operating Income	ROI
0	$20,000	—			
1	10,000	$14,000	$10,000	$4,000	0.20
2	0	12,000	10,000	2,000	0.20

EXHIBIT 23-10
Residual Income Calculated Using a .20 Implicit Interest Rate

	Period 1	Period 2
Operating income	$4,000	$2,000
Less: Implicit interest cost:		
.20 × 20,000	4,000	
.20 × 10,000		2,000
Residual income	$ 0	$ 0

EXHIBIT 23-11
Residual Income Calculated Using .10

	Period 1	Period 2
Operating income	$4,000	$2,000
Less: Implicit interest cost:		
.10 × 20,000	2,000	
.10 × 10,000		1,000
Residual income	$2,000	$1,000

earned a larger ROI than the firm's cost of money (the .10 rate used to compute interest).

If desired, different interest costs could be used for assets acquired at different time periods, for assets with different lives, and for assets with different risks. Using different interest costs is a refinement that, while yielding increased accuracy in assigning capital costs, increases complexity and hence might be omitted. However, it is in principle desirable that the interest cost computed for working capital be based on the current short-term borrowing rate. Decisions involving working capital should be sensitive to the current cost of financing the working capital.

Some critics of residual income claim that it establishes a bias toward large investments because large investments can result in large residual incomes. However, one should remember that larger investments also result in large interest expenses and large depreciation expenses. These expenses act as a counterbalance.

Depreciation Method

The residual income method works best if used in combination with the present-value method of depreciation. If the depreciation method does not reflect the change in value associated with the cash flows anticipated when the asset was obtained, then the residual income can be negative even when the actual results for a desirable investment were exactly as forecasted.

Interest as a Cost of Product

Assume a bottle of wine costs $10 to produce and then must age for two years before it can be sold. With an interest cost of .10 per year what is the cost when the bottle is ready for sale? From an economic viewpoint the cost is $12.10, and this is the relevant cost for managerial decision making.

Through the years accountants have argued whether interest is an inventoriable cost similar in nature to material and labor costs. Although the question is interesting theoretically, and there are arguments both pro and con, the accounting issue is subordinate to the primary question of how interest should be incorporated into the decision-making process. One way or another managers must be charged for the capital they use. The following sections briefly review several techniques for treating interest as a product cost.

One method suggested for incorporating interest into the product-costing accounts is to compute the interest on the assets utilized, allocate this interest to departments, and then absorb it into the cost of product. Assuming a value of money of .20 and assets of $10,000 (all equity financed), the entries to accomplish the inclusion of interest, assuming three-quarters of the inventory has been sold, are given in Exhibit 23-12. Note the *implicit interest cost* and *implicit interest revenue.* Capital tied up in inventory gives rise to a debit called **implicit interest cost** that is exactly matched by a credit called **implicit interest revenue.**

The above entries reflect the fact that 75 percent of the goods worked on during the period were sold and thus 75 percent of the interest is expensed during the period. For the portion of the manufactured product still on hand, interest revenue is not recognized, since the funds are invested in goods not yet sold. Because 75 percent of the goods worked on during the period were sold and one-fourth are still in

---

EXHIBIT 23-12

Entries to Record Implicit Interest

Implicit Interest Cost		*Implicit* *Interest Revenue*	
(1) 2,000	(2) 2,000	(3) 1,500	(1) 2,000

Manufacturing Costs		*Income*	
(2) 2,000	(4) 1,500	(4) 1,500	(3) 1,500

Explanation of entries
(1) Records the interest cost and the interest revenue
     earned on the funds tied up in assets ($10,000 ×
     20%). Part of the credit would be to interest payable
     rather than implicit interest if there is debt outstand-
     ing.
(2) Records the transfer of the $2,000 implicit interest
     to the manufacturing account.
(3) Transfers $1,500 of the manufacturing costs to the
     income account (75% of the inventory has been
     used).
(4) Transfers $1,500 of the interest revenue to the
     income account.

inventory, recognizing only 75 percent of $2,000 (or $1,500) as income for the
period is conservative. Interest cost of $1,500 appears as revenue, and thus the net
effect of implicit interest on the income of the period is zero. The $500 balance in the
implicit interest revenue account could be closed to the manufacturing account (or
to various inventory accounts) or merely subtracted from the inventories.

   If it is desired to present a unit cost of product for decision making and performance measurement, the cost of product should include interest cost on the incremental assets. For assets already owned, the cost measure used should be the interest
on the opportunity cost of employing the resources in other projects. Thus, interest
on any increase in working capital that is required by the project is also relevant.

Inflation

Inflation is defined as a situation where the average price of all goods and services is
increasing. Many countries have been afflicted with rapidly rising prices. When inflation is pronounced or protracted, business managers consider the value of price-level
adjustments in improving their decision making. This section evaluates the use of
cost-based information compared to the use of price-level–adjusted information.

   A cost accounting system that is based on historical cost information can be
effective even during periods of rapidly changing price levels. However, accounting

records are sometimes adjusted for price-level changes. Whether price-level–adjusted information is more useful than cost-based information is the issue to be considered. Inappropriate price-level adjustments can lead to cost-accounting information that is less useful than the unadjusted measures. Price-level adjustments are examined next from the interrelated perspectives of cost control, decision making, and performance measures.

Cost Control

In any price-change situation, overall prices change by one percentage while the price of a specific factor of production usually changes by a different percentage. The difference in the response of specific assets to a general change in the price level complicates the analysis. If all prices changed by the same percentage, the elimination of price-level distortions would be an easy task.

Assume that the general price level increased by .10 in a period in which a firm uses 10,000 units of raw material. The actual cost per unit is $1.30 and the standard cost is $1.00 per unit. There is an unfavorable price variance of

$$10,000(\$1.30 - \$1.00) = \$3,000$$

It can be argued, however, that the standard cost should be adjusted to $1.10 to reflect the .10 inflation. If so, the unfavorable price variance is only $2,000:

$$10,000(\$1.30 - \$1.10) = \$2,000$$

The unadjusted cost numbers show that prices for this material increased by 30 percent while other prices increased by 10 percent on average. Adjusting the standard cost shows that, even after inflation is taken into consideration, actual costs were $2,000 higher because of prices changes specific to this product.

Information of the same basic nature is supplied by both variance measures. It is difficult to argue that one measure is useful but the other is not. The same conclusions can be drawn from either variance measure if the figures are understood and are analyzed using the same basic information.

Measuring Performance and Decisions

The argument sometimes is made that if historical cost information is used, inflation produces inflated income measures and inflated returns on investment. For assets used in different plants and purchased at different times, the cost-based measures may lose their relevance during a period of inflation.

Consider a situation where a firm that requires a .15 return on investment purchases an asset with a three-year life for $3,000. This asset has cash flows (revenues) of $1,600 in period 1, $1,400 in period 2, and $1,200 in period 3. The cash flows result in a .20 internal rate of return. Using straight-line depreciation, for period 1 the depreciation expense is $1,000, and reported income is $600. Because the cost of the investment is $3,000, the firm earns a return on investment of 20 percent ($600/$3,000) in year 1.

Assume now that inflation of .10 was expected and indeed occurred. Suppose both the depreciation expense and the asset's values are adjusted to reflect the .10 change in price level. These are the only price-level adjustments that will be made. The price-level and initial adjusted income statements are given in Exhibit 23-13.

EXHIBIT 23-13

Price-Level Adjusted Income: Year 1

	Not Price-Level Adjusted	Price-Level Adjusted
Revenue	$1,600	$1,600
Depreciation: 1,000(1.10)	1,000	1,100
Income	$ 600	$ 500

The asset's value is adjusted to $3,300 ($1.10 \times $3,000), and the price-level adjusted ROI is:

$$\text{ROI} = \frac{\$\ 500}{\$3,300} = .15$$

In the second year, actual revenues are assumed to be $1,400 and inflation to continue at the .10 rate. The price-level adjusted income statement and price-level adjusted ROI for year 2 are given in Exhibit 23-14.

If inflation continues at .10 in year 3, revenues of $1,200 lead to a loss, as shown in Exhibit 23-15.

EXHIBIT 23-14

Price-Level Adjusted Income and ROI: Year 2

Revenue	$1,400
Depreciation: $1,000 \times (1.10)^2$	1,210
Income	$ 190

$$\text{ROI} = \frac{\$\ 190}{\$2,000(1.21)} = .08$$

EXHIBIT 23-15

Price-Level Adjusted Income: Year 3

Revenue	$1,200
Depreciation: $1,000 \times (1.10)^3$	1,331
Loss	$ 131

EXHIBIT 23-16

Investment Yields 20 Percent Internal Rate of Return

Time	Cash Flows	Present-Value Factors (.20)	Present Values
0	− $3,000	$(1.20)^{-0}$	− $3,000
1	1,600	$(1.20)^{-1}$	1,333
2	1,400	$(1.20)^{-2}$	972
3	1,200	$(1.20)^{-3}$	695
		Net present value	$ 0

If the firm requires an ROI of .15 in each year, the investment fails the test after year 1. The investment fails to meet the firm's target return, and management would reject it using the price-level adjusted calculations.

However, an inspection of the investment's cash flows reveals the investment earned an internal rate of return of .20 (see Exhibit 23-16), and hence it would have a positive net present value using .15 as the discount rate. Conventional accounting in this simplified example would also indicate an ROI for each time period equal to .20 (see Exhibit 23-17).

In this example, the conventional accounting (using straight-line depreciation expense) indicates a performance measure of .20 for each year. This is consistent with the .20 internal rate of return. Equally important, the favorable performance is consistent with the fact that the owners want management to accept this investment.

The price-level adjusted measures, however, all indicate that the investment's performance would not be acceptable. The use of price-level adjustments is inappropriate. The problem is that inflation is already built into the cash-flow forecast and into the discount rate. Adjustment to depreciation expense or to the asset is not necessary.

Discount rates are based on rates for borrowing established in the market by lenders whose expectations of inflation will be reflected in the time-structure of interest rates. Thus, management is predicting the cash flows in column 4 of Exhibit 23-18 in inflation-adjusted dollars. With a forecast of .10 inflation per year, the num-

---

EXHIBIT 23-17

Investment Yields 20 Percent Return on Investment

Period	Cash Flows	Straight-Line Depreciation	Income	Beginning Investment	ROI
1	$1,600	$1,000	$600	$3,000	.20
2	1,400	1,000	400	2,000	.20
3	1,200	1,000	200	1,000	.20

EXHIBIT 23-18

Constant-Dollar Adjustment

(1)	(2) Forecasted Actual (Nominal)	(3)	(4) Constant Dollar
Period	Cash Flows	Inflation Adjustment	(Col. 1 ÷ Col. 2)
1	$1,600	1.100	$1,454.55
2	1,400	1.210	1,157.02
3	1,200	1.331	901.58
	$4,200		$3,513.15

bers reflect management's forecasts in current or nominal dollars, given in column 2. **Nominal cash flows** reflect inflation forecasts but are *not* adjusted to equivalent purchasing power.

Dollars of different time periods, converted to units of equivalent purchasing power, are called **constant dollars.** Using inflation-adjusted (constant-dollar) cash flows and a .15 required return, the investment would have been rejected. The use of the nominal .15 interest rate applied to the constant-dollar forecast is incorrect because the adjusted cash flows exclude inflation while a discount rate of .15 includes the effect of expected inflation. Using the nominal-dollar cash flows under inflation results in accepting the investment, since the IRR is .20, which exceeds the .15 required return.

When management perfectly forecasts the price-level change and uses these forecasts in making decisions, price-level adjustments to the conventional cost-based information distort the resulting figures and can lead to incorrect decisions unless the discount rate is also purged of inflation expectations. The fact that performance measurement is distorted affects management's investment decisions. Good investments may be rejected using price-level adjusted performance measures even when the forecasted results are realized. To the extent that inflation is a surprise, in that it is unexpected, the above criticism of price-level adjustments may not apply. The applicability depends on the use of the calculations and the economic changes that have taken place.

A second limitation to price-level adjustments is that they ignore changes in efficiency. Because conventional accounting for long-lived assets also tends to ignore efficiency changes, price-level adjustments may actually increase the performance-measure distortion.

Consider an asset whose last three years' cash flows were forecasted to be $1,600, then $1,400, then $1,200, similar to the asset in Exhibit 23-17. Assume further that there have been technological or economic changes and, despite a doubling of the price level since the asset was purchased some time ago, the forecasted cash flows for the last three years are now expected to be only $805, $793.50, and $608.35, respec-

EXHIBIT 23-19

Present Value of Remaining Cash Flows

Period	Cash Flow	Present Value Factor	Present Value
1	$805.00	$(1.15)^{-1}$	$ 700
2	793.50	$(1.15)^{-2}$	600
3	608.35	$(1.15)^{-3}$	400
			$1,700

tively. The book value of the asset is $3,000 (cost less depreciation), even though the present value of the actual cash flows at 15 percent is only $1,700. The asset has already given a number of years of service. Assume the accounting depreciation expense per year based on the original cost of the asset is $1,000. If the original forecasts had been realized, the asset would have earned an ROI for each year of .20. If the firm's discount rate is .15, the present value of the remaining cash flows is given in Exhibit 23-19.

With the assumption that the price level has doubled since the asset's acquisition, a price-level adjustment would increase the current $3,000 book value to $6,000 and the annual depreciation expense from $1,000 to $2,000. Given that the asset is not currently worth its book value of $3,000, the price-level adjustments will not contribute to operating management's enthusiasm or to top management's understanding.

Price-Level Adjustments and Unexpected Inflation

Unexpected inflation occurs when the market expects one rate of price increase but the actual price increase is larger. Price-level adjustments may be useful when inflation occurs but is not expected. Consider a situation where price-level adjustments are useful.

Assume that the depreciated cost of an asset is $3,000, and the remaining forecasted cash flows are $1,300 in year 1, $1,200 in year 2, and $1,100 in year 3. The firm uses straight-line depreciation of $1,000 per year. The forecasted incomes and ROIs are given in Exhibit 23-20.

EXHIBIT 23-20

Forecasted Income and ROI

Period	Cash Flows	Depreciation	Income	Beginning Investment	ROI
1	$1,300	$1,000	$300	$3,000	.10
2	1,200	1,000	200	2,000	.10
3	1,100	1,000	100	1,000	.10

EXHIBIT 23-21

Cash Flows with Unexpected Inflation

Period	Original Cash Flows	Price Inflation	New Forecast of Cash Flows
1	$1,300	(1.12)	$1,456
2	1,200	$(1.12)^2$	1,505
3	1,100	$(1.12)^3$	1,545

Assume that the top management requires a .10 ROI per year, so the asset is performing satisfactorily. Now suppose inflation unexpectedly increases to .12 per year, so that the cash flows are as shown in Exhibit 23-21. Note that the value of the asset increases in a manner consistent with the amount of inflation.

The new incomes and ROIs resulting from inflation are shown in Exhibit 23-22.

The ROIs are now much higher solely because of inflation. Some type of price-level adjustment seems to be required if management is to separate the effects of operating efficiency and inflation. In periods of surprise inflation, it is possible that the cash flows, incomes, and ROIs are favorably affected by the inflation. In trying to evaluate managerial performance, it is difficult to separate the effects of increased efficiency, and other real changes, from the income effects resulting purely from inflation.

In the above example, inflation favorably affects the cash flows, but the effect can be negative. For example, assume that a firm has fixed-price contracts to deliver a product but its costs change as the price level changes. Under these conditions the firm is harmed by inflation.

Most important, before assuming that price-level adjustments are desirable for performance measurement, during periods of inflation, it is necessary to consider whether the inflation was forecast by management. Practically, inflation may be partly expected and partly a surprise. The determination of the extent of each is difficult at best.

EXHIBIT 23-22

Incomes and ROIs Resulting from Inflation

Period	Cash Flows	Depreciation	Income	Beginning Investment	ROI
1	$1,456	$1,000	$456	$3,000	.152
2	1,505	1,000	505	2,000	.253
3	1,545	1,000	545	1,000	.545

Capital Budgeting and Inflation

Assume a firm can obtain capital at a cost of .20. Further, assume the firm can invest $1,000 and earn $1,300 of cash flows in one time period. The $1,300 is based on an expected inflation rate of .10 for the year. This investment is acceptable.

The firm can incorporate inflation into the analysis. First, assume an overall inflation rate of .10 and that the firm's prices and costs change differently. Without inflation, suppose the firm would earn a $1,100 cash flow at time 1. Given the capital cost of .20, the firm would reject the investment if the firm forecasted zero inflation, since the asset would earn an internal rate of return of only .10. To be acceptable, the capital cost of .20 would have to be equal to or less than .10. Using the inflation-adjusted cash flows (current dollars of $1,300), the investment is acceptable with a .20 cost of money.

An important consideration in making investment decisions with inflation is that the cash flows must incorporate forecasted inflation. This means that the analysis must include the effects of the inflation on the prices of the firm's products and on the costs of its factors of production. Only if inflation is included in the cash flows will the numbers be consistent with the market-determined discount rate, which also reflects lenders' inflationary expectations.

A second consideration is that if the cash flows properly reflect the forecasted price-level changes, and if the actual (nominal) cost of money (which is a market rate and hence incorporates expected inflation) has been determined, then the net present-value analysis using current dollars will indicate the accept or reject decision without any additional adjustments. More simply, under conditions of inflation it is necessary that the cash-flow stream reflect inflation expectations. If it does, then normal capital-budgeting evaluation techniques may be used.

Segment Performance Evaluation in Multinational Firms

Segment performance evaluation in multinational firms presents special problems. Cultural differences across countries make the behavioral implications of performance evaluation systems unique to specific divisions in each country. Tariff and trade restrictions make evaluation of sales and profit performance more complicated. Changing relationships among foreign currencies and different tax laws introduce complexities into the measurement of the income and investment bases. Differential and changing tax laws create tax incentives that vary across countries. These problems have not been solved completely by many international firms that are struggling with performance evaluation criteria for their multinational operations.[1]

The segment-performance measures of several of Japan's large multinational firms were described by Miller.[2]

1. See W. Abdallah and D. Keller, "Measuring the Multinational's Performance," *Management Accounting* (October 1985): 26–30; and P. Tse, "Evaluating Performance in Multinationals," *Management Accounting* (June 1979): 21–25.

2. E. Miller, *Responsibility Accounting and Performance Evaluations* (New York: Van Nostrand Reinhold, 1982).

Sony Corporation and Mitsui & Co., Ltd.	At Sony Corporation, monthly and annual reports of such measures as sales and profit are made in the local currencies of each division. No adjustments are made for currency translation. Mitsui and Co., Ltd. has 128 foreign affiliates, which are grouped administratively into three regions: America, Europe, and Oceana. Performance data is collected by region and then forwarded to headquarters. All data is generated in terms of the local currencies of the foreign segments.

The problems of evaluating the performance of foreign subsidiaries are illustrated in the following case about the Security Systems Corporation. The case describes an actual situation in a real U.S. company, but the firm's name has been changed, at the request of the company, to protect its confidentiality.[3]

The Security Systems Corporation is searching for the proper method of evaluating its subsidiaries. Of concern is their contribution to the overall earnings of the company and how to evaluate whether the specific goals developed by the subsidiaries' management have been met.

In searching for answers, the company is concerned with the following concepts:

- Analysis of results — should it be in local currency or U.S. dollars?

- Management explanation of variances — in local currency or U.S. dollars?

- What should be the time frame for comparative data — plan or forecast?

Description of the firm.   Security Systems Corporation has six distinctive business segments in the new-residential-housing market, consumer appliance market, commercial nonresidential construction, consumer aftermarket, apparel market, automotive market, and capital goods markets. Last year the company achieved 30 percent of its revenues and 35 percent of its earnings from its international subsidiaries. However, four years ago, when the British pound sterling was at one pound = $2.33 U.S. (whereas now it's one pound = $1.20 U.S.), the company achieved 35 percent of its revenues but more significantly 47 percent of its earnings from its international subsidiaries. During the past five years, although the U.S. dollar equivalent of earnings from the international

3. This case was prepared by the company described for the National Association of Accountants and the Management Accounting Section of the American Accounting Association. It originally appeared in S. Moriarity, ed., *Cases from Management Accounting Practice,* Vol. 1 (Montvale, N.J.: National Association of Accountants, 1985). It is adapted and reproduced here with permission.

subsidiaries has gone down from 47 percent of the total to 35 percent, most of the operations have reported significant, steady gains from year to year in terms of their local currency.

Current reporting system.   All operations report their monthly financial data to the firm's world headquarters in U.S. dollars. They use the existing exchange rate at the close of business on the last day of the month. The comparisons of the monthly financial data are made against a financial plan that uses a predetermined exchange rate for the various months of the year.

Over the past five years, even as the U.S. dollar has steadily strengthened against foreign currencies, the company has been analyzing the financial results of its operations totally in U.S. dollars. Its results are compared to a fixed-plan exchange rate.

The company establishes exchange rates to be used each year, many times optimistically, and then sets an earnings per share target on that basis. Then, if the dollar strengthens even greater, the company finds itself missing its targets. It then makes statements that a particular group missed its planned targets, when, in fact, the group's operations may all have exceeded their local currency plans but are losing on the comparison due to unfavorable exchange rate effects.

Review of the current reporting system.   There are two different approaches for consolidating foreign operations into a parent's financial statements. The approaches differ, depending on whether the foreign operations are considered to be relatively self-contained and independent of the parent company (a manufacturing operation serving a local market) or are considered extensions of the parent's operations (a foreign sales office selling goods manufactured by the parent in the United States).

The Security Systems Corporation considers its foreign operations to be self-contained. Thus, the functional currency is the currency of the country in which each operation is located. When preparing consolidated statements, the assets and liabilities of the foreign operations are translated to dollars at the current exchange rate as of the balance sheet date. Revenue and expense accounts are translated at rates that reflect the exchange rate at the time the transactions occurred. Security Systems Corporation accomplishes the latter by translating revenues and expenses monthly at the then current rate. Thus, the U.S. dollar net income reported in the consolidated statements for a foreign operation is simply the difference between the translated revenues and the translated expenses. Any translation adjustment (required to keep the books in balance after the various translations) is recorded in a special equity account in the firm's consolidated balance sheet. These adjustments (resulting primarily from changes in the translated values of assets and liabilities) do not affect the consolidated income statement.

The effect that changes in exchange rates have on reported income can be illustrated with a simple example. Assume that a British subsidiary had the following results when recorded in pounds.

Sales	$ 5,000,000
Expenses	4,000,000
Net income	$ 1,000,000

If the average exchange rate during the period was 1 = $2.33, the income reported in the parent's consolidated income statement would be

Sales	$11,650,000
Expenses	9,320,000
Net income	$ 2,330,000

But if the exchange rate drops to 1 = $1.20, these results would translate to

Sales	$ 6,000,000
Expenses	4,800,000
Net income	$ 1,200,000

Thus if the subsidiary's budget was set at 1 million pounds when the exchange rate was 1 = $2.33, but the average exchange rate turned out to be 1 = $1.20, the subsidiary would have missed its budgeted income by $1,130,000 even though it met its budget target of £1,000,000.

Most accountants and managers would agree that a subsidiary's performance should be measured in terms of its local currency. Actual results should be compared in local terms against the unit's budget and prior year's performance. This point of view treats exchange-rate fluctuations as an uncontrollable factor. A few people disagree. They argue that changes in exchange rates should alter the opportunities available to the subsidiary (particularly if it sells some of its products to U.S. customers). In this view, an alert management should be able to take advantage of these opportunities to help offset the effects of exchange-rate fluctuations. Unfortunately, as a practical matter, it is unlikely that local management will be able to fully overcome exchange rate fluctuations through changes in operations.

Management should distinguish between the controllable and uncontrollable portions of the deviation between actual results in dollars and planned results in dollars. The accountant can aid this distinction by calculating two variances when comparing actual to budgeted results. The first variance should compare actual results to budget in terms of operations, while the second variance should explain the effect of the change in exchange rates. In most firms the second variance should be ignored when measuring the performance of managers. It is the first variance that reflects any problems that are correctable by the manager.

The firm recognized that it has responsibilities to both its stockholders and its management. For its stockholders the firm must measure its overall performance against its plans in U.S. dollars. For its management the firm must reward excellent performance as measured by the factors that management can control.

To meet these responsibilities, the firm structured its incentive compensation plan to give weight to both local and overall results. Key management of the operating units have incentive bonuses available for achieving earnings targets as measured in the local currency. In addition, there is an incentive bonus available for meeting planned results in terms of U.S. dollars. In this way managers are encouraged to exceed their local currency targets to help make up for any adverse changes in exchange rates.

The firm is still concerned, however, that once a unit meets its targets it tends to slack off its efforts until the beginning of the next year. The company has not developed a good system (other than exhortation) for encouraging one unit to exceed its targets to help cover deficits in another unit.

Summary

The difficulties in performance evaluation include all of the problems of measuring unit costs, income, and assets. Any evaluation of performance must consider the limitations of the measures being used. The most widely used performance measure for an investment center is ROI. There are problems in computing an investment's ROI, but more important, even if correctly computed, the use of ROI as a performance measurement tends to create distortions and hence potential pitfalls in management decisions. The use of ROI as the sole measure of performance makes it likely that management's decisions will not be the decisions that the owners of the firm desire.

The residual-income measure does all that ROI does and does it better. Any desirable investment (with a positive net present value) will increase the present value of the residual income and thus should be accepted by management. This statement is accurate regardless of which method of depreciation is used. Even stronger statements can be made if residual income is used in combination with present-value depreciation.

To the extent that inflation is accurately predicted in the cash flows, more harm than good is done by price-level adjustments for purposes of measuring performance. The adjustment tends to lead managers to reject profitable investments.

The use of value measures dominates the use of either cost-based information (which tends to become irrelevant over time) and price-level adjusted information (which tends to distort the performance evaluation measures). Management must weigh the usefulness and cost of complex information systems against the usefulness and cost of other more simplified systems. The use of price-level adjusted information is likely to be more costly and less useful than alternative approaches.

Key Terms to Review

constant dollars, p. 823
economic depreciation, p. 814
implicit interest cost, p. 818
implicit interest revenue, p. 818

inflation, p. 819
nominal cash flows, p. 823
present-value depreciation, p. 814
unexpected inflation, p. 824

Review Problem

RETURN ON INVESTMENT

Robust Corporation is considering the following investment:

Period	Cash Flows
0	$-60,000
1	23,000
2	26,450
3	30,417.50

The firm requires a .10 return. The first year's return on investment if straight-line depreciation is used will be

$$\text{ROI} = \frac{\$23,000 - \$20,000}{\$60,000} = .05.$$

a. Should the investment be undertaken?

b. What return will be earned in period 1 if the forecasts are realized?

Solution to Review Problem

a. The internal rate of return is .15. This is larger than .10 thus the investment is acceptable.

b. $V_0 = \$60,000$
$V_1 = \underline{\ \ 46,000}$
$\underline{\$14,000}$ Present-value depreciation

Income $= 23,000 - 14,000 = \$9,000$

$$\text{ROI} = \frac{\$\ 9,000}{\$60,000} = .15. \text{ Other answers are possible, but this is our choice.}$$

Suggested Readings

Abdallah, W., and D. Keller. "Measuring the Multinational's Performance," *Management Accounting* (October 1985): 26–30.

Bloom, R., and A. Debessay. *Inflation Accounting: Reporting of General and Specific Price Changes.* New York: Praeger, 1984.

Howell, S. "Planning and Control Systems and Their Evolution During Inflation." In *Management Accounting Research and Practice,* ed., D. Cooper, R. Scapeno, and J. Arnold. London: Institute of Cost and Managerial Accountants, 1983.

Jensen, R. E. "Capital Budgeting Under Risk and Inflation: A Pedagogical Guide." In *Advances in Accounting.* London: JAI, 1986.

Miller, E. *Responsibility Accounting and Performance Evaluations.* New York: Van Nostrand Reinhold, 1982.

Tse, P. "Evaluating Performance in Multinationals," *Management Accounting* (June 1979): 21–25.

Vancil, R. F. *Decentralization: Managerial Ambiguity by Design.* Homewood, Ill.: Irwin, 1978.

Review Questions

23-1 Accountants typically ignore implicit interest in break-even analyses. What is the effect of this behavior? Is the effect important?

23-2 Is the variance of an investment the best measure of the risk of that investment?

23-3 Does a project with uncertain returns necessarily add to the firm's overall risk?

23-4 Can you argue from a risk standpoint that a firm with several divisions might be justified in using different required rates of return for each?

Exercises

23-5 **Rates of Return**   An asset costs $18,594 and will earn proceeds of $10,000 per year for two years. The cash is received at the end of each period.

    a. Compute the internal rate of return.

    b. Compute the depreciation in the value of the asset, the income, and the return on investment for each of the two years of life.

23-6 **Rates of Return**   An asset costs $27,665 and will earn proceeds of $10,000 in year 1 and $20,000 in year 2.

    a. Compute the internal rate of return of the investment.

    b. Compute the present-value depreciation, the income, and return on the investment for each of the two years of life.

23-7 Rates of Return An asset costs $28,118 and will earn proceeds of $20,000 in year 1 and $10,000 in year 2.

  a. Compute the internal rate of return of investment.

  b. Compute the present-value depreciation, the income, and the return on investment for each of the two years of life.

23-8 Rates of Return An asset costs $20,000 and earns proceeds of $11,000 in year 1 and $10,500 in year 2.

  a. Compute the internal rate of return of the investment.

  b. Compute the present-value depreciation, the income, and return on investment for each of the two years of life.

23-9 Rates of Return An asset costs $20,000 and will earn proceeds of $12,000 in year 1 and $11,000 in year 2.

  a. Compute the internal rate of return on the investment.

  b. Compute the present-value depreciation, the income, and the return on investment for each of the two years of life.

23-10 Computing Depreciation, Income, and ROI for an Investment An asset costs $18,594 and will earn cash proceeds of $10,000 per year for two years; the first payment is to be received one year from now. The time value of money is .05. Compute the present-value depreciation, the income, and return on investment for each year of the life of the investment.

23-11 Computing ROI Using Straight-Line Depreciation The Mulligan's Novelty Toy Company is considering an investment that has an internal rate of return of .20. There is an initial outlay of $8,000 followed by benefits of $2,085 per year. The asset has a life of eight years. Compute the ROIs of each year using straight-line depreciation.

23-12 Performance Criteria for an Investment An asset costs $17,355 and will earn proceeds of $10,000 per year for two years. The cash is received at the end of each period. The time value of money is .05.

  a. Compute the internal rate of return of the investment.

  b. Compute the present-value depreciation, income, and return on investment.

  c. Compute the residual income of each year.

23-13 Rates of Return An asset costs $25,619 and will earn proceeds of $10,000 in year 1 and $20,000 in year 2. The time value of money is .05.

  a. Compute the internal rate of return of the investment.

  b. Compute the present-value depreciation, income, and return on investment.

Problems

23-14 **Impact of an Investment on Income and Earnings per Share**   Assume that the Alstar Company is considering the investment described in Exercise 23-13. The company uses a straight-line method of depreciation for financial accounting purposes and management is very sensitive to the effect that an investment will have on income and earnings per share.

REQUIRED:

Should the company undertake the investment, assuming that the cash flows are known with certainty and .05 is an appropriate discount rate?

23-15 **Reporting Income Growth**   It has been suggested that a firm should consider its growth rate of income as reflected in its published accounting statements in its decision making. In particular, the firm may select among investments subject to limitations placed on the minimum percentage growth in earnings to be reported.

REQUIRED:

Is it reasonable for a firm to be concerned about its reported growth in income? What problems do you see in using the suggested procedure? What remedies might you suggest?

23-16 **Accepting New Orders**   Consider a situation in which a firm has received the first order from a new customer. Assume that:

a. The firm has excess capacity at the present time.

b. The marginal revenues exceed variable costs.

c. There are no externality problems.

d. The problems of cost justification under the Robinson-Patman Act can be ignored.

e. The new customer is likely to maintain purchases in periods when unexpected declines occur in the orders from other customers.

REQUIRED:

Present arguments, from a risk standpoint, for accepting the order as well as from the traditional marginal viewpoint.

23-17 **Income and ROI**   An investment has the following cash flows. The firm uses a .10 discount rate.

	Cash Flows	.10	Present Value
0	$-12,930		
1	1,000	.9091	$ 909
2	10,000	.8264	8,264
3	5,000	.7513	3,757
			12,930

REQUIRED:

Prepare tables showing the income and ROI calculations for each year using straight-line depreciation and using present-value depreciation.

23-18 Maintaining ROI   The Select Company is considering buying equipment that is expected to earn an internal rate of return of .20. The expected cash flows are

Time	Cash Flows
0	$−10,000,000
1	2,400,000
2	2,880,000
3	3,456,000
4	4,147,200
5	4,976,640

The firm has a .15 weighted average cost of capital and the investment satisfies the normal discounted cash flow investment criteria.

However, management is upset by the fact that in year 1 the projected return on investment is only .04:

Revenues	$2,400,000
Depreciation	2,000,000
Income	$ 400,000

$$ROI = \frac{\$\ 400,000}{\$10,000,000} = .04$$

Management has had a history of earning a satisfactory ROI, and it does not want to jeopardize its record. What do you recommend?

23-19 Evaluating Investments   To avoid the problems associated with measuring accumulated depreciation, Dorit's Food Company uses gross investments in measuring ROI. No accumulated depreciation is deducted in computing the asset base. Straight-line depreciation expense is deducted in computing the income of the period.

The Dorit Company has set a required return of .18 for undertaking investments and also has set .18 as a target ROI. The following investment is being considered by a division manager:

0	$−10,000
1	4,500
2	4,000
3	3,500
4	3,000

REQUIRED:

You have been asked to advise the decision manager. Prepare the ROIs for each year of life using straight-line depreciation. What advice do you offer?

23-20 The ABC Company is building a plant that is expected to cost $10 million to service the firm's capacity needs for the next three years. For another $2.8 million it can build excess capacity that is expected to fill the needs for the next ten years. It is expected that it will cost $3 million to make the identical changes three years from now. The firm's cost of money is .10.

REQUIRED:

a. Should the excess capacity be purchased?

b. If the $3 million expected cost is in terms of constant dollars (zero inflation) and management expects .06 inflation per year, which decision is better?

23-21 The United Company is considering an investment costing $1 million. The expected IRR is .09. Debt funds can be obtained to finance this investment at a cost of .14. The justification offered for the investment is that inflation is expected to be .09; thus, there will be a gain at the expense of the bondholders (they will be holding fixed dollar claims). The real cost of the debt is less than .09. The .09 IRR of the investment includes appropriate adjustments in cash flows because of the expected inflation. The lives of the investment and the debt are comparable. The cash flows of the investment have been computed to be

Time	Constant Cash Flows	Inflation Factor	Adjusted Dollars
0	$-1,800	1,000	$-1,800
1	1,000	1.09	1,090
2	800	1.09^2	950.48

Should the investment be accepted?

23-22 Management expects there is to be a .06 annual inflation rate for the next two years. It is considering the following investment (the cash flows reflect the inflation expectations):

Time	Cash Flows
0	$-18,000
1	11,700
2	10,350

The investment has a .15 IRR. The firm can borrow at a cost of .113.

REQUIRED:

a. Should the investment be accepted?

b. If the $11,700 is actually earned and if the inflation expectations are realized, present useful performance measures.

24

Transfer Pricing

After studying this chapter, you should be able to:

1 Explain why decentralized firms that sell goods and services internally need transfer pricing.

2 Describe some of the behavioral implications of various transfer-pricing policies.

3 Determine how transfer prices are established by top management using market, marginal, variable, or full cost prices, or negotiation.

4 Discuss the implications of transfer-pricing policies for decision making.

5 Identify some of the special transfer-pricing problems that arise in multinational firms.

*T*he past several decades have seen the development of two interesting business phenomena that are in many respects contradictory. Large numbers of business combinations have resulted in an increase in the complexity of business organizations, at the same time that decentralization or divisionalization has been used increasingly as a means of controlling large corporations. Thus, firms seek the advantages of being large and small, simultaneously. One important issue that arises in decentralized organizations is the transfer of goods and services among divisions. This chapter concerns the pricing and control of such internal transfers.

Benefits of Decentralization

Decentralization refers to the degree to which the subunits of an organization are free to make decisions. The extent to which any organization is decentralized is a function of its history, its environment, and the attitudes and preferences of its senior management. In considering whether the degree of decentralization is appropriate, management should weigh carefully the potential costs and benefits to their organization.

Managers delegate decisions that depend on an understanding of local conditions, including, in particular, those of supply and demand. This frees top management from trying to track events in different product and geographic markets and thereby facilitates a quicker response to changing conditions. Opportunities can be seized, and competitors' actions quickly countered. Top management can develop and orchestrate corporate strategy.[1]

Another advantage of decentralization is that it can trigger factors, such as commitment, that motivate those in middle and lower management to play a more significant role in decision making.[2] This commitment and the accompanying involvement by subunit managers are likely to create an experienced pool of managerial talent on which the firm can draw while simultaneously identifying those who are ineffective. Moreover, when managers feel that "this is my business," they achieve more than when they do not feel in control of the operations for which they are held responsible.

1. This explanation is consistent with the principle of bounded rationality developed by March and Simon. The principle argues that in the face of multiple decision situations, coupled with information, acquisition, and processing costs, managers both delegate and accept satisfactory, rather than maximizing, solutions. J. G. March and H. A. Simon, *Organizations* (New York: Wiley, 1958).

2. C. Argyris, *Personality and Organization* (New York: Harper & Row, 1957); and R. Likert, "Measuring Organizational Performance," in *Studies in Personnel and Industrial Psychology*, edited by E. A. Frishman (Homewood, Ill.: Dorsey, 1961).

Others emphasize improved control through better knowledge of the strengths and weaknesses of specific company activities.[3] The unit and its management can focus on a unique skill, a limited market, or a special set of customers with individual needs. This customizing can pay substantive rewards in the right circumstances.

Costs of Decentralization

The most serious costs associated with decentralization occur when **goal congruence** fails — that is, when the activities of one segment are in conflict with the goals of the organization. When a failure to achieve goal congruence occurs, subunits may end up competing with each other for the same limited resources or for the same customers. In such a case, the advantages to one subunit may be more than offset by costs incurred by another subunit. Similar dysfunctional decisions can occur when one subunit transfers goods to a second; then the cost to the buyer is the revenue to the seller. Both units' performances are influenced and hence so are the decisions made. The evaluation process is complicated because the arm's-length transaction found between separate firms in the market is lacking.

When interfirm transfers occur, information also transfers. For example, the cost of the supplying unit is transferred to the receiving unit. However, the cost information may be incomplete, biased, or even intentionally distorted. Information distortion can be caused by poor accounting methods, or it can be a symptom of a lack of commitment by the transferring unit to the total organization, a potentially serious problem in crisis situations.

Decentralization can also lead to the unnecessary duplication of activities. Legal and accounting groups may well proliferate because each subunit manager desires a loyal and responsive staff.

Need for Transfer Prices

If an automobile company buys its glass from an independent glass company, the price is set by market forces. The automobile executives can determine the cost of glass by looking at quoted prices or, better, purchase orders. If the automobile company creates a glass division to manufacture glass, the assembly division "buys" from the glass division. The price of the glass is set in some way by management, not the market. This is an example of a transfer-pricing situation.

The **transfer price** affects revenues (and therefore the glass division's profit) as well as costs (and therefore the profit of the assembly division) but not the profit of

3. J. Dean, "Decentralization and Intercompany Pricing," *Harvard Business Review* (July–August 1955): 65–74.

the company as a whole. Indirect effects, however, may affect the profitability of the firm.

Conflict of Interests

The goal of the firm is profit maximization, yet decentralization motivates subunit managers to act in the interest of their own units. Ideally, transfer prices should guide the managers of the organization's subunits toward maximization of the income of the organization as a whole. Transfer prices can directly affect the profit of the units involved, however, and maximizing the profits of interrelated subunits does not necessarily maximize the profits of the firm.

Subunit managers acting to maximize the unit's profit do not always act to maximize the profit of the corporation.[4] In part, this is because one subunit may be able to act as a monopolistic buyer or seller (monopsonist) in its dealings with other divisions. For example, a buying unit that is the only potential purchaser for a resource may attempt to pay a lower price for the item than it would on the open market. A subunit manager also may alter production decisions made in the central office and based on the subunit's cost by modifying the subunit's cost structure. Furthermore, it is possible for one subunit (division) to save the firm money (by using an overabundant resource or encouraging a cost-benefiting technological change) or cost the firm money (by using a scarce corporate resource or changing the reward structure) in other divisions.

An intracompany pricing scheme should facilitate the maximization of corporate profit rather than subunit profit. Many executives argue that the best results are obtained in the long run by strengthening decentralization rather than overruling decisions made at the subunit level. These executives believe that in the long run the increase in motivation and coincident understanding plus the greater commitment to the enterprise result in greater company profits.

Uses of Divisionalized Data

The intracompany prices yield the revenue of the selling division and the costs of the purchasing division; thus, the transfer-pricing method directly affects the basic reports of both units. These reports, in turn, may be used for

1. Measuring the performance of division management,

2. Decision making, including:

    a. Make-or-buy decisions,

    b. Pricing policy for the end product,

    c. Output decisions of components and end products,

    d. Capital-budgeting decisions and decisions to drop products.

---

4. J. Hirshleifer, "On the Economics of Transfer Pricing," *Journal of Business* (July 1956): 172–74; P. W. Cook, "New Technique for Intracompany Pricing," *Harvard Business Review* (July–August 1957): 74–80; see also J. R. Gould, "Internal Pricing in Firms Where There Are Costs of Using an Outside Market," *Journal of Business* (January 1964): 61–67.

Transfer-Pricing Alternatives

Intracompany prices may be established in essentially three ways. They are:

1. Market-based price (determined by printed price lists, invoices, price quotations, or other evidence)

2. Cost-based price

   a. Marginal cost

   b. Variable cost

   c. Full cost (either actual or standard and including or excluding a "reasonable" profit)

3. Negotiated price (which, in the extreme, includes prices established by the central office)

Setting the transfer price frequently is approached from the point of view that only one of these procedures is correct, but any of the above alternatives may be reasonable. The choice should be made only after determining the purpose for which the information is to be used and the cost of implementation.

General Transfer-Pricing Rule

Although there is no single best transfer-pricing method for all situations, a useful general rule is that the transfer price should equal the division's marginal (often, approximated by variable) cost directly associated with production and transfer, plus any opportunity cost related to the transfer.

Transfer price = Marginal cost + Opportunity cost

Marginal cost is primarily the cost of direct materials and labor. It is more difficult to establish the opportunity cost associated with the goods or services transferred from one unit to another.

If the selling division can sell all of its output in the external market at a constant price, as would be true in perfect competition, the general rule yields market price as the transfer price. Suppose, for example, that the selling division's product sells for $100 in the external market, and the variable cost of production is $60. Using variable cost to approximate marginal cost and noting that the opportunity cost of selling internally is the margin of ($100 − $60) or $40 lost on the possible market sale, the transfer price should be $60 + ($100 − 60) = $100. This is the market price.

If there is no external market for the selling unit's product, then the opportunity cost associated with the transfer is zero, and the general rule yields a transfer price equal to the variable cost of $60.

Market Price

If the market for the product being transferred (the intermediate product) is perfectly competitive — meaning that any firm can sell all it wants of a homogeneous product at a constant price — the market price should be used as the transfer price. The buying division must pay the same price for the product being purchased internally as it would pay in the external market. Examples of product markets coming close to this ideal case are the markets for oil and coal. No single firm can influence the world or even the United States price for these products.

Consider this example of when the market price should be used as the transfer price. A chemical company explored for oil because it desired a cheap source of raw material. If the market price is $39 per barrel, however, it is better to sell the oil in the market unless the value of oil as raw material is at least $39. If the cost of finding and pumping the oil exceeds the market price of $39 per barrel, the chemical division should not be made to pay in excess of $39 to the exploration and development division. The manager of the chemical division would rather buy oil in the market at $39 than buy internally at a higher price. Moreover, this is best for the firm.

It would seem that production costs are neglected when market price is used. But the relevant costs are implicit in the use of market price. Suppose the oil exploration (more generally the supplying, or manufacturing) division sells to the firm's chemical (more generally the buying or distribution) division. Suppose that oil (the intermediate product) can be bought or sold in a purely competitive market at a price p of $39. The marginal exploration costs of the manufacturing division are given by the increasing marginal cost curve in Exhibit 24-1, which is labeled MC_m and indicates

EXHIBIT 24-1

Manufacturing Division

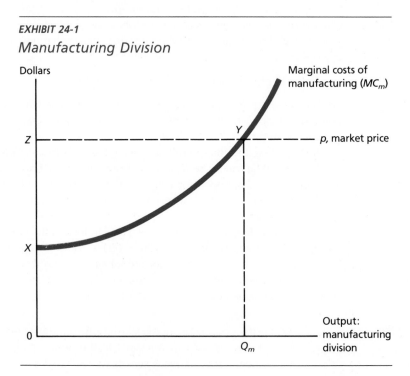

EXHIBIT 24-2

Distribution Division

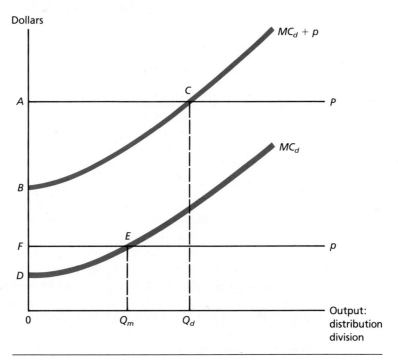

that each additional unit costs more to obtain. Exhibit 24-1 shows that the manufacturing division should produce Q_m units of product and transfer them at a price p to the distribution division.

With Q_m units of output, the marginal cost of the manufacturing division is equal to marginal revenue, the market price p. The manufacturing division should not produce in excess of Q_m units. If the distribution division wants to sell more than Q_m units, it should buy the extra units on the market.

Exhibit 24-2 shows the decision process of the distribution division. The distribution division's marginal cost is MC_d, and it buys the product from the manufacturing division at a price of p. The transfer price is p. The distribution division sells the final product, which may be oil in barrels or gasoline, at a price of P in a competitive market. The distribution division should sell Q_d units. At that output, marginal cost equals marginal revenue, the price P, for the firm. The unit output of the manufacturing division, Q_m, will be equal to or less than the units sold by the distribution division. In this case it would benefit the firm to have the distribution division buy some product from the market to process and sell.

The curves of Exhibits 24-1 and 24-2 are:

$P =$ price of the end product and hence the average revenue (if price is constant across output levels, as it would be in a perfectly competitive market, average revenue equals marginal revenue equals price)

$p =$ market price of the intermediate product

$MC_m =$ marginal-cost curve of the manufacturing division

$MC_d =$ marginal-cost curve of the distribution division

$MC_d + p =$ sum of MC_d plus p, the marginal cost of the distribution division and the intermediate price of the product (the curve is based on the assumption that all products produced at a marginal cost less than the competitive price p have a marginal cost to the distribution division equal to the firm's opportunity cost p)

Management of the manufacturing division would only produce Q_m units because if more were produced, the marginal cost would exceed the market price p. Management of the distribution division would not pay in excess of the market price p to the manufacturing division, since the product could be purchased in the market for that price. Thus, the marginal-cost curve of the distribution division is the sum of the marginal cost of the distribution division, MC_d, and the competitive price p of the intermediate product. The transfer price should be the competitive price p which is also the marginal cost of the manufacturing division at an output of Q_m. Management of the distribution division would buy Q_m units from the manufacturing division, $Q_d - Q_m$ units from outside, and obtain a profit equal to the area denoted *ABC* in Exhibit 24-2. The profit to the manufacturing division is shown in Exhibit 24-1 as the area *XYZ*.[5]

Marginal Cost

Given the restrictive assumptions in the previous section, the market price is the appropriate transfer price. Since the market price is equal to the marginal cost of the selling (manufacturing) division at the best solution, the marginal cost is also the appropriate transfer price.

In a perfectly competitive market for the intermediate product, the transfer price can be set equal to the market price. But perfect intermediate markets seldom exist. The appropriateness of using the market price generally depends on the extent of competition in the market, the existence of idle capacity (which reduces production costs), volume effects on production, alternative facility uses, and degree of interdependence among divisions. Products also differ not only by final use but by quality, delivery conditions, and related factors.

When there is no intermediate market, a transfer price equal to marginal (approx-

5. The areas representing profits in Exhibit 24-1 and 24-2 are not comparable due to a change in scale.

imated in practice by variable) cost is still relevant. However, managers are typically reluctant to transfer goods and services at marginal cost because this tends to reduce their division's profit, which is often used to measure its performance. Such transfer prices may then cause behavioral responses that destroy many of the advantages otherwise attained by decentralization. Further, under certain conditions, marginal-cost pricing is insufficient to obtain an optimal solution. Marginal cost is necessary for a correct economic transfer price, but it may not be sufficient. Even in the previous example, the use of the marginal manufacturing cost as a transfer price does not ensure the right output decision. It is also necessary to use the market price of the intermediate product. Because the marginal cost may be difficult to determine in specific cases, alternative approaches are described next.

Variable Cost

Since marginal cost is often difficult to measure, accountants frequently work with average variable cost as an approximation of the desired marginal cost. Average variable cost (AVC), which is easier to compute, is used as an estimate of the marginal cost required in a transfer-pricing analysis.

When variable cost is used as the transfer price, transfers are often made at the standard variable cost per unit. Where this number affects performance measures, management may permit a separate lump-sum charge to cover fixed costs and profits based on expected (rather than actual) results. Alternatively, the divisions may receive a prorated share of the firm's actual contribution margin based on their standard costs. Thus, for example, if the unit contribution margin on final sale were $3 and if two divisions, A and B, had 12 percent standard costs ($8 and $4, respectively), then division A would be allocated ($8/$12) $3 or $2 for each unit sold while division B would receive ($4/$12) $3 or $1.

Although there is a certain appeal to marginal-cost transfer pricing as approximated by variable cost, the method is not widely used. Market-based and full-cost approaches dominate. Approximately three-fourths of the transfer-pricing systems used in the United States as well as the world are of these two types. Of those other systems in use, most reflect negotiated transfer prices. Let's now examine these more popular approaches.

Full Cost

More firms use full (or absorption) cost for transfer pricing than any other method. When full (absorption) cost is used, there is little incentive for the selling unit to control costs, since such costs can be transferred to the buying unit. The situation is made even worse if absorption costing is combined with a cost-plus transfer price because the selling unit's inefficiencies then allow it an increased return.

Absorption costing also affects decisions inappropriately by causing the fixed costs of the selling unit (hence company fixed costs) to be viewed as variable costs since they are included in the price paid by the buying unit of the same company. Assume, for example, that there are three divisions. Division A buys from B and B buys from C, but each can also buy externally. Suppose further that division A is considering purchasing an intermediate good from division B at a transfer price of $490 per unit. Division *B*'s marginal cost is $490, including $100 per unit paid to *C*.[6] An outside supplier wishing to obtain the business offers to supply the goods at a price of $480 to *A*. Division *C* now supplies *B* at a price of $100 per unit. The $100 is *C*'s full cost of manufacturing a unit of product. Division *C*'s marginal cost is $40 per unit. The $100 is included in *B*'s marginal cost of $490. Division *B*'s other marginal costs total $390.

Division *A* would prefer to buy from the outside at a cost of $480 (which is less than *B*'s marginal cost of $490 and less than the price *B* is charging). The net cost to the firm of buying would be $480 on each unit. But if *A* buys from *B*, the marginal cost to the firm is only $40 + ($490 − $100) = $430. The firm is better off if *A* buys from *B* even though *B*'s marginal cost exceeds the cost of buying on the outside market. Division *B*'s transfer price (at marginal cost) is distorted by the fact that it is being charged full cost by division *C*. Costs that are fixed in division *C* (and hence to the entire firm) are being made to appear variable to division *B*. A transfer price based on *C*'s marginal cost would lead to the proper decision.

If the finished unit can be sold at a price of above $430, the firm's position is improved. The firm would rather have the sale than not have the sale. A transfer price based on division *C*'s marginal cost of $40 would lead to the proper decision. Division *C*'s full cost of $100 is of interest (on the average, sales have to be for $100 for the firm to show a profit), but the full cost is of no help in making the decision of whether the intermediate good should be obtained from another division.

In certain cases a given product or service may appear to be available from several alternative sources, even within the same organization. An example involves the availability of close-substitute courses in a major university. For example, consider the availability of courses in real estate offered in different schools at Cornell University.

Transfer Pricing at Cornell University	Cornell is a private university of roughly 17,000 students located in Ithaca, New York. The university consists of several major academic units designated as colleges, professional schools and departments. When students enroll in a particular academic unit at Cornell, tuition is paid to that college, professional school or department. If a student enrolls in a course taught outside of the college or professional school in which he or she is officially registered, the student's college or professional school pays an "accessory instruction" fee to the unit offering the course. Thus, transfer prices are established to transfer funds among academic units as students enroll in courses across the Cornell campus. The following is a list of accessory instruction fees (transfer prices) paid by the Johnson Graduate School of Management to other academic units when the business students take courses in other academic units.

6. Marginal cost would probably be approximated by using variable cost in practice but marginal cost is the better concept.

Academic Unit	Amount
Architecture	$311.22 per credit hour
Arts and Sciences	245.27 per credit hour
Engineering	290.74 per credit hour
Hotel School	297.13 per credit hour
Law School	240.96 per credit hour
African Studies	363.96 per credit hour
Physical Education	182.36 per credit hour
Agriculture	321.56 per credit hour
Human Ecology	309.22 per credit hour
Industrial and Labor Relations	269.67 per credit hour
Veterinary Medicine	321.56 per credit hour

Students in the Johnson Graduate School of Management may desire to take courses in real estate, a topic not covered in the School. Such courses can be found in the School of Architecture and the School of Hotel Management. Should the student elect a course in the School of Architecture, the cost is $311.22 per credit hour while a similar course in the Hotel School costs $297.13. The student can elect either, and the Johnson Graduate School of Management then makes the transfer payment. The credit-hour transfer price is cost-driven. The market is complex since the product is different in the two alternative situations. Teachers differ as does course content. The transfer prices are cost-plus prices.

Negotiated Price

Even if marginal cost is relevant and full cost is not, there is still room for negotiation between the parties. The use of marginal cost does not set the transfer price in most organizations. The problem with a negotiated price, however, is that different divisions bargain with different skill. The final outcome generally will not maximize the well-being of the firm as it relates to the specific decision considered. Moreover, managers may be rewarded for their intrafirm negotiating ability rather than for their managerial skills in running divisions. Negotiation is also costly: it takes time and can lead to poor working relationships. Arbitration may be necessary.

If central management believes inappropriate transfer pricing decisions are being made, there is a reason and certainly a temptation to step in and set the price from the point of view of maximizing the firm's profits. Each month a schedule of prices might be published by central management, and the divisions would make their decisions based on these prices.

A possible advantage of this procedure is that it could be efficient in that it avoids haggling and other potentially destructive behavior. It is also decisive. A disadvantage is that it removes the pricing decision (hence control) from the manager selling the product. There often will be resentment at having to sell the product at a price that is beyond the manager's control but that nevertheless affects the manager's performance measure. Morever, setting transfer prices centrally undermines the very decentralization that the transfer-pricing method is supposed to facilitate.

Forced Internal Buying versus Autonomy

Coupled with the issue of setting a transfer price is the issue of whether a buying division should be forced to buy materials and components from the firm's other divisions or be free to buy either inside or outside the firm. Current practice on this issue varies widely among companies. One serious problem is in attempting to use outside bids to yield market prices. Bidders will soon tire of making bids on business they never get. There are trade-offs to be considered in developing firm policy as it relates to quality and alternate sources of supply. Autonomy can result in dysfunctional decision making, but forcing internal transfer also can result in significant costs including undermining decentralization. One such instance and its effect is indicated by the following excerpt from the *Wall Street Journal.*

Forced Internal Parts Transfers at General Motors

The *Wall Street Journal* reported that General Motors managers feel obligated to buy automobile parts from other GM divisions, in spite of the fact that high-quality parts can be purchased outside the firm at competitive prices. This situation reduces the incentive of GM's parts operations to produce efficiently.[7]

Measuring Performance

Measuring performance is difficult when transfer prices affect revenue or expenses. If the intermediate market is perfectly competitive, then market price is a good measure to use as the transfer price. In the absence of perfectly competitive markets or an easily determined market price, it may be necessary to use negotiated prices or a combination of market and negotiated prices. The use of market price simulates the market conditions that the divisions would face if the divisions were separate corporate entities rather than subdivisions of one business organization. Unfortunately, it is not always easy to establish the market price. List price is not a reliable indicator in all cases. Market conditions, custom, special terms of payment, quantity concessions, and other factors make it difficult to estimate an equivalent price in the market.

Even if it can be assumed that the market price can be determined, the question still remains as to whether it is a fair price for internal purposes. For example, the

7. "Groping Giant: In a High-Tech Drive, GM Falls Below Rivals in Auto Profit Margins," *Wall Street Journal,* July 22, 1986, pp. 1, 16.

manufacturing division may have a more-or-less captive market, and so have less selling expense than the firms setting the market price. The manufacturing division should not get the entire benefit of these savings.

A troublesome problem also exists when there is no market price. For example, one division may conduct research that is applicable to another division. There is frequently no market price for research, and costs incurred are not the primary factor in setting the value of the research. This makes establishing a price difficult. Here the sale price must be negotiated or possibly fixed by management.

In the absence of a market price, any reports or measures resulting from the intracompany price are more arbitrary than is the case with a normal accounting report. Such reports and measures of efficiency may do more harm than good. A management faced with recurring situations where intracompany transfers cannot be priced objectively should reconsider the pros and cons of decentralized accounting reports aimed at measuring income and return on investment. In situations of this nature, the use of other measures of performance such as standard costs should be considered.

Assuming that an objective is to measure performance, several difficulties arise from basing the transfer price of the manufacturing or selling division on cost. The use of marginal (usually, in practice, variable) cost alone would almost always lead to a deficit for the supplying division unless a cost-plus system were used. The use of cost as the basis of the transfer price also places a large burden on the cost accounting department to establish accurately the relevant values. A by-product of a transfer-pricing system based on cost can be a series of arguments on just what the cost is.

Consider an example where the marginal cost of one division is constant — that is, its marginal-cost curve is a horizontal line that does not increase as production increases. This is illustrated by MC_m in Exhibit 24-3. Assume further that there is no

EXHIBIT 24-3

Transfer Pricing and Constant Efficiency

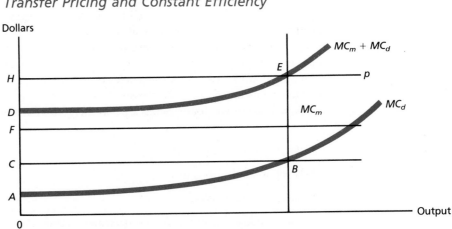

intermediate market for the product. The profit of the distribution division is *ABC*, which is equal to the area *DEH*, the profit of the firm. The manufacturing division makes no profit if it charges a price equal to its marginal cost because its marginal-cost curve is horizontal. This is a case where the best decision is reached using marginal costs but the resulting profit measures make it unattractive to the manager of the manufacturing division. When such a situation is approximated, the manufacturing division is better evaluated using costs rather than profits.

Further issues are raised when a firm uses the profit-center approach. The profit-center manager may not be able to control the number of units sold. Consider a parts division of an automobile company making components of a new model when there is no replacement market. The parts division cannot control the number of units sold, and the transfer price cannot help but be somewhat arbitrary. In a situation of this type, it might be more desirable to measure the performance of the parts division by the cost of the product rather than by a fictitious profit figure at least two steps removed from the correctly measured variables (that is, those that are controllable by the parts division).

The first question raised by management must be whether the use of transfer prices is appropriate at all. Only if the answer to this question is yes should the question of the method of computing and controlling the transfer price be raised.

Decision Making and Transfer Pricing

A division manager can determine how to maximize divisional profit under a given transfer pricing system based on marginal cost. Although the result may not be consistent with the firm's objective of maximizing company profit, a transfer price based on marginal cost may be actually desirable from the point of view of the selling division. For example, the use of marginal cost as a transfer price for the product of the manufacturing division (with costs like those in Exhibit 24-1) allows the manufacturing division to pass cost inefficiencies on to the distribution division. It thereby provides no incentives to reduce costs.

Four general types of decisions are considered here that involve transfer pricing. They are:

- Pricing of an end product,

- Level-of-output decisions,

- Make-or-buy decisions,

- Capital budgeting decisions and decisions to drop products.

All these decisions should be made on the basis of either marginal or differential cost techniques from the point of view of the whole corporation. Pricing and output decisions must be solved using the marginal costs of the several divisions because the individual divisions' best interests may not be the same as those of the corporation. Neither full costs nor market prices can be used as transfer prices in making these decisions. However, the marginal costs should be compared with the relevant market prices in arriving at a final decision. Pricing and output decisions have been discussed at some length already in this and prior chapters.

The manufacturing division should use market price where available to compute revenue. The marginal cost of the manufacturing division should be used to establish the cost of the distribution division. Using the marginal cost of the manufacturing division to establish the transfer price is a necessary but not a sufficient condition for optimal output decisions at the firm level. Further, the advantages of decentralization should not be quickly sacrificed to the transfer-pricing solution without carefully weighing all the costs and benefits.

The make-or-buy decision requires knowledge of those costs that can be avoided by purchasing the product. This requires a cost breakdown that is not supplied by the market price. The same type of information is required for the decision as to whether or not to drop a product. These are nonmarginal decisions and must be made on the basis of differential-revenue and cost techniques.

The transfer price used in capital-budgeting decisions made by a division buying components from another division should be based on the incremental cash inflows and outflows that result from the investment. These flows are tied to variable and semivariable costs.

Thus, for some decision-making purposes (make-or-buy, capital budgeting, or abandoning a product), the differential costs of the goods transferred from division to division should be known. For pricing or output decisions, the marginal cost of the product must be used to determine the best solutions.

The limitations of transfer pricing for decision making should be carefully noted. The fact that using marginal costs as the basis for transfer prices may not lead to the optimal output decision at the division level has been discussed. Indeed, there is no one method of transfer pricing that is best for all varieties of decision making and performance evaluation.

Consider the problem of whether or not to drop division B, which sells parts to division A. Assume that the transfer-pricing system uses marginal costs, that a computation of the income of division B indicates that the income computed in accordance with accounting procedures is negative, and that a computation of the contribution of division A to the recovery of fixed costs directly identified with division B indicates that the division is not making any contribution. Yet it may not be best to abandon division B. The production of parts may have the effect of increasing the profit of division A, which would otherwise have to purchase parts on the open market at a higher price. Thus, to determine whether division B should be dropped, it is necessary to look beyond the information obtained from using transfer pricing to the effect of the abandonment on the income of the entire firm.

Financial Accounting

A firm's general financial accounting reports require that inventories be recorded at cost to conform to generally accepted accounting principles. This cost is full cost, including manufacturing overhead but not including any element of unrealized profit (that is, profit not realized by sale to a party outside the organization). Financial reporting requirements mean that the accounting group in the central office must be supplied with unit cost of product by the selling division so that divisional profit (or loss) can be eliminated from the inventory value of the purchasing division and the income of the selling division in preparing consolidated financial statements.

Multinational Firms

As in segment performance measurement, the transfer-pricing issue presents special problems in multinational firms. Such factors as cultural differences, quotas and import duties, differing marginal tax rates, currency regulations, and foreign exchange rate fluctuations affect the transfer pricing problem.[8] The following quotation illustrates how Honeywell deals with this problem.

International Transfer Pricing at Honeywell	Honeywell has about 100 international subsidiaries and affiliates, all considered profit centers. Honeywell's solution to the foreign-currency-exchange problem in transfer pricing among its foreign subsidiaries was to adopt what the firm calls "dollar indexing." Local currency transfer prices are converted to U.S. dollar transfer prices using a planned exchange rate. When actual exchange rates fluctuate from their predicted levels, U.S. dollar transfer prices are "indexed" to the current exchange rate between the U.S. dollar and the subsidiary's local currency.[9]

Firms might be expected to set transfer prices to maximize the expected after-tax present values of the cash flows. For example, if a firm operates in a country that restricts the repatriation of income back to the home country, transfer prices might

---

8. L. Merville and J. W. Petty, "Transfer Pricing for the Multinational Firm," *Accounting Review* (October 1978): 935–39.

9. D. Malmstrom, "Accommodating Exchange Rate Fluctuations in Intercompany Pricing and Invoicing," *Management Accounting* (September 1977): 24–28.

be increased as a means of moving cash across international boundaries without violating a country's rules on dividend repatriation.

Comparing Transfer-Pricing Methods

No single method of transfer pricing can fill all the needs of a decentralized organization. No pretense of absolute correctness has or can be made for any of the pricing methods. The admitted inaccuracies must be weighted against the gains resulting from having decentralized operations and decision making. The greater the significance of the intradivisional transfers, the more unreliable are the income measures of the divisions involved.

Business considerations beyond those of production and investment are often relevant to transfer-pricing decisions. Differences in tax rates, tariffs, and conversion rates among countries can have an overriding impact on the transfer price selected. Similar considerations can also influence transfer prices within a country. For example, to maximize tax deductions based on percentage-depletion allowances in the extractive industries, firms may wish to use very high transfer prices among subsidiaries. Again, different transfer prices are useful for different objectives. Since internal performance measurement can be accomplished separately from the requirements of external financial reporting, multiple transfer-pricing systems may be appropriate within a single firm. When the above questions arise, ethical considerations as well as economic calculations should influence the final decision. In addition, the effects of the transfer-pricing policy on cooperation among divisions should be considered. For example, in a *Business Week* article, the writer describes how the subunits of Gulf Oil Company attempted to boost their own performance measures at the other subunits' expense through inflated transfer prices.[10]

Summary

Attempting to administer the separate components of one firm as if they were separate competing entities frequently requires the use of transfer prices for both accounting purposes and decision making. The economic analysis of transfer pricing indicates that the solution can become extremely complex if the demand and the production of the products are dependent on each other (technological dependence may also be introduced). However, several observations may be made:

1. There is an entire schedule of marginal costs. The appropriateness of any one marginal cost should not be assumed. The use of marginal costs (particularly as estimated in practice using variable cost) for transfer pricing does not en-

10. "Gulf Oil Goes Back to What It Knows Best," *Business Week* (January 31, 1977): 80.

sure that the company is operating at its optimal output because divisions may act to maximize their own profits to the detriment of the profit of the company. This can occur when competitive prices are used as well.

2. The use of marginal-cost transfer pricing may result in inappropriate actions, such as attempting to decrease efficiency, or having an increasing marginal-cost curve to increase divisional profit (by increasing marginal cost and thus increasing the transfer price of the product).

3. Transfer-pricing procedures do not generally give good results for nonmarginal decisions such as abandoning a plant or make-or-buy decisions. These decisions require a differential-cost and revenue analysis.

The choice of the transfer-pricing method depends on the information available. For certain decisions, transfer prices are not useful at all. The extent to which transfer prices are an artificial compromise should be recognized by the user, so that he or she may be alert to those cases where they cannot be used for decision-making purposes.

It is likely that in many cases firms have created profit centers that require the use of transfer prices when cost centers would have been a more effective means of controlling costs and measuring performance. The use of a profit center requires that revenue be computed, and this in turn requires the use of prices where there may not have been an arm's-length transaction or where the profit-manager cannot control sales.

If an intermediate market exists and there are no important demand or cost dependencies, market price will lead to the maximization of both divisional and company profits. However, if such intermediate markets do not exist, analysis is required to determine the best transfer price. Such prices require some nonmarket imposition that inevitably reduces the division manager's independence. The decision of what transfer-pricing system to use requires a consideration of the expected savings gained in more appropriate operational decisions versus the expected losses from reduced decentralized operations. Such losses reflect, for example, behavioral changes when a manager no longer perceives independence of operation.

In choosing a transfer price a balance must be struck. A useful system should help the firm attain goal congruence while encouraging greater effort and improved performance from managers. To the extent a decentralized system is desired, a well-conceived transfer-pricing system is essential.

Key Terms to Review

decentralization, p. 838.

goal congruence, p. 839

transfer price, p. 839

Review Problem

TRANSFER PRICING

The Barnsville, Ohio, Division of the Trine Company has developed a product requiring a specially made casing. The Altoona, Pennsylvania, Division of Trine has the skill to produce the needed casing, but due to the specific requirements of the special casing, Altoona would need to cut back production of another item by 500 units per month to provide the 400 units per month required by Barnsville. Variable costs for the new casing are estimated at $10 per unit. The specific item to be cut back sells on the market for $37 a unit and is produced at a cost of $30, of which $18 is considered to be variable. The Barnsville division has requested a bid on the project by the Altoona Division. As manager of the Altoona Division, what price would you charge?

Solution to Review Problem

The lost contribution margin on Altoona's current production is ($30 − $18)(500) or $6,000 per month. In terms of the new casing, this works out to be $6,000 ÷ 400 or $15 per unit. The variable cost per unit of the new casing is $10. The bid (transfer price) should be at least $10 + $15 or $25 per unit using variable costs to approximate marginal cost. If the Barnsville Division can secure the same quality and satisfactory delivery conditions for less than $25, it should do so. But if Altoona offers better quality or delivery, it might justify charging a price above $25.

At $25 there is no profit performance incentive for Altoona to accept the offer. Hence, some price negotiation in the form of a markup to cost may be appropriate by which both the firm and the division's profits benefit.

If there were excess capacity in the Altoona plant, a lower bid (transfer) price is appropriate. This price should not drop below the marginal production cost, which is estimated using a variable cost of $10.

Suggested Readings

Argyris, C. *Personality and Organization.* New York: Harper & Row, 1957.

Benke, R., and J. Edwards. *Transfer Pricing: Techniques and Uses.* New York: National Association of Accountants, 1980.

Eccles, R. *The Transfer Pricing Problem: A Theory for Practice.* Lexington, Mass.: Lexington Books, 1985.

Grabski, S. "Transfer Pricing in Complex Organizations: A Review and Integration of Recent Empirical and Analytical Research." *Journal of Accounting Literature* (Spring 1985): 33–75.

Hirshleifer, J. "Economics of the Divisionalized Firm." *Journal of Business* (April 1957): 96–108.

———. "On the Economics of Transfer Pricing." *Journal of Business* (July 1956): 172–84.

Horngren, C., and G. Foster. *Cost Accounting: A Managerial Emphasis*, 6th ed. Englewood Cliffs, N.J.: Prentice-Hall, 1987, chap. 25.

Kaplan, R., and A. Atkinson. *Advanced Management Accounting*, 2nd ed. Englewood Cliffs, N.J.: Prentice-Hall, 1989, chap. 14.

Lucien, K. "Transfer Pricing for the Cost of Funds in a Commercial Bank." *Management Accounting* (January 1979): 23–36.

March, J., and H. Simon. *Organizations.* New York: Wiley, 1958.

Solomons, D. *Divisional Performance: Measurement and Control.* New York: Financial Executives Research Foundation, 1965.

Vancil, R. *Decentralization: Managerial Ambiguity by Design.* New York: Financial Executives Research Foundation, 1979.

Whinston, A. "Price Guides in Decentralized Organizations." In *New Prospectives in Organization Research,* edited by W. Cooper, H. Leavitt, and M. Shelley. New York: Wiley, 1962, pp. 405–8.

Review Questions

24-1 Under a marginal-cost transfer-pricing arrangement, will division management acting to maximize the profits of the division also be maximizing the profits of the corporation?

24-2 What are the advantages and disadvantages of centralization and decentralization of authority?

24-3 What are the three main methods of establishing transfer prices?

24-4 If the manager of a distribution (buying) division acts to maximize the division's profits, what is likely to happen to the firm?

24-5 If the manager of a manufacturing (selling) division acts to maximize the division's profits, what is the likely effect on the firm?

24-6 If the transfer price is set equal to the marginal cost of the manufacturing division, will this lead to decisions that maximize the profits of the firm?

24-7 Assuming the use of marginal cost as the basis of final prices, are transfer prices useful for decisions such as abandoning a division?

24-8 Assuming that a division is performing research for other divisions, at what price should it transfer its completed research? (Assume that the research is one of several products made by the division.)

24-9 If both the distribution and manufacturing divisions act monopolistically, what is the effect on the firm?

24-10 What are the main problems in using full cost as a basis for transfer-price decisions?

24-11 Why isn't marginal cost used commonly as the transfer price?

24-12 Why isn't variable cost alone often used as a transfer price?

24-13 It is often said that one of the purposes of transfer pricing is to promote goal congruence in a decentralized firm. What is meant by *goal congruence*?

24-14 Why might a market-based transfer price not be possible in a given case?

Exercises   **24-15 Use of Performance Measures**   The Elston Company used the market price of a competitive producer as the internal transfer price for an identical product. The manufacturing division claimed that it should be permitted to charge a higher price. The market price was based on a vendor with a more modern and more efficient plant. The manager of the manufacturing plant was forced to operate with an outdated and inefficient plant. Further, he had no authority to make capital investments or otherwise modernize his plant. He believed that he was being penalized for something beyond his control and claimed the practice created bad "managerial psychology." The vice president for finance ruled that "since the primary objective of the intracompany pricing system was to provide a means of measuring performance against known competitive levels, competitive practice with regard to cost and price must be followed."

Comment on this situation in terms of the use to which the performance measures are being put and the appropriateness of the procedure. Can you think of other reasons besides the efficiency of the plant that might cause other divisions under similar plans to object?

24-16 Internal Audit Charges   Assume that the top management of the Argon Company requires all divisions to have their activities audited periodically by the Internal Auditing Division. At what price should the audit services be charged to the divisions?

24-17 Using Marginal Cost as Transfer Price   Draw a set of curves showing what happens to output if the distribution division is forced to buy all product from the manufacturing division and the manufacturing division's marginal cost is used as the transfer price. Assume a constant market price of p for the intermediate product, a constant price of P for the final product, and increasing marginal cost curves.

24-18 Suppose the distribution division must buy only from the manufacturing division. Which of the below statements are true assuming competitive markets and increasing marginal costs?

   a. The competitive (market) price of the intermediate product is not relevant in making the decision.

   b. The relevant cost is the sum of the marginal costs of the manufacturing and distribution divisions.

   c. Sales of the distribution division are reduced.

   d. The firm's profits are reduced.

Problems   **24-19 Production and Pricing Decisions within Companies**   The Regulite Company has two divisions (manufacturing and distribution) acting as profit centers. It is a small company that feels its price is set by its competitors but that it can sell all it can produce at a price of $100 per unit.

The average variable costs (an estimate of variable costs) for the two divisions are:

$$AVC_m = 40 \qquad AVC_d = 10 + 0.005Q$$

The manufacturing division has $5,000 and the distribution division $1,000 of fixed costs. In addition, the corporate headquarters allocates $3,000 of its costs to manufacturing and $2,000 to distribution.

REQUIRED:

a. What is the optimum level of production for the firm? What would be the profit of the firm? What is the marginal cost of manufacturing at the optimal output?

b. If you were in charge of the distribution division, what price would you offer the manufacturing division? What output would result? What would be the profits of the distribution division?

c. Do the profit figures provide useful performance measures? Explain.

24-20 Production and Pricing Decisions within Companies Suppose that the average variable costs for the two divisions of the Regulite Company in Problem 24-19 are:

$$AVC_m = 8 + 0.01Q \qquad AVC_d = 62$$

There are no fixed costs.

REQUIRED:

a. What is the optimum level of production for the firm? What would be the profit of the firm? What is the marginal cost of manufacturing at the optimal output?

b. If you were in charge of the distribution division, what price would you offer the manufacturing division? What output would result?

c. What is the effect of your answer in part **b** on the firm's profits?

d. What profits are shown by the distribution division? Under these assumptions, would the profit figures provide good performance measures?

24-21 Production and Pricing Decisions within Companies Suppose that the average variable costs for the two divisions of the Regulite Company in Problem 24-19 are:

$$AVC_m = 8 + 0.01Q \qquad AVC_d = 2 + 0.005Q$$

There are no fixed costs.

REQUIRED:

a. What is the optimum level of production for the firm? What would be the profit of the firm? What is the marginal cost of manufacturing at the optimal output?

b. If you were in charge of the distribution division, what price would you offer the manufacturing division? What output would result?

c. In **b**, what effect is there on company profits? Are the profit figures of the divisions good indicators of performance in this case?

24-22 Production and Pricing Decisions within Companies Suppose that the average variable costs for the two divisions of the Regulite Company in Problem 24-19 are:

$$AVC_m = 8 + 0.01Q \qquad AVC_d = 2 + 0.005Q$$

The price is $100 - 0.01Q$, and there are no fixed costs.

REQUIRED:

a. What is the optimum level of production for the firm? What is the marginal cost of manufacturing? What is the profit of the firm?

b. If you were in charge of the distribution division, what price would you offer the manufacturing division? What output would result?

c. What is the effect on company profits of your answer in part **b?** Are the profit figures good indicators of performance?

24-23 Continuation of Problem 24-22 If the manufacturing division acts as a monopolist, at what price would it sell its product to the distribution division? What output would result? Which division acting monopolistically has the greater impact? Why?

24-24 An Acquisition's Impact on Profits In 1982 a major chemical company acquired a major oil company. The chemical company used approximately $800,000,000 of oil products in its production operations.

What effect would the acquisition have on the profits of the chemical company? Some analysts argued that acquisition guaranteed a cheap source of raw material for the chemical company. What do you think?

24-25 Constant Marginal Costs Assume a situation where the marginal cost in both the manufacturing and distribution divisions is constant. The firm can expand its production without a significant (measurable) change in efficiency. This assumption has the effect of making the MC_m and MC_d schedules horizontal (see Exhibit 24-7).

EXHIBIT 24-7

Constant Marginal Cost and Perfect Competition

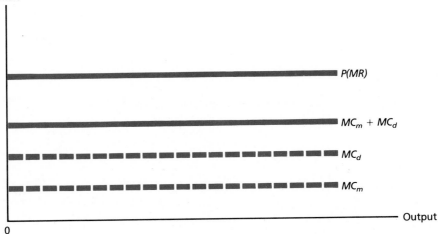

REQUIRED:

a. Is $MR \geq MC_m + MC_d$ necessary for production?

b. If $P \geq MC_m + MC_d$, how much should the firm produce?

c. What will the manufacturing division's profits be?

d. Will optimal output be reached if one division acts as a monopolist?

Special Topics in Cost Accounting

25

Product-Quality Costs and Productivity Measurement

LEARNING OBJECTIVES

After studying this chapter, you should be able to:

1 Define *quality costing*.

2 Understand the difference between quality of conformance and quality of design.

3 List and define the four types of costs associated with quality of conformance.

4 Define *productivity, aggregate productivity,* and *component productivity*.

5 Explain some limitations of summary productivity measures.

6 Describe the multidimensional view of productivity analysis.

B oth manufacturing and service firms are increasingly concerned with the issues of product (or service) quality and productivity. Product and service quality can provide firms with an advantage as they compete to an ever greater extent in a worldwide market. Moreover, product quality is critical to firms that attempt to reduce their materials and parts inventories. Without large inventories on hand, manufacturers must be able to depend on the quality of the materials and parts they do have in stock.

Productivity is a key factor for firms that need to boost their profit margins by generating more units of products or services with the same amount of capital invested. International competition has caused companies to focus on increasing productivity. *Fortune* magazine found in a recent survey of large corporations that 78 percent of the firms' chief executive officers listed productivity improvement and cost control as the most critical aspects of their corporate strategy.[1]

This chapter discusses the methods currently in use for measuring and reporting productivity and the costs of ensuring product quality.

Quality Costing

The benefits from increased product quality come in lower costs for reworking discovered defective units and from more satisfied customers who find fewer defective units. The cost of lowering the tolerance for defective units results from the increased costs of using a better production technology. These costs could be due to using more highly skilled and experienced workers, from using a better grade of materials, or from acquiring updated production equipment.

Some firms have installed a quality-costing system as a part of the cost accounting system. A **quality-costing system** monitors and accumulates the costs incurred by a firm in maintaining or improving product quality. Below is an excerpt from an article in *Management Accounting* that describes the various types of product quality costs (emphasis added).

---

1. M. McComas, "Atop the Fortune 500: A Survey of the C.E.O.'s," *Fortune* (April 28, 1986): 26–31.

Measuring Quality Costs

The quality costs discussed here deal with costs associated with quality of conformance as opposed to costs associated with quality of design. **Quality of design** refers to variations in products which have the same functional use.[2] For example, a Cadillac and a Chevrolet automobile may be used for the same function, transportation, but their design qualities are different. For this type of quality, higher quality generally means higher costs. The same relationship, however, does not exist when cost associated with quality of conformance is considered.

Quality of conformance refers to the degree with which the final product meets its specifications. In other words, quality of conformance refers to the product's fitness for use. If products are sold and they do not meet the consumers' expectations, the company will incur costs because the consumer is unhappy with the product's performance. These costs are one kind of quality costs that will be reduced if higher quality products are produced. Thus, higher quality may mean lower total costs when quality of conformance is considered. Accountants, therefore, should be aware of the costs associated with quality of conformance and how they can be of assistance to management.

The costs associated with quality of conformance generally can be classified into four types: prevention costs, appraisal costs, internal failure costs, and external failure costs.[3] The prevention and appraisal costs occur because a lack of quality of conformance can exist. The internal and external failure costs occur because a lack of quality of conformance does exist.

Prevention costs are the costs associated with designing, implementing, and maintaining the quality system. These costs include engineering quality control systems, quality planning by various departments, and quality training programs.

Appraisal costs are the costs incurred to ensure that materials and products meet quality standards. These costs include inspection of raw materials, laboratory tests, quality audits, and field testing.

Internal failure costs are the costs associated with materials and products that fail to meet quality standards and result in manufacturing losses. They include the cost of scrap, repair, and rework of defective products identified before they are shipped to consumers.

External failure costs are the costs incurred because inferior quality products are shipped to consumers. They include the costs of handling complaints, warranty replacement, repairs of returned products, and so forth.[4]

2. Juran, J. M., and F. M. Gyrna, *Quality Planning and Analysis* (New York: McGraw-Hill, 1971).

3. Quality Cost–Cost Effectiveness Committee: American Society for Quality Control, *Quality Costs — What and How* (Milwaukee: American Society for Quality Control, 1971).

4. Roth, H. P., and W. J. Morse, "Let's Help Measure and Report Quality Costs," *Management Accounting* (August 1983): 50.

The cost of attaining the desired level of product quality can be a significant cost item in many firms. By some estimates the cost of quality in a typical U.S. manufacturing firm ranges from 10 to 20 percent of sales. In contrast, the Japanese automobile industry is reported to show quality costs in the range from 2.5 to 4 percent of sales.[5] Quality costs are also relevant in service industries.

Quality Costs in Banking

Quality costs also occur in service industry firms. The *Banker's Magazine* reported that all checks issued in the United States include a magnetic recognition code designed for automated processing. Yet many of these checks are rejected by the computer as unreadable when automatic processing is attempted. The Bank Administration Institute estimated that in one year alone the nation's banks incurred $435 million in reprocessing costs for faulty checks. This amount was roughly one-half of all of the check processing costs incurred in the United States.[6]

The magnitude of quality costs has prompted many companies to install quality-costing systems to monitor and help reduce the costs of achieving high-quality production.

Reducing Quality Costs at TRW

Business Week reported that TRW has a new accounting system that supports its efforts to reduce the cost of product quality. The system focuses on costs ranging from scrap to warranty costs, and the company's goal is to reduce quality costs by $24 million.[7]

---

5. See J. W. Schmidt and J. F. Jackson, "Measuring the Cost of Product Quality," Proceedings of the February 1982 Meeting of the Society of Automotive Engineers, 1982. See also H. P. Roth and W. J. Morse, "Let's Help Measure and Report Quality Costs," *Management Accounting* (August 1983): 53.

6. W. J. Latzko, "Quality Control for Banks," *Bankers' Magazine* (Autumn 1977): 64–68.

7. "TRW Leads a Revolution in Managing Technology," *Business Week* (November 15, 1982): 124–130.

EXHIBIT 25-1

Typical Quality Cost Report

	Current Month's Cost	Percentage of Total
Prevention costs:		
Quality training	$ 2,000	1.3%
Reliability engineering	10,000	6.5
Pilot studies	5,000	3.3
Systems development	8,000	5.2
Total prevention	$ 25,000	16.3%
Appraisal costs:		
Materials inspection	$ 6,000	3.9%
Supplies inspection	3,000	2.0
Reliability testing	5,000	3.3
Laboratory	25,000	16.3
Total appraisal	39,000	25.5%
Internal failure costs:		
Scrap	$ 15,000	9.8%
Repair	18,000	11.8
Rework	12,000	7.8
Down time	6,000	3.9
Total internal failure	51,000	33.3%
External failure costs:		
Warranty costs	$ 14,000	9.2%
Out of warranty repairs and replacement	6,000	3.9
Customer complaints	3,000	2.0
Product liability	10,000	6.5
Transportation losses	5,000	3.3
Total external failure	38,000	24.9
Total quality costs	$153,000	100.0%

Cost of a Faulty Electrical Component at Hewlett-Packard

Fortune magazine reported on a Hewlett-Packard executive's description of the potential cost of a faulty resistor. If the faulty component is identified before use, it is discarded at a cost of $.02. Once the resistor has been installed in a larger electronic component, it could cost $10 to repair the component. If the faulty resistor is part of a several thousand dollar computer, and the parts must be repaired in the field, the repair cost can exceed the manufacturing cost of the computer.[8]

8. J. Main, "The Battle for Quality Begins," *Fortune* (December 29, 1980): 28–33.

These examples highlight the importance of having a cost-accounting system that regularly monitors and reports on quality costs. A typical quality-costing report is displayed in Exhibit 25-1.[9] The next step is to estimate standard (or budgeted) costs for each line item.

Productivity

The business press has highlighted the need for increases in productivity of U.S. firms in order to compete effectively with foreign firms, most notably Japanese companies. For example, during a recent year the most productive plants in Ford Motor Company produced an average of two engines per day per employee using 777 square feet of plant space. A Toyota plant, on the other hand, produced nine engines per day per employee and used only 454 square feet of floor space.[10]

Can U.S. industries achieve the necessary level of productivity? Some people argue that the superior productivity of some foreign competitors is due solely to cultural factors or historical events. Others, however, believe that these differences need not exist and that the productivity of U.S. firms can be substantially improved. For example, the following anecdotes, originally reported in a variety of business publications and compiled by Kaplan, support the latter view.[11]

General Motors	Changing from railroad deliveries every other day to truck deliveries three times daily facilitated an 80 percent reduction in the inventory of an important part at a Buick plant.

9. The source of this report was H. P. Roth and W. J. Morse, "Let's Help Measure and Report Quality Costs," *Management Accounting* (August 1983): 53.

10. See "The U.S. Competitive Position in the 1980's . . . and Some Things We Can Do About It," a report published by the Center for International Business; T. Murrin, "Rejecting the Traditional Ways of Doing Business" (Chicago: American Production and Inventory Control Society, October 1982); R. Kaplan, "Measuring Manufacturing Performance: A New Challenge for Managerial Accounting Research," *Accounting Review* (October 1983): 686.

11. R. Kaplan, "Measuring Manufacturing Performance: A New Challenge for Managerial Accounting Research," *Accounting Review* (October 1983): 687.

| **Ford Motor Company** | Ford reduced its overall inventory position by $750 million over a two-year period by doing a better job in coordinating deliveries from its suppliers. |

| **Matushita** | Eight years after Matushita acquired a Motorola television plant in the United States, production volume had been increased by 40 percent, and defects had been reduced from 150 per 100 television sets to three per 100 television sets. |

| **Sony and Honda** | These two companies have achieved the lowest defect rates in their respective industries in U.S. plants. |

| **Sanyo** | It took Sanyo only two months to reduce the defect rate by 30 percent in a U.S. television plant it acquired.[12] |

| **Hewlett-Packard** | *Business Week* reported that a division of Hewlett-Packard estimated that it could reduce its factory work force by 33 percent, decrease factory floor space by 25 percent, and reduce inventories by 66 percent if it abandoned the detect-and-fix method of quality control with a zero-defects philosophy.[13] |

12. See H. Takeuchi, "Productivity: Learning from the Japanese," *California Management Review* (Summer 1981): 5–19; R. Schonberger, *Japanese Manufacturing Techniques* (New York: Free Press, 1982).

13. *Business Week* (November 1, 1982): 66.

How can such productivity improvements be facilitated? One way is for the managerial accounting system to be more attuned to the many facets of productivity and to collect productivity data in a systematic way for use by management. Before this can be done effectively, it is important to understand two ideas: (1) the nature of productivity in general and (2) the nature of the production process to which productivity measurements are to be applied.

Productivity Measures

The most common definition of **productivity** is some ratio of output to input. Such ratios can be further categorized as follows:

$$\text{Aggregate (or total) productivity} = \frac{\text{Total output}}{\text{Total input}}$$

$$\text{Component (or partial) productivity} = \frac{\text{Total output}}{\text{Component of input}}$$

Aggregate productivity is an attempt to measure the ratio of all of the organization's output to all of its inputs. Dollar measures are generally used. Total output is the sum, across all products or services, of the number of units produced times the sales price per unit. Inputs are also generally measured in dollar terms and include direct-material, direct labor, overhead, and capital. The material, labor, and overhead measures are straightforward measures of actual costs. The capital measure is more troublesome, and generally depreciation is used as the measure of capital consumed. The aggregate productivity measure is generally calculated during each of several time periods, and comparisons are made across periods. This approach is troublesome because changing price levels make the dollar measures across time noncomparable. In the denominator of the total productivity measure, for example, labor cost is added to depreciation. Labor cost is in terms of current dollars, but depreciation is the time allocation of a historical cost figure. Price-level adjustments can be used to alleviate these difficulties, but such adjustments are complex and can be misleading (see Chapters 19 and 20).

Component productivity is a measure of the relationship between output and one or more components of the organization's inputs. Component productivity measures are computed using both dollar values and physical measures. When dollar measures are used, the dollar value of output is divided by the dollar value of an input component. Sales per labor dollar is an example. Physical component-productivity measures rely on nondollar measures of output and component input. An example would be automobiles produced per labor hour.[14]

---

14. See C. E. Craig and R. C. Harris, "Total Productivity Measurement at the Firm Level," *Sloan Management Review* (Spring 1973): 13–29; J. L. Mammone, "Productivity Measurement: A Conceptual Overview," *Management Accounting* (June 1980): 36–42; J. L. Mammone, "A Practical Approach to Productivity Measurement," *Management Accounting* (July 1980): 40–44.

Illustration of Productivity Measurement in a Governmental Unit

Productivity is an important dimension of success in any organization. Service-industry companies, nonprofit firms, and governmental units must be just as aware of productivity issues as manufacturing firms. The following Harvard Business School case illustrates the measurement of productivity in the New York City Sanitation Department.[15]

Productivity Measurement: New York City Sanitation Department

The Bureau of Motor Equipment of the New York City Sanitation Department had about 1,200 employees and an operating budget of about $38 million. It was responsible for maintaining the department's 5,000 vehicles. It operated seventy-five repair garages located throughout the city and one major central repair facility.

According to a report of the New York State Financial Control Board, conditions in the Bureau of Motor Equipment in 1978 were chaotic. Over half the vehicles it was responsible for servicing were out of service on the average day, resulting in huge amounts of overtime pay for the personnel assigned to the remaining vehicles. Ronald Contino was placed in charge of the bureau in late 1978. Within two years, the bureau was supplying 100 percent of the primary vehicles needed every day. Mr. Contino estimated that $16.5 million of costs had been avoided during that period.

Mr. Contino attributed the change to two main factors: (1) a change in labor management relations and (2) the creation of "profit centers" as a substitute for work standards in the central repair facility.

Mr. Contino set up labor/management committees, each consisting of shop supervisors, tradespeople, and a shop steward. Their mandate was to investigate ways to solve problems, to improve the quality of work life, and to increase productivity. A committee was formed in each of the eight principal departments, called shops, in the central repair facility. (This case focuses only on the central repair facility.) The committees met monthly with the manager of the central repair facility.

In 1978 the central repair facility operated under negotiated work standards that covered practically every job, from rebuilding an engine to fixing a generator. Committee members were concerned that if suggestions for improving productivity were made and implemented, management would subsequently adjust the work standards upward.

After a number of discussions, the following plan was adopted: management would no longer be interested in work standards as applied to specific jobs and individuals; individual records of time spent on jobs would no longer be required. Instead, management would be interested only in whether the shop as a whole was producing at an acceptable level. The "value" of output would be measured by what it

---

15. Copyright © 1983 by the President and Fellows of Harvard College. This case was prepared by Robert N. Anthony as the basis for class discussion rather than to illustrate either effective or ineffective handling of an administrative situation. Reprinted by permission of the Harvard Business School.

would cost to purchase the same items or services from outside vendors, and the total value of output for a period would be compared with the total cost of operating the shop.

The output values were determined by checking outside price lists or by obtaining price quotes for specific jobs. If the electric shop repaired an alternator, for example, the shop would receive a credit equal to what it would cost to buy a rebuilt alternator from a private supplier. The costs included labor costs (salary, fringe benefits, sick pay, vacations, and jury duty), material costs, depreciation of machinery, and other overhead costs. The difference between output values and cost was called "profit" and the eight shops were therefore called profit centers.

According to Mr. Contino, the "profit center" work measurement system had a significant impact on production:

> This system provides a mechanism which measures productivity without threatening the individual worker . . . and labor has responded enthusiastically to this concept. . . . In addition, employees in individual shops can now see how well they are doing compared to the private sector (each shop has a large chart in a visible location) and a degree of competitiveness has developed, further spurring their desire to increase efficiency. The combination of the "profit motive" and the elimination of threats has worked like magic.

As evidence of progress, Mr. Contino referred to the table in Exhibit 25-2. He also had data showing that productivity and profits had improved with the passage of time.

As shown in Exhibit 25-2, all profit centers except the motor room reported a profit in 1981. The situation in the motor room illustrated the difficulty of measuring output. Initially, the shop's credit for rebuilt engines was the same as the cost to buy new motors because reliable data on the price of rebuilt motors was not available.

EXHIBIT 25-2

New York Department of Sanitation Profit Center Status

Profit Center	Number of Weeks in Operation since Inception	Annualized, in $000s			Productivity Factor
		Input	Output	Profit	
Transmission	37	$ 350	$ 716	$ 366	2.05
Unit repair	40	1,280	2,146	866	1.68
Upholstery	35	126	183	57	1.45
Radiator	36	263	438	175	1.67
Machine	23	643	1,562	919	2.43
Passenger cars	30	494	534	40	1.08
Electric	37	603	717	114	1.19
Motor room	43	1,272	822	(451)	.65
Total		$5,031	$7,117	$2,086	1.41

The first reports showed that productivity was less than 1.0, meaning that the city could have purchased new engines for less than it spent rebuilding engines. As a result of decisions made by the shop's labor/management committee, the motor room subsequently doubled its productivity and appeared to be producing at a substantial "profit." However, once a database of the outside price of rebuilt engines had been developed, all the shop's past reports were converted to the rebuilt values, the reports then showed that the shop was operating at a "loss." This led the labor/management committee to take further steps to increase productivity, including the discontinuation of unprofitable products and the transfer of personnel from support functions to line functions. By March 1982 the motor room's productivity factor hit 1.19.

The relatively low productivity in the passenger car shop had a different cause. The problem was that shop employees were required to list the actual time it took to do each job on a "job sheet," and they feared that if they consistently beat readily available industrywide standards, sooner or later management would either require more work from individuals or would track each individual's daily performance. Thus, they tended to omit certain jobs done from their daily work sheet.

After the low productivity became apparent, meetings between the labor/management committee and the entire shop's work force were held, and it was agreed that it would no longer be necessary for employees to list the actual time it took to do a job. The February 1982 report for the shop showed the results: productivity moved from 1.05 to 1.30.

Mr. Contino summarized his impressions of the results of the program as follows:

> I have found that the process of getting labor involved in the running of an operation is not only exciting and rewarding, but also extremely worthwhile in terms of improving productivity and service quality. BME's experience belies the common notions that the government worker cannot be productive or that the output of a government operation cannot be measured. There is no simple formula for succeeding in the change from a traditional approach to the labor/management approach, and there should be no doubt that management's commitment to the process is a critical factor. But given the effort and the true desire to see it succeed, it does work. The simple proof is what has been achieved by BME in operating in this fashion.

Limitation of Summary Productivity Measures

Summary productivity measures aim at providing insights as to the magnitude of the outputs resulting from a given amount of inputs. Although summary measures of productivity are widely used and can provide some information on productivity performance, such measures are flawed in two ways. First, the use of dollar measures introduces valuation problems that obscure measures of changes in productivity. Second, both the dollar measures and the physical measures of productivity are too highly aggregated over heterogeneous outputs and inputs to be meaningful. There is a tendency to view a ratio of total outputs to total inputs as a measure of productive efficiency. However, such an interpretation is problematic, as the following excerpt from a *Management Accounting* article by B. Gold explains.

It is inherently impossible to measure the physical "efficiency" of manufacturing processes, or of most economic activities, for the concept is based on a false analogy. To measure changes in the physical efficiency of a process requires comparing a combined physical measure of all relevant outputs in terms which reflect the primary purposes of the undertaking. Thus, one can calculate an engine's physical efficiency in respect to energy conversion by comparing the energy content of its fuel consumption with the energy equivalent of the useful power delivered by it. But it is not possible to measure the physical "efficiency" of the engine as a whole, nor of the process of producing it. Such determinations are prevented by the absence of any important physical common denominators for combining the input contributions of many kinds of labor, materials, facilities and equipment, and a wide array of technical and managerial activities. Nor are there important physical common denominators for combining the wide range of quality characteristics and service characteristics which differentiate the many available types of engines from one another.

Lacking an economically significant concept of "physical efficiency," managerial efforts to improve operation must be refocused on appraising the effects of changes in various input-output relationships on specified performance objectives subject to management control. Thus, management needs a productivity analysis framework.[16]

A Multidimensional View of Productivity Analysis

Multidimensional productivity analysis measures the effect on productivity of several factors of production using several measures of production. Productivity is a multidimensional concept. Production technologies are complex processes involving many critical facets. It is important to realize that the overall productivity of such a complex system is the result of performance in many important subareas. In order for management to gain insight into the inner workings of the production technology — to see what is going wrong, what is going right, and where the opportunities for improvement are — it is necessary to have multiple physical productivity measures, each concentrating on a critical aspect of the business. Moreover, the identification of these critical dimensions will vary widely across organizations. We would not expect the same issues to be crucial at Texas Instruments, American Airlines, and New York State Electric and Gas Corporation.

Among the critical dimensions that should be regularly monitored in manufacturing firms are the percentage of defective units produced, inventory levels, machine time and labor time per unit produced, physical amounts of various capital resources required per unit produced (such as factory floor space per unit), energy consumption per unit, and a host of other factors.

In some cases, a particular aspect of the production technology may be so critical that it justifies implementation of an elaborate accounting system designed specifically for that purpose. An example is provided by the energy accounting system developed by Dow Chemical USA, which is described in the following excerpt from a *Management Accounting* article.

16. B. Gold, "Practical Productivity Analysis for Management Accountants," *Management Accounting* (May 1980): 32.

Energy Accounting at Dow Chemical USA

The chemical industry, an enormous consumer of energy, has been reporting on energy conservation through the Chemical Manufacturers Assn. (CMA) to the Department of Energy (DOE) since 1975. Indeed, the energy conservation data reported by the chemical and allied products industry comprises more than 90% of the energy for fuel and process use reported to the DOE.

As one of the largest chemical companies and, therefore, user of energy, Dow Chemical USA decided an energy conservation program was in its best interest. . . .

In order to produce energy savings, Dow had to first come up with some way of measuring the amount of energy used in production. It developed an "Energy Accounting System," which was unique in the industry at the time. Today it is considered one of the most comprehensive energy use monitoring systems in existence.

Basic to its conservation program is the principle that every plant and any new capital project operate at maximum energy efficiency. In order to gauge this efficiency at its U.S. location, Dow management developed an energy accounting and reporting system.

It is designed to determine how much energy was consumed during production. Every month, Dow's headquarters in Midland, Mich., receives reports via computer from its seven major divisions which in turn obtain this information from 115 manufacturing plants. This division summary of data or the monthly Btu report measures the production output in Btus.

Each division also calculates the energy value of its input in Btus. This information is reported on the Division Energy Input Report. The calculation includes the Btu value of raw material purchased and transferred and the fuels and power consumed in production. Dow is then able to determine how much energy it has consumed in Btus. Data is compiled from the Division Energy Input Report for reporting to the CMA which ultimately reports the statistics for the entire industry to the Department of Energy.

The energy reporting structure for Dow Chemical USA features monthly comparisons for goal and base year, to the preceding year, to standards, and to other locations. Achievement highlights are also noted. At the division level, individual plants are compared to goals and standards and comparisons are made to other divisions. External reporting is to the federal, state, and local governments, the Department of Energy, and the Chemical Manufacturers Assn. The system not only provides for an analysis of results, but it also encourages the reporting of opportunities for improvement.[17]

17. M. Gartenberg, "How Dow Accounts for Its Energy Use," *Management Accounting* (March 1980): 10, 11.

Managers should beware of simplistic, unidimensional productivity measures. They are too highly aggregated to provide much insight into where the opportunities for improvement lie. By regularly reporting multiple physical measures relating to key aspects of the production technology, managerial accountants can provide the most useful information for management decisions.[18]

Summary

The costs of defective production can be significant, and many firms have installed quality-costing systems to monitor and accumulate the costs of achieving or maintaining quality. Quality costs can be categorized as prevention costs, appraisal costs, internal failure costs, and external failure costs. The first two categories of cost result from a potential lack of conformance quality. The latter two cost categories result from an existing lack of conformance quality.

Productivity measurements attempt to relate production outputs to inputs. Aggregate measures focus on the ratio of total output to total input and are usually computed in dollar terms. Component measures examine the relationship of output to one or more inputs. Component measures are computed in both dollar and physical terms. Such highly simplified and aggregate measures of productivity are of limited usefulness. A more informative approach is to view productivity analysis in terms of multiple, physical measures that focus on the critical aspects of the production technology.

Key Terms to Review

aggregate productivity, p. 870
appraisal costs, p. 865
component productivity, p. 870
external failure costs, p. 865
internal failure costs, p. 865
multidimensional productivity analysis, p. 874

prevention costs, p. 865
productivity, p. 870
quality-costing system, p. 864
quality of conformance, p. 865
quality of design, p. 865
summary productivity measures, p. 873

18. Banker, Datar, and Kaplan have proposed a productivity-measurement system that extends an approach developed by the American Productivity Center. This system relies on aggregations and across-period comparisons of standard cost variances. While such comparisons of standard cost variances across time are useful, this approach is still limited by the valuation problems that dollar measures entail. See R. Banker, S. Datar, and R. Kaplan, "Productivity Measurement and Management Accounting," Working paper, Carnegie-Mellon University and Harvard University, 1987; see also American Productivity Center, *Total Performance Measurement* (Houston: American Productivity Center, 1981).

Review Problem

PRODUCTIVITY

Some of the most important statistics in evaluating the economic affairs of a country are the measures of productivity and the changes in productivity through time.

How would you measure productivity and the changes in a country's productivity for a period of time? What measurement problems do you anticipate?

Solution to Review Problem

a. The measure of productivity is the dollar measure of production divided by the dollar measure of input. The change in productivity is the change in the above measure.

b. Output (we accept dollar measures of completed sales); input (the measure of the capital use is complex; many transactions are not reported).

Suggested Readings

American Productivity Center. *Total Performance Measurement.* Houston: American Productivity Center, 1981.

Banker, R., S. Datar, and R. Kaplan. "Productivity Measurement and Management Accounting." Working paper, Carnegie-Mellon University and Harvard University, 1987.

Buehler, V., and Y. K. Shetty. *Productivity Improvement: Case Studies of Proven Practice.* New York: AMACOM, 1981.

Clark, J. "Costing for Quality at Celanese." *Management Accounting* (March 1985): 42–46.

Eilon, S., B. Gold, and J. Soesan. *Applied Productivity Analysis for Industry.* New York: Permagon Press, 1976.

Gold, B. *Productivity, Technology and Capital: Economic Analysis, Management Strategies, and Government Policies.* Lexington, Mass.: Lexington Books, 1979.

Hayes, R. "Why Japanese Factories Work." *Harvard Business Review* (July-August 1981): 57–66.

Kaplan, R. "Measuring Manufacturing Performance: A New Challenge for Managerial Accounting Research." *Accounting Review* (October 1983): 686–705.

Kendrick, J., and D. Creamer. *Measuring Company Productivity: Handbook with Case Studies,* rev. ed. New York: Conference Board, 1965.

Kraft, K. "Measuring Productivity Efficiency." *Management Accounting* (June 1983): 40–43.

Mammone, J. L. "Productivity Measurement: A Conceptual Overview." *Management Accounting* (June 1980): 36–42.

Morse, W. "Measuring Quality Cost." *Cost and Management* (July–August 1983): 16–20.

Murrin, T. "Rejecting the Traditional Ways of Doing Business." Chicago: American Production and Inventory Control Society, October 1982.

Poe, G., and L. Mechem. "How Total Factor Productivity Works." *Management Accounting* (June 1983): 44–46.

Reich, R. "The Next American Frontier." *Atlantic Monthly* (March 1983): 43–58 and (April 1983): 97–108.

Richardson, P., and J. Gordon. "Measuring Total Manufacturing Performance." *Sloan Management Review* (Winter 1980): 47–58.

Roth, H. P., and W. J. Morse. "Let's Help Measure and Report Quality Costs." *Management Accounting* (August 1983): 50–53.

Smith, L. "Using Labor Information to Measure Productivity." *Management Accounting* (June 1983): 47–49.

Tyson, T. N. "Quality and Profitability: Have Controllers Made the Connection?" *Management Accounting* (November 1987): 38–42.

Review Questions

25-1 What is the purpose of a quality-costing system?

25-2 Define *quality of conformance.*

25-3 What is meant by *quality of design?*

25-4 List four types of costs associated with quality of conformance.

25-5 Define and give an example of *prevention costs.*

25-6 Define and give an example of *appraisal costs.*

25-7 Define and give an example of *internal failure costs.*

25-8 Define and give an example of *external failure costs.*

25-9 Give two reasons why product quality has received increasing attention in recent years.

25-10 Define the term *aggregate productivity.*

25-11 What is meant by the term *component productivity?*

25-12 Discuss two general limitations of summary productivity measures.

25-13 What is meant by *multidimensional productivity analysis?*

Exercises

25-14 Preparation of a Quality-Cost Report   Integrated Systems Company, a small computer software firm, experienced the following costs during November:

Training of quality-control personnel	$1,000
Tests of software products	800
Costs of rework on faulty computer diskettes	1,200
Costs of unsalvageable defective products	600
Replacements of in-warranty products	250
Inspection of materials	900

Prepare a quality-cost report for the month of November.

25-15 Aggregate Productivity Measurement in Agriculture   Suwannee Beef Company raises beef cattle for the meat-packing industry. During March, sales of animals brought in $180,000 of revenue. Costs included animal feed and other materials costing $29,000, direct labor costs of $41,000, and overhead costs of $40,000. Calculate the company's aggregate productivity for March using dollar measures.

25-16 Multidimensional Productivity Measurement   Referring to Exercise 25-15, suggest some physical measures that the Suwannee Beef Company might use in a multidimensional approach to productivity measurement.

25-17 Component Productivity Measurement   Daytona Surf Boards, Inc. manufactures surf boards. During May 20,000 boards were produced using 10,000 direct labor hours, 20,000 machine hours, and 200,000 pounds of direct material in a factory with 8,000 square feet. Using physical units calculate three component productivity measures for the month of May.

Problems

25-18 Productivity Accounting   Productivity, defined as output divided by input, has been the center of attention recently because of the general below-average performance of U.S. industries. Productivity improvement is vital for industry and for increasing the standard of living for the consumer. Additionally, improved productivity is necessary if companies wish to remain competitive and improve their profitability.

Productivity is often directly associated with profitability because both are measures of performance. In addition, improved productivity is assumed to result in improved profits. Although there are many similarities, distinct differences do exist. Profits represent the significant financial measure in a business enterprise, whereas productivity measures represent a significant physical measure.

Because productivity influences the accounting performance measures, and because productivity measures represent one type of performance measure, the management accountant should participate in the development and implementation of productivity measures.

Many companies have already developed measures of productivity. For example, one manufacturing firm employs this rather simplistic measure:

$$\frac{\text{Total revenue}}{\text{Total labor costs}}$$

A company in a regulated industry developed the following productivity evaluation from its work measurement system:

$$\frac{\text{Total applicable standard hours}}{\text{Total actual reported hours}}$$

where total applicable standard hours equals job activity times standard hours allowed per activity.

An equipment manufacturer uses the following productivity measure with values expressed in terms of a base year:

$$\frac{\text{Sales billed}}{\text{Direct costs incurred to produce and sell product or service}}$$

Each of these three measures is an attempt to evaluate the effect of various input factors on physical output.

REQUIRED:

a. Comment on the validity of this statement: "Productivity is just another ratio and, when considered by itself, suffers from the same shortcomings as any other ratio analysis."

b. What criteria should the management accountant consider in the initial implementation of a productivity measurement and analysis program?

c. Discuss the attributes and deficiencies of any two of the three productivity measures presented in the problem. *(CMA adapted)*

25-19 Costs of Maintaining Product Quality; Variances Maidwell Company manufactures washers and dryers on a single assembly line in its main factory. The market has deteriorated over the last five years, and competition has made cost control very important. Management has been concerned about the materials cost of both washers and dryers. There have been no model changes in the past two years, and economic conditions have allowed the company to negotiate price reductions in many key parts.

Maidwell uses a standard cost system in accounting for materials. Purchases are charged to inventory at a standard price with purchase discounts considered an administrative cost reduction. Production is charged at the standard price of the materials used. Thus, the price variance is isolated at time of purchase as the difference between gross contract price and standard price multiplied by the quantity purchased. When a substitute part is used in production rather than the regular part, a price variance equal to the difference in the standard prices of the materials is recognized at the time of substitution in the production process. The quantity variance is the actual quantity used compared to the standard quantity allowed with the difference multiplied by the standard price.

The materials variances for several of the parts Maidwell uses are unfavorable. Part 4121 is one item that has an unfavorable variance. Maidwell knows that some of these parts will be defective and fail. The failure is discovered during production. The normal defective rate is 5 percent of normal input. The original contract price of this part was $.285 per unit; thus, Maidwell set the standard unit price at $.285. The unit contract purchase price of part 4121 was increased $.04 to $.325 from the original $.285 due to a parts specification change. Maidwell chose not to change the standard but instead to treat the increase in price as a price variance. In addition, the contract terms were changed from n/30 to 4/10, n/30 as a consequence of negotiations resulting from changes in the economy.

Data regarding the usage of part 4121 during December is as follows.

Purchases of part 4121	150,000 units
Unit price paid for purchases of part 4121	$.325
Requisitions of part 4121 from stores for use in products	134,000 units
Substitution of part 5125 for part 4121 to use obsolete stock (standard unit price of part 5125 is $.35)	24,000 units
Units of part 4121 and its substitute (part 5125) identified as being defective	9,665 units
Standard allowed usage (including normal defective units) of part 4121 and its substitute based on output for the month	153,300 units

Maidwell's material variances related to part 4121 for December were reported as follows:

Price variance	$7,560.00 U
Quantity variance	1,339.50 U
Total material variances for part 4121	$8,899.50 U

Bob Speck, the purchasing director, claims the unfavorable price variance is misleading. Speck says that his department has worked hard to obtain price concessions and purchase discounts from suppliers. In addition, Speck has indicated that engineering changes have been made in several parts increasing their price even though the part identification has not changed. These price increases are not his department's responsibility. Speck declares that price variances simply no longer measure the purchasing department's performance.

Jim Buddle, the manufacturing manager, thinks that responsibility for the quantity variance should be shared. Buddle states that manufacturing cannot control quality arising from less expensive parts, substitutions of material to use up otherwise obsolete stock, or engineering changes that increased the quantity of materials used.

The accounting manager, Mike Kohl, has suggested that the computation of variances be changed to identify variations from standard with the causes and functional areas responsible for the variances. The following system of materials variances and the method of computation for each was recommended by Kohl.

Variance	Method of Calculation
Economics variance	Quantity purchased times the changes made after setting standards that were the result of negotiations based on changes in the general economy
Engineering change variance	Quantity purchased times change in price due to part specifications changes
Purchase price variance	Quantity purchased times change in contract price due to changes other than parts specifications or the general economy
Substitutions variance	Quantity substituted times the difference in standard price between parts substituted
Excess usage variance	Standard price times the difference between the standard quantity allowed for production minus actual parts used (reduced for abnormal scrap)
Abnormal failure rate variance	Abnormal scrap times standard price

REQUIRED:

a. Discuss the appropriateness of Maidwell Company's current method of variance analysis for materials and indicate whether the claims of Bob Speck and Jim Buddle are valid.

b. Compute the materials variances for part 4121 for December using the system recommended by Mike Kohl.

c. Indicate who would be responsible for each of the variances in Mike Kohl's system of variance analysis for materials. *(CMA adapted)*

25-20 Product Quality and Productivity in a Public Utility; Performance Evaluation and Review System   Harold Small joined Morton Electric Company eight months ago as vice president of personnel administration. Morton Electric Company is a small regional public utility serving 50,000 customers in three communities and the surrounding rural area. Electricity is generated at a central plant, but each community has a substation and its own work crew. The total labor force at the central plant and three substations, exclusive of administrative and clerical personnel, numbers 180 people.

Small designed and introduced a Performance Evaluation and Review System (PERS) shortly after joining Morton. This system is based on a similar system he developed and administered in his prior position with a small company. He thought the system worked well there and could be easily adapted for use at Morton.

The purpose of PERS, as conceived by Small, is to provide a positive feedback system for evaluating employees that is uniform for each class of employees. Thus, the system indicates to employees how they perform on the job and helps them correct any shortcomings. The plant supervisors and field supervisors are responsible for administering the system for the plant workers and the substation crew workers, respectively. The general supervisors are responsible for the plant/field supervisors. Employees get personal PERS reports monthly informing them of their current status, and there is a review and evaluation every six months.

PERS is based on a point system in an attempt to make it uniform for all workers. There are eight categories for evaluation with a maximum number of points for each category and a total of 100 points for the system. The eight categories for the plant and crew workers and the maximum number of points in each category are as follows.

Categories	Points
1. *Quality of work:* Points are deducted if the job must be redone within 48 hours of completion.	15
2. *Productivity:* Points are deducted if the work was not completed within the time specified for the type of job.	15
3. *Safety on the job:* Points are deducted if the employee does not use safe work habits on the job to protect himself and others.	15
4. *Neatness of work area or repair truck:* Points are deducted if the work area or truck is not clean and neat.	15
5. *Cooperation with fellow workers:* Points are deducted if an employee does not work well with others.	10
6. *Courtesy on the job and with the public:* Points are deducted if an employee is rude and unpleasant when there is contact with the public.	10
7. *Appearance:* Points are deducted if an employee does not wear standard work clothing or if the clothing is sloppy and dirty at the beginning of each day.	10
8. *Tardiness/excess absenteeism:* Points are deducted if an employee arrives late or is absent for causes other than illness or death in the immediate family.	10
Total points	100

The list of categories used to evaluate the plant/field supervisors is slightly different.

Each employee begins the year with 100 points. If an infraction in any of the categories is observed, one to five penalty points can be assessed for each infraction. Notification is given to the employee indicating the infraction and the points to be deducted. A worker who is assessed twenty-five points in any one month or loses all the points in any category in one month is subject to immediate review. Likewise, anytime an employee drops below forty points, a review is scheduled. The general supervisor meets with the individual employee and the employee's plant/field supervisor at this review.

If an employee has no infractions during the month, up to twelve points can be restored to the employee's point total — two points each for categories 1 through 4 and one point each for categories 5 through 8. However, at no time can a worker have more than the maximum allowed in each category or more than 100 points in total.

When Small first introduced PERS to the general supervisors, they were not sure they liked the system. Small told them how well it had worked where he had used it before. Small's enthusiasm for the system convinced the general supervisors that the system had merit.

There were a few isolated problems with the system in the first two months. However, Ray Meyer, a crew worker, is very unhappy with the new system, as evidenced by his conversation with Dan Jenkins, a fellow crew worker.

Meyer: Look at this notice of infraction. I've lost twenty-two points. I can't believe it.

Jenkins: How did your supervisor get you for that many points in such a short period?

Meyer: Remember that bad storm we had two weeks ago? He disagreed with me on the work at Elm and Wabash. It was dangerous, and I probably did fly off the handle. It was late at night after I had been working fifteen hours straight. Look what he got me for: five points for lack of cooperation, five points for a dirty uniform, five points for a messy truck including lunch bags and coffee cups in the cab, four points for slow work, and three points for being ten minutes late the next morning. Can you image that? Being docked for ten minutes when I worked a double shift the day before? I didn't get home until 1:00 A.M. I even cleaned the truck up after he left that night — on my own time, no less!

Jenkins: At least you won't get reviewed.

Meyer: Sure, but I bet he planned it to come out less than twenty-five points.

Jenkins: Boy, we worked ourselves to a frazzle that night and the next two days. You know Mike's supervisor? Well, he recommended that his guys get positive points added back to the PERS reports over and above the normal monthly allowances.

REQUIRED:

   a. Without regard to Ray Meyer's recent experience with the system, evaluate the Performance Evaluation and Review System (PERS) in terms of its

   (1) Design for a performance review and evaluation system.

   (2) Value as a motivational device.

   b. What problems might occur in the administration of the Performance Evaluation and Review System, and how might these administrative problems affect employee motivation? Explain your answer. *(CMA adapted)*

26

Behavioral and Economic Implications of Budgeting and Responsibility Accounting

After studying this chapter, you should be able to:

1 List and discuss some behavioral effects of budgets.

2 Discuss the potential implications of standard tightness and budget difficulty.

3 Define and discuss the merits of differential budget standards.

4 Explain the expectancy theory of motivation and its implications for budgeting and responsibility accounting.

5 Define *participatory budgeting* and discuss some of its behavioral implications.

6 List some of the factors that determine the effectiveness of participatory budgeting.

7 Explain a contingency view of managerial accounting.

8 Discuss the design of responsibility accounting systems in hierarchical versus matrix organizations.

*T*he motivational aspects of human activity have a potentially profound impact on the activity of the accountant. Although the importance of interpersonal relationships and individual behavior is not a new area of study, the results have recently begun to affect managerial accounting theory and practice.

Importance of Behavioral Issues

Costs are controlled by people. The **behavioral issues** of cost accounting are those issues that consider how people are likely to act. The traditional approach to cost control compares actual results with budgeted amounts that represent goals for management. Standards and the analysis of variances are used to increase the ability of management to exercise control over performance. The development of cost centers and the decentralization of decision making are, in large part, responses to the need for subunits within a firm that control specific resources and therefore can be evaluated in light of how they use those resources. Central to these developments is the assumption that the more sophisticated the system, the greater the likelihood of success in controlling costs and improving performance. Indeed, there is perhaps a tendency for many firms to expect desirable results merely from the use of the techniques alone.

In recent years, there has developed an increased recognition of the importance of organizational issues and the human-resource assets of the firm. If management uses only conventional measures of revenues, expenses, profits, cost variances, and output, it is possible that short-run economic gains may be achieved at the expense of long-run goals. Failure to consider the impact of control techniques on the individuals responsible for the activity of the firm may adversely affect employee morale, loyalty, trust, and motivation.

Present methods of evaluation often fail to consider how people are motivated. Cost control and other reports measuring performance are often used primarily for punitive purposes (correcting unsatisfactory performance). Several authors have found that there is a strong asymmetrical (different rewards for good and bad performance) reward system connected with performance reports. The fact that the budget is exceeded is just as important as by how much it is exceeded. Equally important, reports may be required and investigations conducted when there are unfavorable variances; these investigations are frequently followed by reprimands and recommendations for corrective action, while favorable reports do not elicit an offsetting favorable response. Control systems may lead to reports of losses, but they usually fail to show the opportunity costs of ventures forgone. The result is conservative behavior on the part of managers, often substantially more conservative than top management desires. These comments suggest that the design of control techniques should include the motivational aspects of human activity as a paramount consideration.

Since many managers will have goals that differ substantially from the goals of the organization, and since these goals will be multidimensional, it is imperative that means be found to obtain goal congruence (all parties are working toward the same goal). Companies must find ways by which a diverse set of individuals with a diverse set of goals can be motivated to seek the goals of the organization.

Behavioral Effects of Budgets

A budget implicitly includes a set of specific goals. A budget is a source of pressure that can, if it becomes too great, create mistrust and hostility and may eventually lead to declining performance. Research suggests that there is a great deal of distrust of the entire budgetary process at the supervisory level.[1] There are several reasons for this distrust by supervisors. These reasons are based on common beliefs that

- Budgets tend to oversimplify the real situation and fail to allow for variations in external factors;

- Budgets do not adequately reflect qualitative variables, such as preparing people for the next higher position;

- Budgets simply confirm what the supervisor already knows or, alternatively, distort the true situation;

- Budgets are too often used to manipulate the supervisor, and therefore the indicated performance measures are suspect;

- Budget reports emphasize results, not reasons;

- Budgets interfere with the supervisor's style of leadership and are thus unwelcome.

Budgets may also produce unwanted side effects. One of these is the formation of small informal groups to combat pressure and reduce tension. Such informal groups usually have their own goals, and they may conflict with those of the organization.

A second undesirable side effect is the overemphasis on departmental performance as compared with firm performance. Important interdepartmental dependencies and economies may be ignored or overlooked in a quest for optimization of the reported performance.

A third effect is the perhaps undue publicity given to individual performance and particularly to "failure." The extensive exposure given to performance reports across

1. C. Argyris, *The Impact of Budgets on People* (New York: Controllership Foundation, 1952). The study is old, but there is no more recent evidence that would cause its conclusions to be suspect.

departments for comparative purposes may increase friction among supervisors as well as between supervisors and the accounting staff.

A fourth and particularly noxious consequence of the budget and performance-evaluation process can be a stifling of initiative. Individuals are often discouraged from trying something new when established ways have a large chance of success and new methods portend a greater degree of uncertainty. Churchill, Cooper, and Sainsbury found that workers who were audited conformed more closely to company policy than those who were not. Furthermore, they did so even when there were more efficient alternatives available.[2]

The problems associated with the budgeting process do not mean that the process should be scrapped but rather that careful consideration is required if it is to have the desired effects. Ideally, the budget provides a plan for achieving a goal or goals that have been accepted by the participants. If the budgeted amounts are reasonable, the projected achievement levels may then become the aspiration levels of the supervisors who must also obtain acceptance of the budget by members of their departments. The manager, according to the aspiration literature, will extend a disproportionate amount of energy to achieve an aspiration level.[3] It seems useful then to investigate various proposals for securing conformance between aspiration levels and firm goals as expressed in budgets.

One of the early empirical studies dealing with the interactions of budgets, aspiration levels, and performance in an accounting context was conducted by Stedry.[4] His pioneer study highlighted the importance of the acceptance of the goals or standards and the relationship between the level of difficulty implied by the standards and the resulting performance. Stedry used several groups of people in controlled experimental situations. Some of these groups were given budgets and some were not. Among the groups given budgets, some were asked to set their own goals prior to receiving the budgets and some were given the budget first. Finally, budget levels were varied; high, medium, and low budgets were used.

The groups that were told a goal existed but were never told its amount performed better than those who were told their budgeted amounts initially. Of those told their budgets first, those groups with attainable (medium at best) goals performed better than those given high (difficult-to-attain) goals.

The level of the budget also had an impact on aspiration levels. Groups given budgets with goals less than their aspiration level tended to lower their aspiration level. The report on actual performance also influenced the aspiration level, the aspiration level tending toward the actual level.

Stedry concluded that budgets should be developed with conscious consideration of the motivational effects. By properly adjusting the budget given to an individ-

2. N. C. Churchill, W. E. Cooper, and T. Sainsbury, "Laboratory and Field Studies of the Behavioral Effects of Audits," in C. P. Bonini, R. K. Jaedicke, and H. Wagner, eds., *Management Controls* (New York: McGraw-Hill, 1964).

3. See S. W. Becker and D. Green, "Budgeting and Employee Behavior," *Journal of Business* (October 1962): 392–402.

4. A. C. Stedry, *Budget Control and Cost Behavior* (Englewood Cliffs, N.J.: Prentice-Hall, 1960).

ual in light of past performance, the individual could be motivated toward better performance. Stedry recognized that it would be necessary for a manager to achieve the aspiration level part of the time.

Although perhaps intuitively appealing, the use of individual budgets to motivate individual managers suffers from several limitations. In the first place, this approach would require a dual record system. Records must be kept of actual performance and expected performance for evaluation and decision making. Simultaneously, a separate set of records must be kept in order to provide the manager with budget levels and performance records that would achieve the desired motivational results.

Not only is this dual reporting system an additional cost, but it could lead to undesirable results in terms of trust, morale, and performance if it became general knowledge.[5] A problem would develop if two individuals with similar tasks under similar conditions discover that they are being measured against different standards. Hence, one could accept the basic hypothesis advanced by Stedry and even admire a motivational system such as he proposes, yet find the problems of implementation insurmountable.

Motivation

Motivation is the means by which people are encouraged to achieve a specific desired result. An organization's goals cannot be achieved unless employees are motivated. Contrary to the assumptions implicit in much cost accounting literature, superiors are seldom in positions of absolute authority and hence are not able to achieve their ends by decree. The consent and cooperation of those in subordinate positions must be attained. Also, it must be recognized that information is not always perfect. For example, a subordinate may have reason to withhold or alter the data transmitted. Moreover, it is unrealistic to assume that even correct information is always accurately processed.

Perhaps the most questionable assumption of traditional control theory is the assumed indifference of the subordinate to the task and to the goals of the organization. The attitude of the subordinate is assumed to be basically negative. The traditional response to this assumption has been that financial rewards combined with an authoritative control system are required. Yet factors such as pride in a job well done and job content can also play an important role in achieving goal congruence.

Researchers in psychology have developed several theories of motivation. Among these are the following: Maslow (hierarchy-of-needs-based theory of motivation), Cyert and March (goals achieved through subordinate efforts), McGregor (Theory X, Theory Y), Herzberg (job content is distinct from its context), Skinner (positive

---

5. Another cost would involve hiring trained psychologists to establish workable means of measuring accurately each employee's aspiration level, assuming that it could be done at all.

reinforcement), and Vroom (expectancy theory).[6] None of the theories advanced by these writers has achieved universal acceptance, yet all have contributed to a better understanding of the motivational process.

Expectancy Theory and the Motivational Impact of Budgets

Several accounting researchers have used the expectancy theory of motivation to investigate the behavioral implications of budgets.

Expectancy Model of Motivation   Under the **expectancy model of motivation,** people are assumed to select actions on the basis of (1) the expectation that the action will result in specific outcomes and (2) the valences (or personal satisfaction) derived from the outcomes.[7] The expectancy model can be expressed mathematically.[8]

According to the expectancy theory, an individual decides how much effort to put forth toward achieving a work goal by estimating the expectancy of accomplishing that goal given his effort. The individual also estimates the expectancy that achievement of the work goal will result in his attainment of various extrinsic rewards, such as recognition, promotion, and pay raises. The individual places values (valences) on the successful performance of the task, the effort required to achieve the task, and the outcomes or extrinsic rewards that are obtained if the work goal is achieved.

A superior can influence the variables in the worker's expectancy framework by (1) determining the extrinsic rewards, (2) altering the individual's expectancy that work-goal accomplishment leads to those rewards, (3) altering the worker's expectancy that effort will result in accomplishment of the task, (4) altering the worker's

---

6. For the references to these works, the reader is referred to the suggested readings at the end of this chapter.

7. Expectancy was originally developed by J. W. Atkinson and V. H. Vroom. See J. W. Atkinson, "Toward Experimental Analysis of Human Motivation in Terms of Motives, Expectations and Incentives," in *Motives in Fantasy, Action and Society,* edited by J. W. Atkinson (New York: Van Nostrand, 1958); V. H. Vroom, *Work and Motivation* (New York: Wiley, 1964). Expectancy theory can be conceived as a special case of expected utility theory. For the relationship between expectancy theory and expected utility theory, see G. Feltham, "Expectancy Theory: A Decision Theory and Economics of Incentives Perspective," unpublished, University of British Columbia, 1978. Applications of expectancy theory to accounting issues have been made by: J. Ronen and L. Livingstone, "An Expectancy Theory Approach to the Motivational Impact of Budgets," *Accounting Review* (October 1975): 671–85; K. Ferris, "A Test of the Expectancy Theory of Motivation in an Accounting Environment," *Accounting Review* (July 1977): 605–15; H. Rockness, "Expectancy Theory in a Budgetary Setting: An Experimental Examination," *Accounting Review* (October 1977): 893–903; and P. Brownell and M. McInnes, "Budgetary Participation, Motivation, and Managerial Performance," *Accounting Review* (October 1986): 587–600.

8. A formulation of the expectancy model is originally due to R. J. House, "A Path-Goal Theory of Leader Effectiveness," *Administrative Science Quarterly* (September 1971): 321–38. This version of the model was used by J. Ronen and L. Livingstone, "An Expectancy Theory Approach to the Motivational Impact of Budgets," *Accounting Review* (October 1975): 671–85, on which our discussion is primarily based, and by P. Brownell and M. McInnes, "Budgetary Participation, Motivation, and Managerial Performance," *Accounting Review* (October 1986): 587–600.

intrinsic value of goal accomplishment by striving to cause the worker to internalize the organization's goals, and (5) altering the workers' valence for goal-directed effort (for example, by reducing the organizational barriers that hamper goal achievement).

Expectancy Model and the Budgeting Process Budgets reflect the expectations of management regarding what constitutes the successful performance of a task. Moreover, budgets often help the subordinate in formulating the extrinsic valences associated with successful task accomplishment. The perceived difficulty in meeting a budget affects the subordinate's expectancy that effort put forth toward meeting the budget will be successful in meeting that objective.

Several widely accepted tenets of budgeting and responsibility accounting may be interpreted in light of the expectancy model. First, it is a common view that budgets should generally be set at reasonably attainable levels. Second, participation by subordinates in the budgetary process is generally viewed, at least in some settings, as benefitting goal accomplishment. In terms of the expectancy model, participatory budgeting may cause the subordinate to internalize the organization's goals, thereby increasing the subordinate's personal satisfaction associated with successful performance of the task. Third, management by exception is a managerial technique that is commonly used in conjunction with budgeting and responsibility accounting systems. Under the expectancy-theory view, nonreinforcement by management when budgetary goals are achieved would lead to a lowering of the subordinate's expectancies that budgetary goal achievement will lead to extrinsic rewards. Finally, it is a widely accepted tenet of responsibility accounting that a subordinate's performance should be judged on the basis of factors under the subordinate's control. In terms of the expectancy model, only factors viewed as controllable by the subordinate will be likely to be associated with the expectancy that the subordinate's effort will result in accomplishment of the budgetary goals.

Thus, the expectancy model of motivation is rich enough to incorporate many of the purposes and features of budgeting and responsibility accounting systems.

Motivating Desired Behavior with Responsibility Accounting

A cost accounting system that records costs so that people can be held responsible for their control is called a **responsibility accounting system.** Responsibility accounting systems are often used by organizations to motivate specific behavior patterns desired by management. If inventory levels are out of hand, for example, management can provide an inducement to operating managers to reduce inventory levels by including a carrying cost for inventory in the costs charged to the offending operating units. A manager can be induced to spend time and effort training subordinates for managerial positions by the inclusion of a bonus in the manager's compensation package that is based on the manager's performance in successfully training subordinates for managerial positions. McDonald's Corporation has used such an incentive plan in the past to compensate the managers of its company-owned restaurants.[9] For

9. See W. E. Sasser and S. H. Pettway, "Case of Big Mac's Pay Plans," *Harvard Business Review* (July–August 1974): 30–36, 44–46, 156–58.

another example, consider the following anecdote concerning rush orders. This event occurred in a real manufacturing firm and was originally reported by Raymond Villers.[10]

Solving the Rush-Order Problem with Responsibility Accounting

When the sales manager requested a rush order, the production scheduler typically claimed that to produce the order on a rushed basis would disrupt normal production and cost a significant amount of money. The sales manager usually responded by asking the production scheduler if the scheduler wanted to take responsibility for losing the customer who had requested the rush order. Since the production scheduler did not want to assume that responsibility, he generally gave in and scheduled the order. The result, however, was considerable ill feeling between the sales manager and the production scheduler.

The problem was eventually solved through responsibility accounting by keeping track of the extra costs associated with the rush order and charging them to the sales department, rather than to the production department. The result was a reduction in the number of rush-order requests by the sales manager and a pleasant acceptance by the production scheduler of the rush-order requests that were made.

The responsibility accounting system ensured that the same individual (in this case the sales manager) would consider both the costs and the benefits of accepting a rush order. Previously, the sales manager had focused on the benefits, while the production scheduler was concerned only with the costs.

Participatory Management

According to the theory behind **participatory management,** if employees participate in goal setting, they will accept the established level of accomplishment and the required sacrifice to achieve it.[11] Participation by itself will not necessarily lead to better performance, however. One problem with the participatory technique is that it may be quite difficult to realize in practice. Argyris describes what he calls pseudo-participation on the part of the supervisors.[12] The supervisors must first perceive that their input is desired, and then the supervisors must supply their knowledge and

---

10. R. E. Villers, "Control and Freedom in a Decentralized Company," *Harvard Business Review* (July–August 1954): 826–96.

11. Becker and Green, op. cit., p. 397.

12. Argyris, op. cit.

expertise to the questions at hand. Thus, the supervisors really must become involved, and not just go through the motions.

Consider, for example, the following comment: "We bring them in [supervisors of budget areas], we tell them that we want their frank opinion, but most of them just sit there and nod their heads. We know they're not coming out with exactly how they feel. I guess budgets scare them."[13] Here is a case where the supervisors do not perceive that their opinions are really desired. The result is a failure of the budget and control process before it begins. Knowledge of this attitude should be a signal to the accounting department of a possibly serious breakdown in the trust and respect of the supervisors for the accounting function. If true, it will almost certainly impair the effectiveness of that department.

It is possible that participation in decisions will cause all levels of employees to join together in an effort to reach and attain the organizational goals (which the employees helped set). The spirit of cooperation that is implicit in participatory management is very attractive to a layman compared to a coercive type of managerial environment implicit in the conventional organizational arrangement. Unfortunately, if pushed too far, participatory management can result in too much discussion and delay and not enough action. Too often events do not wait for organizations to explore fully all alternative decisions. If all parties affected by a decision concur with the decision, then that is ideal, but this is likely to be rare. Even if all parties participate in decisions, we are likely to find irreconcilable differences. In fact, participation might accentuate these differences.

Participatory budgeting is widely used in virtually all types of organizations. The following excerpt from a *Management Accounting* article describes its use at University Community Hospital in Tampa, Florida. It is an application of participatory management.

Participative Budgeting at University Community Hospital

The degree of effectiveness of managers and first-line supervisors at our hospital—or any hospital, for that matter—depends upon many personality traits. One of the most important of these traits is the ability to be motivated by being involved. This trait is essential because the degree of decentralization typical in a hospital setting requires individuals to make timely quality decisions within the scope of established general guidelines. Furthermore, the various departments tend to be so diverse and complex that the department director is the "expert" who must relate to the vice president, a "generalist," in developing and executing a plan of operation. Therefore, the hospital setting is ideal for a high degree of participative budgeting given the diverse departments and individuals and groups of differing ranks.

The participative approach to budgeting has proven very successful at University Community Hospital. Our budget projections have proven to be

---

13. Ibid., p. 28.

extremely accurate because of a combination of good forecasting and willingness to cooperate in taking corrective action to overcome adverse variances. In fact, our overall projections have generally been so close to our actual experience that our finance committee of the board has jokingly suggested the budget was prepared after the fact. It would be difficult to envision our budget effort being accomplished in an effective manner without the participative approach.[14]

Determinants of the Effectiveness of Participative Budgeting

Researchers have found that several characteristics of organizations, societies, and personalities affect the degree to which participative budgeting is successful. Brownell[15] surveyed the literature and listed four classes of variables as being instrumental in moderating the effectiveness of participatory budgeting: cultural, organizational, interpersonal, and individual. Exhibit 26-1 summarizes some of Brownell's conclusions.

A recent study by Chendall[16] provided evidence that the effectiveness of participative budgeting is moderated by the mesh in the personality styles of a superior and subordinate. When the superior-subordinate pairing is homogeneous, in the sense that either both are high authoritarian personalities or both are low authoritarian personalities, the subordinate will have a more positive attitude toward the job and the budget. In heterogeneous pairings, the opposite result will be true. Consider, for example, a high authoritarian superior and a low authoritarian subordinate. The superior prefers personal exchanges based on power and authority, is likely to be autocratic, and is not concerned about group approval. The low authoritarian subordinate, who by definition does not share these attitudes about interpersonal relations, is likely to be frustrated in the interpersonal exchanges necessary for a participative budgeting approach.

Methods of Obtaining Goal Congruence

Managers could be evaluated, at least in part, on the basis of the principles and techniques used in decision making rather than on the consequences of the decisions alone. This method emphasizes the reasonableness of the decision, given the information available at the time the decision had to be made.

Quite often a good procedure can lead to a poor result when decisions must be made under uncertainty. Moreover, poor decision making can occasionally work out for the best. The firm that did not construct a plant in downtown San Francisco just prior to the great earthquake because the payback period was seven years rather than

14. M. Feldbush, "Participative Budgeting in a Hospital Setting," *Management Accounting* (September 1981): 43–46.

15. P. Brownell, "Participation in the Budgeting Process: When It Works and When It Doesn't," *Journal of Accounting Literature* (Spring 1982): 124–53.

16. R. Chenhall, "Authoritarianism and Participative Budgeting: A Dyadic Analysis," *Accounting Review* (April 1986): 263–72.

EXHIBIT 26-1

Variables Moderating Effectiveness of Participatory Management and Budgeting

Variables Moderating the Effectiveness of Participatory Budgeting	Result
Cultural:	
Nationality	Participation is viewed more as a norm in some cultures (such as in Norway) than in others.
Legislative	Participation is mandated in some European countries.
Organizational:	
Environmental stability	Participation is an effective response to turbulent and dynamic environments.
Technology	Complex interdependencies between subunits accompanying technological sophistication are better managed with participation.
Task uncertainty	Tasks characterized by high uncertainty, thereby requiring large amounts of information, are effectively confronted in a participatory manner.
Interpersonal:	
Task stress	Participation is effective in low-stress tasks, but high-stress tasks are managed more effectively with little or no participation.
Group size	The smaller the group being managed, the more effective is participation.
Congruence between task and individual	When working on ambiguous tasks, individuals with a high need for achievement prefer a participative approach; those with a low need for achievement prefer a more authoritarian style.
Intrinsic satisfaction from task	Participatory management is more effective for intrinsically unrewarding tasks.
Individual:	
Personality (locus of control)	People who feel they are in control of their destinies prefer a participative approach; people who rely on luck prefer little or no participation.
External reference points	Individuals with considerable experience relevant to the task prefer to participate in its management.
Perceived emphasis placed on accounting information	Managers who believe their performance is evaluated using budget information prefer to participate.

an arbitrarily imposed limit of five years should congratulate itself on its good fortune and not on the quality of its decision-making process.

Another means of motivating employees is through incentive plans. Several firms have adopted group plans that reward the entire group for gains achieved by any member of that group. The individual may be rewarded separately as well. Some observers believe this may provide a means of circumventing the problems of isolating individual performance in an age characterized by technological dependence.

Some suggestions for improving goal congruence, and hence control procedures, are listed below.

1. Continued attention should be given to the problem of accounting for human resources. Measures are available by which aspects such as trust and loyalty can be measured. Changes in these measures may provide indications of the effects of different policies.

2. Communication and feedback devices need reexamination. It is important for individuals to learn about their success or failure. More frequent feedback is required than is generally supplied. If performance is substantially below expectations, budgetary revisions downward may be in order to prevent the frustrations associated with failure to reach aspiration levels, which in turn leads to lower future performance.

3. Budgets should be based on time periods for which useful input and output figures can be developed. The input-activity measures must be related to the output-activity results if the resulting feedback is to be of any value.

4. Accountants should work more closely with behavioral scientists. Furthermore, accountants should learn more about this area themselves. Encouragement should be given to those on the job to obtain this training. Such an approach will accelerate a total-system's view of the accounting function, a step that will facilitate more goal-oriented control techniques.

5. Participation schemes should be introduced into organizations with due consideration for the implementation problems entailed. Where such plans exist, consideration should be given to improving their effectiveness. When this is done, a system of participation with some goals imposed will improve the setting within which effective control can be exercised. This, it should be emphasized, is a necessary but not sufficient condition for effective control. The accounting department still needs to develop and cultivate the trust of line managers through better measurement techniques if it is to help line managers do a better job.

Finally, we should not overlook the positive incentives that accrue to challenging and enjoyable jobs and to opportunities to learn and advance. These very real incentives contribute to the needs of the subordinate as well as to obtaining the goals of the organization.

Contingency View of Managerial Accounting System Design

Practically all of the research that has been done concerning the behavioral effects of managerial accounting systems suggests that a contingency view of system design is desirable. According to a **contingency view of managerial accounting,** system characteristics are contingent on numerous variables in the organizational environment. Managerial accounting system characteristics such as the extent of participatory budgeting, the tightness of standards, the difficulty of achieving budgets, the restriction of performance evaluation to controllables, and the designation of subunits as cost centers, profit centers, or investment centers all depend on the organizational setting. The personality styles of the people involved, the degree of ambiguity in the task, the stability in the external environment, and the nature of the organization's technology all come to bear on the optimal design of a managerial accounting system. For this reason, there is considerable difference in the types of managerial accounting systems employed by different organizations and by different subunits within the same organization.[17]

The contingency view of managerial accounting implies that different types of organizations will require different managerial accounting systems. As an example of this phenomenon, we consider the difference in the responsibility accounting systems employed in a hierarchical organization versus a matrix organization. Exhibit 26-2 depicts these two forms of organization. In a **hierarchical organization,** each subunit is divided into smaller subunits proceeding down the organization chart. Each subunit falls under the well-defined control of the next subunit up in the chart. In a **matrix organization,** each subunit falls under two or more types of managerial structures, depicted alphabetically and numerically in Exhibit 26-2. An example of a matrix structure is a project team formed to analyze a major new program. The team may consist of an engineer (department 1), a marketing specialist (department 2), a financial analyst (department 3), and a legal expert (department 4). Each of these individuals falls under their department management, but the project team (team A, for example) also has a team manager.

The responsibility accounting system illustrated in Chapter 10 for the Marriott Corporation (see Exhibit 10-3) reflects a hierarchical organization. Each Marriott hotel falls unambiguously under the management of a particular geographical region, each region falls within a particular area, and so on. The responsibility accounting system used at United Airlines reflects more of a matrix approach to the organization. The company has four geographical divisions that are further subdivided into regions. The company also has identified seven major markets. Many flights cross divisional boundaries, and this phenomenon must be reflected in the responsibility accounting system. The geographical divisions are cost centers whose responsibilities include airports, reservations offices, and local sales offices.

---

17. For further reading on the contingency theory of managerial accounting, see D. Hayes, "The Contingency Theory of Managerial Accounting," *Accounting Review* (January 1977): 22–39.

EXHIBIT 26-2

Hierarchical and Matrix Organizations

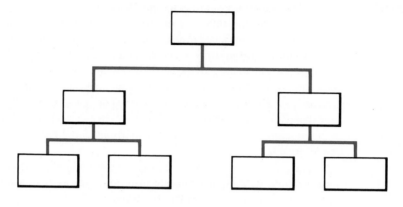

Summary

The history of cost control has been marked by the view that the primary incentive for employees is an economic one. Furthermore, employees have been implicitly viewed, at best, as indifferent and, at worst, as wasteful, lazy, and purposefully inefficient. Modern behavioral theory, on the other hand, recognizes that employees have a host of goals in addition to the economic one. It recognizes that individual behavior is essentially adaptive, problem solving, and decision oriented; and that this behavior is constrained by limited knowledge, limited cognitive ability, and changing value structures. Hence, individuals tend to adopt "satisficing" behavior (or constrained optimization behavior) patterns.

Managerial accounting has traditionally been viewed as the primary means of controlling and reducing costs. Yet organization theorists have argued for some time that this traditional view, with its emphasis on cost variances and the budgeted income and the implied behavioral implications, produces or reinforces the responses of indifference, inefficiency, hostility, and conflict that management wishes to avoid. Management may be more effective when it concentrates on motivating workers rather than directly on cost control. Although a conclusive statement that a reduction in undesirable responses by employees can be attained by moving toward approaches more consistent with a modern behavioral model cannot be made because of the lack of reliable empirical data, there is a strong presumption that this may be the case.

Accountants must understand and apply the motivational aspects of human activity as they relate to budgeting and responsibility accounting. Budgets, which represent a set of specific goals of the company as a whole, may result in behavior on the part of those responsible for implementing the budget that is not goal congruent. Managers who carefully consider the potential behavioral consequences of budgets on their employees can enhance the value of the budgetary process.

Key Terms to Review

behavioral issues, p. 886
contingency view of managerial accounting, p. 897
expectancy model of motivation, p. 890
hierarchical organization, p. 897

matrix organization, p. 897
motivation, p. 889
participatory management, p. 892
responsibility accounting system, p. 891

Review Problem

A COST REDUCTION PROGRAM

The Staley Investment Banking Corporation hired a consulting firm to help it reduce costs. The consulting firm recommended the following goals for each operating unit:

Reduction in direct personnel costs	20%
Reduction in expenses	25%

Each unit appointed a vice president, who was in charge of the cost reduction program. The vice president reported to a central committee chairman but the actual cost reduction program of the unit would have to be approved by the managing director.

Evaluate the program.

Solution to Review Problem

The primary problem with the program is that it concentrates on costs and neglects the effect on revenues and net income. Also, all units are being treated the same. Units that are already efficient will be penalized.

Suggested Readings

Behavioral Studies of Budgeting and Responsibility Accounting

Argyris, C. "Human Problems with Budgets." *Harvard Business Review* (January–February 1953): 97–110.

———. *The Impact of Budgets on People.* New York: Controllership Foundation, 1952.

Becker, S. W., and D. Green. "Budgeting and Employee Behavior." *Journal of Business* (October 1962): 392–402.

Benston, G. "The Role of the Firm's Accounting System for Motivation." *Accounting Review* (April 1963): 347–54.

———. "Participation in the Budgeting Process: When It Works and When It Doesn't." *Journal of Accounting Literature* (Spring 1982): 124–53.

———. "The Role of Accounting Data in Performance Evaluation, Budgetary Participation, and Organizational Effectiveness." *Journal of Accounting Research* (Spring 1982): 12–27.

Brownell, P., and M. McInnes. "Budgetary Participation, Motivation, and Managerial Performance." *Accounting Review* (October 1986): 587–600.

Bruns, W., and J. Waterhouse. "Budgetary Control and Organization Structure." *Journal of Accounting Research* (Autumn 1975): 177–203.

Caplan, E. H. "Behavioral Assumptions of Management Accounting." *Accounting Review* (July 1966): 496–509.

———. "Behavioral Assumptions of Management Accounting—Report of a Field Study." *Accounting Review* (April 1968): 243–362.

Chenhall, R. H. "Authoritarianism and Participative Budgeting: A Dyadic Analysis." *Accounting Review* (April 1986): 263–72.

Ferris, K. R. "A Test of the Expectancy Theory of Motivation in an Accounting Environment." *Accounting Review* (July 1977): 605–15.

Ferris, K. R., and J. L. Livingstone, eds. *Management Planning and Control: The Behavioral Foundations.* Beavercreek, Ohio: Century VII, 1987.

Hayes, D. "The Contingency Theory of Managerial Accounting." *Accounting Review* (January 1977): 22–29.

Kenis, I. "Effects of Budgetary Goal Characteristics on Managerial Attributes and Performance." *Accounting Review* (October 1979): 707–21.

Merchant, K. "The Design of the Corporate Budgeting System: Influences on Managerial Behavior and Performance." *Accounting Review* (October 1981): 813–29.

Rockness, H. O. "Expectancy Theory in a Budgetary Setting: An Experimental Examination." *Accounting Review* (October 1977): 893–903.

Ronen, J., and L. Livingstone. "An Expectancy Theory Approach to the Motivational Impact of Budgets." *Accounting Review* (October 1975): 671–85.

Schiff, M., and A. Lewin. "The Impact of People on Budgets." *Accounting Review* (April 1970): 252–68.

Stedry, A. C. *Budget Control and Cost Behavior.* Englewood Cliffs, N.J.: Prentice-Hall, 1960.

General Theories of Motivation and Organization

Cyert, R., and J. March. *A Behavioral Theory of the Firm.* Englewood Cliffs, N.J.: Prentice-Hall, 1963.

Gregor, W. "An Uneasy Look at Performance Appraisal." *Harvard Business Review* (September–October 1972): 133–39.

Herzberg, F., B. Mausner, and B. Snyderman. *The Motivation to Work.* New York: Wiley, 1959.

Likert, R. *The Human Organization, Its Management and Value.* New York: McGraw-Hill, 1967.

March, J. G., and H. A. Simon. *Organization.* New York: Wiley, 1958.

Maslow, A. *Eupsychian Management: A Journal.* Homewood, Ill.: Irwin, 1965.

Skinner, B. *Science and Human Behavior.* New York: Free Press, 1953.

Steers, R. M., and L. W. Porter. *Motivation and Work Behavior.* New York: McGraw-Hill, 1975, chap. 5.

Vroom, V. *Work and Motivation.* New York: Wiley, 1964.

Review Questions

26-1 Should decisions be made to optimize the well-being of a segment of an organization as a whole?

26-2 Are quantitative measures of dollars of expected profit (or rate of return or present value) good and sufficient bases for making business decisions?

26-3 Is cost accounting the best means of implementing a cost-reduction program?

26-4 Who has responsibility for repair department costs?

26-5 Of the several possible motivational objectives of a cost-accounting system, which are most likely to be successfully achieved?

26-6 Should cost standards be hard or easy to attain?

26-7 Are people more motivated by threats of punishment or by the offer of rewards for accomplishment?

26-8 Assume you have been directed by the president of your firm to improve profits by 10 percent. What alternatives do you have?

26-9 What methods might be used to motivate development and research department personnel toward achieving the firm's objectives?

26-10 How should a class in, say, cost control, tackle its own motivation problem?

Exercises   26-11 Every six months the production manager, I. Makit, and the purchasing manager, D. LeGrump, determine the raw material and other input needs of the production department. LeGrump knows that he is responsible for meeting the general purchasing schedule once it is set up and agreed to by Makit and himself. Eight weeks ago Makit advised LeGrump that he noticed that the supply of one essential input was running low and that he would need the next batch of raw material on time (in accordance with the original production schedule) in four weeks. LeGrump found that the regular supplier could not make delivery in accordance with this schedule. He called a number of places and finally found a supplier who accepted the four-week commitment.

LeGrump followed up by mail and was assured by the supplier that he would receive the material in time. The matter was so important that LeGrump called again a week in advance and was again assured that the material would arrive in time.

The day before the material was to be used LeGrump checked once again and found that the shipment had not been received. Inquiry revealed that the shipment had been misdirected by the railroad and was still in Chicago, 500 miles away, and would not be received for two days.

The material was finally obtained but only after considerable extra expense (only a part of which is recoverable) and substantial down time.

Where do you believe the responsibility lies, and who should bear this cost?

26-12 The Spede Manufacturing Company owns a trucking fleet, has its own utility services, and maintains a repair shop. These are all operated as profit centers. The trucking division has been complaining to the utility division that its wires at one point in the road were too low and did not give the larger trucks enough clearance. The repair shop agreed to make the changes but wanted to know whether the costs of the adjustment were to be charged to the utility division or the trucking division. Both the divisions refused to accept the $1,500 cost of making the adjustment, and the repair shop refused to perform the task unless it could charge the costs of making the adjustment to one of the two divisions. One day the top of a truck caught the wires and ripped them down. The cost of repairing the lines was $2,500, and there was an additional cost to the firm of $4,000 because of the disruption of service. Investigation disclosed that the truck had failed to clamp down its top properly and the extra two inches of height caused the catching of the wire. The trucking division and the utility division both refused to accept the $2,500 repair charges.

Assume that you are the controller in charge of the accounting for the three service divisions (repair, trucking, and utility). What would be your next step?. What is the proper role of responsible accounting in determining the blame for this situation?

26-13 The following letter was received by a new controller. Write a reply.

The Krocks and Potts Company
(Makers of Fine Dinnerware)
Scurry, Ohio

Controller
13 Morningside Avenue
Sashay, Ohio

Dear Controller:

I hesitate to write to you even before your arrival, but a problem has come up in the controller's division about which you should be informed.

As you know, we have recently overhauled our entire organization and brought in a number of new people. One of these new people is Ben Pole, who has taken over our Putter, Pennsylvania, activities. Ben is a good man and well suited to our decentralized activities.

About the time that we hired Ben, U. U. Pusher, one of our extremely bright and young staff members, took over our new performance analysis staff. This staff operates out of the controller's office.

It is Pusher's duty to prepare reports showing budgeted performance, actual performance, and explanations of any differences for both divisions of the plant. Pusher has a staff of two men, one for each division, who operate out of our main plant. They have consulted and are acquainted with their respective division's line and staff executive personnel as well as with the operation.

Until yesterday we thought all was going well. Yesterday afternoon, however, Ben Pole stormed into my office quite unhappy about the whole setup.

I can't recall his exact words, but the gist of his comments indicate that he feels Pusher's staff is usurping his responsibilities. He feels they snoop around asking too many questions and generally waste his staff's time. Ben feels it is his job to analyze and explain his division's performance.

From your experience, can you think of any reason for Ben's position, and what would you suggest we do, if anything, about his complaint?

Sincerely,
I. M. Thebos
Manager

26-14 Consider the following memo to the controller of a manufacturing company. Write a reply.

To: Controller
From: Thebos
Subject: Budgets

Ben Pole has sent me the following budget report, which applies to his manufacturing supervisor:

Period	1		2		3		4		5		6	
Budget	$39,000		$40,000		$39,500		$38,000		$38,500		$38,500	
Actual	41,000		39,500		38,000		39,000		38,500		38,250	
Variance	$ 2,000	U	$ 500	F	$ 1,500	F	$ 1,000	U	$ 0		$ 250	F

The supervisor has a substantial number of men and a large amount of equipment under his control. He is paid a "base" salary that is actually somewhat low for his type of work. However, we have a rather liberal bonus plan that pays him an additional $1,000 per month each time he makes his budget and 2 percent of the saving (amount below budget).

We have been quite pleased so far with the continued improvement in the supervisor's performance and wonder if this might not be a model for the rest of our operations. What do you think?

I. M. Thebos

26-15 The following is a condensation of an actual case. In a particular plant a mistake was made on a customer's special order. The goods were returned at a cost of $3,000, which was paid by the manufacturer. The allocated costs to these goods was $100,000. The customer was so unhappy that he decided to take his entire business elsewhere. This business had been growing and amounted to about 4 percent of the manufacturing firm's total billings over the past fiscal year.

There developed a strong argument over which segment of the firm should receive the charge for the error and how large the charge should be.

There seemed to be general agreement that the problem was poor workmanship. The manufacturing department argued that they had been on overtime the whole period and that the extra workers hired for this particular job were not able to do the job. The personnel department countered by saying that under the tight labor markets, this was the best that could be done and that management knew this when it accepted the special order. Both agreed that the inspection department should have located the error if it had done its job properly. Inspection maintained that perhaps it could have caught the problem even though it was unusual, but even if it had it would have saved only the small transportation expense. Further, its equipment and procedures would have to be changed substantially if the firm wished to ensure that defects such as the present kind would be detected by the inspection department.

The plant manager finally gave up. He decided to charge the error to no department. He explained, "I thought it might be best to put the whole thing in a loss account, otherwise someone would be hurt."

What is the most important issue here? If you were the controller what advice would you give the plant manager? (Indicate the priority attaching to your suggestion.)

26-16 In a behavioral study Stedry hypothesized that if an individual were at least moderately discouraged, the difference between actual and aspired-to cost levels would increase because the individual would then allow actual costs to rise. Do you agree? Why?

26-17 The president of Nifty Novelties Company, a wholesaler, presents you with a comparison of distribution costs for two salespeople and wants to know whether you think the salespeople's compensation plan is working to the detriment of the company. He supplies the following information for the month of June.

	Salespeople	
	Smith	Brown
Gross sales	$25,000	$15,000
Sales returns	2,000	500
Cost of goods sold	18,000	9,000
Reimbursed expenses (e.g., entertainment)	600	200
Other direct charges (e.g., samples)	400	500
Commission rate on gross sales dollars	5%	5%

   a. What inappropriate sales practices might be encouraged by basing commissions on gross sales?

   b. Is there information to support the president's concern? What additional information would be useful before any decisions are made? (*CPA adapted*)

26-18 Some accountants argue that budgets have motivational impact and should therefore be changed from period to period and from person to person for motivational reasons. Comment.

26-19 "Static budgets have no use if large deviations from the budgeted activity level are expected." Comment.

26-20 Suppose a control system is based on the following premise. It is better to set a standard of ten hours knowing it will take fifteen to do the job than to set fifteen hours as the standard if it would then take sixteen hours. It is better to do the job in fifteen hours than in sixteen. Do you agree?

Problems

26-21 **Participative Budgeting**   Scott Weidner, the controller in the Division of Social Services for the state, recognizes the importance of the budgetary process for planning, control, and motivation purposes. He believes that a properly implemented participative budgeting process for planning purposes and a management by exception reporting procedure based on the participative budget will motivate his subordinates to improve productivity within their particular departments. Based on this philosophy, Weidner has implemented the following budget procedures:

1. An appropriation target figure is given to each department manager. This amount is the maximum funding that each department can expect to receive in the next fiscal year.

2. Department managers develop their individual budgets within the following spending constraints as directed by the controller's staff.

   (a) Expenditure requests cannot exceed the appropriation target.

   (b) All fixed expenditures should be included in the budget. Fixed expenditures would include such items as contracts and salaries at current levels.

   (c) All government projects directed by higher authority should be included in the budget in their entirety.

3. The controller's staff consolidates the departmental budget requests from the various departments into one budget that is to be submitted for the entire division.

4. On final budget approval by the legislature, the controller's staff allocates the appropriation to the various departments on instructions from the division manager. However, a specified percentage of each department's appropriation is held back in anticipation of potential budget cuts and special funding needs. The amount and use of this contingency fund is left to the discretion of the division manager.

5. Each department is allowed to adjust its budget when necessary to operate within the reduced appropriation level. However, as stated in the original directive, specific projects authorized by higher authority must remain intact.

6. The final budget is used as the basis of control for a management by exception form of reporting. Excessive expenditures by account for each department are

highlighted on a monthly basis. Department managers are expected to account for all expenditures over budget. Fiscal responsibility is an important factor in the overall performance evaluation of department managers.

Weidner believes his policy of allowing the department managers to participate in the budget process and then holding them accountable for their performance is essential, especially during these times of limited resources. He further believes the department managers will be motivated positively to increase the efficiency and effectiveness of their departments because they have provided input into the initial budgetary process and are required to justify any unfavorable performances.

REQUIRED:

a. Explain the operational and behavioral benefits that generally are attributed to a participative budgeting process.

b. Identify deficiencies in Scott Weidner's participative budgetary policy for planning and performance evaluation purposes. For each deficiency identified, recommend how the deficiency can be corrected. Use the following format in preparing your response. (*CMA adapted*)

Deficiencies	Recommendations
1.	1.

26-22 Behavioral Implications of Merit Pay   Wilson and Associates is a medium-size marketing organization specializing in professional promotion and publicity services. The firm's top management believes it provides quality service as evidenced by the high level of customer satisfaction.

The organization consists of three departments — Print Media, Audio Media, and Visual Media. A senior director is in charge of each department. The company employs eighty clerical staff who are paid on an hourly basis and thirty professional staff who are on salary. A large majority of the employees have an excellent rating in their job skills. All the employees demonstrate above average performance in their job responsibilities. The employees take pride in their achievements and morale is very good.

Salary ranges are established for different job classifications within the clerical staff (clerk, clerk typist, secretary, and administrative assistant) and the professional staff (analyst, manager, and director). A fixed-rate structure is used for all salaries, and there are no provisions for commissions because Wilson does not want its professional staff applying undue sales pressure on the customers. Management is proud that the company does not have to resort to a salary plus commission structure for its professionals to generate sales.

Employees are recognized for superior performances through salary increases and promotions. Management believes that salary increases should be based on merit, and promotions are made from within whenever possible. Top management contends that highly skilled and motivated employees will improve productivity if they are rewarded with annual merit pay raises and if promotions are based on performance.

Top management announced in November that the amount available for pay increases would be ten percent of the actual total salary expenditures for 19x2. All salary increases would be effective January 1, 19x3.

The Print Media Department consisted of twenty clerical employees and eight professional staff on January 1, 19x2. Six clerical employees were added during the year at the rate of about one every two months. Two professional staff were added, one on March 1 and one on August 1. There were three promotions during the year — two secretaries to administrative assistants and one manager to director. The total actual salary expense for the department without regard for employee fringe benefits and employer tax contributions were $548,000. Therefore, the total amount allocated for wage increases for the Print Media Department in 19x3 is designated to be $54,800.

Shortly after the merit pay program was announced, the Print Media Department employees had their year-end evaluation. The evaluation was conducted by each employee's supervisor. The senior director met with each supervisor and received all performance reports. The senior director then announced the merit pay increase for each employee.

On completion of this entire process, several employees complained individually about the inequities of the merit pay program. The senior director was concerned about the employee discontent because the clerical and professional people complaining were some of the highest achievers of the staff. These individuals tended to be at the lower classification levels and were relatively new employees, having been with the company from one to four years. The individuals showed potential and were highly motivated, often working extra hours and assuming additional responsibilities.

The new employees' behavior differed slightly from the employees who had been with the department for a longer period of time. The veteran employees, while highly skilled and competent in their jobs, tended to be reluctant to accept additional responsibility or to work excessive hours on a regular basis.

REQUIRED:

a. Review Wilson and Associates' wage and compensation plan.

(1) Identify and discuss the strengths of the program in general.

(2) Identify and explain the shortcomings in the administration of the merit pay increases that are to become effective in 19x3, and discuss what effect these shortcomings may have on the group of discontented employees in the Print Media Department.

b. Explain how this compensation program would be received by employees who believe in the authoritarian school of management thought versus employees who believe in the participative school of management thought. (*CMA adapted*)

26-23 Decentralization; Participative Management RNB is a bank holding company for a state-wide group of retail consumer-oriented banks. The bank holding company was formed in the early 1960s by a group of young investors who believed in a high level of consumer services. The number of banks owned by the holding company expanded rapidly. These banks gained visibility through their experimentation with innovations such as free-standing twenty-four-hour automated banking machines, automated funds transfer systems, and other advances in banking services.

RNB's earnings performance has been better than most other banks in the state. The founders organized and continue to operate RNB on a highly decentralized basis. As the number of banks owned grew, RNB's executive management delegated more responsibility and authority to individual bank presidents. The bank presidents are viewed by RNB as a "linking pin" to its executive management. Although certain aspects of each bank's operations are standardized (such as procedures for account and loan applications and salary rates), bank presidents have significant autonomy in determining how each individual bank operates.

The decentralization has led each of the banks to develop individual marketing campaigns. Several of them have introduced unique packaged accounts that include a combination of banking services. However, they sometimes fail to notify the other banks in the group as well as the executive office of their plans and programs. One result has been interbank competition for customers where the market areas overlap. Also, the corporate marketing officer had recently begun a statewide advertising campaign that conflicted with some of the individual banks' advertising. Consequently, there have been occasions when customers and tellers have experienced both confusion and frustration, particularly when the customers attempt to receive services at a bank other than their "home" bank.

RNB's executive management is concerned that there will be a slight decline in earnings for the first time in its history. The decline appears to be attributable to reduced customer satisfaction and higher operating costs. The competition among the state's banks is keen. Bank location and consistent high-quality customer service are important. RNB's eighteen banks are well located, and the three new bank acquisitions planned for next year are considered to be in prime locations. The increase in operating costs appears to be directly related to the individual banks' aggressive marketing efforts and new programs. Specifically, expenditures increased for advertising, and for the special materials and added personnel for the packaged accounts.

For the past three months RNB's executive management has been meeting with the individual bank presidents. The purpose of the meetings is to review RNB's recent performance and seek ways to improve it. One recommendation that appeals to RNB's executive management is to change the organization to a more centralized structure. The specific proposal calls for a reduction in individual bank autonomy and creation of a centralized Individual Bank Management Committee. The committee would consist of all bank presidents and be chaired by a newly created position, vice president of individual bank operations. The individual banks' policies, expected to conform to overall RNB plans, would be set by consensus of the committee. RNB's executive management feels that this participative management approach will be a "fair trade" for the loss of autonomy by the individual bank presidents.

REQUIRED:

a. Discuss the advantages attributed to a decentralized organizational structure.

b. Identify disadvantages of a decentralized structure supporting each disadvantage with an example from RNB's situation.

c. The proposed more centralized structure is said by RNB's executive management to include the participative management approach.

   (1) Define the concept *participative management.*

   (2) Does RNB's recommended approach include participative management? Use information from the situation to support your answer. (*CMA adapted*)

26-24 Behavior Implications of Accounting System   The B&B Company manufactures and sells chemicals for agricultural and industrial use. The company has grown significantly over the last ten years but has made few changes in its information gathering and reporting system. Some of the managers have expressed concern that the system is essentially the same as it was when the firm was only half its present size. Others believe that much of the information from the system is not relevant and that more appropriate and timely information should be available.

Dora Hepple, chief accountant, has observed that the actual monthly cost data for most production processes are compared with the actual costs of the same processes for the previous year. Any variance not explained by price changes requires an explanation by the individual in charge of the cost center. She believes that this information is inadequate for good cost control.

George Vector, one of the production supervisors, contends that the system is adequate because it allows for explanation of discrepancies. The current year's costs seldom vary from the previous year's costs (as adjusted for price changes). This indicates that costs are under control.

Vern Hopp, general manager of the Fine Chemical Division, is upset with the current system. He has to request the same information each month regarding recurring operations. This is a problem that he believes should be addressed.

Walter Metts, president, has appointed a System Review Task Force to determine whether the information needs of the internal management of the firm are being met by the existing system. Specific modifications in the existing system or implementation of a new system will be considered only if management's needs are not being met. William Afton, assistant to the president, has been put in charge of the task force.

Shortly after the committee was appointed, Afton overheard one of the cost accountants say, "I've been doing it this way for fifteen years, and now Afton and his committee will try to eliminate my job." Another person replied, "That's the way it looks. John and Brownie in general accounting also think that their positions are going to be eliminated or at least changed significantly." Over the next few days, Afton overheard a middle management person talking about the task force saying, "That's all this company thinks about — maximizing its profits, not the employees." He also overheard a production manager in the Mixing Department say that he believed the system was in need of revision because the most meaningful information he received came from Brad Cummings, a salesperson. He stated, "After they have the monthly sales meeting, Brad stops by the office and indicates what the sales plans and targets are for the next few months. This sure helps me in planning my mixing schedules."

Afton is aware that two problems of paramount importance to be addressed by his System Review Task Force are (1) to determine management's information needs for cost control and decision making purposes and (2) to meet the behavioral needs of the company and its employees.

REQUIRED:

a. Discuss the behavioral implications of having an accounting information system that does not appear to meet the needs of management.

b. Identify and explain the specific problems B&B Company appears to have with regard to the perception of B&B's employees concerning

(1) The accounting information system.

(2) The firm.

c. Assume that the initial review of the System Review Task Force indicates that a new accounting information system should be designed and implemented.

(1) Identify specific behavioral factors that B&B's management should address in the design and implementation of a new system.

(2) For each behavioral factor identified, discuss how B&B's management can address the behavioral factor. (*CMA adapted*)

26-25 Participative versus Imposed Budgets   An effective budget converts the objectives and goals of management into data. The budget often serves as a blueprint that represents management's plan for operating the business.

The budget frequently is the basis for control. Management performance can be evaluated by comparing actual results with the budget.

Thus, creating the budget is essential for the successful operation of an organization. Finding the resources to implement the budget (that is, getting from a starting point to the ultimate goal) requires the extensive use of human resources. The manner in which the people involved perceive their roles in the budget operation is important to the successful use of the budget as an effective management tool for planning, communicating, and controlling.

REQUIRED:

a. Discuss the behavioral implications on budgetary planning and budgetary control when a company's management employs

(1) An imposed budgetary approach.

(2) A participative budgetary approach.

b. Communication plays an important part in the budget operation whether an imposed or participatory budgetary approach is used.

(1) Describe the differences between the communication flows in these two budgetary approaches.

(2) Discuss the behavioral implications of the communication process for each of these budgetary approaches. (*CMA adapted*)

26-26 Management Style, Morale, and Motivation   Linda Fry is the supervisor for the bookkeeping department of Medford Bank and Trust. The department processes 10,000 to 15,000 checks and related items daily. Six clerical employees perform this work under Fry's direct supervision.

The sequence of events in preparing cancelled checks for processing by the bookkeeping department is as follows:

1. Checks are processed through the proof department, where the dollar amount is micro-encoded onto the check and a record of the transaction is input to the computer records.

2. Computer printouts for the daily check processing activities are printed overnight. The printout, along with the cancelled checks, arrives at the bookkeeping department at the beginning of each work day.

Specific operations within the bookkeeping department include the following:

▪ A sample of payor signatures on the checks is verified for authenticity.

▪ All checks over $500 are examined for an endorsement.

▪ All check errors are identified and appropriate special handling provisions are completed.

▪ All stop-payment checks are identified and reversed out of the computer record.

■ Insufficient fund checks are identified and reversed out of the computer records. The check is returned to the endorser and appropriate charges are made to the customer's account.

■ Questions from customers and creditors concerning check verification, account balance, and collected balance are answered via telephone conversations.

Medford's top management believes in exercising tight control and authority over all departments. The nature of the banking business and the need for strong internal control procedures underlie the philosophy put forth by the executives. Top management encourages the interchange of ideas, but the communication process essentially follows a top-down structure.

To facilitate control and performance within the bookkeeping department, authority and decision making reside with Fry. She assigns duties and responsibilities to the clerical workers and carefully reviews the performance of her employees. Fry believes she has the employees' respect and feels she can recognize internal conflict and discontent.

Top management perceives that the employees hired for the bookkeeping department tend to be unskilled and may lack ambition. However, several employees have shown a willingness to learn new skills and are amenable to training programs. The employees function best when there are specific guidelines and directions for a particular job and when the lines of authority are clear. The jobs, however, tend to be somewhat dull and repetitive over time and provide little opportunity to incentive or personal satisfaction.

In spite of the nature of the work and the skill levels of the employees, productivity in the bookkeeping department is good and has been improving. The employees get along and work well with each other. They have retained their current positions from one to three years and are efficient at their specific job functions. However, the employees generally regard the work as an unpleasant task, and the repetitiveness of the work has led to morale and motivation problems.

REQUIRED:

a. Identify the management style that appears to be followed in the bookkeeping department.

   (1) What factors presented in this situation support your selection of this management style?

   (2) Explain whether this style can be a means of promoting effective work flow and improving productivity.

b. Identify circumstances that may have led to the morale and motivation problems of the bookkeeping department employees.

c. Recommend changes Linda Fry may wish to implement in the bookkeeping department to improve employee morale and motivation while at the same time maintaining the desired standards of performance and productivity. (*CMA adapted*)

26-27 Matrix Organizations Reardon Company manufactures and markets radio and sonar detection equipment. The Department of Defense is Reardon's most important customer.

Joseph Reardon founded the company ten years ago to manufacture and market a radio receiver on which he had just received a patent. The company has grown significantly from the early years when it was staffed by a very small group of reliable employees.

In the past year the sales department has complained that certain segments of the product line are not receiving the attention they deserve from the production and research and development departments. The existence of many somewhat diverse products whose purchasers have strict deadlines requires coordination of production and sales. This has not been present in the past year. One result of this lack of coordination has been an increasing inefficiency in the use of resources. There is also a lack of coordination between the sales effort and the research and development programs.

The company is divided into four separate areas of responsibility — marketing, production, research and development, and finance. Joseph Reardon functions as the chief executive officer and also heads the research and development activity. He is concerned that the current organizational structure is the cause of the lack of coordination and the increasing inefficiencies.

He plans to appoint a task force to evaluate alternative organizational structures for Reardon Company. One structure that he has specifically requested to be included in the study is the matrix form of organization.

REQUIRED:

a. Define the *matrix organizational structure.*

b. Identify strengths and weaknesses of the matrix form of organizational structure.

c. Discuss how the matrix form of organization could be applied to the situation described in Reardon Company. (*CMA adapted*)

26-28 Behavioral Effects of Perquisites   HuffCo, Inc. is a large manufacturing company with three operating divisions located in Chicago, St. Louis, and Minneapolis. The corporate headquarters are also located in Chicago.

Employee perquisites are an important element of HuffCo's compensation plan for its professional staff. Certain perquisites are provided to all professional employees regardless of management level. These include the following:

- Company-paid retirement benefits.

- Company-paid basic medical insurance and major medical plan.

- Company-paid term life insurance.

- Company-paid vacation.

- Company-paid holidays.

- Discounts on the purchase of company products.

- Reimbursement of authorized company travel.

These basic perquisites vary to a certain degree among employees. For instance, the retirement benefits and term life insurance coverage are keyed to each employee's salary, and vacation time depends on management level and length of service with the company. Otherwise, these benefits are the same for all professional staff.

Professional staff members classified as executive management have some additional perquisites over and above the basic plan. Those persons qualifying for executive management status are clearly identified — that is, only persons above a designated management level are entitled to this classification. The additional perquisites include the following:

- More comprehensive company-paid medical plan including dental insurance.

- Company-paid disability insurance coverage.

- Company-paid membership to one country/athletic club.

- Access to a company car for business use.

- Special executive privileges, such as an executive rest room and executive dining room.

- Larger offices with more expensive furnishings.

- More liberal travel expense reimbursement.

The differences in the travel expense reimbursement policy between the executive management and the other professional staff members are shown in the following table.

DIFFERENCES IN TRAVEL EXPENSE POLICY		
	Basic	*Executive*
Air travel	Not to exceed coach class; special reduced rates to be used when available	First class allowed
Rental cars	Restricted to compact	No restrictions on type of automobile
Hotel	Actual amount spent up to a maximum of $75 per day unless excess authorized	Actual amount spent
Meals	Actual amount spent up to a maximum of $25 per day unless excess authorized	Actual amount spent
Reserved lounges of airline clubs	None	Payment for one membership to allow admission to reserved lounge of airline club located in terminals of major airports

Although HuffCo has a clearly defined plan for perquisites, some members of the professional staff have received special privileges. Some of the privileges have occurred several times, and others have evolved over time and have tended to become accepted by top management. The following activities or special privileges have been observed.

- Several executives have memberships in two or three country/athletic clubs, and all are company-paid.

- Several executives have company cars assigned to them permanently, and the cars are used for all travel including to and from the office.

- Office size and furnishings do not appear to be applied consistently according to title and rank. For instance, several individuals not classified as executive management have as large or larger offices as some executives. In addition, some offices of executives are remodeled more frequently.

- Several executives receive company products free. The dollar value of the products has never exceeded $300 annually.

- Executives' air travel is not consistent. When an executive and nonexecutive are on the same flight, most executives travel coach with the nonexecutive. However, some executives travel first class while the nonexecutive travels coach, and some executives have the nonexecutive travel first class with the company paying the additional fare.

- The travel expenses of spouses who accompany executives to meetings have been paid by the company on several occasions. This issue is not addressed in the company travel policy.

- Use of personal automobiles for company business is only allowed for short trips when company cars or common carrier service is not available. Several executives have used personal automobiles for long trips when common carriers (airlines) would have been less expensive.

- Several executives have company-paid memberships for two or more airline club lounges.

REQUIRED:

a. Explain the behavioral implications and the effect on employee performance of having two (or more) levels of perquisites for professional employees assuming eligibility is clearly defined and consistently applied.

b. Discuss the possible implications on (1) behavior and (2) cost control when company policy governing perquisites is not clear or is not applied consistently such as has occurred with HuffCo, Inc. Use HuffCo examples in your discussion when applicable. (*CMA adapted*)

27

Learning Curves and Cost Behavior

*F*or many years the Boston Consulting Group (BCG) has been one of the leading business strategy consultant firms in the world. One of the major conclusions of BCG's research is that a firm should attempt to be first in sales in the segment of the industry in which it operates. Such a firm can have lower costs because it accumulates experience as it produces more units of product than its competitors. The original theory behind this corporate strategy recommendation is learning curve theory, which is the topic of this chapter.

Cost Curves

Conventional economics assumes that both the average variable cost and the marginal cost per unit of product are concave (U-shaped) functions as illustrated in Exhibit 27-1. Furthermore, as is indicated in Exhibit 27-1, the marginal cost curve intersects the average variable cost curve from below at its minimum. When the marginal cost curve is below the average cost curve, average cost declines. Once the marginal cost rises

EXHIBIT 27-1

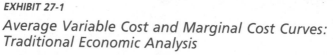

*Average Variable Cost and Marginal Cost Curves:
Traditional Economic Analysis*

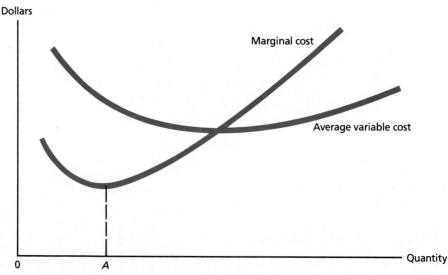

EXHIBIT 27-2

Average Variable Costs and Marginal Costs:
Discrete-Unit Example

Units Produced per Day	Fixed Cost	Total Variable Cost	Total Cost	Marginal Cost	Average Variable Cost
0	$256	$ 0	$256	—	—
1	256	64	320	$ 64	$64
2	256	84	340	20	42
3	256	99	355	15	33
4	256	112	368	13	28
5	256	125	381	13	25
6	256	144	400	19	24
7	256	175	431	31	25
8	256	224	480	49	28
9	256	297	553	73	33
10	256	400	656	103	40

above the average cost curve, average cost increases. These classic relationships are illustrated in Exhibit 27-1 for the continuous case.

The same results are illustrated numerically for a discrete-unit example in Exhibit 27-2. Average variable cost is a minimum at the sixth unit. Up to this point marginal cost is below average variable cost. Marginal cost of the seventh unit exceeds the previous average variable cost of the sixth unit and causes the average variable cost to increase.

The shape of the marginal cost curve reflects increasing efficiency with increasing output to point *A*, followed by increasing marginal costs resulting from inefficiencies. Constant efficiency, a condition often assumed in accounting analyses, would be reflected by a horizontal marginal cost curve and a related horizontal variable cost curve.

The traditional analysis mixes together two factors that should be considered separately. These include the time-rate of production (the number of units produced per unit of time) and the total number of units produced.[1] The marginal cost per unit might, on an a priori basis, be expected to increase as the time-rate of production increases or, perhaps, to exhibit a cost-behavior pattern similar to that in Exhibit 27-1 with the horizontal axis relabeled in terms of the units produced per unit of time.

However, in many situations, such as the production of a new product, the learning phenomenon tends to reduce the marginal cost as the cumulative output increases, and it is difficult to predict the shape of the marginal cost curve. In the initial stages of production, learning is an important factor. Learning may often even be the dominant factor affecting costs.

1. See J. Hirshleifer, "The Firm's Cost Function: A Successful Reconstruction?," *Journal of Business* (July 1962): 235–55; and A. Alchian, "Costs and Outputs," in *The Allocation of Economic Resources: Essays in Honor of B. F. Haley*, edited by M. Abramovitz. (Stanford, Calif.: Stanford University Press, 1959.)

That average labor time per unit of output declines as total output increases has been generally known for many years.[2] The observation that the rate of improvement exhibits regularities for common activities even across firms, and that this regularity repeats itself for new but similar projects, is an important factor in making the effects of the learning phenomenon predictable. Predictability, in turn, has implications for decision making and thereby for accounting.

The Learning-Curve Model

According to the **learning-curve model,** as the amount of experience in performing a task increases, the average time to complete the task declines. This relation can be approximated as a constant percentage reduction in the average direct labor input time required per unit as the cumulative output doubles. For example, assume a labor time reduction rate of 20 percent for the average hours of production and assume that the first unit requires 125 direct labor hours. Then if the total production doubles to two units, the average hours for two units should be 100 direct labor hours, .8(125). A total of 200 direct labor hours for both units is required. The first unit takes 125 direct labor hours and the second unit takes 75 hours to produce. If production is again doubled, the four units would take an average of 80 direct labor hours each, .8(100), a total of 320 hours. This means that 120 hours (320 − 200) must be expended in total to produce the third and fourth units.

One minus the percentage reduction due to learning is known as the **learning rate**. The learning rate in the present example is $1 - 0.2 = 0.8$, or 80 percent.

Exhibit 27-3 shows the average direct labor hours, total direct labor hours, the additional hours for the added units, and the additional hours per added unit for the example.

Doubling the production from one unit to two units reduces the direct labor hours from 125 for the first unit to 75 for the second unit. If production is again doubled to four units, the *average* hours required to produce the two additional units is 60. If production is increased from 16 to 32 units, the average hours for the last sixteen units are reduced to 30.72 hours. Additional production can be expected to further decrease the average hours required per unit.

Mathematically, the learning curve effect is written as

$$Y = aX^b \tag{1}$$

2. Initial applications were made in the airframe industry on the basis of regularities observed as early as 1925. See M. A. Requero, *An Economic Study of the Airframe Industry* (Wright-Patterson Air Force Base, Ohio: Department of the Air Force, October 1957), p. 213; and T. P. Wright, "Factor Affecting the Cost of Airplanes," *Journal of Aeronautical Science* (February 1936): 122–28.

EXHIBIT 27-3

Computation of Hours per Added Unit

Number of Units (X)	Average Direct Labor Hours (Y)	Total Direct Labor Hours (X · Y)	Additional Direct Labor Hours for Doubling Output	Average Additional Direct Labor Hours per Added Units
1	125	125	125	125
2	125 × .8 = 100	200	75	75
4	125 × .8² = 80	320	120	60
8	125 × .8³ = 64	512	192	48
16	125 × .8⁴ = 51.2	819.20	307.20	38.40
32	125 × .8⁵ = 40.96	1,310.72	491.52	30.72

where

Y = the average number of direct labor hours required for X units

a = the number of direct labor hours required for the first unit

X = the cumulative number of units produced

b = the index of learning

If r denotes the learning rate, .8 in the above example, then the value of b in equation (1) is given by the log of the learning rate divided by the log of 2.[3] For the current example, b takes on the value -0.322.

$$b = \frac{\log r}{\log 2} = \frac{\log .8}{\log 2} = -.322$$

3. This can be shown as follows. If the first unit takes a hours, then the average for two units is $(1 - c)a = ra$ hours according to the model where c is the percentage reduction due to learning and r is the learning rate. Since $X = 2$, $Y = aX^b$ gives $ra = a2^b$.

Dividing both sides by a,

$r = 2^b$

Taking logs:

$\log r = b \log 2$

and

$$b = \frac{\log r}{\log 2}$$

See D. Teichroew, *An Introduction to Management Science* (New York: Wiley, 1964): 159–63, for learning formulated in terms of marginal cost rather than average cost. In his model, Y is considered to be the marginal cost for the X-th unit in equation (1).

Equation (1) can be illustrated using the example given in Exhibit 27-3. For $X = 32$, using equation (1) yields:

$$Y = 125(32)^{-.322} = 125(.3276) = 40.96$$

This is the value in the second column for Y in Exhibit 27-3 when X is 32.

Data from a project or similar activity can be used to estimate the value of b in equation (1). Thus, if the records yield values for the time to produce the first unit, a, for total production, X, and for total direct labor hours XY, then b can be estimated.

Taking the log of both sides of equation (1) yields:

$$\log Y = \log a + b \log X \tag{2}$$

$$b = \frac{\log Y - \log a}{\log X}$$

If it is reasonable to assume that b remains constant, equation (1) can be used to compute the average number of direct labor hours, Y, to produce X units. The value of Y is, in turn, useful in predicting the time to complete given production goals and to estimate costs.

Since Y is the average number of labor hours required for X units, the total number of hours required for X units is given by:

$$YX = aX^{b+1} \tag{3}$$

Again if $X = 32$, then:

$$\text{Total hours} = YX = aX^{b+1} = 125(32)^{.678} = 1,310$$

This is the entry in the total hours column, column 3 of Exhibit 27-3, when X is 32.

The learning effect can be graphed. The average number of labor hours required for X units as expressed by equation (1) is graphed on arithmetic scales in Exhibit 27-4 and on log scales in Exhibit 27-5. Equation (1) is linear on the log chart because equation (2) is linear.

An appealing alternative, but equivalent, mathematical description of the learning-curve model given by equation (1) is obtained by altering the formula to incorporate the learning rate explicitly. The result for the present example is:

$$Y = a(.8)^{\log_2 X} \tag{4}$$

Or in general

$$Y = ar^{\log_2 X} \tag{5}$$

The symbols retain their same definitions.[4] The problem with the model in this form is that it is necessary to recompute the exponent for each value of X.

---

4. Mathematically, using equation (2) and where *exp* stands for exponent:

$$b = \log r / \log 2$$

$$\log Y = \log a + (\log X)(\log r)/\log 2$$

$$= \log a + \log r \exp(\log X/\log 2)$$

EXHIBIT 27-4

Average Labor Hours Required for X Units, Arithmetic Scale

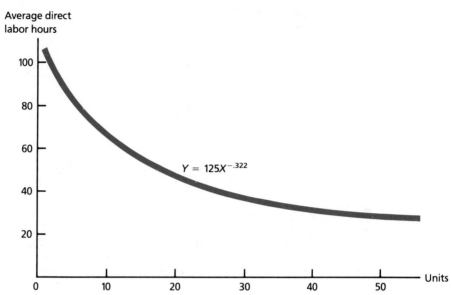

Equation (5) can be reformulated. The log of X to the base 2, $\log_2 X$, is the exponent to which 2 must be raised to obtain X. This is written $2^n = X$. Then

$$Y = a(r)^n \tag{6}$$

For $X = 32$, $n = 5$ (since $2^5 = 32$) and $r = .8$,

$$Y = 125(.8)^5 = 40.96$$

This is the amount shown in column 2 of Exhibit 27-3.

Equation (6) is mathematically equivalent to equation (5), since $n = \log_2 X$ and if many calculations are required, equation (6) is easier to use than equation (5).

Determining the Parameters of the Model

In order to use the model as defined by either equation (1) or equation (5), it is necessary to estimate the parameters a and b (or a and r). This can be done algebraically or graphically. The algebraic solution illustrated for equation (2) relies on the

$$= \log a + \log r \exp(\log X)(\log_2 10)$$

$$= \log a + \log r \exp(\log_2 X)$$

Therefore,

$$Y = a(r)^{\log_2 X}$$

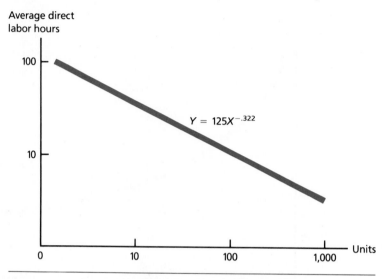

EXHIBIT 27-5

Average Labor Hours Required for X Units, Log Scale

value of a, which is subject to considerable uncertainty since it relates to only a single unit. One possibility is to solve equation (2) simultaneously for two different output levels, (x_1 and x_2).[5] Alternatively, the available data may be plotted on log-log paper, and estimates may be made of the constants a and b.

Assuming data are available for cumulative output and direct labor hours, the data can be plotted on log-log paper, where both axes are in logs. The first step is to plot cumulative output using the horizontal axis and the average number of labor hours using the vertical axis. The final step is to visually fit a straight line to the data and extend it to the left until it crosses the vertical axis. A straight edge may be used. The value on the vertical axis for X equal to one is the estimate of a in equation (2). The value of b in equation (2) is the ratio of the difference in the logs of the vertical rise in the line to the related horizontal change. Using the data in Exhibit 27-3 to illustrate:

- Step 1. Plot the points for X and Y (columns 1 and 2) on a log-log graph as in Exhibit 27-6 (log-log scale).

- Step 2. The value of a is approximated by the value of the line at X equal to one.

5. An alternative would be to consider using groups of units — say, ten, for example — where X stands for a group of ten. Then a is estimated on ten items. Also see the Review Problem (p. 935).

EXHIBIT 27-6

Estimation of Parameters

Average direct
labor hours (Y)

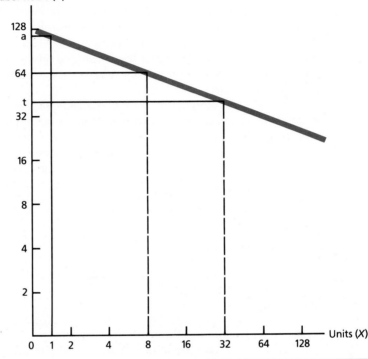

■ Step 3. The value of *b* is approximated by the slope of the line in logs. In this case:

$$\frac{\log t - \log 64}{\log 32 - \log 8}$$

If *t* is estimated to be about 41 then:

$$\frac{1.6128 - 1.8062}{1.5051 - .9031} = -.32$$

This is in close agreement with the example value of *b* calculated earlier.

Usually, this simple construction process is adequate. An alternative and more sophisticated procedure would be to fit a regression equation to the data. Nearly all computer programs involve linear regression models, but both data series need to be converted to logarithms before using this statistical technique. The use of regression equations is discussed in any elementary statistics book, and its use in cost estimation was discussed in Chapter 13.

A manager is well advised to be skeptical of the applicability of the slope coefficient obtained from the data. Significant variations are common in empirical studies.[6] Research suggests that both the learning rate and the slope are directly related to the initial ratio of machine to labor input hours. Where this ratio is three machine hours to one labor hour, the learning rate tends to be near 90 percent. When the ratio is one to one, the learning rate is around 85 percent, and when it is one to three, the rate is about 80 percent. The decline in these figures is intuitively appealing, since as the relative amount of labor in an activity increases, the opportunities for learning can be expected to increase.

An extended example may help understanding of this point. The Gemini Company acts as a subcontractor for parts used in the space program. The company has been requested to bid on a contract for 750 units required in the assembly of the reentry mechanism of a new space vehicle. Thus, the firm is interested in the expected cost of the contract. The company had recently produced 250 of the items at the following costs, as indicated by the accounting records.

Direct materials	$10,000
Direct labor (5,000 hours @ $5)	25,000
Tooling (can be reused)	3,000
Variable overhead	5,000
Fixed overhead (allocated on the basis of one-quarter of direct labor costs)	6,250
Total cost	$49,250

The company has a partial record of the total time required to produce the 250 units. The data are: first unit, 120 hours; 15 units, 735 hours; 100 units, 2,724 hours; and 250 units, 5,000 hours. The learning effect applies to the direct labor time and perhaps to the variable overhead cost if it is a direct function of the direct labor time. The model of learning suggested by equation (1) can be used with b determined by solving equation (2). The value of Y is 20, since $X = 250$, the total hours are 5,000, and $a = 120$. Using equation (2),

$$b = \frac{\log 20 - \log 120}{\log 250}$$

$$= -.325$$

The value of b is based on partial and probably imperfect data. Assume, from this analysis and other information the manager has about the labor intensity of the process, that an 80 percent learning rate is deemed appropriate. (Recall that the b value for an 80 percent learning rate is $-.322$.) With these data the manager may use equation (3) to estimate the total direct labor hours required for the additional 750

6. See N. Baloff, "The Learning Curve—Some Controversial Issues," *Journal of Industrial Economics* (July 1966): 275–82.

units by first finding the labor hours required for the entire output to date, 1,000 units.

$$XY = aX^{b+1} = 120(1000)^{.678} \approx 12,800$$

The additional hours required for 750 units are $12,800 - 5,000 = 7,800$ hours.

Alternatively, the manager may reason as follows. Given an 80 percent learning rate for the time required for the average unit, a doubling of the quantity produced results in a 20 percent reduction in the average time per unit. Given an average time of $5,000/250 = 20$ hours for 250 units, the average time for 500 units is $.8(20)$ or sixteen hours, and the average time for 1,000 units is $.8(16)$ or 12.8 hours. The total time required for the 750 unit contract would be $1,000(12.8)$ or 12,800 hours, less the 5,000 hours put in on the initial 250 units, which yields a requirement of 7,800 additional hours. Assuming the hourly wage rate remains constant, variable overhead remains at 20 percent of direct labor, and other costs change proportionally, the incremental cost of the new contract is given in Exhibit 27-7:

EXHIBIT 27-7

New Contract Incremental Cost

Direct materials	$30,000
Direct labor (7,800 hours @ $5)	39,000
Tooling	0
Variable overhead	7,800
Total incremental cost	$76,800

The firm may still choose to incorporate a fixed-overhead element, but the anticipated incremental cost of the 750-unit order is $76,800. This is less than twice the accounting cost of the initial 250 units, although the new contract is three times as large.

Accumulating Production Data by Production Lot

Production data are often accumulated on a lot-by-lot basis rather than for specific items. The data in Exhibit 27-8 provide an example where each lot includes twenty units.

The data are consistent with a learning curve characterized by an 80 percent learning rate. The average direct labor hours decline by a constant 80 percent as cumulative output doubles. Thus, the equation $Y = aX^b$ (or here $Y = 100X^{-.322}$) applies, where X now represents the lot of twenty units to which the Y applies. Y is the average time per unit in the lot. For example, setting X equal to 4 yields an average direct labor time of 64 hours for each unit in the fourth lot of 20 items. These are items 61 through 80, inclusive, in the firm's cumulative production.

Direct labor hours are computed first. The relationship between direct labor hours and cost is then used to establish dollar values. Although it would be possible to

---

EXHIBIT 27-8

Output and Direct Labor Hours for Twenty-Unit Lots

Number of Lots	Cumulative Units	Cumulative Direct Labor Hours per Lot	Average Direct Labor Hours per Lot	Average Direct Labor Hours per Unit
1	20	2,000	2,000	100.00
2	40	3,200	1,600	80.00
4	80	5,120	1,280	64.00
8	160	8,192	1,024	51.20
16	320	13,107	819	40.96

express the learning curve directly in terms of cost, this is not done for two reasons. First, it hides the basic nature of the relationship between learning and production time. Second, and of more practical concern, not all costs change proportionally with direct labor hours. Those costs that change, but do not change proportionally, would lead to inaccurate estimates of final unit costs.

A Related Model of Learning

A related model of learning, known as the incremental model, is also based on equation (1). All of the variables have the same interpretation except Y. In the incremental model Y is defined as the number of direct labor hours required to produce the X-th unit.

Thus if the learning rate is .80 as before and the first unit takes 125 direct labor hours, then the second unit requires 100 direct labor hours yielding a total of 225 direct labor hours for both units. This is in contrast to the average model, which required 2(.8)(125) or 200 direct labor hours for two units. Similarly, the fourth unit would require eighty direct labor hours under the incremental model whereas eighty direct labor hours would be the average time for four units under the average model.

Learning is assumed to take place slower under the incremental model since the total time required for a given number of units is less than under the average model. However, both models give similar results for large production quantities.

The incremental model has gained a substantial following over the last quarter century, for several reasons. First, it is easier for operating personnel to deal with the time for the next unit than the average time for all units produced to date. Further, the data are more readily available. Finally, the average model tends to hide productivity changes that influence the direct labor hours required.[7]

---

7. See S. Liao, "The Learning Curve: Wright's Model vs. Crawford's Model," *Issues in Accounting Education* (Fall 1988): 302–15.

Use of Learning Curves in Decision Making: An Example

One actual example of applying learning curves to the estimation of costs for decision making involves an aircraft company.[8] The company was faced with a cutback in orders resulting from a stretch-out procurement program by the air force. The company's reaction was to consider cancelling various subcontracts and doing this work in its own plant. One such subcontract involved 372 landing-flap assemblies. However, before cancelling the subcontract, the aircraft company wished to consider the costs of the two alternatives.

The aircraft company had already produced 165 similar assemblies, the last of which took 445 hours. This put the company well along its learning curve. Based on the company's learning curve, a total labor input of 111,000 hours for the 372 additional units was projected. In contrast, the subcontractor was just getting started on its learning curve and, therefore as a more efficient producer, would be able to produce the one hundred sixty-fifth assembly with fewer hours than the aircraft company needed for that assembly. Nevertheless, since at the decision time the subcontractor was higher on its learning curve, the total hours required to produce the 372 assemblies by the subcontractor was predicted to be more than would be required by the aircraft company. The aircraft company elected to cancel the subcontract and take advantage of the savings, which amounted to over $300,000.

Difficulties in Obtaining Data

Perhaps the most serious limitation in using learning curves is in obtaining valid data on which to base their computation. For example, suppose that a firm decreases the planned labor input for a product by increasing the use of purchased parts. The result may be a decline in the actual labor used per unit, but it would not be due to learning. There is a shift of the required labor input to the supplier. Indeed, the effect of ignoring such facts may simultaneously give an apparently declining learning curve coupled with an increasing unit cost. A given learning curve relates to one manufacturing process, and if the process is changed, the learning curve may no longer apply.

The learning-curve phenomenon measures only direct labor. Thus, if more time is spent in, say, designing the product, there may again be an apparent increase in learning, as reflected by the curve, without a decline in total cost. The direct labor is merely shifted to indirect labor or overhead. A similar effect occurs if supervisory labor or new equipment replaces direct labor.

A decline in the labor input can also occur when there are changes in the materials used. Better materials can reduce labor input without necessarily lowering cost. A similar result can be obtained if there is a change in the labor mix. Better but more expensive labor can cause a learning effect, as measured using direct labor hours per unit, unmatched by a reduction in average cost.

These factors can work in the opposite direction as well. For example, a tight labor market may lead to poorer labor quality. The effect of both new and less skilled labor diminishes the learning effect, yet average cost could decline if wages are sufficiently low. Changes in labor mix, overhead, and the associated factors of production, then, can considerably confound the learning-curve effect.

8. The example is adapted from one in an article by F. J. Andress, "The Learning Curve as a Production Tool," *Harvard Business Review* (January–February 1954): 87–97.

Learning-Curve Applications

The applicability of learning curves is more important in cases where the direct labor input in an activity is large and the activity is complex. Since the learning curve is steepest at its start, and since new projects cause recycling of labor, the learning effect is also more pronounced where the rate of product or process innovation is high. Moreover, if learning is expected and planned for, greater use of this phenomenon can be made. If learning is encouraged and expected, a climate may be created where it can and will occur.[9]

Learning may not always occur. The change in capabilities required may be too drastic for worker adaptability. Output may accelerate too quickly, leading to inefficiencies that overcome learning. This seems to have been the case for Lockheed in its Tri Star program. In 1980 and 1981, orders jumped to 25 a year, an eightfold increase over the recent past. Not only was Lockheed forced to pay substantive premiums to suppliers and subcontractors to meet schedules, but the additional labor force required "wrecked havoc with Tri Star's learning curve, dramatically boosting the workhours required to build each airplane."[10]

Conditions conducive to learning are found in many industries, including electronics, home appliance, construction, shipbuilding, and machine shop areas.[11] Moreover even in industries that are capital intensive, such as petroleum refining, the learning curve is of value although to a lesser degree.[12] This can be attributed to the removal of bottlenecks, relaxing preset safety margins, and technological resourcefulness in general.

This extension of the learning concept was carried one step further by the Boston Consulting Group.[13] The concept, now dubbed the **experience curve,** was applied to overall unit costs, not just labor-related costs. A number of firms, including The Norton Company, General Instrument, Texas Instruments, and B. F. Goodrich, have used the experience curve as a major element in formulating business strategy. Experience becomes the combined effect of learning, specialization, scale of operations, and the investment base of the organization. However, cost reductions are enhanced by good management. The learning curve is no substitute for execution.

The views of Bruce Henderson, founder of the Boston Consulting Group, regarding the experience curve were reported in a *Business Week* article.[14]

---

9. An interesting example is supplied by Conway and Schultz, who show that when new workers were put on a task already far down its learning curve, the fresh approach brought by the new group produced a new learning curve. R. W. Conway and A. Schultz, "The Manufacturing Process Function," *Journal of Industrial Engineering* (January–February 1959): 48.

10. See "The Tri Star's Trail of Red Ink," *Business Week* (July 28, 1980): p. 88.

11. Andress, op. cit., pp. 95–97.

12. W. B. Hirschmann, "Profit from the Learning Curve," *Harvard Business Review* (January–February 1964): 125–39.

13. See "The Decline of the Experience Curve," *Fortune* (October 5, 1981): 139–46.

14. "Selling Business a Theory of Economics," *Business Week* (September 8, 1973): 85–90.

<table>
<tr><td>

Value of the Experience Curve

</td><td>

According to Henderson, as reported by *Business Week*, experience curves can be used to calculate precisely the value of an increase in market share of a product because cost behavior can be accurately predicted as production volume increases. Then the company's management can simply weigh the benefit of the increased market share against the cost of the investment necessary to achieve it, along with the predicted reactions of competitors.

</td></tr>
</table>

The experience of B. F. Goodrich Company was reported by an article in *Fortune* magazine.[15]

<table>
<tr><td>

B. F. Goodrich Company

</td><td>

According to the president of B. F. Goodrich, as reported by *Fortune*, the experience curve showed the company's management some things about the tire business that they hadn't realized. The company used what it learned to cut production, realizing that it was not necessary to sell tires to car manufacturers to get enough experience on a tire model to drive down costs. Sufficient production volume to move out on the experience curve could be obtained just by making tires for the more lucrative replacement market.

</td></tr>
</table>

Recently the application of the learning curve (or experience curve) concept has been advocated to determine the productivity benefits obtained from computer-integrated manufacturing (CIM) systems.[16] In this case productivity benefits are expected across the system rather than from a single piece of equipment. Since learning takes place in the absence of CIM, the expectation is that implementing a CIM system increases learning and hence the slope of the learning curve.

Pricing

To the extent that learning curves lead to improved cost predictions, they may be employed in pricing decisions. In some cases involving competitive bidding on government contracts, consideration of learning-curve effects is required. The question is not whether learning curves will be used, but what the appropriate parameters are. An extension of the use of learning-curve data in pricing occurs when buying from a supplier. Sometimes a supplier experiences high initial outlays resulting in part from the fact that the supplier is at the early stage of its learning curve relative to the job. A purchasing firm might be willing initially to pay a higher price if the supplier agrees to

15. "The Decline of the Experience Curve," op. cit., p. 144.
16. See M. Baudin, "Experience Curve Theory: A Technique for Quantifying CIM Benefits," *CIM Review* (Summer 1985): 51–58.

subsequently lower the price per unit.[17] A firm might also consider a strategy of pricing its product lower to achieve market penetration and market share. Increased market share implies larger production runs and hence greater opportunities for learning. The decreased time required for a given cumulative output can lead to lower unit costs and greater profits.

As a caution, however, managers must be wary of changes in the growth rate of an industry that can have implications for the relevance of the experience curve. An article in *Fortune* magazine reported the views of Alan Zakon, who at the time headed the Boston Consulting Group.[18] Zakon used the domestic beer industry to make his point.

Experience Curve in the Domestic Beer Industry

In a low-growth market, the experience curve loses some of its relevance. In the old days of beer production, according to Zakon (as reported by *Fortune*), the industry used very little advertising and brewers were characterized by large differences in size and scale. Over time, the typical plant became larger and its larger production drove down costs. Smaller breweries were driven out of business by high costs, and this left only large breweries. For these companies, costs were already as low as they could go. Then massive advertising was introduced as a way of competing through product differentiation. This changed the focus from cost reduction to marketing, and reduced the importance of the experience curve.

Work Scheduling

Learning curves increase a firm's ability to predict its required labor input and make it possible to forecast labor needs. They also allow production and delivery schedules to be developed with greater accuracy, which, in turn, permit the firm to do a better job scheduling maintenance, quality control, material purchasing, and promotion. Better forecasting and scheduling result in lower costs through better cost control and improved customer relations. Since the effect of learning is most dramatic in reducing incremental costs during start-up periods, the maximum value from using the technique occurs during this time. With a mature production process, further gains in productivity through learning will be minimal unless substantive changes occur in the mode of operations.

Capital Budgeting

The learning effect suggests that unit costs are likely to begin high and taper off. This contrasts with the steady-state, constant unit cost usually assumed in capital-budgeting analyses. Furthermore, the learning curve permits improved estimates of production levels that can be attained and thus has implications for cash flows. These

---

17. See Andress, op. cit., pp. 94–95, for an example.
18. "The Decline of the Experience Curve," op. cit., p. 146.

modifications can be particularly important where the project start-up period is large relative to the life of the project. (Capital budgeting is considered in detail in Chapters 19 and 20.)

Motivation

Costs are often controlled using standards and variances from standards. If these standards are set without regard to the learning phenomenon, meaningless unfavorable variances may occur initially, negatively affecting motivation. Performance reports that show large unfavorable variances that cannot be improved by the manager can erode aspiration and performance levels. Unrealistic standards may even lead to rejection of the standard-setting process, while poorly set standards might lead to rejection of the learning-curve phenomenon and its attendant cost savings.

Sometimes this problem is resolved by recognizing the learning effect through arbitrary adjustments in standards or by making no evaluations until the process "settles down." It would be an improvement if the learning effect could be incorporated directly in standards. Even such decisions as establishing piecework incentive rates should be made considering the learning effect.

The same problem arises when the investigation of an out-of-control cost process leads to corrective action. The time over which the corrective action takes effect often covers several cost-reporting periods. During this period, costs may even rise for awhile before the learning effect takes hold. Simultaneously, management is keeping close tabs on the reaction of costs to new procedures. Hence, it is necessary for management to be aware of the influence of learning during this period and to use standards that consider it.[19]

A similar effect is apparent in evaluating divisional performance. Large activities in their early phases experience relatively higher costs and lower output than at later stages. This should be considered when a division manager's performance is evaluated.

Overtime Decisions

Hiring more workers is not likely to be an easily reversible decision. Once locked into the cost structure, this cost may be difficult to change in the short run. Thus, if an organization is near the beginning of its learning curve, it may prefer to use overtime rather than hire additional workers who will not be needed later.

External Financial Reporting

Learning influences profits through its effects on cost and output. When these effects are important, some attention should be given to them on the firm's annual report. For example, the *Wall Street Journal*, reporting on the consolidation of all subsidiaries by the Phillips Petroleum Company in which it held over a 50 percent interest, stated that "the effect of this [consolidation] will be to reduce earnings from what they would be without such consolidation, because most of the companies being

---

19. The use of learning curves in standard-cost variance analysis is discussed by D. Harvey and S. Soliman, "Standard Cost Variance Analysis in a Learning Environment," *Accounting and Business Research* (Summer 1983): 181–89.

consolidated are ones that are under construction or in the start-up stage, and which therefore are expected to show losses this year."[20]

Assume a situation in which early losses were expected when the decision to undertake these start-ups was made. If financial reports are to be an aid in evaluation and are to be consistent with decision making, some attempt should be made to separate nonrecoverable losses from costs that are incurred as part of the learning process. Where there is reason to believe that learning will take place, an argument can be made for capitalizing some or all of a firm's early losses as assets rather than mislead investors into believing that the financial situation is unfavorable. Admittedly, this procedure could be misused by managers wanting to defer losses that are likely to be nonrecoverable. Such an approach, however, is contrary to present generally accepted accounting principles.

Illustration of Learning-Curve Use in the Aircraft Industry

The Boeing Company is a large aircraft manufacturer. Among its products are the 747 wide-bodied commercial jetliner, the 727 commercial jetliner, and the 707 commercial jet transport. The information presented in this section describes the broad use of learning-curve concepts in Boeing's development of new aircraft.

Aircraft unit costs decrease with each unit manufactured, a phenomenon that Boeing refers to as the **improvement curve**. Production improvement curves at Boeing include specific manufacturing costs that are identifiable on a unit-by-unit basis. Such costs include fabrication (metal and machine operations performed in the manufacture of detailed parts), minor assembly (operations involved in the manufacture of assemblies for assignment to a specific airplane), and major assembly (operations required for the assembly of major body sections and the installation and check-out of nonstructural equipment and systems).

A regression analysis of these unit-identifiable costs yields an improvement curve slope identifying the theoretical cost for the first unit and the slope percentage. The improvement curve is shaped by a number of determinants, such as:

- The degree of completeness and accuracy of the engineering design,

- The extent of engineering changes,

- Type of tooling to be built,

- Whether the program was preceded by prototype production,

- Key management decisions relative to skill allocations, space and equipment requirements, and the establishment of adequate schedules and flow times.

20. Reported in N. Baloff and J. N. Kennelly, "Accounting Implications of Product and Process Start-ups," *Journal of Accounting Research* (Autumn 1967): 142.

All these factors affect the shape of the aircraft improvement curve, but the beginning of each program is where the largest amount of disruption and engineering change activity occurs. As early as possible, fabrication lot sizes are established to take advantage of set-up and run efficiencies. If a large amount of engineering change activity occurs, scrap and rework costs increase. These factors result in shortages affecting the attainment of established schedules and flow times, and result in a high degree of out-of-sequence work and additional costs. It is in the preliminary design phase that engineers and manufacturing personnel working together can have the greatest impact in (1) reducing costs and (2) minimizing the engineering change activity at the front end of the program by accomplishing an effective design-to-cost effort.

Studies indicate that large amounts of rework occur during final assembly, and prior to aircraft delivery, that are directly related to engineering design changes. Analysis of this data indicates that a reduction in change activity can result in significant reductions in production hours resulting in lower unit costs. Other perturbations to the improvement curve also affect the shape of the curve, but they are not as sensitive to improvement by management attention. These are identified as new model and customer introductions, major change proposals adding or deleting major equipment, transferring of work from one division to another, and work force strikes.

Before spending money on a new aircraft production program, Boeing must have accurate estimates of its ability to produce a quality product on schedule at a competitive price. The improvement curve is used to assist management obtain the answers to many manufacturing problems when estimating production costs, manpower requirements, space allocations, and equipment utilization. The accuracy of the improvement curve has been established to the point where Boeing uses it in the following managerial processes:

- Establishing budgets,

- Estimating hardware costs,

- Forecasting manpower requirements,

- Scheduling,

- Purchasing,

- Pricing.

Boeing also uses the curve to chart total production and various elements of production, such as fabrication, subassembly, and major assembly work. Each element of production portrays unique characteristics that result in individual improvement curves.

The production learning curve can be used to estimate the total production costs for a given number of units for a new aircraft program. Detailed estimates for the various production elements of cost are prepared for the first aircraft, then improvement curve history for similar aircraft programs is analyzed to select the curve most comparable to the hardware and program conditions anticipated for the new program. The improvement curve selected is then applied by extending the first new

*Boeing's Improvement Curve for
the KC-135 Jet Tanker*   **BOEING**

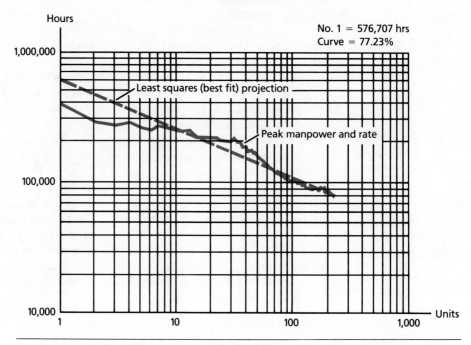

BOEING KC-135 UNIT HOURS
Fabrication + Minor Assembly + Major Assembly,
Units 1–215

aircrafts' cost down the curve slope for the total number of aircraft estimated for the new program. The total production cost is calculated under the curve by multiplying the cost of the first aircraft value by the cumulative curve slope value for the number of units to be estimated.

The improvement curve is an important tool for Boeing management in the aircraft resource decision-making process. Exhibit 27-9 displays the improvement curve developed by Boeing for its KC-135 jet tanker aircraft, a version of the Boeing 707.

Summary

The learning curve concept has many applications. It should be used in cost control, labor requirement planning, and pricing. The true nature of the learning curve associated with a new product or process will never be known for certain a priori. However, a reasonable assumption of its shape is better than the implicit assumption of no learning at all.

Key Terms to Review

experience curve, p. 928   learning-curve model,   learning rate, p. 918
improvement curve,   p. 918
p. 933

Review Problem

LEARNING CURVES

Suppose that the following facts are known:

Cumulative Units	Total Direct Labor Time
4	450 hrs
16	1,012.5 hrs

Assuming a constant learning rate applies, estimate that rate, and estimate the total direct labor time for forty-eight additional units. The review problem is designed to illustrate the relationships in the learning-curve model.

Solution to the Review Problem

This problem can be solved most easily by using the average direct labor times:

For 4 units $450 \div 4 = 112.5$
For 16 units $1012.5 \div 16 = 63.281$

Now, using equation (5):

$ar^2 = 112.5$ and

$ar^4 = 63.281$

Dividing,

$ar^4 \div ar^2 = r^2 = .5625$. Hence $r = .75$.

This implies a constant percentage reduction of .25 and a learning rate of $1 - .25 = .75$, since $.75^2 = .5625$.

Sixteen units plus forty-eight more units gives sixty-four total units. For sixty-four units, we need ar^6. Hence

$$ar^6 = ar^4(r^2) = 63.281(.5625) = 35.59556$$

This is the average time for sixty-four units. The total time for sixty-four units is $64(35.59556) = 2,278$ hrs. Hence the time for forty-eight more units is the total time for sixty-four units minus the total time for sixteen units.

Total time for 64 units	2,278.0 hrs
Total time for 16 units	1,012.5
Time for additional 48 units	1,265.5 hrs

There are other ways to solve the problem.

Suggested Readings

Alchian, A. "Costs and Outputs." In *The Allocation of Economic Resources: Essays in Honor of B. F. Haley*, edited by M. Abramovitz. Stanford, Calif.: Stanford University Press, 1959.

Andress, F. "The Learning Curve as a Production Tool." *Harvard Business Review* (January–February 1954): 87–97.

Baloff, N. "The Learning Curve — Some Controversial Issues." *Journal of Industrial Economics* (July 1966): 275–82.

Baloff, N., and J. Kennelly. "Accounting Implications of Product and Process Start-ups." *Journal of Accounting Research* (Autumn 1967): 142.

Baudin, M. "Experience Curve Theory: A Technique for Quantifying CIM Benefits." *CIM Review* (Summer 1985): 51–58.

Belkaoui, A. *The Learning Curve: A Management Accounting Tool.* Westport, Conn.: Quorum Books, 1986.

Chen, J., and R. Manes. "Distinguishing the Two Forms of the Constant Percentage Learning Curve Model." *Contemporary Accounting Research* (Spring 1985): 242–52.

Conway, R., and A. Schultz. "The Manufacturing Process Function." *Journal of Industrial Engineering* (January–February 1959): 39–53.

Harvey, D., and S. Soliman. "Standard Cost Variance Analysis in a Learning Environment." *Accounting and Business Research* (Summer 1983): 181–89.

Hirschmann, W. "Profit from the Learning Curve." *Harvard Business Review* (January–February 1964): 125–39.

Hirshleifer, J. "The Firm's Cost Function: A Successful Reconstruction?" *Journal of Business* (July 1962): 235–55.

Liao, S. "The Learning Curve: Wright's Model vs. Crawford's Model." *Issues in Accounting Education* (Fall 1988): 302–15.

Requero, M. *An Economic Study of the Airframe Industry.* Wright-Patterson Air Force Base, Ohio: Department of the Air Force, October 1957.

Wright, T. "Factor Affecting the Cost of Airplanes." *Journal of Aeronautical Science* (February 1936): 122–28.

Review Questions

27-1 Modify the following statement so that it is more accurate: "Marginal costs will tend to increase as more units are produced."

27-2 What conditions may cause the average variable cost to decline as

    a. Output per unit of time increases?

    b. Cumulative output increases?

27-3 Accept as a premise that the average labor hours required per unit is reduced 20 percent as the quantity produced doubles. Is it correct to say that "This implies a situation where the second unit requires about 80 percent as much direct labor as the first; the tenth 80 percent as much as the fifth, and so on?"

27-4 If an 80 percent learning model is assumed to apply and labor costs $5 per hour, how much should it cost in direct labor to produce 100 units if the first unit takes eighty hours?

27-5 In plotting learning-curve data, why is log-log paper particularly useful?

27-6 "Learning curves are relatively easy to estimate; however, their influence tends to be of very marginal value." Evaluate this statement.

27-7 Suggest five decisions for which the learning effect may be important.

27-8 What is the most significant feature about the learning curve that makes it useful?

27-9 Discuss how learning-curve techniques may be used in setting standards for control.

27-10 What costs might one expect to be associated with a particular learning curve?

27-11 Does an 80 percent learning curve denote a higher rate of improvement than a 70 percent curve? Explain. Which curve has the more negative slope? (Assume that the first unit would be produced in the same amount of labor using either curve.)

27-12 Draw a graph of an 80 percent learning curve that reaches a steady-state (that is, no more learning takes place) after thirty-two units have been produced. (Assume that the first unit requires 100 direct labor hours.) Use arithmetic scales.

Exercises 27-13 **Balancing Costs** The Sharp Company subcontracts some aircraft parts to the Doit Company because of the greater familiarity of the latter with the task. The manager of Sharp notes that Doit has an 85 percent learning curve, whereas Sharp has an 80 percent curve. However, Doit is far down the curve. Sharp would start at the top of its own curve if it made the part and hence would incur large initial costs. But since it would not need to pay freight or profit to Doit, the manager believes that Sharp, at least from a learning-curve viewpoint, should not subcontract. Do you agree? Why?

27-14 **Adding New Products** A firm plans to begin production of a new desk-top fan and several small electric drills; all are new items for the firm. One manager suggests producing an electric pencil sharpener, which also would be a new item for them. Many factors need to be considered in this example, but can you see any argument from a learning-curve standpoint for adding the electric pencil sharpener?

27-15 **Implications of the Learning Curve in Pricing Decisions** One possible implication of the learning curve is that a firm ought to price low in an attempt to maximize market-share. This would lead in turn to a faster slide down the learning curve and the domination of the market as the low-cost producer.

Do you see any difficulties with this strategy?

27-16 **Additional Costs** The Boxer Company makes parts for ship navigation systems. It has previously made about 10,000 parts exactly like the type ordered by the government for a new type of submarine. A new government order calls for 10,000 parts. The company's records yield the following cost data for the 10,000 parts made to date:

Direct materials	$ 1,000,000
Direct labor (800,000 hours at $8/hr)	6,400,000
Set-up costs (no labor)	60,000
Variable overhead ($4/DLH)	3,200,000
Fixed overhead (allocated at $1/DLH)	800,000
Total costs	$11,460,000

Assuming an 80 percent learning rate on the average time required as production doubles and no change in the unit-labor costs per hour, estimate the company's additional costs from accepting the order.

Problems

27-17 Using Learning Curves   Assume a learning rate of 80 percent — that is, the average number of labor hours required per unit is reduced 20 percent as the quantity produced doubles.

REQUIRED:

    a. If the first 100 units require 100 hours, how many total hours will be required to produce 200 units? How many additional hours are required for the second 100 units?

    b. Suppose the firm has an opportunity to bid on a contract that will raise its total output from 200 to 500 units. How many labor hours will be involved?

27-18 Computing Costs   Use the following costs:

    Direct labor $5 per hour

    Other variable manufacturing costs $4 per direct labor hour

and assume an 80 percent learning curve is applicable.

REQUIRED:

Compute the labor and labor-related costs associated with (assume the first unit produced required 100 labor hours) the following:

    a. The production of three additional units after the first unit has been completed;

    b. The production of eight units after the eighth unit has been completed.

27-19 Price Decisions   Easy Run Motors, Inc., produces electric motors, which it sells to manufacturers of household appliances. The company is currently producing 150 units of a model that a single firm is purchasing for $35 per unit. Variable production costs associated with the 150 units are expected to total $3,000. The firm that is purchasing the 150 units has expressed an interest in contracting for an additional 450 units if the selling price per unit is reduced to $22 per motor.

REQUIRED:

Assuming that all variable production costs fluctuate with labor hours and that a 90 percent learning curve is applicable, should Easy Run lower the price? (Assume that all other variable costs and expenses associated with the product would total $5 per unit.) Learning applies to the average time per unit.

27-20 **Using Learning Curves to Derive Bids**   Manual Machine Company has received an invitation to submit a bid for the production of 800 private-label vacuum cleaners. The company knows that the competition for this contract will be keen, and it wants to find the minimum price it can charge for the 800 units. The planning department of the company has estimated the costs of producing the first 100 units as follows:

Direct labor 400 hours @ $5	$2,000
Direct materials 100 units @ $20 per unit[a]	2,000
Other variable manufacturing costs @ $4 per direct labor hour[b]	1,600
Nonvariable manufacturing costs	4,000
Set-up costs	5,000

[a] Each additional 100 units of direct material can be purchased at a 10 percent discount from the previous 100 until the minimum cost per unit reaches $14.58.

[b] Varies with direct labor.

The nonvariable manufacturing costs and the set-up costs are not expected to change as the units produced are increased from 100 to 800, and selling and administrative expenses associated with the product are negligible.

REQUIRED:

Assuming that a 90 percent learning curve is applicable to average direct labor per unit, what is the lowest price per unit Manual Machine could offer?

27-21 **Total Costs**   Estimate the total cost (outlay) to produce an order for 250 parts given the following information on 750 identical parts that have just been finished. Note: Indicate the learning rate you used and show how you obtained it. You may assume some noise in the data and hence you may use a rounded rate.

TOTAL COST 750 UNITS

Material cost[a] @ $100 per unit (average)	$ 75,000
Direct labor (53,250 hours @ $4)	213,000
Variable overhead[b] @ 2 per direct labor hour	106,500
Set-up costs (required for every 250 units)[c]	75,000
Tooling costs (required for every 500 units)[c]	46,000
Fixed overhead (allocated)	173,000
Total	$688,500

Total time for the first 125 units	15,630 hrs
Total time for the first 250 units	24,985 hrs
Total time for the first 500 units	40,082 hrs

[a] It is estimated that material costs will decline by 10 percent on a unit basis for future units made.

[b] Based on, and variable with, direct labor hours.

[c] No learning assumed. Same level expected.

27-22 **Changes in the Learning Curve**   Suppose that prior to the production of a certain item an 80 percent learning curve is believed to apply to the average labor hours involved in the process with the first unit to be produced estimated at 100 direct labor hours.

REQUIRED:

Indicate how the following events would tend to alter the estimate of the learning curve. Specifically, would the following events result in (a) a shift in the estimated learning curve with no change in the shape of the curve; (b) a change in the shape of the estimated learning curve; or (c) no change? (Treat each event independently of all previous events.)

a. The estimated number of direct labor hours required for the first unit is revised from 100 to 150.

b. The estimated learning rate is changed from 80 to 90 percent.

c. The depreciation that will be applied to the manufacturing equipment used in the process during the production period is increased by 10 percent.

d. The estimate of the hourly wage for direct laborers is increased from $5.00 to $5.25.

e. A new machine is purchased that will replace ten direct laborers. This new machine was not considered in estimating the 80 percent learning curve.

27-23 **Determining Prices**   The GIVRAC Manufacturing Company produces the fire control devices used in nuclear submarines. The first thirty assemblies resulted in the following costs:

	(in $000)
Materials	$ 157
Direct labor (30,000 hrs)	450
Variable overhead	360
Fixed overhead (allocated)	250
Total costs	$1,217

The U.S. Navy has opened bidding for another ninety assemblies. Bob Nixon, president of GIVRAC, wants to ensure a contribution margin of 25 percent on the bid if successful.

REQUIRED:

What price should Nixon quote the U.S. Navy if he believes an 85 percent learning rate is appropriate? What assumptions did you make in your analysis?

27-24 **Labor Hours Based on Production Quantity**   The Lee Regulator Clock Company produces clocks for sale by Limited Editions. They typically produce their clocks in runs of 100 for each 1,000 limited edition. From previous experience the firm expects a 30 percent reduction in average time per unit as production doubles. For the present model, the first 100 clocks will require 3,800 direct labor hours.

REQUIRED:

Prepare a schedule that provides the expected average and total direct labor hours for 200, 400, 800, and 1000 units. What would this schedule be used for by Lee?

27-25 **Assessing Costs** McLaren Inc. makes sports-car frames for a special series of automobiles. Their records indicate that the first 100 assemblies required 57,000 direct labor hours, while for the entire 300 assemblies produced to date, 120,000 direct labor hours were needed. Standard variable costs are estimated at $28.50 per direct labor hour. The firm is now costing an order for a second 300-unit shipment.

REQUIRED:

Estimate the standard variable cost associated with the new order. How much less was it than the cost of the initial 300 units? If the new order was for 500 units instead of being for 300 units, how would the cost be found?

28

Additional Topics in Cost-Variance Investigation

LEARNING OBJECTIVES

After studying this chapter, you should be able to:

1 Describe the costs and benefits of investigating a cost variance.

2 List possible causes of cost variances.

3 Construct a variance-investigation control chart.

4 Formulate and solve a simple decision-theoretic variance-investigation model and describe its limitations and assumptions.

5 Explain the implications of variance investigation in an agency framework.

6 Use ex post variance analysis to analyze performance and understand its potential advantages.

*T*his chapter addresses two additional topics in variance analysis not covered earlier in the text. The first topic concerns the decision to investigate cost variances. The second topic is a different approach to variance analysis that explicitly incorporates the decision effects of changes in parameters.

Cost-Variance Investigation

A common report confronting managers is the periodic performance report. Such reports typically provide substantial detail concerning the manager's budget and deviations from the budget. These deviations are called *variances*. Managers are expected to use this variance information both to improve performance and explain substantive deviations to their superiors. Improved future performance can result from information contained in either positive or negative variations from the standards given by the budget's figures. A performance report, however, will typically present many separate variances. The manager must select from these which ones to investigate.

Variances from budget standards can occur for many reasons and hence require different responses. They can be divided into (1) those that occur before operations begin and the cost is incurred, called ex ante reasons; (2) those that occur after operations begin and while or after the cost is incurred, called ex post reasons; and (3) random deviations:

1. Ex ante reasons

    a. Prediction or forecast errors

    b. Technological and parameter errors in establishing the decision model and the inputs to the model

2. Ex post reasons

    a. Errors in implementation

    b. Errors in measuring and properly recording results

3. Random deviations from budget standards

Prediction or forecast errors — say, in the purchase price of an input, in a wage-rate estimate or in the number of hours needed to produce a unit of product — can lead to inappropriate standards and hence to cost variances. Improving the manager's knowledge of the input-factor markets and the technical requirements of better forecasting methods can, in turn, reduce these variances. Alternatively, cost variances may occur from either omitting important technological aspects of the current operating process or misestimation of the parameter input values to the decision model used to control the process. Both inaccurate cost standards and failure to formulate the decision model correctly will lead to cost variances.

Even when neither of these problems arises prior to the development of the variance control system, difficulties may appear later. First, the process may not be implemented properly whether through inadequate supervision, a lack of motivation, or changes in the quality, timing, or level of inputs to the process. Second, errors in the accounting measurement of the results also can cause cost variances. These accounting errors include mistakes as well as the misclassification in the accounts of properly measured values. Sometimes such values can also be misleading due to accounting convention. For example, when a cost variance is based on FIFO inventory methods in a period of rapidly changing prices, the cost variance will not indicate the impact of the variance in current values.

Because of the manager's inability to forecast the future and because of unplanned inefficiencies, a deviation of actual from planned results is likely. But random variability is also present and only the familiarity of the manager with the process will allow the separation of random from nonrandom deviations. Moreover, even when a manager believes a deviation to be nonrandom, it is still necessary to decide whether the deviation is one about which something can be done and for which the expected benefit from correction exceeds the expected cost of the correction.

Managers must decide where to allocate their attention among the many variances reported to them. To do so, first they will investigate those variances they believe their superiors consider important. This choice is influenced by which cost variances are reported as well as how they are reported. Since this reporting is typically done by accountants, often based on preset procedures established by both managers and accountants, the latter play an important role in determining what variances are ultimately selected for investigation.

In practice, it seems the investigation process is typically governed by rules of thumb. The manager is encouraged to investigate variances exceeding some arbitrary percentage of the budgeted value, often 10 percent. Large absolute deviations may also be highlighted and thereby become candidates for further action. In most cases, managers also have the discretion to investigate other variances should they deem it appropriate. Because managers are busy people, management by exception is the typical approach — that is, not all variances are investigated. (Managers may also delegate some or all of the analysis to the accountants.) Rules of thumb will be tempered by managerial intuition based on familiarity with the process, the expectation of finding and correcting the cause and the net benefit of doing so.

It might seem that firms would use more sophisticated techniques to choose the variances to be investigated. For example, quality-control techniques would appear to be relevant and have been around for a long time. However, these techniques have generated little enthusiasm among managers and accountants concerned with the investigation of cost variances. Perhaps the relative sophistication of quality-control methods discourages their use (despite their adoption in manufacturing settings). Fortunately, there are relatively simple techniques that, if adopted, are helpful.

EXHIBIT 28-1

Probability of an Unfavorable Cost Variance as Large or Larger than the Variance Observed

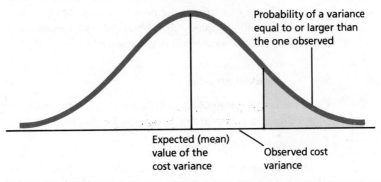

Probability of a variance equal to or larger than the one observed

Expected (mean) value of the cost variance

Observed cost variance

To the extent that expected variability and economic measures of decision significance can be effectively incorporated into cost-variance investigation procedures, the process can be improved. The issue that remains is whether these added procedures are cost-justified. This is essentially an empirical question and remains to be addressed when such techniques are tried in practice.

Before discussing these refinements, it is worth noting that performance reports affect the way individuals behave and perform. These long-run behavioral effects may be both direct and indirect with subsequent impacts on the likelihood of the organization attaining its objectives. For example, if periodic reporting increases the desire of managers to alter the reported data, audits may be required, which in turn have implications for the organization's total costs and profit.

Use of Information on Variability

The simplest modification to using an investigation rule based on a percentage of budget is to incorporate the variability that naturally occurs in the process into the decision. Suppose the expected value and variability (measured using the standard deviation) of the probability distribution for the cost variance are known when the process is in control. An in-control process is one in which deviations from expected results are due only to random causes.[1] Using the expected value of the cost variance and its standard deviation, the probability of observing an observation as unusual as the one obtained is computed using a normal probability distribution. This process is illustrated in Exhibit 28-1 for a cost variance in excess of its expected value — hence unfavorable here. This procedure compares the cost variance to the cost variance expected based on the budgeted cost level.

1. The observed variance is typically not zero, even if there are no inefficiencies, due to measurement error and to the effects of uncontrolled factors such as weather.

As an example, suppose that a plot of the relevant historical data suggests that a normal probability distribution is a reasonable approximation.[2] Suppose further that the expected cost variance is $200 and the standard deviation is $10 (both based on the relevant historical data). A cost variance of $220 is observed. What is the probability of a variance this large if the process is in control — that is, when deviations are due only to random causes? The observed cost variance is two standard deviations from the mean (or expected cost) variance:

$$z = \frac{\text{Observation} - \text{Mean}}{\text{Standard deviation}} = \frac{x - \mu}{\sigma} = \frac{220 - 200}{10} = 2$$

Using the normal probability distribution in the Appendix at the end of the book, the probability of an unfavorable cost variance this large or larger is given by

$$N_z(-z) = N_z(-2) = 0.02275$$

If it is known in advance that the variance will be unfavorable, we should double this probability. Only 50 percent (the right half) of the curve is relevant if it is known in advance that the variance will be unfavorable. The probability of such a large unfavorable variance or one larger is then .0455. If this probability is small — say, less than .05 (depending on the importance the manager attaches to the cost in question) — the particular cost variance is a candidate for investigation: the variance is considered unusual. This approach requires the manager intuitively to combine the probability of a cost variance as large or larger than the one obtained and the dollar amount involved with any knowledge about the correctability of the situation. Further, the manager must then compare the benefits from correction with alternative uses of the resources required to investigate and, if possible, correct the current situation. It is a difficult task for the manager to juggle all of these factors simultaneously. There are, then, a host of reasons a manager may decide not to investigate a particular variance:

- The process is to be changed in the future, making prior data no longer relevant.

- The cost of investigation and correction, if a correctable situation is uncovered, may exceed the expected benefits. (The selection of the probability level that triggers an investigation implicitly reflects management's cost-benefit evaluation. However, management is often not explicit in the way it considers these values.)

- There is substantial likelihood that the cause of the variance will not be found even if an investigation is made.

- Even if found, the cause may be beyond the manager's control.

2. A normal probability distribution is used under the assumption that a number of independent factors influence the observed cost variance. It is somewhat unusual for individual values to follow a normal probability law. Such behavior is not unusual for the means of large samples, but it is seldom the case for individual observations. If a normal distribution does not fit the data reasonably well, other logical choices might be tried, such as a rectangular or triangular probability distribution based on knowledge from existing data for this or similar processes.

- The manager may have better opportunities to use scarce resources.

- The manager's superior may not be perceived to be interested in this variance.

- The manager may be scheduled to switch jobs before any change can benefit the manager's future performance report. Hence, no change is made even though warranted.

- The manager may not properly evaluate the available alternatives.

Nevertheless, the above approach can signal when a process moves beyond levels that might reasonably be expected by chance and therefore merits investigation.

The approach just described is applicable when the cost is estimated by a linear-regression equation. For example, suppose that indirect labor expense y is estimated from relevant past data as a linear function of direct labor hours x, as follows:

$$y = 69.37 + .12x$$

Assume that the standard error of estimate (a measure of the uncertainty in any predicted value) is 8.72. Suppose that indirect labor expense for the period in question was $120.23 and that 300 direct labor hours were used. The expected indirect labor cost, using the above equation and 300 hours, is

$$y = 69.37 + .12(300) = \$105.37$$

Using the standard error of estimate, the actual value of $120.23 is less than two standard-deviation units $[1.70 = (120.23 - 105.37)/8.72]$ from the predicted value, and it might therefore be considered within the normal variability of the process. In other words, the observed difference is due to random fluctuations or measurement error rather than a substantive change in the process.[3] If the statistical assumptions for hypothesis testing are met, deviations less than two standard deviations occur about 95 percent of the time.

Both examples just described presume the underlying distribution for which the cost values are drawn is stable (and thus relevant to the present period's observation) and normal. Although this is unlikely to be precisely the case, the normal distribution is convenient and likely to be an adequate approximation for many cost processes. Normality is a reasonable assumption whenever the underlying probability distribution is essentially symmetrical and unimodal. When this is not the case, the procedure illustrated can lead to errors. The basic approach, however, is applicable to any probability distribution.

Control Charts

The technique described in the previous section is identical to testing whether a batch of product is within tolerance. Quality control engineers have used this idea for many years, and some accountants have suggested adopting these ideas to the cost-

---

3. Using the standard error of estimate understates the probability that a deviation is random. Hence, it is more likely to signal an out-of-control situation than probability theory would indicate. The procedure is conservative. The understatement, however, tends to be relatively minor. A normal probability distribution is used under the assumption that a number of independent factors influence the observed cost variance.

EXHIBIT 28-2

Illustration of a Control Chart for a Cost Process

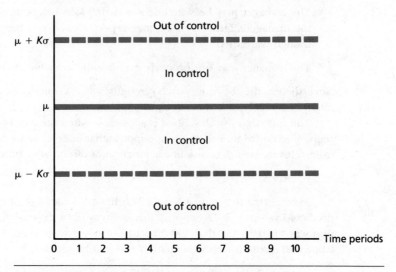

variance investigation decision. In quality control, samples are taken over short periods, often less than an hour, and the important characteristic is recorded on a **control chart,** such as the one shown in Exhibit 28-2. In Exhibit 28-2, μ represents the known or assumed value of this characteristic — say, the mean of the process — and σ is of the process standard deviation estimated using existing data. The value of K is the number of standard deviations around the expected value within which the process is considered to be in control.

The value of μ may be set from specifications, or it may be approximated using data gathered when the process is operating in control. To be useful, probabilistically, the chart's control limits should reflect the operation of the process when it is judged to be in control. The standard deviation is computed on the basis of the sample data during the control period. The assumption made here is that sufficient relevant data exists so that the estimated standard deviation may be assumed to be the actual one.[4]

The value of K is set to establish the desired probability beyond the control limits. For example, if $K = 1.96$, then there is a .05 probability of obtaining a sample value outside the control limits even though the process is in control. The calculation of K requires several important assumptions that may not be reasonable in any specific situation.

---

4. The assumption is made here that the historical information provides a reasonable value of σ. An equally reasonable assumption would consider the data as only an estimate of σ and use a t, rather than a normal, distribution. When the sample size gets large, say over 30, use of the t distribution is typically unnecessary.

EXHIBIT 28-3

Cost Variance Control Chart (.05 Probability)

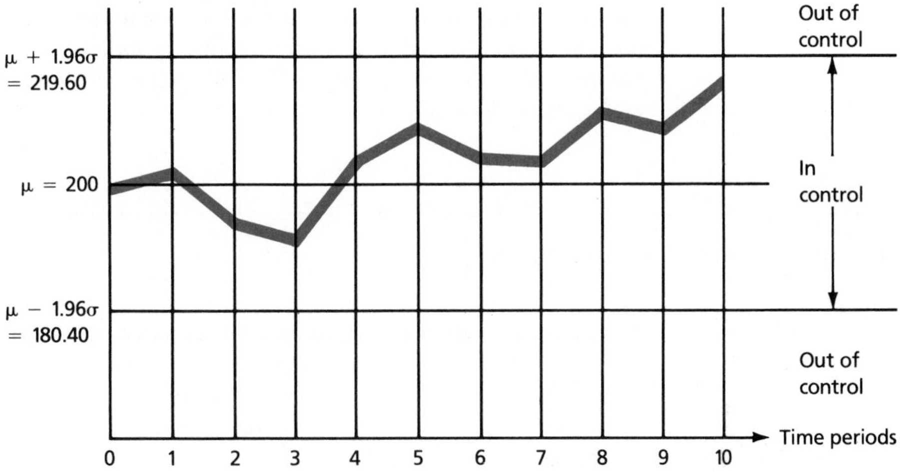

First, the calculation of the process standard deviation based on past data assumes the process's variability remains constant over time. In some processes, this assumption may not be valid, causing the probability of being outside the control limits to change. Second, the approach illustrated in Exhibit 28-2 implicitly assumes that the process to be controlled can be described by a normal probability distribution and that each observation reflects the same amount of information. Neither assumption may be justified. However, the procedure is satisfactory if the violation of either assumption is modest. Data collected over time can be used to verify the adequacy of the assumption.

The control chart has the desirable feature that past observations are retained and trends are more likely to be revealed. For example, in Exhibit 28-3 no sample point alone signals an investigation. However, the trend of values suggests that the process has shifted and an investigation will soon be signaled Hence, the manager may elect to stop the process now rather than waiting for an out-of-control observation.[5]

Control charts have been used to control physical aspects of production processes for years. But can control charts easily be extended to cost variances? Unfortunately, cost variances are not as easily modeled as are physical quality-control procedures. The problems with assuming normality have already been described. In addition, rather than sampling a number of items at one point in time, cost variances occur over substantial periods of time, generally at least a week long. Furthermore, each cost observation may be based on a different, and perhaps difficult to estimate,

5. The likelihood of seven observations in a row above the mean, if the process is in control, is $(.5)^7$ or .008.

level of activity. Each point, then, reflects a different information set. Finally, changes in conditions (activity levels, weather, and so on) can cause changes in process variability that in turn render the established control limits of dubious value. Keeping track of the time-pattern of cost variances can be useful, but care must be exercised to prevent mechanistic approaches from replacing judgment. In general, it is not surprising that control-chart techniques have not been widely embraced for cost-variance investigation decisions.

Ex post Variance Analysis

The traditional variance-analysis procedures outlined in Chapters 7 and 8 have limitations. One of the most important of these limitations is that the analysis is static. The analysis does not explicitly account for the effects of changes in parameters on decisions. Exhibit 28-4 depicts the decision-making process and its relationship to traditional variance analysis.

EXHIBIT 28-4

Decision-Making Process and Traditional Variance Analysis

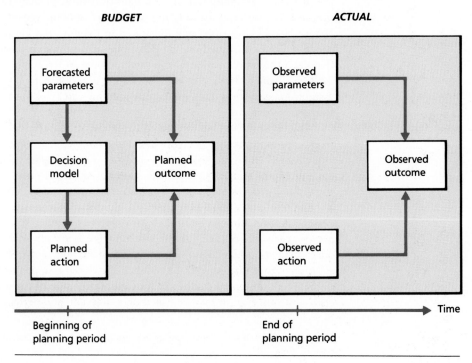

As Exhibit 28-4 shows, a decision model (or any choice process) has parameters as its input and actions as its output. **Parameters** are the inputs to the model estimated by the manager. For example, in a discounted-cash-flow decision model, the parameters are cash flows across several time periods and a discount rate. The decision model is the net-present-value or internal-rate-of-return model. The action is the capital investment project or projects selected. For another example, consider a product-mix decision made using linear programming. The parameters in the example are the unit contribution margins for the firm's products, the technological coefficients that detail how much of the firm's scarce resources are used by one unit of each product, and the amounts of each scarce resource available (the right-hand-sides of the constraints).

Forecasted parameters are put into the decision model, and planned actions emerge. The combination of parameters and actions yields an outcome. In the product-mix example, the forecasted unit contribution margin of a product (a parameter) is multiplied by the planned production quantity for that product (an action) to yield the aggregate contribution margin from that product. Then these aggregate production quantity for that product (an action) to yield the aggregate contribution margin from that product. Then these aggregate contribution margins are summed across products to yield the firm's aggregate contribution margin. This is the outcome.

Traditional variance analysis compares planned or budgeted outcome (such as profit or contribution margin) with the observed or budgeted outcome, and a variance is calculated. A flexible budget is generally used to disaggregate this large variance into two components, as shown in Exhibit 28-5. The flexible budget adjusts for

---

EXHIBIT 28-5

Traditional Variance Analysis

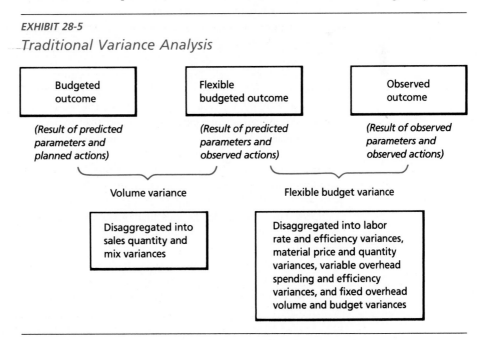

changes in activity. It is based on the observed action (actual activity level) but the predicted parameters (standards). The two resulting variances (volume variance and flexible budget variance) are then further divided into a variety of component variances for control and diagnostic purposes.

In what sense is the traditional variance analysis static? Refer again to Exhibit 28-4. In the right side of the exhibit, there is no decision model represented. Thus, the traditional variance analysis does not explicitly account for the effect of changes in the parameter values on the optimal action, via the decision model. There is no formal consideration, for example, of how a change in the sales price of a product should change the optimal sales mix. The new optimal sales mix, given the sales-price parameter actually observed, is never considered in the analysis. In short, the decision effects of parameter changes are left out of traditional variance analysis.

To remedy this shortcoming, a variance analysis procedure called **ex post variance analysis** can be used[6] to consider the decision effects of parameter changes after those changes are known. Exhibit 28-6 depicts the basic structure of ex post variance analysis.

In the ex post analysis, three sets of variables are used. The forecasted parameters are ex ante parameters (before the fact), and they are placed into the decision model to determine the ex ante action (optimal action given the ex ante parameters). The combination of ex ante parameters and ex ante action yields the ex ante outcome (budgeted outcome). The observed parameters combined with the observed action yield the observed outcome. The new concept is the ex post set of variables. The ex post parameters are the best parameters that could have been achieved in retrospect. Looking back on the period after it is over, each parameter change is classified by the accountant as favorable or unfavorable. Then the accountant classifies any unfavorable parameter changes as avoidable or unavoidable by those implementing the firm's technology. (*Technology* is used broadly to encompass production, sales, financing, and so forth.)

Suppose, for example, that a product has an ex ante (standard) labor usage of one hour per unit, and after the period is over it is determined that the observed labor usage was actually 1.2 hours per unit. First, this parameter change is classified as unfavorable. Because labor usage was greater than expected, the product's unit contribution margin will be lower than expected. Second, the accountant classifies the change in labor usage as avoidable or unavoidable by those implementing the relevant part of the firm's technology. This requires consultation by the accountant with those who know what happened. If, for example, the increase in labor usage was due to poor work habits by production employees, the change was avoidable. On the other hand, the labor-usage change was unavoidable if a bad storm resulted in flooding, which in turn damaged a machine and caused a normally automated task to be done manually.

After all parameter changes have been classified as either favorable or unfavorable and avoidable or unavoidable, the ex post set of parameters can be determined. To adjust the ex ante parameter values to their ex post values, all favorable parameter

6. J. Demski, "An Accounting System Structured on a Linear Programming Model," *Accounting Review* (October 1967): 701–12. See also H. Itami, *Adaptive Behavior: Management Control and Information Analysis* (Sarasota, Fl.: American Accounting Association, 1977).

EXHIBIT 28-6

Ex post Variance Analysis

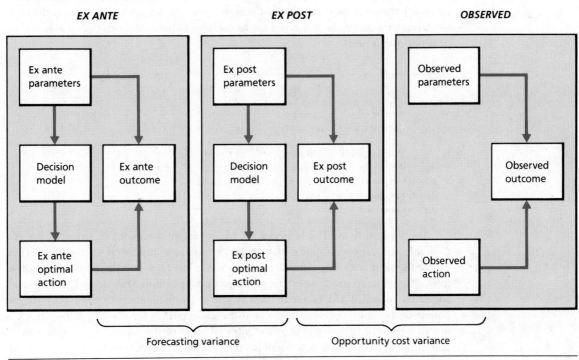

changes and all unfavorable, unavoidable parameter changes are incorporated into the ex post parameter values. Unfavorable, avoidable changes are not incorporated into the ex post parameter values. This is because an observed parameter value that differed from the ex ante (standard) level because of an unfavorable, avoidable change is not the best that could have been achieved in retrospect. If the change was unfavorable and could have been avoided, the firm could have done better in retrospect, with regard to that parameter value. Exhibit 28-7 summarizes the relationship between the ex ante, ex post, and observed values for a particular parameter.

EXHIBIT 28-7

Ex ante, Ex post, and Observed Parameters

	Unfavorable	Favorable
Unavoidable	$c^a \neq c^p = c^o$	$c^a \neq c^p = c^o$
Avoidable	$c^a = c^p \neq c^o$	

c^a denotes ex ante parameter

c^p denotes ex post parameter

c^o denotes observed parameter

Once the ex post set of parameters has been computed, these parameters are placed into the decision model and the ex post optimal action is determined (refer to Exhibit 28-6). Then the ex post outcome is computed as the result of the combined ex post parameters and the ex post action. Since the ex ante and ex post decision models are the same, the following relationships will hold between the ex ante and ex post optimal actions.

Case	Type of Parameter Change	Relationship Among Parameter Sets	Relationship Among Optimal Decisions
I	Unfavorable, unavoidable; or favorable	$c^a \neq c^p = c^o$	$x^a \neq x^p \ ? \ x^o$
II	Unfavorable, avoidable	$c^a = c^p \neq c^o$	$x^a = x^p \ ? \ x^o$

x^a denotes ex ante action
x^p denotes ex post action
x^o denotes observed action

The inequality symbol between x^a and x^p in the unfavorable, unavoidable (or favorable) case is used to mean that x^a and x^p will not, in general, be the same. They can be the same, but only if the decision model is insensitive to the parameter change from c^a to c^p. In contrast, when the parameter change is unfavorable and avoidable, c^a and c^p are identical and, hence, x^a and x^p also must be identical because they are the output of the same decision model and the same parameter set. A question mark is placed between x^p and x^o, since the internal logic of the model is not sufficient to determine this relationship. x^o denotes the observed action, which will be the result of a complex set of technological and environmental factors that occurred during the period.

Now everything is in place to implement the ex post variance analysis. Let m^a, m^p, and m^o denote the ex ante, ex post, and observed outcomes, respectively. The difference between m^a and m^p is the **forecasting variance** (refer again to Exhibit 28-6). It represents the difference between what the firm planned to do (ex ante or budgeted a "forecasting" variance because it is due to (1) errors in forecasting the ex ante parameters, relative to what could have been achieved with respect to those parameters, and (2) the induced effect of these forecasting errors on the firm's decision-making process. Thus, there are a first-order effect and a second-order effect on the outcome as a result of forecasting errors.

The forecasting variance can be further disaggregated into a **forecasting parameter variance** and a **forecasting decision variance,** as depicted in the upper half of Exhibit 28-8.[7] These variances capture the first-order and second-order effects of forecasting errors mentioned above.

7. Demski, note 6, termed these disaggregated variances the *price and efficiency variance* (instead of *parameter variance*) and the *basis variance* (instead of *decision variance*). The terminology used here is intended to be more general, rather than being tied to a particular decision application. (Demski's basis variance, for example, originates from the term *basis* used in linear programming.)

EXHIBIT 28-8

Disaggregation of Ex post Variances

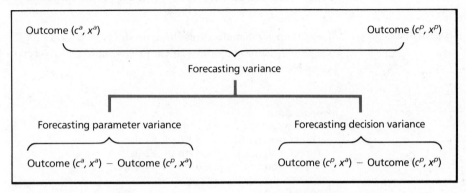

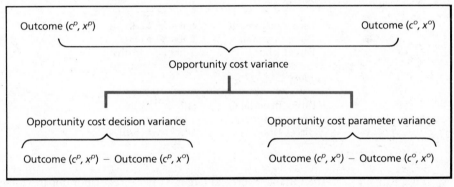

Referring again to Exhibit 28-6, the difference between m^p and m^o is termed the **opportunity cost variance.** It is the difference between the outcome that the firm should have planned to accomplish (the best it could have achieved with accurate forecasting and optimal decision making) and the outcome that it actually did accomplish. It represents the opportunity cost of the firm not having used its resources to optimal advantage during the period. It is caused by (1) the implementation errors (as opposed to forecasting errors) implicit in the unfavorable, avoidable differences between parameters c^p and c^o, and (2) the result of having taken the observed action x^o instead of the ex post optimal action x^p. The opportunity cost variance can be further subdivided, as shown in the lower half of Exhibit 28-8, in an analogous way to the subdivision of the forecasting variance. The resulting variances are termed the **opportunity cost decision variance** and the **opportunity cost parameter variance.**

Ex post analysis, as presented here, also allows for changes that the manager might make during the process. Realization that initial estimates were in error may occur throughout the process. If the manager elects to intervene during the process, the final outcome will be altered. This will be reflected in the actual outcome and perhaps reduce the size of the opportunity cost variance. If this happens, it may suggest that the current reporting system is not sufficiently timely or detailed.

Example

Joel Company manufactures three products, *A*, *B*, and *C*. A linear program is used for the firm's planning model. (Linear programming is covered in Chapter 17.) Standard costs are as follows:

Product A:

Direct material Q	5 lbs @ $3/lb
Direct material R	3 lbs @ $2/lb
Direct labor:	6 hrs @ $15/hr

Product B:

Direct material R	6 lbs @ $2/lb
Direct material S	2 lbs @ $1/lb
Direct labor:	4 hrs @ $15/hr

Product C:

Direct material Q	3 lbs @ $3/lb
Direct material S	4 lbs @ $1/lb
Direct labor:	5 hrs @ $15/hr

The variable overhead rate is $1 per direct labor dollar. Variable selling and administrative costs and selling prices are as follows:

Product	Variable Selling and Administrative	Sales Price
A	$2	$220
B	$7	$150
C	$4	$180

The firm anticipates the following quantities of its raw materials and labor available for the planning period under consideration:

Direct material Q	5,000 lbs
Direct material R	4,000 lbs
Direct material S	3,000 lbs
Direct labor	7,000 hrs

Joel Company's fixed costs can be ignored for this planning exercise because the product-mix decision is a short-run decision, and the optimal decision is unaffected by the fixed costs associated with fixed facilities.

Ex ante Decision Model   The standards, variable selling and administrative costs, sales prices, and resource-availability levels listed above are the firm's ex ante parameter values. The ex ante unit contribution margins are as follows, where c_i^a denotes the ex ante unit contribution margin of product i:

$$c_A^a = \$17 = \$220 - (5)(\$3) - (3)(\$2) - (6)(\$15) - (6)(\$15)(1) - \$2$$

$$c_B^a = \$\,9 = \$150 - (6)(\$2) - (2)(\$1) - (4)(\$15) - (4)(\$15)(1) - \$7$$

$$c_C^a = \$13 = \$180 - (3)(\$3) - (4)(\$1) - (5)(\$15) - (5)(\$15)(1) - \$4$$

Joel Company's ex ante planning model is the following linear program, where x_i^a denotes the ex ante optimal value for the production quantity of product i:

$$\max 17x_A^a + 9x_B^a + 13x_C^a$$

Subject to:

$$5x_A^a \qquad\;\; + 3x_C^a \le 5{,}000$$
$$3x_A^a + 6x_B^a \qquad\quad\;\; \le 4{,}000$$
$$2x_B^a + 4x_C^a \le 3{,}000$$
$$6x_A^a + 4x_B^a + 5x_C^a \le 7{,}000$$
$$x_A^a \;\ge\quad 0$$
$$x_B^a \;\ge\quad 0$$
$$x_C^a \;\ge\quad 0$$

The ex ante optimal solution to the product-mix problem, along with the ex ante outcome (aggregate contribution margin) are given below:[8]

$$x_A^a = 923 \qquad x_B^a = 205 \qquad x_C^a = 128$$

$$m^a = \$19{,}200 = c_A^a x_A^a + c_B^a x_B^a + c_C^a x_C^a$$

Ex post Decision Model   At the end of the period, the following actual results were observed:

- Each unit of *A* required 6 lbs of *Q*

- Each unit of *B* required 5 lbs of *R*

- Each unit of *C* required 6 lbs of *S*

- Labor cost was \$12 per hour

8. The firm's product-mix decision model is a linear program with the optimal solution rounded to whole numbers. The firm believes the possible improvement in the solution from using integer programming would not be worth the cost. In this problem, the differences due to rounding the solution are insignificant.

- All other parameters were equal to their standard levels. The variable overhead rate remained unchanged.

- The usage of direct material Q by product A was an avoidable change. All of the other unfavorable changes were unavoidable.

The ex post unit contribution margins are calculated as follows:

$$c_A^p = \$53 = \$220 - (5)(\$3) - (3)(\$2) - (6)(\$12) - (6)(\$12)(1) - \$2$$

$$c_B^p = \$35 = \$150 - (5)(\$2) - (2)(\$1) - (4)(\$12) - (4)(\$12)(1) - \$7$$

$$c_C^p = \$41 = \$180 - (3)(\$3) - (6)(\$1) - (5)(\$12) - (5)(\$12)(1) - \$4$$

Note that only the favorable and unfavorable, unavoidable parameter changes are reflected in the ex post unit contribution margins. The change in the usage of material Q by product A was avoidable, and therefore the change is not reflected in the ex post contribution margin c_A^p. Instead, the material Q usage by product A remains at 5 pounds per unit rather than 6.

The ex post planning model is the following linear program:

$$\max 53x_A^p + 35x_B^p + 41x_C^p$$

Subject to:

$$
\begin{aligned}
5x_A^p \qquad\quad + 3x_C^p &\leq 5{,}000 \\
3x_A^p + 5x_B^p \qquad\quad &\leq 4{,}000 \\
2x_B^p + 6x_C^p &\leq 3{,}000 \\
6x_A^p + 4x_B^p + 5x_C^p &\leq 7{,}000 \\
x_A^p &\geq \quad 0 \\
x_B^p &\geq \quad 0 \\
x_C^p &\geq \quad 0
\end{aligned}
$$

Again, the unfavorable, avoidable change in the material Q usage by product A is not reflected in the material Q constraint in the ex post planning model. The ex post optimal solution and outcome (aggregate contribution margin) are given below:

$$x_A^p = 958 \qquad x_B^p = 225 \qquad x_C^p = 70$$

$$m^p = \$61{,}519 = c_A^p x_A^p + c_B^p x_B^p + c_C^p x_C^p$$

Observed Results   The observed unit contribution margins, actions, and outcome are the following:

$$c_A^o = \$50 \qquad c_B^o = \$35 \qquad c_C^o = \$41$$

$$x_A^o = 800 \qquad x_B^o = 300 \qquad x_C^o = 60$$

$$m^o = \$52{,}960 = c_A^o x_A^o + c_B^o x_B^o + c_C^o x_C^o$$

The only change between the ex post and observed unit contribution margins is due to the unfavorable, avoidable change in the material Q usage by product A. Since one more pound was used, at \$3 per pound, c_A^o is \$3 less than c_A^p.

Ex post Variance Analysis Now the ex post variances may be calculated as shown below:

Forecasting variance
$$= (\$17)(923) + (\$9)(205) + (\$13)(128)$$
$$- [(\$53)(958) + (\$35)(225) + (\$41)(70)]$$
$$= \$19,200 - 61,519 = (\$42,319)$$

Forecasting parameter variance $= (\$17 - \$53)(923) + (\$9 - \$35)(205) + (\$13 - 41)(128) = (\$42,142)$

Forecasting decision variance $= \$53(923 - 958) + \$35(205 - 225) + \$41(128 - 70) = (\$177)$

Opportunity cost variance
$$= (\$53)(958) + (\$35)(225) + (\$41)(70)$$
$$- [(\$50)(800) + (\$35)(300) + (\$41)(60)]$$
$$= \$8,559$$

Opportunity cost
parameter variance
$$= (\$53 - \$50)(800) + (\$35 - \$35)(300) + (\$41 - \$41)(60) = \$2,400$$

Opportunity cost
decision variance
$$= \$53(958 - 800) + \$35(225 - 300) + \$41(70 - 60)$$
$$= \$6,159$$

The ex post variance analysis reveals that the forecasting variance is considerably larger than the opportunity cost variance. Thus, the firm's planning process is hampered by inaccurate forecasts more than its implementation efforts are hampered by implementation errors. Moreover, the first-order effect of the forecasting errors is much larger than the second-order effect. Since the firm's planning model is relatively insensitive to the forecasting errors, there was not a significant impact on the decisions or the resulting contribution margin.

Evaluation of Ex post Variance Analysis

Ex post variance analysis rests on four assumptions:

1. The firm employs a well-defined planning model (such as linear programming, EOQ inventory models, discounted-cash-flow models);

2. The accountant is able to classify unfavorable parameter changes as unavoidable or avoidable;

3. Feedback information from the model will be useful for future planning;

4. The search for the correct decision can be limited to the planning model in use.

When these assumptions are satisfied, ex post analysis has the potential to yield greater benefits to management than traditional variance analysis because it encompasses more phenomena. Most important, it explicitly provides insight into the decision effects of parameter changes, and it includes the impact of forecasting errors as well as implementation errors in the variance analysis. Since ex post variance analysis is also more costly than the traditional analysis, its use is a cost-benefit issue. Even if the judgment is made that formal ex post variance analysis is not worth implementing, in a cost-benefit sense there are two important reasons for managers to study the technique. First, ex post analysis provides a way of thinking about performance evaluation and diagnosis. It provides a method of thinking critically about the effects of a dynamic and uncertain environment on decisions and outcomes. Second, a study of ex post variance analysis provides insight into the limitations of the traditional analysis.

Use of Ex post Analysis

Ex post variance analysis can conceptually be used in the context of any formal planning model. The analysis was illustrated using a linear-programming formulation of the product-mix decision problem. It could also be implemented in the context of an inventory model, a capital-budgeting model, or any other explicit planning model. Moreover, the concept of ex post analysis, as a way of thinking, is widely applied in a variety of settings by real-world organizations. Two illustrations follow.

Ex post Variance Analysis in an Oil Refinery

In an article in the *Accounting Review,* Demski reported an actual trial run at using ex post variance analysis for production planning in an oil refinery. The application's results were highly encouraging in that the approach proved to be feasible and useful in providing control information that was not generated by traditional variance analysis.[9]

Ex post Analysis at the World Bank

An article in *Forbes* reported on the World Bank's use of the concept of ex post analysis in diagnosing its performance in security trading. According to a World Bank executive, if a security is purchased at par, trades at 105, is sold, and subsequently trades at 110, a mistake has been made. Each such mistake is carefully scrutinized. Management determines what it should have done, what was done, and what would have happened had the Bank made an optimal decision in retrospect. The results of the analysis are used not for reward or punishment but for improving performance.[10]

9. Demski, note 6.
10. B. Weberman, "Smart Answers to Dumb Questions," *Forbes* (May 19, 1986): 110–13.

Summary

A reasonable approach to the variance-investigation decision is to estimate the standard deviation for each cost process and calculate the probability of a cost observation occurring given that the process is in control. Probabilistic rules of thumb (.05 or .01) can be used initially as a decision criterion. As knowledge of the costs and benefits improves, along with an understanding of the process, the decision rules can be refined and perhaps more sophisticated procedures introduced.

Traditional cost-variance analysis does not explicitly recognize the impact of parameter changes on decisions. Ex post variance analysis does allow for such effects and separates the effects due to misforecasts and those due to faulty implementation of the firm's technology. If the analysis can be constrained to a formal decision-model setting, a more complete analysis can be made with payoffs to the diligent manager.

Key Terms to Review

control chart, p. 948
ex post variance analysis, p. 952
forecasting parameter variance, p. 954
opportunity cost variance, p. 955
opportunity cost parameter variance,
   p. 955

parameters p. 951
forecasting variance, p. 954
forecasting decision variance, p. 954
opportunity cost decision variance,
   p. 954

Review Problem

COST CONTROL

Answer the following questions.

1. Explain why the use of an organization's resources for cost control should be considered in a broader context.

2. What do you believe is the most difficult aspect of attaining cost control?

3. How would the means by which a firm designed and implemented a cost-control policy affect the observed cost variances?

Solution to Review Problem

1. This is only one claim on the cash and manpower resources of the firm. In fact, it is part of the firm's overall capital budgeting problem. The relevant planning period would probably differ from the normal reporting period.

2. There are a number of potential candidates for this honor, including obtaining correct cost data, making good forecasts, implementing the program and required changes, designing the appropriate incentive system and others. The more difficult issue will depend on the organization and the situation. We caution that too much credence is often given to the accuracy of the costs as computed and not enough attention is paid to the circumstances surrounding their occurrence.

3. The more individuals understand why the system of cost control is in place, accept its objectives and realize the consequences of cost variances particularly to themselves, the more effective a cost control system will be.

Suggested Readings

Baiman, S., and J. Demski. "Variance Analysis Procedures as Motivational Devices." *Management Science* (August 1980): 840–48.

Boer, G. "Solutions in Search of a Problem: The Case of Budget Variance Investigation Models." *Journal of Accounting Literature* (Spring 1984): 47–69.

Demski, J. "An Accounting System Structured on a Linear Programming Model." *Accounting Review* (October 1967): 701–12.

———. "Optimizing the Search for Cost Deviation Sources." *Management Science* (April 1970): 486–94.

Dittman, D., and P. Prakash. "The Significance and Investigation of Cost Variances: Survey and Extensions." *Journal of Accounting Research* (Autumn 1975): 311–37.

Duvall, R. "Rules for Investigating Cost Variances." *Management Science* (June 1967): 631–41.

Dyckman, T. "The Investigation of Cost Variance." *Journal of Accounting Research* (Fall 1969): 215–44.

Itami, H. *Adaptive Behavior: Management Control and Information Analysis.* Sarasota, Fla.: American Accounting Association, 1977.

Jacobs, F. "When and How to Use Statistical Cost Variance Investigation Techniques." *Cost and Management* (January–February 1983): 26–32.

Jacobs, F., and R. Marshall. "A Note on the Choice Structure of Cost Variance Investigation Models." *Journal of Accounting Literature* (Spring 1984): 73–83.

Kaplan, R. *Advanced Managerial Accounting.* Englewood Cliffs, N.J.: Prentice-Hall, 1982.

———. "Optimal Investigation Strategies with Imperfect Information." *Journal of Accounting Research* (Spring 1969): 32–43.

———. "The Significance and Investigation of Cost Variances: Survey and Extensions." *Journal of Accounting Research* (Autumn 1975): 311–37.

Magee, R. *Advanced Managerial Accounting.* New York: Harper & Row, 1986.

———. "A Simulation Analysis of Alternative Cost Investigation Models." *Accounting Review* (July 1976): 529–44.

Ozan, T., and T. Dyckman. "A Normative Model for Investigation Decisions Involving Multi-Origin Cost Variances." *Journal of Accounting Research* (Spring 1971): 88–115.

Ronen, J. "Nonaggregation vs. Disaggregation of Variances." *Accounting Review* (January 1974): 50–60.

Tomczyk, S., and C. Chatterjee. "The Impact of Outliers and Influential Points on the Cost-Variance Investigation Decision." *Issues in Accounting Education* (Fall 1986): 293–301.

APPENDIX
Decision Theoretic Approaches

The methods discussed in this chapter omit explicit recognition of the costs and benefits to be obtained from investigating cost variances.[11] They are considered to be included intuitively by the manager. Proponents of the control-chart approach advocate intuitively adjusting the control limits to reflect these costs and benefits. The following discussion is designed to incorporate these substantive issues systematically into the decision process. Although such techniques are not being widely used today, considering them formally improves an understanding of the process and helps in making more informed decisions.[12]

Setting Up the Problem

The cost-variance investigation decision involves a multistate process in which information about the states reaches the manager at discrete time intervals. This information concerns the state of the process over which the manager has some, but not complete, control. The manager is in turn faced with the question of whether to intervene in order to exercise that control. Exercising control here means first deciding whether or not to investigate the process prior to the next stage (time period).

If the manager elects to investigate, and an out-of-control state is thought to exist, a further analysis is likely to be made in the hope of finding the cause. If the cause is found and it is correctable, the manager will attempt to do so, subject to cost considerations. Although an actual situation would likely involve many possible state values, some consistent with the process being in control and some not, only two states will be considered in this simple illustration.

s_1　　The in-control state
s_2　　The out-of-control state

Through time, the process being monitored may change from being in control to being out of control, or vice versa. Thus, the process can be described as one in which the state variable is subject to transformation during each stage. These transformations (from in control to out of control and vice versa) are only partially under the

---

11. The discussion in this Appendix is heavily influenced by R. Duvall, "Rules for Investigating Cost Variances," *Management Science* (June 1967): 631–41; R. Kaplan, "Optimal Investigation Strategies with Imperfect Information," *Journal of Accounting Research* (Spring 1969): 32–43; and R. Kaplan, *Advanced Management Accounting* (Englewood Cliffs, N.J.: Prentice-Hall, 1982), pp. 334–41.

12. See R. Magee, "A Simulation Analysis of Alternative Cost Variance Investigation Models," *Accounting Review* (July 1976): 529–44. Using simulation, Magee argues that the simple methods are nearly as cost effective as more complex models.

influence of the manager through the manipulation of decision variables (which are assumed here to remain constant within each stage of the process). Furthermore, knowledge about the process in a given stage is probabilistic. The information available about the process may or may not be indicative of the actual state of the process.

The description of the problem so far implies only a single process. In fact, at each stage the decision maker is monitoring several processes. The task is to select a subset of the processes for investigation given budget and other constraints and a desire to minimize costs. The constraints and cost minimization usually prevent an investigation of all processes at every stage. Furthermore, the investigation action can be dichotomized in practice so that either an exploratory investigation at a substantially reduced cost or a complete investigation may be undertaken initially.

The probabilistic elements in the problem are several. First, the process of transformation from an in-control to an out-of-control state (and vice versa) is in part probabilistic. The state of control shifts from stage to stage according to some random process as well as in response to the actions taken by the decision maker. Decisions to modify the process must be made on the basis of sample information that is also probabilistic. Finally, an investigation, once initiated, may fail to disclose a situation requiring adjustment when one exists. Moreover, adjustment, once undertaken, may fail to restore the desired in-control state.

Some variables often included in a control system are not optimized in the present discussion but, rather, are treated as parameters (their levels are assumed fixed, although perhaps unknown). These parameters are the time interval between cost reports, the lag between measurement and control implementation, the cost of investigation and adjustment, and the accuracy of the information. Decisions are made concerning only the investigation decision and how information can be used to make that decision.

Simple Investigation-Decision Situation

Consider first a very simple one-period problem in which monetary values are used to evaluate each state-action pair. The monetary values are assumed to reflect the consequences to the decision maker of each action under each state. Two states —

s_1 in control
s_2 out of control

— are used, and two possible actions are considered:

a_1 investigate
a_2 do not investigate

There are several implicit assumptions. One of these is that the incurred costs are reported on a periodic basis. Thus, a do-not-investigate action implies that the activity is continued at least until the next cost observation is available. An additional assumption made here is that an investigation always reveals the cause of an out-of-control situation, which is immediately corrected.[13] The in-control state then persists until

13. The problem described can easily be expanded to incorporate probabilistic detection and correction. See T. Dyckman, "The Investigation of Cost Variances," *Journal of Accounting Research* (Fall 1969): 215–44.

the end of the period. The implicit assumption here is that the saving that will be denoted by L, from correcting an out-of-control process, is the saving until the end of the period. In a more realistic case, there are several periods. The process may remain in control for some fraction of the total time horizon considered. An investigation not undertaken in this period may be undertaken in the next. Therefore, the present value of the savings depends on following an optimal decision policy in the future. The one-period benefit, L, used here underestimates the actual benefit obtainable over a multiple investigation-period horizon. A good deal can be learned about the problem from the single-period model while avoiding the mathematics required to deal with a more complex problem statement.

The cost of an investigation is assumed to be an amount C. The cost of correction is M. The value of the savings obtainable from an investigation when the activity is out of control is $L - M$, where $L - M$ is greater than C. If $L - M$ is less than C, investigation would never be warranted. It is important to recognize that it is the value L, rather than the specific cost variance under consideration (although the two may be related), that is important. If the cost variance is caused by conditions that can be corrected, the benefit is the cost saved by the reduction or elimination of the cause of the variance.

Exhibit 28-9 gives the general form of the cost payoff table associated with a two-state, two-action problem. Typically, the values are of a small-enough magnitude so that it can be assumed the decision maker is willing to act on the basis of the expected costs measured in monetary terms. If so, the action with the lowest expected cost is best. The expected cost of each action is obtained by multiplying the payoffs by their probabilities and summing across states. If the probability of the in-control state is denoted p_1 and of the out-of-control state by p_2, respectively, the expected costs are

$$\text{Expected cost of } a_1 = Cp_1 + (C + M)p_2 = C + Mp_2 \tag{1}$$

$$\text{Expected cost of } a_2 = Op_1 + Lp_2 = Lp_2 \tag{2}$$

The cost variance is a candidate for investigation if the expected cost of investigating is less than the expected cost of not investigating (that is, if the expected cost of action a_1 is less than the expected cost of action a_2).

EXHIBIT 28-9

General Cost Payoff Matrix: Two-State Form

Actions: a_i	States: s_i	
	s_1 In Control	s_2 Out of Control
a_1 Investigate	C	$C + M$
a_2 Do not investigate	O	L

If the expected cost of action a_1 is to be less than the expected cost of action a_2, then using equations (1) and (2)

$$C + Mp_2 < Lp_2, \text{ or} \tag{3}$$

$$C - (L - M)p_2 < 0 \tag{4}$$

Suppose, for example, that an out-of-control process leads to an estimated cost of $15,000 for the period. This is the estimated value of L. Assume an investigation cost of $2,000 and a $3,000 cost to correct an out-of-control situation. An in-control process remains in control for the period, and an out-of-control process stays out of control for the entire period unless corrected. Exhibit 28-10 summarizes these assumptions.

For the specific example in Exhibit 28-10, suppose that p_1 = .73 and p_2 = .27. Then inequality (4) yields the following:

$$\$2,000 - \$12,000(.27) = \$-3,240 < 0$$

Investigation is the optimal action if the information and assumptions are accepted as presented.

The analysis assumes that the manager can establish the prior subjective probabilities over the states. These probabilities are required to use inequality (4). This is perhaps a feasible task for someone familiar with the activity, since only two states are involved. The decision maker needs to define the probability of the two states. Care is necessary, however, to provide for changes that may have taken place in the process. This implies that the prior probabilities should be based on relevant historical information adjusted for future differences from past conditions by someone knowledgeable about the activity.

Break-Even Probability

The requirement that the manager be able to estimate the state probabilities is not as critical as it appears. Instead, the manager can first calculate the probability that equates the costs of the two actions. This probability is called the *break-even probability*. The manager can then decide whether the actual probability of the out-of-control state exceeds this value or not. It is not necessary to specify a value but only

---

EXHIBIT 28-10

Specific Cost Payoff Matrix: Two-State Form

	States: s_i	
Actions: a_i	s_1 In Control	s_2 Out of Control
a_1 Investigate	$2,000	$ 5,000
a_2 Do not investigate	0	$15,000

whether p_2 exceeds the break-even value. The procedure also makes it unnecessary to do the expected-value calculations each time an investigation decision is required.

Letting p_b denote the break-even probability, inequality (4) is set equal to zero:

$$C - (L - M)p_b = 0 \tag{5}$$

If p_2 exceeds p_b, the activity is a candidate for investigation. If p_2 is less than p_b, the activity should not be investigated. Solving for p_b yields:

$$p_b = \frac{C}{L - M} \tag{6}$$

If p_2 exceeds $C/(L - M)$, the process should be considered for investigation. Using the probability of the in-control state, p_1, then $1 - p_1$ must exceed $C/(L - M)$ for an investigation to be signaled or, alternatively, p_1 must be less than $1 - [C/(L - M)]$.

In the example, $C/(L - M)$ equals \$2,000/\$12,000 or 1/6. Thus, p_1 must be less than $1 - (1/6) = 5/6 = .83$ for an investigation. Since p_1 was given to be .73, investigation is the preferred action. Note that investigation is preferred here even in a case for which the probability of being in control exceeds .5, as long as the probability is less than .83. Using p_1, an investigation is signaled if p_1 is less than $1 - [C/(L - M)]$; otherwise, it is not. As soon as the probability of being in control drops below $1 - [C/(L - M)]$, an investigation should be undertaken. The larger the cost savings and the smaller the cost of investigation and correction, the larger is the break-even value, as would be expected. The break-even value is independent of the stage at which the process is examined, and it is therefore relevant to all time periods.

Exploratory Investigations and the Value of Information

A firm usually has a choice of conducting at least two levels of investigation. The first level of investigation might be essentially exploratory in nature. It would cost less than a full investigation, but it would have a smaller chance of disclosing the cause of an out-of-control situation. The exploratory investigation should be conducted if the expected benefits from this action exceed both those from waiting and those from a full investigation. The investigation decision can be discussed in terms of the *expected value of perfect information*. This concept from decision theory describes the increased value to the decision maker if the true state of the process were known before the decision were made. In this case, all uncertainty is removed before a decision is required.

Suppose that perfect information is available concerning the actual state of the process. Then, if the state is s_1, no investigation would be undertaken since it is known that the process is in control. This is expected to occur with probability p_1. Alternatively, if the state is s_2, an investigation would be made with cost $C + M$ to find out the cause of the state being out of control and to lay the groundwork for correction. This occurs with probability p_2. Thus, the expected cost with perfect information, denoted by E^*, is given by

$$E^* = 0(p_1) + (C + M)(p_2) \tag{7}$$

$$= (C + M)(p_2) \tag{8}$$

But without perfect information, the manager's expected cost is the cost associated with the best action based on what is known. This minimum cost is given by

$$\text{Min} \begin{cases} C + M(p_2) & \text{investigate} \\ L(p_2) & \text{do not investigate} \end{cases} \tag{9}$$

Thus, the expected value of perfect information, denoted by E_p, and therefore the maximum value of processing additional information, is equal to the value obtained from equation (8) subtracted from the minimum of equation (9). This gives

$$E_p = \begin{cases} C(1 - p_2) = C(p_1), \text{ if investigate is the minimum-cost action} \\ (L - M - C)(p_2), \text{ if do not investigate is the} \\ \qquad\qquad\qquad\qquad\qquad \text{minimum-cost action} \end{cases} \tag{10}$$

Continuing the example described earlier and assuming

$C = \$2,000,\ L = \$15,000,\ M = \$3,000,\ p_1 = .73,\ p_2 = .27$

Hence, $(L - M - C) = \$10,000$

With perfect information the expected cost would be

$E^* = (C + M)(p_2)$

$\qquad = \$5,000 \times .27 = \$1,350$

The expected cost without perfect information is

$$\text{Min} \begin{cases} 2,000 + 3,000(.27) = \$2,810, \text{ investigate} \\ 15,000(.27) = \$4,050, \text{ do not investigate} \end{cases}$$

The better decision is to investigate, with an expected cost of $2,810. Since the investigate decision gives the minimum expected cost, the expected value of perfect information is

$E_p = C(p_1) = 2,000 \times .73 = \$1,460$

Or equivalently,

$E_p = \$2,810 - \$1,350 = \$1,460$

Additional information is worth no more than the difference between the expected cost of the best action without perfect information and the expected cost with perfect information. This difference is $1,460.

Assume now that the records required for an exploratory examination are being kept, that the cost of such an investigation is C', where $C' < C$, and the probability that the cause of an out-of-control situation will be discovered when it exists is h. The alternative of an exploratory investigation should be evaluated in terms of the expected cost associated with its use. The cost from the alternative of an exploratory investigation will amount to C', given state s_1, and $C' + Mh + L(1 - h)$, given state s_2 (where h is less than 1). The value h is the probability that an exploratory investigation will lead to the discovery (and thus correction) of an out-of-control situation when it exists. Such an investigation may be justified even if its cost exceeds the

---

EXHIBIT 28-11

Expected Costs of Three Actions

Case	Action	Expected Cost
a	Do not investigate	$L(p_2)$
b	Exploratory investigation	$C' + [L(1 - b) + bM](p_2)$
c	Full investigation	$C + M(p_2)$

---

expected value of perfect information (that is, even if $C' > E_p$). This is true because perfect information still leads to a cost of C in the out-of-control state. In the example, an b of .95 and a C' of \$1,500 is sufficient to produce this result.

Three cases exist. The expected costs are given in Exhibit 28-11. Setting case a equal to case b and case b equal to case c, two break-even probabilities (call them p_b and p_c) can be determined. Typically, but not necessarily, p_b will exceed p_c. Using these break-even probabilities, the investigation decision can again be based on the probability p_1. The choices are illustrated in Exhibit 28-12. In the example here, assuming that $b = .4$ and $C' = \$200$, p_b is approximately .96 and p_c is about .75.

Suppose that $p_c < p_1 < p_b$, so that an exploratory investigation is made. Assume that the investigation does not uncover any cause for the variance. The process may be either in or out of control at this point. However, before allowing the process to continue another period, the probabilities should be revised for any information provided by this investigation, and the full-investigation action should be compared to the action do not investigate. (This step need not be performed if the revision will increase p_1.)

These results bear directly on the extent of records to be maintained for control purposes. If p_b is less than p_c for some process, a fact that may be ascertained in advance, an exploratory investigation will never be relevant, and the necessary records to conduct one need not be kept. The likelihood of this situation increases as b decreases and as C' approaches C. The larger the difference $p_b - p_c$, the larger b, and the lower C', the more value there is to keeping the necessary records supporting an exploratory investigation.

EXHIBIT 28-12   ·

Investigation Action Choice Using Revised Probability of In-Control State

Full investigation	Exploratory investigation	No investigation

0   p_c p_b 1

Increasing scale for p_1

**Some
Extensions**

The next step would be to consider the cost-investigation problem when the state random variable is continuous rather than discrete. Another extension would examine multiple causes of cost variances, some of them uncontrollable. Further possibilities include relaxing the assumptions on the equal time interval between cost reports, introducing a lag between the investigation and the implementation of control, incorporating uncertainty into the cost estimates and the success of the control action, using dynamic programming to solve the problem created by future dependencies, and developing techniques to estimate the transition probabilities. These and additional issues are covered in the suggested readings listed at the end of the chapter.

**Variance
Investigation in
an Agency
Framework**

The cost-variance investigation techniques discussed in this chapter all have one limitation. These approaches fail to consider the effect on the process generating the costs of the investigation policy itself. The impact of an actual investigation is included in the models, but not the impact of the investigation policy. The investigation policy can be expected to have an effect on the process generating the costs since the process is not purely mechanistic. If, for example, a production process that generates costs is totally automated, then there would be no effect on the cost-generating process from the variance investigation policy. Machines do not react psychologically to a monitoring policy. In contrast, if there are also people working within the process that generates the costs, then the variance-investigation policy can affect their behavior, and this can in turn affect the costs that are incurred. None of the variance-investigation models addressed in this chapter explicitly consider the impact of the investigation policy on the behavior of the people involved.

Although several individuals have conducted research on this issue, not a great deal of headway has been made in developing a practical variance-investigation method that incorporates the reactions of the people affected by the monitoring policy. Some insight into the problem has been provided, however, by analyzing the variance-investigation decision in the context of a principal-agent model. Such analyses have revealed several important insights, including the following:[14]

1. The optimal variance-investigation policy is in general different if the agent's reaction to being monitored is explicitly included in the analysis than if such possible reactions are ignored. Hence, the issue is a nontrivial one.

2. Since monitoring an agent is an imperfect technology, a monitoring policy results in additional uncertainty for the agent about the agent's compensation over and above the uncertainty about that compensation due solely to uncertainty concerning the state of nature. Since agents are, in general, averse to risk, they must be compensated for bearing greater risk by specifying a compensation scheme with higher payments, on average, than would be required otherwise.

---

14. Research on this issue includes R. Lambert, "Variance Investigation in Agency Settings," *Journal of Accounting Research* (Autumn 1985): 633–47; and S. Baiman and J. Demski, "Economically Optimal Performance Evaluation and Control Systems," *Journal of Accounting Research* (Supplement, 1980): 184–220.

3. For a very risk-averse agent it may be optimal to use a policy of investigating only unfavorable variances, rather than a policy of investigating both unfavorable and favorable variances. By focusing only on unfavorable variances, the principal saves on conducting costly investigations and takes advantage of the agent's high risk aversion. The agent will find those actions that make low outcomes (and hence unfavorable variances) more likely, even less attractive than they might otherwise be, due to the potential for the imposition of additional uncertainty (through imperfect monitoring) when unfavorable variances are observed.

   In contrast, if the agent has very low risk aversion, it may be counterproductive to try to overcome this risk tolerance. In this case, the principal may find it desirable to select a policy of investigating only favorable variances. Again the principal saves on costly investigations, and motivates the agent by providing an incentive for the agent to strive for high outcomes (rather than trying to avoid low outcomes).

   Thus, monitoring may be most efficiently used as the basis for punishing the more risk-averse agents while rewarding more risk-tolerant agents.

4. The benefits from conducting a variance investigation increase as the information from the investigation about the agent's action increases. Such benefits are not, however, necessarily greater when a variance is extreme or unusual in a statistical sense.

These conclusions must be regarded as tentative at best, since they are based on highly simplified models that make many restrictive assumptions. They are included here to emphasize the importance of considering the impact on employee behavior of the variance-investigation policy. Considerably more insight is needed into this complex issue.

Review Questions

28-1 What are the basic causes of cost variances?

28-2 What do you feel are the most important aspects of a cost-variance information system?

28-3 What are the most important questions to consider in implementing a statistical cost-variance investigation model?

28-4 Discuss the following questions. If a cost variance is investigated, will the cause of the variance be found? If the cause of the variance is found, will the situation be corrected? If the situation is corrected, is the firm better off because the investigation was conducted? If it is not investigated, will the variance continue in the future?

28-5 Why is expected payoff a reasonable quantity to base decisions on when magnitudes of all possible payoffs are relatively small?

28-6 What does it mean for a process to be in control?

28-7 What important factors does ex post variance analysis allow to be considered?

28-8 The benefits from a cost investigation increase as both the information from the investigation about the agent's action increase and the variance of the cost distribution increases. Comment.

28-9 How does a decision-theory approach to the problem of when to investigate cost variances improve on the often-used control chart procedure (see Appendix)?

28-10 What is the primary lesson available from an agency framework to cost-variance analysis (see Appendix)?

Exercises

28-11 **Explaining Variances** Morse Electronics evaluates all cost variances by the rule that an explanation is required for any variance that exceeds budget by more than ten percent. Evaluate this policy.

28-12 **Controlling Inventory Cost Using Variances** Consider the problem of inventory levels. Many firms use what is known as the economic order quantity (EOQ) model. If management wishes to control inventory cost using investigation decisions based on cost variances, what causes of such variances are possible? Is it important to distinguish between the causes?

28-13 **Using Decision Models** Criticize the following statement: Simple decision models should not be relied on since realistic situations are far too complex for such models to be useful.

28-14 **Controlling Mailing Costs** Ace Mailorder Company is anxious to keep its mailing cost in line. They believe total mailing costs are related to activity that is measured by sales dollars. The manager in charge of mailing has been asked to record mailing costs divided by sales each week. Previous data suggests that the mean of the mailing cost to sales dollars variable is .0830 with a variance of .0001.

During the most recent set of weeks, the following data have been observed.

Week	Mail Costs ÷ Sales
1	.0875
2	.0931
3	.0762
4	.0751
5	.0824
6	.0887
7	.1020
8	.0976

Ace uses a control-chart approach to cost control.

REQUIRED:

a. If the firm is willing to take a 5 percent chance of investigating an in-control situation, should an investigation be taken?

b. Do you believe this process is in control? Explain.

c. How would you criticize the approach used by Ace?

28-15 **Control Procedures in Water Usage** Murray Machine and Foundary is concerned with the amount of water it is using in its cooling activities. The firm has obtained readings on the amounts from city-installed gauges for the last 300 working days and converted it to gallons per hour of activity. The daily data are indicated in the accompanying table as summarized for display to management.

HOURLY WATER CONSUMPTION IN HUNDREDS OF GALLONS PER HOUR

Usage	No. Days	Usage	No. Days
100–102	2	110–112	60
102–104	14	112–114	47
104–106	32	114–116	31
106–108	42	116–118	11
108–110	57	118–120	4

REQUIRED:

a. Are there any important factors to consider before using this data in any control procedures for water usage?

b. Assuming the data is satisfactory, what is the expected daily usage? What is the variance of the daily usage?

c. Compute daily and weekly (five-day) control chart limits that would allow a change in the level of usage to be detected with 95 percent confidence. What statistical assumptions have you made in setting these limits?

d. What information has been lost in the data given in the table that would be of value if one had the individual values recorded by day?

28-16 **Controlling Power Costs** The budgeted power cost is $20,000. The cost is budgeted at the expected amount when the process is in control. The expected cost when the process is out of control is $30,000. Management in charge of controlling the cost has indicated that there is equal likelihood of favorable and unfavorable variances and the standard deviation of the actual cost about the mean value is $6,000 for either state. Assume that the cost is normally distributed. The actual cost for January is $27,000.

REQUIRED:

a. Compute the number of standard deviations the January cost is from the mean amount for both the in-control and out-of-control cases.

b. Compute the probability of January's cost being greater than $27,000, if the in-control state exists (if the cost fluctuations are caused by random factors).

Problems

28-17　Cost Variance Control Charts　The following data are reports for a particular process over three time periods:

Cost report 1	$300
Cost report 2	250
Cost report 3	400

Assume that if the process is in control, the reported cost is normally distributed with mean $200 and standard deviation $100. If the process is out of control, the reported cost is normally distributed with mean $500 and standard deviation $100. At the beginning of period 1 the process had just been corrected, and there is a .7 probability of the in-control state. The cost of conducting an investigation is $200 and the cost of correcting is $100. For this particular process, it is estimated that each out-of-control situation corrected results in a $500 savings at the present value.

REQUIRED:

Construct a cost variance control chart with limits $\mu - 1.96\sigma$ for the three periods. Using this chart, what would have been the decisions for each report?

28-18　Ex post Variance Analysis; Production Planning　Kristin Scott, the production manager of Jackson, Inc., is currently making the production schedule for 19x1. Jackson, Inc. produces three products, denoted by *A, B,* and *C.* The standards for the production of *A* are as follows:

Direct material	$5/lb of product *A*
Direct labor	.2 hrs/lb of product *A*
Direct labor rate	$10/hr (applies to all three products)

Products *B* and *C* are joint products from a single production process that uses an input denoted *Z.* One pound of *Z* input into the joint process yields .6 pounds of *B* and .4 pounds of *C.* Raw material *Z* has a standard cost of $14 per pound of *Z.*

The direct labor standards for the production of products *B* and *C* are the following:

Standard direct labor hours in the joint process	.3 hrs/lb of *Z*
Standard direct labor hours in the separable process for product *B*	.1 hr/lb of *B*
Standard direct labor hours in the separable process for product *C*	.2 hrs/lb of *C*

Jackson's variable overhead rate is $10 per direct labor hour. Jackson's annual fixed cost is $20,000.

Management has decided that at least 10,000 pounds of each product must be produced. Management has also estimated that all of Jackson's production during 19x1 can be sold at the following prices:

A	$13/lb
B	$32/lb
C	$24/lb

Since Jackson's production operation involves highly skilled workers, only 14,000 hours of direct labor are estimated to be available during 19x1.

Jackson has no inventory on January 1, 19x1.

REQUIRED:

a. Formulate and solve Jackson's production planning problem for the year 19x1. Show calculations and support all numbers used in your formulation with computations. (Hint: you might start by thinking about contribution margins.)

b. After the conclusion of 19x1, Jackson noted the following actual results:

A	12,000 pounds
B	16,500 pounds
C	11,000 pounds

Two departures from standard performance were noted during 19x1. Due to unavoidable supply interruptions, the raw material for *A* actually cost $6 per pound instead of the estimated $5 per pound. The labor required to produce *A* averaged .15 hours per pound instead of the standard .2 hours per pound.

Compute the following variances from the traditional variance analysis. Indicate whether each variance is favorable or unfavorable.

(1) Material price variance

(2) Variable overhead efficiency variance

(3) Interpret the variable overhead efficiency variance

c. Given the information in **b** above, and using Demski's ex post variance analysis, compute the following:

(1) Ex post contribution margin per pound of *A*.

(2) Ex post contribution margin per pound of *Z* entered into the joint process.

(3) Ex post optimal production plan. Formulate and solve.

d. Using Demski's ex post variance analysis, compute each of the following variances.

(1) Forecasting decision variance

(2) Forecasting parameter variance

(3) Opportunity cost decision variance

(4) Opportunity cost parameter variance

28-19 **Ex post Variance Analysis; Job Shop**   Job Shop, Inc. began operations on January 1, 19x9 as a special-order metal fabricating plant. The business was very small, employing only five metal workers and one accountant in addition to Cora Nelle, the majority owner and president of the company.

The shop was able to perform four basic metal working activities: cutting (C), molding (M), drilling (D), and shaping (S). Each of the five metal workers employed by Job Shop was able to perform all four activities.

On January 1, the firm had been offered the following jobs, each of which was a subcontract from a larger metal fabricating company. The activity times, labor requirements, and costs were forecast by the company's accountant, Mal Ott. Each activity cost is half material and half labor.

Job Number	Activities Required	Time Required for Activity	Laborers Required for Activity	Activity Cost	Job Price
1	C	2 weeks	2	300	700
	M	2 weeks	3	200	
				500	
2	D	2 weeks	2	200	600
	C	2 weeks	2	300	
				500	
3	M	2 weeks	4	200	800
	S	2 weeks	3	100	
				300	

The activities for each potential job must be performed sequentially in the order shown. No other metal workers are available for Job Shop to hire. The deadline for each job is four weeks away, and Ms. Nelle will not accept a job unless she is confident it can be finished. Overtime is not possible.

Based on Mr. Ott's forecasts, Ms. Nelle did the following analysis and concluded that the firm should accept jobs 1 and 2 and reject job 3: The letter and number in each cell show the type of activity and labor requirement.

If jobs 1, 2, and 3 are accepted:

Job Number	Weeks 1, 2		Weeks 3, 4		Cost	Price
1	C	2	M	3	$500	$700
2	D	2	C	2	500	600
3	M	4	S	3	300	800
Total labor	8[a]		8[a]			
Total cost					$1,300	
Total revenue						$2,100

Total contribution = $2,100 − $1,300 = $800

[a] Infeasible; violates labor constraints.

If jobs 1 and 2 are accepted:

Job Number	Weeks 1, 2		Weeks 3, 4		Cost	Price
1	C	2	M	3	$500	$700
2	D	2	C	2	500	600
Total labor	4		5			
Total cost					$1,000	
Total revenue						$1,300

Total contribution = $1,300 − $1,000 = $300

If jobs 1 and 3 are accepted:

Job Number	Weeks 1, 2		Weeks 3, 4		Cost	Price
1	C	2	M	3	$500	$700
3	M	4	S	3	300	800

Total labor		6[a]		6[a]		
Total cost					$800	
Total revenue						$1,500
Total contribution = $1,500 − $800 = $700						

[a] Infeasible; violates labor constraints.

If jobs 2 and 3 are accepted:

Job Number	Weeks 1, 2		Weeks 3, 4		Cost	Price
2	D	2	C	2	$500	$600
3	M	4	S	3	300	800

Total labor		6[a]		5		
Total cost					$800	
Total revenue						$1,400
Total contribution = $1,400 − $800 = $600						

[a] Infeasible; violates labor constraints.

Because Job Shop is just starting operations, Ms. Nelle does not believe other opportunities will become available during the next four weeks. She is unwilling to lay off idle workers because skilled metal workers are in short supply and business is expected to increase in the future.

On January 1, 19x9, Ms. Nelle gave Mr. Ott a copy of an article explaining ex post variance analysis and asked him to read the article and report on the desirability of implementing such a system at Job Shop, Inc. Having read the article, Mal reported that although the article described a firm whose planning model was a linear program, the concepts were general and were certainly applicable to Job Shop's operation. Ms. Nelle then instructed Mr. Ott to install such a variance-analysis system for Job Shop, Inc.

REQUIRED:

a. What is Job Shop's ex ante optimal program (planning model solution)? What is the ex ante budgeted total contribution?

b. During January the firm completed jobs 1 and 2 on schedule. The actual cost of job 1 was $600 instead of the forecasted $500 because of an increase in the labor cost of the cutting operation for job 1 from $150 to $200 and an increase in the cost of the material used in the molding operation from $100 to $150. (Recall that the cost forecasts given earlier are half labor and half material.) These changes were avoidable.

The actual cost of job 2 was $550 due to an unavoidable increase in the cost of the drilling activity from $200 to $250.

The labor requirement for the molding operation turned out to be only two workers for job 1 instead of the forecasted three. Mr. Ott figured that the molding activity for job 3, if it had been accepted, could have been accomplished with three workers instead of the forecasted four.

All other actual costs and labor requirements were the same as the forecasts.

(1) What is the firm's ex post optimal program (that is, optimal job acceptance and rejection and resulting total contribution)?

(2) What is the forecasting decision variance? Define (in this setting) and show computations.

(3) What is the forecasting parameter variance? Define and show computations.

(4) What is the observed total contribution?

(5) What is the opportunity cost decision variance? Define and show computations.

(6) What is the opportunity cost parameter variance? Define and show computations.

(7) Disaggregate the opportunity cost parameter variance into its components.

(8) The opportunity cost decision variance resulted from (choose one):

    (a) A forecast error.

    (b) An implementation error.

    (c) Both forecast and implementation errors.

28-20 Ex post Variance Analysis; Inventory Problem The controller of the Ezra Company has recently returned from an executive development program where she learned about the ex post variance-analysis system. She found the concepts interesting and wonders whether they can be applied in the Ezra Company. Giving the matter some thought, she realizes that the operations of Ezra Company are diverse and complicated and that no single planning model can be identified for the entire firm's operation. She notes, however, that formal planning models of various kinds are used in various departments. She decides, therefore, to implement the ex post system on a trial basis in just one department.

A certain dry chemical called sushate is a critical element in Ezra's manufacturing process. Because of its unstable nature, the costs of processing orders for sushate and the costs of carrying sushate in inventory are quite large. Consequently, a special department has been established at Ezra Company that does nothing but order and store sushate. The controller chooses this department for her experiment with ex post variance analysis.

The planning model used in the sushate department is a simple economic order quantity (EOQ) model. This model specifies the cost of ordering sushate and carrying it in inventory as follows:

$$C = \frac{BD}{Q} + \frac{QS}{2}$$

where

    B = annual amount of sushate needed

    D = costs associated with placing one order for sushate, regardless of the amount ordered; D does not include the price of the sushate; only the ordering costs are included (clerical, telephone, postage, etc.)

    S = annual cost of carrying one unit of sushate in inventory

    Q = amount of sushate in one order

    C = annual cost of ordering and carrying sushate in inventory

The economic order quantity (value of Q which minimizes C) is given by the EOQ formula:

$$Q^* = \sqrt{\frac{2BD}{S}}$$

For the coming year, the sushate department has made the following forecasts:

Amount of sushate needed during entire year	B	100 units
Costs per order (not including price of sushate itself):		
Clerical		$ 5.00
Telephone		1.00
Other		4.00
Total	D	$10.00
Annual inventory carrying cost per unit of sushate	S	$ 5.00

Using the EOQ formula, the optimal order quantity for each order is

$$Q^* = \sqrt{\frac{(2)(100)(\$10.00)}{\$5.00}}$$

$$= \sqrt{400} = 20$$

The associated cost is:

$$C = \frac{(100)(\$10.00)}{20} + \frac{(20)(\$5.00)}{2}$$

$$= \$50.00 + \$50.00$$

$$= \$100$$

Thus the sushate department's ex ante plan is to order a quantity of twenty units of sushate per order with an expected annual cost of $100.

At the end of the year, the controller observed the following:

Amount of sushate needed during year	B	100 units
Costs per order (not including price of sushate itself):		
Clerical		$ 6.00
Telephone		4.50
Other		4.00
Total	D	$14.50
Annual inventory carrying cost per unit of sushate	S	$ 3.00

During the year, the department placed five orders for twenty units each. Consequently, the observed cost of running the sushate department was

$$C = \frac{(100)(14.50)}{20} + \frac{(20)(3)}{2} = \$102.50$$

The change in the clerical ordering cost was judged by the controller to be avoidable. The change in the telephone ordering cost was judged to be unavoidable.

Note: The EOQ model has nothing to do with the cost of the sushate itself (that is, its purchase price). The cost of running the sushate department consists solely of two items: ordering costs (exclusive of the purchase price) and inventory carrying costs. No information is given about the purchase price of sushate, and none is needed.

Assume that the ex ante, ex post, and observed values of B are all the same, 100 units.

REQUIRED:

a. What are the ex post values of D and S?

b. What is the ex post economic order quantity, Q?

c. What is the ex post cost of operating the sushate department (that is, the ex post value of C)?

d. Calculate the following variances:

(1) Total forecasting variance,

(2) Total opportunity cost variance.

e. Write a formula for a variance that in this context would be analogous to the forecasting parameter variance. Use the following notation:

(1) B amount of sushate needed during year

(2) D^a ex ante cost per order

(3) D^p ex post cost per order

(4) S^a ex ante carrying cost per unit

(5) S^p ex post carrying cost per unit

(6) Q^a ex ante economic order quantity

(7) Q^p ex post economic order quantity

Do not compute the numerical value of the variance.

f. Explain briefly what such a forecasting parameter (price and efficiency) variance would represent. How should it be interpreted?

28-21 Probability of Being in Control as a Function of Previous Cost Variances (see Appendix) The probability that a department will keep its operation within control in week 2 is a function of the reported cost variance in week 1. The following probabilities describe the situation.

Cost Variance in Week 1	Probability of Control in Week 2
Over $600	1.00
Between $600 and $400	.75
Between $400 and $200	.50
Between $200 and $0	.70

REQUIRED:

a. A variance of $350 in week 1 implies the process will be in control in week 2 with what probability?

b. Why does the probability fall and then rise?

c. Within what cost bounds do you think a cost investigation is signaled if the problem is always located and corrected?

d. Explain why the figure of .75 holds between $400 and $600 while 1.00 holds above $600.

28-22 The Value of an Investigation (see Appendix)   A process has an unfavorable variance reported of $7,600. It is estimated that these excess costs will continue if the process is allowed to continue without investigation and if the process is actually out of control. There is .9 probability that the cause of the variance was a peculiarity of the one period and will not recur. This will be known at the end of the period if the variance does not recur. The cost of conducting an investigation is estimated to be $1,000, and the cost of correction is an additional $1,200. Assume that if there is something wrong, an investigation will reveal the problem and it will be corrected. If the variance is not corrected now, and if it recurs, it will be investigated next period.

REQUIRED:

Should the investigation be conducted?

28-23 Expected Costs of Full and Exploratory Investigations (see Appendix)   For a given process, the revised probability of an out-of-control situation is p_2. The cost of a full investigation is $1,000 and the cost of correction is $200. The cost of an exploratory investigation, if undertaken, is $500, and there is a .8 probability it will determine that the process is out of control and at a cost of $200 eliminate the cause of the out-of-control situation. There is a .2 probability that the exploratory investigation will fail to determine that the process is out of control. The value of the savings if the process is corrected is $2,000.

REQUIRED:

a. Graph the following functions of p_2 on the same axes and find the break-even probabilities:

(1) the expected cost of a full investigation

(2) the expected cost of an exploratory investigation

(3) the expected cost of not investigating

b. Graph C' and E_p as functions of p_2.

28-24 Assumptions about Prior-State Probabilities (continuation of Problem 28-17) (see Appendix)   The classical statistical approach to Problem 28-17, part **a**, would not specify the prior odds over the states. What prior knowledge about the states, if any, does it assume?

28-25 Continuation of Problem 28-24 (see Appendix)   What can be done when the manager has imprecise ideas about the prior-state probabilities?

28-26 Value of Correcting an Out-of-Control Process (see Appendix)   The most recent cost report received by a manager of a toy company led her to estimate a .6 probability that the costs on a new line of preschool toys are out of control. From past experience with other preschool lines, she estimates that if the situation is as far out of control as the cost report suggests, the company could save the equivalent of about $2,487 as a direct result of correcting the out-of-control situations. A full investigation to discover the source of the variance would cost $1,000, and it would take another $500 to correct the situation if the process is discovered to be out of control.

REQUIRED:

a. Assuming that the investigation cost would be incurred immediately and that the savings would occur at the end of each year, should an investigation be undertaken?

b. Find the out-of-control state probability such that the manager would be indifferent between investigating and not investigating.

28-27 Graphing Expected Cost of Actions (see Appendix) The cost of investigating a certain process is $1,000, and if it is out of control, the average correction cost is $500. The estimated value of the savings associated with correcting a particular type of cost variance for this process is $5,000.

REQUIRED:

a. Graph the expected cost of each action as a function of p_2, the out-of-control state probability.

b. Find the break-even probability of being out of control.

c. Assume p_2, the probability of being out of control, is .2. Compute the expected cost of investigation and not investigating.

d. Repeat part c assuming $p_2 = .3$.

28-28 Evaluating When Investigation Is Warranted (see Appendix) Assume the probability that a process is in control is .75.

REQUIRED:

a. If C, the cost of investigation, is $100 and M, the cost of correction, is $50, how large must L, the savings from correcting an out-of-control process, be before an investigation is warranted?

b. If L is $2,000 and M is $500, what is the largest value of C for which an investigation is warranted?

c. If C is $500 and L is $5,000, how large can M be such that an investigation is still warranted?

d. Using the parameter values in part c with $M = $2,000, is an investigation desirable?

e. Let h be the probability that the cause for an out-of-control situation will be discovered when it exists. Let $L = $5,000, $M = $2,000, $p_2 = .25$, $C = $500. If h is .9, what is the maximum C' such that an exploratory investigation is justified? (C' is the cost of an exploratory examination.)

28-29 Value of Information (See Appendix) Cilla Company manufactures a line of women's handbags. An operations summary of Cilla's cutting department for May 19x4 included the following analysis:

Standard materials cost of production	$314,000
Materials price variance	0
Unfavorable materials quantity variance	16,000
Actual materials cost of production	$330,000

Donna Cook, cutting department supervisor, gathered the following information for use in deciding whether or not the variance should be investigated:

Estimated cost of investigating the variance	$4,000
Estimated cost of making the necessary changes if the cutting department is operating improperly	$8,000
Estimated present value of future unfavorable variances that would be saved by making the necessary changes if the cutting department is operating improperly	$40,000
Estimated probability of the cutting department operating properly during the current fiscal year	90%

REQUIRED:

a. Recommend whether or not Cilla Company should investigate the unfavorable materials quantity variance. Support your recommendation by

 (1) Preparing a payoff table for use in making the decision.

 (2) Computing the expected value of the cost of each possible action.

b. Donna Cook is uncertain about the probability estimate for proper operation of the cutting department (that is, 90 percent). Determine the probability estimate of the cutting department operating properly that would cause Cilla Company to be indifferent between the two possible actions.

c. Assume a consultant is available to advise Cilla Company and is able to predict accurately the state of the operations in the cutting department. Compute the expected value of the consultant's perfect information. (*CMA adapted*)

29

Cost Accounting and Professional Examinations

After studying this chapter, you should be able to:

1 List the major accounting professional examinations, and give the names of the organizations that administer them.

2 Discuss the role of cost accounting in these examinations.

*T*his chapter discusses selected professional examinations and organizations that are relevant to accountants, many of whom will sit for one or more of the following examinations:

United States:

1. Certified Public Accountant (CPA)

2. Certified Management Accountant (CMA)

Canada:[1]

1. Certified General Accountant (CGA)

2. Society of Management Accounts (SMA)

The CPA examination is a uniform exam given across the United States, but the CPA certificate is issued separately and under different conditions by the individual states. Passing the CPA examination is only one, although a critical, step toward securing the CPA certificate, which is required for all who wish to practice public accounting. Passing the CMA examination leads to designation as a Certified Management Accountant by the National Association of Accountants (NAA).

Most practicing accountants spend time in both the financial and managerial branches of accounting, so those considering an accounting career should take both examinations and should do so as soon as they complete their studies and are allowed to sit for the exams. This is when their knowledge is freshest. If more than a few months elapse between the end of school and the examination date, it is wise to enroll in one of the many review courses available for preparing candidates (including by correspondence).[2] Many accounting programs also offer review courses timed to meet the needs of those taking these exams.[3]

Passing these exams allows successful candidates to become members of the related professional organizations and, in the case of the CPA, to practice as licensed professionals. Membership in such professional organizations can significantly increase the career opportunities available to those trained in accounting. Further, the value of the certificates continues to higher-level appointments, where more global company responsibilities are encountered.

Membership in the American Institute of Certified Public Accountants and the Institute of Certified Management Accountants also provides benefits from the educational programs offered by these associations and from the contacts that can be made

---

1. The Certified General Accountants Association of Canada and the Society of Management Accountants of Canada are the equivalent licensing bodies of Canada for the AICPA and the ICMA in the United States.

2. See a recent issue of the *Journal of Accountancy* for advertisements of CPA review courses.

3. At a later point, the practitioner may also elect to take the exam administered by the Institute of Internal Auditors. However, cost accounting is not as important a topic for this exam.

during meetings. Members also are often selected to serve on special committees of these organizations, the Financial Accounting Standards Board, as well as state and national committees concerned with improving the practice and the profession of accounting.

The construction of these examinations is one method used by the accounting profession to influence what is taught in universities. Recently, concern about the level of professionalism in accounting has increased. In a recent response to the *Report of the National Commission on Fraudulent Financial Reporting,*[4] the American Accounting Association noted the following:[5]

> We find evidence of a growing concern over the erosion of professionalism in this country. This erosion is reflected in and is, we believe, a major contributing factor to the increased incidence of fraudulent financial reporting.

The report goes on to observe:

> The [Treadway] Commission also recognizes the important impact of the CPA Examination on accounting curricula and textbook development. Some substantive portion of the exam should be devoted to professionalism; this would accelerate its incorporation into accounting education.

Exams change over time, and changes in instruction inevitably follow. Although future exams should not be assumed to parallel past exams, nevertheless, past experience is helpful in forming short-run expectations concerning the exams as they relate to cost accounting.

Currently, the CMA exam is divided into five roughly equal parts:

1. Economics and business finance,

2. Organizational behavior, including ethical considerations,

3. Public reporting standards, auditing, and taxes,

4. Internal reporting and analysis,

5. Decision analysis, including modeling and information systems.

Parts 4 and 5 constitute the bulk of what is considered traditional cost accounting. About 40 percent of the CMA exam deals with traditional cost accounting,[6] versus about 5 percent of the CPA exam. The materials and problems included in this book (some selected from the past exams of the certifying organizations) are designed in part to help the reader prepare to pass the cost accounting related sections of this exam.

---

4. National Commission on Fraudulent Financial Reporting, *Report of the National Commission on Fraudulent Financial Reporting* (Washington, D.C.: U.S. Government Printing Office, 1987).

5. American Accounting Association, *Report of the AAA Treadway Commission Task Force* (Cornell University, July 6, 1987). The report also comments directly and negatively on the move toward machine-gradable examinations.

6. See R. DePasquale, "Does the Typical Curriculum Prepare You for the CMA Exam?," *Management Accounting* (November 1985): 44–46.

Information on the state requirements for the CPA exam can be obtained from each state's Board of Public Accountancy located in the capital city for that state. Additional information on the CPA exam can be obtained from

- Director of Examinations
- AICPA
- 1211 Avenue of the Americas
- New York, NY 10036

Information on the CMA exam is available from

- Institute of Certified Management Accountants
- 10 Paragon Drive
- P.O. Box 405
- Montvale, NJ 07645

Students can become student members of the NAA and receive its journal, *Management Accounting*. In addition, students can subscribe at reduced rates to the *Journal of Accountancy* (the publication of the AICPA). Copies of past professional examinations (both for the CPA and CMA) are available from the parent organization at reasonable prices.

Suggested Readings

American Accounting Association. *Report of the AAA Treadway Commission Task Force.* Cornell University, July 6, 1987.

American Accounting Association, "Report of the Committee on Professional Examinations," *Accounting Review* (Supplement to vol. 49): 3–37.

DePasquale, R. "Does the Typical Curriculum Prepare You for the CMA Exam?" *Management Accounting* (November 1985): 44–46.

TABLE A. PRESENT VALUE OF $1[a] $(1 + r)^{-n}$

n/r	1.0%	2.0%	3.0%	4.0%	5.0%	6%	7%	8%	9%	10%	12%	14%	16%	20%	24%
1	.9901	.9804	.9709	.9615	.9524	.9434	.9346	.9259	.9174	.9091	.8929	.8772	.8621	.8333	.8065
2	.9803	.9612	.9426	.9246	.9070	.8900	.8734	.8573	.8417	.8264	.7972	.7695	.7432	.6944	.6504
3	.9706	.9423	.9151	.8890	.8638	.8396	.8163	.7938	.7722	.7513	.7118	.6750	.6407	.5787	.5245
4	.9610	.9238	.8885	.8548	.8227	.7921	.7629	.7350	.7084	.6830	.6355	.5921	.5523	.4823	.4230
5	.9515	.9057	.8626	.8219	.7835	.7473	.7130	.6806	.6499	.6209	.5674	.5194	.4761	.4019	.3411
6	.9420	.8880	.8375	.7903	.7462	.7050	.6663	.6302	.5963	.5645	.5066	.4556	.4104	.3349	.2751
7	.9327	.8706	.8131	.7599	.7107	.6651	.6227	.5835	.5470	.5132	.4523	.3996	.3538	.2791	.2218
8	.9235	.8535	.7894	.7307	.6768	.6274	.5820	.5403	.5019	.4665	.4039	.3506	.3050	.2326	.1789
9	.9143	.8368	.7664	.7026	.6446	.5919	.5439	.5002	.4604	.4241	.3606	.3075	.2630	.1938	.1443
10	.9053	.8203	.7441	.6756	.6139	.5584	.5083	.4632	.4224	.3855	.3220	.2697	.2267	.1615	.1164
11	.8963	.8043	.7224	.6496	.5847	.5268	.4751	.4289	.3875	.3505	.2875	.2366	.1954	.1346	.0938
12	.8874	.7885	.7014	.6246	.5568	.4970	.4440	.3971	.3555	.3186	.2567	.2076	.1685	.1122	.0757
13	.8787	.7730	.6810	.6006	.5303	.4688	.4150	.3677	.3262	.2897	.2292	.1821	.1452	.0935	.0610
14	.8700	.7579	.6611	.5775	.5051	.4423	.3878	.3405	.2992	.2633	.2046	.1597	.1252	.0779	.0492
15	.8613	.7430	.6419	.5553	.4810	.4173	.3624	.3152	.2745	.2394	.1827	.1401	.1079	.0649	.0397
16	.8528	.7284	.6232	.5339	.4581	.3936	.3387	.2919	.2519	.2176	.1631	.1229	.0930	.0541	.0320
17	.8444	.7142	.6050	.5134	.4363	.3714	.3166	.2703	.2311	.1978	.1456	.1078	.0802	.0451	.0258
18	.8360	.7002	.5874	.4936	.4155	.3503	.2959	.2502	.2120	.1799	.1300	.0946	.0691	.0376	.0208
19	.8277	.6864	.5703	.4746	.3957	.3305	.2765	.2317	.1945	.1635	.1161	.0829	.0596	.0313	.0168
20	.8195	.6730	.5537	.4564	.3769	.3118	.2584	.2145	.1784	.1486	.1037	.0728	.0514	.0261	.0135
21	.8114	.6598	.5375	.4388	.3589	.2942	.2415	.1987	.1637	.1351	.0926	.0638	.0443	.0217	.0109
22	.8034	.6468	.5219	.4220	.3418	.2775	.2257	.1839	.1502	.1228	.0826	.0560	.0382	.0181	.0088
23	.7954	.6342	.5067	.4057	.3256	.2618	.2109	.1703	.1378	.1117	.0738	.0491	.0329	.0151	.0071
24	.7876	.6217	.4919	.3901	.3101	.2470	.1971	.1577	.1264	.1015	.0659	.0431	.0284	.0126	.0057
25	.7798	.6095	.4776	.3751	.2953	.2330	.1842	.1460	.1160	.0923	.0588	.0378	.0245	.0105	.0046
26	.7720	.5976	.4637	.3607	.2812	.2198	.1722	.1352	.1064	.0839	.0525	.0331	.0211	.0087	.0037
27	.7644	.5859	.4502	.3468	.2678	.2074	.1609	.1252	.0976	.0763	.0469	.0291	.0182	.0073	.0030
28	.7568	.5744	.4371	.3335	.2551	.1956	.1504	.1159	.0895	.0693	.0419	.0255	.0157	.0061	.0024
29	.7493	.5631	.4243	.3207	.2429	.1846	.1406	.1073	.0822	.0630	.0374	.0224	.0135	.0051	.0020
30	.7419	.5521	.4120	.3083	.2314	.1741	.1314	.0994	.0754	.0573	.0334	.0196	.0116	.0042	.0016
35	.7059	.5000	.3554	.2534	.1813	.1301	.0937	.0676	.0490	.0356	.0189	.0102	.0055	.0017	.0005
40	.6717	.4529	.3066	.2083	.1420	.0972	.0668	.0460	.0318	.0221	.0107	.0053	.0026	.0007	.0002
45	.6391	.410	.2644	.1713	.1112	.0727	.0476	.0313	.0207	.0137	.0061	.0027	.0013	.0003	.0001
50	.6080	.3715	.2281	.1407	.0872	.0543	.0339	.0213	.0134	.0085	.0035	.0014	.0006	.0001	.0000

[a] r is the rate of discount and n is the number of time periods.

TABLE B. FUTURE VALUE $1 $(1 + r)^n$

Number of Periods	1%	2%	3%	4%	5%	6%	7%	8%	9%	10%	12%	14%	16%	20%	24%
1	1.0100	1.0200	1.0300	1.0400	1.0500	1.0600	1.0700	1.0800	1.0900	1.1000	1.1200	1.1400	1.1600	1.2000	1.2400
2	1.0201	1.0404	1.0609	1.0816	1.1025	1.1236	1.1449	1.1664	1.1881	1.2100	1.2544	1.2996	1.3456	1.4400	1.5376
3	1.0303	1.0612	1.0927	1.1249	1.1576	1.1910	1.2250	1.2597	1.2950	1.3310	1.4049	1.4815	1.5609	1.7280	1.9066
4	1.0406	1.0824	1.1255	1.1699	1.2155	1.2625	1.3108	1.3605	1.4116	1.4641	1.5735	1.6890	1.8106	2.0736	2.3642
5	1.0510	1.1041	1.1593	1.2167	1.2763	1.3382	1.4026	1.4693	1.5386	1.6105	1.7623	1.9254	2.1003	2.4883	2.9316
6	1.0615	1.1262	1.1941	1.2653	1.3401	1.4185	1.5007	1.5869	1.6771	1.7716	1.9738	2.1950	2.4364	2.9860	3.6352
7	1.0721	1.1487	1.2299	1.3159	1.4071	1.5036	1.6058	1.7138	1.8280	1.9487	2.2107	2.5023	2.8262	3.5832	4.5077
8	1.0829	1.1717	1.2668	1.3686	1.4775	1.5938	1.7182	1.8509	1.9926	2.1436	2.4760	2.8526	3.2784	4.2998	5.5895
9	1.0937	1.1951	1.3048	1.4233	1.5513	1.6895	1.8385	1.9990	2.1719	2.3579	2.7731	3.2519	3.8030	5.1598	6.9310
10	1.1046	1.2190	1.3439	1.4802	1.6289	1.7908	1.9672	2.1589	2.3674	2.5937	3.1058	3.7072	4.4114	6.1917	8.5944
11	1.1157	1.2434	1.3842	1.5395	1.7103	1.8983	2.1049	2.3316	2.5804	2.8531	3.4785	4.2262	5.1173	7.4301	10.657
12	1.1268	1.2682	1.4258	1.6010	1.7959	2.0122	2.2522	2.5182	2.8127	3.1384	3.8960	4.8179	5.9360	8.9161	13.214
13	1.1381	1.2936	1.4685	1.6651	1.8856	2.1329	2.4098	2.7196	3.0658	3.4523	4.3635	5.4924	6.8858	10.699	16.386
14	1.1495	1.3195	1.5126	1.7317	1.9799	2.2609	2.5785	2.9372	3.3417	3.7975	4.8871	6.2613	7.9875	12.839	20.319
15	1.1610	1.3459	1.5580	1.8009	2.0789	2.3966	2.7590	3.1722	3.6425	4.1772	5.4736	7.1379	9.2655	15.407	25.195
16	1.1726	1.3728	1.6047	1.8730	2.1829	2.5404	2.9522	3.4259	3.9703	4.5950	6.1304	8.1372	10.748	18.486	31.242
17	1.1843	1.4002	1.6528	1.9479	2.2920	2.6928	3.1588	3.7000	4.3276	5.0545	6.8660	9.2765	12.467	22.186	38.740
18	1.1961	1.4282	1.7024	2.0258	2.4066	2.8543	3.3799	3.9960	4.7171	5.5599	7.6900	10.575	14.462	26.623	48.038
19	1.2081	1.4568	1.7535	2.1068	2.5270	3.0256	3.6165	4.3157	5.1417	6.1159	8.6128	12.055	16.776	31.948	59.587
20	1.2202	1.4859	1.8061	2.1911	2.6533	3.2071	3.8697	4.6610	5.6044	6.7275	9.6463	13.743	19.460	38.337	73.864
21	1.2324	1.5157	1.8603	2.2788	2.7860	3.3996	4.1406	5.0338	6.1088	7.4002	10.803	15.667	22.574	46.005	91.591
22	1.2447	1.5460	1.9161	2.3699	2.9253	3.6035	4.4304	5.4365	6.6586	8.1403	12.100	17.861	26.186	55.206	113.57
23	1.2572	1.5769	1.9736	2.4647	3.0715	3.8197	4.7405	5.8715	7.2579	8.9543	13.552	20.361	30.376	66.247	140.83
24	1.2697	1.6084	2.0328	2.5633	3.2251	4.0489	5.0724	6.3412	7.9111	9.8497	15.178	23.212	35.236	79.496	174.63
25	1.2824	1.6406	2.0938	2.6658	3.3864	4.2919	5.4274	6.8485	8.6231	10.834	17.000	26.461	40.874	95.396	216.54
26	1.2953	1.6734	2.1566	2.7725	3.5557	4.5494	5.8074	7.3964	9.3992	11.918	19.040	30.166	47.414	114.47	268.51
27	1.3082	1.7069	2.2213	2.8834	3.7335	4.8223	6.2139	7.9881	10.245	13.110	21.324	34.389	55.000	137.37	332.95
28	1.3213	1.7410	2.2879	2.9987	3.9201	5.1117	6.6488	8.6271	11.167	14.421	23.883	39.204	63.800	164.84	412.86
29	1.3345	1.7758	2.3566	3.1187	4.1161	5.4184	7.1143	9.3173	12.172	15.863	26.749	44.693	74.008	197.81	511.95
30	1.3478	1.8114	2.4273	3.2434	4.3219	5.7435	7.6123	10.062	13.267	17.449	29.959	50.950	85.849	237.37	634.81
40	1.4889	2.2080	3.2620	4.8010	7.0400	10.285	14.974	21.724	31.409	45.259	93.050	188.88	378.72	1468.7	5455.9
50	1.6446	2.6916	4.3839	7.1067	11.467	18.420	29.457	46.901	74.357	117.39	289.00	700.23	1670.7	9100.4	46890.4

TABLE C. PRESENT VALUE OF A $1 ANNUITY $\dfrac{1 - (1 + r)^{-n}}{r}$

n/r	1.0%	2.0%	3.0%	4.0%	5.0%	6%	7%	8%	9%	10%	12%	14%	16%	20%	24%
1	.9901	.9804	.9709	.9615	.9524	.9434	.9346	.9259	.9174	.9091	.8929	.8772	.8621	.8333	.8065
2	1.9704	1.9416	1.9135	1.8861	1.8594	1.8334	1.8080	1.7833	1.7591	1.7355	1.6901	1.6467	1.6052	1.5278	1.4568
3	2.9410	2.8839	2.8286	2.7751	2.7232	2.6730	2.6243	2.5771	2.5313	2.4869	2.4018	2.3216	2.2459	2.1065	1.9813
4	3.9020	3.8077	3.7171	3.6299	3.5459	3.4651	3.3872	3.3121	3.2397	3.1699	3.0373	2.9137	2.7982	2.5887	2.4043
5	4.8534	4.7135	4.5797	4.4518	4.3295	4.2124	4.1002	3.9927	3.8897	3.7908	3.6048	3.4331	3.2743	2.9906	2.7454
6	5.7955	5.6014	5.4172	5.2421	5.0757	4.9173	4.7665	4.6229	4.4859	4.3553	4.1114	3.8887	3.6847	3.3255	3.0205
7	6.7282	6.4720	6.2303	6.0020	5.7864	5.5824	5.3893	5.2064	5.0330	4.8684	4.5638	4.2883	4.0386	3.6046	3.2423
8	7.6517	7.3255	7.0197	6.7327	6.4632	6.2098	5.9713	5.7466	5.5348	5.3349	4.9676	4.6389	4.3436	3.8372	3.4212
9	8.5660	8.1622	7.7861	7.4353	7.1078	6.8017	6.5152	6.2469	5.9952	5.7590	5.3282	4.9464	4.6065	4.0310	3.5655
10	9.4713	8.9826	8.5302	8.1109	7.7217	7.3601	7.0236	6.7101	6.4177	6.1446	5.6502	5.2161	4.8332	4.1925	3.6819
11	10.3676	9.7868	9.2526	8.7605	8.3064	7.8869	7.4987	7.1390	6.8051	6.4951	5.9377	5.4527	5.0286	4.3271	3.7757
12	11.2551	10.5753	9.9540	9.3851	8.8632	8.3838	7.9427	7.5361	7.1607	6.8137	6.1944	5.6603	5.1971	4.4392	3.8514
13	12.1337	11.3484	10.6350	9.9856	9.3936	8.8527	8.3577	7.9038	7.4869	7.1034	6.4235	5.8424	5.3423	4.5327	3.9124
14	13.0037	12.1062	11.2961	10.5631	9.8986	9.2950	8.7455	8.2442	7.7862	7.3667	6.6282	6.0021	5.4075	4.6106	3.9616
15	13.8650	12.8493	11.9379	11.1184	10.3797	9.7122	9.1079	8.5595	8.0607	7.6061	6.8109	6.1422	5.5755	4.6755	4.0013
16	14.7179	13.5777	12.5611	11.6523	10.8378	10.1059	9.4466	8.8514	8.3126	7.8237	6.9740	6.2651	5.6685	4.7296	4.0333
17	15.5622	14.2919	13.1661	12.1657	11.2741	10.4773	9.7632	9.1216	8.5436	8.0216	7.1196	6.3729	5.7487	4.7746	4.0591
18	16.3983	14.9920	13.7535	12.6593	11.6896	10.8276	10.0591	9.3719	8.7556	8.2014	7.2497	6.4674	5.8178	4.8122	4.0799
19	17.2260	15.6785	14.3238	13.1339	12.0853	11.1581	10.3356	9.6036	8.9501	8.3649	7.3658	6.5504	5.8775	4.8435	4.0967
20	18.0455	16.3514	14.8775	13.5903	12.4622	11.4699	10.5940	9.8181	9.1285	8.5136	7.4694	6.6231	5.9288	4.8696	4.1103
21	18.8570	17.0112	15.4150	14.0292	12.8211	11.7641	10.8355	10.0168	9.2922	8.6487	7.5620	6.6870	5.9731	4.8913	4.1212
22	19.6604	17.6580	15.9369	14.4511	13.1630	12.0416	11.0612	10.2007	9.4424	8.7715	7.6446	6.7429	6.0113	4.9094	4.1300
23	20.4558	18.2922	16.4436	14.8568	13.4886	12.3034	11.2722	10.3711	9.5802	8.8832	7.7184	6.7921	6.0442	4.9245	4.1371
24	21.2434	18.9139	16.9355	15.2470	13.7986	12.5504	11.4693	10.5288	9.7066	8.9847	7.7843	6.8351	6.0726	4.9371	4.1428
25	22.0232	19.5235	17.4131	15.6221	14.0939	12.7834	11.6536	10.6748	9.8226	9.0770	7.8431	6.8729	6.0971	4.9476	4.1474
26	22.7952	20.1210	17.8768	15.9828	14.3752	13.0032	11.8258	10.8100	9.9290	9.1609	7.8957	6.9061	6.1182	4.9563	4.1511
27	23.5596	20.7069	18.3270	16.3296	14.6430	13.2105	11.9867	10.9352	10.0266	9.2372	7.9426	6.9352	6.1364	4.9636	4.1542
28	24.3164	21.2813	18.7641	16.6631	14.8981	13.4062	12.1371	11.0511	10.1161	9.3066	7.9844	6.9607	6.1520	4.9697	4.1566
29	25.0658	21.8444	19.1884	16.9837	15.1411	13.5907	12.2777	11.1584	10.1983	9.3696	8.0218	6.9830	6.1656	4.9747	4.1585
30	25.8077	22.3965	19.6004	17.2920	15.3724	13.7648	12.4090	11.2578	10.2737	9.4269	8.0552	7.0027	6.1772	4.9789	4.1601
31	26.5423	22.9377	20.0004	17.5885	15.5928	13.9291	12.5318	11.3498	10.3428	9.4790	8.0850	7.0199	6.1872	4.9824	4.1614
32	27.2696	23.4683	20.3888	17.8735	15.8027	14.0840	12.6466	11.4350	10.4062	9.5264	8.1116	7.0350	6.1959	4.9854	4.1624
33	27.9897	23.9886	20.7658	18.1476	16.0025	14.2302	12.7538	11.5139	10.4644	9.5694	8.1354	7.0482	6.2034	4.9878	4.1632
34	28.7027	24.4986	21.1318	18.4112	16.1929	14.3681	12.8540	11.5869	10.5178	9.6086	8.1566	7.0599	6.2098	4.9898	4.1639
35	29.4086	24.9986	21.4872	18.6646	16.3742	14.4982	12.9477	11.6546	10.5668	9.6442	8.1755	7.0700	6.2153	4.9915	4.1644
40	32.8347	27.3555	23.1148	19.7928	17.1591	15.0463	13.3317	11.9246	10.7574	9.7791	8.2438	7.1050	6.2335	4.9966	4.1659
45	36.0945	29.4902	24.5187	20.7200	17.7741	15.4558	13.6055	12.1084	10.8812	9.8628	8.2825	7.1232	6.2421	4.9986	4.1664
50	39.1961	31.4236	25.7298	21.4822	18.2559	15.7619	13.8007	12.2335	10.9617	9.9148	8.3045	7.1327	6.2463	4.9995	4.1666

TABLE D. FUTURE VALUE OF A $1 ANNUITY $\dfrac{(1+r)^n - 1}{r}$

Number of Periods	1%	2%	3%	4%	5%	6%	7%	8%	9%	10%	12%	14%	16%	20%	24%
1	1.0000	1.0000	1.0000	1.0000	1.0000	1.0000	1.0000	1.0000	1.0000	1.0000	1.0000	1.0000	1.0000	1.0000	1.0000
2	2.0100	2.0200	2.0300	2.0400	2.0500	2.0600	2.0700	2.0800	2.0900	2.1000	2.1200	2.1400	2.1600	2.2000	2.2400
3	3.0301	3.0604	3.0909	3.1216	3.1525	3.1836	3.2149	3.2464	3.2781	3.3100	3.3744	3.4396	3.5056	3.6400	3.7776
4	4.0604	4.1216	4.1836	4.2465	4.3101	4.3746	4.4399	4.5061	4.5731	4.6410	4.7793	4.9211	5.0665	5.3680	5.6842
5	5.1010	5.2040	5.3091	5.4163	5.5256	5.6371	5.7507	5.8666	5.9847	6.1051	6.3528	6.6101	6.8771	7.4416	8.0484
6	6.1520	6.3081	6.4684	6.6330	6.8019	6.9753	7.1533	7.3359	7.5233	7.7156	8.1152	8.5355	8.9775	9.9299	10.980
7	7.2135	7.4343	7.6625	7.8983	8.1420	8.3938	8.6540	8.9228	9.2004	9.4872	10.089	10.730	11.413	12.915	14.615
8	8.2857	8.5830	8.8923	9.2142	9.5491	9.8975	10.259	10.636	11.028	11.435	12.299	13.232	14.240	16.499	19.122
9	9.3685	9.7546	10.159	10.582	11.026	11.491	11.978	12.487	13.021	13.579	14.775	16.085	17.518	20.798	24.712
10	10.462	10.949	11.463	12.006	12.577	13.180	13.816	14.486	15.192	15.937	17.548	19.337	21.321	25.958	31.643
11	11.566	12.168	12.807	13.486	14.206	14.971	15.783	16.645	17.560	18.531	20.654	23.044	25.732	32.150	40.237
12	12.682	13.412	14.192	15.025	15.917	16.869	17.888	18.977	20.140	21.384	24.133	27.270	30.850	39.580	50.894
13	13.809	14.680	15.617	16.626	17.713	18.882	20.140	21.495	22.953	24.522	28.029	32.088	36.786	48.496	64.109
14	14.947	15.973	17.086	18.291	19.598	21.015	22.550	24.214	26.019	27.975	32.392	37.581	43.672	59.195	80.496
15	16.096	17.293	18.598	20.023	21.578	23.276	25.129	27.152	29.360	31.772	37.279	43.842	51.659	72.035	100.81
16	17.257	18.639	20.156	21.824	23.657	25.672	27.888	30.324	33.003	35.949	42.753	50.980	60.925	87.442	126.01
17	18.430	20.012	21.761	23.697	25.840	28.212	30.840	33.750	36.973	40.544	48.883	59.117	71.673	105.93	157.25
18	19.614	21.412	23.414	25.645	28.132	30.905	33.999	37.450	41.301	45.599	55.749	68.394	84.140	128.11	195.99
19	20.810	22.840	25.116	27.671	30.539	33.760	37.379	41.446	46.018	51.159	63.439	78.969	96.603	154.74	244.03
20	22.019	24.297	26.870	29.778	33.066	36.786	40.995	45.762	51.160	57.275	72.052	91.024	115.37	186.68	303.60
21	23.239	25.783	28.676	31.969	35.719	39.992	44.865	50.422	56.765	64.002	81.698	104.76	134.84	225.02	377.46
22	24.471	27.299	30.536	34.248	38.505	43.392	49.005	55.456	62.873	71.402	92.502	120.43	157.41	271.03	469.05
23	25.716	28.845	32.452	36.617	41.430	46.995	53.436	60.893	69.531	79.543	104.60	138.29	183.60	326.23	582.62
24	26.973	30.421	34.426	39.082	44.502	50.815	58.176	66.764	76.789	88.497	118.15	158.65	213.97	392.48	723.46
25	28.243	32.030	36.459	41.645	47.727	54.864	63.249	73.105	84.700	98.347	133.33	181.87	249.21	471.98	898.09
26	29.525	33.670	38.553	44.311	51.113	59.156	68.676	79.954	93.323	109.18	150.33	208.33	290.08	567.37	1114.6
27	30.820	35.344	40.709	47.084	54.669	63.705	74.483	87.350	102.72	121.09	169.37	238.49	337.50	681.85	1383.1
28	32.129	37.051	42.930	49.967	58.402	68.528	80.697	95.338	112.96	134.20	190.69	272.88	392.50	819.22	1716.0
29	33.450	38.792	45.218	52.966	62.322	73.639	87.346	103.96	124.13	148.63	214.58	312.09	456.30	984.06	2128.9
30	34.784	40.568	47.575	56.084	66.438	79.058	94.460	113.28	136.31	164.49	241.33	356.78	530.31	1181.8	2640.9
40	48.886	60.402	75.401	95.025	120.79	154.76	199.63	259.05	337.88	442.59	767.09	1342.0	2360.7	7343.8	22728
50	64.463	84.579	112.79	152.66	209.34	290.33	406.52	573.76	815.08	1163.9	2400.0	4994.5	10435.	45497	195,377

TABLE E   NORMAL PROBABILITY DISTRIBUTION FUNCTION (PROBABILITIES THAT GIVEN STANDARD NORMAL VARIABLES WILL NOT BE EXCEEDED—LEFT TAIL)[a]

$N_z(-z)$. Also $N_z(z) = 1 - N_z(-z)$

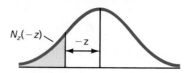

$-z$	0.00	0.01	0.02	0.03	0.04	0.05	0.06	0.07	0.08	0.09
.0	0.50000	0.49601	0.49202	0.48803	0.48405	0.48006	0.47608	0.47210	0.46812	0.46414
.1	0.46017	0.45620	0.45224	0.44828	0.44433	0.44038	0.43644	0.43251	0.42858	0.42465
.2	0.42074	0.41683	0.41294	0.40905	0.40517	0.40129	0.39743	0.39358	0.39874	0.38591
.3	0.38209	0.37828	0.37448	0.37070	0.36693	0.36317	0.35942	0.35569	0.35197	0.34827
.4	0.34458	0.34090	0.33724	0.33360	0.32997	0.32636	0.32276	0.31918	0.31561	0.31207
.5	0.30854	0.30503	0.30153	0.29806	0.29460	0.29116	0.28774	0.28434	0.28096	0.27760
.6	0.27425	0.27093	0.26763	0.26435	0.26109	0.25785	0.25463	0.25143	0.24825	0.24510
.7	0.24196	0.23885	0.23576	0.23270	0.22965	0.22663	0.22363	0.22065	0.21770	0.21476
.8	0.21186	0.20897	0.20611	0.20327	0.20045	0.19766	0.19489	0.19215	0.18943	0.18673
.9	0.18406	0.18141	0.17879	0.17619	0.17361	0.17106	0.16853	0.16602	0.16354	0.16109
1.0	0.15866	0.15625	0.15386	0.15151	0.14917	0.14686	0.14457	0.14231	0.14007	0.13786
1.1	0.13567	0.13350	0.13136	0.12924	0.12714	0.12507	0.12302	0.12100	0.11900	0.11702
1.2	0.11507	0.11314	0.11123	0.10935	0.10749	0.10565	0.10383	0.10204	0.10027	0.09853
1.3	0.09680	0.09510	0.09342	0.09176	0.09012	0.08851	0.08691	0.08534	0.08379	0.08226
1.4	0.08076	0.07927	0.07780	0.07636	0.07493	0.07353	0.07215	0.07078	0.06944	0.06811
1.5	0.06681	0.06552	0.06426	0.06301	0.06178	0.06057	0.05938	0.05821	0.05705	0.05592
1.6	0.05480	0.05370	0.05262	0.05155	0.05050	0.04947	0.04846	0.04746	0.04648	0.04551
1.7	0.04457	0.04363	0.04272	0.04182	0.04093	0.04006	0.03920	0.03836	0.03754	0.03673
1.8	0.03593	0.03515	0.03438	0.03362	0.03288	0.03216	0.03144	0.03074	0.03005	0.02938
1.9	0.02872	0.02807	0.02743	0.02680	0.02619	0.02559	0.02500	0.02442	0.02385	0.02330
2.0	0.02275	0.02216	0.02169	0.02118	0.02068	0.02018	0.01970	0.01923	0.01876	0.01831
2.1	0.01786	0.01743	0.01700	0.01659	0.01618	0.01578	0.01539	0.01500	0.01463	0.01426
2.2	0.01390	0.01355	0.01321	0.01287	0.01255	0.01222	0.01191	0.01160	0.01130	0.01101
2.3	0.01072	0.01044	0.01017	0.00990	0.00964	0.00939	0.00914	0.00889	0.00866	0.00842
2.4	0.00820	0.00798	0.00776	0.00755	0.00734	0.00714	0.00695	0.00676	0.00657	0.00639
2.5	0.00621	0.00604	0.00587	0.00570	0.00554	0.00539	0.00523	0.00508	0.00494	0.00480
2.6	0.00466	0.00453	0.00440	0.00427	0.00415	0.00402	0.00391	0.00379	0.00368	0.00357
2.7	0.00347	0.00336	0.00326	0.00317	0.00307	0.00298	0.00289	0.00280	0.00272	0.00264
2.8	0.00256	0.00248	0.00240	0.00233	0.00226	0.00219	0.00212	0.00205	0.00199	0.00193
2.9	0.00187	0.00181	0.00175	0.00169	0.00164	0.00159	0.00154	0.00149	0.00144	0.00139
3.0	0.00135	0.00131	0.00126	0.00122	0.00118	0.00114	0.00111	0.00107	0.00104	0.00100
3.1	0.00097	0.00094	0.00090	0.00087	0.00084	0.00082	0.00079	0.00076	0.00074	0.00071
3.2	0.00069	0.00066	0.00064	0.00062	0.00060	0.00058	0.00056	0.00054	0.00052	0.00050
3.3	0.00048	0.00047	0.00045	0.00043	0.00042	0.00040	0.00039	0.00038	0.00036	0.00035
3.4	0.00034	0.00032	0.00031	0.00030	0.00029	0.00028	0.00027	0.00026	0.00025	0.00024
3.5	0.00023	0.00022	0.00022	0.00021	0.00020	0.00019	0.00019	0.00018	0.00017	0.00017
3.6	0.00016	0.00015	0.00015	0.00014	0.00014	0.00013	0.00013	0.00012	0.00012	0.00011
3.7	0.00011	0.00010	0.00010	0.00010	0.00009	0.00009	0.00008	0.00008	0.00008	0.00008
3.8	0.00007	0.00007	0.00007	0.00006	0.00006	0.00006	0.00006	0.00005	0.00005	0.00005
3.9	0.00005	0.00005	0.00004	0.00004	0.00004	0.00004	0.00004	0.00004	0.00003	0.00003

[a] By symmetry this table also gives the area in the right tail for $+z$.

TABLE F   DISTRIBUTION OF *t*

This table gives *t* values for *n* degrees of freedom that correspond with the probability that the value of the random variable is greater than or less than the value giving plus or minus the *t* value. The *t* distribution is symmetrical.

n	Probability												
	.9	.8	.7	.6	.5	.4	.3	.2	.1	.05	.02	.01	.001
1	.158	.325	.510	.727	1.000	1.376	1.963	3.078	6.314	12.706	31.821	63.657	636.619
2	.142	.289	.445	.617	.816	1.061	1.386	1.886	2.920	4.303	6.965	9.925	31.598
3	.137	.277	.424	.584	.765	.978	1.250	1.638	2.353	3.182	4.541	5.841	12.924
4	.134	.271	.414	.569	.741	.941	1.190	1.533	2.132	2.776	3.747	4.604	8.610
5	.132	.267	.408	.559	.727	.920	1.156	1.476	2.015	2.571	3.365	4.032	6.869
6	.131	.265	.404	.553	.718	.906	1.134	1.440	1.943	2.447	3.143	3.707	5.959
7	.130	.263	.402	.549	.711	.896	1.119	1.415	1.895	2.365	2.998	3.499	5.408
8	.130	.262	.399	.546	.706	.889	1.108	1.397	1.860	2.306	2.896	3.355	5.041
9	.129	.261	.398	.543	.703	.883	1.100	1.383	1.833	2.262	2.821	3.250	4.781
10	.129	.260	.397	.542	.700	.879	1.093	1.372	1.812	2.228	2.764	3.169	4.587
11	.129	.260	.396	.540	.697	.876	1.088	1.363	1.796	2.201	2.718	3.106	4.437
12	.128	.259	.395	.539	.695	.873	1.083	1.356	1.782	2.179	2.681	3.055	4.318
13	.128	.259	.394	.538	.694	.870	1.079	1.350	1.771	2.160	2.650	3.012	4.221
14	.128	.258	.393	.537	.692	.868	1.076	1.345	1.761	2.145	2.624	2.977	4.140
15	.128	.258	.393	.536	.691	.866	1.074	1.341	1.753	2.131	2.602	2.947	4.073
16	.128	.258	.392	.535	.690	.865	1.071	1.337	1.746	2.120	2.583	2.921	4.015
17	.128	.257	.392	.534	.689	.863	1.069	1.333	1.740	2.110	2.567	2.898	3.965
18	.127	.257	.392	.534	.688	.862	1.067	1.330	1.734	2.101	2.552	2.878	3.922
19	.127	.257	.391	.533	.688	.861	1.066	1.328	1.729	2.093	2.539	2.861	3.883
20	.127	.257	.391	.533	.687	.860	1.064	1.325	1.725	2.086	2.528	2.845	3.850
21	.127	.257	.391	.532	.686	.859	1.063	1.323	1.721	2.080	2.518	2.831	3.819
22	.127	.256	.390	.532	.686	.858	1.061	1.321	1.717	2.074	2.508	2.819	3.792
23	.127	.256	.390	.532	.685	.858	1.060	1.319	1.714	2.069	2.500	2.807	3.767
24	.127	.256	.390	.531	.685	.857	1.059	1.318	1.711	2.064	2.492	2.797	3.745
25	.127	.256	.390	.531	.684	.856	1.058	1.316	1.708	2.060	2.485	2.787	3.725
26	.127	.256	.390	.531	.684	.856	1.058	1.315	1.706	2.056	2.479	2.779	3.707
27	.127	.256	.389	.531	.684	.855	1.057	1.314	1.703	2.052	2.473	2.771	3.690
28	.127	.256	.389	.530	.683	.855	1.056	1.313	1.701	2.048	2.467	2.763	3.674
29	.127	.256	.389	.530	.683	.854	1.055	1.311	1.699	2.045	2.462	2.756	3.659
30	.127	.256	.389	.530	.683	.854	1.055	1.310	1.697	2.042	2.457	2.750	3.646
40	.126	.255	.388	.529	.681	.851	1.050	1.303	1.684	2.021	2.423	2.704	3.551
60	.126	.254	.387	.527	.679	.848	1.046	1.296	1.671	2.000	2.390	2.660	3.460
120	.126	.254	.386	.526	.677	.845	1.041	1.289	1.658	1.980	2.358	2.617	3.373
∞	.126	.253	.385	.524	.674	.842	1.036	1.282	1.645	1.960	2.326	2.576	3.291

Source: This table is reprinted from "Statistical Tables for Biological, Agricultural and Medical Research" by Sir Ronald A. Fisher and Frank Yates (New York: Hafner, 1957). Permission to reprint it was granted by Longman Publishing Company, Longman Group UK, Ltd., London. (Previously published by Oliver and Boyd, Ltd., Edinburgh.)

Note: For $n = 15$ degrees of freedom and $t = 2.602$ there is .02 probability that a random draw from the *t* distribution would give a value less than or greater than $t = 2.602$. Since the *t* distribution is symmetrical there is .01 probability that a random draw from the *t* distribution would give a value equal to or less than $t = -2.602$. There is also a .01 probability that a random draw from the *t* distribution will give a value equal to or greater than $t = 2.602$.

Glossary

Abnormal spoilage   The amount of spoilage above that expected, given the production technology.

Absorption costing   A product-costing system in which both variable and fixed manufacturing overhead are product costs.

Accept or reject decisions   Accept or reject decisions involve independent investments (all the proposals can be undertaken if they are desirable).

Account classification   A technique used to analyze and understand costs by separating the costs into either fixed or variable categories.

Actual activity   The level of output actually achieved during a given period.

Actual costing   A product-costing system in which the actual costs of direct material, direct labor, and overhead are applied to work in process.

Actual overhead   Overhead costs actually incurred (e.g., cost of direct material used or depreciation on machinery).

Administrative cost   Cost of running an organization.

Aggregate productivity   Total output divided by total input.

Allocated costs with traceable benefits   Costs that cannot be directly identified but that have a close correlation with the activity of the unit.

Allocated costs with indirect benefits   Costs that cannot be identified directly with the activity and that have little correlation with changes in the level of the activity.

Allocation base   The measure used to determine how costs are to be allocated (square footage, machine hours, etc.).

Annual equivalent cost   A series of equal annual costs whose present value is also equal to the initial outlay.

Annuity   An annuity is the present value of a dollar per period where there is a constant length of time between each period and each time period has the same interest rate. The symbol $B(n, r)$ is used to represent the present value of a dollar per period for n periods and r interest rate.

Applied overhead   The amount of overhead cost added to the work-in-process inventory account.

Appraisal costs   The costs incurred to ensure that inputs and outputs meet quality standards.

Avoidable fixed cost   A fixed cost that may be eliminated under some circumstances.

Bayes decision rule   A method of choosing the best action that uses probabilities (often subjective) and the utilities of the outcomes.

Behavioral implications   Concern for how the accounting system motivates (affects) workers.

Best of the set decisions   "Best of the set" decisions involve mutually exclusive investments.

Bottom-line calculations   The focus of reported income.

Break-even analysis   Determination of the sales (in units or dollars) required for a company to earn a profit of zero.

Break-even point   The sales level (in units or dollars) at which the firm earns a profit of zero.

Break-even probability   The probability that equates the uncertain costs of two actions.

Budget   A quantitative statement of a plan of action for some specified period of time.

Budget committee   Top-management group appointed to advise the budget director.

Budget director (or budget officer)   The person in charge of an organization's budgeting process.

Budget manual   A document that specifies the procedures to be used in the organization's budgeting process.

Budget variance   Actual fixed overhead minus budgeted fixed overhead.

Burden   Another term for overhead.

By-products   A joint product of relatively small importance to the firm.

Capital asset pricing model   A theoretical construct that relates an asset's required return to the default-free return that can be earned, plus a risk adjustment. The risk adjustment is for the covariance of the asset's return and the market's return.

Capital budget   Quantifies the organization's plans for acquisition and disposal of capital assets, such as buildings and equipment.

Capital budgeting   The process of deciding whether or not to commit resources to projects whose costs and benefits are spread over several time periods, and to relate the benefits to the costs in a reasonable manner that is consistent with an objective of maximizing the stockholders' well-being.

Carrying costs   Storage, insurance, obsolescence, and other costs of holding inventories.

Cash budget   A document showing planned sources and uses of cash.

Cash flow return on investment (ROI)   Some experts advocate using an ROI based on cash flows rather than on income. There are several methods of calculation with different degrees of correctness.

Cash flows   The change in cash during a period of time. The cash-flow procedure assumes that the amount of a cash disbursement or cash receipt is the amount by which the change in financial position associated with an investment should be measured.

Certainty equivalent   The amount of dollars that is equivalent to the value of a complex gamble (or investment).

CLADR   Class life asset depreciation range. A depreciation (cost recovery) system defined by the IRS.

Coefficient of correlation   A measure of the strength of association between the dependent and one (or more) independent variable(s).

Coefficient of determination   The proportion of variability in the dependent variable accounted for by changes in one (or more) independent variable(s).

Common costs   A name for either joint or indirect costs.

Component productivity   Total output divided by some input component (e.g., total automobiles divided by total workers' hours).

Computer-integrated manufacturing (CIM)   The full automation of a manufacturing facility, with computers controlling the entire production process.

Conditional profit   The profit (net gain) for a given action and a given state of nature (event) occurring.

Constant dollars   The nominal (current) dollars are adjusted to real purchasing power using inflation adjustment factors.

Contingency view of managerial accounting   System characteristics are contingent on variables in the organizational environment. The people and the organization determine the accounting system.

Contribution income statement   An income statement emphasizing the contribution to income by an activity or department.

Contribution margin per unit   Unit sales price minus unit variable cost.

Contribution margin ratio   The percentage of each sales dollar available to make a contribution toward covering fixed cost and profit. Unit contribution margin divided by sales price.

Control chart   A graph on which costs are plotted relative to the expected cost and expected cost deviations in order to monitor cost trends visually.

Control system   A set of procedures designed to monitor and regulate some phenomenon.

Controllable cost   Costs that are controlled or heavily influenced by an individual.

Controller (or comptroller)   Chief managerial accountant in an organization. Generally a member of top management.

Conversion costs   Direct labor and manufacturing overhead.

Convex polygon   The set of feasible solutions for a linear programming problem.

Cost accounting   Part of an organization's accounting system that accumulates cost and other quantitative data for the purposes of both financial and managerial accounting.

Cost allocation   The assignment of a cost to two or more cost objectives, such as products, services, or time periods.

Cost-allocation systems   Systems of assigning costs to different cost centers or profit centers.

Cost center   An organizational subunit in which the manager is held responsible for costs.

Cost control   The process of controlling costs by comparing actual costs with some type of standard or budgeted cost.

Cost distribution (or cost allocation)   Assignment of overhead costs to department overhead centers.

Cost driver   An activity or procedure that causes costs to be incurred. For example, the number of invoices will drive the costs of accounts payable.

Cost objective The product, service, or time period receiving allocated costs.

Cost of goods manufactured Cost of beginning work-in-process inventory, plus manufacturing costs incurred during the accounting period, less the cost of ending work-in-process inventory.

Cost of goods sold The cost of manufacturing or purchasing the goods that were sold during an accounting period.

Cost of money This cost is determined by the opportunity to invest the funds and earn a return or the return required by investors. The cost of money provides the rate of discount to be applied to future cash flows. There is an implicit assumption that funds may be borrowed or lent at this same rate.

Cost of a prediction error A type of sensitivity analysis that establishes the cost effect of an error in determining one of the input values.

Cost-performance-reporting (CPR) A CPR system collects data on actual costs incurred, budgeted costs, and the time in which activities are completed.

Cost-plus pricing A method of pricing in which the price is set at product cost plus some profit margin.

Cost pool An accumulation of costs to be allocated to products, services, or time periods.

Cost structure The relative proportions of the various types of cost incurred by an organization.

Cost variance Difference between actual cost and standard cost.

Cost-volume-profit analysis An overview of the relationships between cost and revenue and sales volume, with an emphasis on the impact of these variables on profit.

Cross-sectional data Data collected across activities at a single point in time.

Current dollars Dollars that reflect inflation but are not adjusted to "real" or "constant" amounts. This is a nominal dollar measure.

DCF Discounted cash flow.

Decentralization Refers to the degree to which the subunits of an organization are allowed to make decisions affecting production, investment, and marketing.

Decision model A simplified, mathematical representation of a decision situation.

Decision trees A pictorial presentation showing the different feasible decisions and the possible events (outcomes) with their probabilities. The branches make the picture look like a tree.

Denominator activity The activity measure used in the denominator of a predetermined overhead rate.

Departmental overhead rate An overhead rate computed for a particular department (in contrast to a plantwide overhead rate).

Dependent demand The demand for components or raw materials as a function of the demand for the final product.

Dependent projects The cash flows associated with an investment are affected by the decision to accept or reject a second investment.

Differential budget standards Budgets are set at varying levels of difficulty to best motivate the different individuals.

Differential cost analysis The process of selecting the least cost alternative ignoring costs that are the same across alternatives.

Direct cost A cost that can be traced to a particular cost objective.

Direct costing See *Variable costing*.

Direct labor The cost of wages, salaries, and fringe benefits of employees who work directly on a manufactured product.

Direct material Raw material that is incorporated as a physical part of the product.

Direct pricing Cost-based pricing based on variable costs only.

Discount for risk The difference between the expected monetary value and the certainty equivalent for a specific investor or for the market.

Discounted cash flow (DCF) methods Investment procedures that make use of the cash flows of the investments and consider the time value of money.

Discretionary fixed costs Fixed costs that can be avoided at the decision maker's election.

Divestment decision The decision of a firm to sell or not sell an asset presently owned.

Dual problem The alternate mathematical statement of a primal linear programming problem. If the primal is a maximization problem, the dual is a minimization problem and vice versa.

Earnings-per-share (EPS) Earnings to the common stockholders divided by the number of shares outstanding. The EPS is complicated since accountants may have more than one income calculation for each period.

Economic break-even point (EBE) A breakeven point that includes the interest cost on the capital that is used.

Economic depreciation See *Present-value depreciation*.

Economic order quantity formula (EOQ) A solution to the basic inventory problem if certainty is assumed. The formula is $Q = \sqrt{\dfrac{2KD}{k}}$ where Q is the amount to be ordered, K is the fixed costs of placing an order, D is the amount needed per unit of time, and k is the carrying cost per unit of time.

Efficiency variance Standard variable overhead rate times the difference between actual hours and standard hours.

EMV See *Expected monetary value*.

EOQ See *Economic order quantity formula*.

Equivalent units A measure of the amount of productive input required to complete one unit of output.

Ex post variance analysis A procedure that examines variances considering the effect on the decision process of changes in the parameter values after the model has been implemented.

Expectancy theory of motivation The theory that actions are selected on the basis of the likelihood of specific outcomes (the expectancy) and the utility (valences) of the outcomes.

Expected activity   The level of output anticipated for a particular period.

Expected monetary value   The sum of the products of the monetary outcomes times the probability of their occurring.

Expected profit   The sum of all the products of the conditional profits times the probability of their occurring.

Expected utility   The sum of the products of the outcome's utility and the probability of the outcome for all outcomes of a decision.

Expected value of perfect information   The increased value to the decision maker if the true state of the process were known before a decision is required.

Expense   The cost of an asset that has been used up or sold for the purpose of generating revenue.

External failure costs   The costs incurred because inferior quality products are shipped to customers.

Financial accounting   The process of providing financial information to users outside an organization, such as stockholders, lenders, and governmental agencies.

Financial budget   Specifies the organization's plans for financing its activities.

Finished goods   Completed products.

First-in, first-out (FIFO)   A method of process costing in which the cost of the period's beginning work-in-process inventory is kept separate from the current period's production costs. Also, an inventory flow assumption in which the oldest goods obtained are the first to be charged as an expense.

Fixed cost   A cost that does not change in total when the volume of activity changes.

Fixed overhead activity variance   Fixed overhead rate times the difference between budgeted hours and actual hours.

Fixed overhead efficiency variance   Fixed overhead rate times the difference between actual hours and standard hours allowed.

Flexible budget   A budget that includes different cost levels for different levels of activity.

Flexible manufacturing system   Integrated systems for automatic random processing.

Forecasting decision variance   The difference between the ex post outcome the firm should have planned, and the outcome based on the ex post parameter value and the ex ante action.

Forecasting parameter variance   The difference between the ex ante planned outcome, and the outcome based on the ex ante action and ex post parameter value.

Forecasting variance   The difference between the ex ante planned outcome and, ex post, what the firm should have planned.

Full costing   See *Absorption costing*.

Goal congruence   Meshing of individual and organizational goals.

Gross investment   Investment with no deduction for accumulated depreciation.

Hierarchical organizations   Organizations in which each unit controls a group of subunits, which may in turn control other subunits.

High-low method   The use of a line drawn between the cost at a high level and the cost at a low level of activity to estimate costs at other activity levels.

Homoscedasticity   The condition in which the conditional distribution of the dependent variable around the regression line is the same at all values of the independent variable.

Hurdle rate   The return required for an investment.

Hybrid costing system   A product-costing system that bears some characteristics of two or more basic costing systems (for example, both job-order and process costing).

Implicit interest cost   The capital cost associated with equity capital is not normally recorded. This is the recognition that equity capital has a cost, and if equity capital is used in manufacturing a product there is an interest cost. There is an explicit interest cost with debt.

Implicit interest revenue   If there is an implicit interest cost associated with using equity capital, there is also implicit interest revenue.

Incremental cost   The additional cost that will be incurred if an action is taken.

Incremental-cost analysis   An analysis of the increase in revenue and expense resulting from an action.

Independent projects   An investment is economically independent if the cash flows (or more generally the costs and benefits) expected from the investment would be the same regardless of whether a second investment were accepted or rejected.

Indirect cost   A cost that cannot be traced to a particular cost objective is an indirect cost, with respect to that cost objective.

Indirect costs   Costs that by management decision result in two or more products.

Indirect labor   The cost of compensating employees who are necessary for production but do not work directly on the product.

Indirect material   The cost of material that is consumed in production, but is not physically incorporated in the product. Also, the cost of minor materials used in production, even if they are a physical part of the product.

Inflation   The upward change in overall (average) prices.

Internal failure costs   The costs associated with products that fail to meet quality standards.

Internal-rate-of-return (IRR) method   The internal rate of return is the rate of interest that causes the present value of the cash flows of a project to be equal to zero. This rate of interest is also the average return on investment earned through the life of the project, where the average is of a very special type. If the IRR is larger than the cost of money, and if the cash flows are an investment type of cash flows, the investment is acceptable. Other terms applied to the same measure are the yield, return on investment, and time-adjusted rate of return.

Inventoriable cost (or product cost)   A cost that is identified with goods manufactured or purchased for resale.

Inventory master file A computerized listing of all inventory items, used in MRP systems.

Investment center An organizational subunit in which the manager is held responsible for both profit and its relationship to invested capital.

Investment turnover The sales of a period divided by the average investment.

Investment type of cash flows Negative flow(s) followed by positive inflow ($- + + +$).

Job-cost sheet A document containing a detailed listing of the costs of producing a particular production job.

Job-order costing A product-costing system in which costs are assigned to batches of products called jobs.

Joint costs Costs that by their nature result in two or more products.

Joint price/quantity variance The difference between actual price and standard price times the difference between actual quantity and standard quantity.

Joint process A process resulting in two or more outputs or products.

Joint products Separate products that emerge in predictable portions from a joint process.

Just-in-time inventory policy A policy under which items are produced or received on order when needed for sale or completion of other items.

Labor distribution document A source document used to trace direct labor costs to the appropriate job-cost sheets.

Learning curve model A model that describes the reduction in the average direct labor input as a constant percentage reduction when cumulative output doubles.

Learning rate One minus the constant percentage reduction in direct labor time per unit as cumulative output doubles.

Last in, first out (LIFO) With LIFO, the oldest goods purchased are the last goods to be charged as an expense.

Linear utility function The utility function (a straight line) is consistent with the use of expected monetary values to make decisions.

Loan type of cash flows Positive flow(s) followed by negative outflows ($+ - - -$).

Management by exception A management technique in which managers investigate only significant deviations from expected performance.

Management by objectives (MBO) A management approach in which the organization's mission or primary goal is broken down into specific objectives.

Managerial accounting The process of providing financial information to users inside the organization, for the purposes of planning, control, and decision making.

Manufacturing cost Cost of manufacturing a product for resale.

Manufacturing overhead See *Overhead.*

Marginal cost The cost of producing one more unit during a specified time period.

Marketing costs (or selling costs) Costs of marketing the organization's product or service.

Master budget   Ties together all of an organization's budgets into a unified plan.

Material requirements planning (MRP)   A method for coordinating detailed production plans in multistage production systems involving many products.

Material requirements planning II (MRP II)   A detailed production planning system for multiple products linked to the financial system of the organization.

Material requisition   A source document used to authorize the release of materials to production and trace their costs to the appropriate job-cost sheets.

Matrix organizations   Each subunit is controlled by two or more types of managerial units.

Merchandise cost   Cost of acquiring merchandise for resale.

Mix variance (material mix variance)   A variance that shows the effect on direct-material costs of changes in the mix of materials used.

Mix variance (sales-mix variance)   A variance that captures the impact on profit of changes in the sales mix.

Monte Carlo simulation   A process of simulation where outcomes are determined by a random draw (selection) for each stochastic event, and the overall outcome is computed using these inputs.

Motivational aspects   How the accounting system motivates the workers being reported on.

Multidimensional productivity analysis   Productivity measured using a variety of different input measures.

Multiple regression   A mathematical approach that measures the extent to which a dependent variable changes in relation to changes in several independent variables.

Mutually exclusive investments   When the potential benefits to be derived from the first investment will completely disappear if the second investment is accepted, or when it would be technically impossible to undertake the first if the second were accepted, the two investments are said to be mutually exclusive.

Net present value method   The net present value method applies a rate of discount (interest rate) to future cash flows to bring them back to the present (finding present value equivalents). The present values are then added. The net present value of an investment is the amount the firm could afford to pay in excess of the cost of the investment and still break even on the investment.

Net realizable value   Selling price less costs of completion and sale.

Nominal dollars   See *Current dollars*.

Nonconventional cash flows   Cash flows with more than one sign change ($- + + -$).

Nonsystematic risk   Using the capital asset pricing model, the risk that is independent of the market fluctuations is not relevant to decisions, since it has been assumed that individual investors have diversified their investments so as to eliminate this type of risk.

Normal (or average) activity   The level of output required to satisfy average consumer demand.

Normal costing   A product-costing system in which the actual costs of direct material and direct labor are applied to work in process. Overhead is applied to work in process on the basis of a predetermined overhead rate.

Normal pricing   Cost-based pricing based on product costs measured under absorption costing.

Normal spoilage   The amount of spoilage expected, given the production technology.

Normal standard   A standard that is equal to expected performance, considering likely working conditions.

Objective function   The mathematical statement to be optimized in a linear programming problem.

Operating budget   Specifies the organization's plan for carrying out its operating activities such as production and sales.

Operating expenses   Period costs of conducting operations. Included are selling and administrative costs and the costs of operating a service-industry organization.

Operating rate   Operating profit divided by dollars of sales.

Operation costing   A hybrid product-costing system. Direct labor and overhead costs are accounted for using process-costing methods, but direct material costs are accounted for using job-order costing methods.

Operational control   This is defined to be control measures that are physical in nature. Pounds of output per pounds of input would be an illustration.

Opportunity cost   The cost of one course of action, measured in terms of the value of opportunities that are precluded by taking that course of action.

Opportunity cost decision variance   The difference between the ex post outcome the firm should have planned, and the outcome based on the ex post parameter value and the observed action.

Opportunity cost parameter variance   The difference between the observed result, and the outcome based on the ex post parameter value and observed action.

Opportunity cost variance   The difference between the ex post outcome the firm should have planned and the observed outcome.

Ordering costs   Handling, shipping, inspections, and other costs incurred in obtaining inventory.

Out-of-pocket cost (or *outlay cost*)   Costs that actually require the payment of money.

Overapplied overhead   The amount by which applied overhead exceeds actual overhead.

Overhead   All manufacturing costs except for direct material and direct labor. Includes indirect labor, indirect material, and other manufacturing costs.

Overhead absorption   See *Overhead application*.

Overhead application (or *absorption*)   Assignment of manufacturing overhead costs to products.

Parameters   Values selected by the decision maker as inputs to the decision model.

Participative budgeting   Involving subordinates in the budget process (for example, in setting goals).

Payback method The length of time required to recover the initial investment is computed, and this measure is compared to the maximum payback period.

Perfect information The decision maker knows what the outcome is to be.

Performance report A document showing a person's or a responsibility accounting center's budgeted and actual performance.

Period cost A cost that is identified with a period of time, rather than a product.

Perpetuity A series of constant cash flows, equally spaced, continuing for an infinite number of time periods.

Plantwide overhead rate An overhead rate computed for an entire production facility (in contrast to a departmental overhead rate).

Post audit The process of comparing, after an investment has been placed in operation, the actual results to estimated results that formed the basis for the capital-budgeting decision; any variances should be explained. Also called *reappraisal*.

Practical (or *attainable*) capacity The activity level at which long-run or short-run marginal costs are equal.

Practical standard (or *attainable standard*) A standard that is difficult to attain but can be attained by skilled personnel with diligence under expected conditions.

Precautionary level of inventory Level of inventory needed to avoid the cost of being caught short, often called safety stock.

Predetermined overhead rate Budgeted manufacturing overhead divided by the budgeted level of the activity base or denominator activity.

Present-value distribution A distribution of present-value outcomes derived from a simulation process.

Present-value depreciation The periodic depreciation expense for an asset is defined as the change in the value of the asset, where value is computed using the asset's cash flows. To avoid complications, we assume that the actual decrease in value for each period is the same as the expected decrease.

Present-value index A variant of the present-value approach. The index is frequently computed by dividing the present value of the cash proceeds, exclusive of the initial investment, by the investment.

Present-value profile The plot of the net present value of the investment over a wide range of discount rates. The resulting graph is called a present-value profile.

Prevention costs The costs of designing, implementing, and maintaining the quality system.

Price-level adjusted income The income that results from the adjustment to depreciation expense for inflation.

Price variance (*direct-material price variance*) Actual quantity used times the difference between actual price and standard price.

Primal problem The initial mathematical form of the linear programming problem including the function to be optimized and the constraints.

Process control The control of a process using directly controllable costs.

Process costing A product-costing system in which costs are assigned to departments and then applied to equivalent units of production activity.

Product cost (or inventoriable cost) A cost that is identified with goods manufactured or purchased for resale.

Product costing The process of accumulating and classifying costs and then assigning those costs to products or services.

Product structure file A listing of the material and parts requirements for all manufactured items, used in MRP systems.

Productivity Amount of output divided by amount of input.

Profit center An organizational subunit in which the manager is held responsible for profit.

Profit-volume chart A graph showing the firm's profit as a function of sales volume.

Programmed costs Administrative costs that are fixed in the short run.

Pro forma financial statements Budgeted financial statements (such as an income statement and balance sheet).

Proration (cost variance proration) The allocation of cost variances to the manufacturing accounts: work-in-process inventory, finished-goods inventory, and cost of goods sold.

Purchase-price variance Actual quantity purchased times the difference between actual price and standard price.

Pure price variance Standard quantity times the difference between actual price and standard price.

Quality costing The process of controlling the cost of maintaining or improving product quality.

Quality of conformance The degree to which the output meets specifications.

Quality of design Similar products (automobiles, for example) may have different design characteristics (such as Chevrolets and Cadillacs).

Quantity variance (direct material quantity variance) Standard price times the difference between actual quantity and standard quantity.

Quantity variance (sales-quantity variance) A variance that holds constant the sales mix at a predetermined mix, and focuses on the total quantity of products sold.

Real-time information system Instantaneous generation of data, even as the relevant events occur.

Reciprocal service The situation where two or more service departments supply service to each other.

Regression analysis A mathematical approach that measures the extent to which a dependent variable changes in relation to changes in one (or more) independent variable(s).

Regression coefficient The mathematical constant that gives the change in the dependent variable for a unit change in the independent variable.

Regression equation The expression that gives the mathematical relation between the dependent and the independent variable(s).

Relevant cost   A relevant cost is a cash flow that differs across available alternatives.

Relevant range   The range of activity (independent variable), within which activity is expected in the future.

Residual income   The income before capital costs, minus an implicit interest cost on all capital being employed. Residual income measures return after allowing for a return on equity as well as debt.

Responsibility accounting   The identification of subunits in an organization and the individuals who will be held accountable for the performance of those subunits.

Responsibility accounting systems   Assigning costs to the unit responsible for the magnitude of the costs.

Return on investment (ROI)   The income divided by the beginning or average investment. Rather than the depreciated investment (that is, a figure based on the depreciated plant assets) some companies use the initial investment (undepreciated plant assets). ROI can be computed by dividing income by average investment or by multiplying the investment turnover (sales divided by average investment) by the operating rate (operating profit divided by sales):

$$\text{ROI} = \frac{\text{Sales}}{\text{Average investment}} \times \frac{\text{Operating profit}}{\text{Sales}} = \frac{\text{Operating profit}}{\text{Average investment}}$$

Return-on-investment pricing   A method of pricing in which the price is set in order to achieve the profit required to earn a certain return on investment.

Revenue center   An organizational subunit in which the manager is held responsible for revenue.

Revolving budget (or rolling budget)   A budgeting system in which a new budget is periodically developed for a time period longer than the period between new budgets.

Reworked units   Products that do not initially meet product-quality standards but have subsequently been reworked so that they may be sold as good units.

Risk aversion   A common attitude toward risk that leads to valuing an alternative at less than its expected monetary value.

Robinson-Patman amendment   An amendment to the Clayton Act that prohibits unlawful price discrimination.

ROI   See *Return on investment.*

Rolling budget   See *Revolving budget.*

Safety stock   Level of inventory required to avoid being short of a needed item, also called precautionary inventory.

Sales mix   The relative proportions of sales of each of a firm's products.

Scatter plot   A plot of data points often used to search for variables that may be related to one another.

Scrap   Part of the raw material that is not usable in making a product. An example is the unusable end of a metal bar that remains after pieces are cut for production.

Semivariable cost A cost that has both a fixed component and a variable component.

Sensitivity analysis An analysis that determines how a calculated result changes if there are errors in predicting one or more of the input values to the calculation.

Separable costs Costs other than joint costs that can be identified directly with the final product.

Service costing The process of accumulating and classifying costs and then assigning those costs to the services produced by the organization.

Service department A department that is necessary for production but does not work directly on the organization's product or service (an equipment maintenance department, for example).

Service department cost allocation Allocation of costs from service departments to production departments.

Shadow price The economic cost of a factor of production.

Simple regression analysis A mathematical approach that measures the extent to which a dependent variable changes in relation to changes in a single independent variable.

Speculative level of inventory A change in the level of inventory made to take advantage of expected changes in prices.

Spending variance Actual variable overhead minus the product of actual hours and the standard variable overhead rate.

Spoilage Raw material or finished products discovered to be unusable due to defects.

St. Petersburg paradox A classic gamble illustrating the drastic discounting for events with large outcomes but very small probabilities.

Standard cost A predetermined cost. The cost that should be incurred in some activity.

Standard-cost accounting system (or ***standard costing***) A product-costing and cost-control system in which predetermined (or standard) costs are used instead of actual costs.

Standard costing A product-costing and cost-control system in which standard costs of direct material, direct labor, and overhead are applied to work in process.

Standard error of estimate A measure of the variation of the individual sample points about the mean value. In regression, the variation is measured about the regression line.

Standard error of the average of the dependent variable A measure of the variability in the average of the dependent variable.

Standard error of the average value A measure of the variation of the average of the individual sample points.

Statistical decision theory The process of obtaining information about which state of nature is true, using evidence to adjust the probability distribution of the states of nature to arrive at new probabilities, taking into consideration the possible losses (or costs or profits) associated with each act, and choosing the optimal act.

Statistically dependent cash flows   The outcomes of earlier years affect the cash flows of the later years.

Statistically independent cash flows   The yearly cash flows are considered to be independent events. Knowing the cash flows of one year does not help in predicting the cash flows of the other years.

Step-fixed cost   A cost that is constant over a given range of activity, but the total cost jumps to a new level with any further increase in activity.

Source document   A document used as the basis for an accounting entry (such as material requisition forms and labor time cards).

Split-off point   The point in the production process when a joint product can be separately identified.

Summary productivity measures   Total dollar measures of output (of a collection of products) divided by total dollar measures of inputs.

Sunk cost   A cost incurred in the past, that cannot be changed by any future course of action.

Terminal value   The value as of the end of a project's life. The terminal value at time n is equal to the present value times $(1 + r)^n$.

***Theoretical capacity* (or *ideal capacity*)**   The level of activity that could be achieved by operating at peak maintainable output.

***Theoretical standard* (or *ideal standard*)**   A standard that can be attained only under the best of conditions.

***Three-way analysis* (of overhead variances)**   A presentation of overhead variances in which the fixed overhead budget variance and the variable overhead spending variance are combined into a single variance, usually called a budget variance. The other two variances in the presentation are the fixed overhead volume variance and the variable overhead efficiency variance.

Time-series data   Data sequenced in time.

Time value   Money has value and a dollar in hand today is worth more than a dollar to be received one year from today. We define $(1 + r)^n$ to be the accumulation factor and $(1 + r)^{-n}$ to be the present value factor.

Transactional level of inventory   The level of inventory required to satisfy demand.

Treasurer   An accountant in the organization's top management who is responsible for the custody of funds and other assets, arranging financing, and managing investments and receivables.

Underapplied overhead   The amount by which actual overhead exceeds applied overhead.

Unit contribution margin   The excess of the product's sales price over its unit variable cost.

Utility function   The systematic assignment of numerical values to monetary outcomes taking into account a person's risk attitude. The utility function should be consistent with the person's psychological reaction to the outcomes.

Value of perfect information   The best action under conditions of uncertainty has an expected monetary value. There is also an expected value with the decision maker choosing the best action for each state of nature (as when there is perfect information). The improvement in these two expected values is the value of perfect information.

Variable cost A cost that changes proportionately with changes in activity.

Variable costing A product-costing system in which variable manufacturing overhead is a product cost, but fixed manufacturing overhead is a period cost.

Volume variance Difference between applied fixed overhead and budgeted fixed overhead.

Waste Portion of material inputs that disappears in the production process. Examples include evaporated liquids, sawdust, or metal shavings.

Weighted average A method of process costing in which the cost of the period's beginning work-in-process inventory is averaged with the current period's production costs.

Weighted-average cost of capital A measure frequently used by firms as the required return for investments (it has some severe limitations in this use) and equal to the weighted average of the costs of each capital using the relative importance of each capital source in the firm's capital structures.

Work in process Partially completed products.

Work measurement A systematic analysis of a task for the purpose of determining standards for the performance of the task.

Yield variance A variance that holds the mix of direct materials constant at a predetermined mix and focuses on the total quantity of materials used.

Zero-base budgeting. A budgeting technique in which each budgeted expense is initially set at zero. Then justification must be provided for increasing the budgeted amount.

Index